EPIC COLLECTION

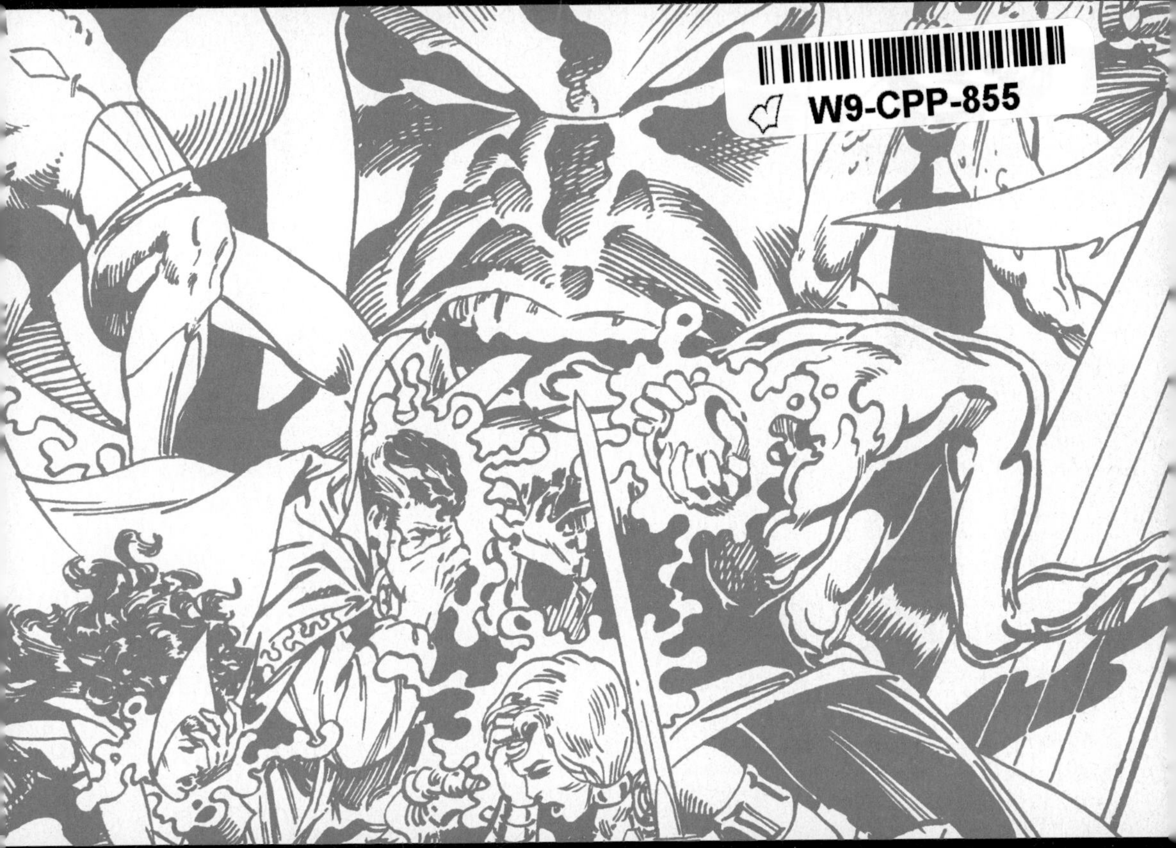

THE DEFENDERS

ASHES, ASHES...

VOLUME 7

1982-1983

DEFENDERS #110-125 AND AVENGERS ANNUAL #11

DEFENDERS

WRITERS:
J.M. DeMATTEIS
WITH **DON PERLIN** & **STEVEN GRANT**

BREAKDOWNS/PENCILERS:
DON PERLIN
WITH **SAL BUSCEMA** & **AL MILGROM**

FINISHERS/INKERS:
**KIM DeMULDER,
JACK ABEL,
MIKE GUSTOVICH
& ANDY MUSHYNSKY**
WITH **MIKE ESPOSITO,
HILARY BARTA,
AL MILGROM,
ALAN KUPPERBERG
& DIVERSE HANDS**

LETTERERS:
**SHELLY LEFERMAN
& JANICE CHIANG**
WITH **DIVERSE HANDS**

COLORISTS:
**GEORGE ROUSSOS
& CHRISTIE SCHEELE**
WITH **CARL GAFFORD**

ASSISTANT EDITORS:
ANN NOCENTI
WITH **MIKE CARLIN**

EDITORS:
AL MILGROM
WITH **CARL POTTS
& MARK GRUENWALD**

FRONT COVER ART:
BRENT ANDERSON WITH
COLORS BY **DEAN WHITE**

BACK COVER ART:
DON PERLIN &
AL MILGROM WITH COLORS
BY **GEORGE ROUSSOS**

COLLECTION EDITOR: CORY SEDLMEIER
BOOK DESIGNER: NICKEL DESIGNWORKS
COLOR RESTORATION: TOM MULLIN WITH COLORTEK

SVP PRINT, SALES & MARKETING: DAVID GABRIEL
EDITOR IN CHIEF: AXEL ALONSO   **CHIEF CREATIVE OFFICER:** JOE QUESADA
PRESIDENT: DAN BUCKLEY   **EXECUTIVE PRODUCER:** ALAN FINE

DEFENDERS EPIC COLLECTION: ASHES, ASHES... Contains material originally published in magazine form as DEFENDERS #110-125 and AVENGERS ANNUAL #11. First printing 2017. ISBN# 978
1-302-90428-9. Published by MARVEL WORLDWIDE, INC., a subsidiary of MARVEL ENTERTAINMENT, LLC. OFFICE OF PUBLICATION: 135 West 50th Street, New York, NY 10020. Copyright © 2017
MARVEL No similarity between any of the names, characters, persons, and/or institutions in this magazine with those of any living or dead person or institution is intended, and any such similarity
which may exist is purely coincidental. **Printed in the U.S.A.** DAN BUCKLEY, President, Marvel Entertainment; JOE QUESADA, Chief Creative Officer; TOM BREVOORT, SVP of Publishing; DAVID
BOGART, SVP of Business Affairs & Operations, Publishing & Partnership; C.B. CEBULSKI, VP of Brand Management & Development, Asia; DAVID GABRIEL, SVP of Sales & Marketing, Publishing; JEFF
YOUNGQUIST, VP of Production & Special Projects; DAN CARR, Executive Director of Publishing Technology; ALEX MORALES, Director of Publishing Operations; SUSAN CRESPI, Production Manager;
STAN LEE, Chairman Emeritus. For information regarding advertising in Marvel Comics or on Marvel.com, please contact Vit DeBellis, Integrated Sales Manager, at vdebellis@marvel.com. For Marvel
subscription inquiries, please call 888-511-5480. **Manufactured between 7/7/2017 and 8/8/2017 by LSC COMMUNICATIONS INC., KENDALLVILLE, IN, USA.**

10 9 8 7 6 5 4 3 2 1

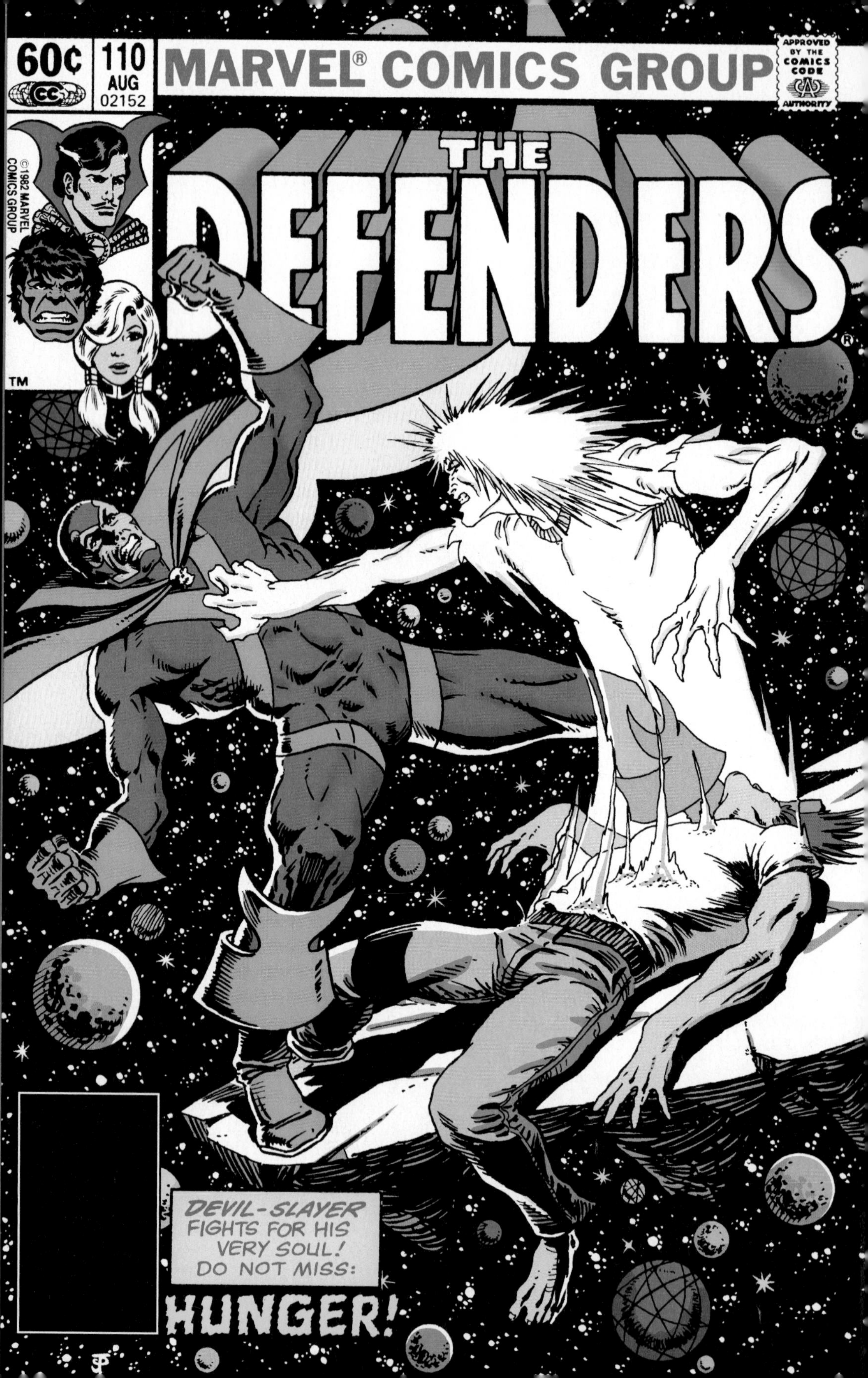
60¢
110
AUG
02152
MARVEL® COMICS GROUP
APPROVED BY THE COMICS CODE AUTHORITY
THE DEFENDERS®
©1982 MARVEL COMICS GROUP
TM
DEVIL-SLAYER FIGHTS FOR HIS VERY SOUL! DO NOT MISS:
HUNGER!

STAN LEE PRESENTS: **THE DYNAMIC DEFENDERS!**™

J. M. DE MATTEIS scripter	DON PERLIN layouts	MIKE ESPOSITO finisher	SHELLY LEFERMAN letterer	GEORGE ROUSSOS colorist	ALLEN MILGROM editor	JIM SHOOTER editor-in-chief

"THERE ARE SO MANY WORLDS TO WALK, SO MANY WONDERS TO BEHOLD, AND--IN ALL THE LIMITLESS COSMOS--ONLY I HAVE ACCESS TO THESE MYRIAD REALMS.

"FOR ONLY I--AMONG ALL BEINGS --POSSESS THE DIMENSION-SPANNING SHADOW CLOAK!

"WHY, THEN, HAVE I CHOSEN TO COME HERE--TO THIS BLEAK AND AWFUL PLACE MEN CALL THE NEGATIVE ZONE? WHY, THEN, DO I SIT ON A BARREN PIECE OF ROCK, CRADLING THE LIFELESS, BLANK-EYED BODY OF A MAN I HARDLY KNEW?

"WHY? BECAUSE I AM ERIC SIMON PAYNE.

"WHY? BECAUSE I AM-- THE DEVIL-SLAYER!

"WHY? BECAUSE I...

HUNGER...

"IF ONLY I KNEW--WHAT IT WAS I HUNGERED FOR...

5

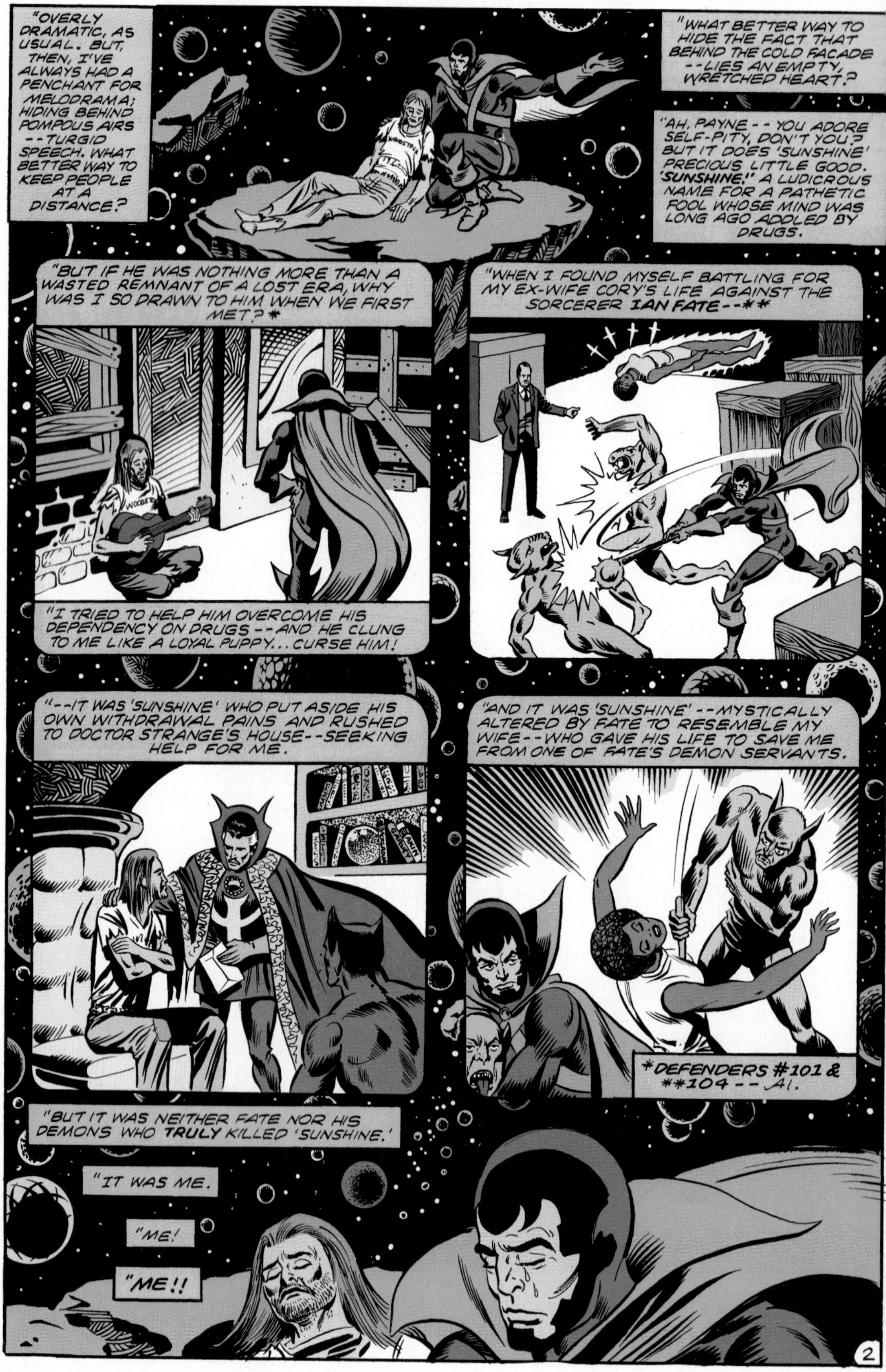
"OVERLY DRAMATIC, AS USUAL. BUT, THEN, I'VE ALWAYS HAD A PENCHANT FOR MELODRAMA; HIDING BEHIND POMPOUS AIRS --TURGID SPEECH. WHAT BETTER WAY TO KEEP PEOPLE AT A DISTANCE?
"WHAT BETTER WAY TO HIDE THE FACT THAT BEHIND THE COLD FACADE --LIES AN EMPTY, WRETCHED HEART?
"AH, PAYNE -- YOU ADORE SELF-PITY, DON'T YOU? BUT IT DOES 'SUNSHINE' PRECIOUS LITTLE GOOD. 'SUNSHINE!' A LUDICROUS NAME FOR A PATHETIC FOOL WHOSE MIND WAS LONG AGO ADDLED BY DRUGS.
"BUT IF HE WAS NOTHING MORE THAN A WASTED REMNANT OF A LOST ERA, WHY WAS I SO DRAWN TO HIM WHEN WE FIRST MET? *
"I TRIED TO HELP HIM OVERCOME HIS DEPENDENCY ON DRUGS -- AND HE CLUNG TO ME LIKE A LOYAL PUPPY... CURSE HIM!
"WHEN I FOUND MYSELF BATTLING FOR MY EX-WIFE CORY'S LIFE AGAINST THE SORCERER IAN FATE -- **
"--IT WAS 'SUNSHINE' WHO PUT ASIDE HIS OWN WITHDRAWAL PAINS AND RUSHED TO DOCTOR STRANGE'S HOUSE--SEEKING HELP FOR ME.
"AND IT WAS 'SUNSHINE' -- MYSTICALLY ALTERED BY FATE TO RESEMBLE MY WIFE--WHO GAVE HIS LIFE TO SAVE ME FROM ONE OF FATE'S DEMON SERVANTS.
*DEFENDERS #101 & **104 -- AL.
"BUT IT WAS NEITHER FATE NOR HIS DEMONS WHO TRULY KILLED 'SUNSHINE.'
"IT WAS ME.
"ME!
"ME!!
2

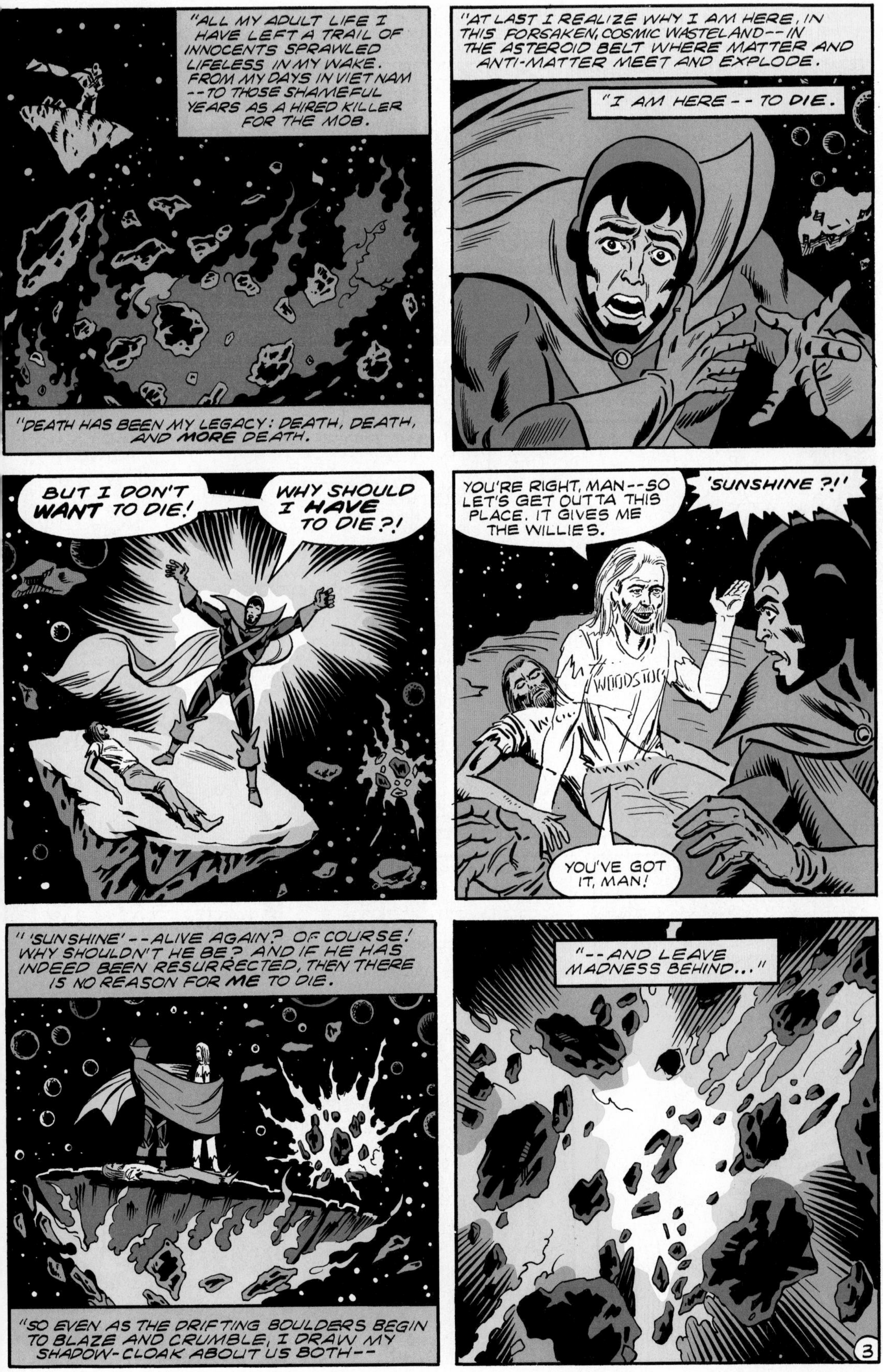
"ALL MY ADULT LIFE I HAVE LEFT A TRAIL OF INNOCENTS SPRAWLED LIFELESS IN MY WAKE. FROM MY DAYS IN VIET NAM --TO THOSE SHAMEFUL YEARS AS A HIRED KILLER FOR THE MOB.
"DEATH HAS BEEN MY LEGACY: DEATH, DEATH, AND MORE DEATH.
"AT LAST I REALIZE WHY I AM HERE, IN THIS FORSAKEN, COSMIC WASTELAND-- IN THE ASTEROID BELT WHERE MATTER AND ANTI-MATTER MEET AND EXPLODE.
"I AM HERE -- TO DIE.
BUT I DON'T WANT TO DIE!
WHY SHOULD I HAVE TO DIE?!
YOU'RE RIGHT, MAN--SO LET'S GET OUTTA THIS PLACE. IT GIVES ME THE WILLIES.
'SUNSHINE?!'
WOODSTO
YOU'VE GOT IT, MAN!
" 'SUNSHINE' --ALIVE AGAIN? OF COURSE! WHY SHOULDN'T HE BE? AND IF HE HAS INDEED BEEN RESURRECTED, THEN THERE IS NO REASON FOR ME TO DIE.
"SO EVEN AS THE DRIFTING BOULDERS BEGIN TO BLAZE AND CRUMBLE, I DRAW MY SHADOW-CLOAK ABOUT US BOTH--
"--AND LEAVE MADNESS BEHIND..."
3

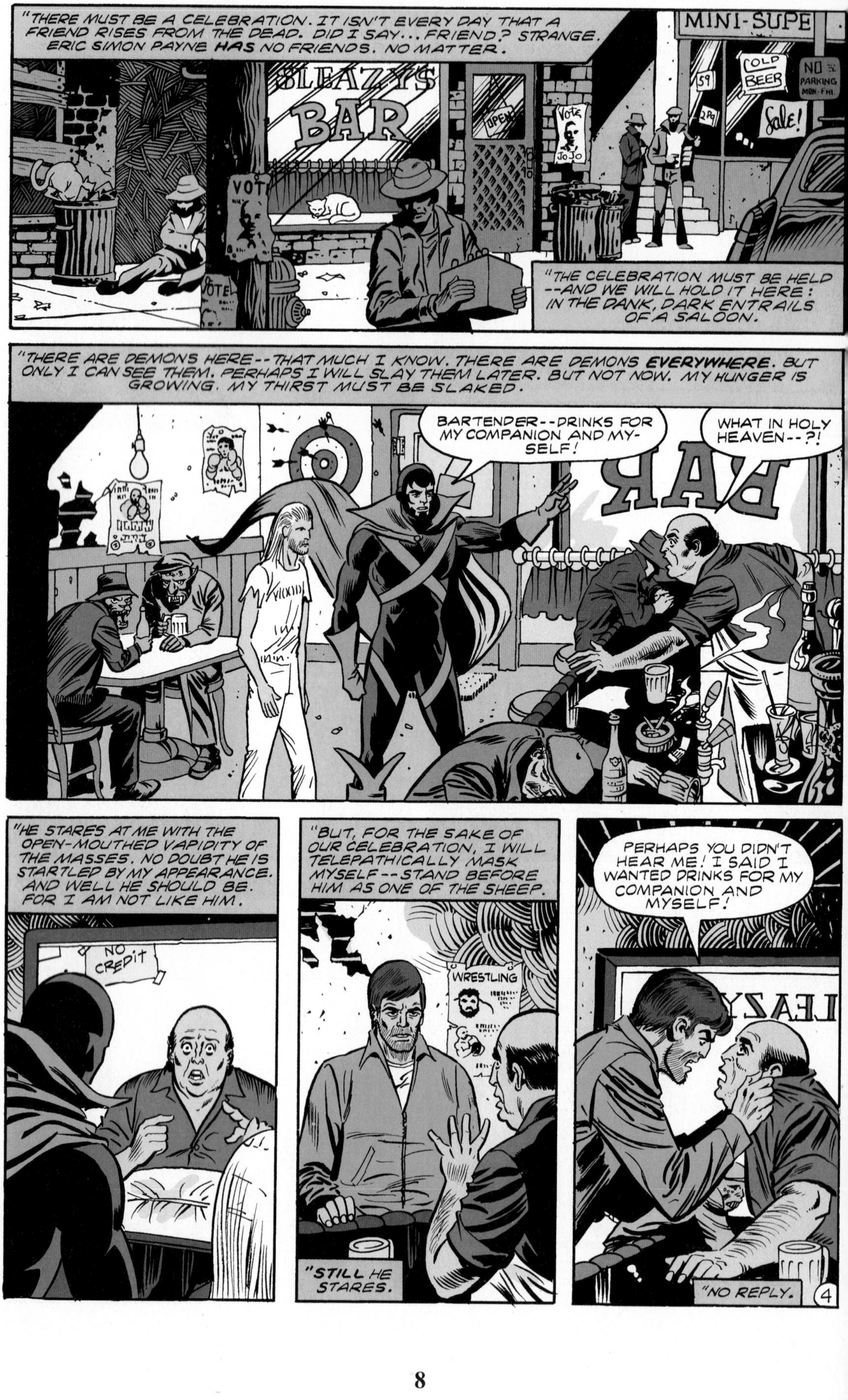

"THERE MUST BE A CELEBRATION. IT ISN'T EVERY DAY THAT A FRIEND RISES FROM THE DEAD. DID I SAY... FRIEND? STRANGE. ERIC SIMON PAYNE HAS NO FRIENDS. NO MATTER.
MINI-SUPE
SLEAZY'S BAR
OPEN
COLD BEER
NO PARKING MON-FRI
Sale!
Vote JoJo
"THE CELEBRATION MUST BE HELD --AND WE WILL HOLD IT HERE: IN THE DANK, DARK ENTRAILS OF A SALOON.
"THERE ARE DEMONS HERE--THAT MUCH I KNOW. THERE ARE DEMONS EVERYWHERE. BUT ONLY I CAN SEE THEM. PERHAPS I WILL SLAY THEM LATER. BUT NOT NOW. MY HUNGER IS GROWING. MY THIRST MUST BE SLAKED.
BARTENDER--DRINKS FOR MY COMPANION AND MY-SELF!
WHAT IN HOLY HEAVEN--?!
"HE STARES AT ME WITH THE OPEN-MOUTHED VAPIDITY OF THE MASSES. NO DOUBT HE IS STARTLED BY MY APPEARANCE. AND WELL HE SHOULD BE. FOR I AM NOT LIKE HIM.
NO CREDIT
"BUT, FOR THE SAKE OF OUR CELEBRATION, I WILL TELEPATHICALLY MASK MYSELF--STAND BEFORE HIM AS ONE OF THE SHEEP.
WRESTLING
"STILL HE STARES.
PERHAPS YOU DIDN'T HEAR ME! I SAID I WANTED DRINKS FOR MY COMPANION AND MYSELF!
"NO REPLY.
4

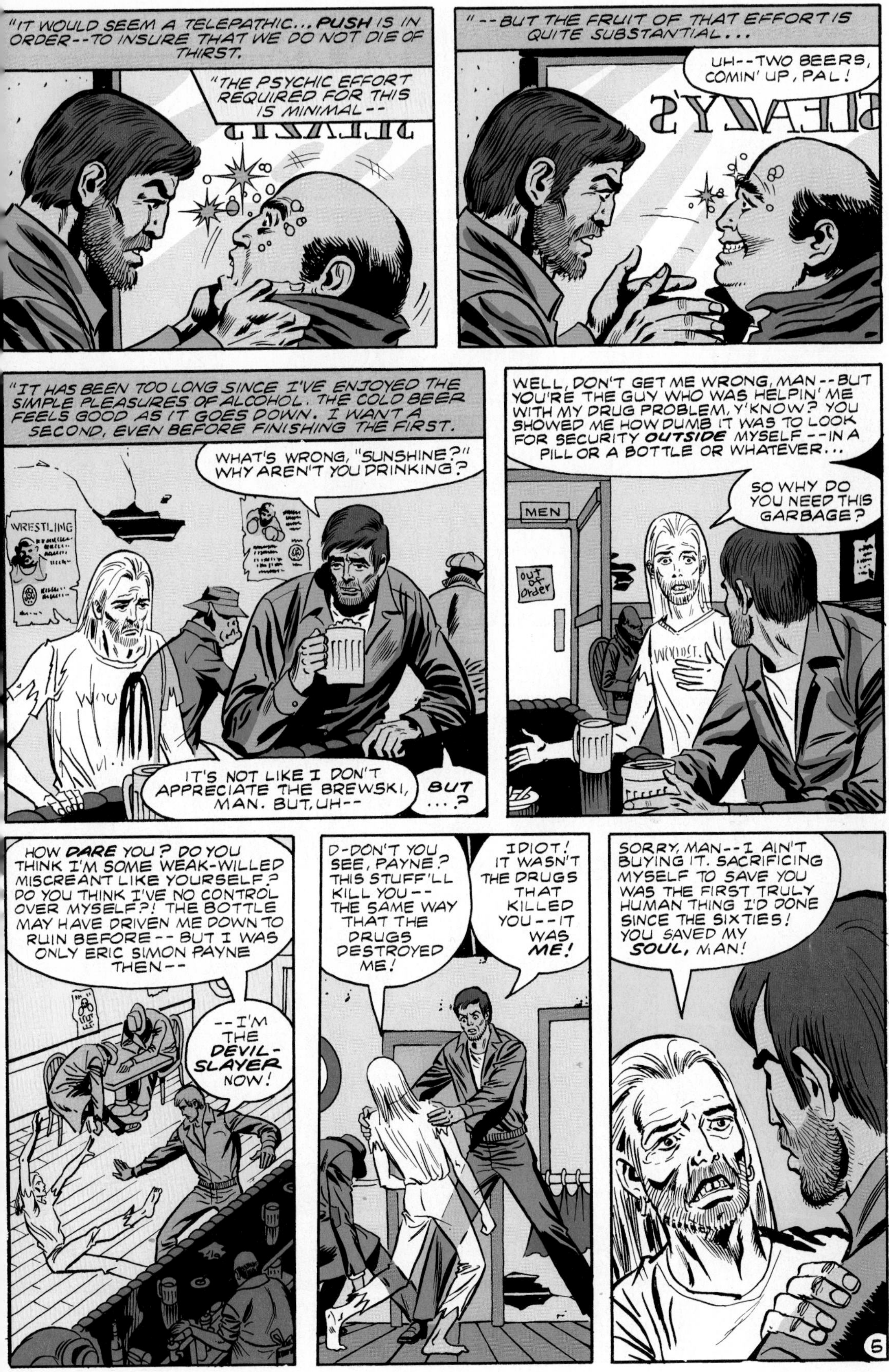
"IT WOULD SEEM A TELEPATHIC... PUSH IS IN ORDER--TO INSURE THAT WE DO NOT DIE OF THIRST.
"THE PSYCHIC EFFORT REQUIRED FOR THIS IS MINIMAL--
" --BUT THE FRUIT OF THAT EFFORT IS QUITE SUBSTANTIAL...
UH--TWO BEERS, COMIN' UP, PAL!
SLEAZY'S
"IT HAS BEEN TOO LONG SINCE I'VE ENJOYED THE SIMPLE PLEASURES OF ALCOHOL. THE COLD BEER FEELS GOOD AS IT GOES DOWN. I WANT A SECOND, EVEN BEFORE FINISHING THE FIRST.
WHAT'S WRONG, "SUNSHINE?" WHY AREN'T YOU DRINKING?
WRESTLING
IT'S NOT LIKE I DON'T APPRECIATE THE BREWSKI, MAN. BUT, UH--
BUT ...?
WELL, DON'T GET ME WRONG, MAN--BUT YOU'RE THE GUY WHO WAS HELPIN' ME WITH MY DRUG PROBLEM, Y'KNOW? YOU SHOWED ME HOW DUMB IT WAS TO LOOK FOR SECURITY OUTSIDE MYSELF--IN A PILL OR A BOTTLE OR WHATEVER...
SO WHY DO YOU NEED THIS GARBAGE?
MEN
out of order
HOW DARE YOU? DO YOU THINK I'M SOME WEAK-WILLED MISCREANT LIKE YOURSELF? DO YOU THINK I'VE NO CONTROL OVER MYSELF?! THE BOTTLE MAY HAVE DRIVEN ME DOWN TO RUIN BEFORE--BUT I WAS ONLY ERIC SIMON PAYNE THEN--
--I'M THE DEVIL-SLAYER NOW!
D-DON'T YOU SEE, PAYNE? THIS STUFF'LL KILL YOU--THE SAME WAY THAT THE DRUGS DESTROYED ME!
IDIOT! IT WASN'T THE DRUGS THAT KILLED YOU--IT WAS ME!
SORRY, MAN--I AIN'T BUYING IT. SACRIFICING MYSELF TO SAVE YOU WAS THE FIRST TRULY HUMAN THING I'D DONE SINCE THE SIXTIES! YOU SAVED MY SOUL, MAN!
6

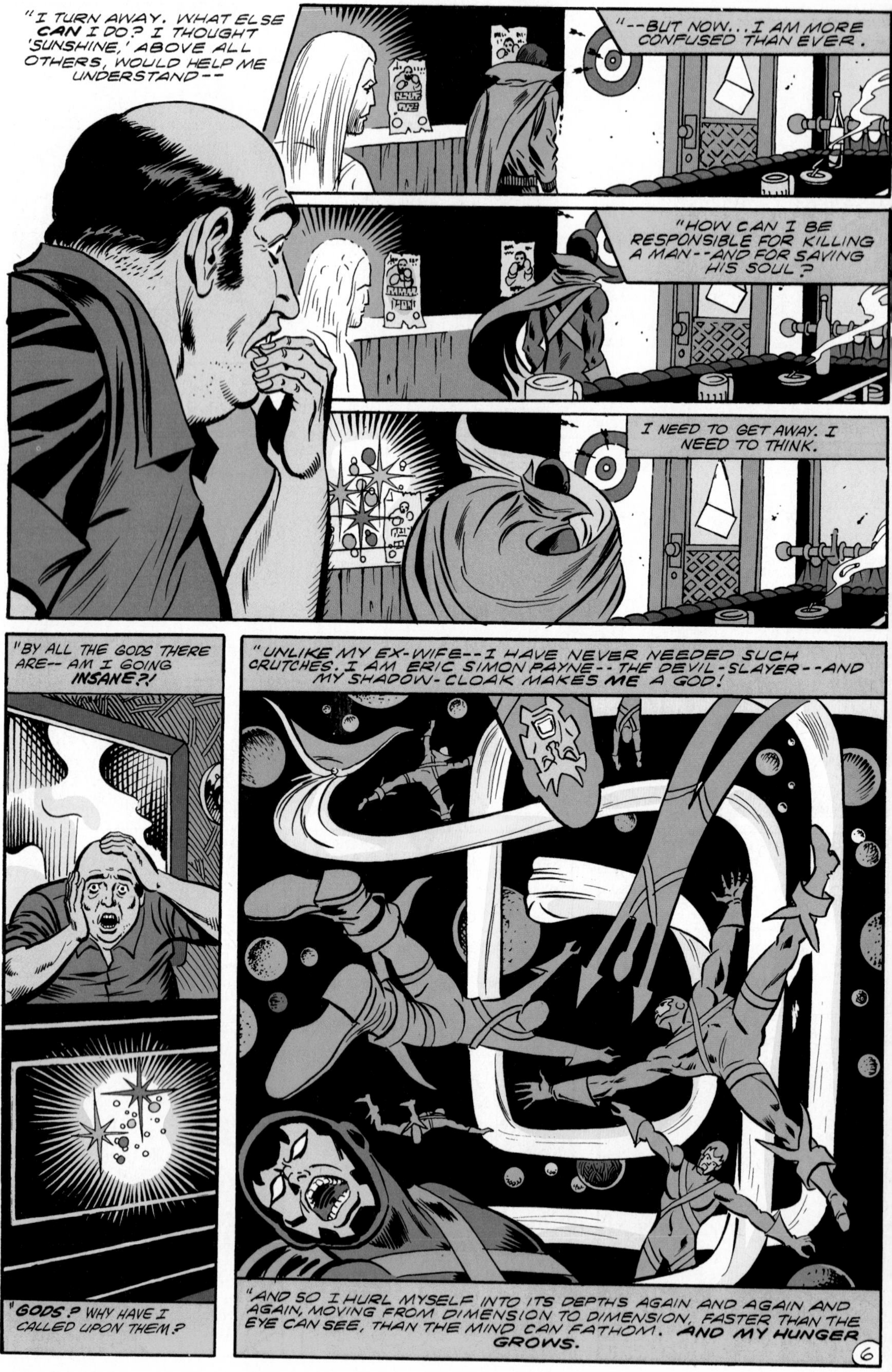
"I TURN AWAY. WHAT ELSE CAN I DO? I THOUGHT 'SUNSHINE,' ABOVE ALL OTHERS, WOULD HELP ME UNDERSTAND--
"--BUT NOW... I AM MORE CONFUSED THAN EVER.
"HOW CAN I BE RESPONSIBLE FOR KILLING A MAN--AND FOR SAVING HIS SOUL?
I NEED TO GET AWAY. I NEED TO THINK.
"BY ALL THE GODS THERE ARE--AM I GOING INSANE?!
"GODS? WHY HAVE I CALLED UPON THEM?
"UNLIKE MY EX-WIFE--I HAVE NEVER NEEDED SUCH CRUTCHES. I AM ERIC SIMON PAYNE--THE DEVIL-SLAYER--AND MY SHADOW-CLOAK MAKES ME A GOD!
"AND SO I HURL MYSELF INTO ITS DEPTHS AGAIN AND AGAIN AND AGAIN, MOVING FROM DIMENSION TO DIMENSION, FASTER THAN THE EYE CAN SEE, THAN THE MIND CAN FATHOM. AND MY HUNGER GROWS.
6

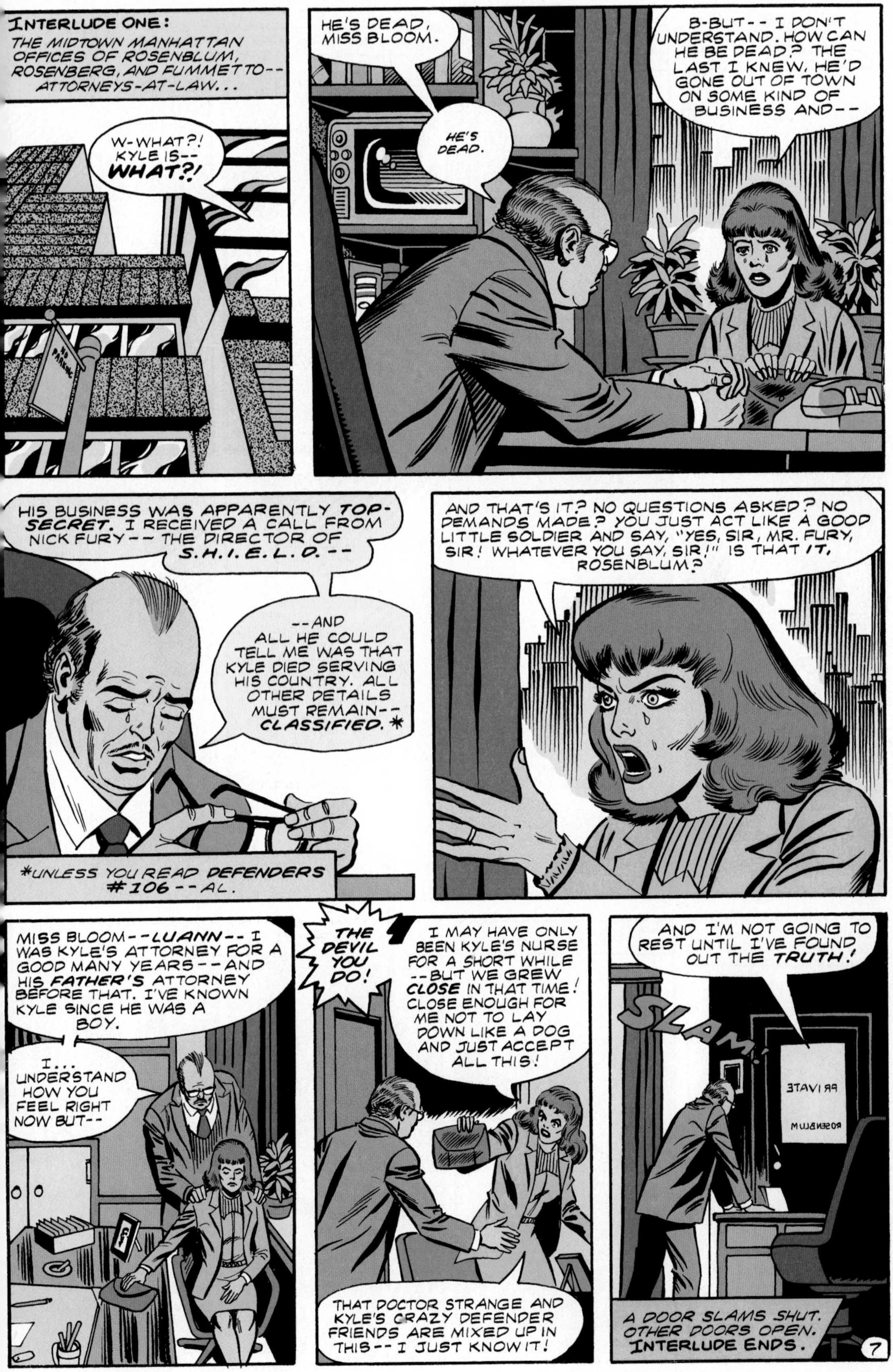
INTERLUDE ONE:
THE MIDTOWN MANHATTAN OFFICES OF ROSENBLUM, ROSENBERG, AND FUMMETTO-- ATTORNEYS-AT-LAW...
W-WHAT?! KYLE IS-- WHAT?!
HE'S DEAD, MISS BLOOM.
HE'S DEAD.
B-BUT-- I DON'T UNDERSTAND. HOW CAN HE BE DEAD? THE LAST I KNEW, HE'D GONE OUT OF TOWN ON SOME KIND OF BUSINESS AND--
HIS BUSINESS WAS APPARENTLY TOP-SECRET. I RECEIVED A CALL FROM NICK FURY-- THE DIRECTOR OF S.H.I.E.L.D.--
--AND ALL HE COULD TELL ME WAS THAT KYLE DIED SERVING HIS COUNTRY. ALL OTHER DETAILS MUST REMAIN-- CLASSIFIED.*
*UNLESS YOU READ DEFENDERS #106 --AL.
AND THAT'S IT? NO QUESTIONS ASKED? NO DEMANDS MADE? YOU JUST ACT LIKE A GOOD LITTLE SOLDIER AND SAY, "YES, SIR, MR. FURY, SIR! WHATEVER YOU SAY, SIR!" IS THAT IT, ROSENBLUM?
MISS BLOOM--LUANN-- I WAS KYLE'S ATTORNEY FOR A GOOD MANY YEARS--AND HIS FATHER'S ATTORNEY BEFORE THAT. I'VE KNOWN KYLE SINCE HE WAS A BOY.
I... UNDERSTAND HOW YOU FEEL RIGHT NOW BUT--
THE DEVIL YOU DO!
I MAY HAVE ONLY BEEN KYLE'S NURSE FOR A SHORT WHILE --BUT WE GREW CLOSE IN THAT TIME! CLOSE ENOUGH FOR ME NOT TO LAY DOWN LIKE A DOG AND JUST ACCEPT ALL THIS!
THAT DOCTOR STRANGE AND KYLE'S CRAZY DEFENDER FRIENDS ARE MIXED UP IN THIS-- I JUST KNOW IT!
AND I'M NOT GOING TO REST UNTIL I'VE FOUND OUT THE TRUTH!
SLAM!
A DOOR SLAMS SHUT. OTHER DOORS OPEN. INTERLUDE ENDS.
7

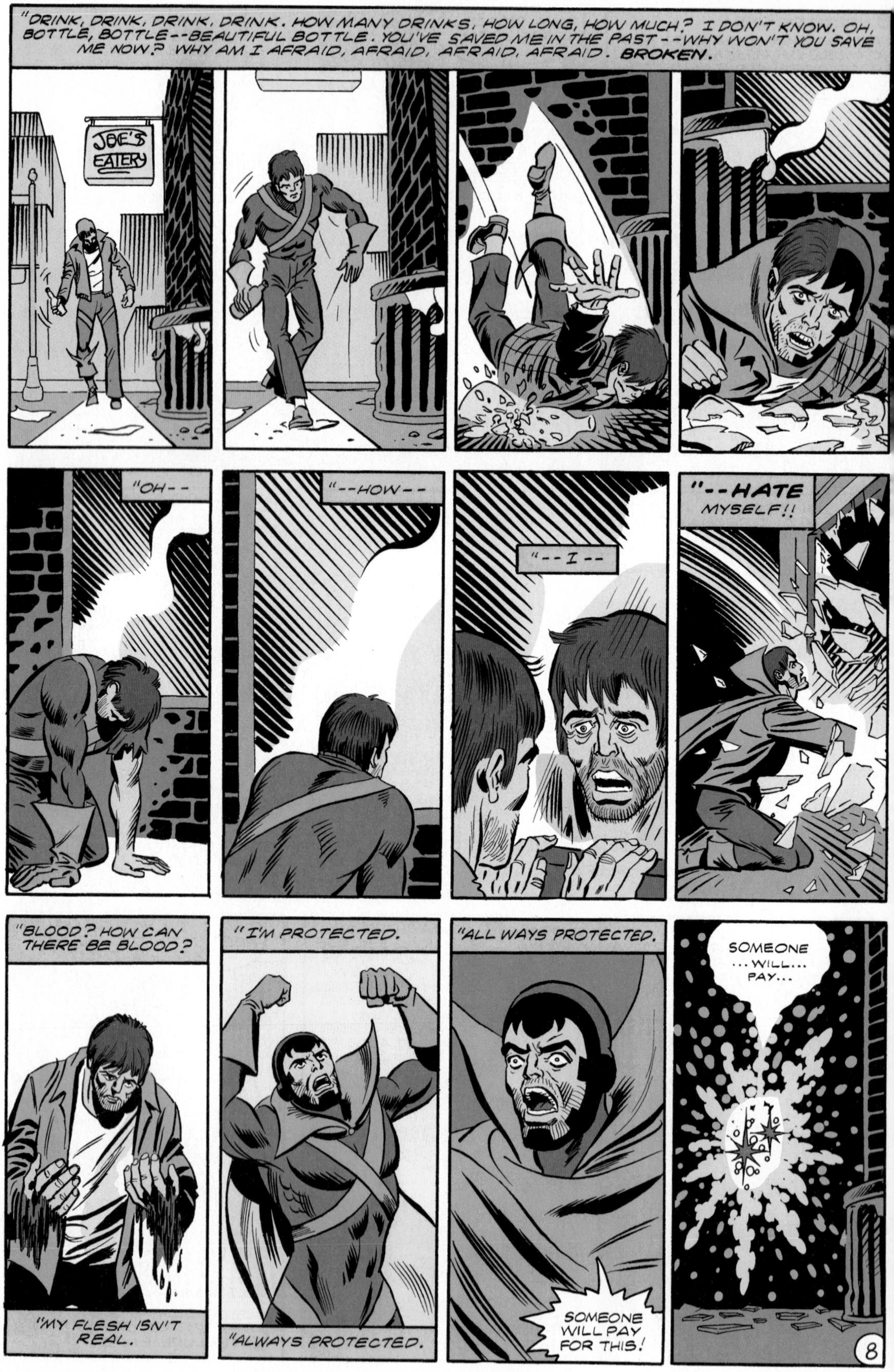
"DRINK, DRINK, DRINK, DRINK. HOW MANY DRINKS, HOW LONG, HOW MUCH? I DON'T KNOW. OH, BOTTLE, BOTTLE--BEAUTIFUL BOTTLE. YOU'VE SAVED ME IN THE PAST--WHY WON'T YOU SAVE ME NOW? WHY AM I AFRAID, AFRAID, AFRAID, AFRAID. BROKEN.
JOE'S EATERY
"OH--
"--HOW--
"--I--
"--HATE MYSELF!!
"BLOOD? HOW CAN THERE BE BLOOD?
"MY FLESH ISN'T REAL.
"I'M PROTECTED.
"ALWAYS PROTECTED.
"ALL WAYS PROTECTED.
SOMEONE WILL PAY FOR THIS!
SOMEONE ...WILL... PAY...
8

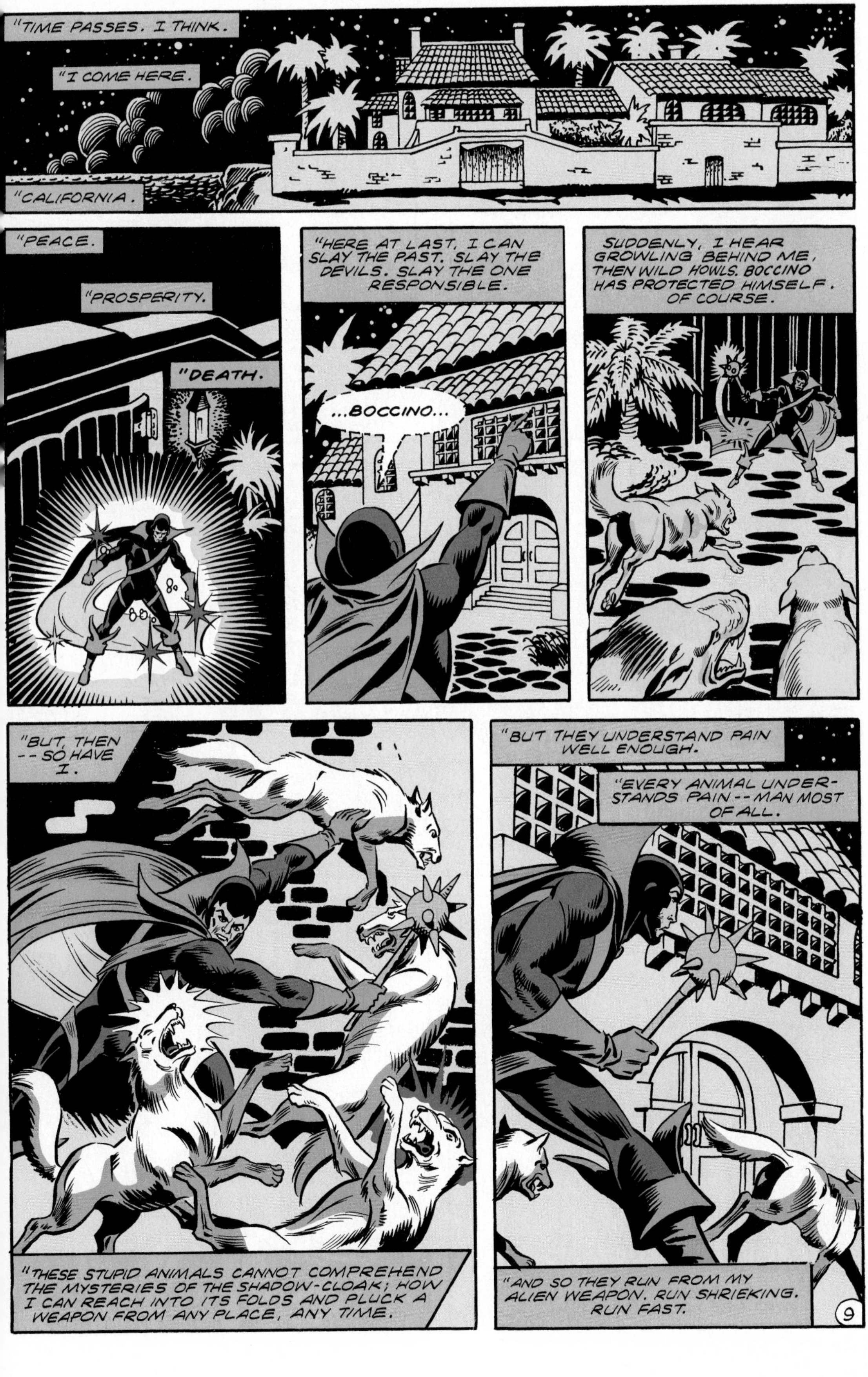
"TIME PASSES. I THINK.
"I COME HERE.
"CALIFORNIA.
"PEACE.
"PROSPERITY.
"DEATH.
"HERE AT LAST, I CAN SLAY THE PAST. SLAY THE DEVILS. SLAY THE ONE RESPONSIBLE.
...BOCCINO...
SUDDENLY, I HEAR GROWLING BEHIND ME, THEN WILD HOWLS. BOCCINO HAS PROTECTED HIMSELF. OF COURSE.
"BUT, THEN -- SO HAVE I.
"THESE STUPID ANIMALS CANNOT COMPREHEND THE MYSTERIES OF THE SHADOW-CLOAK; HOW I CAN REACH INTO ITS FOLDS AND PLUCK A WEAPON FROM ANY PLACE, ANY TIME.
"BUT THEY UNDERSTAND PAIN WELL ENOUGH.
"EVERY ANIMAL UNDERSTANDS PAIN -- MAN MOST OF ALL.
"AND SO THEY RUN FROM MY ALIEN WEAPON. RUN SHRIEKING. RUN FAST.
9

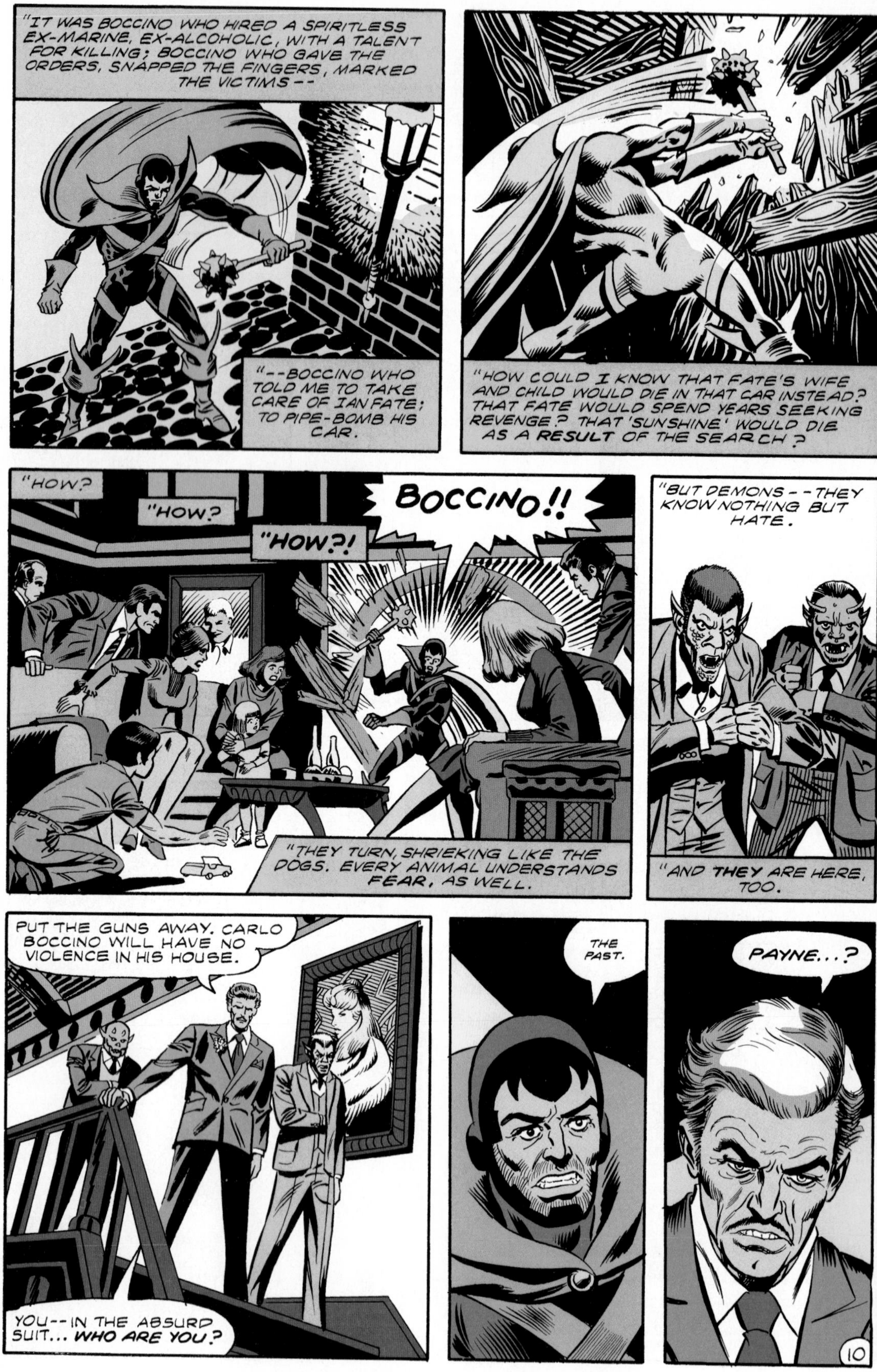

"IT WAS BOCCINO WHO HIRED A SPIRITLESS EX-MARINE, EX-ALCOHOLIC, WITH A TALENT FOR KILLING; BOCCINO WHO GAVE THE ORDERS, SNAPPED THE FINGERS, MARKED THE VICTIMS--
"--BOCCINO WHO TOLD ME TO TAKE CARE OF IAN FATE: TO PIPE-BOMB HIS CAR.
"HOW COULD I KNOW THAT FATE'S WIFE AND CHILD WOULD DIE IN THAT CAR INSTEAD? THAT FATE WOULD SPEND YEARS SEEKING REVENGE? THAT 'SUNSHINE' WOULD DIE AS A RESULT OF THE SEARCH?
"HOW?
"HOW?
"HOW?!
BOCCINO!!
"THEY TURN, SHRIEKING LIKE THE DOGS. EVERY ANIMAL UNDERSTANDS FEAR, AS WELL.
"BUT DEMONS--THEY KNOW NOTHING BUT HATE.
"AND THEY ARE HERE, TOO.
PUT THE GUNS AWAY. CARLO BOCCINO WILL HAVE NO VIOLENCE IN HIS HOUSE.
YOU--IN THE ABSURD SUIT... WHO ARE YOU?
THE PAST.
PAYNE...?
10

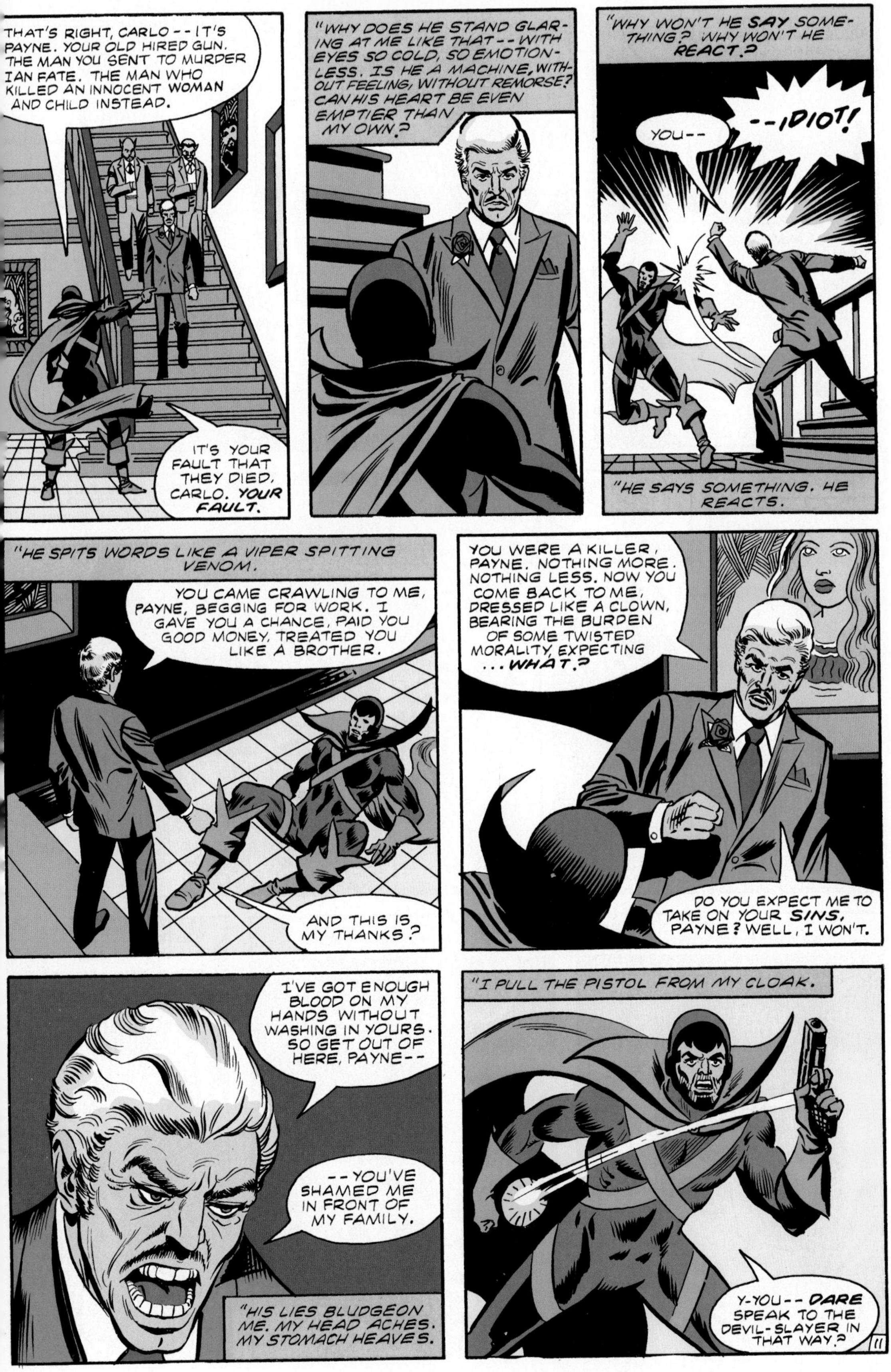
THAT'S RIGHT, CARLO -- IT'S PAYNE. YOUR OLD HIRED GUN. THE MAN YOU SENT TO MURDER IAN FATE. THE MAN WHO KILLED AN INNOCENT WOMAN AND CHILD INSTEAD.
IT'S YOUR FAULT THAT THEY DIED, CARLO. YOUR FAULT.
"WHY DOES HE STAND GLARING AT ME LIKE THAT -- WITH EYES SO COLD, SO EMOTIONLESS. IS HE A MACHINE, WITHOUT FEELING, WITHOUT REMORSE? CAN HIS HEART BE EVEN EMPTIER THAN MY OWN?
"WHY WON'T HE SAY SOMETHING? WHY WON'T HE REACT?
YOU--
--IDIOT!
"HE SAYS SOMETHING. HE REACTS.
"HE SPITS WORDS LIKE A VIPER SPITTING VENOM.
YOU CAME CRAWLING TO ME, PAYNE, BEGGING FOR WORK. I GAVE YOU A CHANCE, PAID YOU GOOD MONEY, TREATED YOU LIKE A BROTHER.
AND THIS IS MY THANKS?
YOU WERE A KILLER, PAYNE. NOTHING MORE. NOTHING LESS. NOW YOU COME BACK TO ME, DRESSED LIKE A CLOWN, BEARING THE BURDEN OF SOME TWISTED MORALITY, EXPECTING ...WHAT?
DO YOU EXPECT ME TO TAKE ON YOUR SINS, PAYNE? WELL, I WON'T.
I'VE GOT ENOUGH BLOOD ON MY HANDS WITHOUT WASHING IN YOURS. SO GET OUT OF HERE, PAYNE--
--YOU'VE SHAMED ME IN FRONT OF MY FAMILY.
"HIS LIES BLUDGEON ME. MY HEAD ACHES. MY STOMACH HEAVES.
"I PULL THE PISTOL FROM MY CLOAK.
Y-YOU-- DARE SPEAK TO THE DEVIL-SLAYER IN THAT WAY?
11

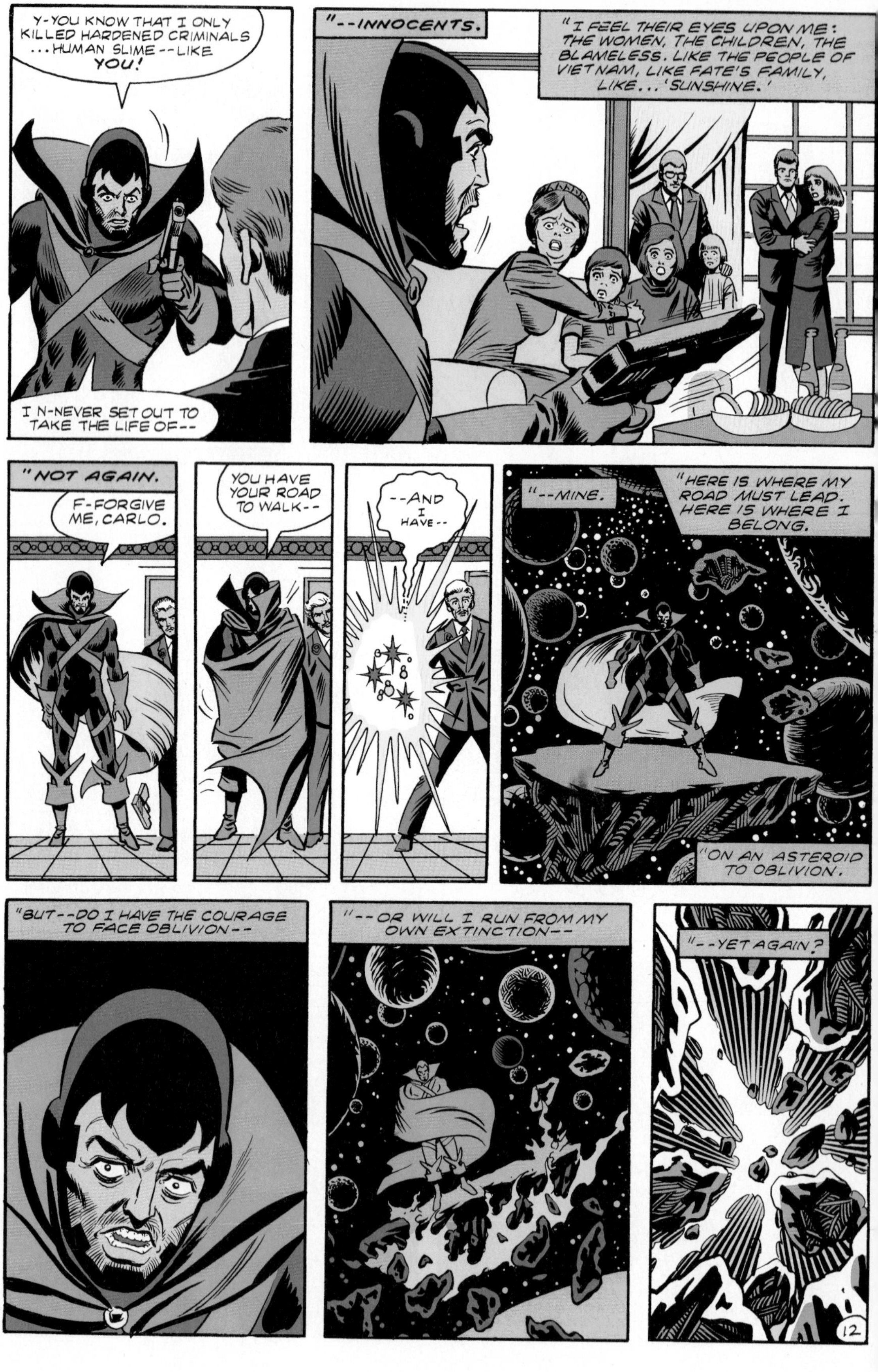
Y-YOU KNOW THAT I ONLY KILLED HARDENED CRIMINALS ...HUMAN SLIME--LIKE YOU!
I N-NEVER SET OUT TO TAKE THE LIFE OF--
"--INNOCENTS.
"I FEEL THEIR EYES UPON ME: THE WOMEN, THE CHILDREN, THE BLAMELESS. LIKE THE PEOPLE OF VIETNAM, LIKE FATE'S FAMILY, LIKE...'SUNSHINE.'
"NOT AGAIN.
F-FORGIVE ME, CARLO.
YOU HAVE YOUR ROAD TO WALK--
--AND I HAVE--
"--MINE.
"HERE IS WHERE MY ROAD MUST LEAD. HERE IS WHERE I BELONG.
"ON AN ASTEROID TO OBLIVION.
"BUT--DO I HAVE THE COURAGE TO FACE OBLIVION--
"--OR WILL I RUN FROM MY OWN EXTINCTION--
"--YET AGAIN?
12

INTERLUDE TWO:

WASHINGTON D.C. ON A CLEAR SPRING AFTERNOON.

THE PRESIDENTIAL MOTORCADE MAKES ITS WAY DOWN PENNSYLVANIA AVENUE-- BUT THE CROWDS ARE SPARSE.

THERE IS TENSION IN THE AIR --THICK AS SMOKE-- AND A BRIGHT FEAR THAT SHINES IN EVERY EYE.

THAT FEAR IS DIRECTED TOWARD THE OCCUPANT OF ONE LIMOUSINE IN PARTICULAR...

...TOWARD THE MAN WHOSE FACE IS HIDDEN BEHIND THE TINTED, BULLET-PROOF GLASS...

...TOWARD THE PRESIDENT OF THE UNITED STATES...

...KYLE RICHMOND?!

INTERLUDE TWO ENDS.

"MY HUNGER HAS BE-COME RAVENOUS. HOW LONG HAS IT BEEN SINCE I'VE LAST EATEN? I DON'T KNOW. AND I DON'T CARE. WHY SHOULD I CARE? BETTER STILL--

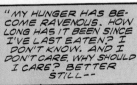

"--WHY HAVE I COME HERE?

"QUEENSTOWN, ILLINOIS IS THE TOWN THAT BIRTHED ME. THE PLACE WHERE MY FATHER DRANK AND GAVE SUF-FERING AND MY MOTHER PRAYED AND SUFFERED.

"WHERE I SOUGHT SALVATION IN ENTHRALLING BOOKS AND MINDLESS VIOLENCE, IN PRETTY GIRLS AND PETTY CRIMES.

"AND, OCCASIONALLY, IN THE SIMPLE PLEASURES OF FRIEND-SHIP...

...I'LL BE DONE IN JUST A MINUTE, PAL!

WELL HURRY IT UP, DAD! I WANNA BEAT THE PANTS OFF YOU IN A GOOD GAME OF ONE-ON-ONE!

13

17

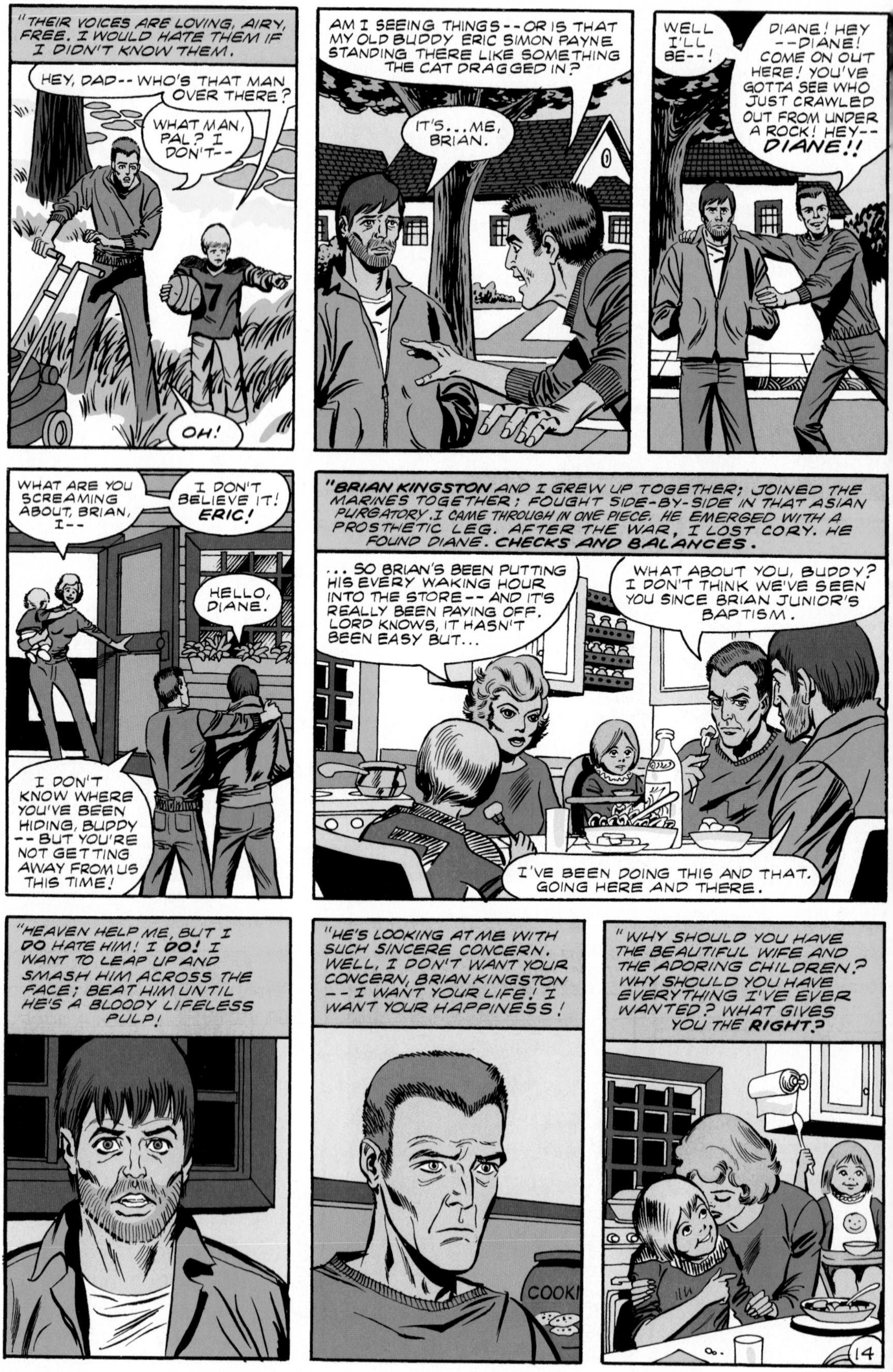
"THEIR VOICES ARE LOVING, AIRY, FREE. I WOULD HATE THEM IF I DIDN'T KNOW THEM.
HEY, DAD-- WHO'S THAT MAN OVER THERE?
WHAT MAN, PAL? I DON'T--
OH!
AM I SEEING THINGS--OR IS THAT MY OLD BUDDY ERIC SIMON PAYNE STANDING THERE LIKE SOMETHING THE CAT DRAGGED IN?
IT'S...ME, BRIAN.
WELL I'LL BE--!
DIANE! HEY --DIANE! COME ON OUT HERE! YOU'VE GOTTA SEE WHO JUST CRAWLED OUT FROM UNDER A ROCK! HEY-- DIANE!!
WHAT ARE YOU SCREAMING ABOUT, BRIAN, I--
I DON'T BELIEVE IT! ERIC!
HELLO, DIANE.
I DON'T KNOW WHERE YOU'VE BEEN HIDING, BUDDY --BUT YOU'RE NOT GETTING AWAY FROM US THIS TIME!
"BRIAN KINGSTON AND I GREW UP TOGETHER; JOINED THE MARINES TOGETHER; FOUGHT SIDE-BY-SIDE IN THAT ASIAN PURGATORY. I CAME THROUGH IN ONE PIECE. HE EMERGED WITH A PROSTHETIC LEG. AFTER THE WAR, I LOST CORY. HE FOUND DIANE. CHECKS AND BALANCES.
...SO BRIAN'S BEEN PUTTING HIS EVERY WAKING HOUR INTO THE STORE--AND IT'S REALLY BEEN PAYING OFF. LORD KNOWS, IT HASN'T BEEN EASY BUT...
WHAT ABOUT YOU, BUDDY? I DON'T THINK WE'VE SEEN YOU SINCE BRIAN JUNIOR'S BAPTISM.
I'VE BEEN DOING THIS AND THAT. GOING HERE AND THERE.
"HEAVEN HELP ME, BUT I DO HATE HIM! I DO! I WANT TO LEAP UP AND SMASH HIM ACROSS THE FACE; BEAT HIM UNTIL HE'S A BLOODY LIFELESS PULP!
"HE'S LOOKING AT ME WITH SUCH SINCERE CONCERN. WELL, I DON'T WANT YOUR CONCERN, BRIAN KINGSTON --I WANT YOUR LIFE! I WANT YOUR HAPPINESS!
COOKI
"WHY SHOULD YOU HAVE THE BEAUTIFUL WIFE AND THE ADORING CHILDREN? WHY SHOULD YOU HAVE EVERYTHING I'VE EVER WANTED? WHAT GIVES YOU THE RIGHT?
14

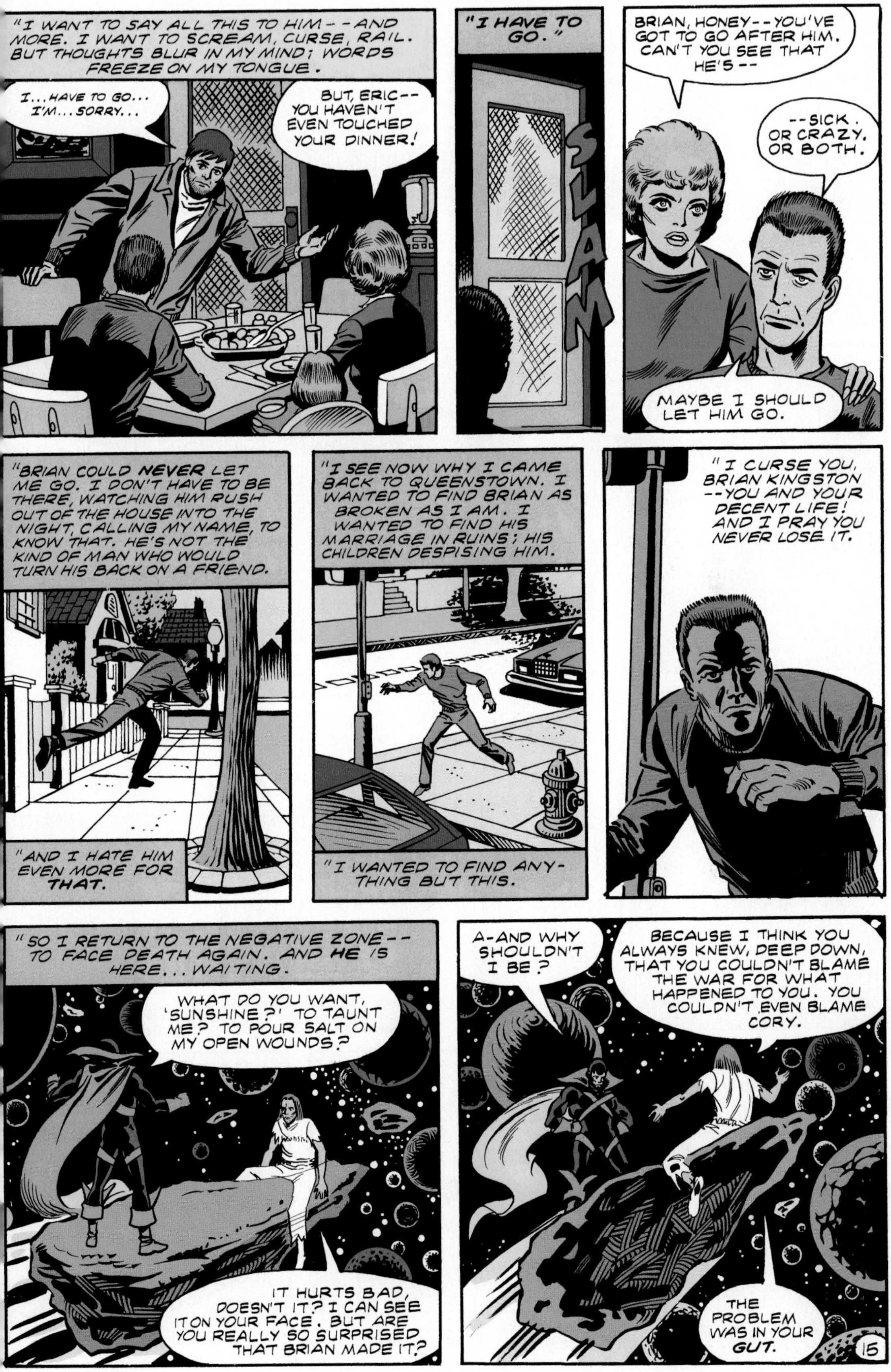
"I WANT TO SAY ALL THIS TO HIM--AND MORE. I WANT TO SCREAM, CURSE, RAIL. BUT THOUGHTS BLUR IN MY MIND; WORDS FREEZE ON MY TONGUE.
I...HAVE TO GO... I'M...SORRY...
BUT, ERIC-- YOU HAVEN'T EVEN TOUCHED YOUR DINNER!
"I HAVE TO GO."
SLAM
BRIAN, HONEY--YOU'VE GOT TO GO AFTER HIM. CAN'T YOU SEE THAT HE'S --
--SICK. OR CRAZY. OR BOTH.
MAYBE I SHOULD LET HIM GO.
"BRIAN COULD NEVER LET ME GO. I DON'T HAVE TO BE THERE, WATCHING HIM RUSH OUT OF THE HOUSE INTO THE NIGHT, CALLING MY NAME, TO KNOW THAT. HE'S NOT THE KIND OF MAN WHO WOULD TURN HIS BACK ON A FRIEND.
"AND I HATE HIM EVEN MORE FOR THAT.
"I SEE NOW WHY I CAME BACK TO QUEENSTOWN. I WANTED TO FIND BRIAN AS BROKEN AS I AM. I WANTED TO FIND HIS MARRIAGE IN RUINS; HIS CHILDREN DESPISING HIM.
"I WANTED TO FIND ANYTHING BUT THIS.
"I CURSE YOU, BRIAN KINGSTON --YOU AND YOUR DECENT LIFE! AND I PRAY YOU NEVER LOSE IT.
"SO I RETURN TO THE NEGATIVE ZONE-- TO FACE DEATH AGAIN. AND HE IS HERE...WAITING.
WHAT DO YOU WANT, 'SUNSHINE?' TO TAUNT ME? TO POUR SALT ON MY OPEN WOUNDS?
IT HURTS BAD, DOESN'T IT? I CAN SEE IT ON YOUR FACE. BUT ARE YOU REALLY SO SURPRISED THAT BRIAN MADE IT?
A-AND WHY SHOULDN'T I BE?
BECAUSE I THINK YOU ALWAYS KNEW, DEEP DOWN, THAT YOU COULDN'T BLAME THE WAR FOR WHAT HAPPENED TO YOU. YOU COULDN'T EVEN BLAME CORY.
THE PROBLEM WAS IN YOUR GUT.
15

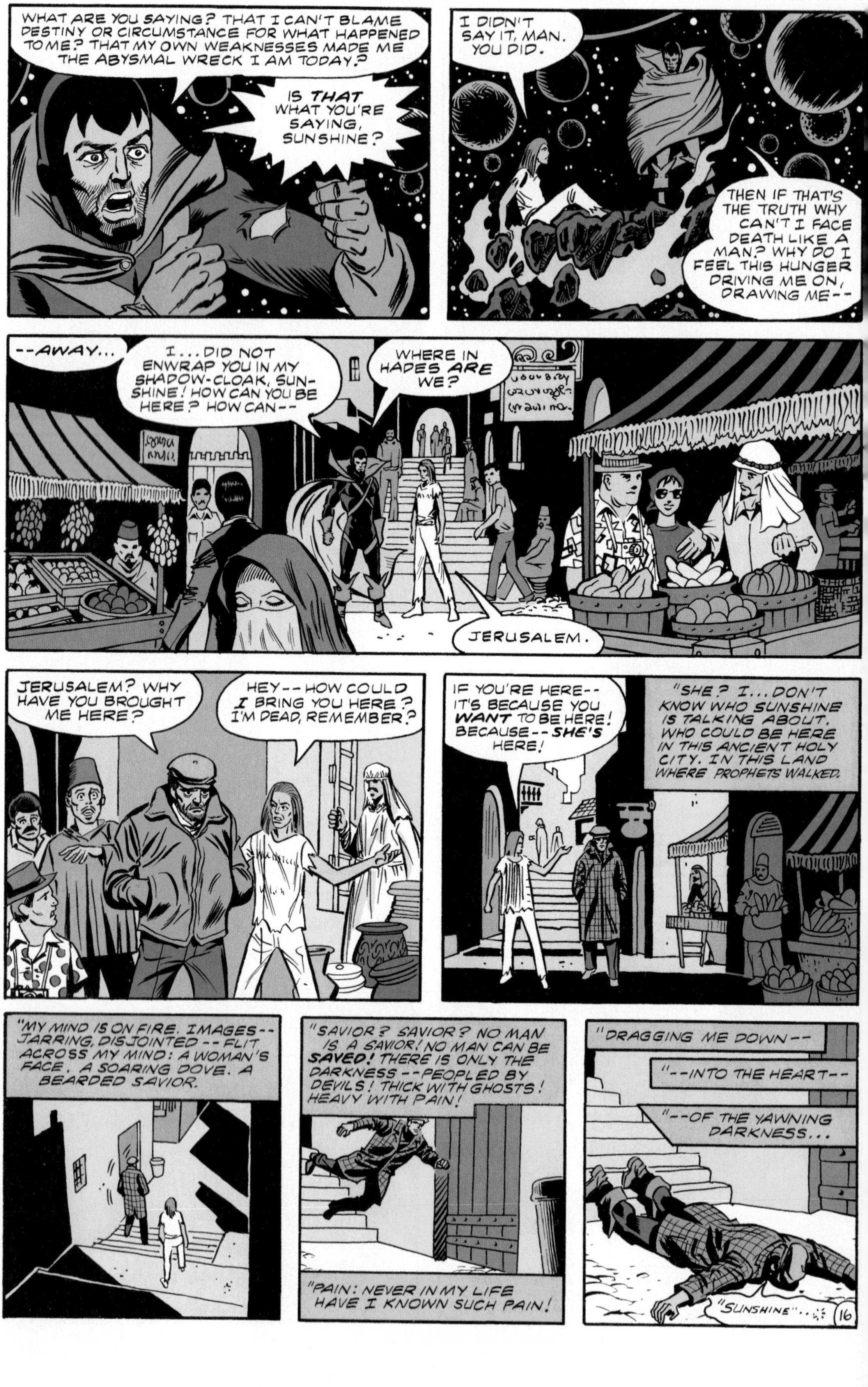
WHAT ARE YOU SAYING? THAT I CAN'T BLAME DESTINY OR CIRCUMSTANCE FOR WHAT HAPPENED TO ME? THAT MY OWN WEAKNESSES MADE ME THE ABYSMAL WRECK I AM TODAY?
IS THAT WHAT YOU'RE SAYING, SUNSHINE?
I DIDN'T SAY IT, MAN. YOU DID.
THEN IF THAT'S THE TRUTH WHY CAN'T I FACE DEATH LIKE A MAN? WHY DO I FEEL THIS HUNGER DRIVING ME ON, DRAWING ME--
--AWAY...
I...DID NOT ENWRAP YOU IN MY SHADOW-CLOAK, SUNSHINE! HOW CAN YOU BE HERE? HOW CAN--
WHERE IN HADES ARE WE?
JERUSALEM.
JERUSALEM? WHY HAVE YOU BROUGHT ME HERE?
HEY--HOW COULD I BRING YOU HERE? I'M DEAD, REMEMBER?
IF YOU'RE HERE--IT'S BECAUSE YOU WANT TO BE HERE! BECAUSE--SHE'S HERE!
"SHE? I...DON'T KNOW WHO SUNSHINE IS TALKING ABOUT. WHO COULD BE HERE IN THIS ANCIENT HOLY CITY. IN THIS LAND WHERE PROPHETS WALKED.
"MY MIND IS ON FIRE. IMAGES--JARRING, DISJOINTED--FLIT ACROSS MY MIND: A WOMAN'S FACE. A SOARING DOVE. A BEARDED SAVIOR.
"SAVIOR? SAVIOR? NO MAN IS A SAVIOR! NO MAN CAN BE SAVED! THERE IS ONLY THE DARKNESS--PEOPLED BY DEVILS! THICK WITH GHOSTS! HEAVY WITH PAIN!
"PAIN: NEVER IN MY LIFE HAVE I KNOWN SUCH PAIN!
"DRAGGING ME DOWN--
"--INTO THE HEART--
"--OF THE YAWNING DARKNESS...
"SUNSHINE"...
16

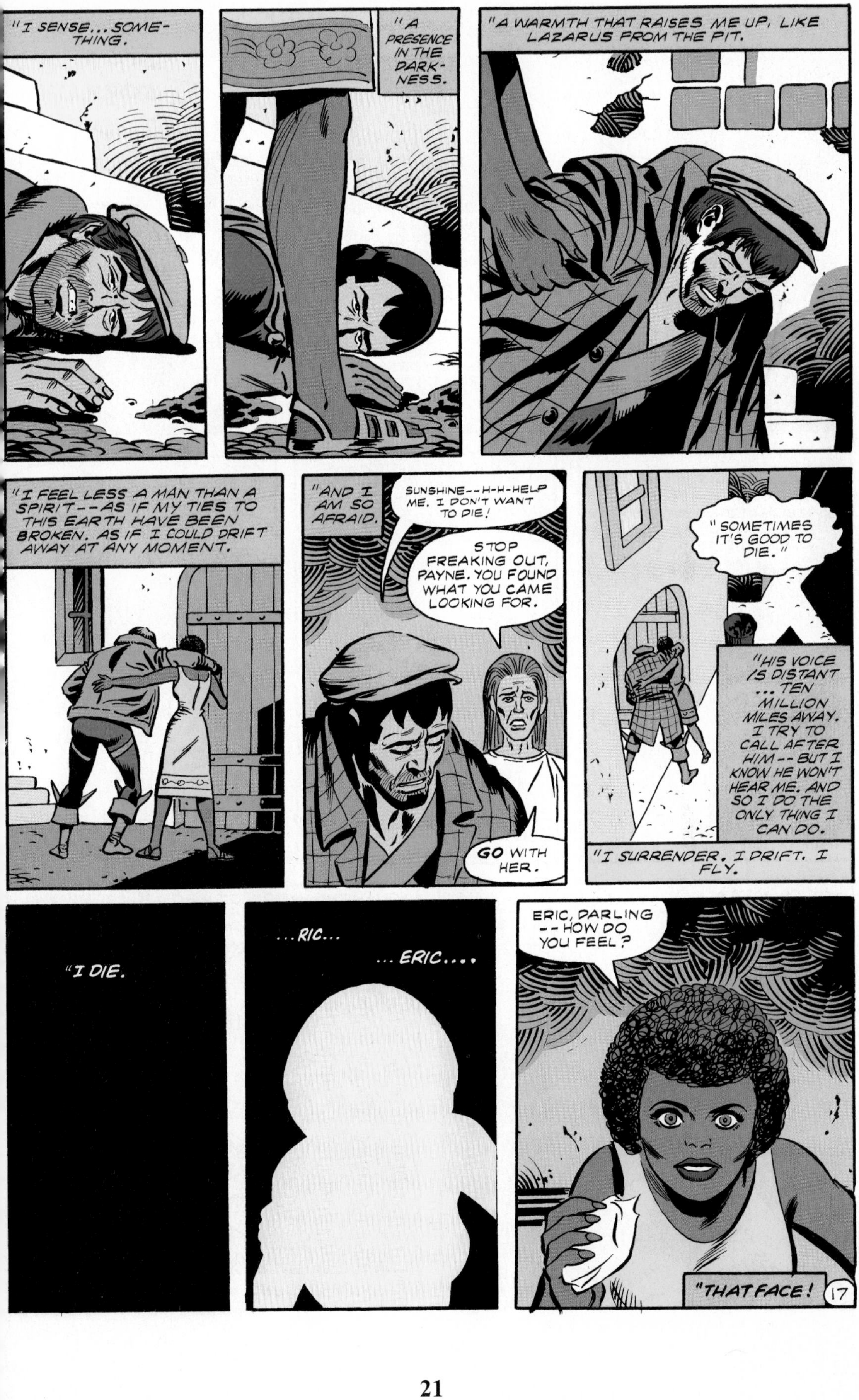
"I SENSE... SOMETHING.
"A PRESENCE IN THE DARKNESS.
"A WARMTH THAT RAISES ME UP, LIKE LAZARUS FROM THE PIT.
"I FEEL LESS A MAN THAN A SPIRIT--AS IF MY TIES TO THIS EARTH HAVE BEEN BROKEN. AS IF I COULD DRIFT AWAY AT ANY MOMENT.
"AND I AM SO AFRAID.
SUNSHINE--H-H-HELP ME. I DON'T WANT TO DIE!
STOP FREAKING OUT, PAYNE. YOU FOUND WHAT YOU CAME LOOKING FOR.
GO WITH HER.
"SOMETIMES IT'S GOOD TO DIE."
"HIS VOICE IS DISTANT ...TEN MILLION MILES AWAY. I TRY TO CALL AFTER HIM--BUT I KNOW HE WON'T HEAR ME. AND SO I DO THE ONLY THING I CAN DO.
"I SURRENDER. I DRIFT. I FLY.
"I DIE.
...RIC...
...ERIC....
ERIC, DARLING --HOW DO YOU FEEL?
"THAT FACE!
17

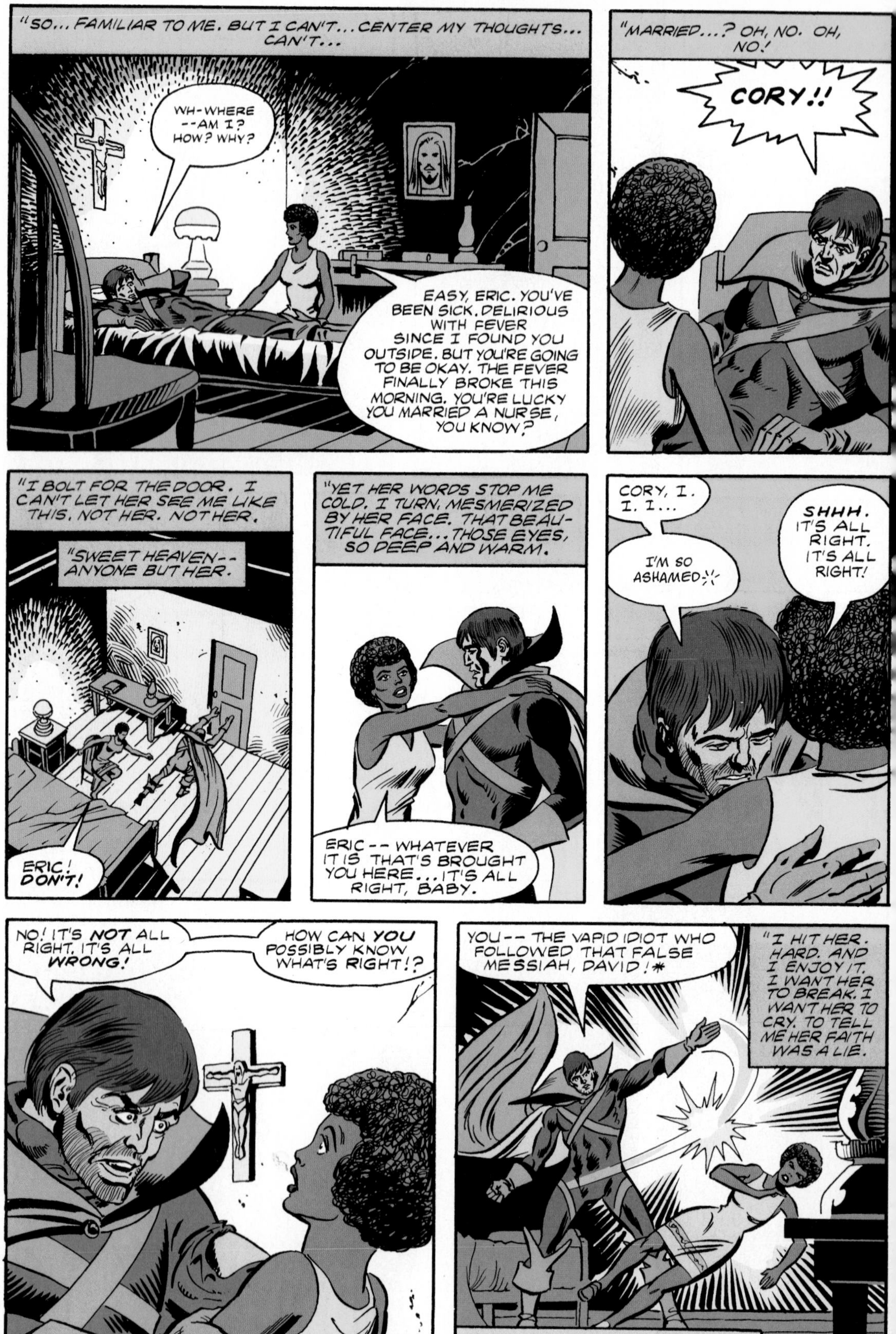
"SO... FAMILIAR TO ME. BUT I CAN'T... CENTER MY THOUGHTS... CAN'T...
WH-WHERE --AM I? HOW? WHY?
EASY, ERIC. YOU'VE BEEN SICK, DELIRIOUS WITH FEVER SINCE I FOUND YOU OUTSIDE. BUT YOU'RE GOING TO BE OKAY. THE FEVER FINALLY BROKE THIS MORNING. YOU'RE LUCKY YOU MARRIED A NURSE, YOU KNOW?
"MARRIED...? OH, NO. OH, NO!
CORY!!
"I BOLT FOR THE DOOR. I CAN'T LET HER SEE ME LIKE THIS. NOT HER. NOT HER.
"SWEET HEAVEN-- ANYONE BUT HER.
ERIC! DON'T!
"YET HER WORDS STOP ME COLD. I TURN, MESMERIZED BY HER FACE. THAT BEAUTIFUL FACE... THOSE EYES, SO DEEP AND WARM.
ERIC -- WHATEVER IT IS THAT'S BROUGHT YOU HERE... IT'S ALL RIGHT, BABY.
CORY, I. I. I...
I'M SO ASHAMED!
SHHH. IT'S ALL RIGHT. IT'S ALL RIGHT!
NO! IT'S NOT ALL RIGHT. IT'S ALL WRONG!
HOW CAN YOU POSSIBLY KNOW WHAT'S RIGHT!?
YOU -- THE VAPID IDIOT WHO FOLLOWED THAT FALSE MESSIAH, DAVID!*
"I HIT HER. HARD. AND I ENJOY IT. I WANT HER TO BREAK. I WANT HER TO CRY. TO TELL ME HER FAITH WAS A LIE.
*SEE DEFENDERS #97 -- AL.
18

"BUT SHE WON'T.

THAT'S TRUE, ERIC. DAVID *WAS* A FALSE MESSIAH. I *WAS*... MISLED.

BUT THAT DOESN'T CHANGE THE FACT THAT WHAT DAVID *STOOD FOR* WAS REAL--

--THAT ALL THE HOPES, PRAYERS, AND PRECIOUS DREAMS WERE *REAL!*

I STAYED A WHILE WITH THE FEW OF DAVID'S FOLLOWERS THAT REMAINED-- THEN I KNEW I HAD TO LEAVE. I REALIZED THAT I WAS HERE IN THIS HOLIEST OF LANDS--

--AND THAT, IF I COULDN'T FIND THE ESSENCE, THE CORE BEHIND ALL THE RELIGIOUS FACADES *HERE*-- I'D NEVER FIND IT ANYWHERE!

AND I *DID* FIND IT HERE, ERIC. I FOUND SOMETHING IN MY OWN HEART: A FAITH IN SOMETHING BIGGER. NO, MORE THAN A FAITH-- A *PROOF*.

A PROOF THAT'S RENEWED WITH EVERY DAWN-- WITH EVERY BREATH I TAKE...

"HER WORDS ARE SO CLEAR, SO CERTAIN, THAT THEY CALM MY OWN MAUNDERING THOUGHTS. I SEE WITH EQUAL CLARITY; SPEAK WITH EQUAL CERTAINTY.

CORY-- DON'T YOU THINK I WOULD LIKE TO BELIEVE THAT THERE IS A BENIFICENT DEITY WHO'S WILLING TO FORGIVE ME FOR MY SINS? BUT I *CAN'T!*

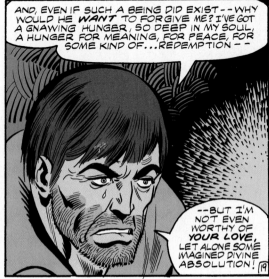

AND, EVEN IF SUCH A BEING DID EXIST--WHY WOULD HE *WANT* TO FORGIVE ME? I'VE GOT A GNAWING HUNGER, SO DEEP IN MY SOUL, A HUNGER FOR MEANING, FOR PEACE, FOR SOME KIND OF...REDEMPTION--

--BUT I'M NOT EVEN WORTHY OF *YOUR LOVE*, LET ALONE SOME IMAGINED DIVINE ABSOLUTION!

19

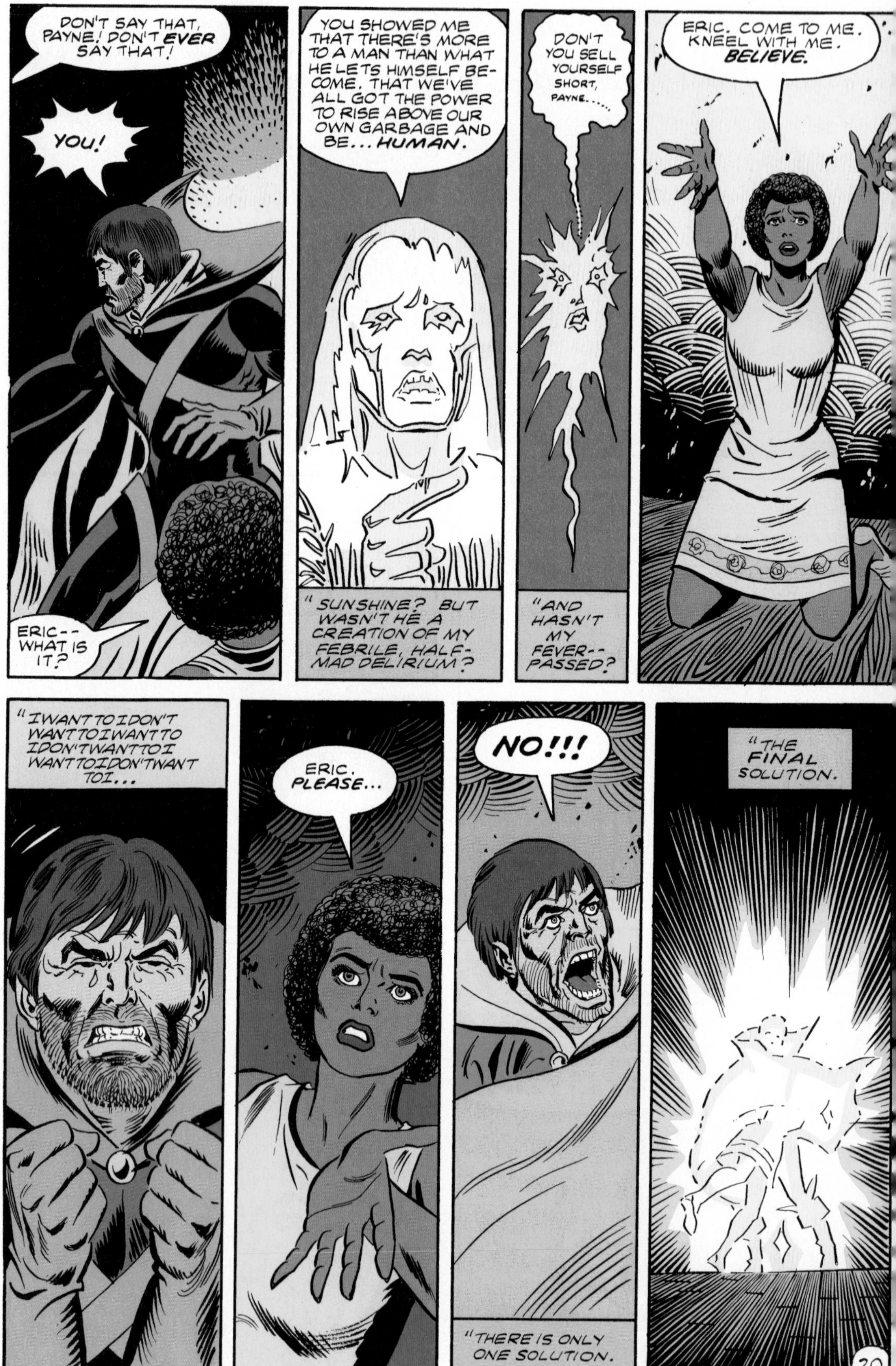
DON'T SAY THAT, PAYNE! DON'T EVER SAY THAT!
YOU!
ERIC-- WHAT IS IT?
YOU SHOWED ME THAT THERE'S MORE TO A MAN THAN WHAT HE LETS HIMSELF BE-COME. THAT WE'VE ALL GOT THE POWER TO RISE ABOVE OUR OWN GARBAGE AND BE... HUMAN.
"SUNSHINE? BUT WASN'T HE A CREATION OF MY FEBRILE, HALF-MAD DELIRIUM?
DON'T YOU SELL YOURSELF SHORT, PAYNE.....
"AND HASN'T MY FEVER--PASSED?
ERIC. COME TO ME. KNEEL WITH ME. BELIEVE.
"IWANTTOIDON'T WANTTOIWANTTO IDON'TWANTTOI WANTTOIDON'TWANT TOI...
ERIC. PLEASE...
NO!!!
"THERE IS ONLY ONE SOLUTION.
"THE FINAL SOLUTION.
20

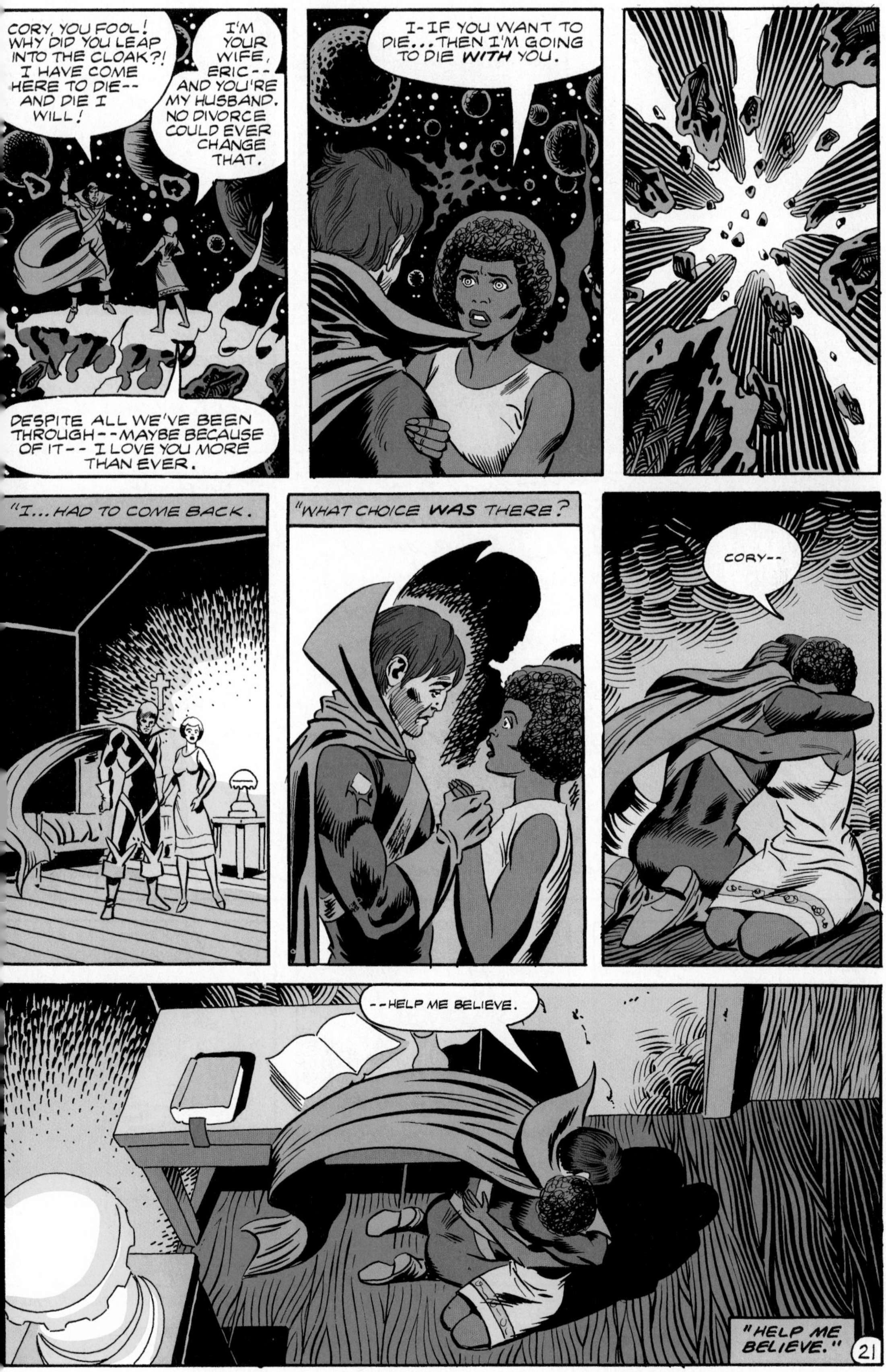
CORY, YOU FOOL! WHY DID YOU LEAP INTO THE CLOAK?! I HAVE COME HERE TO DIE-- AND DIE I WILL!
I'M YOUR WIFE, ERIC-- AND YOU'RE MY HUSBAND. NO DIVORCE COULD EVER CHANGE THAT.
DESPITE ALL WE'VE BEEN THROUGH--MAYBE BECAUSE OF IT-- I LOVE YOU MORE THAN EVER.
I-IF YOU WANT TO DIE... THEN I'M GOING TO DIE WITH YOU.
"I... HAD TO COME BACK.
"WHAT CHOICE WAS THERE?
CORY--
--HELP ME BELIEVE.
"HELP ME BELIEVE."
21

EPILOGUE:
FOUR MONTHS LATER...

Dear Doctor Strange...

It's been hard for us since that night in Jerusalem; that night that seems like centuries ago.

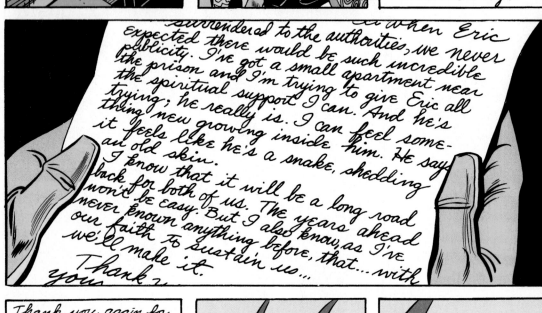

...when Eric surrendered to the authorities, we never expected there would be such incredible publicity. I've got a small apartment near the prison and I'm trying to give Eric all the spiritual support I can. And he's trying; he really is. I can feel something new growing inside him. He says it feels like he's a snake, shedding an old skin.

I know that it will be a long road back for both of us. The years ahead won't be easy. But I also know, as I've never known anything before, that...with our faith to sustain us... we'll make it.

Thank y...
yours

Thank you again for your kindness and concern. Sincerely, Cory Payne

Next HELLCAT GOES IT ALONE AS HER SEARCH FOR THE TRUTH ABOUT HER HERITAGE COMES TO AN END. DON'T MISS...
"FATHERS AND DAUGHTERS!"

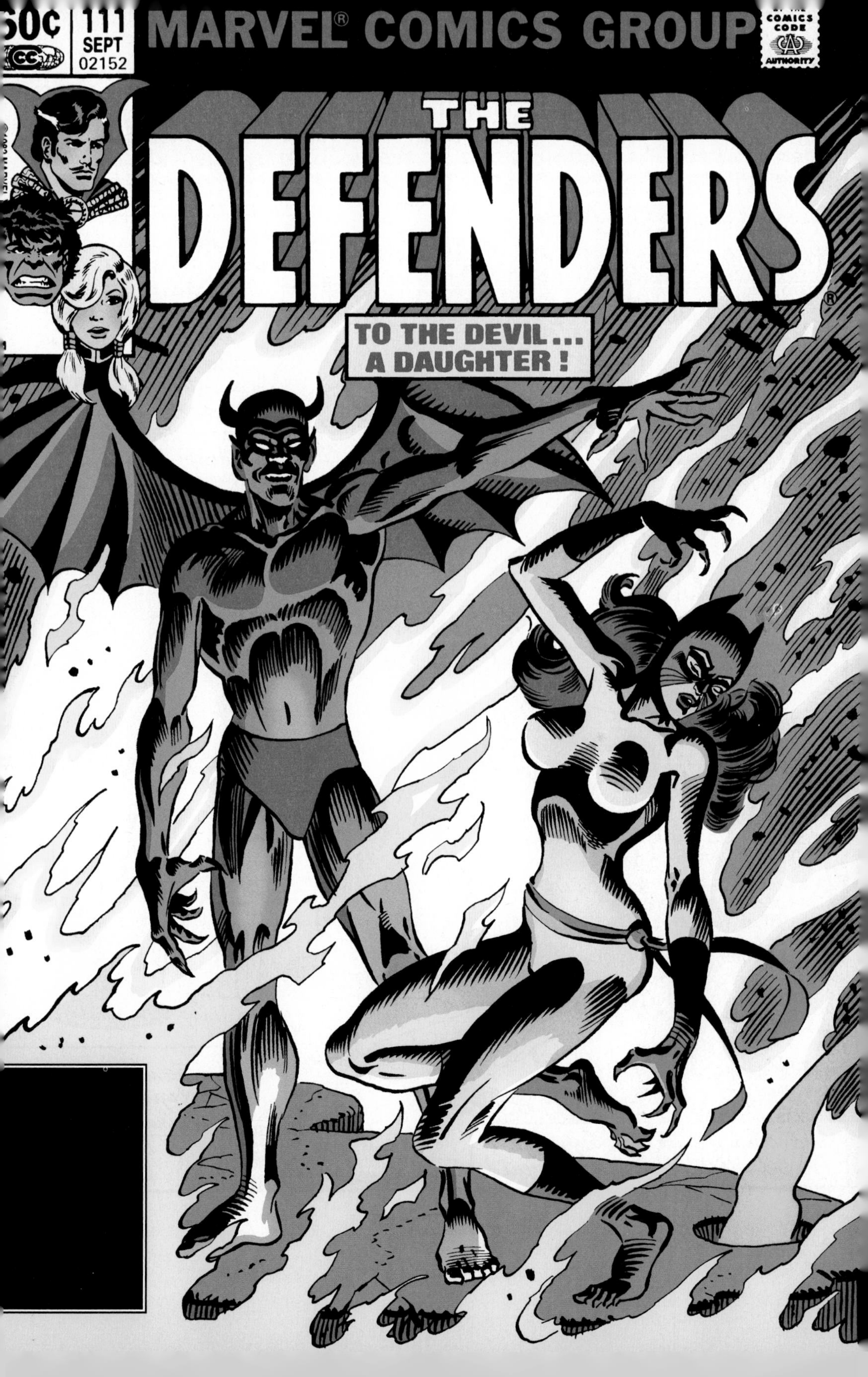
60¢
111
SEPT
02152
MARVEL® COMICS GROUP
COMICS CODE
AUTHORITY
THE DEFENDERS®
TO THE DEVIL... A DAUGHTER!

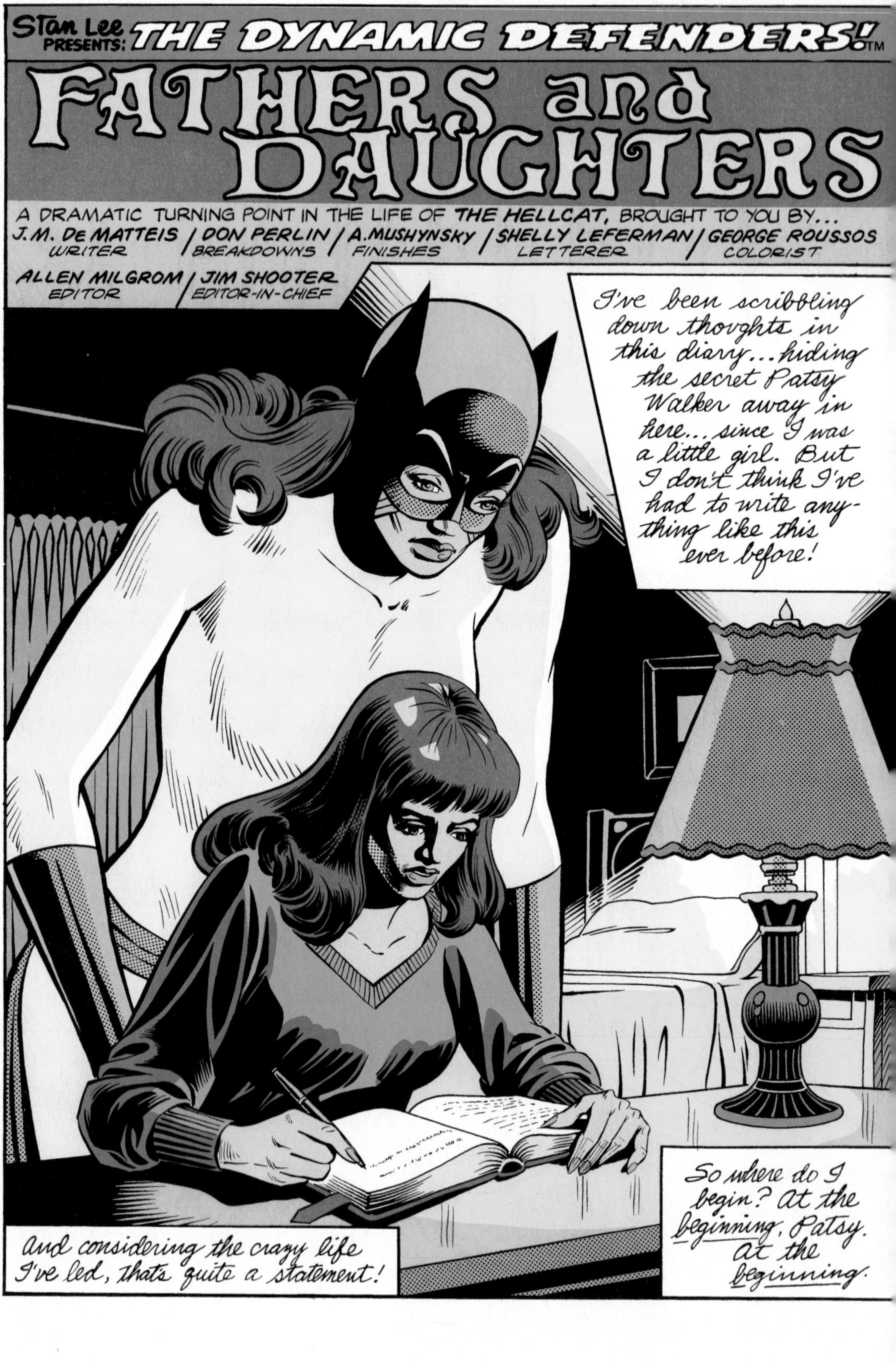

Stan Lee PRESENTS: THE DYNAMIC DEFENDERS!™
FATHERS and DAUGHTERS
A DRAMATIC TURNING POINT IN THE LIFE OF THE HELLCAT, BROUGHT TO YOU BY...
J.M. DeMATTEIS WRITER / DON PERLIN BREAKDOWNS / A. MUSHYNSKY FINISHES / SHELLY LEFERMAN LETTERER / GEORGE ROUSSOS COLORIST
ALLEN MILGROM EDITOR / JIM SHOOTER EDITOR-IN-CHIEF
I've been scribbling down thoughts in this diary... hiding the secret Patsy Walker away in here... since I was a little girl. But I don't think I've had to write anything like this ever before!
And considering the crazy life I've led, that's quite a statement!
So where do I begin? At the beginning, Patsy. At the beginning.

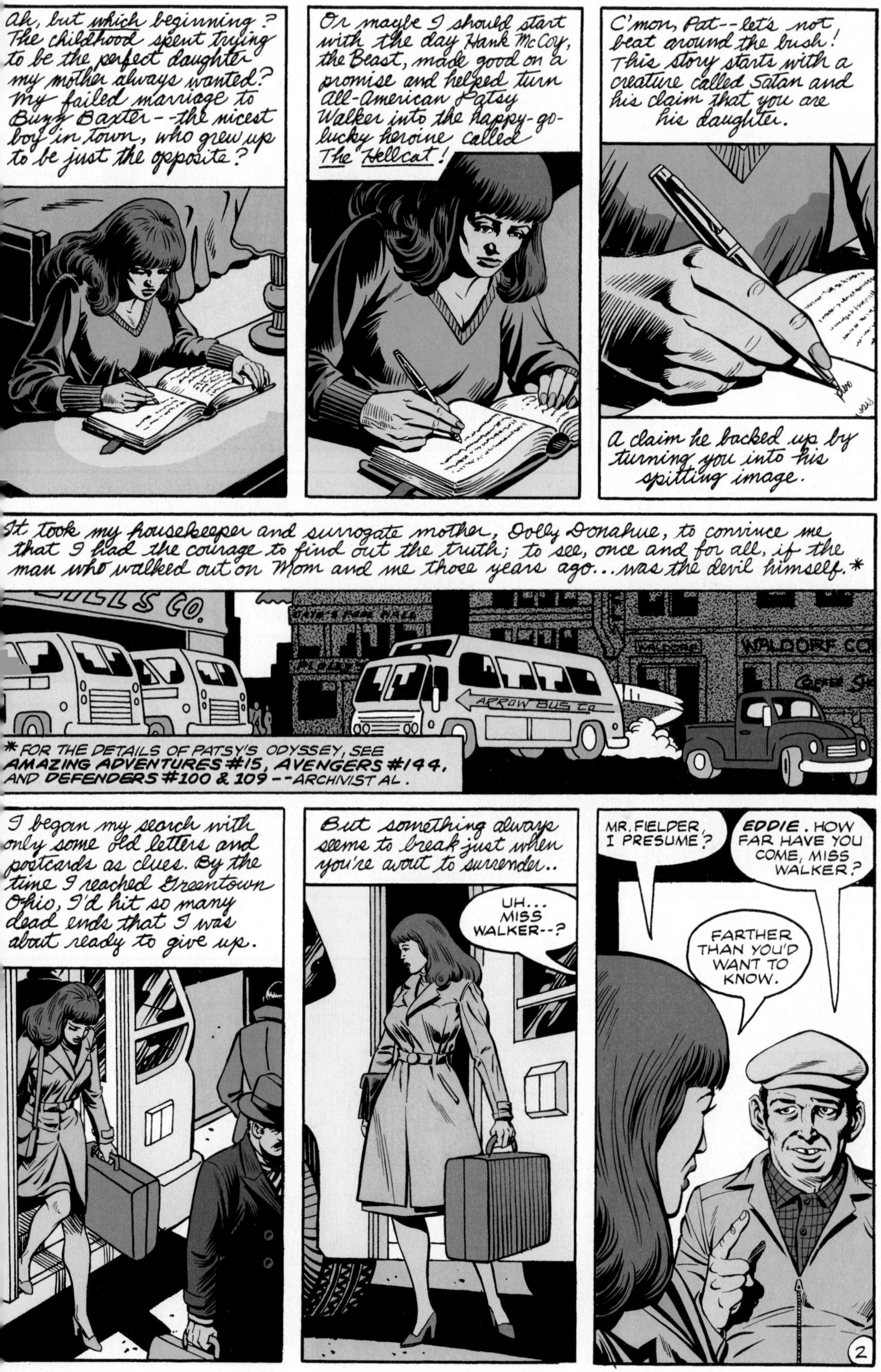
Ah, but which beginning? The childhood spent trying to be the perfect daughter my mother always wanted? My failed marriage to Buzz Baxter--the nicest boy in town, who grew up to be just the opposite?
Or maybe I should start with the day Hank McCoy, the Beast, made good on a promise and helped turn All-American Patsy Walker into the happy-go-lucky heroine called The Hellcat!
C'mon, Pat--let's not beat around the bush! This story starts with a creature called Satan and his claim that you are his daughter.
A claim he backed up by turning you into his spitting image.
It took my housekeeper and surrogate mother, Dolly Donahue, to convince me that I had the courage to find out the truth; to see, once and for all, if the man who walked out on Mom and me those years ago...was the devil himself.*
ARROW BUS CO.
WALDORF
*FOR THE DETAILS OF PATSY'S ODYSSEY, SEE AMAZING ADVENTURES #15, AVENGERS #144, AND DEFENDERS #100 & 109--ARCHIVIST AL.
I began my search with only some old letters and postcards as clues. By the time I reached Greentown Ohio, I'd hit so many dead ends that I was about ready to give up.
But something always seems to break just when you're about to surrender..
UH... MISS WALKER--?
MR. FIELDER, I PRESUME?
EDDIE. HOW FAR HAVE YOU COME, MISS WALKER?
FARTHER THAN YOU'D WANT TO KNOW.
2

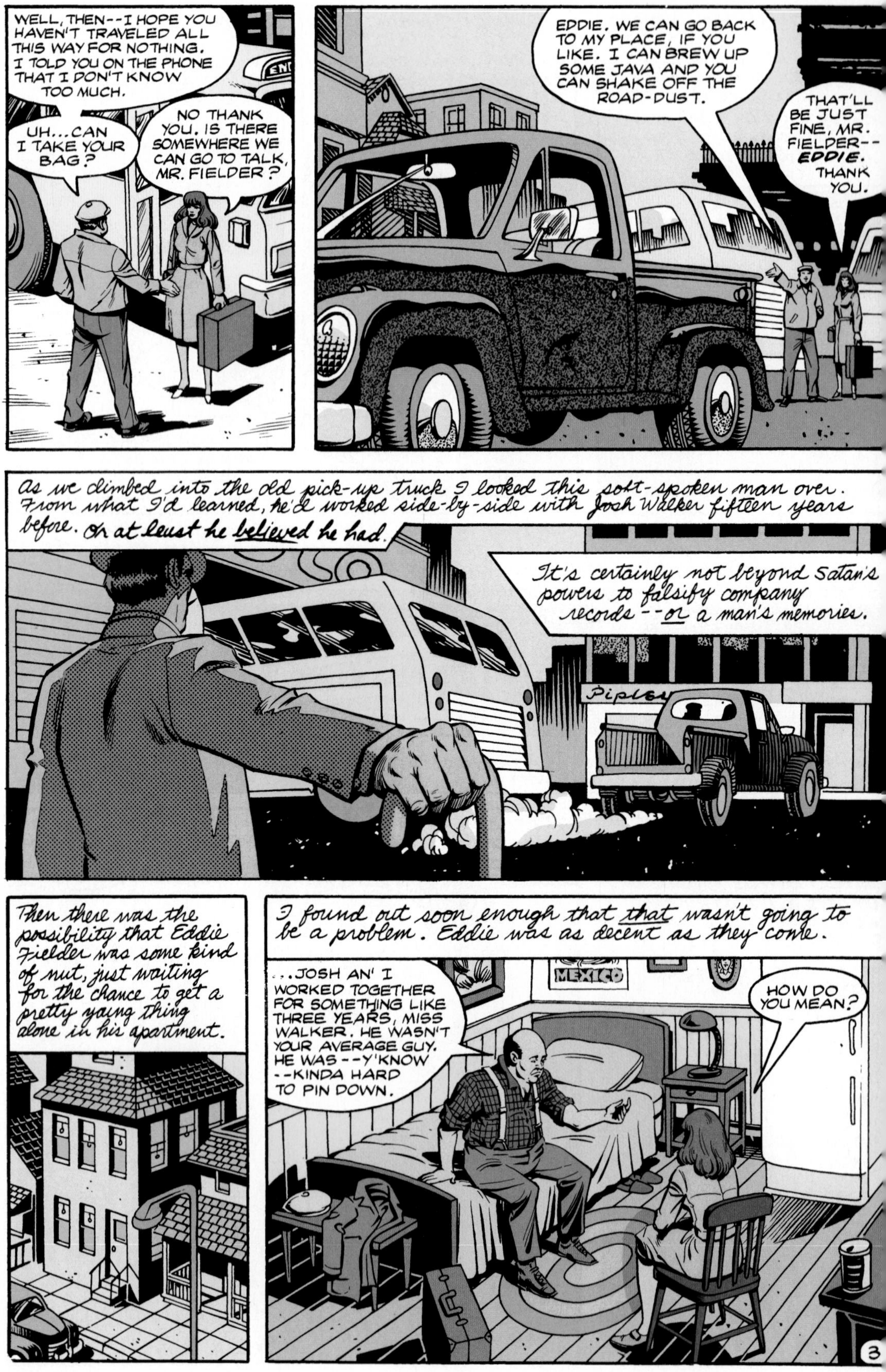
WELL, THEN--I HOPE YOU HAVEN'T TRAVELED ALL THIS WAY FOR NOTHING. I TOLD YOU ON THE PHONE THAT I DON'T KNOW TOO MUCH.
UH...CAN I TAKE YOUR BAG?
NO THANK YOU. IS THERE SOMEWHERE WE CAN GO TO TALK, MR. FIELDER?
EDDIE. WE CAN GO BACK TO MY PLACE, IF YOU LIKE. I CAN BREW UP SOME JAVA AND YOU CAN SHAKE OFF THE ROAD-DUST.
THAT'LL BE JUST FINE, MR. FIELDER--EDDIE. THANK YOU.
As we climbed into the old pick-up truck I looked this soft-spoken man over. From what I'd learned, he'd worked side-by-side with Josh Walker fifteen years before. Or at least he believed he had.
It's certainly not beyond Satan's powers to falsify company records--or a man's memories.
Then there was the possibility that Eddie Fielder was some kind of nut, just waiting for the chance to get a pretty young thing alone in his apartment.
I found out soon enough that that wasn't going to be a problem. Eddie was as decent as they come.
MEXICO
...JOSH AN' I WORKED TOGETHER FOR SOMETHING LIKE THREE YEARS, MISS WALKER. HE WASN'T YOUR AVERAGE GUY. HE WAS--Y'KNOW--KINDA HARD TO PIN DOWN.
HOW DO YOU MEAN?
3

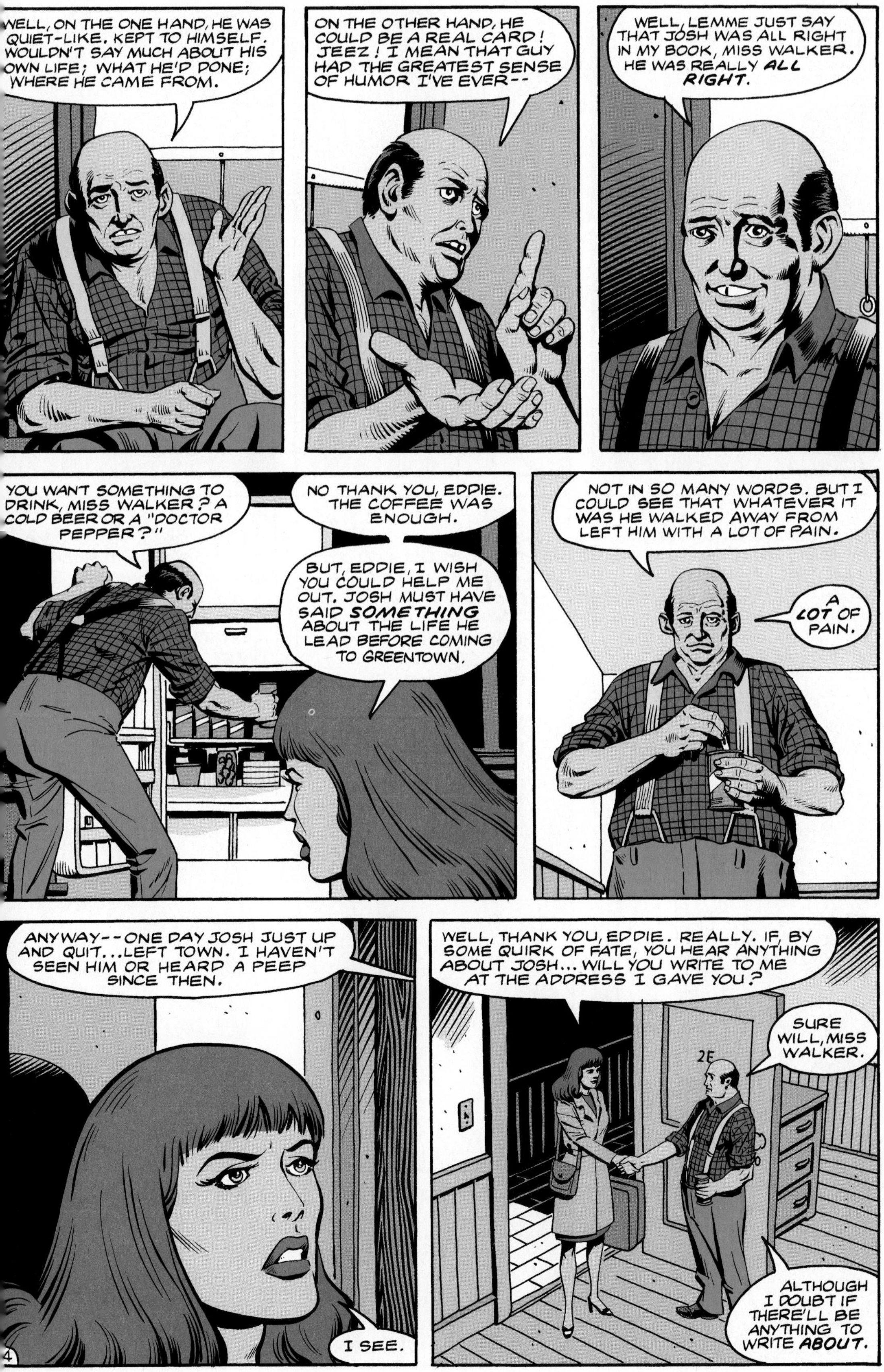
WELL, ON THE ONE HAND, HE WAS QUIET-LIKE. KEPT TO HIMSELF. WOULDN'T SAY MUCH ABOUT HIS OWN LIFE; WHAT HE'D DONE; WHERE HE CAME FROM.
ON THE OTHER HAND, HE COULD BE A REAL CARD! JEEZ! I MEAN THAT GUY HAD THE GREATEST SENSE OF HUMOR I'VE EVER--
WELL, LEMME JUST SAY THAT JOSH WAS ALL RIGHT IN MY BOOK, MISS WALKER. HE WAS REALLY ***ALL RIGHT***.
YOU WANT SOMETHING TO DRINK, MISS WALKER? A COLD BEER OR A "DOCTOR PEPPER?"
NO THANK YOU, EDDIE. THE COFFEE WAS ENOUGH.
BUT, EDDIE, I WISH YOU COULD HELP ME OUT. JOSH MUST HAVE SAID ***SOMETHING*** ABOUT THE LIFE HE LEAD BEFORE COMING TO GREENTOWN.
NOT IN SO MANY WORDS. BUT I COULD SEE THAT WHATEVER IT WAS HE WALKED AWAY FROM LEFT HIM WITH A LOT OF PAIN.
A ***LOT*** OF PAIN.
ANYWAY--ONE DAY JOSH JUST UP AND QUIT...LEFT TOWN. I HAVEN'T SEEN HIM OR HEARD A PEEP SINCE THEN.
I SEE.
WELL, THANK YOU, EDDIE. REALLY. IF, BY SOME QUIRK OF FATE, YOU HEAR ANYTHING ABOUT JOSH... WILL YOU WRITE TO ME AT THE ADDRESS I GAVE YOU?
2E
SURE WILL, MISS WALKER.
ALTHOUGH I DOUBT IF THERE'LL BE ANYTHING TO WRITE ***ABOUT***.

UH...ONE THING, MISS WALKER. YOU SAID ON THE PHONE THAT YOU WERE A RELATIVE OF JOSH'S. WHY IS IT YOU'RE SO DESPERATE TO FIND HIM?

IS THERE A SICKNESS IN THE FAMILY?

YOU COULD SAY THAT, EDDIE.

YOU COULD SAY THAT.

I was in a fog as I walked down those rickety old stairs and out into the gray streets of Greentown. Eddie Fielder's description of his co-worker fit in so well with my memories of my father; memories of a man who could be so, so serious-- and then break me up with his wild jokes. Mom always said I got my sense of humor from Dad.

But other memories kept cropping up as well. Memories of the web of deceit spun around the Defenders by Satan and the demons of the Six-Fingered Hand. A web of lies within lies... spun by the Lord of Lies.

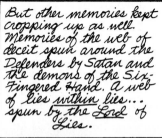

For all I knew, Eddie Fielder could have been one of Satan's demons, sent to trip me up. Sent to do...heaven-knows-what! Oh, I was paranoid. Paranoid to the nth degree. And I had darn good reason to be.

32

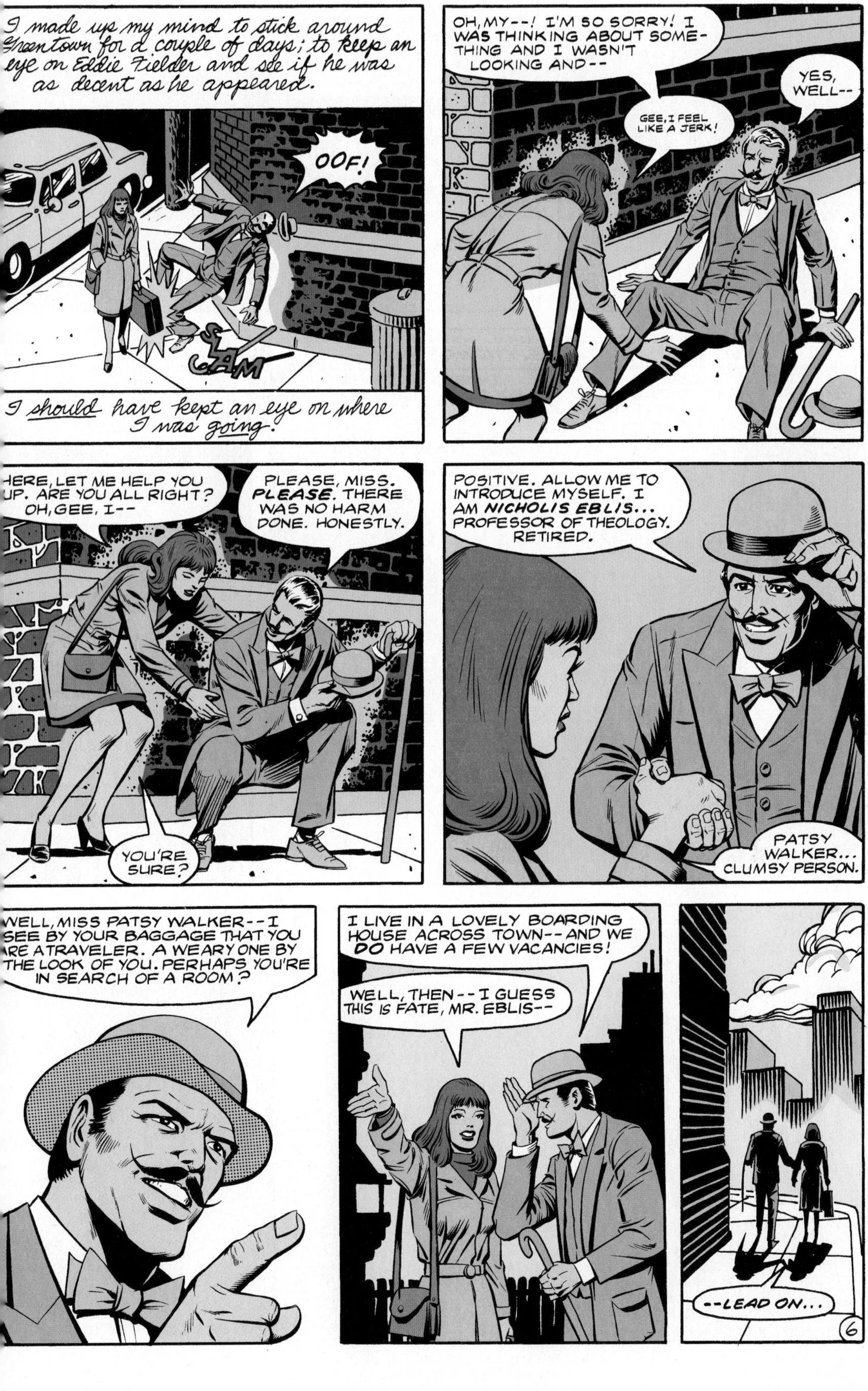
I made up my mind to stick around Greentown for a couple of days; to keep an eye on Eddie Fielder and see if he was as decent as he appeared.
OOF!
WHAM
I should have kept an eye on where I was going.
OH, MY--! I'M SO SORRY! I WAS THINKING ABOUT SOMETHING AND I WASN'T LOOKING AND--
YES, WELL--
GEE, I FEEL LIKE A JERK!
HERE, LET ME HELP YOU UP. ARE YOU ALL RIGHT? OH, GEE, I--
PLEASE, MISS. PLEASE. THERE WAS NO HARM DONE. HONESTLY.
YOU'RE SURE?
POSITIVE. ALLOW ME TO INTRODUCE MYSELF. I AM NICHOLIS EBLIS... PROFESSOR OF THEOLOGY. RETIRED.
PATSY WALKER... CLUMSY PERSON.
WELL, MISS PATSY WALKER--I SEE BY YOUR BAGGAGE THAT YOU ARE A TRAVELER. A WEARY ONE BY THE LOOK OF YOU. PERHAPS YOU'RE IN SEARCH OF A ROOM?
I LIVE IN A LOVELY BOARDING HOUSE ACROSS TOWN--AND WE DO HAVE A FEW VACANCIES!
WELL, THEN--I GUESS THIS IS FATE, MR. EBLIS--
--LEAD ON...
6

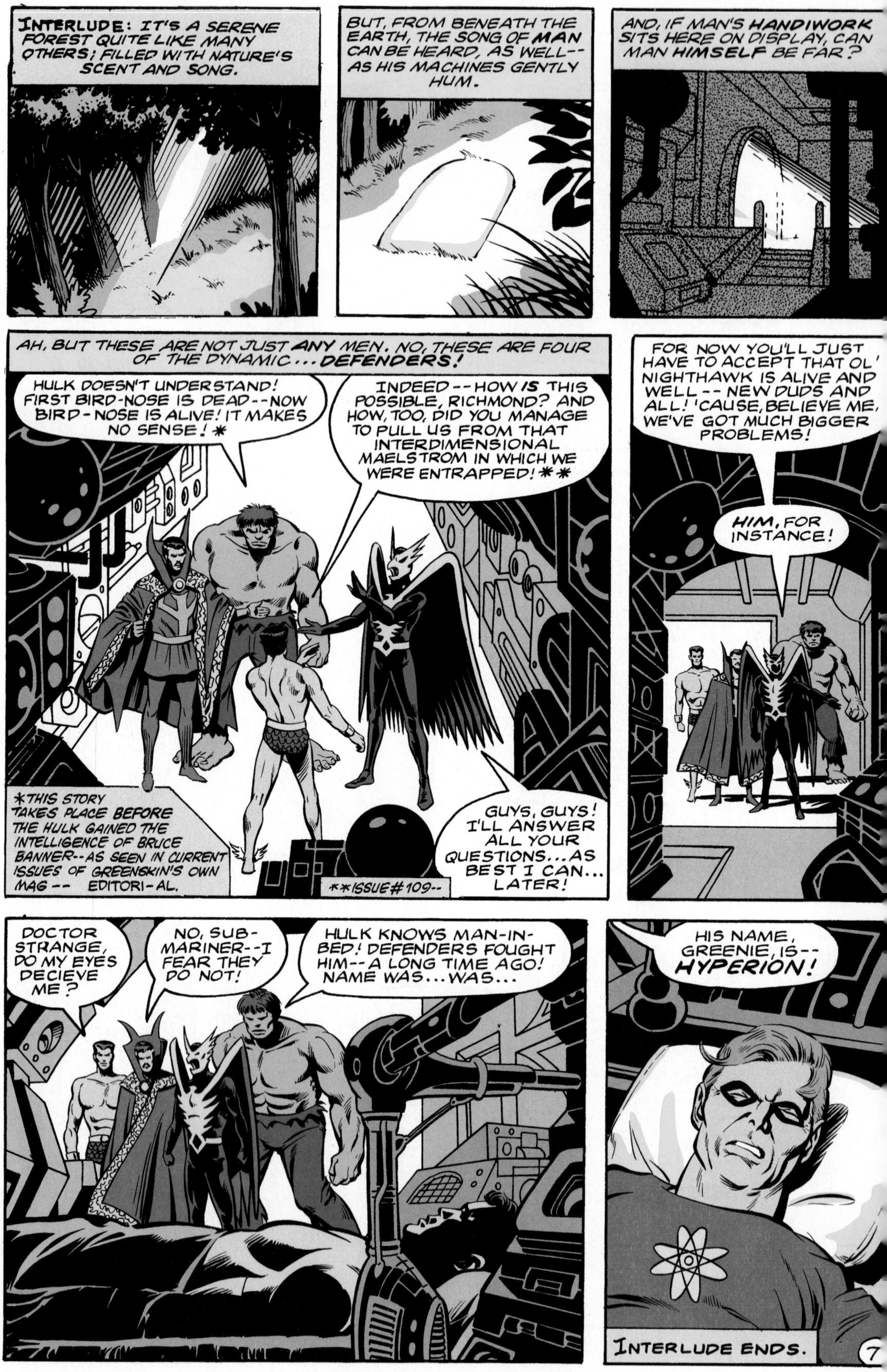
INTERLUDE: IT'S A SERENE FOREST QUITE LIKE MANY OTHERS; FILLED WITH NATURE'S SCENT AND SONG.
BUT, FROM BENEATH THE EARTH, THE SONG OF MAN CAN BE HEARD, AS WELL-- AS HIS MACHINES GENTLY HUM.
AND, IF MAN'S HANDIWORK SITS HERE ON DISPLAY, CAN MAN HIMSELF BE FAR?
AH, BUT THESE ARE NOT JUST ANY MEN. NO, THESE ARE FOUR OF THE DYNAMIC... DEFENDERS!
HULK DOESN'T UNDERSTAND! FIRST BIRD-NOSE IS DEAD--NOW BIRD-NOSE IS ALIVE! IT MAKES NO SENSE! *
INDEED--HOW IS THIS POSSIBLE, RICHMOND? AND HOW, TOO, DID YOU MANAGE TO PULL US FROM THAT INTERDIMENSIONAL MAELSTROM IN WHICH WE WERE ENTRAPPED! **
GUYS, GUYS! I'LL ANSWER ALL YOUR QUESTIONS... AS BEST I CAN... LATER!
*THIS STORY TAKES PLACE BEFORE THE HULK GAINED THE INTELLIGENCE OF BRUCE BANNER--AS SEEN IN CURRENT ISSUES OF GREENSKIN'S OWN MAG -- EDITORI-AL.
**ISSUE #109--
FOR NOW YOU'LL JUST HAVE TO ACCEPT THAT OL' NIGHTHAWK IS ALIVE AND WELL -- NEW DUDS AND ALL! 'CAUSE, BELIEVE ME, WE'VE GOT MUCH BIGGER PROBLEMS!
HIM, FOR INSTANCE!
DOCTOR STRANGE, DO MY EYES DECIEVE ME?
NO, SUB-MARINER--I FEAR THEY DO NOT!
HULK KNOWS MAN-IN-BED! DEFENDERS FOUGHT HIM--A LONG TIME AGO! NAME WAS... WAS...
HIS NAME, GREENIE, IS-- HYPERION!
INTERLUDE ENDS.
7

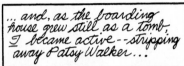
Night...

...and, as the boarding house grew still as a tomb, I became active--stripping away Patsy Walker...

...and becoming something more...
...the Hellcat!

Once, the idea of being a super heroine was my life's dream; my secret obsession.

It's funny how dreams can turn on you like that.

I sat in the window, ready to begin my closer investigation of Eddie Fielder....ready to prowl.

But something was wrong.

I was dizzy...queasy... the strain of the past weeks (maybe the past months) was catching up with me.

But I couldn't let a case of the jitters stop me.

Since the afternoon, I'd been swept up in a strange feeling... call it woman's intuition

I knew that Greentown was important to me...

...that it held the solution to the riddle of Josh Walker...

8

35

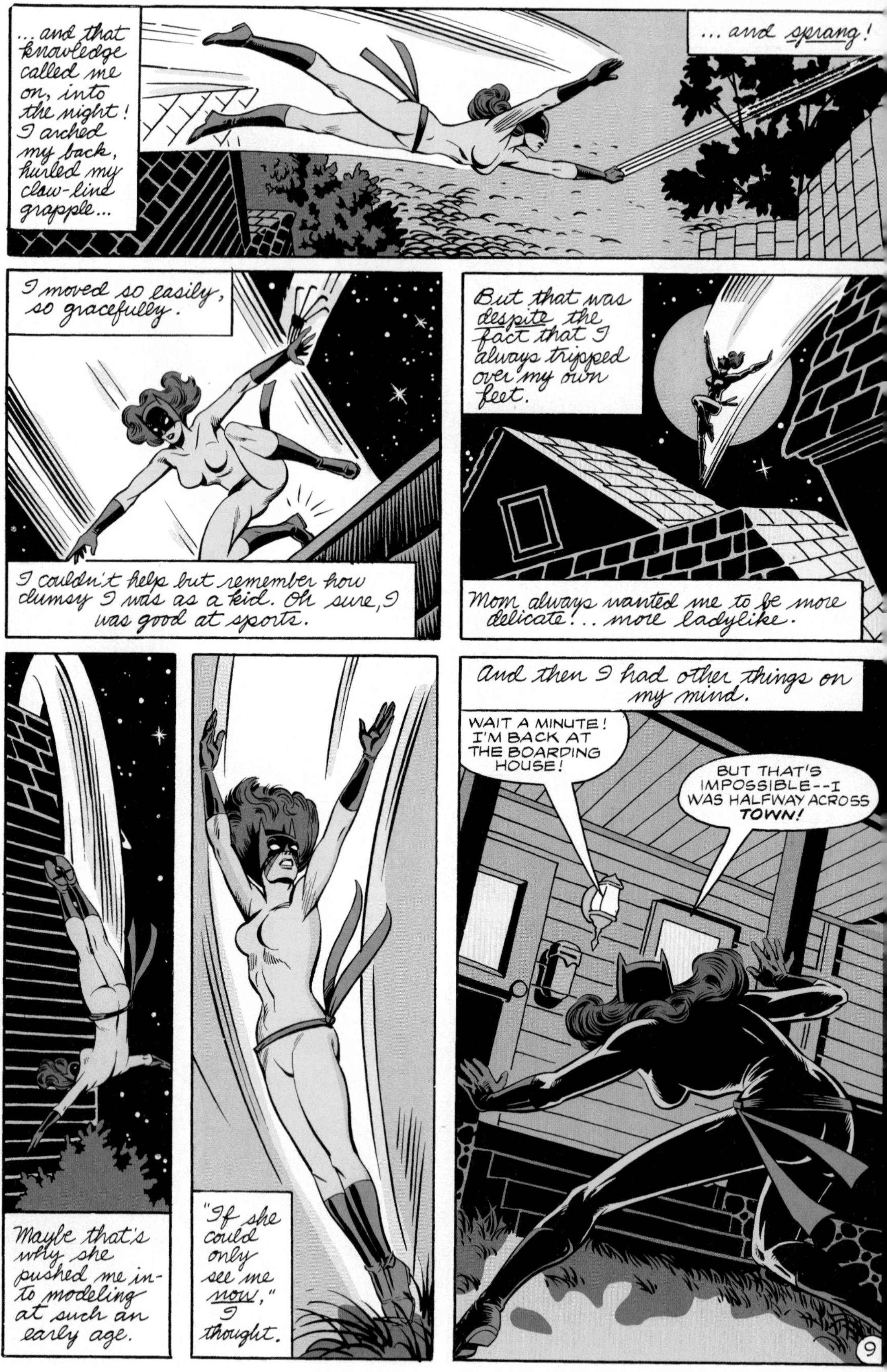
...and that knowledge called me on, into the night! I arched my back, hurled my claw-line grapple...
...and sprang!
I moved so easily, so gracefully.
I couldn't help but remember how clumsy I was as a kid. Oh sure, I was good at sports.
But that was despite the fact that I always tripped over my own feet.
Mom always wanted me to be more delicate!... more ladylike.
Maybe that's why she pushed me into modeling at such an early age.
"If she could only see me now," I thought.
And then I had other things on my mind.
WAIT A MINUTE! I'M BACK AT THE BOARDING HOUSE!
BUT THAT'S IMPOSSIBLE--I WAS HALFWAY ACROSS TOWN!
9

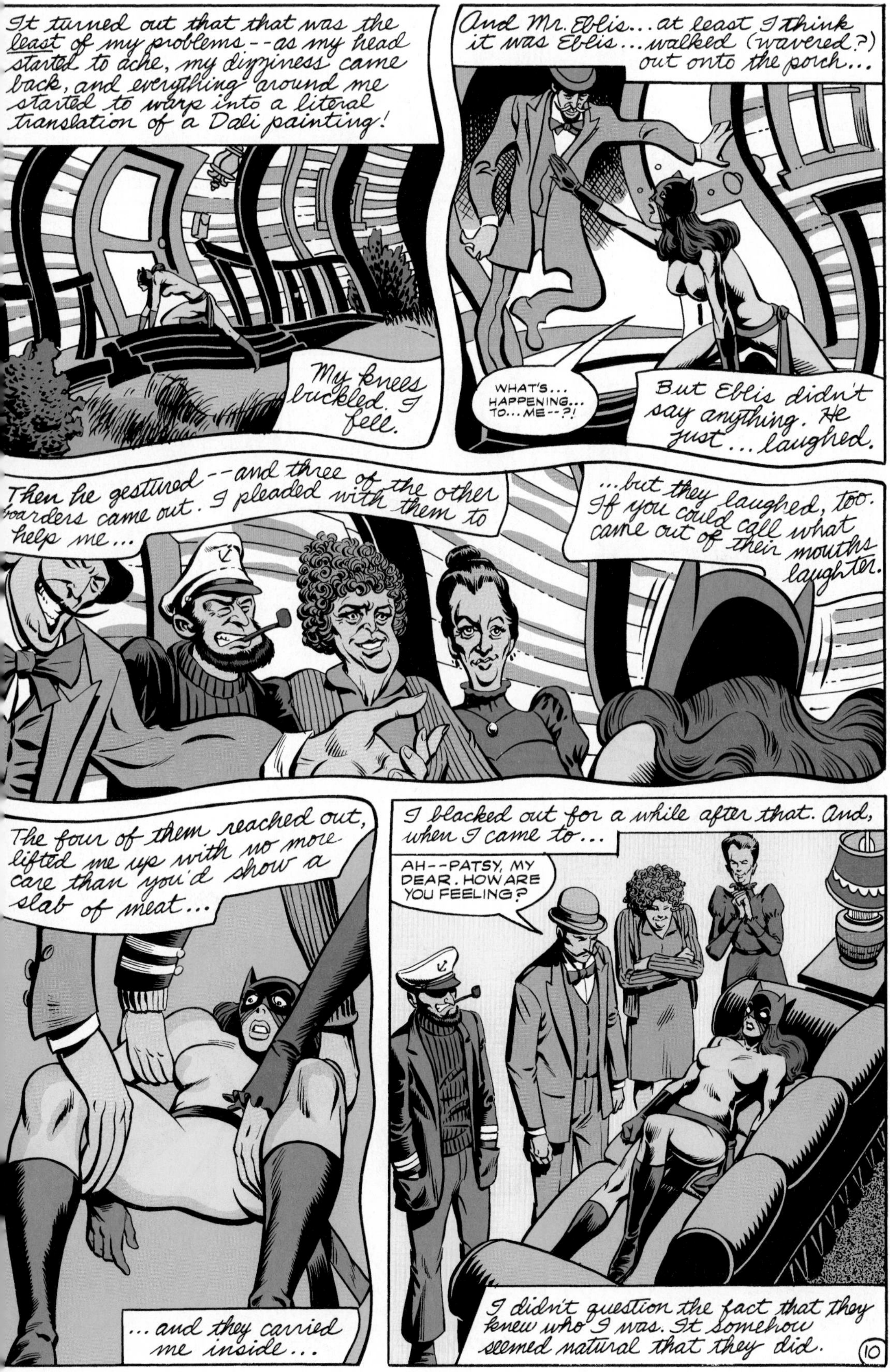
It turned out that that was the least of my problems--as my head started to ache, my dizziness came back, and everything around me started to warp into a literal translation of a Dali painting!
My knees buckled. I fell.
And Mr. Eblis... at least I think it was Eblis... walked (wavered?) out onto the porch...
WHAT'S... HAPPENING... TO... ME--?!
But Eblis didn't say anything. He just... laughed.
Then he gestured--and three of the other boarders came out. I pleaded with them to help me...
...but they laughed, too. If you could call what came out of their mouths laughter.
The four of them reached out, lifted me up with no more care than you'd show a slab of meat...
...and they carried me inside...
I blacked out for a while after that. And, when I came to...
AH--PATSY, MY DEAR. HOW ARE YOU FEELING?
I didn't question the fact that they knew who I was. It somehow seemed natural that they did.
10

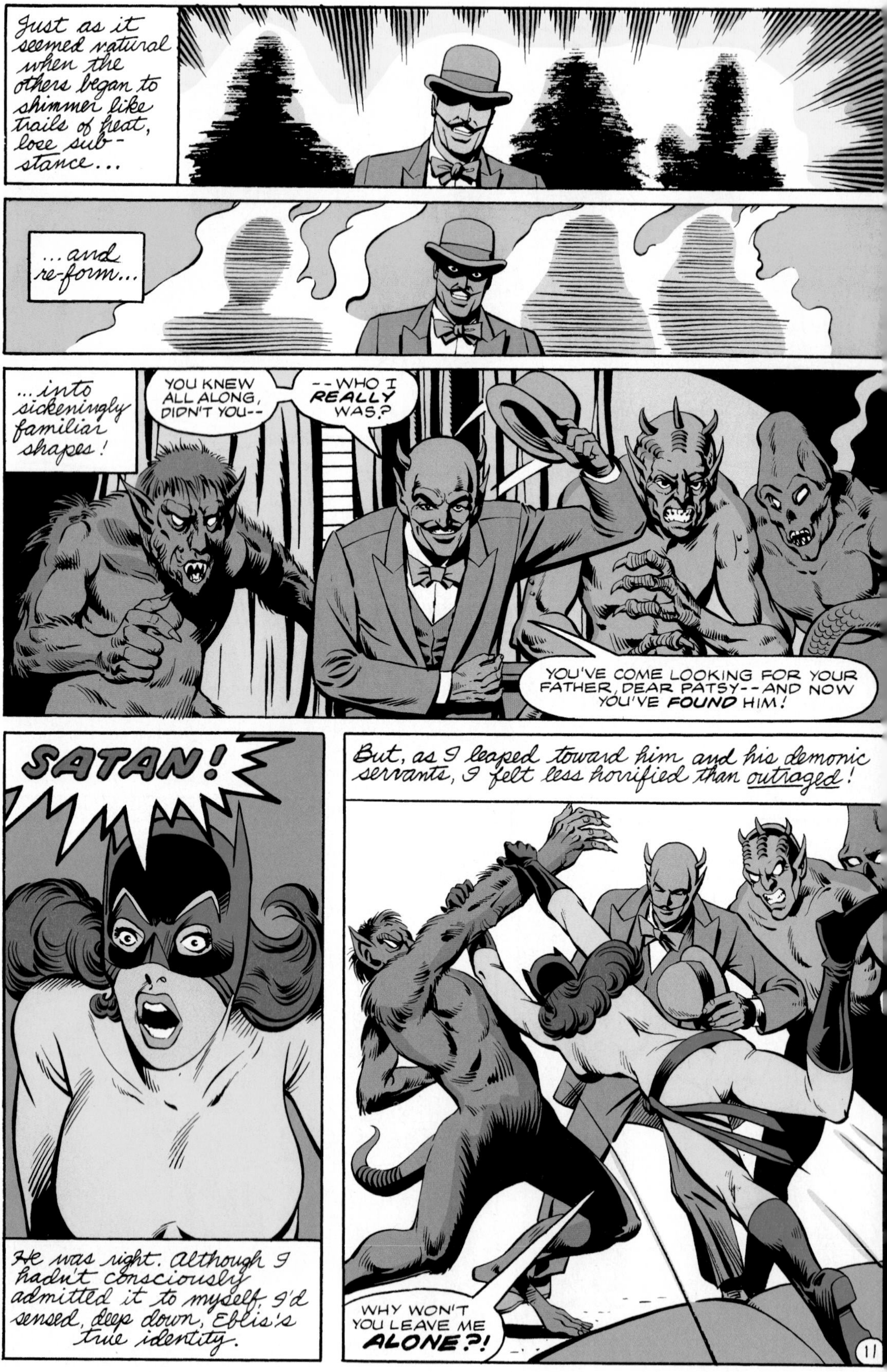
Just as it seemed natural when the others began to shimmer like trails of heat, lose sub-stance...
...and re-form...
...into sickeningly familiar shapes!
YOU KNEW ALL ALONG, DIDN'T YOU--
--WHO I REALLY WAS?
YOU'VE COME LOOKING FOR YOUR FATHER, DEAR PATSY--AND NOW YOU'VE FOUND HIM!
SATAN!
He was right. Although I hadn't consciously admitted it to myself, I'd sensed, deep down, Eblis's true identity.
But, as I leaped toward him and his demonic servants, I felt less horrified than outraged!
WHY WON'T YOU LEAVE ME ALONE?!
11

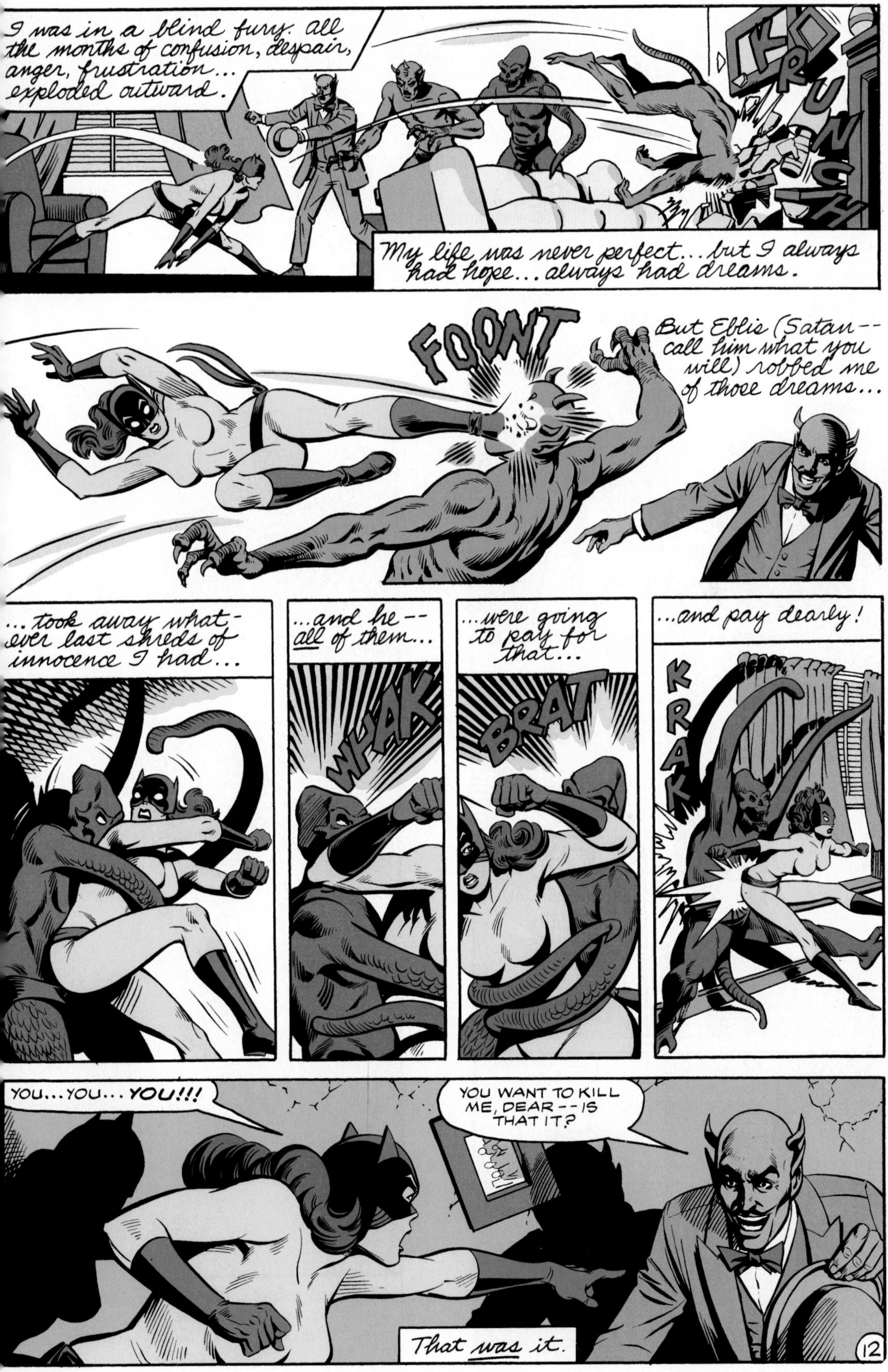
I was in a blind fury. All the months of confusion, despair, anger, frustration... exploded outward.
KRUNCH
My life was never perfect... but I always had hope... always had dreams.
FOONT
But Eblis (Satan--call him what you will) robbed me of those dreams...
...took away whatever last shreds of innocence I had...
...and he--all of them...
WHAK
...were going to pay for that...
BRAT
...and pay dearly!
KRAK
YOU...YOU...YOU!!!
YOU WANT TO KILL ME, DEAR--IS THAT IT?
That was it.
12

YOU'RE NOT MY FATHER, SATAN! YOU'RE NOT!

YOU'RE NOT!

YOU'RE NOT!

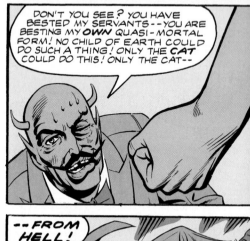

DON'T YOU SEE? YOU HAVE BESTED MY SERVANTS--YOU ARE BESTING MY OWN QUASI-MORTAL FORM! NO CHILD OF EARTH COULD DO SUCH A THING! ONLY THE CAT COULD DO THIS! ONLY THE CAT--

SMAK

THARK

--FROM HELL!

KRAK

OF COURSE I AM.

I stood there, transformed again into a sub-human demon-thing. And I didn't care. All I wanted was his death.

40

I stood on a precipice of the soul, looking down...

...and I thank God that I found the courage...

...not to jump.

NO. **NO!**

I KNOW NOW ...I CAN FEEL IT AS I'VE NEVER FELT IT BEFORE. I'M NO DAUGHTER OF **YOURS,** EBLIS.

I'M A **WOMAN!**

INDEED YOU ARE, PATSY WALKER--AND A FINE EXAMPLE AT THAT! BUT KNOW THIS: HAD YOU NOT TURNED AWAY--OF YOUR OWN WILL-- FROM YOUR DARKER SELF...

...YOUR SOUL WOULD HAVE BEEN MINE--AND YOUR HUMANITY WOULD HAVE BEEN BURIED--**FOREVER!**

BUT, NOW THAT YOU HAVE PROVED YOUR WORTH, YOU HAVE ALSO EARNED THE HONOR OF--

--AN EXPLANATION!

He stood there in that form through which he first revealed himself to me... *

...and he reached out. I felt a rush of cold fire as we passed, like wisps of smoke, through the dimensions...

...to **Hell!**

I wish I could say that all the Defenders' battles with demonic forces had made sights like this mundane... but it just wasn't so!

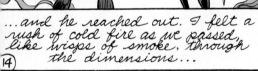

*DEFENDERS #99--AL.

I was scared witless!

(14)

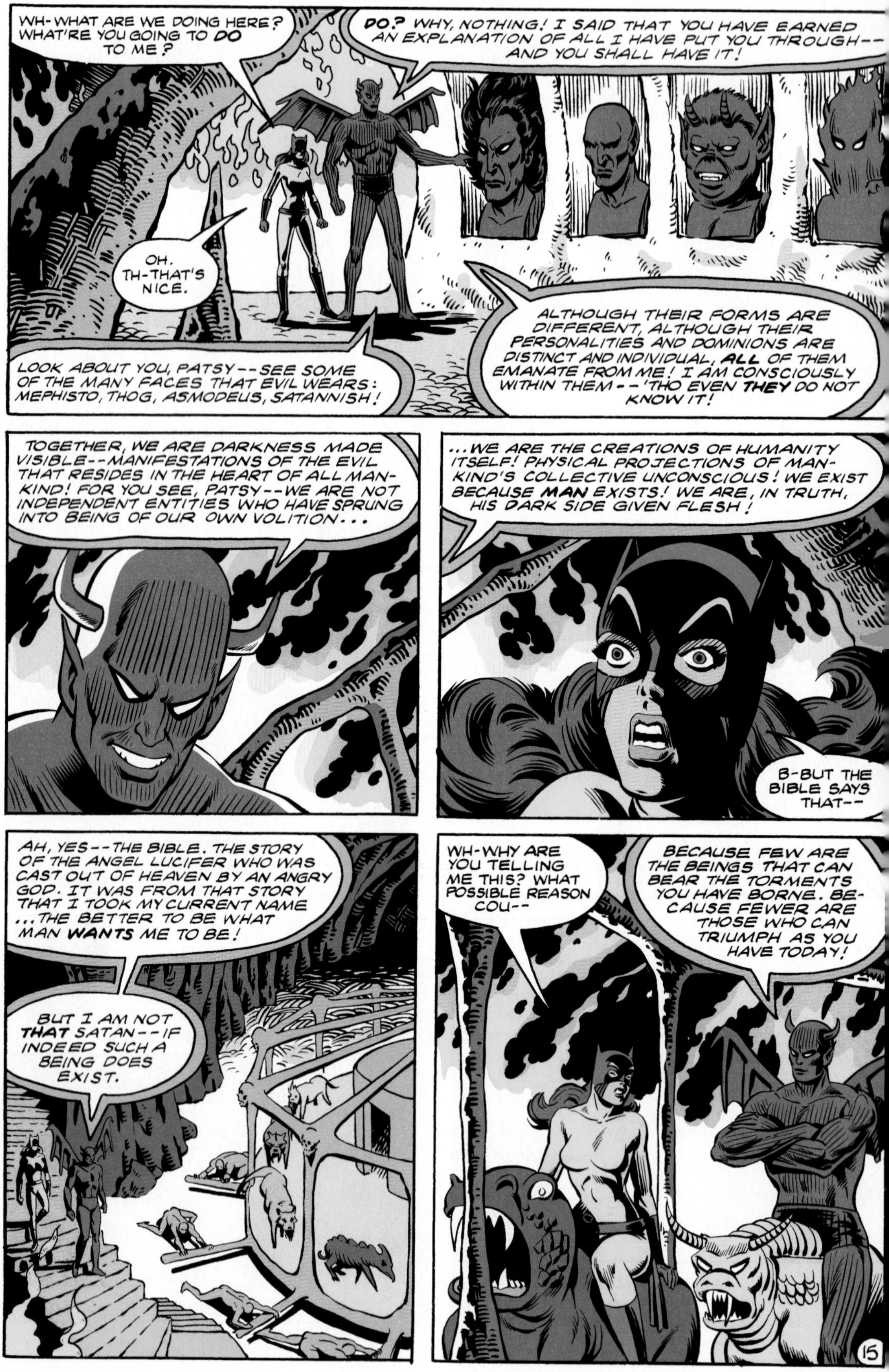
WH-WHAT ARE WE DOING HERE? WHAT'RE YOU GOING TO DO TO ME?
DO? WHY, NOTHING! I SAID THAT YOU HAVE EARNED AN EXPLANATION OF ALL I HAVE PUT YOU THROUGH-- AND YOU SHALL HAVE IT!
OH. TH-THAT'S NICE.
LOOK ABOUT YOU, PATSY--SEE SOME OF THE MANY FACES THAT EVIL WEARS: MEPHISTO, THOG, ASMODEUS, SATANNISH!
ALTHOUGH THEIR FORMS ARE DIFFERENT, ALTHOUGH THEIR PERSONALITIES AND DOMINIONS ARE DISTINCT AND INDIVIDUAL, ALL OF THEM EMANATE FROM ME! I AM CONSCIOUSLY WITHIN THEM--'THO EVEN THEY DO NOT KNOW IT!
TOGETHER, WE ARE DARKNESS MADE VISIBLE--MANIFESTATIONS OF THE EVIL THAT RESIDES IN THE HEART OF ALL MANKIND! FOR YOU SEE, PATSY--WE ARE NOT INDEPENDENT ENTITIES WHO HAVE SPRUNG INTO BEING OF OUR OWN VOLITION...
...WE ARE THE CREATIONS OF HUMANITY ITSELF! PHYSICAL PROJECTIONS OF MANKIND'S COLLECTIVE UNCONSCIOUS! WE EXIST BECAUSE MAN EXISTS! WE ARE, IN TRUTH, HIS DARK SIDE GIVEN FLESH!
B-BUT THE BIBLE SAYS THAT--
AH, YES--THE BIBLE. THE STORY OF THE ANGEL LUCIFER WHO WAS CAST OUT OF HEAVEN BY AN ANGRY GOD. IT WAS FROM THAT STORY THAT I TOOK MY CURRENT NAME ...THE BETTER TO BE WHAT MAN WANTS ME TO BE!
BUT I AM NOT THAT SATAN--IF INDEED SUCH A BEING DOES EXIST.
WH-WHY ARE YOU TELLING ME THIS? WHAT POSSIBLE REASON COU--
BECAUSE FEW ARE THE BEINGS THAT CAN BEAR THE TORMENTS YOU HAVE BORNE. BECAUSE FEWER ARE THOSE WHO CAN TRIUMPH AS YOU HAVE TODAY!
15

BUT, WAIT--THERE IS ONE MORE DEVIL I HAVE NOT TOLD YOU OF: THE MOST DANGEROUS DEVIL OF ALL!

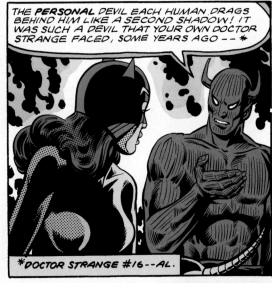

THE *PERSONAL* DEVIL EACH HUMAN DRAGS BEHIND HIM LIKE A SECOND SHADOW! IT WAS SUCH A DEVIL THAT YOUR OWN DOCTOR STRANGE FACED, SOME YEARS AGO -- *

*DOCTOR STRANGE #16--AL.

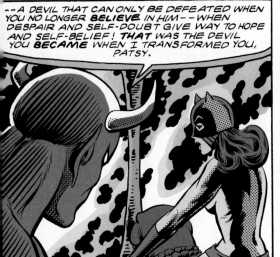

--A DEVIL THAT CAN ONLY BE DEFEATED WHEN YOU NO LONGER *BELIEVE* IN HIM--WHEN DESPAIR AND SELF-DOUBT GIVE WAY TO HOPE AND SELF-BELIEF! *THAT* WAS THE DEVIL YOU *BECAME* WHEN I TRANSFORMED YOU, PATSY.

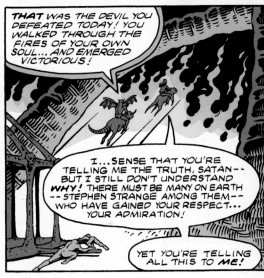

THAT WAS THE DEVIL YOU DEFEATED TODAY! YOU WALKED THROUGH THE FIRES OF YOUR OWN SOUL....AND EMERGED VICTORIOUS!

I...SENSE THAT YOU'RE TELLING ME THE TRUTH, SATAN-- BUT I STILL DON'T UNDERSTAND *WHY!* THERE MUST BE MANY ON EARTH --STEPHEN STRANGE AMONG THEM-- WHO HAVE GAINED YOUR RESPECT... YOUR ADMIRATION!

YET YOU'RE TELLING ALL THIS TO *ME!*

YOU ARE A SPECIAL ONE, PATSY WALKER! YOU BEGAN LIFE LIKE SO MANY OTHERS-- EYES LOCKED ON THE FINITE, ON WHAT SO MANY FOOLS ASSUME TO BE...*REALITY!* YET YOU GREW TO BECOME A TRUE HEROINE! YOU WERE WORTHY OF BEING TRAINED BY THE DEMI-GODS OF TITAN! *

YOU ARE THAT RARE ONE IN A MILLION WITH THE AWARENESS TO TRULY *KNOW* LIFE --IN ALL ITS MYRIAD LEVELS! YOU HAVE LATENT WITHIN YOU THE POWER TO TRANSCEND EVERY PERCEPTION AND PEER INTO THE HEART OF THE INFINITE!

B-BUT I WOULD THINK THAT...*EVERY-ONE* HAS THAT POTENTIAL!

INDEED. BUT FEW HAVE THE COURAGE TO *TRY!* IT WAS THAT COURAGE THAT THE TITANIAN GODDESS, MOONDRAGON, SAW WITHIN YOU!

*IN AVENGERS #151--AL.

THESE ARE STRANGE THINGS FOR "EVIL PERSONIFIED" TO BE TELLING ME--!

16

43

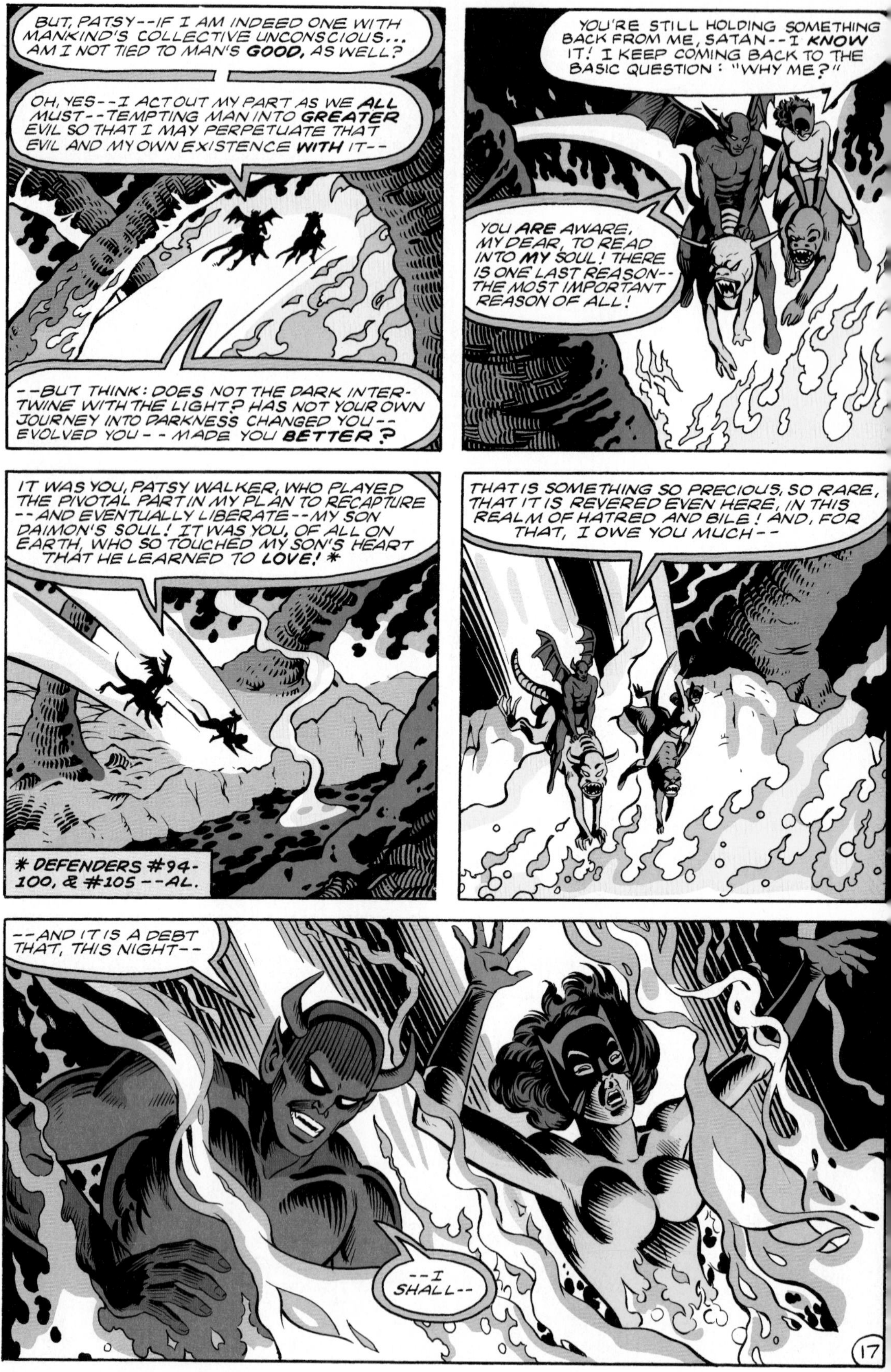
BUT, PATSY--IF I AM INDEED ONE WITH MANKIND'S COLLECTIVE UNCONSCIOUS... AM I NOT TIED TO MAN'S GOOD, AS WELL?
OH, YES--I ACT OUT MY PART AS WE ALL MUST--TEMPTING MAN INTO GREATER EVIL SO THAT I MAY PERPETUATE THAT EVIL AND MY OWN EXISTENCE WITH IT--
--BUT THINK: DOES NOT THE DARK INTERTWINE WITH THE LIGHT? HAS NOT YOUR OWN JOURNEY INTO DARKNESS CHANGED YOU--EVOLVED YOU--MADE YOU BETTER?
YOU'RE STILL HOLDING SOMETHING BACK FROM ME, SATAN--I KNOW IT! I KEEP COMING BACK TO THE BASIC QUESTION: "WHY ME?"
YOU ARE AWARE, MY DEAR, TO READ INTO MY SOUL! THERE IS ONE LAST REASON--THE MOST IMPORTANT REASON OF ALL!
IT WAS YOU, PATSY WALKER, WHO PLAYED THE PIVOTAL PART IN MY PLAN TO RECAPTURE--AND EVENTUALLY LIBERATE--MY SON DAIMON'S SOUL! IT WAS YOU, OF ALL ON EARTH, WHO SO TOUCHED MY SON'S HEART THAT HE LEARNED TO LOVE! *
* DEFENDERS #94-100, & #105--AL.
THAT IS SOMETHING SO PRECIOUS, SO RARE, THAT IT IS REVERED EVEN HERE, IN THIS REALM OF HATRED AND BILE! AND, FOR THAT, I OWE YOU MUCH--
--AND IT IS A DEBT THAT, THIS NIGHT--
--I SHALL--
17

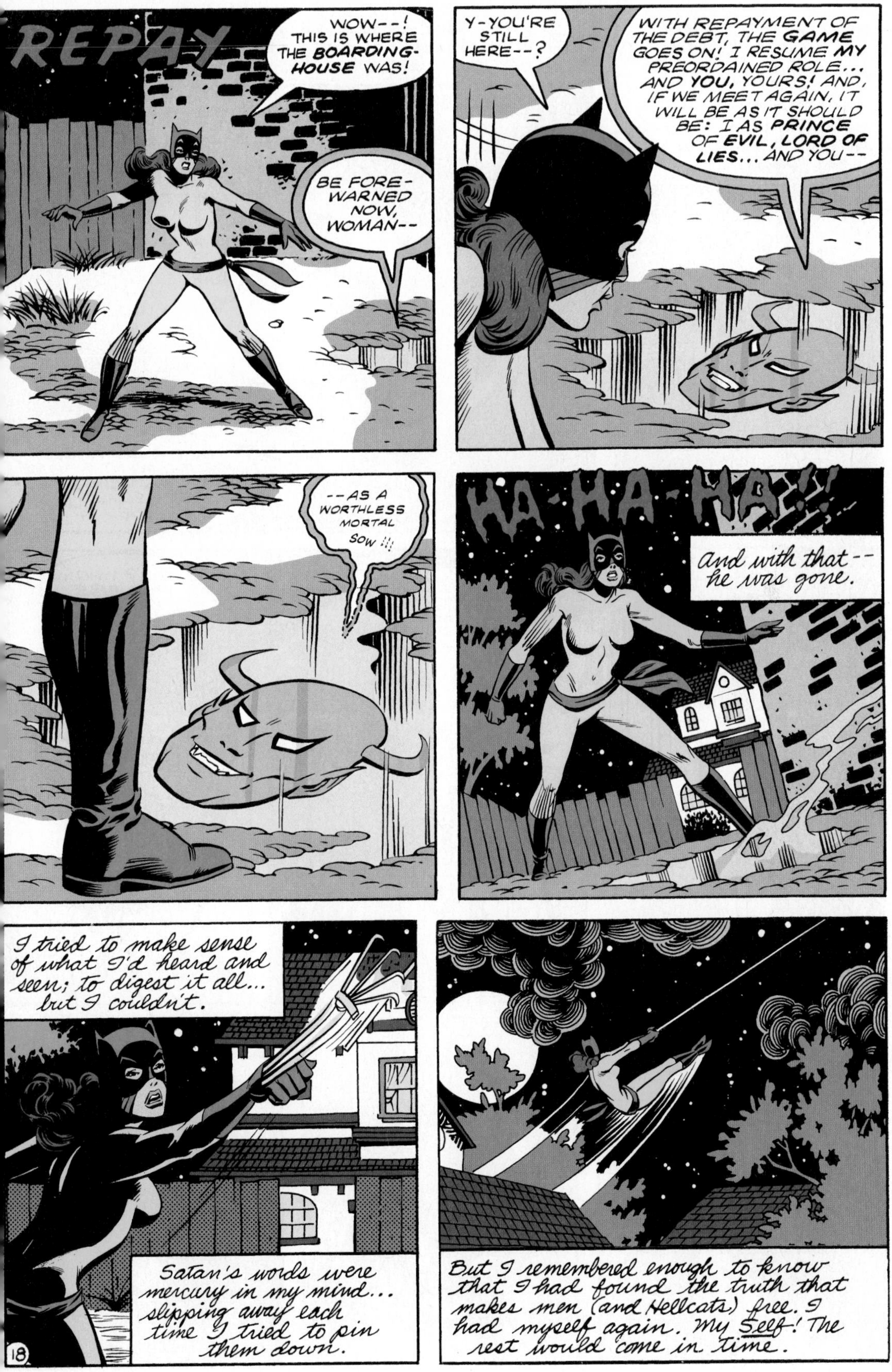
REPAY
WOW--! THIS IS WHERE THE BOARDING-HOUSE WAS!
BE FORE-WARNED NOW, WOMAN--
Y-YOU'RE STILL HERE--?
WITH REPAYMENT OF THE DEBT, THE GAME GOES ON! I RESUME MY PREORDAINED ROLE... AND YOU, YOURS! AND, IF WE MEET AGAIN, IT WILL BE AS IT SHOULD BE: I AS PRINCE OF EVIL, LORD OF LIES... AND YOU--
--AS A WORTHLESS MORTAL SOW !!!
HA-HA-HA!!
and with that-- he was gone.
I tried to make sense of what I'd heard and seen; to digest it all... but I couldn't.
Satan's words were mercury in my mind... slipping away each time I tried to pin them down.
18
But I remembered enough to know that I had found the truth that makes men (and Hellcats) free. I had myself again. My Self! The rest would come in time.

As I swung across Greentown, my mind felt clearer than it had since Moondragon stripped me of my Titan-spawned mental powers.* And I realized two things...

*DEFENDERS #77--AL.

One: That those powers had never left me...only my belief in them had. Two: that Eddie Fielder wouldn't be alone in his apartment.

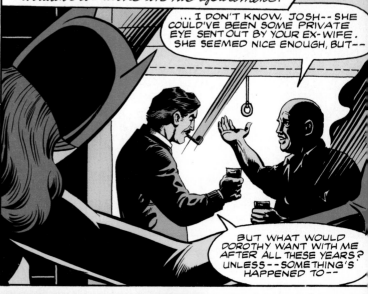

...I DON'T KNOW, JOSH-- SHE COULD'VE BEEN SOME PRIVATE EYE SENT OUT BY YOUR EX-WIFE. SHE SEEMED NICE ENOUGH, BUT--

BUT WHAT WOULD DOROTHY WANT WITH ME AFTER ALL THESE YEARS? UNLESS--SOMETHING'S HAPPENED TO--

JOSHUA WALKER--?

YES? WHO... WHO ARE YOU?

I-IT'S ME.

IT'S PATSY.

19

46

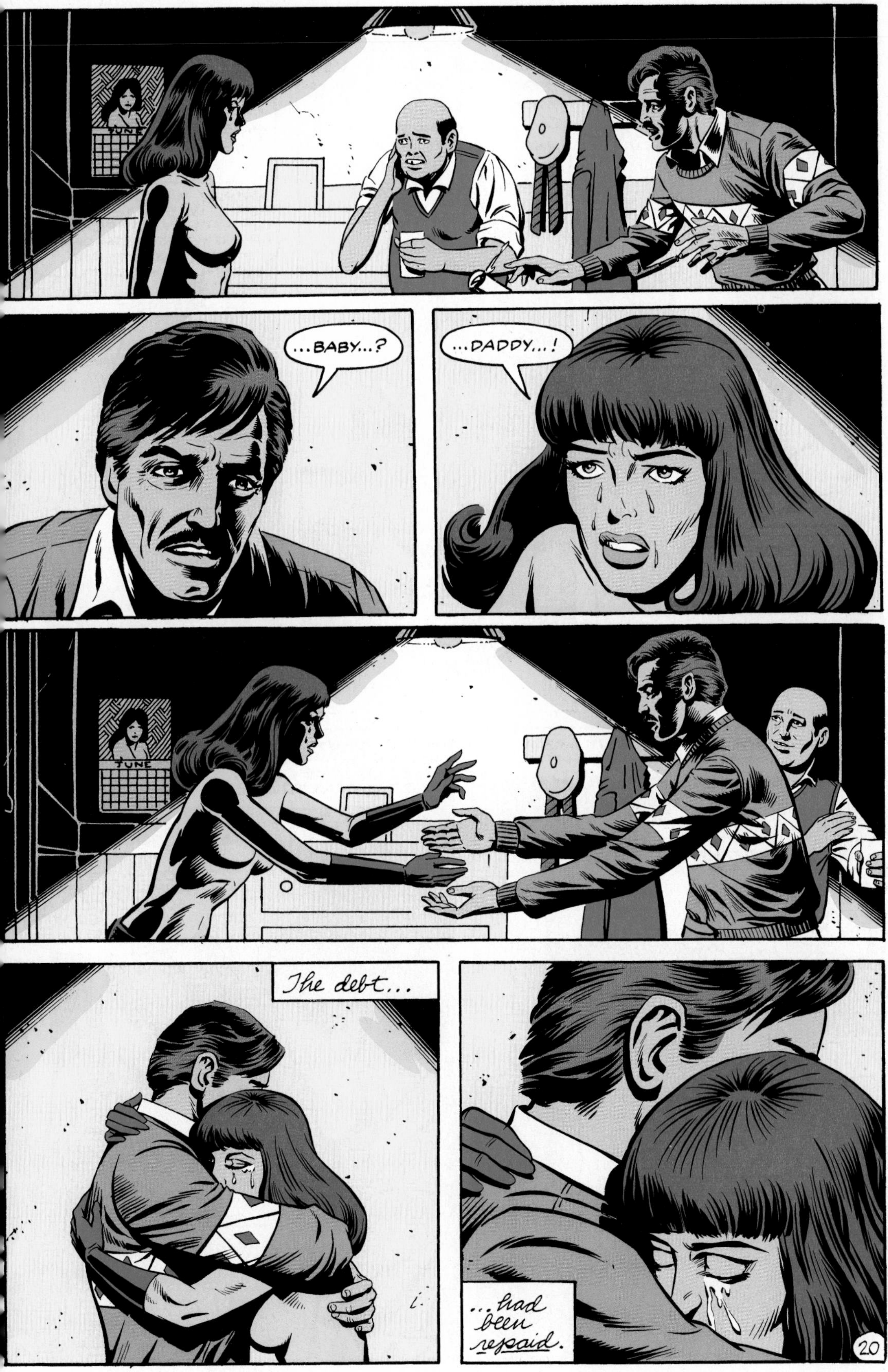
JUNE
...BABY...?
...DADDY...!
JUNE
The debt...
...had been repaid.
20

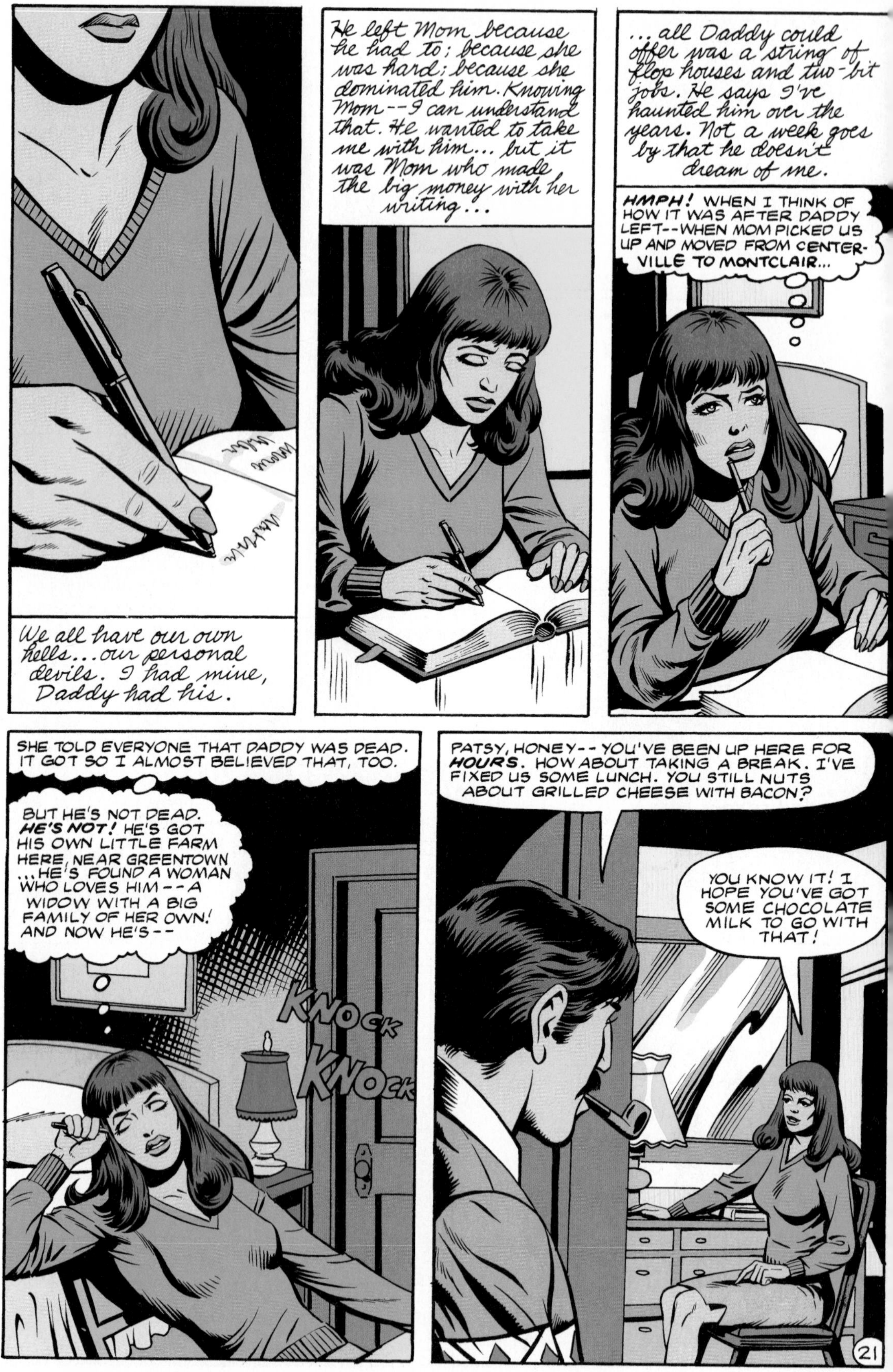
We all have our own hells... our personal devils. I had mine, Daddy had his.
He left Mom because he had to; because she was hard; because she dominated him. Knowing Mom -- I can understand that. He wanted to take me with him... but it was Mom who made the big money with her writing...
...all Daddy could offer was a string of flop houses and two-bit jobs. He says I've haunted him over the years. Not a week goes by that he doesn't dream of me.
HMPH! WHEN I THINK OF HOW IT WAS AFTER DADDY LEFT--WHEN MOM PICKED US UP AND MOVED FROM CENTERVILLE TO MONTCLAIR...
SHE TOLD EVERYONE THAT DADDY WAS DEAD. IT GOT SO I ALMOST BELIEVED THAT, TOO.
BUT HE'S NOT DEAD. HE'S NOT! HE'S GOT HIS OWN LITTLE FARM HERE, NEAR GREENTOWN ...HE'S FOUND A WOMAN WHO LOVES HIM -- A WIDOW WITH A BIG FAMILY OF HER OWN! AND NOW HE'S --
KNOCK KNOCK
PATSY, HONEY-- YOU'VE BEEN UP HERE FOR HOURS. HOW ABOUT TAKING A BREAK. I'VE FIXED US SOME LUNCH. YOU STILL NUTS ABOUT GRILLED CHEESE WITH BACON?
YOU KNOW IT! I HOPE YOU'VE GOT SOME CHOCOLATE MILK TO GO WITH THAT!
21

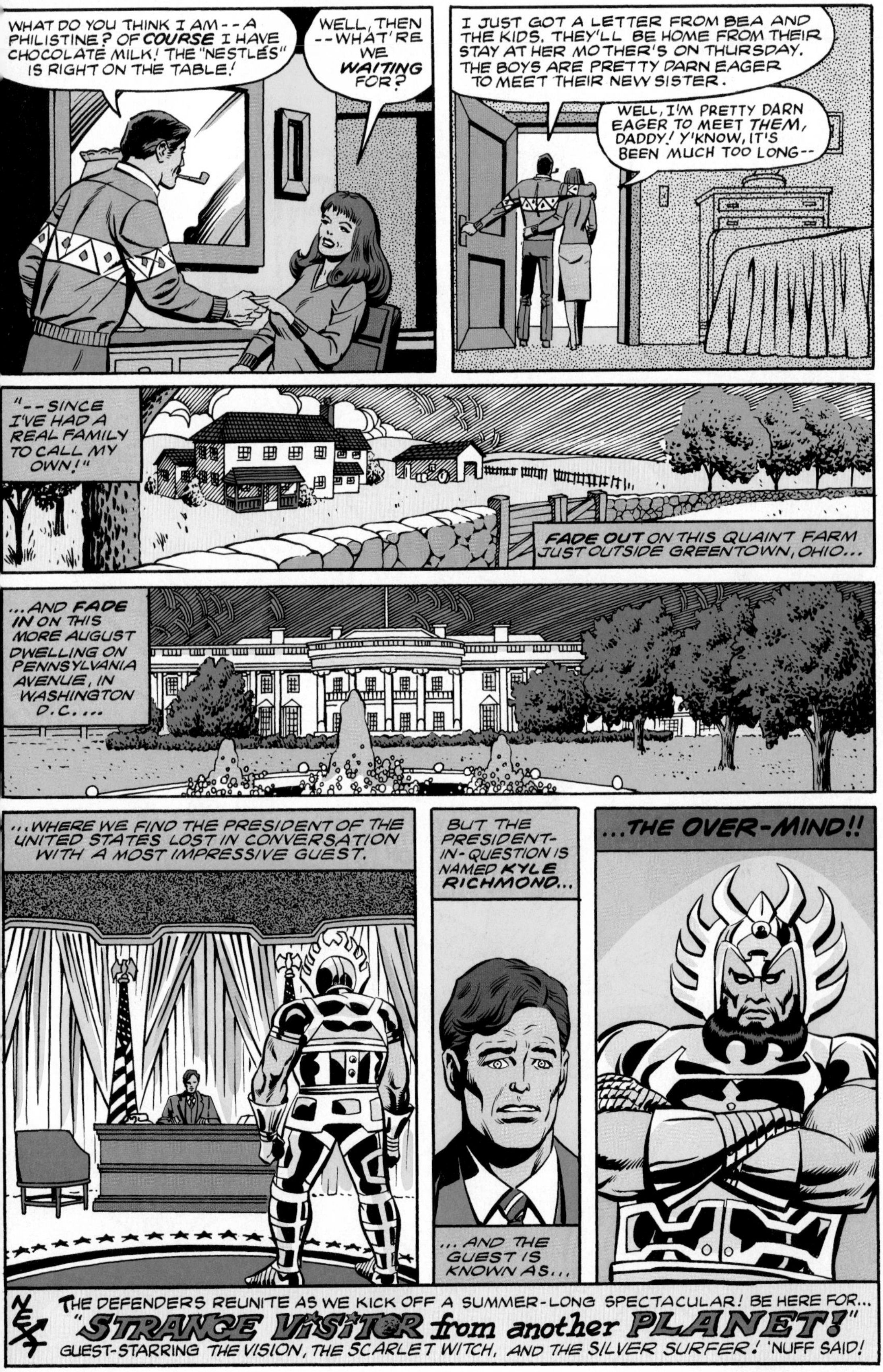
WHAT DO YOU THINK I AM--A PHILISTINE? OF COURSE I HAVE CHOCOLATE MILK! THE "NESTLÉS" IS RIGHT ON THE TABLE!
WELL, THEN --WHAT'RE WE WAITING FOR?
I JUST GOT A LETTER FROM BEA AND THE KIDS. THEY'LL BE HOME FROM THEIR STAY AT HER MOTHER'S ON THURSDAY. THE BOYS ARE PRETTY DARN EAGER TO MEET THEIR NEW SISTER.
WELL, I'M PRETTY DARN EAGER TO MEET THEM, DADDY! Y'KNOW, IT'S BEEN MUCH TOO LONG--
"--SINCE I'VE HAD A REAL FAMILY TO CALL MY OWN!"
FADE OUT ON THIS QUAINT FARM JUST OUTSIDE GREENTOWN, OHIO...
...AND FADE IN ON THIS MORE AUGUST DWELLING ON PENNSYLVANIA AVENUE, IN WASHINGTON D.C....
...WHERE WE FIND THE PRESIDENT OF THE UNITED STATES LOST IN CONVERSATION WITH A MOST IMPRESSIVE GUEST.
BUT THE PRESIDENT-IN-QUESTION IS NAMED KYLE RICHMOND...
...AND THE GUEST IS KNOWN AS...
...THE OVER-MIND!!
NEXT
THE DEFENDERS REUNITE AS WE KICK OFF A SUMMER-LONG SPECTACULAR! BE HERE FOR...
"STRANGE VISITOR from another PLANET!"
GUEST-STARRING THE VISION, THE SCARLET WITCH, AND THE SILVER SURFER! 'NUFF SAID!

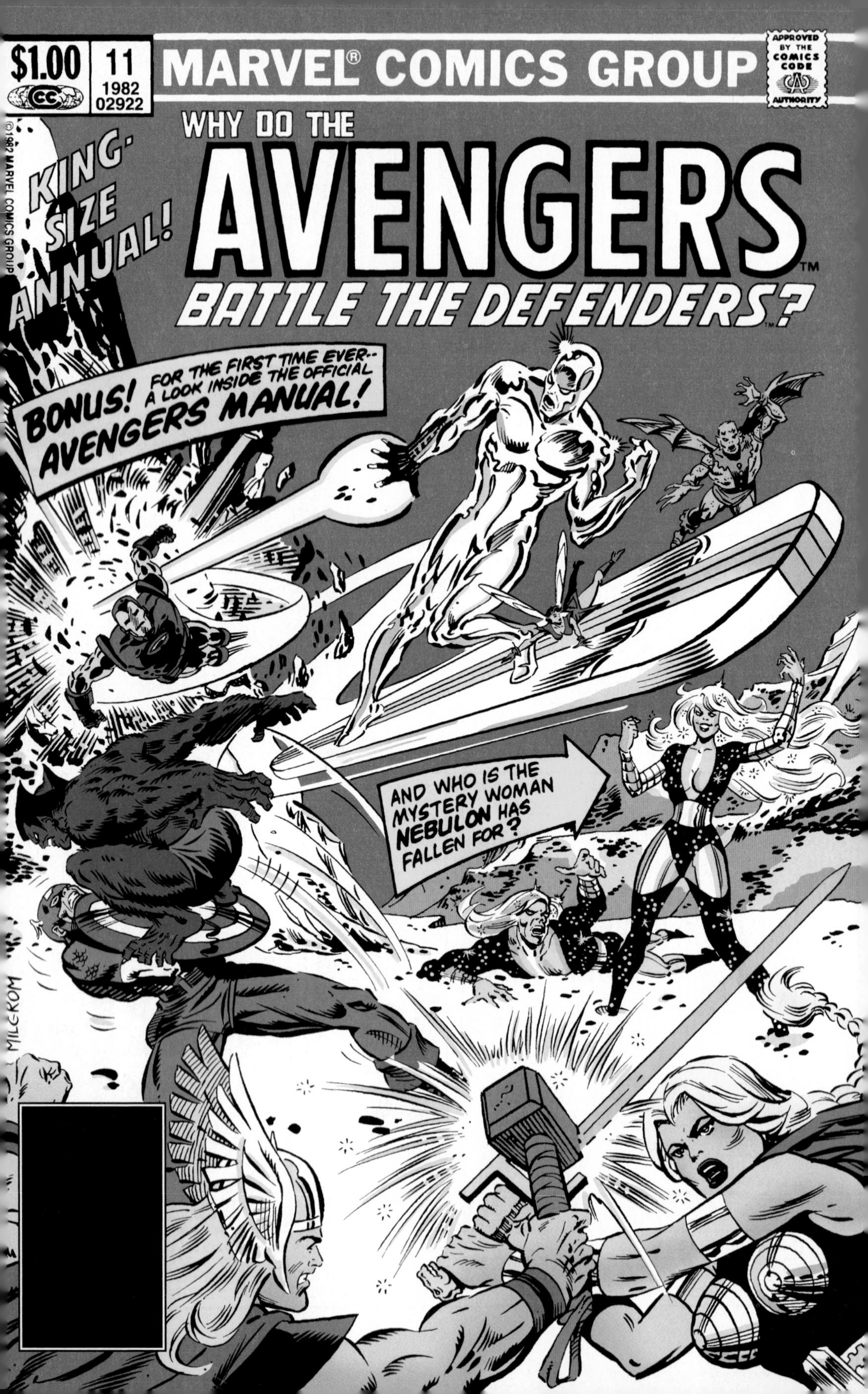

$1.00
11
1982
02922
MARVEL® COMICS GROUP
APPROVED BY THE COMICS CODE AUTHORITY
WHY DO THE
AVENGERS™
BATTLE THE DEFENDERS?™
KING-SIZE ANNUAL!
BONUS! FOR THE FIRST TIME EVER-- A LOOK INSIDE THE OFFICIAL AVENGERS MANUAL!
AND WHO IS THE MYSTERY WOMAN NEBULON HAS FALLEN FOR?
©1982 MARVEL COMICS GROUP
MILGROM

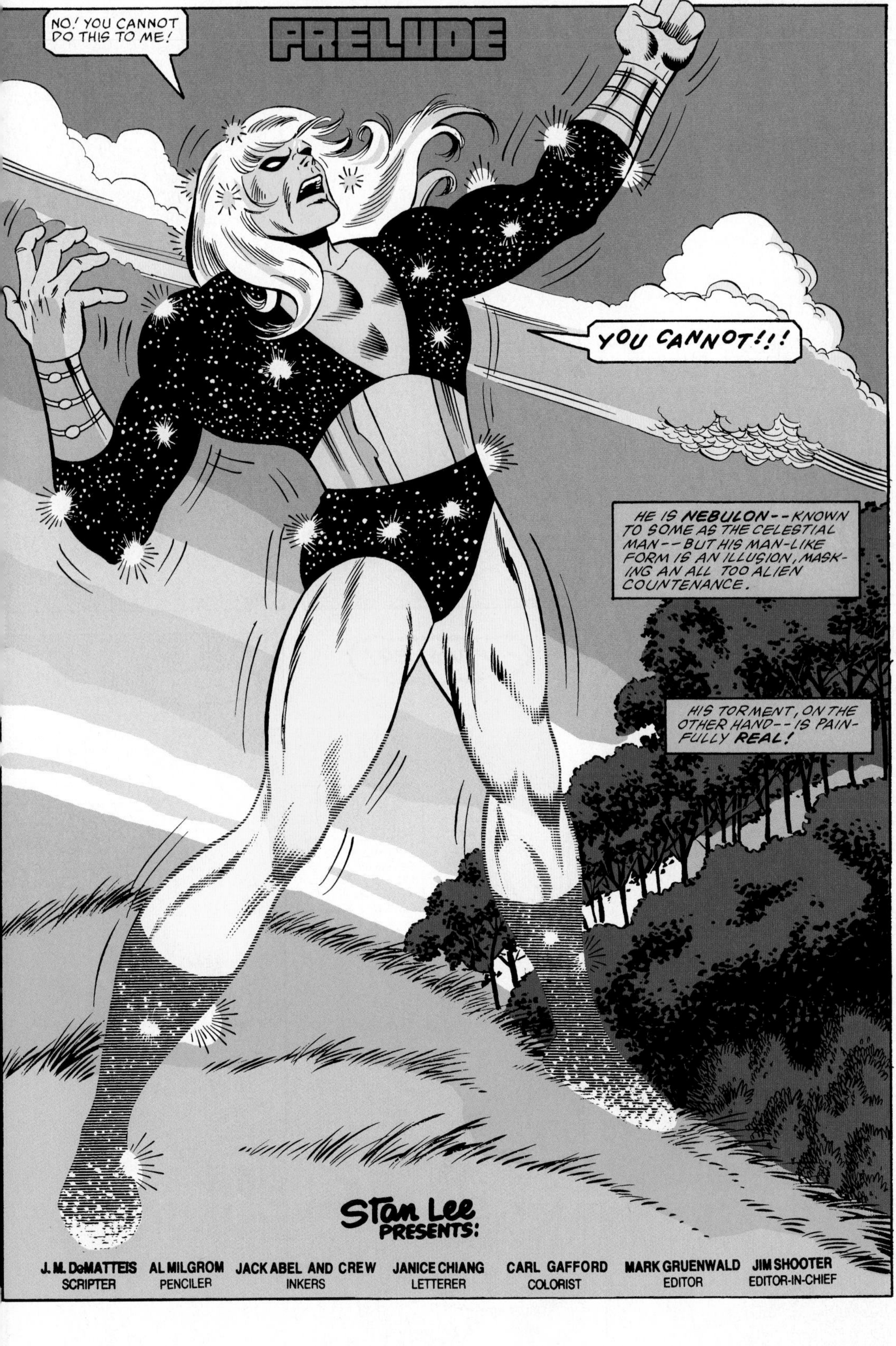
PRELUDE
NO! YOU CANNOT DO THIS TO ME!
YOU CANNOT!!!
HE IS NEBULON--KNOWN TO SOME AS THE CELESTIAL MAN--BUT HIS MAN-LIKE FORM IS AN ILLUSION, MASKING AN ALL TOO ALIEN COUNTENANCE.
HIS TORMENT, ON THE OTHER HAND--IS PAINFULLY REAL!
STAN LEE PRESENTS:
J. M. DeMATTEIS SCRIPTER
AL MILGROM PENCILER
JACK ABEL AND CREW INKERS
JANICE CHIANG LETTERER
CARL GAFFORD COLORIST
MARK GRUENWALD EDITOR
JIM SHOOTER EDITOR-IN-CHIEF

NEBULON—THESE HISTRIONICS WILL DO YOU LITTLE GOOD!

BUT, YOUR LORDSHIP—!

SILENCE! YOU WERE TRIED AND CONVICTED BY THE HIGH TRIBUNAL—

—AND NOW YOU MUST PAY THE PENALTY!

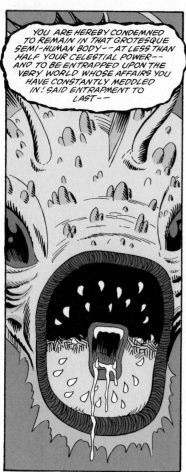

YOU ARE HEREBY CONDEMNED TO REMAIN IN THAT GROTESQUE SEMI-HUMAN BODY—AT LESS THAN HALF YOUR CELESTIAL POWER—AND TO BE ENTRAPPED UPON THE VERY WORLD WHOSE AFFAIRS YOU HAVE CONSTANTLY MEDDLED IN! SAID ENTRAPMENT TO LAST—

—FOREVER!

B-BUT, YOUR LORDSHIP... SURELY THE PUNISHMENT IS TOO—EXTREME! SURELY YOU CAN FIND IT IN YOUR NOBLE HEART TO—

I SAID—

—SILENCE!

2

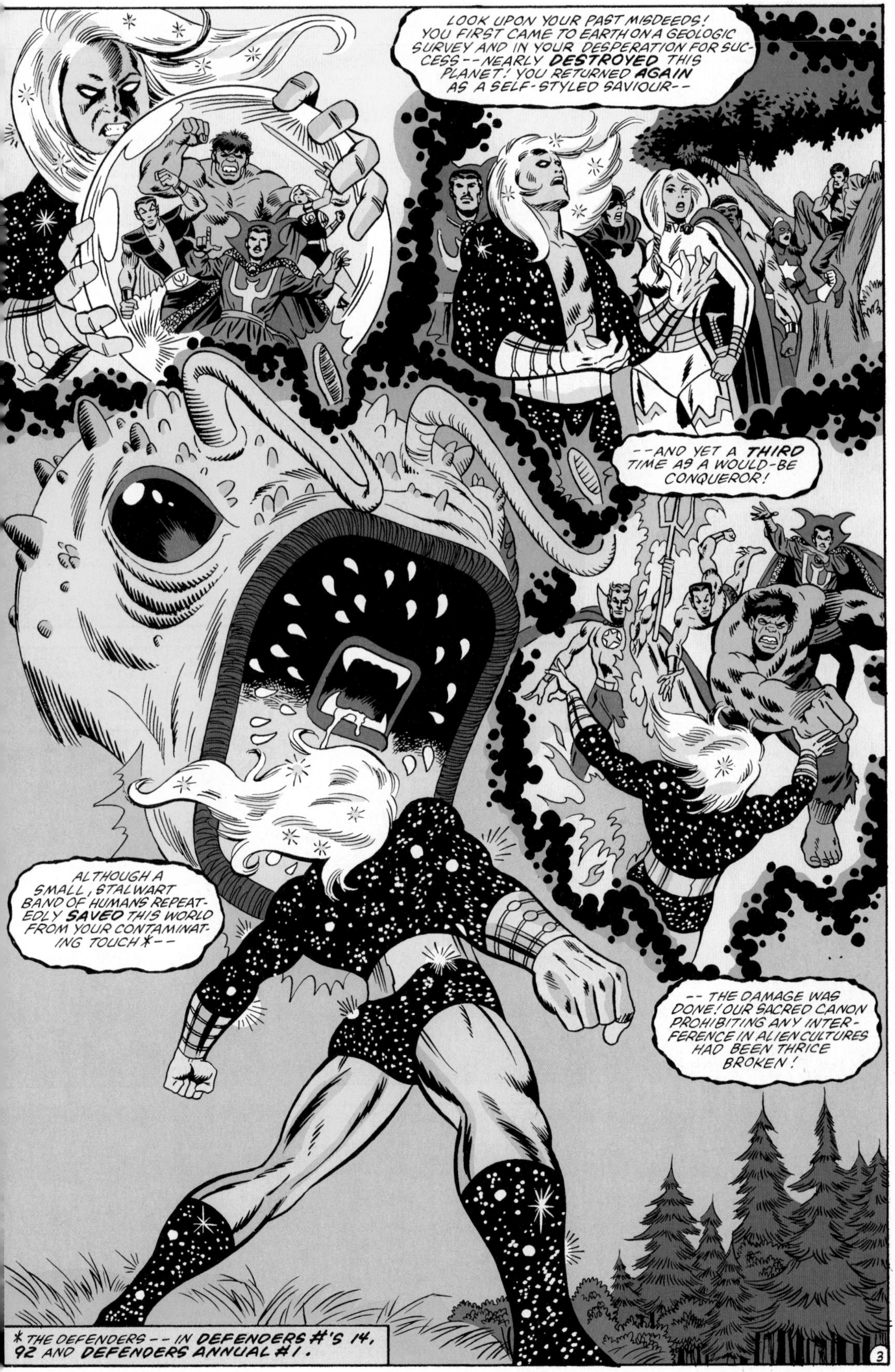
LOOK UPON YOUR PAST MISDEEDS! YOU FIRST CAME TO EARTH ON A GEOLOGIC SURVEY AND IN YOUR DESPERATION FOR SUCCESS--NEARLY DESTROYED THIS PLANET! YOU RETURNED AGAIN AS A SELF-STYLED SAVIOUR--
--AND YET A THIRD TIME AS A WOULD-BE CONQUEROR!
ALTHOUGH A SMALL, STALWART BAND OF HUMANS REPEATEDLY SAVED THIS WORLD FROM YOUR CONTAMINATING TOUCH*--
--THE DAMAGE WAS DONE! OUR SACRED CANON PROHIBITING ANY INTERFERENCE IN ALIEN CULTURES HAD BEEN THRICE BROKEN!
*THE DEFENDERS--IN DEFENDERS #'S 14, 92 AND DEFENDERS ANNUAL #1.
3

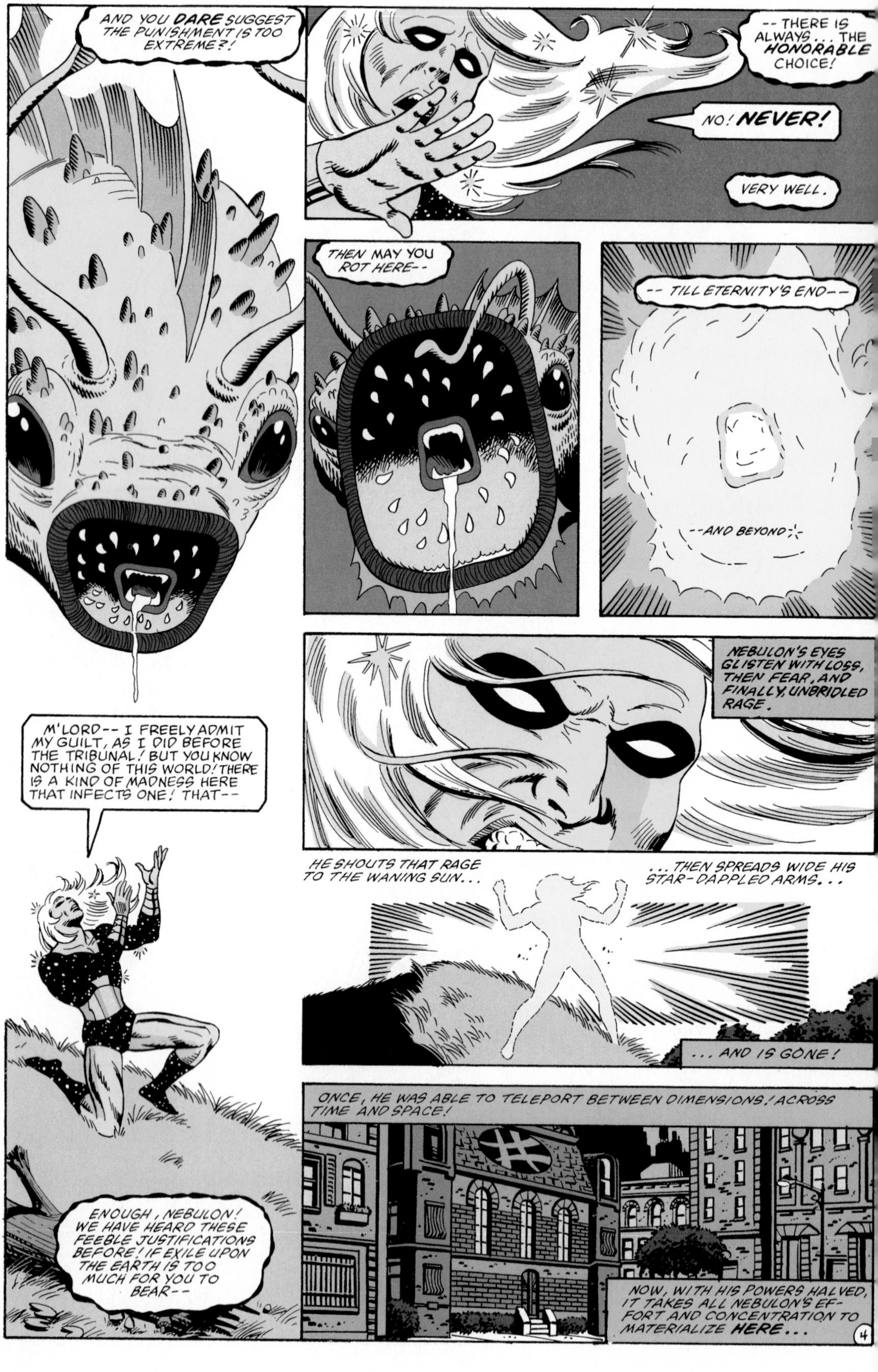

AND YOU DARE SUGGEST THE PUNISHMENT IS TOO EXTREME?!
--THERE IS ALWAYS... THE HONORABLE CHOICE!
NO! NEVER!
VERY WELL.
THEN MAY YOU ROT HERE--
--TILL ETERNITY'S END--
--AND BEYOND!
NEBULON'S EYES GLISTEN WITH LOSS, THEN FEAR, AND FINALLY, UNBRIDLED RAGE.
M'LORD-- I FREELY ADMIT MY GUILT, AS I DID BEFORE THE TRIBUNAL! BUT YOU KNOW NOTHING OF THIS WORLD! THERE IS A KIND OF MADNESS HERE THAT INFECTS ONE! THAT--
ENOUGH, NEBULON! WE HAVE HEARD THESE FEEBLE JUSTIFICATIONS BEFORE! IF EXILE UPON THE EARTH IS TOO MUCH FOR YOU TO BEAR--
HE SHOUTS THAT RAGE TO THE WANING SUN...
...THEN SPREADS WIDE HIS STAR-DAPPLED ARMS...
...AND IS GONE!
ONCE, HE WAS ABLE TO TELEPORT BETWEEN DIMENSIONS! ACROSS TIME AND SPACE!
NOW, WITH HIS POWERS HALVED, IT TAKES ALL NEBULON'S EFFORT AND CONCENTRATION TO MATERIALIZE HERE...
4

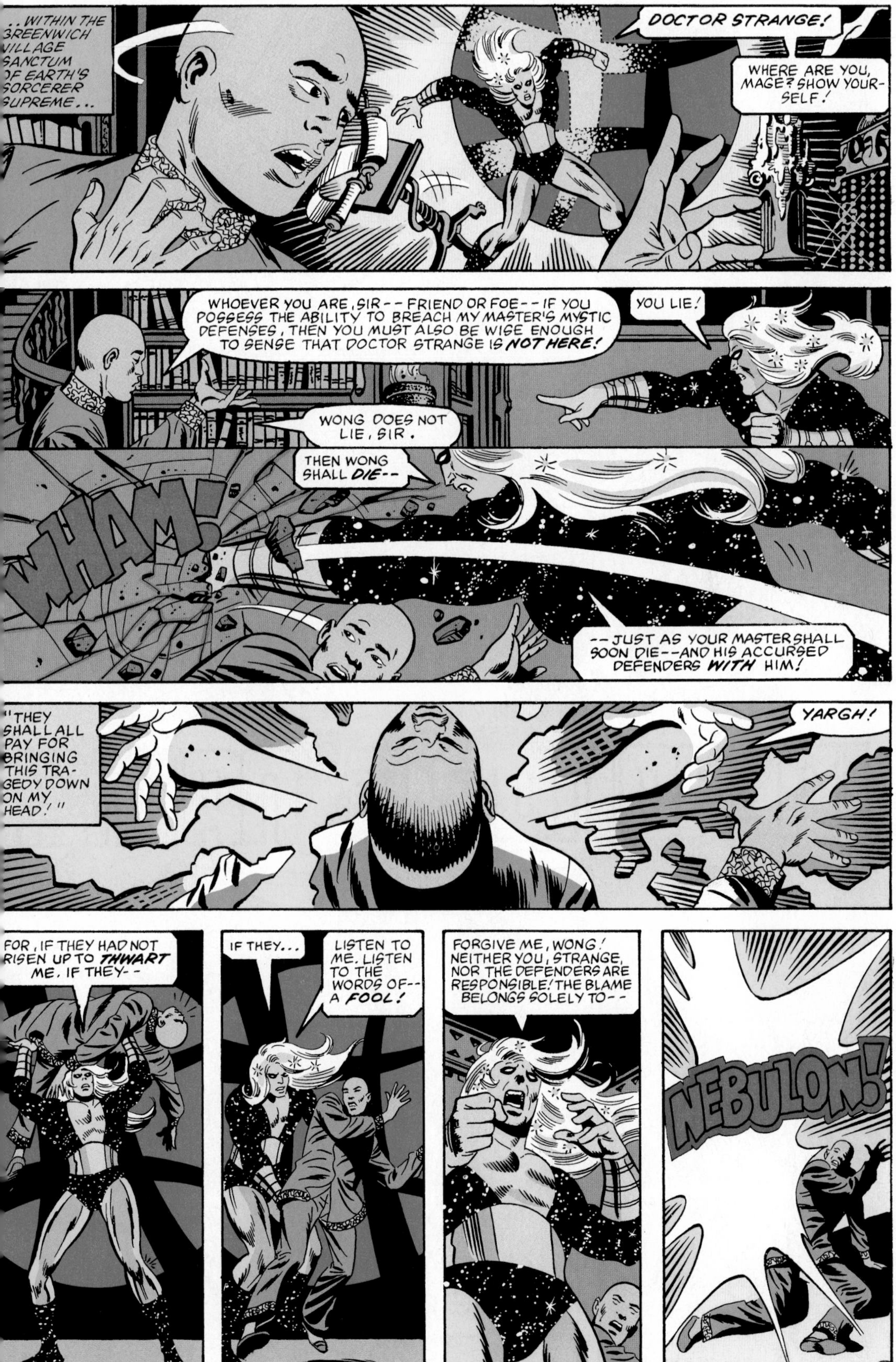

..WITHIN THE GREENWICH VILLAGE SANCTUM OF EARTH'S SORCERER SUPREME...
DOCTOR STRANGE!
WHERE ARE YOU, MAGE? SHOW YOURSELF!
WHOEVER YOU ARE, SIR--FRIEND OR FOE--IF YOU POSSESS THE ABILITY TO BREACH MY MASTER'S MYSTIC DEFENSES, THEN YOU MUST ALSO BE WISE ENOUGH TO SENSE THAT DOCTOR STRANGE IS NOT HERE!
YOU LIE!
WONG DOES NOT LIE, SIR.
THEN WONG SHALL DIE--
WHAM!
--JUST AS YOUR MASTER SHALL SOON DIE--AND HIS ACCURSED DEFENDERS WITH HIM!
"THEY SHALL ALL PAY FOR BRINGING THIS TRAGEDY DOWN ON MY HEAD!"
YARGH!
FOR, IF THEY HAD NOT RISEN UP TO THWART ME, IF THEY--
IF THEY...
LISTEN TO ME. LISTEN TO THE WORDS OF--A FOOL!
FORGIVE ME, WONG! NEITHER YOU, STRANGE, NOR THE DEFENDERS ARE RESPONSIBLE! THE BLAME BELONGS SOLELY TO--
NEBULON!
5

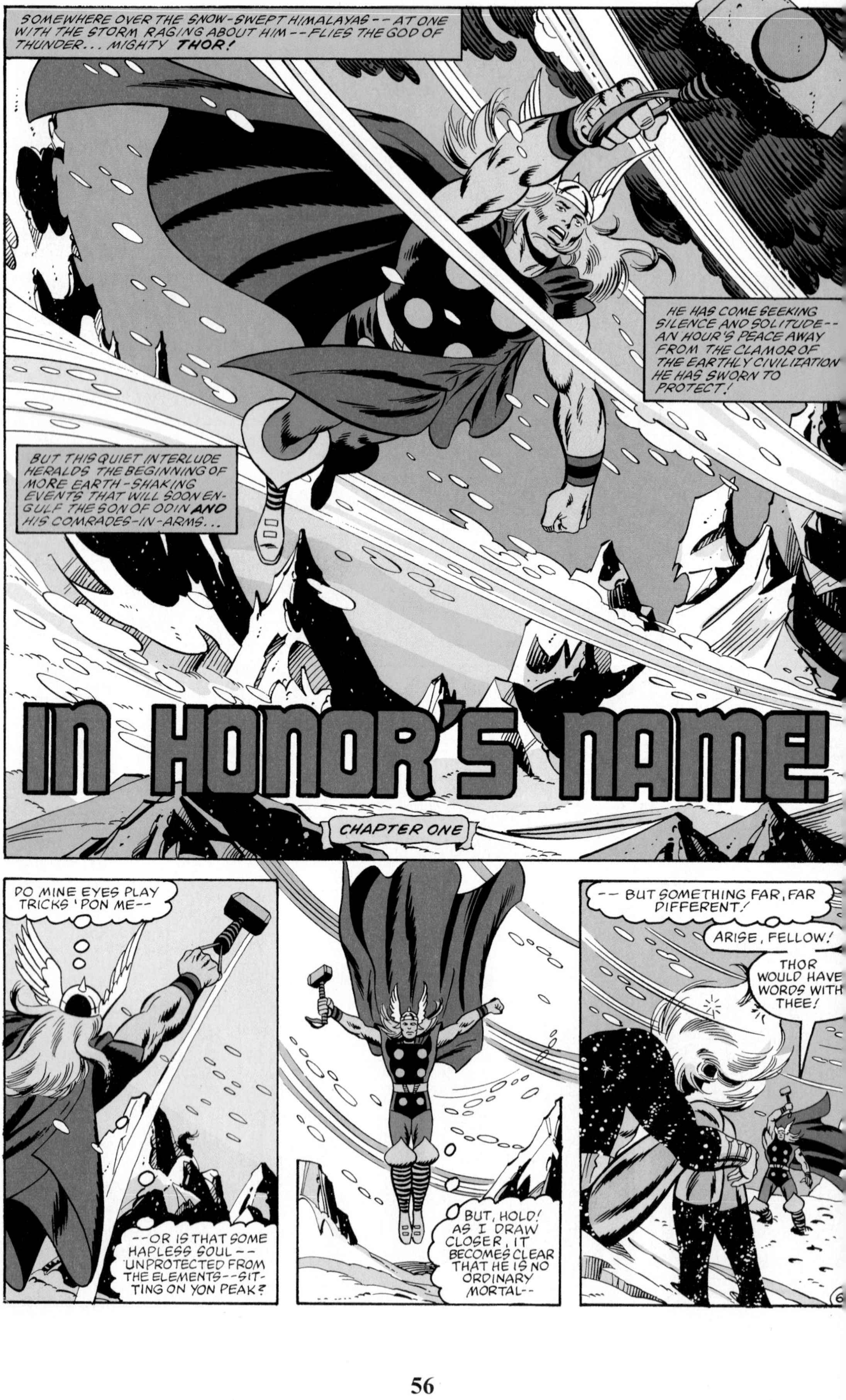
SOMEWHERE OVER THE SNOW-SWEPT HIMALAYAS--AT ONE WITH THE STORM RAGING ABOUT HIM--FLIES THE GOD OF THUNDER... MIGHTY THOR!
HE HAS COME SEEKING SILENCE AND SOLITUDE--AN HOUR'S PEACE AWAY FROM THE CLAMOR OF THE EARTHLY CIVILIZATION HE HAS SWORN TO PROTECT!
BUT THIS QUIET INTERLUDE HERALDS THE BEGINNING OF MORE EARTH-SHAKING EVENTS THAT WILL SOON ENGULF THE SON OF ODIN AND HIS COMRADES-IN-ARMS...
IN HONOR'S NAME!
CHAPTER ONE
DO MINE EYES PLAY TRICKS 'PON ME--
--OR IS THAT SOME HAPLESS SOUL--UNPROTECTED FROM THE ELEMENTS--SITTING ON YON PEAK?
BUT, HOLD! AS I DRAW CLOSER, IT BECOMES CLEAR THAT HE IS NO ORDINARY MORTAL--
--BUT SOMETHING FAR, FAR DIFFERENT!
ARISE, FELLOW!
THOR WOULD HAVE WORDS WITH THEE!

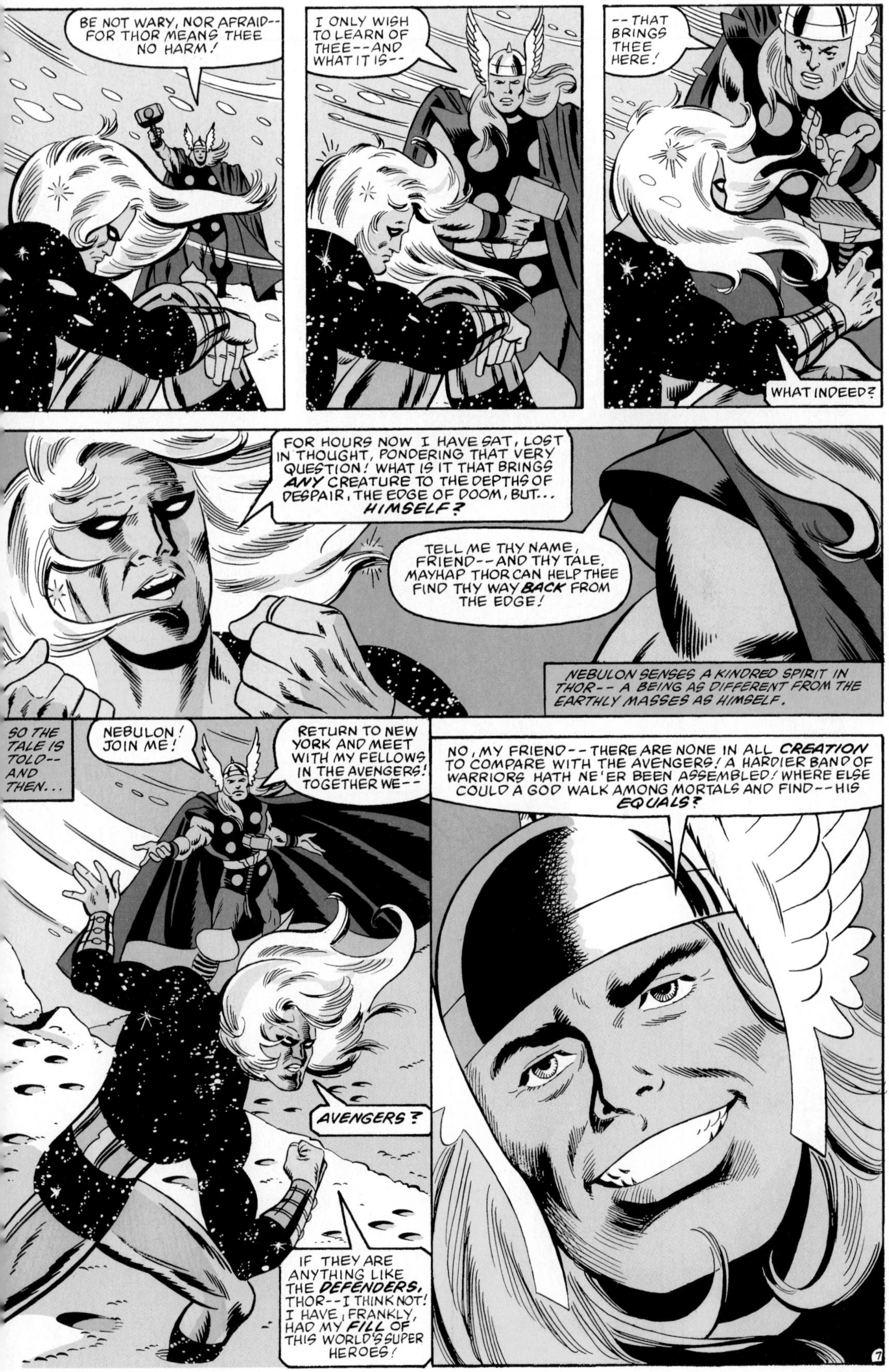

BE NOT WARY, NOR AFRAID-- FOR THOR MEANS THEE NO HARM!
I ONLY WISH TO LEARN OF THEE--AND WHAT IT IS--
--THAT BRINGS THEE HERE!
WHAT INDEED?
FOR HOURS NOW I HAVE SAT, LOST IN THOUGHT, PONDERING THAT VERY QUESTION! WHAT IS IT THAT BRINGS ANY CREATURE TO THE DEPTHS OF DESPAIR, THE EDGE OF DOOM, BUT... HIMSELF?
TELL ME THY NAME, FRIEND--AND THY TALE. MAYHAP THOR CAN HELP THEE FIND THY WAY BACK FROM THE EDGE!
NEBULON SENSES A KINDRED SPIRIT IN THOR-- A BEING AS DIFFERENT FROM THE EARTHLY MASSES AS HIMSELF.
SO THE TALE IS TOLD-- AND THEN...
NEBULON! JOIN ME!
RETURN TO NEW YORK AND MEET WITH MY FELLOWS IN THE AVENGERS! TOGETHER WE--
AVENGERS?
IF THEY ARE ANYTHING LIKE THE DEFENDERS, THOR--I THINK NOT! I HAVE, FRANKLY, HAD MY FILL OF THIS WORLD'S SUPER HEROES!
NO, MY FRIEND--THERE ARE NONE IN ALL CREATION TO COMPARE WITH THE AVENGERS! A HARDIER BAND OF WARRIORS HATH NE'ER BEEN ASSEMBLED! WHERE ELSE COULD A GOD WALK AMONG MORTALS AND FIND--HIS EQUALS?
7

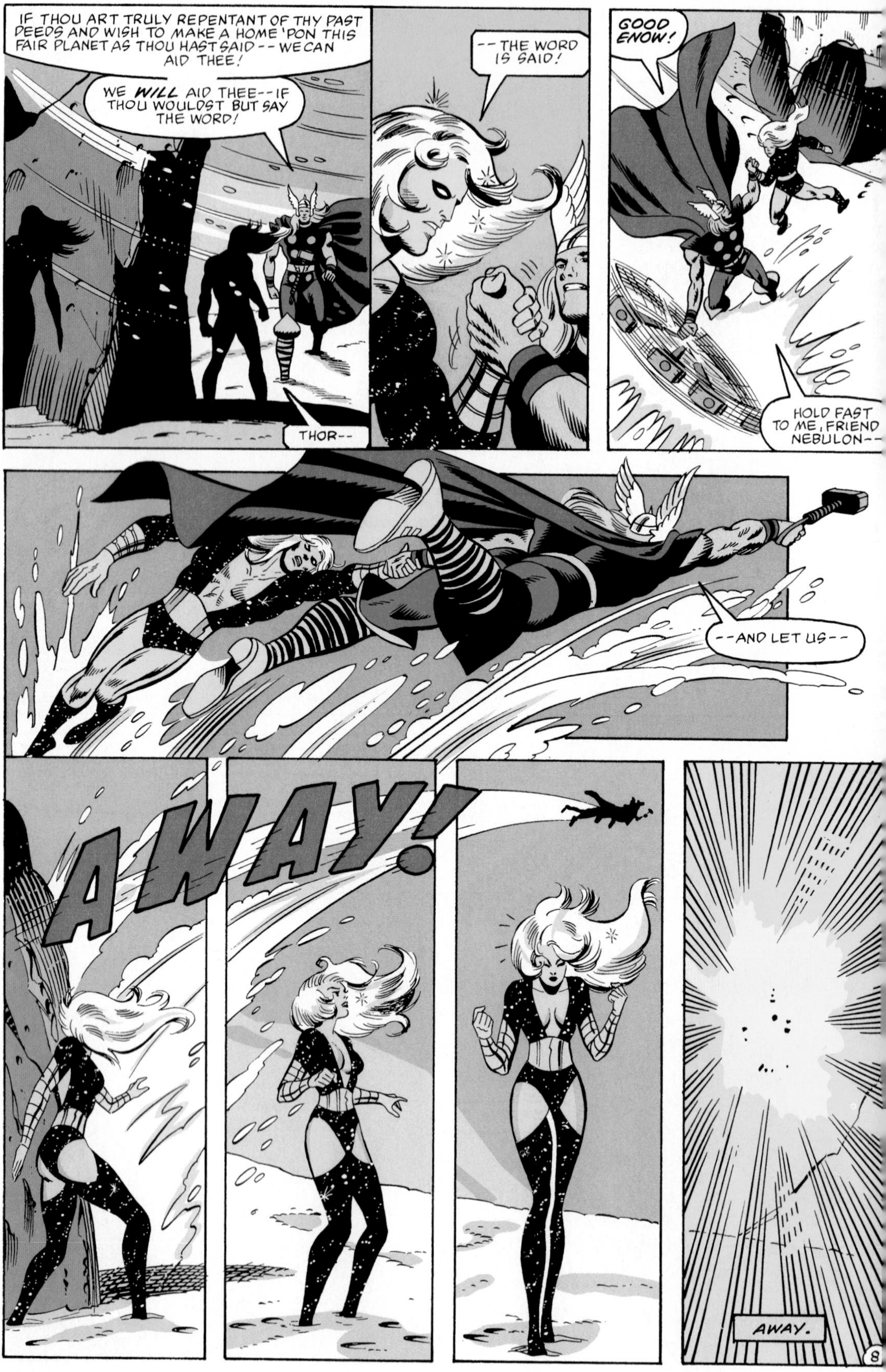
IF THOU ART TRULY REPENTANT OF THY PAST DEEDS AND WISH TO MAKE A HOME 'PON THIS FAIR PLANET AS THOU HAST SAID -- WE CAN AID THEE!
WE WILL AID THEE--IF THOU WOULDST BUT SAY THE WORD!
THOR--
-- THE WORD IS SAID!
GOOD ENOW!
HOLD FAST TO ME, FRIEND NEBULON--
--AND LET US--
AWAY!
AWAY.
8

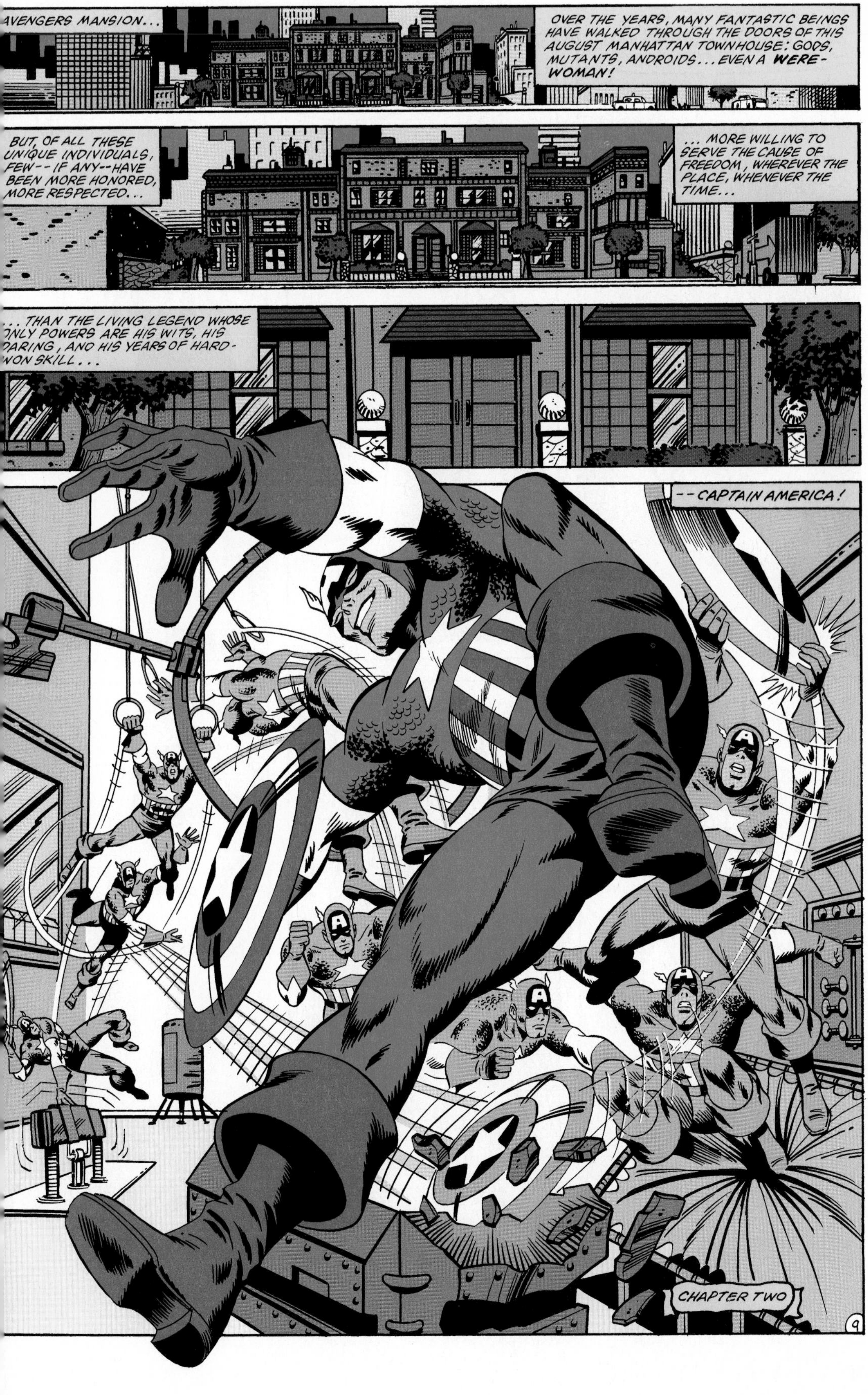
AVENGERS MANSION...
OVER THE YEARS, MANY FANTASTIC BEINGS HAVE WALKED THROUGH THE DOORS OF THIS AUGUST MANHATTAN TOWNHOUSE: GODS, MUTANTS, ANDROIDS... EVEN A WERE-WOMAN!
BUT, OF ALL THESE UNIQUE INDIVIDUALS, FEW--IF ANY--HAVE BEEN MORE HONORED, MORE RESPECTED...
...MORE WILLING TO SERVE THE CAUSE OF FREEDOM, WHEREVER THE PLACE, WHENEVER THE TIME...
...THAN THE LIVING LEGEND WHOSE ONLY POWERS ARE HIS WITS, HIS DARING, AND HIS YEARS OF HARD-WON SKILL...
--CAPTAIN AMERICA!
CHAPTER TWO
9

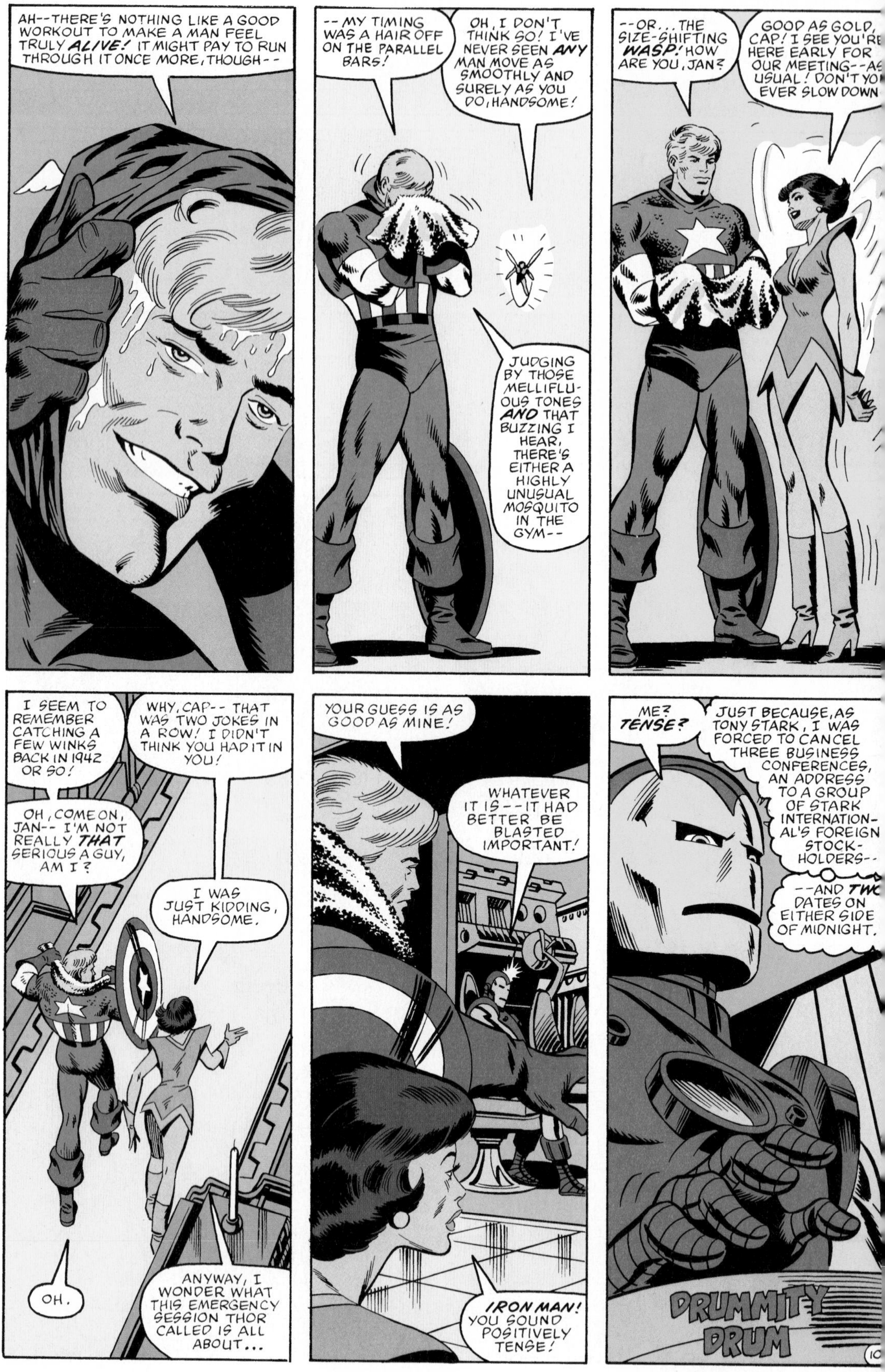
AH--THERE'S NOTHING LIKE A GOOD WORKOUT TO MAKE A MAN FEEL TRULY ALIVE! IT MIGHT PAY TO RUN THROUGH IT ONCE MORE, THOUGH--
--MY TIMING WAS A HAIR OFF ON THE PARALLEL BARS!
OH, I DON'T THINK SO! I'VE NEVER SEEN ANY MAN MOVE AS SMOOTHLY AND SURELY AS YOU DO, HANDSOME!
JUDGING BY THOSE MELLIFLUOUS TONES AND THAT BUZZING I HEAR, THERE'S EITHER A HIGHLY UNUSUAL MOSQUITO IN THE GYM--
--OR...THE SIZE-SHIFTING WASP! HOW ARE YOU, JAN?
GOOD AS GOLD, CAP! I SEE YOU'RE HERE EARLY FOR OUR MEETING--AS USUAL! DON'T YOU EVER SLOW DOWN
I SEEM TO REMEMBER CATCHING A FEW WINKS BACK IN 1942 OR SO!
WHY, CAP-- THAT WAS TWO JOKES IN A ROW! I DIDN'T THINK YOU HAD IT IN YOU!
OH, COME ON, JAN-- I'M NOT REALLY THAT SERIOUS A GUY, AM I?
I WAS JUST KIDDING, HANDSOME.
OH.
ANYWAY, I WONDER WHAT THIS EMERGENCY SESSION THOR CALLED IS ALL ABOUT...
YOUR GUESS IS AS GOOD AS MINE!
WHATEVER IT IS--IT HAD BETTER BE BLASTED IMPORTANT!
IRON MAN! YOU SOUND POSITIVELY TENSE!
ME? TENSE?
JUST BECAUSE, AS TONY STARK, I WAS FORCED TO CANCEL THREE BUSINESS CONFERENCES, AN ADDRESS TO A GROUP OF STARK INTERNATIONAL'S FOREIGN STOCK-HOLDERS--
--AND TW DATES ON EITHER SIDE OF MIDNIGHT.
DRUMMITY DRUM
10

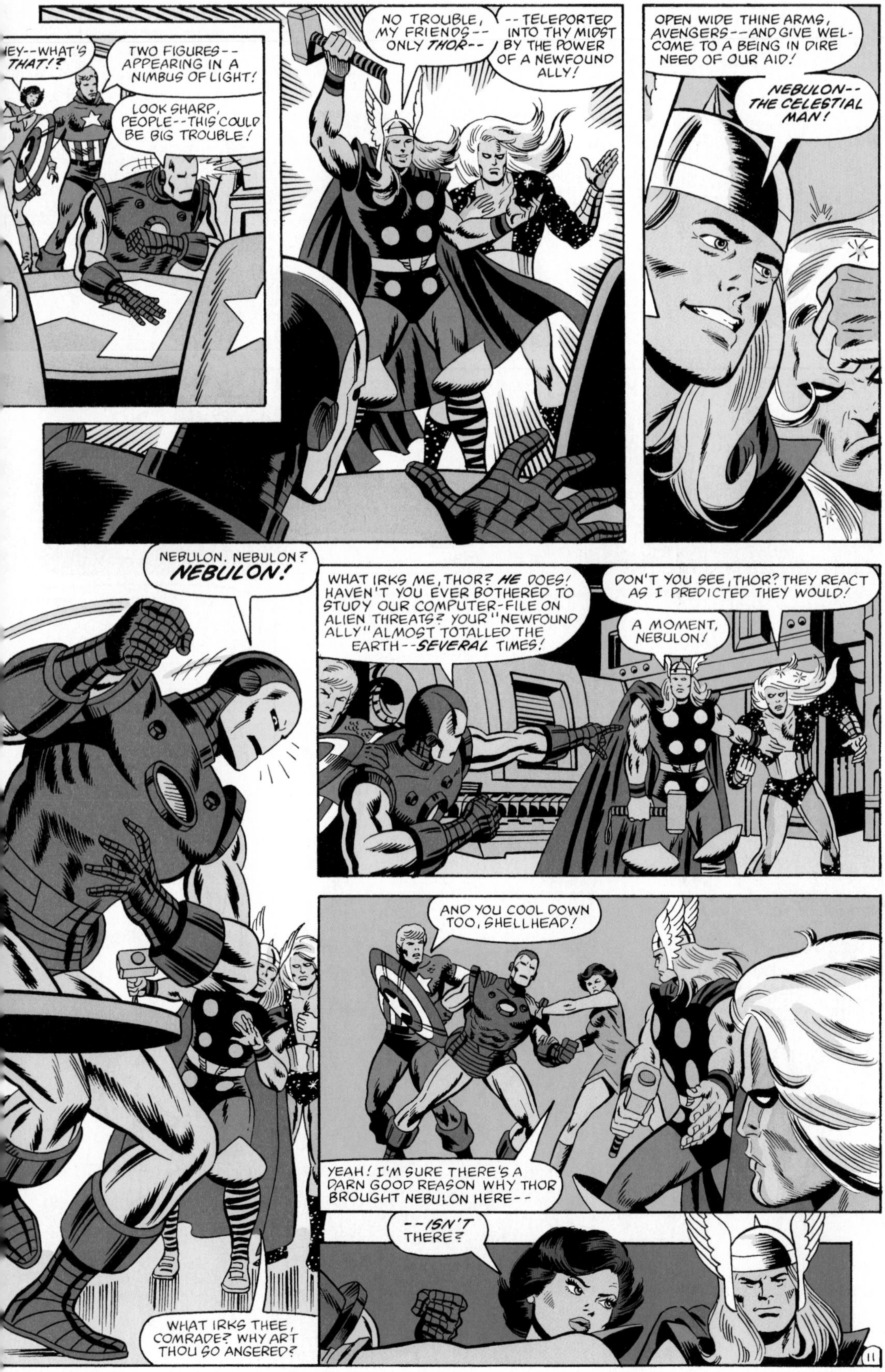
HEY--WHAT'S THAT!?
TWO FIGURES--APPEARING IN A NIMBUS OF LIGHT!
LOOK SHARP, PEOPLE--THIS COULD BE BIG TROUBLE!
NO TROUBLE, MY FRIENDS--ONLY THOR--
--TELEPORTED INTO THY MIDST BY THE POWER OF A NEWFOUND ALLY!
OPEN WIDE THINE ARMS, AVENGERS--AND GIVE WELCOME TO A BEING IN DIRE NEED OF OUR AID!
NEBULON--THE CELESTIAL MAN!
NEBULON. NEBULON? NEBULON!
WHAT IRKS THEE, COMRADE? WHY ART THOU SO ANGERED?
WHAT IRKS ME, THOR? HE DOES! HAVEN'T YOU EVER BOTHERED TO STUDY OUR COMPUTER-FILE ON ALIEN THREATS? YOUR "NEWFOUND ALLY" ALMOST TOTALLED THE EARTH--SEVERAL TIMES!
DON'T YOU SEE, THOR? THEY REACT AS I PREDICTED THEY WOULD!
A MOMENT, NEBULON!
AND YOU COOL DOWN TOO, SHELLHEAD!
YEAH! I'M SURE THERE'S A DARN GOOD REASON WHY THOR BROUGHT NEBULON HERE--
--ISN'T THERE?
11

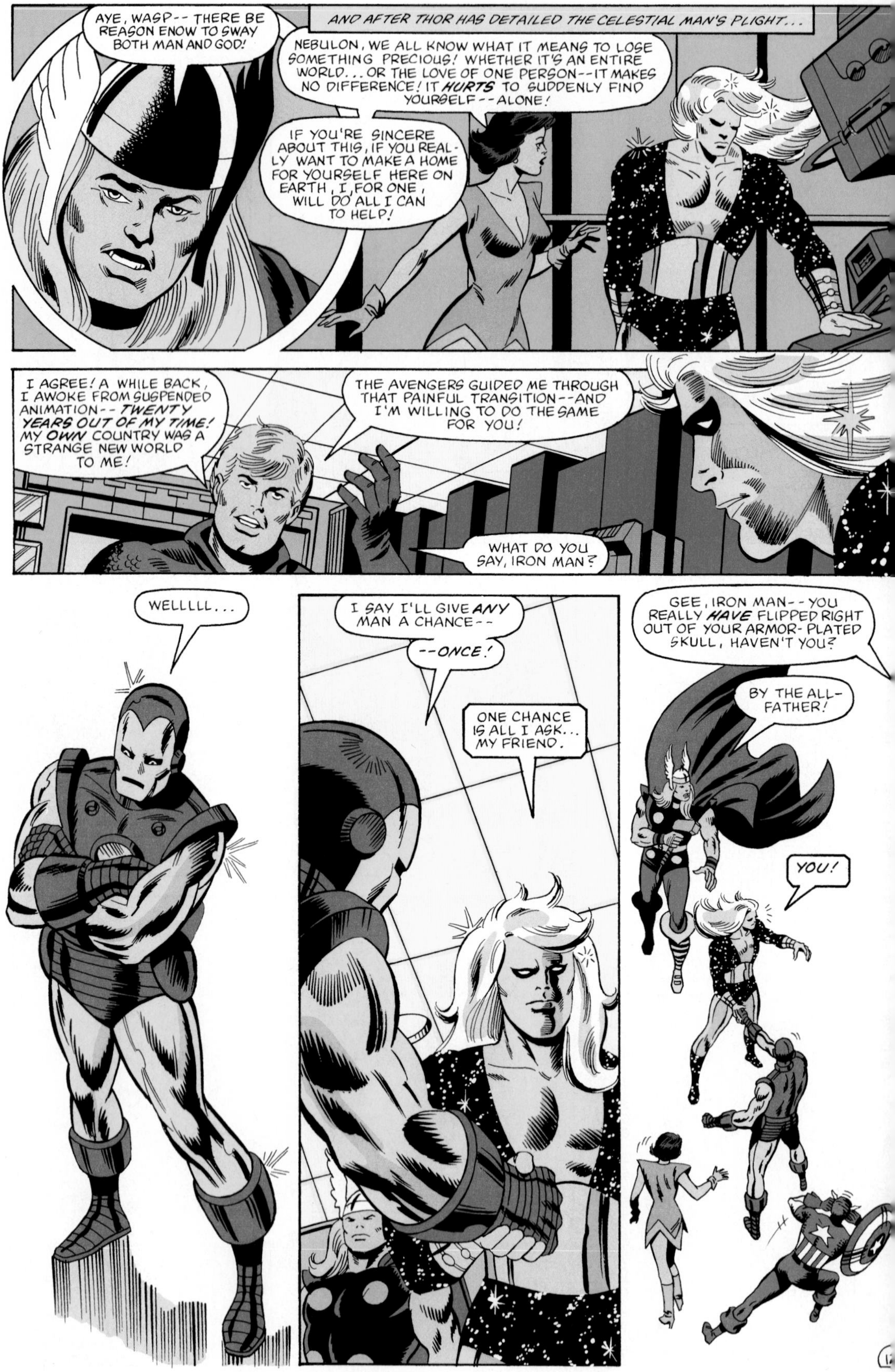
AYE, WASP-- THERE BE REASON ENOW TO SWAY BOTH MAN AND GOD!
AND AFTER THOR HAS DETAILED THE CELESTIAL MAN'S PLIGHT...
NEBULON, WE ALL KNOW WHAT IT MEANS TO LOSE SOMETHING PRECIOUS! WHETHER IT'S AN ENTIRE WORLD... OR THE LOVE OF ONE PERSON--IT MAKES NO DIFFERENCE! IT HURTS TO SUDDENLY FIND YOURSELF--ALONE!
IF YOU'RE SINCERE ABOUT THIS, IF YOU REALLY WANT TO MAKE A HOME FOR YOURSELF HERE ON EARTH, I, FOR ONE, WILL DO ALL I CAN TO HELP!
I AGREE! A WHILE BACK, I AWOKE FROM SUSPENDED ANIMATION--TWENTY YEARS OUT OF MY TIME! MY OWN COUNTRY WAS A STRANGE NEW WORLD TO ME!
THE AVENGERS GUIDED ME THROUGH THAT PAINFUL TRANSITION--AND I'M WILLING TO DO THE SAME FOR YOU!
WHAT DO YOU SAY, IRON MAN?
WELLLLL...
I SAY I'LL GIVE ANY MAN A CHANCE--
--ONCE!
ONE CHANCE IS ALL I ASK... MY FRIEND.
GEE, IRON MAN--YOU REALLY HAVE FLIPPED RIGHT OUT OF YOUR ARMOR-PLATED SKULL, HAVEN'T YOU?
BY THE ALL-FATHER!
YOU!

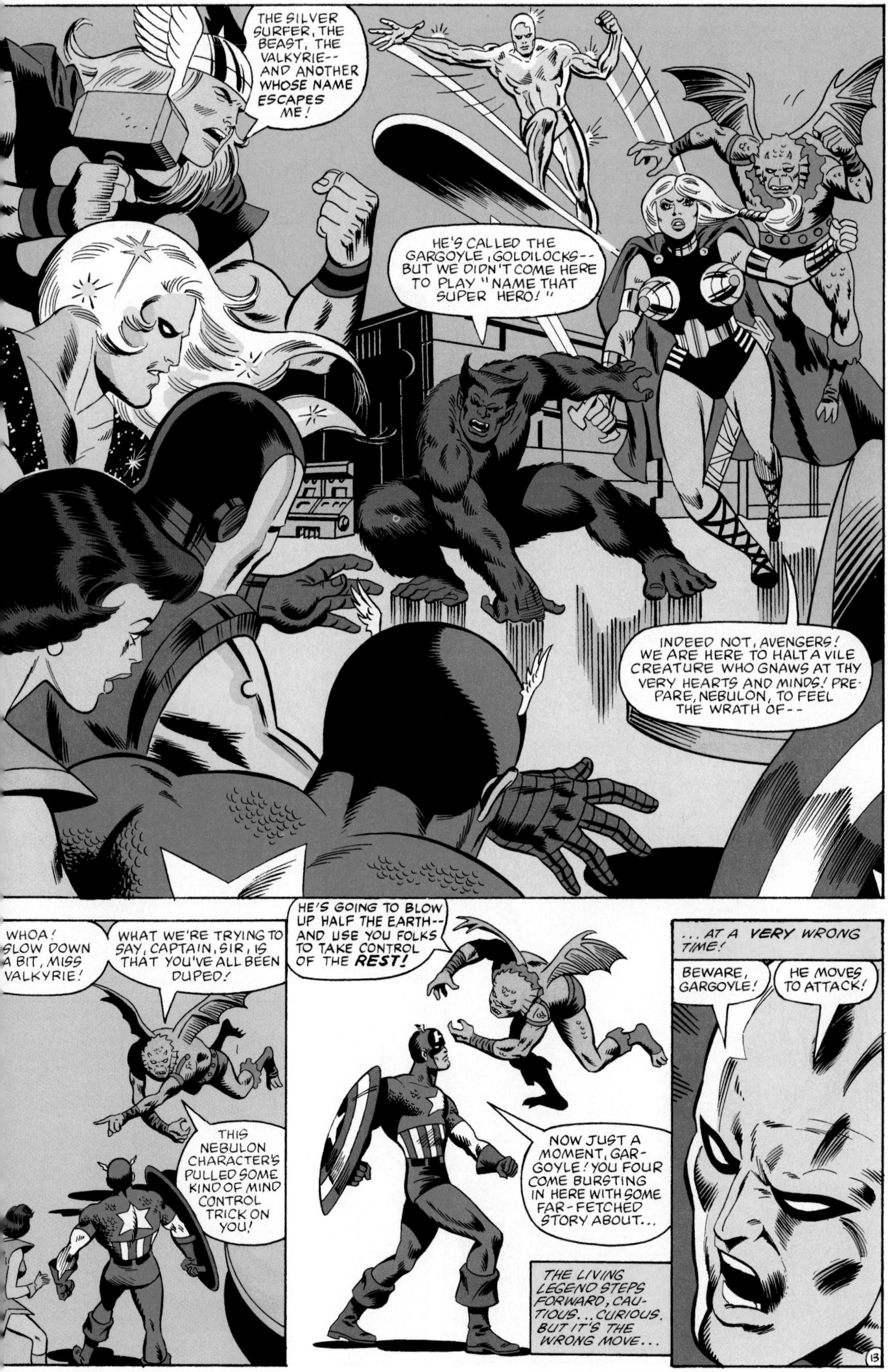

THE SILVER SURFER, THE BEAST, THE VALKYRIE-- AND ANOTHER WHOSE NAME ESCAPES ME!
HE'S CALLED THE GARGOYLE, GOLDILOCKS-- BUT WE DIDN'T COME HERE TO PLAY "NAME THAT SUPER HERO!"
INDEED NOT, AVENGERS! WE ARE HERE TO HALT A VILE CREATURE WHO GNAWS AT THY VERY HEARTS AND MINDS! PREPARE, NEBULON, TO FEEL THE WRATH OF--
WHOA! SLOW DOWN A BIT, MISS VALKYRIE!
WHAT WE'RE TRYING TO SAY, CAPTAIN, SIR, IS THAT YOU'VE ALL BEEN DUPED!
THIS NEBULON CHARACTER'S PULLED SOME KIND OF MIND CONTROL TRICK ON YOU!
HE'S GOING TO BLOW UP HALF THE EARTH-- AND USE YOU FOLKS TO TAKE CONTROL OF THE **REST!**
NOW JUST A MOMENT, GARGOYLE! YOU FOUR COME BURSTING IN HERE WITH SOME FAR-FETCHED STORY ABOUT...
THE LIVING LEGEND STEPS FORWARD, CAUTIOUS... CURIOUS. BUT IT'S THE WRONG MOVE...
...AT A **VERY WRONG** TIME!
BEWARE, GARGOYLE!
HE MOVES TO ATTACK!
13

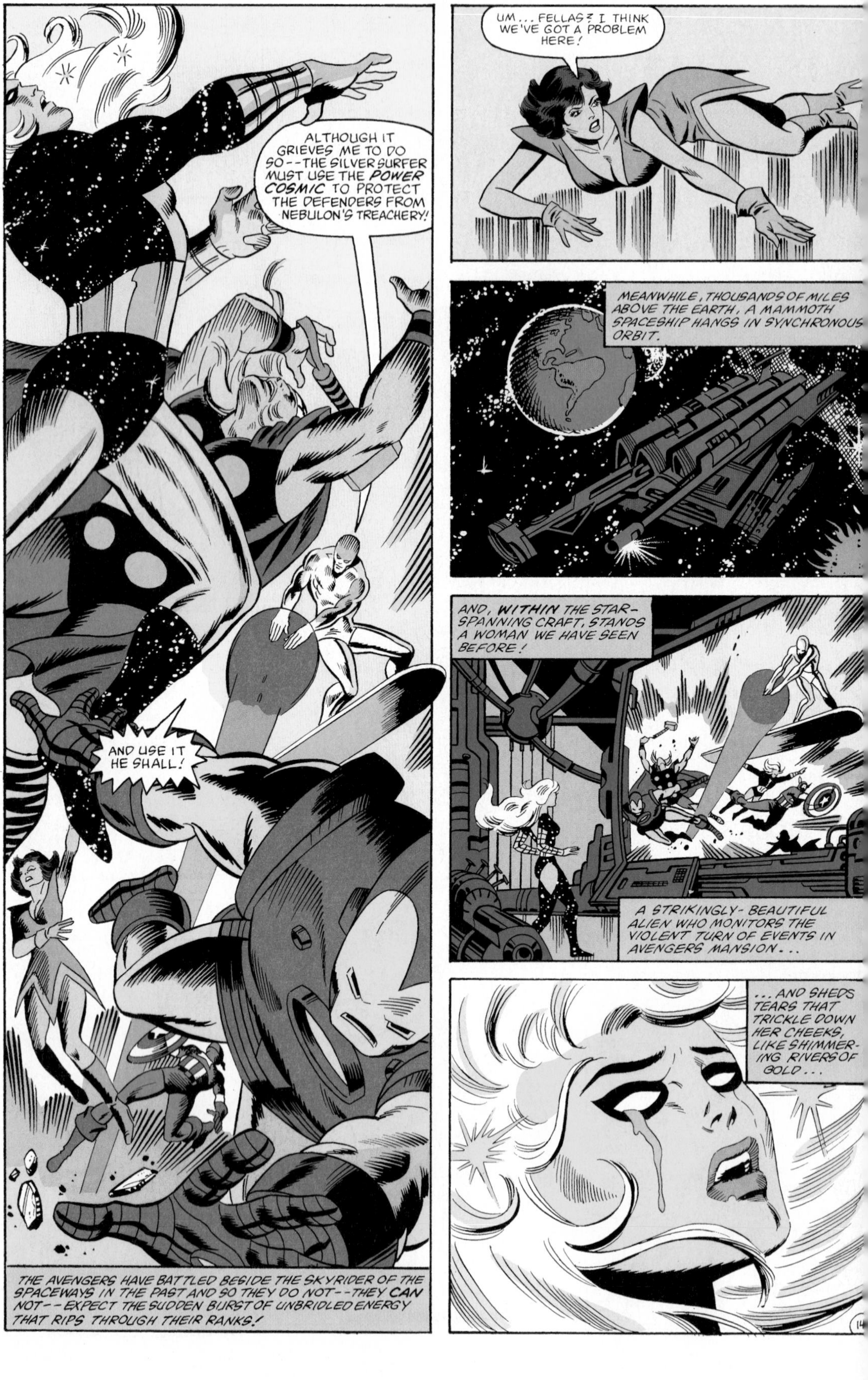
ALTHOUGH IT GRIEVES ME TO DO SO--THE SILVER SURFER MUST USE THE POWER COSMIC TO PROTECT THE DEFENDERS FROM NEBULON'S TREACHERY!
AND USE IT HE SHALL!
THE AVENGERS HAVE BATTLED BESIDE THE SKYRIDER OF THE SPACEWAYS IN THE PAST AND SO THEY DO NOT--THEY CAN NOT--EXPECT THE SUDDEN BURST OF UNBRIDLED ENERGY THAT RIPS THROUGH THEIR RANKS!
UM... FELLAS? I THINK WE'VE GOT A PROBLEM HERE!
MEANWHILE, THOUSANDS OF MILES ABOVE THE EARTH, A MAMMOTH SPACESHIP HANGS IN SYNCHRONOUS ORBIT.
AND, WITHIN THE STAR-SPANNING CRAFT, STANDS A WOMAN WE HAVE SEEN BEFORE!
A STRIKINGLY-BEAUTIFUL ALIEN WHO MONITORS THE VIOLENT TURN OF EVENTS IN AVENGERS MANSION...
...AND SHEDS TEARS THAT TRICKLE DOWN HER CHEEKS, LIKE SHIMMERING RIVERS OF GOLD...

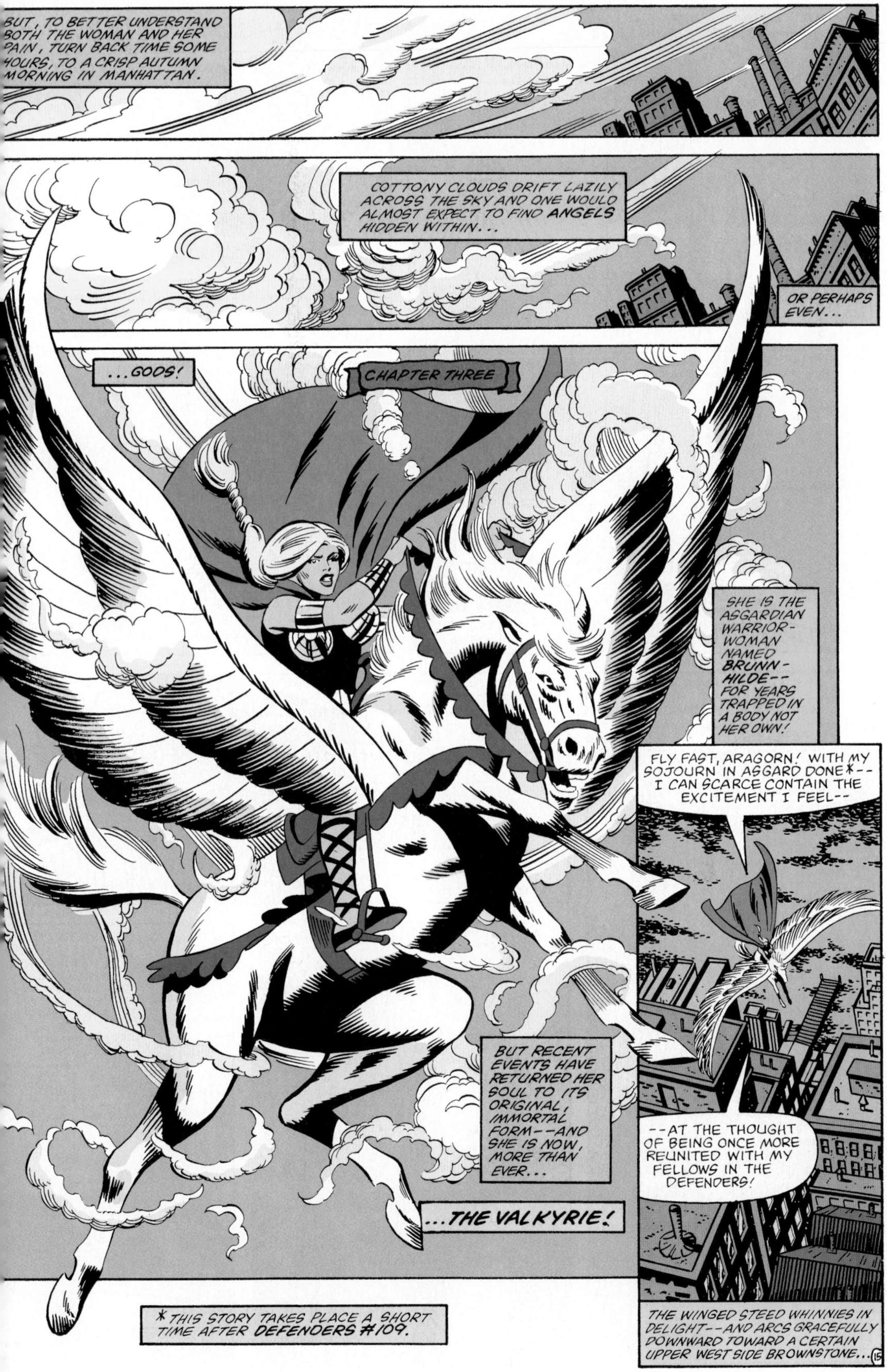
BUT, TO BETTER UNDERSTAND BOTH THE WOMAN AND HER PAIN, TURN BACK TIME SOME HOURS, TO A CRISP AUTUMN MORNING IN MANHATTAN.
COTTONY CLOUDS DRIFT LAZILY ACROSS THE SKY AND ONE WOULD ALMOST EXPECT TO FIND ANGELS HIDDEN WITHIN...
OR PERHAPS EVEN...
...GODS!
CHAPTER THREE
SHE IS THE ASGARDIAN WARRIOR-WOMAN NAMED BRUNN-HILDE--FOR YEARS TRAPPED IN A BODY NOT HER OWN!
BUT RECENT EVENTS HAVE RETURNED HER SOUL TO ITS ORIGINAL, IMMORTAL FORM--AND SHE IS NOW, MORE THAN EVER...
...THE VALKYRIE!
FLY FAST, ARAGORN! WITH MY SOJOURN IN ASGARD DONE*--I CAN SCARCE CONTAIN THE EXCITEMENT I FEEL--
--AT THE THOUGHT OF BEING ONCE MORE REUNITED WITH MY FELLOWS IN THE DEFENDERS!
THE WINGED STEED WHINNIES IN DELIGHT--AND ARCS GRACEFULLY DOWNWARD TOWARD A CERTAIN UPPER WEST SIDE BROWNSTONE...
15
*THIS STORY TAKES PLACE A SHORT TIME AFTER DEFENDERS #109.

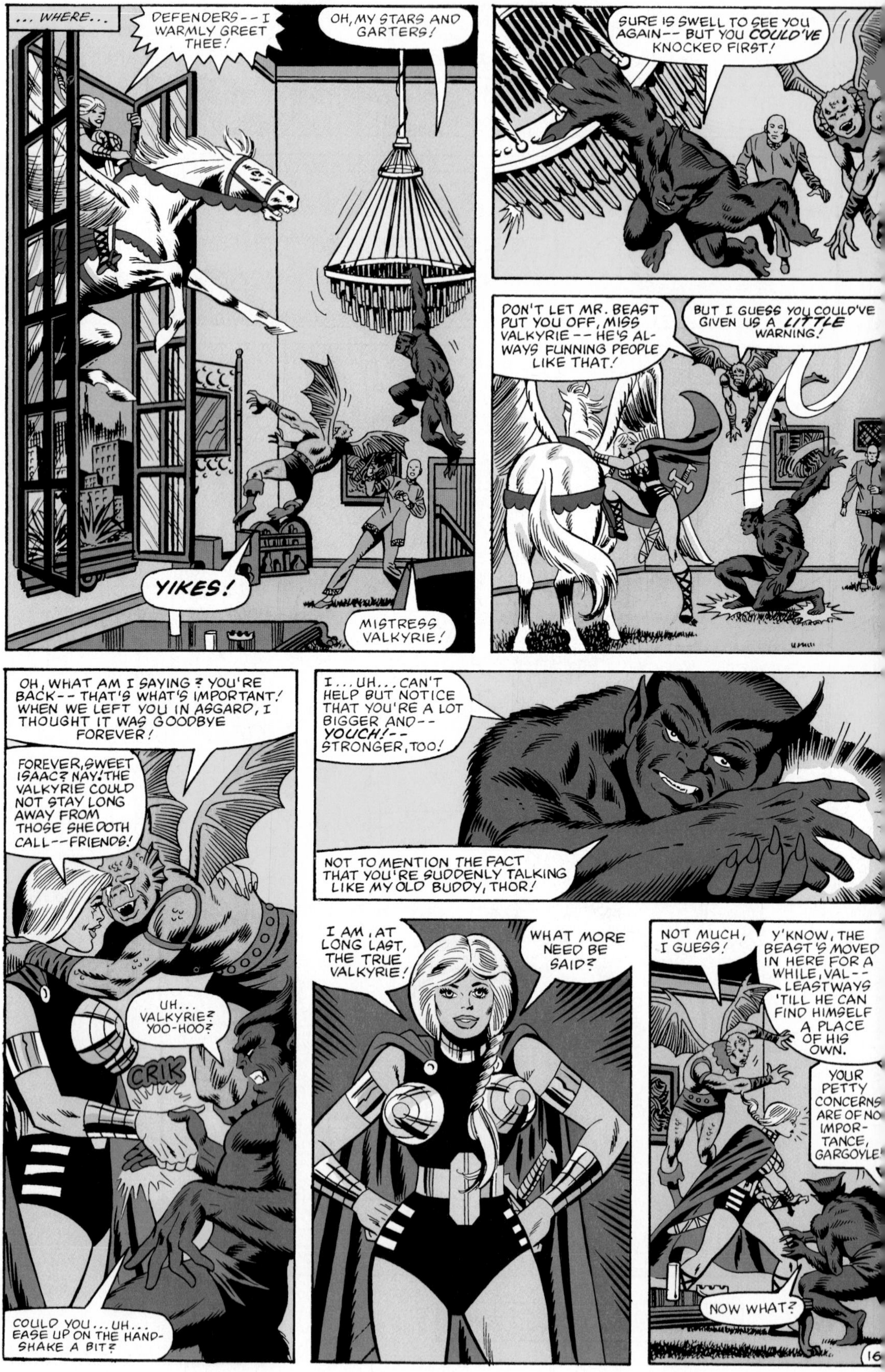

... WHERE...
DEFENDERS--I WARMLY GREET THEE!
OH, MY STARS AND GARTERS!
YIKES!
MISTRESS VALKYRIE!
SURE IS SWELL TO SEE YOU AGAIN-- BUT YOU COULD'VE KNOCKED FIRST!
DON'T LET MR. BEAST PUT YOU OFF, MISS VALKYRIE--HE'S ALWAYS FUNNING PEOPLE LIKE THAT!
BUT I GUESS YOU COULD'VE GIVEN US A LITTLE WARNING!
OH, WHAT AM I SAYING? YOU'RE BACK--THAT'S WHAT'S IMPORTANT! WHEN WE LEFT YOU IN ASGARD, I THOUGHT IT WAS GOODBYE FOREVER!
FOREVER, SWEET ISAAC? NAY! THE VALKYRIE COULD NOT STAY LONG AWAY FROM THOSE SHE DOTH CALL--FRIENDS!
UH... VALKYRIE? YOO-HOO?
CRIK
COULD YOU...UH... EASE UP ON THE HANDSHAKE A BIT?
I...UH...CAN'T HELP BUT NOTICE THAT YOU'RE A LOT BIGGER AND-- YOUCH!-- STRONGER, TOO!
NOT TO MENTION THE FACT THAT YOU'RE SUDDENLY TALKING LIKE MY OLD BUDDY, THOR!
I AM, AT LONG LAST, THE TRUE VALKYRIE!
WHAT MORE NEED BE SAID?
NOT MUCH, I GUESS!
Y'KNOW, THE BEAST'S MOVED IN HERE FOR A WHILE, VAL--LEASTWAYS 'TILL HE CAN FIND HIMSELF A PLACE OF HIS OWN.
YOUR PETTY CONCERNS ARE OF NO IMPORTANCE, GARGOYLE!
NOW WHAT?
16

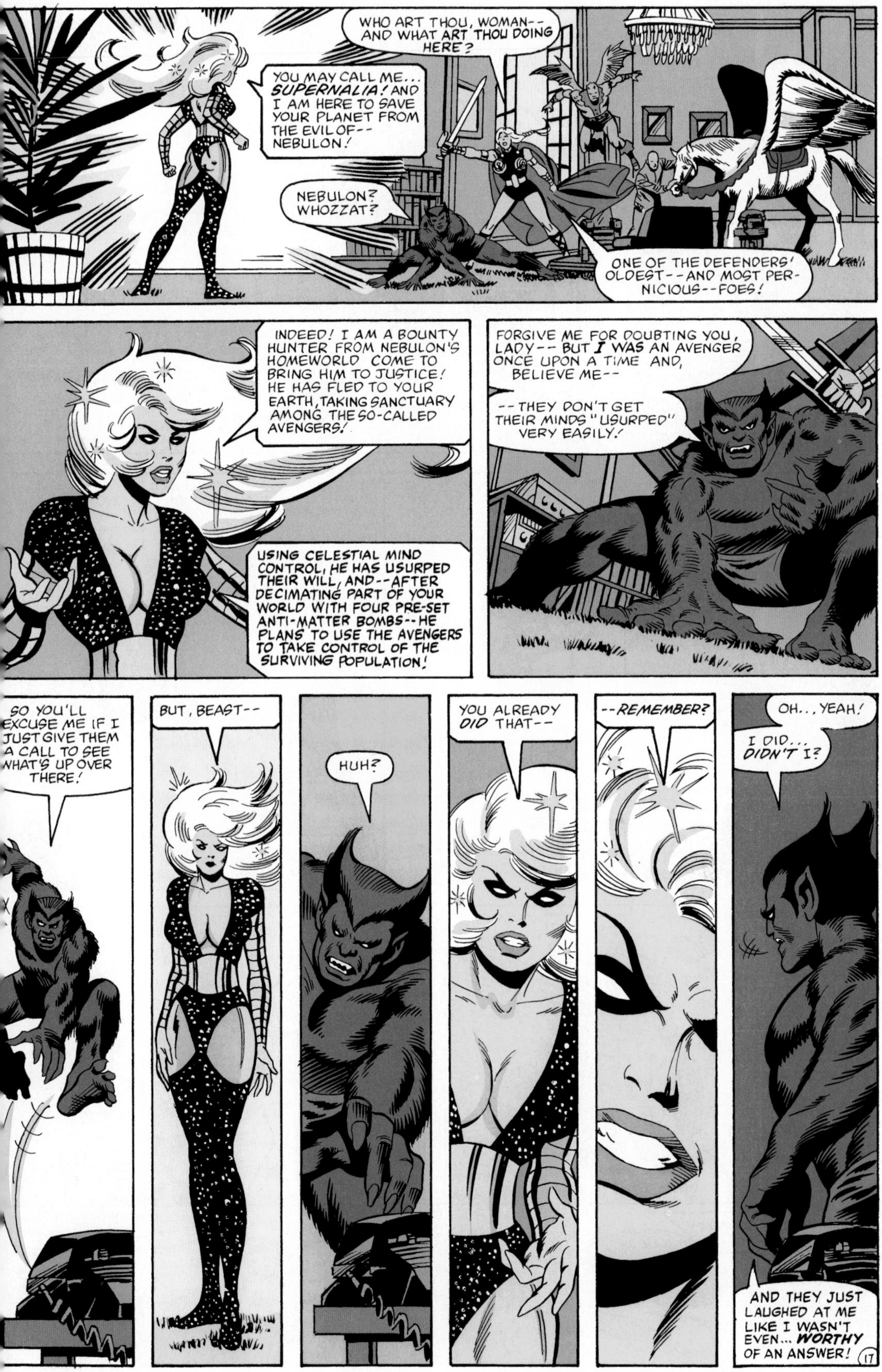

WHO ART THOU, WOMAN-- AND WHAT ART THOU DOING HERE?
YOU MAY CALL ME... SUPERNALIA! AND I AM HERE TO SAVE YOUR PLANET FROM THE EVIL OF-- NEBULON!
NEBULON? WHOZZAT?
ONE OF THE DEFENDERS' OLDEST--AND MOST PERNICIOUS--FOES!
INDEED! I AM A BOUNTY HUNTER FROM NEBULON'S HOMEWORLD COME TO BRING HIM TO JUSTICE! HE HAS FLED TO YOUR EARTH, TAKING SANCTUARY AMONG THE SO-CALLED AVENGERS!
USING CELESTIAL MIND CONTROL, HE HAS USURPED THEIR WILL, AND--AFTER DECIMATING PART OF YOUR WORLD WITH FOUR PRE-SET ANTI-MATTER BOMBS--HE PLANS TO USE THE AVENGERS TO TAKE CONTROL OF THE SURVIVING POPULATION!
FORGIVE ME FOR DOUBTING YOU, LADY-- BUT I WAS AN AVENGER ONCE UPON A TIME AND, BELIEVE ME--
--THEY DON'T GET THEIR MINDS "USURPED" VERY EASILY!
SO YOU'LL EXCUSE ME IF I JUST GIVE THEM A CALL TO SEE WHAT'S UP OVER THERE!
BUT, BEAST--
HUH?
YOU ALREADY DID THAT--
--REMEMBER?
OH.., YEAH!
I DID... DIDN'T I?
AND THEY JUST LAUGHED AT ME LIKE I WASN'T EVEN... WORTHY OF AN ANSWER!
17

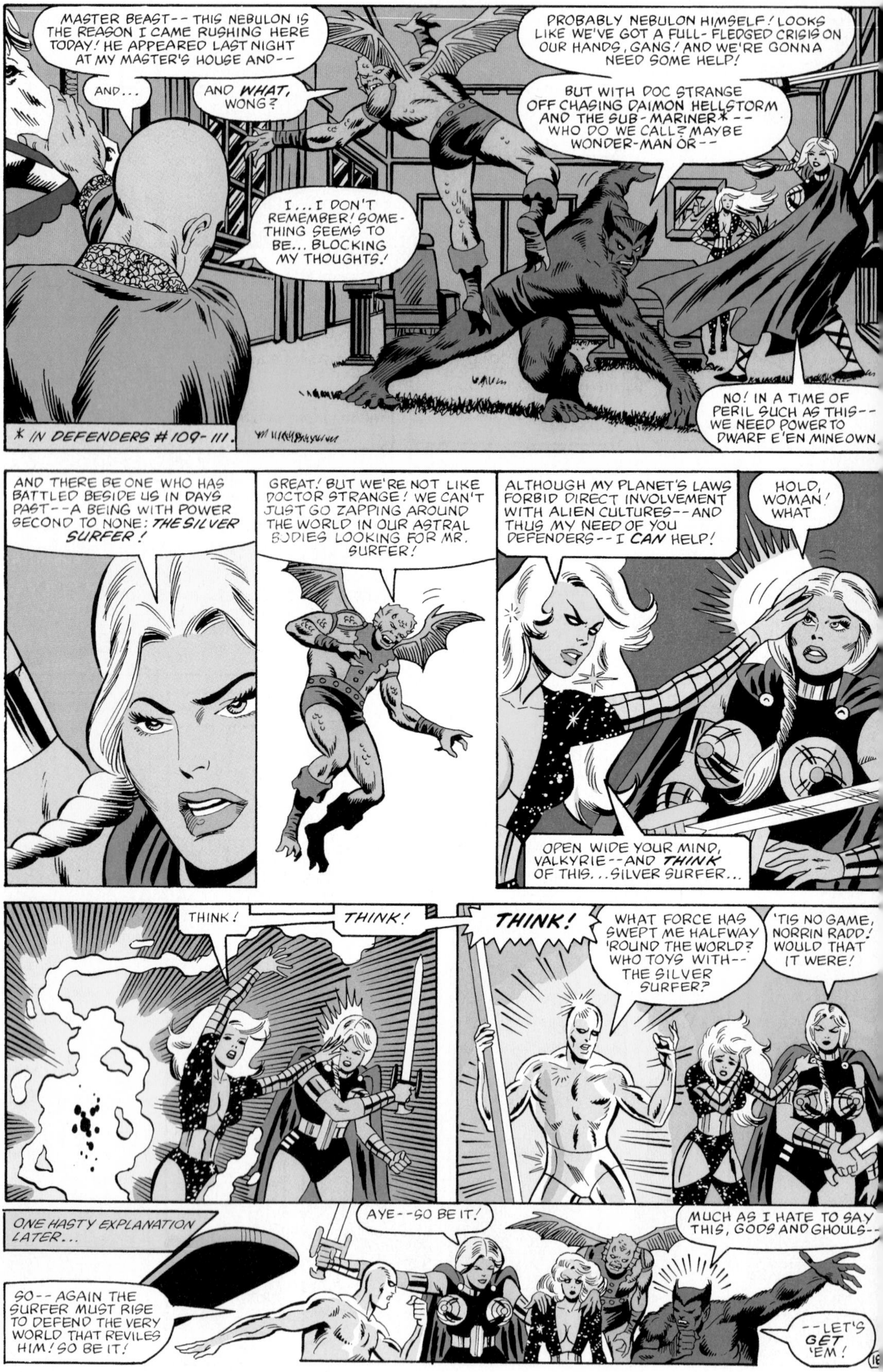
MASTER BEAST-- THIS NEBULON IS THE REASON I CAME RUSHING HERE TODAY! HE APPEARED LAST NIGHT AT MY MASTER'S HOUSE AND--
AND...
AND WHAT, WONG?
I... I DON'T REMEMBER! SOME-THING SEEMS TO BE... BLOCKING MY THOUGHTS!
PROBABLY NEBULON HIMSELF! LOOKS LIKE WE'VE GOT A FULL-FLEDGED CRISIS ON OUR HANDS, GANG! AND WE'RE GONNA NEED SOME HELP!
BUT WITH DOC STRANGE OFF CHASING DAIMON HELLSTORM AND THE SUB-MARINER*-- WHO DO WE CALL? MAYBE WONDER-MAN OR--
NO! IN A TIME OF PERIL SUCH AS THIS-- WE NEED POWER TO DWARF E'EN MINE OWN.
* IN DEFENDERS #109-111.
AND THERE BE ONE WHO HAS BATTLED BESIDE US IN DAYS PAST--A BEING WITH POWER SECOND TO NONE: THE SILVER SURFER!
GREAT! BUT WE'RE NOT LIKE DOCTOR STRANGE! WE CAN'T JUST GO ZAPPING AROUND THE WORLD IN OUR ASTRAL BODIES LOOKING FOR MR. SURFER!
ALTHOUGH MY PLANET'S LAWS FORBID DIRECT INVOLVEMENT WITH ALIEN CULTURES--AND THUS MY NEED OF YOU DEFENDERS--I CAN HELP!
HOLD, WOMAN! WHAT
OPEN WIDE YOUR MIND, VALKYRIE--AND THINK OF THIS...SILVER SURFER...
THINK!
THINK!
THINK!
WHAT FORCE HAS SWEPT ME HALFWAY 'ROUND THE WORLD? WHO TOYS WITH-- THE SILVER SURFER?
'TIS NO GAME, NORRIN RADD! WOULD THAT IT WERE!
ONE HASTY EXPLANATION LATER...
AYE--SO BE IT!
SO-- AGAIN THE SURFER MUST RISE TO DEFEND THE VERY WORLD THAT REVILES HIM! SO BE IT!
MUCH AS I HATE TO SAY THIS, GODS AND GHOULS--
--LET'S GET 'EM!
18

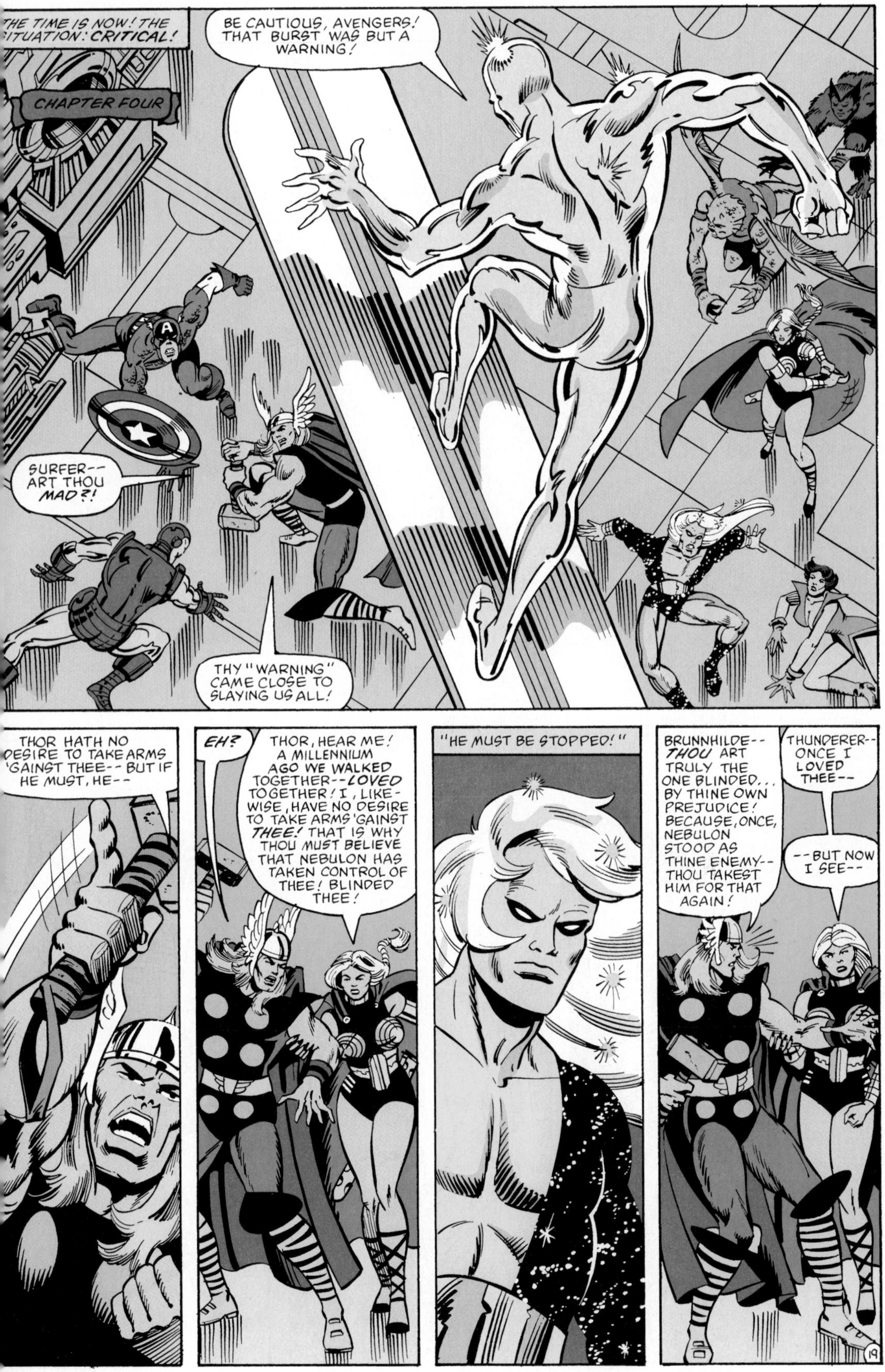
THE TIME IS NOW! THE SITUATION: CRITICAL!
CHAPTER FOUR
BE CAUTIOUS, AVENGERS! THAT BURST WAS BUT A WARNING!
SURFER-- ART THOU MAD?!
THY "WARNING" CAME CLOSE TO SLAYING US ALL!
THOR HATH NO DESIRE TO TAKE ARMS 'GAINST THEE-- BUT IF HE MUST, HE--
EH?
THOR, HEAR ME! A MILLENNIUM AGO WE WALKED TOGETHER--LOVED TOGETHER! I, LIKE-WISE, HAVE NO DESIRE TO TAKE ARMS 'GAINST THEE! THAT IS WHY THOU MUST BELIEVE THAT NEBULON HAS TAKEN CONTROL OF THEE! BLINDED THEE!
"HE MUST BE STOPPED!"
BRUNNHILDE-- THOU ART TRULY THE ONE BLINDED... BY THINE OWN PREJUDICE! BECAUSE, ONCE, NEBULON STOOD AS THINE ENEMY-- THOU TAKEST HIM FOR THAT AGAIN!
THUNDERER-- ONCE I LOVED THEE--
--BUT NOW I SEE--
19

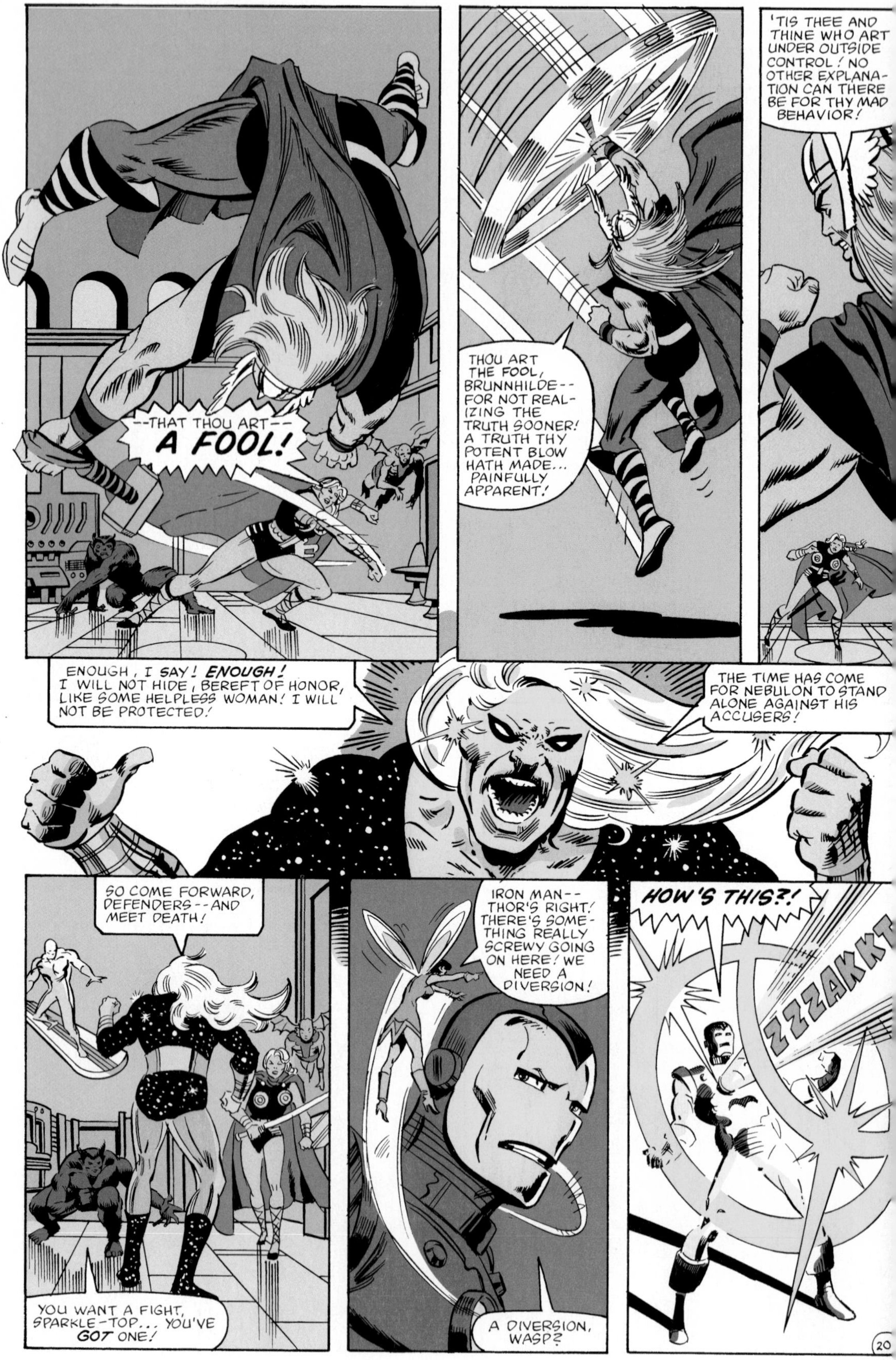
--THAT THOU ART--
A FOOL!
THOU ART THE FOOL, BRUNNHILDE--FOR NOT REALIZING THE TRUTH SOONER! A TRUTH THY POTENT BLOW HATH MADE... PAINFULLY APPARENT!
'TIS THEE AND THINE WHO ART UNDER OUTSIDE CONTROL! NO OTHER EXPLANATION CAN THERE BE FOR THY MAD BEHAVIOR!
ENOUGH, I SAY! ENOUGH! I WILL NOT HIDE, BEREFT OF HONOR, LIKE SOME HELPLESS WOMAN! I WILL NOT BE PROTECTED!
THE TIME HAS COME FOR NEBULON TO STAND ALONE AGAINST HIS ACCUSERS!
SO COME FORWARD, DEFENDERS--AND MEET DEATH!
YOU WANT A FIGHT, SPARKLE-TOP... YOU'VE GOT ONE!
IRON MAN--THOR'S RIGHT! THERE'S SOMETHING REALLY SCREWY GOING ON HERE! WE NEED A DIVERSION!
A DIVERSION, WASP?
HOW'S THIS?!
ZZZAKKT
20

KRA-KOOM!

WAIT TILL TONY STARK GETS THE *BILL* FOR THIS!

AYE! THY REPULSORS ARE INDEED... FORMIDABLE!

WE RETREAT? WHY?

BECAUSE THERE'S NO POINT IN STICKING AROUND TO FIGHT WHEN WE CAN GET OUR TAILS OUT OF HERE AND *PLAN!*

RIGHT! IT DOESN'T TAKE A GENIUS TO FIGURE OUT THAT SOMEONE'S MANIPULATING THE DEFENDERS!

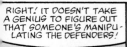

A GENTLE-SOULED BEING LIKE THE SURFER WOULD *NEVER* HAVE ATTACKED LIKE THAT—*IF* HE WAS IN HIS RIGHT MIND!

HOW CAN YOU BE *SO* CERTAIN OF THE DEFENDERS' INNOCENCE?

NEBULON— THE BEAST AND THE SILVER SURFER HAVE BEEN THOR'S COMRADES IN BATTLE! BRUNNHILDE HAS BEEN... E'EN *MORE!*

I AM CERTAIN... BECAUSE MY HEART *TELLS* ME SO!

TO FOLLOW THE URGINGS OF THE HEART, THUNDERER—

—IS OFTEN TO COURT DISASTER!

PERHAPS,' BUT, FOR THOR, THERE HATH NE'ER BEEN ANOTHER WAY!

NOW, QUICKLY, CANST THOU USE THY POWER TO TELEPORT US TO A DISTANT PLACE OF SAFETY?

YOU HAVE TRUSTED ME, THOR—I CAN DO LITTLE ELSE BUT TRUST *YOU!*

IF WE NEED A PLACE TO PLAN, TO FERRET OUT THE VILLAIN YOU BELIEVE IS BEHIND ALL THIS—

21

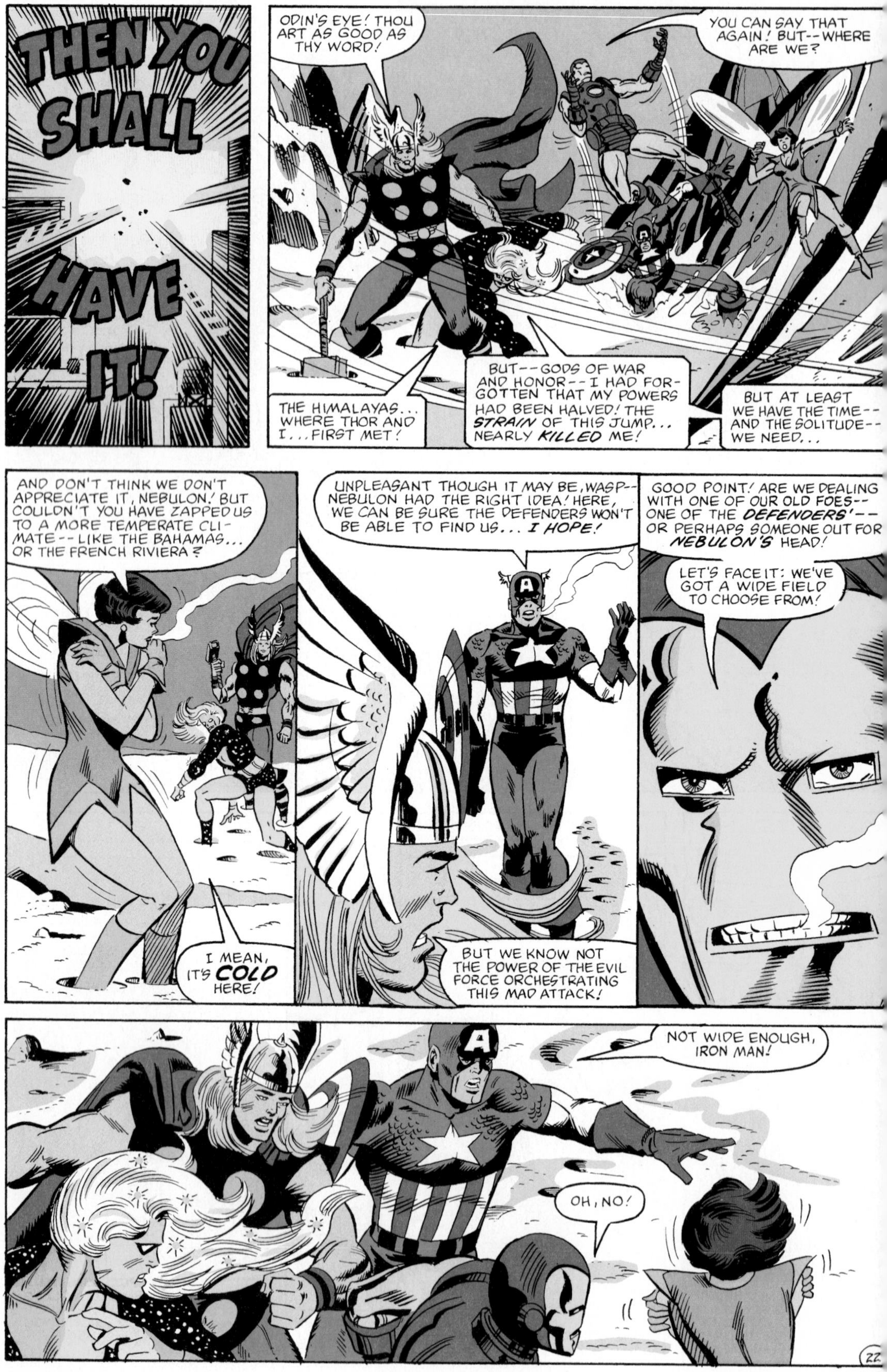
THEN YOU SHALL HAVE IT!
ODIN'S EYE! THOU ART AS GOOD AS THY WORD!
YOU CAN SAY THAT AGAIN! BUT--WHERE ARE WE?
THE HIMALAYAS... WHERE THOR AND I... FIRST MET!
BUT--GODS OF WAR AND HONOR--I HAD FORGOTTEN THAT MY POWERS HAD BEEN HALVED! THE STRAIN OF THIS JUMP... NEARLY KILLED ME!
BUT AT LEAST WE HAVE THE TIME--AND THE SOLITUDE--WE NEED...
AND DON'T THINK WE DON'T APPRECIATE IT, NEBULON! BUT COULDN'T YOU HAVE ZAPPED US TO A MORE TEMPERATE CLIMATE--LIKE THE BAHAMAS... OR THE FRENCH RIVIERA?
I MEAN, IT'S COLD HERE!
UNPLEASANT THOUGH IT MAY BE, WASP--NEBULON HAD THE RIGHT IDEA! HERE, WE CAN BE SURE THE DEFENDERS WON'T BE ABLE TO FIND US... I HOPE!
BUT WE KNOW NOT THE POWER OF THE EVIL FORCE ORCHESTRATING THIS MAD ATTACK!
GOOD POINT! ARE WE DEALING WITH ONE OF OUR OLD FOES--ONE OF THE DEFENDERS'--OR PERHAPS SOMEONE OUT FOR NEBULON'S HEAD!
LET'S FACE IT: WE'VE GOT A WIDE FIELD TO CHOOSE FROM!
NOT WIDE ENOUGH, IRON MAN!
OH, NO!
22

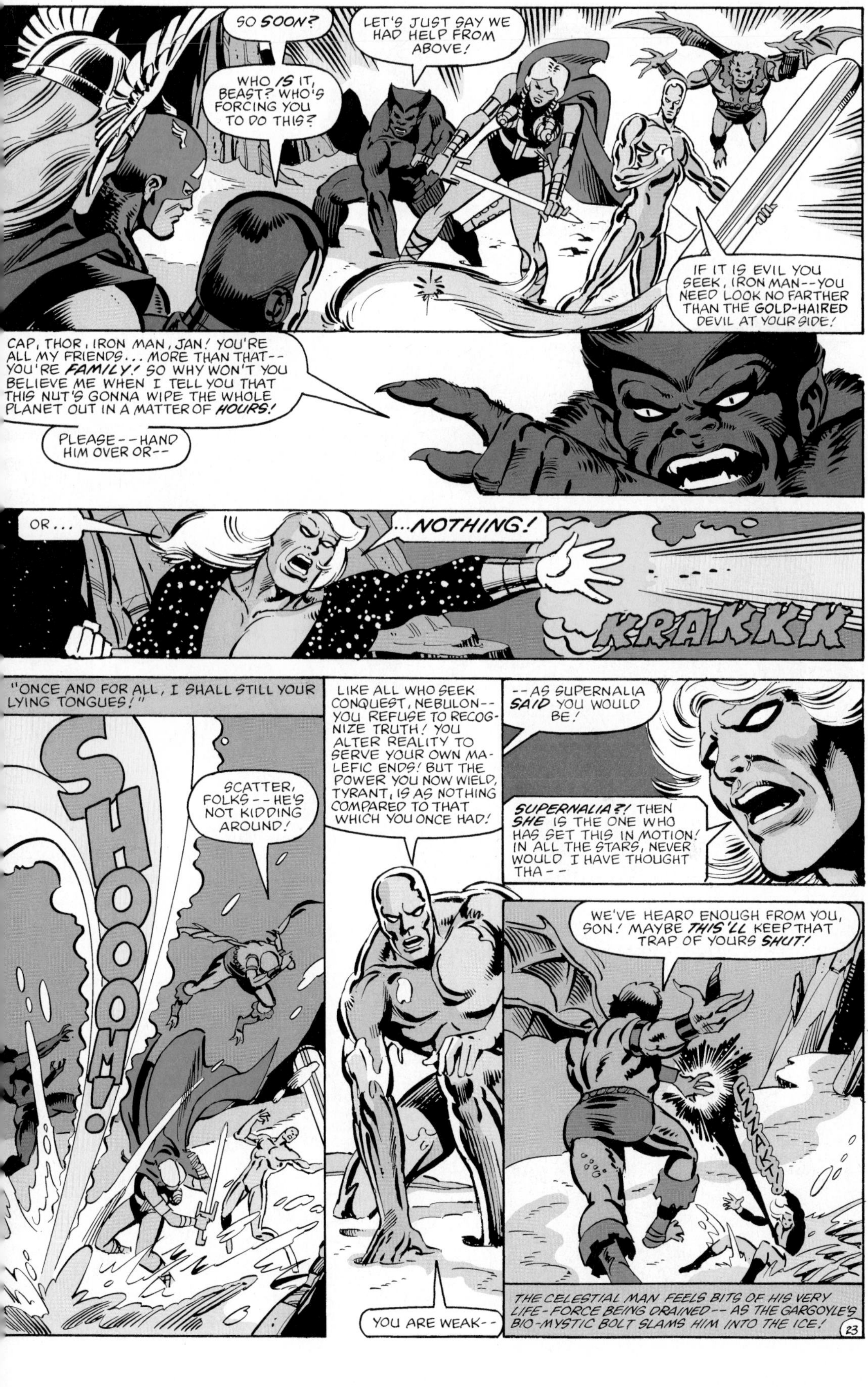
SO SOON?
LET'S JUST SAY WE HAD HELP FROM ABOVE!
WHO IS IT, BEAST? WHO'S FORCING YOU TO DO THIS?
IF IT IS EVIL YOU SEEK, IRON MAN--YOU NEED LOOK NO FARTHER THAN THE GOLD-HAIRED DEVIL AT YOUR SIDE!
CAP, THOR, IRON MAN, JAN! YOU'RE ALL MY FRIENDS... MORE THAN THAT--YOU'RE FAMILY! SO WHY WON'T YOU BELIEVE ME WHEN I TELL YOU THAT THIS NUT'S GONNA WIPE THE WHOLE PLANET OUT IN A MATTER OF HOURS!
PLEASE--HAND HIM OVER OR--
OR...
...NOTHING!
KRAKKK
"ONCE AND FOR ALL, I SHALL STILL YOUR LYING TONGUES!"
SHOOOM!
SCATTER, FOLKS--HE'S NOT KIDDING AROUND!
LIKE ALL WHO SEEK CONQUEST, NEBULON--YOU REFUSE TO RECOGNIZE TRUTH! YOU ALTER REALITY TO SERVE YOUR OWN MALEFIC ENDS! BUT THE POWER YOU NOW WIELD, TYRANT, IS AS NOTHING COMPARED TO THAT WHICH YOU ONCE HAD!
YOU ARE WEAK--
--AS SUPERNALIA SAID YOU WOULD BE!
SUPERNALIA?! THEN SHE IS THE ONE WHO HAS SET THIS IN MOTION! IN ALL THE STARS, NEVER WOULD I HAVE THOUGHT THA--
WE'VE HEARD ENOUGH FROM YOU, SON! MAYBE THIS'LL KEEP THAT TRAP OF YOURS SHUT!
ZNNAKK!
THE CELESTIAL MAN FEELS BITS OF HIS VERY LIFE-FORCE BEING DRAINED--AS THE GARGOYLE'S BIO-MYSTIC BOLT SLAMS HIM INTO THE ICE!
23

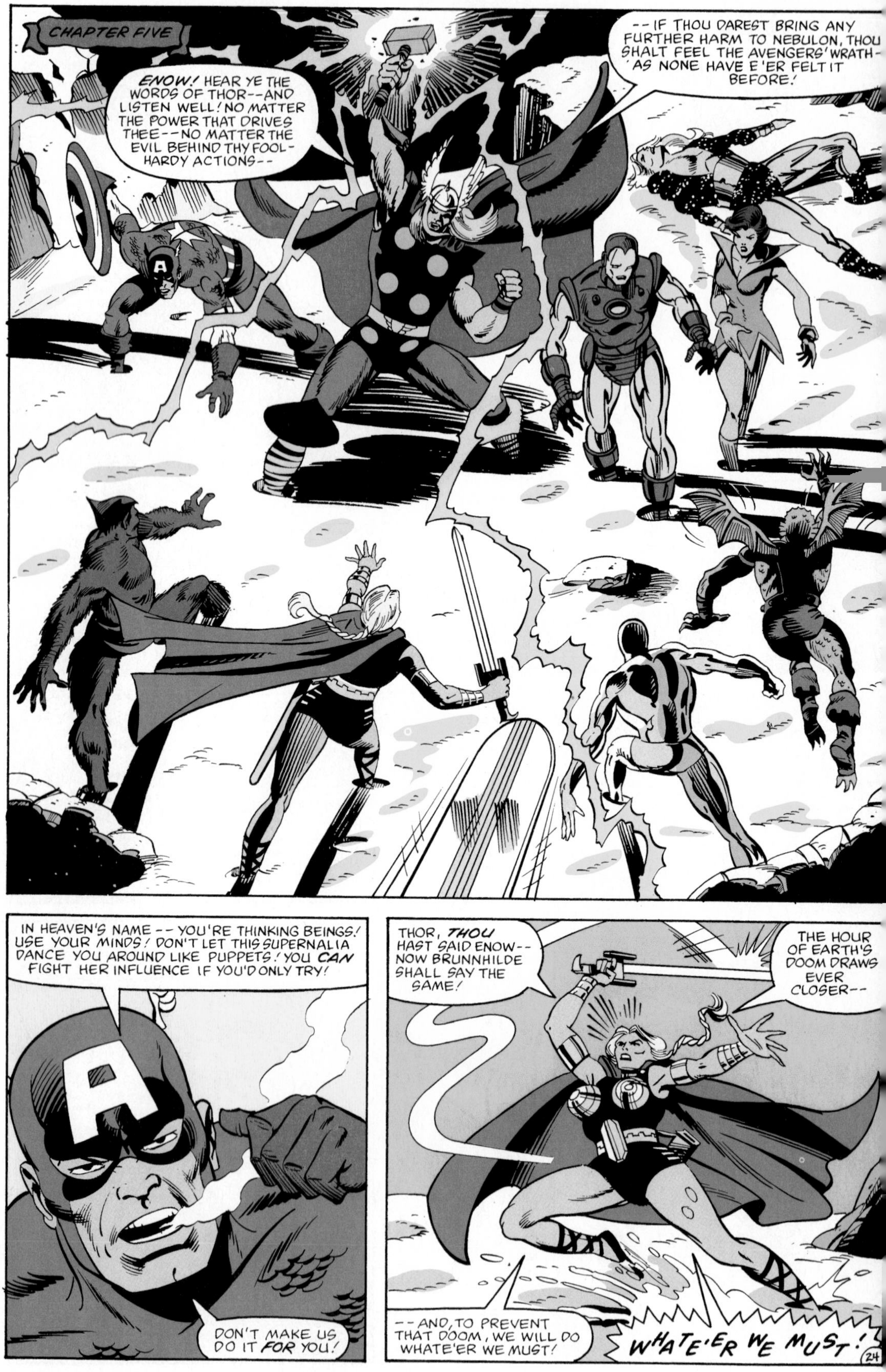
CHAPTER FIVE
ENOW! HEAR YE THE WORDS OF THOR--AND LISTEN WELL! NO MATTER THE POWER THAT DRIVES THEE--NO MATTER THE EVIL BEHIND THY FOOL-HARDY ACTIONS--
--IF THOU DAREST BRING ANY FURTHER HARM TO NEBULON, THOU SHALT FEEL THE AVENGERS' WRATH--AS NONE HAVE E'ER FELT IT BEFORE!
IN HEAVEN'S NAME -- YOU'RE THINKING BEINGS! USE YOUR MINDS! DON'T LET THIS SUPERNALIA DANCE YOU AROUND LIKE PUPPETS! YOU CAN FIGHT HER INFLUENCE IF YOU'D ONLY TRY!
DON'T MAKE US DO IT FOR YOU!
THOR, THOU HAST SAID ENOW--NOW BRUNNHILDE SHALL SAY THE SAME!
THE HOUR OF EARTH'S DOOM DRAWS EVER CLOSER--
--AND, TO PREVENT THAT DOOM, WE WILL DO WHATE'ER WE MUST!
WHATE'ER WE MUST!
24

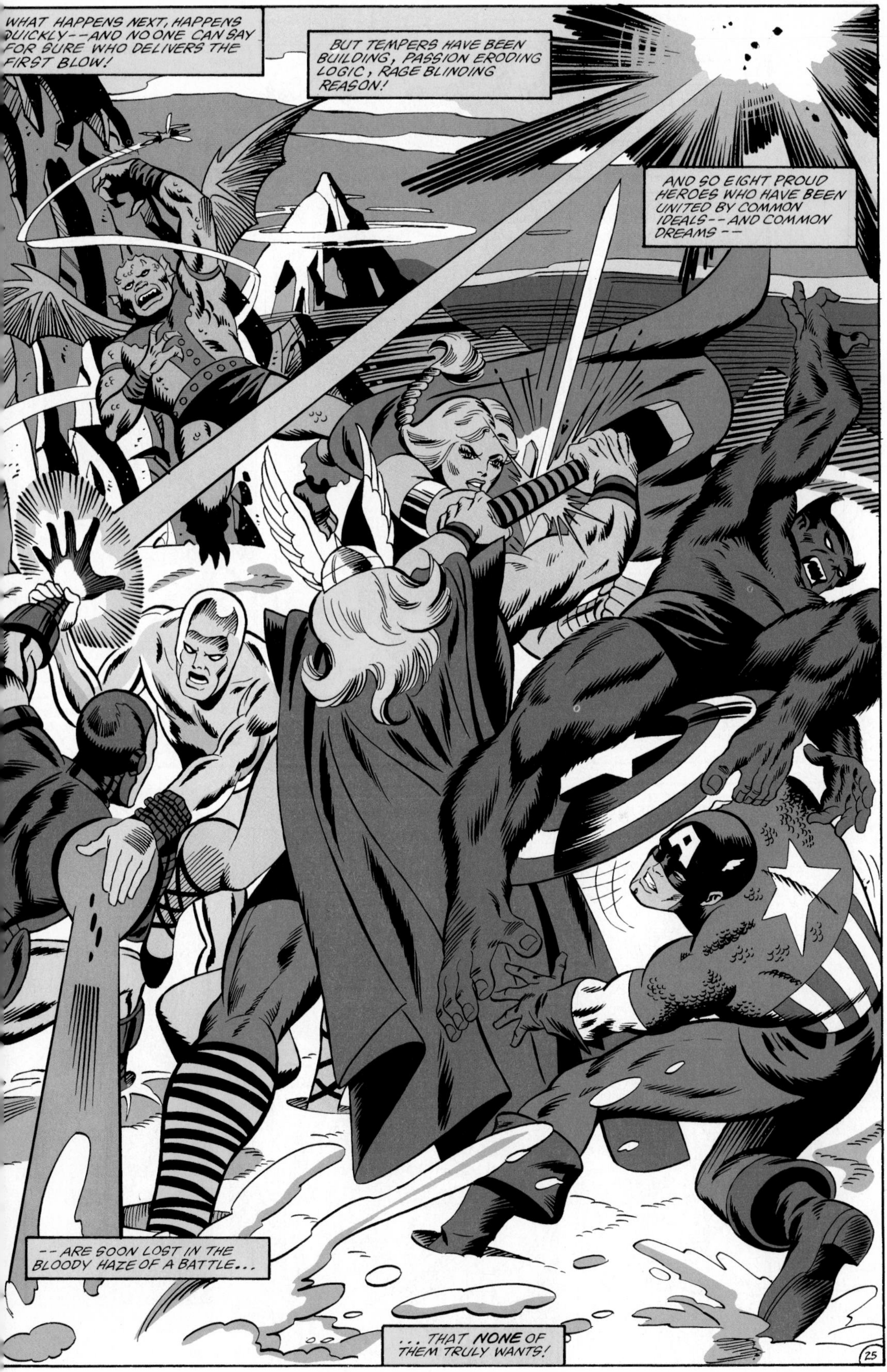
WHAT HAPPENS NEXT, HAPPENS QUICKLY--AND NO ONE CAN SAY FOR SURE WHO DELIVERS THE FIRST BLOW!
BUT TEMPERS HAVE BEEN BUILDING, PASSION ERODING LOGIC, RAGE BLINDING REASON!
AND SO EIGHT PROUD HEROES WHO HAVE BEEN UNITED BY COMMON IDEALS--AND COMMON DREAMS--
--ARE SOON LOST IN THE BLOODY HAZE OF A BATTLE...
...THAT **NONE** OF THEM TRULY WANTS!
25

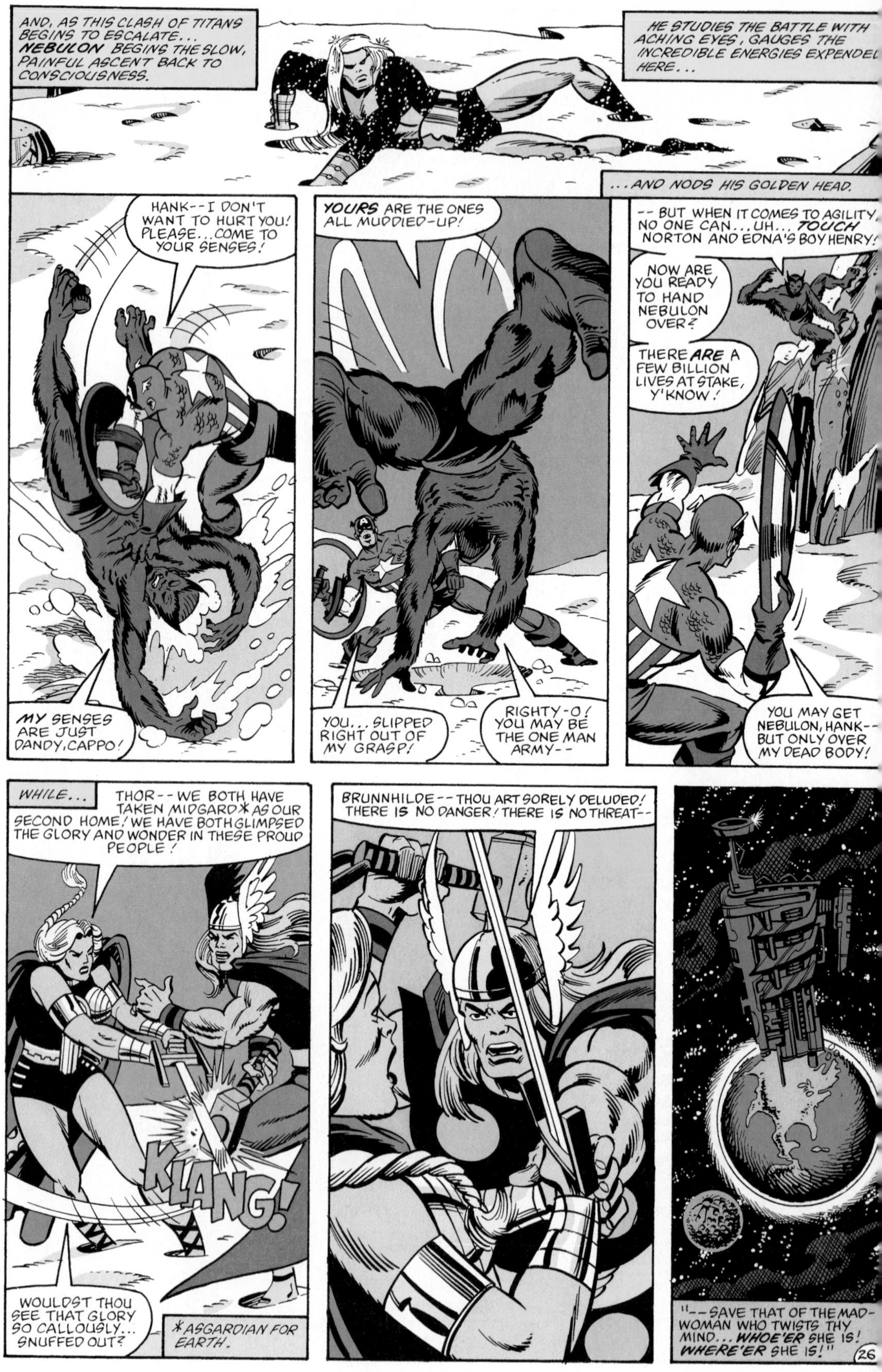
AND, AS THIS CLASH OF TITANS BEGINS TO ESCALATE... NEBULON BEGINS THE SLOW, PAINFUL ASCENT BACK TO CONSCIOUSNESS.
HE STUDIES THE BATTLE WITH ACHING EYES, GAUGES THE INCREDIBLE ENERGIES EXPENDED HERE...
...AND NODS HIS GOLDEN HEAD.
HANK--I DON'T WANT TO HURT YOU! PLEASE...COME TO YOUR SENSES!
MY SENSES ARE JUST DANDY, CAPPO!
YOURS ARE THE ONES ALL MUDDIED-UP!
YOU... SLIPPED RIGHT OUT OF MY GRASP!
RIGHTY-O! YOU MAY BE THE ONE MAN ARMY--
--BUT WHEN IT COMES TO AGILITY NO ONE CAN...UH... TOUCH NORTON AND EDNA'S BOY HENRY!
NOW ARE YOU READY TO HAND NEBULON OVER?
THERE ARE A FEW BILLION LIVES AT STAKE, Y'KNOW!
YOU MAY GET NEBULON, HANK--BUT ONLY OVER MY DEAD BODY!
WHILE...
THOR--WE BOTH HAVE TAKEN MIDGARD* AS OUR SECOND HOME! WE HAVE BOTH GLIMPSED THE GLORY AND WONDER IN THESE PROUD PEOPLE!
KLANG!
WOULDST THOU SEE THAT GLORY SO CALLOUSLY... SNUFFED OUT?
*ASGARDIAN FOR EARTH.
BRUNNHILDE--THOU ART SORELY DELUDED! THERE IS NO DANGER! THERE IS NO THREAT--
"--SAVE THAT OF THE MAD-WOMAN WHO TWISTS THY MIND... WHOE'ER SHE IS! WHERE'ER SHE IS!"
26

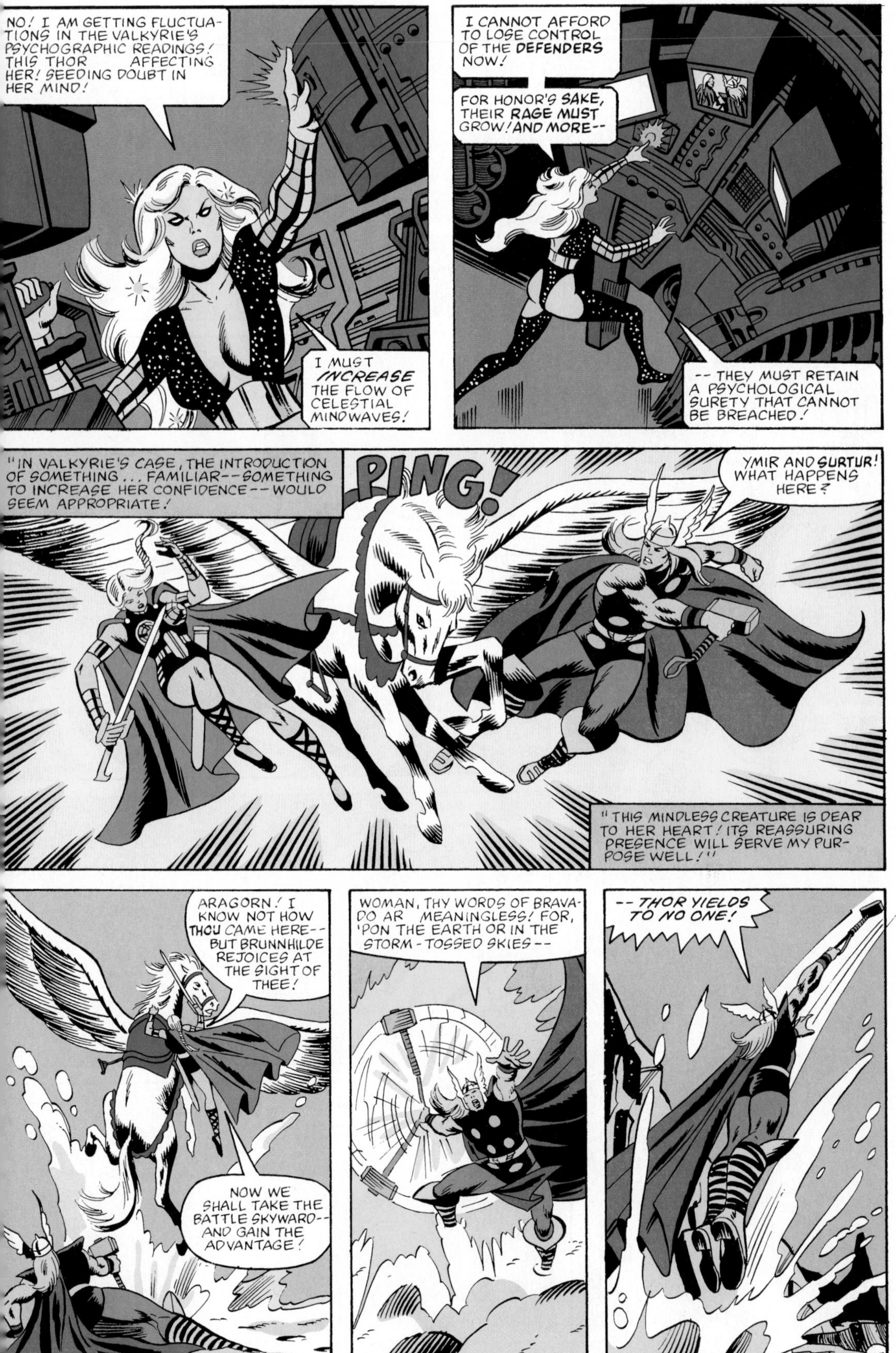
NO! I AM GETTING FLUCTUATIONS IN THE VALKYRIE'S PSYCHOGRAPHIC READINGS! THIS THOR AFFECTING HER! SEEDING DOUBT IN HER MIND!
I MUST INCREASE THE FLOW OF CELESTIAL MINDWAVES!
I CANNOT AFFORD TO LOSE CONTROL OF THE DEFENDERS NOW!
FOR HONOR'S SAKE, THEIR RAGE MUST GROW! AND MORE--
--THEY MUST RETAIN A PSYCHOLOGICAL SURETY THAT CANNOT BE BREACHED!
"IN VALKYRIE'S CASE, THE INTRODUCTION OF SOMETHING... FAMILIAR--SOMETHING TO INCREASE HER CONFIDENCE--WOULD SEEM APPROPRIATE!
PING!
YMIR AND SURTUR! WHAT HAPPENS HERE?
"THIS MINDLESS CREATURE IS DEAR TO HER HEART! ITS REASSURING PRESENCE WILL SERVE MY PURPOSE WELL!"
ARAGORN! I KNOW NOT HOW THOU CAME HERE--BUT BRUNNHILDE REJOICES AT THE SIGHT OF THEE!
NOW WE SHALL TAKE THE BATTLE SKYWARD--AND GAIN THE ADVANTAGE!
WOMAN, THY WORDS OF BRAVADO AR MEANINGLESS! FOR, 'PON THE EARTH OR IN THE STORM-TOSSED SKIES--
--THOR YIELDS TO NO ONE!
27

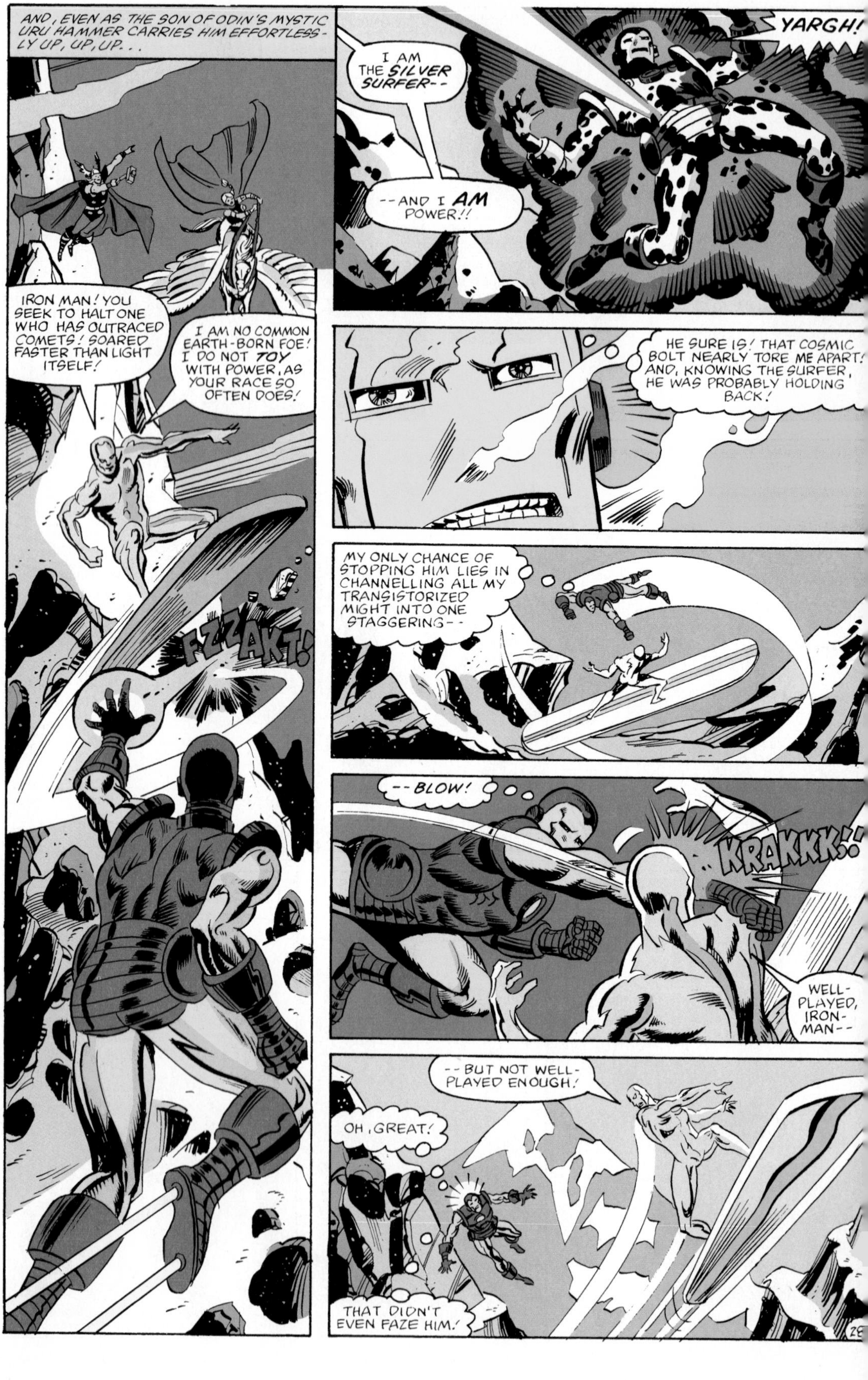

AND, EVEN AS THE SON OF ODIN'S MYSTIC URU HAMMER CARRIES HIM EFFORTLESSLY UP, UP, UP...
I AM THE SILVER SURFER--
YARGH!
--AND I AM POWER!!
IRON MAN! YOU SEEK TO HALT ONE WHO HAS OUTRACED COMETS! SOARED FASTER THAN LIGHT ITSELF!
I AM NO COMMON EARTH-BORN FOE! I DO NOT TOY WITH POWER, AS YOUR RACE SO OFTEN DOES!
FZZAKT!
HE SURE IS! THAT COSMIC BOLT NEARLY TORE ME APART! AND, KNOWING THE SURFER, HE WAS PROBABLY HOLDING BACK!
MY ONLY CHANCE OF STOPPING HIM LIES IN CHANNELLING ALL MY TRANSISTORIZED MIGHT INTO ONE STAGGERING--
--BLOW!
KRAKKK!!
WELL-PLAYED, IRON-MAN--
--BUT NOT WELL-PLAYED ENOUGH!
OH, GREAT!
THAT DIDN'T EVEN FAZE HIM!

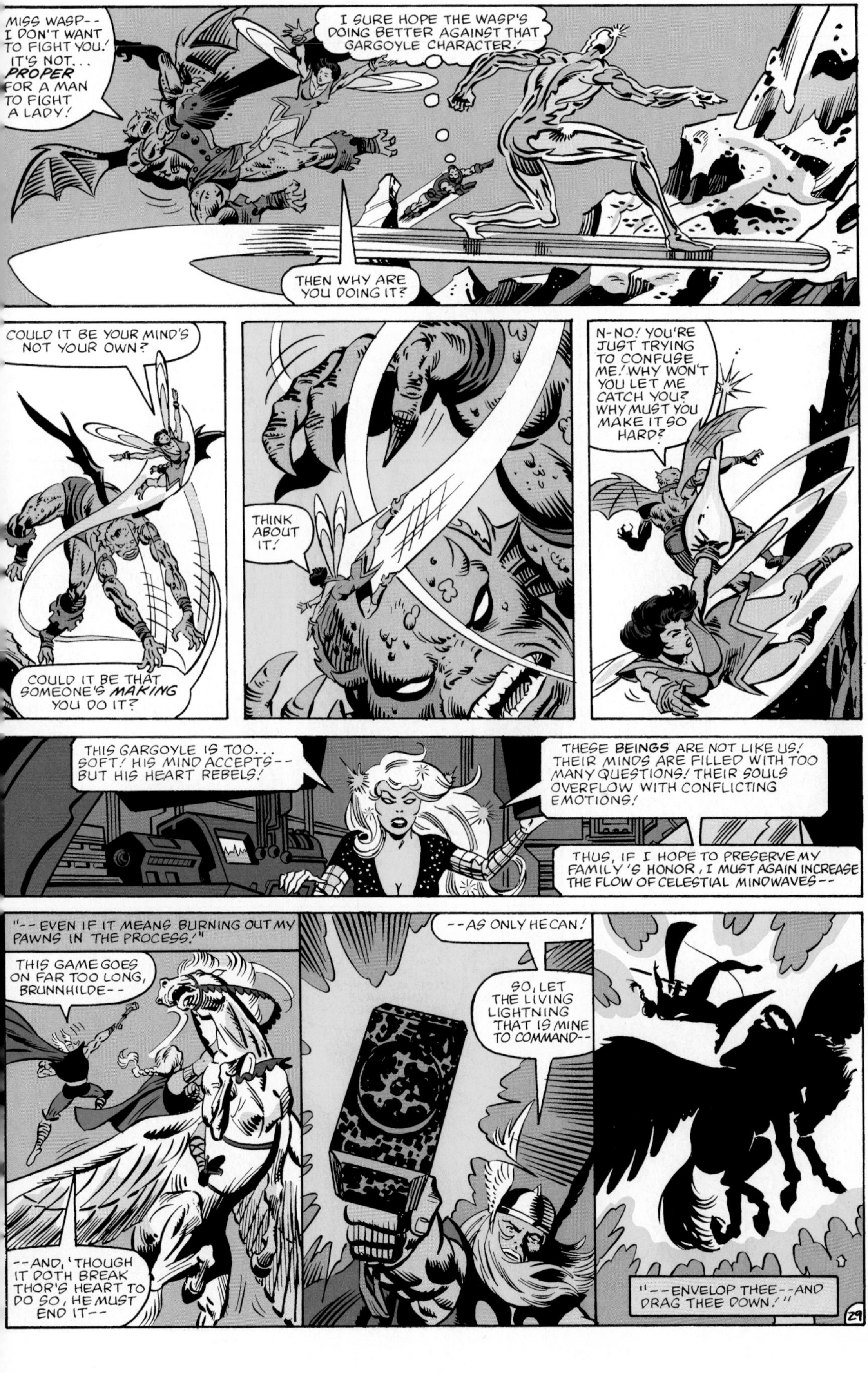
MISS WASP-- I DON'T WANT TO FIGHT YOU! IT'S NOT... *PROPER* FOR A MAN TO FIGHT A LADY!
I SURE HOPE THE WASP'S DOING BETTER AGAINST THAT GARGOYLE CHARACTER!
THEN WHY ARE YOU DOING IT?
COULD IT BE YOUR MIND'S NOT YOUR OWN?
COULD IT BE THAT SOMEONE'S *MAKING* YOU DO IT?
THINK ABOUT IT!
N-NO! YOU'RE JUST TRYING TO CONFUSE ME! WHY WON'T YOU LET ME CATCH YOU? WHY MUST YOU MAKE IT SO HARD?
THIS GARGOYLE IS TOO... SOFT! HIS MIND ACCEPTS-- BUT HIS HEART REBELS!
THESE **BEINGS** ARE NOT LIKE US! THEIR MINDS ARE FILLED WITH TOO MANY QUESTIONS! THEIR SOULS OVERFLOW WITH CONFLICTING EMOTIONS!
THUS, IF I HOPE TO PRESERVE MY FAMILY'S HONOR, I MUST AGAIN INCREASE THE FLOW OF CELESTIAL MINDWAVES--
"--EVEN IF IT MEANS BURNING OUT MY PAWNS IN THE PROCESS!"
THIS GAME GOES ON FAR TOO LONG, BRUNNHILDE--
--AND, 'THOUGH IT DOTH BREAK THOR'S HEART TO DO SO, HE MUST END IT--
--AS ONLY HE CAN!
SO, LET THE LIVING LIGHTNING THAT IS MINE TO COMMAND--
"--ENVELOP THEE--AND DRAG THEE DOWN!"
29

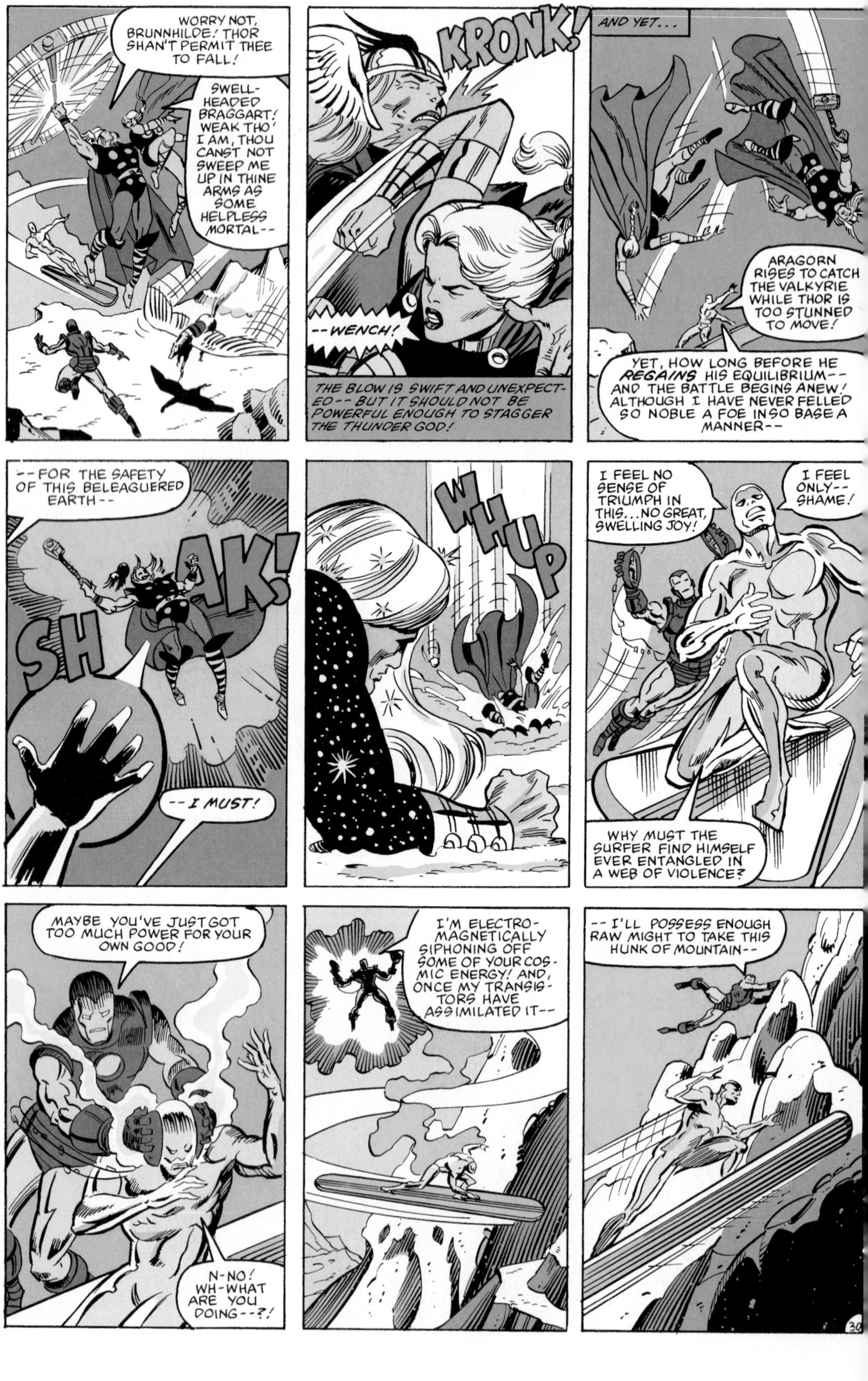
WORRY NOT, BRUNNHILDE! THOR SHAN'T PERMIT THEE TO FALL!
SWELL-HEADED BRAGGART! WEAK THO' I AM, THOU CANST NOT SWEEP ME UP IN THINE ARMS AS SOME HELPLESS MORTAL--
KRONK!
--WENCH!
THE BLOW IS SWIFT AND UNEXPECTED-- BUT IT SHOULD NOT BE POWERFUL ENOUGH TO STAGGER THE THUNDER GOD!
AND YET...
ARAGORN RISES TO CATCH THE VALKYRIE WHILE THOR IS TOO STUNNED TO MOVE!
YET, HOW LONG BEFORE HE REGAINS HIS EQUILIBRIUM-- AND THE BATTLE BEGINS ANEW! ALTHOUGH I HAVE NEVER FELLED SO NOBLE A FOE IN SO BASE A MANNER--
--FOR THE SAFETY OF THIS BELEAGUERED EARTH--
SHAK!
--I MUST!
WHUP
I FEEL NO SENSE OF TRIUMPH IN THIS... NO GREAT, SWELLING JOY!
I FEEL ONLY-- SHAME!
WHY MUST THE SURFER FIND HIMSELF EVER ENTANGLED IN A WEB OF VIOLENCE?
MAYBE YOU'VE JUST GOT TOO MUCH POWER FOR YOUR OWN GOOD!
N-NO! WH-WHAT ARE YOU DOING--?!
I'M ELECTRO-MAGNETICALLY SIPHONING OFF SOME OF YOUR COSMIC ENERGY! AND, ONCE MY TRANSISTORS HAVE ASSIMILATED IT--
--I'LL POSSESS ENOUGH RAW MIGHT TO TAKE THIS HUNK OF MOUNTAIN--
30

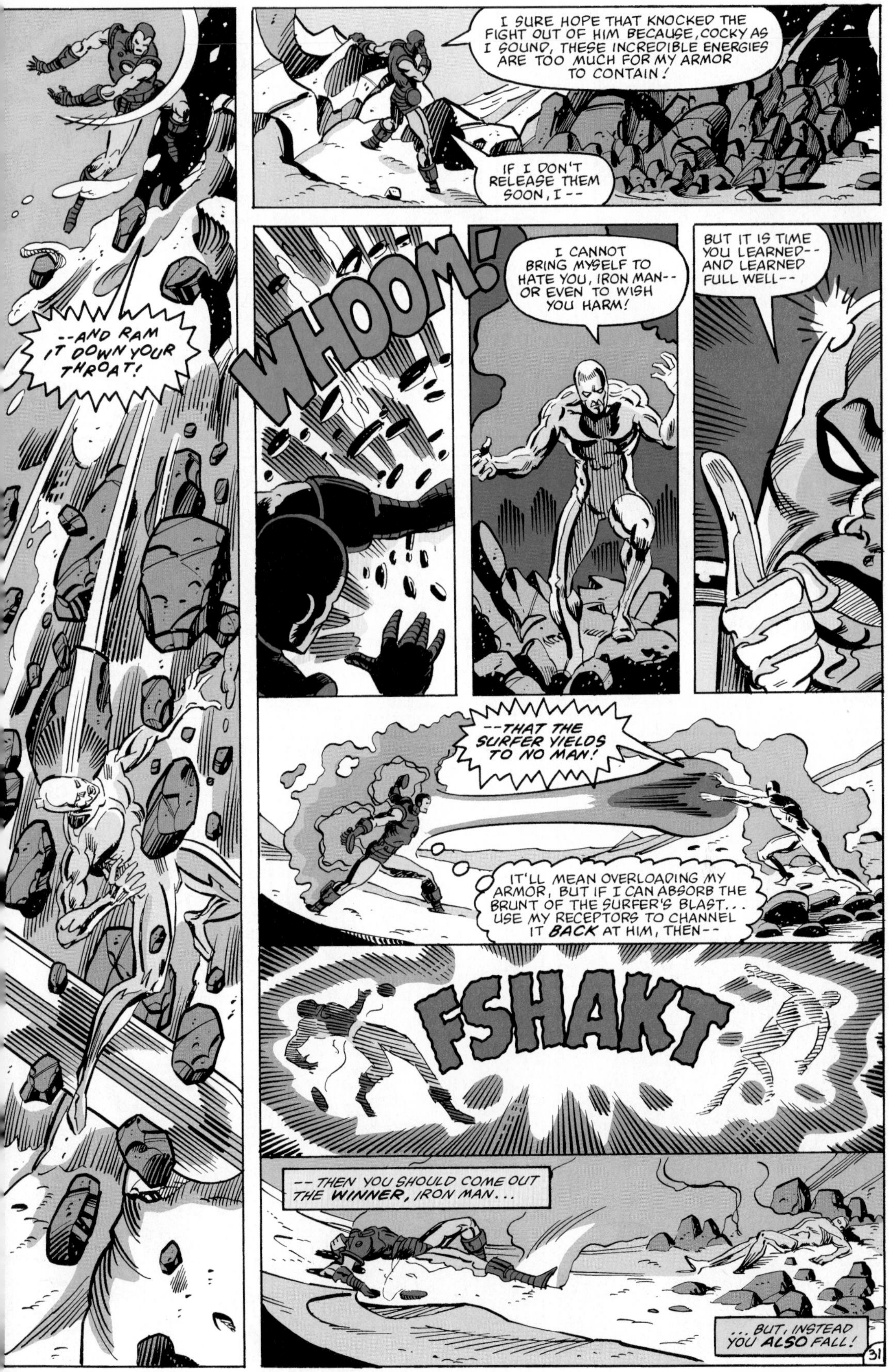
--AND RAM IT DOWN YOUR THROAT!
I SURE HOPE THAT KNOCKED THE FIGHT OUT OF HIM BECAUSE, COCKY AS I SOUND, THESE INCREDIBLE ENERGIES ARE TOO MUCH FOR MY ARMOR TO CONTAIN!
IF I DON'T RELEASE THEM SOON, I--
WHOOM!
I CANNOT BRING MYSELF TO HATE YOU, IRON MAN--OR EVEN TO WISH YOU HARM!
BUT IT IS TIME YOU LEARNED--AND LEARNED FULL WELL--
--THAT THE SURFER YIELDS TO NO MAN!
IT'LL MEAN OVERLOADING MY ARMOR, BUT IF I CAN ABSORB THE BRUNT OF THE SURFER'S BLAST... USE MY RECEPTORS TO CHANNEL IT BACK AT HIM, THEN--
FSHAKT
--THEN YOU SHOULD COME OUT THE WINNER, IRON MAN...
...BUT, INSTEAD YOU ALSO FALL!
31

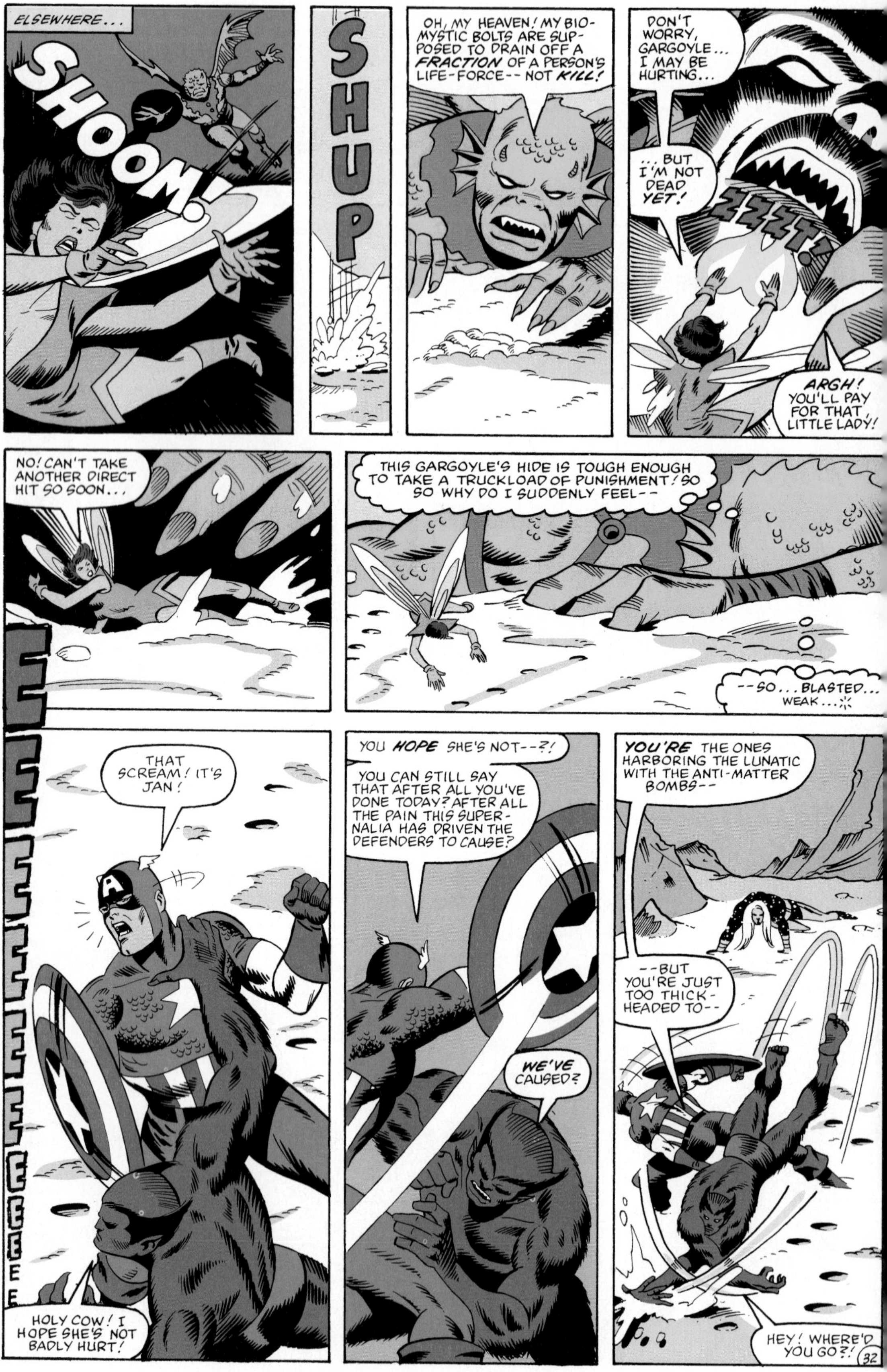

ELSEWHERE...
SHOOOM!
SHUP
OH, MY HEAVEN! MY BIO-MYSTIC BOLTS ARE SUPPOSED TO DRAIN OFF A FRACTION OF A PERSON'S LIFE-FORCE-- NOT KILL!
DON'T WORRY, GARGOYLE... I MAY BE HURTING...
...BUT I'M NOT DEAD YET!
ZZZT!
ARGH! YOU'LL PAY FOR THAT, LITTLE LADY!
NO! CAN'T TAKE ANOTHER DIRECT HIT SO SOON...
THIS GARGOYLE'S HIDE IS TOUGH ENOUGH TO TAKE A TRUCKLOAD OF PUNISHMENT! SO SO WHY DO I SUDDENLY FEEL--
--SO...BLASTED... WEAK...
EEEEEEEEEEEEEE
THAT SCREAM! IT'S JAN!
HOLY COW! I HOPE SHE'S NOT BADLY HURT!
YOU HOPE SHE'S NOT--?!
YOU CAN STILL SAY THAT AFTER ALL YOU'VE DONE TODAY? AFTER ALL THE PAIN THIS SUPER-NALIA HAS DRIVEN THE DEFENDERS TO CAUSE?
WE'VE CAUSED?
YOU'RE THE ONES HARBORING THE LUNATIC WITH THE ANTI-MATTER BOMBS--
--BUT YOU'RE JUST TOO THICK-HEADED TO--
HEY! WHERE'D YOU GO?!
32

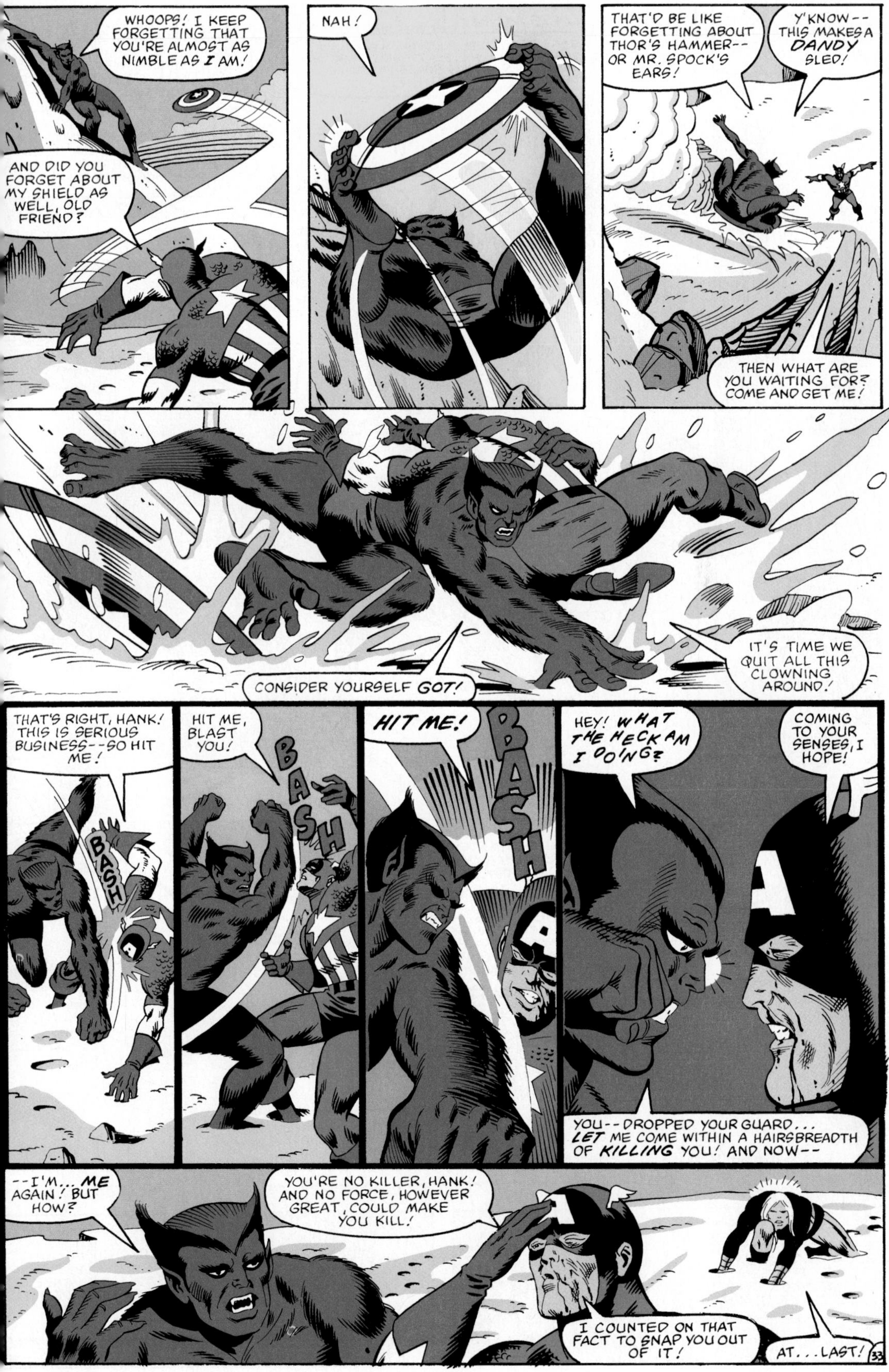
WHOOPS! I KEEP FORGETTING THAT YOU'RE ALMOST AS NIMBLE AS I AM!
AND DID YOU FORGET ABOUT MY SHIELD AS WELL, OLD FRIEND?
NAH!
THAT'D BE LIKE FORGETTING ABOUT THOR'S HAMMER-- OR MR. SPOCK'S EARS!
Y'KNOW-- THIS MAKES A DANDY SLED!
THEN WHAT ARE YOU WAITING FOR? COME AND GET ME!
CONSIDER YOURSELF GOT!
IT'S TIME WE QUIT ALL THIS CLOWNING AROUND!
THAT'S RIGHT, HANK! THIS IS SERIOUS BUSINESS--SO HIT ME!
BASH
HIT ME, BLAST YOU!
BASH
HIT ME!
BASH
HEY! WHAT THE HECK AM I DOING?
COMING TO YOUR SENSES, I HOPE!
YOU--DROPPED YOUR GUARD... LET ME COME WITHIN A HAIRSBREADTH OF KILLING YOU! AND NOW--
--I'M... ME AGAIN! BUT HOW?
YOU'RE NO KILLER, HANK! AND NO FORCE, HOWEVER GREAT, COULD MAKE YOU KILL!
I COUNTED ON THAT FACT TO SNAP YOU OUT OF IT!
AT...LAST!
33

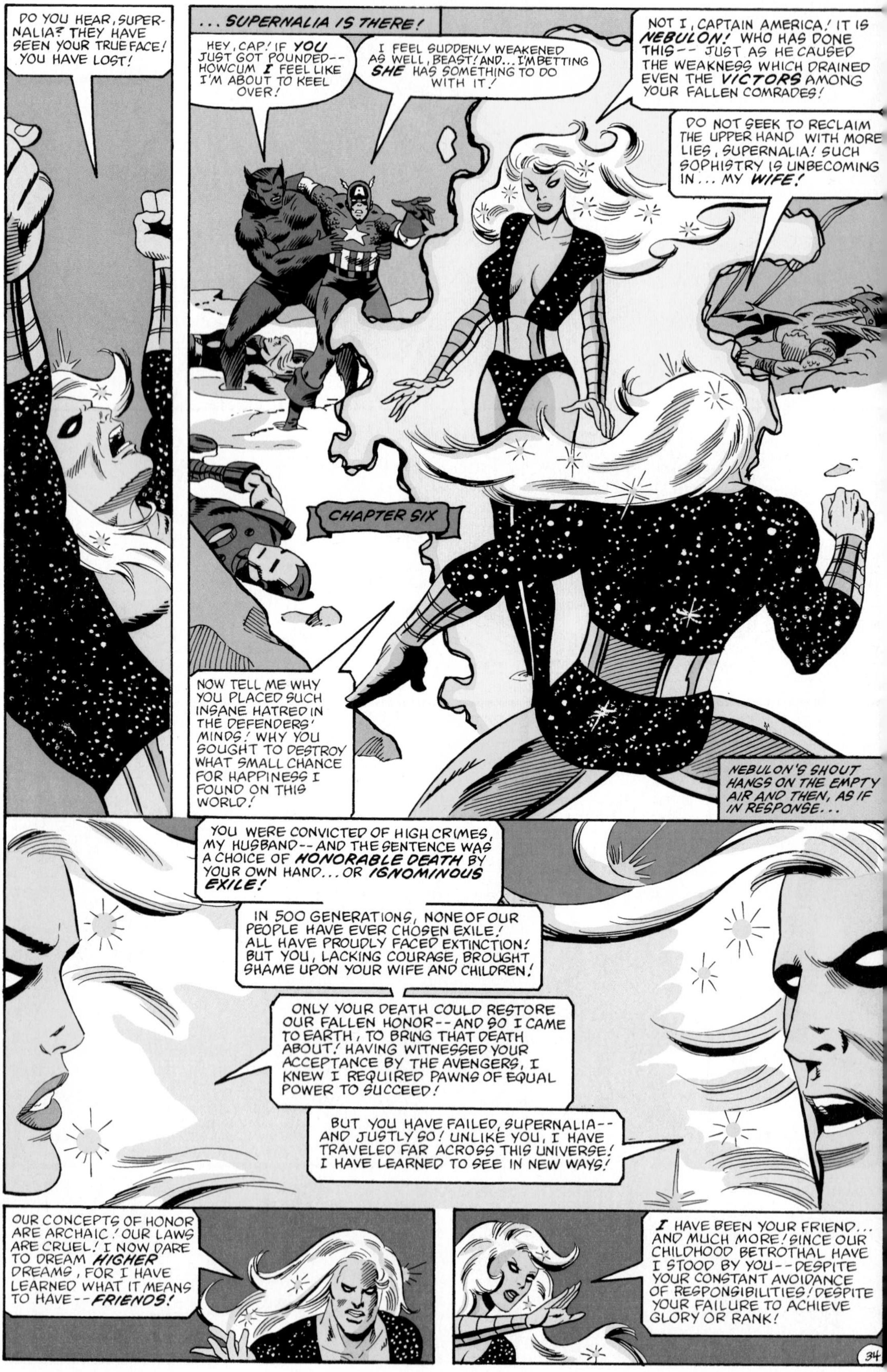
DO YOU HEAR, SUPERNALIA? THEY HAVE SEEN YOUR TRUE FACE! YOU HAVE LOST!
...SUPERNALIA IS THERE!
HEY, CAP! IF YOU JUST GOT POUNDED--HOWCUM I FEEL LIKE I'M ABOUT TO KEEL OVER!
I FEEL SUDDENLY WEAKENED AS WELL, BEAST! AND... I'M BETTING SHE HAS SOMETHING TO DO WITH IT!
NOT I, CAPTAIN AMERICA! IT IS NEBULON! WHO HAS DONE THIS-- JUST AS HE CAUSED THE WEAKNESS WHICH DRAINED EVEN THE VICTORS AMONG YOUR FALLEN COMRADES!
DO NOT SEEK TO RECLAIM THE UPPER HAND WITH MORE LIES, SUPERNALIA! SUCH SOPHISTRY IS UNBECOMING IN... MY WIFE!
CHAPTER SIX
NOW TELL ME WHY YOU PLACED SUCH INSANE HATRED IN THE DEFENDERS' MINDS! WHY YOU SOUGHT TO DESTROY WHAT SMALL CHANCE FOR HAPPINESS I FOUND ON THIS WORLD!
NEBULON'S SHOUT HANGS ON THE EMPTY AIR AND THEN, AS IF IN RESPONSE...
YOU WERE CONVICTED OF HIGH CRIMES, MY HUSBAND--AND THE SENTENCE WAS A CHOICE OF HONORABLE DEATH BY YOUR OWN HAND... OR IGNOMINOUS EXILE!
IN 500 GENERATIONS, NONE OF OUR PEOPLE HAVE EVER CHOSEN EXILE! ALL HAVE PROUDLY FACED EXTINCTION! BUT YOU, LACKING COURAGE, BROUGHT SHAME UPON YOUR WIFE AND CHILDREN!
ONLY YOUR DEATH COULD RESTORE OUR FALLEN HONOR--AND SO I CAME TO EARTH, TO BRING THAT DEATH ABOUT! HAVING WITNESSED YOUR ACCEPTANCE BY THE AVENGERS, I KNEW I REQUIRED PAWNS OF EQUAL POWER TO SUCCEED!
BUT YOU HAVE FAILED, SUPERNALIA--AND JUSTLY SO! UNLIKE YOU, I HAVE TRAVELED FAR ACROSS THIS UNIVERSE! I HAVE LEARNED TO SEE IN NEW WAYS!
OUR CONCEPTS OF HONOR ARE ARCHAIC! OUR LAWS ARE CRUEL! I NOW DARE TO DREAM HIGHER DREAMS, FOR I HAVE LEARNED WHAT IT MEANS TO HAVE--FRIENDS!
I HAVE BEEN YOUR FRIEND... AND MUCH MORE! SINCE OUR CHILDHOOD BETROTHAL HAVE I STOOD BY YOU--DESPITE YOUR CONSTANT AVOIDANCE OF RESPONSIBILITIES! DESPITE YOUR FAILURE TO ACHIEVE GLORY OR RANK!
34

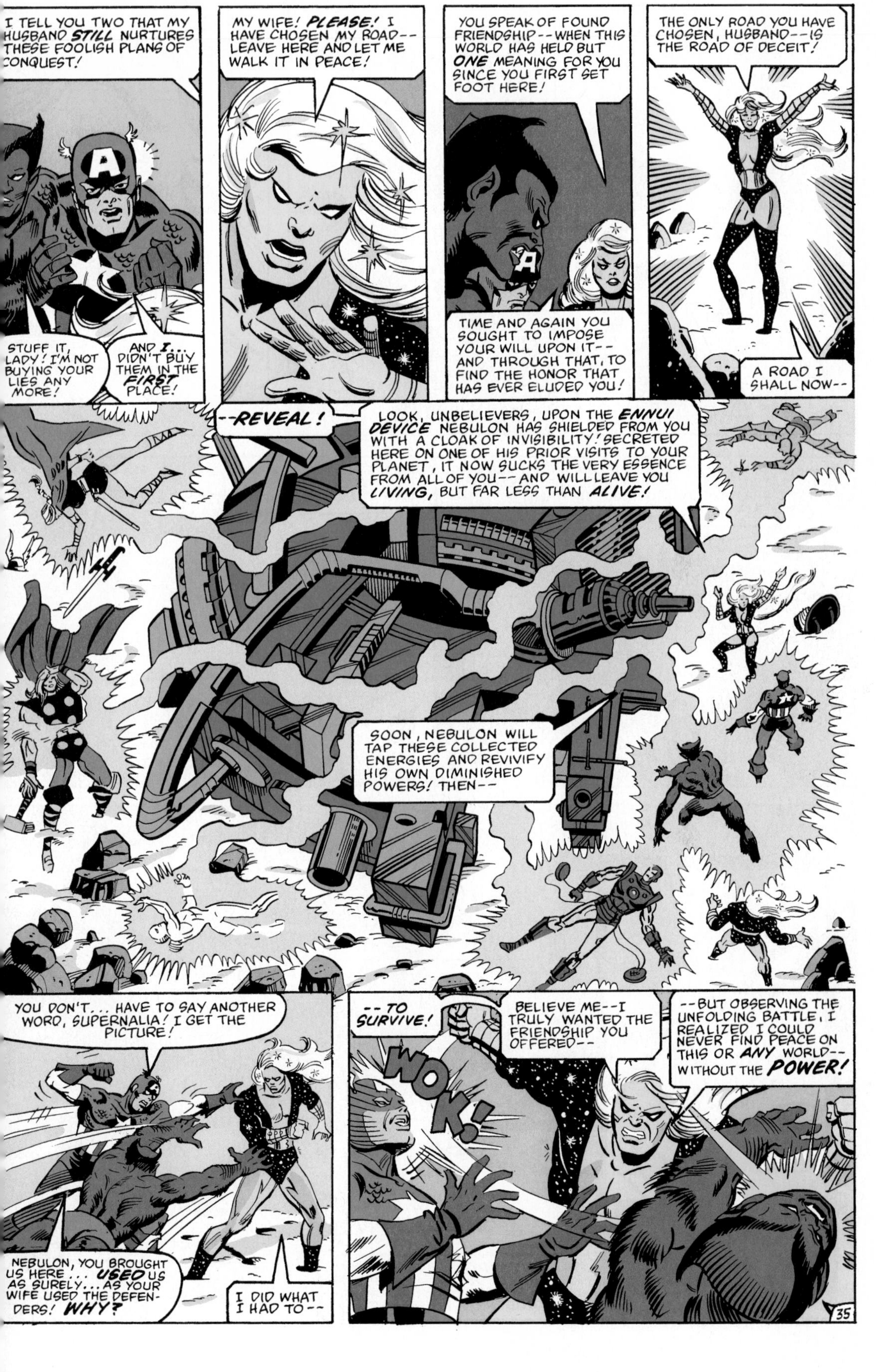
I TELL YOU TWO THAT MY HUSBAND STILL NURTURES THESE FOOLISH PLANS OF CONQUEST!
STUFF IT, LADY! I'M NOT BUYING YOUR LIES ANY MORE!
AND I... DIDN'T BUY THEM IN THE FIRST PLACE!
MY WIFE! PLEASE! I HAVE CHOSEN MY ROAD-- LEAVE HERE AND LET ME WALK IT IN PEACE!
YOU SPEAK OF FOUND FRIENDSHIP--WHEN THIS WORLD HAS HELD BUT ONE MEANING FOR YOU SINCE YOU FIRST SET FOOT HERE!
TIME AND AGAIN YOU SOUGHT TO IMPOSE YOUR WILL UPON IT-- AND THROUGH THAT, TO FIND THE HONOR THAT HAS EVER ELUDED YOU!
THE ONLY ROAD YOU HAVE CHOSEN, HUSBAND--IS THE ROAD OF DECEIT!
A ROAD I SHALL NOW--
--REVEAL!
LOOK, UNBELIEVERS, UPON THE ENNUI DEVICE NEBULON HAS SHIELDED FROM YOU WITH A CLOAK OF INVISIBILITY! SECRETED HERE ON ONE OF HIS PRIOR VISITS TO YOUR PLANET, IT NOW SUCKS THE VERY ESSENCE FROM ALL OF YOU-- AND WILL LEAVE YOU LIVING, BUT FAR LESS THAN ALIVE!
SOON, NEBULON WILL TAP THESE COLLECTED ENERGIES AND REVIVIFY HIS OWN DIMINISHED POWERS! THEN--
YOU DON'T... HAVE TO SAY ANOTHER WORD, SUPERNALIA! I GET THE PICTURE!
NEBULON, YOU BROUGHT US HERE... USED US AS SURELY... AS YOUR WIFE USED THE DEFEN-DERS! WHY?
I DID WHAT I HAD TO--
--TO SURVIVE!
WOK!
BELIEVE ME--I TRULY WANTED THE FRIENDSHIP YOU OFFERED--
--BUT OBSERVING THE UNFOLDING BATTLE, I REALIZED I COULD NEVER FIND PEACE ON THIS OR ANY WORLD-- WITHOUT THE POWER!
35

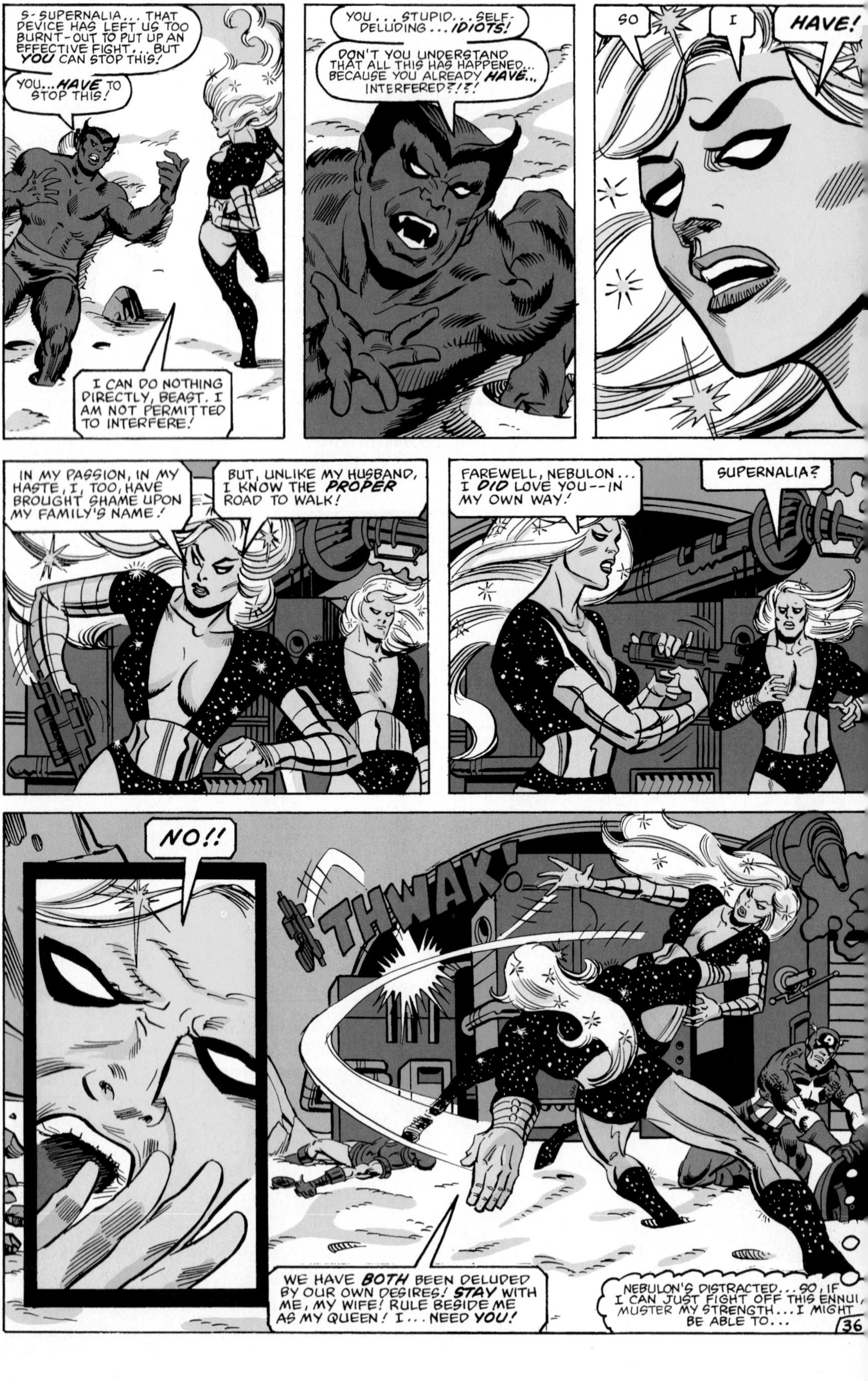
S-SUPERNALIA... THAT DEVICE HAS LEFT US TOO BURNT-OUT TO PUT UP AN EFFECTIVE FIGHT... BUT YOU CAN STOP THIS!
YOU...HAVE TO STOP THIS!
I CAN DO NOTHING DIRECTLY, BEAST. I AM NOT PERMITTED TO INTERFERE!
YOU... STUPID... SELF-DELUDING... IDIOTS!
DON'T YOU UNDERSTAND THAT ALL THIS HAS HAPPENED.. BECAUSE YOU ALREADY HAVE... INTERFERED?!?!
SO
I
HAVE!
IN MY PASSION, IN MY HASTE, I, TOO, HAVE BROUGHT SHAME UPON MY FAMILY'S NAME!
BUT, UNLIKE MY HUSBAND, I KNOW THE PROPER ROAD TO WALK!
FAREWELL, NEBULON... I DID LOVE YOU--IN MY OWN WAY!
SUPERNALIA?
NO!!
THWAK!
WE HAVE BOTH BEEN DELUDED BY OUR OWN DESIRES! STAY WITH ME, MY WIFE! RULE BESIDE ME AS MY QUEEN! I... NEED YOU!
NEBULON'S DISTRACTED... SO, IF I CAN JUST FIGHT OFF THIS ENNUI, MUSTER MY STRENGTH... I MIGHT BE ABLE TO...
36

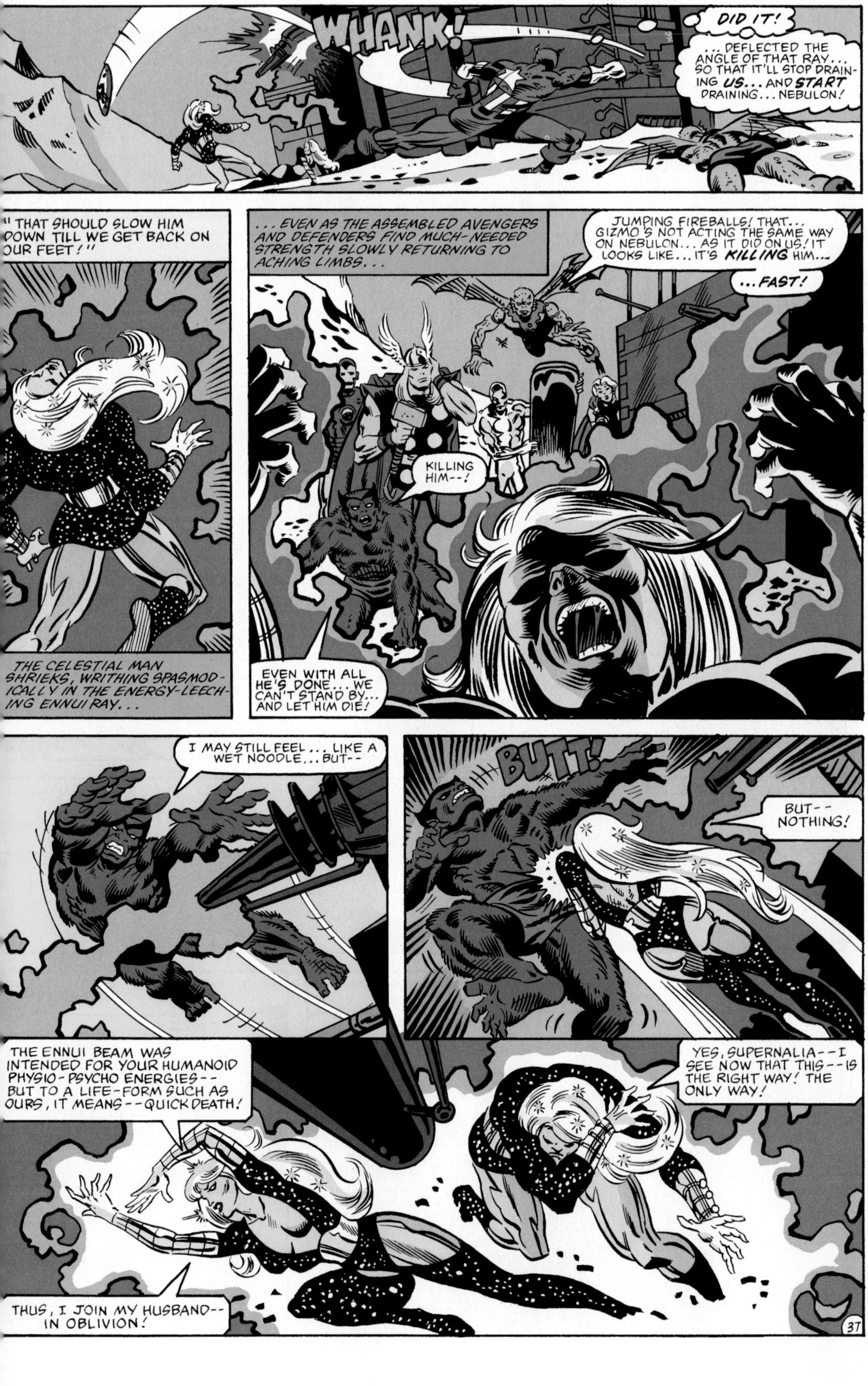
WHANK!
DID IT!
... DEFLECTED THE ANGLE OF THAT RAY... SO THAT IT'LL STOP DRAINING US... AND START DRAINING... NEBULON!
" THAT SHOULD SLOW HIM DOWN TILL WE GET BACK ON OUR FEET! "
THE CELESTIAL MAN SHRIEKS, WRITHING SPASMODICALLY IN THE ENERGY-LEECHING ENNUI RAY...
... EVEN AS THE ASSEMBLED AVENGERS AND DEFENDERS FIND MUCH-NEEDED STRENGTH SLOWLY RETURNING TO ACHING LIMBS...
JUMPING FIREBALLS! THAT... GIZMO'S NOT ACTING THE SAME WAY ON NEBULON... AS IT DID ON US! IT LOOKS LIKE... IT'S KILLING HIM...
...FAST!
KILLING HIM--!
EVEN WITH ALL HE'S DONE... WE CAN'T STAND BY... AND LET HIM DIE!
I MAY STILL FEEL... LIKE A WET NOODLE... BUT--
BUTT!
BUT-- NOTHING!
THE ENNUI BEAM WAS INTENDED FOR YOUR HUMANOID PHYSIO-PSYCHO ENERGIES-- BUT TO A LIFE-FORM SUCH AS OURS, IT MEANS--QUICK DEATH!
YES, SUPERNALIA--I SEE NOW THAT THIS--IS THE RIGHT WAY! THE ONLY WAY!
THUS, I JOIN MY HUSBAND-- IN OBLIVION!
37

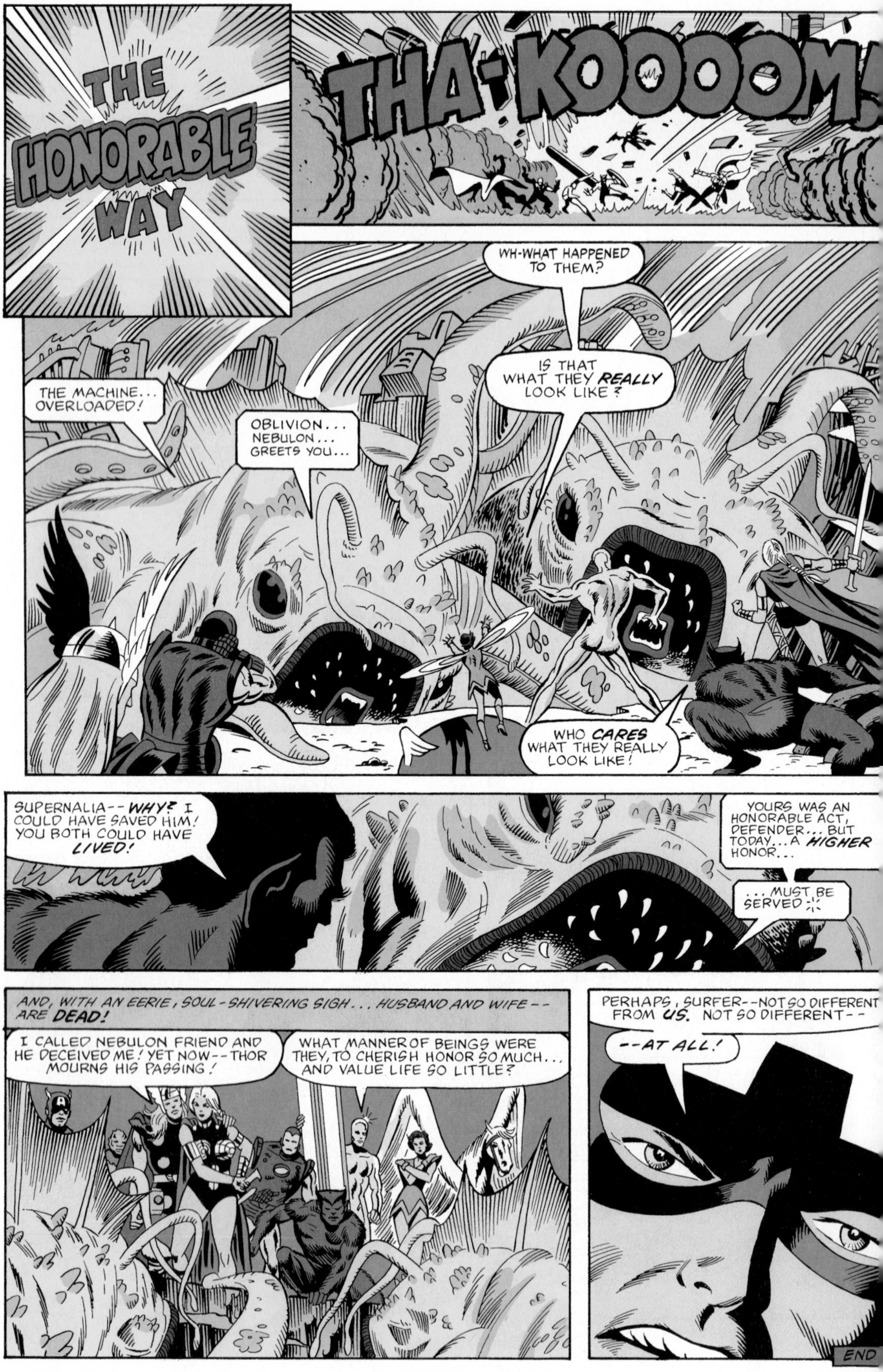
THE HONORABLE WAY
THA-KOOOOM!
WH-WHAT HAPPENED TO THEM?
IS THAT WHAT THEY REALLY LOOK LIKE?
THE MACHINE... OVERLOADED!
OBLIVION... NEBULON... GREETS YOU...
WHO CARES WHAT THEY REALLY LOOK LIKE!
SUPERNALIA--WHY? I COULD HAVE SAVED HIM! YOU BOTH COULD HAVE LIVED!
YOURS WAS AN HONORABLE ACT, DEFENDER... BUT TODAY...A HIGHER HONOR...
...MUST BE SERVED
AND, WITH AN EERIE, SOUL-SHIVERING SIGH... HUSBAND AND WIFE--ARE DEAD!
I CALLED NEBULON FRIEND AND HE DECEIVED ME! YET NOW--THOR MOURNS HIS PASSING!
WHAT MANNER OF BEINGS WERE THEY, TO CHERISH HONOR SO MUCH... AND VALUE LIFE SO LITTLE?
PERHAPS, SURFER--NOT SO DIFFERENT FROM US. NOT SO DIFFERENT--
--AT ALL!
END

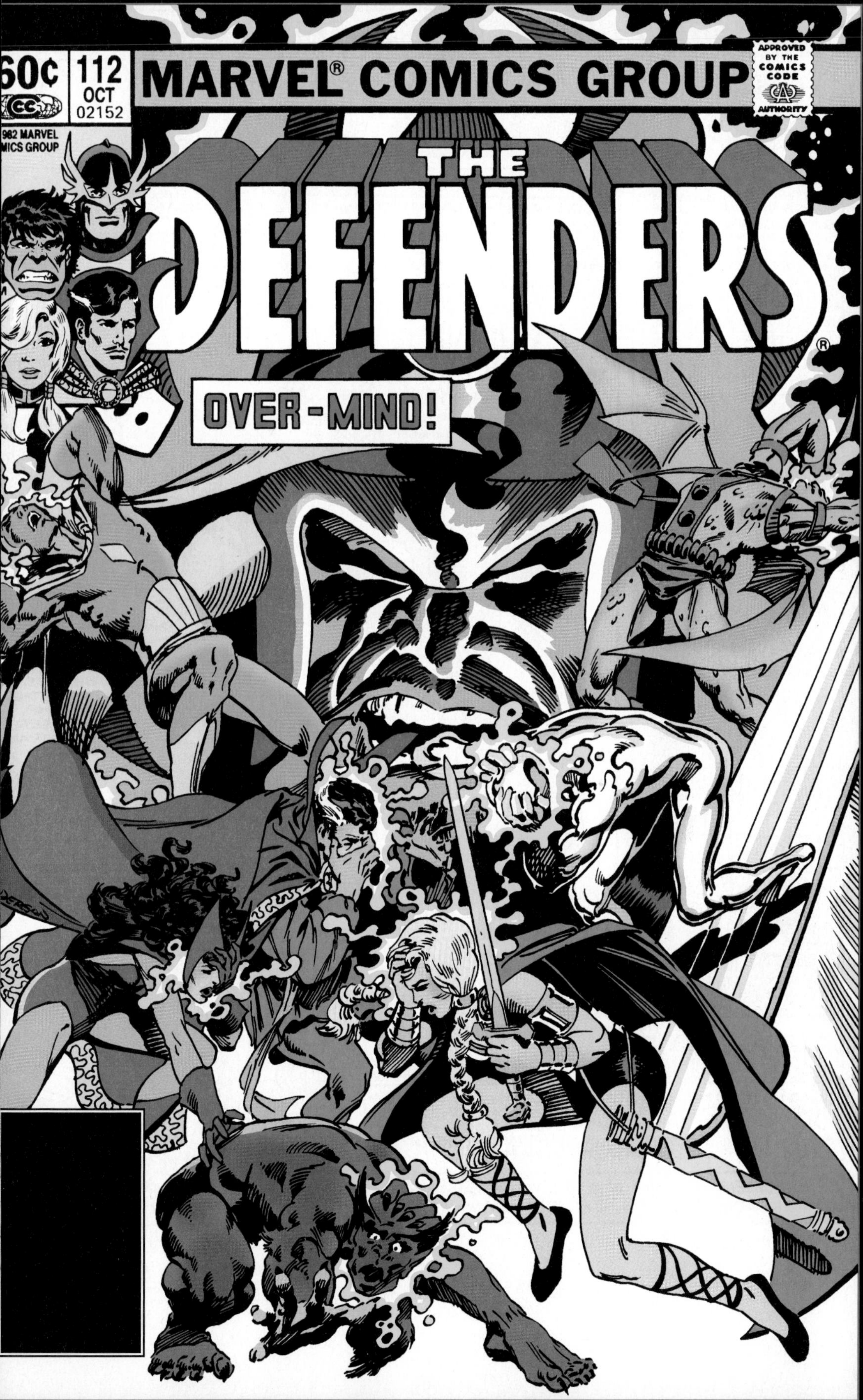
60¢
112
OCT
02152
MARVEL® COMICS GROUP
APPROVED BY THE COMICS CODE AUTHORITY
1982 MARVEL
MICS GROUP
THE
DEFENDERS®
OVER-MIND!

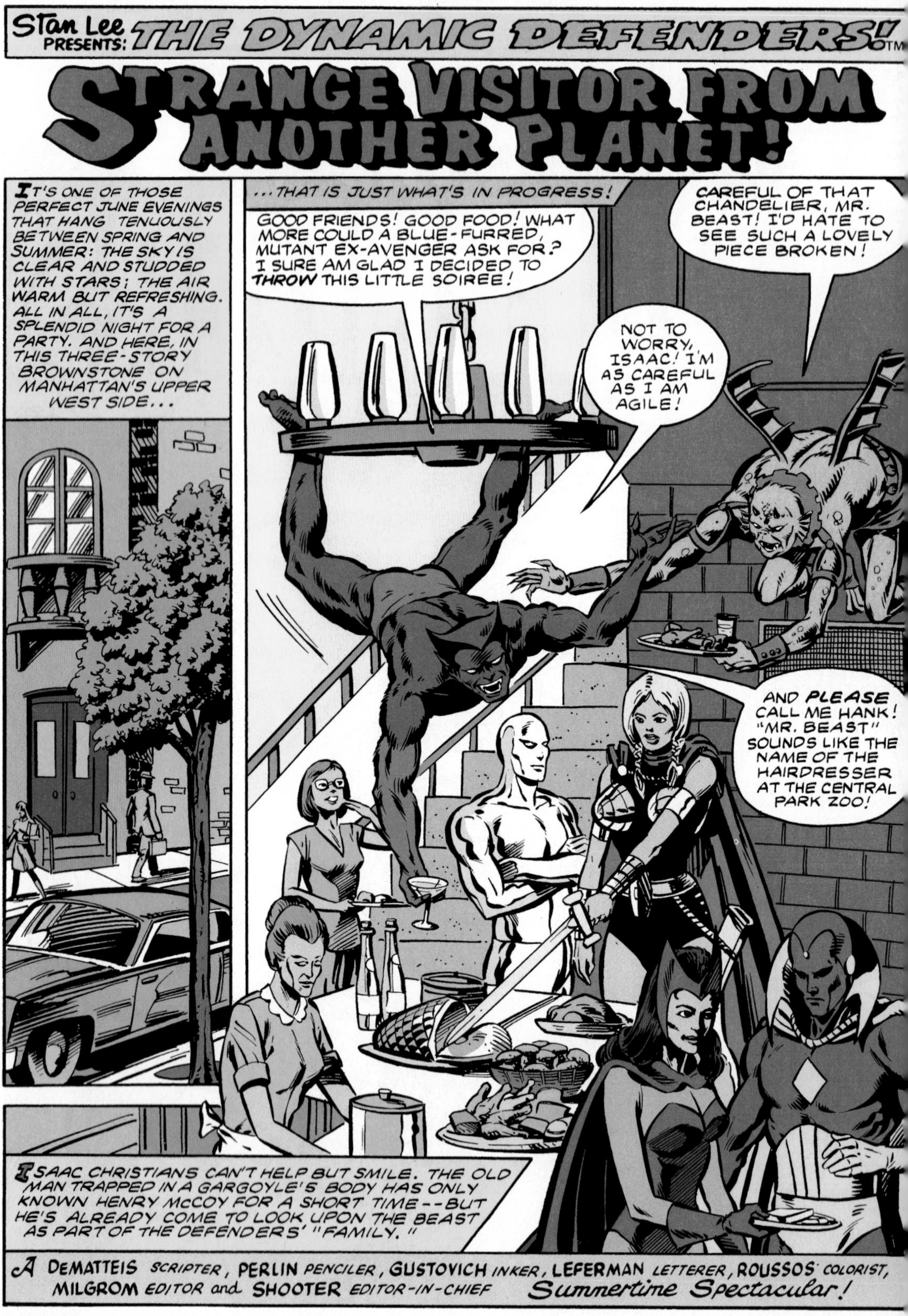
Stan Lee PRESENTS: THE DYNAMIC DEFENDERS!™
STRANGE VISITOR FROM ANOTHER PLANET!
IT'S ONE OF THOSE PERFECT JUNE EVENINGS THAT HANG TENUOUSLY BETWEEN SPRING AND SUMMER: THE SKY IS CLEAR AND STUDDED WITH STARS; THE AIR WARM BUT REFRESHING. ALL IN ALL, IT'S A SPLENDID NIGHT FOR A PARTY. AND HERE, IN THIS THREE-STORY BROWNSTONE ON MANHATTAN'S UPPER WEST SIDE...
...THAT IS JUST WHAT'S IN PROGRESS!
GOOD FRIENDS! GOOD FOOD! WHAT MORE COULD A BLUE-FURRED, MUTANT EX-AVENGER ASK FOR? I SURE AM GLAD I DECIDED TO THROW THIS LITTLE SOIREE!
CAREFUL OF THAT CHANDELIER, MR. BEAST! I'D HATE TO SEE SUCH A LOVELY PIECE BROKEN!
NOT TO WORRY, ISAAC! I'M AS CAREFUL AS I AM AGILE!
AND PLEASE CALL ME HANK! "MR. BEAST" SOUNDS LIKE THE NAME OF THE HAIRDRESSER AT THE CENTRAL PARK ZOO!
ISAAC CHRISTIANS CAN'T HELP BUT SMILE. THE OLD MAN TRAPPED IN A GARGOYLE'S BODY HAS ONLY KNOWN HENRY McCOY FOR A SHORT TIME--BUT HE'S ALREADY COME TO LOOK UPON THE BEAST AS PART OF THE DEFENDERS' "FAMILY."
A DEMATTEIS SCRIPTER, PERLIN PENCILER, GUSTOVICH INKER, LEFERMAN LETTERER, ROUSSOS COLORIST, MILGROM EDITOR and SHOOTER EDITOR-IN-CHIEF Summertime Spectacular!

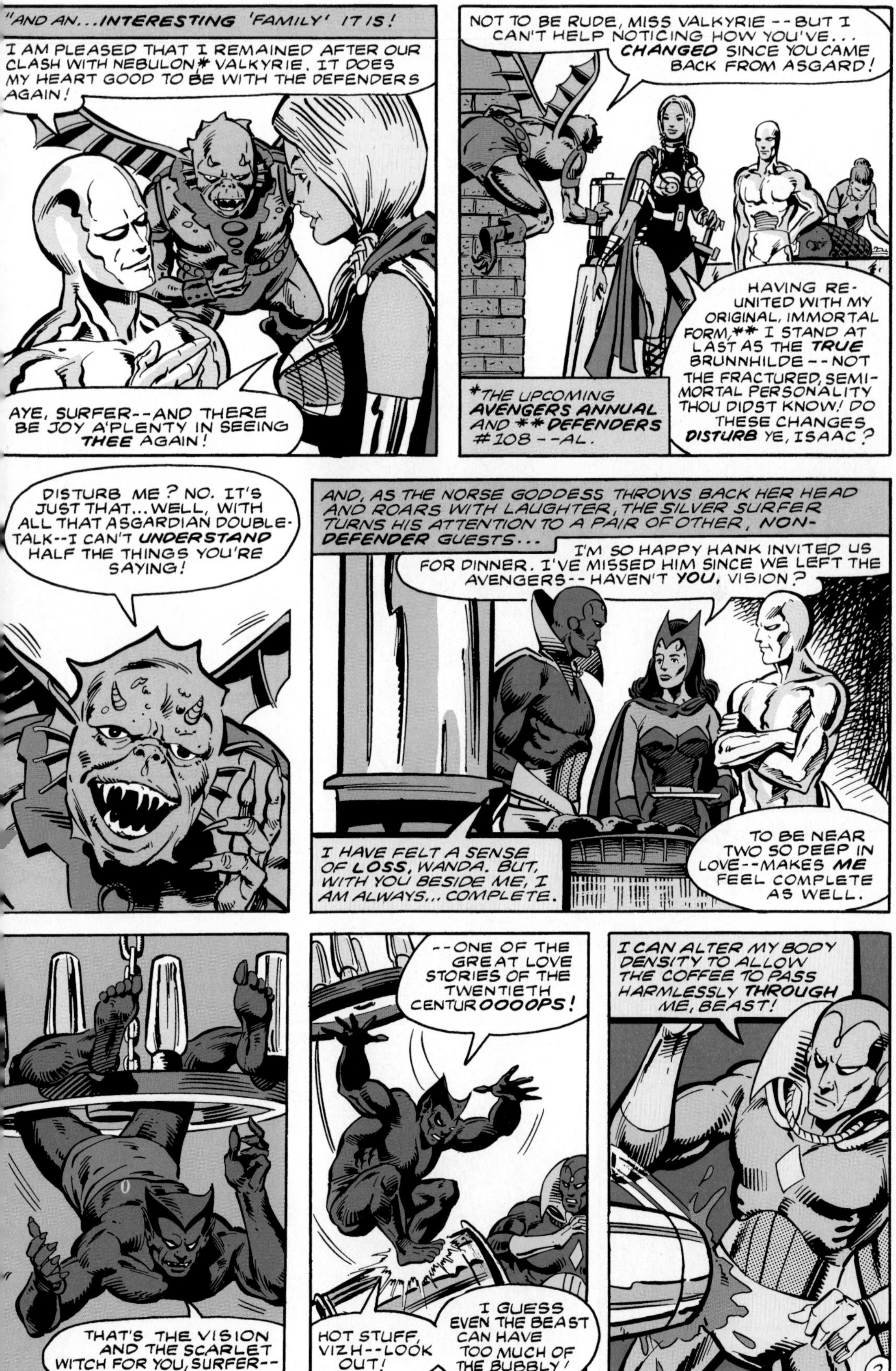
"AND AN... INTERESTING 'FAMILY' IT IS!
I AM PLEASED THAT I REMAINED AFTER OUR CLASH WITH NEBULON* VALKYRIE. IT DOES MY HEART GOOD TO BE WITH THE DEFENDERS AGAIN!
AYE, SURFER--AND THERE BE JOY A'PLENTY IN SEEING THEE AGAIN!
NOT TO BE RUDE, MISS VALKYRIE--BUT I CAN'T HELP NOTICING HOW YOU'VE... CHANGED SINCE YOU CAME BACK FROM ASGARD!
HAVING RE-UNITED WITH MY ORIGINAL, IMMORTAL FORM,** I STAND AT LAST AS THE TRUE BRUNNHILDE--NOT THE FRACTURED, SEMI-MORTAL PERSONALITY THOU DIDST KNOW! DO THESE CHANGES DISTURB YE, ISAAC?
*THE UPCOMING AVENGERS ANNUAL AND **DEFENDERS #108--AL.
DISTURB ME? NO. IT'S JUST THAT... WELL, WITH ALL THAT ASGARDIAN DOUBLE-TALK--I CAN'T UNDERSTAND HALF THE THINGS YOU'RE SAYING!
AND, AS THE NORSE GODDESS THROWS BACK HER HEAD AND ROARS WITH LAUGHTER, THE SILVER SURFER TURNS HIS ATTENTION TO A PAIR OF OTHER, NON-DEFENDER GUESTS...
I'M SO HAPPY HANK INVITED US FOR DINNER. I'VE MISSED HIM SINCE WE LEFT THE AVENGERS--HAVEN'T YOU, VISION?
I HAVE FELT A SENSE OF LOSS, WANDA. BUT, WITH YOU BESIDE ME, I AM ALWAYS... COMPLETE.
TO BE NEAR TWO SO DEEP IN LOVE--MAKES ME FEEL COMPLETE AS WELL.
THAT'S THE VISION AND THE SCARLET WITCH FOR YOU, SURFER--
--ONE OF THE GREAT LOVE STORIES OF THE TWENTIETH CENTUROOOOPS!
HOT STUFF, VIZH--LOOK OUT!
I GUESS EVEN THE BEAST CAN HAVE TOO MUCH OF THE BUBBLY!
I CAN ALTER MY BODY DENSITY TO ALLOW THE COFFEE TO PASS HARMLESSLY THROUGH ME, BEAST!
2

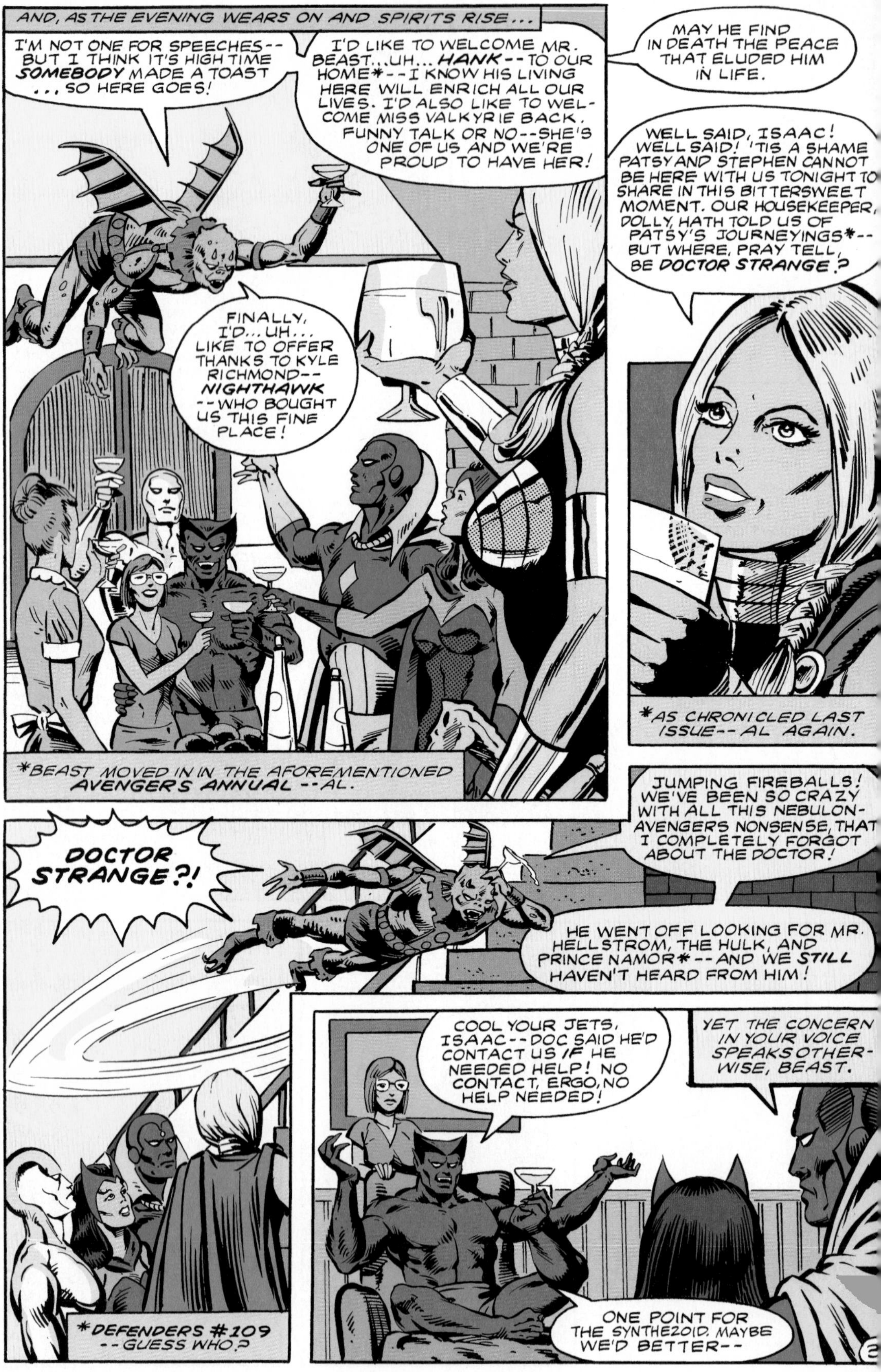
AND, AS THE EVENING WEARS ON AND SPIRITS RISE...
I'M NOT ONE FOR SPEECHES-- BUT I THINK IT'S HIGH TIME SOMEBODY MADE A TOAST ... SO HERE GOES!
I'D LIKE TO WELCOME MR. BEAST...UH... HANK--TO OUR HOME*--I KNOW HIS LIVING HERE WILL ENRICH ALL OUR LIVES. I'D ALSO LIKE TO WELCOME MISS VALKYRIE BACK.
FUNNY TALK OR NO--SHE'S ONE OF US AND WE'RE PROUD TO HAVE HER!
FINALLY, I'D...UH... LIKE TO OFFER THANKS TO KYLE RICHMOND-- NIGHTHAWK --WHO BOUGHT US THIS FINE PLACE!
*BEAST MOVED IN IN THE AFOREMENTIONED AVENGER'S ANNUAL--AL.
MAY HE FIND IN DEATH THE PEACE THAT ELUDED HIM IN LIFE.
WELL SAID, ISAAC! WELL SAID! 'TIS A SHAME PATSY AND STEPHEN CANNOT BE HERE WITH US TONIGHT TO SHARE IN THIS BITTERSWEET MOMENT. OUR HOUSEKEEPER, DOLLY, HATH TOLD US OF PATSY'S JOURNEYINGS*-- BUT WHERE, PRAY TELL, BE DOCTOR STRANGE?
*AS CHRONICLED LAST ISSUE--AL AGAIN.
DOCTOR STRANGE?!
JUMPING FIREBALLS! WE'VE BEEN SO CRAZY WITH ALL THIS NEBULON-AVENGERS NONSENSE, THAT I COMPLETELY FORGOT ABOUT THE DOCTOR!
HE WENT OFF LOOKING FOR MR. HELLSTROM, THE HULK, AND PRINCE NAMOR*--AND WE STILL HAVEN'T HEARD FROM HIM!
*DEFENDERS #109 --GUESS WHO?
COOL YOUR JETS, ISAAC--DOC SAID HE'D CONTACT US IF HE NEEDED HELP! NO CONTACT, ERGO, NO HELP NEEDED!
YET THE CONCERN IN YOUR VOICE SPEAKS OTHERWISE, BEAST.
ONE POINT FOR THE SYNTHEZOID. MAYBE WE'D BETTER--

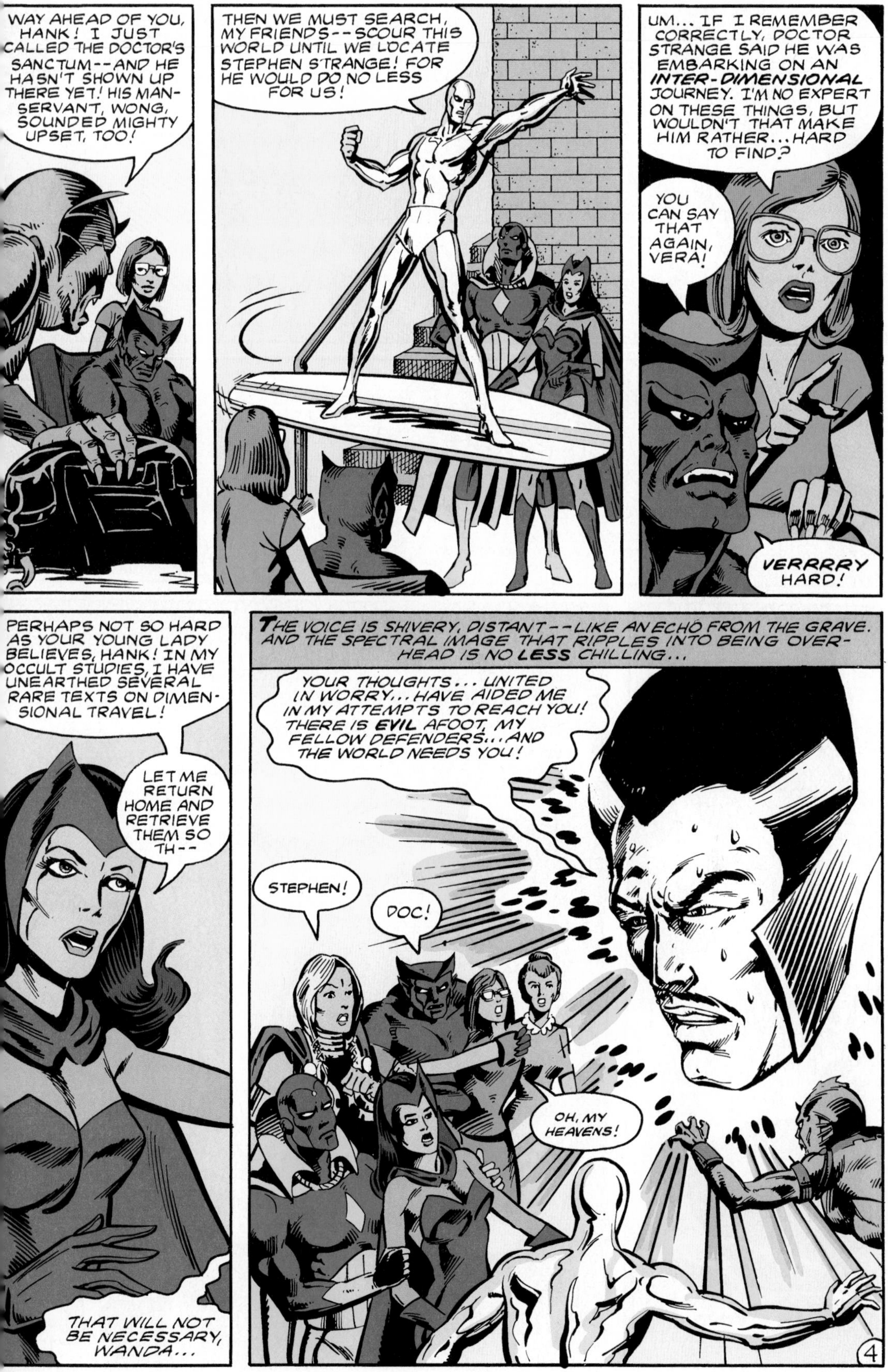

WAY AHEAD OF YOU, HANK! I JUST CALLED THE DOCTOR'S SANCTUM--AND HE HASN'T SHOWN UP THERE YET! HIS MAN-SERVANT, WONG, SOUNDED MIGHTY UPSET, TOO!
THEN WE MUST SEARCH, MY FRIENDS--SCOUR THIS WORLD UNTIL WE LOCATE STEPHEN STRANGE! FOR HE WOULD DO NO LESS FOR US!
UM... IF I REMEMBER CORRECTLY, DOCTOR STRANGE SAID HE WAS EMBARKING ON AN INTER-DIMENSIONAL JOURNEY. I'M NO EXPERT ON THESE THINGS, BUT WOULDN'T THAT MAKE HIM RATHER... HARD TO FIND?
YOU CAN SAY THAT AGAIN, VERA!
VERRRRY HARD!
PERHAPS NOT SO HARD AS YOUR YOUNG LADY BELIEVES, HANK! IN MY OCCULT STUDIES, I HAVE UNEARTHED SEVERAL RARE TEXTS ON DIMEN-SIONAL TRAVEL!
LET ME RETURN HOME AND RETRIEVE THEM SO TH--
THAT WILL NOT BE NECESSARY, WANDA...
THE VOICE IS SHIVERY, DISTANT--LIKE AN ECHO FROM THE GRAVE. AND THE SPECTRAL IMAGE THAT RIPPLES INTO BEING OVER-HEAD IS NO LESS CHILLING...
YOUR THOUGHTS... UNITED IN WORRY... HAVE AIDED ME IN MY ATTEMPTS TO REACH YOU! THERE IS EVIL AFOOT, MY FELLOW DEFENDERS... AND THE WORLD NEEDS YOU!
STEPHEN!
DOC!
OH, MY HEAVENS!
4

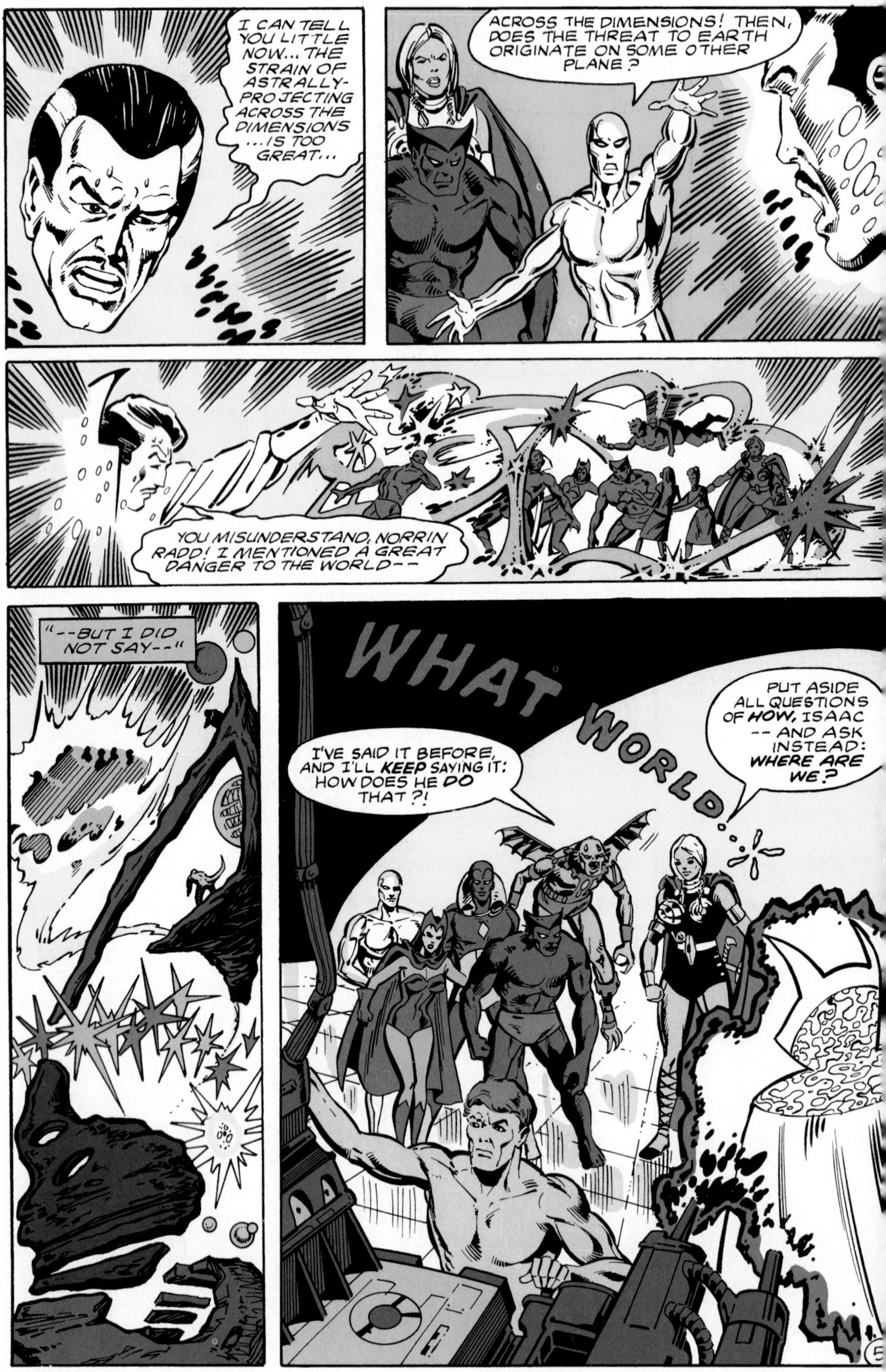

I CAN TELL YOU LITTLE NOW... THE STRAIN OF ASTRALLY-PROJECTING ACROSS THE DIMENSIONS ...IS TOO GREAT...
ACROSS THE DIMENSIONS! THEN, DOES THE THREAT TO EARTH ORIGINATE ON SOME OTHER PLANE?
YOU MISUNDERSTAND, NORRIN RADD! I MENTIONED A GREAT DANGER TO THE WORLD--
"--BUT I DID NOT SAY--"
WHAT WORLD...
I'VE SAID IT BEFORE, AND I'LL KEEP SAYING IT: HOW DOES HE DO THAT?!
PUT ASIDE ALL QUESTIONS OF HOW, ISAAC -- AND ASK INSTEAD: WHERE ARE WE?

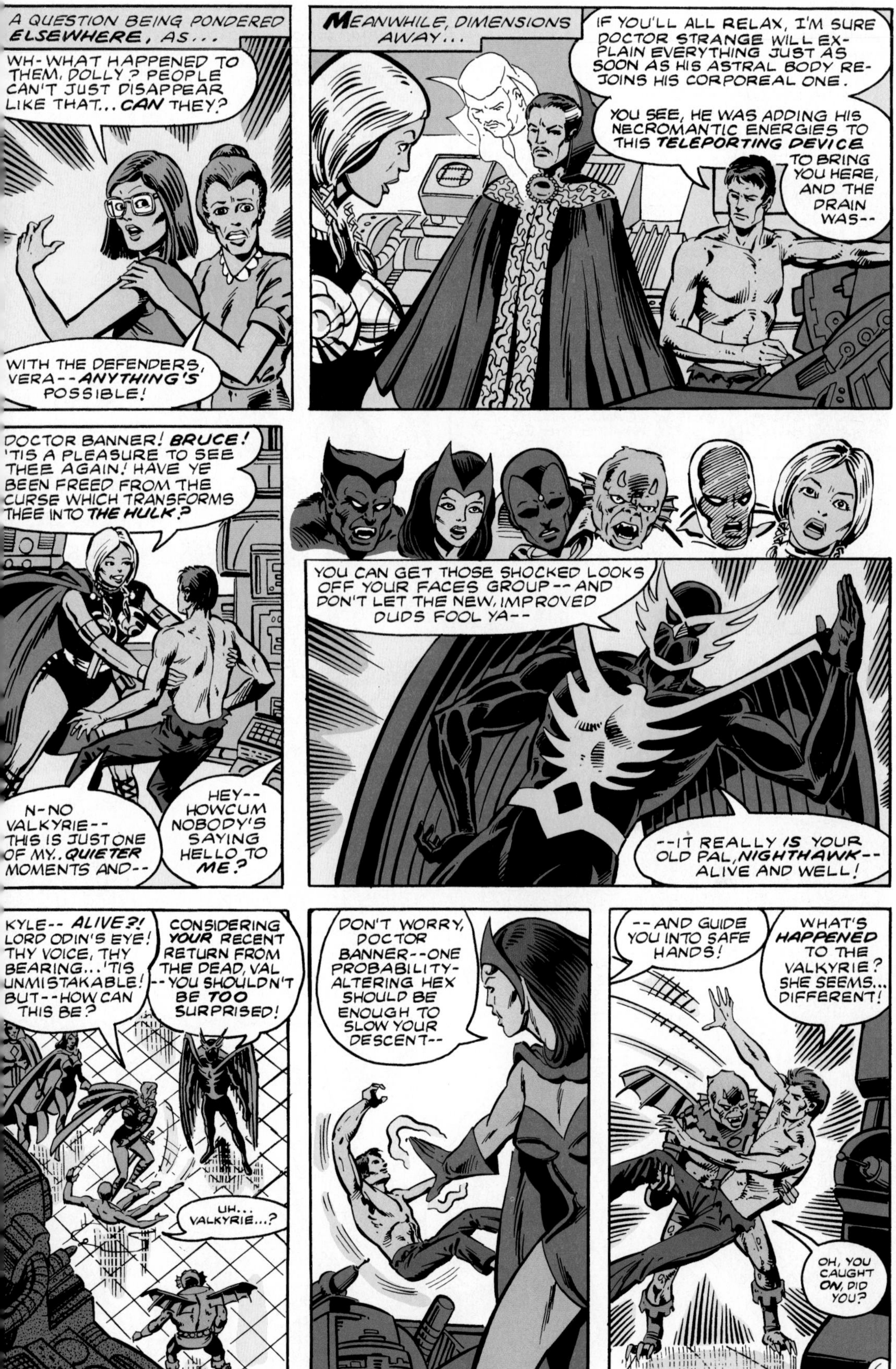

A QUESTION BEING PONDERED ELSEWHERE, AS...
WH-WHAT HAPPENED TO THEM, DOLLY? PEOPLE CAN'T JUST DISAPPEAR LIKE THAT... CAN THEY?
WITH THE DEFENDERS, VERA--ANYTHING'S POSSIBLE!
MEANWHILE, DIMENSIONS AWAY...
IF YOU'LL ALL RELAX, I'M SURE DOCTOR STRANGE WILL EXPLAIN EVERYTHING JUST AS SOON AS HIS ASTRAL BODY REJOINS HIS CORPOREAL ONE.
YOU SEE, HE WAS ADDING HIS NECROMANTIC ENERGIES TO THIS TELEPORTING DEVICE
TO BRING YOU HERE, AND THE DRAIN WAS--
DOCTOR BANNER! BRUCE! 'TIS A PLEASURE TO SEE THEE AGAIN! HAVE YE BEEN FREED FROM THE CURSE WHICH TRANSFORMS THEE INTO THE HULK?
N-NO VALKYRIE--THIS IS JUST ONE OF MY..QUIETER MOMENTS AND--
HEY--HOWCUM NOBODY'S SAYING HELLO TO ME?
YOU CAN GET THOSE SHOCKED LOOKS OFF YOUR FACES GROUP--AND DON'T LET THE NEW, IMPROVED DUDS FOOL YA--
--IT REALLY IS YOUR OLD PAL, NIGHTHAWK--ALIVE AND WELL!
KYLE--ALIVE?! LORD ODIN'S EYE! THY VOICE, THY BEARING...'TIS UNMISTAKABLE! BUT--HOW CAN THIS BE?
CONSIDERING YOUR RECENT RETURN FROM THE DEAD, VAL--YOU SHOULDN'T BE TOO SURPRISED!
UH... VALKYRIE...?
DON'T WORRY, DOCTOR BANNER--ONE PROBABILITY-ALTERING HEX SHOULD BE ENOUGH TO SLOW YOUR DESCENT--
--AND GUIDE YOU INTO SAFE HANDS!
WHAT'S HAPPENED TO THE VALKYRIE? SHE SEEMS... DIFFERENT!
OH, YOU CAUGHT ON, DID YOU?
6

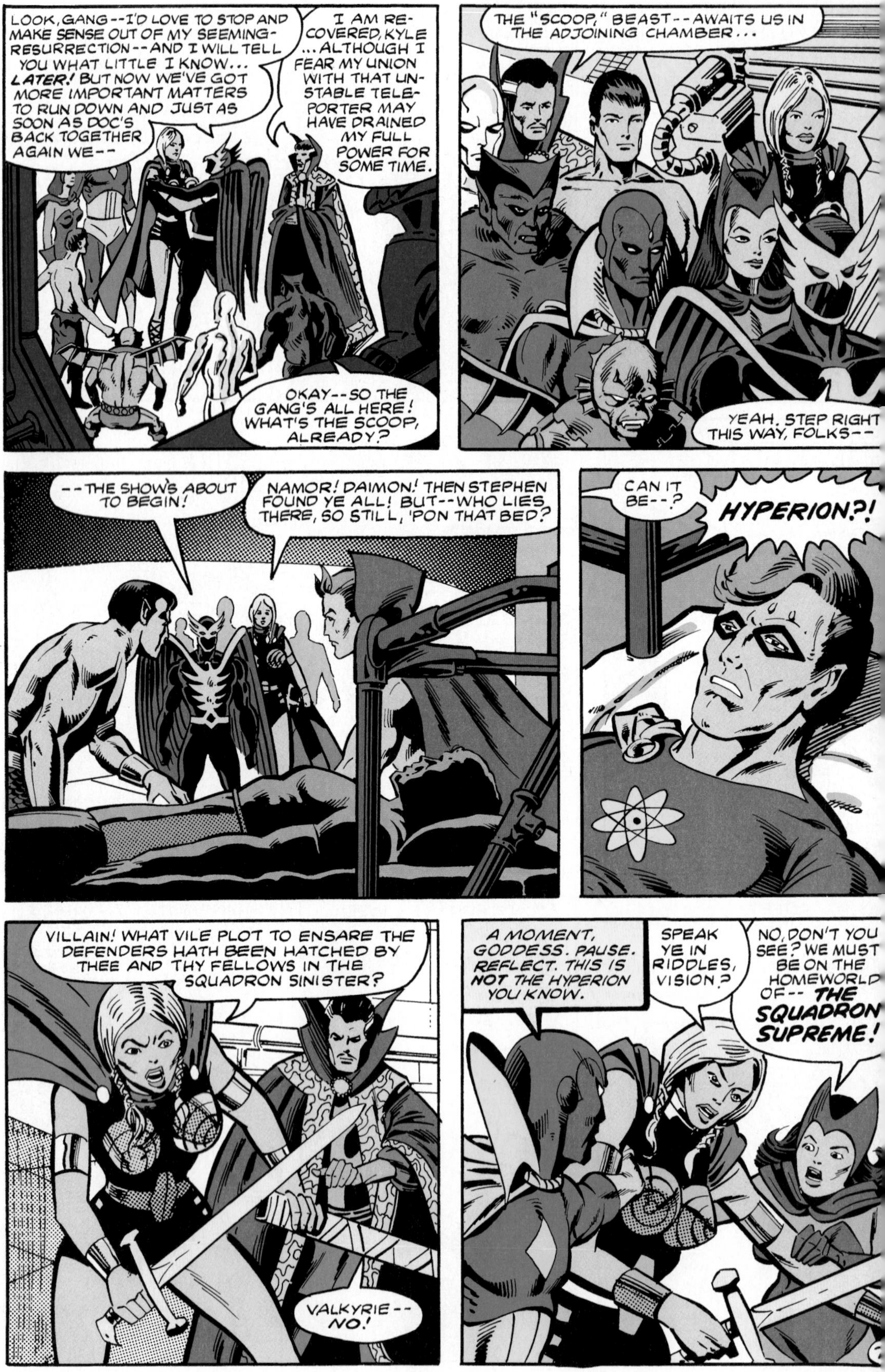
LOOK, GANG--I'D LOVE TO STOP AND MAKE SENSE OUT OF MY SEEMING-RESURRECTION--AND I WILL TELL YOU WHAT LITTLE I KNOW... LATER! BUT NOW WE'VE GOT MORE IMPORTANT MATTERS TO RUN DOWN AND JUST AS SOON AS DOC'S BACK TOGETHER AGAIN WE--
I AM RECOVERED, KYLE ...ALTHOUGH I FEAR MY UNION WITH THAT UNSTABLE TELEPORTER MAY HAVE DRAINED MY FULL POWER FOR SOME TIME.
OKAY--SO THE GANG'S ALL HERE! WHAT'S THE SCOOP, ALREADY?
THE "SCOOP," BEAST--AWAITS US IN THE ADJOINING CHAMBER...
YEAH. STEP RIGHT THIS WAY, FOLKS--
--THE SHOW'S ABOUT TO BEGIN!
NAMOR! DAIMON! THEN STEPHEN FOUND YE ALL! BUT--WHO LIES THERE, SO STILL, 'PON THAT BED?
CAN IT BE--?
HYPERION?!
VILLAIN! WHAT VILE PLOT TO ENSARE THE DEFENDERS HATH BEEN HATCHED BY THEE AND THY FELLOWS IN THE SQUADRON SINISTER?
VALKYRIE--NO!
A MOMENT, GODDESS. PAUSE. REFLECT. THIS IS NOT THE HYPERION YOU KNOW.
SPEAK YE IN RIDDLES, VISION?
NO, DON'T YOU SEE? WE MUST BE ON THE HOMEWORLD OF--THE SQUADRON SUPREME!

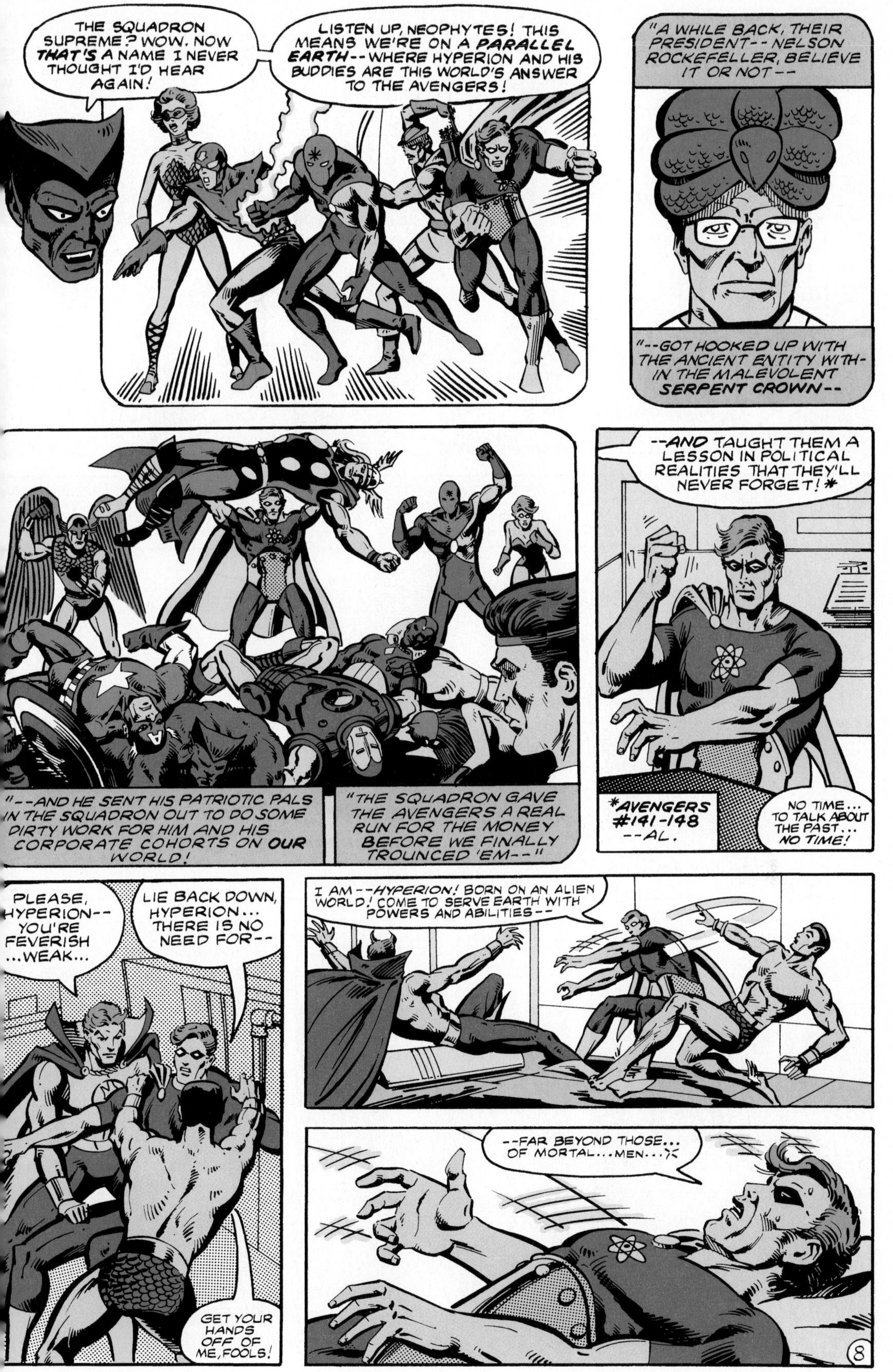
THE SQUADRON SUPREME? WOW. NOW THAT'S A NAME I NEVER THOUGHT I'D HEAR AGAIN!
LISTEN UP, NEOPHYTES! THIS MEANS WE'RE ON A PARALLEL EARTH--WHERE HYPERION AND HIS BUDDIES ARE THIS WORLD'S ANSWER TO THE AVENGERS!
"A WHILE BACK, THEIR PRESIDENT--NELSON ROCKEFELLER, BELIEVE IT OR NOT--
"--GOT HOOKED UP WITH THE ANCIENT ENTITY WITHIN THE MALEVOLENT SERPENT CROWN--
"--AND HE SENT HIS PATRIOTIC PALS IN THE SQUADRON OUT TO DO SOME DIRTY WORK FOR HIM AND HIS CORPORATE COHORTS ON OUR WORLD!
"THE SQUADRON GAVE THE AVENGERS A REAL RUN FOR THE MONEY BEFORE WE FINALLY TROUNCED 'EM--"
--AND TAUGHT THEM A LESSON IN POLITICAL REALITIES THAT THEY'LL NEVER FORGET! *
*AVENGERS #141-148 --AL.
NO TIME... TO TALK ABOUT THE PAST... NO TIME!
PLEASE, HYPERION--YOU'RE FEVERISH ...WEAK...
LIE BACK DOWN, HYPERION... THERE IS NO NEED FOR--
GET YOUR HANDS OFF OF ME, FOOLS!
I AM--HYPERION! BORN ON AN ALIEN WORLD! COME TO SERVE EARTH WITH POWERS AND ABILITIES--
--FAR BEYOND THOSE... OF MORTAL...MEN...
8

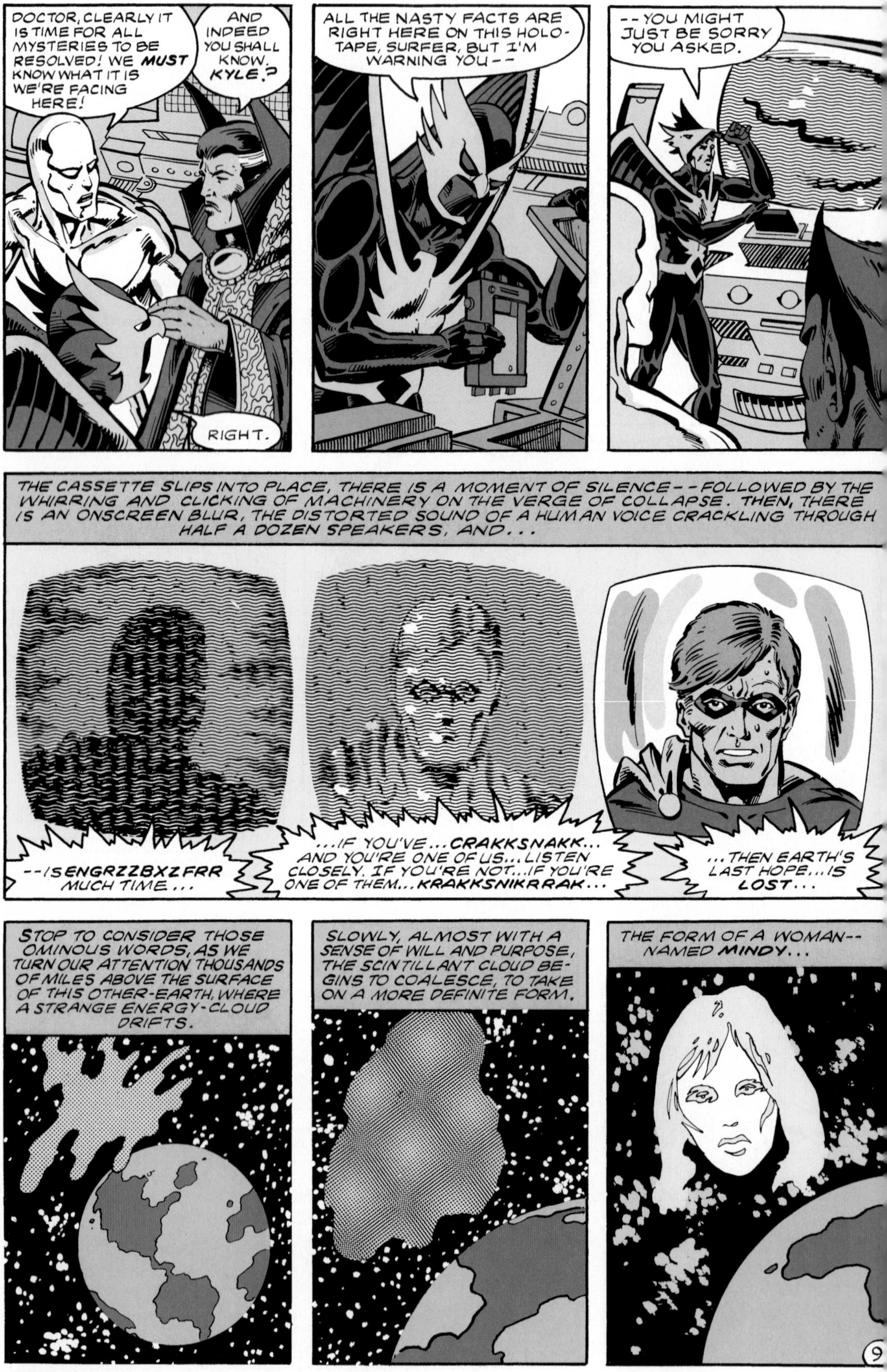

DOCTOR, CLEARLY IT IS TIME FOR ALL MYSTERIES TO BE RESOLVED! WE MUST KNOW WHAT IT IS WE'RE FACING HERE!
AND INDEED YOU SHALL KNOW. KYLE?
RIGHT.
ALL THE NASTY FACTS ARE RIGHT HERE ON THIS HOLO-TAPE, SURFER, BUT I'M WARNING YOU--
--YOU MIGHT JUST BE SORRY YOU ASKED.
THE CASSETTE SLIPS INTO PLACE, THERE IS A MOMENT OF SILENCE--FOLLOWED BY THE WHIRRING AND CLICKING OF MACHINERY ON THE VERGE OF COLLAPSE. THEN, THERE IS AN ONSCREEN BLUR, THE DISTORTED SOUND OF A HUMAN VOICE CRACKLING THROUGH HALF A DOZEN SPEAKERS, AND...
--ISENGRZZBXZFRR MUCH TIME...
...IF YOU'VE...CRAKKSNAKK... AND YOU'RE ONE OF US...LISTEN CLOSELY. IF YOU'RE NOT...IF YOU'RE ONE OF THEM...KRAKKSNIKRRAK...
...THEN EARTH'S LAST HOPE...IS LOST...
STOP TO CONSIDER THOSE OMINOUS WORDS, AS WE TURN OUR ATTENTION THOUSANDS OF MILES ABOVE THE SURFACE OF THIS OTHER-EARTH, WHERE A STRANGE ENERGY-CLOUD DRIFTS.
SLOWLY, ALMOST WITH A SENSE OF WILL AND PURPOSE, THE SCINTILLANT CLOUD BEGINS TO COALESCE, TO TAKE ON A MORE DEFINITE FORM.
THE FORM OF A WOMAN-- NAMED MINDY...
9

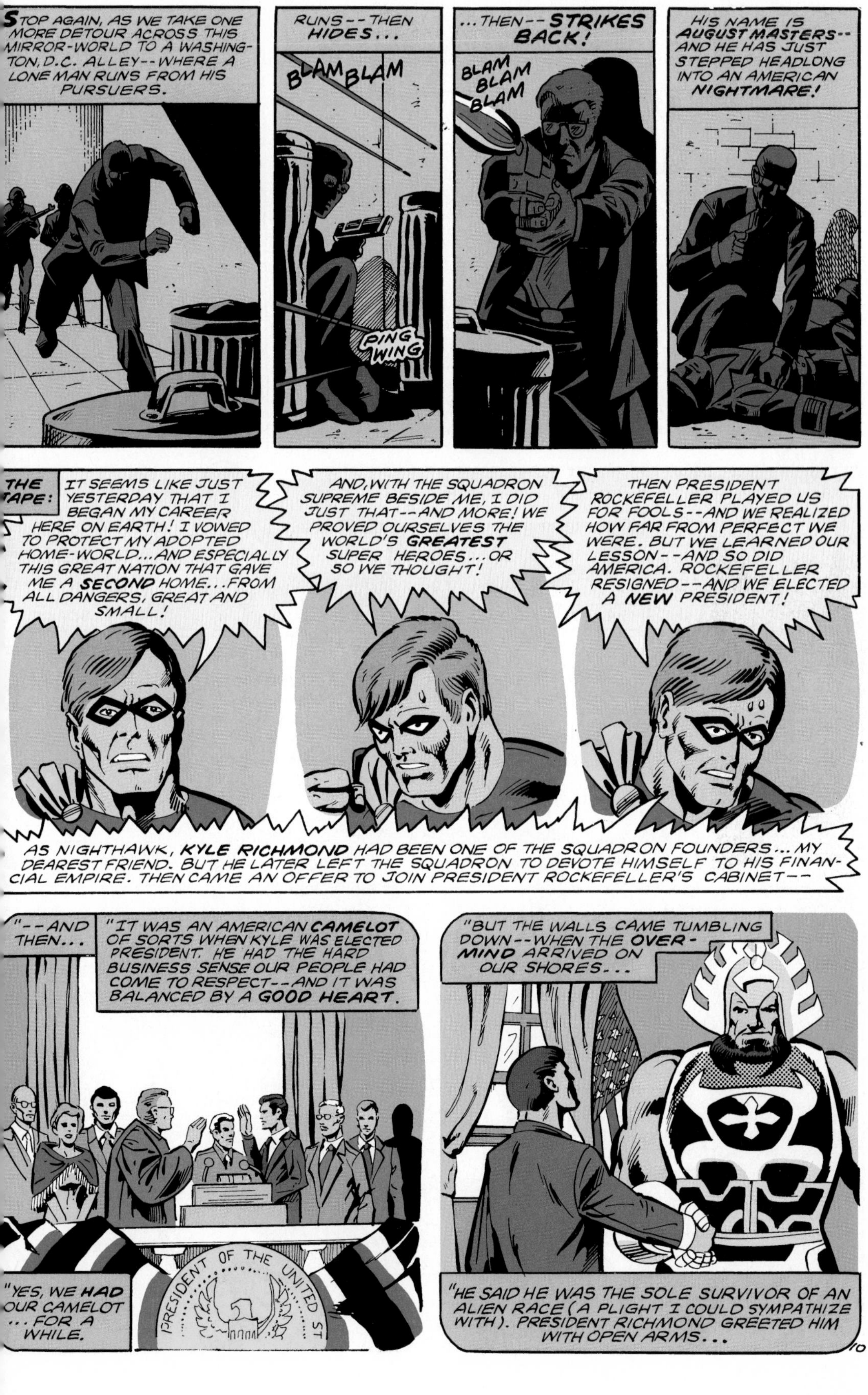
STOP AGAIN, AS WE TAKE ONE MORE DETOUR ACROSS THIS MIRROR-WORLD TO A WASHINGTON, D.C. ALLEY--WHERE A LONE MAN RUNS FROM HIS PURSUERS.
RUNS--THEN HIDES...
BLAM BLAM
PING WING
...THEN--STRIKES BACK!
BLAM BLAM BLAM
HIS NAME IS AUGUST MASTERS--AND HE HAS JUST STEPPED HEADLONG INTO AN AMERICAN NIGHTMARE!
THE TAPE:
IT SEEMS LIKE JUST YESTERDAY THAT I BEGAN MY CAREER HERE ON EARTH! I VOWED TO PROTECT MY ADOPTED HOME-WORLD...AND ESPECIALLY THIS GREAT NATION THAT GAVE ME A SECOND HOME...FROM ALL DANGERS, GREAT AND SMALL!
AND, WITH THE SQUADRON SUPREME BESIDE ME, I DID JUST THAT--AND MORE! WE PROVED OURSELVES THE WORLD'S GREATEST SUPER HEROES...OR SO WE THOUGHT!
THEN PRESIDENT ROCKEFELLER PLAYED US FOR FOOLS--AND WE REALIZED HOW FAR FROM PERFECT WE WERE. BUT WE LEARNED OUR LESSON--AND SO DID AMERICA. ROCKEFELLER RESIGNED--AND WE ELECTED A NEW PRESIDENT!
AS NIGHTHAWK, KYLE RICHMOND HAD BEEN ONE OF THE SQUADRON FOUNDERS... MY DEAREST FRIEND. BUT HE LATER LEFT THE SQUADRON TO DEVOTE HIMSELF TO HIS FINANCIAL EMPIRE. THEN CAME AN OFFER TO JOIN PRESIDENT ROCKEFELLER'S CABINET--
"--AND THEN...
"IT WAS AN AMERICAN CAMELOT OF SORTS WHEN KYLE WAS ELECTED PRESIDENT. HE HAD THE HARD BUSINESS SENSE OUR PEOPLE HAD COME TO RESPECT--AND IT WAS BALANCED BY A GOOD HEART.
PRESIDENT OF THE UNITED ST
"YES, WE HAD OUR CAMELOT ...FOR A WHILE.
"BUT THE WALLS CAME TUMBLING DOWN--WHEN THE OVER-MIND ARRIVED ON OUR SHORES...
"HE SAID HE WAS THE SOLE SURVIVOR OF AN ALIEN RACE (A PLIGHT I COULD SYMPATHIZE WITH). PRESIDENT RICHMOND GREETED HIM WITH OPEN ARMS...
10

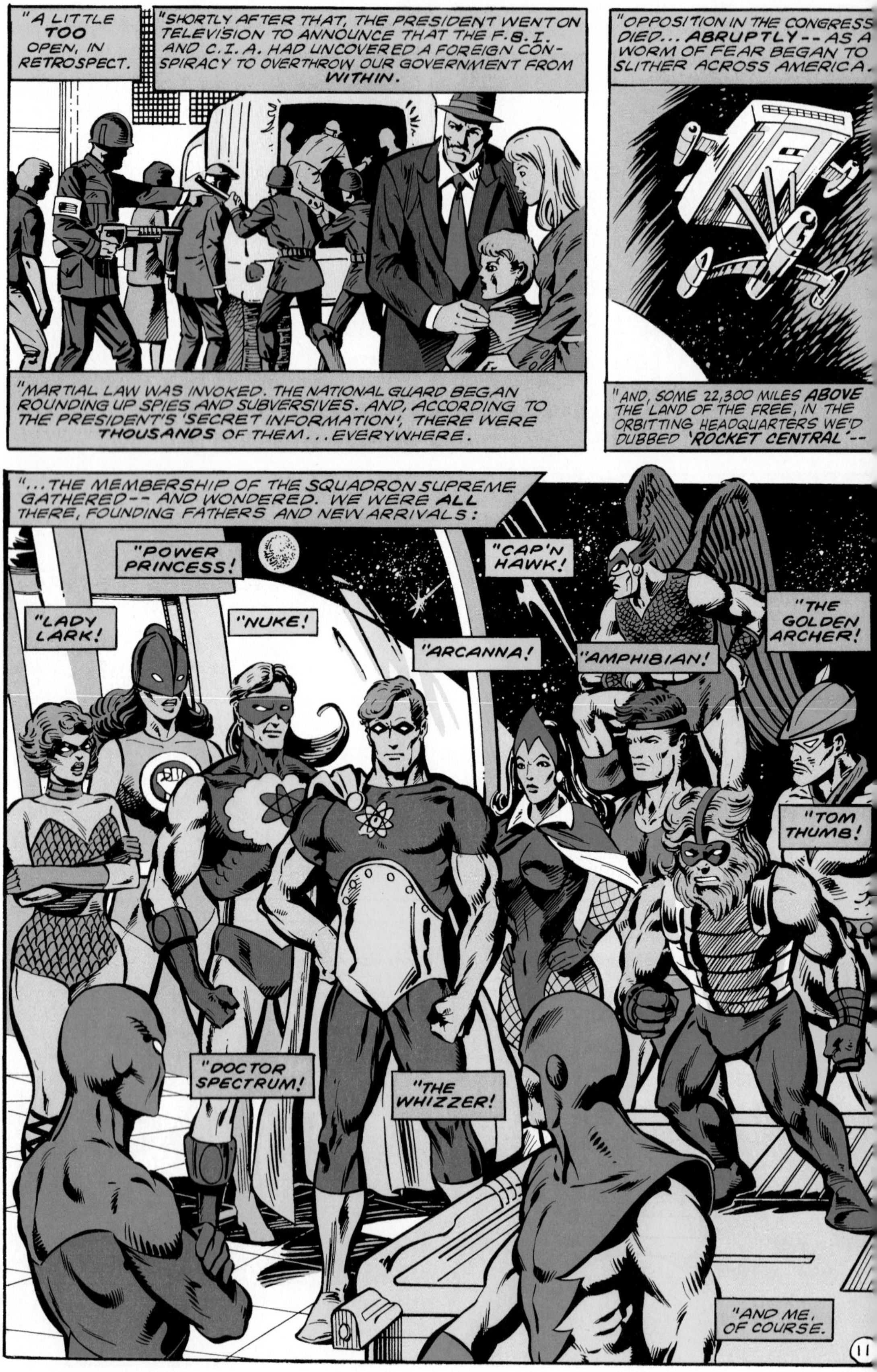

"A LITTLE TOO OPEN, IN RETROSPECT.
"SHORTLY AFTER THAT, THE PRESIDENT WENT ON TELEVISION TO ANNOUNCE THAT THE F.B.I. AND C.I.A. HAD UNCOVERED A FOREIGN CONSPIRACY TO OVERTHROW OUR GOVERNMENT FROM WITHIN.
"MARTIAL LAW WAS INVOKED. THE NATIONAL GUARD BEGAN ROUNDING UP SPIES AND SUBVERSIVES. AND, ACCORDING TO THE PRESIDENT'S 'SECRET INFORMATION', THERE WERE THOUSANDS OF THEM... EVERYWHERE.
"OPPOSITION IN THE CONGRESS DIED... ABRUPTLY-- AS A WORM OF FEAR BEGAN TO SLITHER ACROSS AMERICA.
"AND, SOME 22,300 MILES ABOVE THE LAND OF THE FREE, IN THE ORBITTING HEADQUARTERS WE'D DUBBED 'ROCKET CENTRAL'--
"...THE MEMBERSHIP OF THE SQUADRON SUPREME GATHERED-- AND WONDERED. WE WERE ALL THERE, FOUNDING FATHERS AND NEW ARRIVALS:
"POWER PRINCESS!
"CAP'N HAWK!
"LADY LARK!
"NUKE!
"ARCANNA!
"AMPHIBIAN!
"THE GOLDEN ARCHER!
"TOM THUMB!
"DOCTOR SPECTRUM!
"THE WHIZZER!
"AND ME, OF COURSE.
11

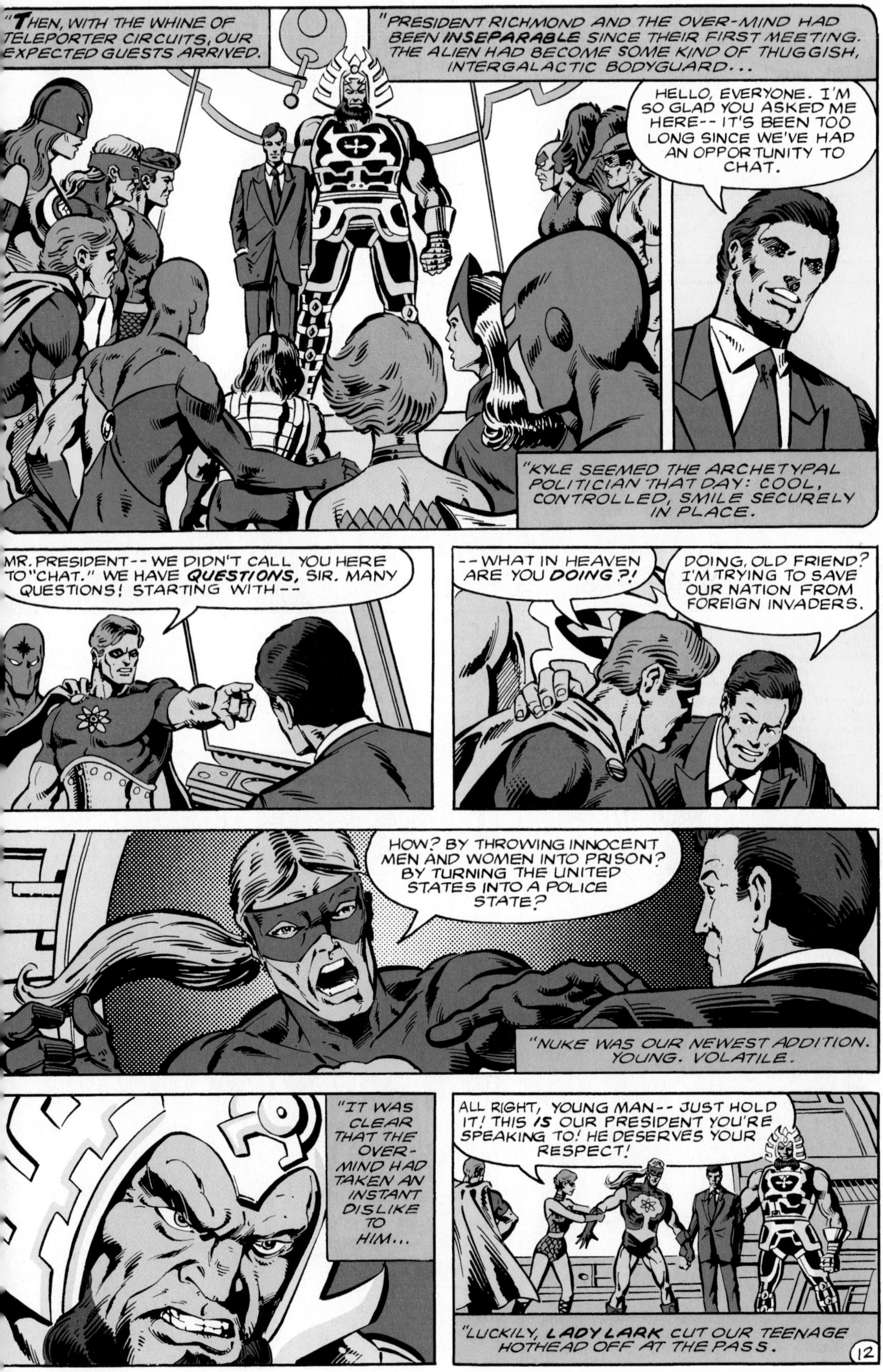
"THEN, WITH THE WHINE OF TELEPORTER CIRCUITS, OUR EXPECTED GUESTS ARRIVED.
"PRESIDENT RICHMOND AND THE OVER-MIND HAD BEEN INSEPARABLE SINCE THEIR FIRST MEETING. THE ALIEN HAD BECOME SOME KIND OF THUGGISH, INTERGALACTIC BODYGUARD...
HELLO, EVERYONE. I'M SO GLAD YOU ASKED ME HERE-- IT'S BEEN TOO LONG SINCE WE'VE HAD AN OPPORTUNITY TO CHAT.
"KYLE SEEMED THE ARCHETYPAL POLITICIAN THAT DAY: COOL, CONTROLLED, SMILE SECURELY IN PLACE.
MR. PRESIDENT-- WE DIDN'T CALL YOU HERE TO "CHAT." WE HAVE QUESTIONS, SIR. MANY QUESTIONS! STARTING WITH--
--WHAT IN HEAVEN ARE YOU DOING?!
DOING, OLD FRIEND? I'M TRYING TO SAVE OUR NATION FROM FOREIGN INVADERS.
HOW? BY THROWING INNOCENT MEN AND WOMEN INTO PRISON? BY TURNING THE UNITED STATES INTO A POLICE STATE?
"NUKE WAS OUR NEWEST ADDITION. YOUNG. VOLATILE.
"IT WAS CLEAR THAT THE OVER-MIND HAD TAKEN AN INSTANT DISLIKE TO HIM...
ALL RIGHT, YOUNG MAN-- JUST HOLD IT! THIS IS OUR PRESIDENT YOU'RE SPEAKING TO! HE DESERVES YOUR RESPECT!
"LUCKILY, LADY LARK CUT OUR TEENAGE HOTHEAD OFF AT THE PASS.
12

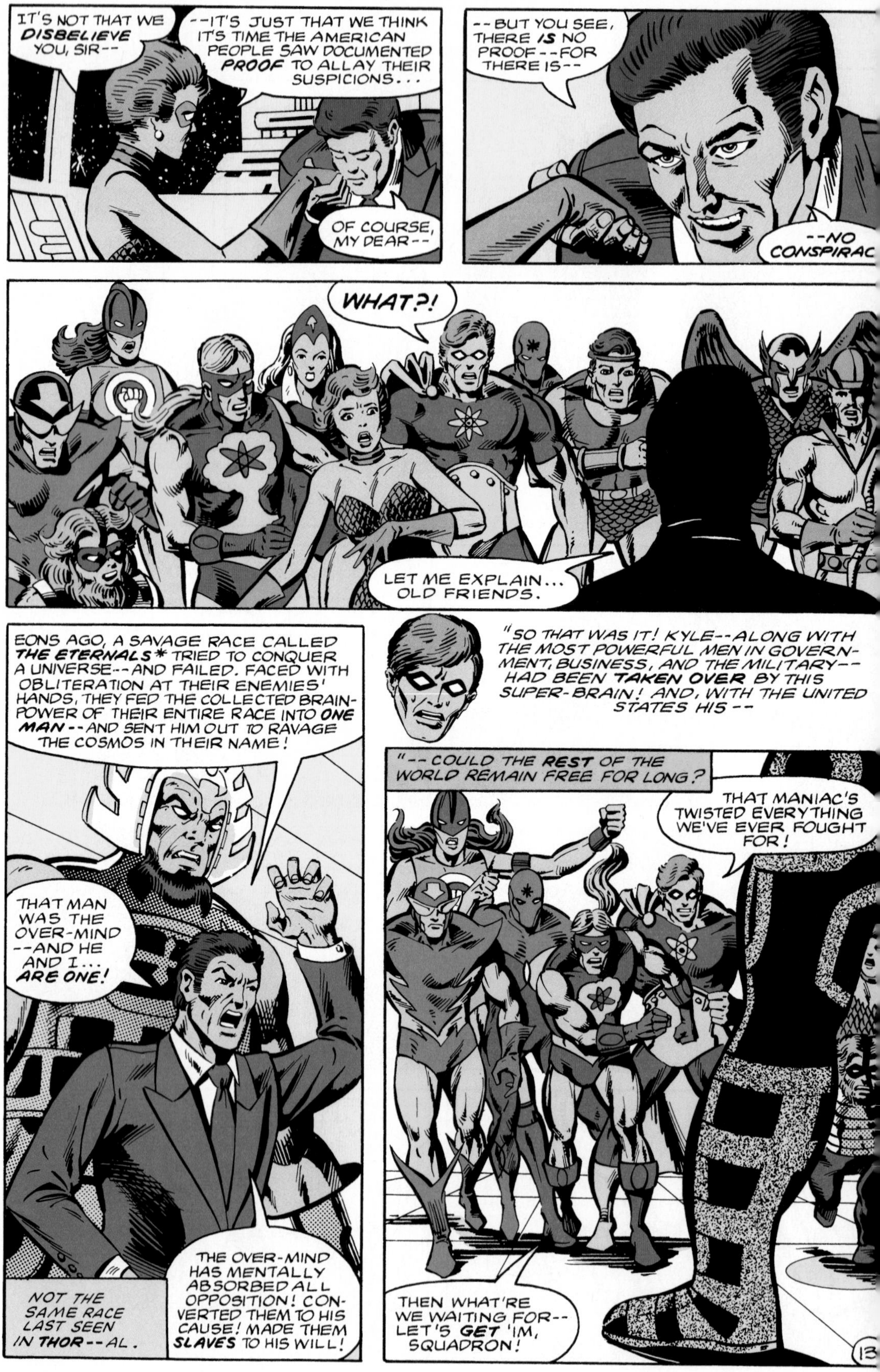
IT'S NOT THAT WE DISBELIEVE YOU, SIR--
--IT'S JUST THAT WE THINK IT'S TIME THE AMERICAN PEOPLE SAW DOCUMENTED PROOF TO ALLAY THEIR SUSPICIONS...
OF COURSE, MY DEAR--
--BUT YOU SEE, THERE IS NO PROOF--FOR THERE IS--
--NO CONSPIRAC
WHAT?!
LET ME EXPLAIN... OLD FRIENDS.
EONS AGO, A SAVAGE RACE CALLED THE ETERNALS* TRIED TO CONQUER A UNIVERSE--AND FAILED. FACED WITH OBLITERATION AT THEIR ENEMIES' HANDS, THEY FED THE COLLECTED BRAIN-POWER OF THEIR ENTIRE RACE INTO ONE MAN--AND SENT HIM OUT TO RAVAGE THE COSMOS IN THEIR NAME!
THAT MAN WAS THE OVER-MIND --AND HE AND I... ARE ONE!
THE OVER-MIND HAS MENTALLY ABSORBED ALL OPPOSITION! CONVERTED THEM TO HIS CAUSE! MADE THEM SLAVES TO HIS WILL!
*NOT THE SAME RACE LAST SEEN IN THOR--AL.
"SO THAT WAS IT! KYLE--ALONG WITH THE MOST POWERFUL MEN IN GOVERNMENT, BUSINESS, AND THE MILITARY--HAD BEEN TAKEN OVER BY THIS SUPER-BRAIN! AND, WITH THE UNITED STATES HIS--
"--COULD THE REST OF THE WORLD REMAIN FREE FOR LONG?
THAT MANIAC'S TWISTED EVERYTHING WE'VE EVER FOUGHT FOR!
THEN WHAT'RE WE WAITING FOR--LET'S GET 'IM, SQUADRON!
13

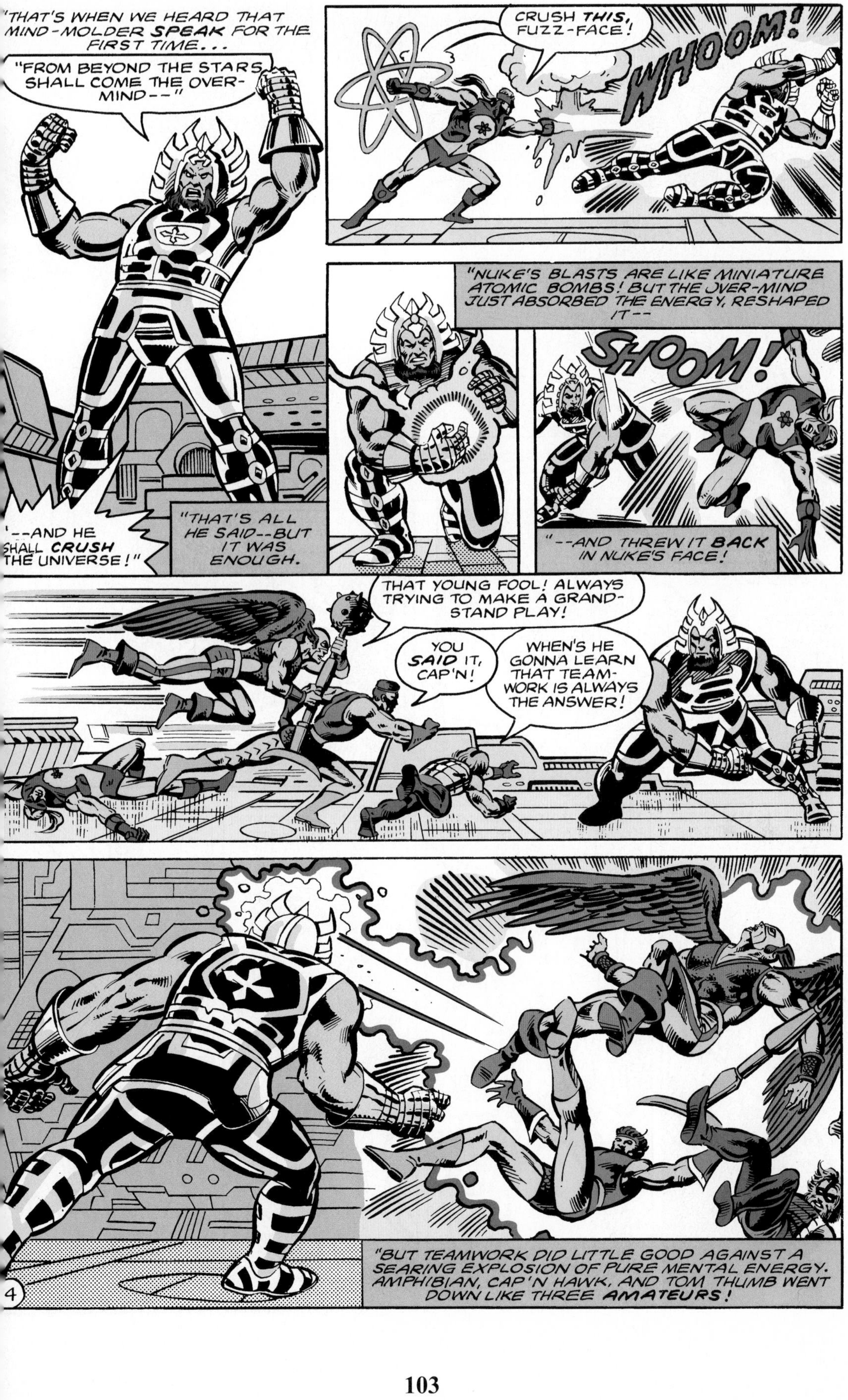
"THAT'S WHEN WE HEARD THAT MIND-MOLDER SPEAK FOR THE FIRST TIME...
"FROM BEYOND THE STARS SHALL COME THE OVER-MIND--"
"--AND HE SHALL CRUSH THE UNIVERSE!"
"THAT'S ALL HE SAID--BUT IT WAS ENOUGH.
CRUSH THIS, FUZZ-FACE!
WHOOM!
"NUKE'S BLASTS ARE LIKE MINIATURE ATOMIC BOMBS! BUT THE OVER-MIND JUST ABSORBED THE ENERGY, RESHAPED IT--
SHOOM!
"--AND THREW IT BACK IN NUKE'S FACE!
THAT YOUNG FOOL! ALWAYS TRYING TO MAKE A GRAND-STAND PLAY!
YOU SAID IT, CAP'N!
WHEN'S HE GONNA LEARN THAT TEAM-WORK IS ALWAYS THE ANSWER!
"BUT TEAMWORK DID LITTLE GOOD AGAINST A SEARING EXPLOSION OF PURE MENTAL ENERGY. AMPHIBIAN, CAP'N HAWK, AND TOM THUMB WENT DOWN LIKE THREE AMATEURS!
4

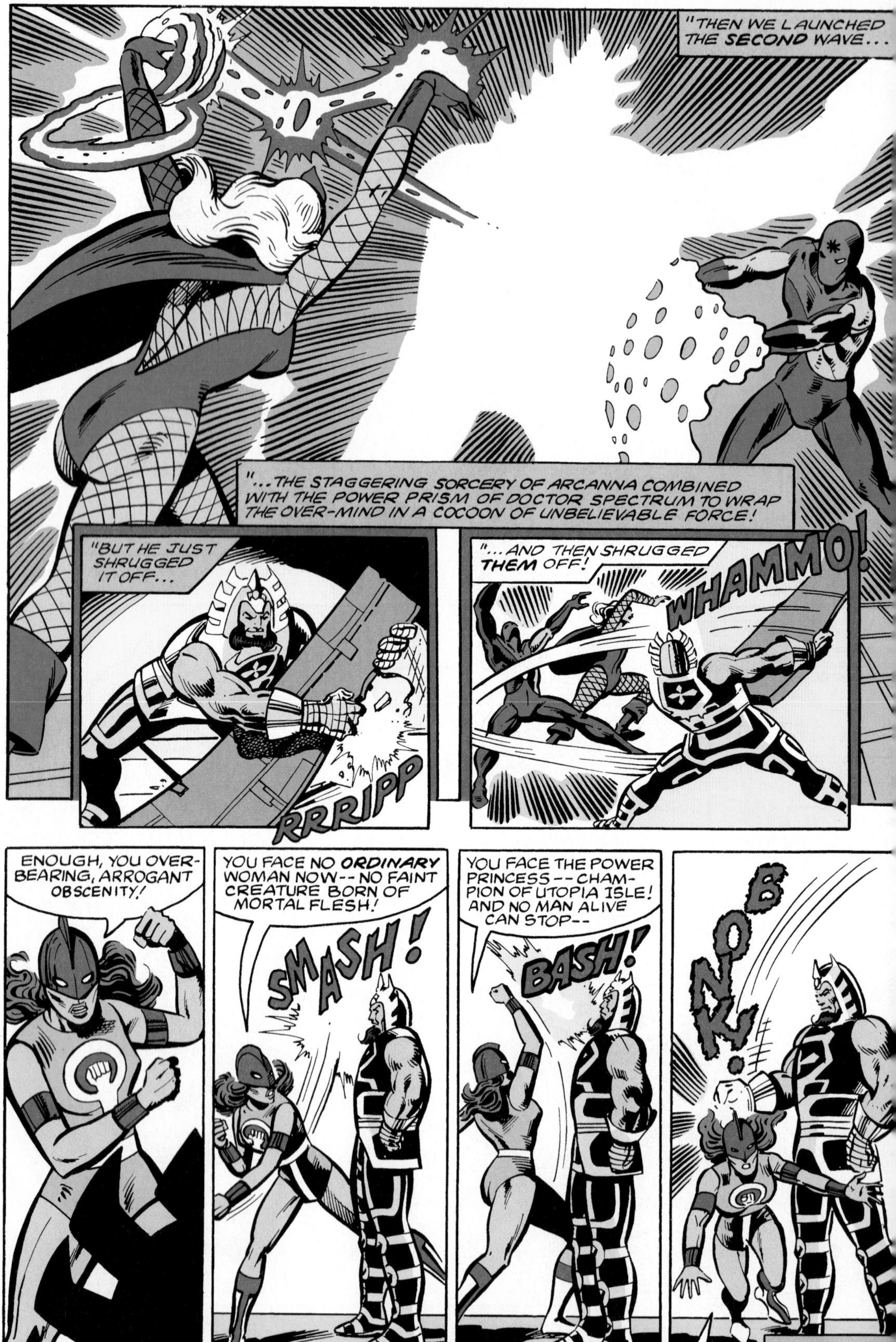
"THEN WE LAUNCHED THE SECOND WAVE...
"...THE STAGGERING SORCERY OF ARCANNA COMBINED WITH THE POWER PRISM OF DOCTOR SPECTRUM TO WRAP THE OVER-MIND IN A COCOON OF UNBELIEVABLE FORCE!
"BUT HE JUST SHRUGGED IT OFF...
RRRIPP
"...AND THEN SHRUGGED THEM OFF!
WHAMMO!
ENOUGH, YOU OVER-BEARING, ARROGANT OBSCENITY!
15
YOU FACE NO ORDINARY WOMAN NOW--NO FAINT CREATURE BORN OF MORTAL FLESH!
SMASH!
YOU FACE THE POWER PRINCESS--CHAMPION OF UTOPIA ISLE! AND NO MAN ALIVE CAN STOP--
BASH!
KNOB
--ME...
"SO MUCH FOR RHETORIC.

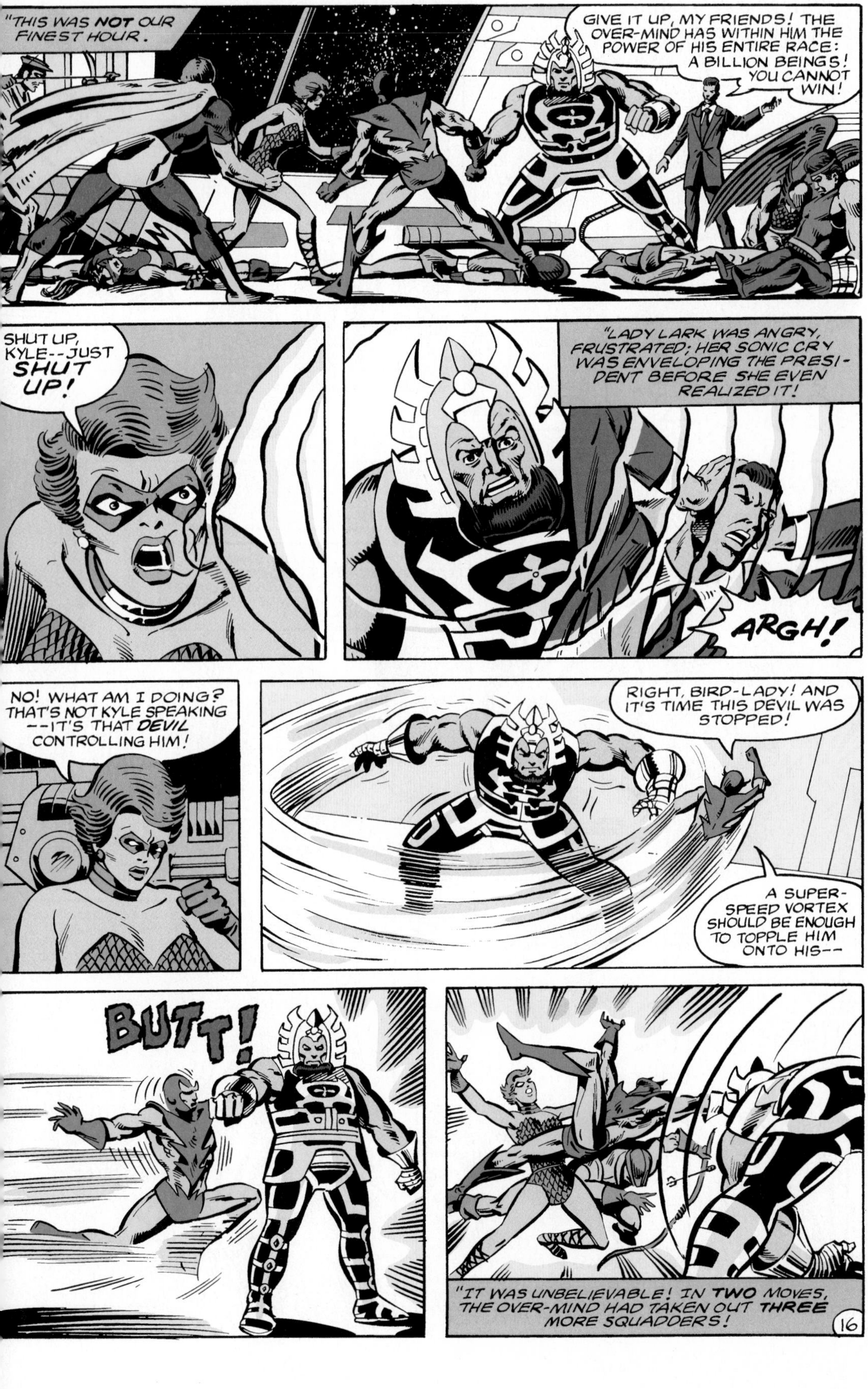

"THIS WAS NOT OUR FINEST HOUR.
GIVE IT UP, MY FRIENDS! THE OVER-MIND HAS WITHIN HIM THE POWER OF HIS ENTIRE RACE: A BILLION BEINGS! YOU CANNOT WIN!
SHUT UP, KYLE--JUST SHUT UP!
"LADY LARK WAS ANGRY, FRUSTRATED; HER SONIC CRY WAS ENVELOPING THE PRESIDENT BEFORE SHE EVEN REALIZED IT!
ARGH!
NO! WHAT AM I DOING? THAT'S NOT KYLE SPEAKING --IT'S THAT DEVIL CONTROLLING HIM!
RIGHT, BIRD-LADY! AND IT'S TIME THIS DEVIL WAS STOPPED!
A SUPER-SPEED VORTEX SHOULD BE ENOUGH TO TOPPLE HIM ONTO HIS--
BUTT!
"IT WAS UNBELIEVABLE! IN TWO MOVES, THE OVER-MIND HAD TAKEN OUT THREE MORE SQUADDERS!
16

"THE MOMENT OF TRUTH HAD ARRIVED. IT WAS UP TO ME, AND ME ALONE TO STOP THE OVER-MIND AND FREE KYLE AND I KNEW I COULD *DO* IT--

--GIVEN THE CHANCE.

"BUT IT WAS A CHANCE--

"--I WASN'T--

"--GOING TO *GET*!

ARGONITE!

"THE ONE SUBSTANCE IN ALL THE UNIVERSE THAT COULD PROVE *FATAL* TO ME!

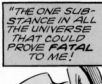

"IN AGONY, I COLLAPSED--

"--AND SAW HOW *TOTALLY* THE OVER-MIND HAD TAKEN CONTROL OF MY PRESIDENT ...MY FRIEND!

"FOR KYLE RICHMOND SIMPLY STOOD THERE, SMIRKING, AS THE ARGONITE RAYS ENVELOPED ME, DRAINING MY LIFE-FORCE AWAY...

"HOW IRONIC THAT A RADIOACTIVE FRAGMENT OF THE WORLD THAT BIRTHED ME WOULD ALSO *BURY* ME! BUT MY DEATH NOW, I REALIZED, WOULD *ALSO* SIGNAL THE END FOR EARTH!

"AND I COULDN'T LET THAT HAPPEN!

"MUSTERING WHAT LITTLE STRENGTH I HAD REMAINING, I SLAMMED PAST THE PRESIDENT AND BOLTED FOR THE SQUADRON'S TELEPORTER.

"IT HAD BEEN BADLY DAMAGED DURING OUR BATTLE WITH OVER-MIND --BUT I PRAYED THAT THERE WAS ENOUGH POWER LEFT TO GET ME THE DEVIL OUT OF THERE.

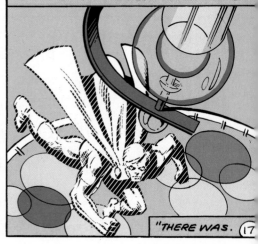

"THERE WAS. (17)

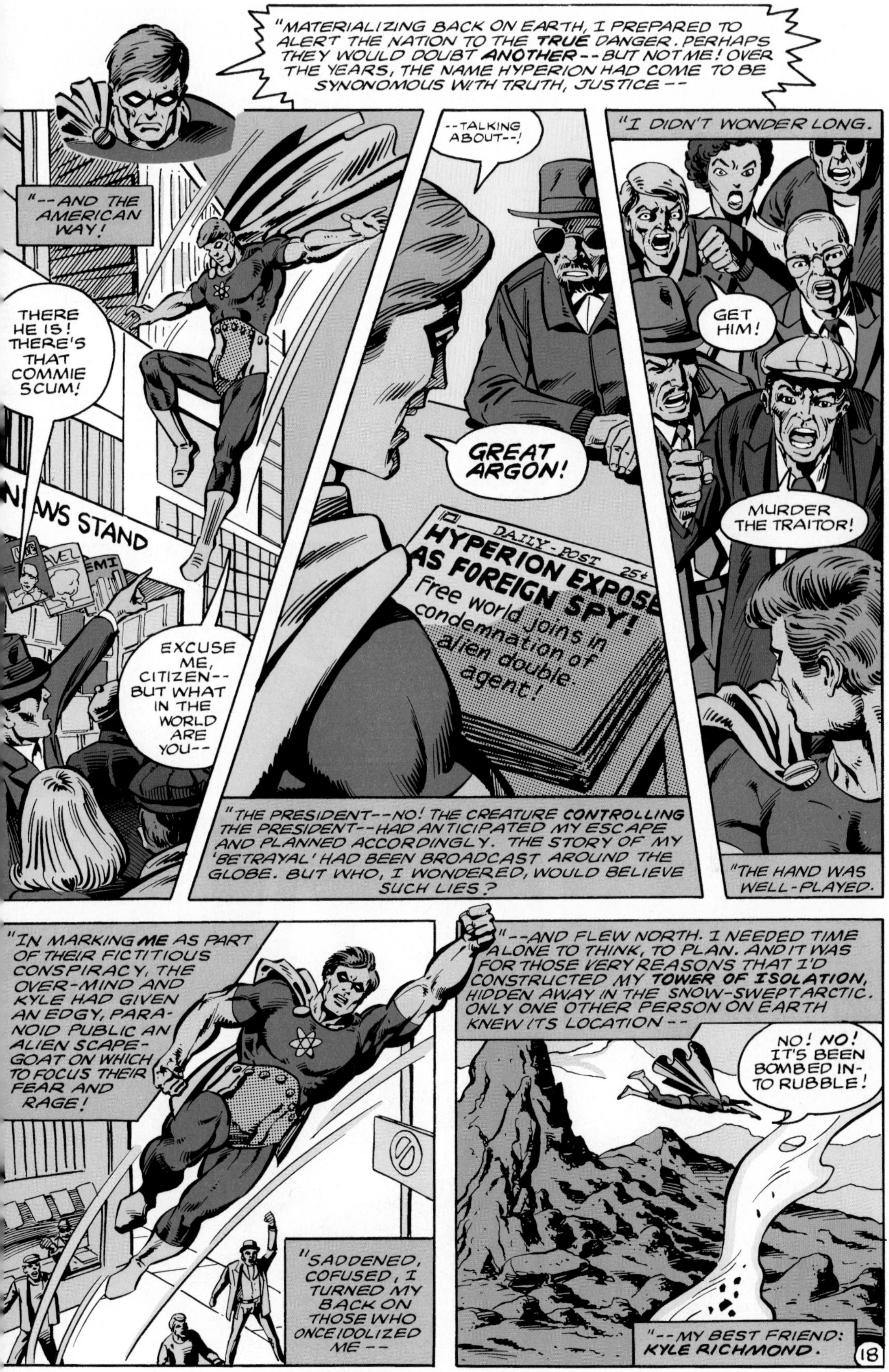
"MATERIALIZING BACK ON EARTH, I PREPARED TO ALERT THE NATION TO THE TRUE DANGER. PERHAPS THEY WOULD DOUBT ANOTHER--BUT NOT ME! OVER THE YEARS, THE NAME HYPERION HAD COME TO BE SYNONOMOUS WITH TRUTH, JUSTICE--
"--AND THE AMERICAN WAY!
THERE HE IS! THERE'S THAT COMMIE SCUM!
NEWS STAND
EXCUSE ME, CITIZEN--BUT WHAT IN THE WORLD ARE YOU--
--TALKING ABOUT--!
GREAT ARGON!
DAILY-POST 25¢
HYPERION EXPOSED AS FOREIGN SPY!
Free world joins in condemnation of alien double-agent!
"I DIDN'T WONDER LONG.
GET HIM!
MURDER THE TRAITOR!
"THE PRESIDENT--NO! THE CREATURE CONTROLLING THE PRESIDENT--HAD ANTICIPATED MY ESCAPE AND PLANNED ACCORDINGLY. THE STORY OF MY 'BETRAYAL' HAD BEEN BROADCAST AROUND THE GLOBE. BUT WHO, I WONDERED, WOULD BELIEVE SUCH LIES?
"THE HAND WAS WELL-PLAYED.
"IN MARKING ME AS PART OF THEIR FICTITIOUS CONSPIRACY, THE OVER-MIND AND KYLE HAD GIVEN AN EDGY, PARANOID PUBLIC AN ALIEN SCAPEGOAT ON WHICH TO FOCUS THEIR FEAR AND RAGE!
"SADDENED, COFUSED, I TURNED MY BACK ON THOSE WHO ONCE IDOLIZED ME--
"--AND FLEW NORTH. I NEEDED TIME ALONE TO THINK, TO PLAN. AND IT WAS FOR THOSE VERY REASONS THAT I'D CONSTRUCTED MY TOWER OF ISOLATION, HIDDEN AWAY IN THE SNOW-SWEPT ARCTIC. ONLY ONE OTHER PERSON ON EARTH KNEW ITS LOCATION--
NO! NO! IT'S BEEN BOMBED INTO RUBBLE!
"--MY BEST FRIEND: KYLE RICHMOND.
18

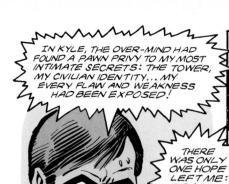

IN KYLE, THE OVER-MIND HAD FOUND A PAWN PRIVY TO MY MOST INTIMATE SECRETS: THE TOWER, MY CIVILIAN IDENTITY... MY EVERY FLAW AND WEAKNESS HAD BEEN EXPOSED!

THERE WAS ONLY ONE HOPE LEFT ME: SPACE!

"THE STARS COULD PROVIDE THE SOLITUDE I NEEDED; THE PRECIOUS *TIME* TO PLAN THAT WAS GROWING MORE AND *MORE* PRECIOUS.

"BUT, NO SOONER HAD I STREAKED HEAVENWARD THAN I FOUND MYSELF BATHED IN AN EERIE, FAMILIAR GLOW!

MY DEATH WAS NOW AN INEVITABILITY -- BUT HOW COULD I DIE KNOWING I'D LET MY ADOPTED HOMEWORLD DOWN?

"AGAIN I HAD BEEN OUTWITTED!

"FOR, CIRCLING THE EARTH, WAS A BELT OF RECENTLY-LAUNCHED SATELLITES THAT WASHED THE WORLD IN CONCENTRATED ARGONITE RAYS! IN SECONDS, MY BLOODSTREAM WAS SATURATED WITH RADIATION!

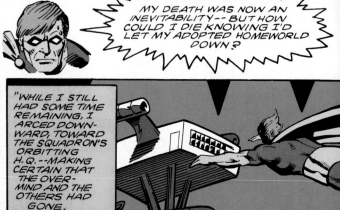

"WHILE I STILL HAD SOME TIME REMAINING, I ARCED DOWNWARD, TOWARD THE SQUADRON'S ORBITING H.Q. --MAKING CERTAIN THAT THE OVERMIND AND THE OTHERS HAD GONE.

"THEN, WORKING AT SUPERSPEED, I BEGAN TO DISMANTLE 'ROCKET CENTRAL'--

"--AND, USING ITS LEAD-LINED WALLS TO PROTECT ME FROM THE DEADLY RAYS, I RETURNED TO EARTH AND HASTILY CONSTRUCTED THIS UNDERGROUND COMPLEX...

(19)

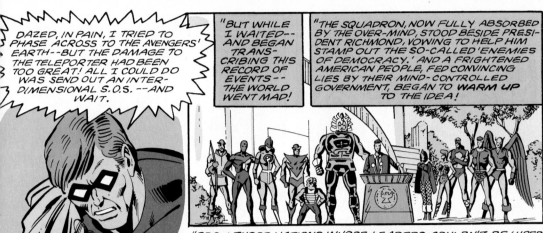

DAZED, IN PAIN, I TRIED TO PHASE ACROSS TO THE AVENGERS' EARTH--BUT THE DAMAGE TO THE TELEPORTER HAD BEEN TOO GREAT! ALL I COULD DO WAS SEND OUT AN INTERDIMENSIONAL S.O.S.--AND WAIT.

"BUT WHILE I WAITED-- AND BEGAN TRANS- CRIBING THIS RECORD OF EVENTS-- THE WORLD WENT MAD!"

"THE SQUADRON, NOW FULLY ABSORBED BY THE OVER-MIND, STOOD BESIDE PRESI- DENT RICHMOND, VOWING TO HELP HIM STAMP OUT THE SO-CALLED 'ENEMIES OF DEMOCRACY.' AND A FRIGHTENED AMERICAN PEOPLE, FED CONVINCING LIES BY THEIR MIND-CONTROLLED GOVERNMENT, BEGAN TO WARM UP TO THE IDEA!"

"SOON, THOSE NATIONS WHOSE LEADERS COULDN'T BE LURED TO THE WHITE HOUSE FOR PSYCHIC-ASSIMILATION --

"--FOUND THEMSELVES UNDER ATTACK BY THE MOST POWERFUL FIGHTING FORCE ON EARTH!

"BACKED BY THE U.S. MILITARY MACHINE AND THE MENTAL MIGHT OF THAT ALIEN MONSTER, THE SQUADRON SUPREME...CONQUERED THE WORLD! AND NOW, PLANET EARTH BELONGS TO THE OVER-MIND!"

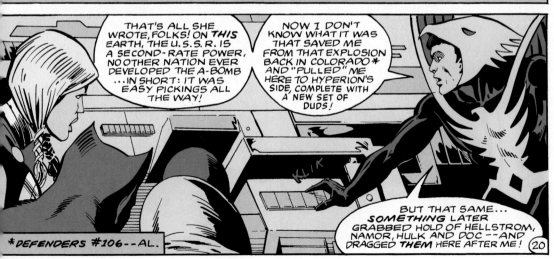

THAT'S ALL SHE WROTE, FOLKS! ON THIS EARTH, THE U.S.S.R. IS A SECOND-RATE POWER, NO OTHER NATION EVER DEVELOPED THE A-BOMB ...IN SHORT: IT WAS EASY PICKINGS ALL THE WAY!

NOW I DON'T KNOW WHAT IT WAS THAT SAVED ME FROM THAT EXPLOSION * AND "PULLED" ME HERE TO HYPERION'S SIDE, COMPLETE WITH A NEW SET OF DUDS!

BUT THAT SAME... SOMETHING LATER GRABBED HOLD OF HELLSTROM, NAMOR, HULK AND DOC--AND DRAGGED THEM HERE AFTER ME!

*DEFENDERS #106--AL.

20

109

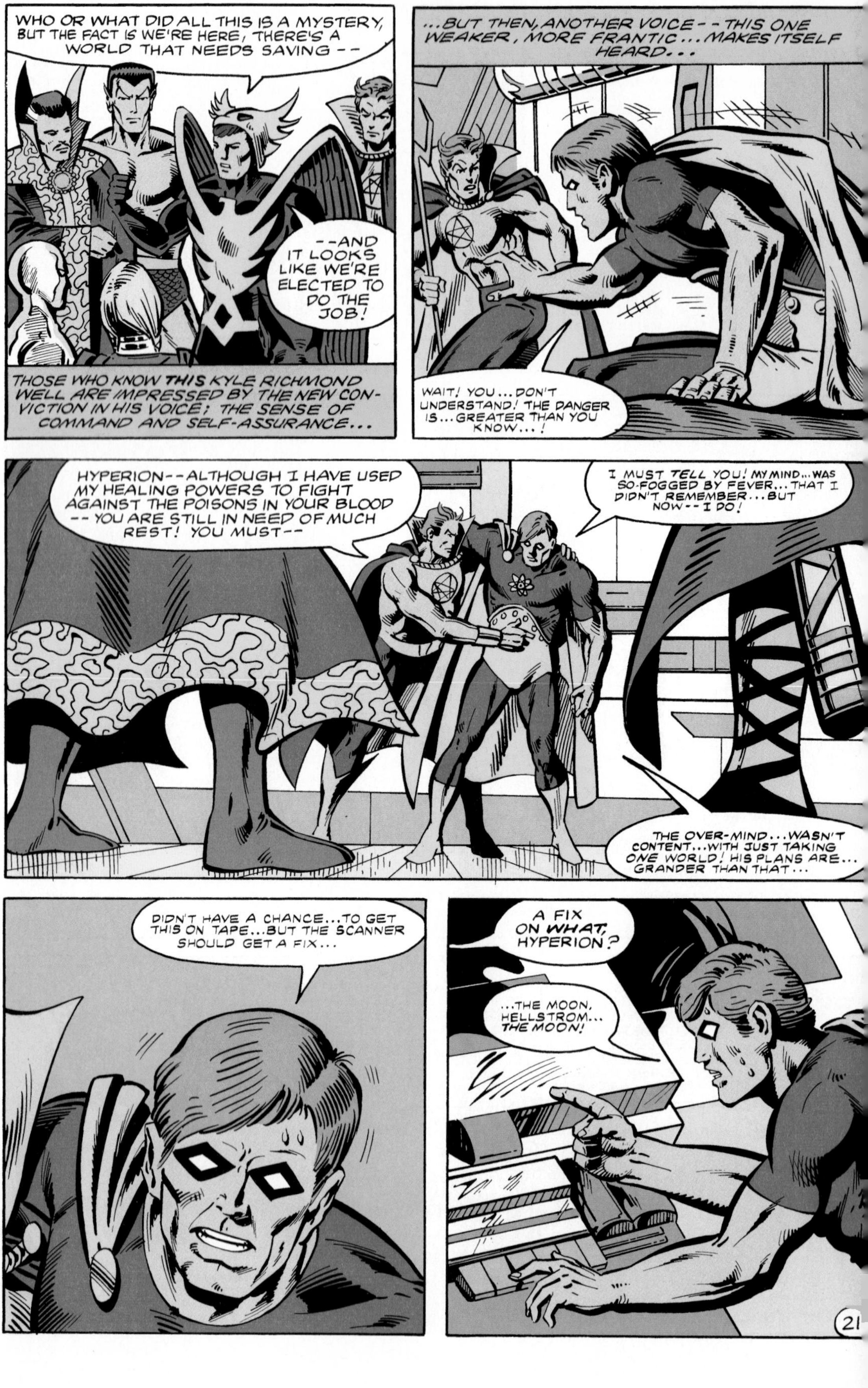

WHO OR WHAT DID ALL THIS IS A MYSTERY, BUT THE FACT IS WE'RE HERE, THERE'S A WORLD THAT NEEDS SAVING --
--AND IT LOOKS LIKE WE'RE ELECTED TO DO THE JOB!
THOSE WHO KNOW THIS KYLE RICHMOND WELL ARE IMPRESSED BY THE NEW CONVICTION IN HIS VOICE: THE SENSE OF COMMAND AND SELF-ASSURANCE...
...BUT THEN, ANOTHER VOICE -- THIS ONE WEAKER, MORE FRANTIC... MAKES ITSELF HEARD...
WAIT! YOU... DON'T UNDERSTAND! THE DANGER IS... GREATER THAN YOU KNOW...!
HYPERION -- ALTHOUGH I HAVE USED MY HEALING POWERS TO FIGHT AGAINST THE POISONS IN YOUR BLOOD -- YOU ARE STILL IN NEED OF MUCH REST! YOU MUST--
I MUST TELL YOU! MY MIND... WAS SO-FOGGED BY FEVER... THAT I DIDN'T REMEMBER... BUT NOW -- I DO!
THE OVER-MIND... WASN'T CONTENT... WITH JUST TAKING ONE WORLD! HIS PLANS ARE... GRANDER THAN THAT...
DIDN'T HAVE A CHANCE... TO GET THIS ON TAPE... BUT THE SCANNER SHOULD GET A FIX...
A FIX ON WHAT, HYPERION?
...THE MOON, HELLSTROM... THE MOON!
21

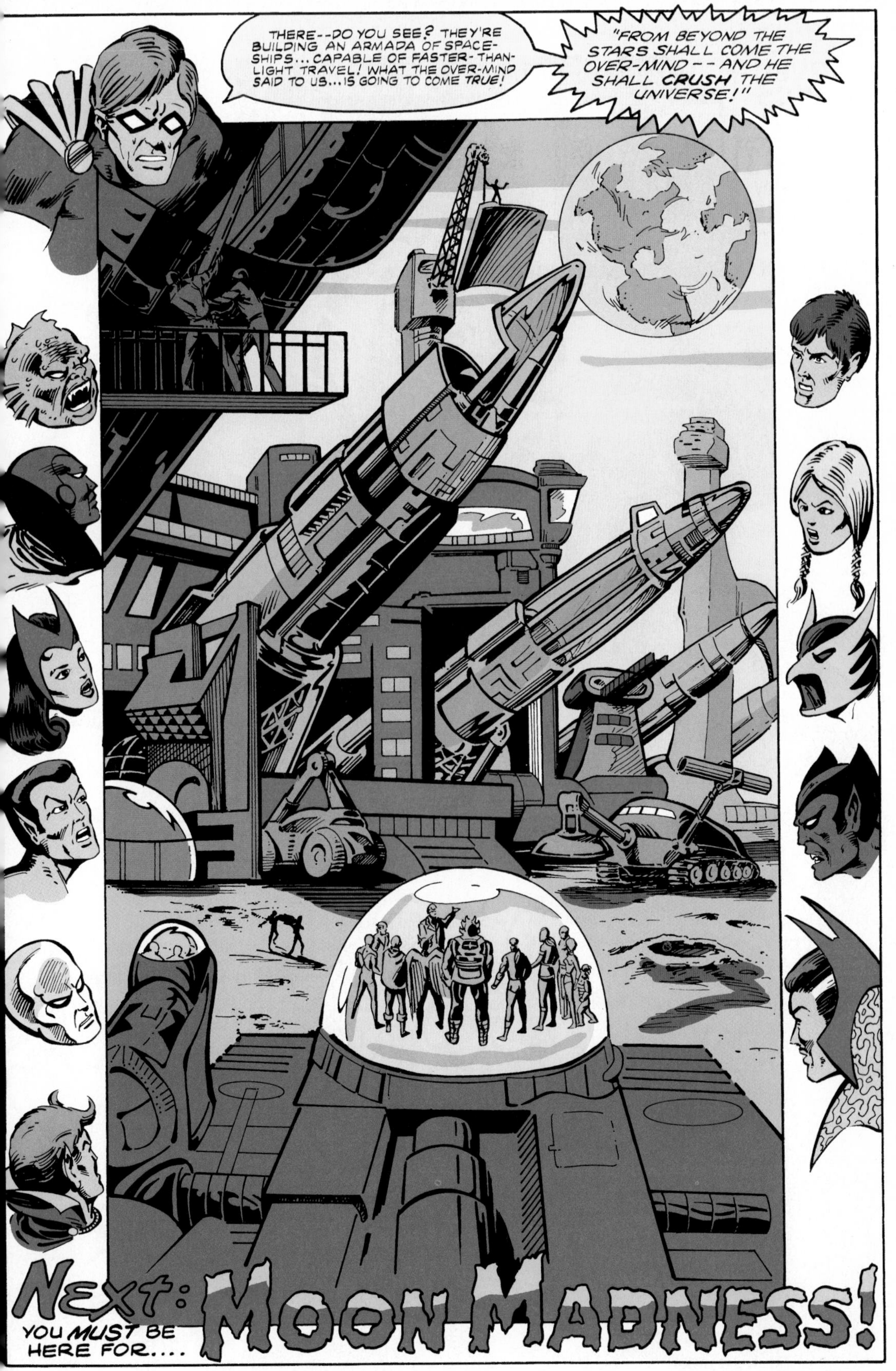
THERE--DO YOU SEE? THEY'RE BUILDING AN ARMADA OF SPACE-SHIPS... CAPABLE OF FASTER-THAN-LIGHT TRAVEL! WHAT THE OVER-MIND SAID TO US... IS GOING TO COME TRUE!
"FROM BEYOND THE STARS SHALL COME THE OVER-MIND -- AND HE SHALL CRUSH THE UNIVERSE!"
NEXT: YOU MUST BE HERE FOR....
MOON MADNESS!

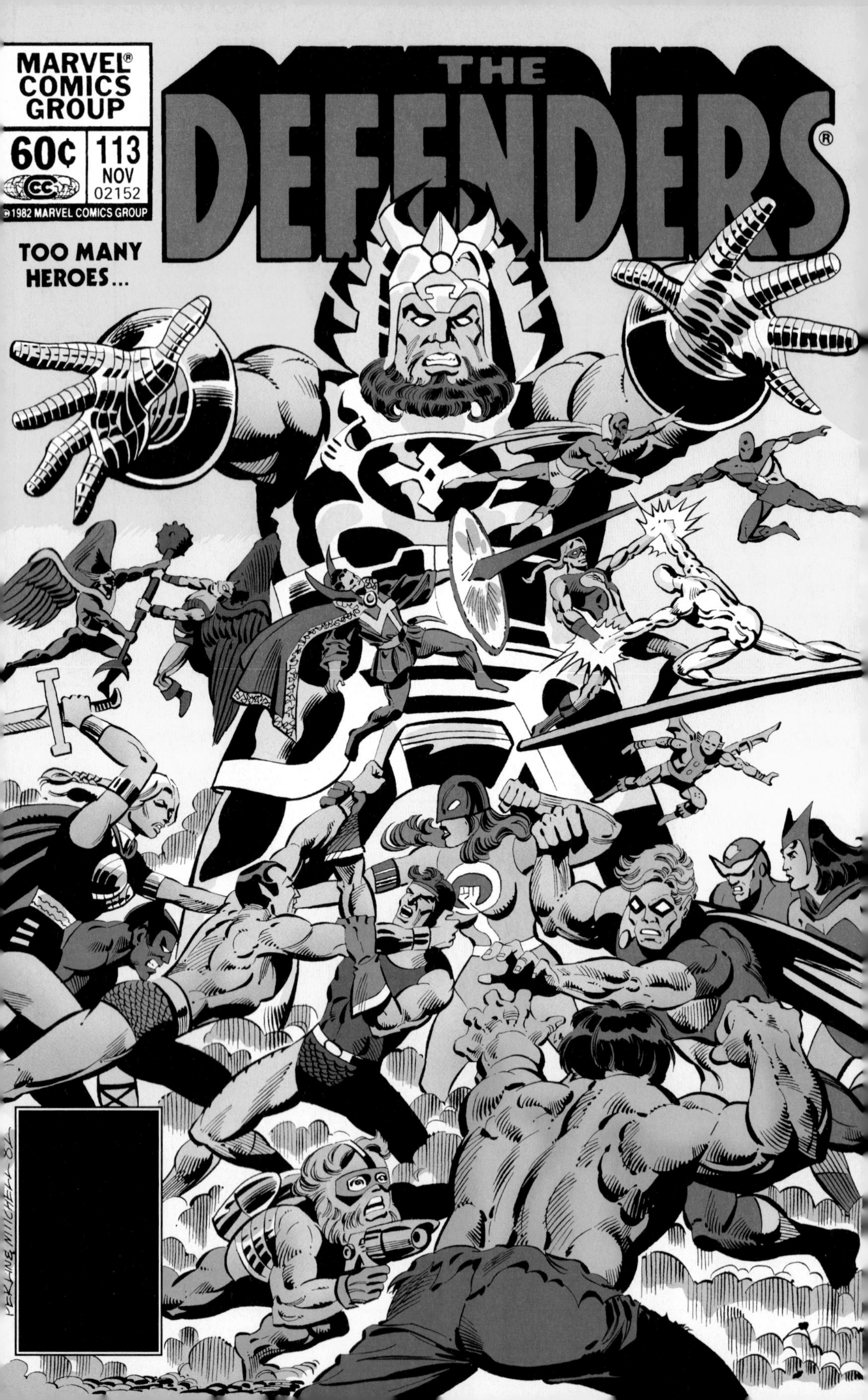
MARVEL® COMICS GROUP
60¢
113
NOV
02152
©1982 MARVEL COMICS GROUP
THE DEFENDERS®
TOO MANY HEROES...

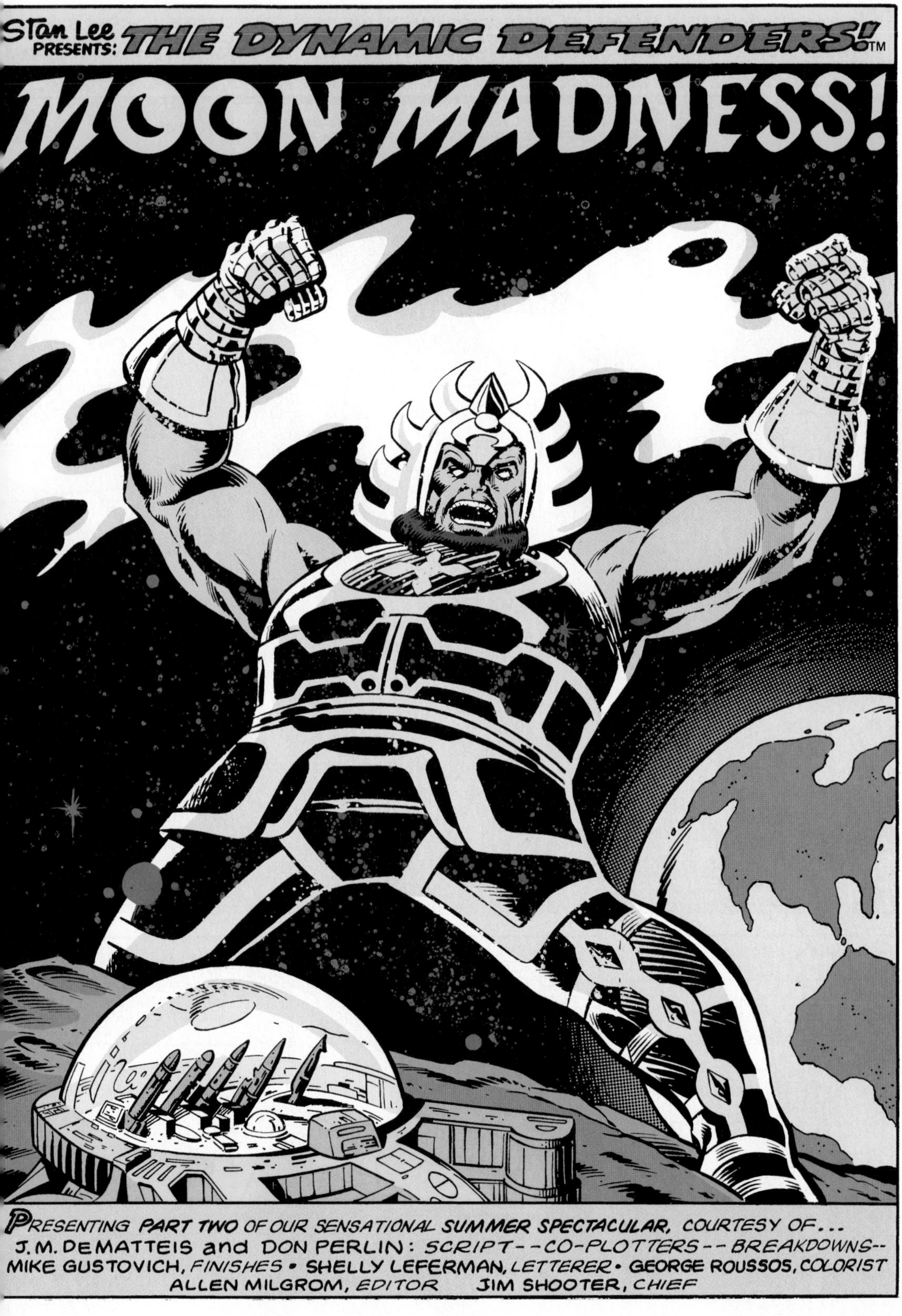
STAN LEE PRESENTS: THE DYNAMIC DEFENDERS!™
MOON MADNESS!
PRESENTING PART TWO OF OUR SENSATIONAL SUMMER SPECTACULAR, COURTESY OF...
J.M. DEMATTEIS and DON PERLIN: SCRIPT--CO-PLOTTERS--BREAKDOWNS--
MIKE GUSTOVICH, FINISHES • SHELLY LEFERMAN, LETTERER • GEORGE ROUSSOS, COLORIST
ALLEN MILGROM, EDITOR JIM SHOOTER, CHIEF

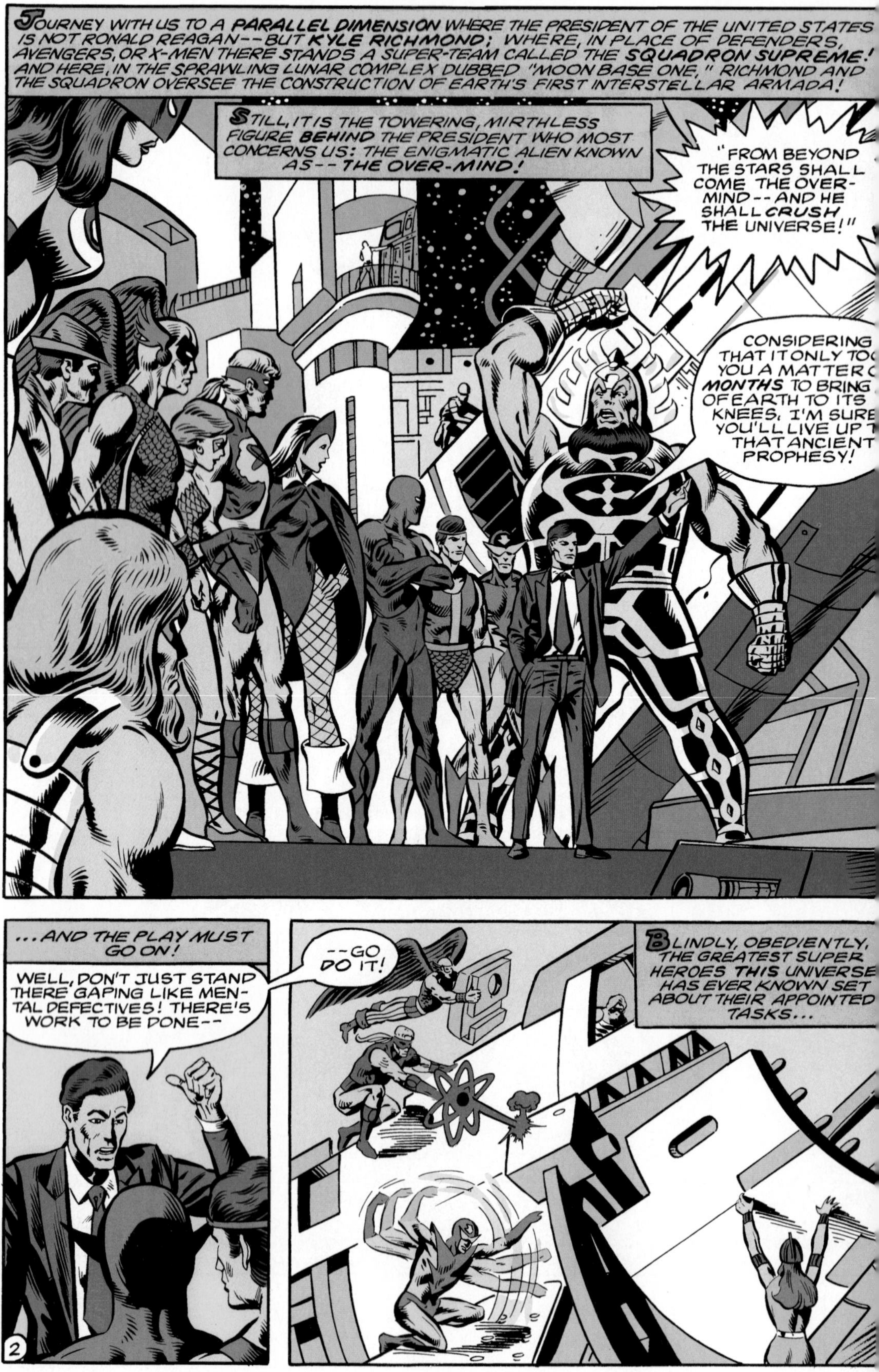
JOURNEY WITH US TO A PARALLEL DIMENSION WHERE THE PRESIDENT OF THE UNITED STATES IS NOT RONALD REAGAN--BUT KYLE RICHMOND; WHERE, IN PLACE OF DEFENDERS, AVENGERS, OR X-MEN THERE STANDS A SUPER-TEAM CALLED THE SQUADRON SUPREME! AND HERE, IN THE SPRAWLING LUNAR COMPLEX DUBBED "MOON BASE ONE," RICHMOND AND THE SQUADRON OVERSEE THE CONSTRUCTION OF EARTH'S FIRST INTERSTELLAR ARMADA!
STILL, IT IS THE TOWERING, MIRTHLESS FIGURE BEHIND THE PRESIDENT WHO MOST CONCERNS US: THE ENIGMATIC ALIEN KNOWN AS--THE OVER-MIND!
"FROM BEYOND THE STARS SHALL COME THE OVER-MIND--AND HE SHALL CRUSH THE UNIVERSE!"
CONSIDERING THAT IT ONLY TO YOU A MATTER MONTHS TO BRING OF EARTH TO ITS KNEES, I'M SURE YOU'LL LIVE UP THAT ANCIENT PROPHESY!
...AND THE PLAY MUST GO ON!
WELL, DON'T JUST STAND THERE GAPING LIKE MEN-TAL DEFECTIVES! THERE'S WORK TO BE DONE--
--GO DO IT!
BLINDLY, OBEDIENTLY, THE GREATEST SUPER HEROES THIS UNIVERSE HAS EVER KNOWN SET ABOUT THEIR APPOINTED TASKS...
2

LET'S FACE IT: ANYONE WHO CAN SO EASILY HOLD ALL THE WORLD'S LEADERS *AND* THE SQUADRON SUPREME UNDER HIS MENTAL COMMAND IS *NOT* TO BE DOUBTED!

DESPITE THE CASUALNESS OF HIS WORDS, THE DEAD *TONE* OF PRESIDENT RICHMOND'S VOICE MAKES IT CLEAR THAT HE, TOO, IS UNDER OUTSIDE CONTROL. BUT HE HAS BEEN CHOSEN TO ACT THE PART OF *LEADER* IN THIS COSMIC TRAGEDY...

...ALL QUESTIONS, ALL RESISTANCE, HAVING BEEN DRAINED FROM THEM.

THE WORK GOES WELL! GUIDED BY THE ADVANCED SCIENCE OF YOUR LONG-DEAD RACE, WE'VE MANAGED TO BUILD A FLEET OF STARSHIPS THAT WILL PROVE UNBEATABLE!

REVENGE--!

YES! YOU'LL HAVE THE VENGEANCE YOUR PEOPLE, *THE ETERNALS,** CRAVED WHEN THEIR PLAN TO CONQUER THE COSMOS WAS THWARTED EONS AGO! WHEN THEY POURED THE BRAIN POWER OF A BILLION BEINGS INTO YOU AND SENT YOU OUT TO RAVAGE THE UNIVERSE IN THEIR NAME!

*NOT TO BE CONFUSED WITH EARTH'S ETERNALS LAST SEEN IN THE PAGES OF *THOR*-- AL.

"FROM BEYOND THE STARS SHALL COME THE OVER-MIND-- AND HE SHALL *CRUSH* THE UNIVERSE!"

INDEED.

③

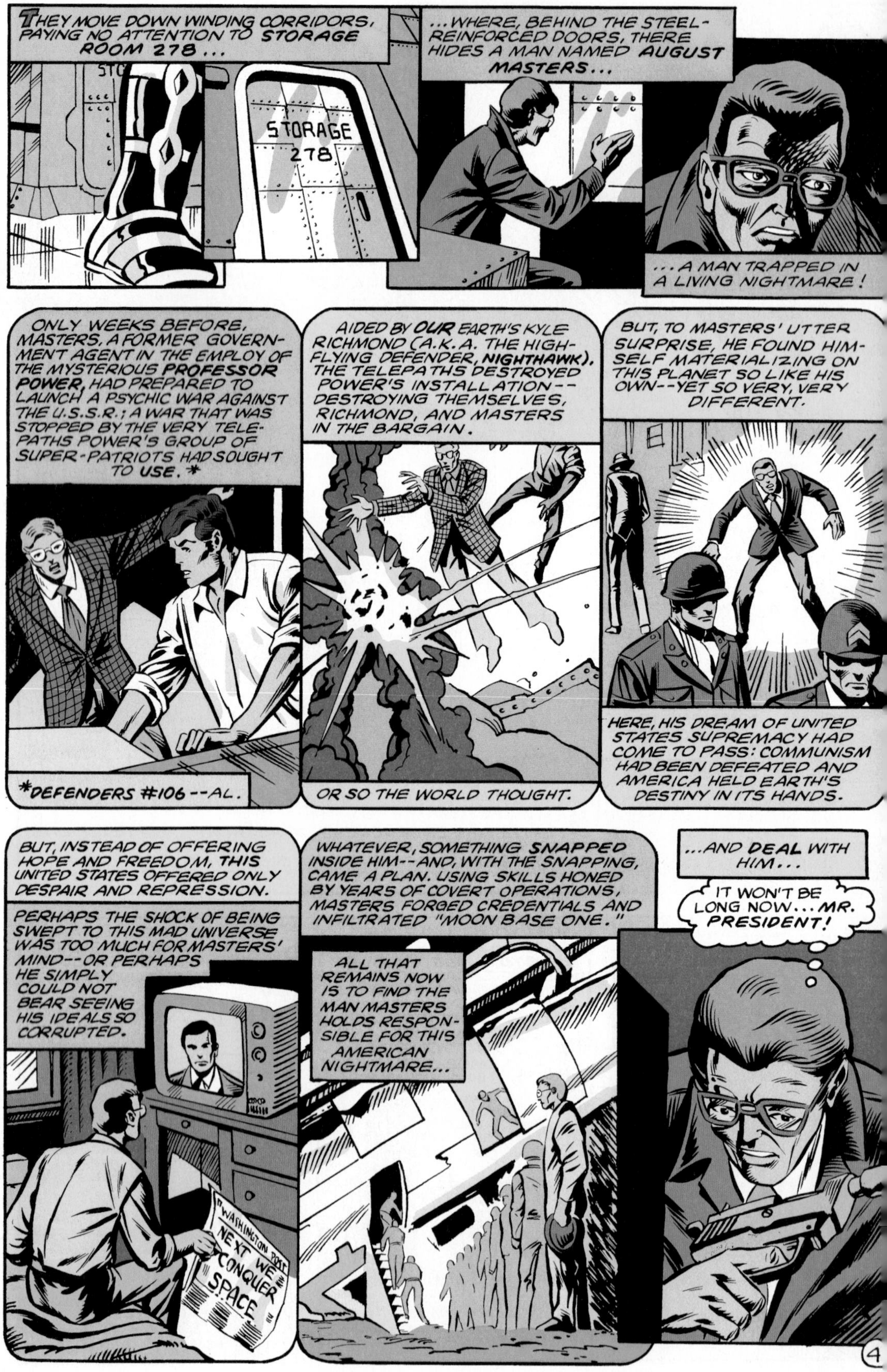
THEY MOVE DOWN WINDING CORRIDORS, PAYING NO ATTENTION TO STORAGE ROOM 278...
STORAGE 278
...WHERE, BEHIND THE STEEL-REINFORCED DOORS, THERE HIDES A MAN NAMED AUGUST MASTERS...
...A MAN TRAPPED IN A LIVING NIGHTMARE!
ONLY WEEKS BEFORE, MASTERS, A FORMER GOVERNMENT AGENT IN THE EMPLOY OF THE MYSTERIOUS PROFESSOR POWER, HAD PREPARED TO LAUNCH A PSYCHIC WAR AGAINST THE U.S.S.R.; A WAR THAT WAS STOPPED BY THE VERY TELEPATHS POWER'S GROUP OF SUPER-PATRIOTS HAD SOUGHT TO USE.*
*DEFENDERS #106--AL.
AIDED BY OUR EARTH'S KYLE RICHMOND (A.K.A. THE HIGH-FLYING DEFENDER, NIGHTHAWK), THE TELEPATHS DESTROYED POWER'S INSTALLATION--DESTROYING THEMSELVES, RICHMOND, AND MASTERS IN THE BARGAIN.
OR SO THE WORLD THOUGHT.
BUT, TO MASTERS' UTTER SURPRISE, HE FOUND HIMSELF MATERIALIZING ON THIS PLANET SO LIKE HIS OWN--YET SO VERY, VERY DIFFERENT.
HERE, HIS DREAM OF UNITED STATES SUPREMACY HAD COME TO PASS: COMMUNISM HAD BEEN DEFEATED AND AMERICA HELD EARTH'S DESTINY IN ITS HANDS.
BUT, INSTEAD OF OFFERING HOPE AND FREEDOM, THIS UNITED STATES OFFERED ONLY DESPAIR AND REPRESSION.
PERHAPS THE SHOCK OF BEING SWEPT TO THIS MAD UNIVERSE WAS TOO MUCH FOR MASTERS' MIND--OR PERHAPS HE SIMPLY COULD NOT BEAR SEEING HIS IDEALS SO CORRUPTED.
WASHINGTON POST
NEXT WE CONQUER SPACE
WHATEVER, SOMETHING SNAPPED INSIDE HIM--AND, WITH THE SNAPPING, CAME A PLAN. USING SKILLS HONED BY YEARS OF COVERT OPERATIONS, MASTERS FORGED CREDENTIALS AND INFILTRATED "MOON BASE ONE."
ALL THAT REMAINS NOW IS TO FIND THE MAN MASTERS HOLDS RESPONSIBLE FOR THIS AMERICAN NIGHTMARE...
...AND DEAL WITH HIM...
IT WON'T BE LONG NOW...MR. PRESIDENT!
4

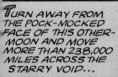 TURN AWAY FROM THE POCK-MARKED FACE OF THIS OTHER-MOON AND MOVE MORE THAN 238,000 MILES ACROSS THE STARRY VOID...

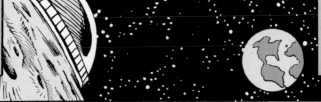 ...TO AN EARTH THAT (FROM SPACE AT LEAST) LOOKS NO WORSE FOR THE TURMOIL ITS PEOPLE HAVE LATELY KNOWN.

LISTEN CAREFULLY AS WE ENTER THIS DREAM-LIKE FOREST IN THE HEART OF NEW ENGLAND; HEAR THE SOUNDS OF STRANGE MACHINES, HUMMING WITHIN THE EARTH...

...AND IMAGINE WHAT COULD BE LURKING THERE, IN CAVERNS UNDERGROUND! DEMONS, PERHAPS? OR ELVES? TROLLS MOLDING HAMMERS AT THEIR FIERY FORGES?

OR PERHAPS...ELEVEN EQUALLY-FANTASTIC HEROES LOOSELY JOINED TOGETHER AS --THE DEFENDERS!

THERE ARE NO WORDS EXCHANGED AS THE ELEVEN GATHER AROUND A TWELFTH -- HYPERION: THE ONE SQUADRON SUPREME MEMBER TO SUCCESSFULLY RESIST THE OVER-MIND AND HIS PRESIDENTIAL PAWN. HE ALMOST PAID FOR THAT RESISTANCE WITH HIS LIFE -- A LIFE THE SON OF SATAN WILL NOT LET SLIP AWAY!

5

ALTHOUGH BORN A CHILD OF HADES, DAIMON HELLSTROM HAS BEEN BLESSED WITH THE *HEALER'S* TOUCH.

WITH A TENDERNESS MANY WOULD THINK HIM INCAPABLE OF, HE LETS THE LIGHT OF REGENERATION PASS *THROUGH* HIM...

...AND THE *MIRACULOUS* OCCURS!

I HAVE DONE WHAT I CAN TO EASE YOUR RADIATION SICKNESS, HYPERION.

YOUR FORMIDABLE RECUPERATIVE POWERS SHOULD DO THE REST!

I HATE TO SOUND UNGRATEFUL, MR. HELLSTROM -- BUT WHAT'S THE POINT OF SAVING *ME* FROM ARGONITE POISONING WHEN THE WORLD I'M PLEDGED TO PROTECT IS IN *CHAINS*?

I'M GLAD *DOCTOR STRANGE* MYSTICALLY ZAPPED YOU DEFENDERS HERE TO HELP MY EARTH OUT OF THIS MESS*--

-- BUT, GREAT ARGON-- TIME'S RUNNING OUT!

*LAST ISSUE--AL.

BE AT EASE, HYPERION. ALTHOUGH THE DAY IS DARK, EMOTIONALISM WILL NOT PROVIDE ANSWERS. WE MUST SEEK HARD FACTS AND, THROUGH THEM, ARRIVE AT A COURSE OF ACTION.

YOUR LOGIC IS AS IMPECCABLE AS EVER, *VISION*! BUT WHAT ELSE CAN A GUY EXPECT FROM AN ANDROID?

SYNTHEZOID, BEAST!

WHATEVER! THE POINT IS -- WE ALREADY *KNOW* WHAT TO DO!

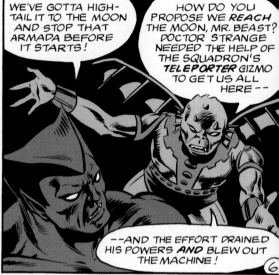

WE'VE GOTTA HIGH-TAIL IT TO THE MOON AND STOP THAT ARMADA BEFORE IT STARTS!

HOW DO YOU PROPOSE WE *REACH* THE MOON, MR. BEAST? DOCTOR STRANGE NEEDED THE HELP OF THE SQUADRON'S *TELEPORTER* GIZMO TO GET US ALL HERE --

--AND THE EFFORT DRAINED HIS POWERS *AND* BLEW OUT THE MACHINE!

6

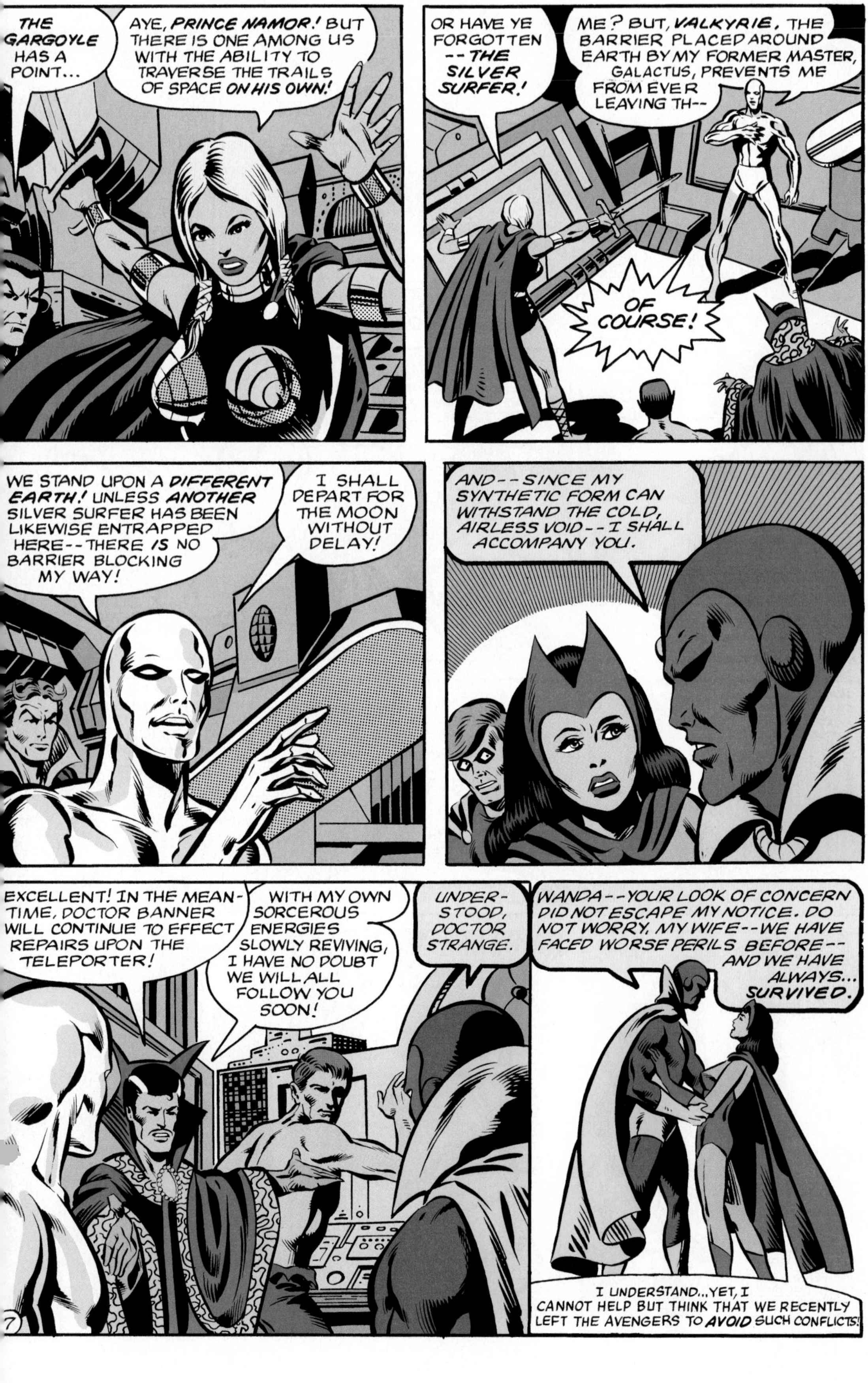
THE GARGOYLE HAS A POINT...
AYE, PRINCE NAMOR! BUT THERE IS ONE AMONG US WITH THE ABILITY TO TRAVERSE THE TRAILS OF SPACE ON HIS OWN!
OR HAVE YE FORGOTTEN --THE SILVER SURFER!
ME? BUT, VALKYRIE, THE BARRIER PLACED AROUND EARTH BY MY FORMER MASTER, GALACTUS, PREVENTS ME FROM EVER LEAVING TH--
OF COURSE!
WE STAND UPON A DIFFERENT EARTH! UNLESS ANOTHER SILVER SURFER HAS BEEN LIKEWISE ENTRAPPED HERE--THERE IS NO BARRIER BLOCKING MY WAY!
I SHALL DEPART FOR THE MOON WITHOUT DELAY!
AND--SINCE MY SYNTHETIC FORM CAN WITHSTAND THE COLD, AIRLESS VOID--I SHALL ACCOMPANY YOU.
EXCELLENT! IN THE MEANTIME, DOCTOR BANNER WILL CONTINUE TO EFFECT REPAIRS UPON THE TELEPORTER!
WITH MY OWN SORCEROUS ENERGIES SLOWLY REVIVING, I HAVE NO DOUBT WE WILL ALL FOLLOW YOU SOON!
UNDERSTOOD, DOCTOR STRANGE.
7
WANDA--YOUR LOOK OF CONCERN DID NOT ESCAPE MY NOTICE. DO NOT WORRY, MY WIFE--WE HAVE FACED WORSE PERILS BEFORE--AND WE HAVE ALWAYS... SURVIVED.
I UNDERSTAND...YET, I CANNOT HELP BUT THINK THAT WE RECENTLY LEFT THE AVENGERS TO AVOID SUCH CONFLICTS!

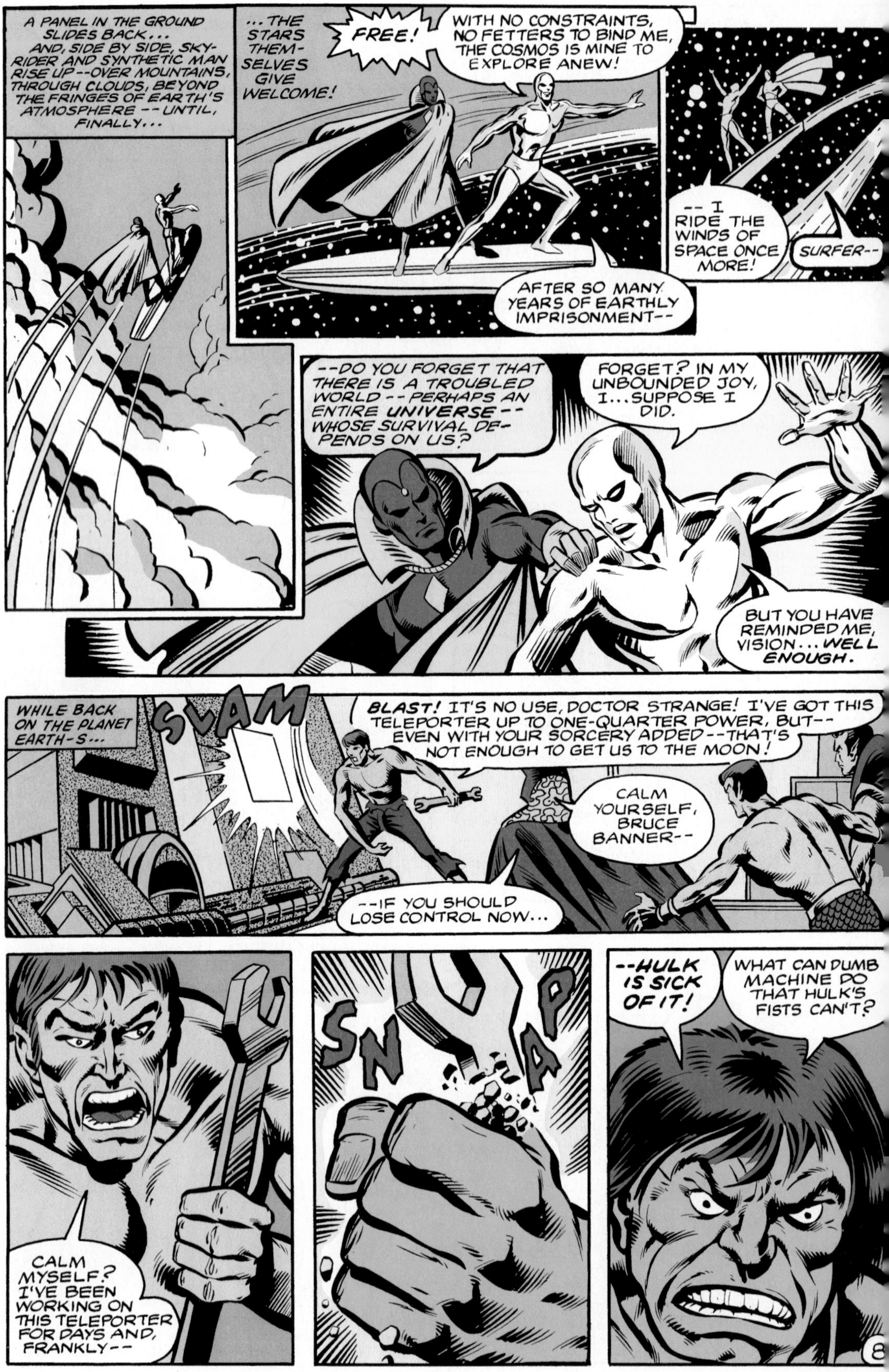
A PANEL IN THE GROUND SLIDES BACK... AND, SIDE BY SIDE, SKY-RIDER AND SYNTHETIC MAN RISE UP--OVER MOUNTAINS, THROUGH CLOUDS, BEYOND THE FRINGES OF EARTH'S ATMOSPHERE -- UNTIL, FINALLY...
...THE STARS THEMSELVES GIVE WELCOME!
FREE!
WITH NO CONSTRAINTS, NO FETTERS TO BIND ME, THE COSMOS IS MINE TO EXPLORE ANEW!
AFTER SO MANY YEARS OF EARTHLY IMPRISONMENT--
-- I RIDE THE WINDS OF SPACE ONCE MORE!
SURFER--
--DO YOU FORGET THAT THERE IS A TROUBLED WORLD -- PERHAPS AN ENTIRE UNIVERSE -- WHOSE SURVIVAL DEPENDS ON US?
FORGET? IN MY UNBOUNDED JOY, I...SUPPOSE I DID.
BUT YOU HAVE REMINDED ME, VISION... WELL ENOUGH.
WHILE BACK ON THE PLANET EARTH-S...
SLAM
BLAST! IT'S NO USE, DOCTOR STRANGE! I'VE GOT THIS TELEPORTER UP TO ONE-QUARTER POWER, BUT-- EVEN WITH YOUR SORCERY ADDED--THAT'S NOT ENOUGH TO GET US TO THE MOON!
CALM YOURSELF, BRUCE BANNER--
--IF YOU SHOULD LOSE CONTROL NOW...
CALM MYSELF? I'VE BEEN WORKING ON THIS TELEPORTER FOR DAYS AND, FRANKLY--
SNAP
--HULK IS SICK OF IT!
WHAT CAN DUMB MACHINE DO THAT HULK'S FISTS CAN'T?
8

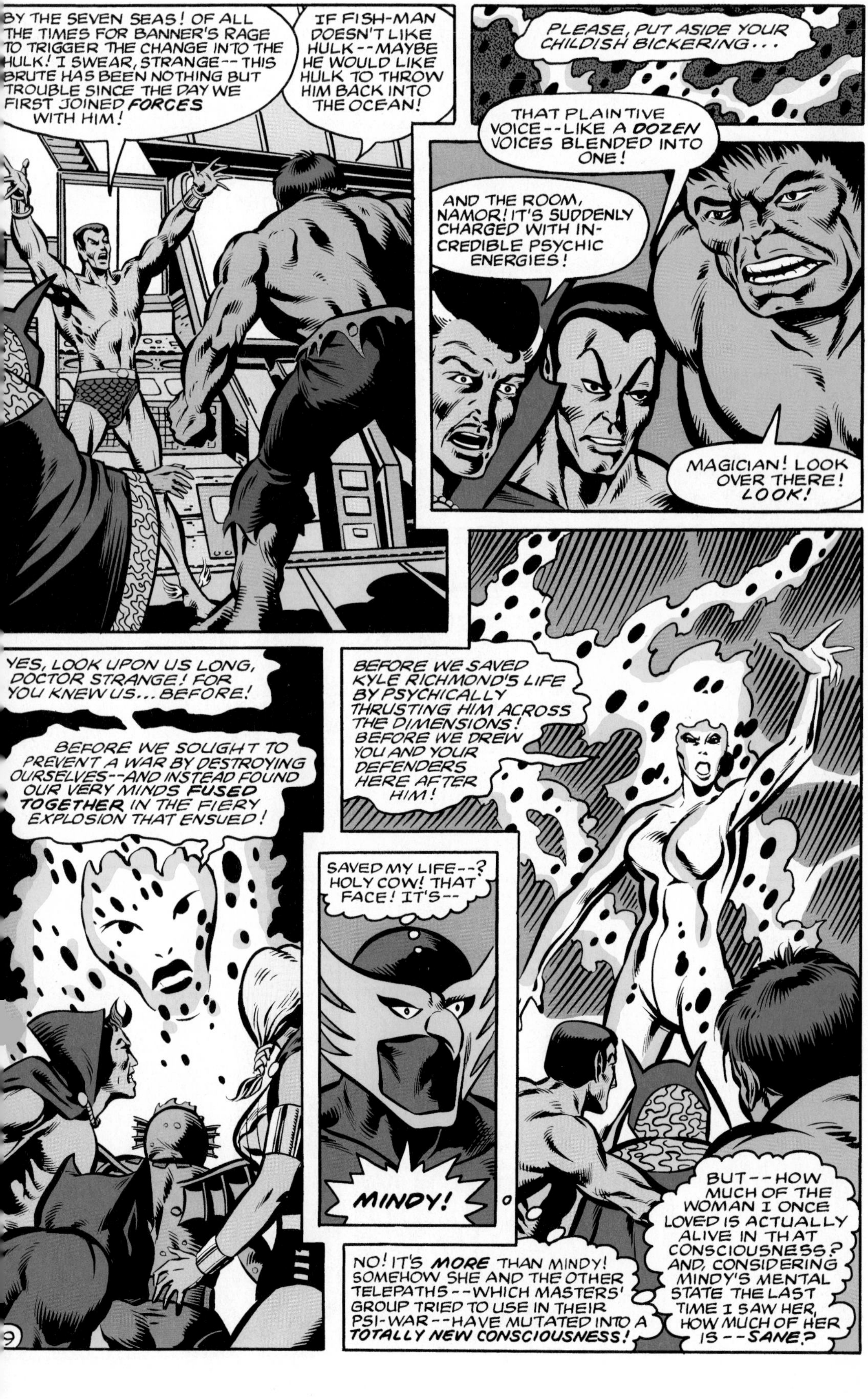
BY THE SEVEN SEAS! OF ALL THE TIMES FOR BANNER'S RAGE TO TRIGGER THE CHANGE INTO THE HULK! I SWEAR, STRANGE-- THIS BRUTE HAS BEEN NOTHING BUT TROUBLE SINCE THE DAY WE FIRST JOINED FORCES WITH HIM!
IF FISH-MAN DOESN'T LIKE HULK--MAYBE HE WOULD LIKE HULK TO THROW HIM BACK INTO THE OCEAN!
PLEASE, PUT ASIDE YOUR CHILDISH BICKERING...
THAT PLAINTIVE VOICE--LIKE A DOZEN VOICES BLENDED INTO ONE!
AND THE ROOM, NAMOR! IT'S SUDDENLY CHARGED WITH INCREDIBLE PSYCHIC ENERGIES!
MAGICIAN! LOOK OVER THERE! LOOK!
YES, LOOK UPON US LONG, DOCTOR STRANGE! FOR YOU KNEW US... BEFORE!
BEFORE WE SOUGHT TO PREVENT A WAR BY DESTROYING OURSELVES--AND INSTEAD FOUND OUR VERY MINDS FUSED TOGETHER IN THE FIERY EXPLOSION THAT ENSUED!
BEFORE WE SAVED KYLE RICHMOND'S LIFE BY PSYCHICALLY THRUSTING HIM ACROSS THE DIMENSIONS! BEFORE WE DREW YOU AND YOUR DEFENDERS HERE AFTER HIM!
SAVED MY LIFE--? HOLY COW! THAT FACE! IT'S--
MINDY!
NO! IT'S MORE THAN MINDY! SOMEHOW SHE AND THE OTHER TELEPATHS--WHICH MASTERS' GROUP TRIED TO USE IN THEIR PSI-WAR--HAVE MUTATED INTO A TOTALLY NEW CONSCIOUSNESS!
BUT--HOW MUCH OF THE WOMAN I ONCE LOVED IS ACTUALLY ALIVE IN THAT CONSCIOUSNESS? AND, CONSIDERING MINDY'S MENTAL STATE THE LAST TIME I SAW HER, HOW MUCH OF HER IS--SANE?
9

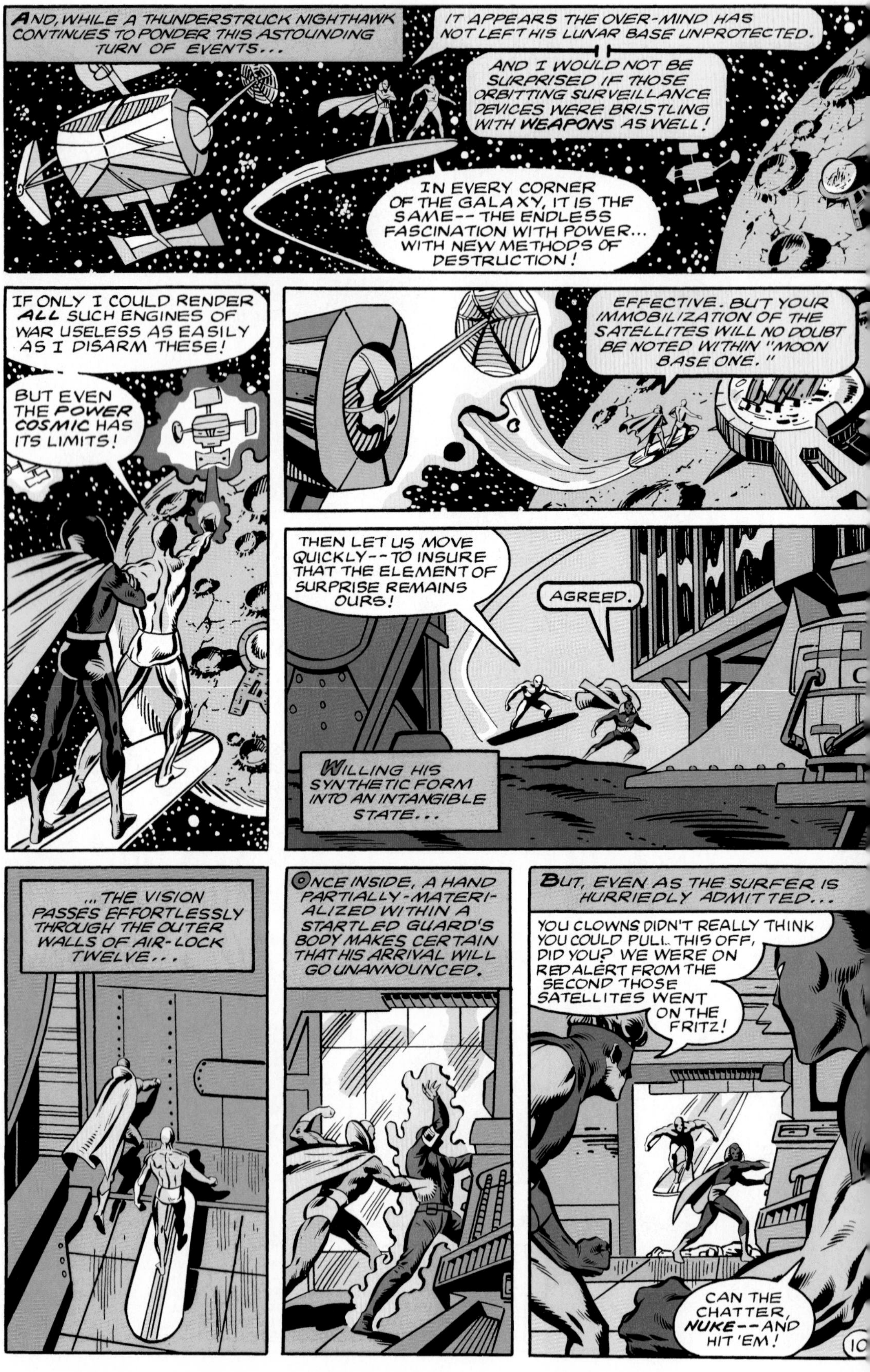
AND, WHILE A THUNDERSTRUCK NIGHTHAWK CONTINUES TO PONDER THIS ASTOUNDING TURN OF EVENTS...
IT APPEARS THE OVER-MIND HAS NOT LEFT HIS LUNAR BASE UNPROTECTED.
AND I WOULD NOT BE SURPRISED IF THOSE ORBITTING SURVEILLANCE DEVICES WERE BRISTLING WITH WEAPONS AS WELL!
IN EVERY CORNER OF THE GALAXY, IT IS THE SAME-- THE ENDLESS FASCINATION WITH POWER... WITH NEW METHODS OF DESTRUCTION!
IF ONLY I COULD RENDER ALL SUCH ENGINES OF WAR USELESS AS EASILY AS I DISARM THESE!
BUT EVEN THE POWER COSMIC HAS ITS LIMITS!
EFFECTIVE. BUT YOUR IMMOBILIZATION OF THE SATELLITES WILL NO DOUBT BE NOTED WITHIN "MOON BASE ONE."
THEN LET US MOVE QUICKLY--TO INSURE THAT THE ELEMENT OF SURPRISE REMAINS OURS!
AGREED.
WILLING HIS SYNTHETIC FORM INTO AN INTANGIBLE STATE...
...THE VISION PASSES EFFORTLESSLY THROUGH THE OUTER WALLS OF AIR-LOCK TWELVE...
ONCE INSIDE, A HAND PARTIALLY-MATERIALIZED WITHIN A STARTLED GUARD'S BODY MAKES CERTAIN THAT HIS ARRIVAL WILL GO UNANNOUNCED.
BUT, EVEN AS THE SURFER IS HURRIEDLY ADMITTED...
YOU CLOWNS DIDN'T REALLY THINK YOU COULD PULL THIS OFF, DID YOU? WE WERE ON RED ALERT FROM THE SECOND THOSE SATELLITES WENT ON THE FRITZ!
CAN THE CHATTER, NUKE--AND HIT 'EM!
10

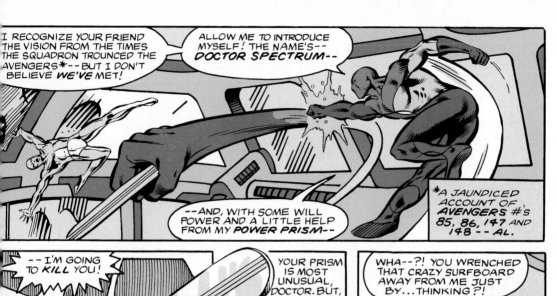

I RECOGNIZE YOUR FRIEND THE VISION FROM THE TIMES THE SQUADRON TROUNCED THE AVENGERS*--BUT I DON'T BELIEVE WE'VE MET!

ALLOW ME TO INTRODUCE MYSELF! THE NAME'S-- DOCTOR SPECTRUM--

--AND, WITH SOME WILL POWER AND A LITTLE HELP FROM MY POWER PRISM--

*A JAUNDICED ACCOUNT OF AVENGERS #'s 85, 86, 147 AND 148--AL.

--I'M GOING TO KILL YOU!

YOUR PRISM IS MOST UNUSUAL, DOCTOR. BUT, AS HERALD TO GALACTUS, I ENCOUNTERED DEADLY FORCES THAT WOULD DWARF YOUR STONE! AND, STILL, THE SURFER LIVES!

TO ME, MY BOARD!

SBAMM

WHA--?! YOU WRENCHED THAT CRAZY SURFBOARD AWAY FROM ME JUST BY...THINKING?!

LIKE YOUR GEM, MY BOARD RESPONDS TO A FLEETING THOUGHT!

BUT, UNLIKE YOU, I DO NOT DEPEND UPON OUTSIDE CONSTRUCTS!

THE SURFER'S TRUE POWER ...IS WITHIN!

YARGH!

BY FEEDING YOUR JEWEL'S RAW ENERGY BACK INTO YOU, I CAN END THIS NEEDLESS CONFLICT BEFORE IT'S TRULY BEGUN!

FORGIVE ME, DOCTOR SPECTRUM --FOR I KNOW YOUR ACTIONS ...WERE NOT YOUR OWN!

DOC!

WHUD!

11

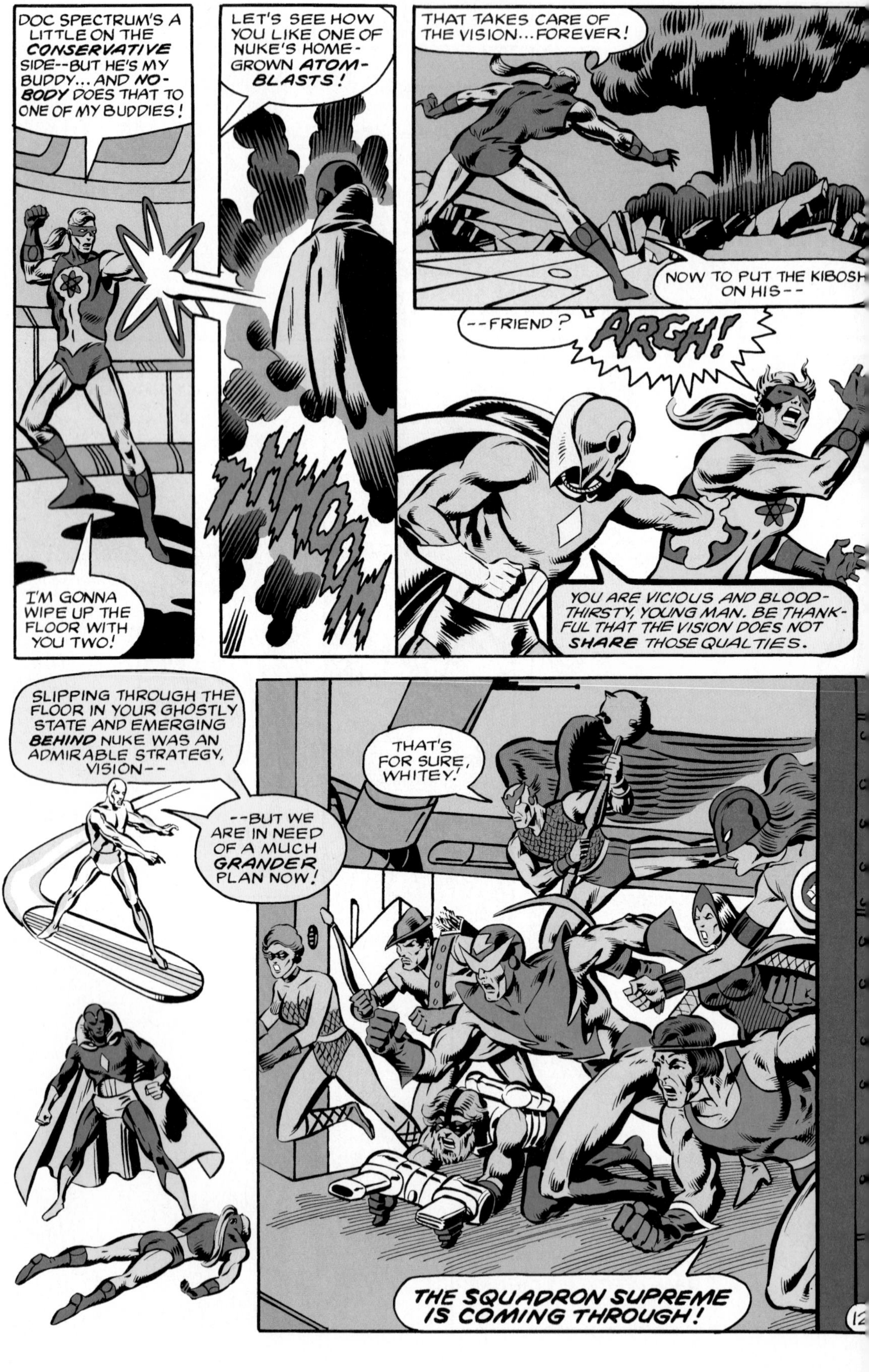
DOC SPECTRUM'S A LITTLE ON THE CONSERVATIVE SIDE--BUT HE'S MY BUDDY... AND NOBODY DOES THAT TO ONE OF MY BUDDIES!
I'M GONNA WIPE UP THE FLOOR WITH YOU TWO!
LET'S SEE HOW YOU LIKE ONE OF NUKE'S HOME-GROWN ATOM-BLASTS!
ZZHOOM
THAT TAKES CARE OF THE VISION... FOREVER!
NOW TO PUT THE KIBOSH ON HIS--
--FRIEND?
ARGH!
YOU ARE VICIOUS AND BLOOD-THIRSTY, YOUNG MAN. BE THANKFUL THAT THE VISION DOES NOT SHARE THOSE QUALTIES.
SLIPPING THROUGH THE FLOOR IN YOUR GHOSTLY STATE AND EMERGING BEHIND NUKE WAS AN ADMIRABLE STRATEGY, VISION--
--BUT WE ARE IN NEED OF A MUCH GRANDER PLAN NOW!
THAT'S FOR SURE, WHITEY!
THE SQUADRON SUPREME IS COMING THROUGH!
12

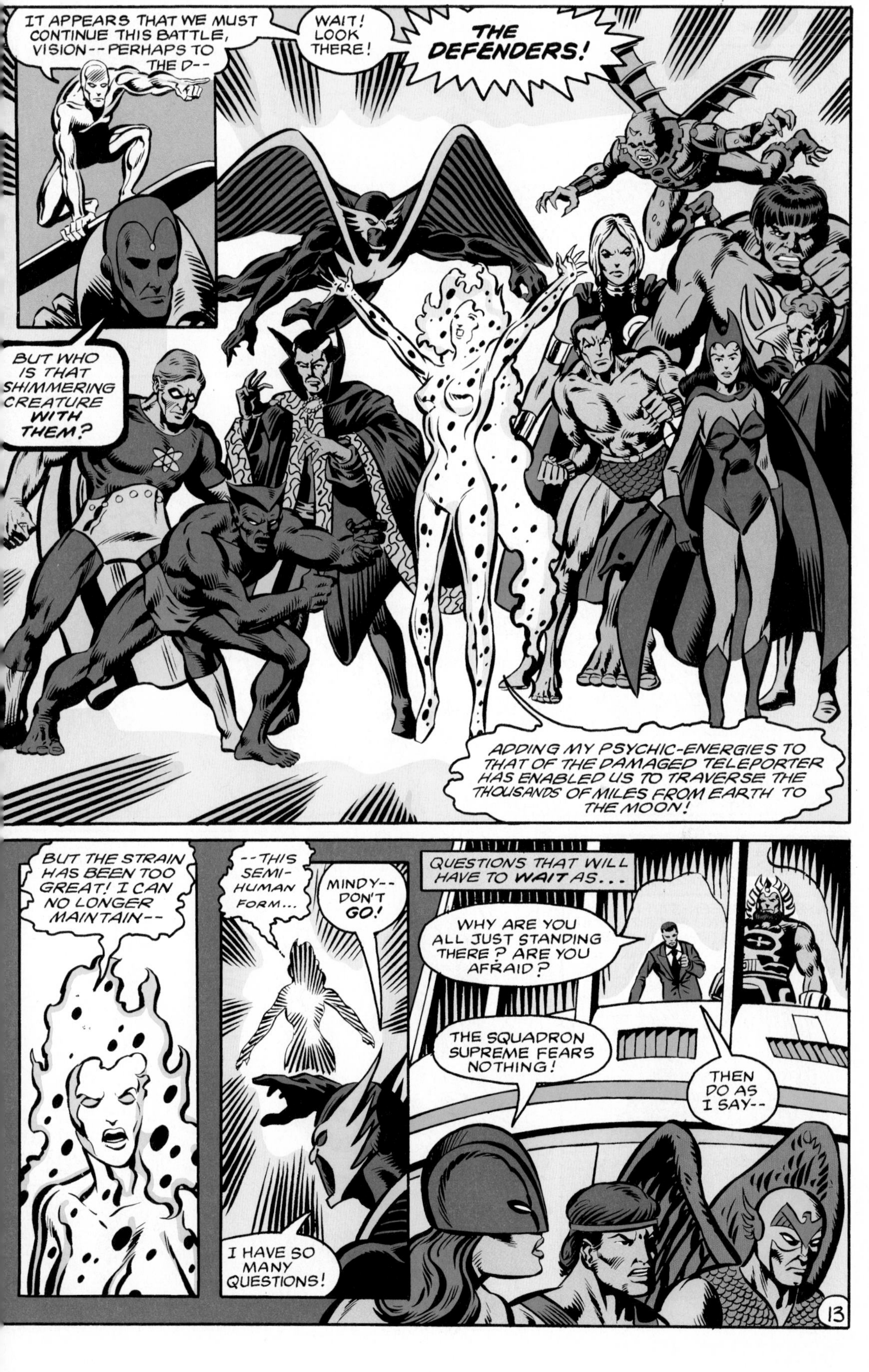
IT APPEARS THAT WE MUST CONTINUE THIS BATTLE, VISION--PERHAPS TO THE D--
WAIT! LOOK THERE!
THE DEFENDERS!
BUT WHO IS THAT SHIMMERING CREATURE WITH THEM?
ADDING MY PSYCHIC-ENERGIES TO THAT OF THE DAMAGED TELEPORTER HAS ENABLED US TO TRAVERSE THE THOUSANDS OF MILES FROM EARTH TO THE MOON!
BUT THE STRAIN HAS BEEN TOO GREAT! I CAN NO LONGER MAINTAIN--
--THIS SEMI-HUMAN FORM...
MINDY--DON'T GO!
I HAVE SO MANY QUESTIONS!
QUESTIONS THAT WILL HAVE TO WAIT AS...
WHY ARE YOU ALL JUST STANDING THERE? ARE YOU AFRAID?
THE SQUADRON SUPREME FEARS NOTHING!
THEN DO AS I SAY--
13

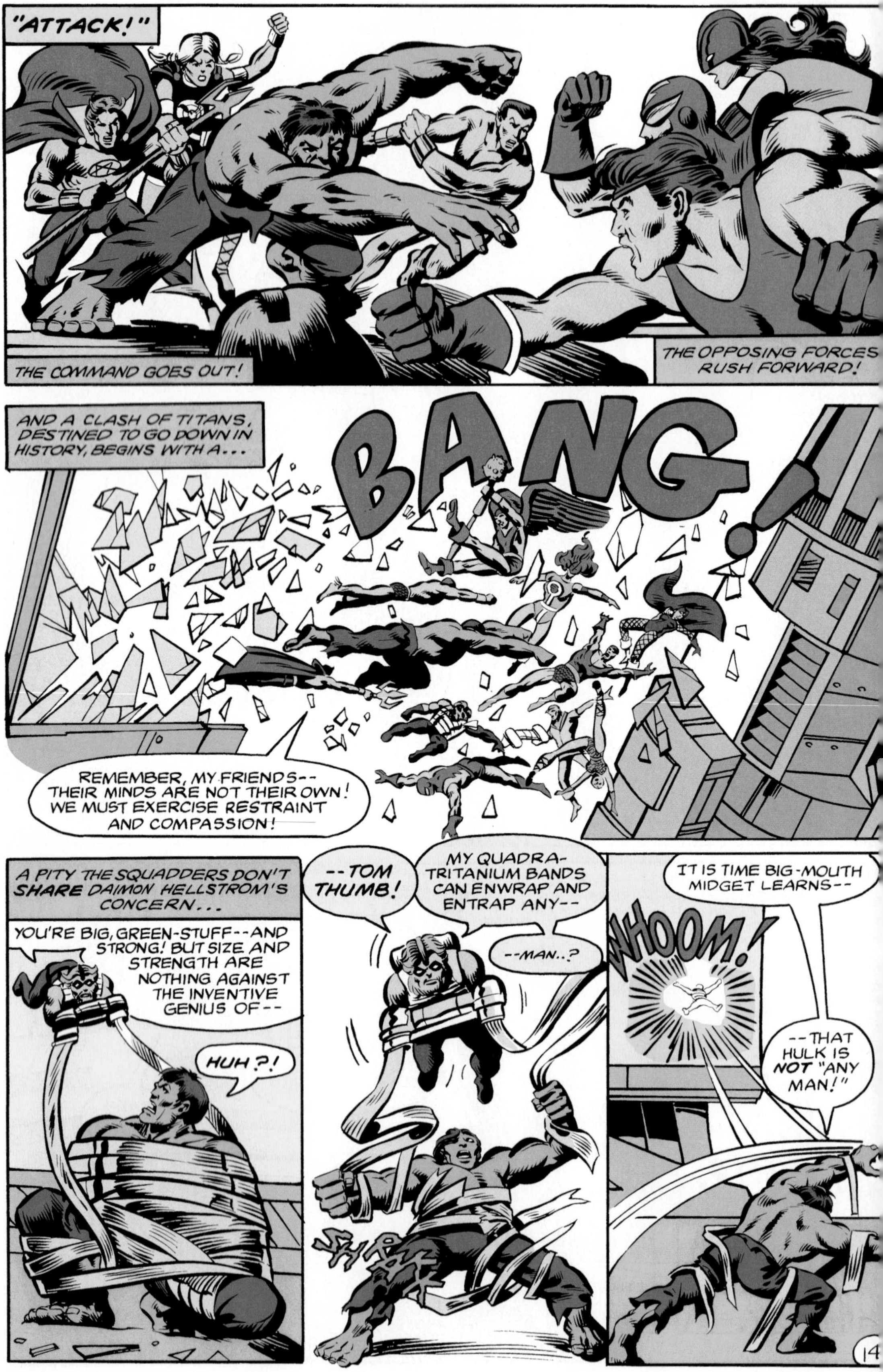
"ATTACK!"
THE COMMAND GOES OUT!
THE OPPOSING FORCES RUSH FORWARD!
AND A CLASH OF TITANS, DESTINED TO GO DOWN IN HISTORY, BEGINS WITH A...
BANG!
REMEMBER, MY FRIENDS-- THEIR MINDS ARE NOT THEIR OWN! WE MUST EXERCISE RESTRAINT AND COMPASSION!
A PITY THE SQUADDERS DON'T SHARE DAIMON HELLSTROM'S CONCERN...
YOU'RE BIG, GREEN-STUFF--AND STRONG! BUT SIZE AND STRENGTH ARE NOTHING AGAINST THE INVENTIVE GENIUS OF--
HUH?!
--TOM THUMB!
MY QUADRA-TRITANIUM BANDS CAN ENWRAP AND ENTRAP ANY--
--MAN..?
IT IS TIME BIG-MOUTH MIDGET LEARNS--
WHOOM!
--THAT HULK IS NOT "ANY MAN!"
14

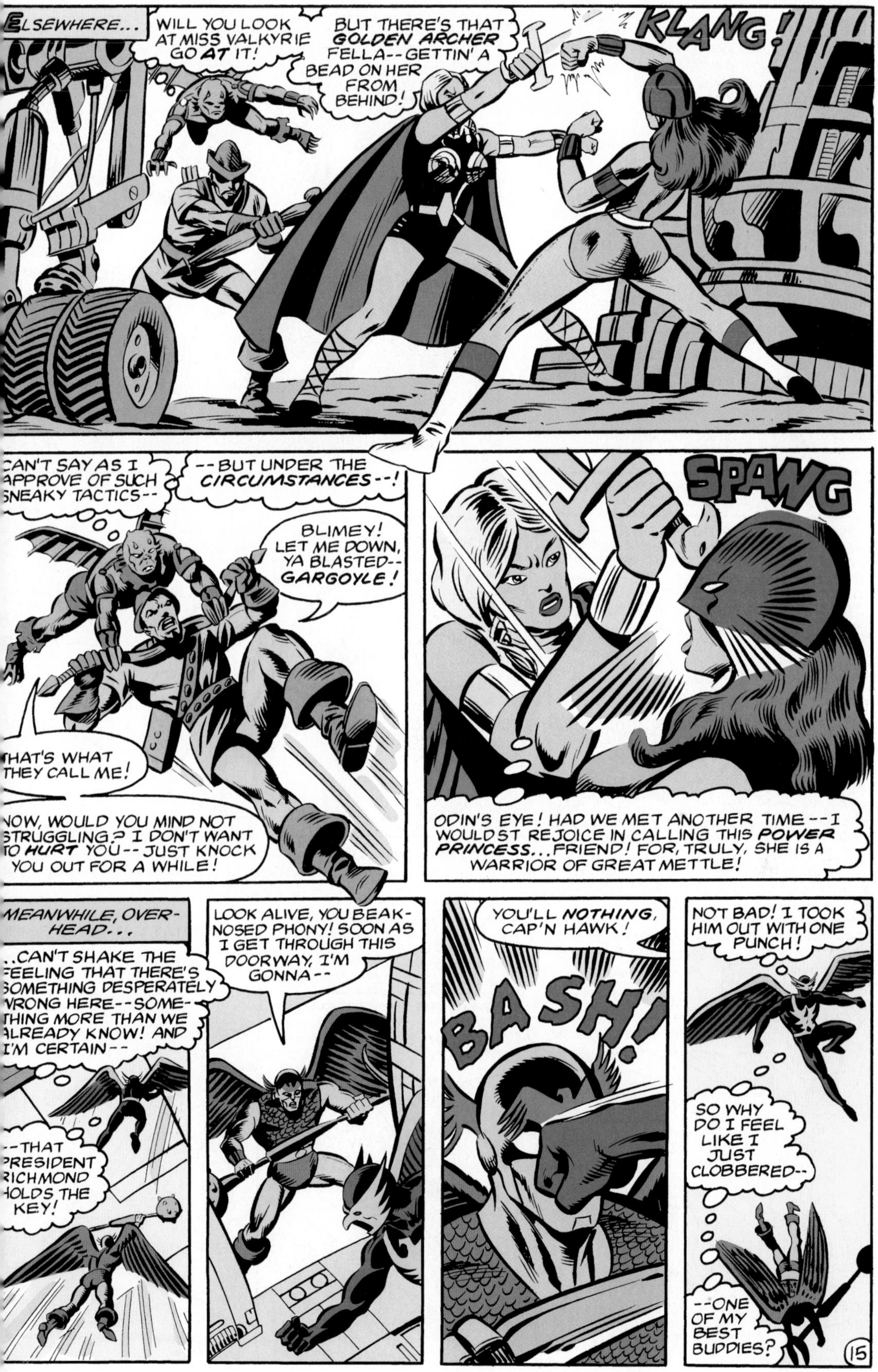
ELSEWHERE...
WILL YOU LOOK AT MISS VALKYRIE GO AT IT!
BUT THERE'S THAT GOLDEN ARCHER FELLA--GETTIN' A BEAD ON HER FROM BEHIND!
KLANG!
CAN'T SAY AS I APPROVE OF SUCH SNEAKY TACTICS--
--BUT UNDER THE CIRCUMSTANCES--!
BLIMEY! LET ME DOWN, YA BLASTED--GARGOYLE!
THAT'S WHAT THEY CALL ME!
NOW, WOULD YOU MIND NOT STRUGGLING? I DON'T WANT TO HURT YOU--JUST KNOCK YOU OUT FOR A WHILE!
SPANG
ODIN'S EYE! HAD WE MET ANOTHER TIME--I WOULDST REJOICE IN CALLING THIS POWER PRINCESS...FRIEND! FOR, TRULY, SHE IS A WARRIOR OF GREAT METTLE!
MEANWHILE, OVERHEAD...
..CAN'T SHAKE THE FEELING THAT THERE'S SOMETHING DESPERATELY WRONG HERE--SOMETHING MORE THAN WE ALREADY KNOW! AND I'M CERTAIN--
--THAT PRESIDENT RICHMOND HOLDS THE KEY!
LOOK ALIVE, YOU BEAK-NOSED PHONY! SOON AS I GET THROUGH THIS DOORWAY, I'M GONNA--
YOU'LL NOTHING, CAP'N HAWK!
BASH!
NOT BAD! I TOOK HIM OUT WITH ONE PUNCH!
SO WHY DO I FEEL LIKE I JUST CLOBBERED--
--ONE OF MY BEST BUDDIES?
15

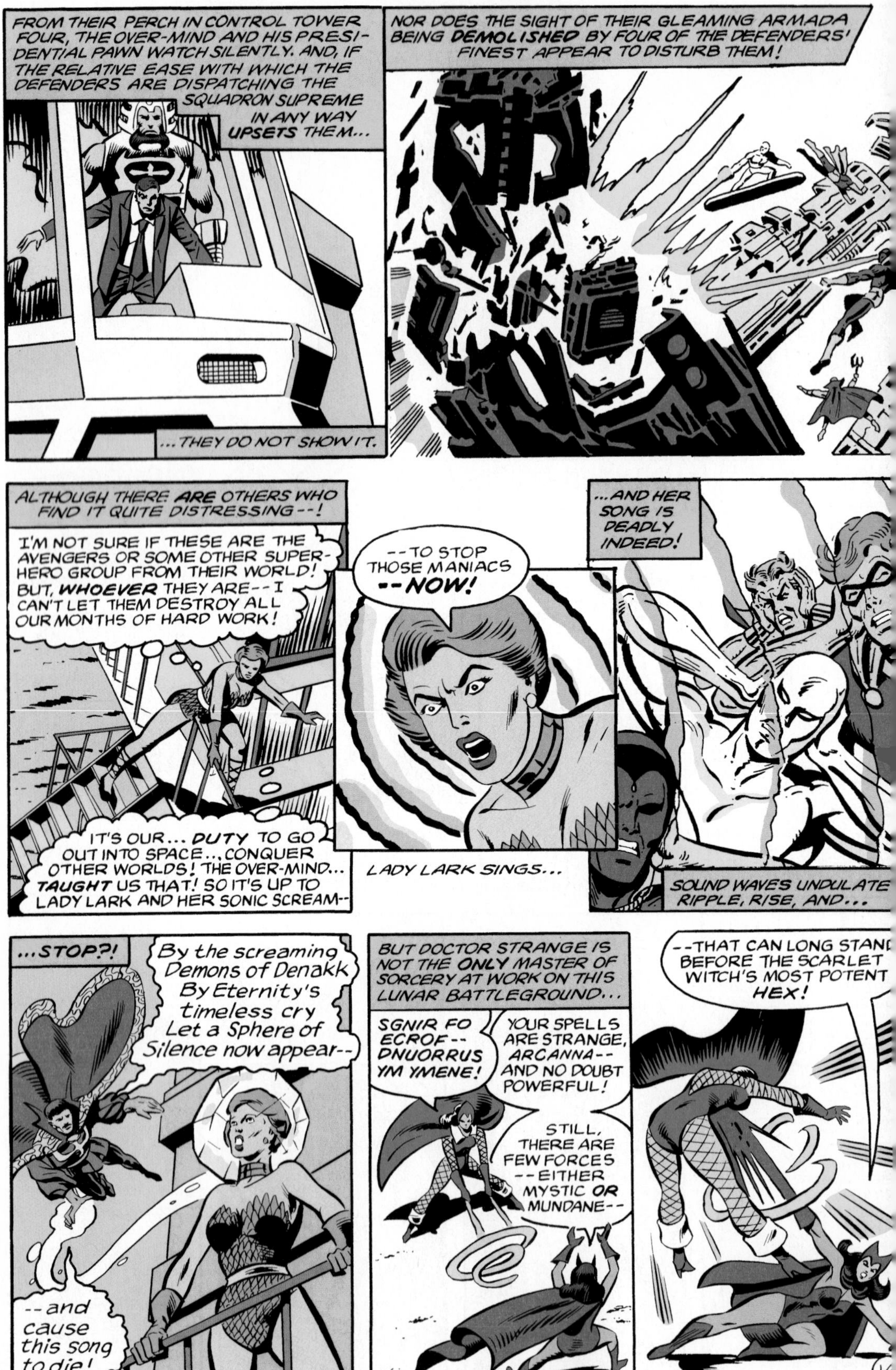
FROM THEIR PERCH IN CONTROL TOWER FOUR, THE OVER-MIND AND HIS PRESIDENTIAL PAWN WATCH SILENTLY. AND, IF THE RELATIVE EASE WITH WHICH THE DEFENDERS ARE DISPATCHING THE SQUADRON SUPREME IN ANY WAY UPSETS THEM...
...THEY DO NOT SHOW IT.
NOR DOES THE SIGHT OF THEIR GLEAMING ARMADA BEING DEMOLISHED BY FOUR OF THE DEFENDERS' FINEST APPEAR TO DISTURB THEM!
ALTHOUGH THERE ARE OTHERS WHO FIND IT QUITE DISTRESSING--!
I'M NOT SURE IF THESE ARE THE AVENGERS OR SOME OTHER SUPER-HERO GROUP FROM THEIR WORLD! BUT, WHOEVER THEY ARE--I CAN'T LET THEM DESTROY ALL OUR MONTHS OF HARD WORK!
IT'S OUR... DUTY TO GO OUT INTO SPACE..., CONQUER OTHER WORLDS! THE OVER-MIND... TAUGHT US THAT! SO IT'S UP TO LADY LARK AND HER SONIC SCREAM--
--TO STOP THOSE MANIACS --NOW!
LADY LARK SINGS...
...AND HER SONG IS DEADLY INDEED!
SOUND WAVES UNDULATE RIPPLE, RISE, AND...
...STOP?!
By the screaming Demons of Denakk By Eternity's timeless cry Let a Sphere of Silence now appear--
--and cause this song to die!
BUT DOCTOR STRANGE IS NOT THE ONLY MASTER OF SORCERY AT WORK ON THIS LUNAR BATTLEGROUND...
SGNIR FO ECROF-- DNUORRUS YM YMENE!
YOUR SPELLS ARE STRANGE, ARCANNA--AND NO DOUBT POWERFUL!
STILL, THERE ARE FEW FORCES --EITHER MYSTIC OR MUNDANE--
--THAT CAN LONG STAND BEFORE THE SCARLET WITCH'S MOST POTENT HEX!

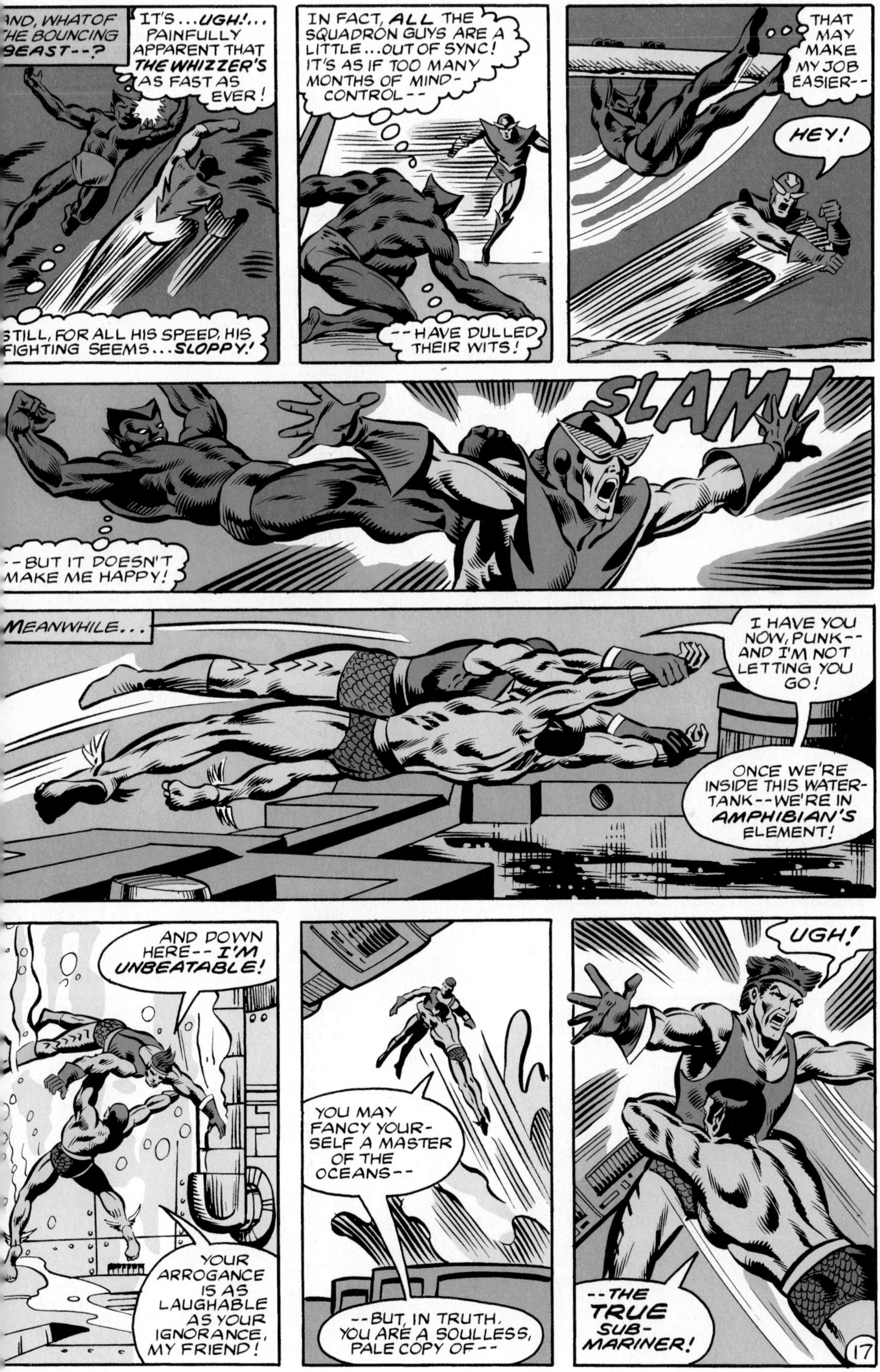
AND, WHAT OF THE BOUNCING BEAST--?
IT'S...UGH!... PAINFULLY APPARENT THAT THE WHIZZER'S AS FAST AS EVER!
STILL, FOR ALL HIS SPEED, HIS FIGHTING SEEMS...SLOPPY!
IN FACT, ALL THE SQUADRON GUYS ARE A LITTLE...OUT OF SYNC! IT'S AS IF TOO MANY MONTHS OF MIND-CONTROL--
--HAVE DULLED THEIR WITS!
THAT MAY MAKE MY JOB EASIER--
HEY!
SLAM!
--BUT IT DOESN'T MAKE ME HAPPY!
MEANWHILE...
I HAVE YOU NOW, PUNK--AND I'M NOT LETTING YOU GO!
ONCE WE'RE INSIDE THIS WATER-TANK--WE'RE IN AMPHIBIAN'S ELEMENT!
AND DOWN HERE--I'M UNBEATABLE!
YOUR ARROGANCE IS AS LAUGHABLE AS YOUR IGNORANCE, MY FRIEND!
YOU MAY FANCY YOURSELF A MASTER OF THE OCEANS--
--BUT, IN TRUTH, YOU ARE A SOULLESS, PALE COPY OF--
UGH!
--THE TRUE SUB-MARINER!
17

HMMM. WE SEEM TO HAVE A MINOR PROBLEM. THE HOUR OF TRANSFORMATION HAS NOT YET COME--

"--AND THE DEFENDERS HAVE *ALREADY* DEFEATED THE *ENTIRE* SQUADRON SUPREME!

"OVER-MIND--

"--GET *OUT* THERE!

WHOOM

ALTHOUGH *HE* IS SUPPOSED TO BE THE MASTER HERE -- THE OVER-MIND BLINDLY OBEYS HIS PAWN'S COMMAND...

"FROM BEYOND THE STARS SHALL COME THE OVER-MIND--

"--AND HE SHALL *CRUSH* THE UNIVERSE!"

Y'KNOW, GUYS 'N' GALS--

--HE'S *VERRRRY* BIG!

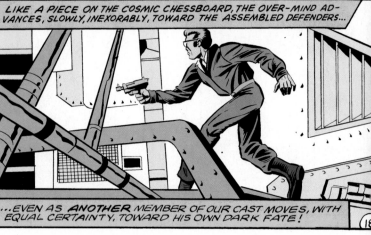

LIKE A PIECE ON THE COSMIC CHESSBOARD, THE OVER-MIND ADVANCES, SLOWLY, INEXORABLY, TOWARD THE ASSEMBLED DEFENDERS...

...EVEN AS *ANOTHER* MEMBER OF OUR CAST MOVES, WITH EQUAL CERTAINTY, TOWARD HIS OWN DARK FATE!

18

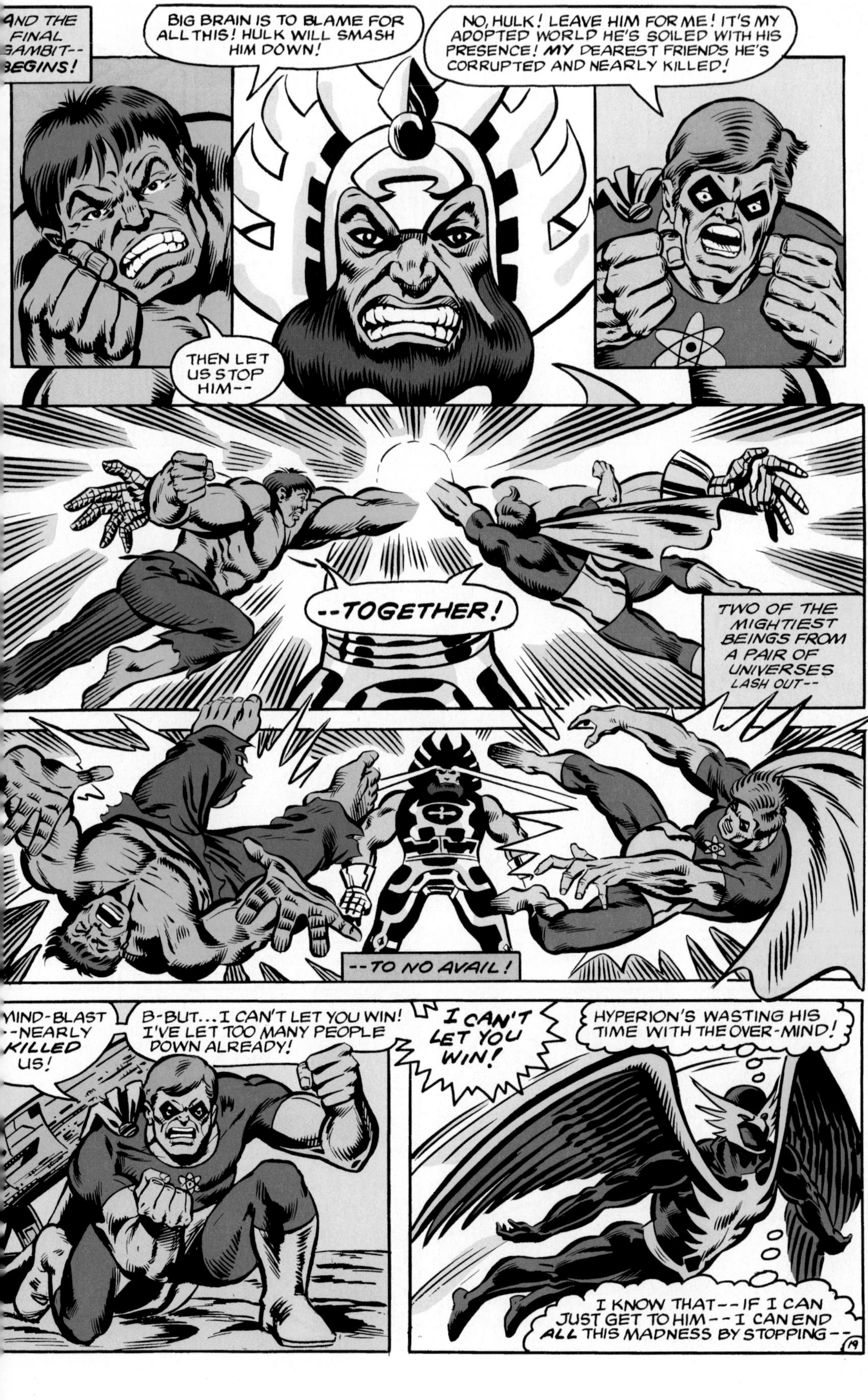
AND THE FINAL GAMBIT-- BEGINS!
BIG BRAIN IS TO BLAME FOR ALL THIS! HULK WILL SMASH HIM DOWN!
NO, HULK! LEAVE HIM FOR ME! IT'S MY ADOPTED WORLD HE'S SOILED WITH HIS PRESENCE! MY DEAREST FRIENDS HE'S CORRUPTED AND NEARLY KILLED!
THEN LET US STOP HIM--
--TOGETHER!
TWO OF THE MIGHTIEST BEINGS FROM A PAIR OF UNIVERSES LASH OUT--
--TO NO AVAIL!
MIND-BLAST --NEARLY KILLED US!
B-BUT... I CAN'T LET YOU WIN! I'VE LET TOO MANY PEOPLE DOWN ALREADY!
I CAN'T LET YOU WIN!
HYPERION'S WASTING HIS TIME WITH THE OVER-MIND!
I KNOW THAT-- IF I CAN JUST GET TO HIM-- I CAN END ALL THIS MADNESS BY STOPPING--
19

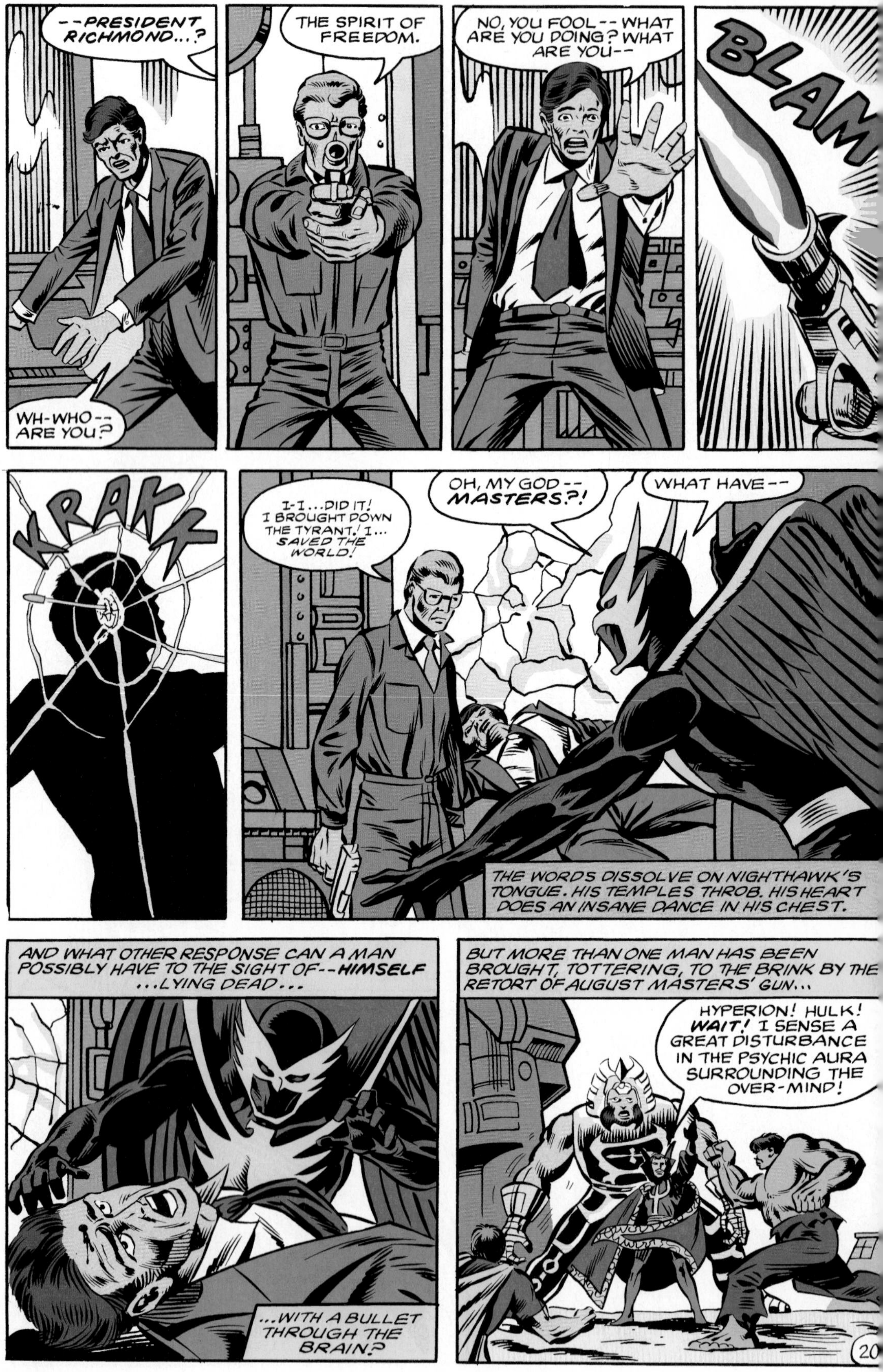
--PRESIDENT RICHMOND...?
WH-WHO-- ARE YOU?
THE SPIRIT OF FREEDOM.
NO, YOU FOOL--WHAT ARE YOU DOING? WHAT ARE YOU--
BLAM
KRAKK
I-I...DID IT! I BROUGHT DOWN THE TYRANT! I... SAVED THE WORLD!
OH, MY GOD-- MASTERS?!
WHAT HAVE--
THE WORDS DISSOLVE ON NIGHTHAWK'S TONGUE. HIS TEMPLES THROB. HIS HEART DOES AN INSANE DANCE IN HIS CHEST.
AND WHAT OTHER RESPONSE CAN A MAN POSSIBLY HAVE TO THE SIGHT OF--HIMSELF ...LYING DEAD...
...WITH A BULLET THROUGH THE BRAIN?
BUT MORE THAN ONE MAN HAS BEEN BROUGHT, TOTTERING, TO THE BRINK BY THE RETORT OF AUGUST MASTERS' GUN...
HYPERION! HULK! WAIT! I SENSE A GREAT DISTURBANCE IN THE PSYCHIC AURA SURROUNDING THE OVER-MIND!
20

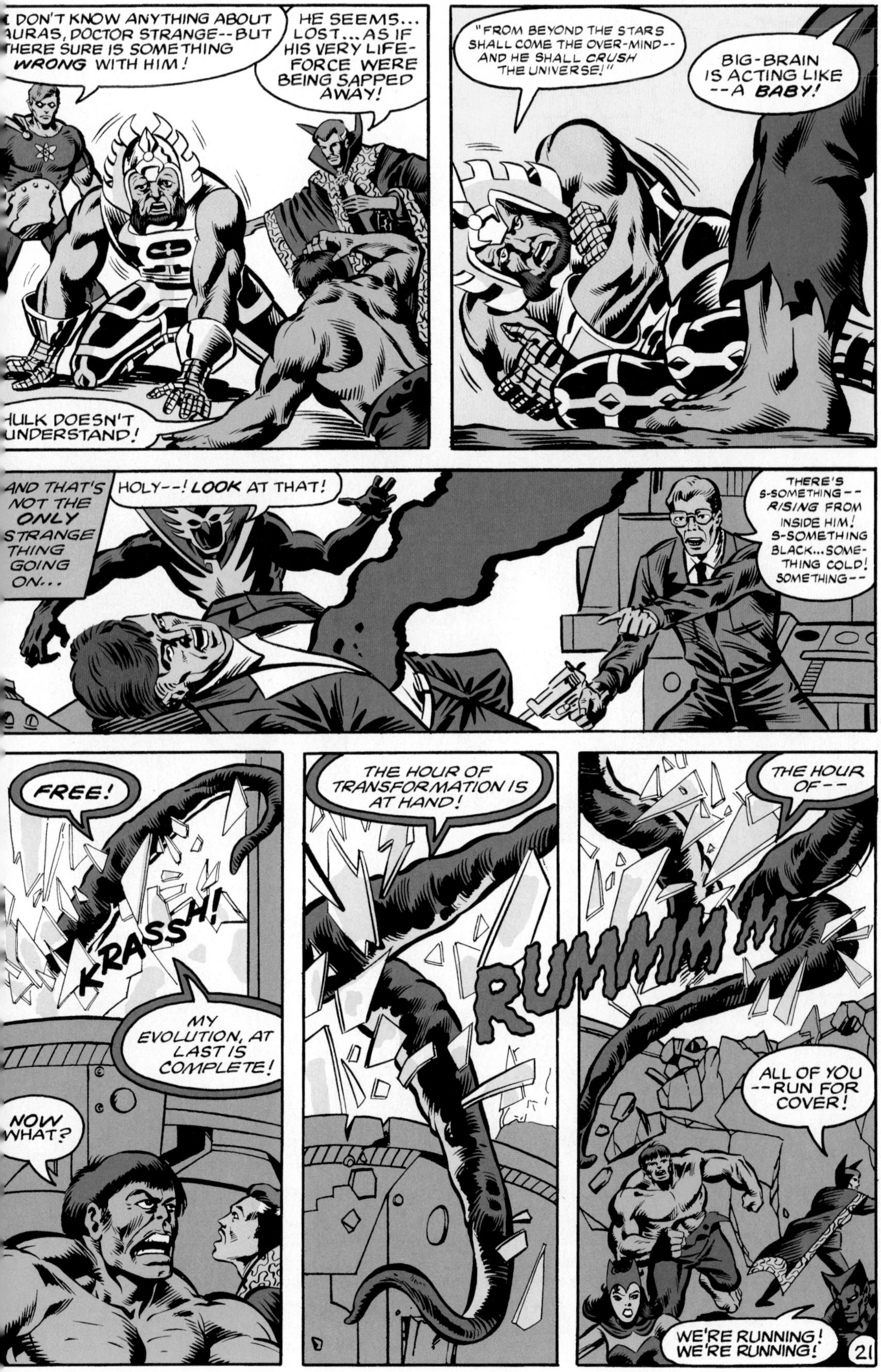
I DON'T KNOW ANYTHING ABOUT AURAS, DOCTOR STRANGE--BUT THERE SURE IS SOMETHING WRONG WITH HIM!
HE SEEMS... LOST... AS IF HIS VERY LIFE-FORCE WERE BEING SAPPED AWAY!
HULK DOESN'T UNDERSTAND!
"FROM BEYOND THE STARS SHALL COME THE OVER-MIND--AND HE SHALL CRUSH THE UNIVERSE!"
BIG-BRAIN IS ACTING LIKE --A BABY!
AND THAT'S NOT THE ONLY STRANGE THING GOING ON...
HOLY--! LOOK AT THAT!
THERE'S-- S-SOMETHING--RISING FROM INSIDE HIM! S-SOMETHING BLACK... SOMETHING COLD! SOMETHING--
FREE!
KRASSH!
MY EVOLUTION, AT LAST IS COMPLETE!
NOW WHAT?
THE HOUR OF TRANSFORMATION IS AT HAND!
RUMMMM
THE HOUR OF--
ALL OF YOU --RUN FOR COVER!
WE'RE RUNNING! WE'RE RUNNING!
21

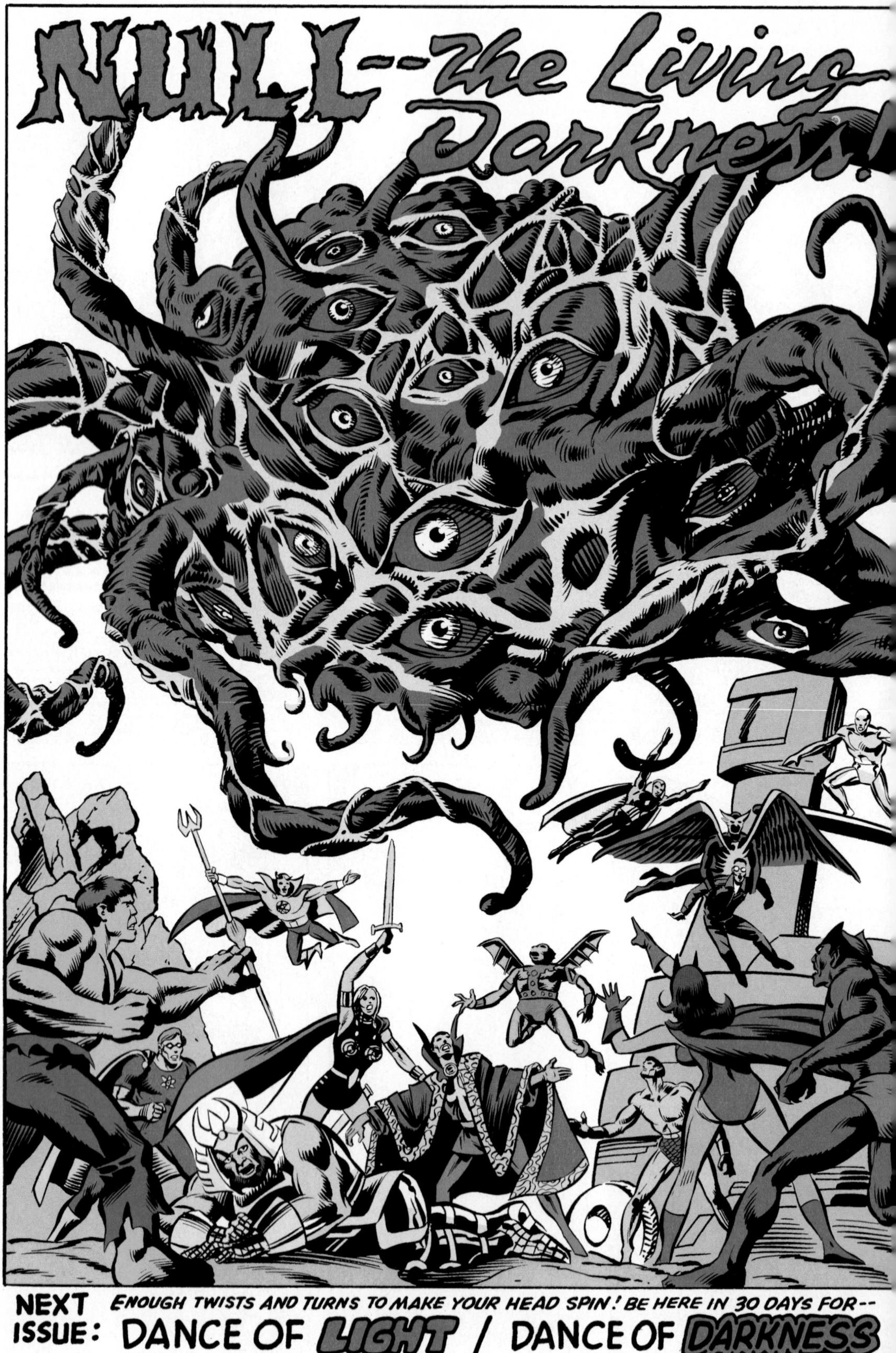
NULL--the Living Darkness!
NEXT ISSUE: ENOUGH TWISTS AND TURNS TO MAKE YOUR HEAD SPIN! BE HERE IN 30 DAYS FOR--
DANCE OF LIGHT / DANCE OF DARKNESS
AND DON'T SAY WE DIDN'T WARN YOU!

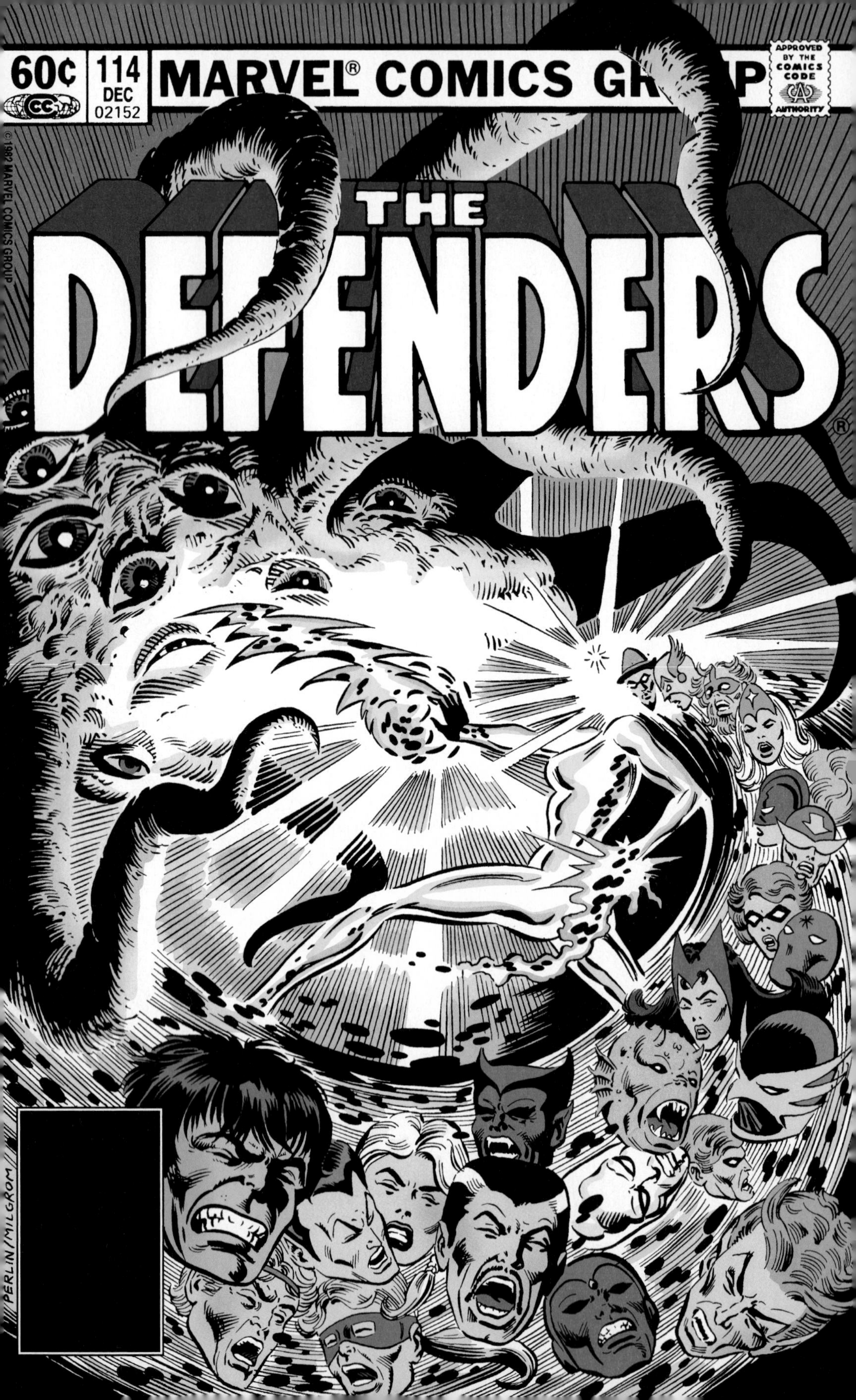

60¢
114
DEC
02152
MARVEL® COMICS GR P
APPROVED BY THE COMICS CODE AUTHORITY
© 1982 MARVEL COMICS GROUP
THE
DEFENDERS®
PERLIN/MILGROM

STAN LEE PRESENTS: THE DYNAMIC DEFENDERS!™

DANCE of DARKNESS! DANCE of LIGHT!

J.M. DeMATTEIS & DON PERLIN SCRIPT PENCILS CO-PLOTTERS	MIKE GUSTOVICH INKER	SHELLY LEFERMAN LETTERER	GEORGE ROUSSOS COLORIST	AL MILGROM EDITOR	JIM SHOOTER CHIEF

THE PLACE: A MOON MUCH LIKE OUR OWN, SOME 238,000 MILES ABOVE THE PARALLEL WORLD CALLED EARTH-S!

THE PLAYERS: THE DYNAMIC DEFENDERS AND THE ASSEMBLED MEMBERSHIP OF THE SQUADRON SUPREME!

THE FOE: WELL, THEY'D THOUGHT IT WAS THE ALIEN CALLED THE OVER-MIND -- BUT IT APPEARS IT WAS REALLY THE MONSTROUS...

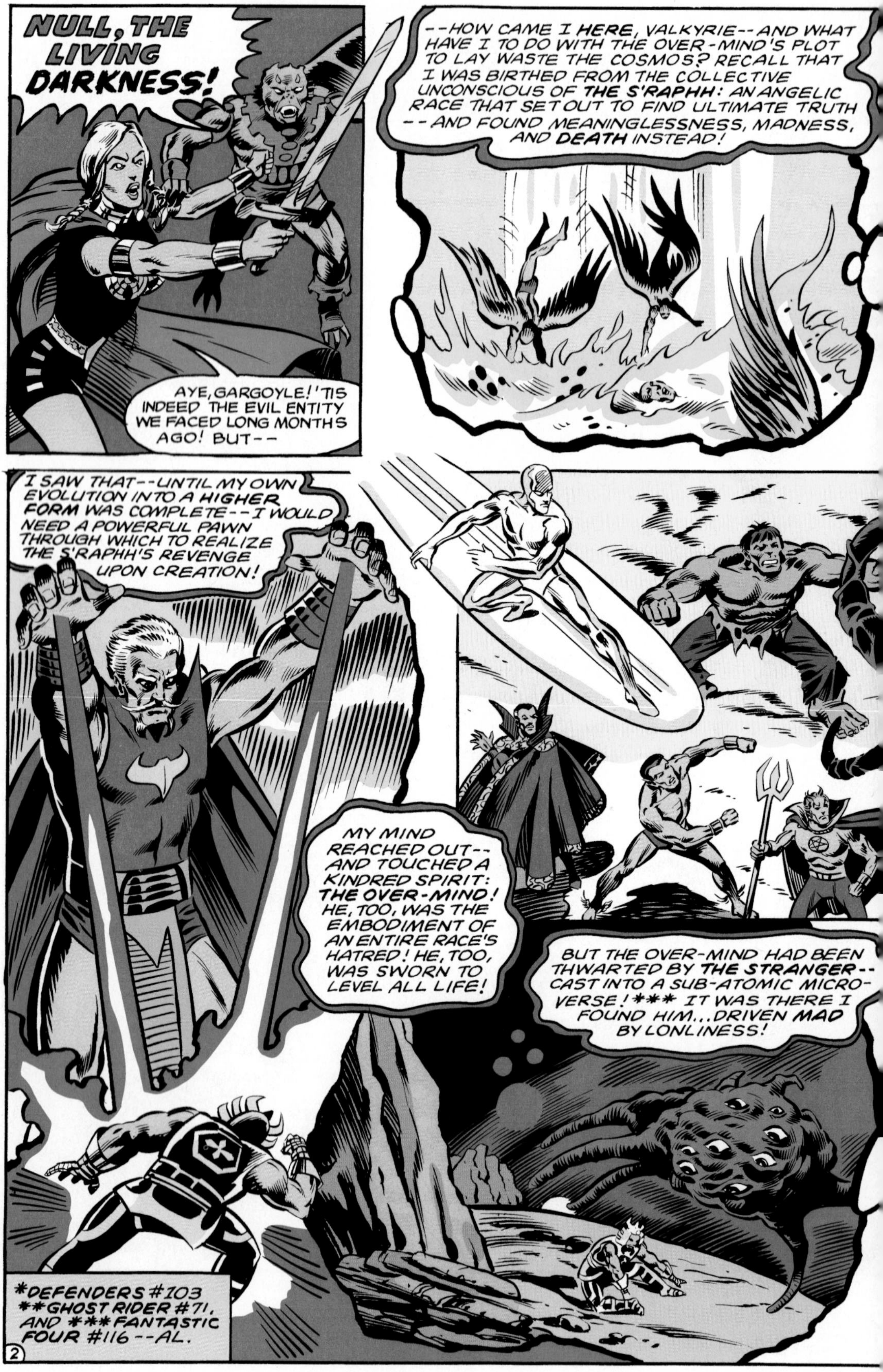
NULL, THE LIVING DARKNESS!
AYE, GARGOYLE! 'TIS INDEED THE EVIL ENTITY WE FACED LONG MONTHS AGO! BUT--
--HOW CAME I HERE, VALKYRIE--AND WHAT HAVE I TO DO WITH THE OVER-MIND'S PLOT TO LAY WASTE THE COSMOS? RECALL THAT I WAS BIRTHED FROM THE COLLECTIVE UNCONSCIOUS OF THE S'RAPHH: AN ANGELIC RACE THAT SET OUT TO FIND ULTIMATE TRUTH --AND FOUND MEANINGLESSNESS, MADNESS, AND DEATH INSTEAD!
I SAW THAT--UNTIL MY OWN EVOLUTION INTO A HIGHER FORM WAS COMPLETE--I WOULD NEED A POWERFUL PAWN THROUGH WHICH TO REALIZE THE S'RAPHH'S REVENGE UPON CREATION!
MY MIND REACHED OUT--AND TOUCHED A KINDRED SPIRIT: THE OVER-MIND! HE, TOO, WAS THE EMBODIMENT OF AN ENTIRE RACE'S HATRED! HE, TOO, WAS SWORN TO LEVEL ALL LIFE!
BUT THE OVER-MIND HAD BEEN THWARTED BY THE STRANGER--CAST INTO A SUB-ATOMIC MICRO-VERSE! *** IT WAS THERE I FOUND HIM...DRIVEN MAD BY LONLINESS!
*DEFENDERS #103 **GHOST RIDER #71, AND ***FANTASTIC FOUR #116--AL.
2

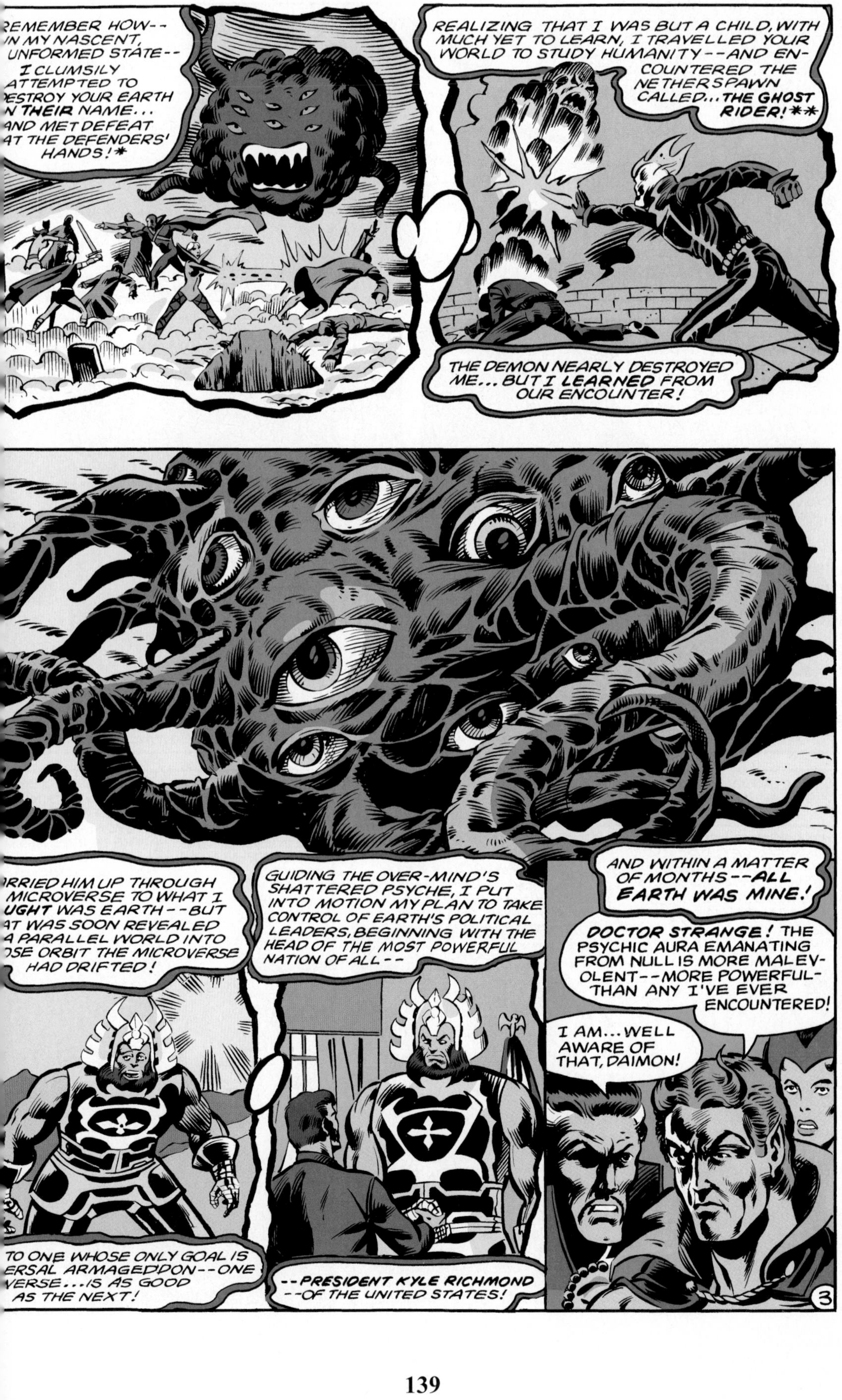
REMEMBER HOW-- N MY NASCENT, UNFORMED STATE-- I CLUMSILY ATTEMPTED TO ESTROY YOUR EARTH N THEIR NAME... AND MET DEFEAT AT THE DEFENDERS' HANDS!*
REALIZING THAT I WAS BUT A CHILD, WITH MUCH YET TO LEARN, I TRAVELLED YOUR WORLD TO STUDY HUMANITY--AND ENCOUNTERED THE NETHERSPAWN CALLED... THE GHOST RIDER!**
THE DEMON NEARLY DESTROYED ME... BUT I LEARNED FROM OUR ENCOUNTER!
RRIED HIM UP THROUGH MICROVERSE TO WHAT I UGHT WAS EARTH--BUT AT WAS SOON REVEALED A PARALLEL WORLD INTO OSE ORBIT THE MICROVERSE HAD DRIFTED!
TO ONE WHOSE ONLY GOAL IS ERSAL ARMAGEDDON--ONE VERSE... IS AS GOOD AS THE NEXT!
GUIDING THE OVER-MIND'S SHATTERED PSYCHE, I PUT INTO MOTION MY PLAN TO TAKE CONTROL OF EARTH'S POLITICAL LEADERS, BEGINNING WITH THE HEAD OF THE MOST POWERFUL NATION OF ALL--
--PRESIDENT KYLE RICHMOND --OF THE UNITED STATES!
AND WITHIN A MATTER OF MONTHS--ALL EARTH WAS MINE!
DOCTOR STRANGE! THE PSYCHIC AURA EMANATING FROM NULL IS MORE MALEVOLENT--MORE POWERFUL-THAN ANY I'VE EVER ENCOUNTERED!
I AM... WELL AWARE OF THAT, DAIMON!
3

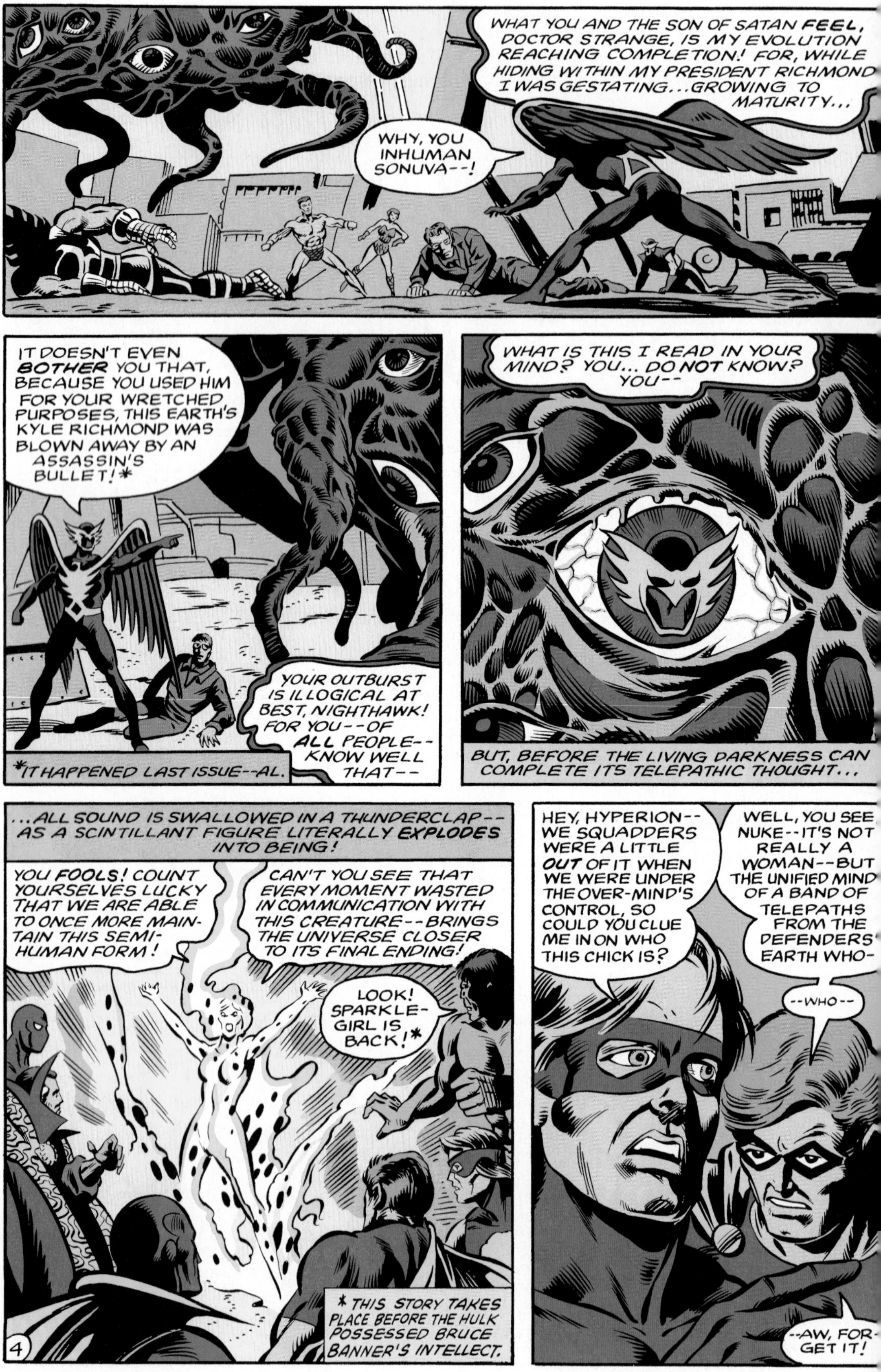
WHAT YOU AND THE SON OF SATAN FEEL, DOCTOR STRANGE, IS MY EVOLUTION REACHING COMPLETION! FOR, WHILE HIDING WITHIN MY PRESIDENT RICHMOND I WAS GESTATING... GROWING TO MATURITY...
WHY, YOU INHUMAN SONUVA--!
IT DOESN'T EVEN BOTHER YOU THAT, BECAUSE YOU USED HIM FOR YOUR WRETCHED PURPOSES, THIS EARTH'S KYLE RICHMOND WAS BLOWN AWAY BY AN ASSASSIN'S BULLET!*
YOUR OUTBURST IS ILLOGICAL AT BEST, NIGHTHAWK! FOR YOU--OF ALL PEOPLE--KNOW WELL THAT--
*IT HAPPENED LAST ISSUE--AL.
WHAT IS THIS I READ IN YOUR MIND? YOU... DO NOT KNOW? YOU--
BUT, BEFORE THE LIVING DARKNESS CAN COMPLETE ITS TELEPATHIC THOUGHT...
...ALL SOUND IS SWALLOWED IN A THUNDERCLAP--AS A SCINTILLANT FIGURE LITERALLY EXPLODES INTO BEING!
YOU FOOLS! COUNT YOURSELVES LUCKY THAT WE ARE ABLE TO ONCE MORE MAINTAIN THIS SEMI-HUMAN FORM!
CAN'T YOU SEE THAT EVERY MOMENT WASTED IN COMMUNICATION WITH THIS CREATURE--BRINGS THE UNIVERSE CLOSER TO ITS FINAL ENDING!
LOOK! SPARKLE-GIRL IS BACK!*
* THIS STORY TAKES PLACE BEFORE THE HULK POSSESSED BRUCE BANNER'S INTELLECT.
4
HEY, HYPERION--WE SQUADDERS WERE A LITTLE OUT OF IT WHEN WE WERE UNDER THE OVER-MIND'S CONTROL, SO COULD YOU CLUE ME IN ON WHO THIS CHICK IS?
WELL, YOU SEE NUKE--IT'S NOT REALLY A WOMAN--BUT THE UNIFIED MIND OF A BAND OF TELEPATHS FROM THE DEFENDERS' EARTH WHO-
--WHO--
--AW, FORGET IT!

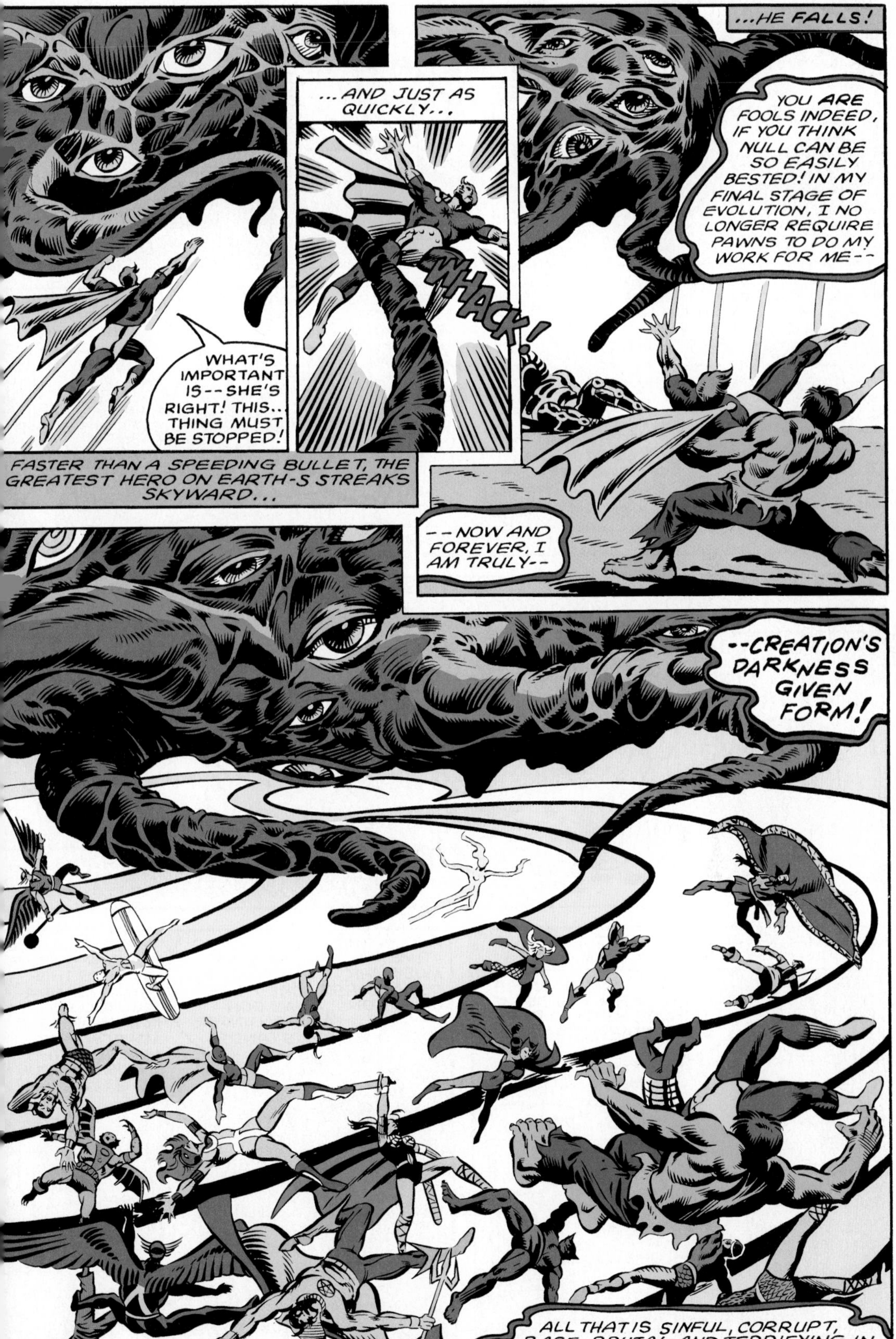
WHAT'S IMPORTANT IS--SHE'S RIGHT! THIS.. THING MUST BE STOPPED!
FASTER THAN A SPEEDING BULLET, THE GREATEST HERO ON EARTH-S STREAKS SKYWARD...
...AND JUST AS QUICKLY...
WHACK!
...HE FALLS!
YOU ARE FOOLS INDEED, IF YOU THINK NULL CAN BE SO EASILY BESTED! IN MY FINAL STAGE OF EVOLUTION, I NO LONGER REQUIRE PAWNS TO DO MY WORK FOR ME--
--NOW AND FOREVER, I AM TRULY--
--CREATION'S DARKNESS GIVEN FORM!
ALL THAT IS SINFUL, CORRUPT, BASE, BRUTAL AND TERRIFYING IN THIS UNIVERSE--IS ALIVE WITHIN ME--
5

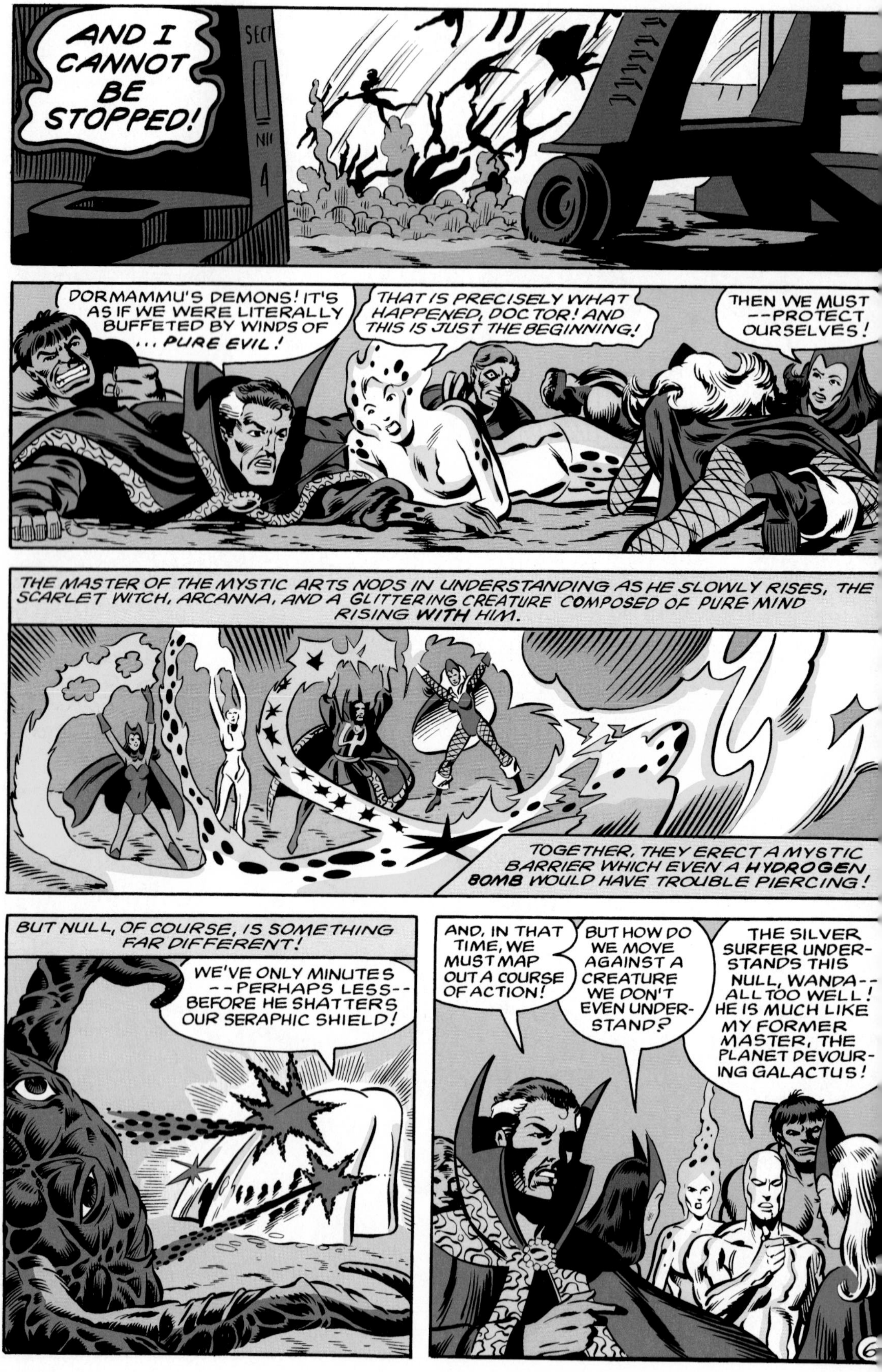
AND I CANNOT BE STOPPED!
DORMAMMU'S DEMONS! IT'S AS IF WE WERE LITERALLY BUFFETED BY WINDS OF ... PURE EVIL!
THAT IS PRECISELY WHAT HAPPENED, DOCTOR! AND THIS IS JUST THE BEGINNING!
THEN WE MUST --PROTECT OURSELVES!
THE MASTER OF THE MYSTIC ARTS NODS IN UNDERSTANDING AS HE SLOWLY RISES, THE SCARLET WITCH, ARCANNA, AND A GLITTERING CREATURE COMPOSED OF PURE MIND RISING WITH HIM.
TOGETHER, THEY ERECT A MYSTIC BARRIER WHICH EVEN A HYDROGEN BOMB WOULD HAVE TROUBLE PIERCING!
BUT NULL, OF COURSE, IS SOMETHING FAR DIFFERENT!
WE'VE ONLY MINUTES --PERHAPS LESS-- BEFORE HE SHATTERS OUR SERAPHIC SHIELD!
AND, IN THAT TIME, WE MUST MAP OUT A COURSE OF ACTION!
BUT HOW DO WE MOVE AGAINST A CREATURE WE DON'T EVEN UNDERSTAND?
THE SILVER SURFER UNDERSTANDS THIS NULL, WANDA--ALL TOO WELL! HE IS MUCH LIKE MY FORMER MASTER, THE PLANET DEVOURING GALACTUS!
6

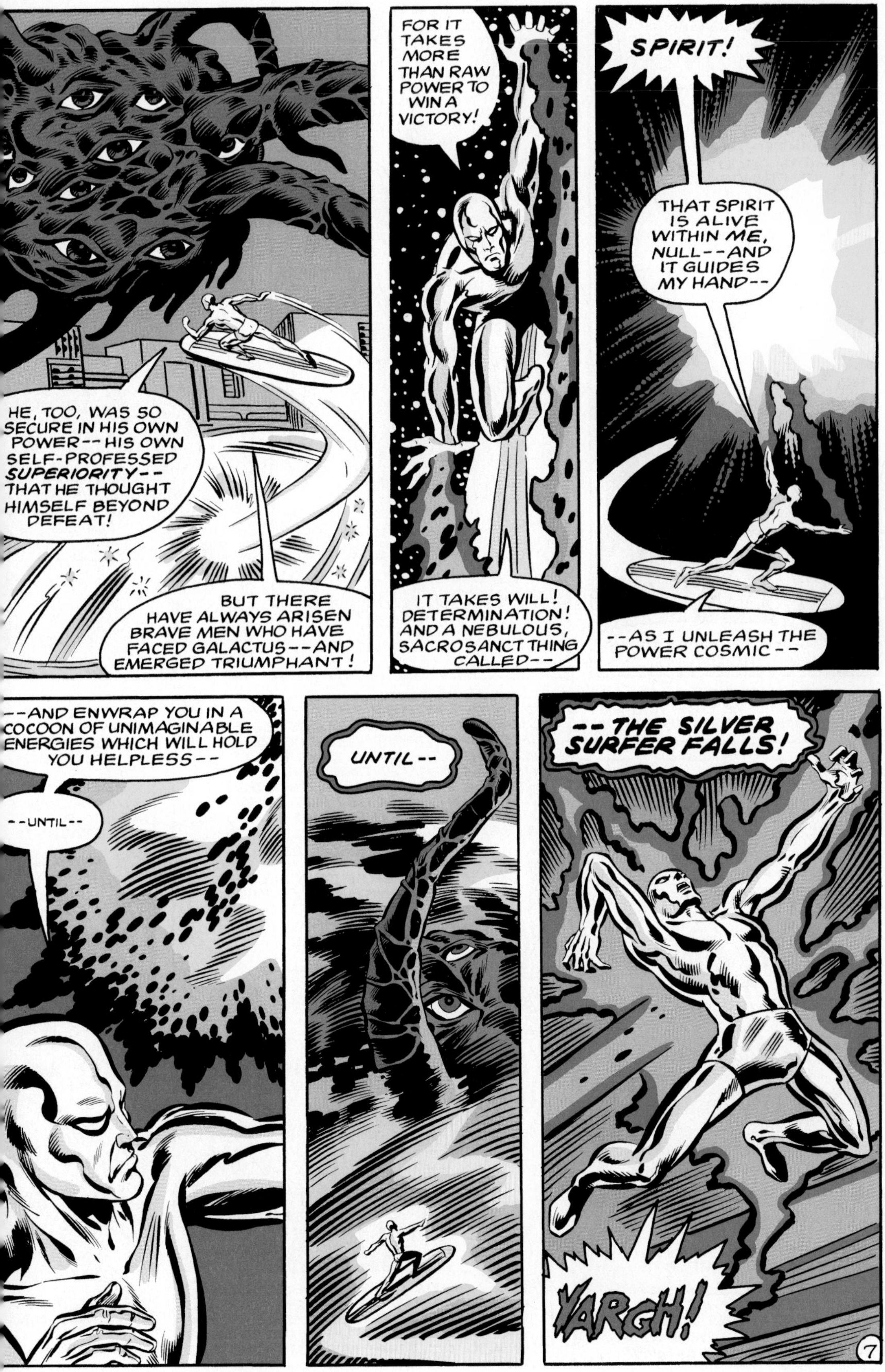
HE, TOO, WAS SO SECURE IN HIS OWN POWER--HIS OWN SELF-PROFESSED SUPERIORITY--THAT HE THOUGHT HIMSELF BEYOND DEFEAT!
BUT THERE HAVE ALWAYS ARISEN BRAVE MEN WHO HAVE FACED GALACTUS--AND EMERGED TRIUMPHANT!
FOR IT TAKES MORE THAN RAW POWER TO WIN A VICTORY!
IT TAKES WILL! DETERMINATION! AND A NEBULOUS, SACROSANCT THING CALLED--
SPIRIT!
THAT SPIRIT IS ALIVE WITHIN ME, NULL--AND IT GUIDES MY HAND--
--AS I UNLEASH THE POWER COSMIC--
--AND ENWRAP YOU IN A COCOON OF UNIMAGINABLE ENERGIES WHICH WILL HOLD YOU HELPLESS--
--UNTIL--
UNTIL--
--THE SILVER SURFER FALLS!
YARGH!
7

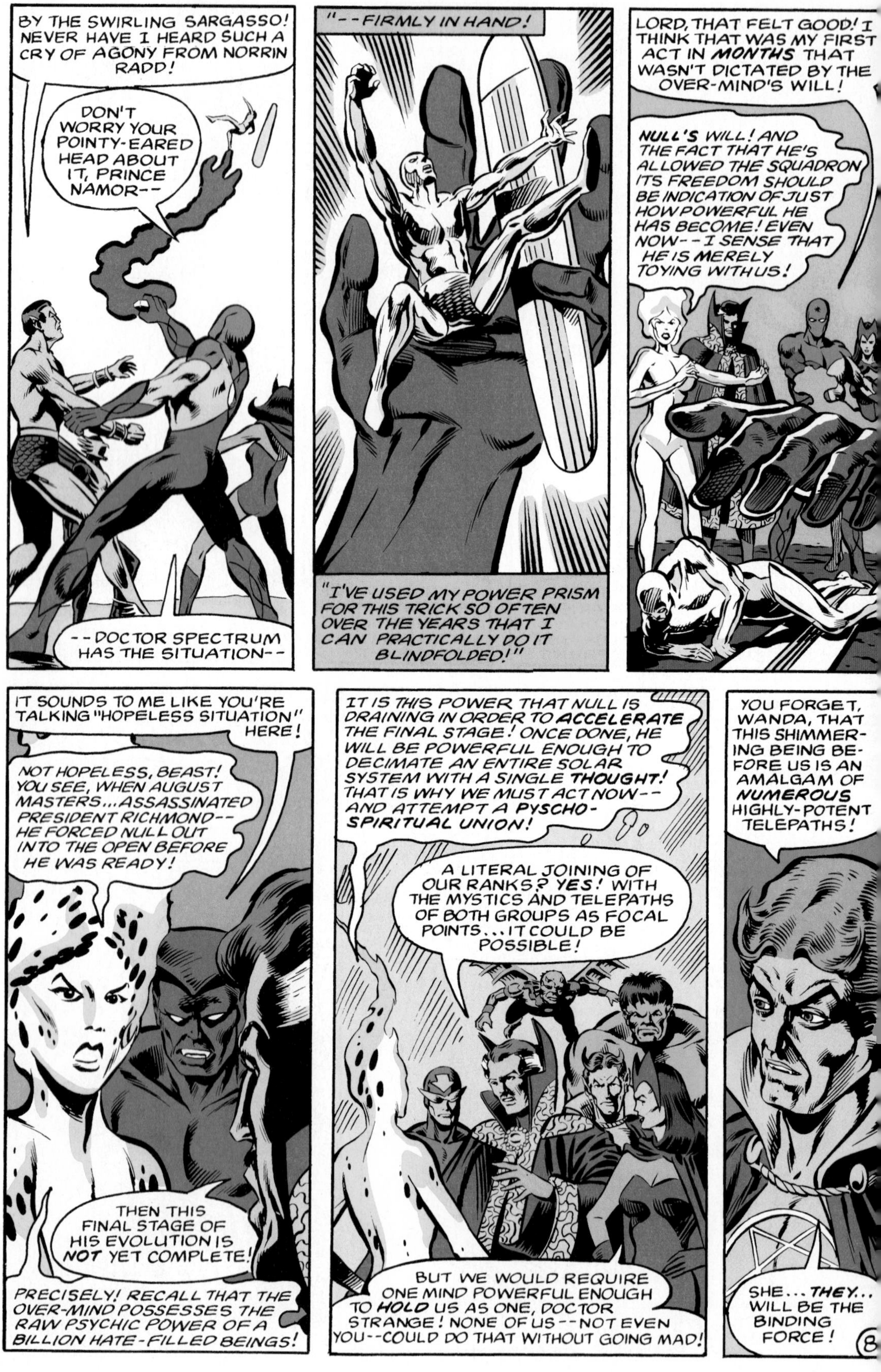
BY THE SWIRLING SARGASSO! NEVER HAVE I HEARD SUCH A CRY OF AGONY FROM NORRIN RADD!
DON'T WORRY YOUR POINTY-EARED HEAD ABOUT IT, PRINCE NAMOR--
--DOCTOR SPECTRUM HAS THE SITUATION--
"--FIRMLY IN HAND!
"I'VE USED MY POWER PRISM FOR THIS TRICK SO OFTEN OVER THE YEARS THAT I CAN PRACTICALLY DO IT BLINDFOLDED!"
LORD, THAT FELT GOOD! I THINK THAT WAS MY FIRST ACT IN MONTHS THAT WASN'T DICTATED BY THE OVER-MIND'S WILL!
NULL'S WILL! AND THE FACT THAT HE'S ALLOWED THE SQUADRON ITS FREEDOM SHOULD BE INDICATION OF JUST HOW POWERFUL HE HAS BECOME! EVEN NOW--I SENSE THAT HE IS MERELY TOYING WITH US!
IT SOUNDS TO ME LIKE YOU'RE TALKING "HOPELESS SITUATION" HERE!
NOT HOPELESS, BEAST! YOU SEE, WHEN AUGUST MASTERS...ASSASSINATED PRESIDENT RICHMOND--HE FORCED NULL OUT INTO THE OPEN BEFORE HE WAS READY!
THEN THIS FINAL STAGE OF HIS EVOLUTION IS NOT YET COMPLETE!
PRECISELY! RECALL THAT THE OVER-MIND POSSESSES THE RAW PSYCHIC POWER OF A BILLION HATE-FILLED BEINGS!
IT IS THIS POWER THAT NULL IS DRAINING IN ORDER TO ACCELERATE THE FINAL STAGE! ONCE DONE, HE WILL BE POWERFUL ENOUGH TO DECIMATE AN ENTIRE SOLAR SYSTEM WITH A SINGLE THOUGHT! THAT IS WHY WE MUST ACT NOW--AND ATTEMPT A PYSCHO-SPIRITUAL UNION!
A LITERAL JOINING OF OUR RANKS? YES! WITH THE MYSTICS AND TELEPATHS OF BOTH GROUPS AS FOCAL POINTS...IT COULD BE POSSIBLE!
BUT WE WOULD REQUIRE ONE MIND POWERFUL ENOUGH TO HOLD US AS ONE, DOCTOR STRANGE! NONE OF US--NOT EVEN YOU--COULD DO THAT WITHOUT GOING MAD!
YOU FORGET, WANDA, THAT THIS SHIMMERING BEING BEFORE US IS AN AMALGAM OF NUMEROUS HIGHLY-POTENT TELEPATHS!
SHE...THEY...WILL BE THE BINDING FORCE!
8

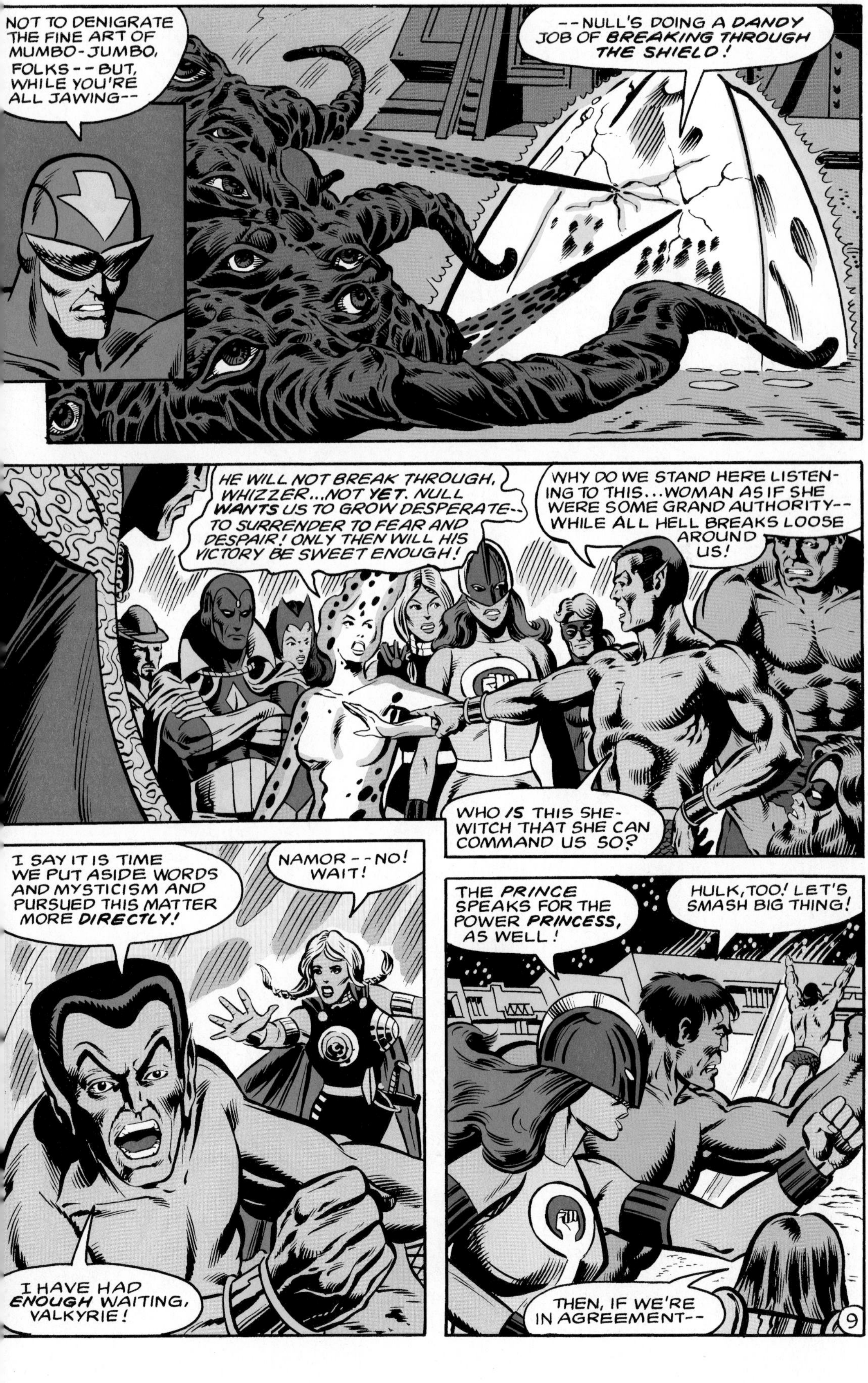
NOT TO DENIGRATE THE FINE ART OF MUMBO-JUMBO, FOLKS--BUT, WHILE YOU'RE ALL JAWING--
--NULL'S DOING A DANDY JOB OF BREAKING THROUGH THE SHIELD!
HE WILL NOT BREAK THROUGH, WHIZZER...NOT YET. NULL WANTS US TO GROW DESPERATE--TO SURRENDER TO FEAR AND DESPAIR! ONLY THEN WILL HIS VICTORY BE SWEET ENOUGH!
WHY DO WE STAND HERE LISTENING TO THIS...WOMAN AS IF SHE WERE SOME GRAND AUTHORITY--WHILE ALL HELL BREAKS LOOSE AROUND US!
WHO IS THIS SHE-WITCH THAT SHE CAN COMMAND US SO?
I SAY IT IS TIME WE PUT ASIDE WORDS AND MYSTICISM AND PURSUED THIS MATTER MORE DIRECTLY!
NAMOR--NO! WAIT!
I HAVE HAD ENOUGH WAITING, VALKYRIE!
THE PRINCE SPEAKS FOR THE POWER PRINCESS, AS WELL!
HULK, TOO! LET'S SMASH BIG THING!
THEN, IF WE'RE IN AGREEMENT--
9

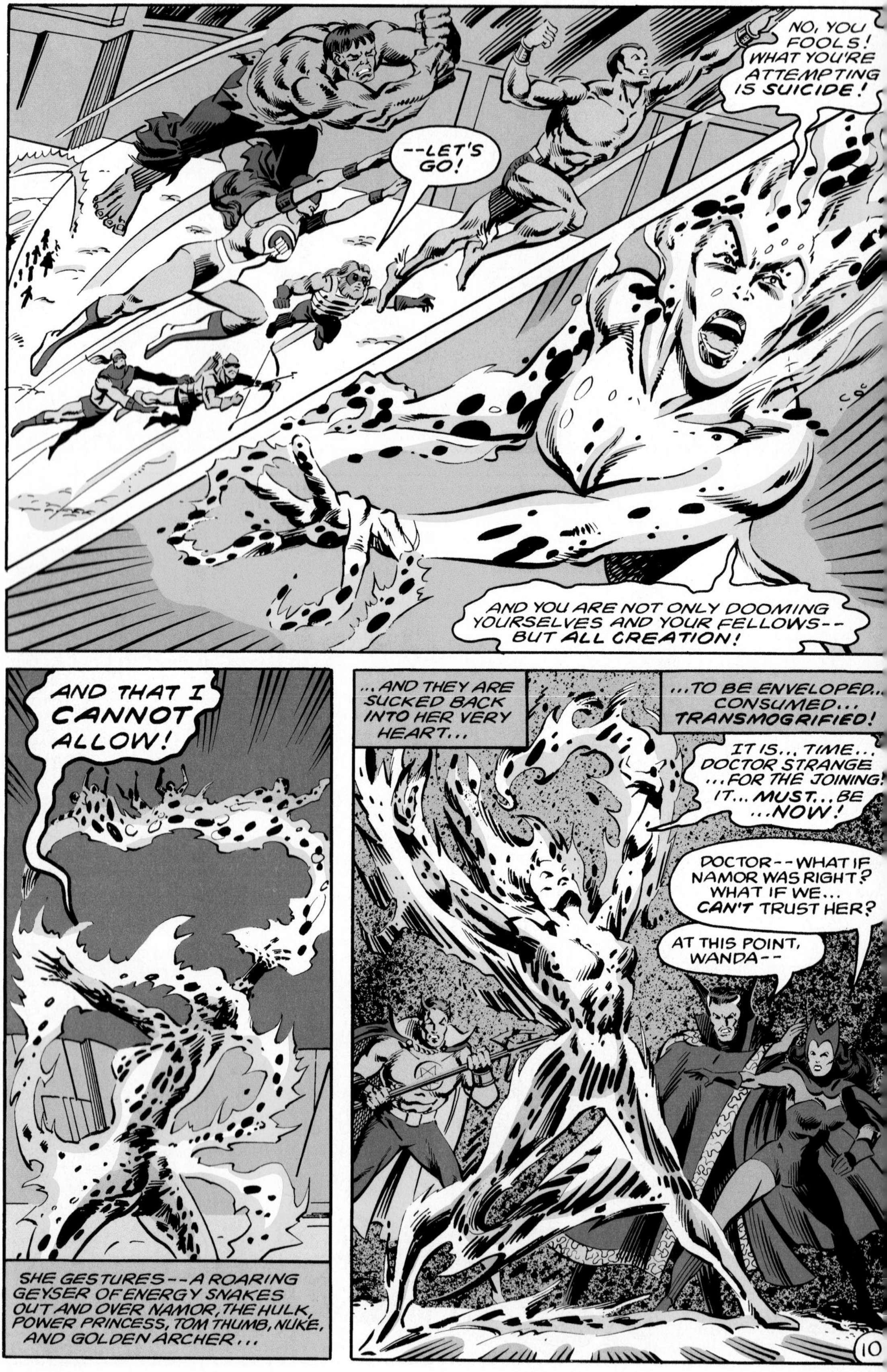
NO, YOU FOOLS! WHAT YOU'RE ATTEMPTING IS SUICIDE!
--LET'S GO!
AND YOU ARE NOT ONLY DOOMING YOURSELVES AND YOUR FELLOWS-- BUT ALL CREATION!
AND THAT I CANNOT ALLOW!
SHE GESTURES--A ROARING GEYSER OF ENERGY SNAKES OUT AND OVER NAMOR, THE HULK, POWER PRINCESS, TOM THUMB, NUKE, AND GOLDEN ARCHER...
...AND THEY ARE SUCKED BACK INTO HER VERY HEART...
...TO BE ENVELOPED... CONSUMED... TRANSMOGRIFIED!
IT IS... TIME... DOCTOR STRANGE ...FOR THE JOINING! IT... MUST... BE ...NOW!
DOCTOR--WHAT IF NAMOR WAS RIGHT? WHAT IF WE... CAN'T TRUST HER?
AT THIS POINT, WANDA--
10

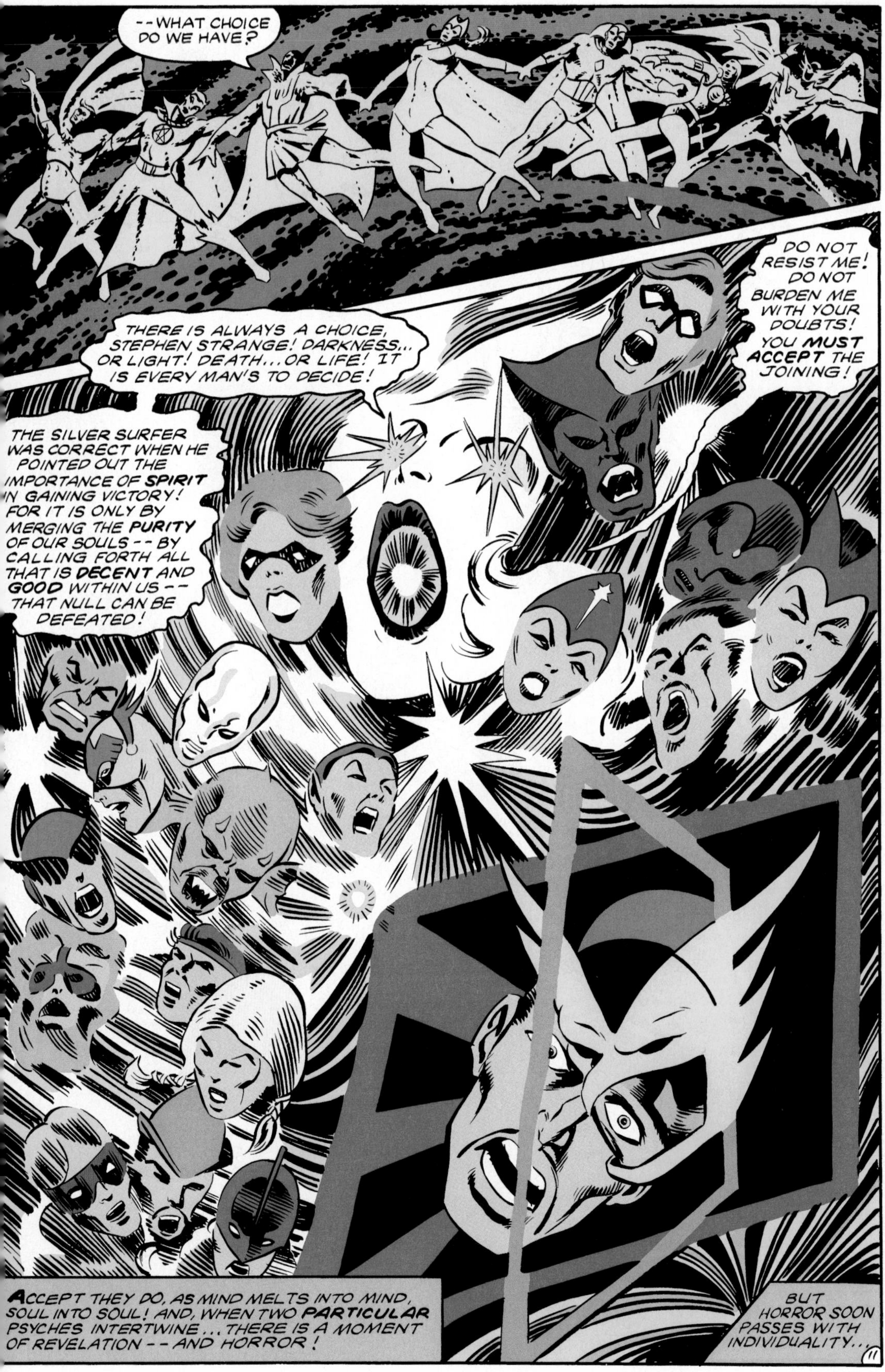
--WHAT CHOICE DO WE HAVE?
THERE IS ALWAYS A CHOICE, STEPHEN STRANGE! DARKNESS... OR LIGHT! DEATH...OR LIFE! IT IS EVERY MAN'S TO DECIDE!
DO NOT RESIST ME! DO NOT BURDEN ME WITH YOUR DOUBTS! YOU MUST ACCEPT THE JOINING!
THE SILVER SURFER WAS CORRECT WHEN HE POINTED OUT THE IMPORTANCE OF SPIRIT IN GAINING VICTORY! FOR IT IS ONLY BY MERGING THE PURITY OF OUR SOULS -- BY CALLING FORTH ALL THAT IS DECENT AND GOOD WITHIN US -- THAT NULL CAN BE DEFEATED!
ACCEPT THEY DO, AS MIND MELTS INTO MIND, SOUL INTO SOUL! AND, WHEN TWO PARTICULAR PSYCHES INTERTWINE... THERE IS A MOMENT OF REVELATION -- AND HORROR!
BUT HORROR SOON PASSES WITH INDIVIDUALITY...
11

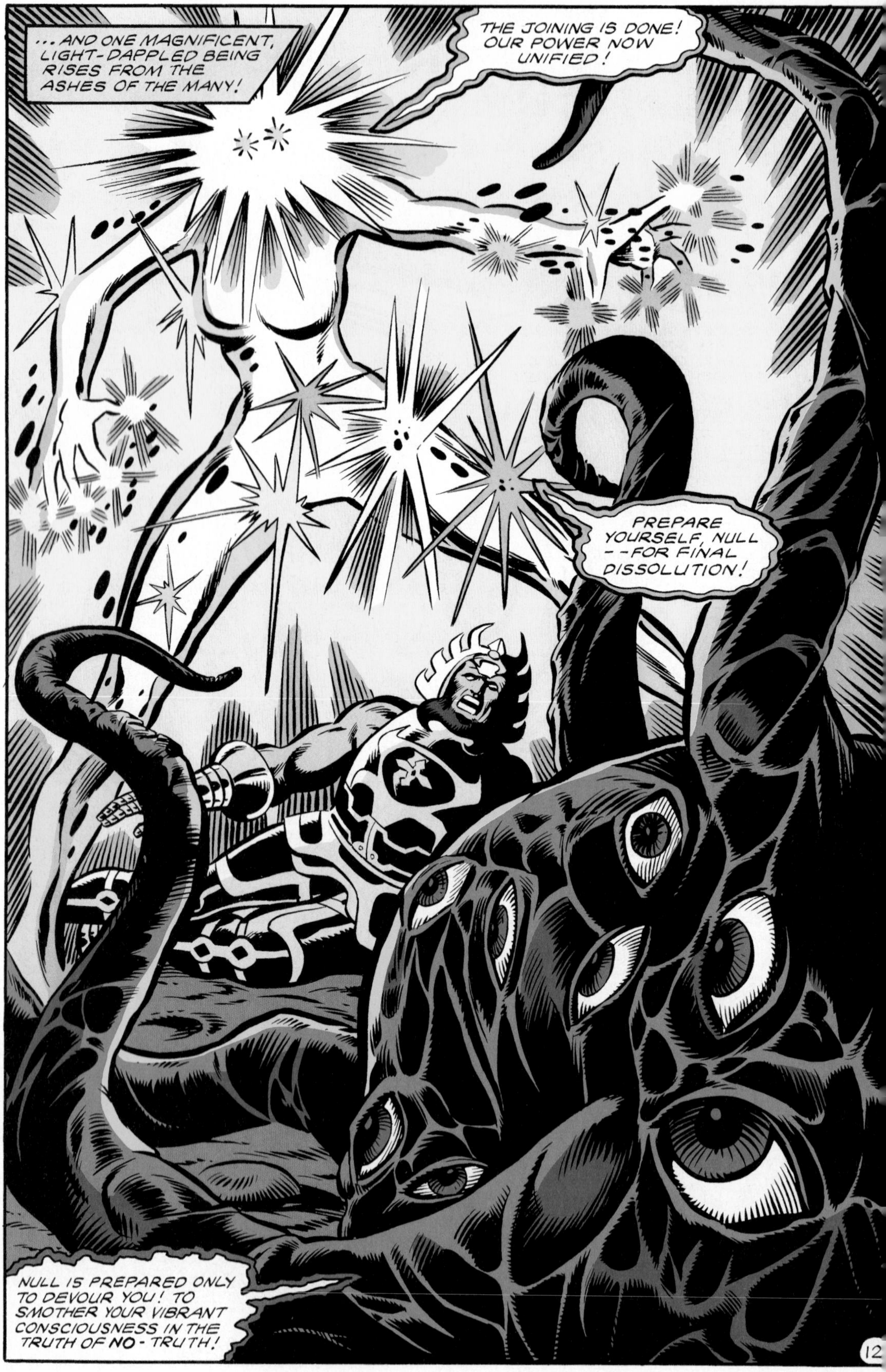
...AND ONE MAGNIFICENT, LIGHT-DAPPLED BEING RISES FROM THE ASHES OF THE MANY!
THE JOINING IS DONE! OUR POWER NOW UNIFIED!
PREPARE YOURSELF, NULL --FOR FINAL DISSOLUTION!
NULL IS PREPARED ONLY TO DEVOUR YOU! TO SMOTHER YOUR VIBRANT CONSCIOUSNESS IN THE TRUTH OF NO-TRUTH!
12

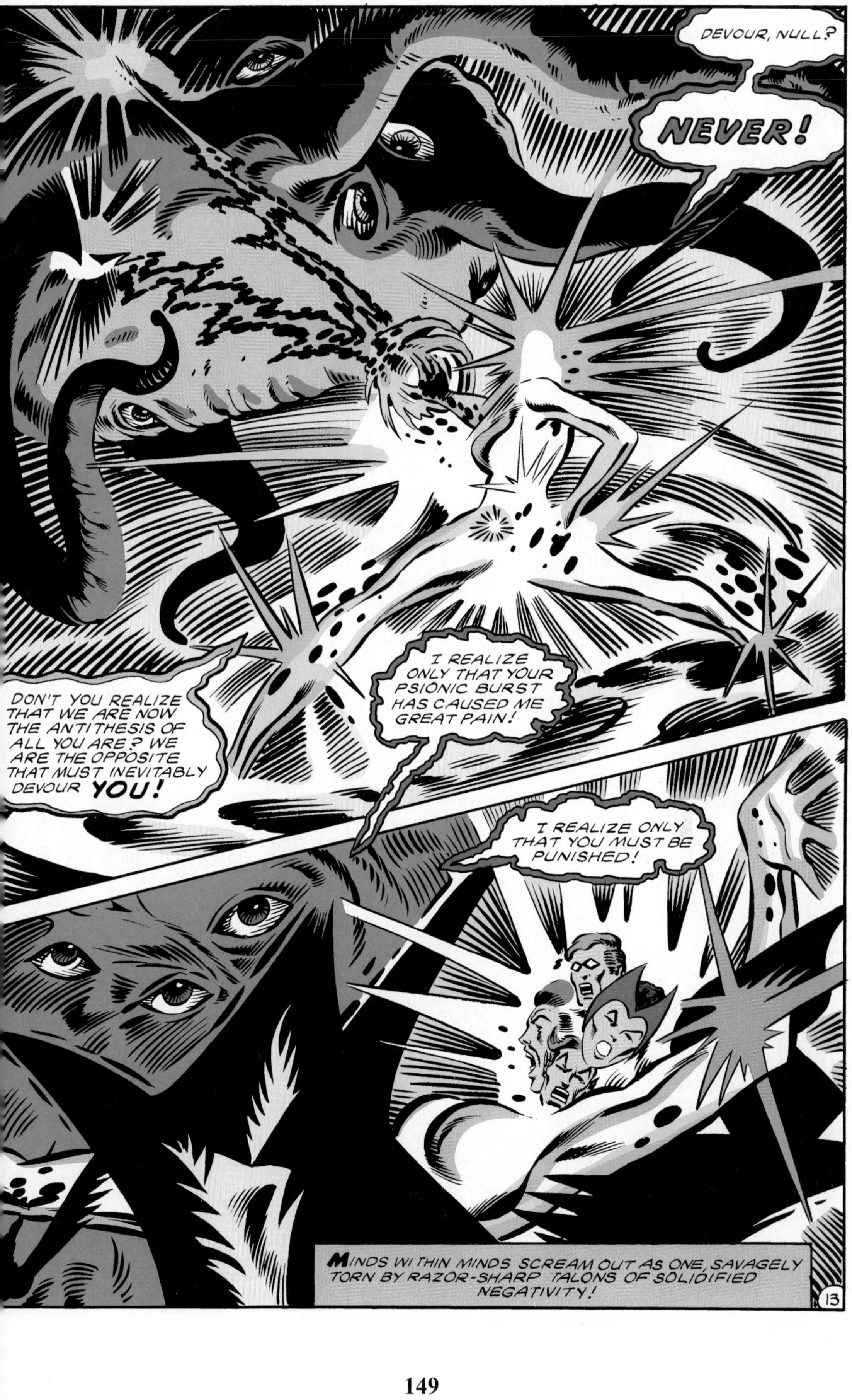
DEVOUR, NULL?
NEVER!
DON'T YOU REALIZE THAT WE ARE NOW THE ANTITHESIS OF ALL YOU ARE? WE ARE THE OPPOSITE THAT MUST INEVITABLY DEVOUR **YOU!**
I REALIZE ONLY THAT YOUR PSIONIC BURST HAS CAUSED ME GREAT PAIN!
I REALIZE ONLY THAT YOU MUST BE PUNISHED!
MINDS WITHIN MINDS SCREAM OUT AS ONE, SAVAGELY TORN BY RAZOR-SHARP TALONS OF SOLIDIFIED NEGATIVITY!
13

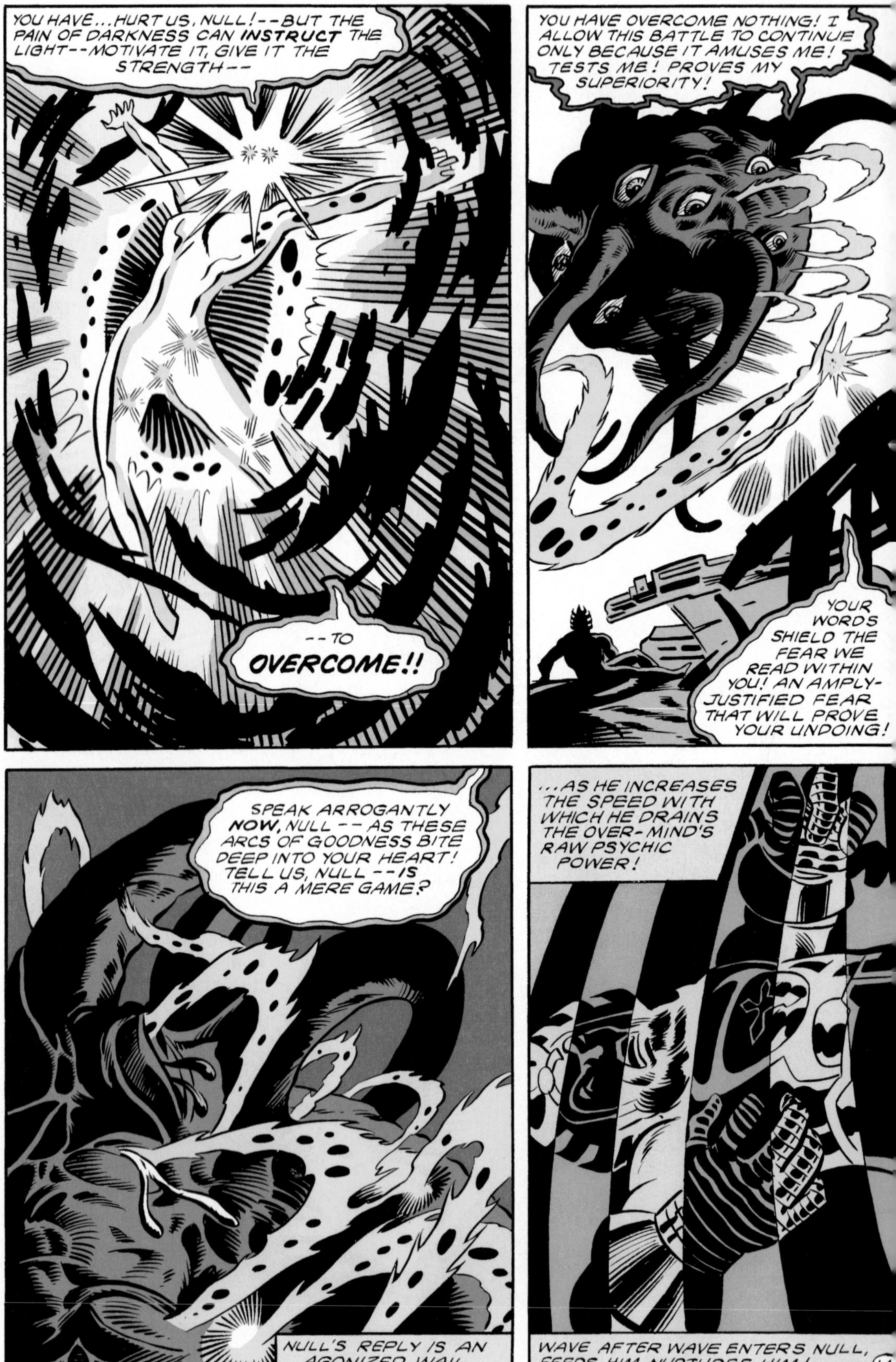

YOU HAVE...HURT US, NULL!--BUT THE PAIN OF DARKNESS CAN INSTRUCT THE LIGHT--MOTIVATE IT, GIVE IT THE STRENGTH--
--TO OVERCOME!!
YOU HAVE OVERCOME NOTHING! I ALLOW THIS BATTLE TO CONTINUE ONLY BECAUSE IT AMUSES ME! TESTS ME! PROVES MY SUPERIORITY!
YOUR WORDS SHIELD THE FEAR WE READ WITHIN YOU! AN AMPLY-JUSTIFIED FEAR THAT WILL PROVE YOUR UNDOING!
SPEAK ARROGANTLY NOW, NULL--AS THESE ARCS OF GOODNESS BITE DEEP INTO YOUR HEART! TELL US, NULL--IS THIS A MERE GAME?
NULL'S REPLY IS AN AGONIZED WAIL...
...AS HE INCREASES THE SPEED WITH WHICH HE DRAINS THE OVER-MIND'S RAW PSYCHIC POWER!
WAVE AFTER WAVE ENTERS NULL, FEEDS HIM, NURTURES HIM!
14

AND THE RESULT...

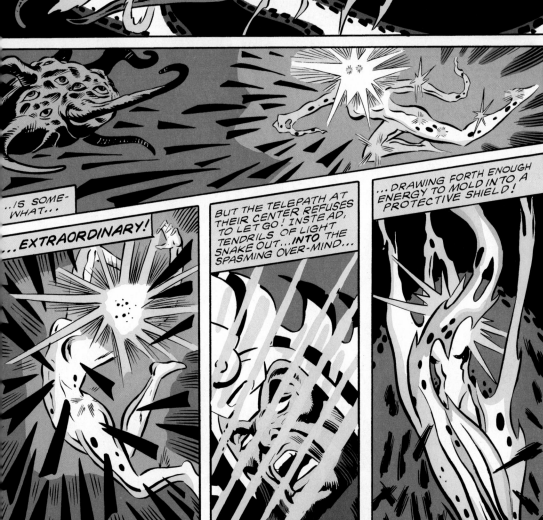

...IS SOME-WHAT...

...EXTRAORDINARY!

BUT THE TELEPATH AT THEIR CENTER REFUSES TO LET GO! INSTEAD, TENDRILS OF LIGHT SNAKE OUT...*INTO* THE SPASMING OVER-MIND...

...DRAWING FORTH ENOUGH ENERGY TO MOLD INTO A PROTECTIVE SHIELD!

PIERCED BY A THOUSAND ASTRAL DAGGERS, THE UNIFIED MINDS OF THE DEFENDERS AND THE SQUADRON SUPREME NEARLY SPLIT APART!

15

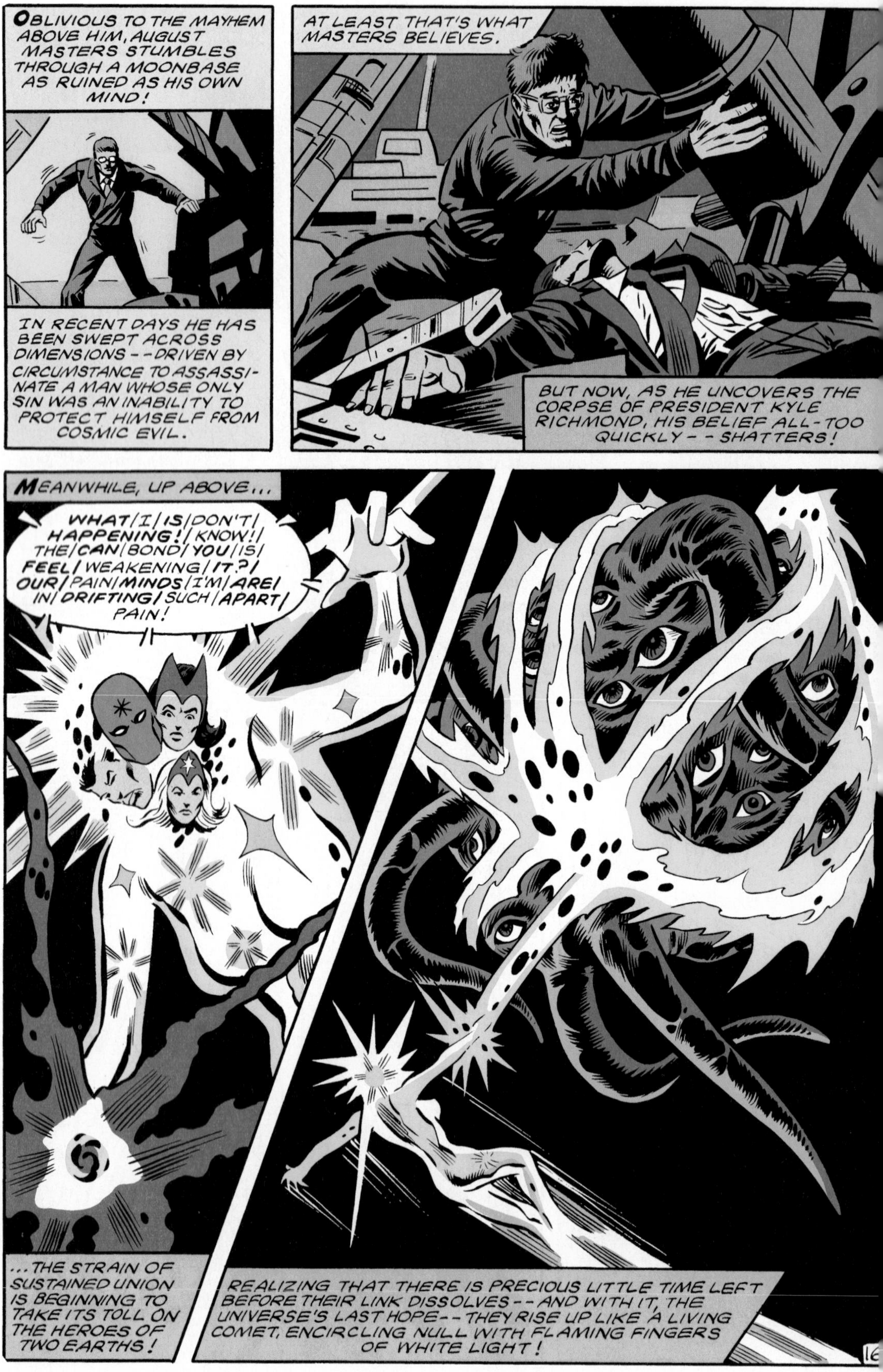

OBLIVIOUS TO THE MAYHEM ABOVE HIM, AUGUST MASTERS STUMBLES THROUGH A MOONBASE AS RUINED AS HIS OWN MIND!
IN RECENT DAYS HE HAS BEEN SWEPT ACROSS DIMENSIONS--DRIVEN BY CIRCUMSTANCE TO ASSASSI-NATE A MAN WHOSE ONLY SIN WAS AN INABILITY TO PROTECT HIMSELF FROM COSMIC EVIL.
AT LEAST THAT'S WHAT MASTERS BELIEVES.
BUT NOW, AS HE UNCOVERS THE CORPSE OF PRESIDENT KYLE RICHMOND, HIS BELIEF ALL-TOO QUICKLY--SHATTERS!
MEANWHILE, UP ABOVE...
WHAT/I/IS/DON'T/HAPPENING!/KNOW!/THE/CAN/BOND/YOU/IS/FEEL/WEAKENING/IT?/OUR/PAIN/MINDS/I'M/ARE/IN/DRIFTING/SUCH/APART/PAIN!
...THE STRAIN OF SUSTAINED UNION IS BEGINNING TO TAKE ITS TOLL ON THE HEROES OF TWO EARTHS!
REALIZING THAT THERE IS PRECIOUS LITTLE TIME LEFT BEFORE THEIR LINK DISSOLVES--AND WITH IT, THE UNIVERSE'S LAST HOPE--THEY RISE UP LIKE A LIVING COMET, ENCIRCLING NULL WITH FLAMING FINGERS OF WHITE LIGHT!
16

BUT DARKNESS GROWS DEEPER, EVEN AS LIGHT FALTERS!

...UNSTOPPABLE!

EVEN NOW, HE SHRUGS OFF THEIR ATTACK WITHOUT SO MUCH AS A WORD...

...AS NEARLY TWO DOZEN PSYCHES REEL -- FOR THE FIRST TIME CONSIDERING...DEFEAT!

THERE | YES | IS | DOCTOR | BUT | I | ONE | AGREE | CHOICE! | WE | BUT | MUST | IT | USE | IS | WHATEVER | EXTREMELY | POWER | DANGEROUS | WE | IT | HAVE | COULD | LEFT | LEAVE | FOR | US | ONE | ALL | LAST | DEAD | STRIKE!

IN A MATTER OF MINUTES, THE LAST OF THE OVER-MIND'S HATE-FILLED ENERGIES WILL BE DRAINED -- AND NULL WILL BE --

FATE SEEMS TO HOLD HER BREATH, AS EACH PLAYER PREPARES FOR THE FINAL GAMBIT!

OH, MY GOD! IT CAN'T BE! IT CAN'T BE!

HE'S JUST... MELTING AWAY!

HE'S NOT EVEN HUMAN!

THE TIME HAS COME...

17

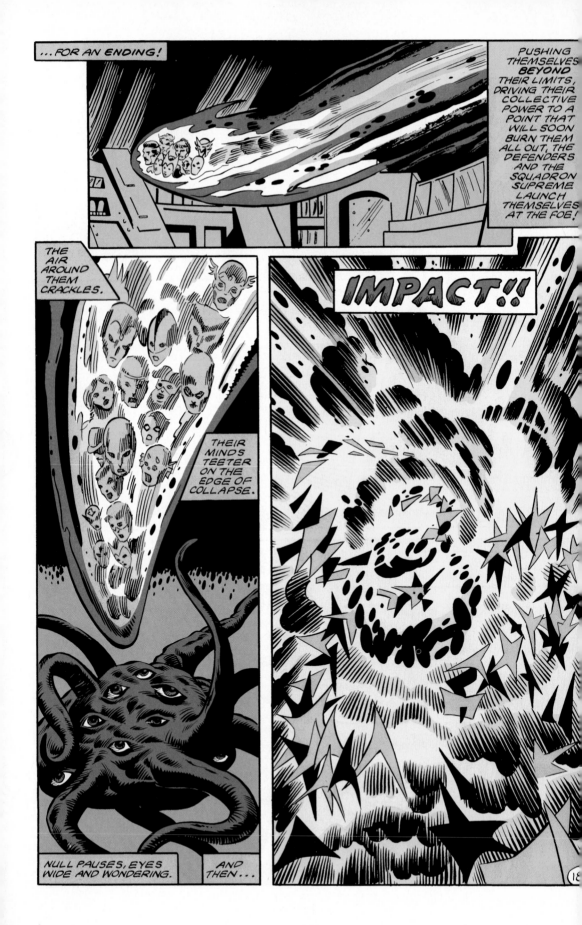

...FOR AN ENDING!

PUSHING THEMSELVES *BEYOND* THEIR LIMITS, DRIVING THEIR COLLECTIVE POWER TO A POINT THAT WILL SOON BURN THEM ALL OUT, THE DEFENDERS AND THE SQUADRON SUPREME LAUNCH THEMSELVES AT THE FOE!

THE AIR AROUND THEM CRACKLES.

THEIR MINDS TEETER ON THE EDGE OF COLLAPSE.

NULL PAUSES, EYES WIDE AND WONDERING.

AND THEN...

IMPACT!!

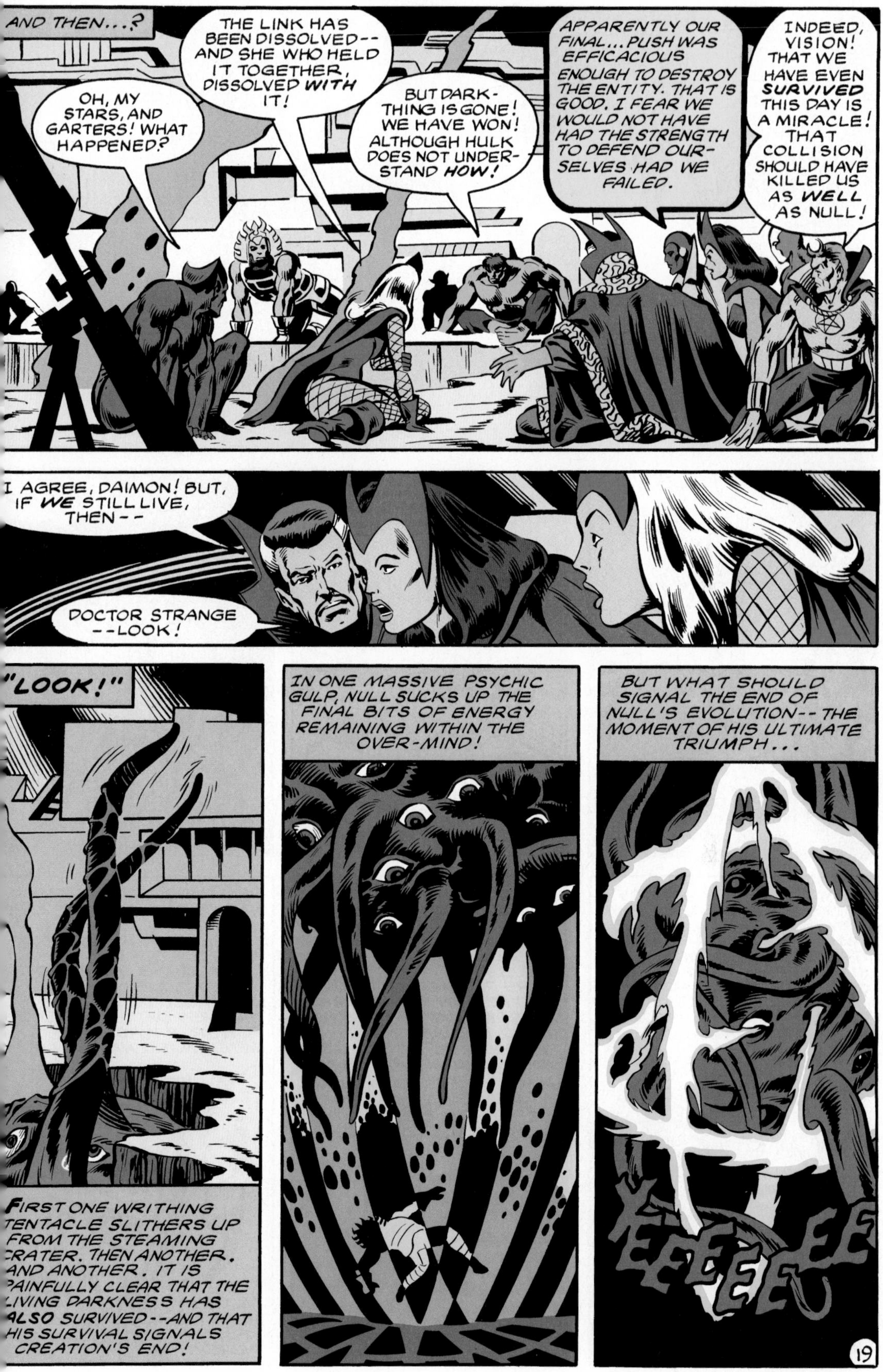

AND THEN...?
OH, MY STARS, AND GARTERS! WHAT HAPPENED?
THE LINK HAS BEEN DISSOLVED-- AND SHE WHO HELD IT TOGETHER, DISSOLVED WITH IT!
BUT DARK-THING IS GONE! WE HAVE WON! ALTHOUGH HULK DOES NOT UNDERSTAND HOW!
APPARENTLY OUR FINAL... PUSH WAS EFFICACIOUS ENOUGH TO DESTROY THE ENTITY. THAT IS GOOD. I FEAR WE WOULD NOT HAVE HAD THE STRENGTH TO DEFEND OURSELVES HAD WE FAILED.
INDEED, VISION! THAT WE HAVE EVEN SURVIVED THIS DAY IS A MIRACLE! THAT COLLISION SHOULD HAVE KILLED US AS WELL AS NULL!
I AGREE, DAIMON! BUT, IF WE STILL LIVE, THEN--
DOCTOR STRANGE --LOOK!
"LOOK!"
FIRST ONE WRITHING TENTACLE SLITHERS UP FROM THE STEAMING CRATER. THEN ANOTHER. AND ANOTHER. IT IS PAINFULLY CLEAR THAT THE LIVING DARKNESS HAS ALSO SURVIVED--AND THAT HIS SURVIVAL SIGNALS CREATION'S END!
IN ONE MASSIVE PSYCHIC GULP, NULL SUCKS UP THE FINAL BITS OF ENERGY REMAINING WITHIN THE OVER-MIND!
BUT WHAT SHOULD SIGNAL THE END OF NULL'S EVOLUTION-- THE MOMENT OF HIS ULTIMATE TRIUMPH...
YEEEEEEE
19

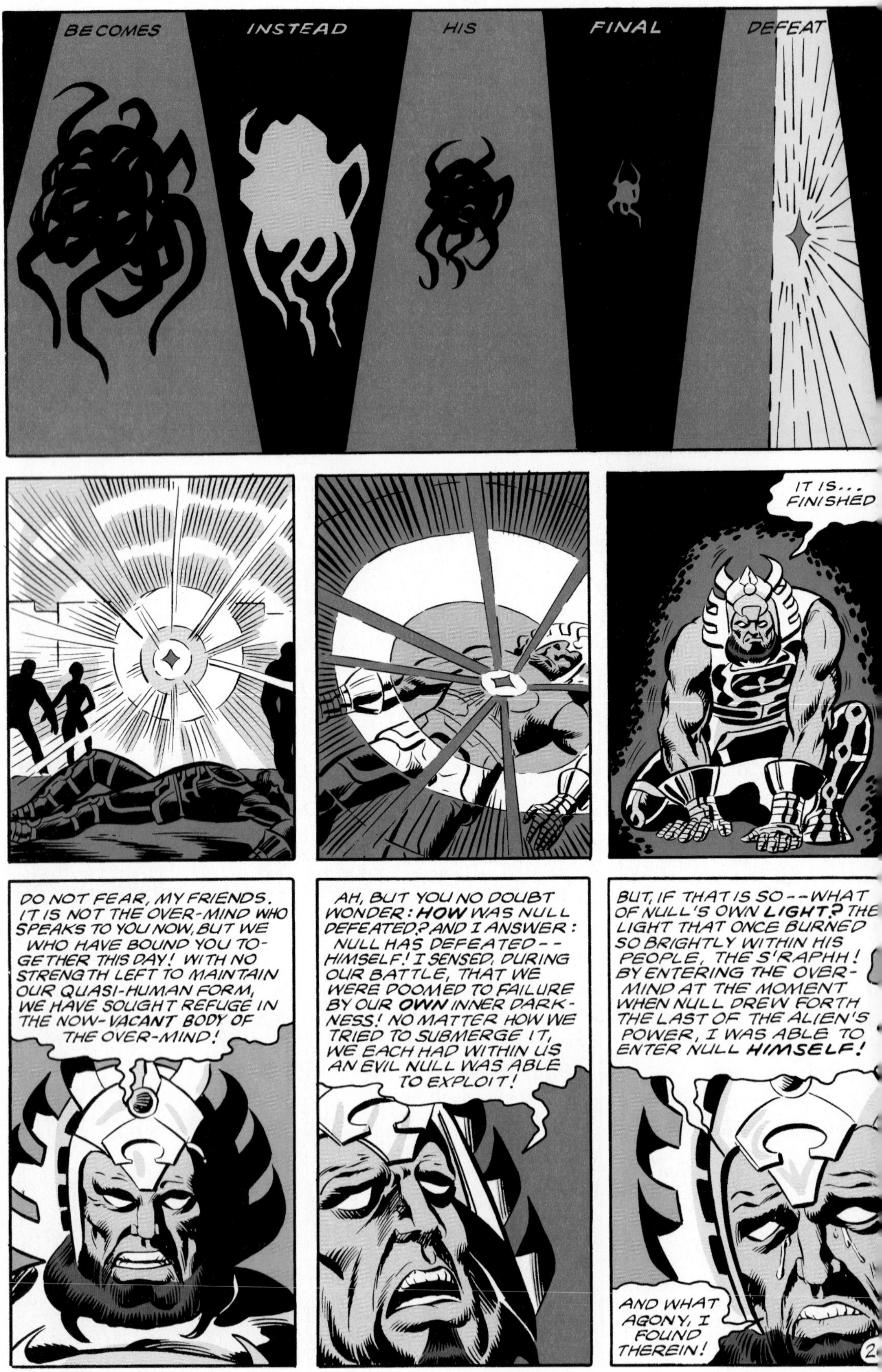
BECOMES
INSTEAD
HIS
FINAL
DEFEAT
IT IS... FINISHED
DO NOT FEAR, MY FRIENDS. IT IS NOT THE OVER-MIND WHO SPEAKS TO YOU NOW, BUT WE WHO HAVE BOUND YOU TOGETHER THIS DAY! WITH NO STRENGTH LEFT TO MAINTAIN OUR QUASI-HUMAN FORM, WE HAVE SOUGHT REFUGE IN THE NOW-VACANT BODY OF THE OVER-MIND!
AH, BUT YOU NO DOUBT WONDER: HOW WAS NULL DEFEATED? AND I ANSWER: NULL HAS DEFEATED--HIMSELF! I SENSED, DURING OUR BATTLE, THAT WE WERE DOOMED TO FAILURE BY OUR OWN INNER DARKNESS! NO MATTER HOW WE TRIED TO SUBMERGE IT, WE EACH HAD WITHIN US AN EVIL NULL WAS ABLE TO EXPLOIT!
BUT, IF THAT IS SO--WHAT OF NULL'S OWN LIGHT? THE LIGHT THAT ONCE BURNED SO BRIGHTLY WITHIN HIS PEOPLE, THE S'RAPHH! BY ENTERING THE OVER-MIND AT THE MOMENT WHEN NULL DREW FORTH THE LAST OF THE ALIEN'S POWER, I WAS ABLE TO ENTER NULL HIMSELF!
AND WHAT AGONY, I FOUND THEREIN!

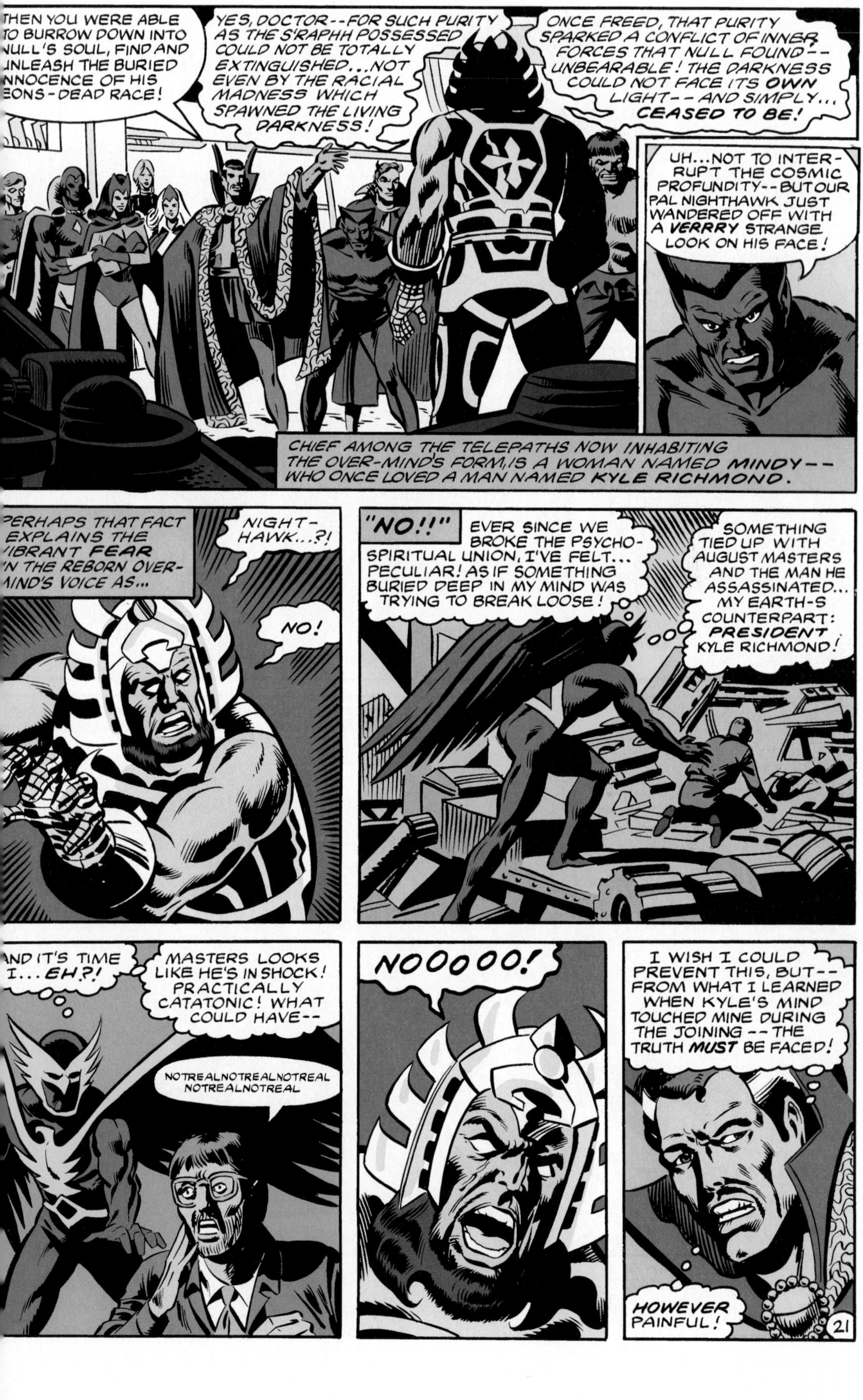

THEN YOU WERE ABLE TO BURROW DOWN INTO NULL'S SOUL, FIND AND UNLEASH THE BURIED INNOCENCE OF HIS EONS-DEAD RACE!
YES, DOCTOR--FOR SUCH PURITY AS THE S'RAPHH POSSESSED COULD NOT BE TOTALLY EXTINGUISHED...NOT EVEN BY THE RACIAL MADNESS WHICH SPAWNED THE LIVING DARKNESS!
ONCE FREED, THAT PURITY SPARKED A CONFLICT OF INNER FORCES THAT NULL FOUND--UNBEARABLE! THE DARKNESS COULD NOT FACE ITS OWN LIGHT--AND SIMPLY... CEASED TO BE!
UH...NOT TO INTERRUPT THE COSMIC PROFUNDITY--BUT OUR PAL NIGHTHAWK JUST WANDERED OFF WITH A VERRRY STRANGE LOOK ON HIS FACE!
CHIEF AMONG THE TELEPATHS NOW INHABITING THE OVER-MIND'S FORM, IS A WOMAN NAMED MINDY--WHO ONCE LOVED A MAN NAMED KYLE RICHMOND.
PERHAPS THAT FACT EXPLAINS THE VIBRANT FEAR IN THE REBORN OVER-MIND'S VOICE AS...
NIGHT-HAWK...?!
NO!
"NO!!"
EVER SINCE WE BROKE THE PSYCHO-SPIRITUAL UNION, I'VE FELT... PECULIAR! AS IF SOMETHING BURIED DEEP IN MY MIND WAS TRYING TO BREAK LOOSE!
SOMETHING TIED UP WITH AUGUST MASTERS AND THE MAN HE ASSASSINATED... MY EARTH-S COUNTERPART: PRESIDENT KYLE RICHMOND!
AND IT'S TIME I... EH?!
MASTERS LOOKS LIKE HE'S IN SHOCK! PRACTICALLY CATATONIC! WHAT COULD HAVE--
NOTREALNOTREALNOTREAL NOTREALNOTREAL
NOOOOO!
I WISH I COULD PREVENT THIS, BUT--FROM WHAT I LEARNED WHEN KYLE'S MIND TOUCHED MINE DURING THE JOINING--THE TRUTH MUST BE FACED!
HOWEVER PAINFUL!
21

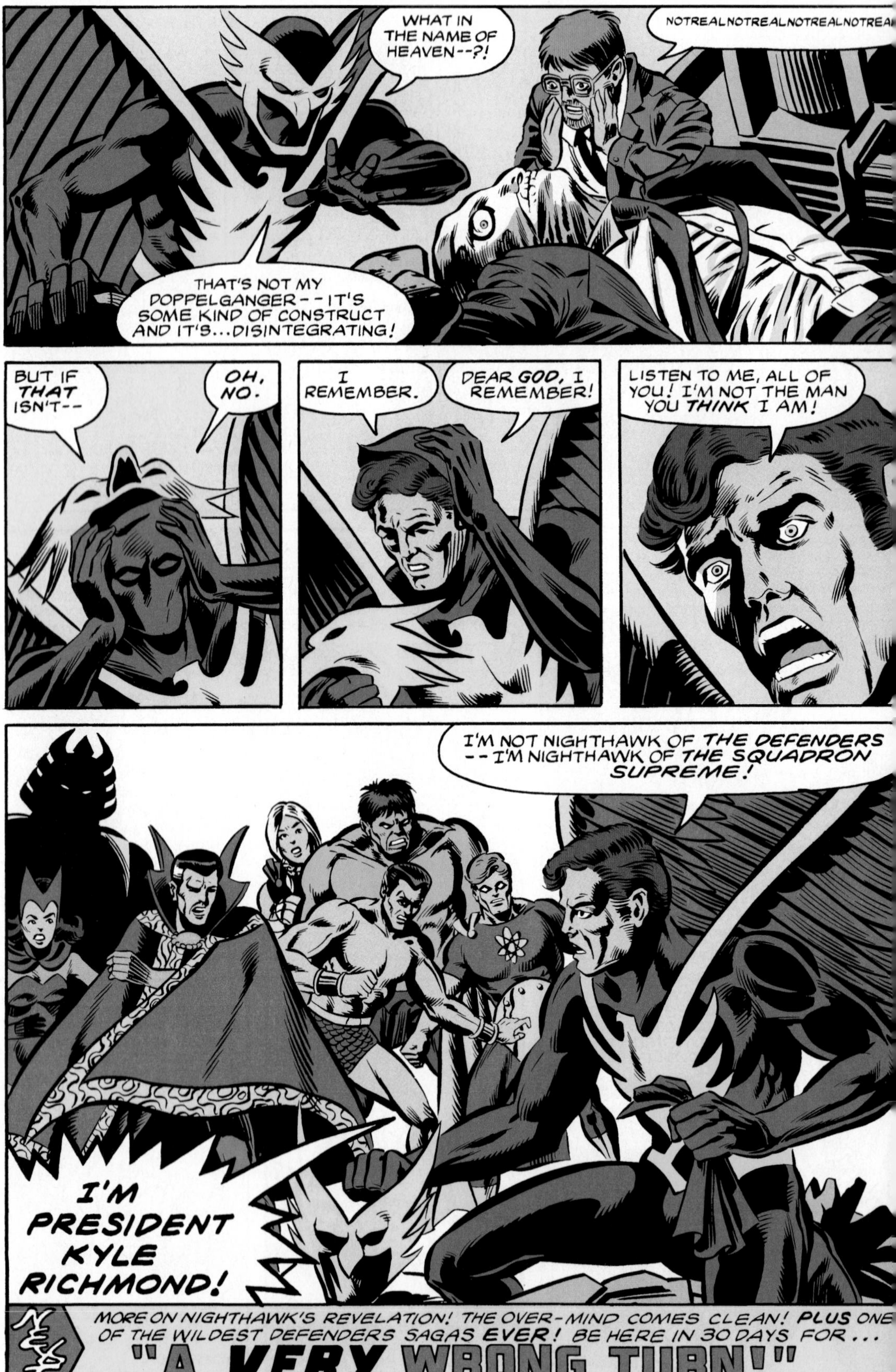
WHAT IN THE NAME OF HEAVEN--?!
NOTREALNOTREALNOTREALNOTREA
THAT'S NOT MY DOPPELGANGER--IT'S SOME KIND OF CONSTRUCT AND IT'S...DISINTEGRATING!
BUT IF THAT ISN'T--
OH, NO.
I REMEMBER.
DEAR GOD, I REMEMBER!
LISTEN TO ME, ALL OF YOU! I'M NOT THE MAN YOU THINK I AM!
I'M NOT NIGHTHAWK OF THE DEFENDERS --I'M NIGHTHAWK OF THE SQUADRON SUPREME!
I'M PRESIDENT KYLE RICHMOND!
MORE ON NIGHTHAWK'S REVELATION! THE OVER-MIND COMES CLEAN! PLUS ONE OF THE WILDEST DEFENDERS SAGAS EVER! BE HERE IN 30 DAYS FOR...
"A VERY WRONG TURN!"

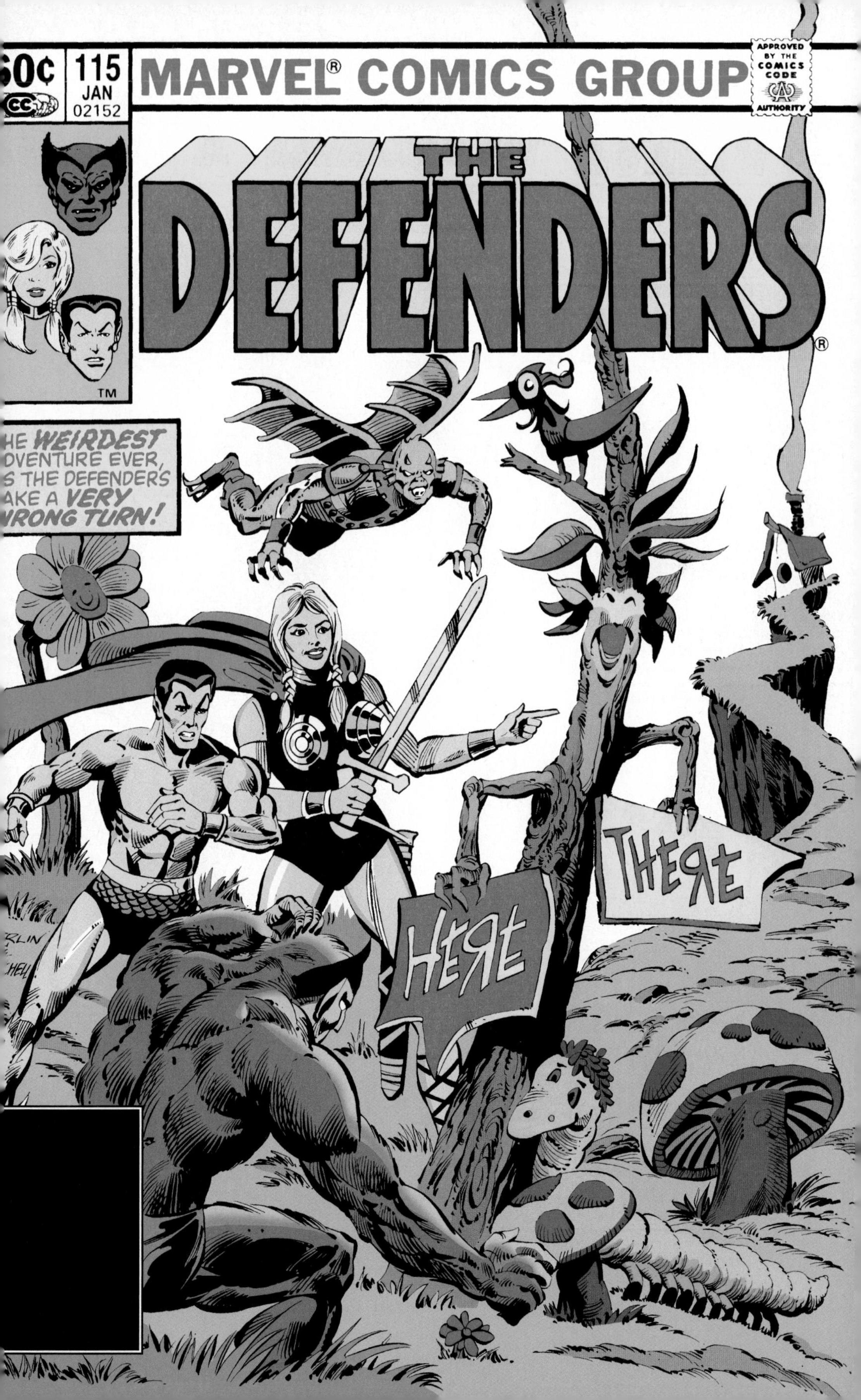
60¢
115
JAN
02152
MARVEL® COMICS GROUP
APPROVED BY THE COMICS CODE AUTHORITY
THE DEFENDERS®
TM
HE WEIRDEST
DVENTURE EVER,
S THE DEFENDER'S
AKE A VERY
RONG TURN!
THERE
HERE

IN A SHORT WHILE, FOUR OF *THE DEFENDERS* WILL BE TAKING...

A VERY WRONG TURN!

J.M. DeMATTEIS SCRIPT	*	DON PERLIN PENCILS	*	HILARY BARTA INKS	*	SHELLY LEFERMAN LETTERER	*	GEORGE ROUSSOS COLORIST	*	AL MILGROM EDITOR	*	JIM SHOOTER EDITOR-IN-CHIEF

BUT, FIRST--THERE'S A PRESSING QUESTION TO BE ANSWERED...

WHO AM I?!?

THE PLACE: THE PARALLEL PLANET CALLED EARTH-S WHERE, HOURS AGO, THE DEFENDERS AND THIS WORLD'S PREMIER SUPER-TEAM, THE SQUADRON SUPREME, DEFEATED THE MONSTROUS NULL--THE LIVING DARKNESS!

THE SPEAKER: KYLE RICHMOND, THE HIGH-FLYING NIGHTHAWK!

HIS PROBLEM? LISTEN...

I-I *THOUGHT* I KNEW WHO I WAS: A MILLIONAIRE... A DEFENDER... A SUPER HERO WHO BARELY ESCAPED A FIERY DEATH BY BEING MIRACULOUSLY TELEPORTED TO THIS EARTH!

BUT, UP THERE ON THE MOON, WHERE WE STOPPED NULL, SOMETHING ...SNAPPED INSIDE ME--

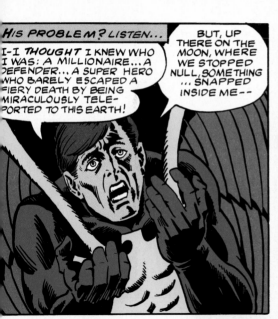

--AND I REMEMBERED!

AT LEAST I *THINK* I REMEMBER!

I'M *NOT* NIGHTHAWK! I'M THE KYLE RICHMOND OF *THIS* EARTH! BUT, HOW CAN THAT BE WHEN HE WAS...

--ASSASSINATED, KYLE? SHOT DOWN BY A MADMAN WHO THOUGHT HE WAS LIBERATING THE WORLD FROM A CORRUPT POLITICAL LEADER?

BUT YOU SAW FOR YOURSELF-- YOU *ALL* SAW--THAT *THAT* KYLE RICHMOND WAS NOTHING BUT A BIOLOGIC CONSTRUCT WHICH NULL USED AS A HIDING PLACE UNTIL HIS EVOLUTION WAS COMPLETE!

YOU ARE-- PRESIDENT KYLE RICHMOND!

THE OTHER KYLE-- THE *DEFENDERS'* KYLE--IS DEAD, AS HE HAS BEEN ALL THESE WEEKS!*

*SINCE DEFENDERS #106, TO BE EXACT --AL.

BUT-- HOW CAN SUCH A THING BE POSSIBLE?

NO, KYLE -- YOUR MEMORIES ARE CORRECT! SET THEM LOOSE--LISTEN TO THEM. YOU ARE WHO YOU BELIEVE YOU ARE!

IT IS POSSIBLE, SILVER SURFER, BECAUSE WE *MADE* IT POSSIBLE! ALTHOUGH WE INHABIT THE VACANT BODY OF THE ALIEN *OVER-MIND*, YOU KNOW THAT WE ARE, IN TRUTH, THE UNITED CONSCIOUSNESSES OF HALF A DOZEN TELEPATHIC MINDS --FUSED TOGETHER IN THE SAME EXPLOSION THAT KILLED KYLE.

"AND PERHAPS YOU ALSO KNOW THAT, CHIEF AMONG OUR JOINED MINDS, IS THAT OF AN UNSTABLE WOMAN NAMED *MINDY*-- WHO LOVED KYLE WITH ALL HER SOUL!"

ALL WRONG. ALL WRONG. ALL WRONG.

2

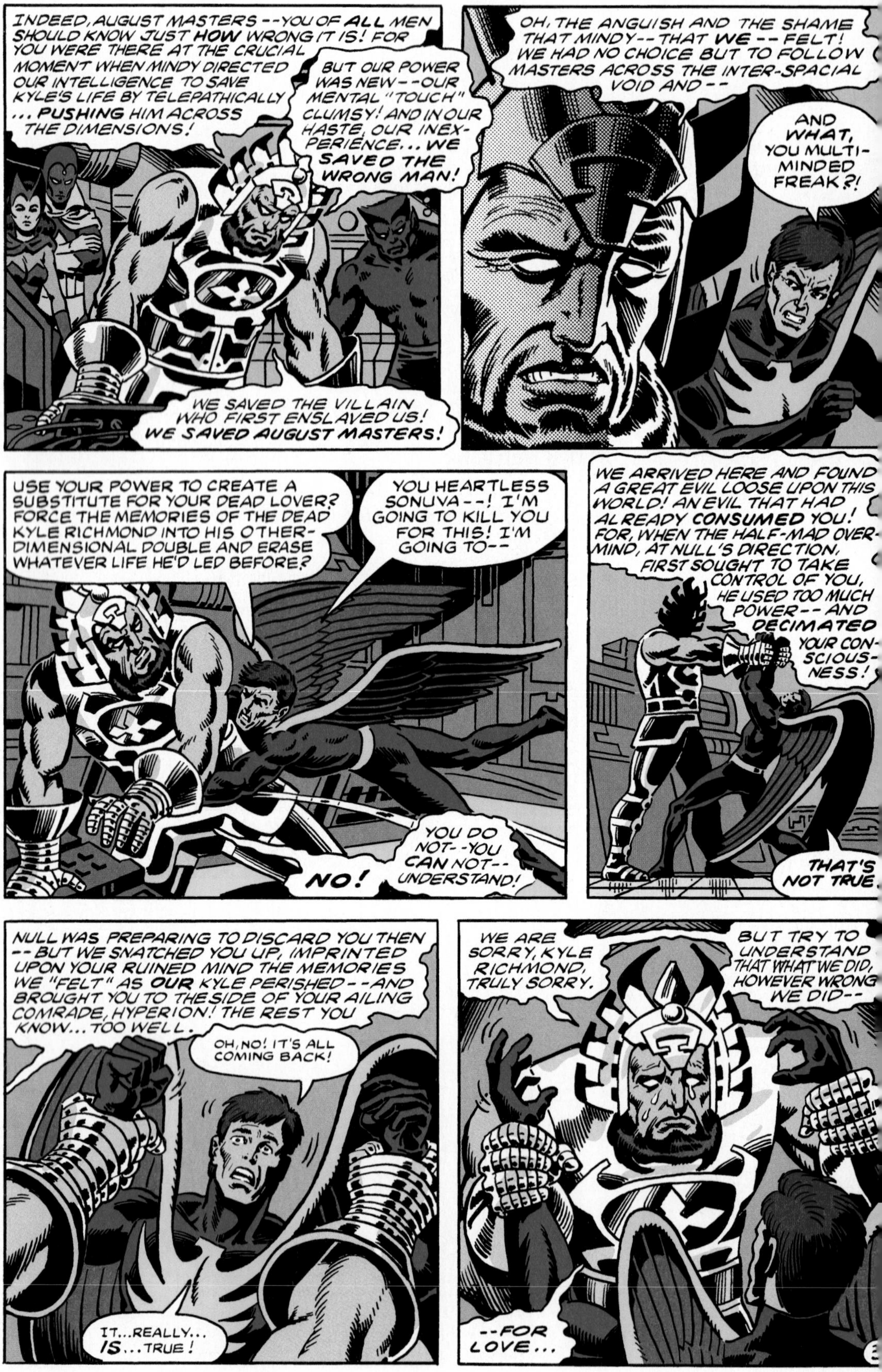
INDEED, AUGUST MASTERS --YOU OF ALL MEN SHOULD KNOW JUST HOW WRONG IT IS! FOR YOU WERE THERE AT THE CRUCIAL MOMENT WHEN MINDY DIRECTED OUR INTELLIGENCE TO SAVE KYLE'S LIFE BY TELEPATHICALLY ... PUSHING HIM ACROSS THE DIMENSIONS!
BUT OUR POWER WAS NEW--OUR MENTAL "TOUCH" CLUMSY! AND IN OUR HASTE, OUR INEXPERIENCE... WE SAVED THE WRONG MAN!
WE SAVED THE VILLAIN WHO FIRST ENSLAVED US! WE SAVED AUGUST MASTERS!
OH, THE ANGUISH AND THE SHAME THAT MINDY--THAT WE--FELT! WE HAD NO CHOICE BUT TO FOLLOW MASTERS ACROSS THE INTER-SPACIAL VOID AND--
AND WHAT, YOU MULTI-MINDED FREAK?!
USE YOUR POWER TO CREATE A SUBSTITUTE FOR YOUR DEAD LOVER? FORCE THE MEMORIES OF THE DEAD KYLE RICHMOND INTO HIS OTHER-DIMENSIONAL DOUBLE AND ERASE WHATEVER LIFE HE'D LED BEFORE?
YOU HEARTLESS SONUVA--! I'M GOING TO KILL YOU FOR THIS! I'M GOING TO--
NO!
YOU DO NOT--YOU CAN NOT--UNDERSTAND!
WE ARRIVED HERE AND FOUND A GREAT EVIL LOOSE UPON THIS WORLD! AN EVIL THAT HAD ALREADY CONSUMED YOU! FOR, WHEN THE HALF-MAD OVER-MIND, AT NULL'S DIRECTION, FIRST SOUGHT TO TAKE CONTROL OF YOU, HE USED TOO MUCH POWER--AND DECIMATED YOUR CONSCIOUSNESS!
THAT'S NOT TRUE
NULL WAS PREPARING TO DISCARD YOU THEN --BUT WE SNATCHED YOU UP, IMPRINTED UPON YOUR RUINED MIND THE MEMORIES WE "FELT" AS OUR KYLE PERISHED--AND BROUGHT YOU TO THE SIDE OF YOUR AILING COMRADE, HYPERION! THE REST YOU KNOW... TOO WELL.
OH, NO! IT'S ALL COMING BACK!
IT...REALLY... IS...TRUE!
WE ARE SORRY, KYLE RICHMOND, TRULY SORRY.
BUT TRY TO UNDERSTAND THAT WHAT WE DID, HOWEVER WRONG WE DID--
--FOR LOVE...

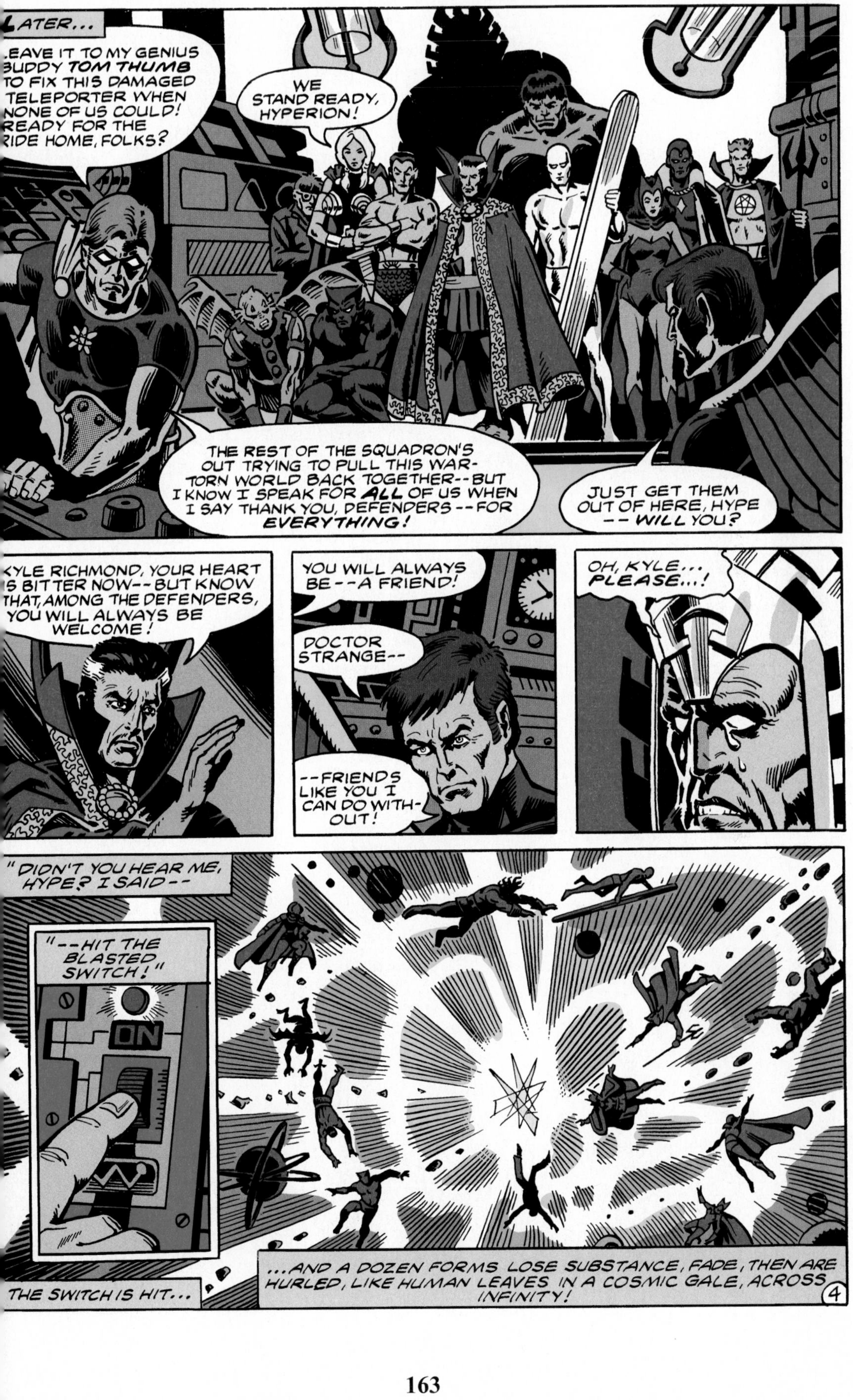
LATER...
LEAVE IT TO MY GENIUS BUDDY TOM THUMB TO FIX THIS DAMAGED TELEPORTER WHEN NONE OF US COULD! READY FOR THE RIDE HOME, FOLKS?
WE STAND READY, HYPERION!
THE REST OF THE SQUADRON'S OUT TRYING TO PULL THIS WAR-TORN WORLD BACK TOGETHER--BUT I KNOW I SPEAK FOR ALL OF US WHEN I SAY THANK YOU, DEFENDERS--FOR EVERYTHING!
JUST GET THEM OUT OF HERE, HYPE--WILL YOU?
KYLE RICHMOND, YOUR HEART IS BITTER NOW--BUT KNOW THAT, AMONG THE DEFENDERS, YOU WILL ALWAYS BE WELCOME!
YOU WILL ALWAYS BE--A FRIEND!
DOCTOR STRANGE--
--FRIENDS LIKE YOU I CAN DO WITHOUT!
OH, KYLE... PLEASE...!
"DIDN'T YOU HEAR ME, HYPE? I SAID--
"--HIT THE BLASTED SWITCH!"
ON
THE SWITCH IS HIT...
...AND A DOZEN FORMS LOSE SUBSTANCE, FADE, THEN ARE HURLED, LIKE HUMAN LEAVES IN A COSMIC GALE, ACROSS INFINITY!
4

BUT INFINITY ENCOMPASSES ALL CREATION, BOTH GREAT...

...AND SMALL.

AND EVEN THE MOST RANDOM, SEEMINGLY-INSIGNIFICANT EVENT...

PHASE TIMER

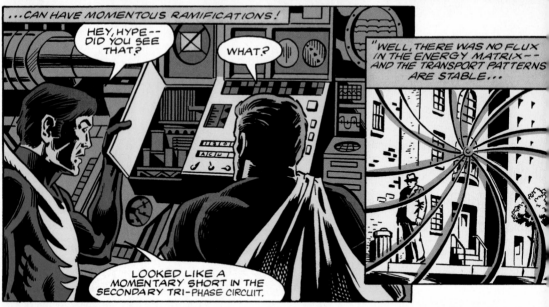
...CAN HAVE MOMENTOUS RAMIFICATIONS!

HEY, HYPE-- DID YOU SEE THAT?

WHAT?

"WELL, THERE WAS NO FLUX IN THE ENERGY MATRIX-- AND THE TRANSPORT PATTERNS ARE STABLE..."

LOOKED LIKE A MOMENTARY SHORT IN THE SECONDARY TRI-PHASE CIRCUIT.

"I'M SURE THERE WAS NO HARM DONE!"

HULK NEVER THOUGHT HE WOULD SAY IT-- BUT HE IS HAPPY TO BE BACK!

POSTPONE YOUR JOY A MOMENT, HULK! THERE IS SOMETHING AMISS HERE!

"FOUR OF OUR NUMBER DID NOT MATERIALIZE WITH US!"

OH, MY STARS AND GARTERS!

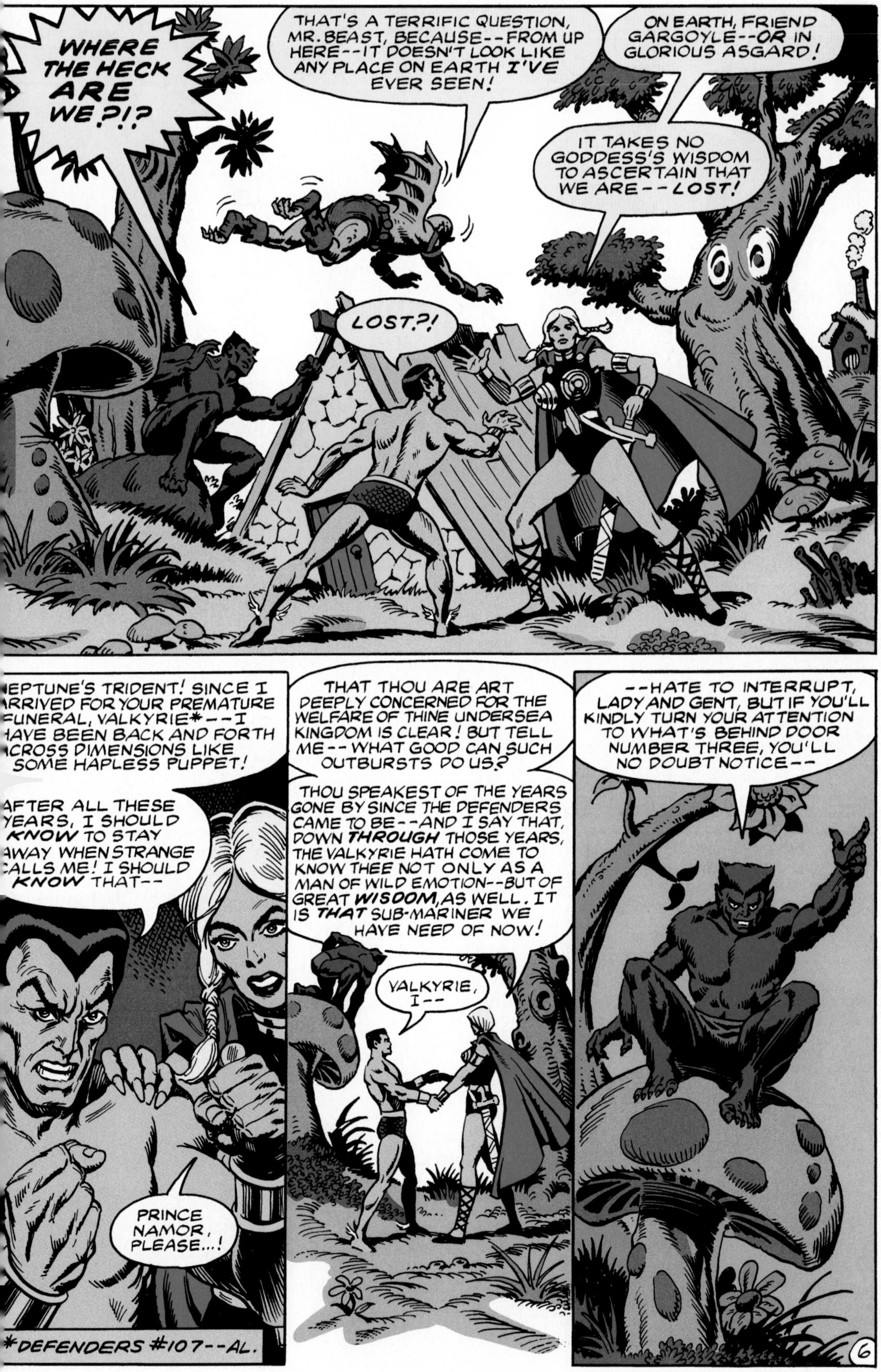

WHERE THE HECK ARE WE?!?
THAT'S A TERRIFIC QUESTION, MR. BEAST, BECAUSE--FROM UP HERE--IT DOESN'T LOOK LIKE ANY PLACE ON EARTH I'VE EVER SEEN!
ON EARTH, FRIEND GARGOYLE--OR IN GLORIOUS ASGARD!
IT TAKES NO GODDESS'S WISDOM TO ASCERTAIN THAT WE ARE--LOST!
LOST?!
EPTUNE'S TRIDENT! SINCE I RRIVED FOR YOUR PREMATURE FUNERAL, VALKYRIE*--I HAVE BEEN BACK AND FORTH CROSS DIMENSIONS LIKE SOME HAPLESS PUPPET!
AFTER ALL THESE YEARS, I SHOULD KNOW TO STAY AWAY WHEN STRANGE CALLS ME! I SHOULD KNOW THAT--
PRINCE NAMOR, PLEASE...!
*DEFENDERS #107--AL.
THAT THOU ARE ART DEEPLY CONCERNED FOR THE WELFARE OF THINE UNDERSEA KINGDOM IS CLEAR! BUT TELL ME--WHAT GOOD CAN SUCH OUTBURSTS DO US?
THOU SPEAKEST OF THE YEARS GONE BY SINCE THE DEFENDERS CAME TO BE--AND I SAY THAT, DOWN THROUGH THOSE YEARS, THE VALKYRIE HATH COME TO KNOW THEE NOT ONLY AS A MAN OF WILD EMOTION--BUT OF GREAT WISDOM, AS WELL. IT IS THAT SUB-MARINER WE HAVE NEED OF NOW!
VALKYRIE, I--
--HATE TO INTERRUPT, LADY AND GENT, BUT IF YOU'LL KINDLY TURN YOUR ATTENTION TO WHAT'S BEHIND DOOR NUMBER THREE, YOU'LL NO DOUBT NOTICE--
6

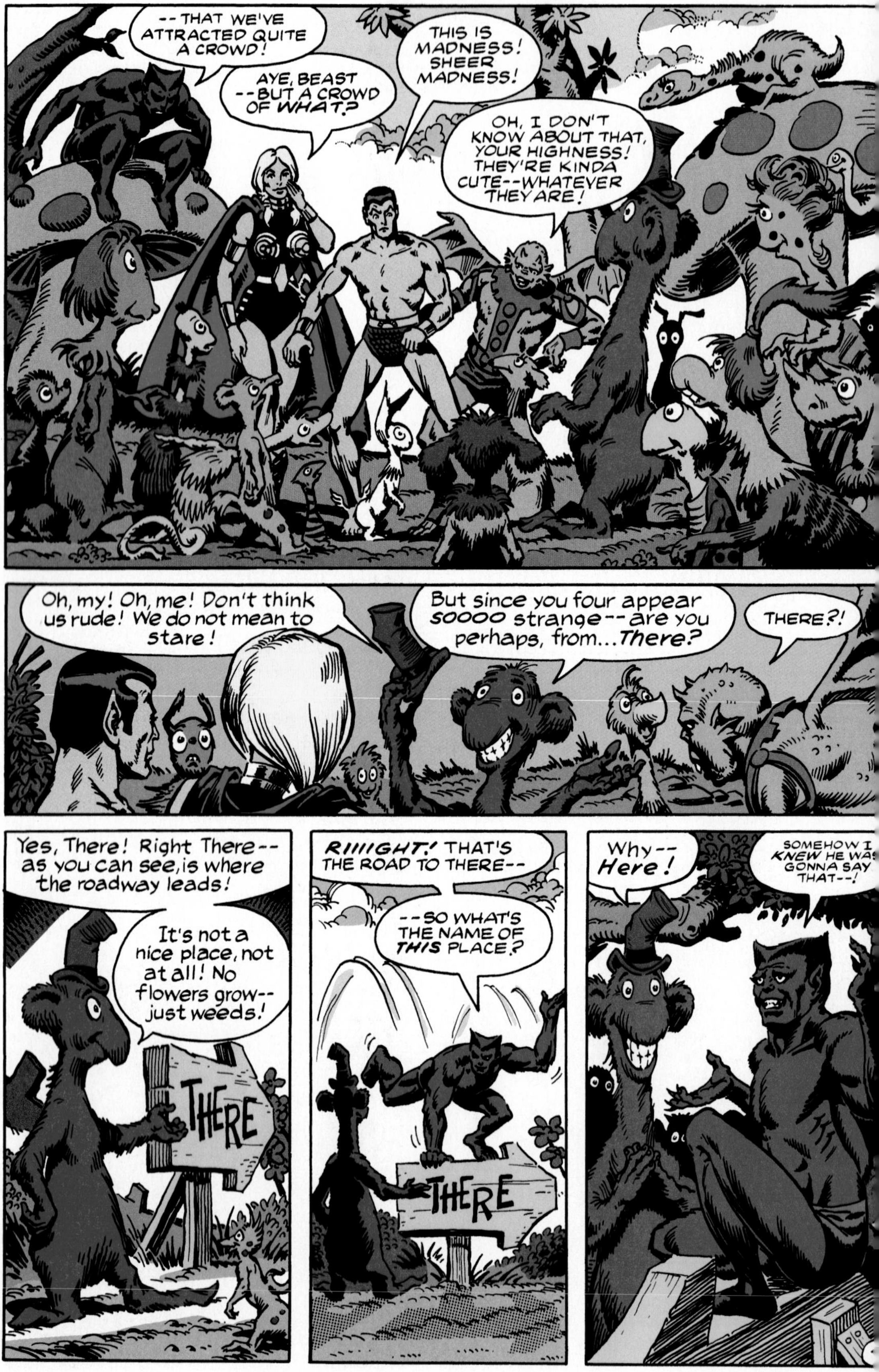

--THAT WE'VE ATTRACTED QUITE A CROWD!
AYE, BEAST --BUT A CROWD OF WHAT?
THIS IS MADNESS! SHEER MADNESS!
OH, I DON'T KNOW ABOUT THAT, YOUR HIGHNESS! THEY'RE KINDA CUTE--WHATEVER THEY ARE!
Oh, my! Oh, me! Don't think us rude! We do not mean to stare!
But since you four appear soooo strange--are you perhaps, from...There?
THERE?!
Yes, There! Right There--as you can see, is where the roadway leads!
It's not a nice place, not at all! No flowers grow--just weeds!
THERE
RIIIGHT! THAT'S THE ROAD TO THERE--
--SO WHAT'S THE NAME OF THIS PLACE?
THERE
Why--Here!
SOMEHOW I KNEW HE WAS GONNA SAY THAT--!

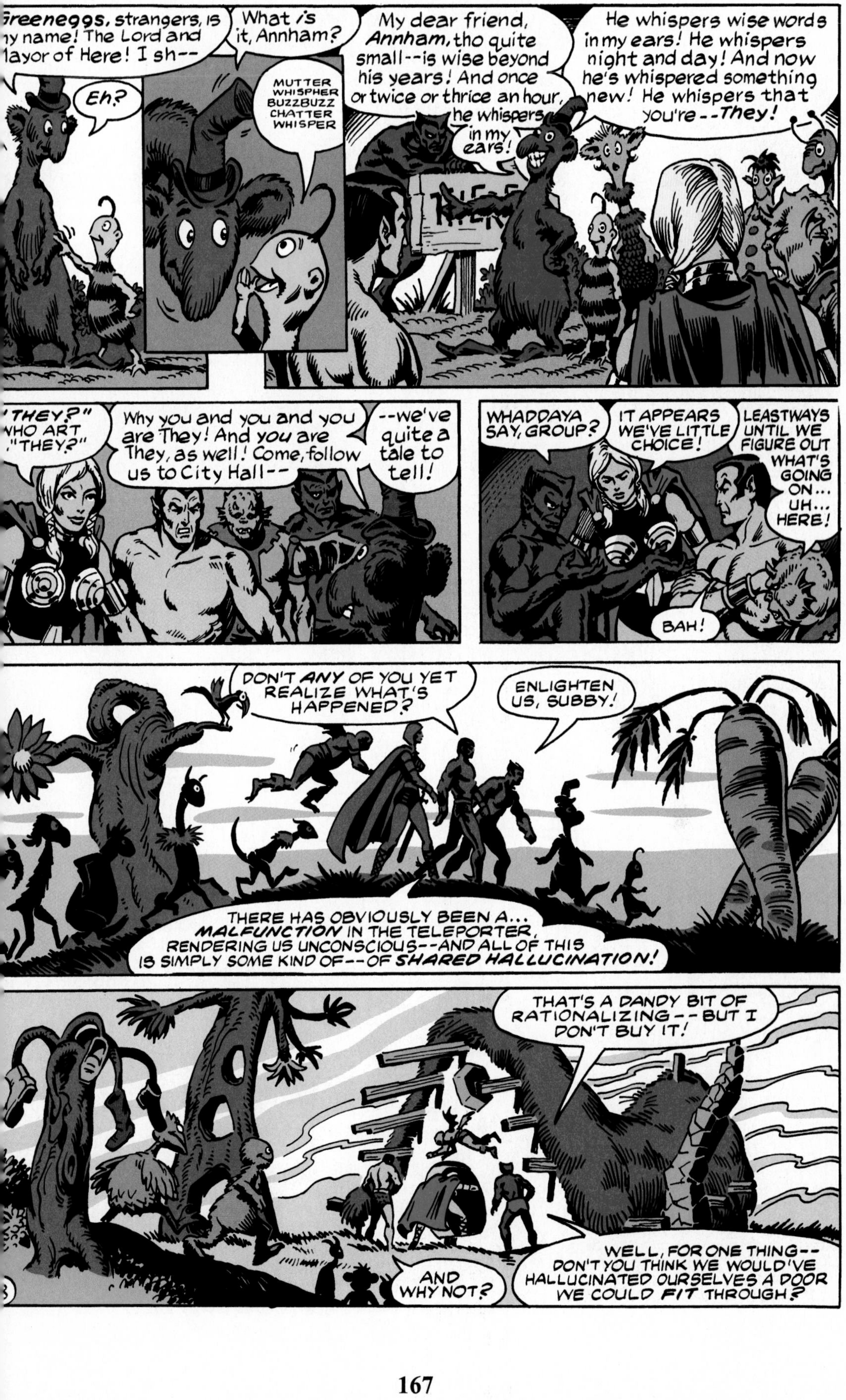
Greeneggs, strangers, is my name! The Lord and Mayor of Here! I sh--
Eh?
What is it, Annham?
MUTTER WHISPHER BUZZBUZZ CHATTER WHISPER
My dear friend, Annham, tho quite small--is wise beyond his years! And once or twice or thrice an hour, he whispers in my ears!
He whispers wise words in my ears! He whispers night and day! And now he's whispered something new! He whispers that you're --They!
"THEY?" WHO ART "THEY?"
Why you and you and you are They! And you are They, as well! Come, follow us to City Hall--
--we've quite a tale to tell!
WHADDAYA SAY, GROUP?
IT APPEARS WE'VE LITTLE CHOICE!
LEASTWAYS UNTIL WE FIGURE OUT WHAT'S GOING ON... UH... HERE!
BAH!
DON'T ANY OF YOU YET REALIZE WHAT'S HAPPENED?
ENLIGHTEN US, SUBBY!
THERE HAS OBVIOUSLY BEEN A... MALFUNCTION IN THE TELEPORTER, RENDERING US UNCONSCIOUS--AND ALL OF THIS IS SIMPLY SOME KIND OF--OF SHARED HALLUCINATION!
THAT'S A DANDY BIT OF RATIONALIZING--BUT I DON'T BUY IT!
AND WHY NOT?
WELL, FOR ONE THING--DON'T YOU THINK WE WOULD'VE HALLUCINATED OURSELVES A DOOR WE COULD FIT THROUGH?

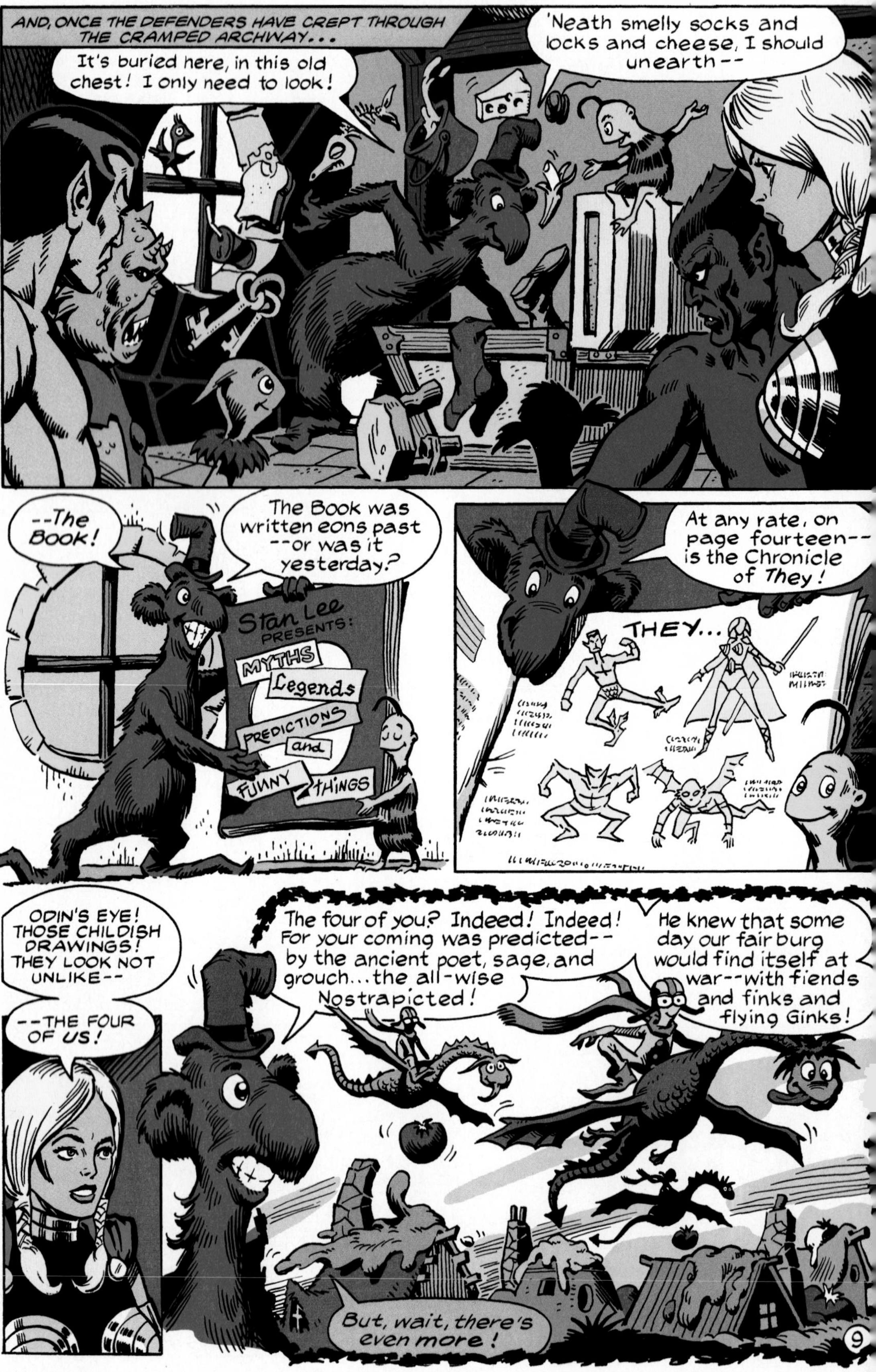
AND, ONCE THE DEFENDERS HAVE CREPT THROUGH THE CRAMPED ARCHWAY...
It's buried here, in this old chest! I only need to look!
'Neath smelly socks and locks and cheese, I should unearth --
--The Book!
The Book was written eons past --or was it yesterday?
Stan Lee PRESENTS: MYTHS Legends PREDICTIONS and FUNNY THINGS
At any rate, on page fourteen-- is the Chronicle of They!
THEY...
ODIN'S EYE! THOSE CHILDISH DRAWINGS! THEY LOOK NOT UNLIKE--
--THE FOUR OF US!
The four of you? Indeed! Indeed! For your coming was predicted-- by the ancient poet, sage, and grouch... the all-wise Nostrapicted!
He knew that some day our fair burg would find itself at war--with fiends and finks and flying Ginks!
But, wait, there's even more!
9

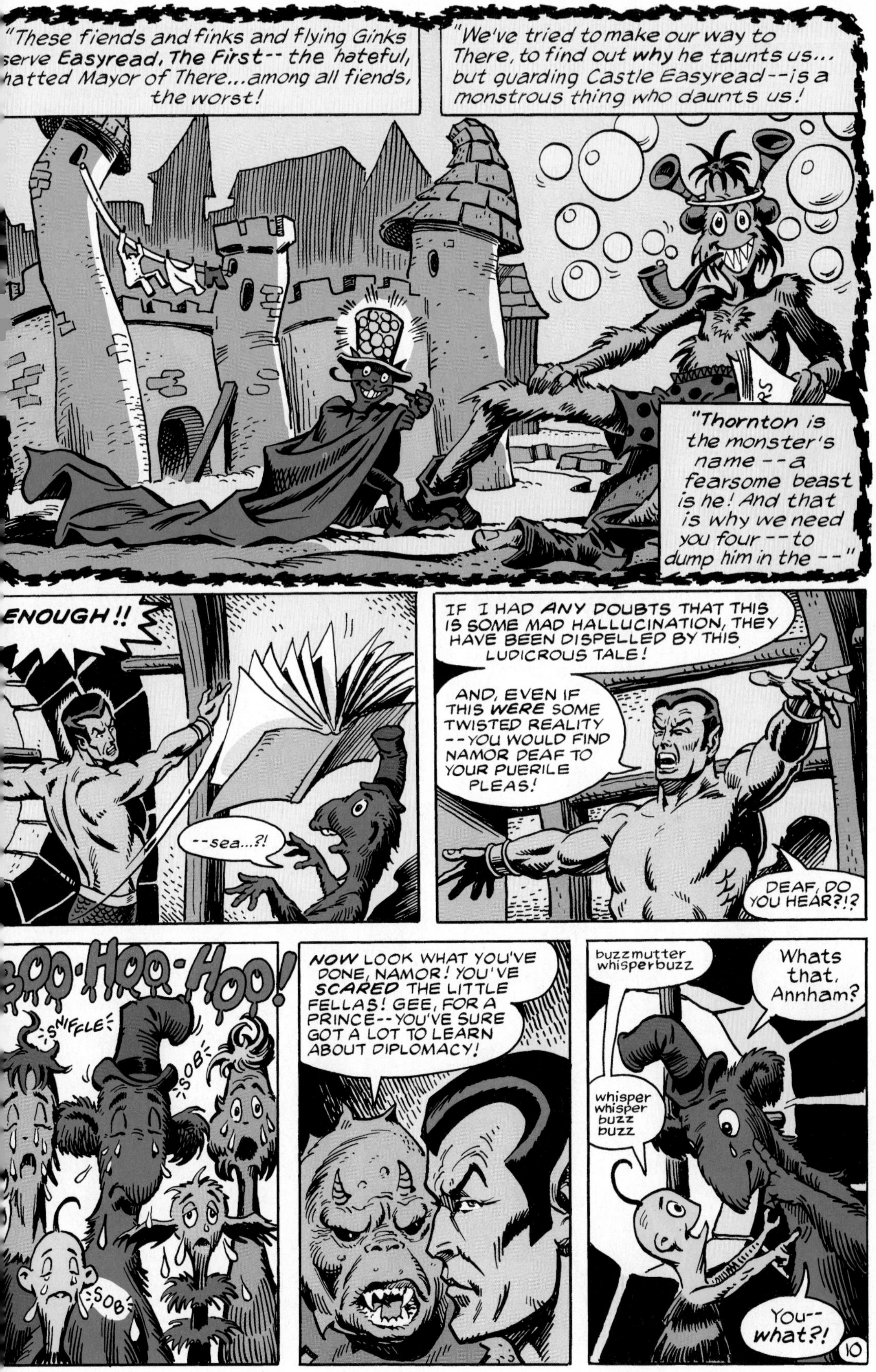
"These fiends and finks and flying Ginks serve Easyread, The First-- the hateful, hatted Mayor of There...among all fiends, the worst!
"We've tried to make our way to There, to find out why he taunts us... but guarding Castle Easyread--is a monstrous thing who daunts us!
"Thornton is the monster's name--a fearsome beast is he! And that is why we need you four--to dump him in the--"
ENOUGH!!
--sea...?!
IF I HAD ANY DOUBTS THAT THIS IS SOME MAD HALLUCINATION, THEY HAVE BEEN DISPELLED BY THIS LUDICROUS TALE!
AND, EVEN IF THIS WERE SOME TWISTED REALITY--YOU WOULD FIND NAMOR DEAF TO YOUR PUERILE PLEAS!
DEAF, DO YOU HEAR?!?
BOO-HOO-HOO!
SNIFFLE
SOB
SOB
NOW LOOK WHAT YOU'VE DONE, NAMOR! YOU'VE SCARED THE LITTLE FELLAS! GEE, FOR A PRINCE--YOU'VE SURE GOT A LOT TO LEARN ABOUT DIPLOMACY!
buzzmutter whisperbuzz
Whats that, Annham?
whisper whisper buzz buzz
You--what?!
10

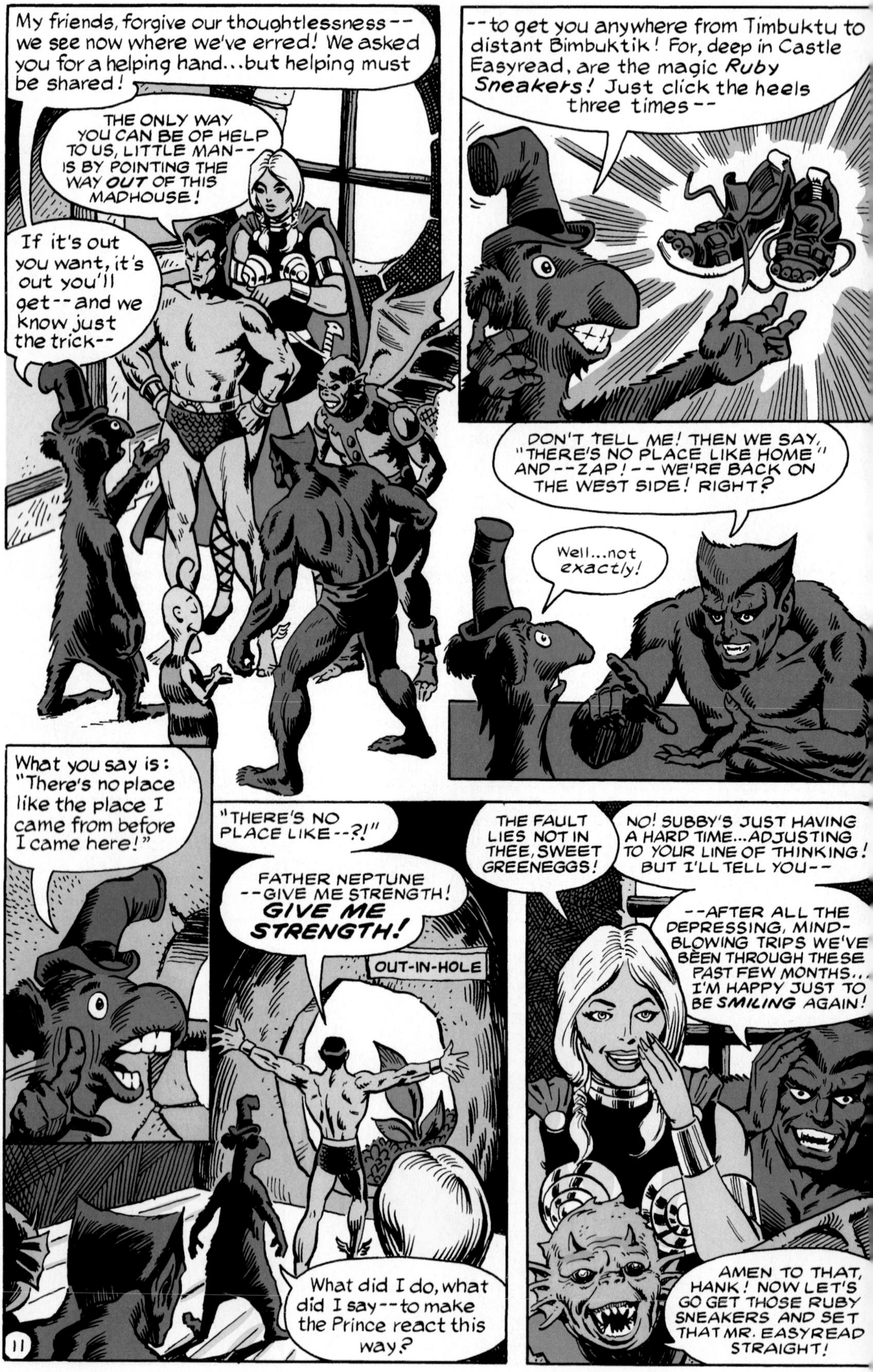
My friends, forgive our thoughtlessness -- we see now where we've erred! We asked you for a helping hand...but helping must be shared!
THE ONLY WAY YOU CAN BE OF HELP TO US, LITTLE MAN-- IS BY POINTING THE WAY OUT OF THIS MADHOUSE!
If it's out you want, it's out you'll get--and we know just the trick--
--to get you anywhere from Timbuktu to distant Bimbuktik! For, deep in Castle Easyread, are the magic Ruby Sneakers! Just click the heels three times--
DON'T TELL ME! THEN WE SAY, "THERE'S NO PLACE LIKE HOME" AND --ZAP!-- WE'RE BACK ON THE WEST SIDE! RIGHT?
Well...not exactly!
What you say is: "There's no place like the place I came from before I came here!"
"THERE'S NO PLACE LIKE--?!"
FATHER NEPTUNE --GIVE ME STRENGTH! GIVE ME STRENGTH!
OUT-IN-HOLE
What did I do, what did I say--to make the Prince react this way?
11
THE FAULT LIES NOT IN THEE, SWEET GREENEGGS!
NO! SUBBY'S JUST HAVING A HARD TIME...ADJUSTING TO YOUR LINE OF THINKING! BUT I'LL TELL YOU--
--AFTER ALL THE DEPRESSING, MIND-BLOWING TRIPS WE'VE BEEN THROUGH THESE PAST FEW MONTHS... I'M HAPPY JUST TO BE SMILING AGAIN!
AMEN TO THAT, HANK! NOW LET'S GO GET THOSE RUBY SNEAKERS AND SET THAT MR. EASYREAD STRAIGHT!

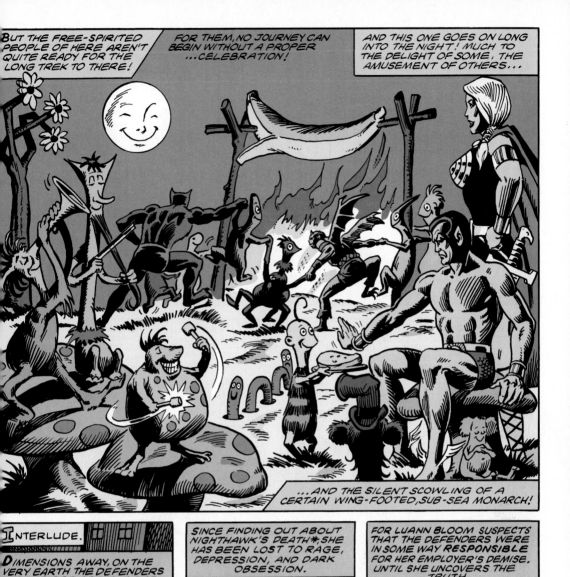

BUT THE FREE-SPIRITED PEOPLE OF HERE AREN'T QUITE READY FOR THE LONG TREK TO THERE!

FOR THEM, NO JOURNEY CAN BEGIN WITHOUT A PROPER ...CELEBRATION!

AND THIS ONE GOES ON LONG INTO THE NIGHT! MUCH TO THE DELIGHT OF SOME, THE AMUSEMENT OF OTHERS...

...AND THE SILENT SCOWLING OF A CERTAIN WING-FOOTED, SUB-SEA MONARCH!

INTERLUDE.

DIMENSIONS AWAY, ON THE VERY EARTH THE DEFENDERS WISH TO SEE AGAIN, A SAD-EYED YOUNG WOMAN PACES NERVOUSLY.

HER NAME IS LUANN BLOOM-- UNTIL RECENTLY, KYLE RICHMOND'S LIVE-IN NURSE... AND FRIEND.

SINCE FINDING OUT ABOUT NIGHTHAWK'S DEATH*, SHE HAS BEEN LOST TO RAGE, DEPRESSION, AND DARK OBSESSION.

*DEFENDERS #110 -- AL

FOR LUANN BLOOM SUSPECTS THAT THE DEFENDERS WERE IN SOME WAY RESPONSIBLE FOR HER EMPLOYER'S DEMISE. UNTIL SHE UNCOVERS THE TRUTH...

...SHE WILL NOT REST EASY.

12

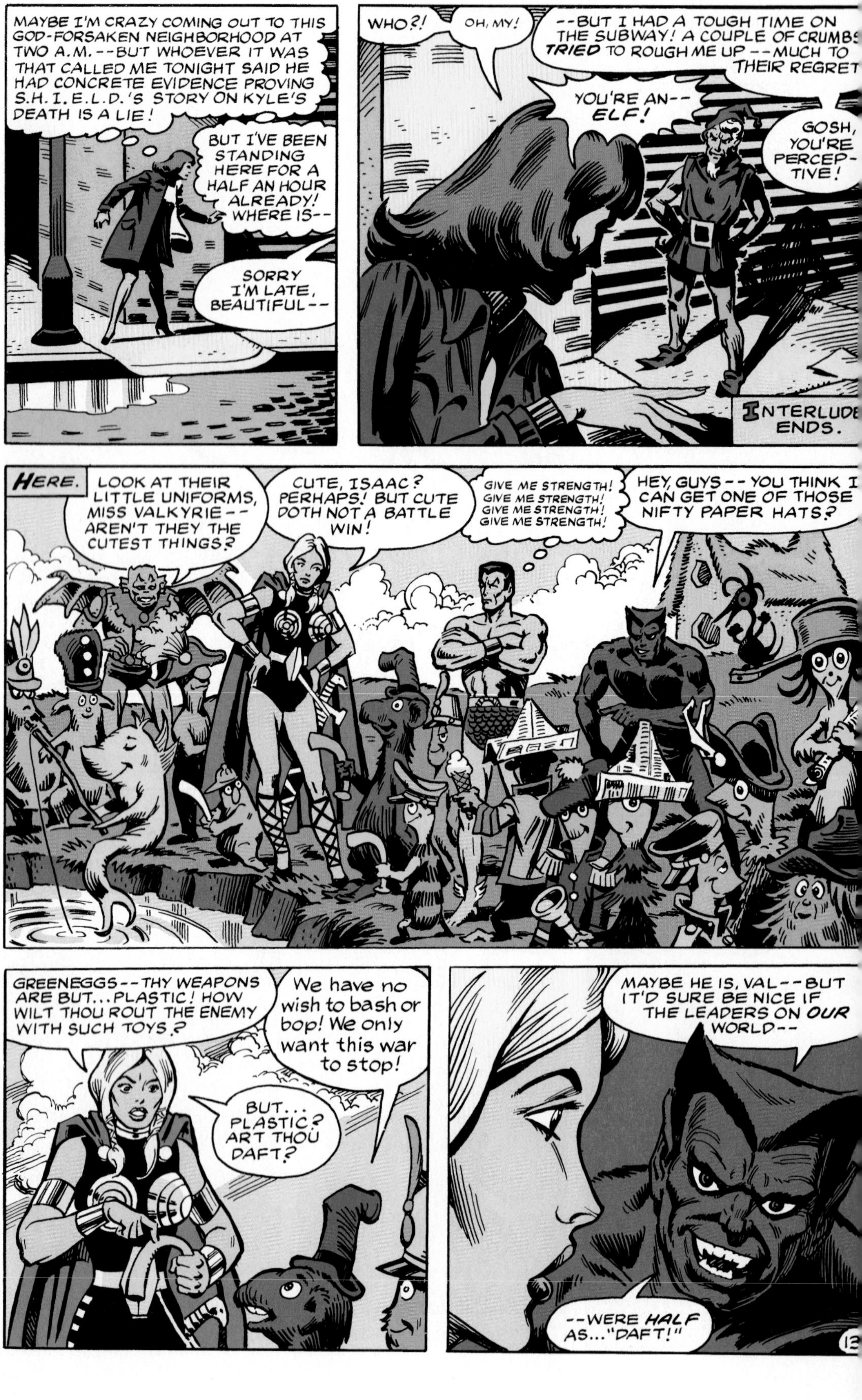
MAYBE I'M CRAZY COMING OUT TO THIS GOD-FORSAKEN NEIGHBORHOOD AT TWO A.M.--BUT WHOEVER IT WAS THAT CALLED ME TONIGHT SAID HE HAD CONCRETE EVIDENCE PROVING S.H.I.E.L.D.'S STORY ON KYLE'S DEATH IS A LIE!
BUT I'VE BEEN STANDING HERE FOR A HALF AN HOUR ALREADY! WHERE IS--
SORRY I'M LATE, BEAUTIFUL--
WHO?!
OH, MY!
--BUT I HAD A TOUGH TIME ON THE SUBWAY! A COUPLE OF CRUMBS TRIED TO ROUGH ME UP--MUCH TO THEIR REGRET
YOU'RE AN--ELF!
GOSH, YOU'RE PERCEPTIVE!
INTERLUDE ENDS.
HERE.
LOOK AT THEIR LITTLE UNIFORMS, MISS VALKYRIE--AREN'T THEY THE CUTEST THINGS?
CUTE, ISAAC? PERHAPS! BUT CUTE DOTH NOT A BATTLE WIN!
GIVE ME STRENGTH! GIVE ME STRENGTH! GIVE ME STRENGTH! GIVE ME STRENGTH!
HEY, GUYS--YOU THINK I CAN GET ONE OF THOSE NIFTY PAPER HATS?
GREENEGGS--THY WEAPONS ARE BUT...PLASTIC! HOW WILT THOU ROUT THE ENEMY WITH SUCH TOYS?
We have no wish to bash or bop! We only want this war to stop!
BUT... PLASTIC? ART THOU DAFT?
MAYBE HE IS, VAL--BUT IT'D SURE BE NICE IF THE LEADERS ON OUR WORLD--
--WERE HALF AS..."DAFT!"
13

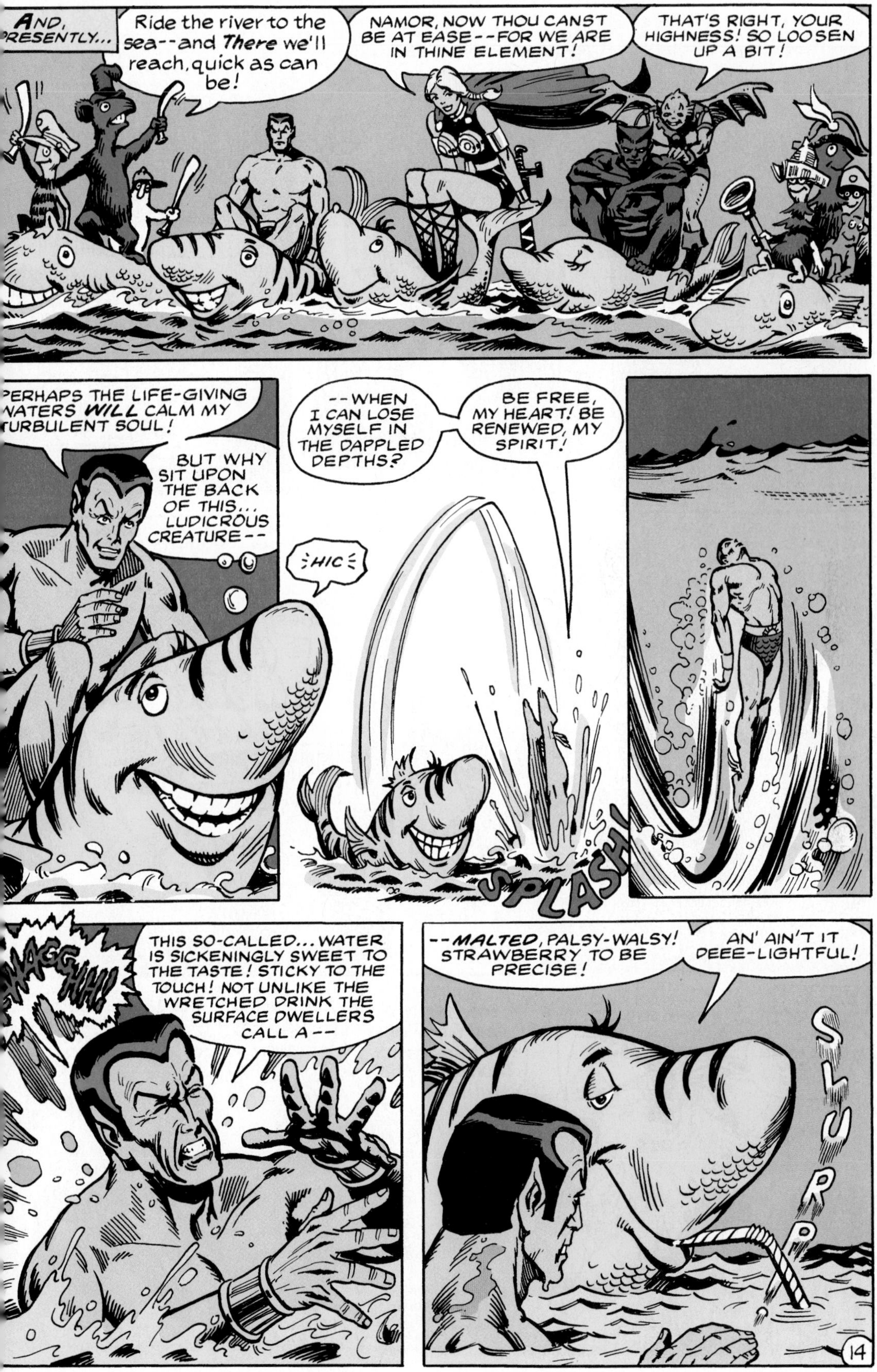
AND, PRESENTLY...
Ride the river to the sea--and There we'll reach, quick as can be!
NAMOR, NOW THOU CANST BE AT EASE--FOR WE ARE IN THINE ELEMENT!
THAT'S RIGHT, YOUR HIGHNESS! SO LOOSEN UP A BIT!
PERHAPS THE LIFE-GIVING WATERS WILL CALM MY TURBULENT SOUL!
BUT WHY SIT UPON THE BACK OF THIS... LUDICROUS CREATURE--
HIC
--WHEN I CAN LOSE MYSELF IN THE DAPPLED DEPTHS?
BE FREE, MY HEART! BE RENEWED, MY SPIRIT!
SPLASH!
HAGGHH!
THIS SO-CALLED... WATER IS SICKENINGLY SWEET TO THE TASTE! STICKY TO THE TOUCH! NOT UNLIKE THE WRETCHED DRINK THE SURFACE DWELLERS CALL A--
--MALTED, PALSY-WALSY! STRAWBERRY TO BE PRECISE!
AN' AIN'T IT DEEE-LIGHTFUL!
SLURP
14

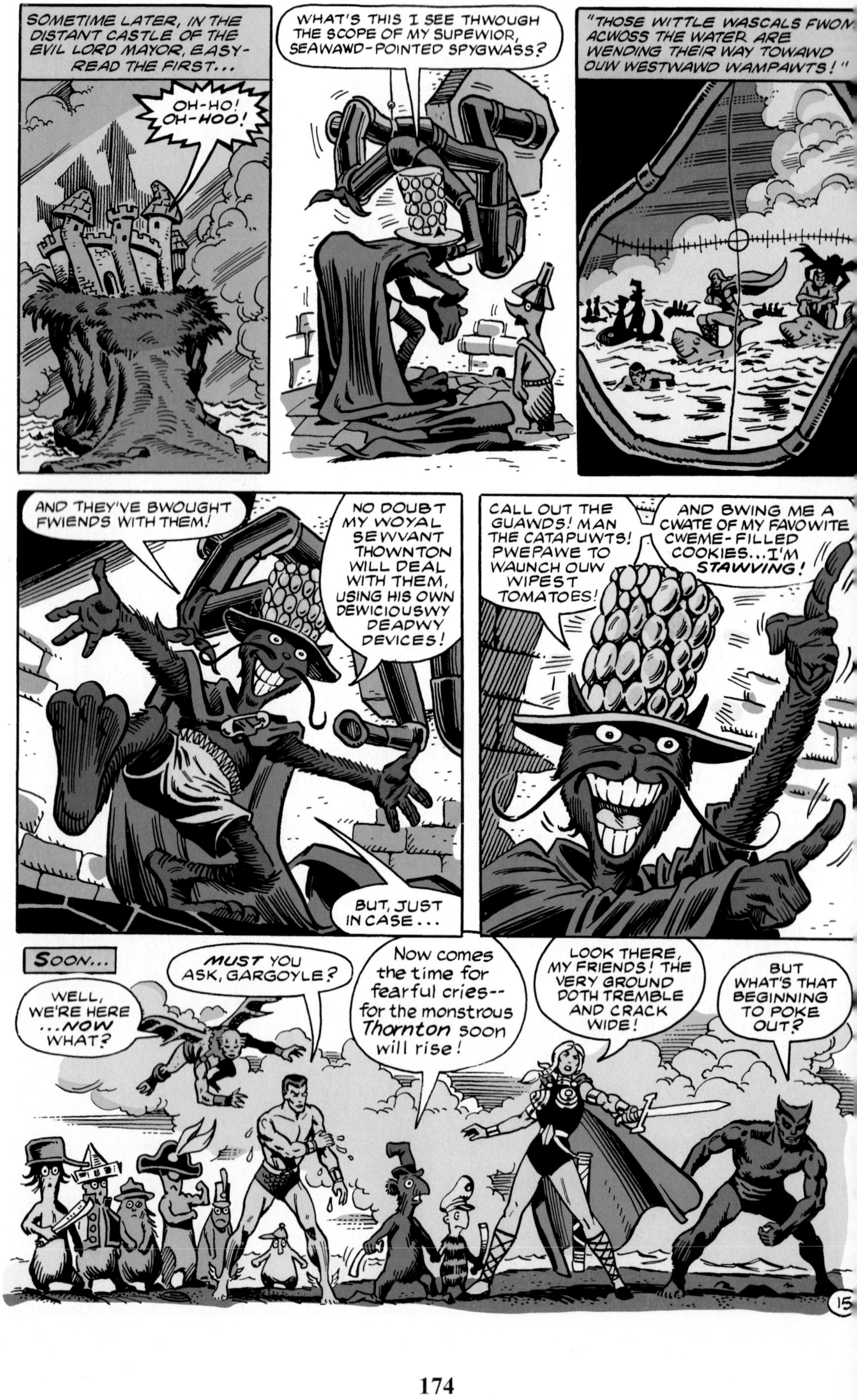
SOMETIME LATER, IN THE DISTANT CASTLE OF THE EVIL LORD MAYOR, EASY-READ THE FIRST...
OH-HO! OH-HOO!
WHAT'S THIS I SEE THWOUGH THE SCOPE OF MY SUPEWIOR, SEAWAWD-POINTED SPYGWASS?
"THOSE WITTLE WASCALS FWOM ACWOSS THE WATER ARE WENDING THEIR WAY TOWAWD OUW WESTWAWD WAMPAWTS!"
AND THEY'VE BWOUGHT FWIENDS WITH THEM!
NO DOUBT MY WOYAL SEWVANT THOWNTON WILL DEAL WITH THEM, USING HIS OWN DEWICIOUSWY DEADWY DEVICES!
BUT, JUST IN CASE...
CALL OUT THE GUAWDS! MAN THE CATAPUWTS! PWEPAWE TO WAUNCH OUW WIPEST TOMATOES!
AND BWING ME A CWATE OF MY FAVOWITE CWEME-FILLED COOKIES...I'M STAWVING!
SOON...
WELL, WE'RE HERE ...NOW WHAT?
MUST YOU ASK, GARGOYLE?
Now comes the time for fearful cries-- for the monstrous Thornton soon will rise!
LOOK THERE, MY FRIENDS! THE VERY GROUND DOTH TREMBLE AND CRACK WIDE!
BUT WHAT'S THAT BEGINNING TO POKE OUT?
15

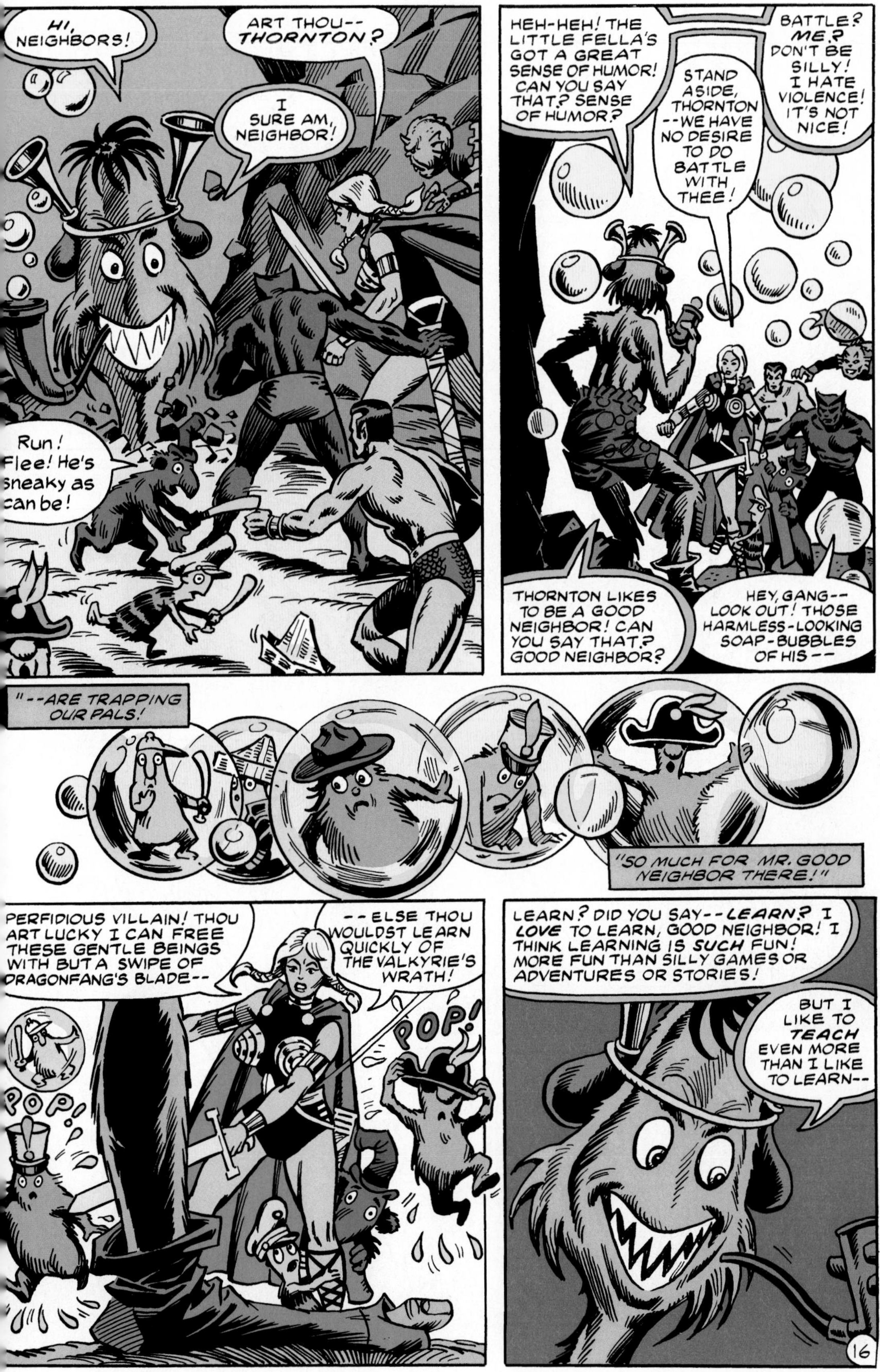

HI, NEIGHBORS!
ART THOU-- THORNTON?
I SURE AM, NEIGHBOR!
Run! Flee! He's sneaky as can be!
HEH-HEH! THE LITTLE FELLA'S GOT A GREAT SENSE OF HUMOR! CAN YOU SAY THAT? SENSE OF HUMOR?
STAND ASIDE, THORNTON --WE HAVE NO DESIRE TO DO BATTLE WITH THEE!
BATTLE? ME? DON'T BE SILLY! I HATE VIOLENCE! IT'S NOT NICE!
THORNTON LIKES TO BE A GOOD NEIGHBOR! CAN YOU SAY THAT? GOOD NEIGHBOR?
HEY, GANG-- LOOK OUT! THOSE HARMLESS-LOOKING SOAP-BUBBLES OF HIS--
"--ARE TRAPPING OUR PALS!
"SO MUCH FOR MR. GOOD NEIGHBOR THERE!"
PERFIDIOUS VILLAIN! THOU ART LUCKY I CAN FREE THESE GENTLE BEINGS WITH BUT A SWIPE OF DRAGONFANG'S BLADE--
--ELSE THOU WOULDST LEARN QUICKLY OF THE VALKYRIE'S WRATH!
POP!
POP!
LEARN? DID YOU SAY--LEARN? I LOVE TO LEARN, GOOD NEIGHBOR! I THINK LEARNING IS SUCH FUN! MORE FUN THAN SILLY GAMES OR ADVENTURES OR STORIES!
BUT I LIKE TO TEACH EVEN MORE THAN I LIKE TO LEARN--
16

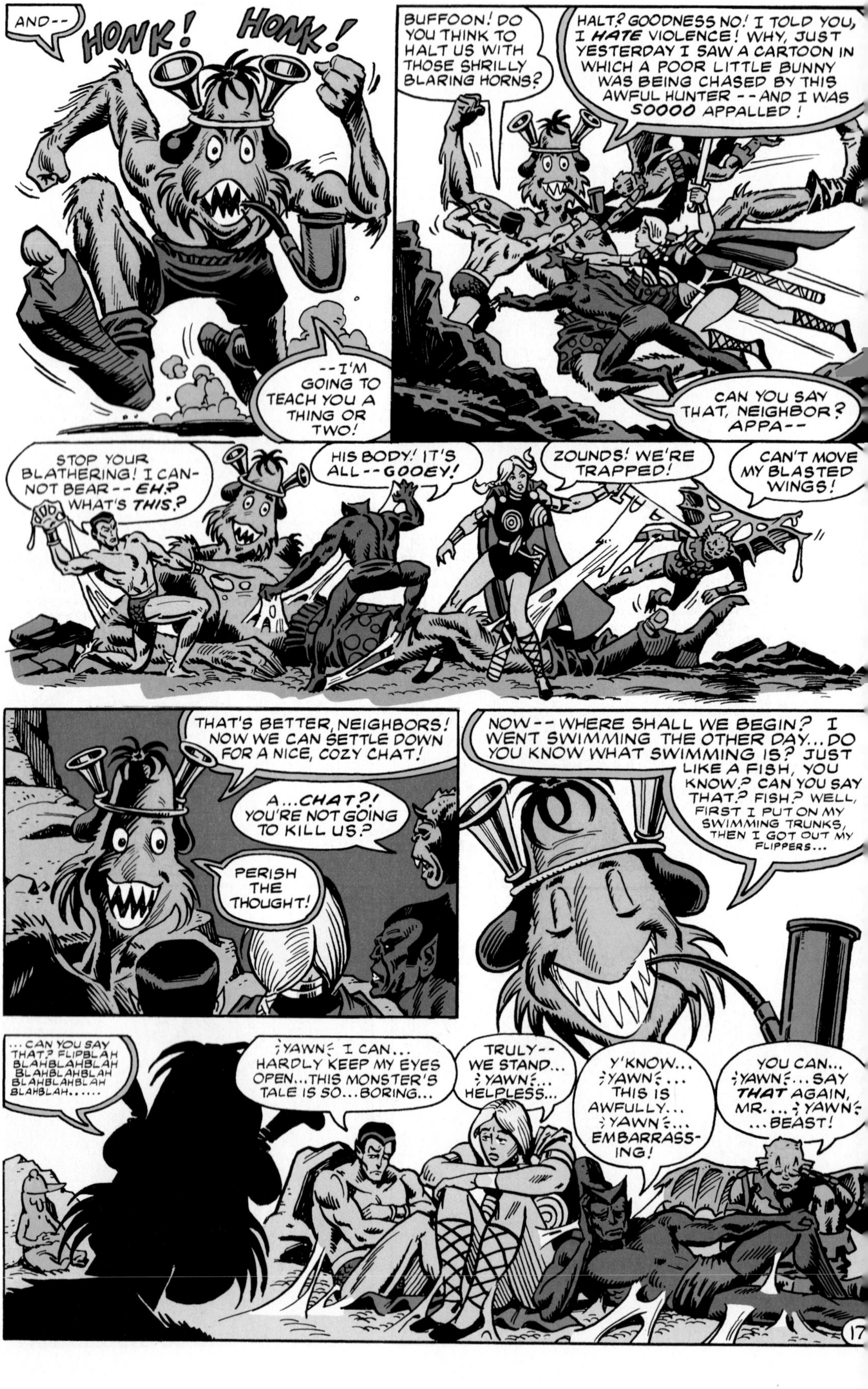

AND--
HONK! HONK!
--I'M GOING TO TEACH YOU A THING OR TWO!
BUFFOON! DO YOU THINK TO HALT US WITH THOSE SHRILLY BLARING HORNS?
HALT? GOODNESS NO! I TOLD YOU, I HATE VIOLENCE! WHY, JUST YESTERDAY I SAW A CARTOON IN WHICH A POOR LITTLE BUNNY WAS BEING CHASED BY THIS AWFUL HUNTER -- AND I WAS SOOOO APPALLED!
CAN YOU SAY THAT, NEIGHBOR? APPA--
STOP YOUR BLATHERING! I CANNOT BEAR -- EH? WHAT'S THIS?
HIS BODY! IT'S ALL -- GOOEY!
ZOUNDS! WE'RE TRAPPED!
CAN'T MOVE MY BLASTED WINGS!
THAT'S BETTER, NEIGHBORS! NOW WE CAN SETTLE DOWN FOR A NICE, COZY CHAT!
A...CHAT?! YOU'RE NOT GOING TO KILL US?
PERISH THE THOUGHT!
NOW -- WHERE SHALL WE BEGIN? I WENT SWIMMING THE OTHER DAY... DO YOU KNOW WHAT SWIMMING IS? JUST LIKE A FISH, YOU KNOW? CAN YOU SAY THAT? FISH? WELL, FIRST I PUT ON MY SWIMMING TRUNKS, THEN I GOT OUT MY FLIPPERS...
...CAN YOU SAY THAT? FLIPBLAH BLAHBLAHBLAH BLAHBLAHBLAH BLAHBLAHBLAH BLAHBLAH.....
YAWN I CAN... HARDLY KEEP MY EYES OPEN... THIS MONSTER'S TALE IS SO... BORING...
TRULY -- WE STAND... YAWN... HELPLESS...
Y'KNOW... YAWN... THIS IS AWFULLY... YAWN... EMBARRASSING!
YOU CAN... YAWN... SAY THAT AGAIN, MR.... YAWN... BEAST!
17

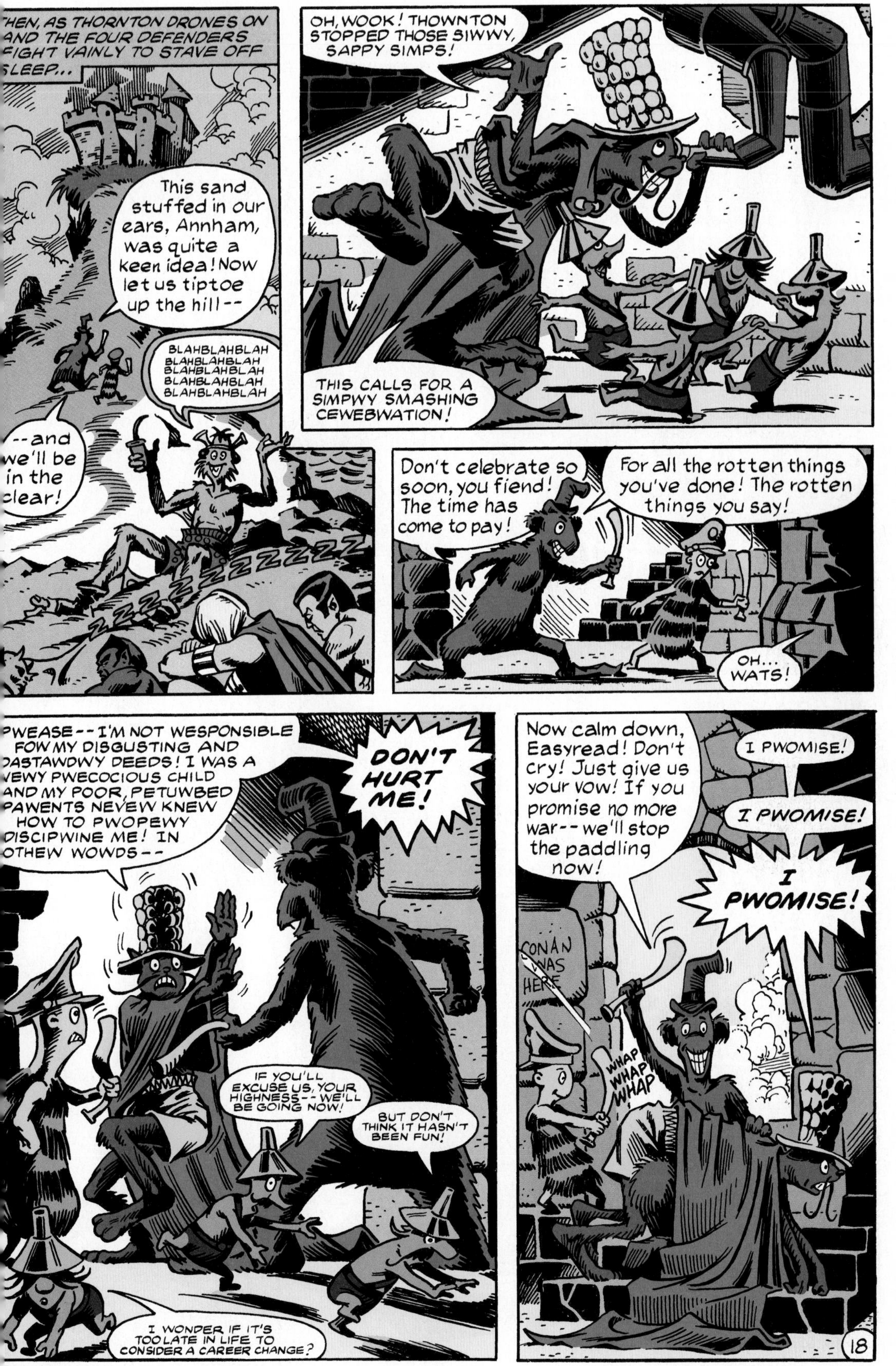

THEN, AS THORNTON DRONES ON AND THE FOUR DEFENDERS FIGHT VAINLY TO STAVE OFF SLEEP...
This sand stuffed in our ears, Annham, was quite a keen idea! Now let us tiptoe up the hill--
BLAHBLAHBLAH BLAHBLAHBLAH BLAHBLAHBLAH BLAHBLAHBLAH BLAHBLAHBLAH
--and we'll be in the clear!
OH, WOOK! THOWNTON STOPPED THOSE SIWWY, SAPPY SIMPS!
THIS CALLS FOR A SIMPWY SMASHING CEWEBWATION!
Don't celebrate so soon, you fiend! The time has come to pay!
For all the rotten things you've done! The rotten things you say!
OH... WATS!
PWEASE-- I'M NOT WESPONSIBLE FOW MY DISGUSTING AND DASTAWDWY DEEDS! I WAS A VEWY PWECOCIOUS CHILD AND MY POOR, PETUWBED PAWENTS NEVEW KNEW HOW TO PWOPEWY DISCIPWINE ME! IN OTHEW WOWDS--
DON'T HURT ME!
IF YOU'LL EXCUSE US, YOUR HIGHNESS-- WE'LL BE GOING NOW!
BUT DON'T THINK IT HASN'T BEEN FUN!
I WONDER IF IT'S TOO LATE IN LIFE TO CONSIDER A CAREER CHANGE?
Now calm down, Easyread! Don't cry! Just give us your vow! If you promise no more war-- we'll stop the paddling now!
I PWOMISE!
I PWOMISE!
I PWOMISE!
CONAN WAS HERE
WHAP WHAP WHAP
18

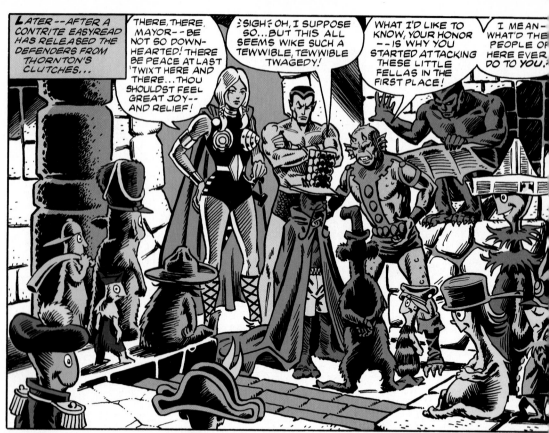

LATER--AFTER A CONTRITE EASYREAD HAS RELEASED THE DEFENDERS FROM THORNTON'S CLUTCHES...

THERE, THERE, MAYOR-- BE NOT SO DOWN-HEARTED! THERE BE PEACE AT LAST 'TWIXT HERE AND THERE...THOU SHOULDST FEEL GREAT JOY-- AND RELIEF!

≥SIGH≤ OH, I SUPPOSE SO...BUT THIS ALL SEEMS WIKE SUCH A TEWWIBLE, TEWWIBLE TWAGEDY!

WHAT I'D LIKE TO KNOW, YOUR HONOR --IS WHY YOU STARTED ATTACKING THESE LITTLE FELLAS IN THE FIRST PLACE!

I MEAN-- WHAT'D THE PEOPLE OF HERE EVER DO TO YOU.

BUT--DON'T YOU SEE? YOU'VE JUST PUT YOUR FINGER ON THE POINT THAT CAUSED THE PAINFUL PWOBWEM!

THEY KEEP INSISTING THAT THEY WIVE HERE--

--WHEN ANYONE IN THEIR WIGHT MINDS CAN CWEAWY SEE WE WIVE HERE--

--AND THEY WIVE--THERE!

THEY LIVE--? YOU LIVE--? AND THAT WAS THE CAUSE OF THIS WAR!?

19

178

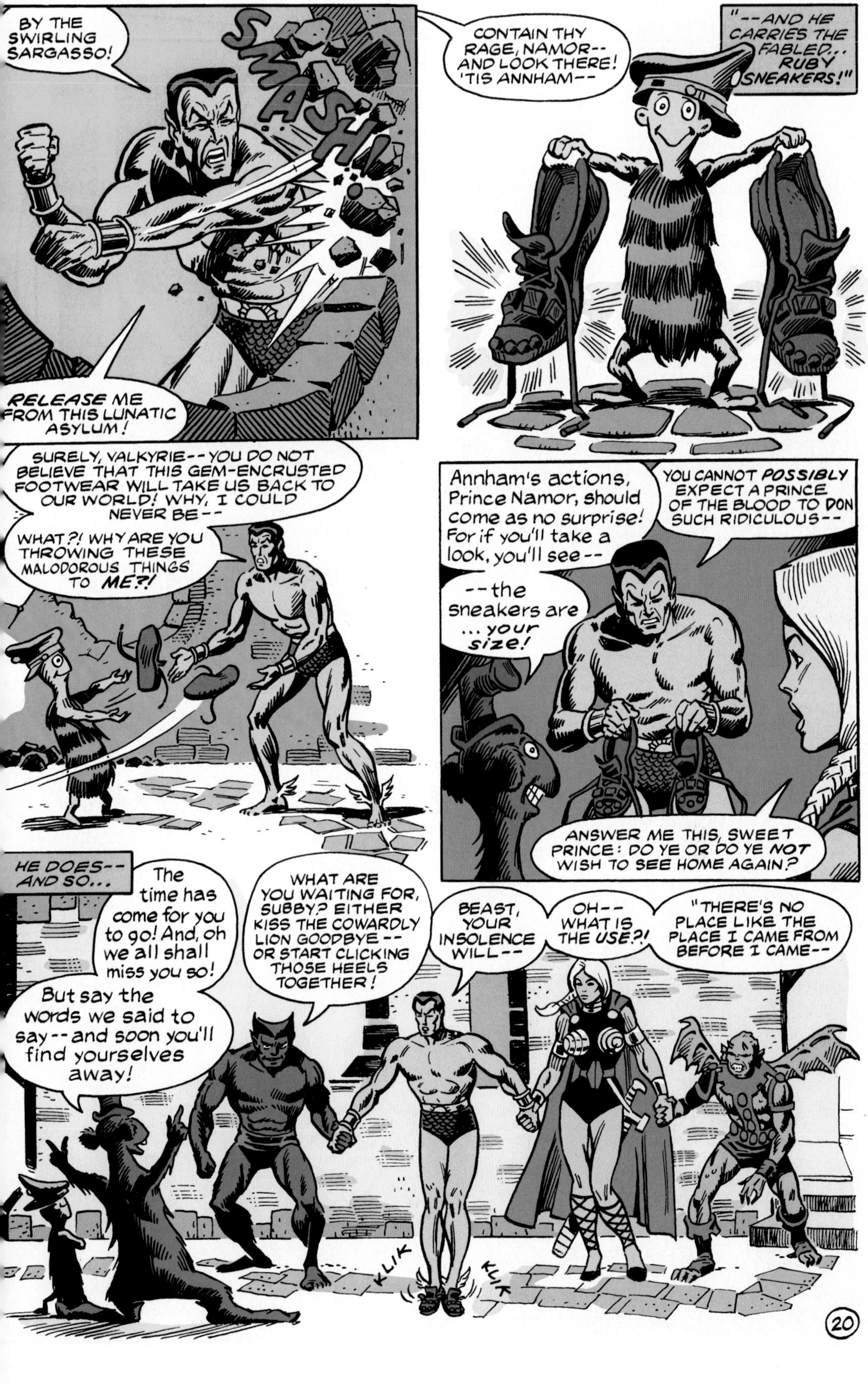

BY THE SWIRLING SARGASSO!
SMASH!
RELEASE ME FROM THIS LUNATIC ASYLUM!
CONTAIN THY RAGE, NAMOR-- AND LOOK THERE! 'TIS ANNHAM--
"--AND HE CARRIES THE FABLED... RUBY SNEAKERS!"
SURELY, VALKYRIE-- YOU DO NOT BELIEVE THAT THIS GEM-ENCRUSTED FOOTWEAR WILL TAKE US BACK TO OUR WORLD! WHY, I COULD NEVER BE--
WHAT?! WHY ARE YOU THROWING THESE MALODOROUS THINGS TO ME?!
Annham's actions, Prince Namor, should come as no surprise! For if you'll take a look, you'll see--
--the sneakers are ...your size!
YOU CANNOT POSSIBLY EXPECT A PRINCE OF THE BLOOD TO DON SUCH RIDICULOUS--
ANSWER ME THIS, SWEET PRINCE: DO YE OR DO YE NOT WISH TO SEE HOME AGAIN?
HE DOES-- AND SO...
The time has come for you to go! And, oh we all shall miss you so!
But say the words we said to say--and soon you'll find yourselves away!
WHAT ARE YOU WAITING FOR, SUBBY? EITHER KISS THE COWARDLY LION GOODBYE-- OR START CLICKING THOSE HEELS TOGETHER!
BEAST, YOUR INSOLENCE WILL--
OH-- WHAT IS THE USE?!
"THERE'S NO PLACE LIKE THE PLACE I CAME FROM BEFORE I CAME--
KLIK
KLIK
20

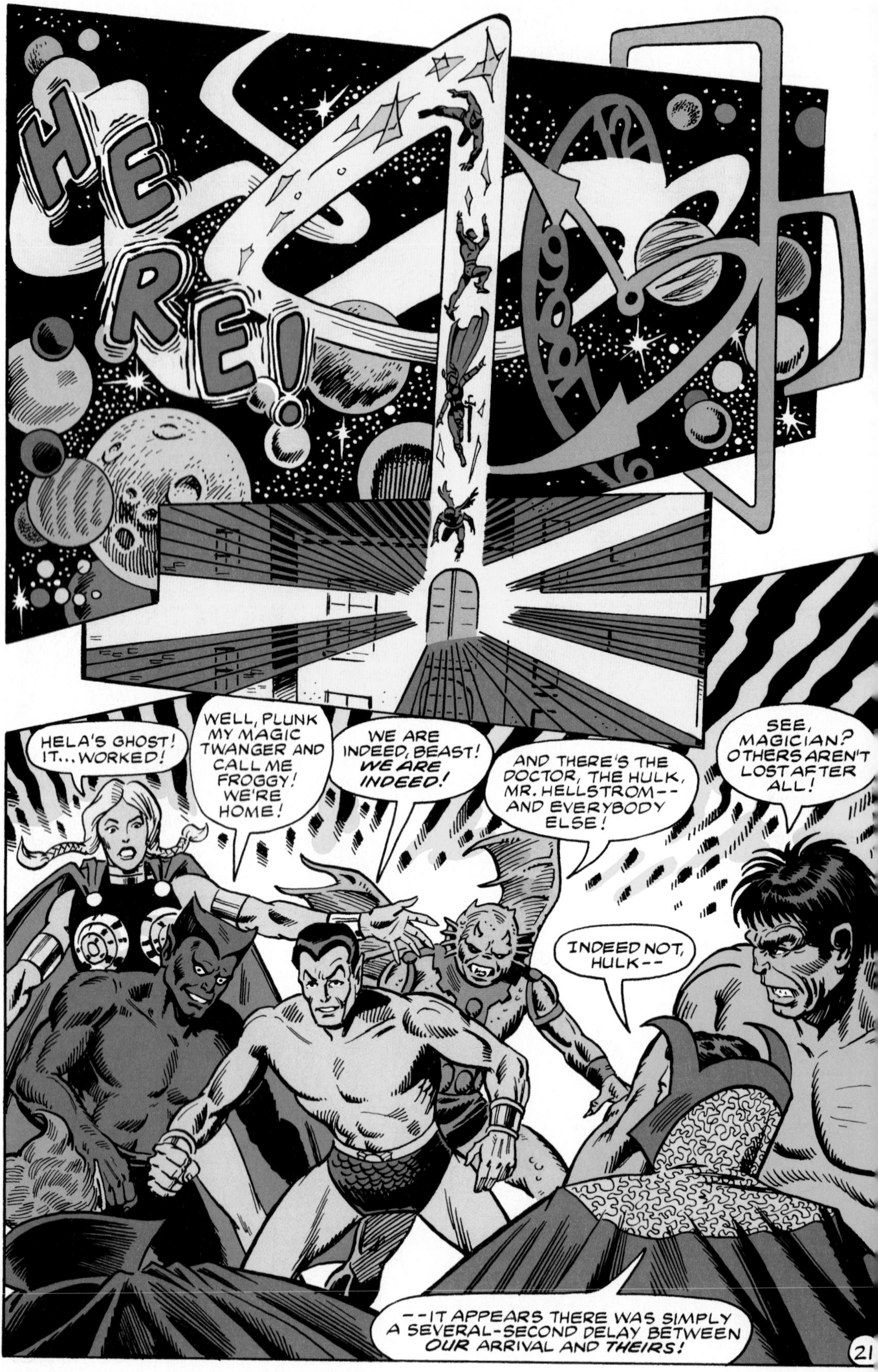
HERE!
HELA'S GHOST! IT... WORKED!
WELL, PLUNK MY MAGIC TWANGER AND CALL ME FROGGY! WE'RE HOME!
WE ARE INDEED, BEAST! WE ARE INDEED!
AND THERE'S THE DOCTOR, THE HULK, MR. HELLSTROM-- AND EVERYBODY ELSE!
SEE, MAGICIAN? OTHERS AREN'T LOST AFTER ALL!
INDEED NOT, HULK--
--IT APPEARS THERE WAS SIMPLY A SEVERAL-SECOND DELAY BETWEEN OUR ARRIVAL AND THEIRS!
21

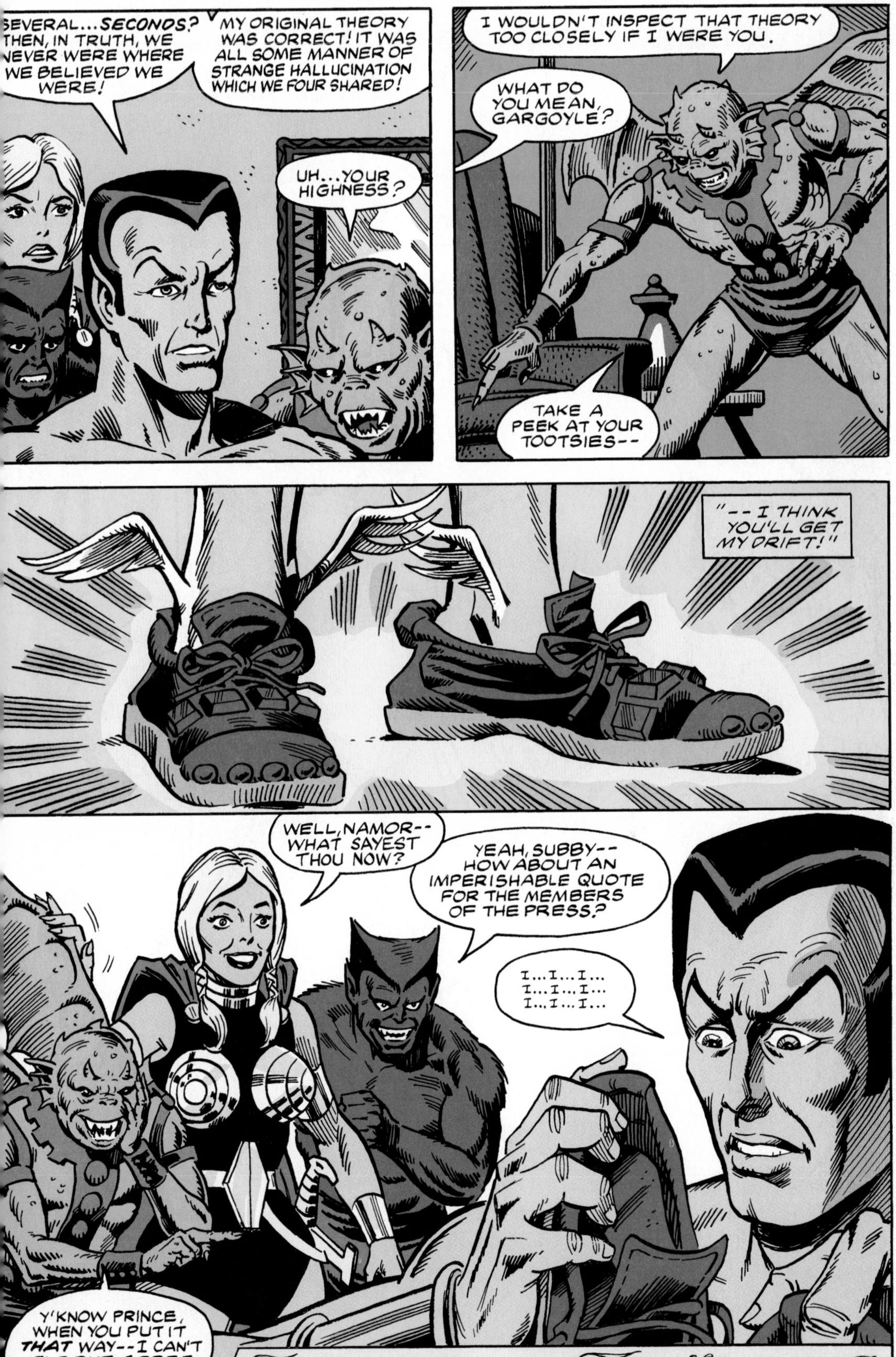
SEVERAL... SECONDS? THEN, IN TRUTH, WE NEVER WERE WHERE WE BELIEVED WE WERE!
MY ORIGINAL THEORY WAS CORRECT! IT WAS ALL SOME MANNER OF STRANGE HALLUCINATION WHICH WE FOUR SHARED!
UH... YOUR HIGHNESS?
I WOULDN'T INSPECT THAT THEORY TOO CLOSELY IF I WERE YOU.
WHAT DO YOU MEAN, GARGOYLE?
TAKE A PEEK AT YOUR TOOTSIES--
"--I THINK YOU'LL GET MY DRIFT!"
WELL, NAMOR--WHAT SAYEST THOU NOW?
YEAH, SUBBY--HOW ABOUT AN IMPERISHABLE QUOTE FOR THE MEMBERS OF THE PRESS?
I... I... I... I... I... I... I... I... I...
Y'KNOW PRINCE, WHEN YOU PUT IT THAT WAY--I CAN'T HELP BUT AGREE WITH YOU!
This story is dedicated to Theodor Geisel, M.D.

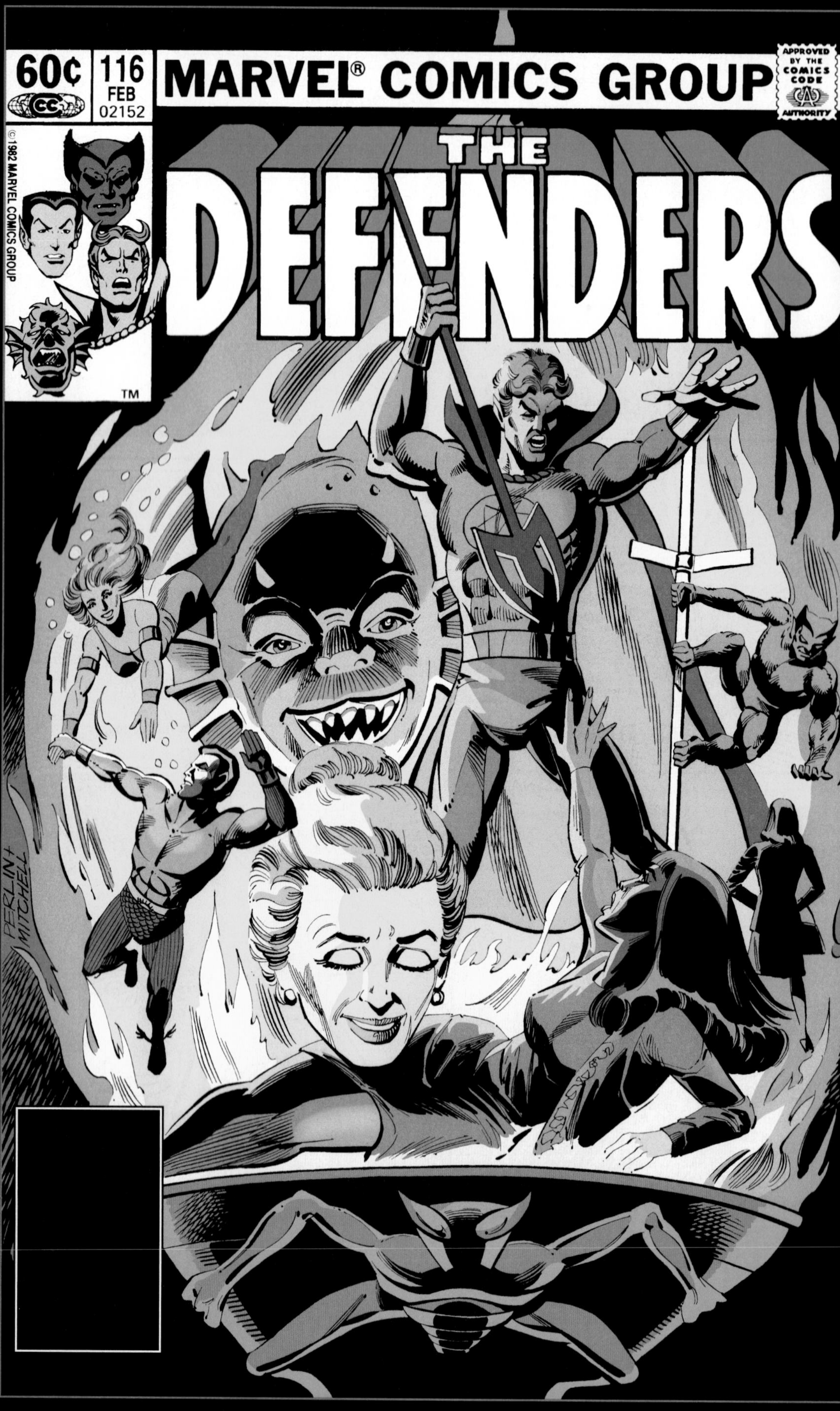

60¢
116
FEB
02152
MARVEL® COMICS GROUP
APPROVED BY THE COMICS CODE AUTHORITY
THE DEFENDERS
© 1982 MARVEL COMICS GROUP
TM
PERLIN + MITCHELL

THE DEFENDERS TWO BY TWO

STan Lee PRESENTS:

| J.M. DE MATTEIS SCRIPTER | DON PERLIN PENCILER | DIVERSE HANDS INKER | JANICE CHIANG LETTERER | GEORGE ROUSSOS COLORIST | AL MILGROM EDITOR | JIM SHOOTER EDITOR-IN-CHIEF |

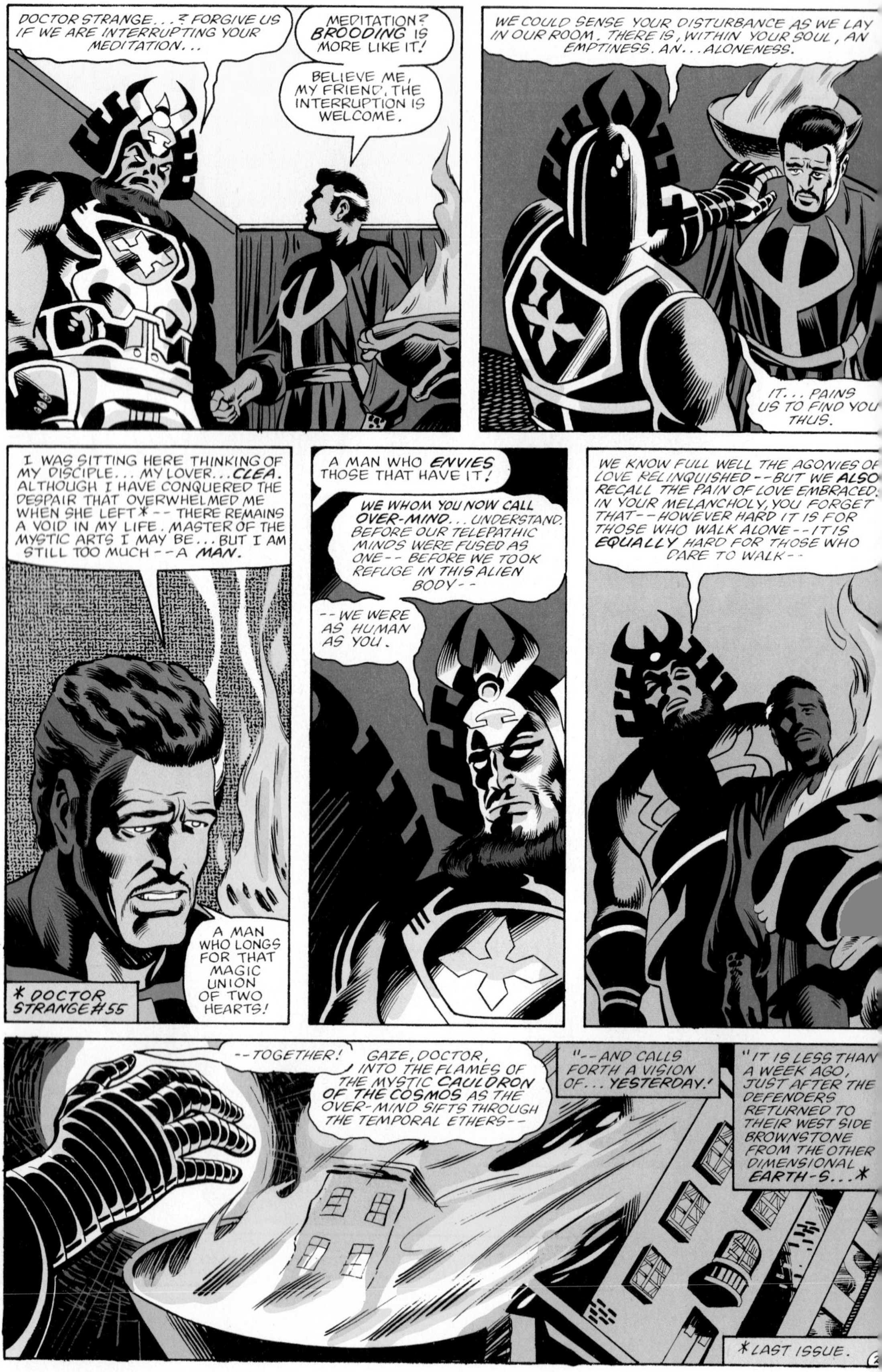
DOCTOR STRANGE...? FORGIVE US IF WE ARE INTERRUPTING YOUR MEDITATION...
MEDITATION? BROODING IS MORE LIKE IT!
BELIEVE ME, MY FRIEND, THE INTERRUPTION IS WELCOME.
WE COULD SENSE YOUR DISTURBANCE AS WE LAY IN OUR ROOM. THERE IS, WITHIN YOUR SOUL, AN EMPTINESS. AN...ALONENESS.
IT...PAINS US TO FIND YOU THUS.
I WAS SITTING HERE THINKING OF MY DISCIPLE... MY LOVER... CLEA. ALTHOUGH I HAVE CONQUERED THE DESPAIR THAT OVERWHELMED ME WHEN SHE LEFT* -- THERE REMAINS A VOID IN MY LIFE. MASTER OF THE MYSTIC ARTS I MAY BE... BUT I AM STILL TOO MUCH -- A MAN.
A MAN WHO LONGS FOR THAT MAGIC UNION OF TWO HEARTS!
*DOCTOR STRANGE #55
A MAN WHO ENVIES THOSE THAT HAVE IT!
WE WHOM YOU NOW CALL OVER-MIND... UNDERSTAND. BEFORE OUR TELEPATHIC MINDS WERE FUSED AS ONE -- BEFORE WE TOOK REFUGE IN THIS ALIEN BODY --
-- WE WERE AS HUMAN AS YOU.
WE KNOW FULL WELL THE AGONIES OF LOVE RELINQUISHED -- BUT WE ALSO RECALL THE PAIN OF LOVE EMBRACED. IN YOUR MELANCHOLY, YOU FORGET THAT -- HOWEVER HARD IT IS FOR THOSE WHO WALK ALONE -- IT IS EQUALLY HARD FOR THOSE WHO DARE TO WALK --
-- TOGETHER!
GAZE, DOCTOR, INTO THE FLAMES OF THE MYSTIC CAULDRON OF THE COSMOS AS THE OVER-MIND SIFTS THROUGH THE TEMPORAL ETHERS --
"-- AND CALLS FORTH A VISION OF... YESTERDAY."
"IT IS LESS THAN A WEEK AGO, JUST AFTER THE DEFENDERS RETURNED TO THEIR WEST SIDE BROWNSTONE FROM THE OTHER DIMENSIONAL EARTH-S...*
*LAST ISSUE.

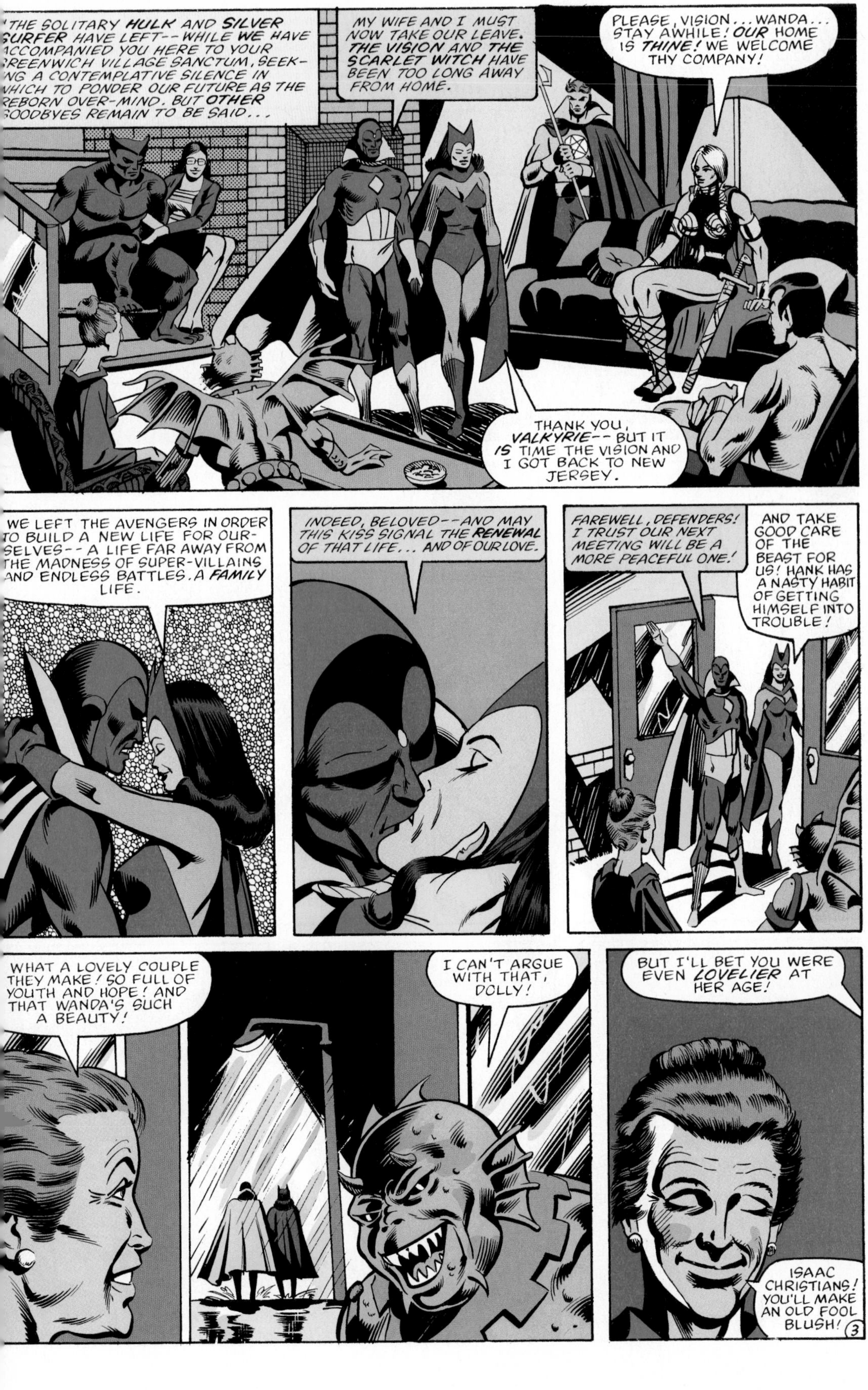
THE SOLITARY HULK AND SILVER SURFER HAVE LEFT-- WHILE WE HAVE ACCOMPANIED YOU HERE TO YOUR GREENWICH VILLAGE SANCTUM, SEEKING A CONTEMPLATIVE SILENCE IN WHICH TO PONDER OUR FUTURE AS THE REBORN OVER-MIND. BUT OTHER GOODBYES REMAIN TO BE SAID...
MY WIFE AND I MUST NOW TAKE OUR LEAVE. THE VISION AND THE SCARLET WITCH HAVE BEEN TOO LONG AWAY FROM HOME.
PLEASE, VISION... WANDA... STAY AWHILE! OUR HOME IS THINE! WE WELCOME THY COMPANY!
THANK YOU, VALKYRIE-- BUT IT IS TIME THE VISION AND I GOT BACK TO NEW JERSEY.
WE LEFT THE AVENGERS IN ORDER TO BUILD A NEW LIFE FOR OURSELVES-- A LIFE FAR AWAY FROM THE MADNESS OF SUPER-VILLAINS AND ENDLESS BATTLES. A FAMILY LIFE.
INDEED, BELOVED--AND MAY THIS KISS SIGNAL THE RENEWAL OF THAT LIFE... AND OF OUR LOVE.
FAREWELL, DEFENDERS! I TRUST OUR NEXT MEETING WILL BE A MORE PEACEFUL ONE!
AND TAKE GOOD CARE OF THE BEAST FOR US! HANK HAS A NASTY HABIT OF GETTING HIMSELF INTO TROUBLE!
WHAT A LOVELY COUPLE THEY MAKE! SO FULL OF YOUTH AND HOPE! AND THAT WANDA'S SUCH A BEAUTY!
I CAN'T ARGUE WITH THAT, DOLLY!
BUT I'LL BET YOU WERE EVEN LOVELIER AT HER AGE!
ISAAC CHRISTIANS! YOU'LL MAKE AN OLD FOOL BLUSH!
3

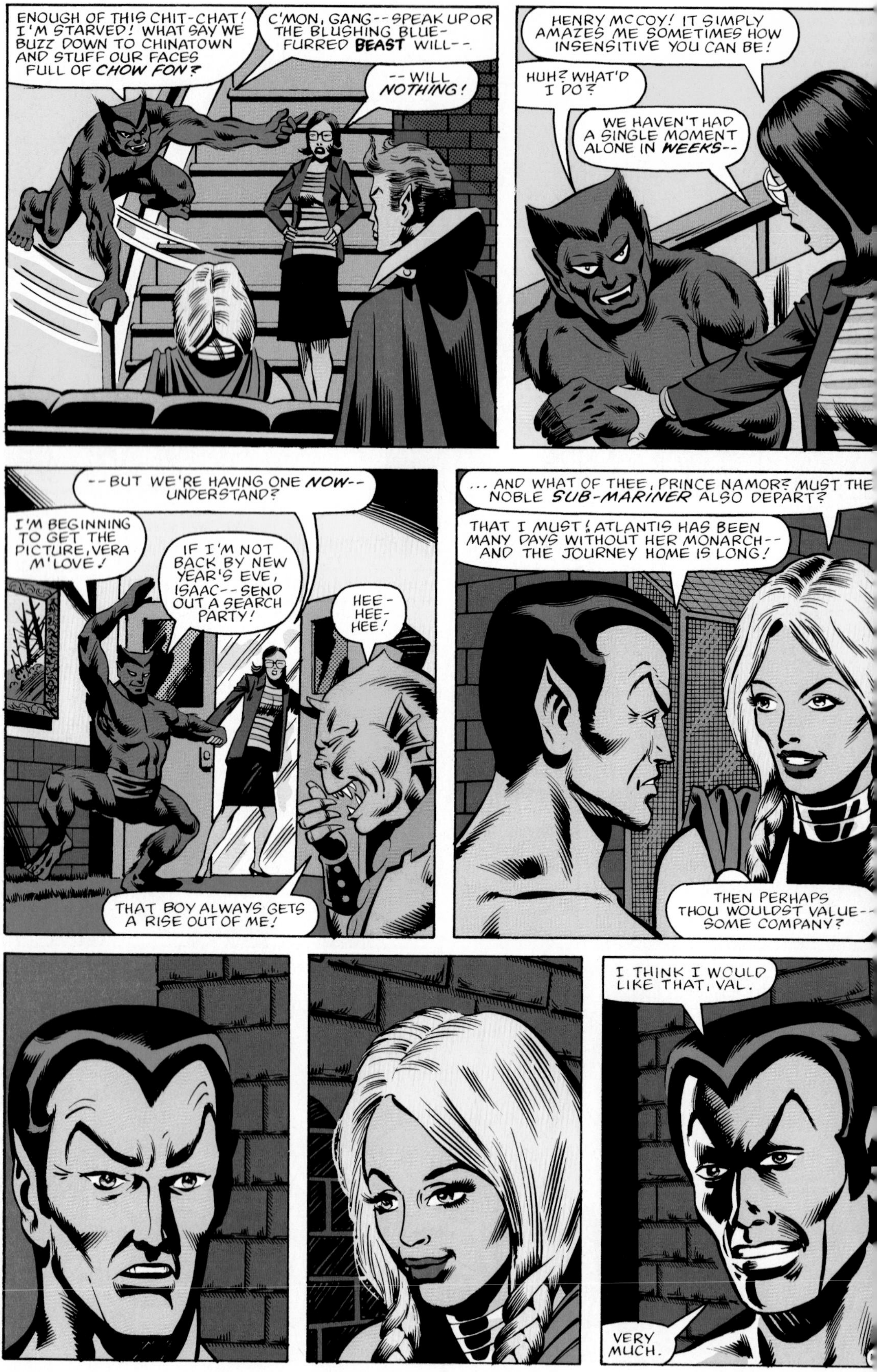

ENOUGH OF THIS CHIT-CHAT! I'M STARVED! WHAT SAY WE BUZZ DOWN TO CHINATOWN AND STUFF OUR FACES FULL OF CHOW FON?
C'MON, GANG--SPEAK UP OR THE BLUSHING BLUE-FURRED BEAST WILL--
--WILL NOTHING!
HENRY McCOY! IT SIMPLY AMAZES ME SOMETIMES HOW INSENSITIVE YOU CAN BE!
HUH? WHAT'D I DO?
WE HAVEN'T HAD A SINGLE MOMENT ALONE IN WEEKS--
--BUT WE'RE HAVING ONE NOW--UNDERSTAND?
I'M BEGINNING TO GET THE PICTURE, VERA M'LOVE!
IF I'M NOT BACK BY NEW YEAR'S EVE, ISAAC--SEND OUT A SEARCH PARTY!
HEE-HEE-HEE!
THAT BOY ALWAYS GETS A RISE OUT OF ME!
... AND WHAT OF THEE, PRINCE NAMOR? MUST THE NOBLE SUB-MARINER ALSO DEPART?
THAT I MUST! ATLANTIS HAS BEEN MANY DAYS WITHOUT HER MONARCH--AND THE JOURNEY HOME IS LONG!
THEN PERHAPS THOU WOULDST VALUE--SOME COMPANY?
I THINK I WOULD LIKE THAT, VAL.
VERY MUCH.

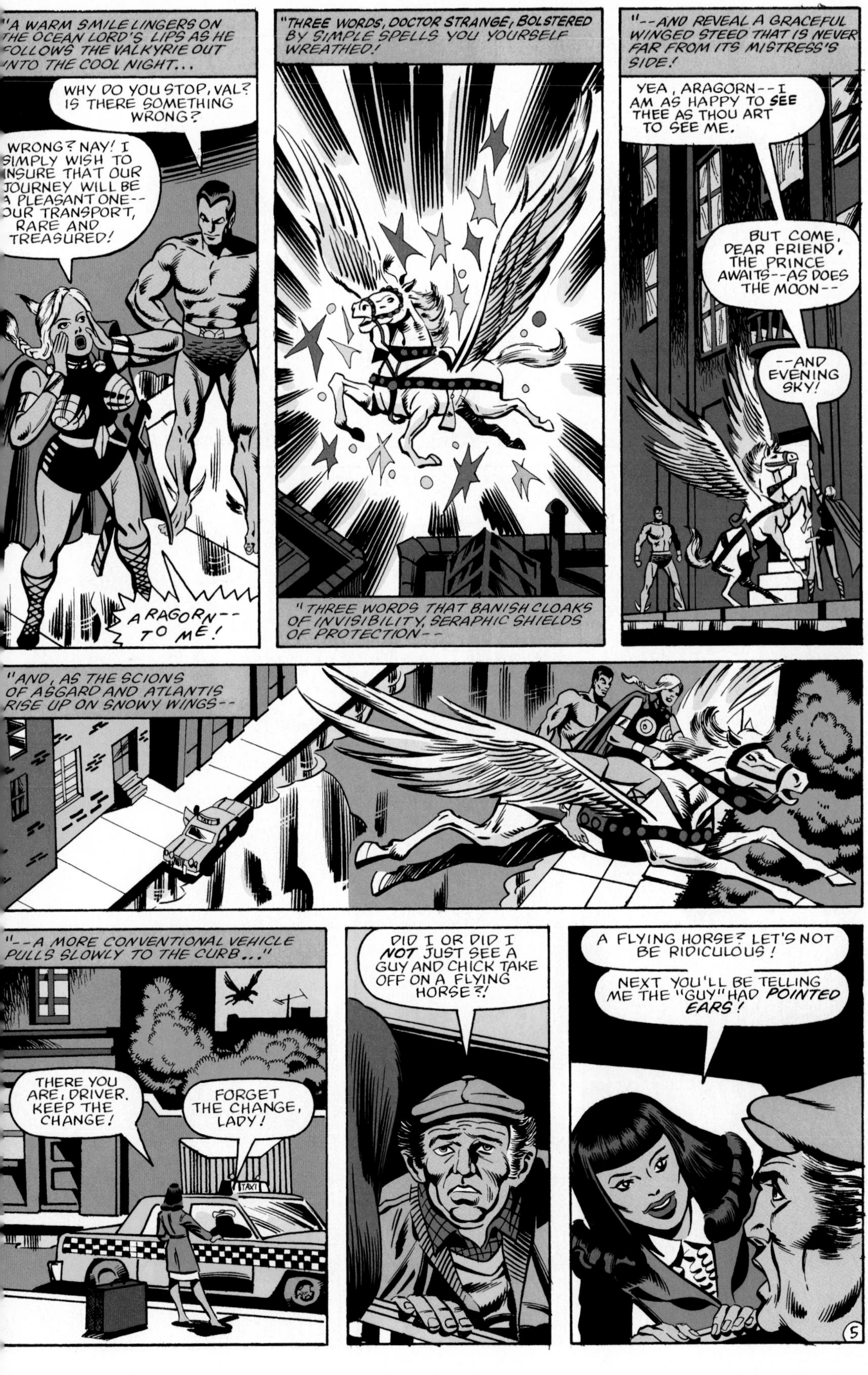
"A WARM SMILE LINGERS ON THE OCEAN LORD'S LIPS AS HE FOLLOWS THE VALKYRIE OUT INTO THE COOL NIGHT...
WHY DO YOU STOP, VAL? IS THERE SOMETHING WRONG?
WRONG? NAY! I SIMPLY WISH TO INSURE THAT OUR JOURNEY WILL BE A PLEASANT ONE-- OUR TRANSPORT, RARE AND TREASURED!
ARAGORN-- TO ME!
"THREE WORDS, DOCTOR STRANGE, BOLSTERED BY SIMPLE SPELLS YOU YOURSELF WREATHED!
"THREE WORDS THAT BANISH CLOAKS OF INVISIBILITY, SERAPHIC SHIELDS OF PROTECTION--
"--AND REVEAL A GRACEFUL WINGED STEED THAT IS NEVER FAR FROM ITS MISTRESS'S SIDE!
YEA, ARAGORN--I AM AS HAPPY TO SEE THEE AS THOU ART TO SEE ME.
BUT COME, DEAR FRIEND, THE PRINCE AWAITS--AS DOES THE MOON--
--AND EVENING SKY!
"AND, AS THE SCIONS OF ASGARD AND ATLANTIS RISE UP ON SNOWY WINGS--
TAXI
"--A MORE CONVENTIONAL VEHICLE PULLS SLOWLY TO THE CURB..."
THERE YOU ARE, DRIVER. KEEP THE CHANGE!
FORGET THE CHANGE, LADY!
TAXI
DID I OR DID I NOT JUST SEE A GUY AND CHICK TAKE OFF ON A FLYING HORSE?!
A FLYING HORSE? LET'S NOT BE RIDICULOUS!
NEXT YOU'LL BE TELLING ME THE "GUY" HAD POINTED EARS!
5

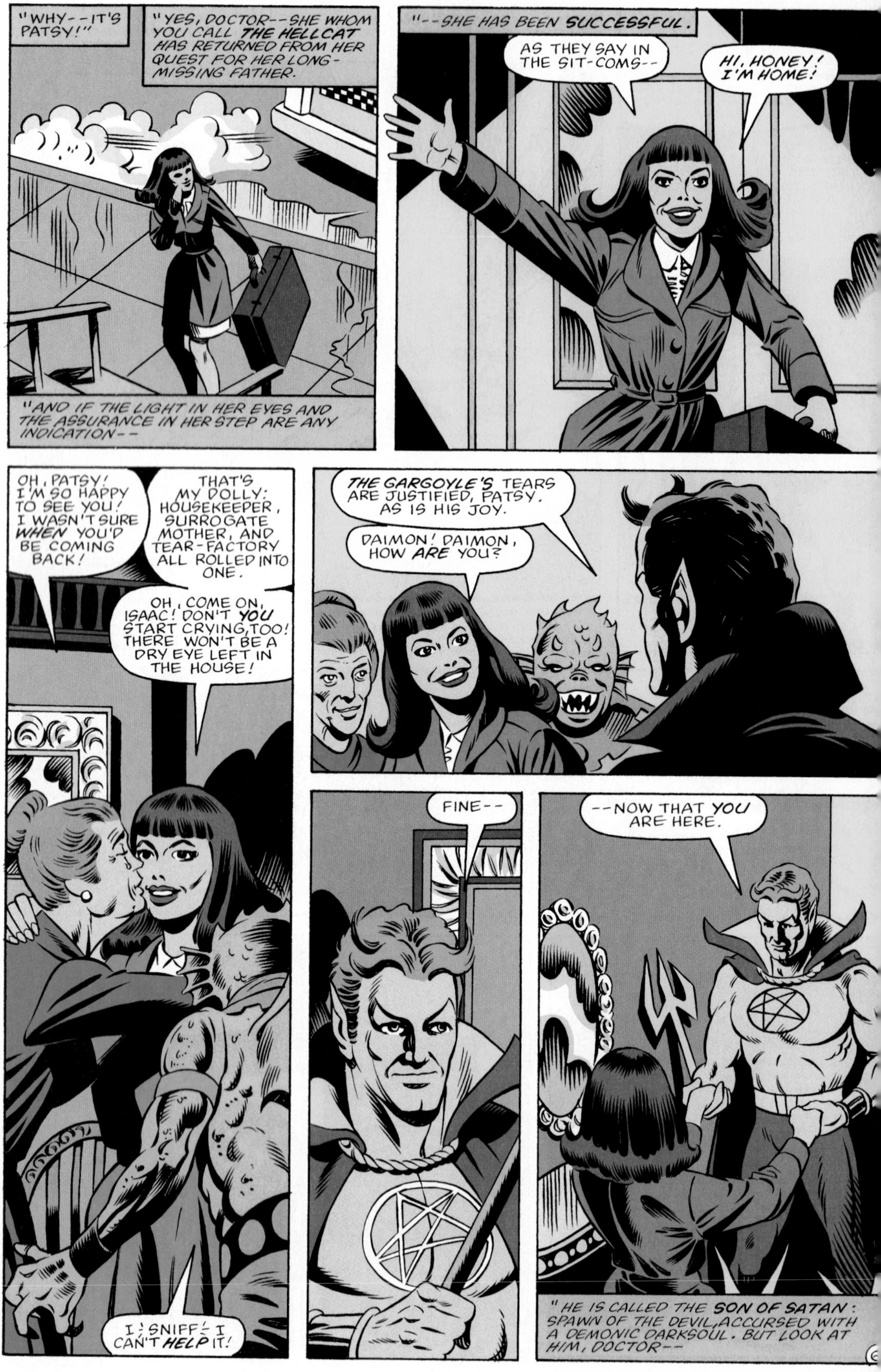
"WHY--IT'S PATSY!"
"YES, DOCTOR--SHE WHOM YOU CALL THE HELLCAT HAS RETURNED FROM HER QUEST FOR HER LONG-MISSING FATHER.
"AND IF THE LIGHT IN HER EYES AND THE ASSURANCE IN HER STEP ARE ANY INDICATION--
"--SHE HAS BEEN SUCCESSFUL.
AS THEY SAY IN THE SIT-COMS--
HI, HONEY! I'M HOME!
OH, PATSY! I'M SO HAPPY TO SEE YOU! I WASN'T SURE WHEN YOU'D BE COMING BACK!
THAT'S MY DOLLY: HOUSEKEEPER, SURROGATE MOTHER, AND TEAR-FACTORY ALL ROLLED INTO ONE.
OH, COME ON, ISAAC! DON'T YOU START CRYING, TOO! THERE WON'T BE A DRY EYE LEFT IN THE HOUSE!
I-SNIFF-I CAN'T HELP IT!
DAIMON! DAIMON, HOW ARE YOU?
THE GARGOYLE'S TEARS ARE JUSTIFIED, PATSY. AS IS HIS JOY.
FINE--
--NOW THAT YOU ARE HERE.
"HE IS CALLED THE SON OF SATAN: SPAWN OF THE DEVIL, ACCURSED WITH A DEMONIC DARKSOUL. BUT LOOK AT HIM, DOCTOR--

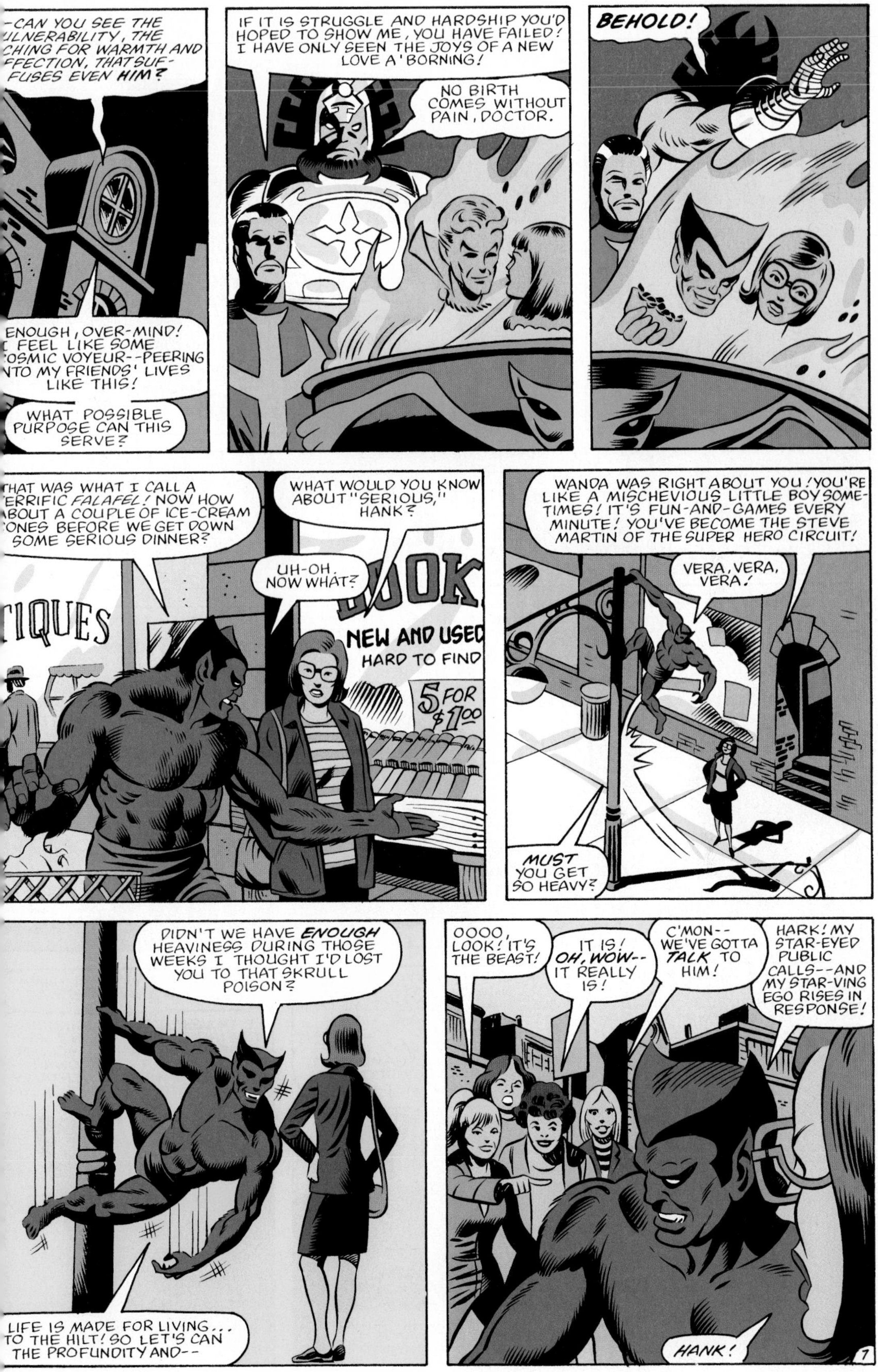
-CAN YOU SEE THE
ULNERABILITY, THE
CHING FOR WARMTH AND
FFECTION, THAT SUF-
FUSES EVEN HIM?
ENOUGH, OVER-MIND! I FEEL LIKE SOME COSMIC VOYEUR--PEERING INTO MY FRIENDS' LIVES LIKE THIS!
WHAT POSSIBLE PURPOSE CAN THIS SERVE?
IF IT IS STRUGGLE AND HARDSHIP YOU'D HOPED TO SHOW ME, YOU HAVE FAILED! I HAVE ONLY SEEN THE JOYS OF A NEW LOVE A'BORNING!
NO BIRTH COMES WITHOUT PAIN, DOCTOR.
BEHOLD!
THAT WAS WHAT I CALL A TERRIFIC FALAFEL! NOW HOW ABOUT A COUPLE OF ICE-CREAM CONES BEFORE WE GET DOWN SOME SERIOUS DINNER?
WHAT WOULD YOU KNOW ABOUT "SERIOUS," HANK?
UH-OH. NOW WHAT?
TIQUES
NEW AND USED
HARD TO FIND
5 FOR $1.00
WANDA WAS RIGHT ABOUT YOU! YOU'RE LIKE A MISCHEVIOUS LITTLE BOY SOME-TIMES! IT'S FUN-AND-GAMES EVERY MINUTE! YOU'VE BECOME THE STEVE MARTIN OF THE SUPER HERO CIRCUIT!
VERA, VERA, VERA!
MUST YOU GET SO HEAVY?
DIDN'T WE HAVE ENOUGH HEAVINESS DURING THOSE WEEKS I THOUGHT I'D LOST YOU TO THAT SKRULL POISON?
LIFE IS MADE FOR LIVING... TO THE HILT! SO LET'S CAN THE PROFUNDITY AND--
OOOO, LOOK! IT'S THE BEAST!
IT IS! OH, WOW-- IT REALLY IS!
C'MON-- WE'VE GOTTA TALK TO HIM!
HARK! MY STAR-EYED PUBLIC CALLS--AND MY STAR-VING EGO RISES IN RESPONSE!
HANK!
7

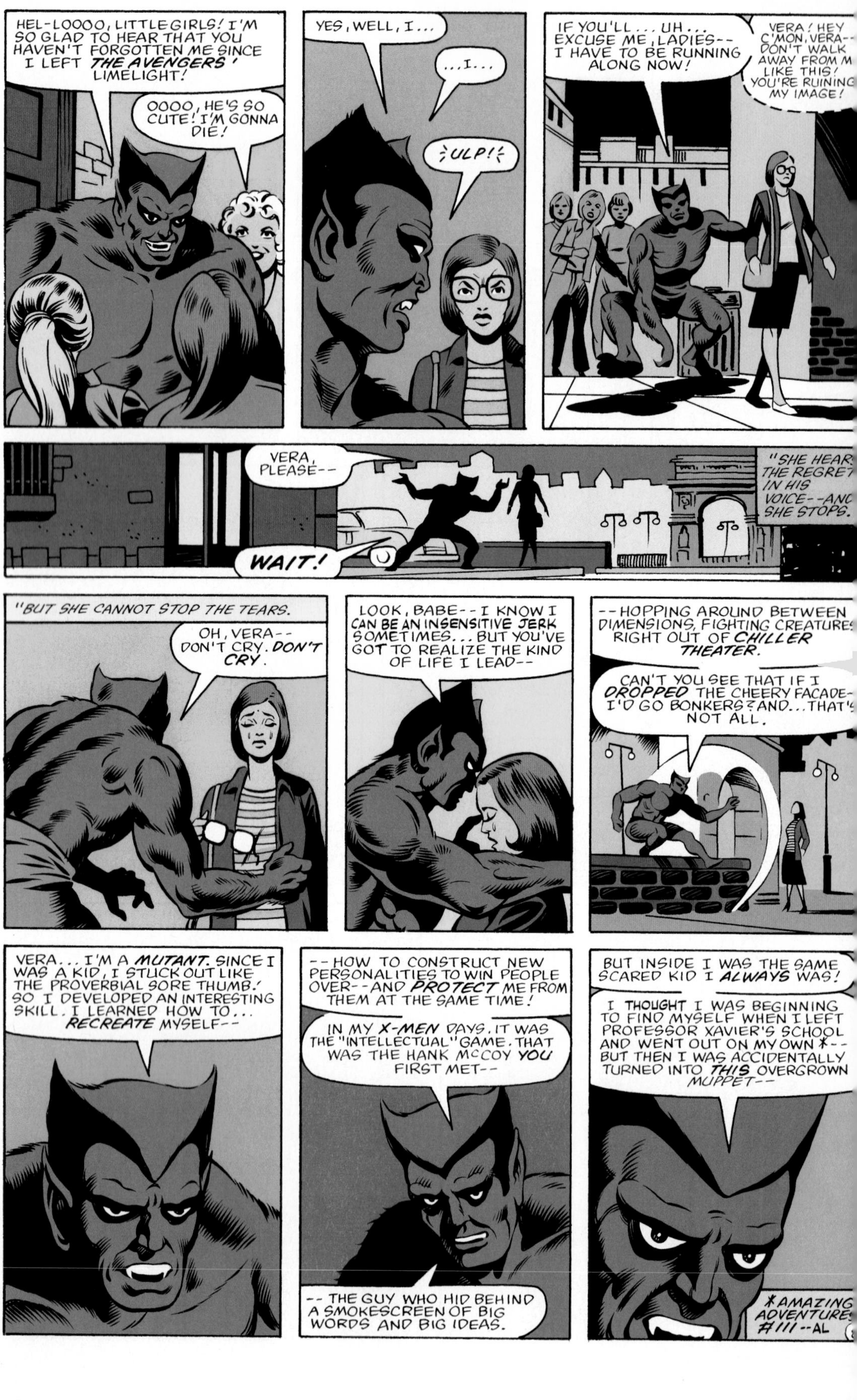

HEL-LOOOO, LITTLE GIRLS! I'M SO GLAD TO HEAR THAT YOU HAVEN'T FORGOTTEN ME SINCE I LEFT THE AVENGERS' LIMELIGHT!
OOOO, HE'S SO CUTE! I'M GONNA DIE!
YES, WELL, I...
...I...
ULP!
IF YOU'LL... UH... EXCUSE ME, LADIES-- I HAVE TO BE RUNNING ALONG NOW!
VERA! HEY C'MON, VERA-- DON'T WALK AWAY FROM M LIKE THIS! YOU'RE RUINING MY IMAGE!
VERA, PLEASE--
WAIT!
"SHE HEAR THE REGRET IN HIS VOICE--AND SHE STOPS.
"BUT SHE CANNOT STOP THE TEARS.
OH, VERA-- DON'T CRY. DON'T CRY.
LOOK, BABE-- I KNOW I CAN BE AN INSENSITIVE JERK SOMETIMES... BUT YOU'VE GOT TO REALIZE THE KIND OF LIFE I LEAD--
--HOPPING AROUND BETWEEN DIMENSIONS, FIGHTING CREATURES RIGHT OUT OF CHILLER THEATER.
CAN'T YOU SEE THAT IF I DROPPED THE CHEERY FACADE-- I'D GO BONKERS? AND... THAT'S NOT ALL.
VERA... I'M A MUTANT. SINCE I WAS A KID, I STUCK OUT LIKE THE PROVERBIAL SORE THUMB! SO I DEVELOPED AN INTERESTING SKILL. I LEARNED HOW TO... RECREATE MYSELF--
--HOW TO CONSTRUCT NEW PERSONALITIES TO WIN PEOPLE OVER--AND PROTECT ME FROM THEM AT THE SAME TIME!
IN MY X-MEN DAYS, IT WAS THE "INTELLECTUAL" GAME. THAT WAS THE HANK McCOY YOU FIRST MET--
--THE GUY WHO HID BEHIND A SMOKESCREEN OF BIG WORDS AND BIG IDEAS.
BUT INSIDE I WAS THE SAME SCARED KID I ALWAYS WAS!
I THOUGHT I WAS BEGINNING TO FIND MYSELF WHEN I LEFT PROFESSOR XAVIER'S SCHOOL AND WENT OUT ON MY OWN*-- BUT THEN I WAS ACCIDENTALLY TURNED INTO THIS OVERGROWN MUPPET--
*AMAZING ADVENTURES #11 --AL

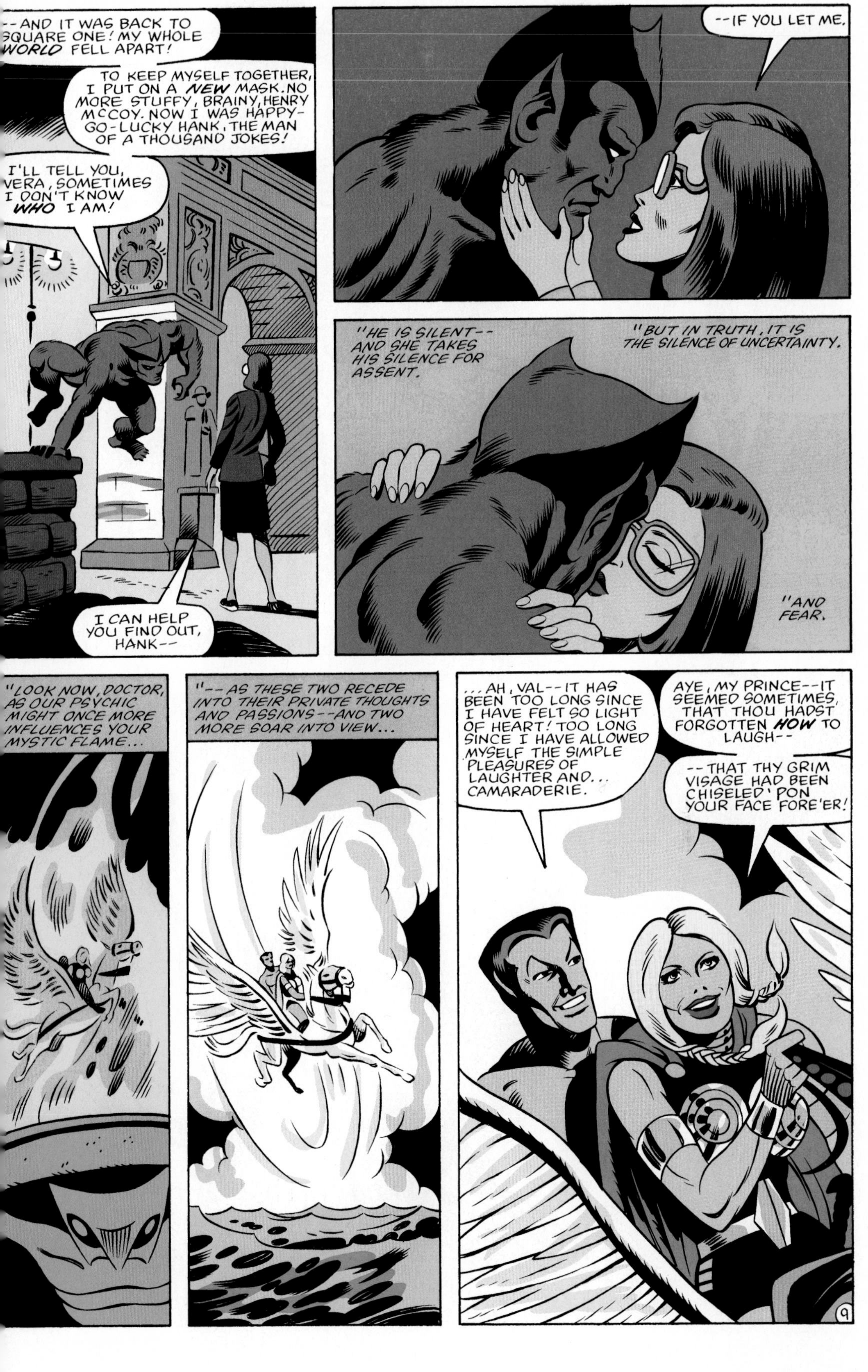
--AND IT WAS BACK TO SQUARE ONE! MY WHOLE WORLD FELL APART!
TO KEEP MYSELF TOGETHER, I PUT ON A NEW MASK. NO MORE STUFFY, BRAINY, HENRY McCOY. NOW I WAS HAPPY-GO-LUCKY HANK, THE MAN OF A THOUSAND JOKES!
I'LL TELL YOU, VERA, SOMETIMES I DON'T KNOW WHO I AM!
I CAN HELP YOU FIND OUT, HANK--
--IF YOU LET ME.
"HE IS SILENT--AND SHE TAKES HIS SILENCE FOR ASSENT.
"BUT IN TRUTH, IT IS THE SILENCE OF UNCERTAINTY.
"AND FEAR.
"LOOK NOW, DOCTOR, AS OUR PSYCHIC MIGHT ONCE MORE INFLUENCES YOUR MYSTIC FLAME...
"--AS THESE TWO RECEDE INTO THEIR PRIVATE THOUGHTS AND PASSIONS--AND TWO MORE SOAR INTO VIEW...
...AH, VAL--IT HAS BEEN TOO LONG SINCE I HAVE FELT SO LIGHT OF HEART! TOO LONG SINCE I HAVE ALLOWED MYSELF THE SIMPLE PLEASURES OF LAUGHTER AND... CAMARADERIE.
AYE, MY PRINCE--IT SEEMED SOMETIMES, THAT THOU HADST FORGOTTEN HOW TO LAUGH--
--THAT THY GRIM VISAGE HAD BEEN CHISELED 'PON YOUR FACE FORE'ER!
9

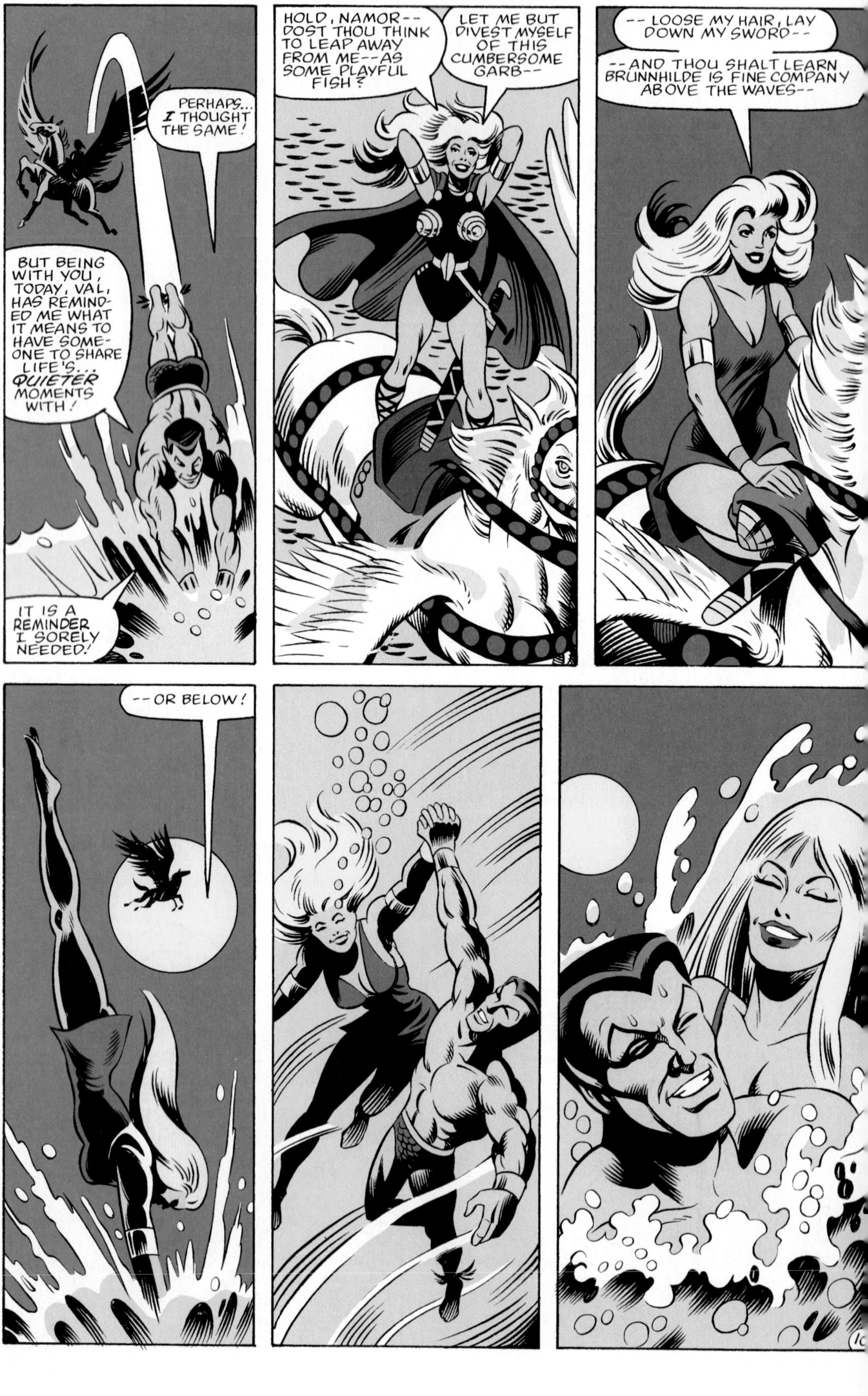
PERHAPS... I THOUGHT THE SAME!
BUT BEING WITH YOU, TODAY, VAL, HAS REMINDED ME WHAT IT MEANS TO HAVE SOMEONE TO SHARE LIFE'S... QUIETER MOMENTS WITH!
IT IS A REMINDER I SORELY NEEDED!
HOLD, NAMOR--DOST THOU THINK TO LEAP AWAY FROM ME--AS SOME PLAYFUL FISH?
LET ME BUT DIVEST MYSELF OF THIS CUMBERSOME GARB--
--LOOSE MY HAIR, LAY DOWN MY SWORD--
--AND THOU SHALT LEARN BRUNNHILDE IS FINE COMPANY ABOVE THE WAVES--
--OR BELOW!

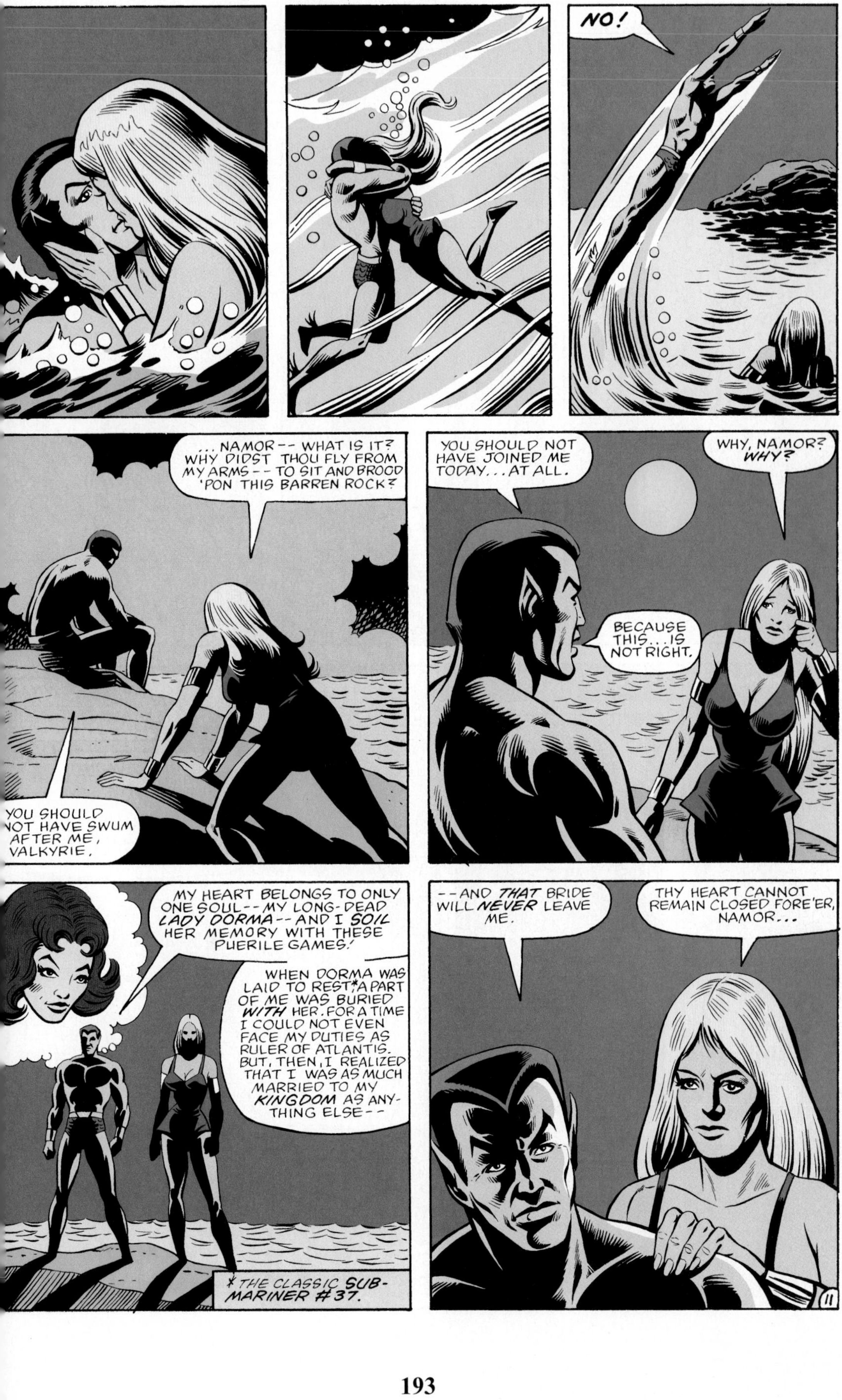
NO!
...NAMOR-- WHAT IS IT? WHY DIDST THOU FLY FROM MY ARMS-- TO SIT AND BROOD 'PON THIS BARREN ROCK?
YOU SHOULD NOT HAVE SWUM AFTER ME, VALKYRIE.
YOU SHOULD NOT HAVE JOINED ME TODAY...AT ALL.
WHY, NAMOR? WHY?
BECAUSE THIS...IS NOT RIGHT.
MY HEART BELONGS TO ONLY ONE SOUL-- MY LONG-DEAD LADY DORMA-- AND I SOIL HER MEMORY WITH THESE PUERILE GAMES!
WHEN DORMA WAS LAID TO REST,* A PART OF ME WAS BURIED WITH HER. FOR A TIME I COULD NOT EVEN FACE MY DUTIES AS RULER OF ATLANTIS. BUT, THEN, I REALIZED THAT I WAS AS MUCH MARRIED TO MY KINGDOM AS ANYTHING ELSE--
*THE CLASSIC SUB-MARINER #37.
--AND THAT BRIDE WILL NEVER LEAVE ME.
THY HEART CANNOT REMAIN CLOSED FORE'ER, NAMOR...
11

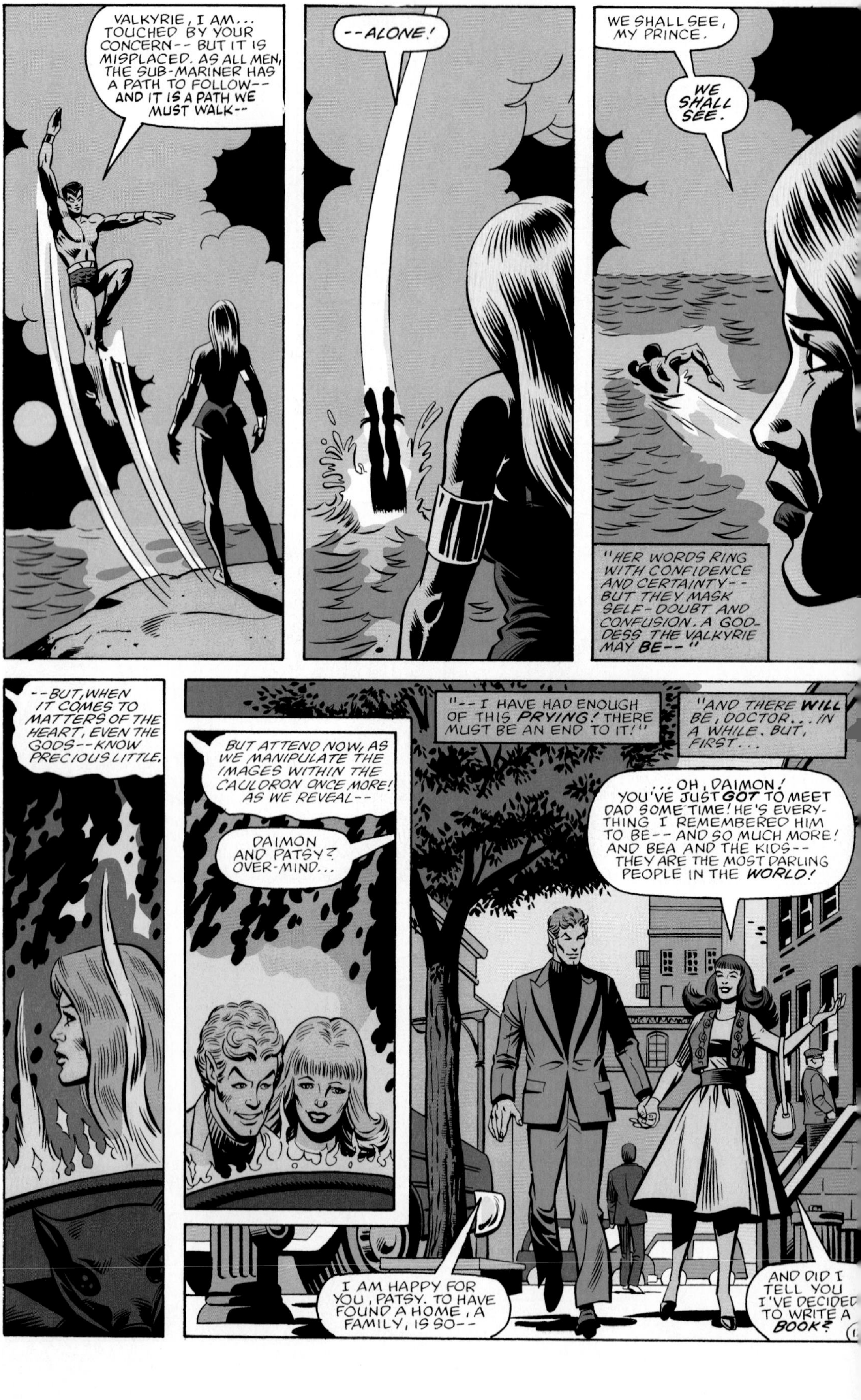

VALKYRIE, I AM... TOUCHED BY YOUR CONCERN-- BUT IT IS MISPLACED. AS ALL MEN, THE SUB-MARINER HAS A PATH TO FOLLOW-- AND IT IS A PATH WE MUST WALK--
--ALONE!
WE SHALL SEE, MY PRINCE.
WE SHALL SEE.
"HER WORDS RING WITH CONFIDENCE AND CERTAINTY-- BUT THEY MASK SELF-DOUBT AND CONFUSION. A GODDESS THE VALKYRIE MAY BE--"
--BUT, WHEN IT COMES TO MATTERS OF THE HEART, EVEN THE GODS--KNOW PRECIOUS LITTLE.
BUT ATTEND NOW, AS WE MANIPULATE THE IMAGES WITHIN THE CAULDRON ONCE MORE! AS WE REVEAL--
DAIMON AND PATSY? OVER-MIND...
"--I HAVE HAD ENOUGH OF THIS PRYING! THERE MUST BE AN END TO IT!"
"AND THERE WILL BE, DOCTOR... IN A WHILE. BUT, FIRST...
...OH, DAIMON! YOU'VE JUST GOT TO MEET DAD SOME TIME! HE'S EVERYTHING I REMEMBERED HIM TO BE-- AND SO MUCH MORE! AND BEA AND THE KIDS-- THEY ARE THE MOST DARLING PEOPLE IN THE WORLD!
I AM HAPPY FOR YOU, PATSY. TO HAVE FOUND A HOME, A FAMILY, IS SO--
AND DID I TELL YOU I'VE DECIDED TO WRITE A BOOK?

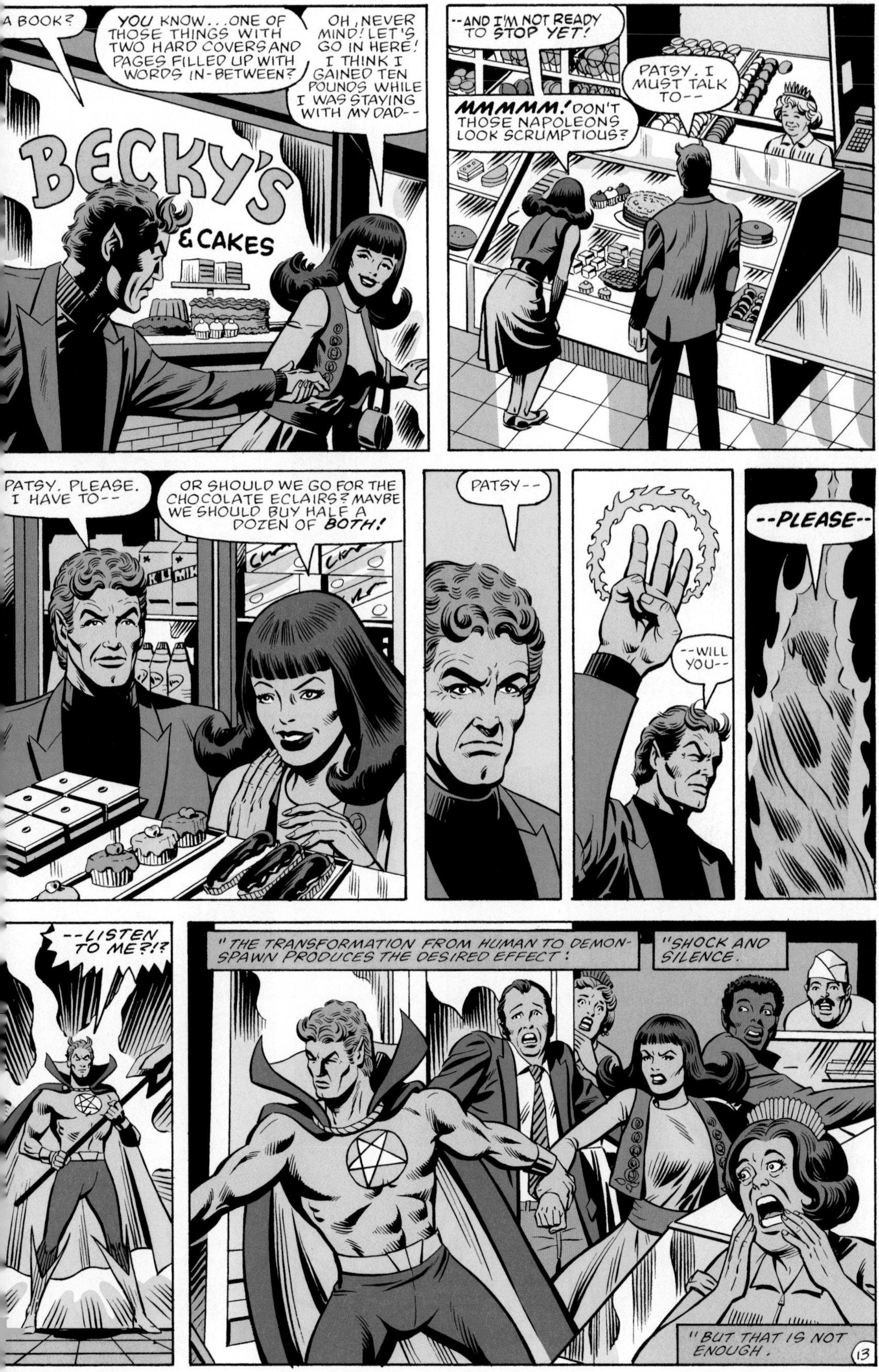
A BOOK?
YOU KNOW...ONE OF THOSE THINGS WITH TWO HARD COVERS AND PAGES FILLED UP WITH WORDS IN-BETWEEN?
OH, NEVER MIND! LET'S GO IN HERE! I THINK I GAINED TEN POUNDS WHILE I WAS STAYING WITH MY DAD--
BECKY'S
& CAKES
--AND I'M NOT READY TO STOP YET!
MMMMM! DON'T THOSE NAPOLEONS LOOK SCRUMPTIOUS?
PATSY. I MUST TALK TO--
PATSY. PLEASE. I HAVE TO--
OR SHOULD WE GO FOR THE CHOCOLATE ECLAIRS? MAYBE WE SHOULD BUY HALF A DOZEN OF BOTH!
PATSY--
--WILL YOU--
--PLEASE--
--LISTEN TO ME?!?
"THE TRANSFORMATION FROM HUMAN TO DEMON-SPAWN PRODUCES THE DESIRED EFFECT:
"SHOCK AND SILENCE.
"BUT THAT IS NOT ENOUGH.
13

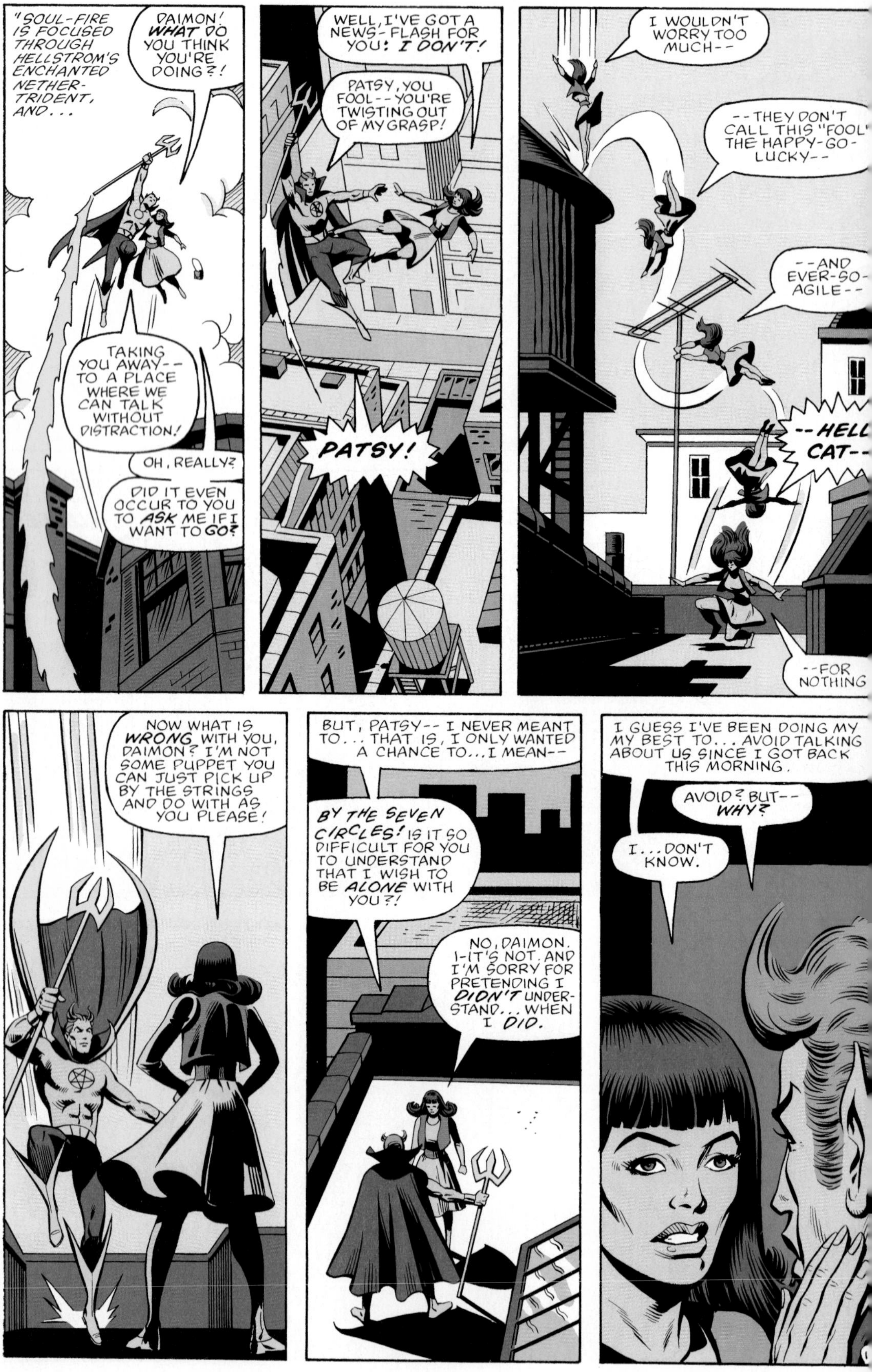
"SOUL-FIRE IS FOCUSED THROUGH HELLSTROM'S ENCHANTED NETHER-TRIDENT, AND...
DAIMON! WHAT DO YOU THINK YOU'RE DOING?!
TAKING YOU AWAY-- TO A PLACE WHERE WE CAN TALK WITHOUT DISTRACTION!
OH, REALLY?
DID IT EVEN OCCUR TO YOU TO ASK ME IF I WANT TO GO?
WELL, I'VE GOT A NEWS-FLASH FOR YOU: I DON'T!
PATSY, YOU FOOL--YOU'RE TWISTING OUT OF MY GRASP!
PATSY!
I WOULDN'T WORRY TOO MUCH--
--THEY DON'T CALL THIS "FOOL" THE HAPPY-GO-LUCKY--
--AND EVER-SO-AGILE--
--HELL CAT--
--FOR NOTHING
NOW WHAT IS WRONG WITH YOU, DAIMON? I'M NOT SOME PUPPET YOU CAN JUST PICK UP BY THE STRINGS AND DO WITH AS YOU PLEASE!
BUT, PATSY-- I NEVER MEANT TO... THAT IS, I ONLY WANTED A CHANCE TO... I MEAN--
BY THE SEVEN CIRCLES! IS IT SO DIFFICULT FOR YOU TO UNDERSTAND THAT I WISH TO BE ALONE WITH YOU?!
NO, DAIMON. I-IT'S NOT. AND I'M SORRY FOR PRETENDING I DIDN'T UNDERSTAND... WHEN I DID.
I GUESS I'VE BEEN DOING MY MY BEST TO... AVOID TALKING ABOUT US SINCE I GOT BACK THIS MORNING.
AVOID? BUT-- WHY?
I...DON'T KNOW.

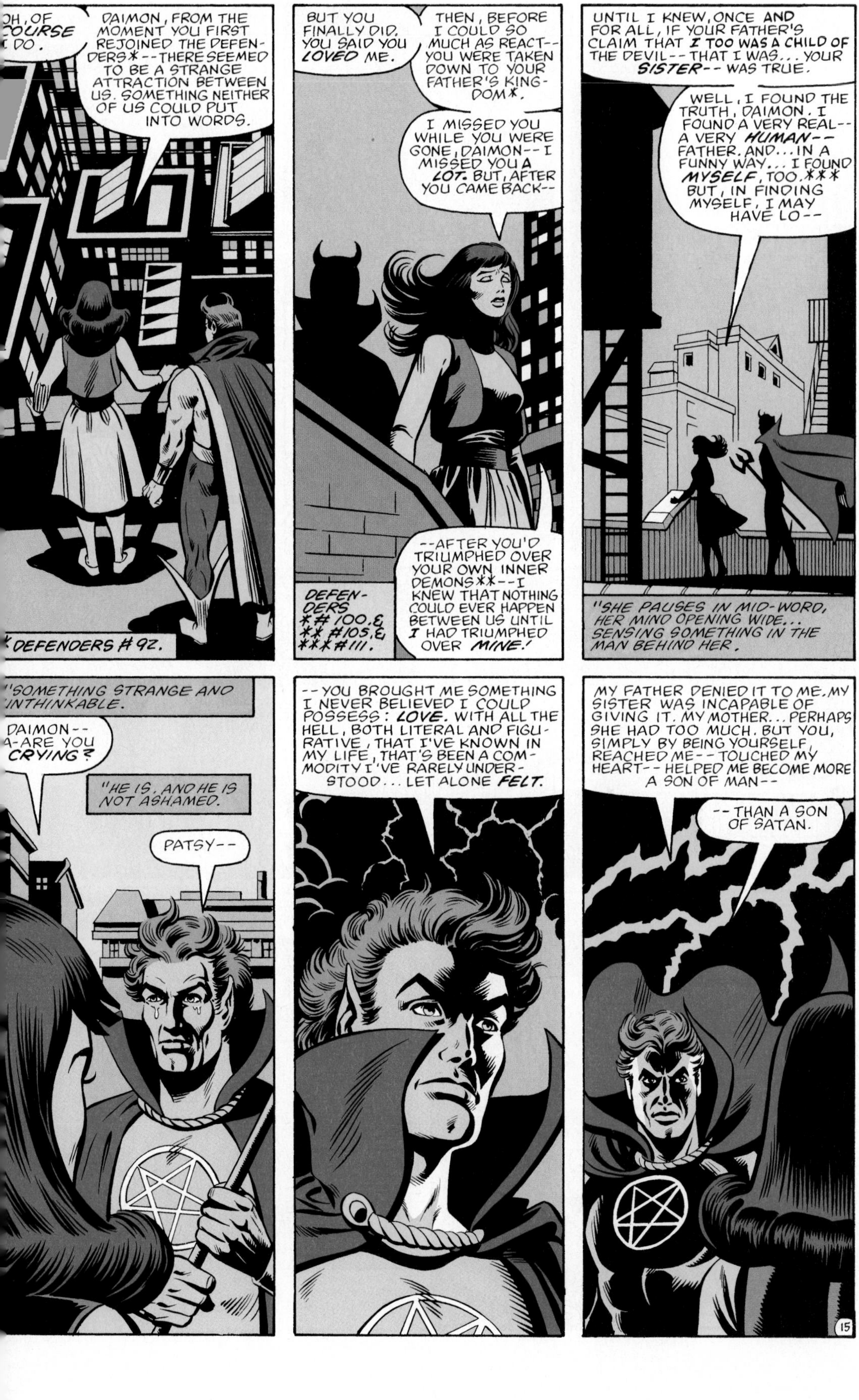
OH, OF COURSE I DO.
DAIMON, FROM THE MOMENT YOU FIRST REJOINED THE DEFENDERS* -- THERE SEEMED TO BE A STRANGE ATTRACTION BETWEEN US. SOMETHING NEITHER OF US COULD PUT INTO WORDS.
*DEFENDERS #92.
BUT YOU FINALLY DID. YOU SAID YOU LOVED ME.
THEN, BEFORE I COULD SO MUCH AS REACT -- YOU WERE TAKEN DOWN TO YOUR FATHER'S KINGDOM*.
I MISSED YOU WHILE YOU WERE GONE, DAIMON -- I MISSED YOU A LOT. BUT, AFTER YOU CAME BACK --
-- AFTER YOU'D TRIUMPHED OVER YOUR OWN INNER DEMONS** -- I KNEW THAT NOTHING COULD EVER HAPPEN BETWEEN US UNTIL I HAD TRIUMPHED OVER MINE!
DEFENDERS *#100, & **#105, & ***#111.
UNTIL I KNEW, ONCE AND FOR ALL, IF YOUR FATHER'S CLAIM THAT I TOO WAS A CHILD OF THE DEVIL -- THAT I WAS... YOUR SISTER -- WAS TRUE.
WELL, I FOUND THE TRUTH, DAIMON. I FOUND A VERY REAL -- A VERY HUMAN -- FATHER. AND... IN A FUNNY WAY... I FOUND MYSELF, TOO.*** BUT, IN FINDING MYSELF, I MAY HAVE LO --
"SHE PAUSES IN MID-WORD, HER MIND OPENING WIDE... SENSING SOMETHING IN THE MAN BEHIND HER.
"SOMETHING STRANGE AND UNTHINKABLE.
DAIMON -- A-ARE YOU CRYING?
"HE IS. AND HE IS NOT ASHAMED.
PATSY --
-- YOU BROUGHT ME SOMETHING I NEVER BELIEVED I COULD POSSESS: LOVE. WITH ALL THE HELL, BOTH LITERAL AND FIGURATIVE, THAT I'VE KNOWN IN MY LIFE, THAT'S BEEN A COMMODITY I'VE RARELY UNDERSTOOD... LET ALONE FELT.
MY FATHER DENIED IT TO ME. MY SISTER WAS INCAPABLE OF GIVING IT. MY MOTHER... PERHAPS SHE HAD TOO MUCH. BUT YOU, SIMPLY BY BEING YOURSELF, REACHED ME -- TOUCHED MY HEART -- HELPED ME BECOME MORE A SON OF MAN --
-- THAN A SON OF SATAN.
15

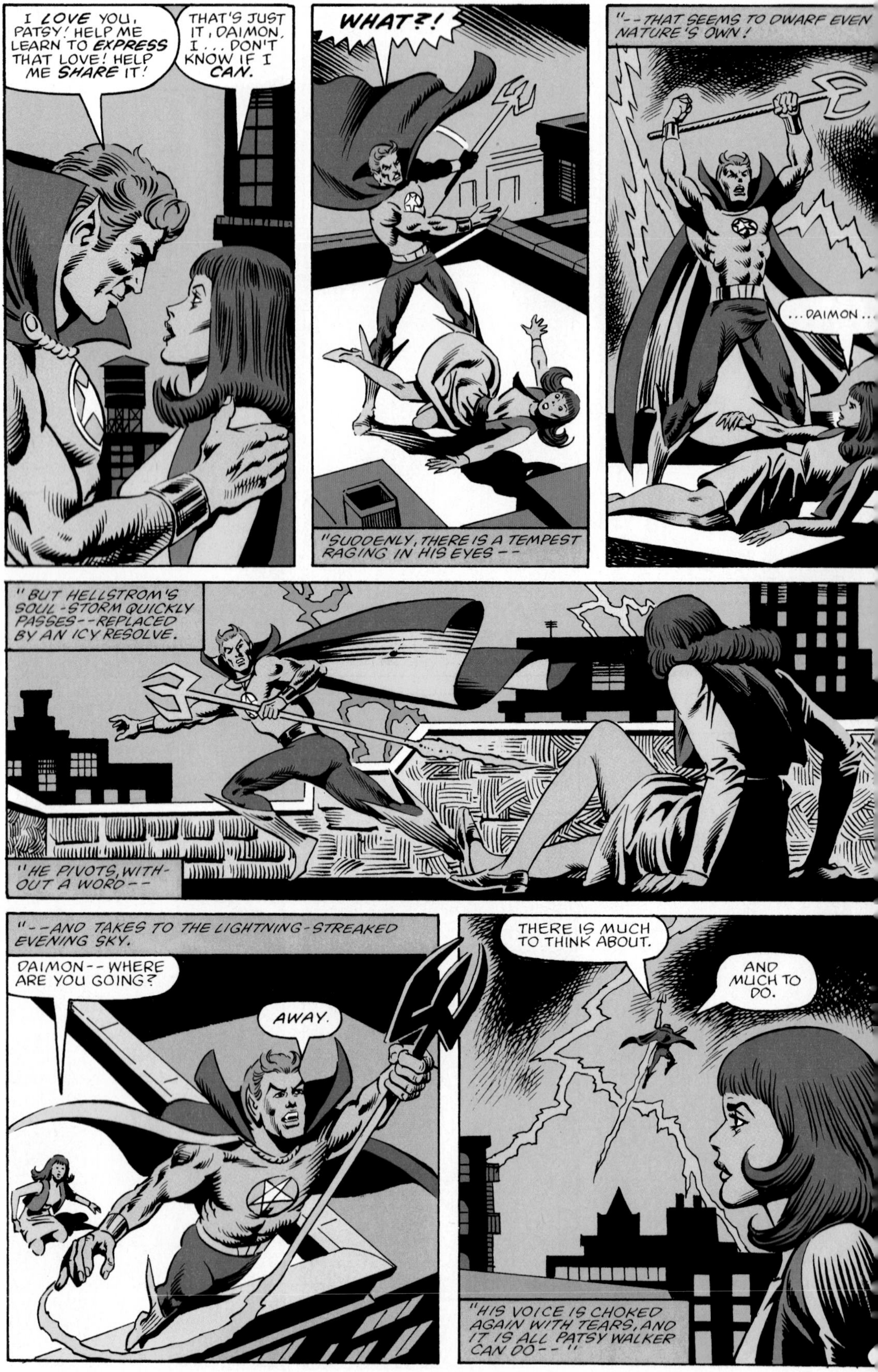
I LOVE YOU, PATSY! HELP ME LEARN TO EXPRESS THAT LOVE! HELP ME SHARE IT!
THAT'S JUST IT, DAIMON, I... DON'T KNOW IF I CAN.
WHAT?!
"SUDDENLY, THERE IS A TEMPEST RAGING IN HIS EYES--
"--THAT SEEMS TO DWARF EVEN NATURE'S OWN!
...DAIMON...
"BUT HELLSTROM'S SOUL-STORM QUICKLY PASSES--REPLACED BY AN ICY RESOLVE.
"HE PIVOTS, WITHOUT A WORD--
"--AND TAKES TO THE LIGHTNING-STREAKED EVENING SKY.
DAIMON--WHERE ARE YOU GOING?
AWAY.
THERE IS MUCH TO THINK ABOUT.
AND MUCH TO DO.
"HIS VOICE IS CHOKED AGAIN WITH TEARS, AND IT IS ALL PATSY WALKER CAN DO--"

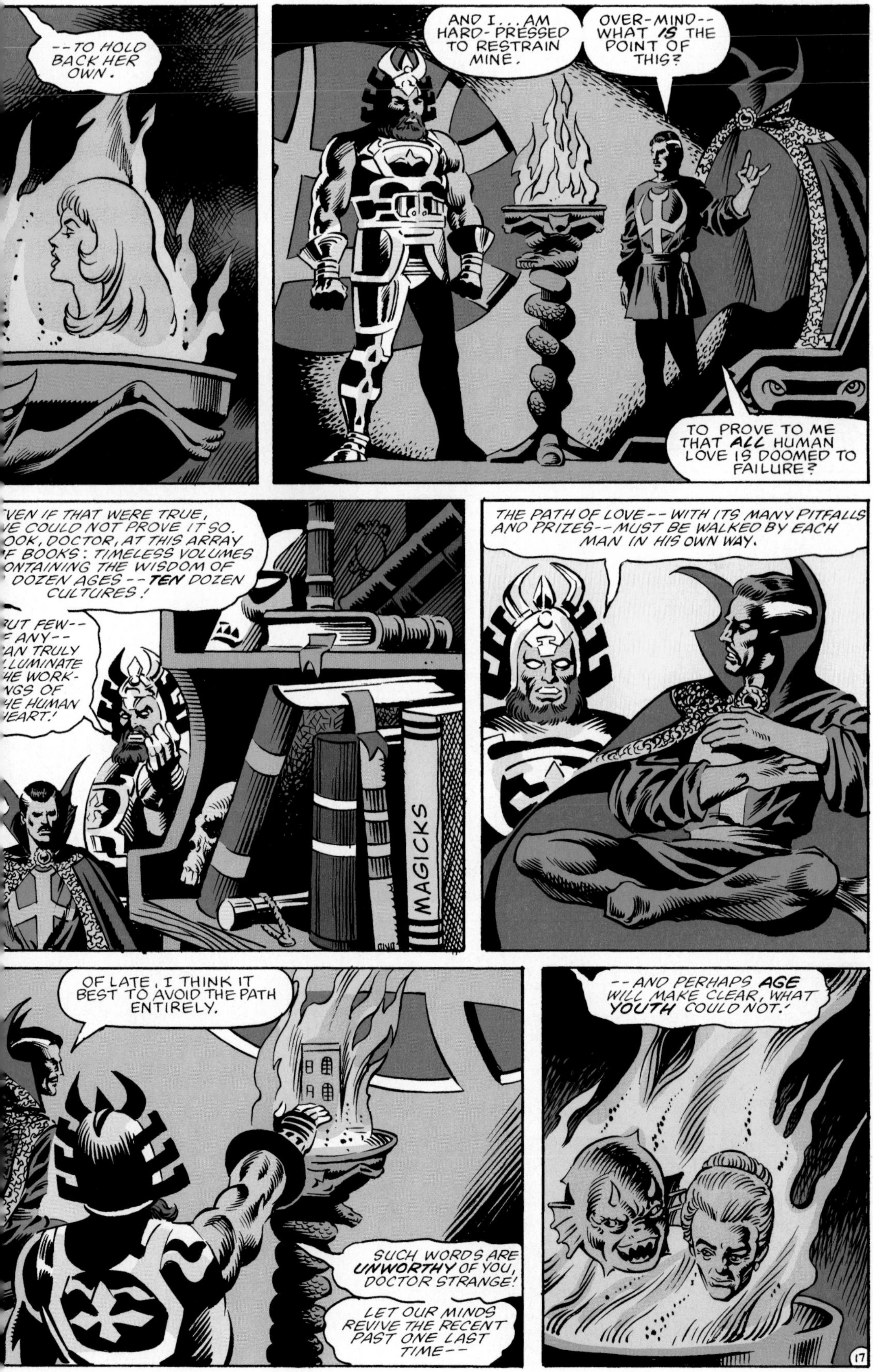
--TO HOLD BACK HER OWN.
AND I... AM HARD-PRESSED TO RESTRAIN MINE.
OVER-MIND--WHAT IS THE POINT OF THIS?
TO PROVE TO ME THAT ALL HUMAN LOVE IS DOOMED TO FAILURE?
VEN IF THAT WERE TRUE, E COULD NOT PROVE IT SO. OOK, DOCTOR, AT THIS ARRAY F BOOKS: TIMELESS VOLUMES ONTAINING THE WISDOM OF DOZEN AGES--TEN DOZEN CULTURES!
UT FEW-- ANY-- AN TRULY LUMINATE HE WORK-NGS OF HE HUMAN EART!
MAGICKS
THE PATH OF LOVE--WITH ITS MANY PITFALLS AND PRIZES--MUST BE WALKED BY EACH MAN IN HIS OWN WAY.
OF LATE, I THINK IT BEST TO AVOID THE PATH ENTIRELY.
SUCH WORDS ARE UNWORTHY OF YOU, DOCTOR STRANGE!
LET OUR MINDS REVIVE THE RECENT PAST ONE LAST TIME--
--AND PERHAPS AGE WILL MAKE CLEAR, WHAT YOUTH COULD NOT!
17

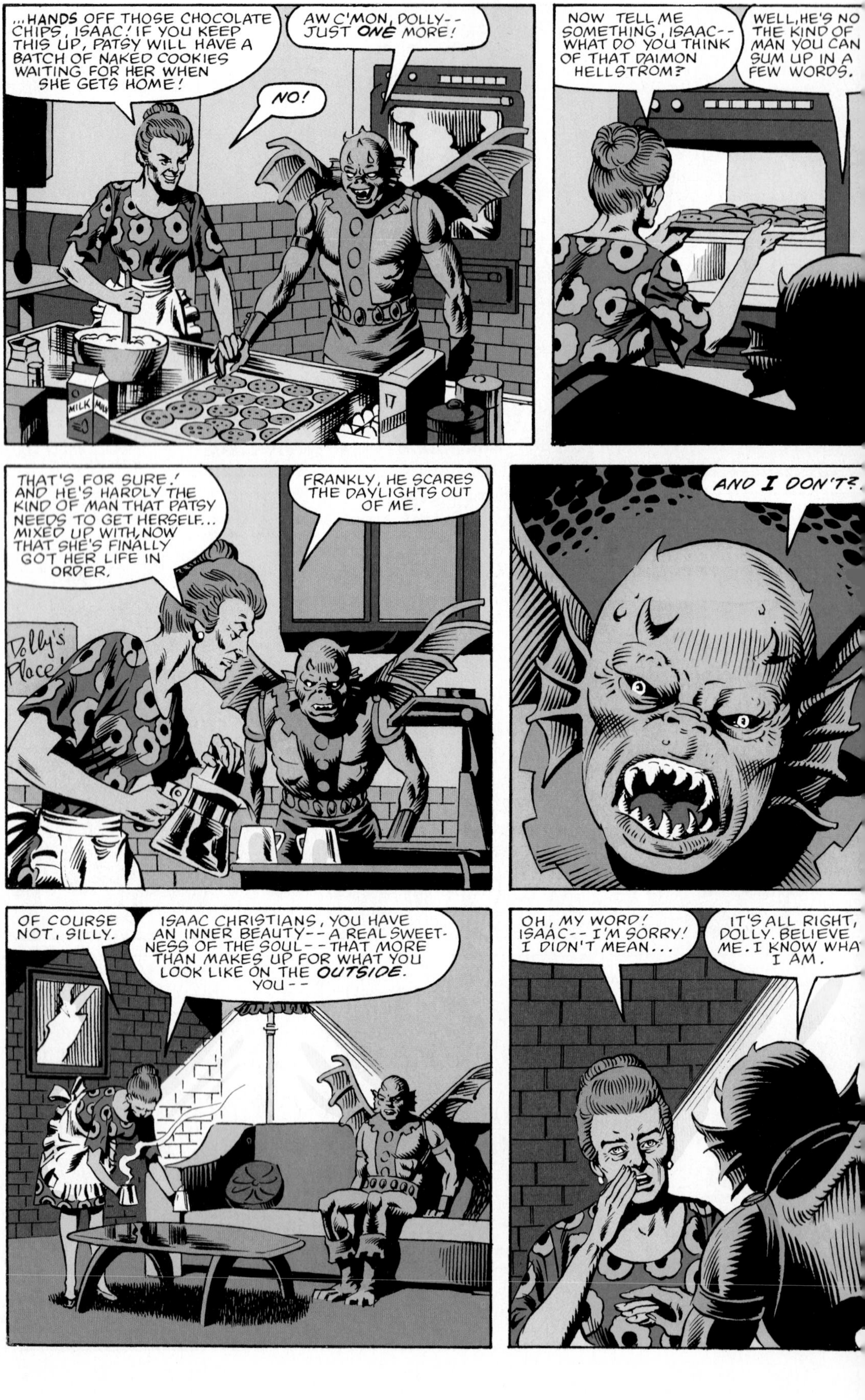
...HANDS OFF THOSE CHOCOLATE CHIPS, ISAAC! IF YOU KEEP THIS UP, PATSY WILL HAVE A BATCH OF NAKED COOKIES WAITING FOR HER WHEN SHE GETS HOME!
AW C'MON, DOLLY-- JUST ONE MORE!
NO!
MILK
NOW TELL ME SOMETHING, ISAAC-- WHAT DO YOU THINK OF THAT DAIMON HELLSTROM?
WELL, HE'S NO THE KIND OF MAN YOU CAN SUM UP IN A FEW WORDS.
THAT'S FOR SURE! AND HE'S HARDLY THE KIND OF MAN THAT PATSY NEEDS TO GET HERSELF... MIXED UP WITH, NOW THAT SHE'S FINALLY GOT HER LIFE IN ORDER.
FRANKLY, HE SCARES THE DAYLIGHTS OUT OF ME.
Dolly's Place
AND I DON'T?
OF COURSE NOT, SILLY.
ISAAC CHRISTIANS, YOU HAVE AN INNER BEAUTY-- A REAL SWEETNESS OF THE SOUL--THAT MORE THAN MAKES UP FOR WHAT YOU LOOK LIKE ON THE OUTSIDE. YOU--
OH, MY WORD! ISAAC-- I'M SORRY! I DIDN'T MEAN...
IT'S ALL RIGHT, DOLLY. BELIEVE ME. I KNOW WHA I AM.

AND I LIKE WHAT YOU SAID.

Y'KNOW -- IT SURE IS NICE HAVING SOMEONE CLOSE TO MY OWN AGE TO TALK TO... TO BE WITH. HECK, I *LOVE* THE KIDS IN THE DEFENDERS --

-- I GUESS I THINK OF THEM AS THE CHILDREN I NEVER HAD, BACK WHEN I WAS STILL... A MAN.

BUT, SOMETIMES, IT'S JUST PLAIN TIRESOME TRYING TO BRIDGE THE GAP OF YEARS.

WHAT I MEAN TO SAY, DOLLY, IS *THANK YOU* -- FOR BEING HERE FOR ME. FOR CARING.

OH, AND THANK *YOU*, ISAAC. SO MUCH.

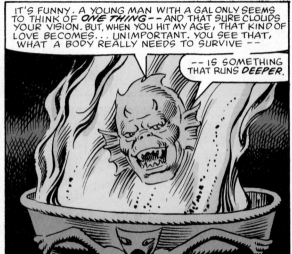

IT'S FUNNY. A YOUNG MAN WITH A GAL ONLY SEEMS TO THINK OF *ONE THING* -- AND THAT SURE CLOUDS YOUR VISION. BUT, WHEN YOU HIT MY AGE, THAT KIND OF LOVE BECOMES... UNIMPORTANT. YOU SEE THAT, WHAT A BODY REALLY NEEDS TO SURVIVE --

-- IS SOMETHING THAT RUNS *DEEPER*.

I'VE NEVER BEEN MARRIED, MYSELF -- BUT THE MARRIAGES I'VE SEEN WORK, WORKED BECAUSE FOLKS WERE *FRIENDS* FIRST -- AND *LOVERS* SECOND.

LET'S FACE IT: PASSION COMES AND GOES LIKE THE TIDE --

-- BUT THAT *DEEPER* LOVE... YOU CAN HANG ONTO IT FOREVER.

-- OR DARN CLOSE TO IT

19

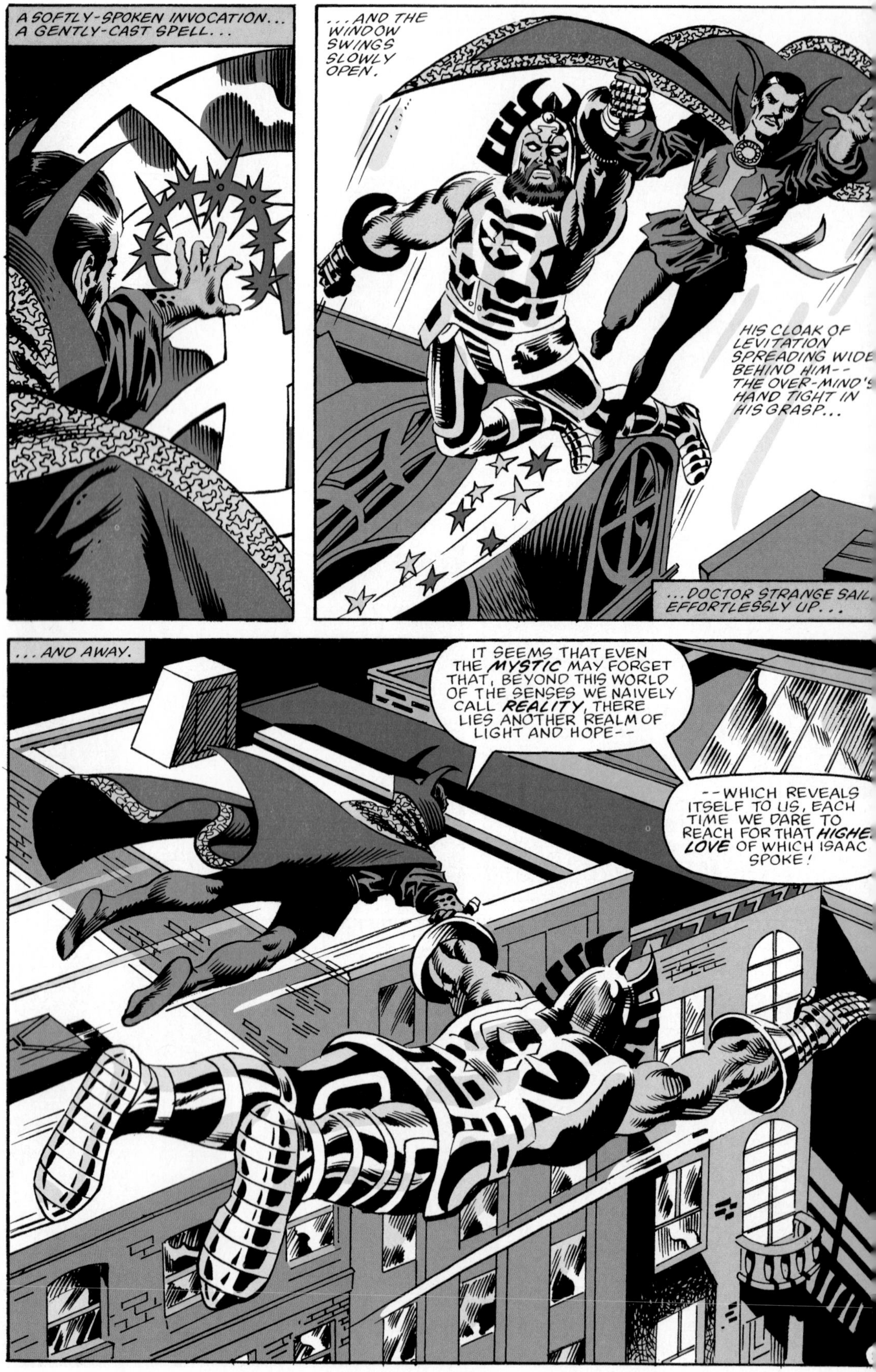
A SOFTLY-SPOKEN INVOCATION... A GENTLY-CAST SPELL...
...AND THE WINDOW SWINGS SLOWLY OPEN.
HIS CLOAK OF LEVITATION SPREADING WIDE BEHIND HIM-- THE OVER-MIND'S HAND TIGHT IN HIS GRASP...
...DOCTOR STRANGE SAILS EFFORTLESSLY UP...
...AND AWAY.
IT SEEMS THAT EVEN THE MYSTIC MAY FORGET THAT, BEYOND THIS WORLD OF THE SENSES WE NAIVELY CALL REALITY, THERE LIES ANOTHER REALM OF LIGHT AND HOPE--
--WHICH REVEALS ITSELF TO US, EACH TIME WE DARE TO REACH FOR THAT HIGHER LOVE OF WHICH ISAAC SPOKE!

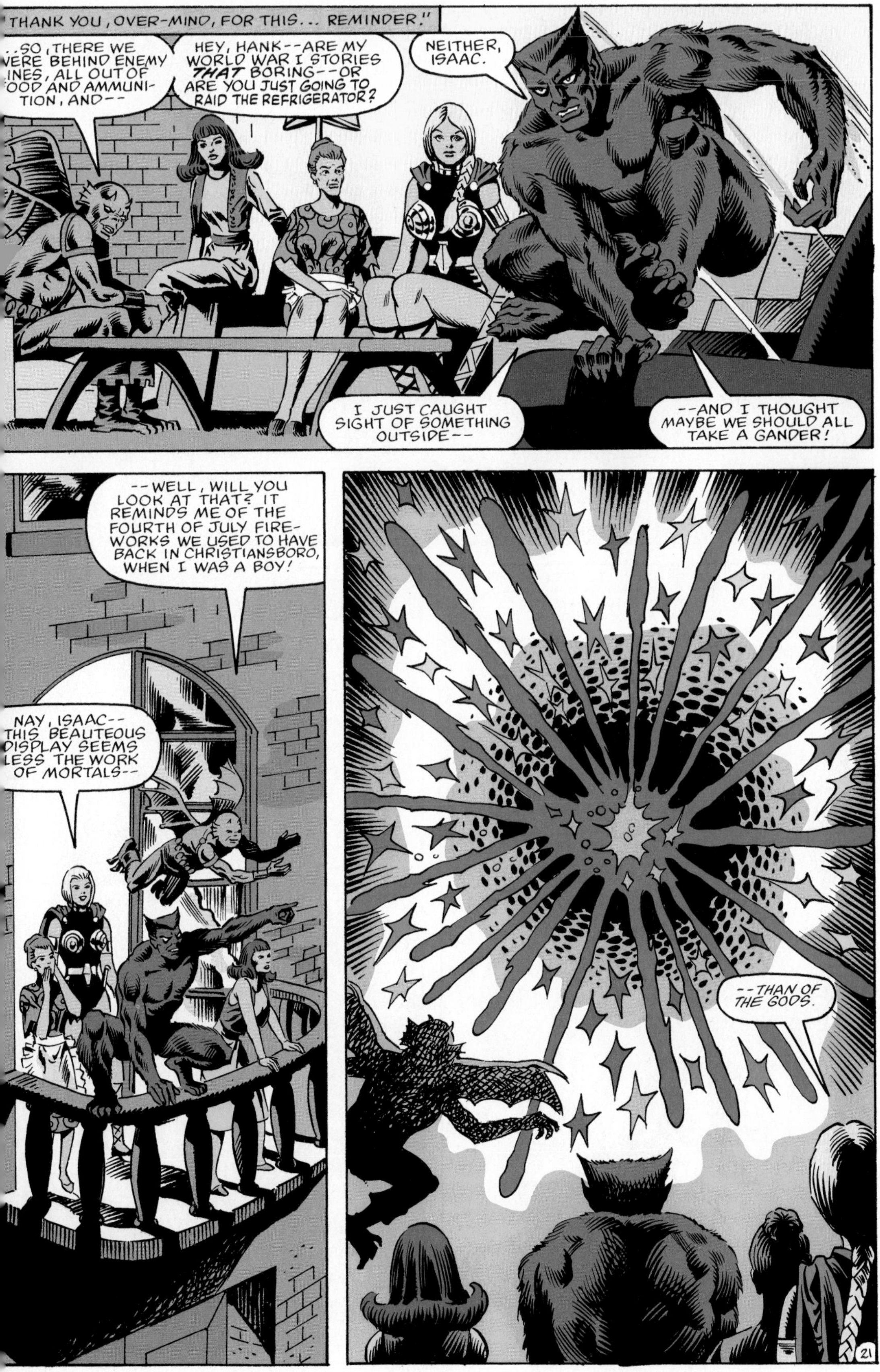
"THANK YOU, OVER-MIND, FOR THIS... REMINDER."
..SO, THERE WE WERE BEHIND ENEMY LINES, ALL OUT OF FOOD AND AMMUNITION, AND--
HEY, HANK--ARE MY WORLD WAR I STORIES THAT BORING--OR ARE YOU JUST GOING TO RAID THE REFRIGERATOR?
NEITHER, ISAAC.
I JUST CAUGHT SIGHT OF SOMETHING OUTSIDE--
--AND I THOUGHT MAYBE WE SHOULD ALL TAKE A GANDER!
--WELL, WILL YOU LOOK AT THAT? IT REMINDS ME OF THE FOURTH OF JULY FIREWORKS WE USED TO HAVE BACK IN CHRISTIANSBORO, WHEN I WAS A BOY!
NAY, ISAAC--THIS BEAUTEOUS DISPLAY SEEMS LESS THE WORK OF MORTALS--
--THAN OF THE GODS.
21

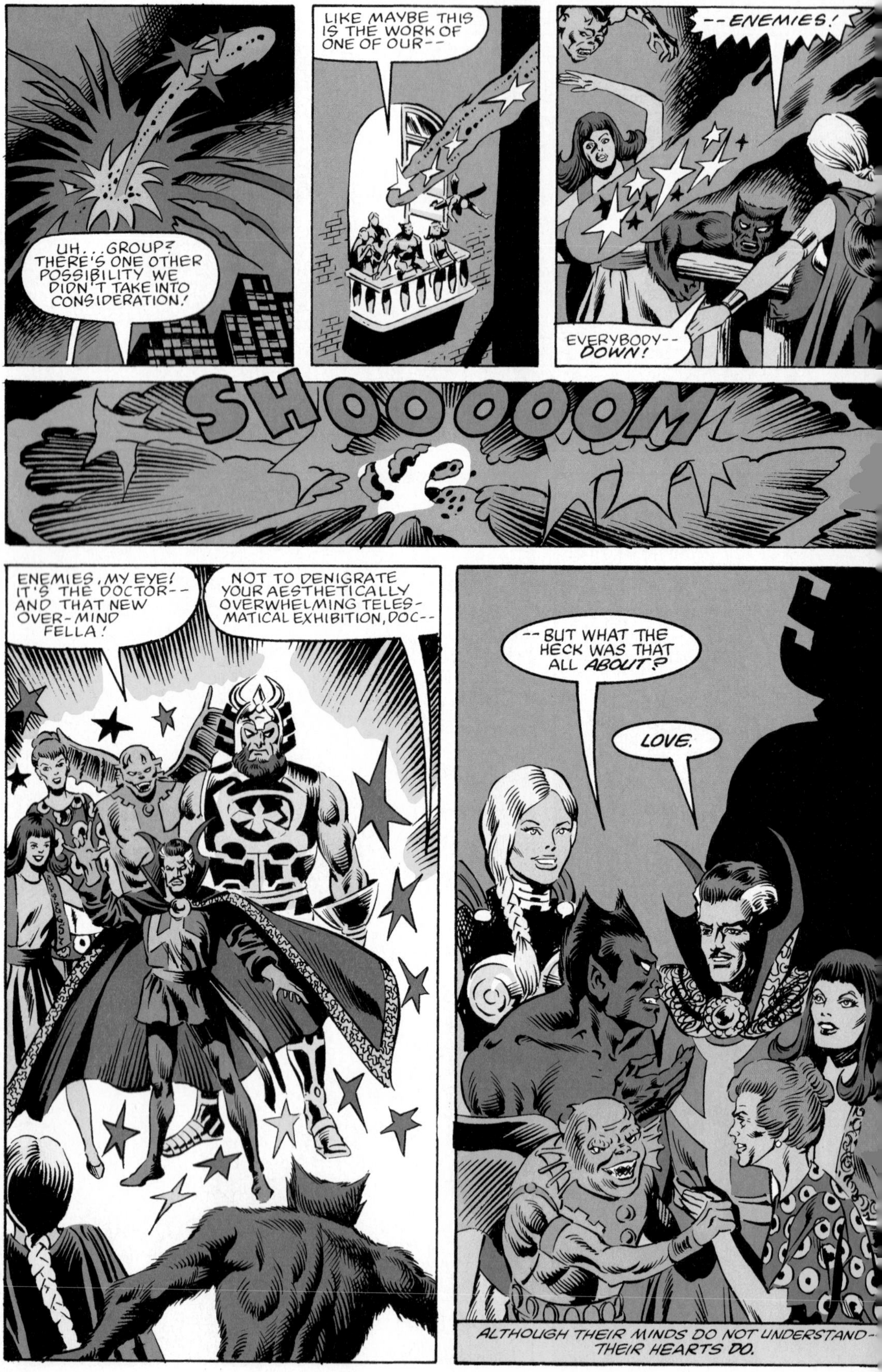
UH...GROUP? THERE'S ONE OTHER POSSIBILITY WE DIDN'T TAKE INTO CONSIDERATION!
LIKE MAYBE THIS IS THE WORK OF ONE OF OUR--
--ENEMIES!
EVERYBODY--DOWN!
SHOOOOOM
ENEMIES, MY EYE! IT'S THE DOCTOR--AND THAT NEW OVER-MIND FELLA!
NOT TO DENIGRATE YOUR AESTHETICALLY OVERWHELMING TELES-MATICAL EXHIBITION, DOC--
--BUT WHAT THE HECK WAS THAT ALL ABOUT?
LOVE.
ALTHOUGH THEIR MINDS DO NOT UNDERSTAND-- THEIR HEARTS DO.

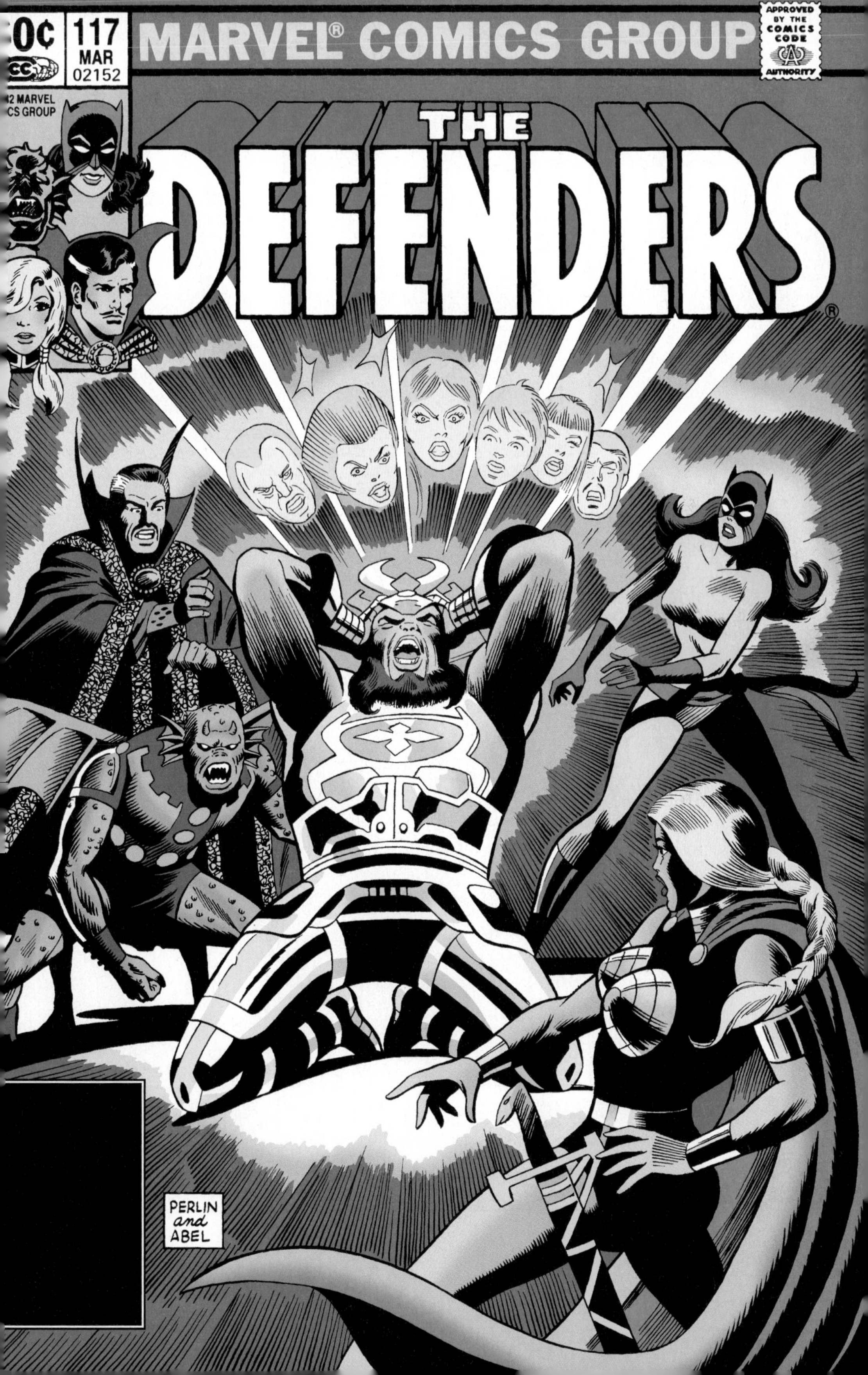

0¢ 117 MAR 02152
CC
MARVEL® COMICS GROUP
APPROVED BY THE COMICS CODE AUTHORITY
2 MARVEL CS GROUP
THE DEFENDERS®
PERLIN and ABEL

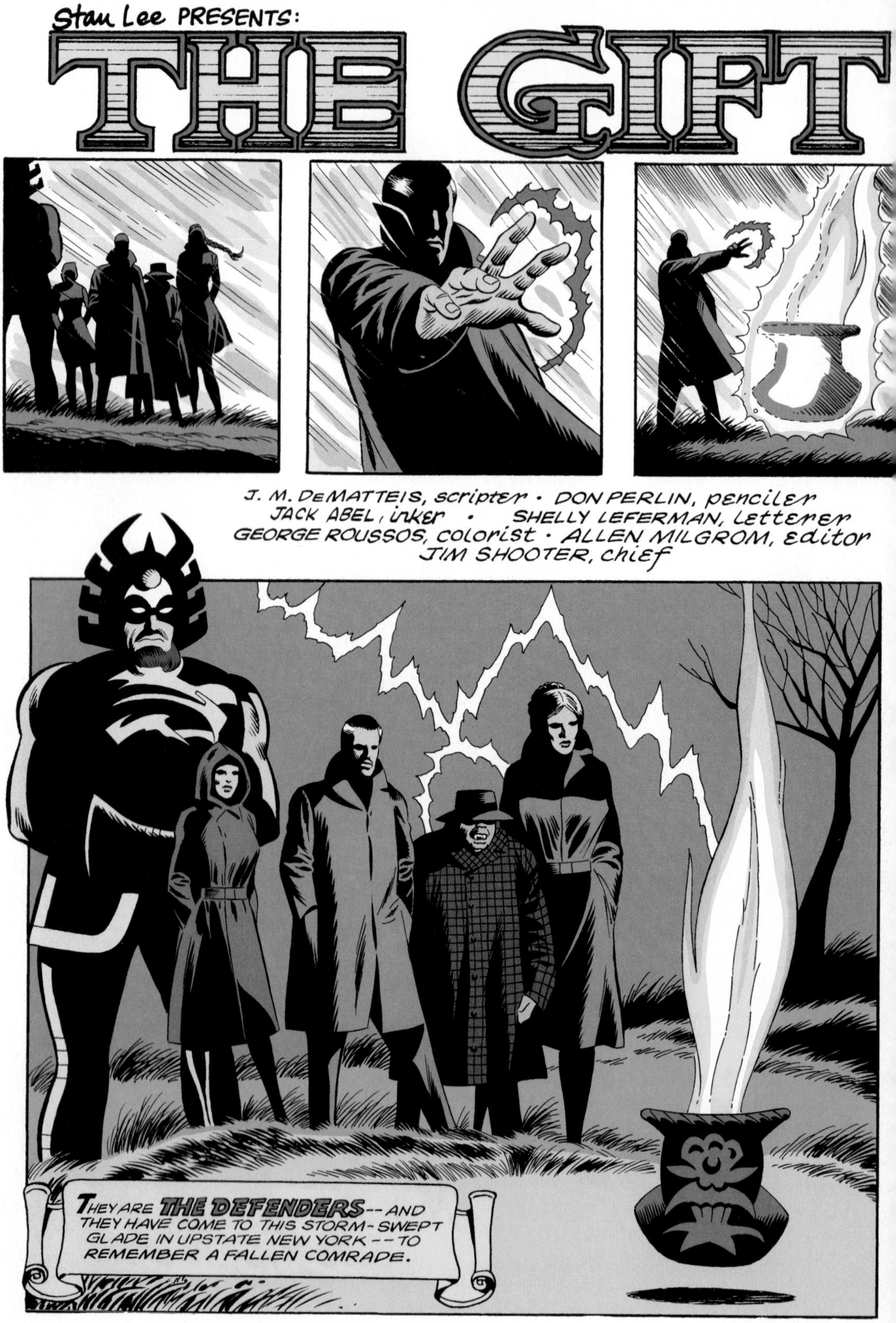
Stan Lee PRESENTS:
THE GIFT
J. M. DeMATTEIS, scripter • DON PERLIN, penciler
JACK ABEL, inker • SHELLY LEFERMAN, letterer
GEORGE ROUSSOS, colorist • ALLEN MILGROM, editor
JIM SHOOTER, chief
THEY ARE THE DEFENDERS-- AND THEY HAVE COME TO THIS STORM-SWEPT GLADE IN UPSTATE NEW YORK -- TO REMEMBER A FALLEN COMRADE.

NIGHTHAWK, I'D LIKE TO THINK THAT-- WHEREVER YOUR DEPARTED SPIRIT HAS JOURNEYED-- YOU CAN HEAR THE WORDS OF DOCTOR STRANGE.

THIS MYSTIC FLAME HAS BURNED, CONCEALED BY MY SPELLS, SINCE YOUR DEATH. AND IT SHALL BURN TILL TIME'S END.

AS SHALL OUR LOVE FOR YOU!

HIS WORDS SPEAK FOR ALL OF THEM...

..BUT ONE...

MEN HAVE CALLED ME...THE OVER-MIND!

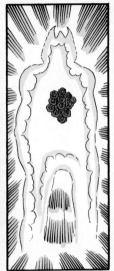

BUT THIS ALIEN FORM IS MERELY A SHELL, HOUSING THE UNITED CONSCIOUSNESS OF SIX TELEPATHS-- ONE OF WHOM WAS A WOMAN NAMED MINDY--

--WHO LOVED YOU, KYLE RICHMOND--

--SO VERY, VERY MUCH...

THAT LOVE DROVE ME MAD, KYLE...AND IT'S TAKEN THIS FUSION-- THIS REBIRTH AS A NEW LIFE-FORM-- TO BRING ME THE BALANCE AND CLARITY THAT ALWAYS SEEMED TO ELUDE ME.

I'VE FOUND HAPPINESS, KYLE. BUT I HAD TO TAKE THIS FORM-- OR AT LEAST THE ILLUSION OF FORM-- ONE LAST TIME--

--TO TELL YOU THAT I'M SORRY FOR THE PAIN I CAUSED YOU... AND THAT THE MEMORY OF OUR DAYS TOGETHER WILL LIGHT MY HEART--

--BEYOND TIME'S END...

2

207

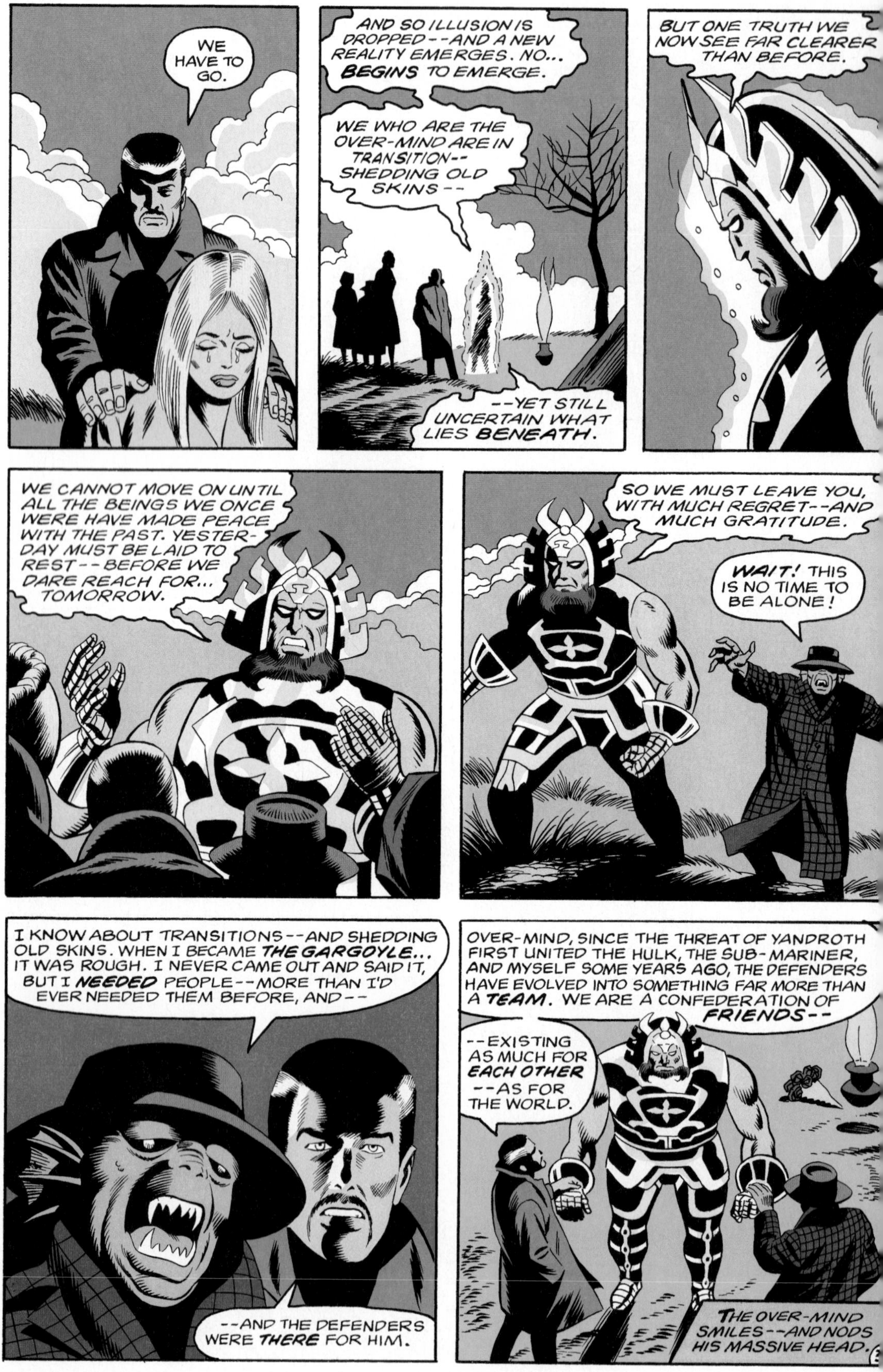
WE HAVE TO GO.
AND SO ILLUSION IS DROPPED--AND A NEW REALITY EMERGES. NO... BEGINS TO EMERGE.
WE WHO ARE THE OVER-MIND ARE IN TRANSITION--SHEDDING OLD SKINS--
--YET STILL UNCERTAIN WHAT LIES BENEATH.
BUT ONE TRUTH WE NOW SEE FAR CLEARER THAN BEFORE.
WE CANNOT MOVE ON UNTIL ALL THE BEINGS WE ONCE WERE HAVE MADE PEACE WITH THE PAST. YESTERDAY MUST BE LAID TO REST--BEFORE WE DARE REACH FOR... TOMORROW.
SO WE MUST LEAVE YOU, WITH MUCH REGRET--AND MUCH GRATITUDE.
WAIT! THIS IS NO TIME TO BE ALONE!
I KNOW ABOUT TRANSITIONS--AND SHEDDING OLD SKINS. WHEN I BECAME THE GARGOYLE... IT WAS ROUGH. I NEVER CAME OUT AND SAID IT, BUT I NEEDED PEOPLE--MORE THAN I'D EVER NEEDED THEM BEFORE, AND--
--AND THE DEFENDERS WERE THERE FOR HIM.
OVER-MIND, SINCE THE THREAT OF YANDROTH FIRST UNITED THE HULK, THE SUB-MARINER, AND MYSELF SOME YEARS AGO, THE DEFENDERS HAVE EVOLVED INTO SOMETHING FAR MORE THAN A TEAM. WE ARE A CONFEDERATION OF FRIENDS--
--EXISTING AS MUCH FOR EACH OTHER--AS FOR THE WORLD.
THE OVER-MIND SMILES--AND NODS HIS MASSIVE HEAD.

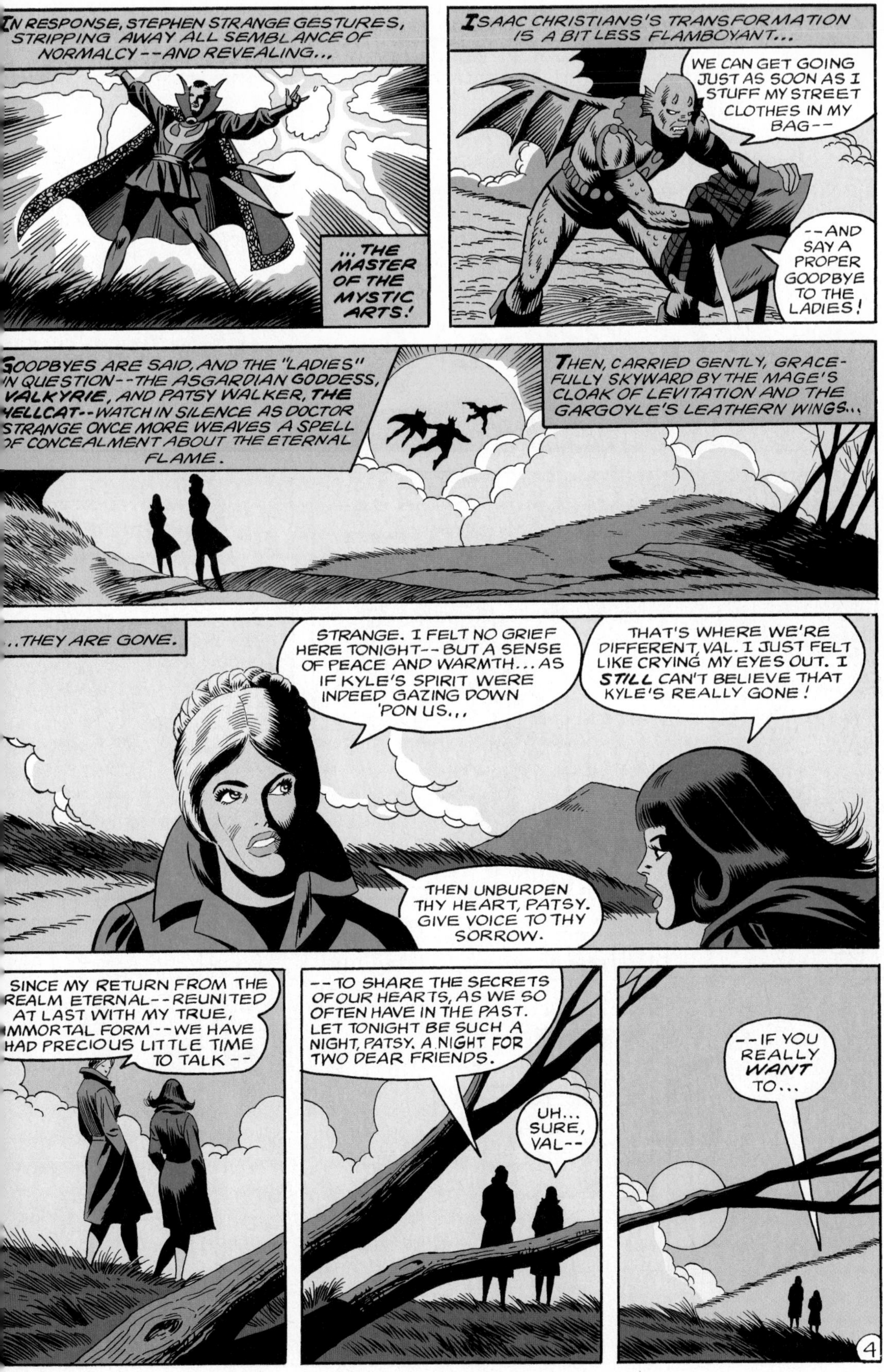
IN RESPONSE, STEPHEN STRANGE GESTURES, STRIPPING AWAY ALL SEMBLANCE OF NORMALCY--AND REVEALING...
...THE MASTER OF THE MYSTIC ARTS!
ISAAC CHRISTIANS'S TRANSFORMATION IS A BIT LESS FLAMBOYANT...
WE CAN GET GOING JUST AS SOON AS I STUFF MY STREET CLOTHES IN MY BAG--
--AND SAY A PROPER GOODBYE TO THE LADIES!
GOODBYES ARE SAID, AND THE "LADIES" IN QUESTION--THE ASGARDIAN GODDESS, VALKYRIE, AND PATSY WALKER, THE HELLCAT--WATCH IN SILENCE AS DOCTOR STRANGE ONCE MORE WEAVES A SPELL OF CONCEALMENT ABOUT THE ETERNAL FLAME.
THEN, CARRIED GENTLY, GRACEFULLY SKYWARD BY THE MAGE'S CLOAK OF LEVITATION AND THE GARGOYLE'S LEATHERN WINGS...
...THEY ARE GONE.
STRANGE. I FELT NO GRIEF HERE TONIGHT--BUT A SENSE OF PEACE AND WARMTH... AS IF KYLE'S SPIRIT WERE INDEED GAZING DOWN 'PON US...
THAT'S WHERE WE'RE DIFFERENT, VAL. I JUST FELT LIKE CRYING MY EYES OUT. I STILL CAN'T BELIEVE THAT KYLE'S REALLY GONE!
THEN UNBURDEN THY HEART, PATSY. GIVE VOICE TO THY SORROW.
SINCE MY RETURN FROM THE REALM ETERNAL--REUNITED AT LAST WITH MY TRUE, IMMORTAL FORM--WE HAVE HAD PRECIOUS LITTLE TIME TO TALK--
--TO SHARE THE SECRETS OF OUR HEARTS, AS WE SO OFTEN HAVE IN THE PAST. LET TONIGHT BE SUCH A NIGHT, PATSY. A NIGHT FOR TWO DEAR FRIENDS.
UH... SURE, VAL--
--IF YOU REALLY WANT TO...
4

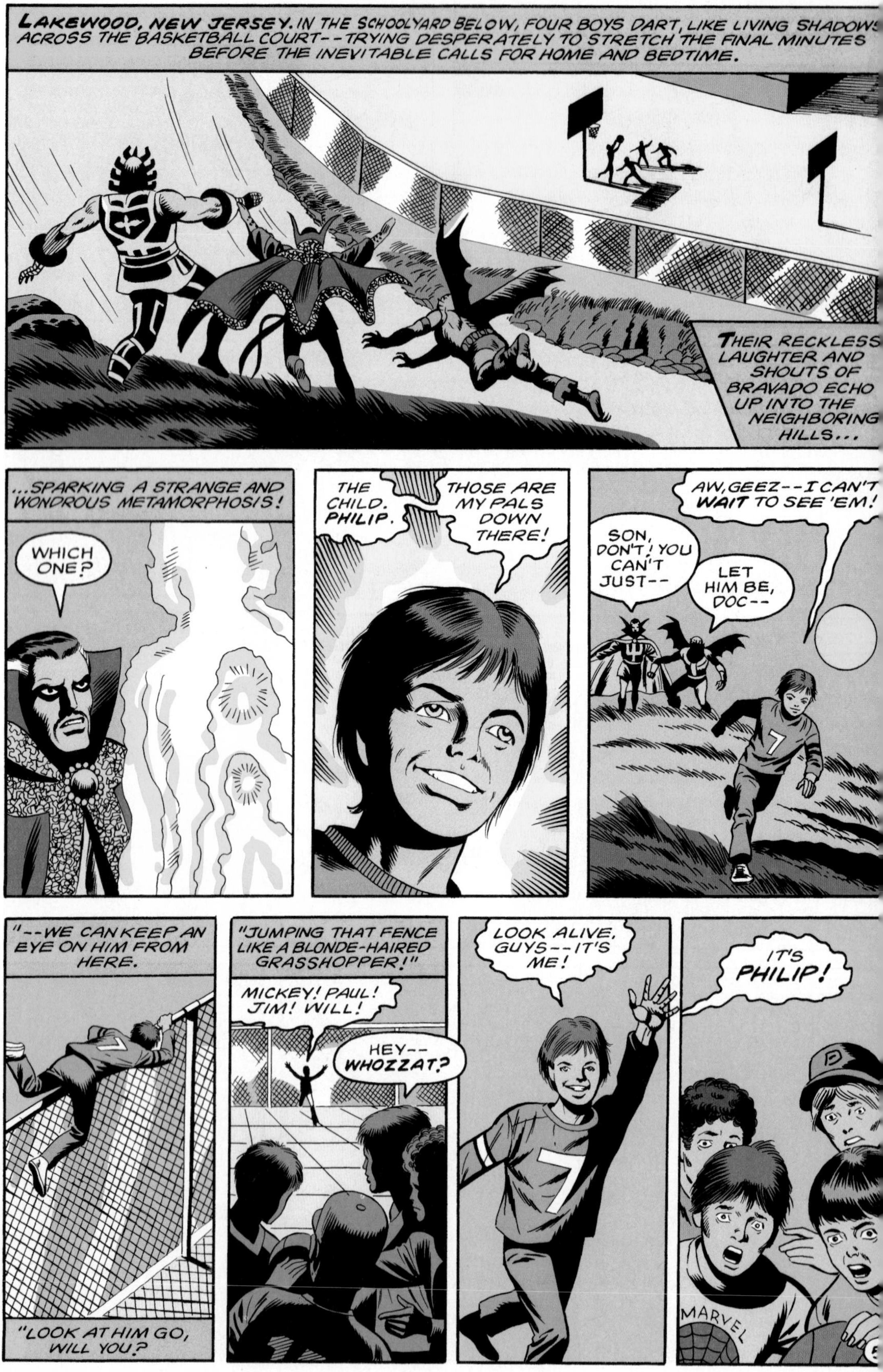
LAKEWOOD, NEW JERSEY. IN THE SCHOOLYARD BELOW, FOUR BOYS DART, LIKE LIVING SHADOWS ACROSS THE BASKETBALL COURT--TRYING DESPERATELY TO STRETCH THE FINAL MINUTES BEFORE THE INEVITABLE CALLS FOR HOME AND BEDTIME.
THEIR RECKLESS LAUGHTER AND SHOUTS OF BRAVADO ECHO UP INTO THE NEIGHBORING HILLS...
...SPARKING A STRANGE AND WONDROUS METAMORPHOSIS!
WHICH ONE?
THE CHILD. PHILIP.
THOSE ARE MY PALS DOWN THERE!
AW, GEEZ--I CAN'T WAIT TO SEE 'EM!
SON, DON'T! YOU CAN'T JUST--
LET HIM BE, DOC--
"--WE CAN KEEP AN EYE ON HIM FROM HERE.
"LOOK AT HIM GO, WILL YOU?
"JUMPING THAT FENCE LIKE A BLONDE-HAIRED GRASSHOPPER!"
MICKEY! PAUL! JIM! WILL!
HEY--WHOZZAT?
LOOK ALIVE, GUYS--IT'S ME!
IT'S PHILIP!
MARVEL

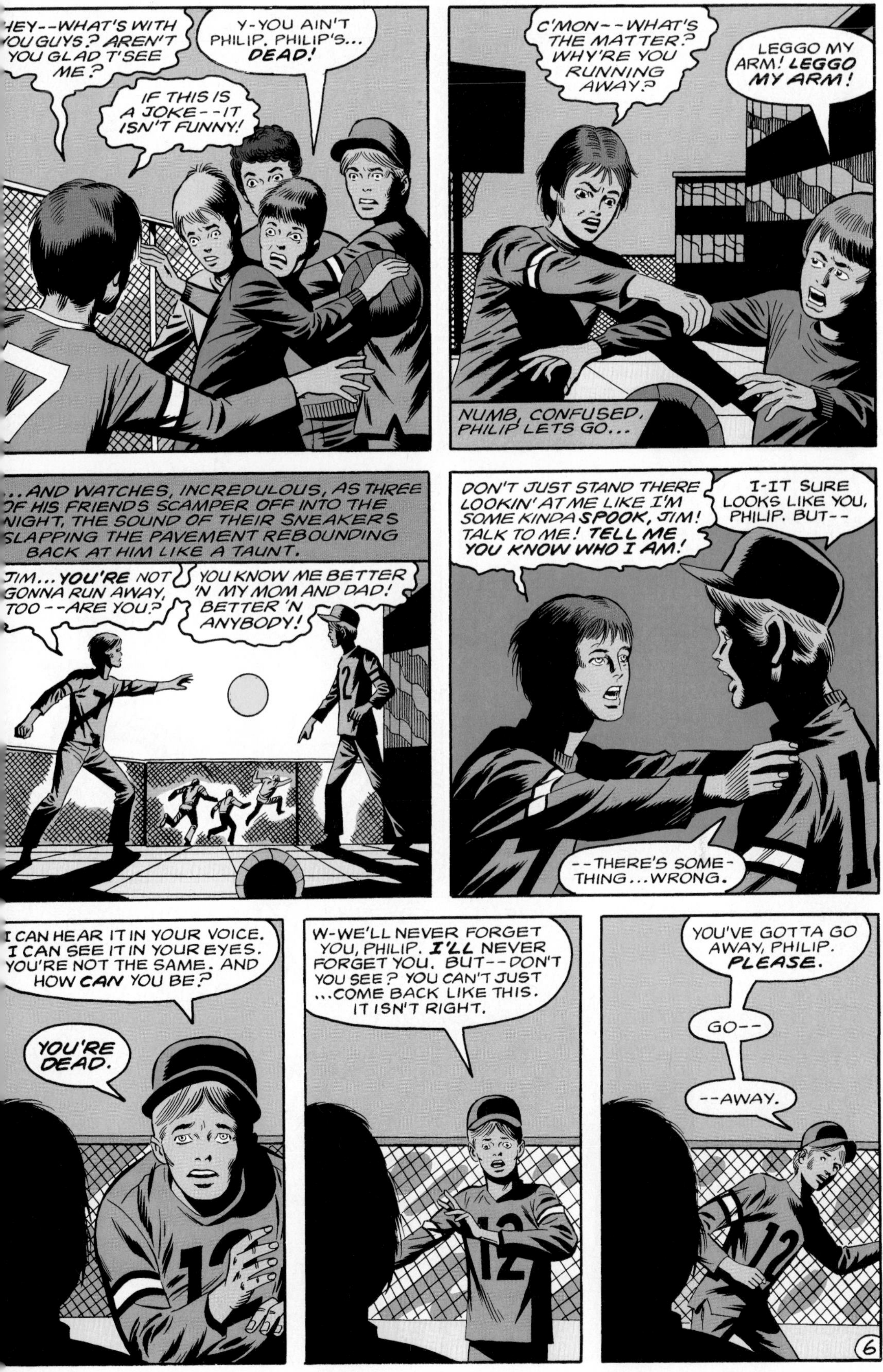
HEY--WHAT'S WITH YOU GUYS? AREN'T YOU GLAD T'SEE ME?
Y-YOU AIN'T PHILIP. PHILIP'S... DEAD!
IF THIS IS A JOKE--IT ISN'T FUNNY!
C'MON--WHAT'S THE MATTER? WHY'RE YOU RUNNING AWAY?
LEGGO MY ARM! LEGGO MY ARM!
NUMB, CONFUSED, PHILIP LETS GO...
...AND WATCHES, INCREDULOUS, AS THREE OF HIS FRIENDS SCAMPER OFF INTO THE NIGHT, THE SOUND OF THEIR SNEAKERS SLAPPING THE PAVEMENT REBOUNDING BACK AT HIM LIKE A TAUNT.
JIM... YOU'RE NOT GONNA RUN AWAY, TOO--ARE YOU?
YOU KNOW ME BETTER 'N MY MOM AND DAD! BETTER 'N ANYBODY!
DON'T JUST STAND THERE LOOKIN' AT ME LIKE I'M SOME KINDA SPOOK, JIM! TALK TO ME! TELL ME YOU KNOW WHO I AM!
I-IT SURE LOOKS LIKE YOU, PHILIP. BUT--
--THERE'S SOMETHING... WRONG.
I CAN HEAR IT IN YOUR VOICE. I CAN SEE IT IN YOUR EYES. YOU'RE NOT THE SAME. AND HOW CAN YOU BE?
YOU'RE DEAD.
W-WE'LL NEVER FORGET YOU, PHILIP. I'LL NEVER FORGET YOU. BUT--DON'T YOU SEE? YOU CAN'T JUST ...COME BACK LIKE THIS. IT ISN'T RIGHT.
YOU'VE GOTTA GO AWAY, PHILIP. PLEASE.
GO--
--AWAY.
6

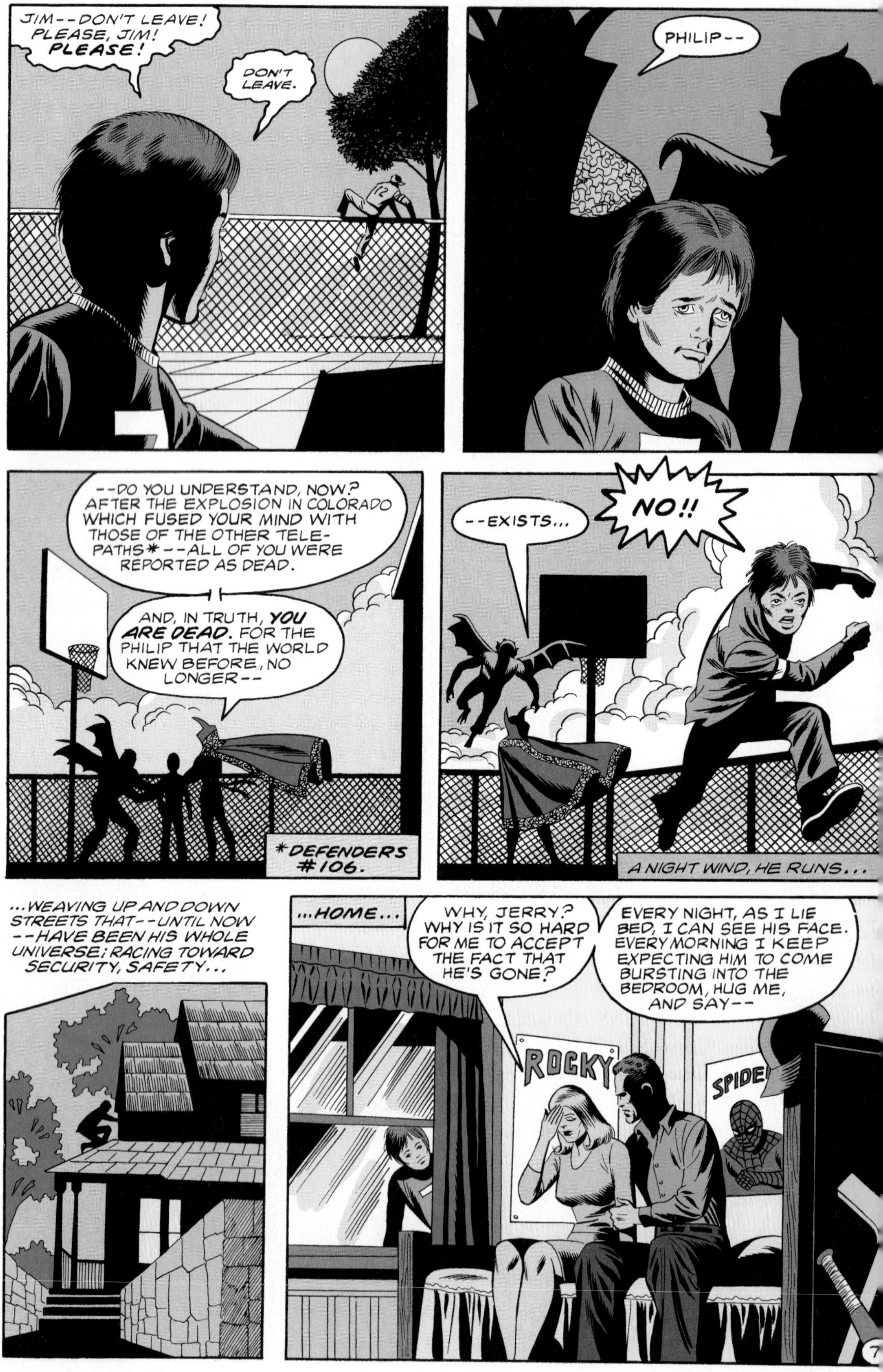

JIM--DON'T LEAVE! PLEASE, JIM! PLEASE!
DON'T LEAVE.
PHILIP--
--DO YOU UNDERSTAND, NOW? AFTER THE EXPLOSION IN COLORADO WHICH FUSED YOUR MIND WITH THOSE OF THE OTHER TELE-PATHS*--ALL OF YOU WERE REPORTED AS DEAD.
AND, IN TRUTH, YOU ARE DEAD. FOR THE PHILIP THAT THE WORLD KNEW BEFORE, NO LONGER--
*DEFENDERS #106.
--EXISTS...
NO!!
A NIGHT WIND, HE RUNS...
...WEAVING UP AND DOWN STREETS THAT--UNTIL NOW--HAVE BEEN HIS WHOLE UNIVERSE; RACING TOWARD SECURITY, SAFETY...
...HOME...
WHY, JERRY? WHY IS IT SO HARD FOR ME TO ACCEPT THE FACT THAT HE'S GONE?
EVERY NIGHT, AS I LIE BED, I CAN SEE HIS FACE. EVERY MORNING I KEEP EXPECTING HIM TO COME BURSTING INTO THE BEDROOM, HUG ME, AND SAY--
ROCKY
SPIDE
7

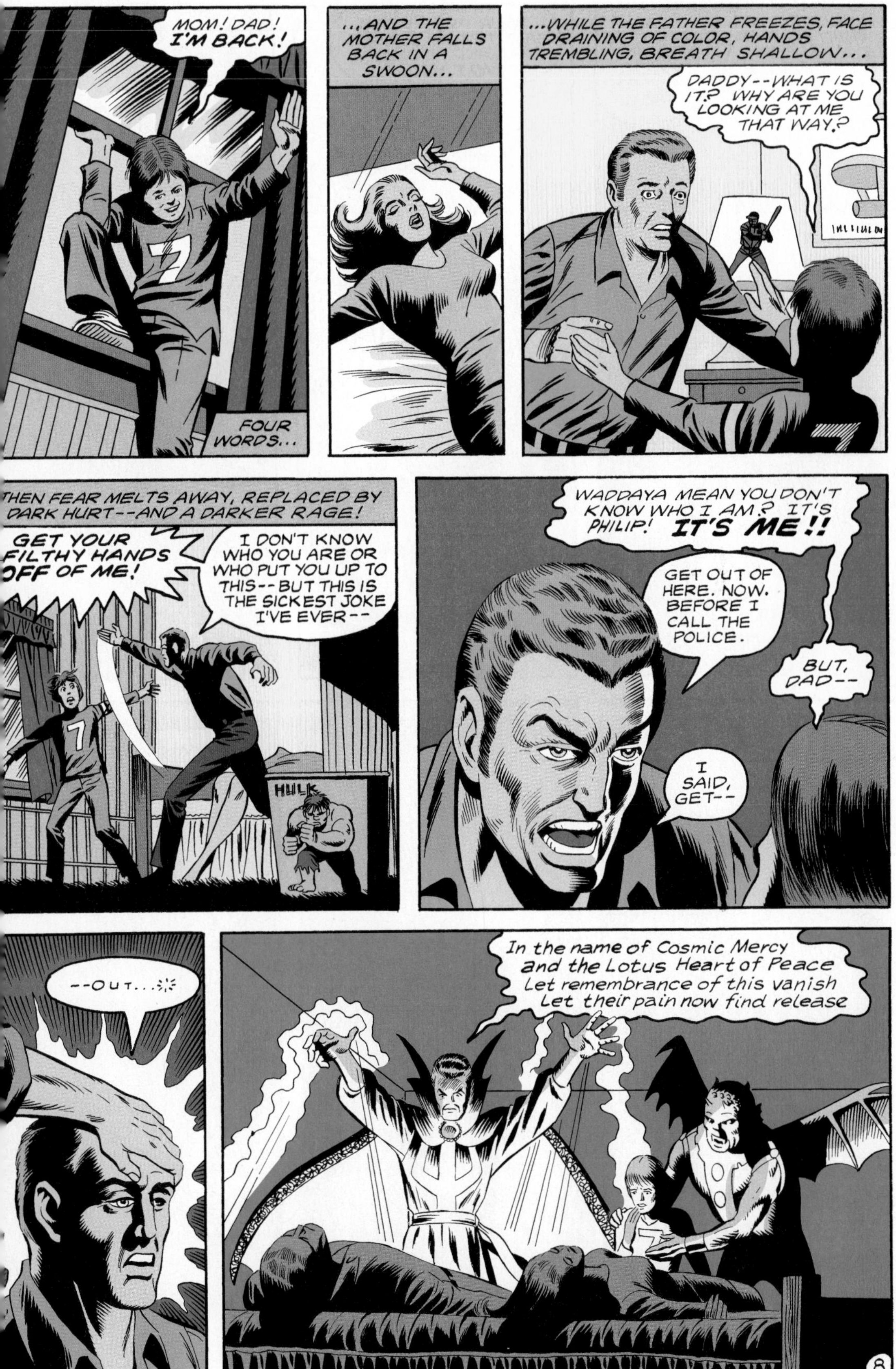

MOM! DAD! I'M BACK!
FOUR WORDS...
...AND THE MOTHER FALLS BACK IN A SWOON...
...WHILE THE FATHER FREEZES, FACE DRAINING OF COLOR, HANDS TREMBLING, BREATH SHALLOW...
DADDY--WHAT IS IT? WHY ARE YOU LOOKING AT ME THAT WAY?
THEN FEAR MELTS AWAY, REPLACED BY DARK HURT--AND A DARKER RAGE!
GET YOUR FILTHY HANDS OFF OF ME!
I DON'T KNOW WHO YOU ARE OR WHO PUT YOU UP TO THIS--BUT THIS IS THE SICKEST JOKE I'VE EVER--
HULK
WADDAYA MEAN YOU DON'T KNOW WHO I AM? IT'S PHILIP! IT'S ME!!
GET OUT OF HERE. NOW. BEFORE I CALL THE POLICE.
BUT, DAD--
I SAID, GET--
--OUT...
In the name of Cosmic Mercy
and the Lotus Heart of Peace
Let remembrance of this vanish
Let their pain now find release
8

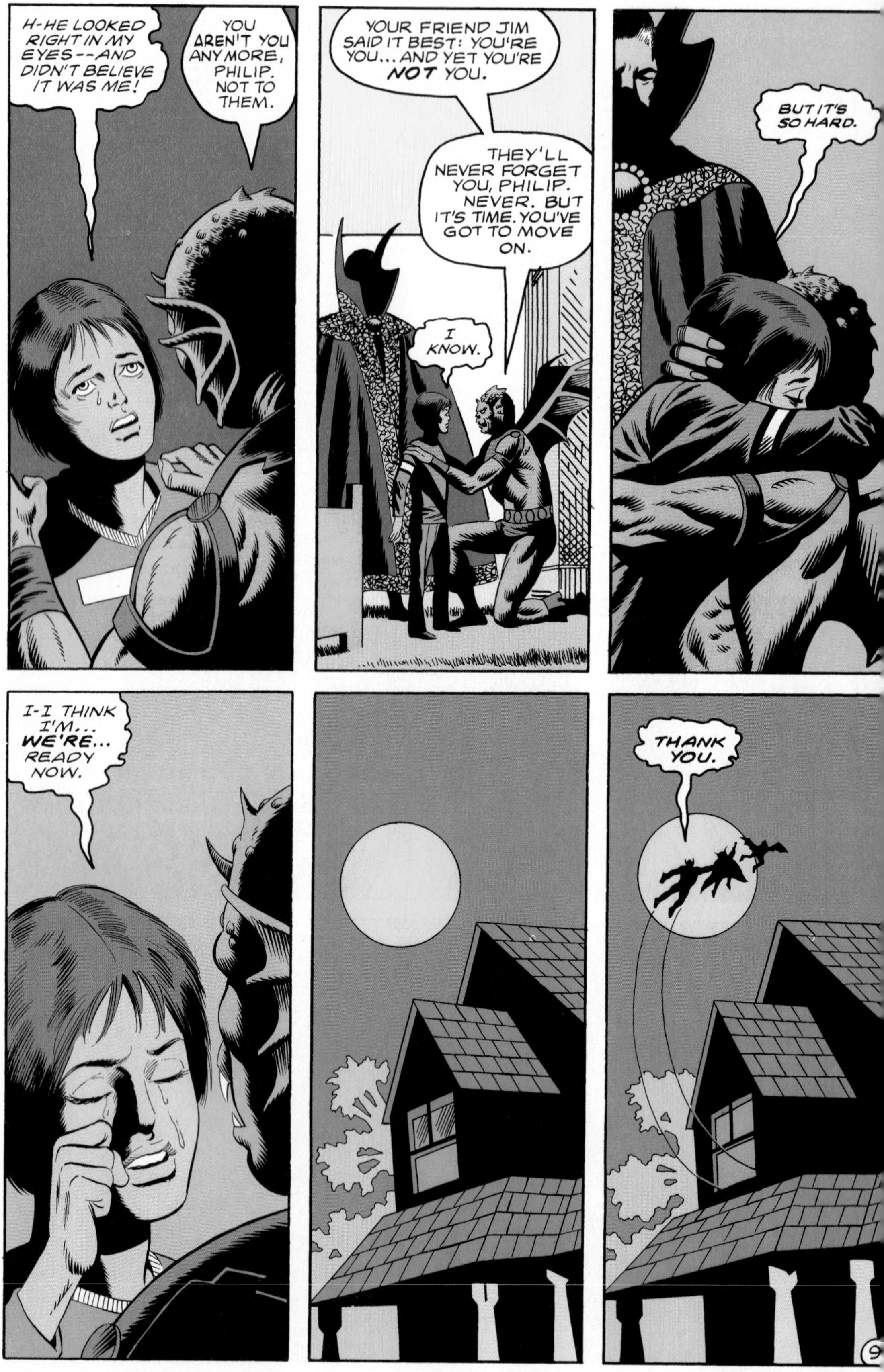
H-HE LOOKED RIGHT IN MY EYES--AND DIDN'T BELIEVE IT WAS ME!
YOU AREN'T YOU ANYMORE, PHILIP. NOT TO THEM.
YOUR FRIEND JIM SAID IT BEST: YOU'RE YOU... AND YET YOU'RE NOT YOU.
THEY'LL NEVER FORGET YOU, PHILIP. NEVER. BUT IT'S TIME. YOU'VE GOT TO MOVE ON.
I KNOW.
BUT IT'S SO HARD.
I-I THINK I'M... WE'RE... READY NOW.
THANK YOU.
9

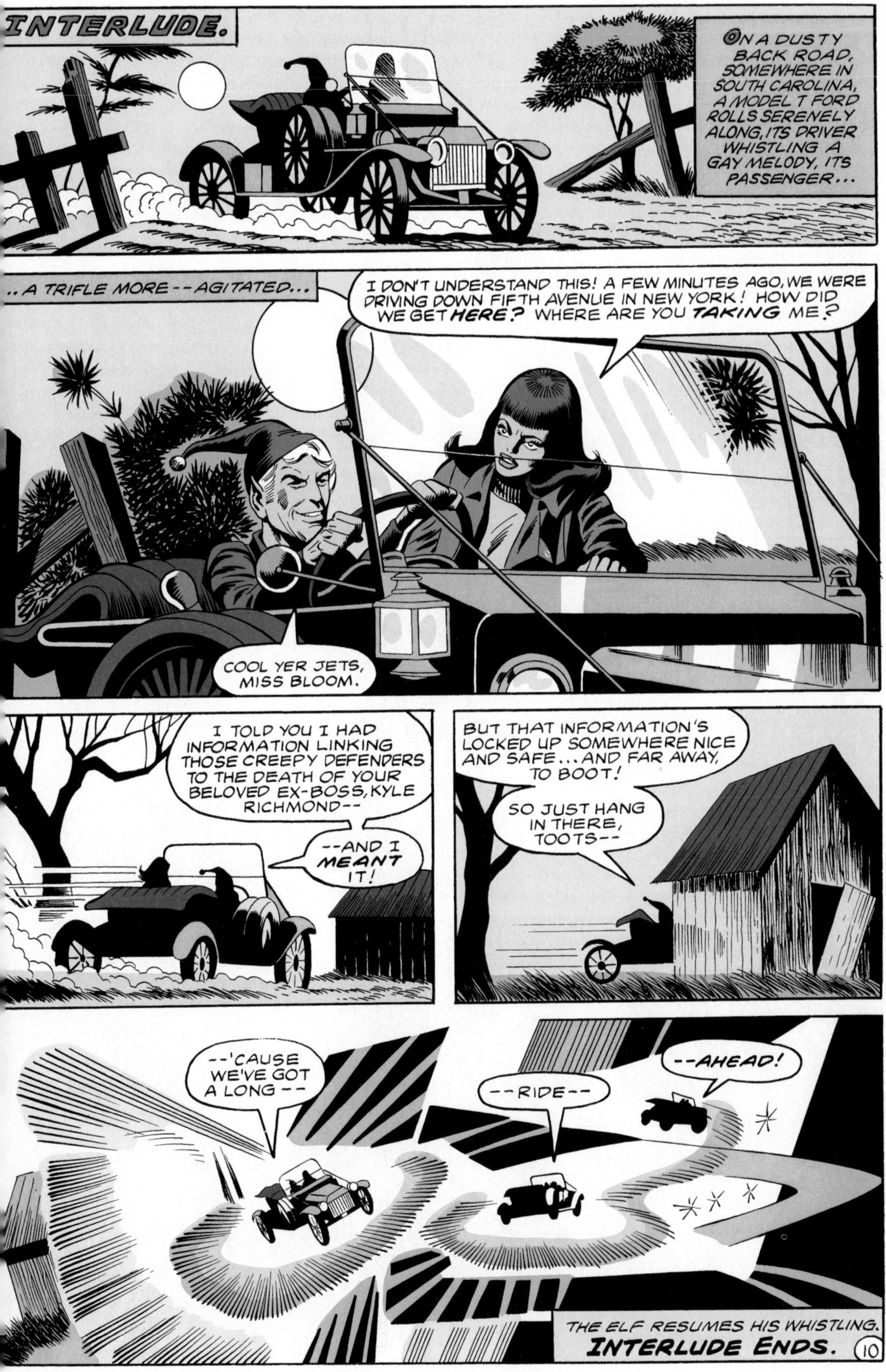
INTERLUDE.
ON A DUSTY BACK ROAD, SOMEWHERE IN SOUTH CAROLINA, A MODEL T FORD ROLLS SERENELY ALONG, ITS DRIVER WHISTLING A GAY MELODY, ITS PASSENGER...
..A TRIFLE MORE--AGITATED...
I DON'T UNDERSTAND THIS! A FEW MINUTES AGO, WE WERE DRIVING DOWN FIFTH AVENUE IN NEW YORK! HOW DID WE GET HERE? WHERE ARE YOU TAKING ME?
COOL YER JETS, MISS BLOOM.
I TOLD YOU I HAD INFORMATION LINKING THOSE CREEPY DEFENDERS TO THE DEATH OF YOUR BELOVED EX-BOSS, KYLE RICHMOND--
--AND I MEANT IT!
BUT THAT INFORMATION'S LOCKED UP SOMEWHERE NICE AND SAFE... AND FAR AWAY, TO BOOT!
SO JUST HANG IN THERE, TOOTS--
--'CAUSE WE'VE GOT A LONG--
--RIDE--
--AHEAD!
THE ELF RESUMES HIS WHISTLING. INTERLUDE ENDS.
10

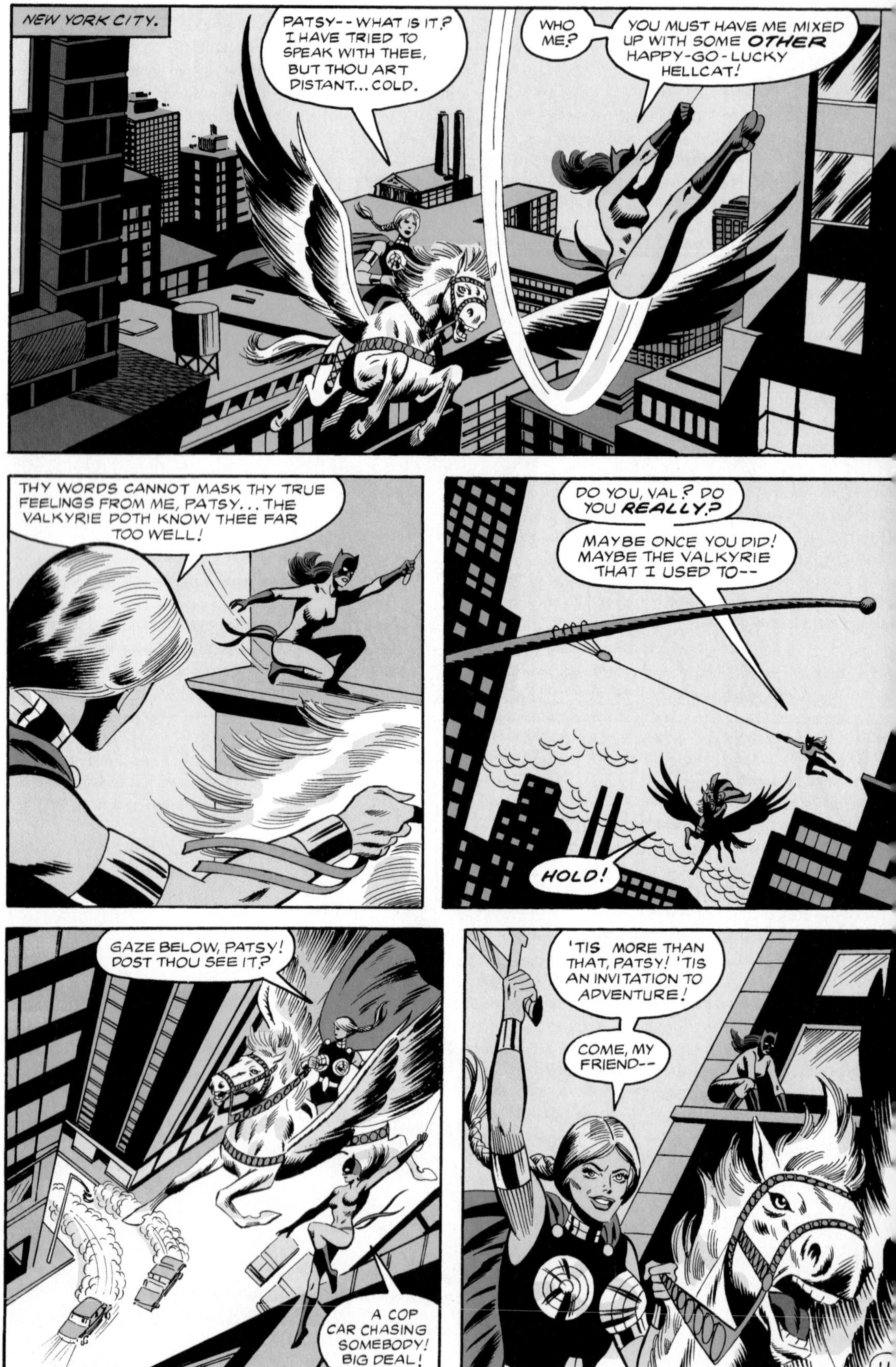
NEW YORK CITY.
PATSY--WHAT IS IT? I HAVE TRIED TO SPEAK WITH THEE, BUT THOU ART DISTANT... COLD.
WHO ME?
YOU MUST HAVE ME MIXED UP WITH SOME OTHER HAPPY-GO-LUCKY HELLCAT!
THY WORDS CANNOT MASK THY TRUE FEELINGS FROM ME, PATSY... THE VALKYRIE DOTH KNOW THEE FAR TOO WELL!
DO YOU, VAL? DO YOU REALLY?
MAYBE ONCE YOU DID! MAYBE THE VALKYRIE THAT I USED TO--
HOLD!
GAZE BELOW, PATSY! DOST THOU SEE IT?
A COP CAR CHASING SOMEBODY! BIG DEAL!
'TIS MORE THAN THAT, PATSY! 'TIS AN INVITATION TO ADVENTURE!
COME, MY FRIEND--
11

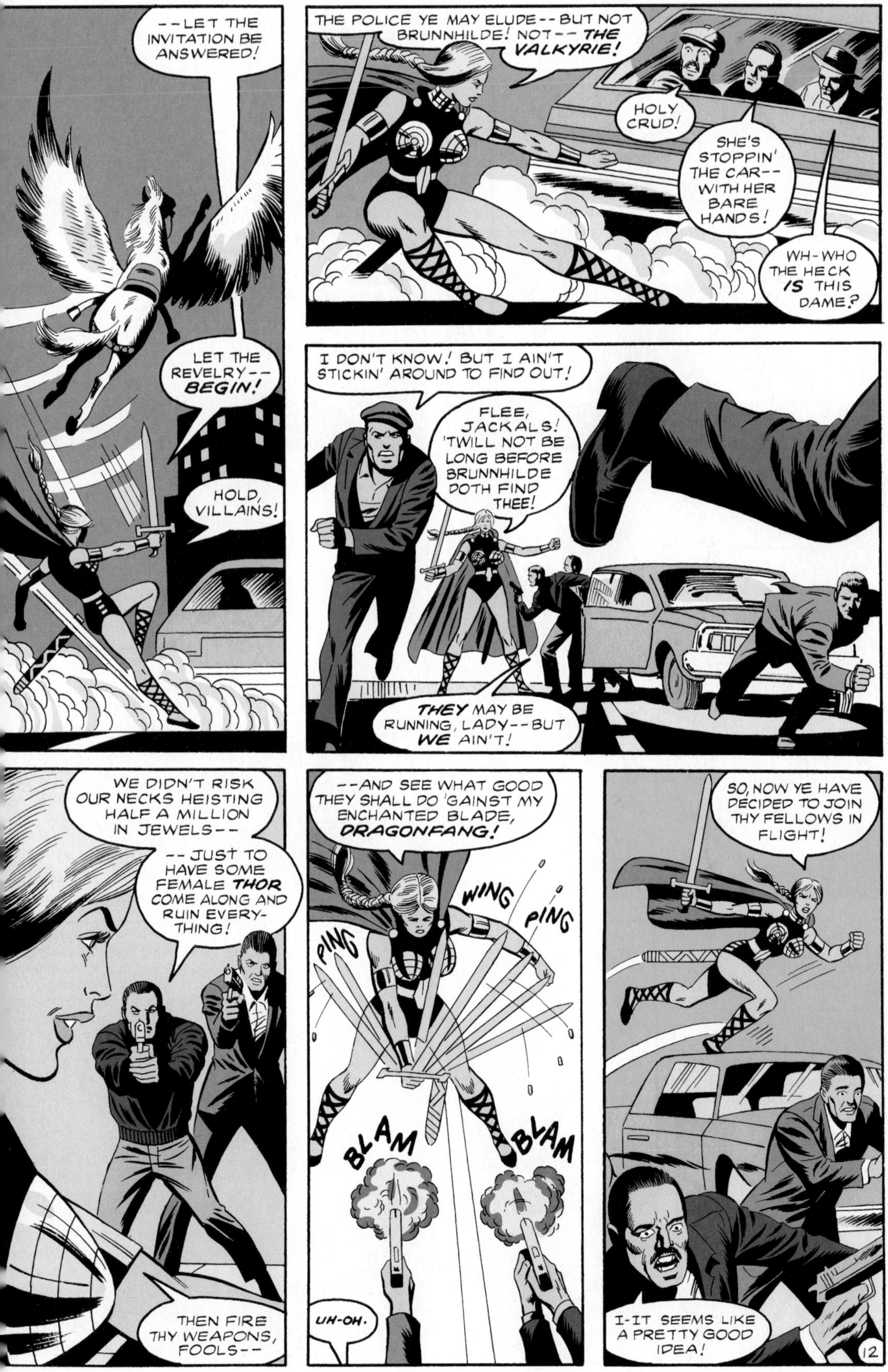
--LET THE INVITATION BE ANSWERED!
LET THE REVELRY--BEGIN!
HOLD, VILLAINS!
THE POLICE YE MAY ELUDE--BUT NOT BRUNNHILDE! NOT--THE VALKYRIE!
HOLY CRUD!
SHE'S STOPPIN' THE CAR--WITH HER BARE HANDS!
WH-WHO THE HECK IS THIS DAME?
I DON'T KNOW! BUT I AIN'T STICKIN' AROUND TO FIND OUT!
FLEE, JACKALS! 'TWILL NOT BE LONG BEFORE BRUNNHILDE DOTH FIND THEE!
THEY MAY BE RUNNING, LADY--BUT WE AIN'T!
WE DIDN'T RISK OUR NECKS HEISTING HALF A MILLION IN JEWELS--
--JUST TO HAVE SOME FEMALE THOR COME ALONG AND RUIN EVERYTHING!
THEN FIRE THY WEAPONS, FOOLS--
--AND SEE WHAT GOOD THEY SHALL DO 'GAINST MY ENCHANTED BLADE, DRAGONFANG!
WING
PING
PING
BLAM
BLAM
UH-OH.
SO, NOW YE HAVE DECIDED TO JOIN THY FELLOWS IN FLIGHT!
I-IT SEEMS LIKE A PRETTY GOOD IDEA!
12

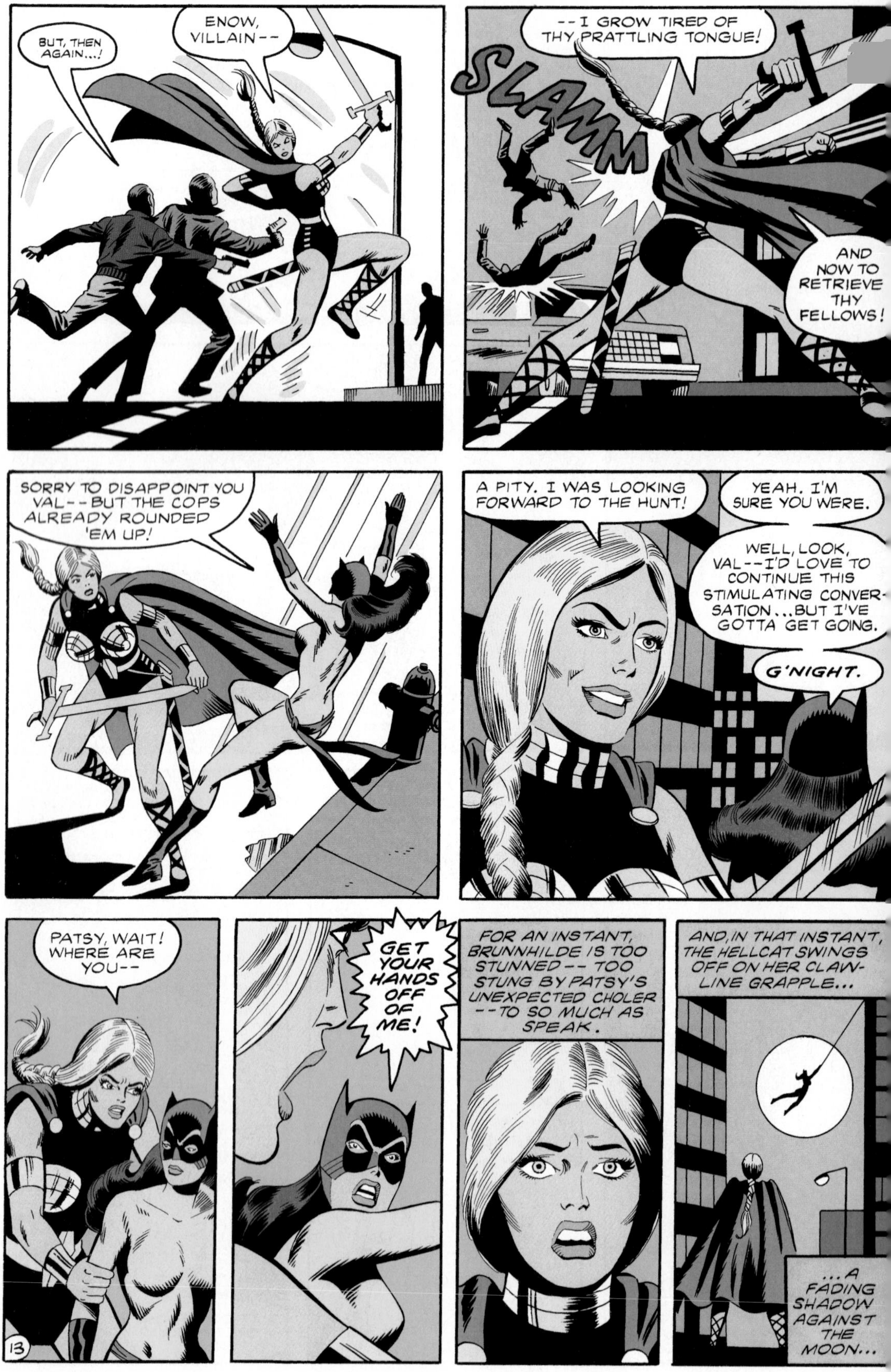
BUT, THEN AGAIN...!
ENOW, VILLAIN--
--I GROW TIRED OF THY PRATTLING TONGUE!
SLAMM
AND NOW TO RETRIEVE THY FELLOWS!
SORRY TO DISAPPOINT YOU VAL--BUT THE COPS ALREADY ROUNDED 'EM UP!
A PITY. I WAS LOOKING FORWARD TO THE HUNT!
YEAH. I'M SURE YOU WERE.
WELL, LOOK, VAL--I'D LOVE TO CONTINUE THIS STIMULATING CONVERSATION...BUT I'VE GOTTA GET GOING.
G'NIGHT.
PATSY, WAIT! WHERE ARE YOU--
GET YOUR HANDS OFF OF ME!
FOR AN INSTANT, BRUNNHILDE IS TOO STUNNED -- TOO STUNG BY PATSY'S UNEXPECTED CHOLER --TO SO MUCH AS SPEAK.
AND, IN THAT INSTANT, THE HELLCAT SWINGS OFF ON HER CLAW-LINE GRAPPLE...
...A FADING SHADOW AGAINST THE MOON...
13

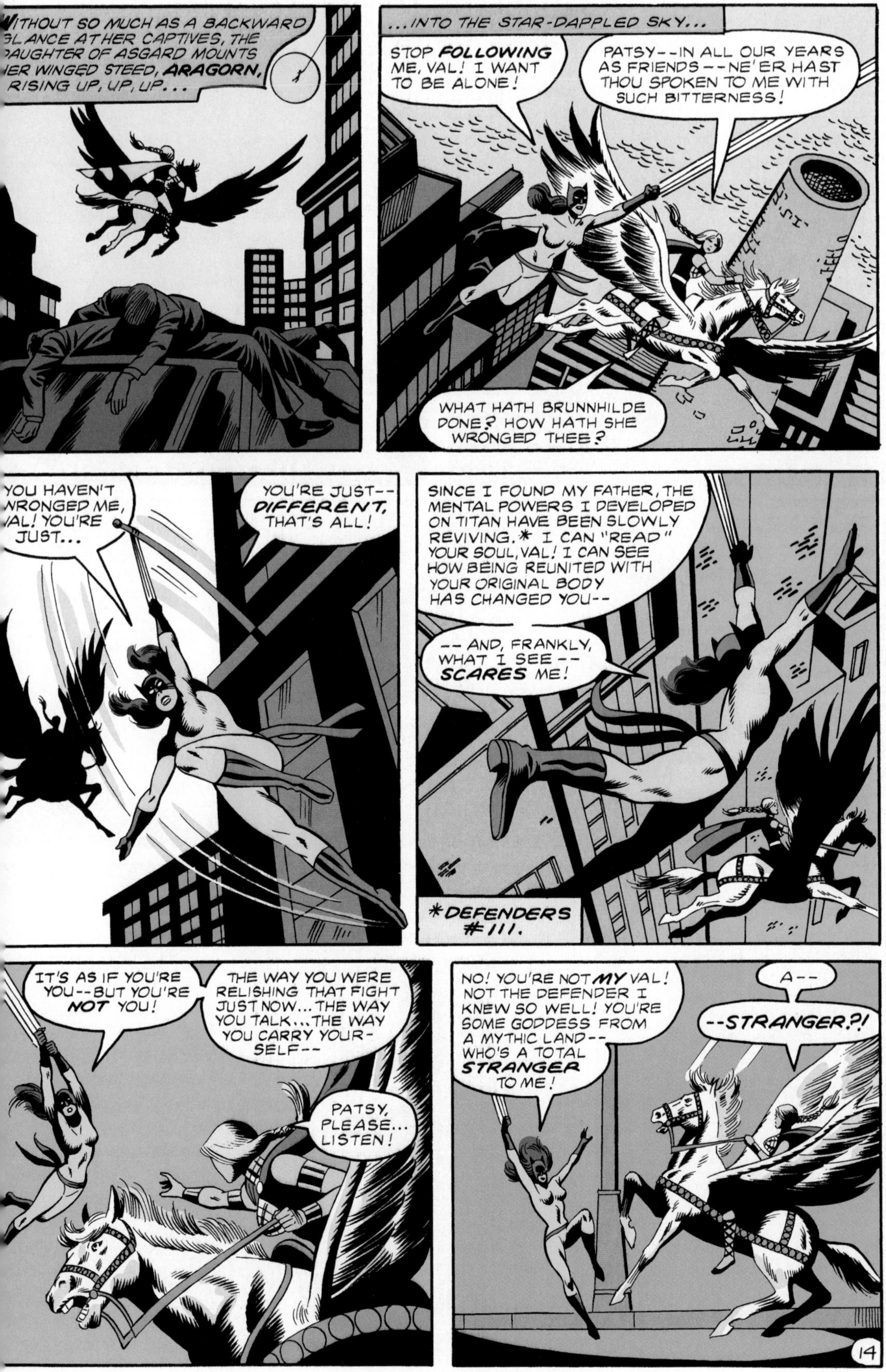
WITHOUT SO MUCH AS A BACKWARD GLANCE AT HER CAPTIVES, THE DAUGHTER OF ASGARD MOUNTS HER WINGED STEED, ARAGORN, RISING UP, UP, UP...
...INTO THE STAR-DAPPLED SKY...
STOP FOLLOWING ME, VAL! I WANT TO BE ALONE!
PATSY--IN ALL OUR YEARS AS FRIENDS--NE'ER HAST THOU SPOKEN TO ME WITH SUCH BITTERNESS!
WHAT HATH BRUNNHILDE DONE? HOW HATH SHE WRONGED THEE?
YOU HAVEN'T WRONGED ME, VAL! YOU'RE JUST...
YOU'RE JUST--DIFFERENT, THAT'S ALL!
SINCE I FOUND MY FATHER, THE MENTAL POWERS I DEVELOPED ON TITAN HAVE BEEN SLOWLY REVIVING.* I CAN "READ" YOUR SOUL, VAL! I CAN SEE HOW BEING REUNITED WITH YOUR ORIGINAL BODY HAS CHANGED YOU--
--AND, FRANKLY, WHAT I SEE--SCARES ME!
*DEFENDERS #111.
IT'S AS IF YOU'RE YOU--BUT YOU'RE NOT YOU!
THE WAY YOU WERE RELISHING THAT FIGHT JUST NOW... THE WAY YOU TALK... THE WAY YOU CARRY YOURSELF--
PATSY, PLEASE... LISTEN!
NO! YOU'RE NOT MY VAL! NOT THE DEFENDER I KNEW SO WELL! YOU'RE SOME GODDESS FROM A MYTHIC LAND--WHO'S A TOTAL STRANGER TO ME!
A--
--STRANGER?!
14

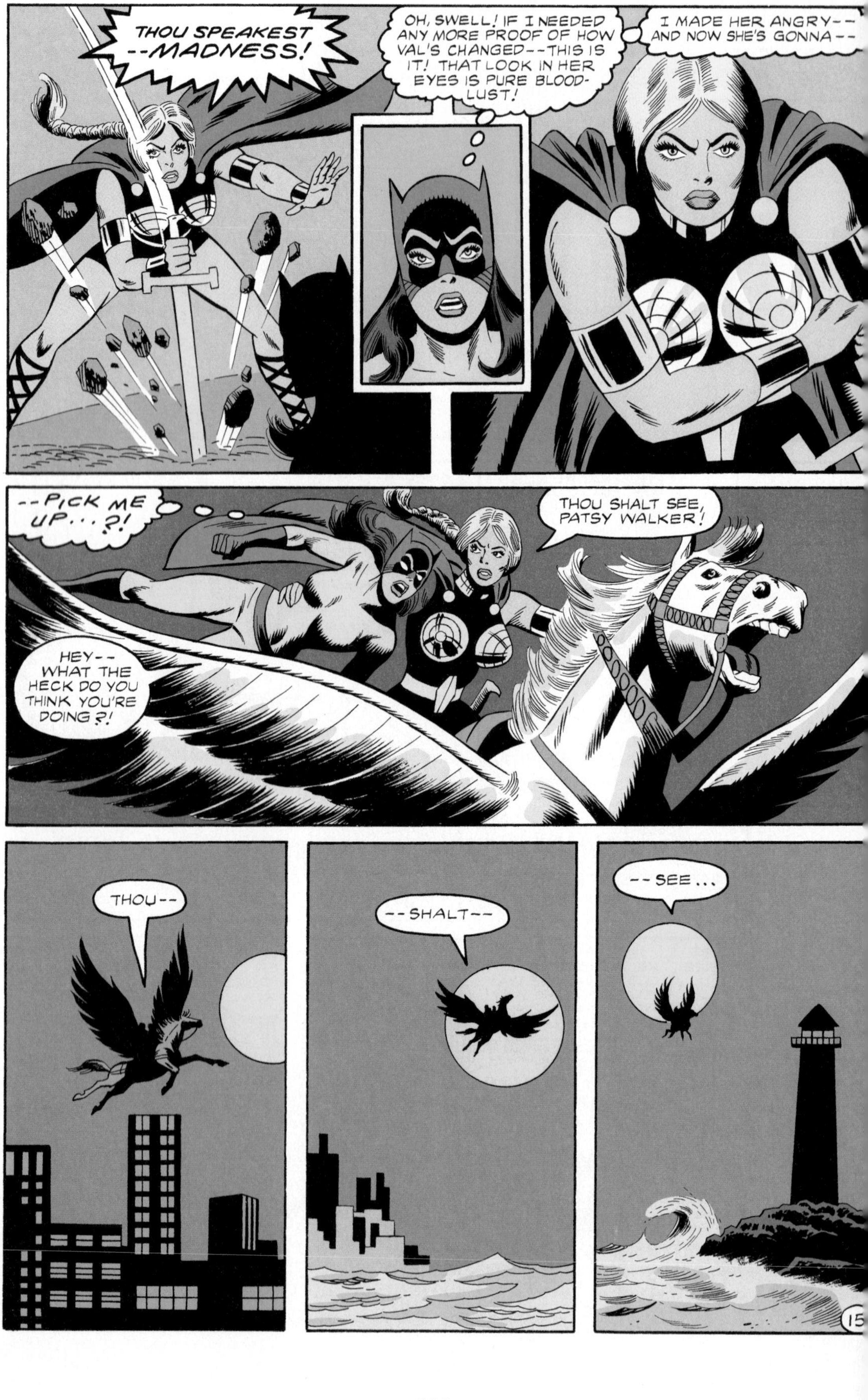
THOU SPEAKEST --MADNESS!
OH, SWELL! IF I NEEDED ANY MORE PROOF OF HOW VAL'S CHANGED--THIS IS IT! THAT LOOK IN HER EYES IS PURE BLOOD-LUST!
I MADE HER ANGRY-- AND NOW SHE'S GONNA--
--PICK ME UP...?!
THOU SHALT SEE, PATSY WALKER!
HEY-- WHAT THE HECK DO YOU THINK YOU'RE DOING?!
THOU--
--SHALT--
--SEE...
15

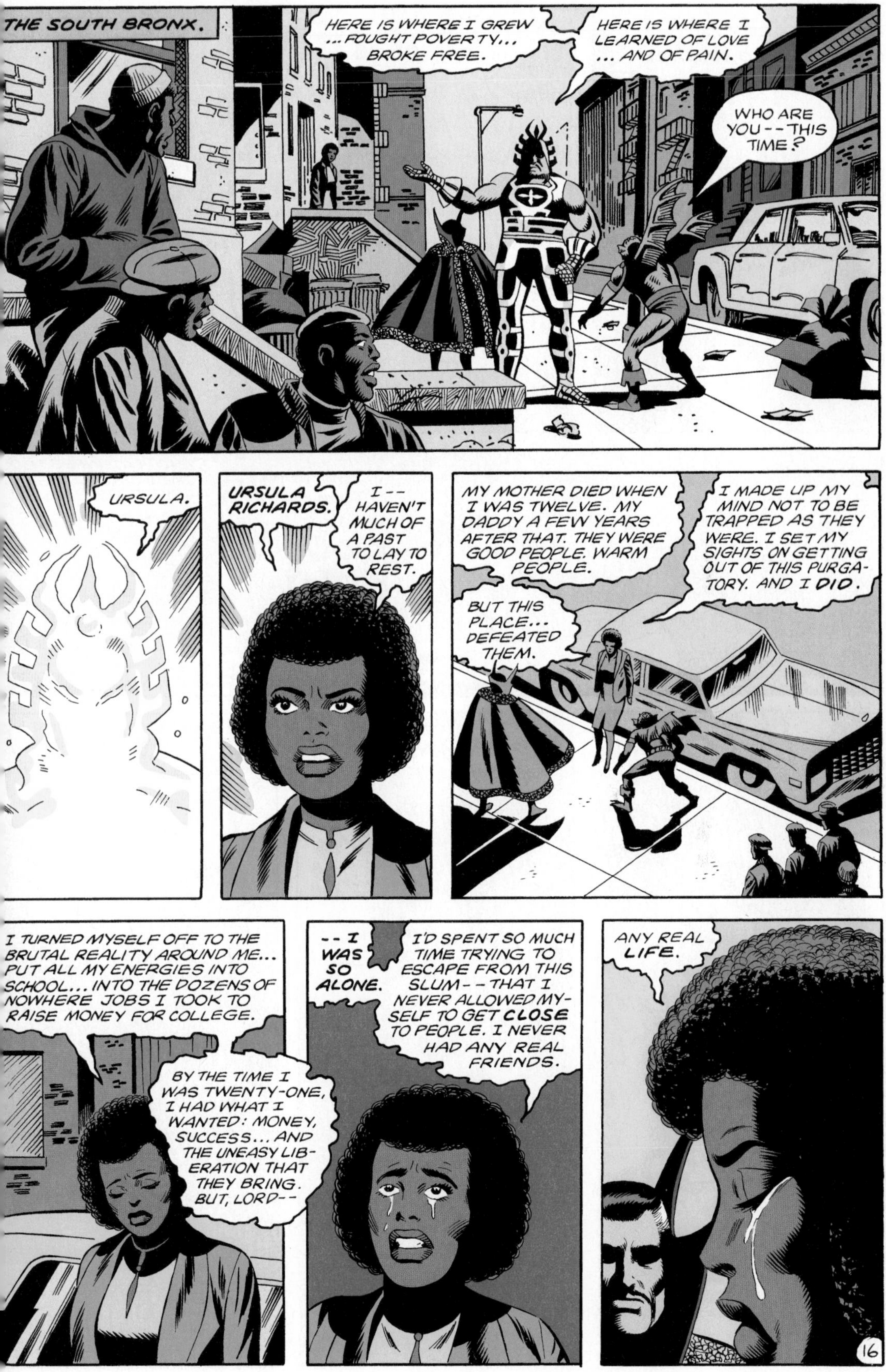
THE SOUTH BRONX.
HERE IS WHERE I GREW ...FOUGHT POVERTY... BROKE FREE.
HERE IS WHERE I LEARNED OF LOVE ... AND OF PAIN.
WHO ARE YOU--THIS TIME?
URSULA.
URSULA RICHARDS.
I -- HAVEN'T MUCH OF A PAST TO LAY TO REST.
MY MOTHER DIED WHEN I WAS TWELVE. MY DADDY A FEW YEARS AFTER THAT. THEY WERE GOOD PEOPLE. WARM PEOPLE.
BUT THIS PLACE... DEFEATED THEM.
I MADE UP MY MIND NOT TO BE TRAPPED AS THEY WERE. I SET MY SIGHTS ON GETTING OUT OF THIS PURGATORY. AND I DID.
I TURNED MYSELF OFF TO THE BRUTAL REALITY AROUND ME... PUT ALL MY ENERGIES INTO SCHOOL... INTO THE DOZENS OF NOWHERE JOBS I TOOK TO RAISE MONEY FOR COLLEGE.
BY THE TIME I WAS TWENTY-ONE, I HAD WHAT I WANTED: MONEY, SUCCESS... AND THE UNEASY LIBERATION THAT THEY BRING. BUT, LORD--
-- I WAS SO ALONE.
I'D SPENT SO MUCH TIME TRYING TO ESCAPE FROM THIS SLUM--THAT I NEVER ALLOWED MYSELF TO GET CLOSE TO PEOPLE. I NEVER HAD ANY REAL FRIENDS.
ANY REAL LIFE.
16

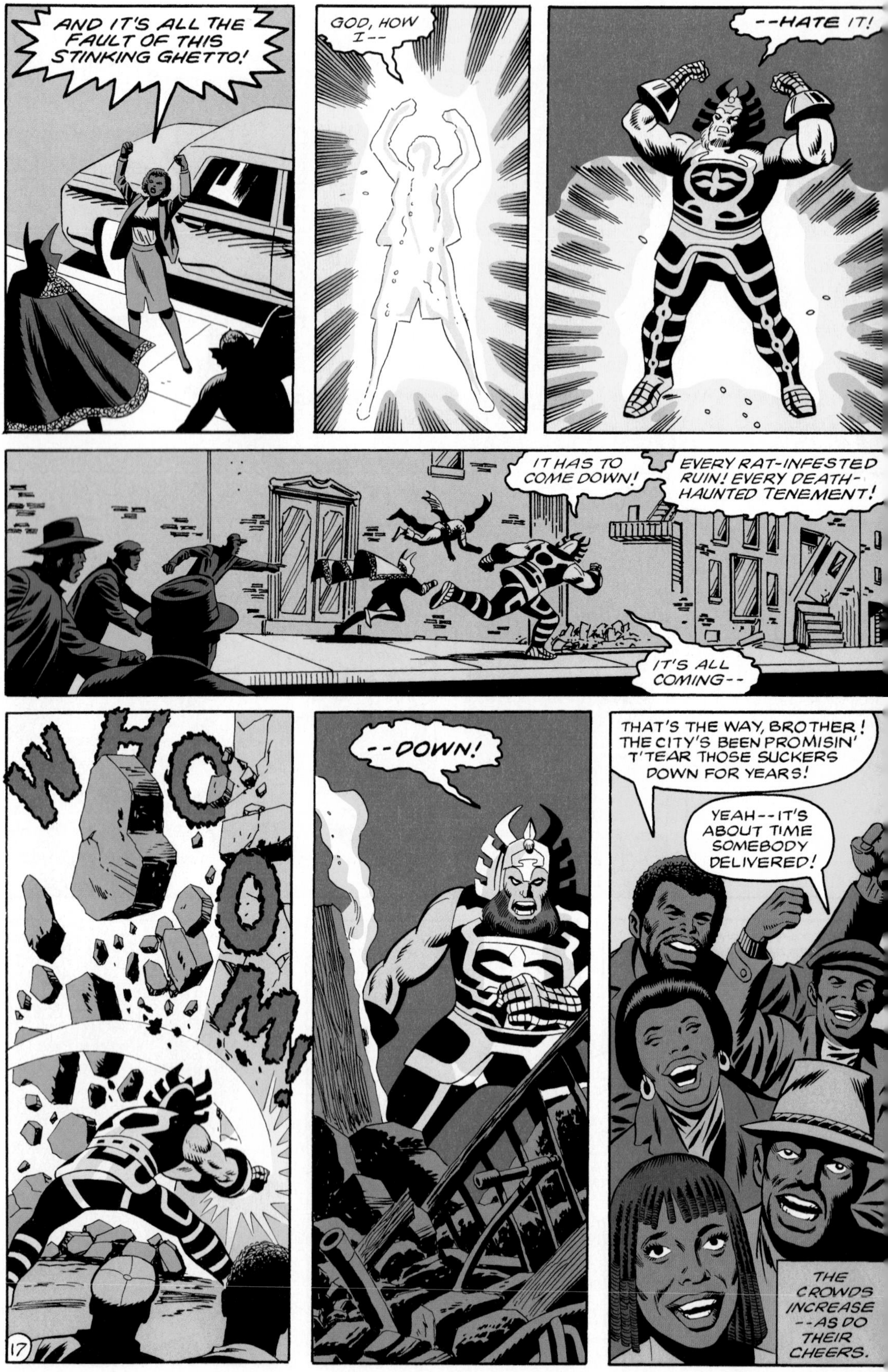
AND IT'S ALL THE FAULT OF THIS STINKING GHETTO!
GOD, HOW I--
--HATE IT!
IT HAS TO COME DOWN!
EVERY RAT-INFESTED RUIN! EVERY DEATH-HAUNTED TENEMENT!
IT'S ALL COMING--
WHOOOM!
--DOWN!
THAT'S THE WAY, BROTHER! THE CITY'S BEEN PROMISIN' T'TEAR THOSE SUCKERS DOWN FOR YEARS!
YEAH--IT'S ABOUT TIME SOMEBODY DELIVERED!
THE CROWDS INCREASE --AS DO THEIR CHEERS.
17

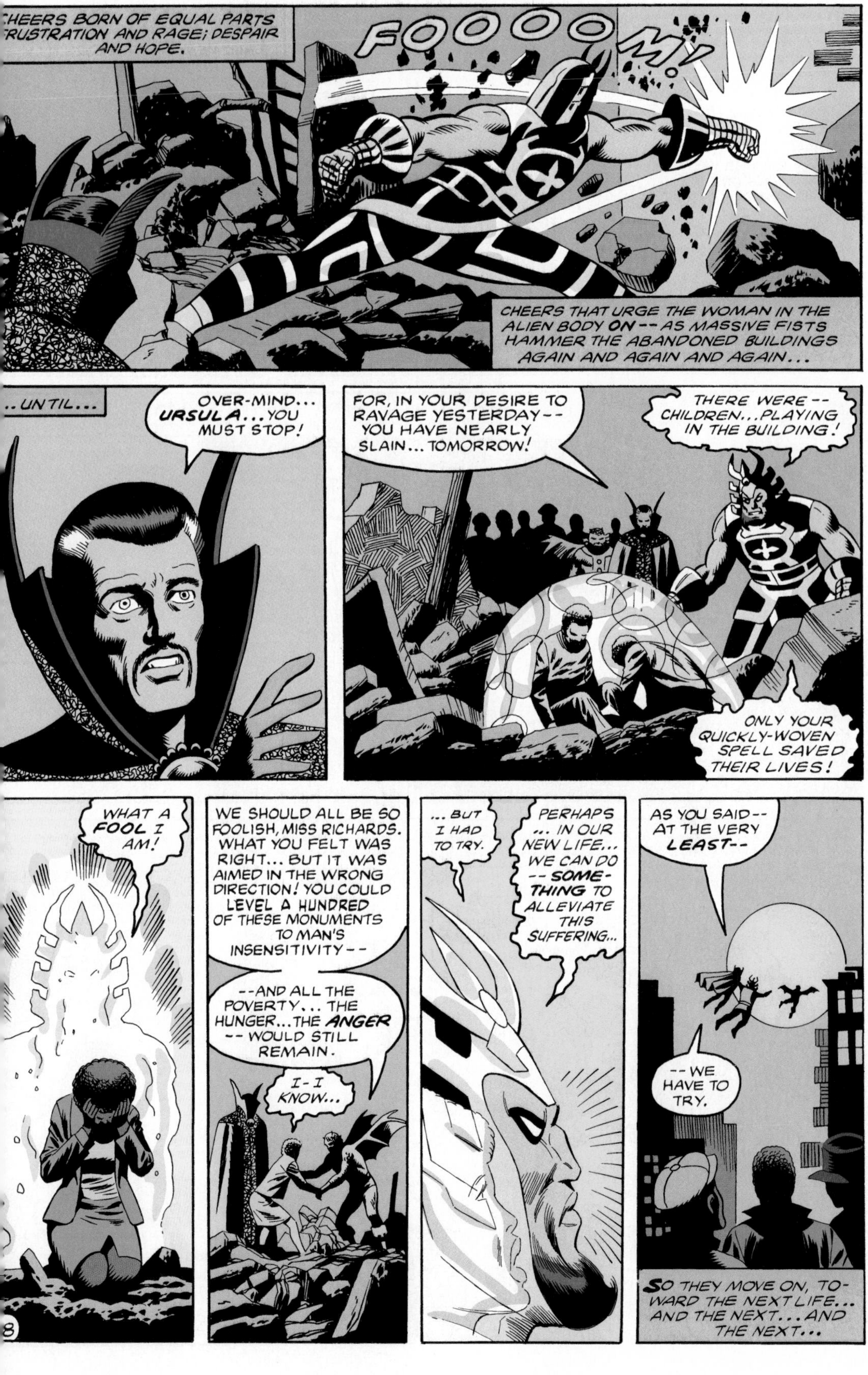

CHEERS BORN OF EQUAL PARTS FRUSTRATION AND RAGE; DESPAIR AND HOPE.
FOOOOM!
CHEERS THAT URGE THE WOMAN IN THE ALIEN BODY ON -- AS MASSIVE FISTS HAMMER THE ABANDONED BUILDINGS AGAIN AND AGAIN AND AGAIN...
..UNTIL...
OVER-MIND... URSULA... YOU MUST STOP!
FOR, IN YOUR DESIRE TO RAVAGE YESTERDAY-- YOU HAVE NEARLY SLAIN... TOMORROW!
THERE WERE -- CHILDREN... PLAYING IN THE BUILDING!
ONLY YOUR QUICKLY-WOVEN SPELL SAVED THEIR LIVES!
WHAT A FOOL I AM!
8
WE SHOULD ALL BE SO FOOLISH, MISS RICHARDS. WHAT YOU FELT WAS RIGHT... BUT IT WAS AIMED IN THE WRONG DIRECTION! YOU COULD LEVEL A HUNDRED OF THESE MONUMENTS TO MAN'S INSENSITIVITY --
--AND ALL THE POVERTY... THE HUNGER... THE ANGER -- WOULD STILL REMAIN.
I-I KNOW...
... BUT I HAD TO TRY.
PERHAPS ... IN OUR NEW LIFE... WE CAN DO -- SOME-THING TO ALLEVIATE THIS SUFFERING...
AS YOU SAID-- AT THE VERY LEAST--
-- WE HAVE TO TRY.
SO THEY MOVE ON, TOWARD THE NEXT LIFE... AND THE NEXT... AND THE NEXT...

POINT PROMONTORY, MAINE.

ALL RIGHT, VAL-- WHY'D YOU BRING ME HERE?

DOST THOU RECOGNIZE THIS PLACE, PATSY?

SURE. THIS IS WHERE WE TOOK ON THAT OMEGATRON GIZMO.*

*DEFENDERS #69.

FOR THEE-- 'TWAS THE FIRST TIME. BUT BRUNNHILDE DIDST BATTLE THE EVIL YANDROTH'S CREATION BEFORE!*

'TWAS MY BAPTISM OF FIRE WITH THE DEFENDERS! MY FIRST-- AND PERHAPS PROUDEST-- MOMENT ON EARTH!

*DEFENDERS #5.

'TWAS THEN THAT THE WOMAN I WAS-- STRIPPED BARE OF ALL MEMORY, ALL IDENTITY BY THE MAGICKS OF THE ENCHANTRESS --

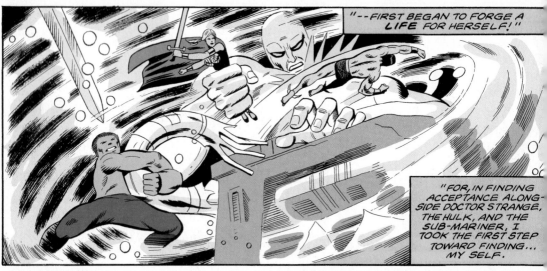

"-- FIRST BEGAN TO FORGE A LIFE FOR HERSELF!"

"FOR, IN FINDING ACCEPTANCE ALONG-SIDE DOCTOR STRANGE, THE HULK, AND THE SUB-MARINER, I TOOK THE FIRST STEP TOWARD FINDING... MY SELF."

"AS THE MONTHS AND YEARS FELL AWAY, THE BLANK SLATE THAT WAS THE VALKYRIE WAS INSCRIBED WITH TALES OF WONDER AND DREAD! MANY WERE THE EVILS ENCOUNTERED --"

-- AND MANY THE JOYS REVEALED!

19

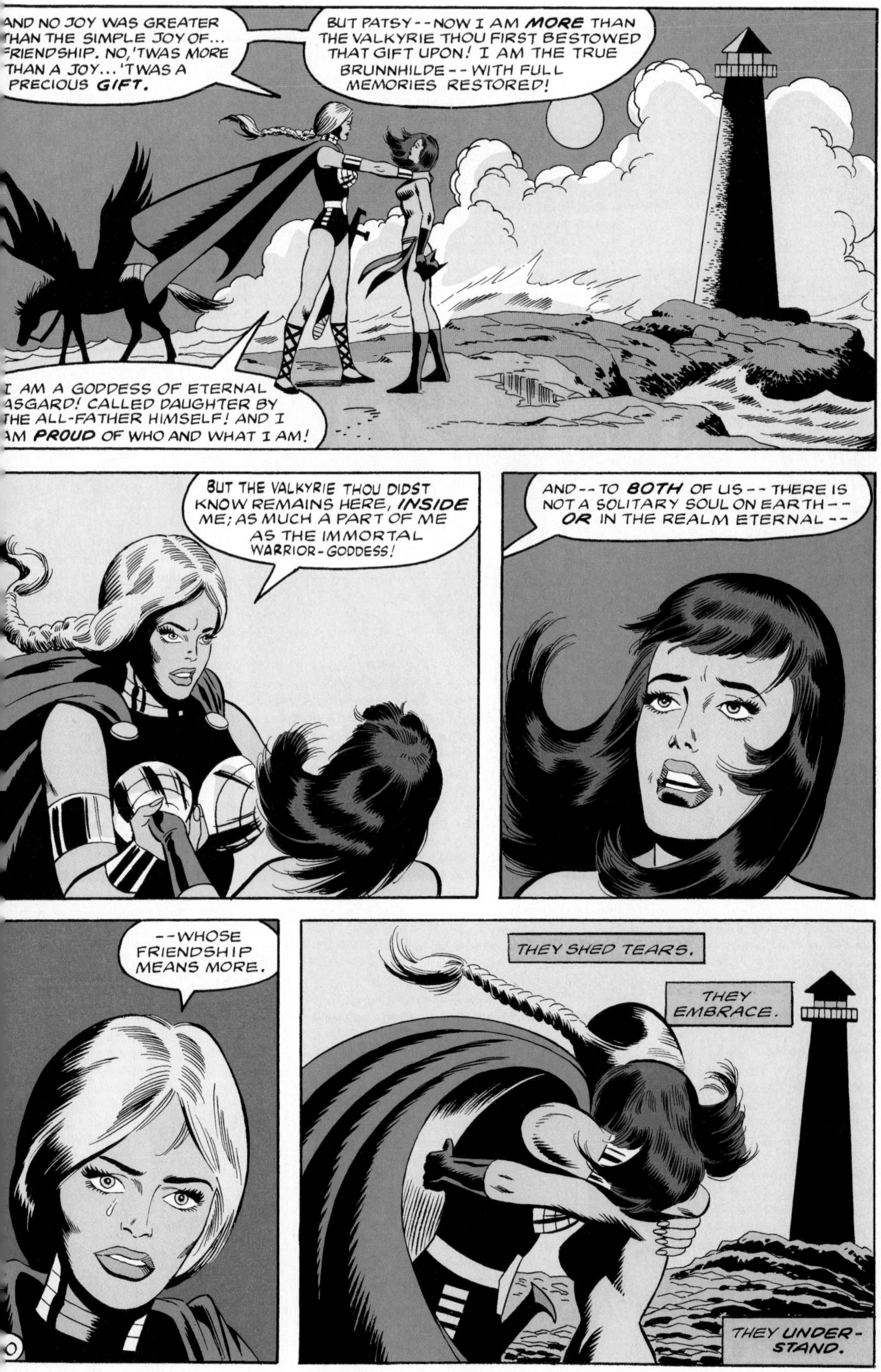
AND NO JOY WAS GREATER THAN THE SIMPLE JOY OF... FRIENDSHIP. NO, 'TWAS MORE THAN A JOY... 'TWAS A PRECIOUS GIFT.
BUT PATSY--NOW I AM MORE THAN THE VALKYRIE THOU FIRST BESTOWED THAT GIFT UPON! I AM THE TRUE BRUNNHILDE--WITH FULL MEMORIES RESTORED!
I AM A GODDESS OF ETERNAL ASGARD! CALLED DAUGHTER BY THE ALL-FATHER HIMSELF! AND I AM PROUD OF WHO AND WHAT I AM!
BUT THE VALKYRIE THOU DIDST KNOW REMAINS HERE, INSIDE ME; AS MUCH A PART OF ME AS THE IMMORTAL WARRIOR-GODDESS!
AND--TO BOTH OF US--THERE IS NOT A SOLITARY SOUL ON EARTH--OR IN THE REALM ETERNAL--
--WHOSE FRIENDSHIP MEANS MORE.
THEY SHED TEARS.
THEY EMBRACE.
THEY UNDER-STAND.

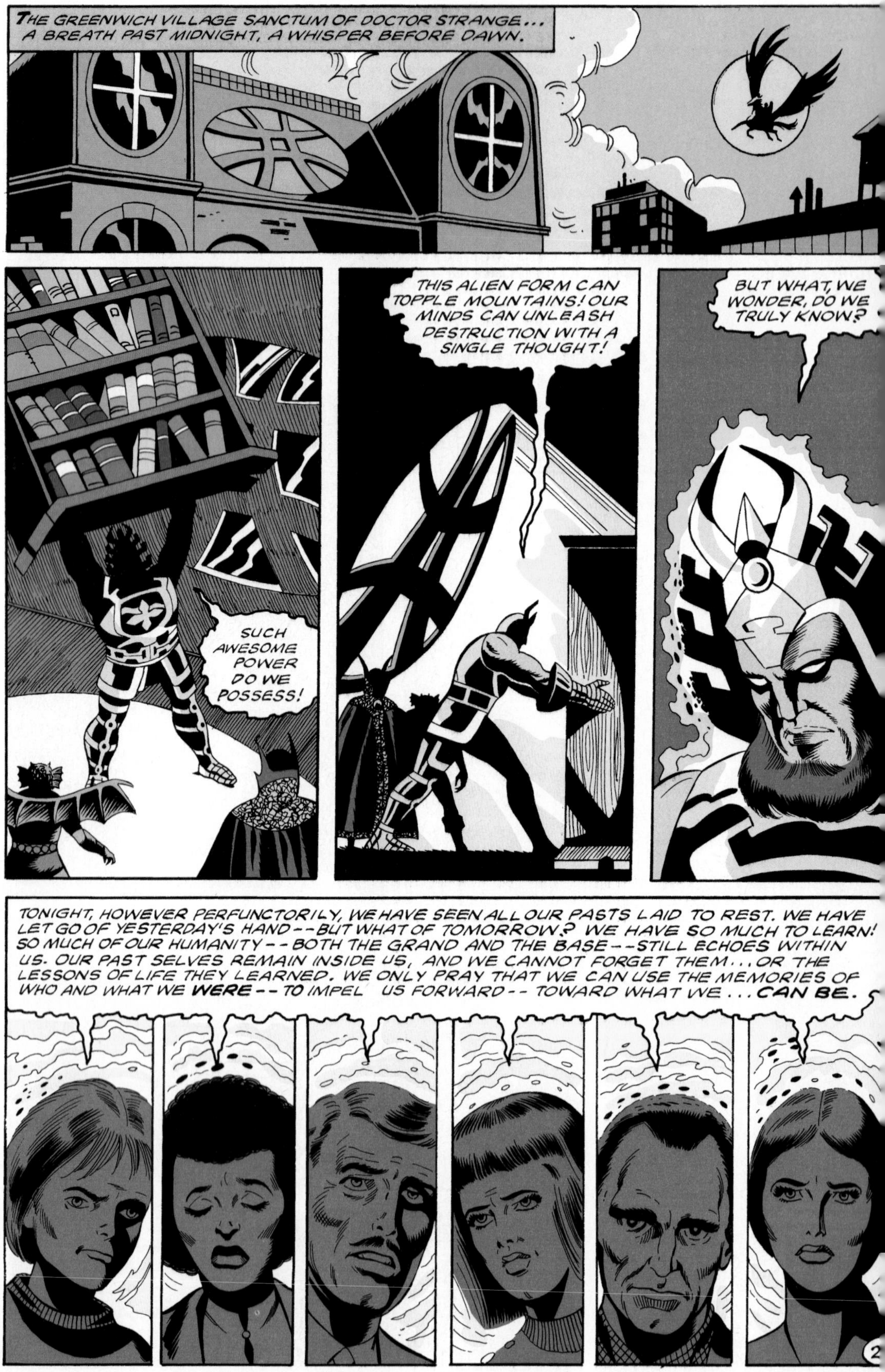
THE GREENWICH VILLAGE SANCTUM OF DOCTOR STRANGE... A BREATH PAST MIDNIGHT, A WHISPER BEFORE DAWN.
SUCH AWESOME POWER DO WE POSSESS!
THIS ALIEN FORM CAN TOPPLE MOUNTAINS! OUR MINDS CAN UNLEASH DESTRUCTION WITH A SINGLE THOUGHT!
BUT WHAT, WE WONDER, DO WE TRULY KNOW?
TONIGHT, HOWEVER PERFUNCTORILY, WE HAVE SEEN ALL OUR PASTS LAID TO REST. WE HAVE LET GO OF YESTERDAY'S HAND--BUT WHAT OF TOMORROW? WE HAVE SO MUCH TO LEARN! SO MUCH OF OUR HUMANITY--BOTH THE GRAND AND THE BASE--STILL ECHOES WITHIN US. OUR PAST SELVES REMAIN INSIDE US, AND WE CANNOT FORGET THEM...OR THE LESSONS OF LIFE THEY LEARNED. WE ONLY PRAY THAT WE CAN USE THE MEMORIES OF WHO AND WHAT WE WERE--TO IMPEL US FORWARD--TOWARD WHAT WE...CAN BE.

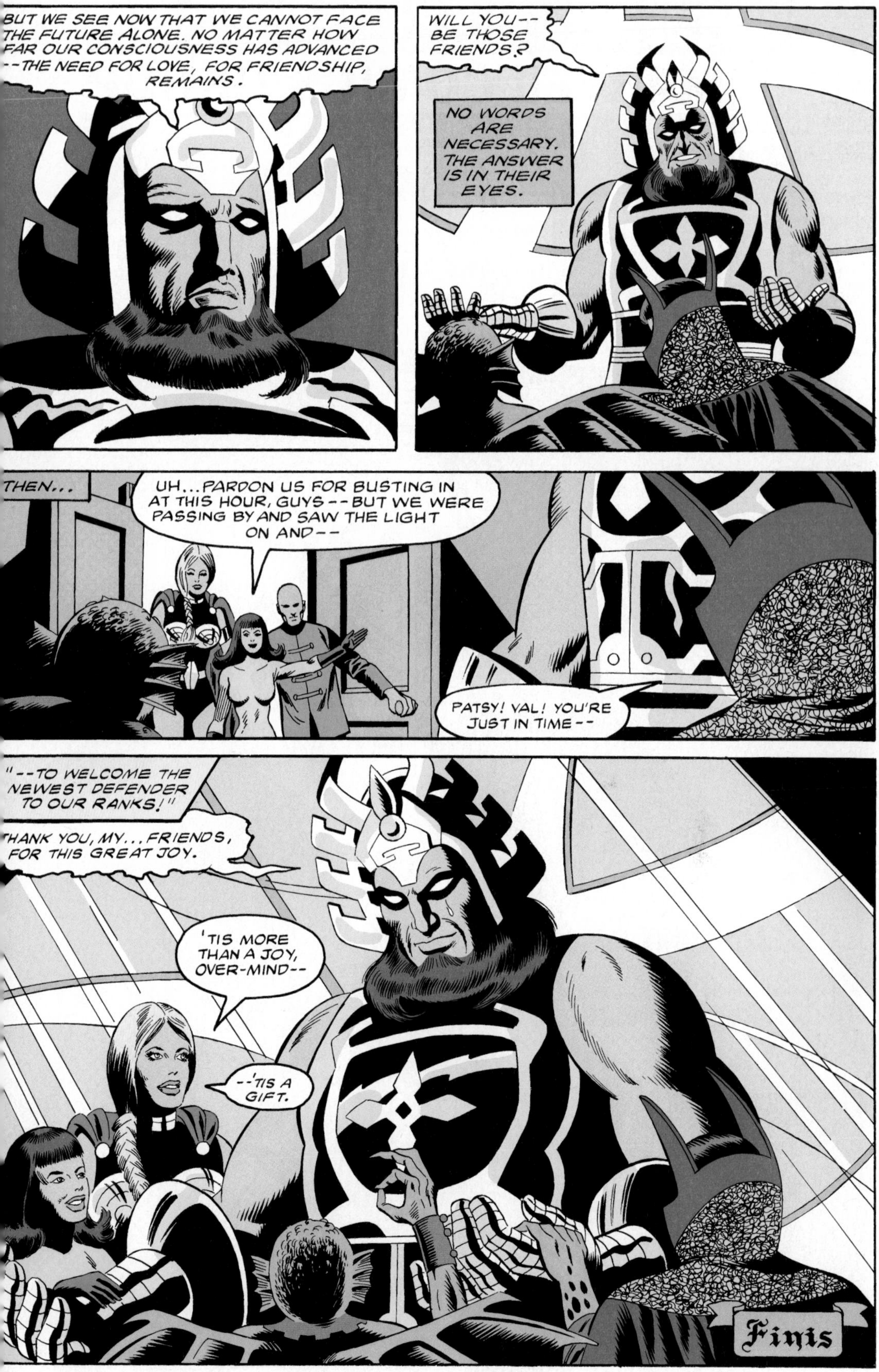
BUT WE SEE NOW THAT WE CANNOT FACE THE FUTURE ALONE. NO MATTER HOW FAR OUR CONSCIOUSNESS HAS ADVANCED --THE NEED FOR LOVE, FOR FRIENDSHIP, REMAINS.
WILL YOU-- BE THOSE FRIENDS?
NO WORDS ARE NECESSARY. THE ANSWER IS IN THEIR EYES.
THEN...
UH...PARDON US FOR BUSTING IN AT THIS HOUR, GUYS--BUT WE WERE PASSING BY AND SAW THE LIGHT ON AND--
PATSY! VAL! YOU'RE JUST IN TIME--
"--TO WELCOME THE NEWEST DEFENDER TO OUR RANKS!"
THANK YOU, MY...FRIENDS, FOR THIS GREAT JOY.
'TIS MORE THAN A JOY, OVER-MIND--
--'TIS A GIFT.
Finis

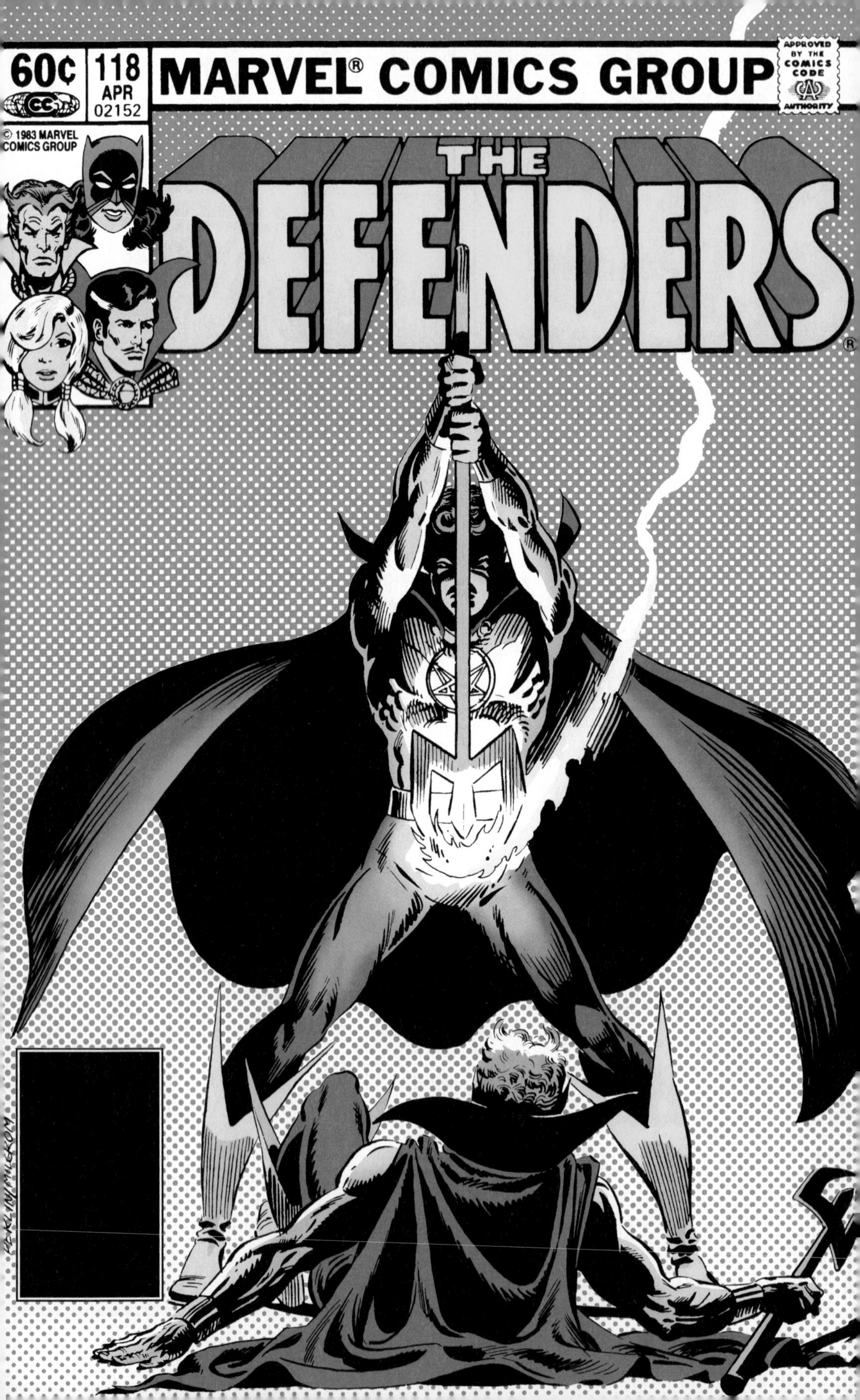
60¢
118
APR
02152
MARVEL® COMICS GROUP
APPROVED BY THE COMICS CODE AUTHORITY
© 1983 MARVEL COMICS GROUP
THE DEFENDERS®

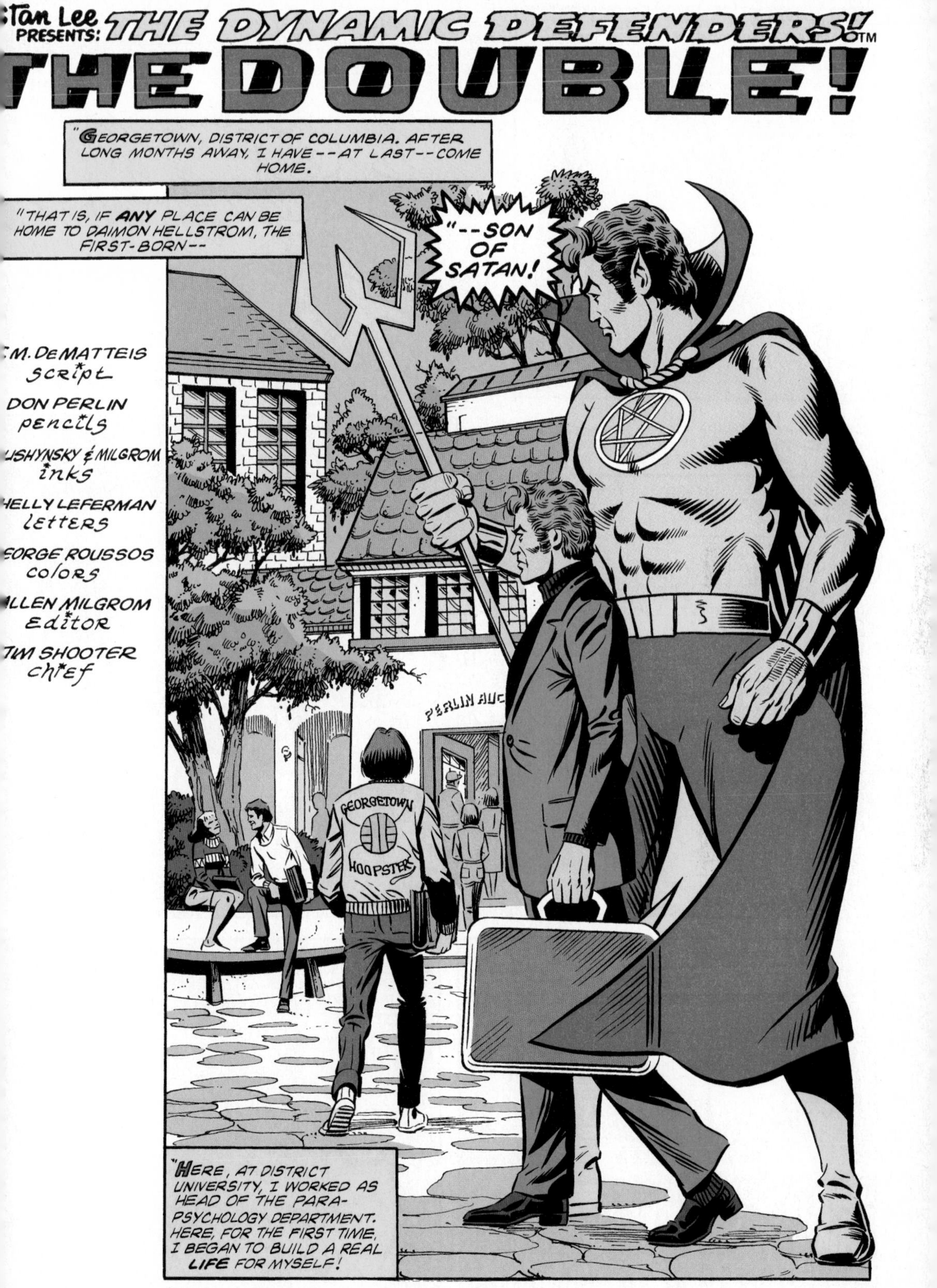

Tan Lee PRESENTS: THE DYNAMIC DEFENDERS!™
THE DOUBLE!
"GEORGETOWN, DISTRICT OF COLUMBIA. AFTER LONG MONTHS AWAY, I HAVE--AT LAST--COME HOME.
"THAT IS, IF ANY PLACE CAN BE HOME TO DAIMON HELLSTROM, THE FIRST-BORN--
"--SON OF SATAN!
M. DeMATTEIS script
DON PERLIN pencils
USHYNSKY & MILGROM inks
HELLY LEFERMAN letters
EORGE ROUSSOS colors
LLEN MILGROM Editor
IM SHOOTER chief
PERLIN AUC
GEORGETOWN HOOPSTERS
"HERE, AT DISTRICT UNIVERSITY, I WORKED AS HEAD OF THE PARA-PSYCHOLOGY DEPARTMENT. HERE, FOR THE FIRST TIME, I BEGAN TO BUILD A REAL LIFE FOR MYSELF!

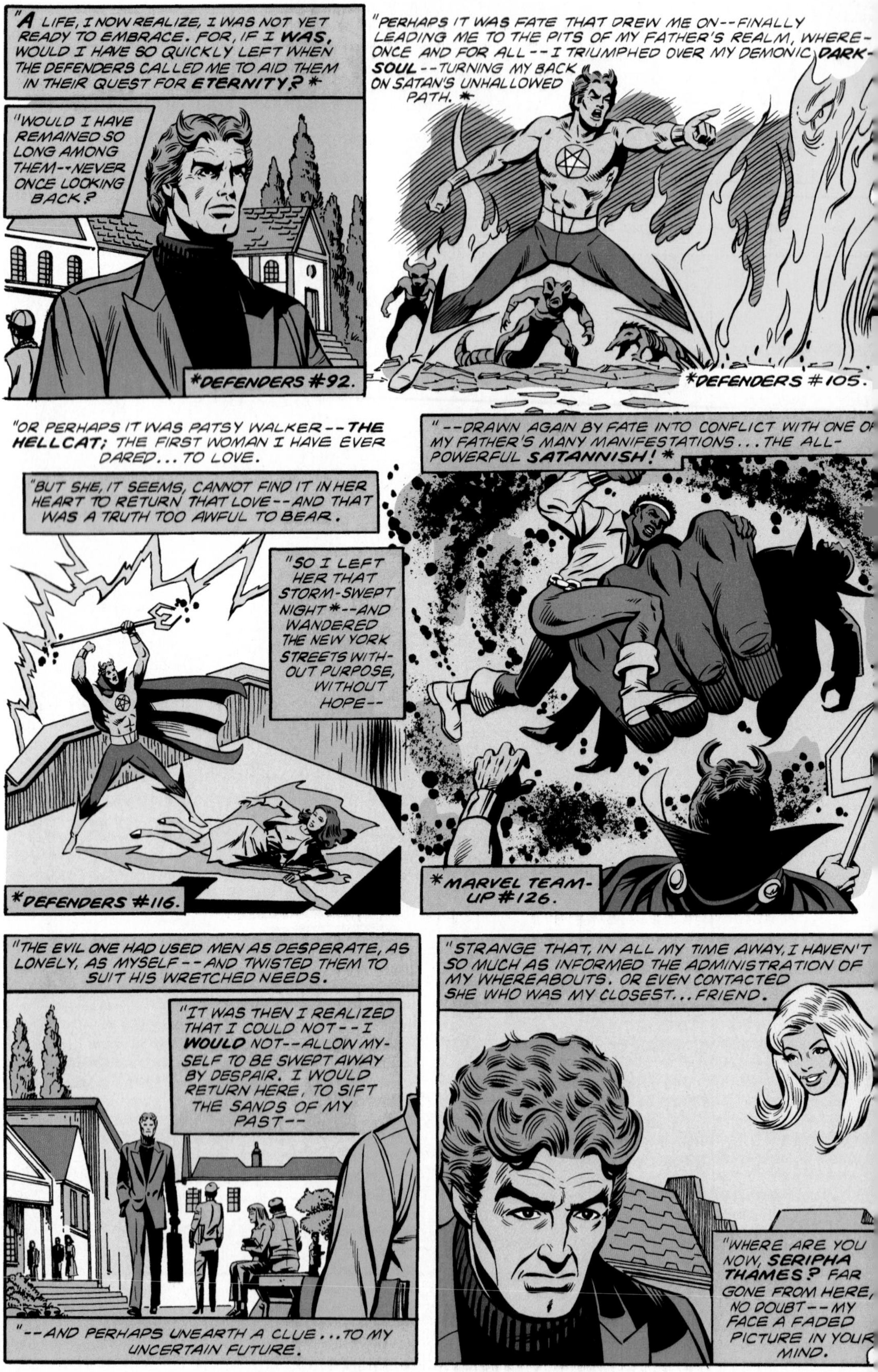
"A LIFE, I NOW REALIZE, I WAS NOT YET READY TO EMBRACE. FOR, IF I WAS, WOULD I HAVE SO QUICKLY LEFT WHEN THE DEFENDERS CALLED ME TO AID THEM IN THEIR QUEST FOR ETERNITY? *
"WOULD I HAVE REMAINED SO LONG AMONG THEM--NEVER ONCE LOOKING BACK?
*DEFENDERS #92.
"PERHAPS IT WAS FATE THAT DREW ME ON--FINALLY LEADING ME TO THE PITS OF MY FATHER'S REALM, WHERE-ONCE AND FOR ALL--I TRIUMPHED OVER MY DEMONIC DARK-SOUL--TURNING MY BACK ON SATAN'S UNHALLOWED PATH. *
*DEFENDERS #105.
"OR PERHAPS IT WAS PATSY WALKER--THE HELLCAT; THE FIRST WOMAN I HAVE EVER DARED... TO LOVE.
"BUT SHE, IT SEEMS, CANNOT FIND IT IN HER HEART TO RETURN THAT LOVE--AND THAT WAS A TRUTH TOO AWFUL TO BEAR.
"SO I LEFT HER THAT STORM-SWEPT NIGHT*--AND WANDERED THE NEW YORK STREETS WITHOUT PURPOSE, WITHOUT HOPE--
*DEFENDERS #116.
"--DRAWN AGAIN BY FATE INTO CONFLICT WITH ONE OF MY FATHER'S MANY MANIFESTATIONS... THE ALL-POWERFUL SATANNISH! *
*MARVEL TEAM-UP #126.
"THE EVIL ONE HAD USED MEN AS DESPERATE, AS LONELY, AS MYSELF--AND TWISTED THEM TO SUIT HIS WRETCHED NEEDS.
"IT WAS THEN I REALIZED THAT I COULD NOT--I WOULD NOT--ALLOW MYSELF TO BE SWEPT AWAY BY DESPAIR. I WOULD RETURN HERE, TO SIFT THE SANDS OF MY PAST--
"--AND PERHAPS UNEARTH A CLUE...TO MY UNCERTAIN FUTURE.
"STRANGE THAT, IN ALL MY TIME AWAY, I HAVEN'T SO MUCH AS INFORMED THE ADMINISTRATION OF MY WHEREABOUTS. OR EVEN CONTACTED SHE WHO WAS MY CLOSEST... FRIEND.
"WHERE ARE YOU NOW, SERIPHA THAMES? FAR GONE FROM HERE, NO DOUBT--MY FACE A FADED PICTURE IN YOUR MIND.

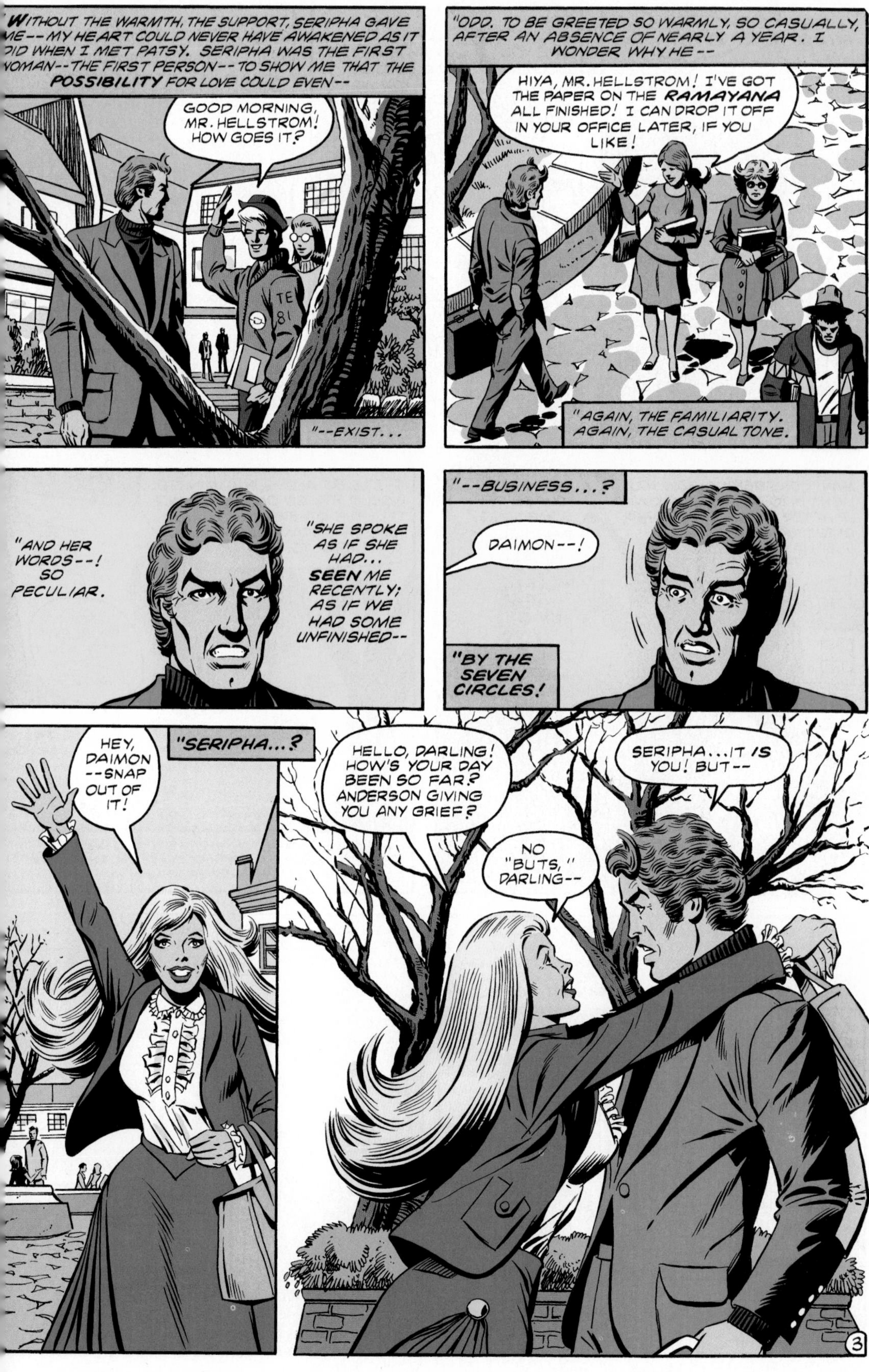

"WITHOUT THE WARMTH, THE SUPPORT, SERIPHA GAVE ME-- MY HEART COULD NEVER HAVE AWAKENED AS IT DID WHEN I MET PATSY. SERIPHA WAS THE FIRST WOMAN--THE FIRST PERSON--TO SHOW ME THAT THE POSSIBILITY FOR LOVE COULD EVEN--
GOOD MORNING, MR. HELLSTROM! HOW GOES IT?
"--EXIST...
"ODD. TO BE GREETED SO WARMLY, SO CASUALLY, AFTER AN ABSENCE OF NEARLY A YEAR. I WONDER WHY HE--
HIYA, MR. HELLSTROM! I'VE GOT THE PAPER ON THE RAMAYANA ALL FINISHED! I CAN DROP IT OFF IN YOUR OFFICE LATER, IF YOU LIKE!
"AGAIN, THE FAMILIARITY. AGAIN, THE CASUAL TONE.
"AND HER WORDS--! SO PECULIAR.
"SHE SPOKE AS IF SHE HAD... SEEN ME RECENTLY; AS IF WE HAD SOME UNFINISHED--
"--BUSINESS...?
DAIMON--!
"BY THE SEVEN CIRCLES!
"SERIPHA...?
HEY, DAIMON --SNAP OUT OF IT!
HELLO, DARLING! HOW'S YOUR DAY BEEN SO FAR? ANDERSON GIVING YOU ANY GRIEF?
SERIPHA...IT IS YOU! BUT--
NO "BUTS," DARLING--
3

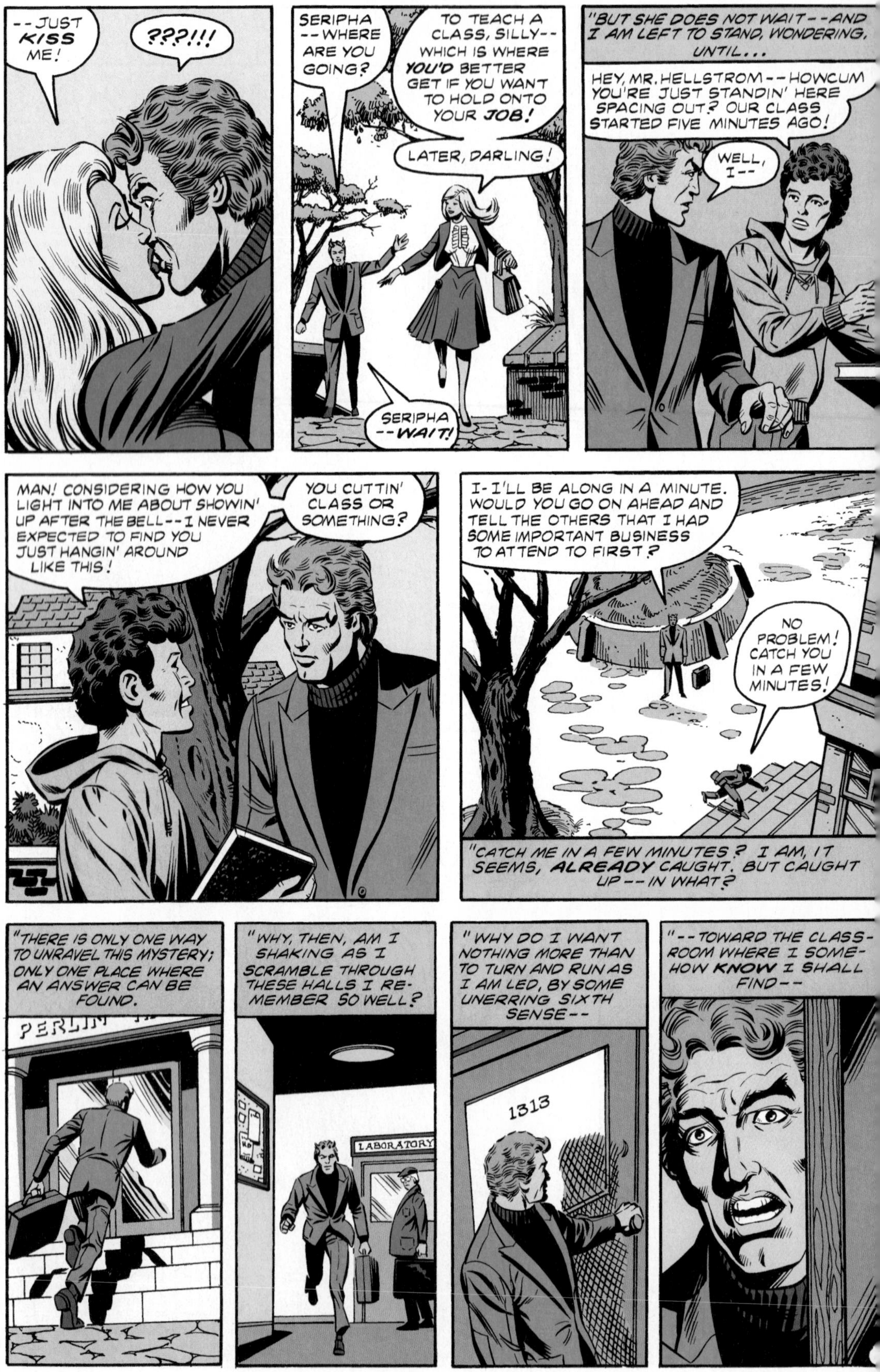
--JUST KISS ME!
???!!!
SERIPHA --WHERE ARE YOU GOING?
TO TEACH A CLASS, SILLY-- WHICH IS WHERE YOU'D BETTER GET IF YOU WANT TO HOLD ONTO YOUR JOB!
LATER, DARLING!
SERIPHA --WAIT!
"BUT SHE DOES NOT WAIT--AND I AM LEFT TO STAND, WONDERING, UNTIL...
HEY, MR. HELLSTROM--HOWCUM YOU'RE JUST STANDIN' HERE SPACING OUT? OUR CLASS STARTED FIVE MINUTES AGO!
WELL, I--
MAN! CONSIDERING HOW YOU LIGHT INTO ME ABOUT SHOWIN' UP AFTER THE BELL--I NEVER EXPECTED TO FIND YOU JUST HANGIN' AROUND LIKE THIS!
YOU CUTTIN' CLASS OR SOMETHING?
I-I'LL BE ALONG IN A MINUTE. WOULD YOU GO ON AHEAD AND TELL THE OTHERS THAT I HAD SOME IMPORTANT BUSINESS TO ATTEND TO FIRST?
NO PROBLEM! CATCH YOU IN A FEW MINUTES!
"CATCH ME IN A FEW MINUTES? I AM, IT SEEMS, ALREADY CAUGHT. BUT CAUGHT UP--IN WHAT?
"THERE IS ONLY ONE WAY TO UNRAVEL THIS MYSTERY; ONLY ONE PLACE WHERE AN ANSWER CAN BE FOUND.
"WHY, THEN, AM I SHAKING AS I SCRAMBLE THROUGH THESE HALLS I REMEMBER SO WELL?
LABORATORY
"WHY DO I WANT NOTHING MORE THAN TO TURN AND RUN AS I AM LED, BY SOME UNERRING SIXTH SENSE--
1313
"--TOWARD THE CLASSROOM WHERE I SOMEHOW KNOW I SHALL FIND--

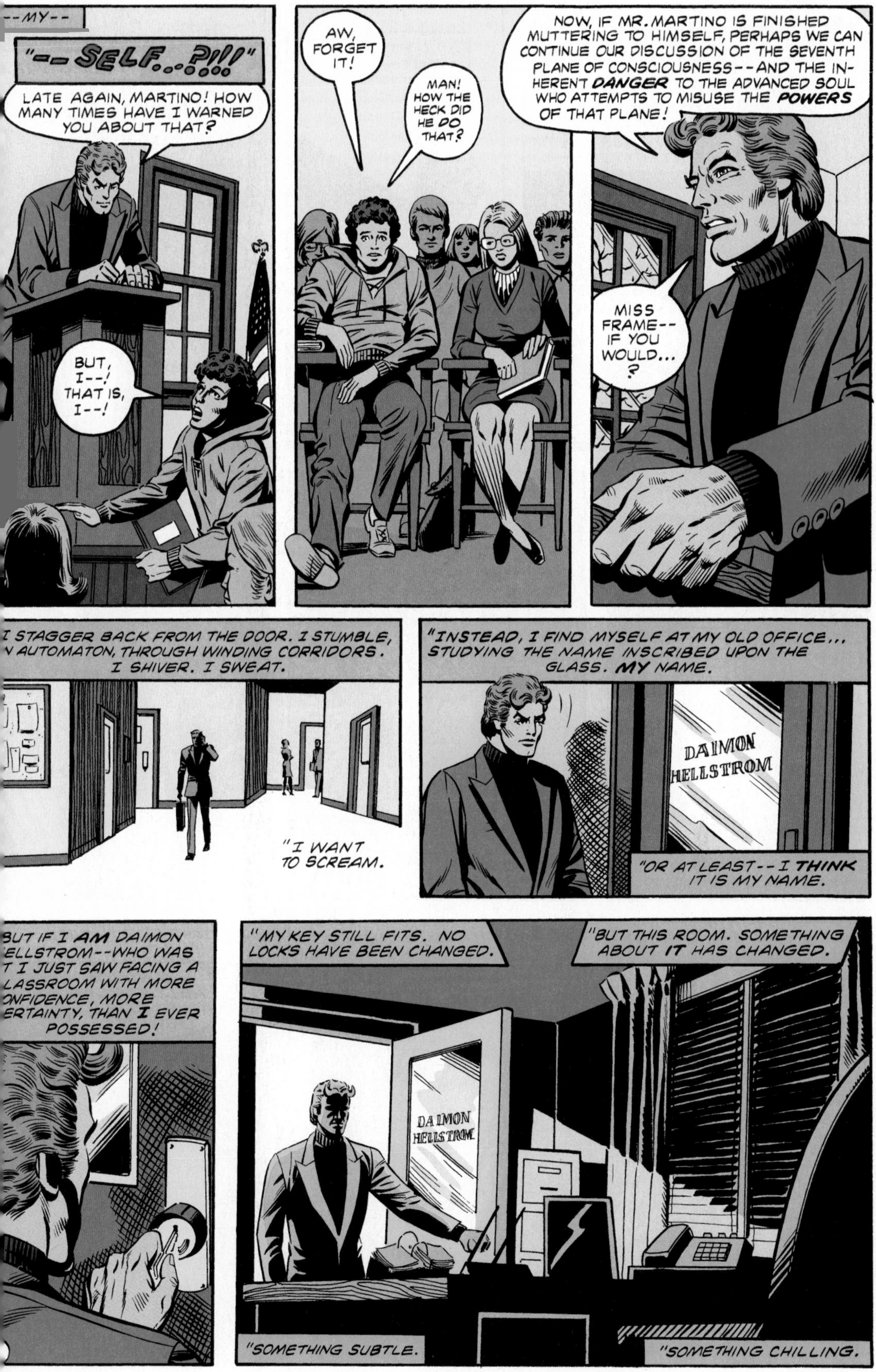
--MY--
"--SELF...?!!"
LATE AGAIN, MARTINO! HOW MANY TIMES HAVE I WARNED YOU ABOUT THAT?
BUT, I--! THAT IS, I--!
AW, FORGET IT!
MAN! HOW THE HECK DID HE DO THAT?
NOW, IF MR. MARTINO IS FINISHED MUTTERING TO HIMSELF, PERHAPS WE CAN CONTINUE OUR DISCUSSION OF THE SEVENTH PLANE OF CONSCIOUSNESS--AND THE INHERENT DANGER TO THE ADVANCED SOUL WHO ATTEMPTS TO MISUSE THE POWERS OF THAT PLANE!
MISS FRAME--IF YOU WOULD...?
I STAGGER BACK FROM THE DOOR. I STUMBLE, AN AUTOMATON, THROUGH WINDING CORRIDORS. I SHIVER. I SWEAT.
"I WANT TO SCREAM.
"INSTEAD, I FIND MYSELF AT MY OLD OFFICE... STUDYING THE NAME INSCRIBED UPON THE GLASS. MY NAME.
DAIMON HELLSTROM
"OR AT LEAST--I THINK IT IS MY NAME.
BUT IF I AM DAIMON HELLSTROM--WHO WAS IT I JUST SAW FACING A CLASSROOM WITH MORE CONFIDENCE, MORE CERTAINTY, THAN I EVER POSSESSED!
"MY KEY STILL FITS. NO LOCKS HAVE BEEN CHANGED.
"BUT THIS ROOM. SOMETHING ABOUT IT HAS CHANGED.
DAIMON HELLSTROM
"SOMETHING SUBTLE.
"SOMETHING CHILLING.

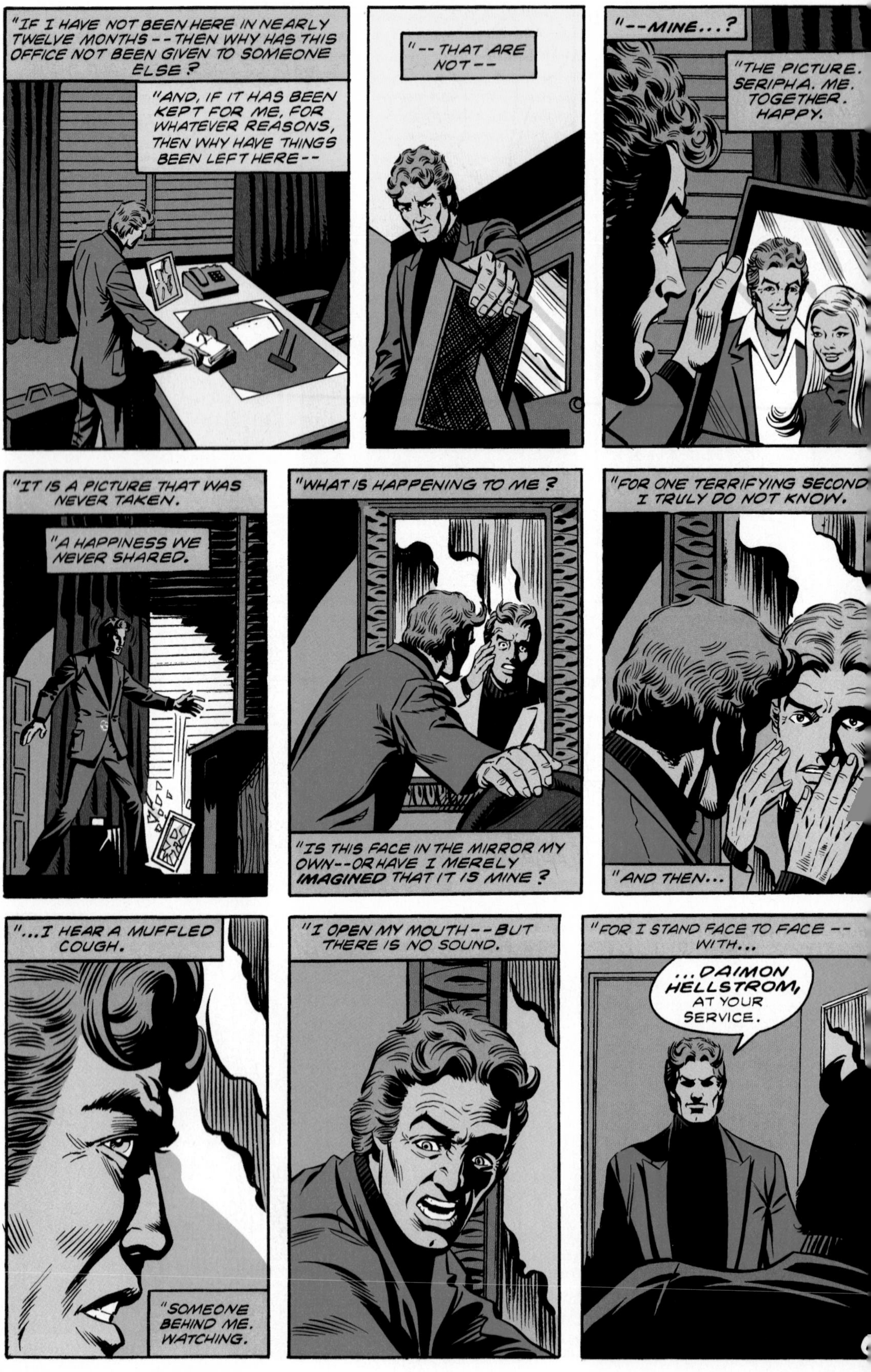
"IF I HAVE NOT BEEN HERE IN NEARLY TWELVE MONTHS --THEN WHY HAS THIS OFFICE NOT BEEN GIVEN TO SOMEONE ELSE?
"AND, IF IT HAS BEEN KEPT FOR ME, FOR WHATEVER REASONS, THEN WHY HAVE THINGS BEEN LEFT HERE--
"--THAT ARE NOT--
"--MINE...?
"THE PICTURE. SERIPHA. ME. TOGETHER. HAPPY.
"IT IS A PICTURE THAT WAS NEVER TAKEN.
"A HAPPINESS WE NEVER SHARED.
"WHAT IS HAPPENING TO ME?
"IS THIS FACE IN THE MIRROR MY OWN--OR HAVE I MERELY IMAGINED THAT IT IS MINE?
"FOR ONE TERRIFYING SECOND I TRULY DO NOT KNOW.
"AND THEN...
"...I HEAR A MUFFLED COUGH.
"SOMEONE BEHIND ME. WATCHING.
"I OPEN MY MOUTH--BUT THERE IS NO SOUND.
"FOR I STAND FACE TO FACE -- WITH...
...DAIMON HELLSTROM, AT YOUR SERVICE.

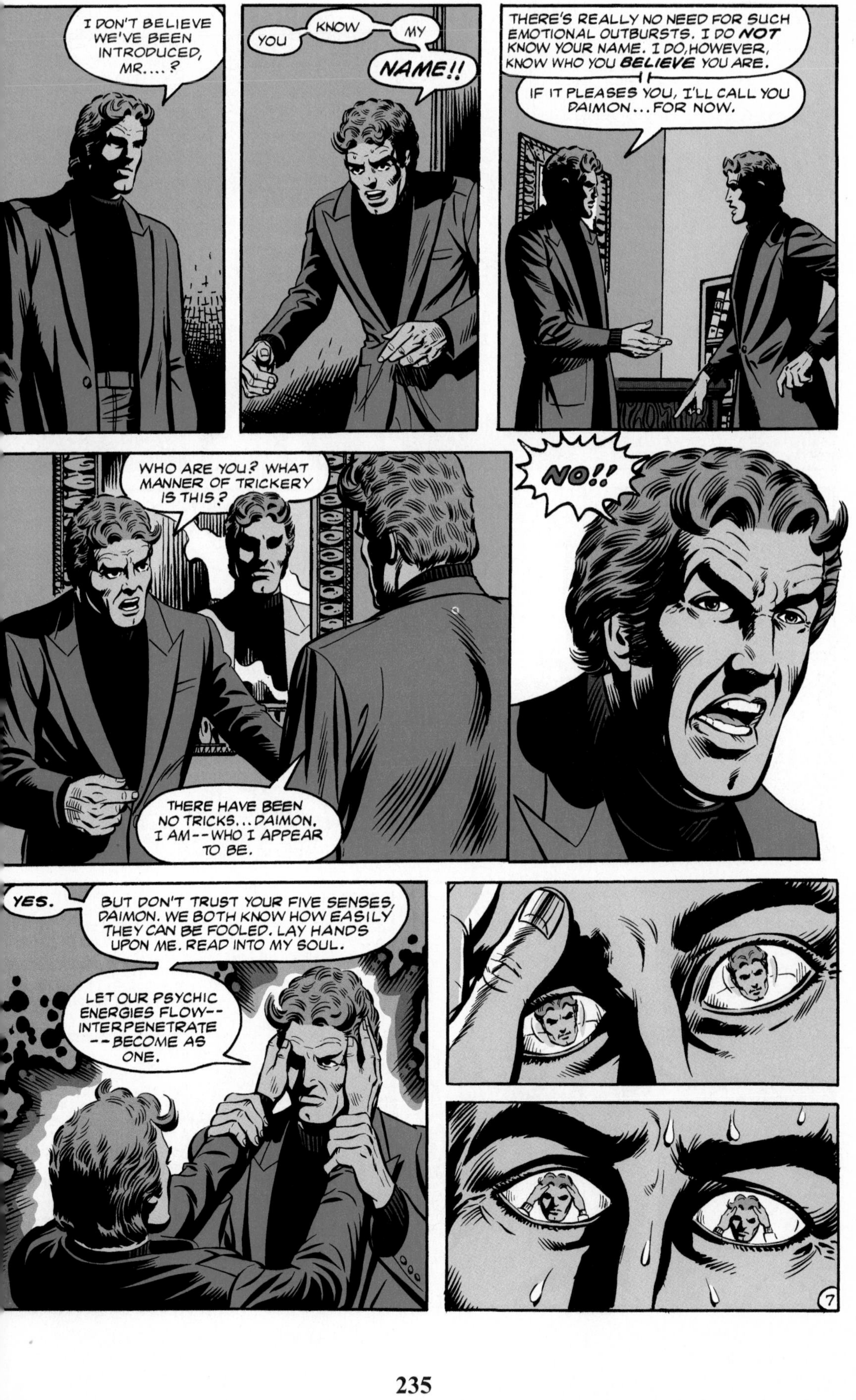
I DON'T BELIEVE WE'VE BEEN INTRODUCED, MR....?
YOU KNOW MY NAME!!
THERE'S REALLY NO NEED FOR SUCH EMOTIONAL OUTBURSTS. I DO NOT KNOW YOUR NAME. I DO, HOWEVER, KNOW WHO YOU BELIEVE YOU ARE.
IF IT PLEASES YOU, I'LL CALL YOU DAIMON... FOR NOW.
WHO ARE YOU? WHAT MANNER OF TRICKERY IS THIS?
THERE HAVE BEEN NO TRICKS... DAIMON. I AM--WHO I APPEAR TO BE.
NO!!
YES.
BUT DON'T TRUST YOUR FIVE SENSES, DAIMON. WE BOTH KNOW HOW EASILY THEY CAN BE FOOLED. LAY HANDS UPON ME. READ INTO MY SOUL.
LET OUR PSYCHIC ENERGIES FLOW--INTERPENETRATE--BECOME AS ONE.
7

"I, WHO HAVE FACED THE LORDS OF HELL WITHOUT FEAR, RECOIL IN ABJECT HORROR.

"FOR WHAT SEEMS AN ETERNITY, I STAND RAPT, MY GAZE LOCKED UPON THIS SHADOW-SELF.

"BUT HE IS *NOT A* SHADOW-SELF. HE IS *REAL.* FOR WHAT I SAW AS I GAZED DOWN INTO THE PITS OF HIS BEING... *WAS MY OWN SOUL!*

"DAZED, DISORIENTED, I LEAVE.

"*HE* REMAINS.

GO. *PLEASE.*

JUST...GO... AWAY...

INTERLUDE.

*F*ROM THE CANYONS OF THE SPIRIT, TO THE CANYONS OF MANHATTAN: THE UPPER WEST SIDE BROWNSTONE HOME OF THE DYNAMIC *DEFENDERS,* TO BE PRECISE...

...WHERE A FRUSTRATED *PATSY WALKER* HAS REACHED THE END OF HER ROPE...OR SHOULD WE SAY...*TYPEWRITER?*

FOUR HOURS! FOUR HOURS ON ONE CRUMMY PARAGRAPH!

JEEZ -- IT READS LIKE A THIRD-GRADER WROTE IT! IT'S AWFUL!

AH, THE TRIALS AND TRAVAILS OF THE BUDDING WORDSMITH!

WHO? OH-- *ISAAC!*

WRITING'S NOT QUITE AS EASY AS YOU THOUGHT IT'D BE, IS IT?

8

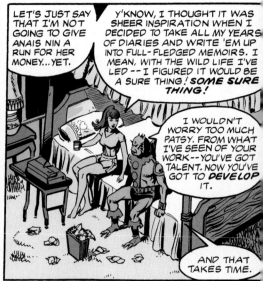

LET'S JUST SAY THAT I'M NOT GOING TO GIVE ANAIS NIN A RUN FOR HER MONEY...YET.

Y'KNOW, I THOUGHT IT WAS SHEER INSPIRATION WHEN I DECIDED TO TAKE ALL MY YEARS OF DIARIES AND WRITE 'EM UP INTO FULL-FLEDGED MEMOIRS. I MEAN, WITH THE WILD LIFE I'VE LED -- I FIGURED IT WOULD BE A SURE THING! *SOME SURE THING!*

I WOULDN'T WORRY TOO MUCH PATSY. FROM WHAT I'VE SEEN OF YOUR WORK -- YOU'VE GOT TALENT. NOW YOU'VE GOT TO *DEVELOP* IT.

AND THAT TAKES TIME.

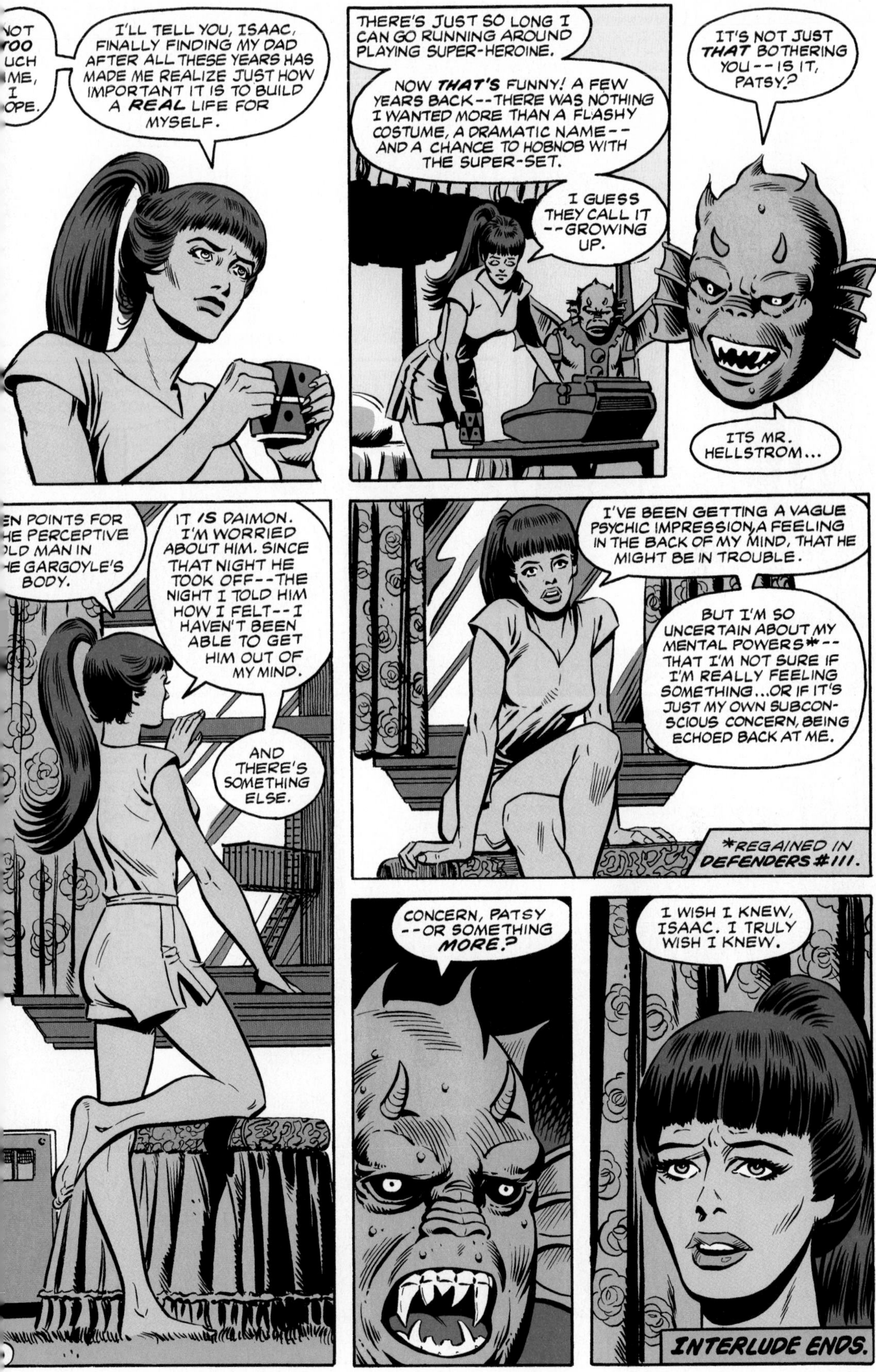

NOT TOO UCH ME, I OPE.
I'LL TELL YOU, ISAAC, FINALLY FINDING MY DAD AFTER ALL THESE YEARS HAS MADE ME REALIZE JUST HOW IMPORTANT IT IS TO BUILD A REAL LIFE FOR MYSELF.
THERE'S JUST SO LONG I CAN GO RUNNING AROUND PLAYING SUPER-HEROINE.
NOW THAT'S FUNNY! A FEW YEARS BACK--THERE WAS NOTHING I WANTED MORE THAN A FLASHY COSTUME, A DRAMATIC NAME--AND A CHANCE TO HOBNOB WITH THE SUPER-SET.
I GUESS THEY CALL IT --GROWING UP.
IT'S NOT JUST THAT BOTHERING YOU--IS IT, PATSY?
ITS MR. HELLSTROM...
EN POINTS FOR HE PERCEPTIVE LD MAN IN HE GARGOYLE'S BODY.
IT IS DAIMON. I'M WORRIED ABOUT HIM. SINCE THAT NIGHT HE TOOK OFF--THE NIGHT I TOLD HIM HOW I FELT--I HAVEN'T BEEN ABLE TO GET HIM OUT OF MY MIND.
AND THERE'S SOMETHING ELSE.
I'VE BEEN GETTING A VAGUE PSYCHIC IMPRESSION, A FEELING IN THE BACK OF MY MIND, THAT HE MIGHT BE IN TROUBLE.
BUT I'M SO UNCERTAIN ABOUT MY MENTAL POWERS*--THAT I'M NOT SURE IF I'M REALLY FEELING SOMETHING...OR IF IT'S JUST MY OWN SUBCONSCIOUS CONCERN, BEING ECHOED BACK AT ME.
*REGAINED IN DEFENDERS #111.
CONCERN, PATSY --OR SOMETHING MORE?
I WISH I KNEW, ISAAC. I TRULY WISH I KNEW.
INTERLUDE ENDS.

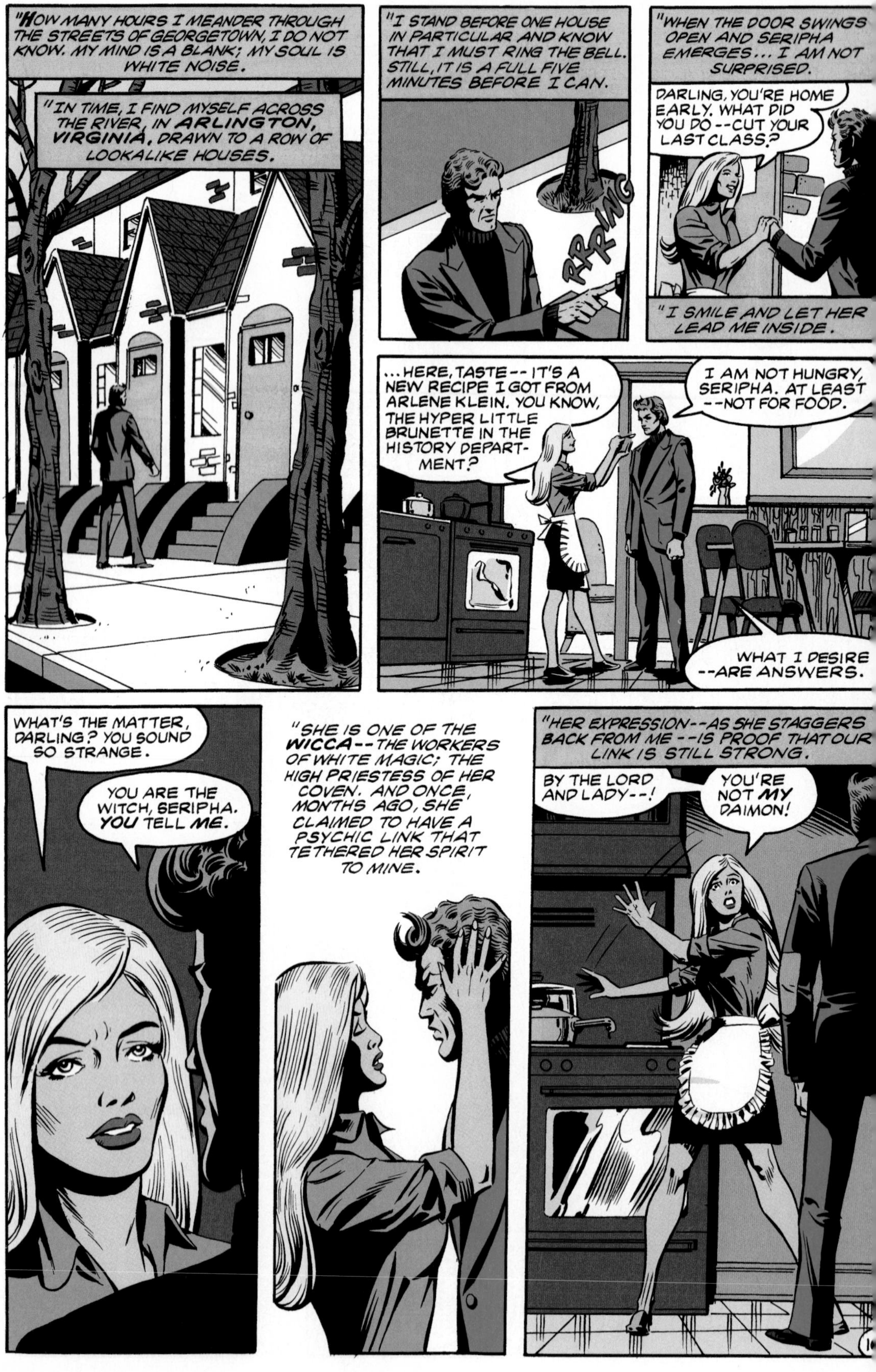

"HOW MANY HOURS I MEANDER THROUGH THE STREETS OF GEORGETOWN, I DO NOT KNOW. MY MIND IS A BLANK; MY SOUL IS WHITE NOISE.
"IN TIME, I FIND MYSELF ACROSS THE RIVER, IN ARLINGTON, VIRGINIA, DRAWN TO A ROW OF LOOKALIKE HOUSES.
"I STAND BEFORE ONE HOUSE IN PARTICULAR AND KNOW THAT I MUST RING THE BELL. STILL, IT IS A FULL FIVE MINUTES BEFORE I CAN.
RRRING
"WHEN THE DOOR SWINGS OPEN AND SERIPHA EMERGES... I AM NOT SURPRISED.
DARLING, YOU'RE HOME EARLY. WHAT DID YOU DO--CUT YOUR LAST CLASS?
"I SMILE AND LET HER LEAD ME INSIDE.
...HERE, TASTE-- IT'S A NEW RECIPE I GOT FROM ARLENE KLEIN. YOU KNOW, THE HYPER LITTLE BRUNETTE IN THE HISTORY DEPARTMENT?
I AM NOT HUNGRY, SERIPHA. AT LEAST --NOT FOR FOOD.
WHAT I DESIRE --ARE ANSWERS.
WHAT'S THE MATTER, DARLING? YOU SOUND SO STRANGE.
YOU ARE THE WITCH, SERIPHA. YOU TELL ME.
"SHE IS ONE OF THE WICCA--THE WORKERS OF WHITE MAGIC; THE HIGH PRIESTESS OF HER COVEN. AND ONCE, MONTHS AGO, SHE CLAIMED TO HAVE A PSYCHIC LINK THAT TETHERED HER SPIRIT TO MINE.
"HER EXPRESSION--AS SHE STAGGERS BACK FROM ME--IS PROOF THAT OUR LINK IS STILL STRONG.
BY THE LORD AND LADY--!
YOU'RE NOT MY DAIMON!

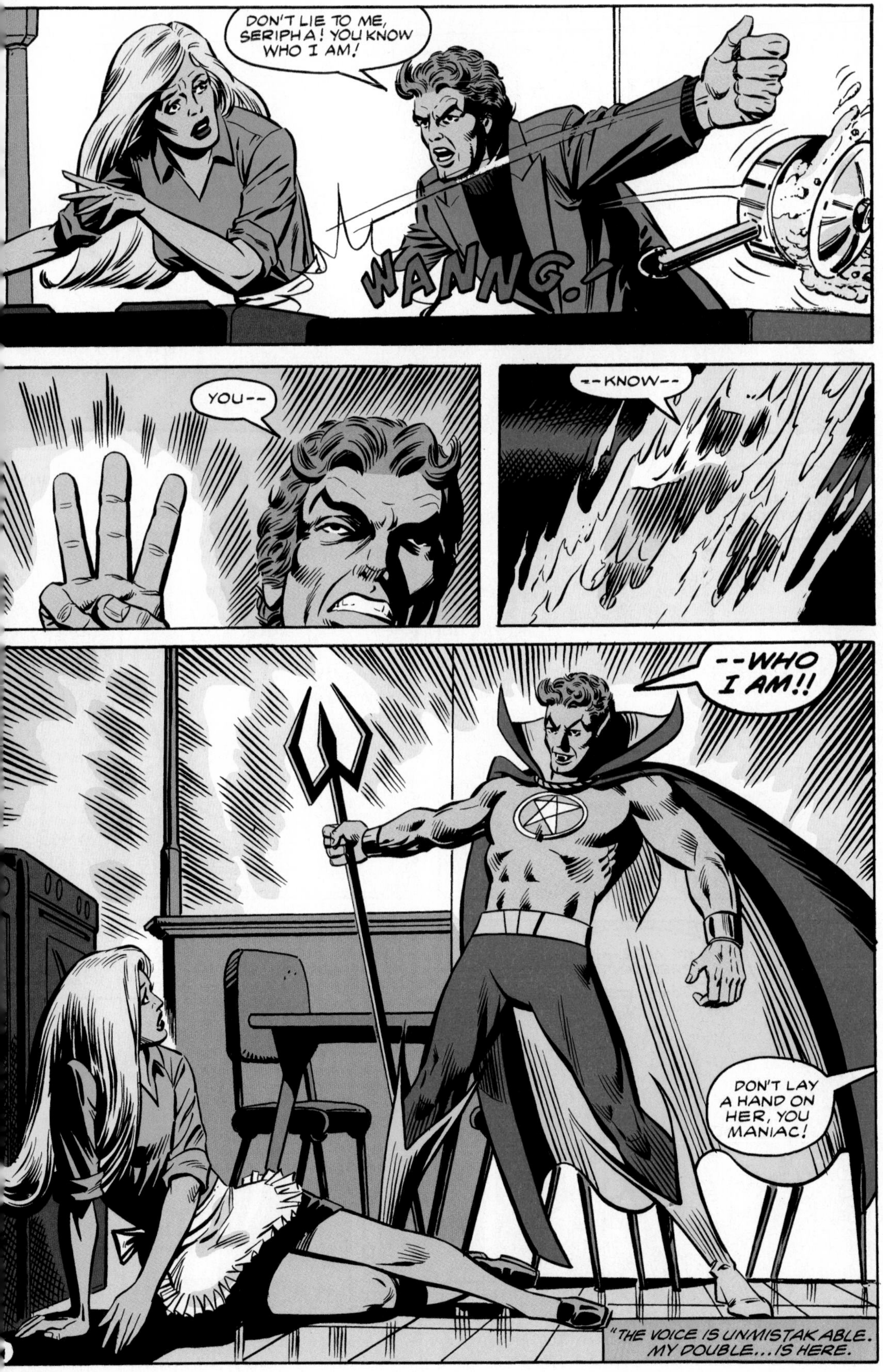
DON'T LIE TO ME, SERIPHA! YOU KNOW WHO I AM!
WANNG
YOU--
--KNOW--
--WHO I AM!!
DON'T LAY A HAND ON HER, YOU MANIAC!
"THE VOICE IS UNMISTAKABLE. MY DOUBLE...IS HERE.

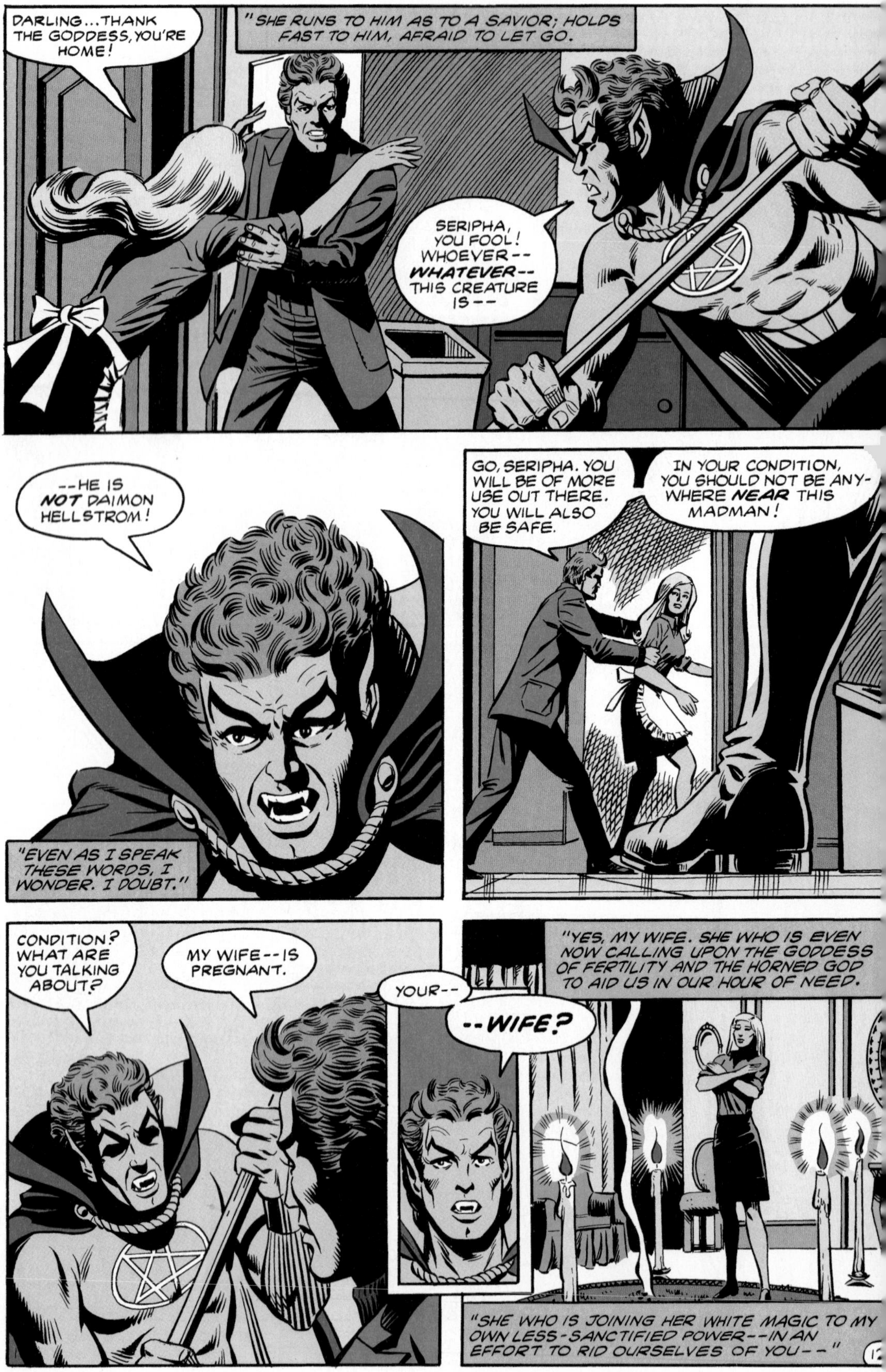
DARLING...THANK THE GODDESS, YOU'RE HOME!
"SHE RUNS TO HIM AS TO A SAVIOR; HOLDS FAST TO HIM, AFRAID TO LET GO.
SERIPHA, YOU FOOL! WHOEVER-- WHATEVER-- THIS CREATURE IS--
--HE IS NOT DAIMON HELLSTROM!
"EVEN AS I SPEAK THESE WORDS, I WONDER. I DOUBT."
GO, SERIPHA. YOU WILL BE OF MORE USE OUT THERE. YOU WILL ALSO BE SAFE.
IN YOUR CONDITION, YOU SHOULD NOT BE ANY-WHERE NEAR THIS MADMAN!
CONDITION? WHAT ARE YOU TALKING ABOUT?
MY WIFE--IS PREGNANT.
YOUR--
--WIFE?
"YES, MY WIFE. SHE WHO IS EVEN NOW CALLING UPON THE GODDESS OF FERTILITY AND THE HORNED GOD TO AID US IN OUR HOUR OF NEED.
"SHE WHO IS JOINING HER WHITE MAGIC TO MY OWN LESS-SANCTIFIED POWER--IN AN EFFORT TO RID OURSELVES OF YOU--"
12

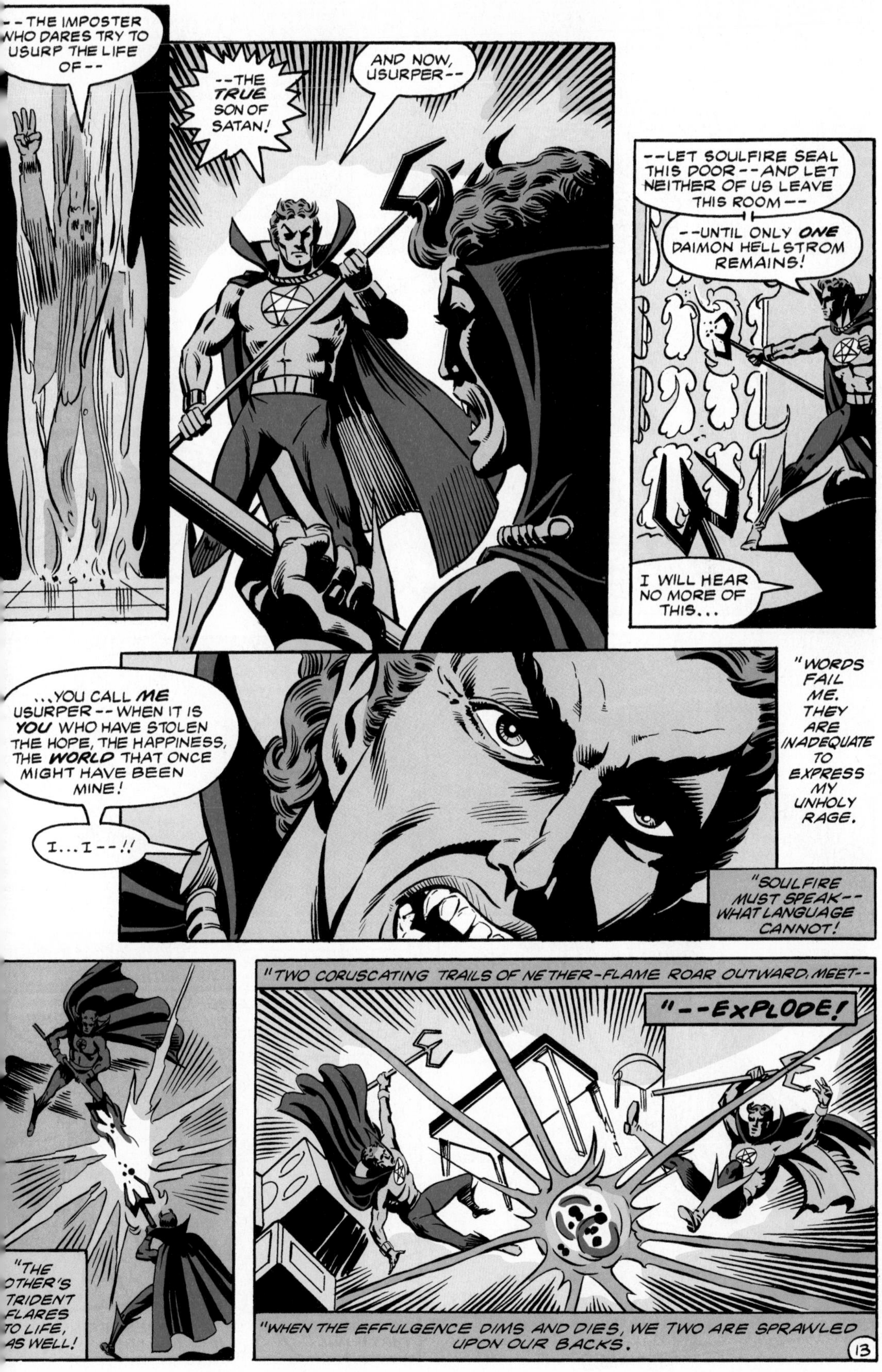
--THE IMPOSTER WHO DARES TRY TO USURP THE LIFE OF--
--THE TRUE SON OF SATAN!
AND NOW, USURPER--
--LET SOULFIRE SEAL THIS DOOR--AND LET NEITHER OF US LEAVE THIS ROOM--
--UNTIL ONLY ONE DAIMON HELLSTROM REMAINS!
I WILL HEAR NO MORE OF THIS...
...YOU CALL ME USURPER--WHEN IT IS YOU WHO HAVE STOLEN THE HOPE, THE HAPPINESS, THE WORLD THAT ONCE MIGHT HAVE BEEN MINE!
I...I--!!
"WORDS FAIL ME. THEY ARE INADEQUATE TO EXPRESS MY UNHOLY RAGE.
"SOULFIRE MUST SPEAK--WHAT LANGUAGE CANNOT!
"THE OTHER'S TRIDENT FLARES TO LIFE, AS WELL!
"TWO CORUSCATING TRAILS OF NETHER-FLAME ROAR OUTWARD, MEET--
"--EXPLODE!
"WHEN THE EFFULGENCE DIMS AND DIES, WE TWO ARE SPRAWLED UPON OUR BACKS.
13

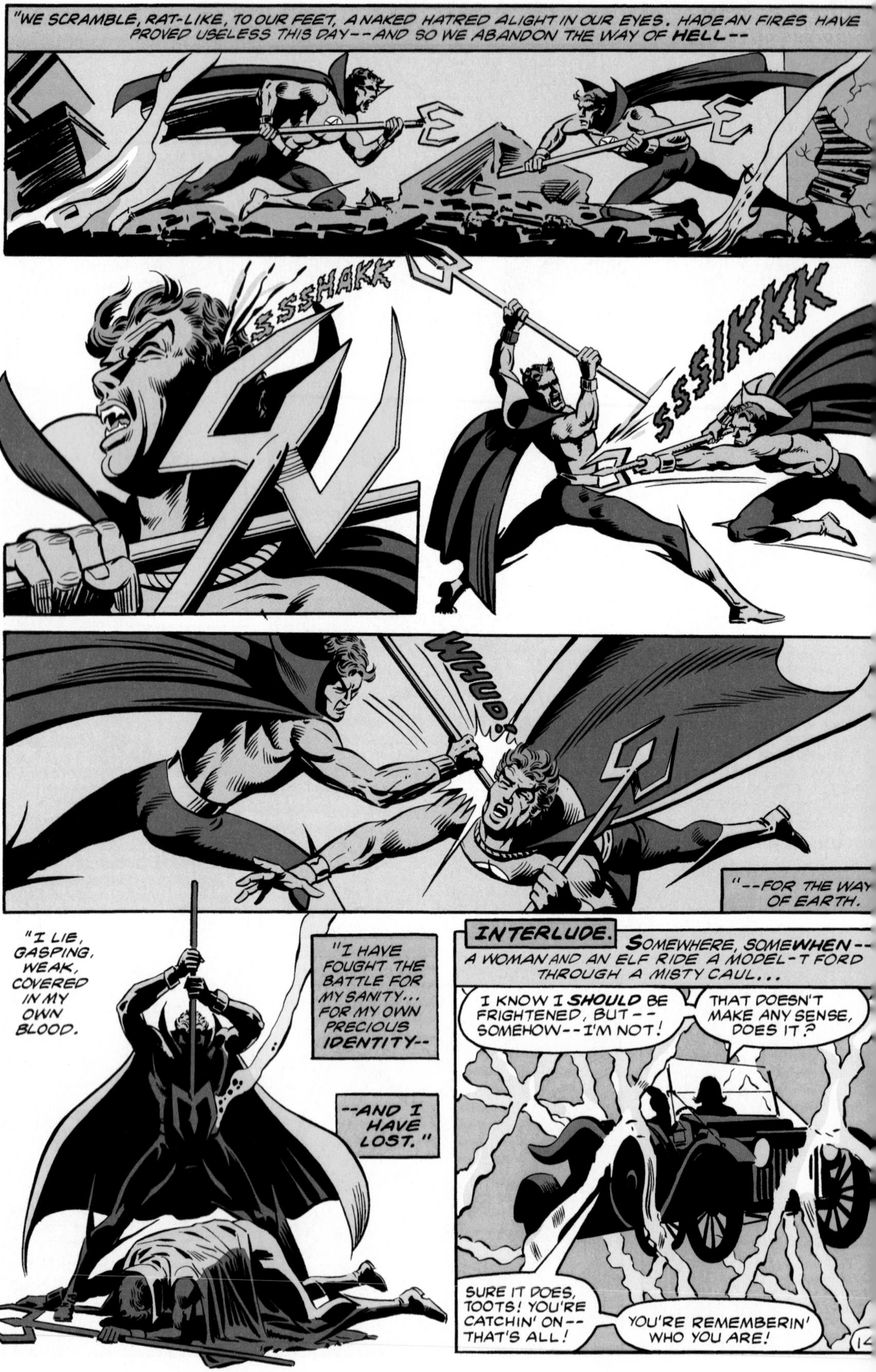
"WE SCRAMBLE, RAT-LIKE, TO OUR FEET, A NAKED HATRED ALIGHT IN OUR EYES. HADEAN FIRES HAVE PROVED USELESS THIS DAY--AND SO WE ABANDON THE WAY OF HELL--
SSSHAKK
SSSIKKK
WHUD
"--FOR THE WAY OF EARTH.
"I LIE, GASPING, WEAK, COVERED IN MY OWN BLOOD.
"I HAVE FOUGHT THE BATTLE FOR MY SANITY... FOR MY OWN PRECIOUS IDENTITY--
--AND I HAVE LOST."
INTERLUDE. SOMEWHERE, SOMEWHEN-- A WOMAN AND AN ELF RIDE A MODEL-T FORD THROUGH A MISTY CAUL...
I KNOW I SHOULD BE FRIGHTENED, BUT-- SOMEHOW--I'M NOT!
THAT DOESN'T MAKE ANY SENSE, DOES IT?
SURE IT DOES, TOOTS! YOU'RE CATCHIN' ON-- THAT'S ALL!
YOU'RE REMEMBERIN' WHO YOU ARE!

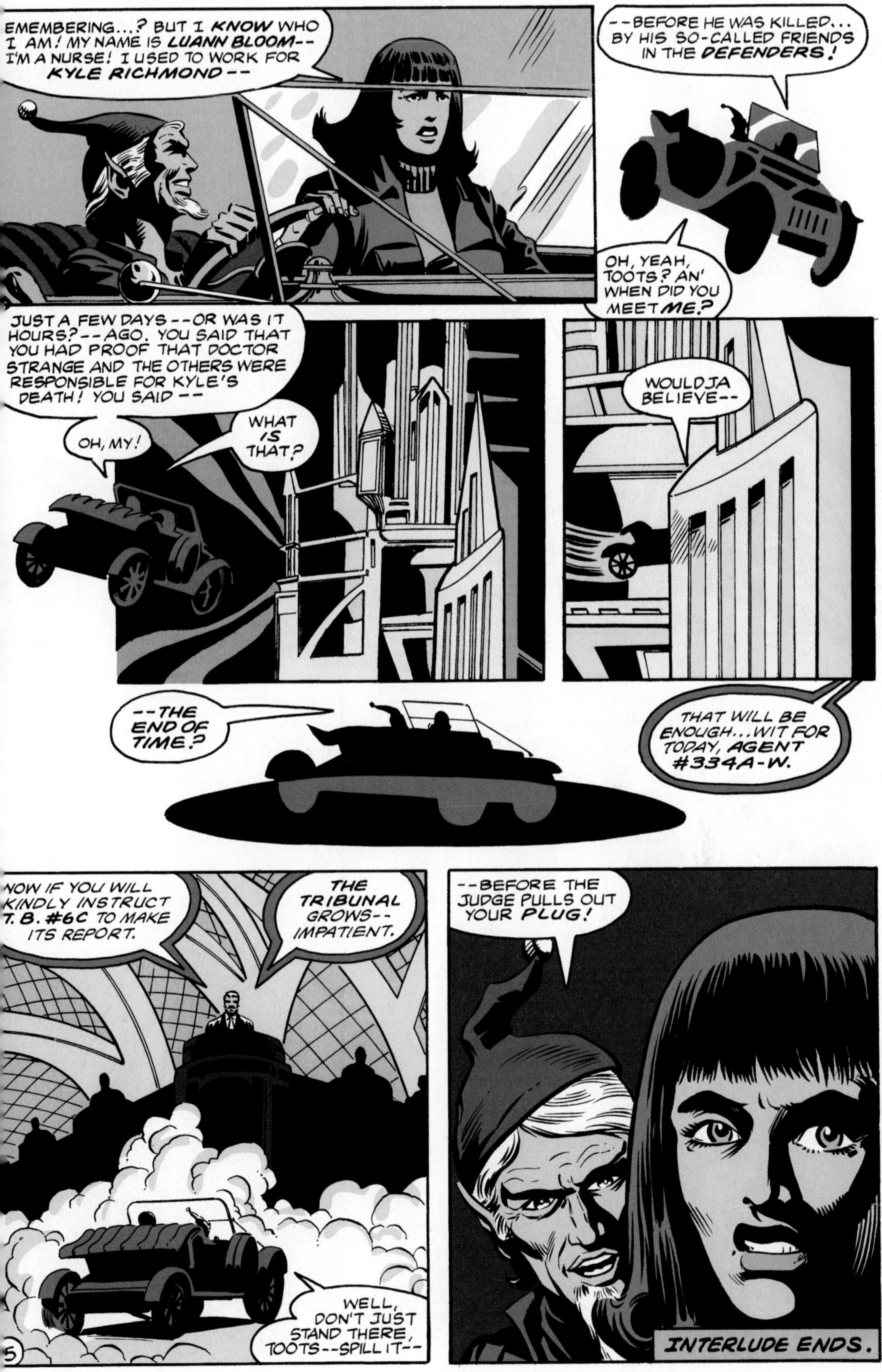
EMEMBERING...? BUT I KNOW WHO I AM! MY NAME IS LUANN BLOOM-- I'M A NURSE! I USED TO WORK FOR KYLE RICHMOND --
--BEFORE HE WAS KILLED... BY HIS SO-CALLED FRIENDS IN THE DEFENDERS!
OH, YEAH, TOOTS? AN' WHEN DID YOU MEET ME?
JUST A FEW DAYS--OR WAS IT HOURS?--AGO. YOU SAID THAT YOU HAD PROOF THAT DOCTOR STRANGE AND THE OTHERS WERE RESPONSIBLE FOR KYLE'S DEATH! YOU SAID --
OH, MY!
WHAT IS THAT?
WOULDJA BELIEVE--
--THE END OF TIME?
THAT WILL BE ENOUGH...WIT FOR TODAY, AGENT #334A-W.
NOW IF YOU WILL KINDLY INSTRUCT T. B. #6C TO MAKE ITS REPORT.
THE TRIBUNAL GROWS-- IMPATIENT.
WELL, DON'T JUST STAND THERE, TOOTS--SPILL IT--
5
--BEFORE THE JUDGE PULLS OUT YOUR PLUG!
INTERLUDE ENDS.

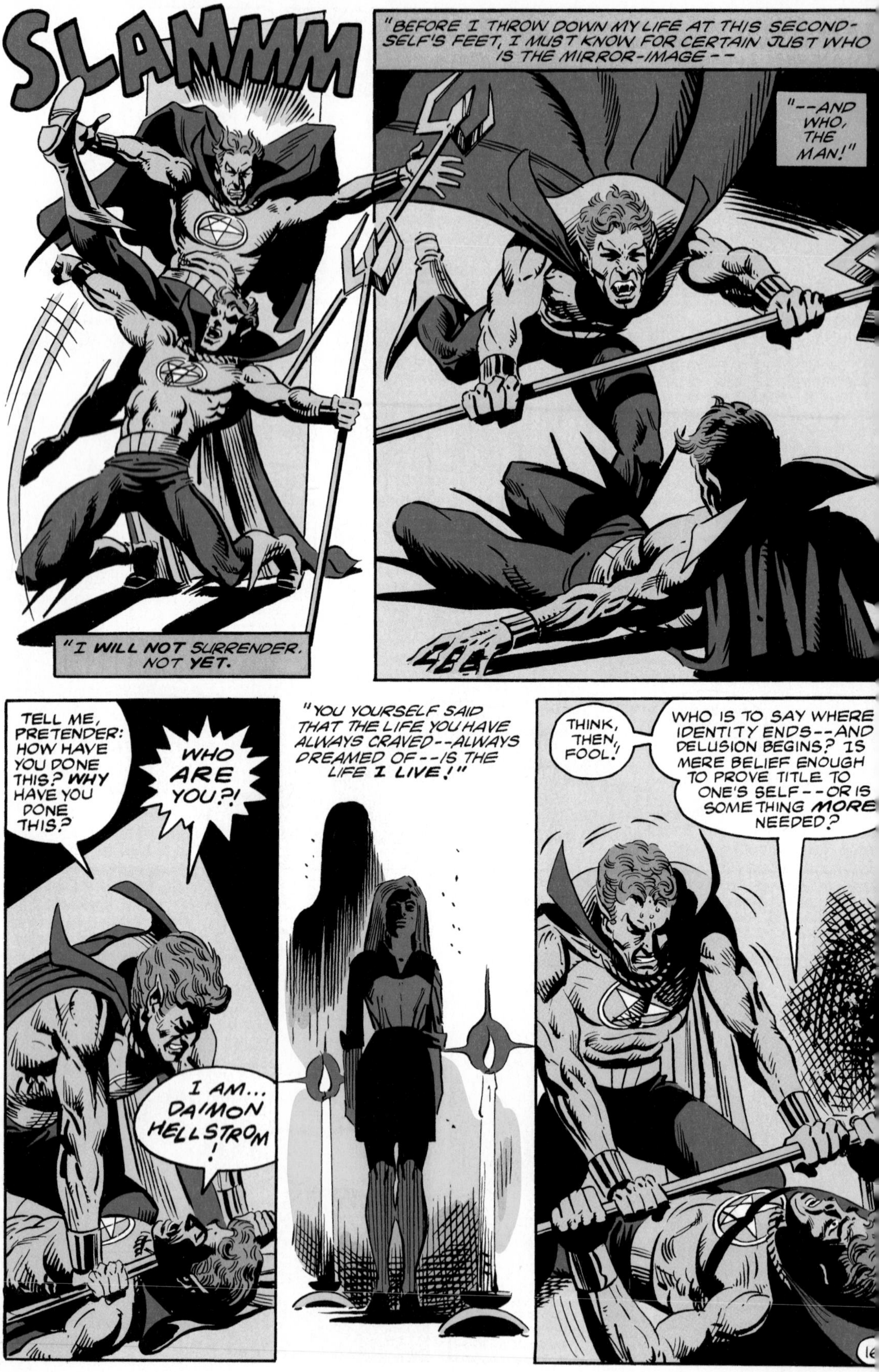
SLAMMM
"BEFORE I THROW DOWN MY LIFE AT THIS SECOND-SELF'S FEET, I MUST KNOW FOR CERTAIN JUST WHO IS THE MIRROR-IMAGE--
"--AND WHO, THE MAN!"
"I WILL NOT SURRENDER. NOT YET.
TELL ME, PRETENDER: HOW HAVE YOU DONE THIS? WHY HAVE YOU DONE THIS?
WHO ARE YOU?!
I AM... DAIMON HELLSTROM!
"YOU YOURSELF SAID THAT THE LIFE YOU HAVE ALWAYS CRAVED--ALWAYS DREAMED OF--IS THE LIFE I LIVE!"
THINK, THEN, FOOL!
WHO IS TO SAY WHERE IDENTITY ENDS--AND DELUSION BEGINS? IS MERE BELIEF ENOUGH TO PROVE TITLE TO ONE'S SELF--OR IS SOMETHING MORE NEEDED?
16

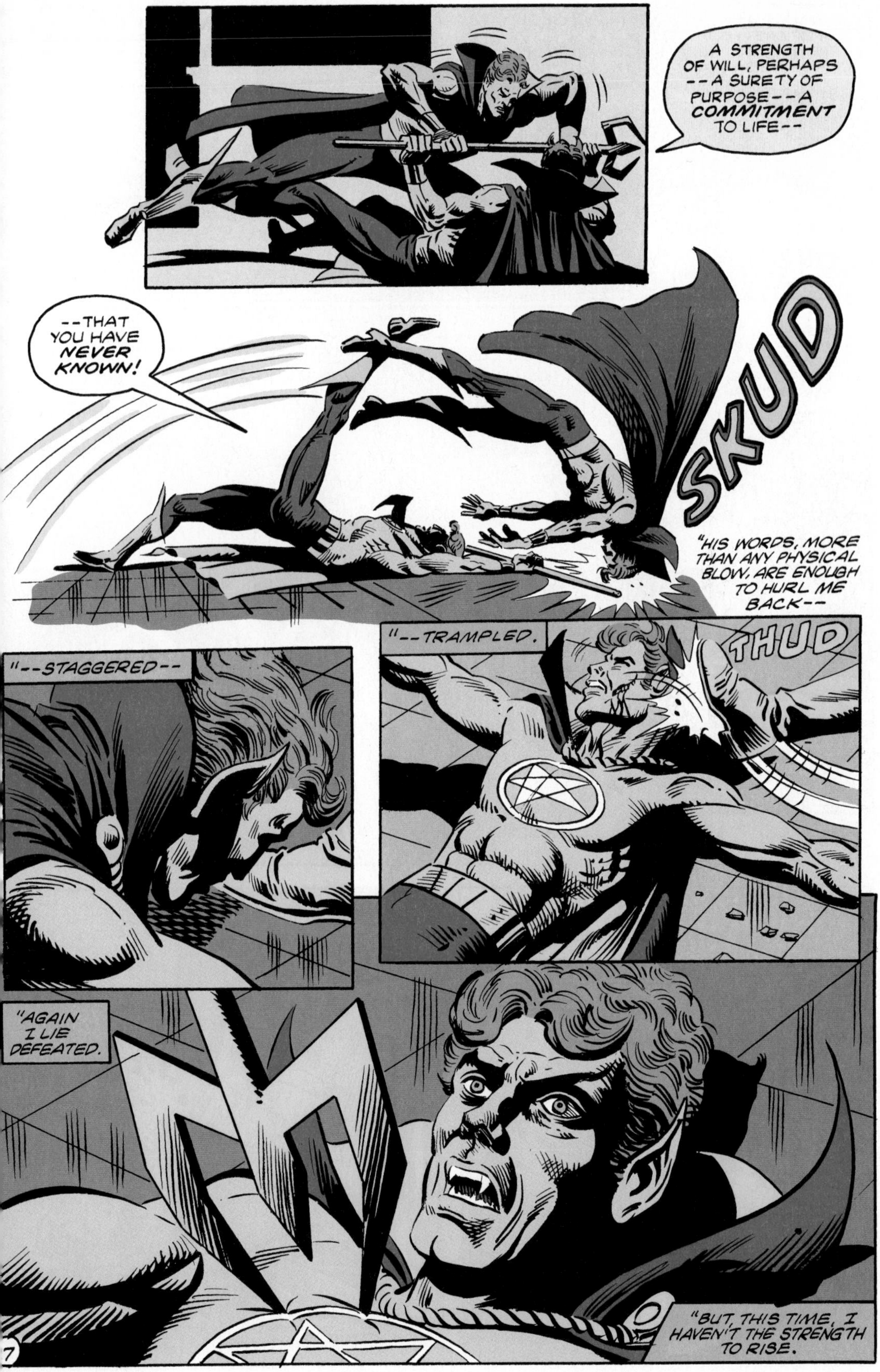
A STRENGTH OF WILL, PERHAPS --A SURETY OF PURPOSE--A COMMITMENT TO LIFE--
--THAT YOU HAVE NEVER KNOWN!
SKUD
"HIS WORDS, MORE THAN ANY PHYSICAL BLOW, ARE ENOUGH TO HURL ME BACK--
"--STAGGERED--
"--TRAMPLED.
THUD
"AGAIN I LIE DEFEATED.
"BUT, THIS TIME, I HAVEN'T THE STRENGTH TO RISE.
7

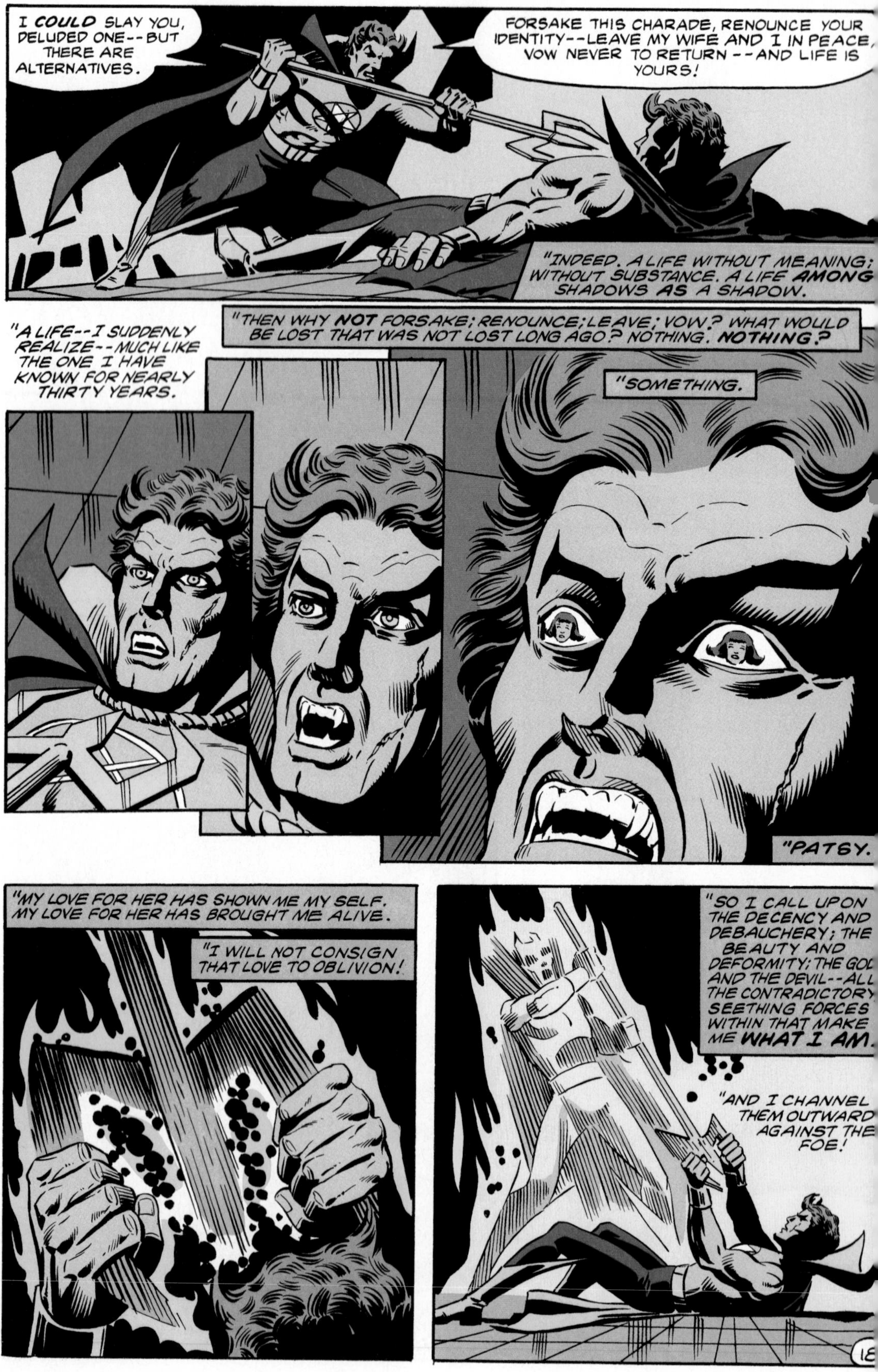

I COULD SLAY YOU, DELUDED ONE--BUT THERE ARE ALTERNATIVES.
FORSAKE THIS CHARADE, RENOUNCE YOUR IDENTITY--LEAVE MY WIFE AND I IN PEACE, VOW NEVER TO RETURN--AND LIFE IS YOURS!
"INDEED. A LIFE WITHOUT MEANING; WITHOUT SUBSTANCE. A LIFE AMONG SHADOWS AS A SHADOW.
"A LIFE--I SUDDENLY REALIZE--MUCH LIKE THE ONE I HAVE KNOWN FOR NEARLY THIRTY YEARS.
"THEN WHY NOT FORSAKE; RENOUNCE; LEAVE; VOW? WHAT WOULD BE LOST THAT WAS NOT LOST LONG AGO? NOTHING. NOTHING?
"SOMETHING.
"PATSY.
"MY LOVE FOR HER HAS SHOWN ME MY SELF. MY LOVE FOR HER HAS BROUGHT ME ALIVE.
"I WILL NOT CONSIGN THAT LOVE TO OBLIVION!
"SO I CALL UPON THE DECENCY AND DEBAUCHERY; THE BEAUTY AND DEFORMITY; THE GOD AND THE DEVIL--ALL THE CONTRADICTORY SEETHING FORCES WITHIN THAT MAKE ME WHAT I AM.
"AND I CHANNEL THEM OUTWARD AGAINST THE FOE!

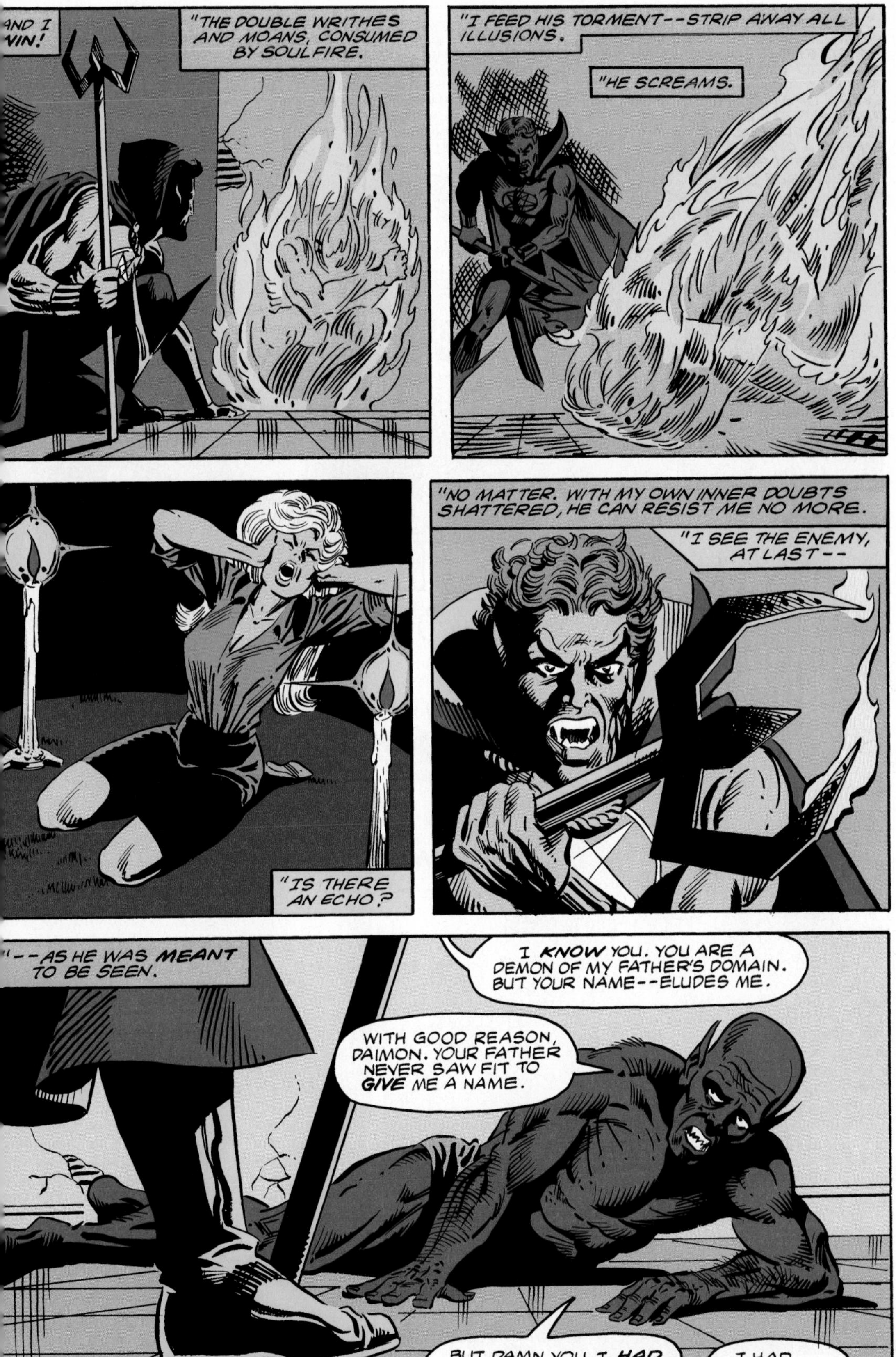
AND I
WIN!
"THE DOUBLE WRITHES AND MOANS, CONSUMED BY SOULFIRE.
"I FEED HIS TORMENT--STRIP AWAY ALL ILLUSIONS.
"HE SCREAMS.
"IS THERE AN ECHO?
"NO MATTER. WITH MY OWN INNER DOUBTS SHATTERED, HE CAN RESIST ME NO MORE.
"I SEE THE ENEMY, AT LAST--
"--AS HE WAS MEANT TO BE SEEN.
I KNOW YOU. YOU ARE A DEMON OF MY FATHER'S DOMAIN. BUT YOUR NAME--ELUDES ME.
WITH GOOD REASON, DAIMON. YOUR FATHER NEVER SAW FIT TO GIVE ME A NAME.
BUT, DAMN YOU, I HAD A NAME...UNTIL TODAY.
I HAD... YOUR NAME.
19

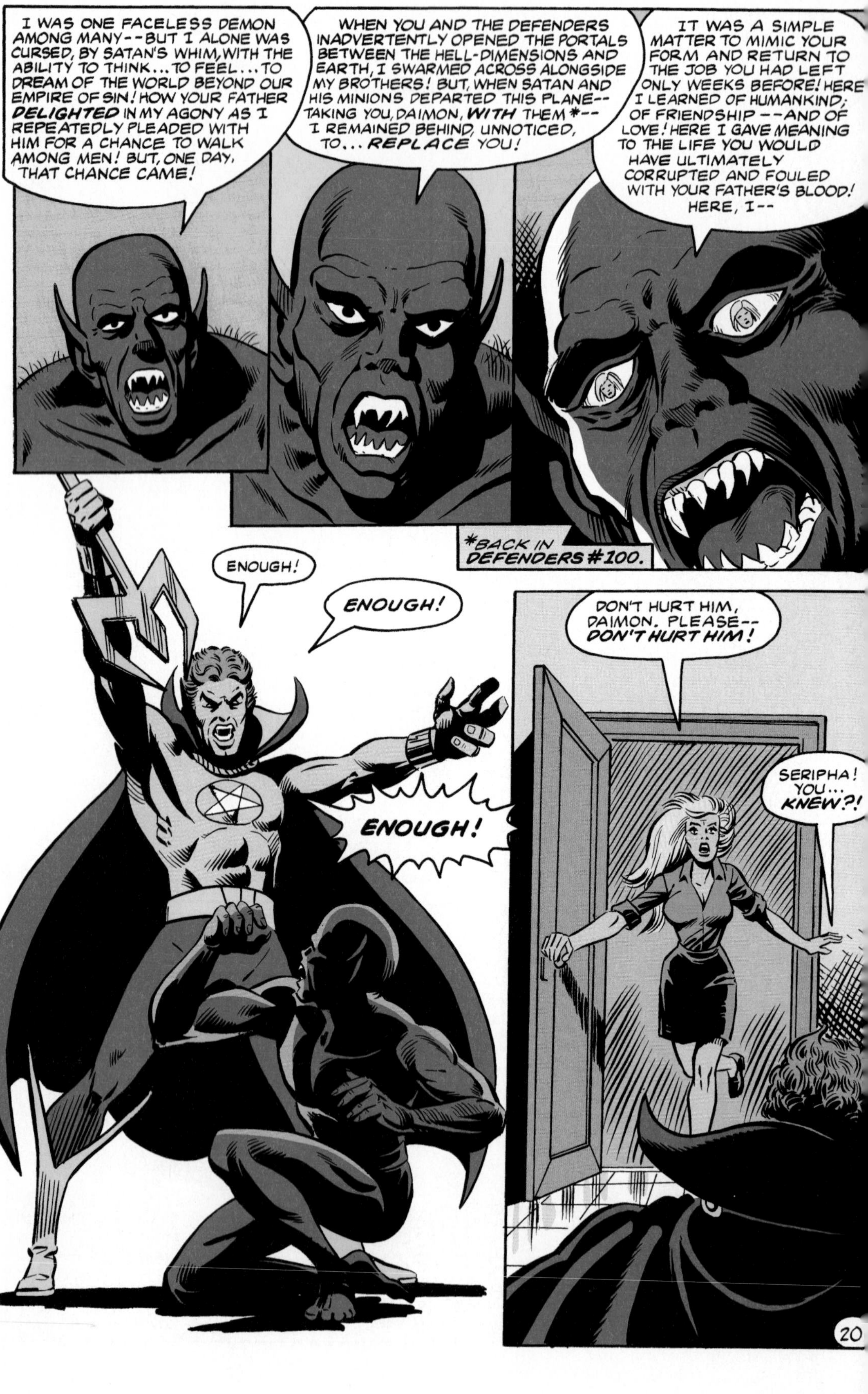
I WAS ONE FACELESS DEMON AMONG MANY--BUT I ALONE WAS CURSED, BY SATAN'S WHIM, WITH THE ABILITY TO THINK... TO FEEL... TO DREAM OF THE WORLD BEYOND OUR EMPIRE OF SIN! HOW YOUR FATHER DELIGHTED IN MY AGONY AS I REPEATEDLY PLEADED WITH HIM FOR A CHANCE TO WALK AMONG MEN! BUT, ONE DAY, THAT CHANCE CAME!
WHEN YOU AND THE DEFENDERS INADVERTENTLY OPENED THE PORTALS BETWEEN THE HELL-DIMENSIONS AND EARTH, I SWARMED ACROSS ALONGSIDE MY BROTHERS! BUT, WHEN SATAN AND HIS MINIONS DEPARTED THIS PLANE--TAKING YOU, DAIMON, WITH THEM*--I REMAINED BEHIND, UNNOTICED, TO... REPLACE YOU!
IT WAS A SIMPLE MATTER TO MIMIC YOUR FORM AND RETURN TO THE JOB YOU HAD LEFT ONLY WEEKS BEFORE! HERE I LEARNED OF HUMANKIND; OF FRIENDSHIP --AND OF LOVE! HERE I GAVE MEANING TO THE LIFE YOU WOULD HAVE ULTIMATELY CORRUPTED AND FOULED WITH YOUR FATHER'S BLOOD! HERE, I--
*BACK IN DEFENDERS #100.
ENOUGH!
ENOUGH!
ENOUGH!
DON'T HURT HIM, DAIMON. PLEASE--DON'T HURT HIM!
SERIPHA! YOU... KNEW?!
20

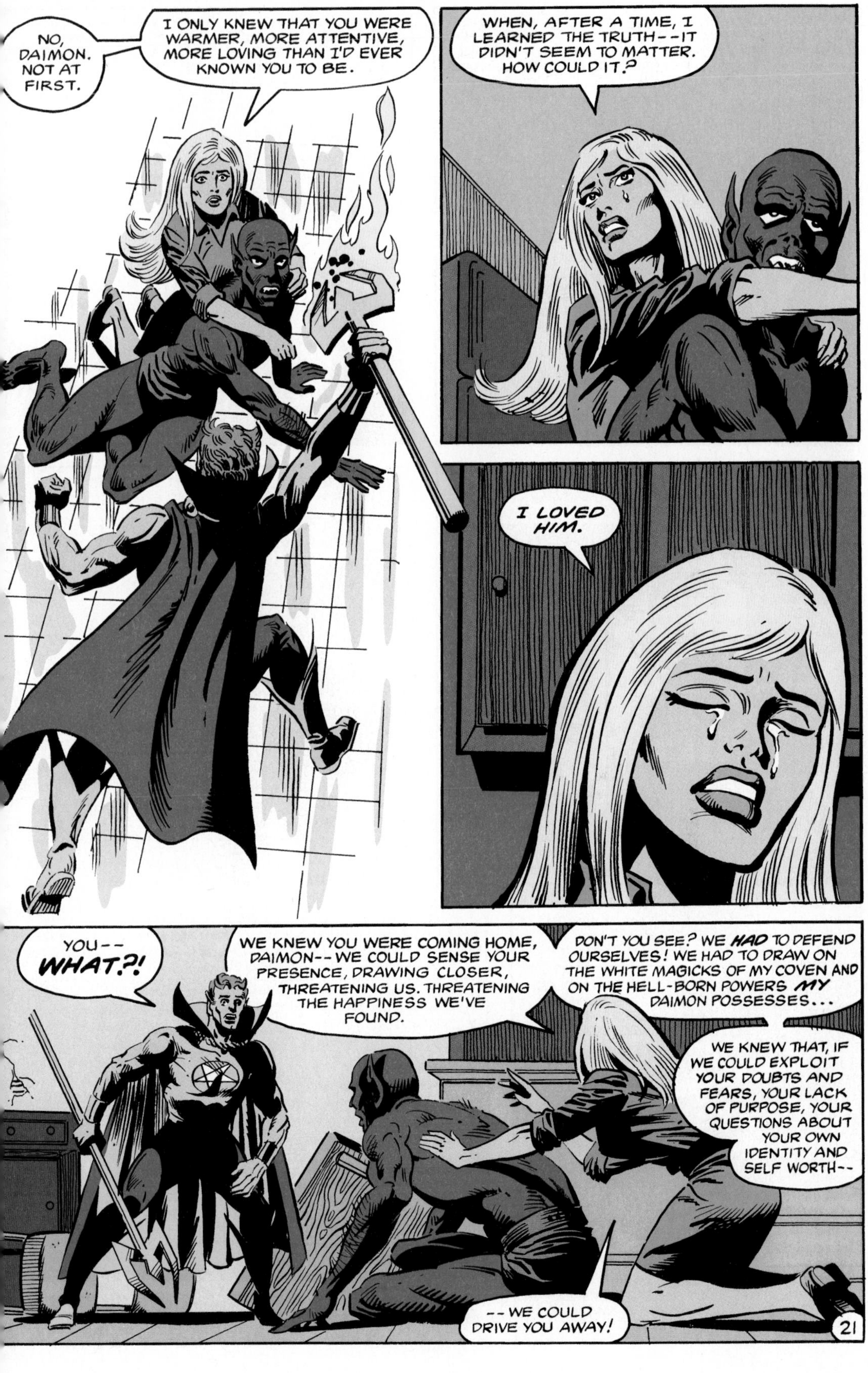

NO, DAIMON. NOT AT FIRST.
I ONLY KNEW THAT YOU WERE WARMER, MORE ATTENTIVE, MORE LOVING THAN I'D EVER KNOWN YOU TO BE.
WHEN, AFTER A TIME, I LEARNED THE TRUTH--IT DIDN'T SEEM TO MATTER. HOW COULD IT?
I LOVED HIM.
YOU-- WHAT?!
WE KNEW YOU WERE COMING HOME, DAIMON--WE COULD SENSE YOUR PRESENCE, DRAWING CLOSER, THREATENING US. THREATENING THE HAPPINESS WE'VE FOUND.
DON'T YOU SEE? WE HAD TO DEFEND OURSELVES! WE HAD TO DRAW ON THE WHITE MAGICKS OF MY COVEN AND ON THE HELL-BORN POWERS MY DAIMON POSSESSES...
WE KNEW THAT, IF WE COULD EXPLOIT YOUR DOUBTS AND FEARS, YOUR LACK OF PURPOSE, YOUR QUESTIONS ABOUT YOUR OWN IDENTITY AND SELF WORTH--
--WE COULD DRIVE YOU AWAY!
21

BUT YOU KNOW YOUR-SELF BETTER THAN WE'D DREAMED, DAIMON, AND --BELIEVE IT OR NOT --I'M GLAD.

WE... DIDN'T **WANT** TO HURT YOU.

BUT LOVE HAS A WAY OF MAKING MEN--AND DEMONS-- DESPERATE.

"AS WELL I KNOW.

I SEE NOW THAT MY WIFE AND I CANNOT CONTINUE LIVING A LIE. SO I DISCARD YOUR FORM, PRINCE OF HADES.

WE SHALL LEAVE HERE--BEGIN LIFE ANEW IN SOME OTHER PLACE. AND WE WILL BE HAPPY --FOR WE WILL HAVE... **EACH OTHER.**

DAIMON....?

GOODBYE, SERIPHA.

"GOODBYE.

"THE NIGHT SEEMS TO OPEN WIDE ITS ARMS IN WELCOME, THE DARKNESS REJOICING AT MY COMING.

" I AM AT HOME IN THE DARK--AS I HAVE ALWAYS BEEN.

"FOR IN DARKNESS MAN IS BLIND TO HIS SURROUNDINGS; BLIND TO HIMSELF.

"NOW. MORE THAN EVER, I FEAR THE COMING OF THE LIGHT.

"HOW LONG I WALK, I DO NOT KNOW. THE SKIN OF THE SATAN-SPAWN IS SHED; THE HUMAN BENEATH ONCE MORE EMERGES.

"BUT WHO **IS** THIS HUMAN CALLED DAIMON HELLSTROM?

"SERIPHA THAMES SAID I KNEW MY-SELF BETTER THAN SHE'D DREAMED-- BUT TONIGHT I SEE THAT I KNOW MYSELF... NOT AT ALL.

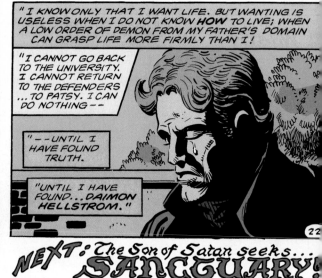

" I KNOW ONLY THAT I WANT LIFE. BUT WANTING IS USELESS WHEN I DO NOT KNOW **HOW** TO LIVE; WHEN A LOW ORDER OF DEMON FROM MY FATHER'S DOMAIN CAN GRASP LIFE MORE FIRMLY THAN I !

"I CANNOT GO BACK TO THE UNIVERSITY. I CANNOT RETURN TO THE DEFENDERS ...TO PATSY. I CAN DO NOTHING --

"--UNTIL I HAVE FOUND TRUTH.

"UNTIL I HAVE FOUND...DAIMON HELLSTROM."

22

NEXT: The Son of Satan seeks... SANCTUARY!

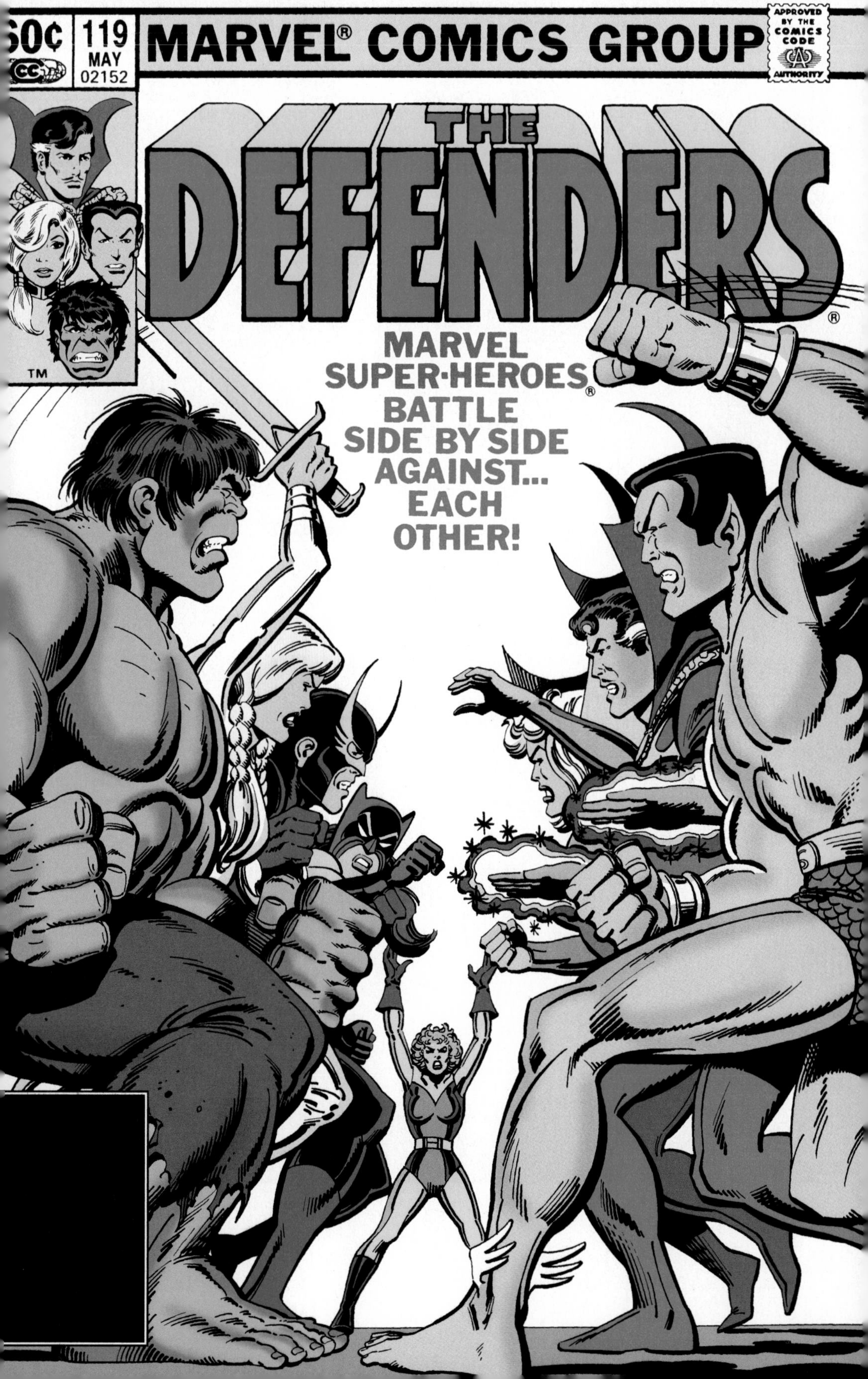
60¢
119
MAY
02152
MARVEL® COMICS GROUP
APPROVED BY THE COMICS CODE AUTHORITY
THE DEFENDERS®
TM
MARVEL SUPER-HEROES® BATTLE SIDE BY SIDE AGAINST... EACH OTHER!

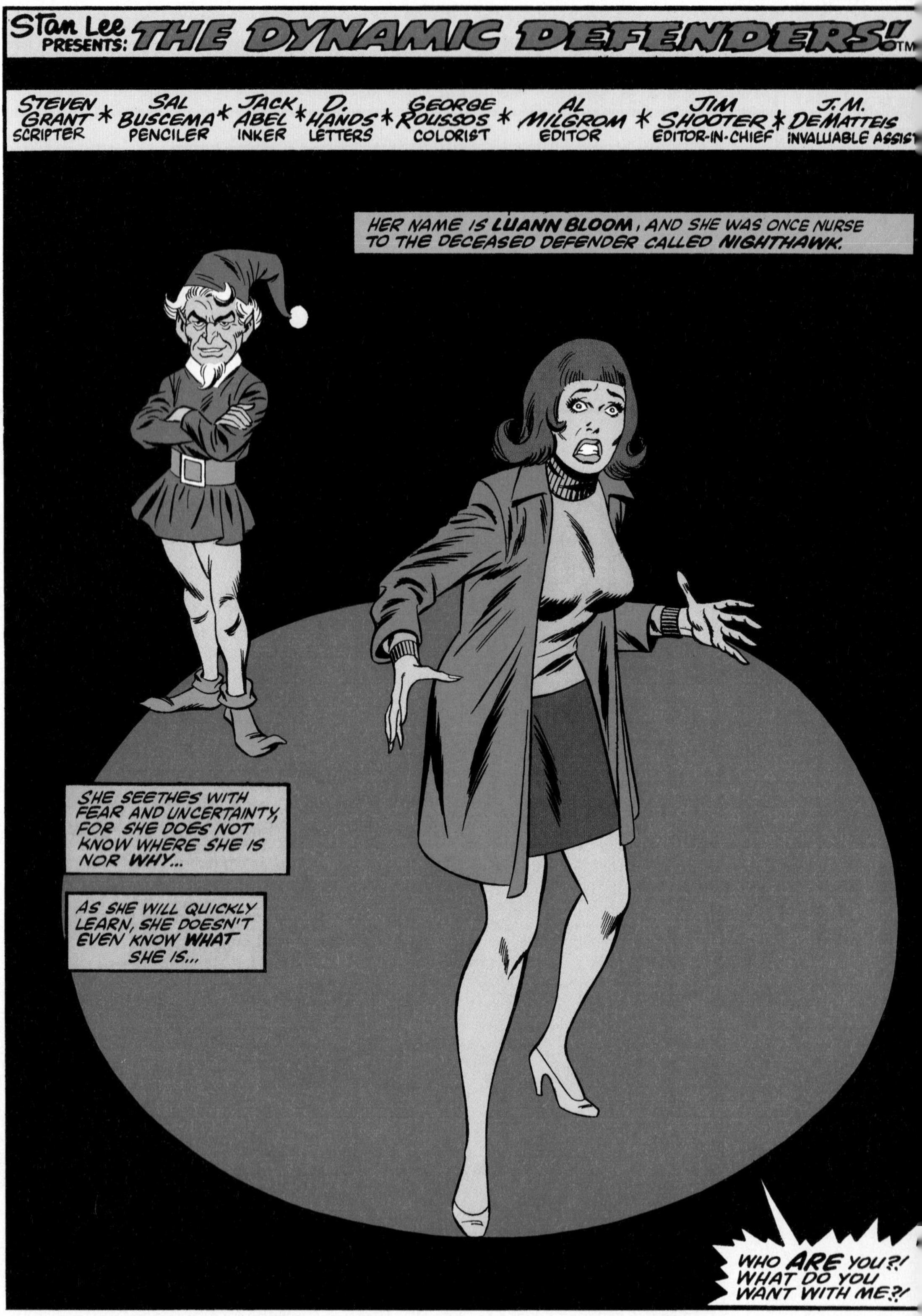
Stan Lee PRESENTS: THE DYNAMIC DEFENDERS!™
STEVEN GRANT SCRIPTER * SAL BUSCEMA PENCILER * JACK ABEL INKER * D. HANDS LETTERS * GEORGE ROUSSOS COLORIST * AL MILGROM EDITOR * JIM SHOOTER EDITOR-IN-CHIEF * J.M. DeMATTEIS INVALUABLE ASSIST
HER NAME IS LUANN BLOOM, AND SHE WAS ONCE NURSE TO THE DECEASED DEFENDER CALLED NIGHTHAWK.
SHE SEETHES WITH FEAR AND UNCERTAINTY, FOR SHE DOES NOT KNOW WHERE SHE IS NOR WHY...
AS SHE WILL QUICKLY LEARN, SHE DOESN'T EVEN KNOW WHAT SHE IS...
WHO ARE YOU?! WHAT DO YOU WANT WITH ME?!

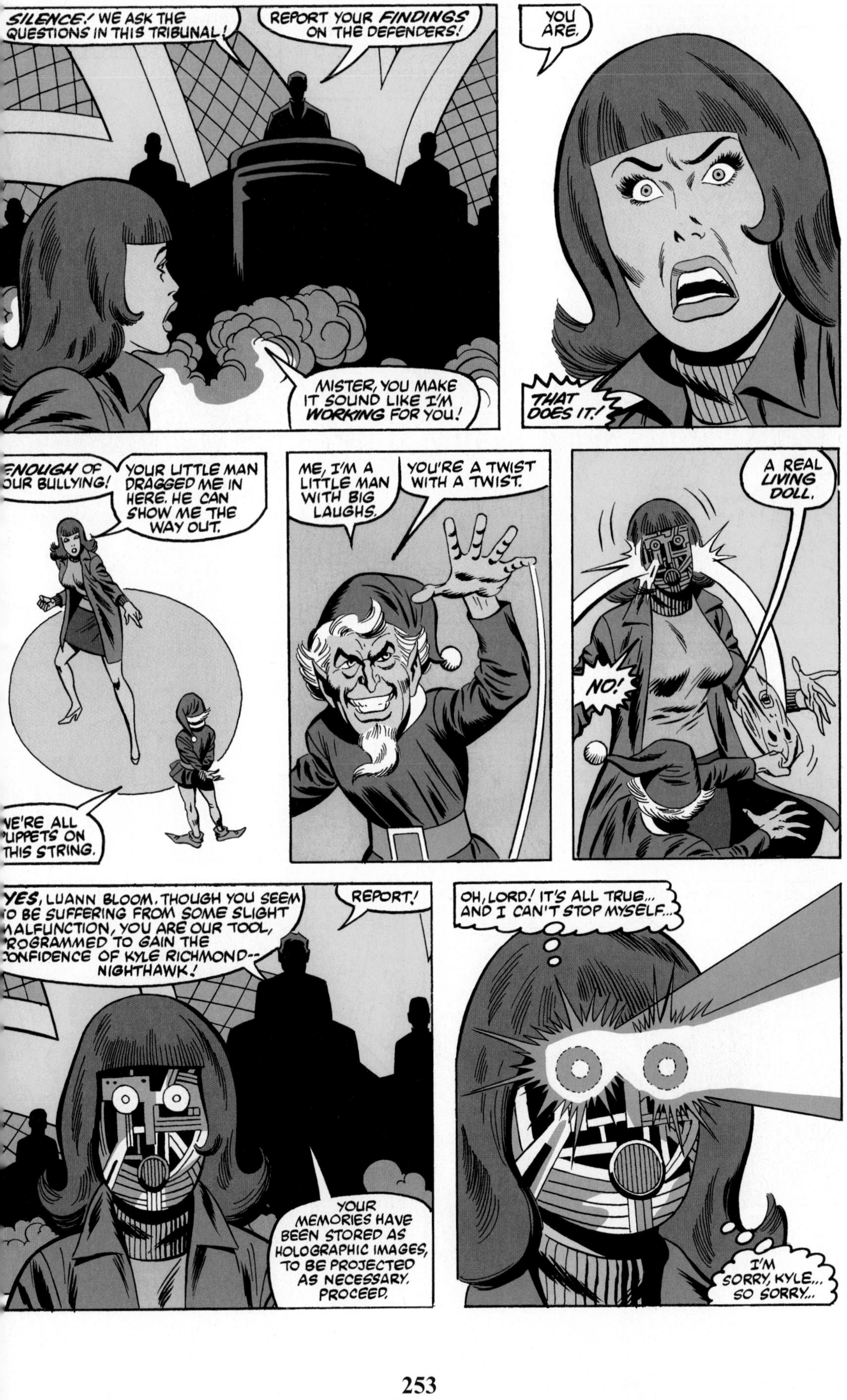
SILENCE! WE ASK THE QUESTIONS IN THIS TRIBUNAL!
REPORT YOUR FINDINGS ON THE DEFENDERS!
MISTER, YOU MAKE IT SOUND LIKE I'M WORKING FOR YOU!
YOU ARE.
THAT DOES IT!
ENOUGH OF YOUR BULLYING!
YOUR LITTLE MAN DRAGGED ME IN HERE. HE CAN SHOW ME THE WAY OUT.
WE'RE ALL PUPPETS ON THIS STRING.
ME, I'M A LITTLE MAN WITH BIG LAUGHS.
YOU'RE A TWIST WITH A TWIST.
A REAL LIVING DOLL.
NO!
YES, LUANN BLOOM. THOUGH YOU SEEM TO BE SUFFERING FROM SOME SLIGHT MALFUNCTION, YOU ARE OUR TOOL, PROGRAMMED TO GAIN THE CONFIDENCE OF KYLE RICHMOND-- NIGHTHAWK!
REPORT!
YOUR MEMORIES HAVE BEEN STORED AS HOLOGRAPHIC IMAGES, TO BE PROJECTED AS NECESSARY. PROCEED.
OH, LORD! IT'S ALL TRUE... AND I CAN'T STOP MYSELF...
I'M SORRY, KYLE... SO SORRY...

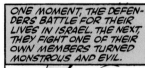

FAMILIAR SCENES TAKE FORM AND PLAY THEMSELVES OUT.

ONE MOMENT, THE DEFENDERS BATTLE FOR THEIR LIVES IN ISRAEL. THE NEXT, THEY FIGHT ONE OF THEIR OWN MEMBERS TURNED MONSTROUS AND EVIL.

THE HISTORY OF THE GROUP UNFOLDS LIKE A FLOWER. THE WAR AGAINST THE MUTANT MANDRILL IS REPLAYED...

IN ANGER, NIGHTHAWK DISBANDS THE DEFENDERS...

ALL THIS IS KNOWN TO US. HAVE YOU NOTHING NEW TO SHOW?

WAIT! THE PICTURE NOW COMING INTO FOCUS--TELL US MORE!

KYLE TOLD ME THIS STORY--ABOUT A SCIENTIST THE DEFENDERS... ONCE FOUGHT...

"...YANDROTH!*

"MY CIRCUITRY CAN TRANSFORM HIS SPOKEN WORD INTO VISUAL IMAGES!"

A COLD VOICE MURMURS "CONTINUE."

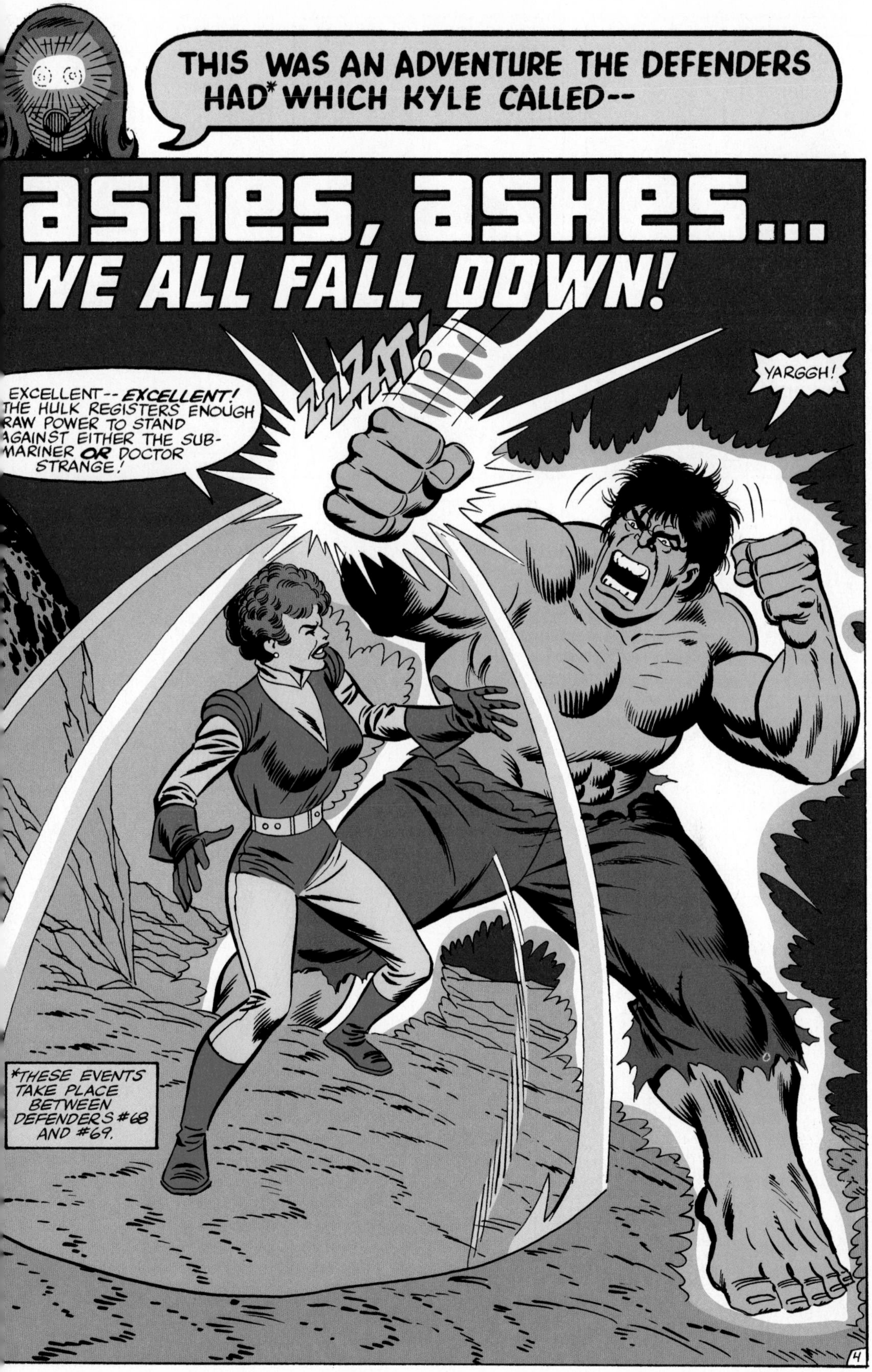
THIS WAS AN ADVENTURE THE DEFENDERS HAD* WHICH KYLE CALLED--
ASHES, ASHES... WE ALL FALL DOWN!
ZZZAT!
EXCELLENT-- EXCELLENT! THE HULK REGISTERS ENOUGH RAW POWER TO STAND AGAINST EITHER THE SUB-MARINER OR DOCTOR STRANGE!
YARGGH!
*THESE EVENTS TAKE PLACE BETWEEN DEFENDERS #68 AND #69.
4

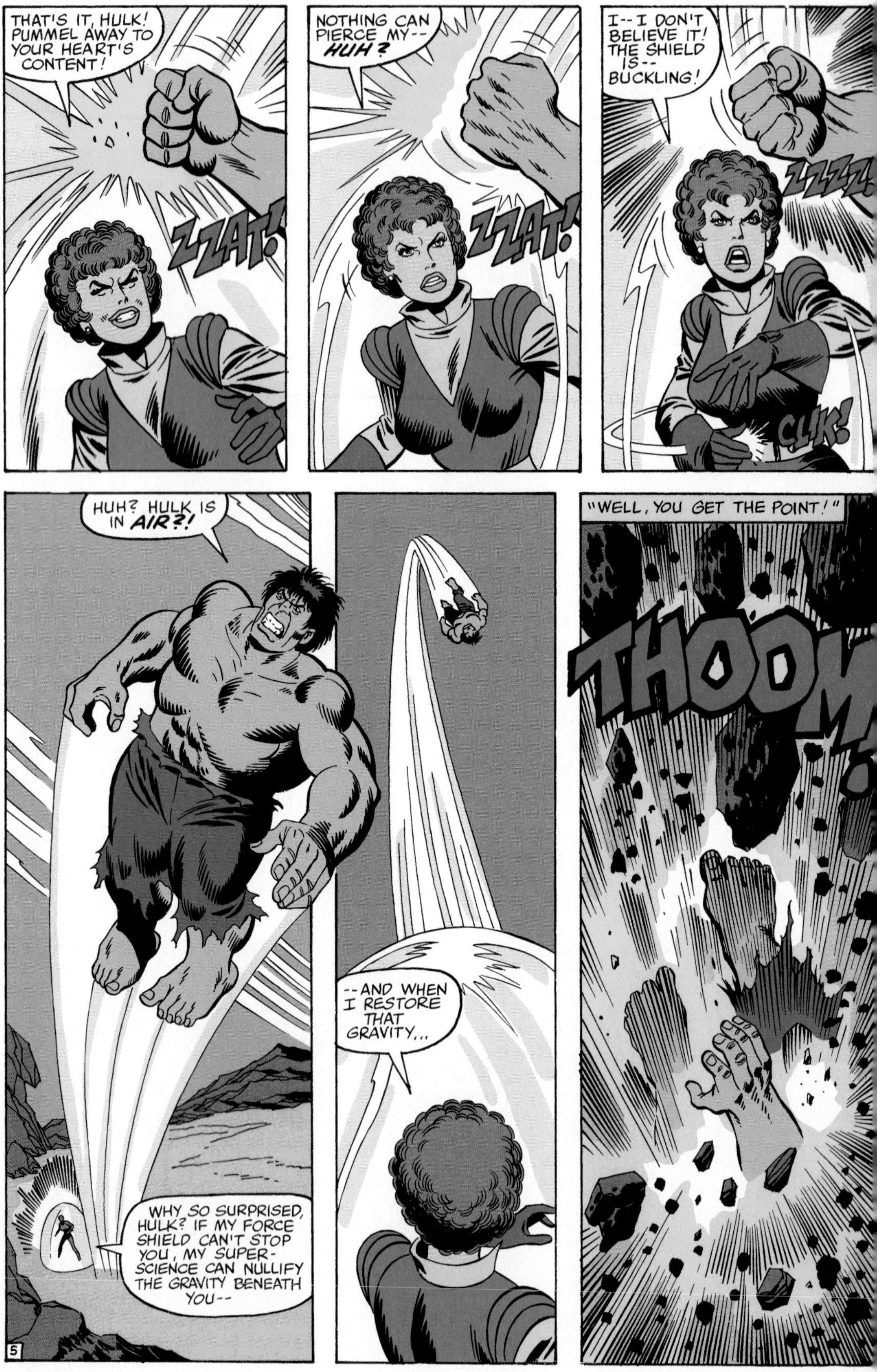
THAT'S IT, HULK! PUMMEL AWAY TO YOUR HEART'S CONTENT!
ZZAT!
NOTHING CAN PIERCE MY-- HUH?
ZZAT!
I--I DON'T BELIEVE IT! THE SHIELD IS--BUCKLING!
CLIK!
HUH? HULK IS IN AIR?!
WHY SO SURPRISED, HULK? IF MY FORCE SHIELD CAN'T STOP YOU, MY SUPER-SCIENCE CAN NULLIFY THE GRAVITY BENEATH YOU--
--AND WHEN I RESTORE THAT GRAVITY...
"WELL, YOU GET THE POINT!"
THOOM

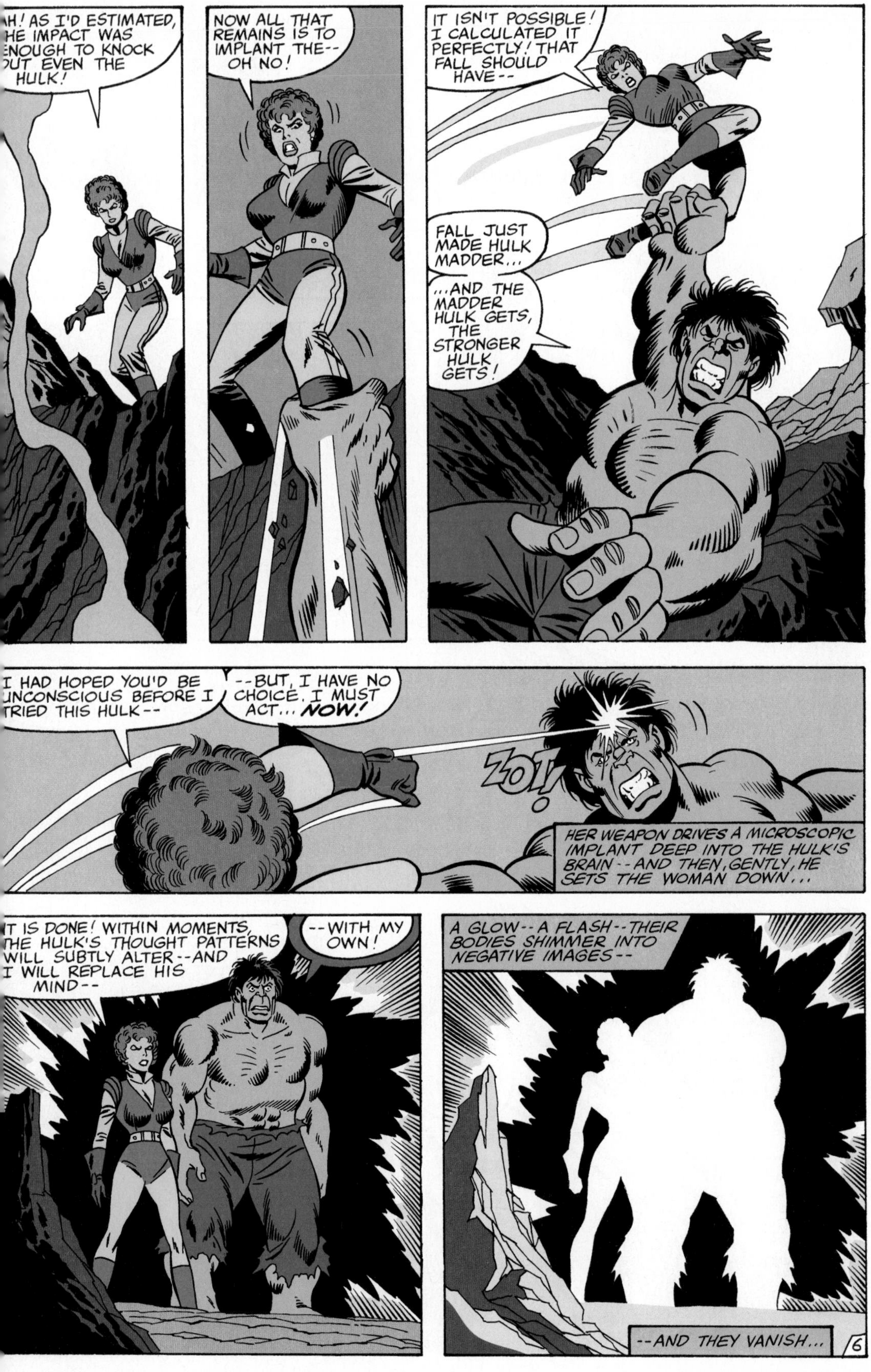
AH! AS I'D ESTIMATED, THE IMPACT WAS ENOUGH TO KNOCK OUT EVEN THE HULK!
NOW ALL THAT REMAINS IS TO IMPLANT THE-- OH NO!
IT ISN'T POSSIBLE! I CALCULATED IT PERFECTLY! THAT FALL SHOULD HAVE--
FALL JUST MADE HULK MADDER...
...AND THE MADDER HULK GETS, THE STRONGER HULK GETS!
I HAD HOPED YOU'D BE UNCONSCIOUS BEFORE I TRIED THIS HULK--
--BUT, I HAVE NO CHOICE. I MUST ACT... NOW!
ZOT!
HER WEAPON DRIVES A MICROSCOPIC IMPLANT DEEP INTO THE HULK'S BRAIN--AND THEN, GENTLY, HE SETS THE WOMAN DOWN...
IT IS DONE! WITHIN MOMENTS, THE HULK'S THOUGHT PATTERNS WILL SUBTLY ALTER--AND I WILL REPLACE HIS MIND--
--WITH MY OWN!
A GLOW--A FLASH--THEIR BODIES SHIMMER INTO NEGATIVE IMAGES--
--AND THEY VANISH...
6

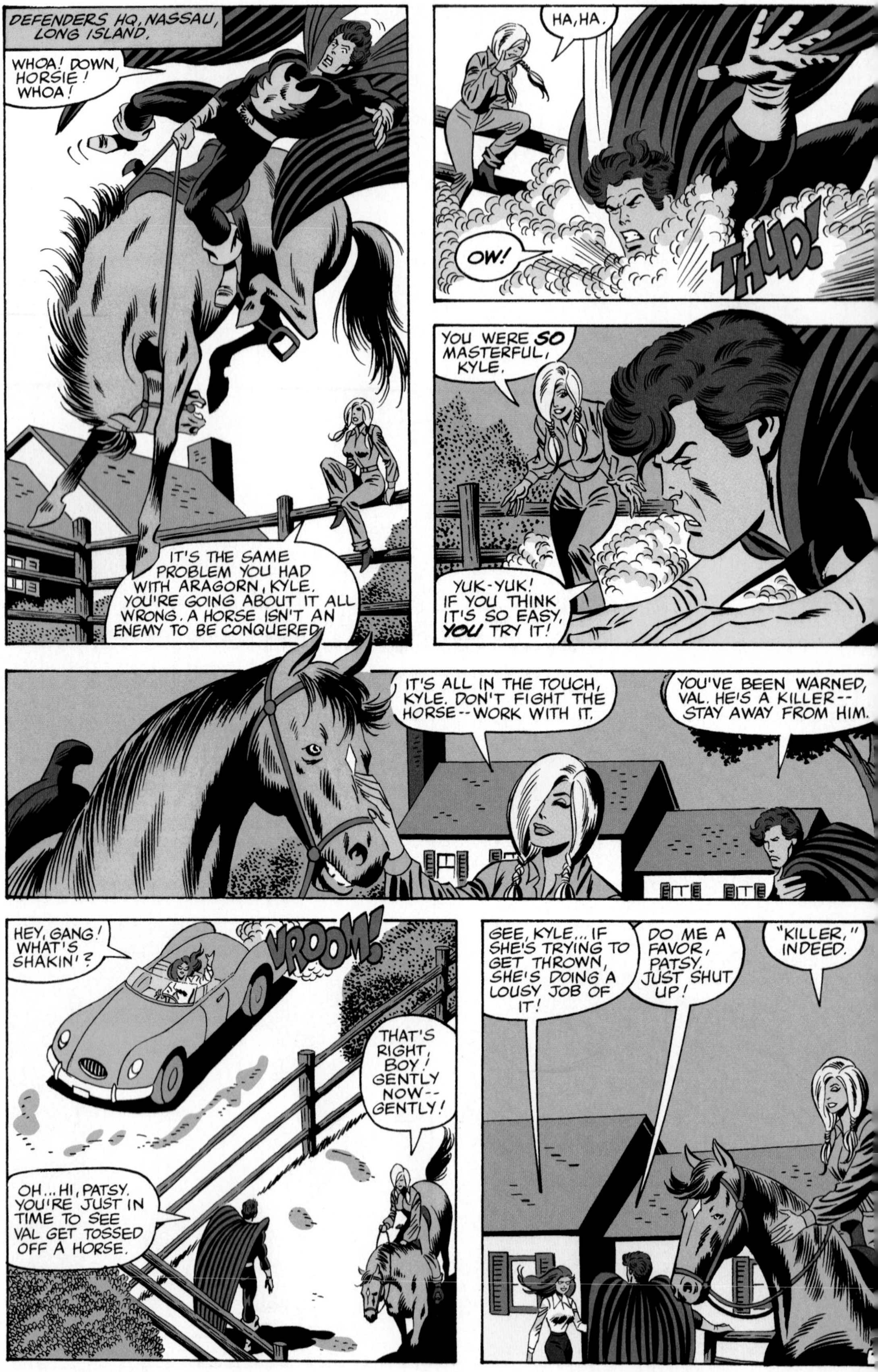
DEFENDERS HQ, NASSAU, LONG ISLAND.
WHOA! DOWN, HORSIE! WHOA!
IT'S THE SAME PROBLEM YOU HAD WITH ARAGORN, KYLE. YOU'RE GOING ABOUT IT ALL WRONG. A HORSE ISN'T AN ENEMY TO BE CONQUERED.
HA, HA.
OW!
THUD!
YOU WERE SO MASTERFUL, KYLE.
YUK-YUK! IF YOU THINK IT'S SO EASY, YOU TRY IT!
IT'S ALL IN THE TOUCH, KYLE. DON'T FIGHT THE HORSE--WORK WITH IT.
YOU'VE BEEN WARNED, VAL. HE'S A KILLER--STAY AWAY FROM HIM.
HEY, GANG! WHAT'S SHAKIN'?
VROOM!
THAT'S RIGHT, BOY! GENTLY NOW--GENTLY!
OH...HI, PATSY. YOU'RE JUST IN TIME TO SEE VAL GET TOSSED OFF A HORSE.
GEE, KYLE... IF SHE'S TRYING TO GET THROWN, SHE'S DOING A LOUSY JOB OF IT!
DO ME A FAVOR, PATSY. JUST SHUT UP!
"KILLER," INDEED.

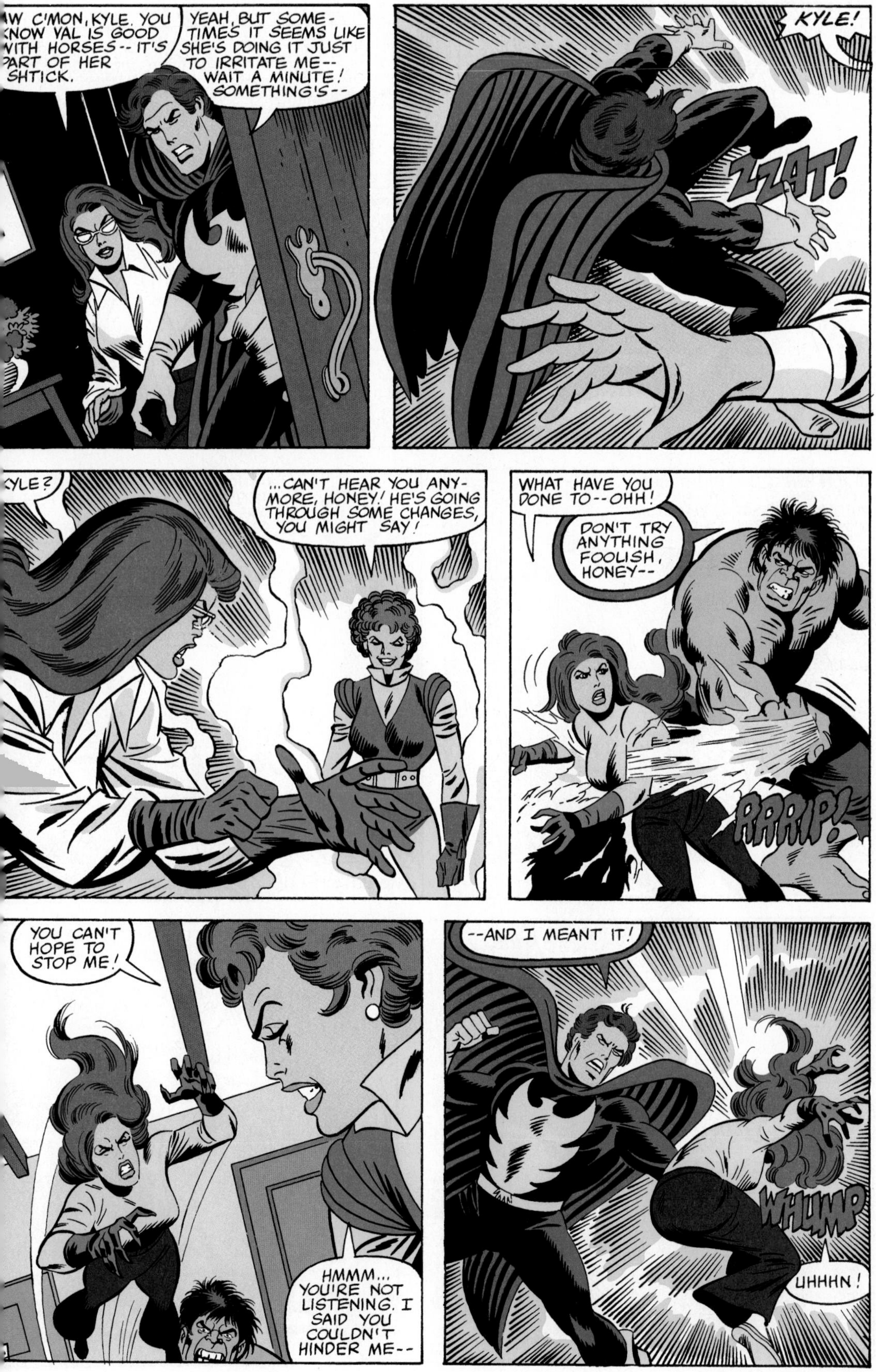
AW C'MON, KYLE. YOU KNOW VAL IS GOOD WITH HORSES -- IT'S PART OF HER SHTICK.
YEAH, BUT SOMETIMES IT SEEMS LIKE SHE'S DOING IT JUST TO IRRITATE ME -- WAIT A MINUTE! SOMETHING'S --
KYLE!
ZZAT!
KYLE?
...CAN'T HEAR YOU ANYMORE, HONEY! HE'S GOING THROUGH SOME CHANGES, YOU MIGHT SAY!
WHAT HAVE YOU DONE TO--OHH!
DON'T TRY ANYTHING FOOLISH, HONEY--
RRRIP!
YOU CAN'T HOPE TO STOP ME!
HMMM... YOU'RE NOT LISTENING. I SAID YOU COULDN'T HINDER ME--
--AND I MEANT IT!
WHUMP
UHHHN!

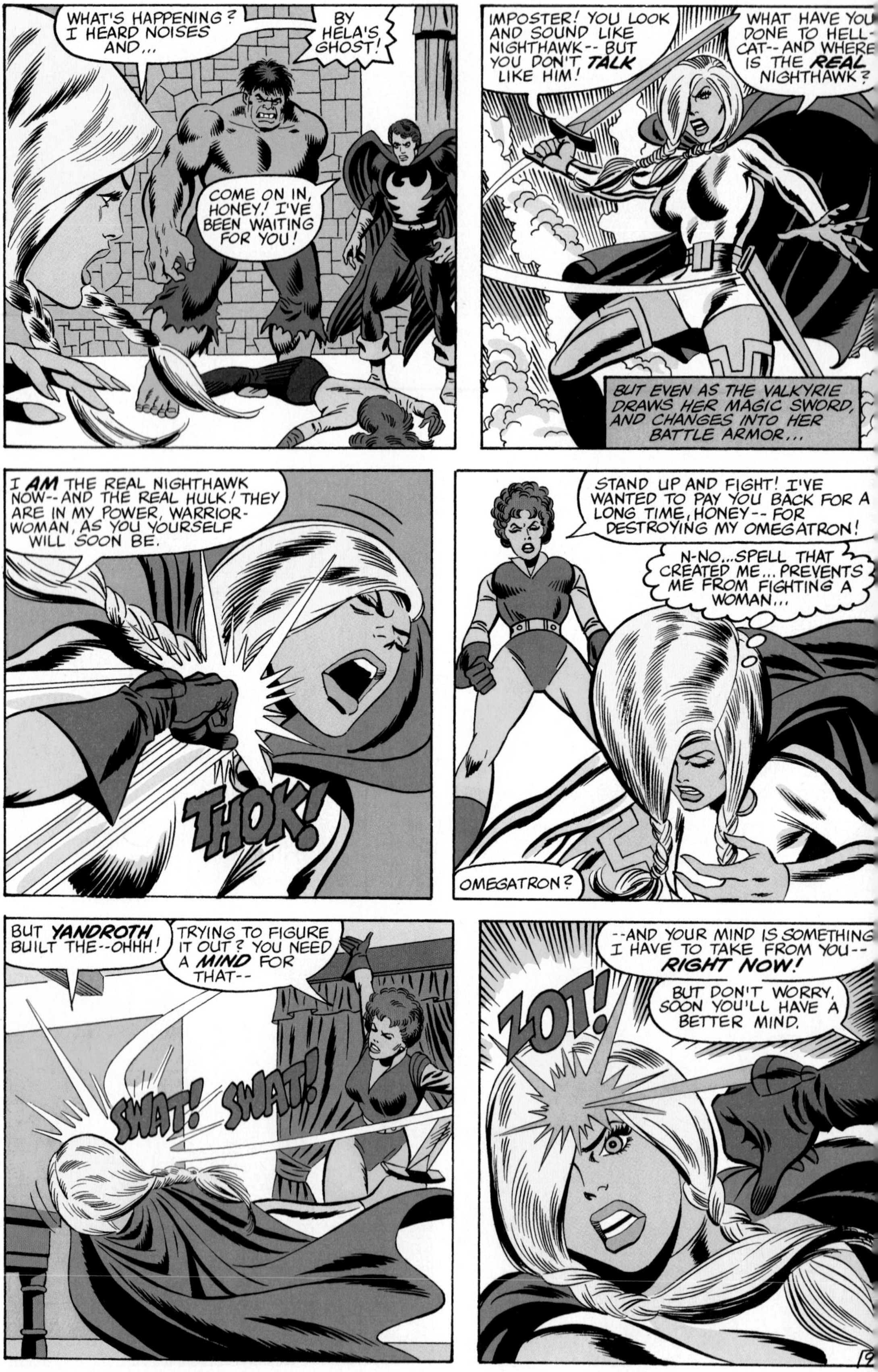
WHAT'S HAPPENING? I HEARD NOISES AND...
BY HELA'S GHOST!
COME ON IN, HONEY! I'VE BEEN WAITING FOR YOU!
IMPOSTER! YOU LOOK AND SOUND LIKE NIGHTHAWK-- BUT YOU DON'T TALK LIKE HIM!
WHAT HAVE YOU DONE TO HELL-CAT--AND WHERE IS THE REAL NIGHTHAWK?
BUT EVEN AS THE VALKYRIE DRAWS HER MAGIC SWORD, AND CHANGES INTO HER BATTLE ARMOR...
I AM THE REAL NIGHTHAWK NOW--AND THE REAL HULK! THEY ARE IN MY POWER, WARRIOR-WOMAN, AS YOU YOURSELF WILL SOON BE.
THOK!
STAND UP AND FIGHT! I'VE WANTED TO PAY YOU BACK FOR A LONG TIME, HONEY-- FOR DESTROYING MY OMEGATRON!
N-NO...SPELL THAT CREATED ME... PREVENTS ME FROM FIGHTING A WOMAN...
OMEGATRON?
BUT YANDROTH BUILT THE--OHHH!
TRYING TO FIGURE IT OUT? YOU NEED A MIND FOR THAT--
SWAT! SWAT!
--AND YOUR MIND IS SOMETHING I HAVE TO TAKE FROM YOU-- RIGHT NOW!
BUT DON'T WORRY, SOON YOU'LL HAVE A BETTER MIND.
ZOT!
9

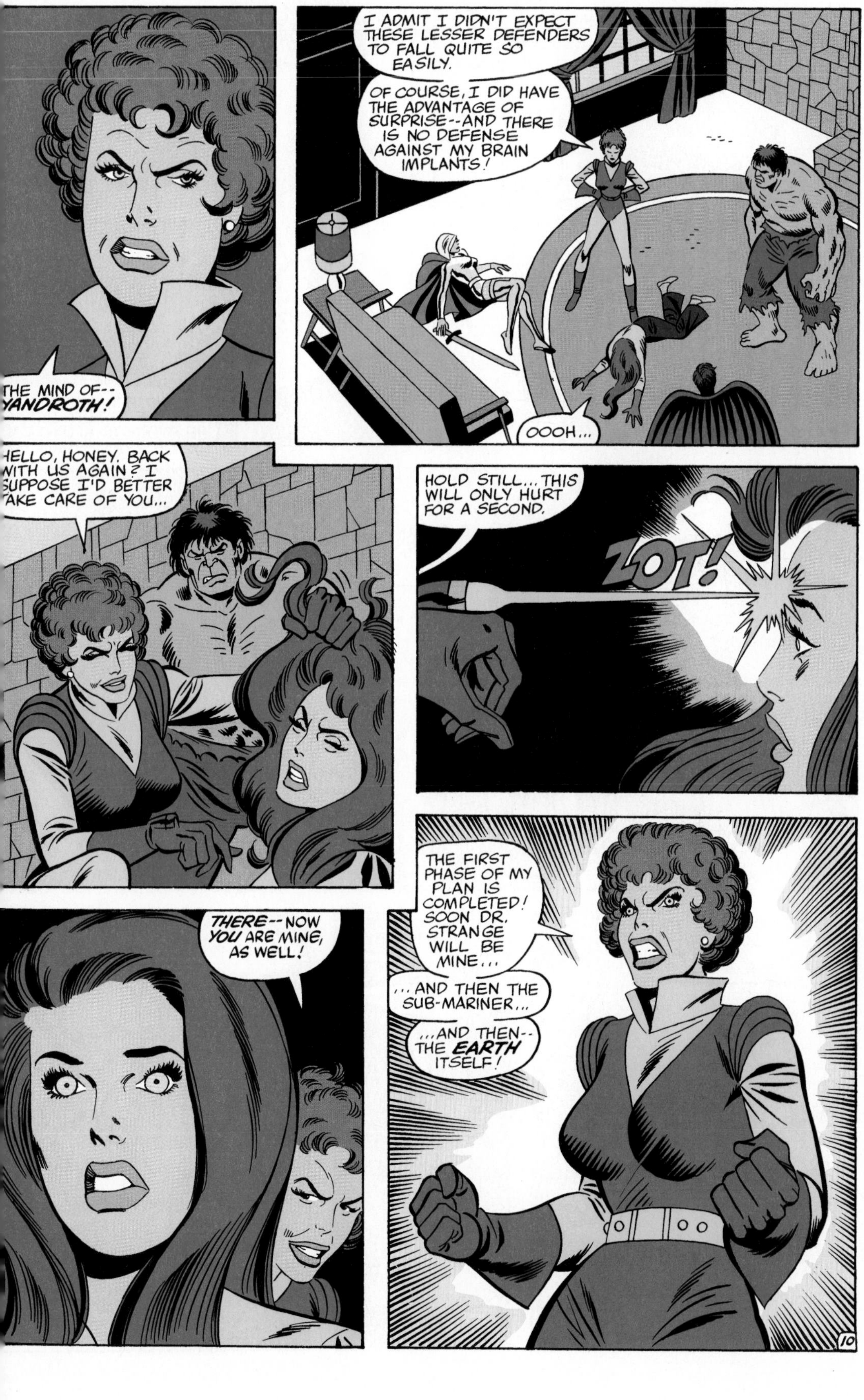
THE MIND OF-- YANDROTH!
I ADMIT I DIDN'T EXPECT THESE LESSER DEFENDERS TO FALL QUITE SO EASILY.
OF COURSE, I DID HAVE THE ADVANTAGE OF SURPRISE--AND THERE IS NO DEFENSE AGAINST MY BRAIN IMPLANTS!
OOOH...
HELLO, HONEY. BACK WITH US AGAIN? I SUPPOSE I'D BETTER TAKE CARE OF YOU...
HOLD STILL... THIS WILL ONLY HURT FOR A SECOND.
ZOT!
THERE--NOW YOU ARE MINE, AS WELL!
THE FIRST PHASE OF MY PLAN IS COMPLETED! SOON DR. STRANGE WILL BE MINE...
...AND THEN THE SUB-MARINER...
...AND THEN-- THE EARTH ITSELF!
10

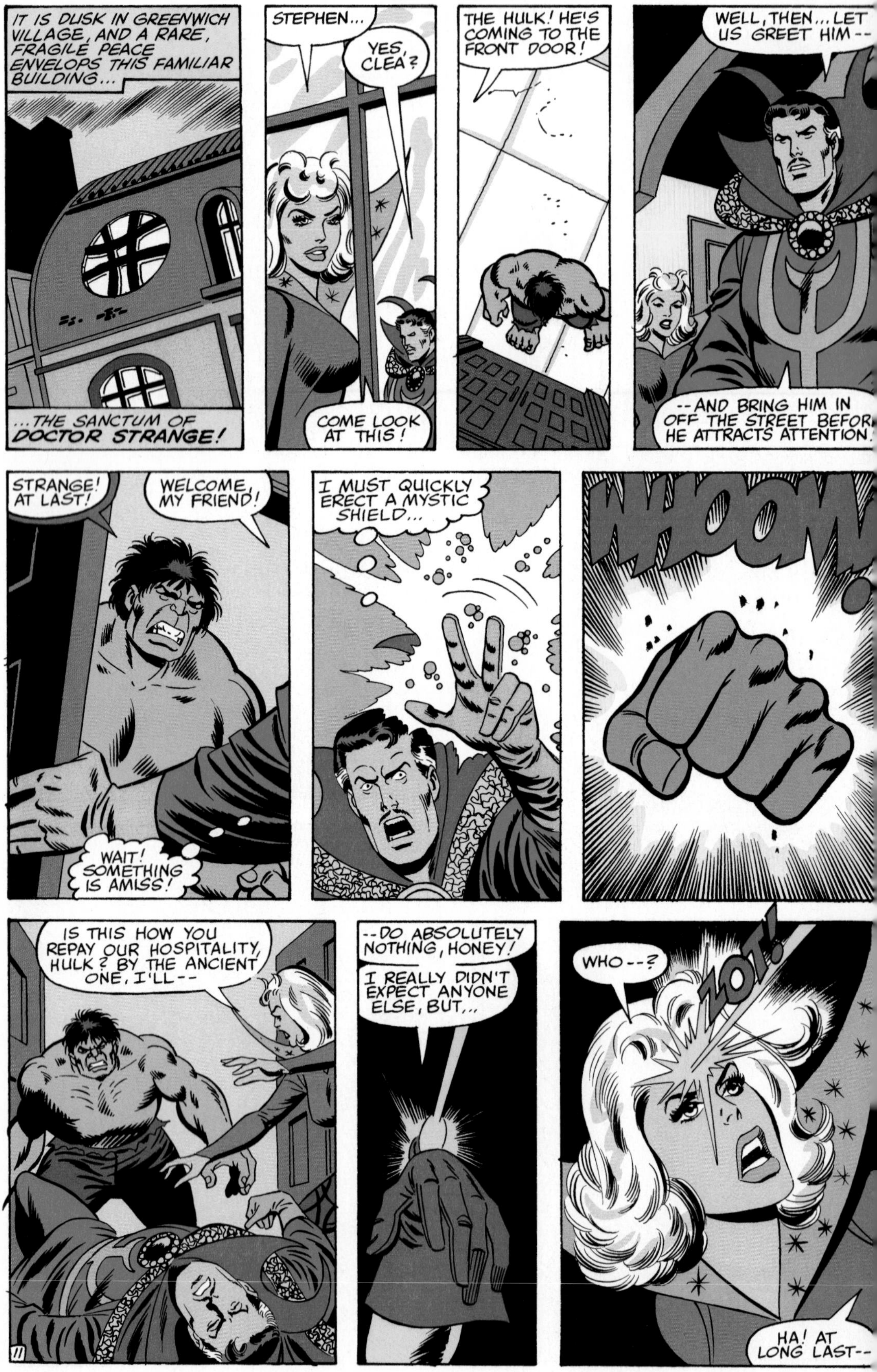
IT IS DUSK IN GREENWICH VILLAGE, AND A RARE, FRAGILE PEACE ENVELOPS THIS FAMILIAR BUILDING...
...THE SANCTUM OF DOCTOR STRANGE!
STEPHEN...
YES, CLEA?
COME LOOK AT THIS!
THE HULK! HE'S COMING TO THE FRONT DOOR!
WELL, THEN... LET US GREET HIM--
--AND BRING HIM IN OFF THE STREET BEFOR HE ATTRACTS ATTENTION.
STRANGE! AT LAST!
WELCOME, MY FRIEND!
WAIT! SOMETHING IS AMISS!
I MUST QUICKLY ERECT A MYSTIC SHIELD...
WHOOM
IS THIS HOW YOU REPAY OUR HOSPITALITY, HULK? BY THE ANCIENT ONE, I'LL--
--DO ABSOLUTELY NOTHING, HONEY!
I REALLY DIDN'T EXPECT ANYONE ELSE, BUT...
WHO--?
ZOT!
HA! AT LONG LAST--
11

--THE DEFENDERS ARE MINE!

PARDON THE DRUGS, STRANGE. I WANT TO KEEP YOU CONSCIOUS, BUT I REALLY DON'T WANT YOU TO FIGHT YOU.

BY THE WAY, MY NAME IS *YANDROTH!*

I HAVE RETURNED IN TIME, THEY DO NOT YET SUSPECT...

HAT MY CONSCIOUSNESS EVADED THE EFFECTS OF THE HULK'S BLOW BY SHIFTING TO MY ASTRAL FORM. BUT WHAT IS THIS WOMAN SAYING?

MUST EXERT ENOUGH CONTROL OVER MY PHYSICAL FORM TO TALK -- BUT STILL KEEP MY MIND FREE OF THE DRUGS.

IM.... POSSIBLE. YANDROTH IS...

DEAD? YES--

--AND *NO!*

"YOU WILL RECALL, DR. STRANGE, THAT YANDROTH CALLED YOU WITH HIS DYING BREATH -- AND THAT ACT BROUGHT TOGETHER THE DEFENDERS FOR THE FIRST TIME.* YET YANDROTH WAS AN ALIEN -- AND HIS DEATH WAS NOT A HUMAN DEATH...

MARVEL FEATURE #1 -- AL.

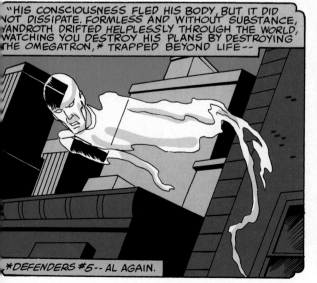

"HIS CONSCIOUSNESS FLED HIS BODY, BUT IT DID NOT DISSIPATE. FORMLESS AND WITHOUT SUBSTANCE, YANDROTH DRIFTED HELPLESSLY THROUGH THE WORLD, WATCHING YOU DESTROY HIS PLANS BY DESTROYING THE OMEGATRON,* TRAPPED BEYOND LIFE--

DEFENDERS #5-- AL AGAIN.

"--UNTIL HE FOUND ME!

"I HAD BEEN WORKING IN A LAB, TRAPPED IN A MENIAL POSITION BY IDIOTS WHO COULDN'T COMPREHEND MY GENIUS. IT WAS A DEAD END -- AND THEN YANDROTH CAME TO ME.

12

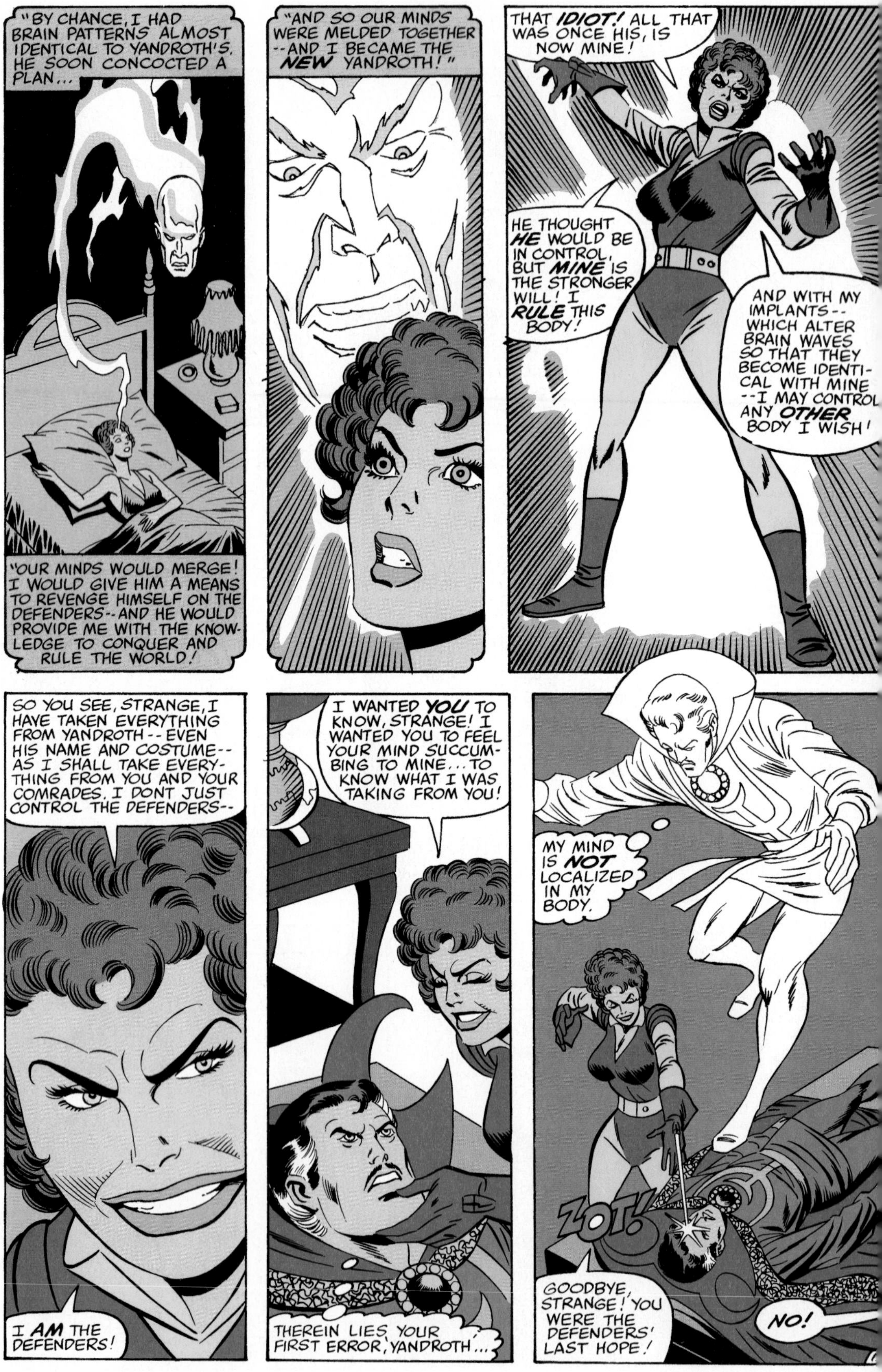
"BY CHANCE, I HAD BRAIN PATTERNS ALMOST IDENTICAL TO YANDROTH'S. HE SOON CONCOCTED A PLAN...
"OUR MINDS WOULD MERGE! I WOULD GIVE HIM A MEANS TO REVENGE HIMSELF ON THE DEFENDERS--AND HE WOULD PROVIDE ME WITH THE KNOWLEDGE TO CONQUER AND RULE THE WORLD!
"AND SO OUR MINDS WERE MELDED TOGETHER --AND I BECAME THE NEW YANDROTH!"
THAT IDIOT! ALL THAT WAS ONCE HIS, IS NOW MINE!
HE THOUGHT HE WOULD BE IN CONTROL, BUT MINE IS THE STRONGER WILL! I RULE THIS BODY!
AND WITH MY IMPLANTS--WHICH ALTER BRAIN WAVES SO THAT THEY BECOME IDENTICAL WITH MINE --I MAY CONTROL ANY OTHER BODY I WISH!
SO YOU SEE, STRANGE, I HAVE TAKEN EVERYTHING FROM YANDROTH--EVEN HIS NAME AND COSTUME--AS I SHALL TAKE EVERYTHING FROM YOU AND YOUR COMRADES. I DONT JUST CONTROL THE DEFENDERS--
I AM THE DEFENDERS!
I WANTED YOU TO KNOW, STRANGE! I WANTED YOU TO FEEL YOUR MIND SUCCUMBING TO MINE...TO KNOW WHAT I WAS TAKING FROM YOU!
THEREIN LIES YOUR FIRST ERROR, YANDROTH...
MY MIND IS NOT LOCALIZED IN MY BODY.
ZOT!
GOODBYE, STRANGE! YOU WERE THE DEFENDERS' LAST HOPE!
NO!

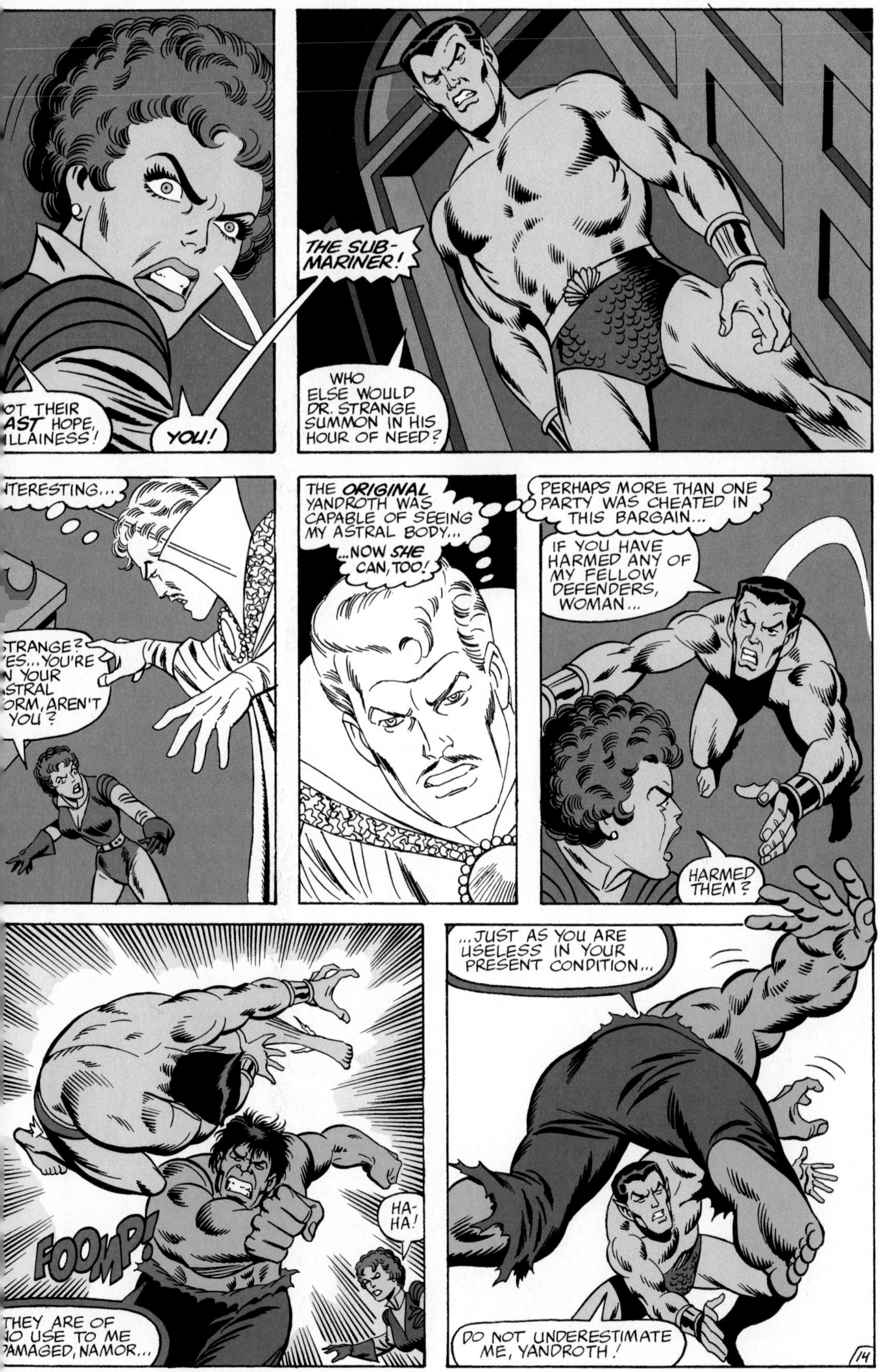

OT THEIR
LAST HOPE,
ILLAINESS!
YOU!
THE SUB-
MARINER!
WHO
ELSE WOULD
DR. STRANGE
SUMMON IN HIS
HOUR OF NEED?
NTERESTING...
STRANGE?
YES...YOU'RE
N YOUR
ASTRAL
ORM, AREN'T
YOU?
THE ORIGINAL
YANDROTH WAS
CAPABLE OF SEEING
MY ASTRAL BODY...
...NOW SHE
CAN, TOO!
PERHAPS MORE THAN ONE
PARTY WAS CHEATED IN
THIS BARGAIN...
IF YOU HAVE
HARMED ANY OF
MY FELLOW
DEFENDERS,
WOMAN...
HARMED
THEM?
FOOMP!
HA-
HA!
THEY ARE OF
NO USE TO ME
DAMAGED, NAMOR...
...JUST AS YOU ARE
USELESS IN YOUR
PRESENT CONDITION...
DO NOT UNDERESTIMATE
ME, YANDROTH!
14

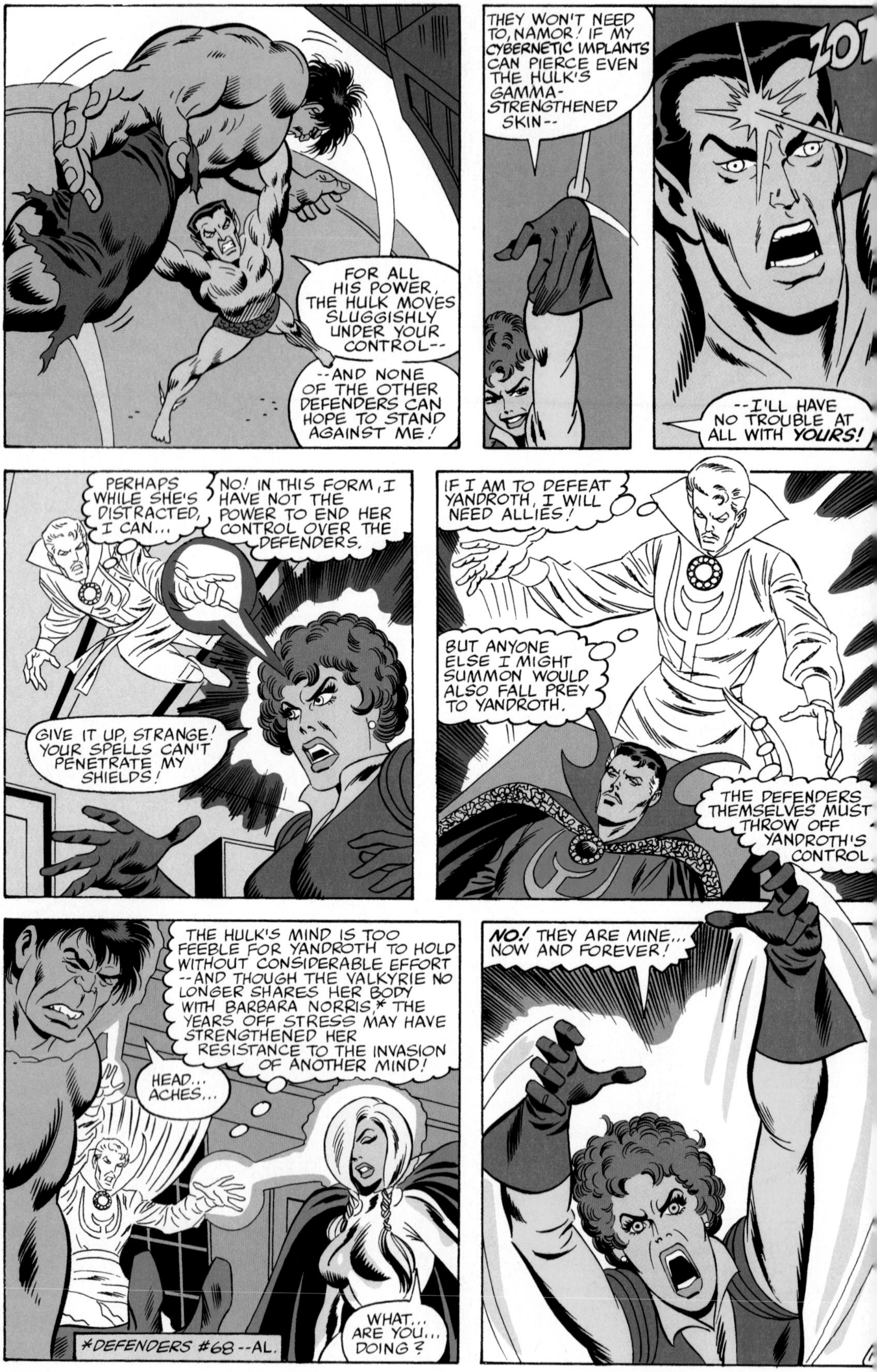
FOR ALL HIS POWER, THE HULK MOVES SLUGGISHLY UNDER YOUR CONTROL--
--AND NONE OF THE OTHER DEFENDERS CAN HOPE TO STAND AGAINST ME!
THEY WON'T NEED TO, NAMOR! IF MY CYBERNETIC IMPLANTS CAN PIERCE EVEN THE HULK'S GAMMA-STRENGTHENED SKIN--
ZOT
--I'LL HAVE NO TROUBLE AT ALL WITH YOURS!
PERHAPS WHILE SHE'S DISTRACTED, I CAN...
NO! IN THIS FORM, I HAVE NOT THE POWER TO END HER CONTROL OVER THE DEFENDERS.
GIVE IT UP, STRANGE! YOUR SPELLS CAN'T PENETRATE MY SHIELDS!
IF I AM TO DEFEAT YANDROTH, I WILL NEED ALLIES!
BUT ANYONE ELSE I MIGHT SUMMON WOULD ALSO FALL PREY TO YANDROTH.
THE DEFENDERS THEMSELVES MUST THROW OFF YANDROTH'S CONTROL.
THE HULK'S MIND IS TOO FEEBLE FOR YANDROTH TO HOLD WITHOUT CONSIDERABLE EFFORT --AND THOUGH THE VALKYRIE NO LONGER SHARES HER BODY WITH BARBARA NORRIS,* THE YEARS OFF STRESS MAY HAVE STRENGTHENED HER RESISTANCE TO THE INVASION OF ANOTHER MIND!
HEAD... ACHES...
WHAT... ARE YOU... DOING?
*DEFENDERS #68--AL.
NO! THEY ARE MINE... NOW AND FOREVER!

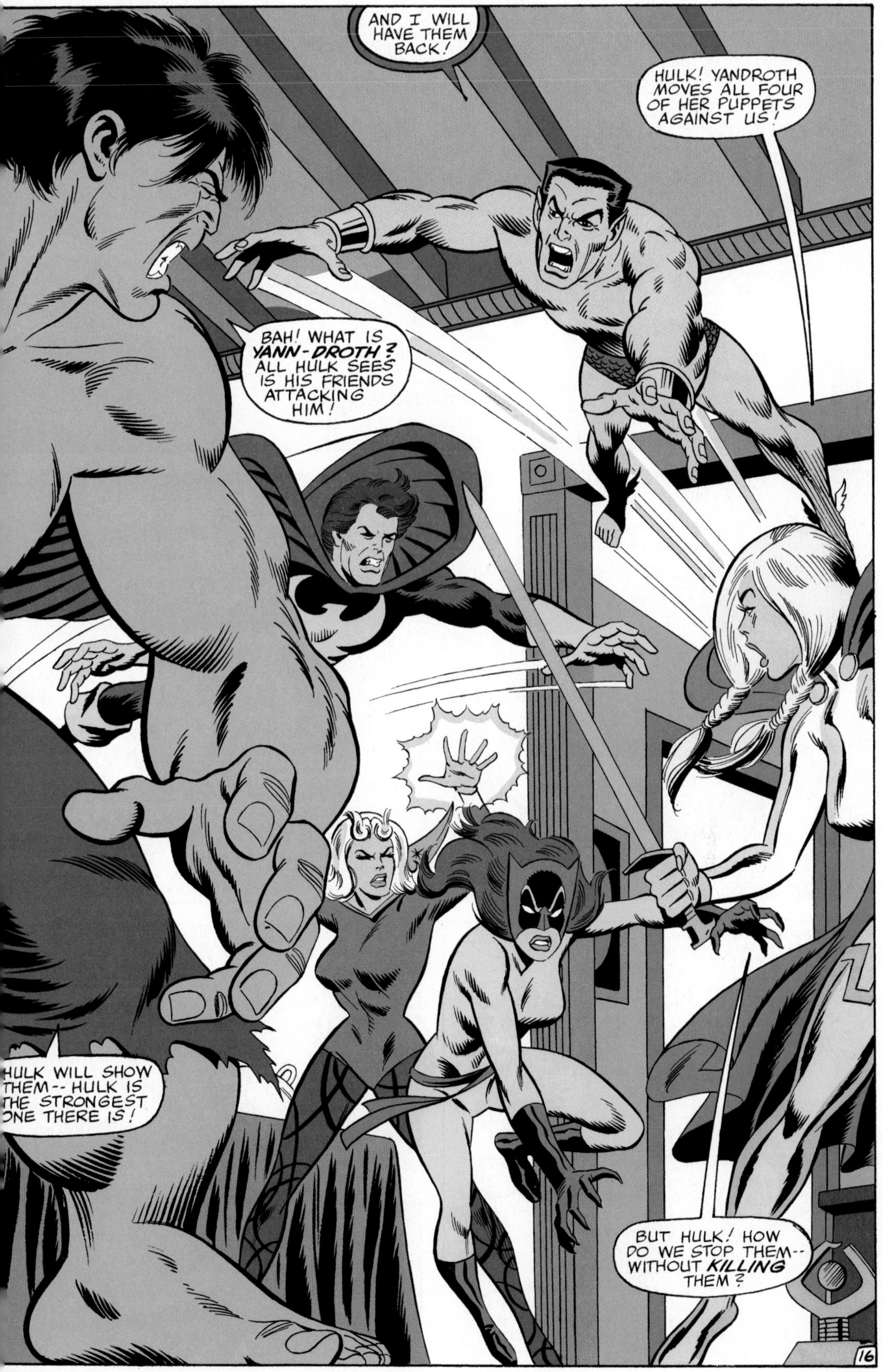
AND I WILL HAVE THEM BACK!
HULK! YANDROTH MOVES ALL FOUR OF HER PUPPETS AGAINST US!
BAH! WHAT IS YANN-DROTH? ALL HULK SEES IS HIS FRIENDS ATTACKING HIM!
HULK WILL SHOW THEM-- HULK IS THE STRONGEST ONE THERE IS!
BUT HULK! HOW DO WE STOP THEM-- WITHOUT KILLING THEM?
16

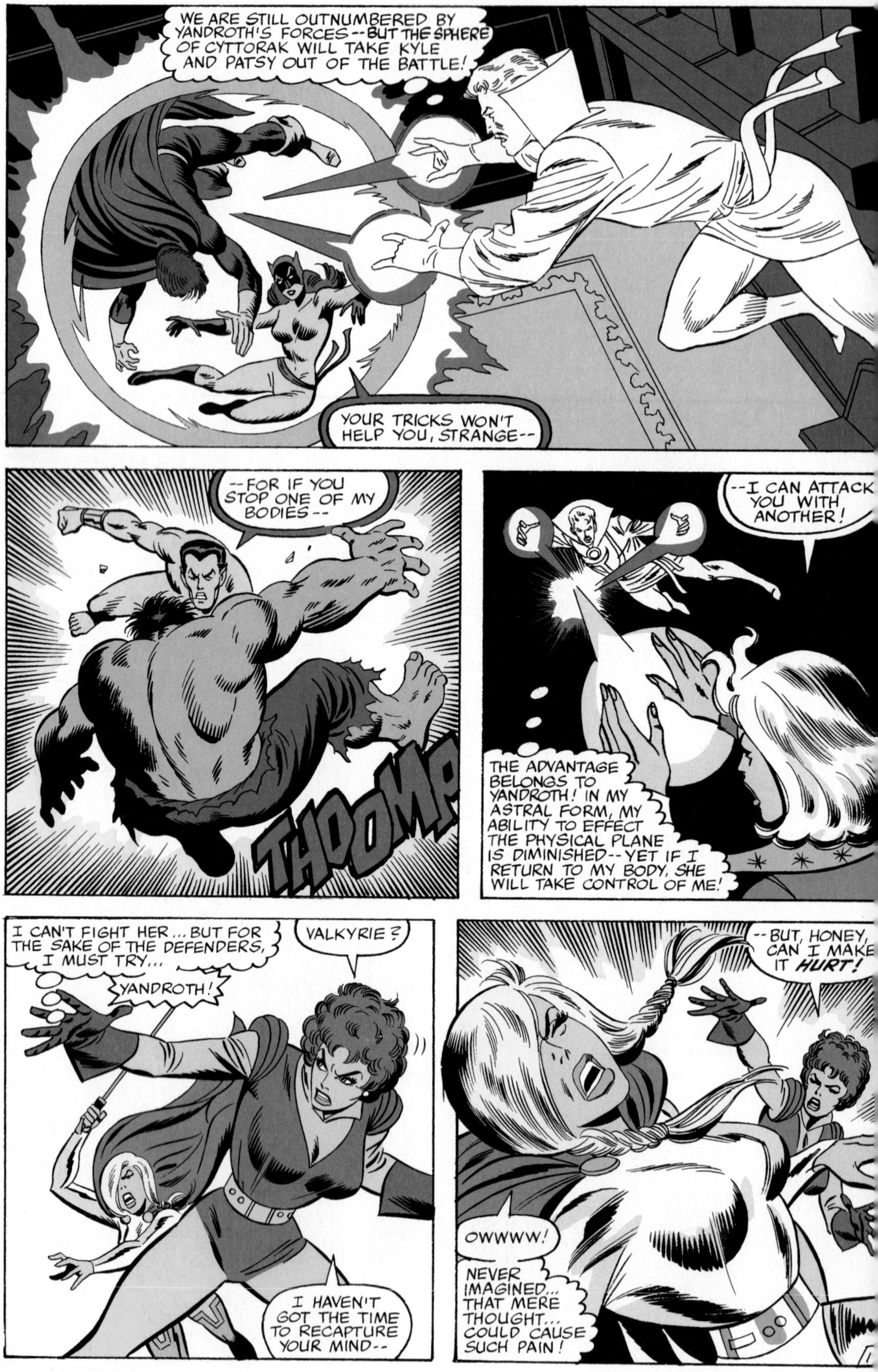
WE ARE STILL OUTNUMBERED BY YANDROTH'S FORCES--BUT THE SPHERE OF CYTTORAK WILL TAKE KYLE AND PATSY OUT OF THE BATTLE!
YOUR TRICKS WON'T HELP YOU, STRANGE--
--FOR IF YOU STOP ONE OF MY BODIES--
THOOMP
--I CAN ATTACK YOU WITH ANOTHER!
THE ADVANTAGE BELONGS TO YANDROTH! IN MY ASTRAL FORM, MY ABILITY TO EFFECT THE PHYSICAL PLANE IS DIMINISHED--YET IF I RETURN TO MY BODY, SHE WILL TAKE CONTROL OF ME!
I CAN'T FIGHT HER... BUT FOR THE SAKE OF THE DEFENDERS, I MUST TRY...
YANDROTH!
VALKYRIE?
I HAVEN'T GOT THE TIME TO RECAPTURE YOUR MIND--
--BUT, HONEY, CAN I MAKE IT HURT!
OWWWW!
NEVER IMAGINED... THAT MERE THOUGHT... COULD CAUSE SUCH PAIN!

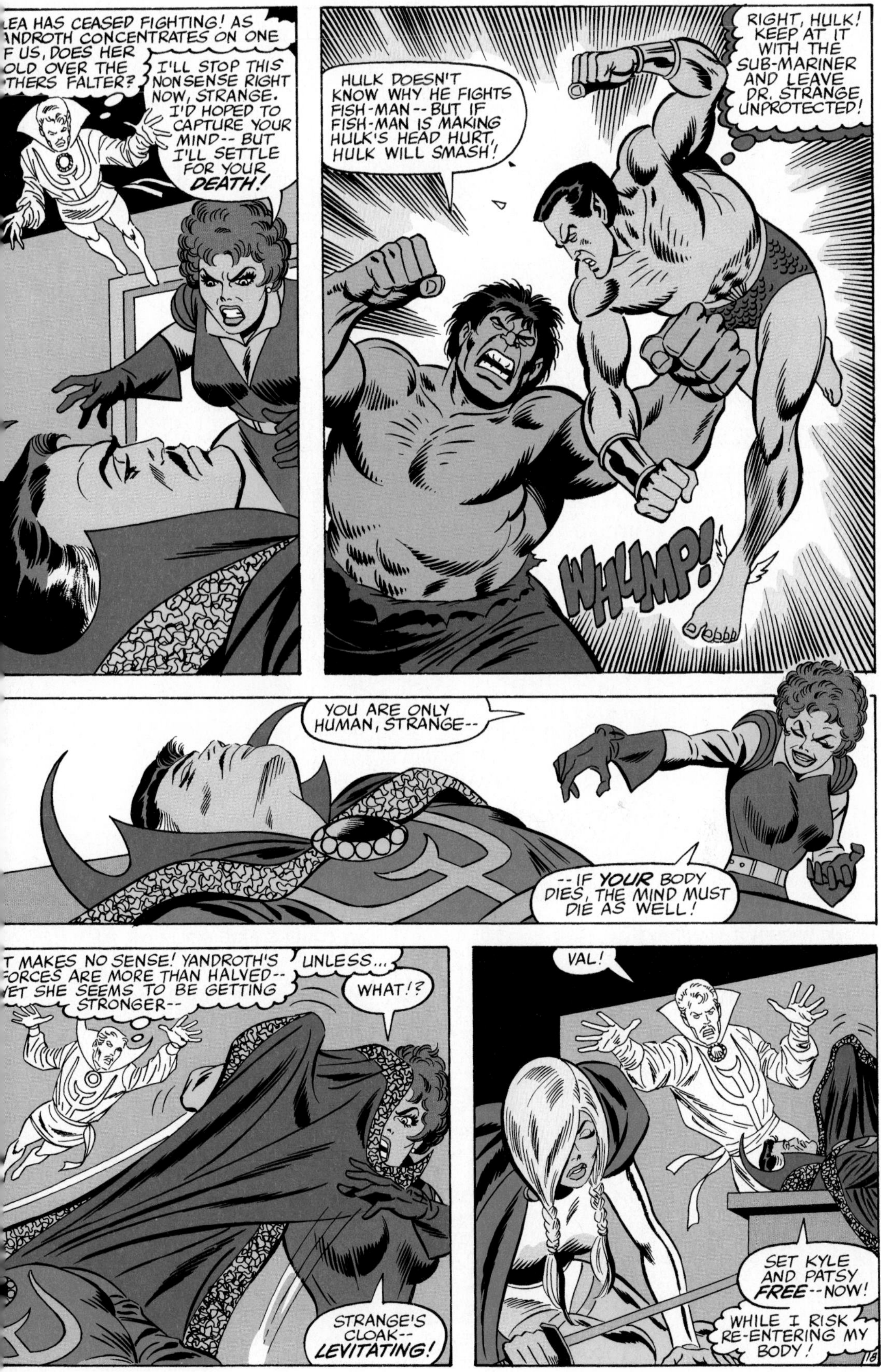

LEA HAS CEASED FIGHTING! AS ANDROTH CONCENTRATES ON ONE F US, DOES HER OLD OVER THE THERS FALTER?
I'LL STOP THIS NONSENSE RIGHT NOW, STRANGE. I'D HOPED TO CAPTURE YOUR MIND-- BUT I'LL SETTLE FOR YOUR DEATH!
HULK DOESN'T KNOW WHY HE FIGHTS FISH-MAN--BUT IF FISH-MAN IS MAKING HULK'S HEAD HURT, HULK WILL SMASH!
RIGHT, HULK! KEEP AT IT WITH THE SUB-MARINER AND LEAVE DR. STRANGE UNPROTECTED!
WHUMP!
YOU ARE ONLY HUMAN, STRANGE--
--IF YOUR BODY DIES, THE MIND MUST DIE AS WELL!
T MAKES NO SENSE! YANDROTH'S FORCES ARE MORE THAN HALVED-- YET SHE SEEMS TO BE GETTING STRONGER--
UNLESS...
WHAT!?
STRANGE'S CLOAK-- LEVITATING!
VAL!
SET KYLE AND PATSY FREE--NOW!
WHILE I RISK RE-ENTERING MY BODY!
18

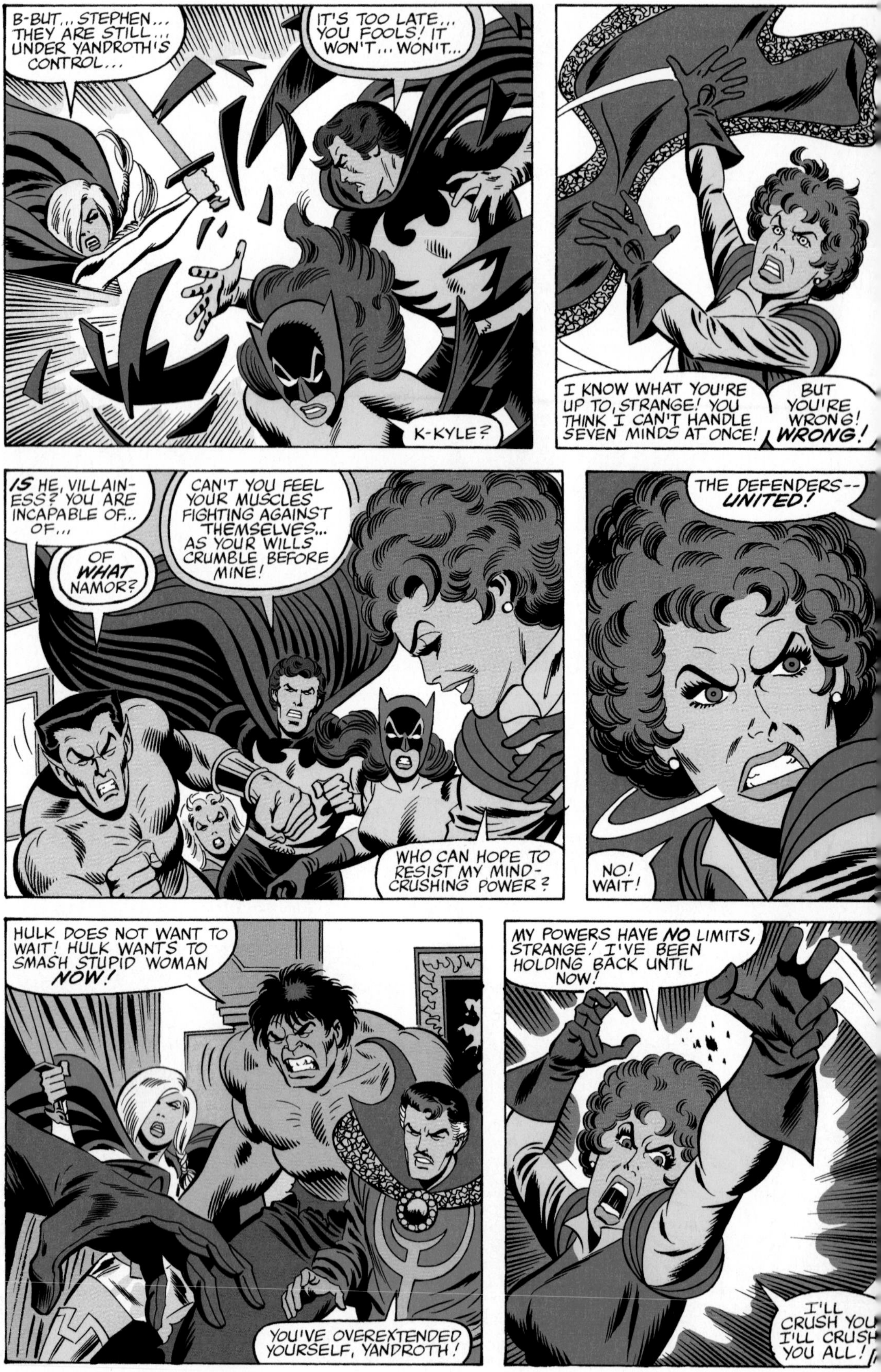
B-BUT... STEPHEN... THEY ARE STILL... UNDER YANDROTH'S CONTROL...
IT'S TOO LATE... YOU FOOLS! IT WON'T... WON'T...
K-KYLE?
I KNOW WHAT YOU'RE UP TO, STRANGE! YOU THINK I CAN'T HANDLE SEVEN MINDS AT ONCE!
BUT YOU'RE WRONG! WRONG!
IS HE, VILLAIN-ESS? YOU ARE INCAPABLE OF... OF...
OF WHAT NAMOR?
CAN'T YOU FEEL YOUR MUSCLES FIGHTING AGAINST THEMSELVES... AS YOUR WILLS CRUMBLE BEFORE MINE!
WHO CAN HOPE TO RESIST MY MIND-CRUSHING POWER?
THE DEFENDERS-- UNITED!
NO! WAIT!
HULK DOES NOT WANT TO WAIT! HULK WANTS TO SMASH STUPID WOMAN NOW!
YOU'VE OVEREXTENDED YOURSELF, YANDROTH!
MY POWERS HAVE NO LIMITS, STRANGE! I'VE BEEN HOLDING BACK UNTIL NOW!
I'LL CRUSH YOU I'LL CRUSH YOU ALL!

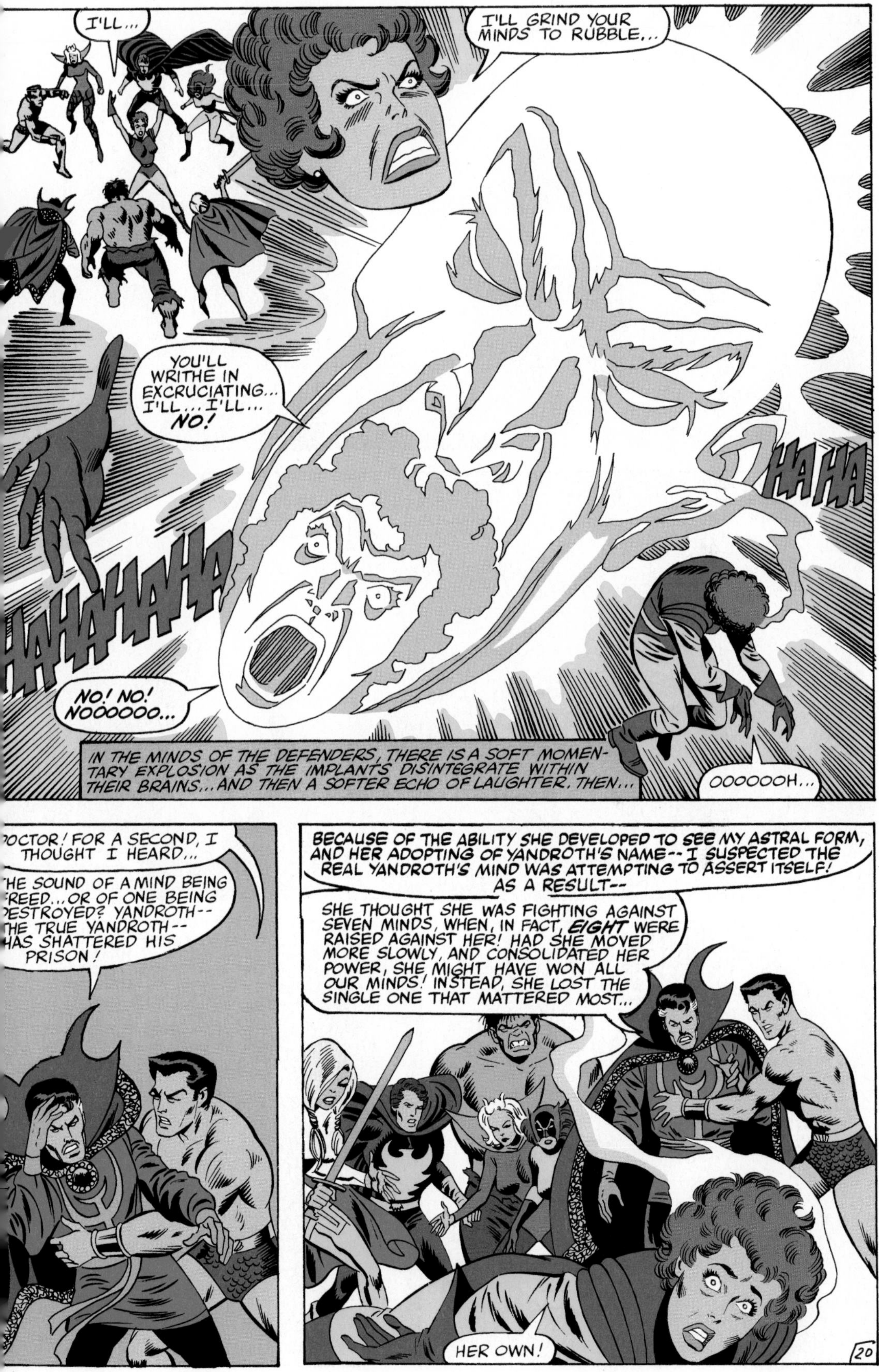
I'LL...
I'LL GRIND YOUR MINDS TO RUBBLE...
YOU'LL WRITHE IN EXCRUCIATING... I'LL... I'LL... NO!
HAHA
HAHAHAHA
NO! NO! NOOOOOO...
IN THE MINDS OF THE DEFENDERS, THERE IS A SOFT MOMENTARY EXPLOSION AS THE IMPLANTS DISINTEGRATE WITHIN THEIR BRAINS... AND THEN A SOFTER ECHO OF LAUGHTER. THEN...
OOOOOOH...
DOCTOR! FOR A SECOND, I THOUGHT I HEARD...
THE SOUND OF A MIND BEING FREED... OR OF ONE BEING DESTROYED? YANDROTH-- THE TRUE YANDROTH-- HAS SHATTERED HIS PRISON!
BECAUSE OF THE ABILITY SHE DEVELOPED TO SEE MY ASTRAL FORM, AND HER ADOPTING OF YANDROTH'S NAME-- I SUSPECTED THE REAL YANDROTH'S MIND WAS ATTEMPTING TO ASSERT ITSELF! AS A RESULT--
SHE THOUGHT SHE WAS FIGHTING AGAINST SEVEN MINDS, WHEN, IN FACT, EIGHT WERE RAISED AGAINST HER! HAD SHE MOVED MORE SLOWLY, AND CONSOLIDATED HER POWER, SHE MIGHT HAVE WON ALL OUR MINDS! INSTEAD, SHE LOST THE SINGLE ONE THAT MATTERED MOST...
HER OWN!
20

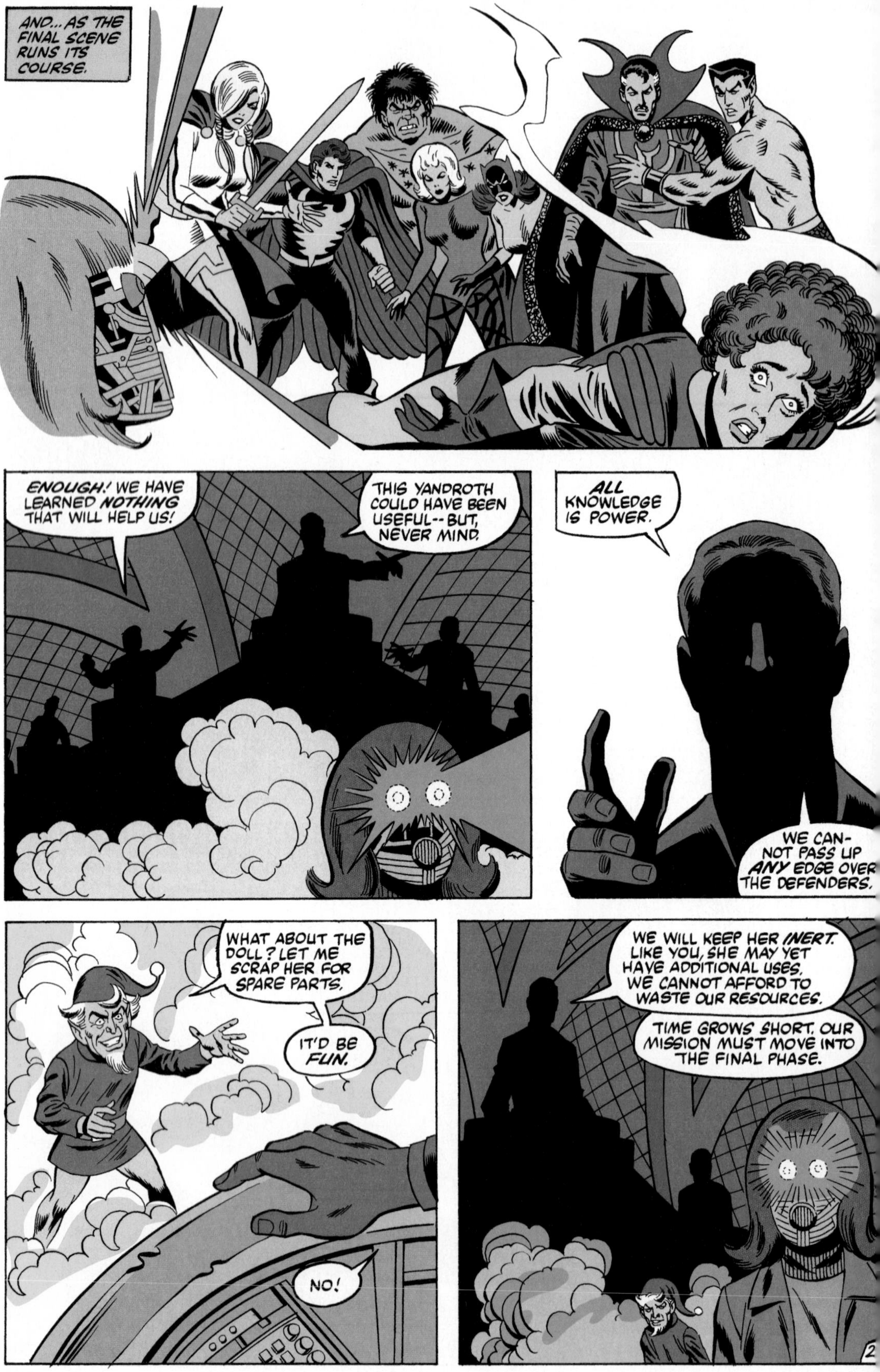
AND... AS THE FINAL SCENE RUNS ITS COURSE.
ENOUGH! WE HAVE LEARNED NOTHING THAT WILL HELP US!
THIS YANDROTH COULD HAVE BEEN USEFUL-- BUT, NEVER MIND.
ALL KNOWLEDGE IS POWER.
WE CAN-NOT PASS UP ANY EDGE OVER THE DEFENDERS.
WHAT ABOUT THE DOLL? LET ME SCRAP HER FOR SPARE PARTS.
IT'D BE FUN.
NO!
WE WILL KEEP HER INERT. LIKE YOU, SHE MAY YET HAVE ADDITIONAL USES. WE CANNOT AFFORD TO WASTE OUR RESOURCES.
TIME GROWS SHORT. OUR MISSION MUST MOVE INTO THE FINAL PHASE.

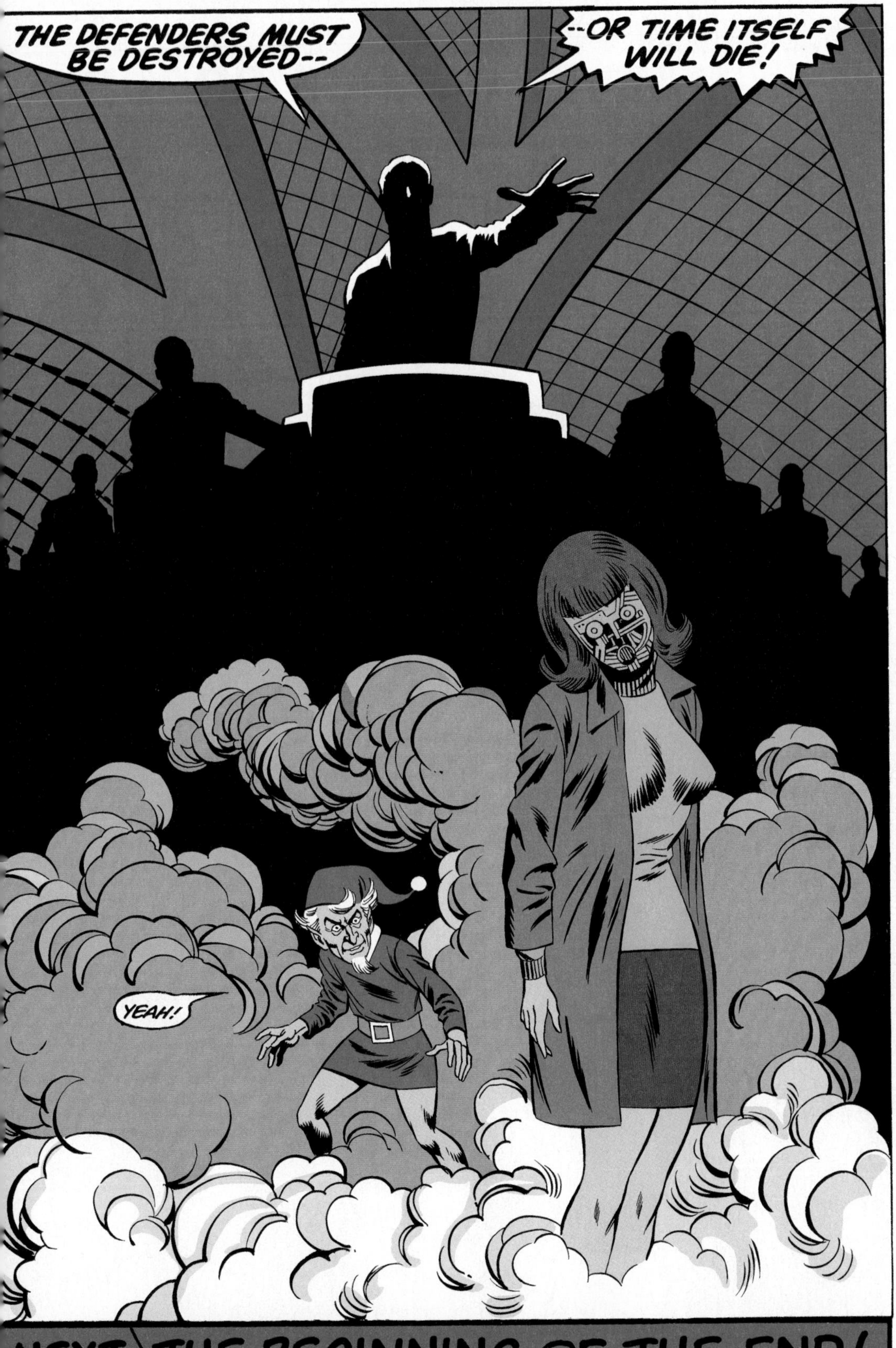
THE DEFENDERS MUST BE DESTROYED--
--OR TIME ITSELF WILL DIE!
YEAH!
NEXT: THE BEGINNING OF THE END!

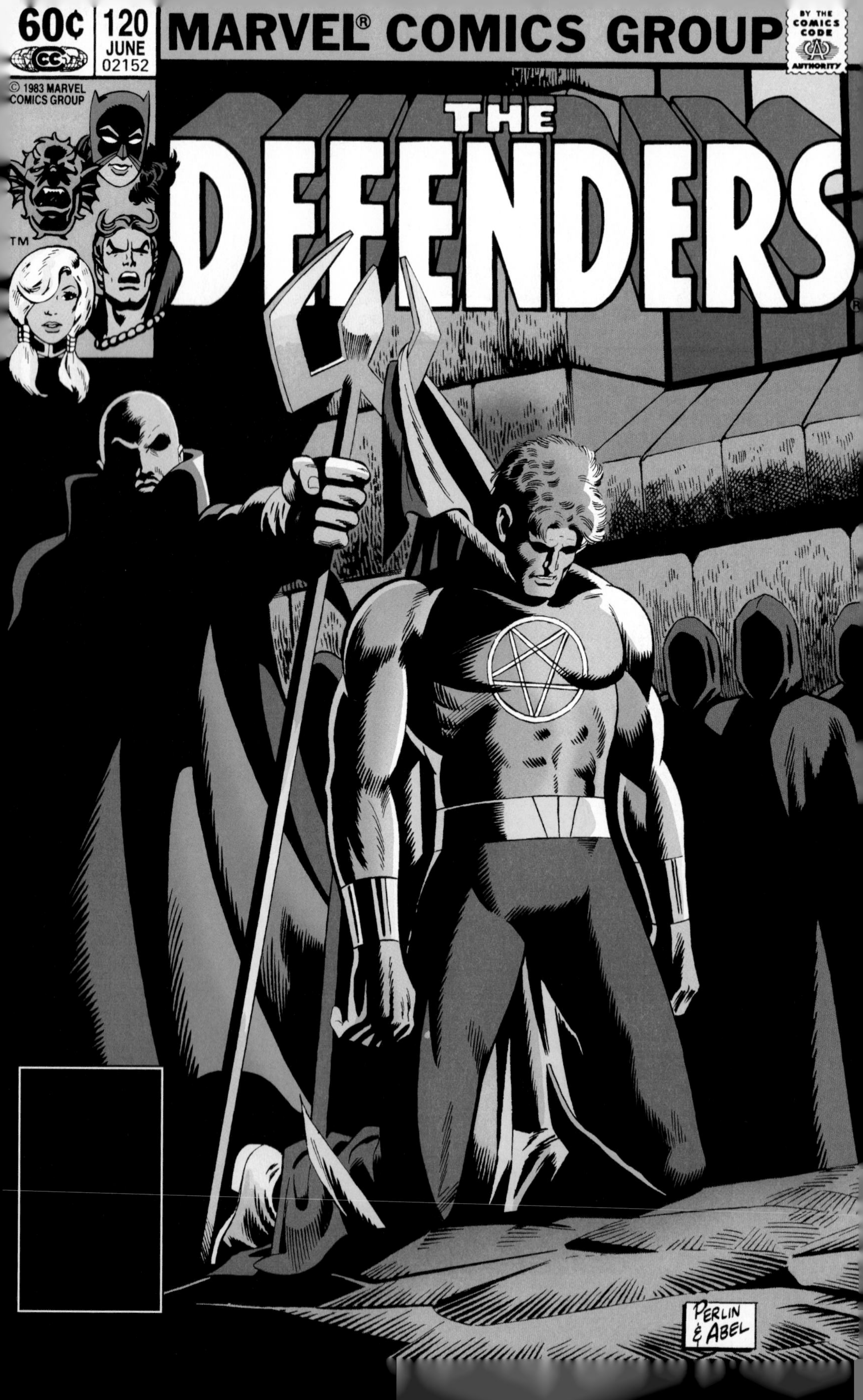

60¢
120
JUNE
02152
MARVEL® COMICS GROUP
BY THE COMICS CODE AUTHORITY
© 1983 MARVEL COMICS GROUP
TM
THE DEFENDERS®
PERLIN & ABEL

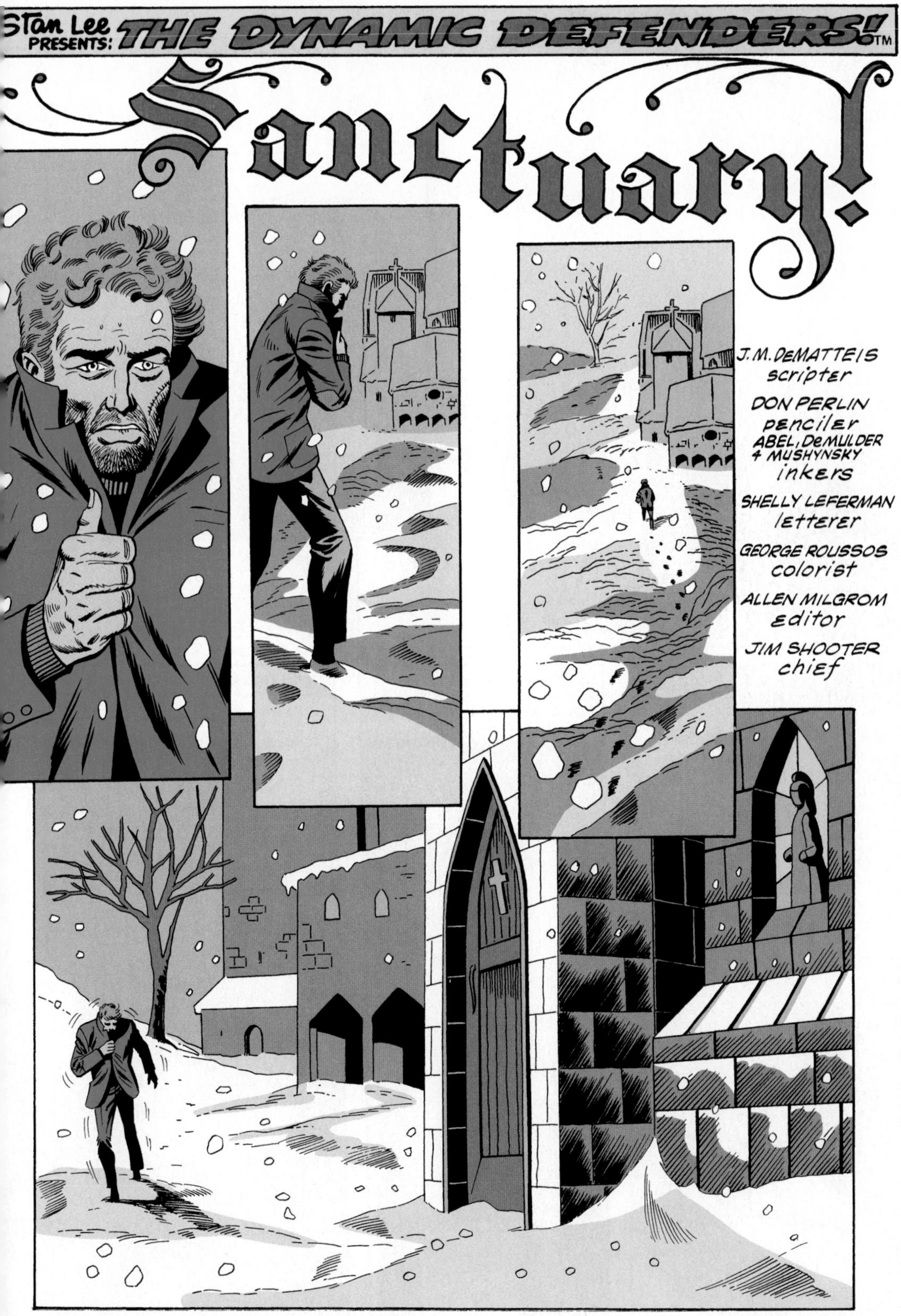
Stan Lee PRESENTS: THE DYNAMIC DEFENDERS!™
Sanctuary!
J.M. DEMATTEIS scripter
DON PERLIN penciler
ABEL, DeMULDER & MUSHYNSKY inkers
SHELLY LEFERMAN letterer
GEORGE ROUSSOS colorist
ALLEN MILGROM editor
JIM SHOOTER chief

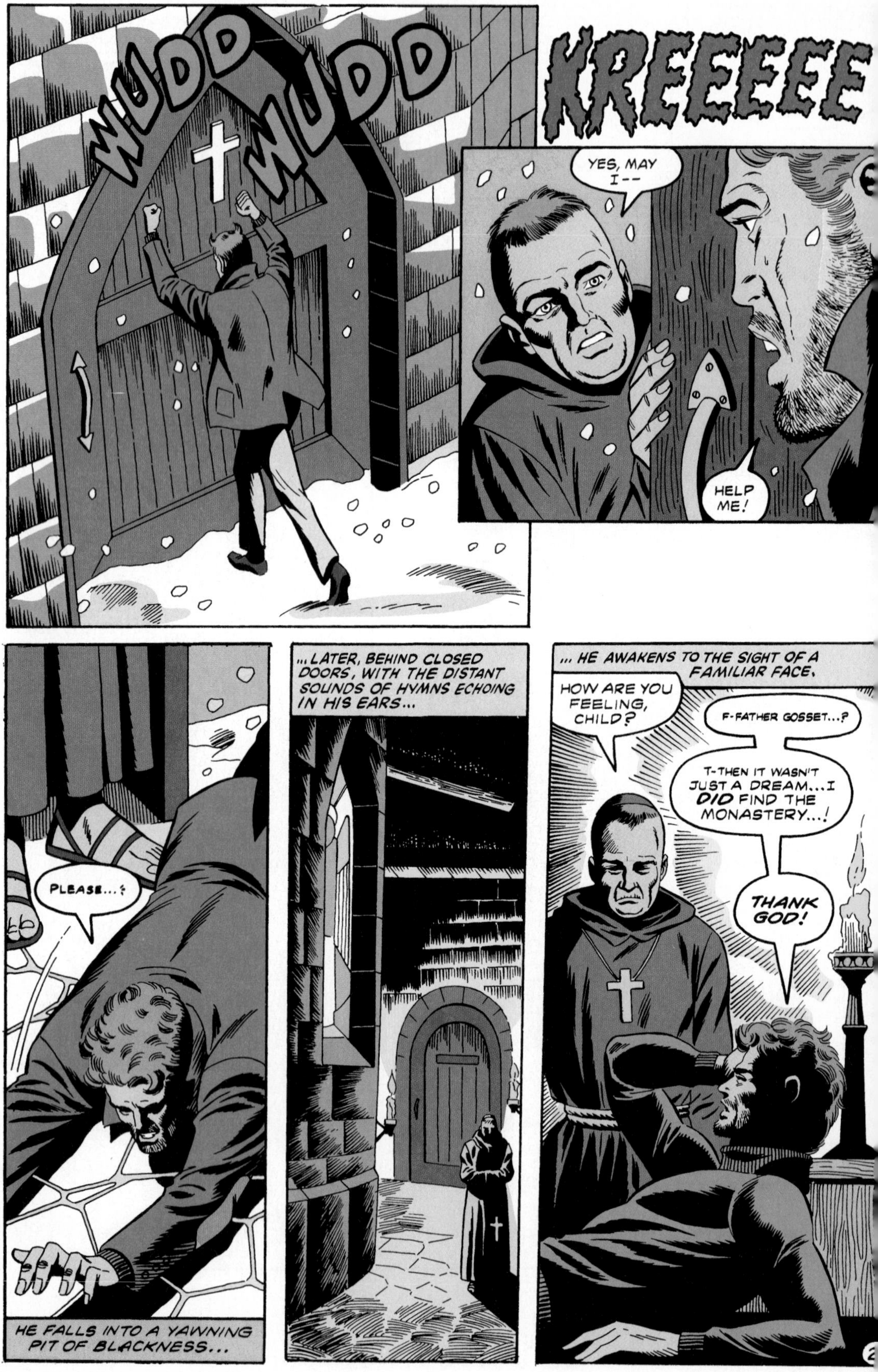
WUDD WUDD
KREEEEE
YES, MAY I--
HELP ME!
PLEASE...
HE FALLS INTO A YAWNING PIT OF BLACKNESS...
...LATER, BEHIND CLOSED DOORS, WITH THE DISTANT SOUNDS OF HYMNS ECHOING IN HIS EARS...
... HE AWAKENS TO THE SIGHT OF A FAMILIAR FACE.
HOW ARE YOU FEELING, CHILD?
F-FATHER GOSSET...?
T-THEN IT WASN'T JUST A DREAM... I DID FIND THE MONASTERY...!
THANK GOD!

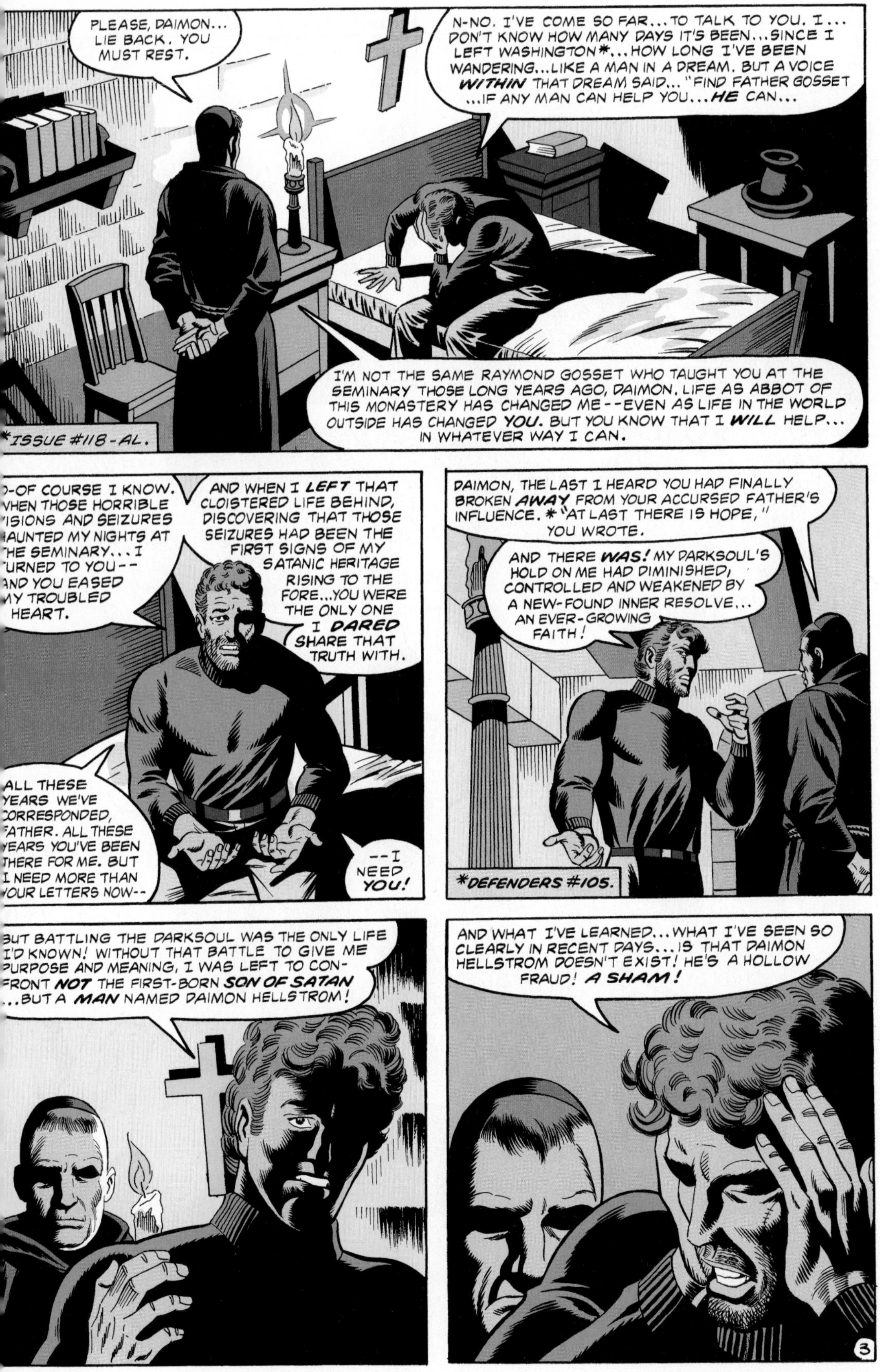
PLEASE, DAIMON... LIE BACK. YOU MUST REST.
N-NO. I'VE COME SO FAR... TO TALK TO YOU. I... DON'T KNOW HOW MANY DAYS IT'S BEEN... SINCE I LEFT WASHINGTON*... HOW LONG I'VE BEEN WANDERING... LIKE A MAN IN A DREAM. BUT A VOICE WITHIN THAT DREAM SAID... "FIND FATHER GOSSET ...IF ANY MAN CAN HELP YOU... HE CAN...
I'M NOT THE SAME RAYMOND GOSSET WHO TAUGHT YOU AT THE SEMINARY THOSE LONG YEARS AGO, DAIMON. LIFE AS ABBOT OF THIS MONASTERY HAS CHANGED ME--EVEN AS LIFE IN THE WORLD OUTSIDE HAS CHANGED YOU. BUT YOU KNOW THAT I WILL HELP... IN WHATEVER WAY I CAN.
*ISSUE #118-AL.
O-OF COURSE I KNOW. WHEN THOSE HORRIBLE VISIONS AND SEIZURES HAUNTED MY NIGHTS AT THE SEMINARY... I TURNED TO YOU-- AND YOU EASED MY TROUBLED HEART.
AND WHEN I LEFT THAT CLOISTERED LIFE BEHIND, DISCOVERING THAT THOSE SEIZURES HAD BEEN THE FIRST SIGNS OF MY SATANIC HERITAGE RISING TO THE FORE... YOU WERE THE ONLY ONE I DARED SHARE THAT TRUTH WITH.
ALL THESE YEARS WE'VE CORRESPONDED, FATHER. ALL THESE YEARS YOU'VE BEEN THERE FOR ME. BUT I NEED MORE THAN YOUR LETTERS NOW--
--I NEED YOU!
DAIMON, THE LAST I HEARD YOU HAD FINALLY BROKEN AWAY FROM YOUR ACCURSED FATHER'S INFLUENCE.* "AT LAST THERE IS HOPE," YOU WROTE.
AND THERE WAS! MY DARKSOUL'S HOLD ON ME HAD DIMINISHED, CONTROLLED AND WEAKENED BY A NEW-FOUND INNER RESOLVE... AN EVER-GROWING FAITH!
*DEFENDERS #105.
BUT BATTLING THE DARKSOUL WAS THE ONLY LIFE I'D KNOWN! WITHOUT THAT BATTLE TO GIVE ME PURPOSE AND MEANING, I WAS LEFT TO CONFRONT NOT THE FIRST-BORN SON OF SATAN ...BUT A MAN NAMED DAIMON HELLSTROM!
AND WHAT I'VE LEARNED... WHAT I'VE SEEN SO CLEARLY IN RECENT DAYS... IS THAT DAIMON HELLSTROM DOESN'T EXIST! HE'S A HOLLOW FRAUD! A SHAM!
3

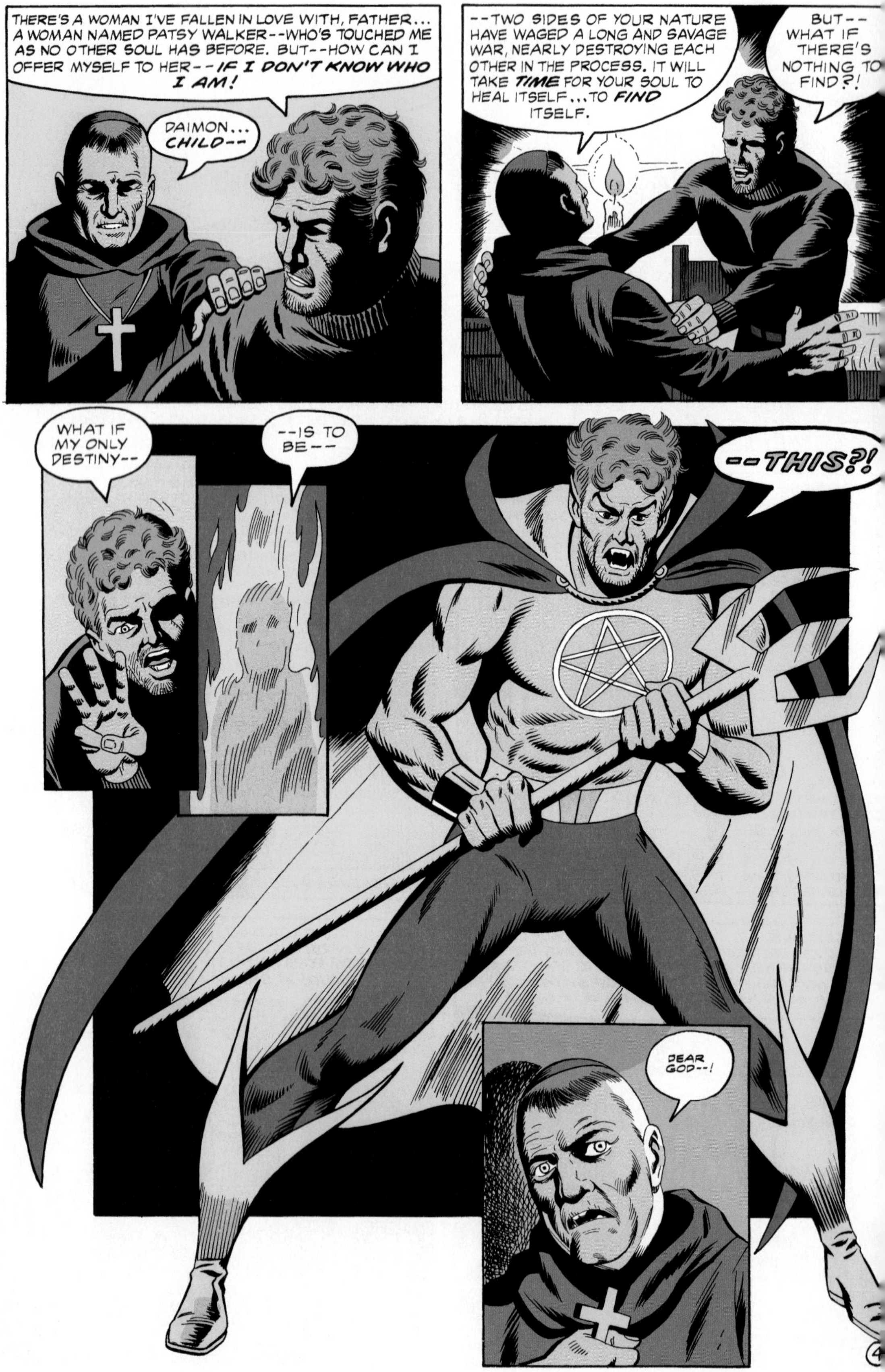
THERE'S A WOMAN I'VE FALLEN IN LOVE WITH, FATHER... A WOMAN NAMED PATSY WALKER--WHO'S TOUCHED ME AS NO OTHER SOUL HAS BEFORE. BUT--HOW CAN I OFFER MYSELF TO HER--IF I DON'T KNOW WHO I AM!
DAIMON... CHILD--
--TWO SIDES OF YOUR NATURE HAVE WAGED A LONG AND SAVAGE WAR, NEARLY DESTROYING EACH OTHER IN THE PROCESS. IT WILL TAKE TIME FOR YOUR SOUL TO HEAL ITSELF...TO FIND ITSELF.
BUT--WHAT IF THERE'S NOTHING TO FIND?!
WHAT IF MY ONLY DESTINY--
--IS TO BE--
--THIS?!
DEAR GOD--!

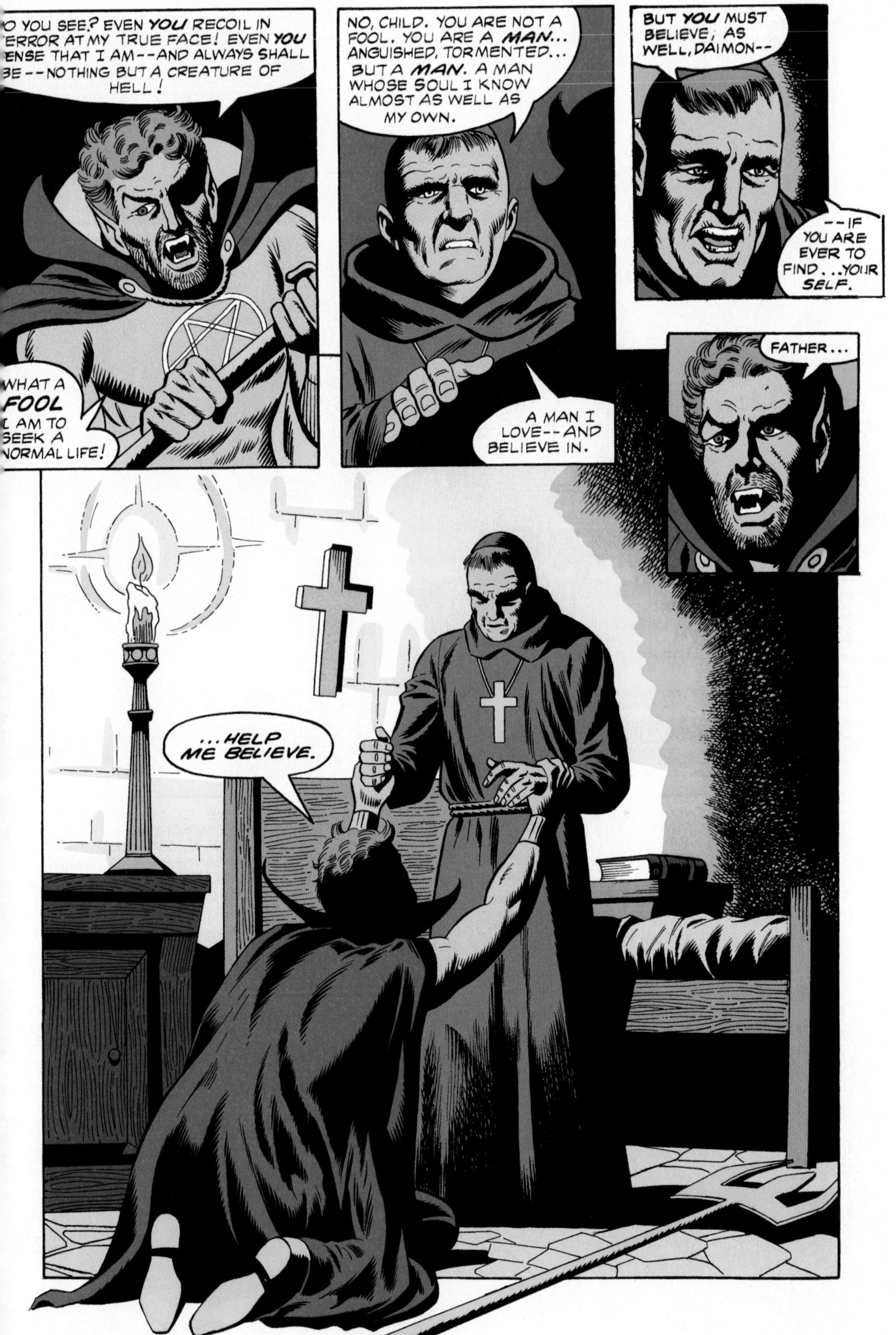
O YOU SEE? EVEN YOU RECOIL IN ERROR AT MY TRUE FACE! EVEN YOU ENSE THAT I AM--AND ALWAYS SHALL BE--NOTHING BUT A CREATURE OF HELL!
WHAT A FOOL I AM TO SEEK A NORMAL LIFE!
NO, CHILD. YOU ARE NOT A FOOL. YOU ARE A MAN... ANGUISHED, TORMENTED... BUT A MAN. A MAN WHOSE SOUL I KNOW ALMOST AS WELL AS MY OWN.
A MAN I LOVE--AND BELIEVE IN.
BUT YOU MUST BELIEVE, AS WELL, DAIMON--
--IF YOU ARE EVER TO FIND...YOUR SELF.
FATHER...
...HELP ME BELIEVE.
5

A NEW DAWN.

EXCUSE ME, MY FRIEND--

--ARE YOU DAIMON...THE ABBOT'S OLD STUDENT--WHO'S COME TO STAY WITH US FOR A WHILE?

I AM.

I'M--*BROTHER JOSHUA*. I JUST WANTED TO INTRODUCE MYSELF...AND OFFER WHATEVER HELP I CAN TO MAKE YOUR STAY WITH US A FRUITFUL ONE.

BUT I MUST BE DISTURBING YOU. WE CAN TALK LATER, WHEN--

NO, BROTHER--YOU WEREN'T DISTURBING ME. I WAS ONLY WATCHING THE MONKS IN MEDITATION...DRINKING IN THE SILENCE--AND THE PEACE.

WELL, THEN--WOULD YOU CARE TO JOIN ME FOR A WALK? SOME PLACE WHERE OUR CHATTER WON'T BOTHER THE OTHERS?

I'D LIKE THAT VERY MUCH.

HAVE YOU BEEN HERE LONG, JOSHUA?

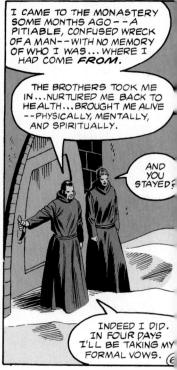

I CAME TO THE MONASTERY SOME MONTHS AGO--A PITIABLE, CONFUSED WRECK OF A MAN--WITH NO MEMORY OF WHO I WAS...WHERE I HAD COME *FROM*.

THE BROTHERS TOOK ME IN...NURTURED ME BACK TO HEALTH...BROUGHT ME ALIVE --PHYSICALLY, MENTALLY, AND SPIRITUALLY.

AND YOU STAYED?

INDEED I DID. IN FOUR DAYS I'LL BE TAKING MY FORMAL VOWS.

280

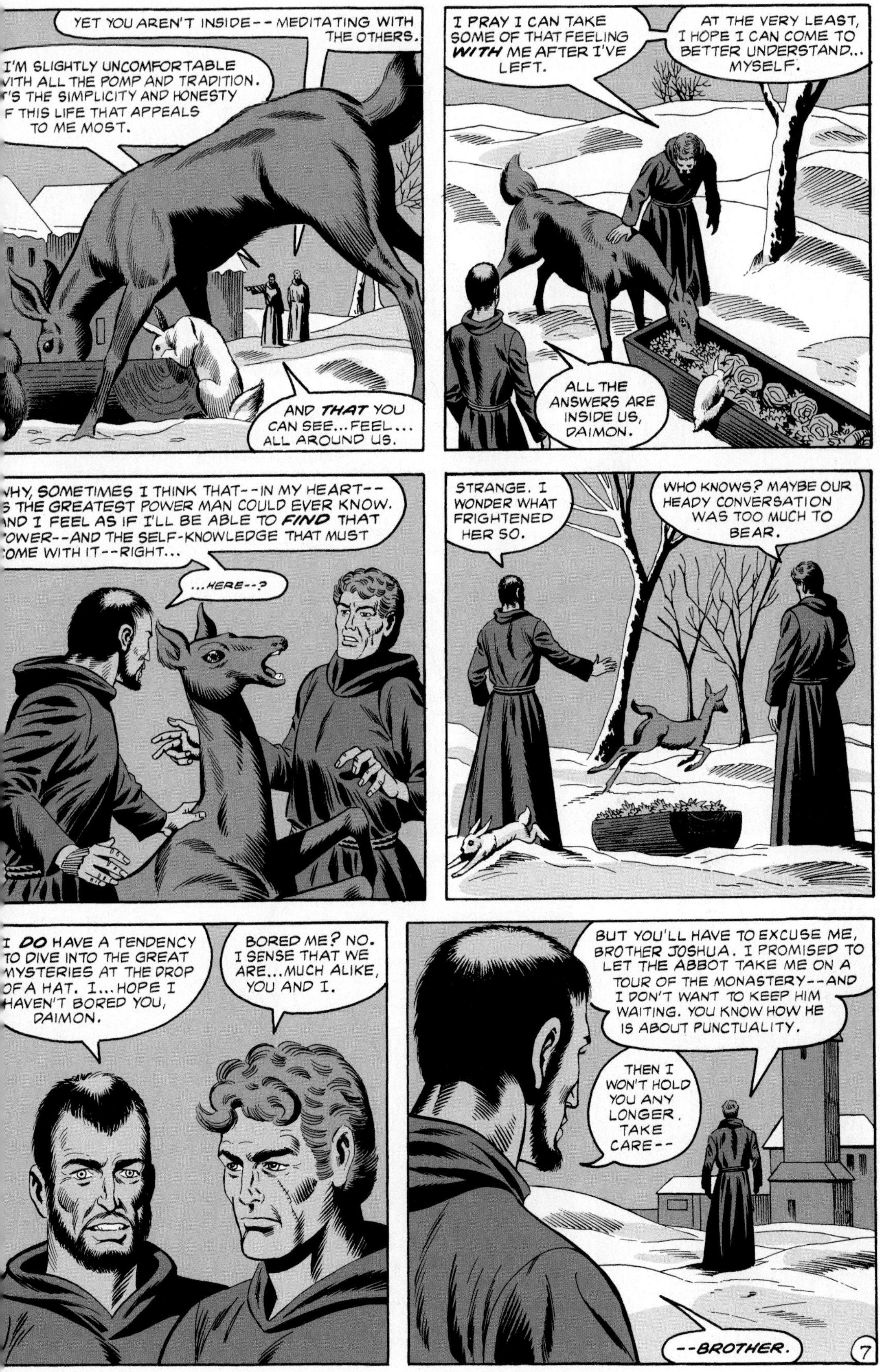
YET YOU AREN'T INSIDE-- MEDITATING WITH THE OTHERS.
I'M SLIGHTLY UNCOMFORTABLE WITH ALL THE POMP AND TRADITION. IT'S THE SIMPLICITY AND HONESTY OF THIS LIFE THAT APPEALS TO ME MOST.
AND THAT YOU CAN SEE...FEEL... ALL AROUND US.
I PRAY I CAN TAKE SOME OF THAT FEELING WITH ME AFTER I'VE LEFT.
AT THE VERY LEAST, I HOPE I CAN COME TO BETTER UNDERSTAND... MYSELF.
ALL THE ANSWERS ARE INSIDE US, DAIMON.
WHY, SOMETIMES I THINK THAT--IN MY HEART--IS THE GREATEST POWER MAN COULD EVER KNOW. AND I FEEL AS IF I'LL BE ABLE TO FIND THAT POWER--AND THE SELF-KNOWLEDGE THAT MUST COME WITH IT--RIGHT...
...HERE--?
STRANGE. I WONDER WHAT FRIGHTENED HER SO.
WHO KNOWS? MAYBE OUR HEADY CONVERSATION WAS TOO MUCH TO BEAR.
I DO HAVE A TENDENCY TO DIVE INTO THE GREAT MYSTERIES AT THE DROP OF A HAT. I...HOPE I HAVEN'T BORED YOU, DAIMON.
BORED ME? NO. I SENSE THAT WE ARE...MUCH ALIKE, YOU AND I.
BUT YOU'LL HAVE TO EXCUSE ME, BROTHER JOSHUA. I PROMISED TO LET THE ABBOT TAKE ME ON A TOUR OF THE MONASTERY--AND I DON'T WANT TO KEEP HIM WAITING. YOU KNOW HOW HE IS ABOUT PUNCTUALITY.
THEN I WON'T HOLD YOU ANY LONGER. TAKE CARE--
--BROTHER.
7

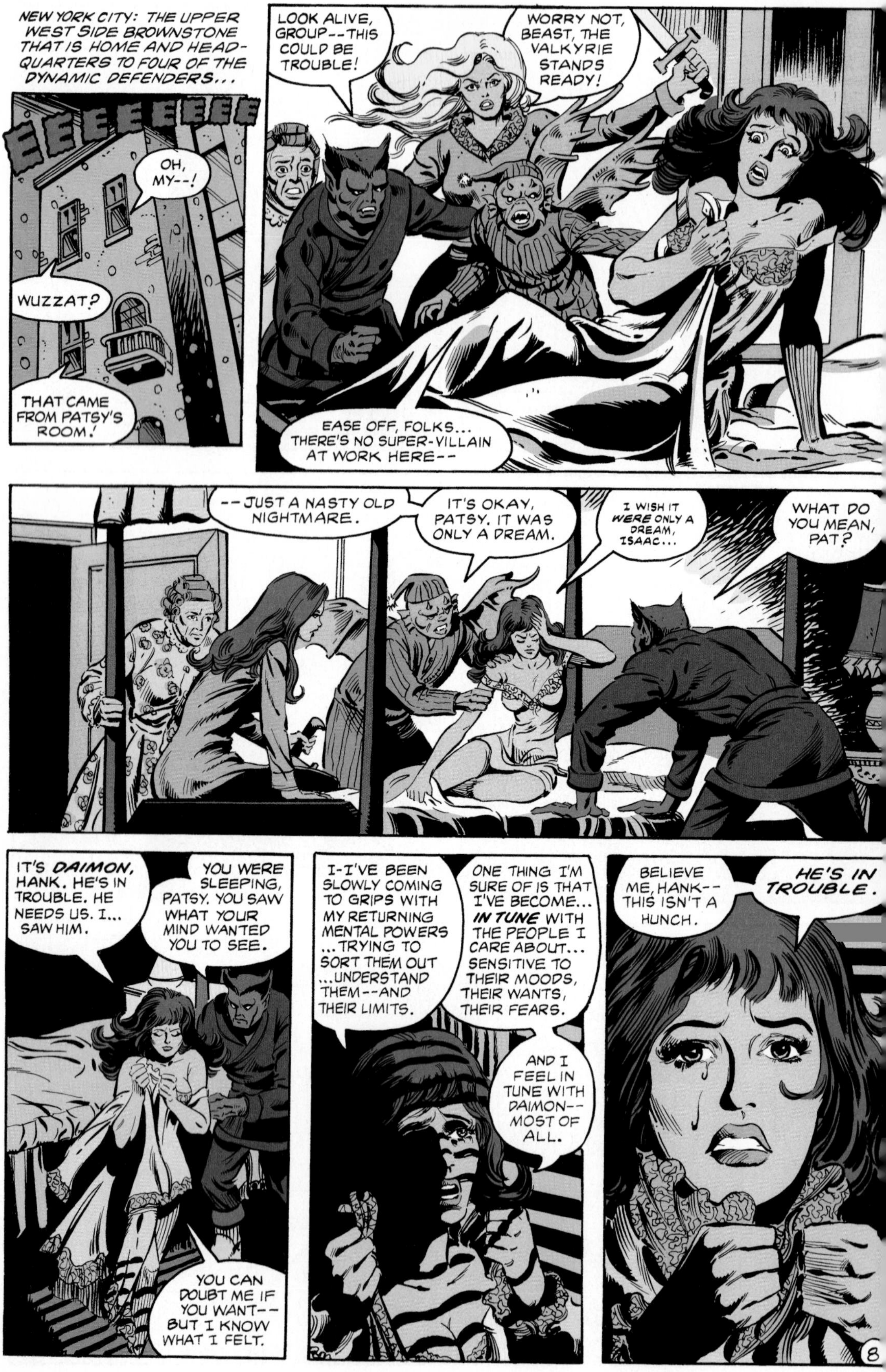

NEW YORK CITY: THE UPPER WEST SIDE BROWNSTONE THAT IS HOME AND HEAD-QUARTERS TO FOUR OF THE DYNAMIC DEFENDERS...
EEEEEEEEE
OH, MY--!
WUZZAT?
THAT CAME FROM PATSY'S ROOM!
LOOK ALIVE, GROUP--THIS COULD BE TROUBLE!
WORRY NOT, BEAST, THE VALKYRIE STANDS READY!
EASE OFF, FOLKS... THERE'S NO SUPER-VILLAIN AT WORK HERE--
--JUST A NASTY OLD NIGHTMARE.
IT'S OKAY, PATSY. IT WAS ONLY A DREAM.
I WISH IT WERE ONLY A DREAM, ISAAC...
WHAT DO YOU MEAN, PAT?
IT'S DAIMON, HANK. HE'S IN TROUBLE. HE NEEDS US. I... SAW HIM.
YOU WERE SLEEPING, PATSY. YOU SAW WHAT YOUR MIND WANTED YOU TO SEE.
YOU CAN DOUBT ME IF YOU WANT--BUT I KNOW WHAT I FELT.
I-I'VE BEEN SLOWLY COMING TO GRIPS WITH MY RETURNING MENTAL POWERS ...TRYING TO SORT THEM OUT ...UNDERSTAND THEM--AND THEIR LIMITS.
ONE THING I'M SURE OF IS THAT I'VE BECOME... IN TUNE WITH THE PEOPLE I CARE ABOUT... SENSITIVE TO THEIR MOODS, THEIR WANTS, THEIR FEARS.
AND I FEEL IN TUNE WITH DAIMON--MOST OF ALL.
BELIEVE ME, HANK--THIS ISN'T A HUNCH.
HE'S IN TROUBLE.
8

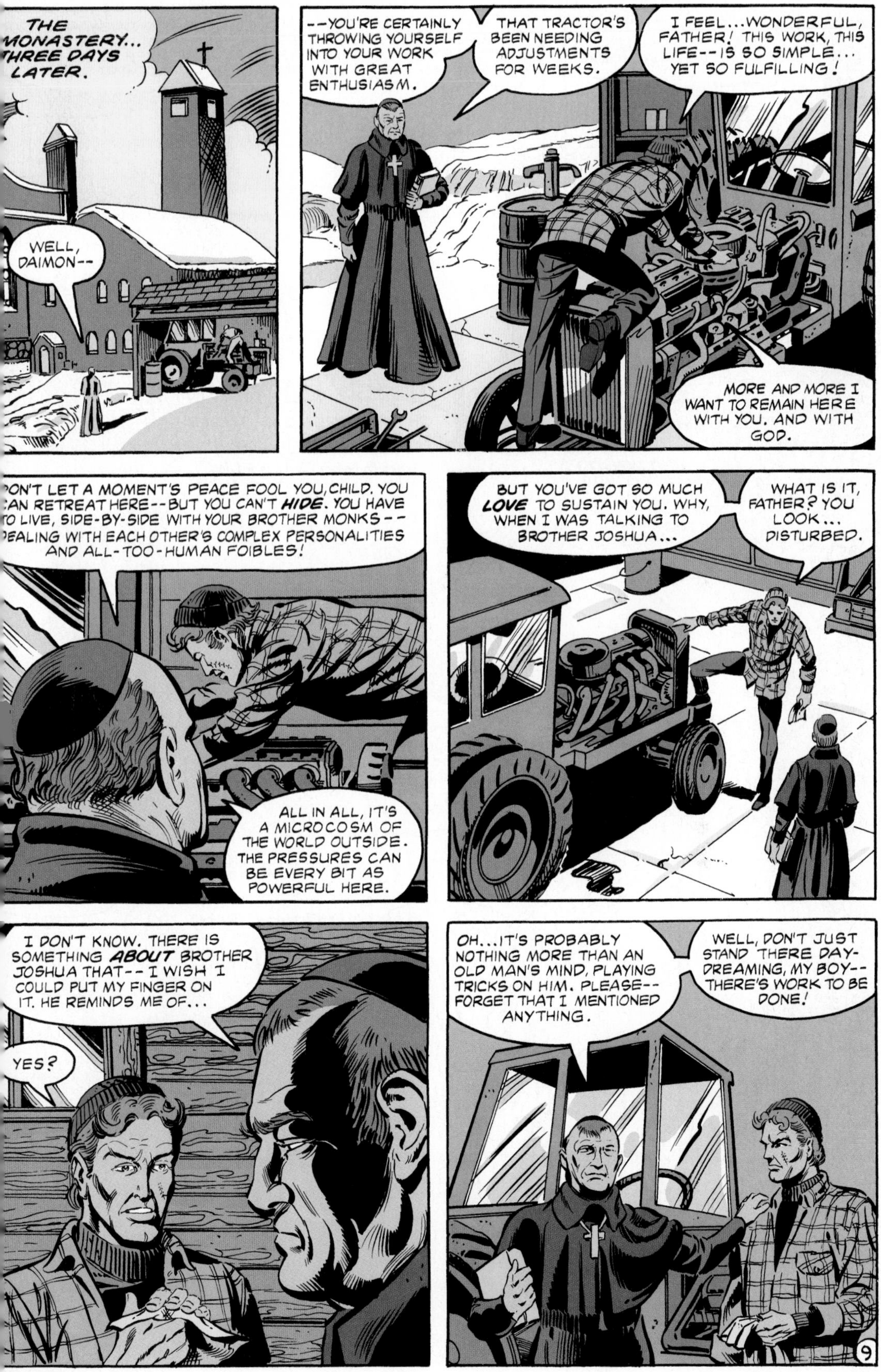
THE MONASTERY... THREE DAYS LATER.
WELL, DAIMON--
--YOU'RE CERTAINLY THROWING YOURSELF INTO YOUR WORK WITH GREAT ENTHUSIASM.
THAT TRACTOR'S BEEN NEEDING ADJUSTMENTS FOR WEEKS.
I FEEL...WONDERFUL, FATHER! THIS WORK, THIS LIFE--IS SO SIMPLE... YET SO FULFILLING!
MORE AND MORE I WANT TO REMAIN HERE WITH YOU. AND WITH GOD.
DON'T LET A MOMENT'S PEACE FOOL YOU, CHILD. YOU CAN RETREAT HERE--BUT YOU CAN'T HIDE. YOU HAVE TO LIVE, SIDE-BY-SIDE WITH YOUR BROTHER MONKS--DEALING WITH EACH OTHER'S COMPLEX PERSONALITIES AND ALL-TOO-HUMAN FOIBLES!
ALL IN ALL, IT'S A MICROCOSM OF THE WORLD OUTSIDE. THE PRESSURES CAN BE EVERY BIT AS POWERFUL HERE.
BUT YOU'VE GOT SO MUCH LOVE TO SUSTAIN YOU. WHY, WHEN I WAS TALKING TO BROTHER JOSHUA...
WHAT IS IT, FATHER? YOU LOOK... DISTURBED.
I DON'T KNOW. THERE IS SOMETHING ABOUT BROTHER JOSHUA THAT--I WISH I COULD PUT MY FINGER ON IT. HE REMINDS ME OF...
YES?
OH...IT'S PROBABLY NOTHING MORE THAN AN OLD MAN'S MIND, PLAYING TRICKS ON HIM. PLEASE--FORGET THAT I MENTIONED ANYTHING.
WELL, DON'T JUST STAND THERE DAY-DREAMING, MY BOY--THERE'S WORK TO BE DONE!
9

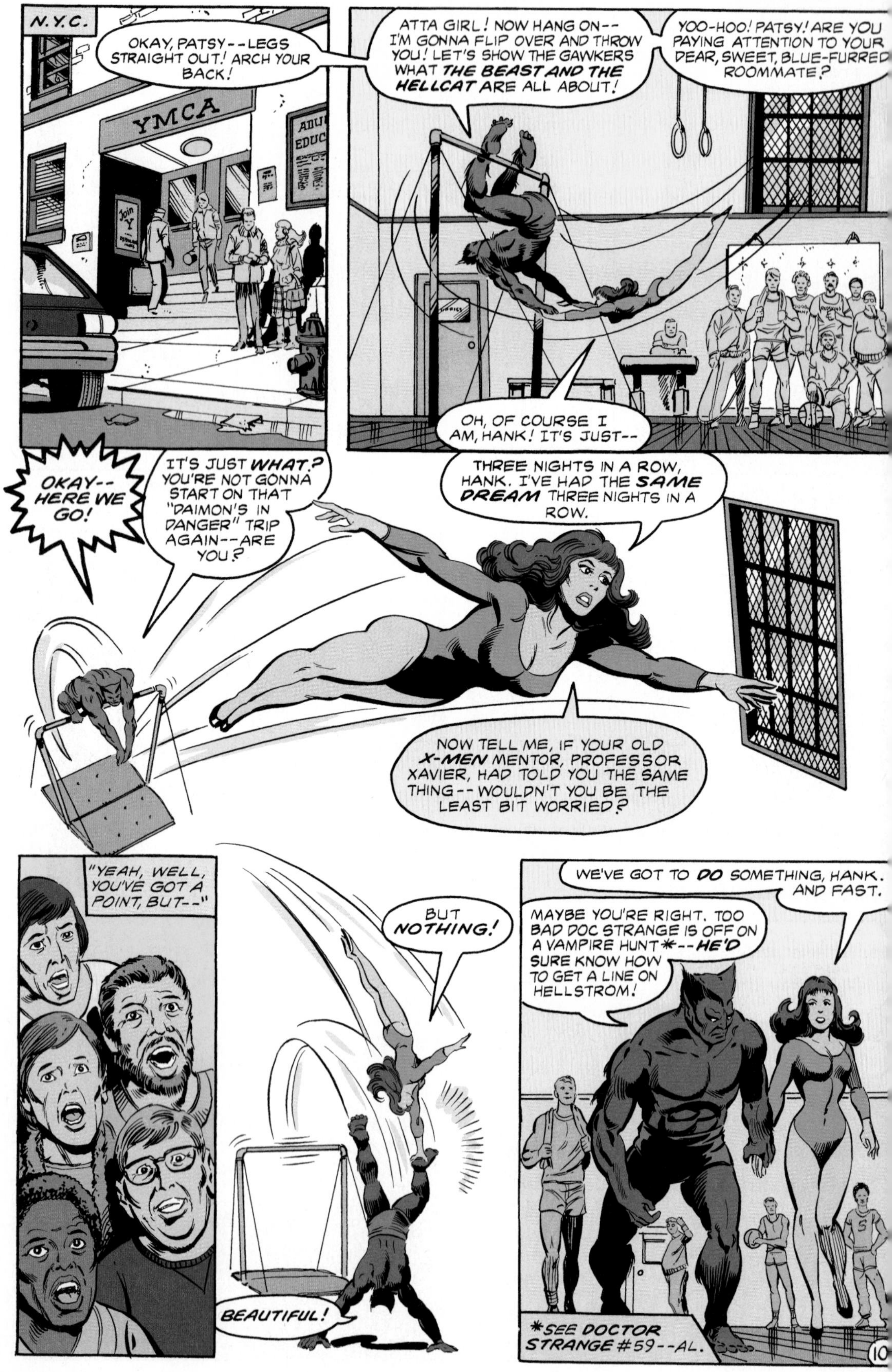
N.Y.C.
OKAY, PATSY--LEGS STRAIGHT OUT! ARCH YOUR BACK!
YMCA
ATTA GIRL! NOW HANG ON--I'M GONNA FLIP OVER AND THROW YOU! LET'S SHOW THE GAWKERS WHAT THE BEAST AND THE HELLCAT ARE ALL ABOUT!
YOO-HOO! PATSY! ARE YOU PAYING ATTENTION TO YOUR DEAR, SWEET, BLUE-FURRED ROOMMATE?
OH, OF COURSE I AM, HANK! IT'S JUST--
OKAY--HERE WE GO!
IT'S JUST WHAT? YOU'RE NOT GONNA START ON THAT "DAIMON'S IN DANGER" TRIP AGAIN--ARE YOU?
THREE NIGHTS IN A ROW, HANK. I'VE HAD THE SAME DREAM THREE NIGHTS IN A ROW.
NOW TELL ME, IF YOUR OLD X-MEN MENTOR, PROFESSOR XAVIER, HAD TOLD YOU THE SAME THING--WOULDN'T YOU BE THE LEAST BIT WORRIED?
"YEAH, WELL, YOU'VE GOT A POINT, BUT--"
BUT NOTHING!
BEAUTIFUL!
WE'VE GOT TO DO SOMETHING, HANK. AND FAST.
MAYBE YOU'RE RIGHT. TOO BAD DOC STRANGE IS OFF ON A VAMPIRE HUNT*--HE'D SURE KNOW HOW TO GET A LINE ON HELLSTROM!
*SEE DOCTOR STRANGE #59--AL.
10

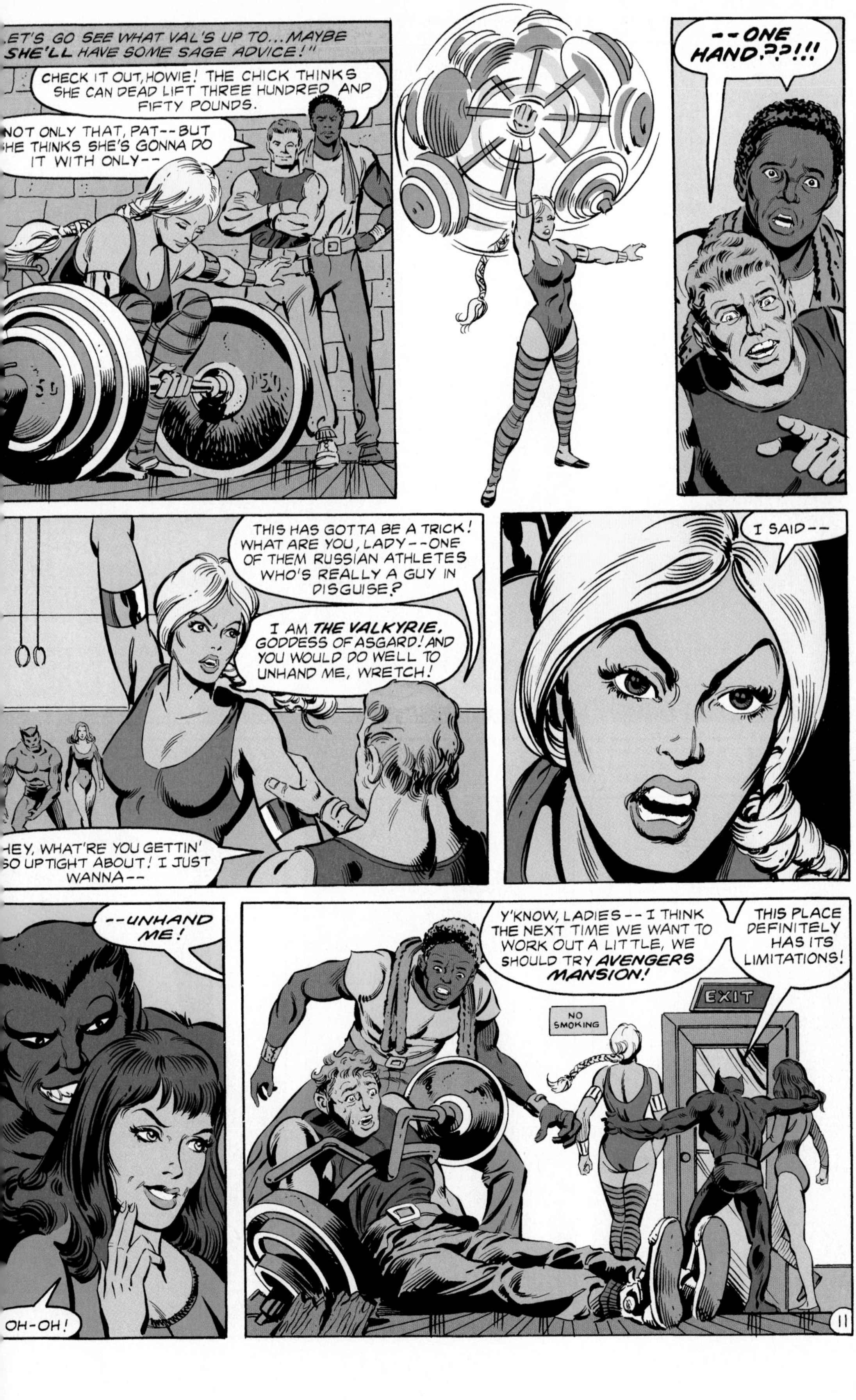

...LET'S GO SEE WHAT VAL'S UP TO... MAYBE SHE'LL HAVE SOME SAGE ADVICE!"
CHECK IT OUT, HOWIE! THE CHICK THINKS SHE CAN DEAD LIFT THREE HUNDRED AND FIFTY POUNDS.
NOT ONLY THAT, PAT--BUT SHE THINKS SHE'S GONNA DO IT WITH ONLY--
--ONE HAND???!!!
THIS HAS GOTTA BE A TRICK! WHAT ARE YOU, LADY--ONE OF THEM RUSSIAN ATHLETES WHO'S REALLY A GUY IN DISGUISE?
I AM THE VALKYRIE, GODDESS OF ASGARD! AND YOU WOULD DO WELL TO UNHAND ME, WRETCH!
HEY, WHAT'RE YOU GETTIN' SO UPTIGHT ABOUT! I JUST WANNA--
I SAID--
--UNHAND ME!
OH-OH!
Y'KNOW, LADIES--I THINK THE NEXT TIME WE WANT TO WORK OUT A LITTLE, WE SHOULD TRY AVENGERS MANSION!
THIS PLACE DEFINITELY HAS ITS LIMITATIONS!
NO SMOKING
EXIT
11

MIDNIGHT--AND THE MONASTERY IS WRAPPED IN BLANKETS OF SILENCE AND SLEEP.

BUT THERE IS ONE TO WHOM SLEEP IS A STRANGER THIS NIGHT...

...AND WHO BREAKS THE SILENCE WITH A TORRENT OF WORDS.

WORDS OF ADJURATION. WORDS OF PRAYER.

FOR THE FIRST TIME IN OVER A DECADE, DAIMON HELLSTROM HAS KNEELED BEFORE HIS GOD, AND ASKED FOR HELP. FOR GUIDANCE.

FOR A SIGN.

SUDDENLY--AS IF IN RESPONSE TO HIS ENTREATY--HELL-STROM'S LUNGS SEEM TO SHRIVEL UP...

...HIS BREATH COMES HARD--IN SHALLOW GASPS...

...AND RAZOR-TIPPED FINGERS OF PAIN DIG DEEP INTO HIS HEART, SLAMMING HIM DOWN LIKE SOME WEIGHTLESS DOLL.

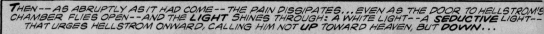

THEN--AS ABRUPTLY AS IT HAD COME--THE PAIN DISSIPATES...EVEN AS THE DOOR TO HELLSTROM'S CHAMBER FLIES OPEN--AND THE *LIGHT* SHINES THROUGH: A WHITE LIGHT--A *SEDUCTIVE* LIGHT-- THAT URGES HELLSTROM ONWARD, CALLING HIM NOT *UP* TOWARD HEAVEN, BUT *DOWN*...

12

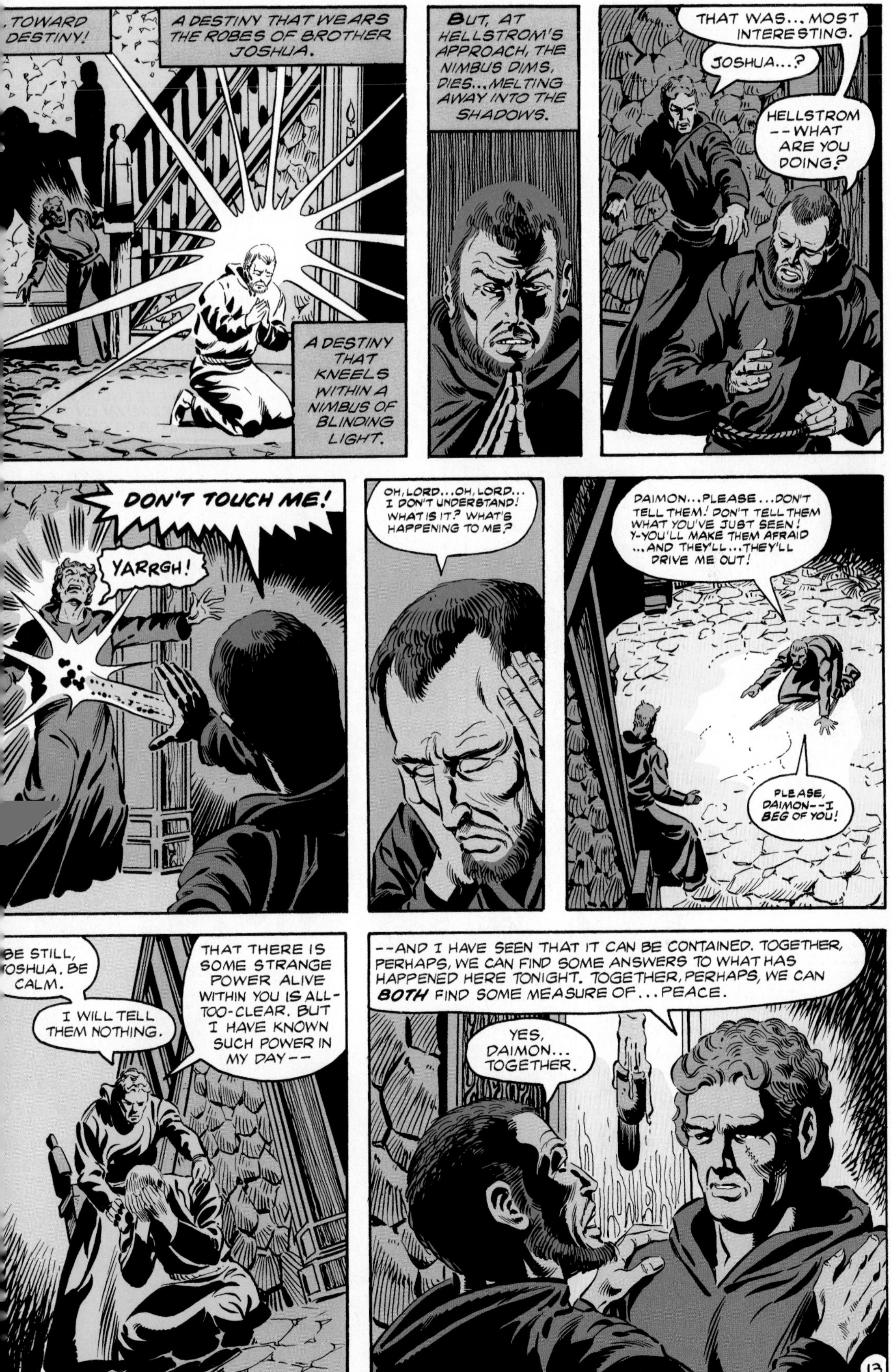
...TOWARD DESTINY!
A DESTINY THAT WEARS THE ROBES OF BROTHER JOSHUA.
A DESTINY THAT KNEELS WITHIN A NIMBUS OF BLINDING LIGHT.
BUT, AT HELLSTROM'S APPROACH, THE NIMBUS DIMS, DIES... MELTING AWAY INTO THE SHADOWS.
THAT WAS... MOST INTERESTING.
JOSHUA...?
HELLSTROM --WHAT ARE YOU DOING?
DON'T TOUCH ME!
YARRGH!
OH, LORD... OH, LORD... I DON'T UNDERSTAND! WHAT IS IT? WHAT'S HAPPENING TO ME?
DAIMON... PLEASE... DON'T TELL THEM! DON'T TELL THEM WHAT YOU'VE JUST SEEN! Y-YOU'LL MAKE THEM AFRAID ...AND THEY'LL... THEY'LL DRIVE ME OUT!
PLEASE, DAIMON--I BEG OF YOU!
BE STILL, JOSHUA. BE CALM.
I WILL TELL THEM NOTHING.
THAT THERE IS SOME STRANGE POWER ALIVE WITHIN YOU IS ALL-TOO-CLEAR. BUT I HAVE KNOWN SUCH POWER IN MY DAY--
--AND I HAVE SEEN THAT IT CAN BE CONTAINED. TOGETHER, PERHAPS, WE CAN FIND SOME ANSWERS TO WHAT HAS HAPPENED HERE TONIGHT. TOGETHER, PERHAPS, WE CAN BOTH FIND SOME MEASURE OF... PEACE.
YES, DAIMON... TOGETHER.
13

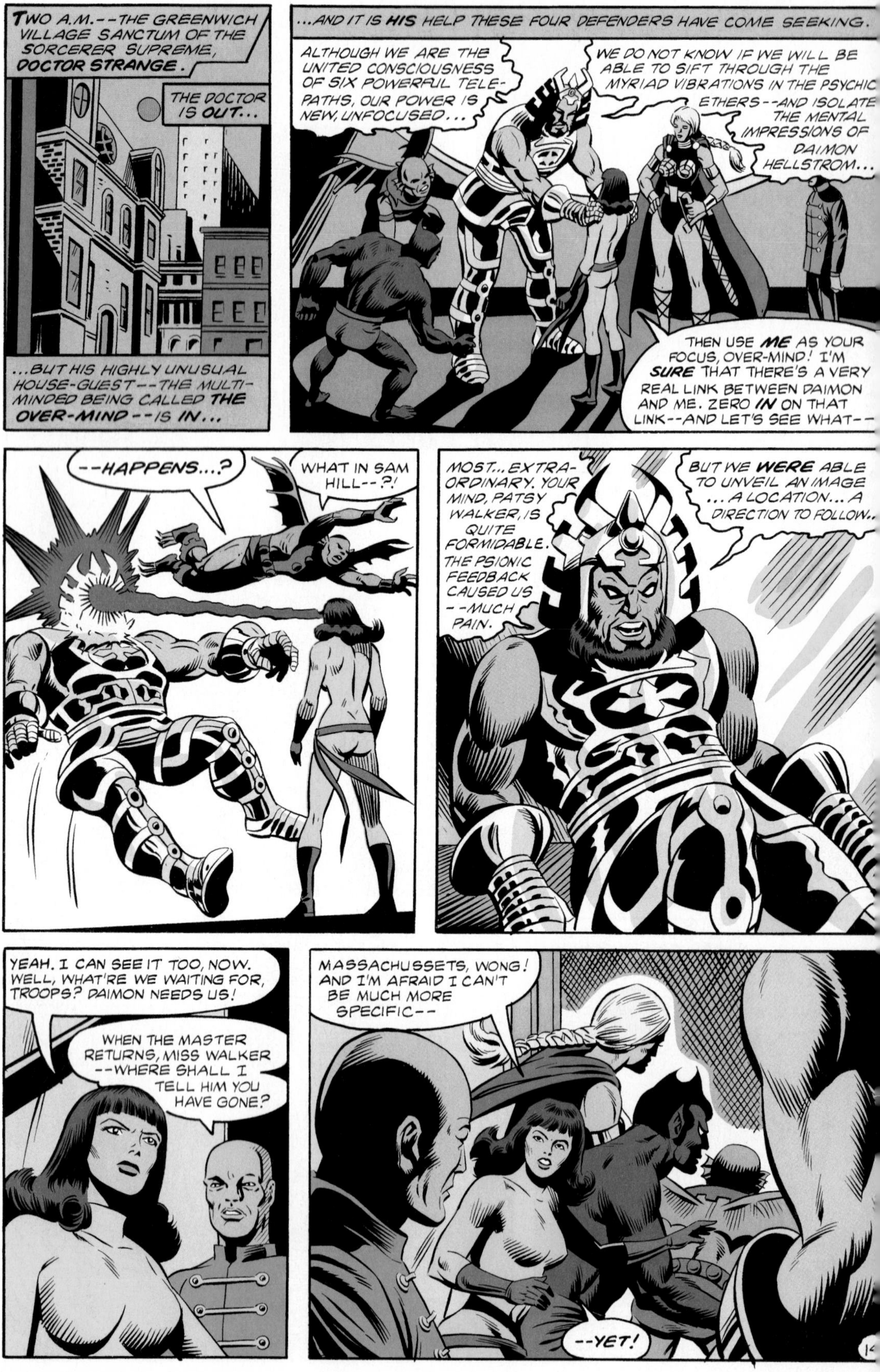

TWO A.M.--THE GREENWICH VILLAGE SANCTUM OF THE SORCERER SUPREME, DOCTOR STRANGE.
THE DOCTOR IS OUT...
...BUT HIS HIGHLY UNUSUAL HOUSE-GUEST--THE MULTI-MINDED BEING CALLED THE OVER-MIND--IS IN...
...AND IT IS HIS HELP THESE FOUR DEFENDERS HAVE COME SEEKING.
ALTHOUGH WE ARE THE UNITED CONSCIOUSNESS OF SIX POWERFUL TELEPATHS, OUR POWER IS NEW, UNFOCUSED...
WE DO NOT KNOW IF WE WILL BE ABLE TO SIFT THROUGH THE MYRIAD VIBRATIONS IN THE PSYCHIC ETHERS--AND ISOLATE THE MENTAL IMPRESSIONS OF DAIMON HELLSTROM...
THEN USE ME AS YOUR FOCUS, OVER-MIND! I'M SURE THAT THERE'S A VERY REAL LINK BETWEEN DAIMON AND ME. ZERO IN ON THAT LINK--AND LET'S SEE WHAT--
--HAPPENS...?
WHAT IN SAM HILL--?!
MOST... EXTRA-ORDINARY. YOUR MIND, PATSY WALKER, IS QUITE FORMIDABLE. THE PSIONIC FEEDBACK CAUSED US--MUCH PAIN.
BUT WE WERE ABLE TO UNVEIL AN IMAGE ...A LOCATION... A DIRECTION TO FOLLOW...
YEAH. I CAN SEE IT TOO, NOW. WELL, WHAT'RE WE WAITING FOR, TROOPS? DAIMON NEEDS US!
WHEN THE MASTER RETURNS, MISS WALKER--WHERE SHALL I TELL HIM YOU HAVE GONE?
MASSACHUSSETS, WONG! AND I'M AFRAID I CAN'T BE MUCH MORE SPECIFIC--
--YET!

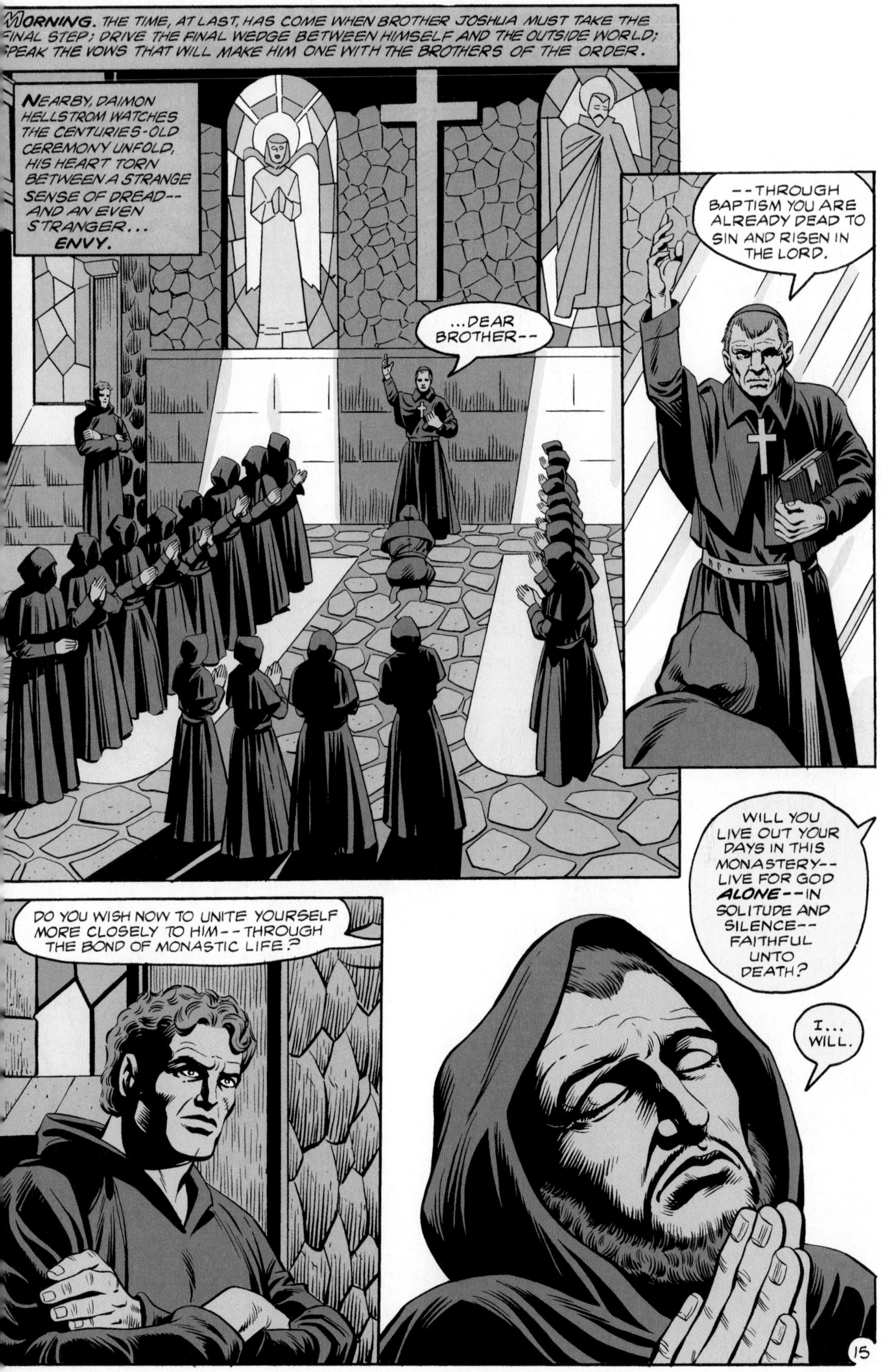
MORNING. THE TIME, AT LAST, HAS COME WHEN BROTHER JOSHUA MUST TAKE THE FINAL STEP; DRIVE THE FINAL WEDGE BETWEEN HIMSELF AND THE OUTSIDE WORLD; SPEAK THE VOWS THAT WILL MAKE HIM ONE WITH THE BROTHERS OF THE ORDER.
NEARBY, DAIMON HELLSTROM WATCHES THE CENTURIES-OLD CEREMONY UNFOLD, HIS HEART TORN BETWEEN A STRANGE SENSE OF DREAD-- AND AN EVEN STRANGER... ENVY.
...DEAR BROTHER--
--THROUGH BAPTISM YOU ARE ALREADY DEAD TO SIN AND RISEN IN THE LORD.
DO YOU WISH NOW TO UNITE YOURSELF MORE CLOSELY TO HIM--THROUGH THE BOND OF MONASTIC LIFE?
WILL YOU LIVE OUT YOUR DAYS IN THIS MONASTERY-- LIVE FOR GOD ALONE--IN SOLITUDE AND SILENCE-- FAITHFUL UNTO DEATH?
I... WILL.
15

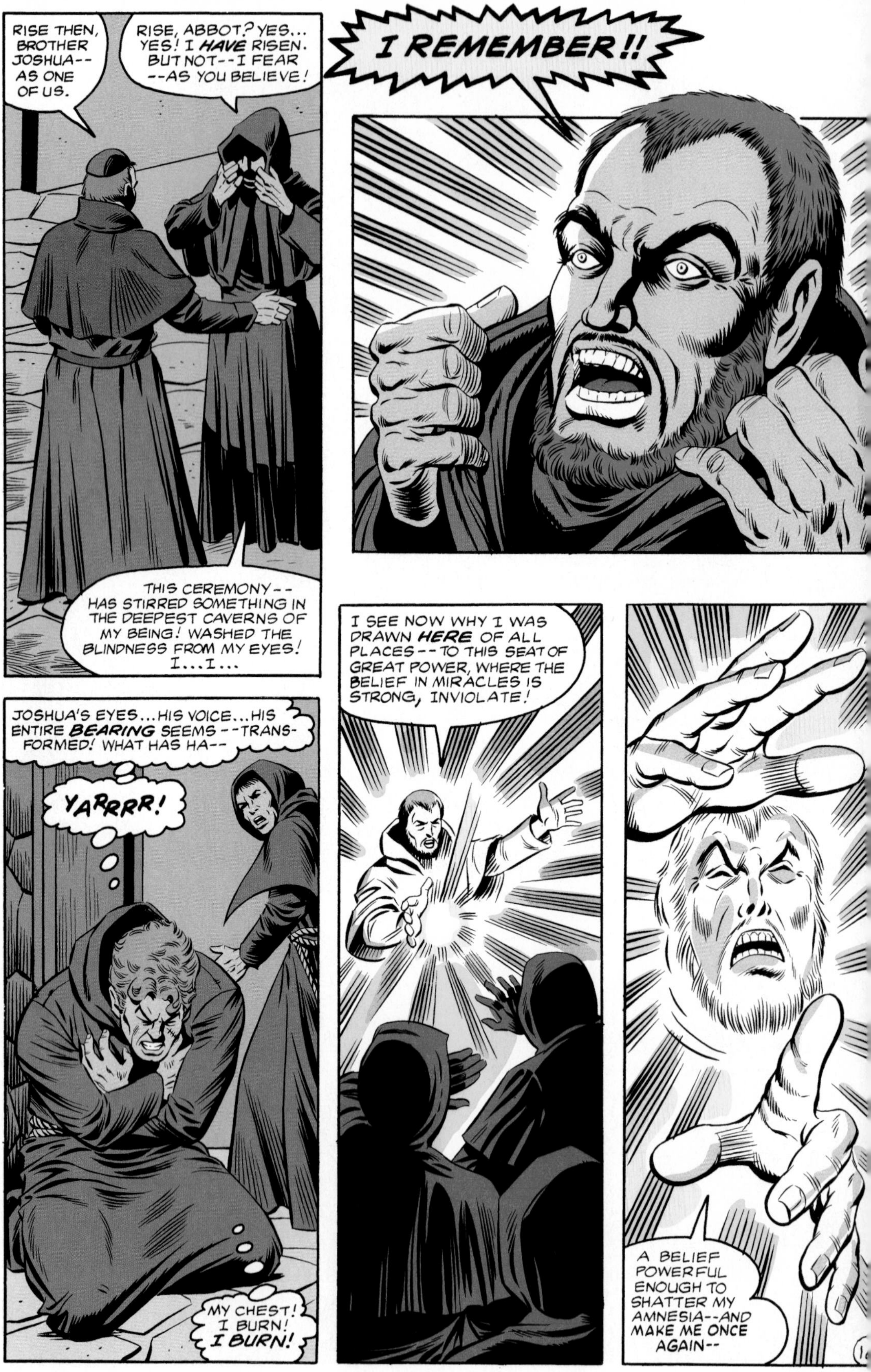

RISE THEN, BROTHER JOSHUA-- AS ONE OF US.
RISE, ABBOT? YES... YES! I HAVE RISEN. BUT NOT--I FEAR --AS YOU BELIEVE!
THIS CEREMONY-- HAS STIRRED SOMETHING IN THE DEEPEST CAVERNS OF MY BEING! WASHED THE BLINDNESS FROM MY EYES! I...I...
I REMEMBER!!
JOSHUA'S EYES...HIS VOICE...HIS ENTIRE BEARING SEEMS--TRANSFORMED! WHAT HAS HA--
YARRRR!
MY CHEST! I BURN! I BURN!
I SEE NOW WHY I WAS DRAWN HERE OF ALL PLACES--TO THIS SEAT OF GREAT POWER, WHERE THE BELIEF IN MIRACLES IS STRONG, INVIOLATE!
A BELIEF POWERFUL ENOUGH TO SHATTER MY AMNESIA--AND MAKE ME ONCE AGAIN--

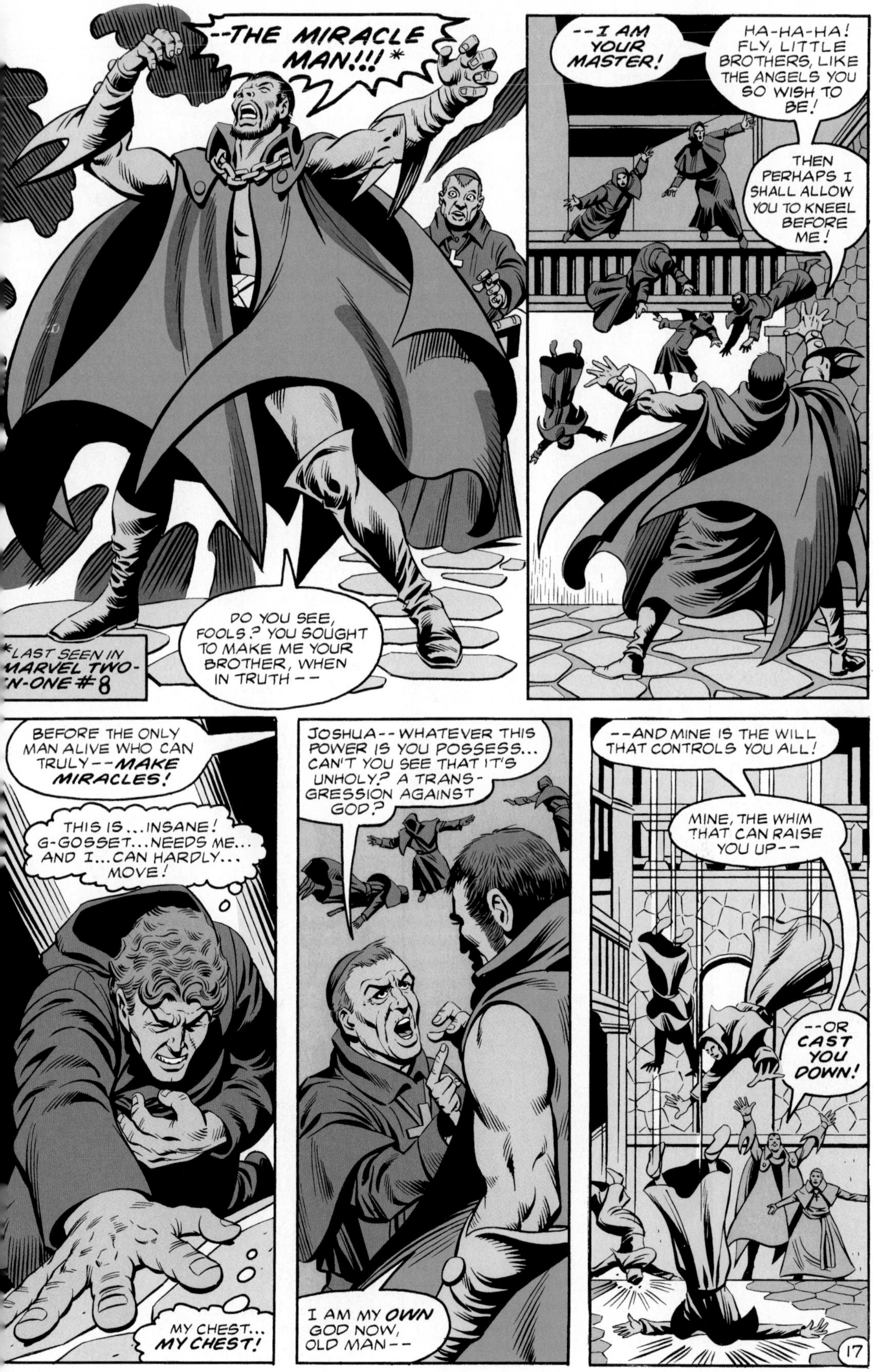
--THE MIRACLE MAN!!! *
DO YOU SEE, FOOLS? YOU SOUGHT TO MAKE ME YOUR BROTHER, WHEN IN TRUTH --
*LAST SEEN IN MARVEL TWO-IN-ONE #8
--I AM YOUR MASTER!
HA-HA-HA! FLY, LITTLE BROTHERS, LIKE THE ANGELS YOU SO WISH TO BE!
THEN PERHAPS I SHALL ALLOW YOU TO KNEEL BEFORE ME!
BEFORE THE ONLY MAN ALIVE WHO CAN TRULY--MAKE MIRACLES!
THIS IS...INSANE! G-GOSSET...NEEDS ME... AND I...CAN HARDLY... MOVE!
MY CHEST... MY CHEST!
JOSHUA--WHATEVER THIS POWER IS YOU POSSESS... CAN'T YOU SEE THAT IT'S UNHOLY? A TRANS-GRESSION AGAINST GOD?
I AM MY OWN GOD NOW, OLD MAN--
--AND MINE IS THE WILL THAT CONTROLS YOU ALL!
MINE, THE WHIM THAT CAN RAISE YOU UP--
--OR CAST YOU DOWN!
17

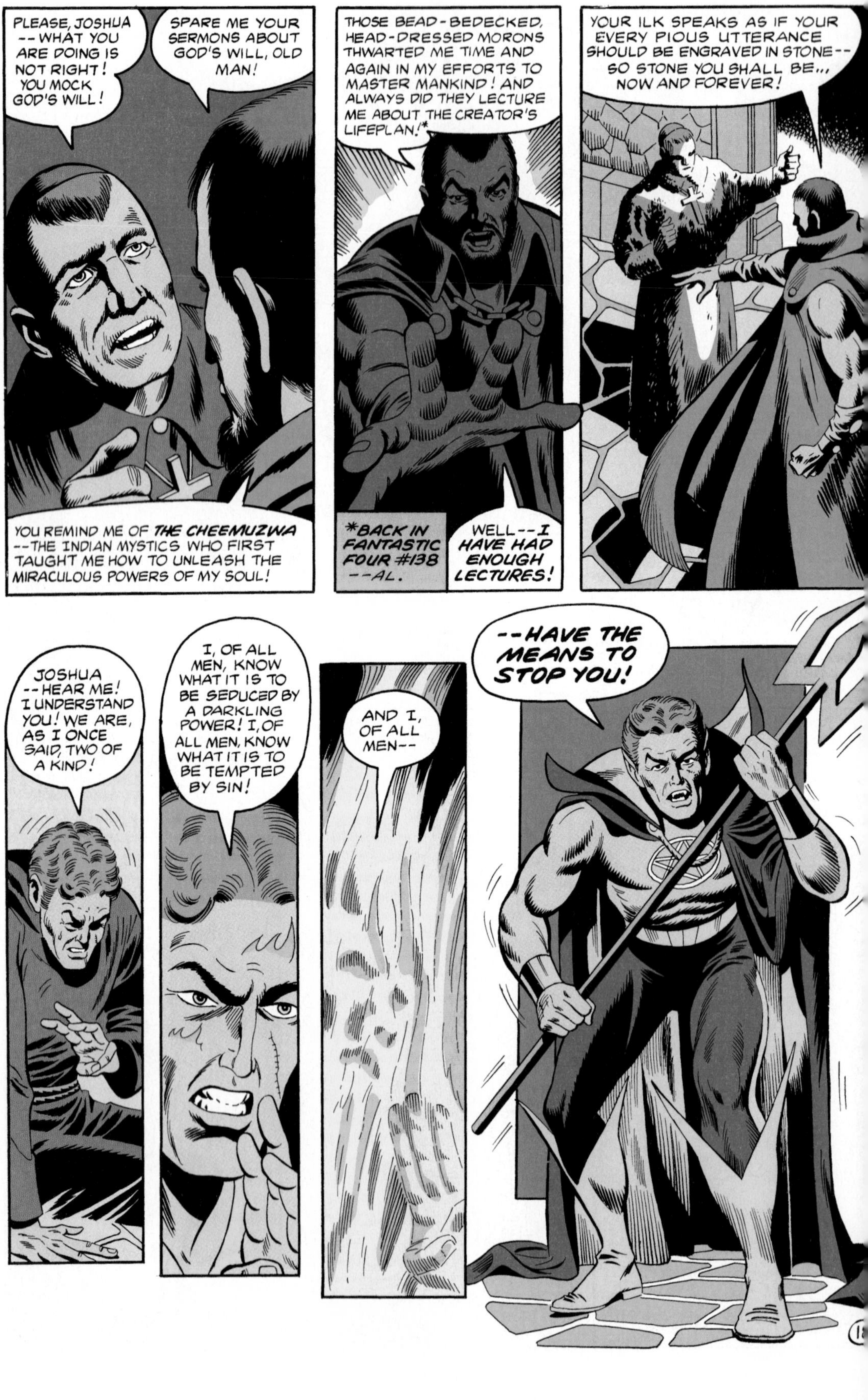

PLEASE, JOSHUA --WHAT YOU ARE DOING IS NOT RIGHT! YOU MOCK GOD'S WILL!
SPARE ME YOUR SERMONS ABOUT GOD'S WILL, OLD MAN!
YOU REMIND ME OF THE CHEEMUZWA --THE INDIAN MYSTICS WHO FIRST TAUGHT ME HOW TO UNLEASH THE MIRACULOUS POWERS OF MY SOUL!
THOSE BEAD-BEDECKED, HEAD-DRESSED MORONS THWARTED ME TIME AND AGAIN IN MY EFFORTS TO MASTER MANKIND! AND ALWAYS DID THEY LECTURE ME ABOUT THE CREATOR'S LIFEPLAN!*
*BACK IN FANTASTIC FOUR #138 --AL.
WELL--I HAVE HAD ENOUGH LECTURES!
YOUR ILK SPEAKS AS IF YOUR EVERY PIOUS UTTERANCE SHOULD BE ENGRAVED IN STONE-- SO STONE YOU SHALL BE..., NOW AND FOREVER!
JOSHUA --HEAR ME! I UNDERSTAND YOU! WE ARE, AS I ONCE SAID, TWO OF A KIND!
I, OF ALL MEN, KNOW WHAT IT IS TO BE SEDUCED BY A DARKLING POWER! I, OF ALL MEN, KNOW WHAT IT IS TO BE TEMPTED BY SIN!
AND I, OF ALL MEN--
--HAVE THE MEANS TO STOP YOU!

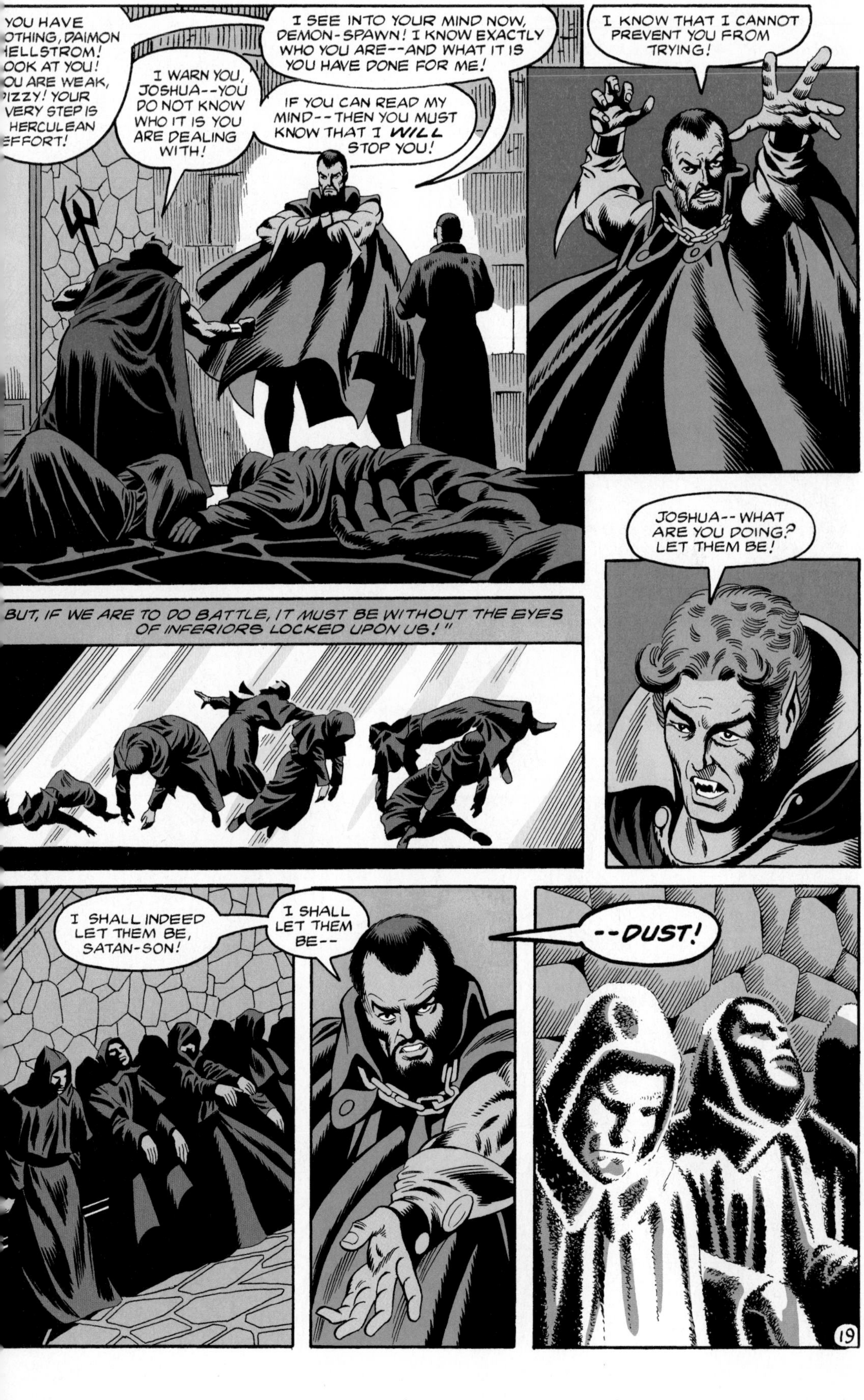
YOU HAVE OTHING, DAIMON HELLSTROM! OOK AT YOU! OU ARE WEAK, IZZY! YOUR VERY STEP IS HERCULEAN EFFORT!
I WARN YOU, JOSHUA--YOU DO NOT KNOW WHO IT IS YOU ARE DEALING WITH!
I SEE INTO YOUR MIND NOW, DEMON-SPAWN! I KNOW EXACTLY WHO YOU ARE--AND WHAT IT IS YOU HAVE DONE FOR ME!
IF YOU CAN READ MY MIND--THEN YOU MUST KNOW THAT I WILL STOP YOU!
I KNOW THAT I CANNOT PREVENT YOU FROM TRYING!
BUT, IF WE ARE TO DO BATTLE, IT MUST BE WITHOUT THE EYES OF INFERIORS LOCKED UPON US!"
JOSHUA--WHAT ARE YOU DOING? LET THEM BE!
I SHALL INDEED LET THEM BE, SATAN-SON!
I SHALL LET THEM BE--
--DUST!
19

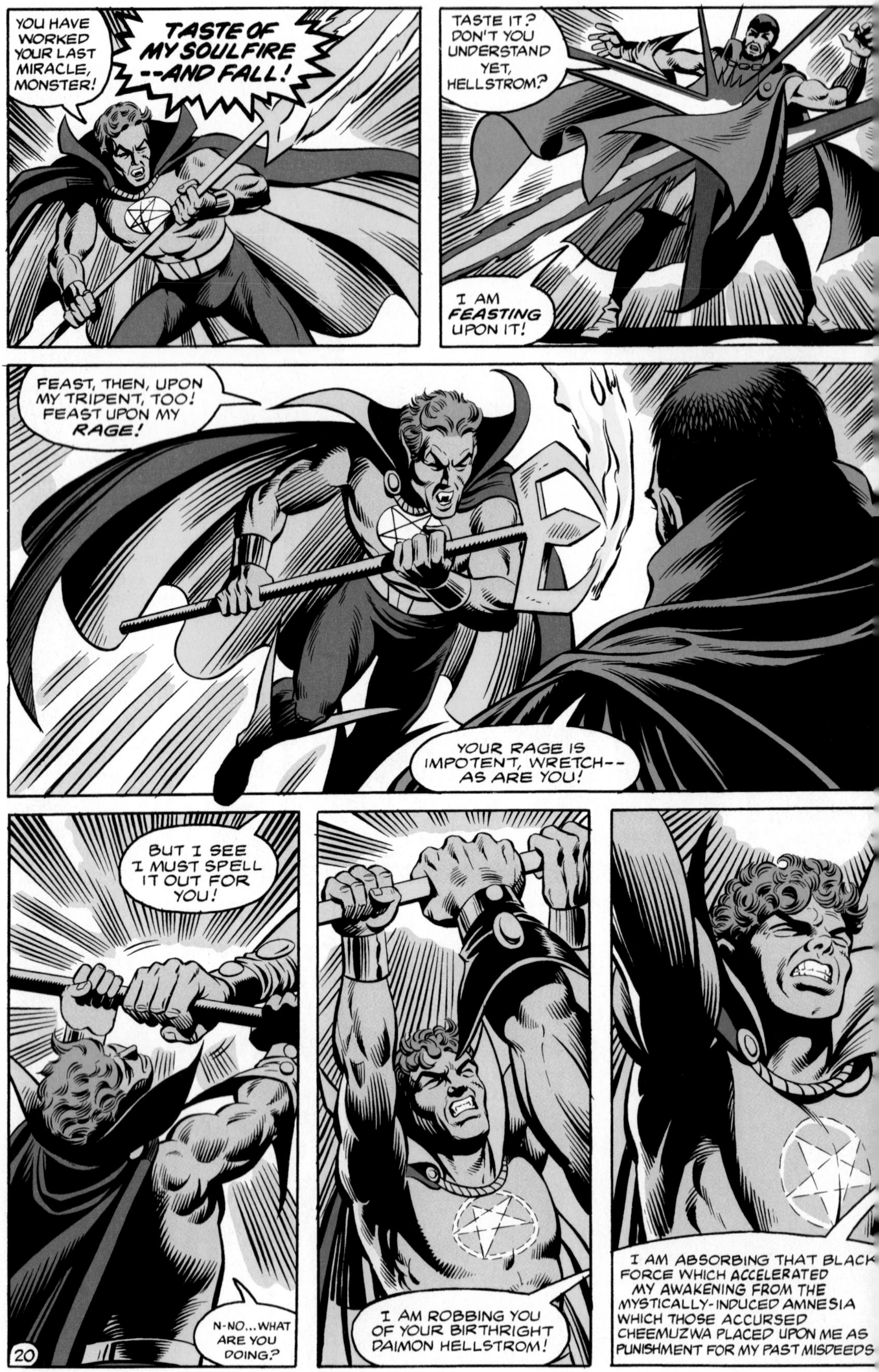
YOU HAVE WORKED YOUR LAST MIRACLE, MONSTER!
TASTE OF MY SOULFIRE --AND FALL!
TASTE IT? DON'T YOU UNDERSTAND YET, HELLSTROM?
I AM FEASTING UPON IT!
FEAST, THEN, UPON MY TRIDENT, TOO! FEAST UPON MY RAGE!
YOUR RAGE IS IMPOTENT, WRETCH-- AS ARE YOU!
BUT I SEE I MUST SPELL IT OUT FOR YOU!
N-NO... WHAT ARE YOU DOING?
20
I AM ROBBING YOU OF YOUR BIRTHRIGHT DAIMON HELLSTROM!
I AM ABSORBING THAT BLACK FORCE WHICH ACCELERATED MY AWAKENING FROM THE MYSTICALLY-INDUCED AMNESIA WHICH THOSE ACCURSED CHEEMUZWA PLACED UPON ME AS PUNISHMENT FOR MY PAST MISDEEDS

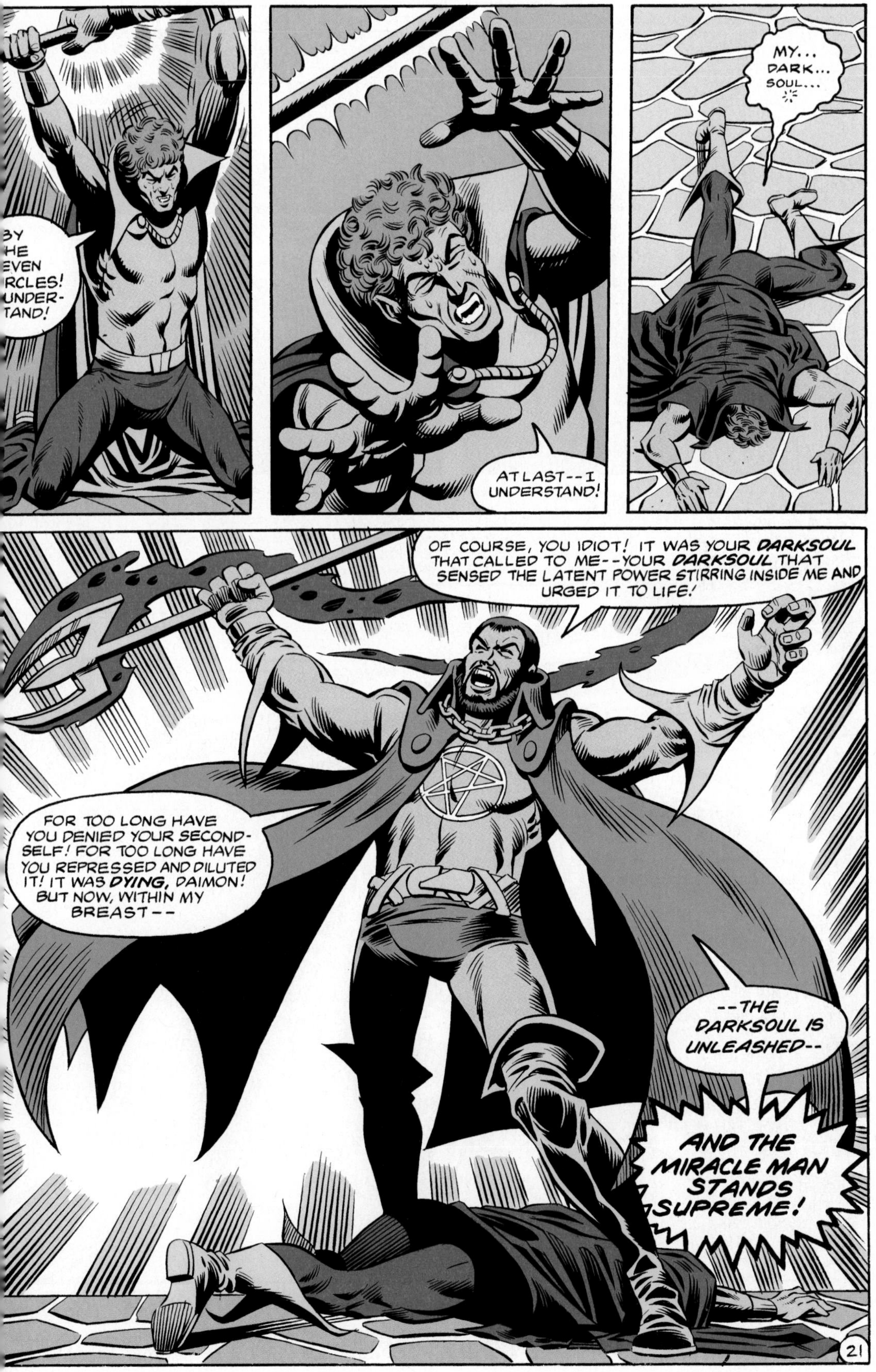
BY
THE
SEVEN
CIRCLES!
I UNDER-
STAND!
AT LAST--I UNDERSTAND!
MY... DARK... SOUL...
OF COURSE, YOU IDIOT! IT WAS YOUR DARKSOUL THAT CALLED TO ME--YOUR DARKSOUL THAT SENSED THE LATENT POWER STIRRING INSIDE ME AND URGED IT TO LIFE!
FOR TOO LONG HAVE YOU DENIED YOUR SECOND-SELF! FOR TOO LONG HAVE YOU REPRESSED AND DILUTED IT! IT WAS DYING, DAIMON! BUT NOW, WITHIN MY BREAST--
--THE DARKSOUL IS UNLEASHED--
AND THE MIRACLE MAN STANDS SUPREME!
21

ELSEWHERE--A HASTILY-BORROWED AVENGERS QUINJET ARCS GRACEFULLY THROUGH THE STARLIT SKY.

IT'S A BEAUTIFUL SIGHT...MOONLIGHT GLINTING OFF THE SHIP'S SURFACE, ITS SLEEK SILVERY FORM DOING AIR-DANCES OVER THE EAST RIVER.

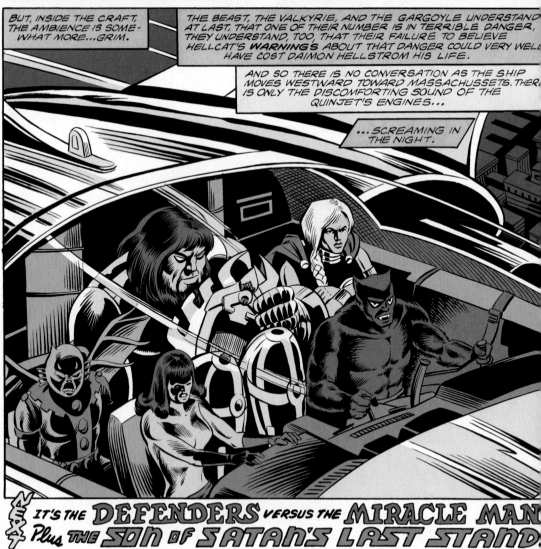

BUT, INSIDE THE CRAFT, THE AMBIENCE IS SOMEWHAT MORE...GRIM.

THE BEAST, THE VALKYRIE, AND THE GARGOYLE UNDERSTAND AT LAST, THAT ONE OF THEIR NUMBER IS IN TERRIBLE DANGER, THEY UNDERSTAND, TOO, THAT THEIR FAILURE TO BELIEVE HELLCAT'S *WARNINGS* ABOUT THAT DANGER COULD VERY WELL HAVE COST DAIMON HELLSTROM HIS LIFE.

AND SO THERE IS NO CONVERSATION AS THE SHIP MOVES WESTWARD TOWARD MASSACHUSSETS. THERE IS ONLY THE DISCOMFORTING SOUND OF THE QUINJET'S ENGINES...

...SCREAMING IN THE NIGHT.

NEXT: IT'S THE **DEFENDERS** VERSUS THE **MIRACLE MAN** Plus THE **SON** OF **SATAN'S LAST STAND!**

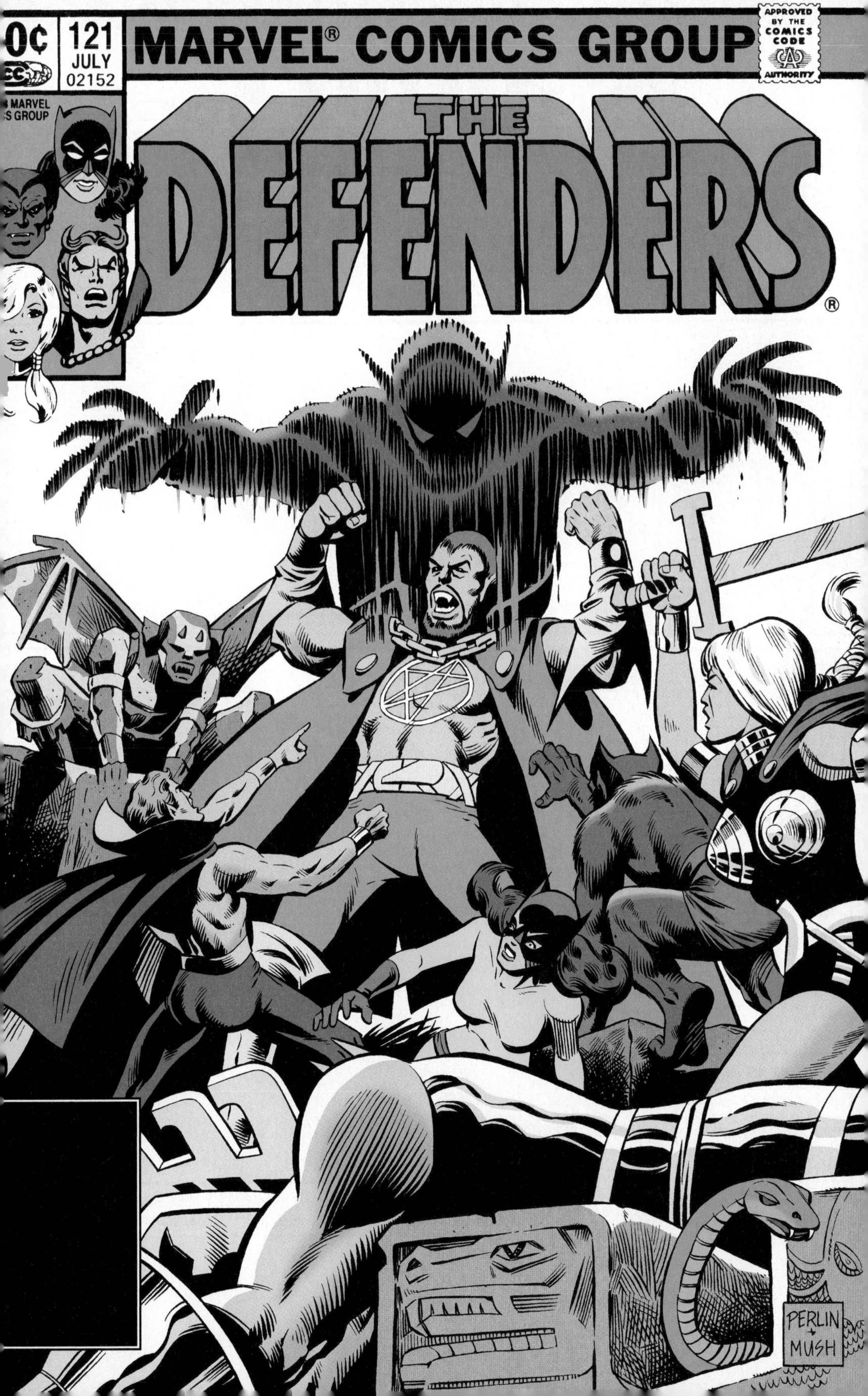
0¢
121
JULY
02152
MARVEL® COMICS GROUP
APPROVED BY THE COMICS CODE AUTHORITY
THE
DEFENDERS®
PERLIN + MUSH

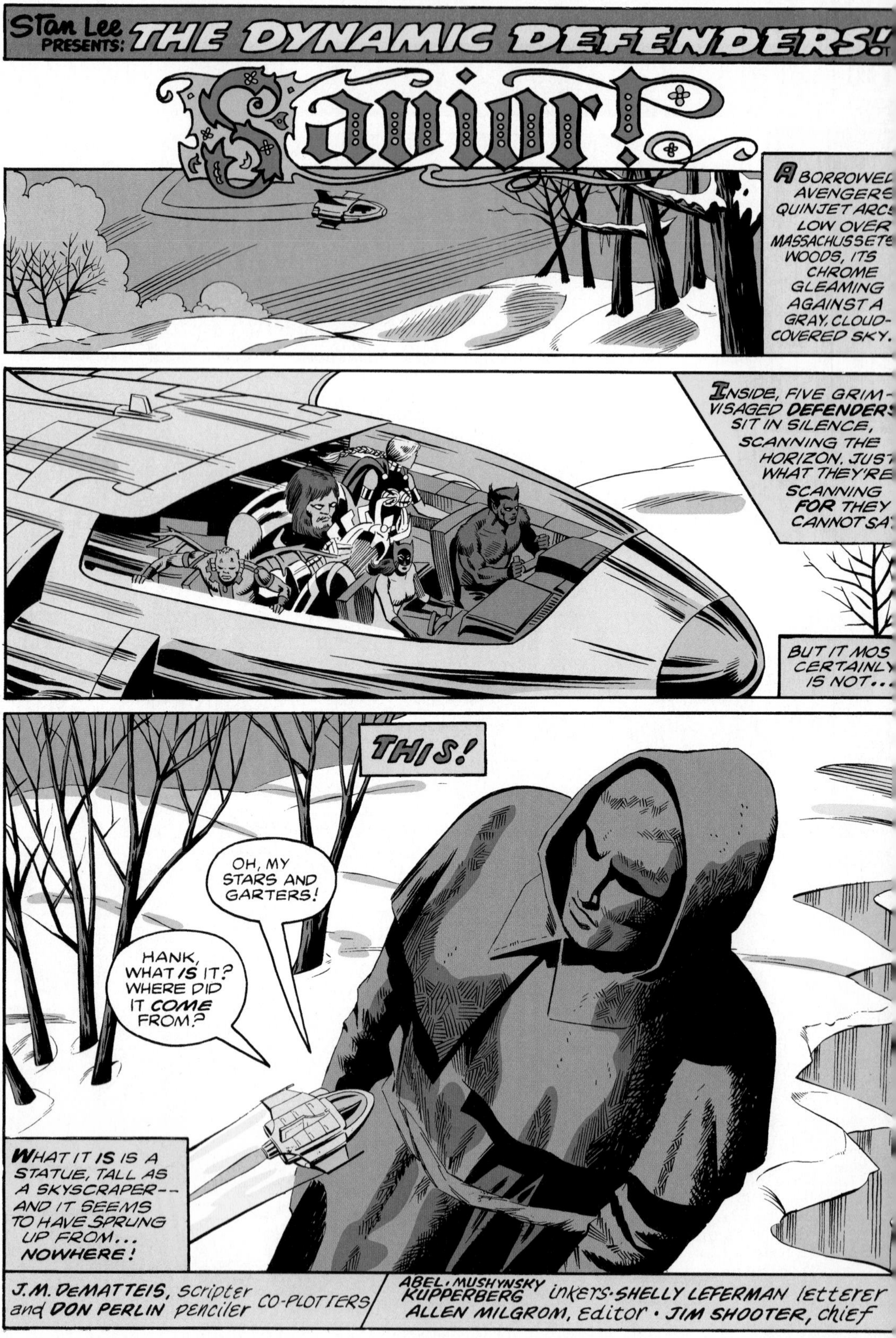

Stan Lee PRESENTS: THE DYNAMIC DEFENDERS!
Savior!
A BORROWED AVENGERS QUINJET ARCS LOW OVER MASSACHUSETTS WOODS, ITS CHROME GLEAMING AGAINST A GRAY, CLOUD-COVERED SKY.
INSIDE, FIVE GRIM-VISAGED DEFENDERS SIT IN SILENCE, SCANNING THE HORIZON. JUST WHAT THEY'RE SCANNING FOR THEY CANNOT SAY.
BUT IT MOST CERTAINLY IS NOT...
THIS!
OH, MY STARS AND GARTERS!
HANK, WHAT IS IT? WHERE DID IT COME FROM?
WHAT IT IS IS A STATUE, TALL AS A SKYSCRAPER-- AND IT SEEMS TO HAVE SPRUNG UP FROM... NOWHERE!
J.M. DeMATTEIS, scripter and DON PERLIN penciler CO-PLOTTERS
ABEL, MUSHYNSKY KUPPERBERG inkers · SHELLY LEFERMAN letterer
ALLEN MILGROM, Editor · JIM SHOOTER, chief

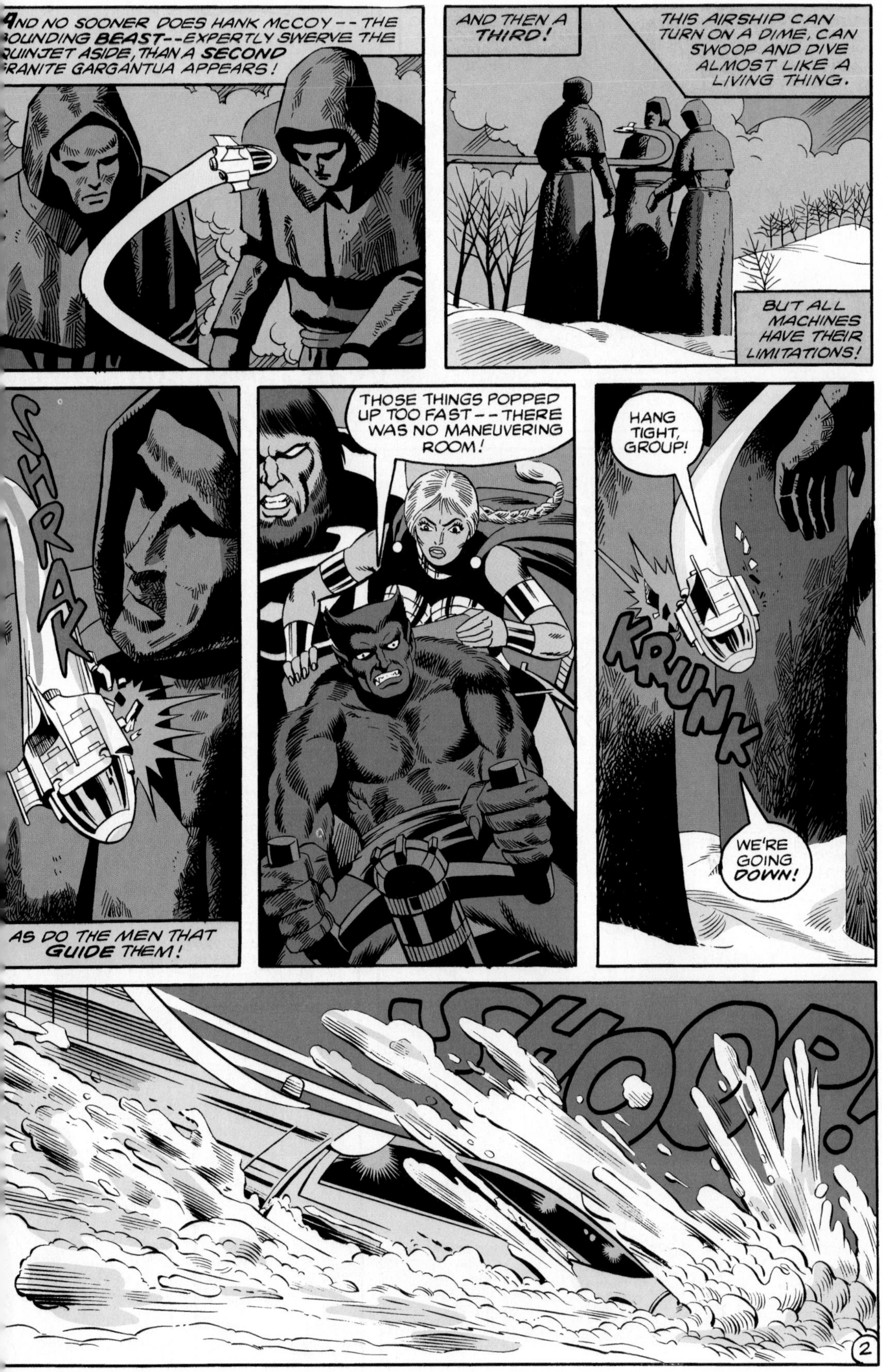
AND NO SOONER DOES HANK McCOY -- THE BOUNDING BEAST--EXPERTLY SWERVE THE QUINJET ASIDE, THAN A SECOND GRANITE GARGANTUA APPEARS!
AND THEN A THIRD!
THIS AIRSHIP CAN TURN ON A DIME, CAN SWOOP AND DIVE ALMOST LIKE A LIVING THING.
BUT ALL MACHINES HAVE THEIR LIMITATIONS!
SHRAK
AS DO THE MEN THAT GUIDE THEM!
THOSE THINGS POPPED UP TOO FAST -- THERE WAS NO MANEUVERING ROOM!
HANG TIGHT, GROUP!
KRUNK
WE'RE GOING DOWN!
SHOOP!
2

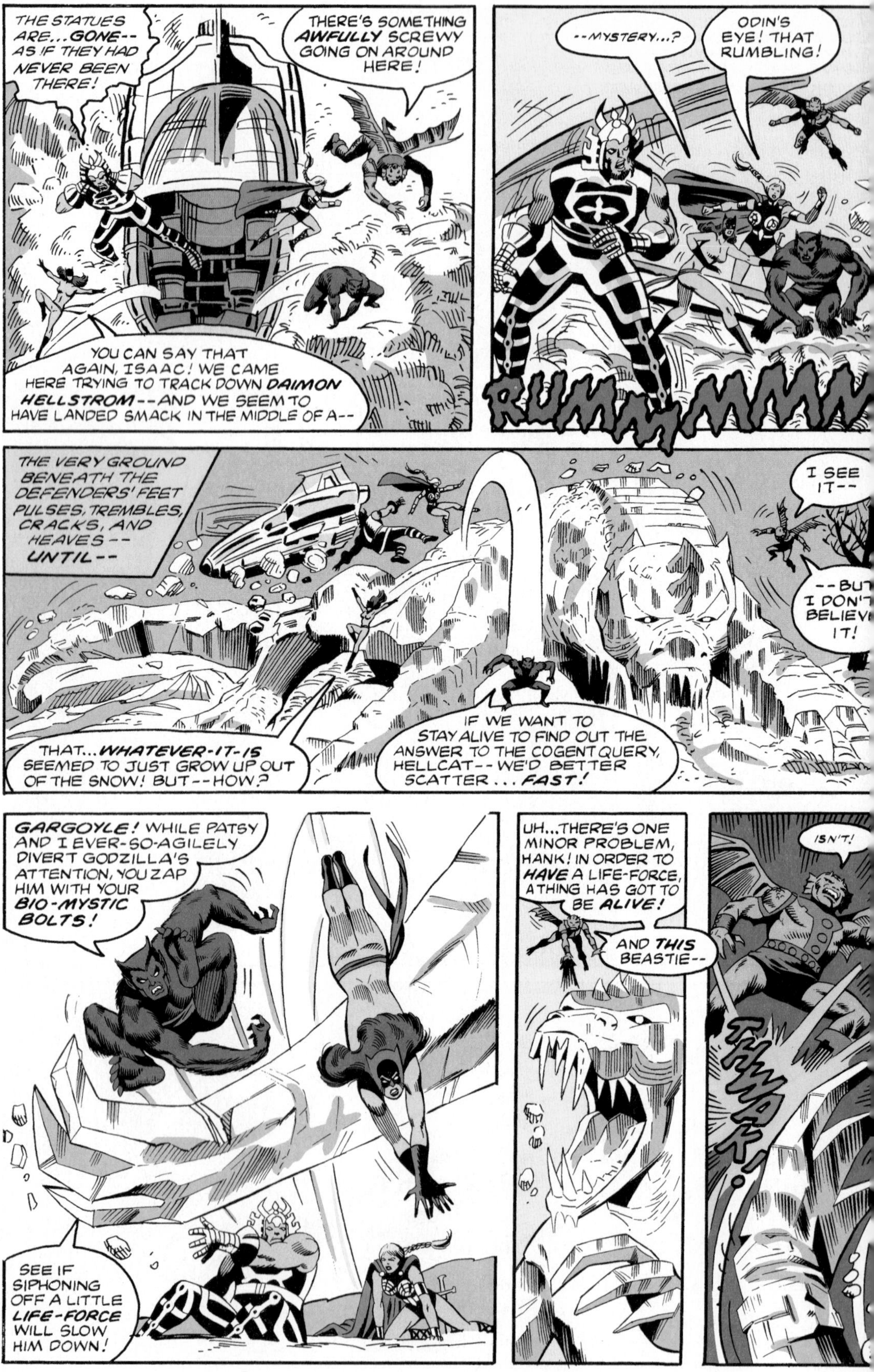
THE STATUES ARE... GONE-- AS IF THEY HAD NEVER BEEN THERE!
THERE'S SOMETHING AWFULLY SCREWY GOING ON AROUND HERE!
YOU CAN SAY THAT AGAIN, ISAAC! WE CAME HERE TRYING TO TRACK DOWN DAIMON HELLSTROM--AND WE SEEM TO HAVE LANDED SMACK IN THE MIDDLE OF A--
--MYSTERY...?
ODIN'S EYE! THAT RUMBLING!
RUMMMMMN
THE VERY GROUND BENEATH THE DEFENDERS' FEET PULSES, TREMBLES, CRACKS, AND HEAVES -- UNTIL--
I SEE IT--
--BUT I DON'T BELIEVE IT!
THAT... WHATEVER-IT-IS SEEMED TO JUST GROW UP OUT OF THE SNOW! BUT--HOW?
IF WE WANT TO STAY ALIVE TO FIND OUT THE ANSWER TO THE COGENT QUERY, HELLCAT-- WE'D BETTER SCATTER... FAST!
GARGOYLE! WHILE PATSY AND I EVER-SO-AGILELY DIVERT GODZILLA'S ATTENTION, YOU ZAP HIM WITH YOUR BIO-MYSTIC BOLTS!
SEE IF SIPHONING OFF A LITTLE LIFE-FORCE WILL SLOW HIM DOWN!
UH...THERE'S ONE MINOR PROBLEM, HANK! IN ORDER TO HAVE A LIFE-FORCE, A THING HAS GOT TO BE ALIVE!
AND THIS BEASTIE--
ISN'T!
THWAK!

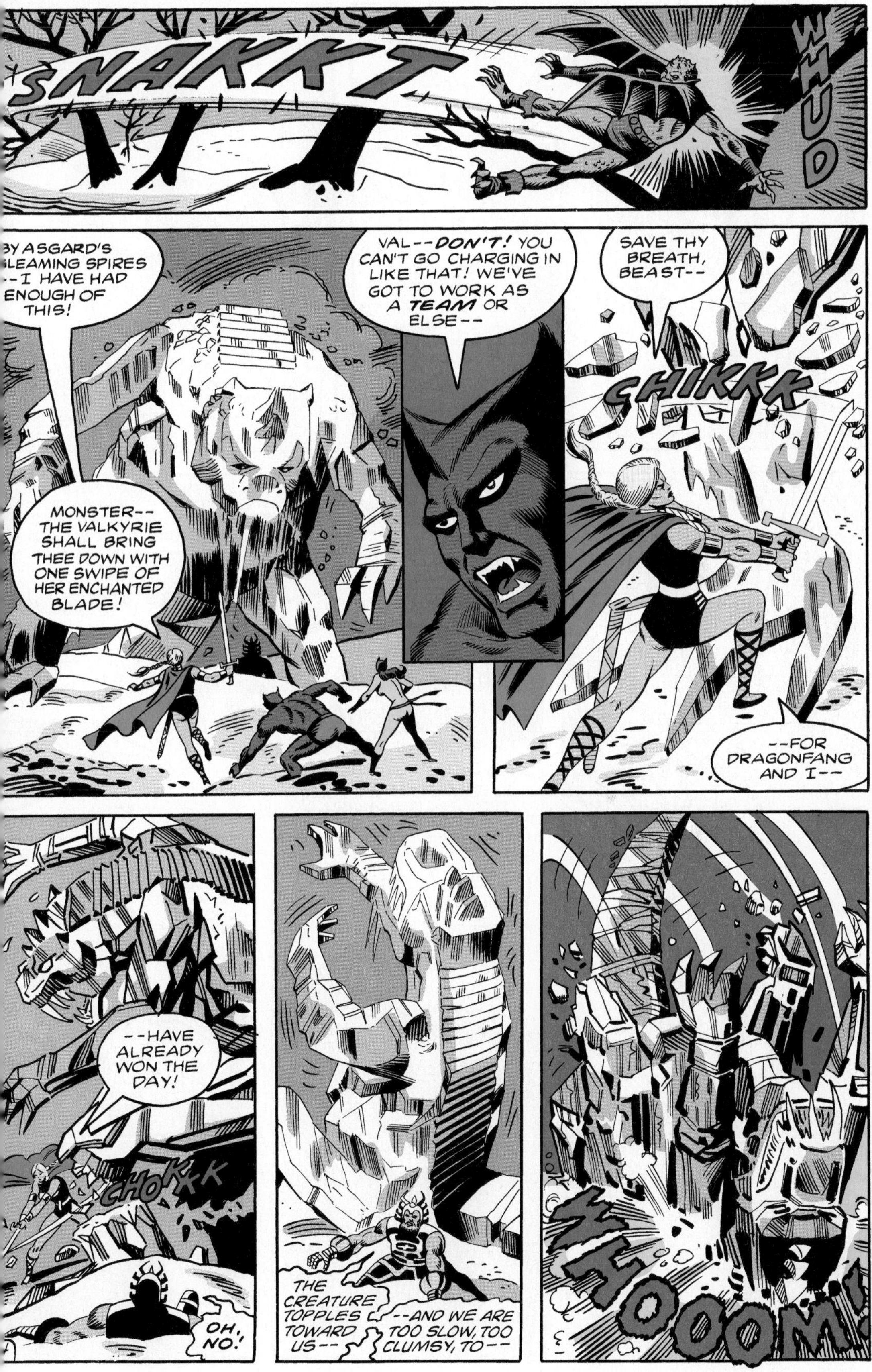
SNAKKT
WHUD
BY ASGARD'S GLEAMING SPIRES--I HAVE HAD ENOUGH OF THIS!
MONSTER--THE VALKYRIE SHALL BRING THEE DOWN WITH ONE SWIPE OF HER ENCHANTED BLADE!
VAL--DON'T! YOU CAN'T GO CHARGING IN LIKE THAT! WE'VE GOT TO WORK AS A TEAM OR ELSE--
SAVE THY BREATH, BEAST--
CHIKKK
--FOR DRAGONFANG AND I--
--HAVE ALREADY WON THE DAY!
CHOKKK
OH, NO!
THE CREATURE TOPPLES TOWARD US--
--AND WE ARE TOO SLOW, TOO CLUMSY, TO--
WHOOOM!

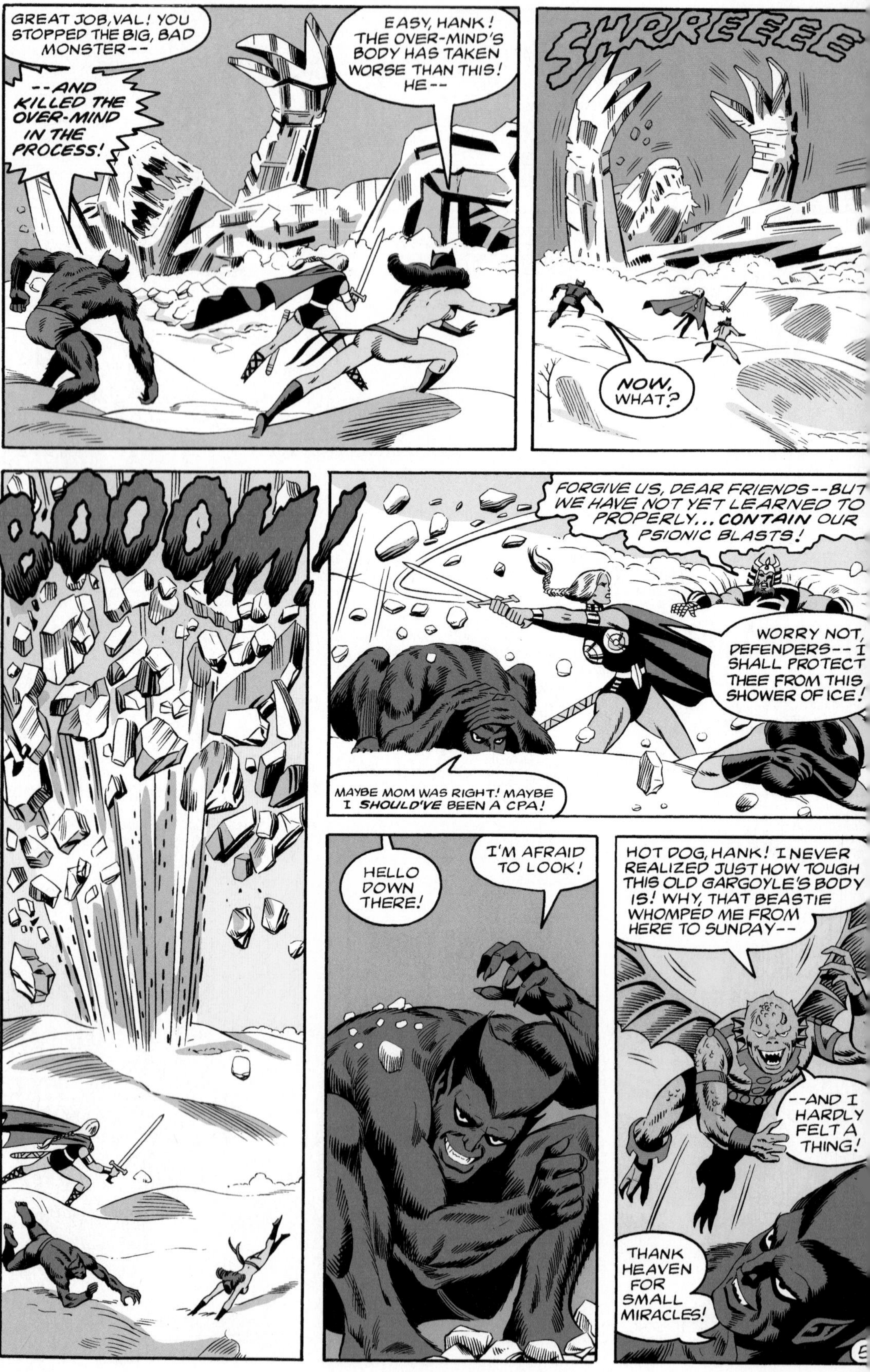
GREAT JOB, VAL! YOU STOPPED THE BIG, BAD MONSTER--
--AND KILLED THE OVER-MIND IN THE PROCESS!
EASY, HANK! THE OVER-MIND'S BODY HAS TAKEN WORSE THAN THIS! HE--
SHREEEEE
NOW, WHAT?
BOOOM!
FORGIVE US, DEAR FRIENDS--BUT WE HAVE NOT YET LEARNED TO PROPERLY... CONTAIN OUR PSIONIC BLASTS!
WORRY NOT, DEFENDERS--I SHALL PROTECT THEE FROM THIS SHOWER OF ICE!
MAYBE MOM WAS RIGHT! MAYBE I SHOULD'VE BEEN A CPA!
HELLO DOWN THERE!
I'M AFRAID TO LOOK!
HOT DOG, HANK! I NEVER REALIZED JUST HOW TOUGH THIS OLD GARGOYLE'S BODY IS! WHY, THAT BEASTIE WHOMPED ME FROM HERE TO SUNDAY--
--AND I HARDLY FELT A THING!
THANK HEAVEN FOR SMALL MIRACLES!
5

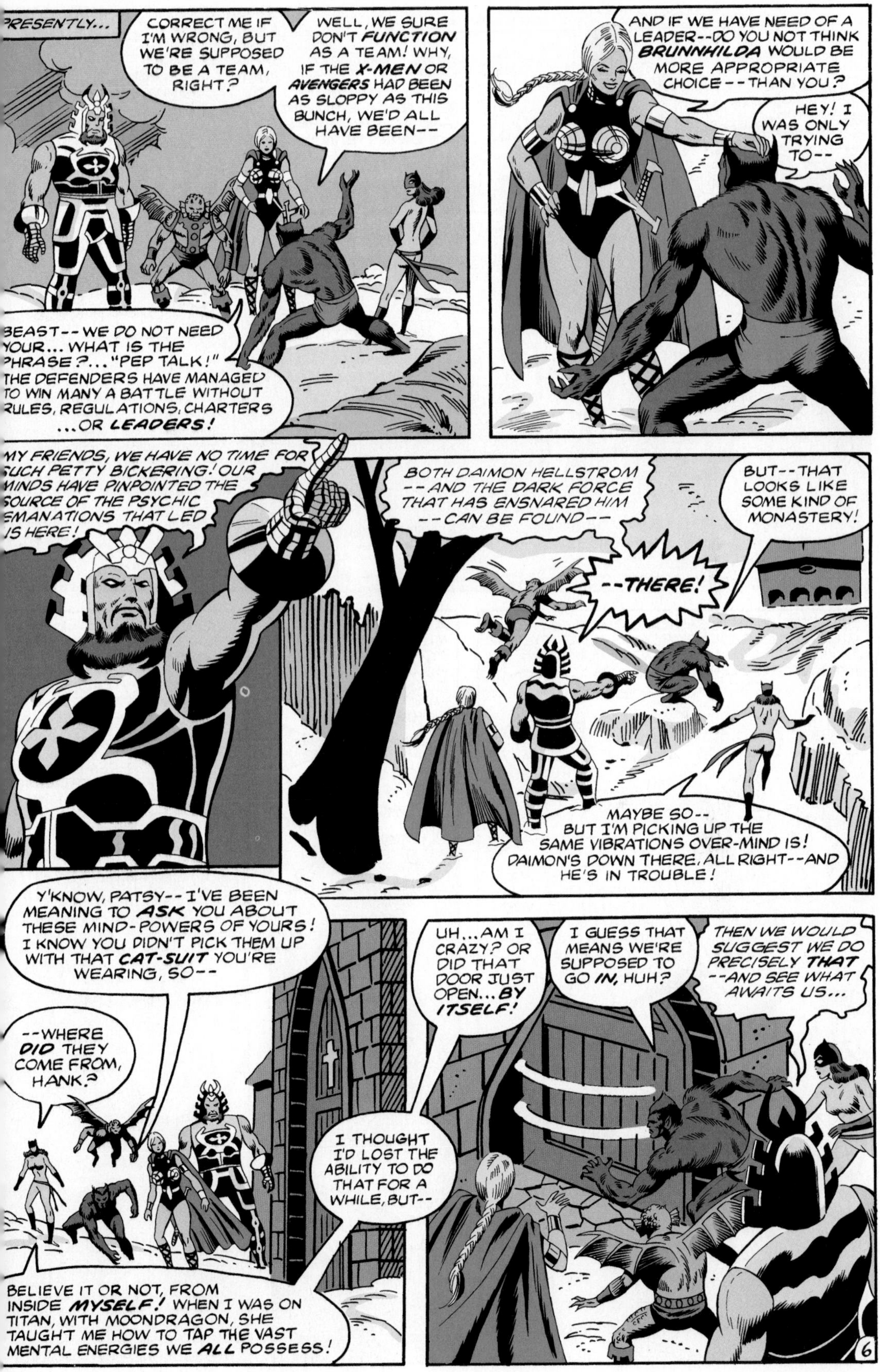
PRESENTLY...
CORRECT ME IF I'M WRONG, BUT WE'RE SUPPOSED TO BE A TEAM, RIGHT?
WELL, WE SURE DON'T FUNCTION AS A TEAM! WHY, IF THE X-MEN OR AVENGERS HAD BEEN AS SLOPPY AS THIS BUNCH, WE'D ALL HAVE BEEN--
BEAST--WE DO NOT NEED YOUR... WHAT IS THE PHRASE?... "PEP TALK!" THE DEFENDERS HAVE MANAGED TO WIN MANY A BATTLE WITHOUT RULES, REGULATIONS, CHARTERS ...OR LEADERS!
AND IF WE HAVE NEED OF A LEADER--DO YOU NOT THINK BRUNNHILDA WOULD BE MORE APPROPRIATE CHOICE--THAN YOU?
HEY! I WAS ONLY TRYING TO--
MY FRIENDS, WE HAVE NO TIME FOR SUCH PETTY BICKERING! OUR MINDS HAVE PINPOINTED THE SOURCE OF THE PSYCHIC EMANATIONS THAT LED US HERE!
BOTH DAIMON HELLSTROM --AND THE DARK FORCE THAT HAS ENSNARED HIM --CAN BE FOUND--
--THERE!
BUT--THAT LOOKS LIKE SOME KIND OF MONASTERY!
MAYBE SO-- BUT I'M PICKING UP THE SAME VIBRATIONS OVER-MIND IS! DAIMON'S DOWN THERE, ALL RIGHT--AND HE'S IN TROUBLE!
Y'KNOW, PATSY--I'VE BEEN MEANING TO ASK YOU ABOUT THESE MIND-POWERS OF YOURS! I KNOW YOU DIDN'T PICK THEM UP WITH THAT CAT-SUIT YOU'RE WEARING, SO--
--WHERE DID THEY COME FROM, HANK?
BELIEVE IT OR NOT, FROM INSIDE MYSELF! WHEN I WAS ON TITAN, WITH MOONDRAGON, SHE TAUGHT ME HOW TO TAP THE VAST MENTAL ENERGIES WE ALL POSSESS!
UH...AM I CRAZY? OR DID THAT DOOR JUST OPEN...BY ITSELF!
I THOUGHT I'D LOST THE ABILITY TO DO THAT FOR A WHILE, BUT--
I GUESS THAT MEANS WE'RE SUPPOSED TO GO IN, HUH?
THEN WE WOULD SUGGEST WE DO PRECISELY THAT --AND SEE WHAT AWAITS US...
6

"...ON THE OTHER SIDE!"

GREETINGS, MY FRIENDS! GREETINGS!

I COULD SENSE YOUR COMING --AND SO PREPARED A PROPER FETE IN YOUR HONOR!

WELL, DON'T JUS STAND THERE-- COME IN! COME IN

WE FEEL WAVES OF INCREDIBLE POWER RADIATING FROM THIS ONE! HE IS THE SOURCE OF EVIL; THE FOCAL POINT WE HAVE BEEN SEARCHING FOR!

THEN WHY DO WE DALLY? LET US ATTACK... NOW!

VAL-- WILL YOU RELAX! WE'RE DEALING WITH UNKNOWNS HERE! LET'S TAKE THINGS ONE STEP AT A TIME!

A SPLENDID IDEA, MISTER McCOY! OR DO YOU PREFER ... BEAST? AH, YES! I KNOW YOU ALL! AND YOU-- SHALL KNOW ME!

FOR I AM-- THE MIRACLE MAN!

MIRACLE MAN?! HANK-- I READ UP ON HIM BACK IN MY AVENGERS DAYS! HE'S AN ALL-POWERFUL LUNATIC WHO NEARLY TROUNCED THE FANTASTIC FOUR A COUPLE OF TIMES!

YEAH... I REMEMBER THE THING TELLING ME ABOUT HIM ONCE --AT A POKER GAME!

...AND NO DOUBT WHAT HE TOLD YOU WAS *TRUE!* BUT THAT WAS THE MAN I ONCE *WAS*...A DELUDED MEGALOMANIAC WHOSE FRAGILE EGO COULD NOT HANDLE THE EARTH-SHATTERING POWERS BESTOWED UPON HIM BY THE INDIAN MYSTICS CALLED *THE CHEEMUZWA!*

THAT MAN--IS NO MORE! FOR HERE, IN THIS MONASTERY, I HAVE BEEN...*REBORN!*

GLAD T'HEAR IT. NOW DO YOU MIND TELLING US WHERE IN BLAZES *DAIMON HELLSTROM* IS?

YOU MEAN THE SO-CALLED *SON OF SATAN?* STEP THIS WAY--AND I'LL GLADLY TAKE YOU TO HIM!

NO, NO-- AFTER *YOU!*

HANK...?

VALKYRIE-- THOSE *MONKS--!*

I SEE, OVER-MIND! THEY SIT, BLANK-EYED, OPEN-MOUTHED, AS IF... ENTRANCED!

IT'S *HIS* GAME, PAT-- SO, FOR NOW, WE PLAY BY HIS *RULES!*

I BELIEVE THE ONE YOU'RE SEARCHING FOR IS RIGHT HERE!

BUT THAT-- IS A STATUE!

INDEED! I'M AFRAID I HAD NO RECOURSE BUT TO CHANGE HIM *INTO* ONE!

YOU *WHAT??* !!!

THERE, THERE, BEAST-- NO NEED TO GET SO EXCITED!

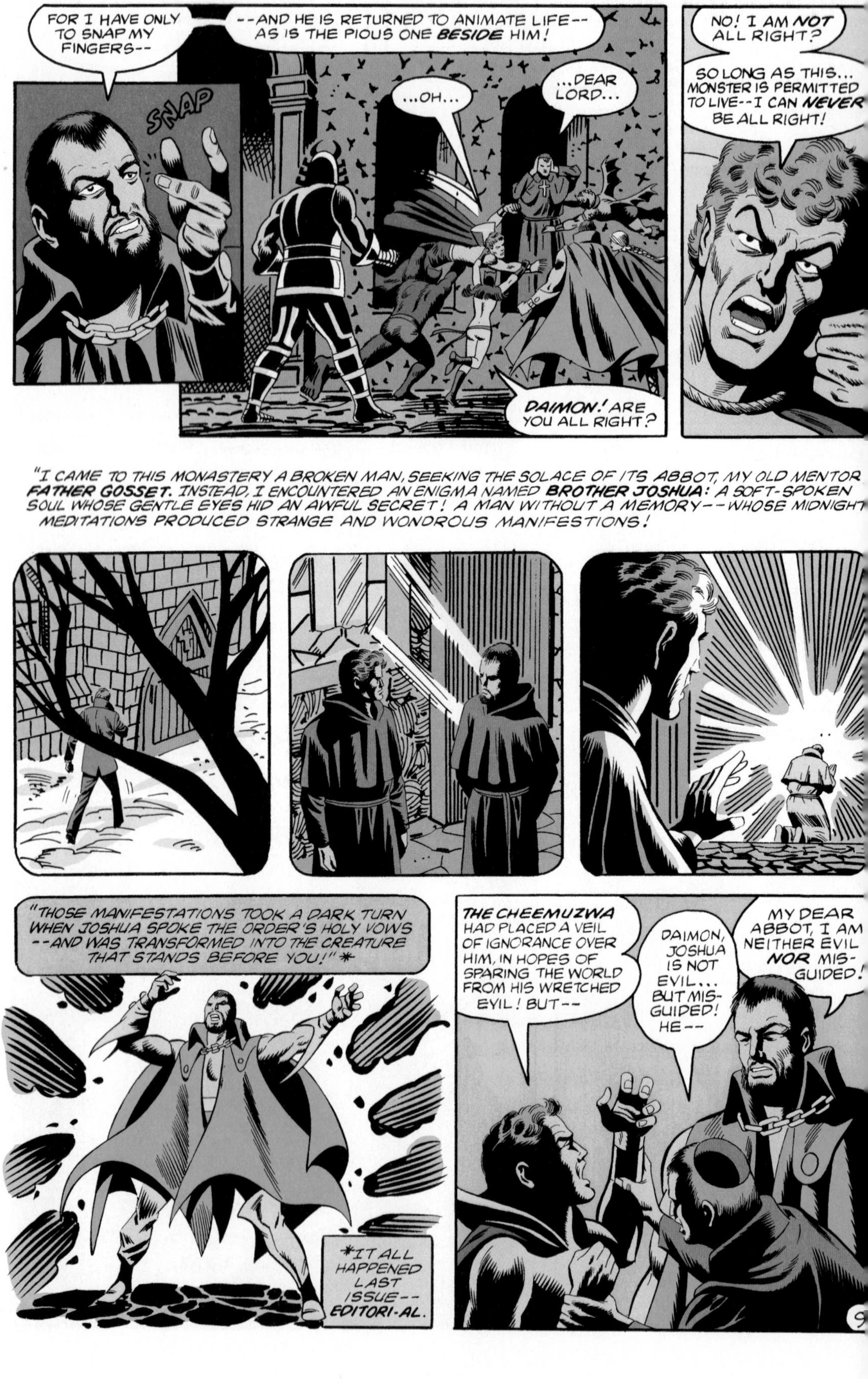
FOR I HAVE ONLY TO SNAP MY FINGERS--
--AND HE IS RETURNED TO ANIMATE LIFE-- AS IS THE PIOUS ONE BESIDE HIM!
SNAP
...OH...
...DEAR LORD...
DAIMON! ARE YOU ALL RIGHT?
NO! I AM NOT ALL RIGHT?
SO LONG AS THIS... MONSTER IS PERMITTED TO LIVE--I CAN NEVER BE ALL RIGHT!
"I CAME TO THIS MONASTERY A BROKEN MAN, SEEKING THE SOLACE OF ITS ABBOT, MY OLD MENTOR FATHER GOSSET. INSTEAD, I ENCOUNTERED AN ENIGMA NAMED BROTHER JOSHUA: A SOFT-SPOKEN SOUL WHOSE GENTLE EYES HID AN AWFUL SECRET! A MAN WITHOUT A MEMORY--WHOSE MIDNIGHT MEDITATIONS PRODUCED STRANGE AND WONDROUS MANIFESTIONS!
"THOSE MANIFESTATIONS TOOK A DARK TURN WHEN JOSHUA SPOKE THE ORDER'S HOLY VOWS --AND WAS TRANSFORMED INTO THE CREATURE THAT STANDS BEFORE YOU!"*
*IT ALL HAPPENED LAST ISSUE--EDITORI-AL.
THE CHEEMUZWA HAD PLACED A VEIL OF IGNORANCE OVER HIM, IN HOPES OF SPARING THE WORLD FROM HIS WRETCHED EVIL! BUT--
DAIMON, JOSHUA IS NOT EVIL... BUT MIS-GUIDED! HE--
MY DEAR ABBOT, I AM NEITHER EVIL NOR MIS-GUIDED!
9

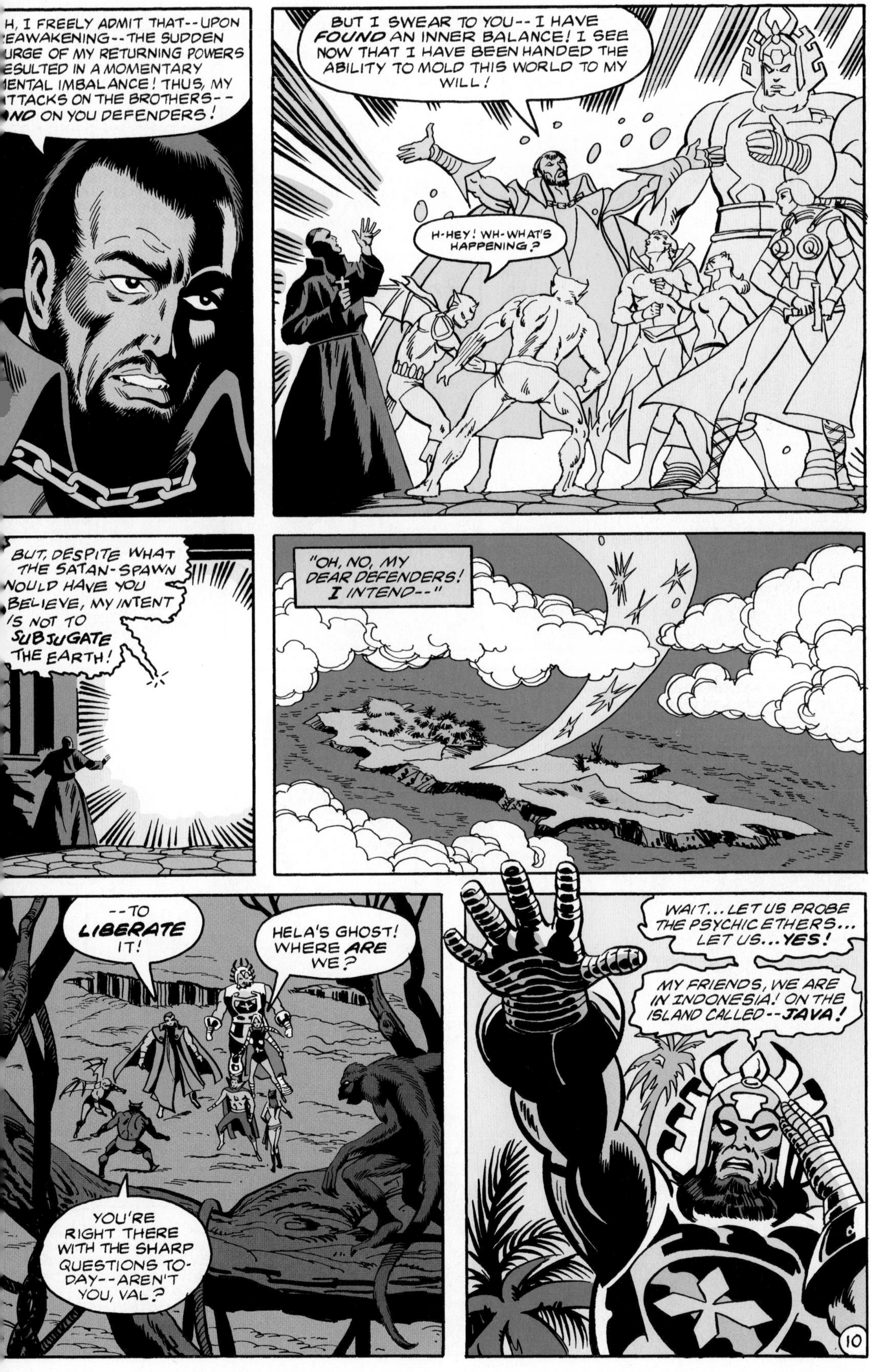
H, I FREELY ADMIT THAT--UPON
EAWAKENING--THE SUDDEN
URGE OF MY RETURNING POWERS
ESULTED IN A MOMENTARY
MENTAL IMBALANCE! THUS, MY
TTACKS ON THE BROTHERS--
ND ON YOU DEFENDERS!
BUT I SWEAR TO YOU--I HAVE FOUND AN INNER BALANCE! I SEE NOW THAT I HAVE BEEN HANDED THE ABILITY TO MOLD THIS WORLD TO MY WILL!
H-HEY! WH-WHAT'S HAPPENING?
BUT, DESPITE WHAT THE SATAN-SPAWN WOULD HAVE YOU BELIEVE, MY INTENT IS NOT TO SUBJUGATE THE EARTH!
"OH, NO, MY DEAR DEFENDERS! I INTEND--"
--TO LIBERATE IT!
HELA'S GHOST! WHERE ARE WE?
YOU'RE RIGHT THERE WITH THE SHARP QUESTIONS TO-DAY--AREN'T YOU, VAL?
WAIT... LET US PROBE THE PSYCHIC ETHERS... LET US... YES!
MY FRIENDS, WE ARE IN INDONESIA! ON THE ISLAND CALLED--JAVA!
10

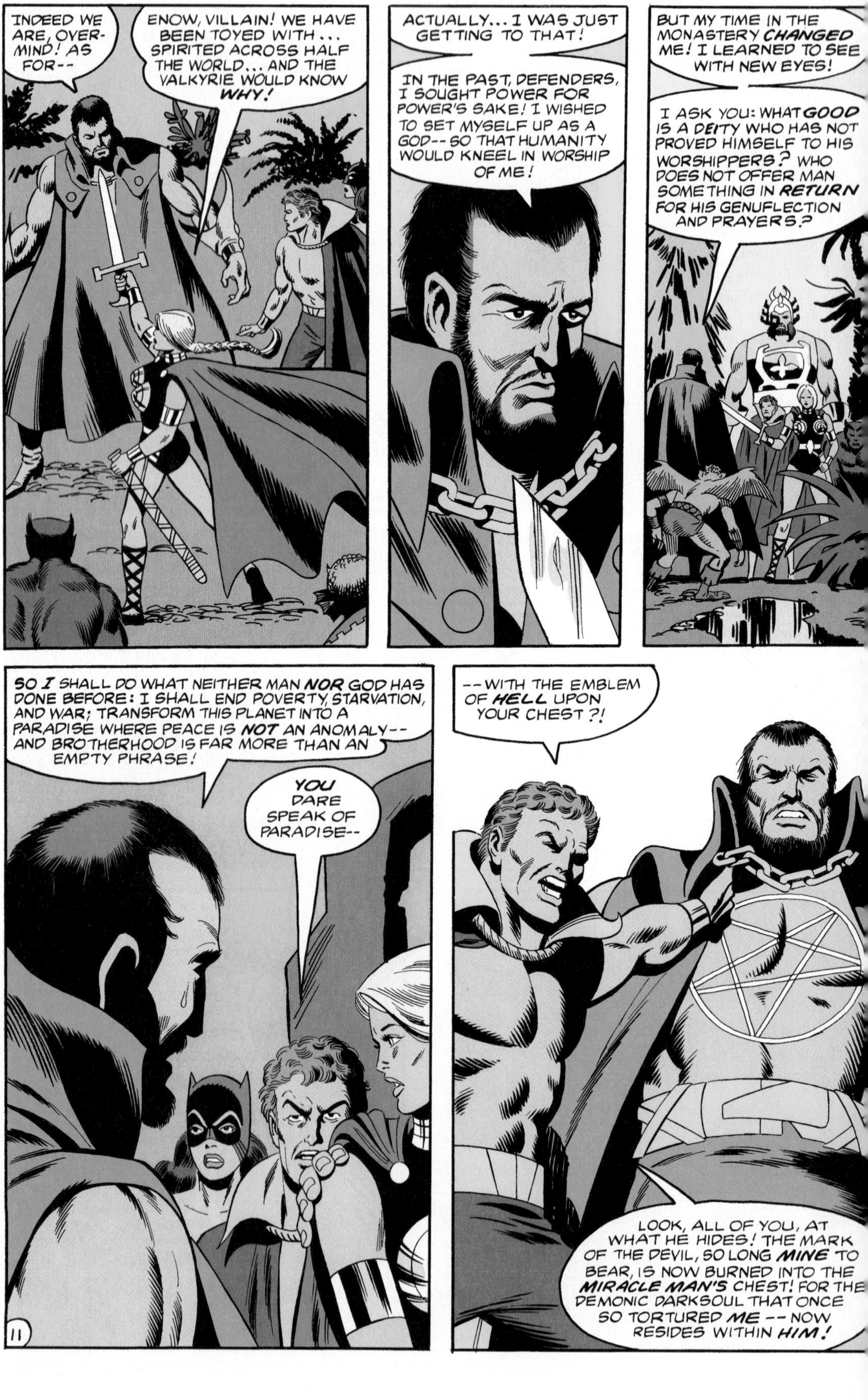
INDEED WE ARE, OVER-MIND! AS FOR--
ENOW, VILLAIN! WE HAVE BEEN TOYED WITH... SPIRITED ACROSS HALF THE WORLD... AND THE VALKYRIE WOULD KNOW WHY!
ACTUALLY... I WAS JUST GETTING TO THAT!
IN THE PAST, DEFENDERS, I SOUGHT POWER FOR POWER'S SAKE! I WISHED TO SET MYSELF UP AS A GOD-- SO THAT HUMANITY WOULD KNEEL IN WORSHIP OF ME!
BUT MY TIME IN THE MONASTERY CHANGED ME! I LEARNED TO SEE WITH NEW EYES!
I ASK YOU: WHAT GOOD IS A DEITY WHO HAS NOT PROVED HIMSELF TO HIS WORSHIPPERS? WHO DOES NOT OFFER MAN SOMETHING IN RETURN FOR HIS GENUFLECTION AND PRAYERS?
SO I SHALL DO WHAT NEITHER MAN NOR GOD HAS DONE BEFORE: I SHALL END POVERTY, STARVATION, AND WAR; TRANSFORM THIS PLANET INTO A PARADISE WHERE PEACE IS NOT AN ANOMALY-- AND BROTHERHOOD IS FAR MORE THAN AN EMPTY PHRASE!
YOU DARE SPEAK OF PARADISE--
--WITH THE EMBLEM OF HELL UPON YOUR CHEST?!
LOOK, ALL OF YOU, AT WHAT HE HIDES! THE MARK OF THE DEVIL, SO LONG MINE TO BEAR, IS NOW BURNED INTO THE MIRACLE MAN'S CHEST! FOR THE DEMONIC DARKSOUL THAT ONCE SO TORTURED ME -- NOW RESIDES WITHIN HIM!
11

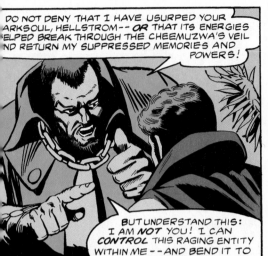

DO NOT DENY THAT I HAVE USURPED YOUR DARKSOUL, HELLSTROM-- *OR* THAT ITS ENERGIES HELPED BREAK THROUGH THE CHEEMUZWA'S VEIL AND RETURN MY SUPPRESSED MEMORIES AND POWERS!

BUT UNDERSTAND THIS: I AM *NOT* YOU! I CAN *CONTROL* THIS RAGING ENTITY WITHIN ME--AND BEND IT TO MY WILL!

WHY DO WE STAND HERE LISTENING TO THIS PARADE OF LIES? DEFENDERS --WE MUST BRING THIS ANIMAL DOWN!

BUT, HELLSTROM-- HE HAS NOT COMMITTED ANY TRUE CRIME!

WHAT.?!

I'M WITH OVER-MIND. WE WAIT. *FOR NOW.*

EXCELLENT! THEN PLEASE JOIN ME FOR A TOUR OF THIS SMALL SECTION OF POOR, BELEAGUERED JAVA--AND SEE THE PURGATORY I SHALL SOON... TRANSFORM!

WE WALK, DEFENDERS, THROUGH *RANNGKASBITUNG:* A COLLECTION OF VILLAGES SOME 150 MILES WEST OF JAKARTA.

THESE PEOPLE SUFFER FROM OVERPOPULATION... MALNUTRITION...LACK OF HOUSING! UP TO THREE FAMILIES ARE OFTEN CROWDED INTO ONE PATHETIC THATCHED HUT!

THEY HAVE NO ELECTRICITY! NO RUNNING WATER! THERE ARE ONLY 32 LATRINES TO PROVIDE FOR THE NEEDS OF 9,000 PEOPLE!

"IN SHORT: IT IS THE PERFECT TESTING GROUND FOR ME TO PROVE BOTH MY INTENTIONS --*AND* MY ABILITIES!"

WE WHO HAVE KNOWN SIMILAR AGONIES IN OUR FORMER LIVES-- CANNOT HELP BUT BE DEEPLY *MOVED* BY THIS!

HANK--DO YOU REALLY THINK HE *COULD* CHANGE THINGS HERE?

I DON'T KNOW, PATS. I JUST DON'T KNOW!

12

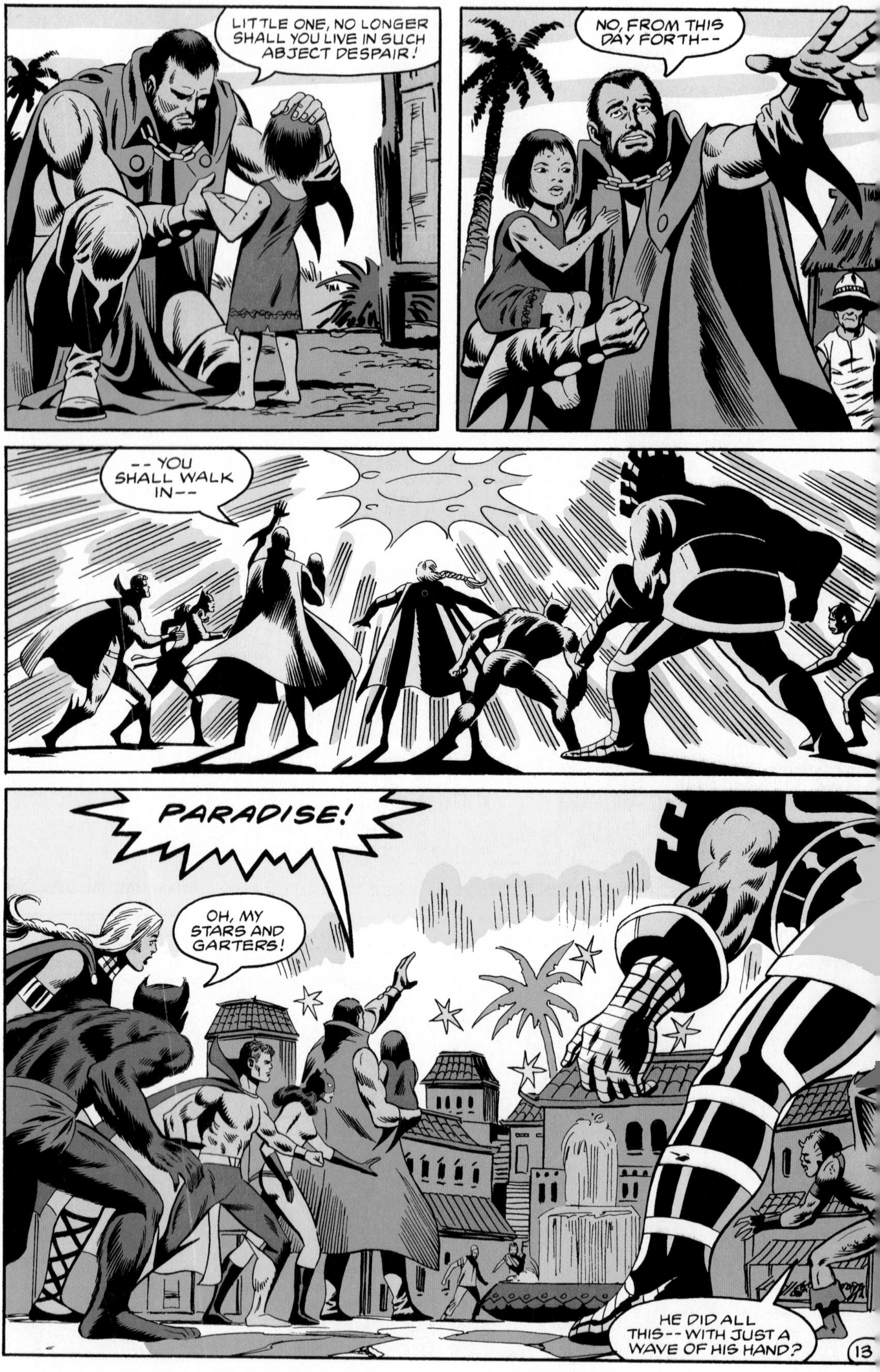
LITTLE ONE, NO LONGER SHALL YOU LIVE IN SUCH ABJECT DESPAIR!
NO, FROM THIS DAY FORTH--
--YOU SHALL WALK IN--
PARADISE!
OH, MY STARS AND GARTERS!
HE DID ALL THIS--WITH JUST A WAVE OF HIS HAND?
13

VALKYRIE--LISTEN TO THE JOYOUS CRIES OF THE PEOPLE! THEY SENSE THAT THE DOORS OF AN EARTHLY HEAVEN HAVE BEEN OPENED WIDE TO THEM; THAT THEY WILL NEVER AGAIN KNOW HUNGER...OR FEAR!

IF THE MIRACLE MAN COULD WORK SUCH WONDERMENT ALL ACROSS THE GLOBE-- IT COULD BE THE BEGINNING OF A VERITABLE... GOLDEN AGE!

OVER-MIND, YOU ARE YOUNG IN MANY WAYS! DO YOU NOT THINK ASGARD'S LORD ODIN COULD BRING SUCH A..."MIRACLE" ABOUT IF HE SO DESIRED? IT IS WELL WITHIN HIS REACH --BUT HE REFRAINS!

FOR WE GODS LEARNED LONG AGO THAT MAN MUST MAKE HIS OWN HEAVEN! TO HAVE IT IMPOSED UPON HIM FROM WITHOUT RESULTS ONLY IN CHAOS-- AND IN DEATH!

THE VALKYRIE SPEAKS WISELY! WE CAN'T ALLOW THIS TRAVESTY TO CONTINUE!

DAIMON, LOOK AROUND! LOOK AT THE HAPPINESS REFLECTED ON ALL THOSE FACES! DO WE HAVE THE RIGHT TO TAKE THIS AWAY FROM THEM--BECAUSE OF A VAGUE MORAL QUESTION?

I DON'T THINK IT'S SO VAGUE, PATSY! WHO ARE WE TO GO MUCKING AROUND WITH THE DIVINE PLAN?

I DON'T KNOW IF I EVEN BELIEVE IN ANY DIVINE PLAN, ISAAC-- BUT THERE'S SOMETHING ABOUT THIS THAT DOESN'T SIT RIGHT WITH ME!

SAVE YOUR DEBATES, DEFENDERS! THERE IS WORK YET TO BE DONE!

AN IMPERIOUS CLAP OF THE HANDS...

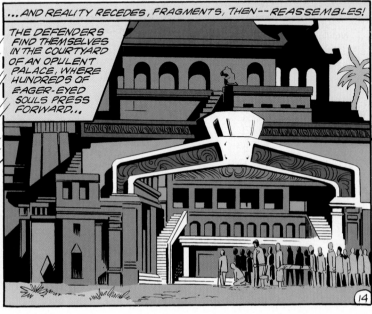

...AND REALITY RECEDES, FRAGMENTS, THEN--REASSEMBLES!

THE DEFENDERS FIND THEMSELVES IN THE COURTYARD OF AN OPULENT PALACE, WHERE HUNDREDS OF EAGER-EYED SOULS PRESS FORWARD...

14

311

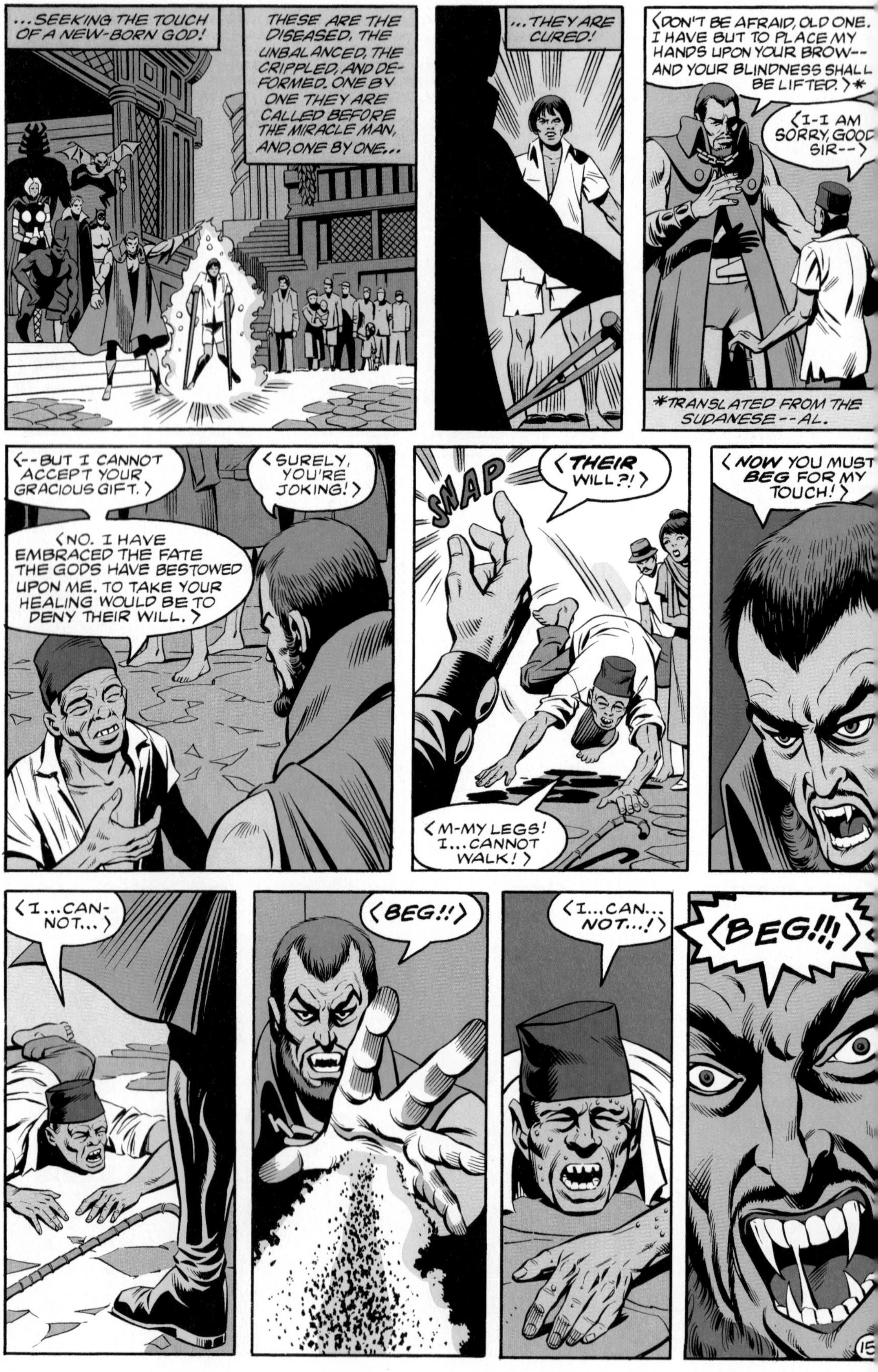
...SEEKING THE TOUCH OF A NEW-BORN GOD!
THESE ARE THE DISEASED, THE UNBALANCED, THE CRIPPLED, AND DEFORMED. ONE BY ONE THEY ARE CALLED BEFORE THE MIRACLE MAN, AND, ONE BY ONE...
...THEY ARE CURED!
⟨DON'T BE AFRAID, OLD ONE. I HAVE BUT TO PLACE MY HANDS UPON YOUR BROW-- AND YOUR BLINDNESS SHALL BE LIFTED.⟩*
⟨I-I AM SORRY, GOOD SIR--⟩
*TRANSLATED FROM THE SUDANESE--AL.
⟨--BUT I CANNOT ACCEPT YOUR GRACIOUS GIFT.⟩
⟨SURELY, YOU'RE JOKING!⟩
⟨NO. I HAVE EMBRACED THE FATE THE GODS HAVE BESTOWED UPON ME. TO TAKE YOUR HEALING WOULD BE TO DENY THEIR WILL.⟩
SNAP
⟨THEIR WILL?!⟩
⟨M-MY LEGS! I...CANNOT WALK!⟩
⟨NOW YOU MUST BEG FOR MY TOUCH!⟩
⟨I...CANNOT...⟩
⟨BEG!!⟩
⟨I...CAN...NOT...!⟩
⟨BEG!!!⟩
15

...UH...GROUP WE SEEM TO HAVE A MAJOR PROBLEM ON OUR HANDS!

INDEED. IT IS THE *DARKSOUL'S* INFLUENCE, FURTHER CORRUPTING HIM.

COULD BE. OR MAYBE IT'S JUST THAT OUT-OF-CONTROL *EGO* HE SAID HE'D TRANSCENDED!

GNAT! WHY DO YOU JUST LIE THERE? DOES YOUR LIFE MEAN SO *LITTLE* TO YOU?!

WE'RE WAY PAST THE POINT OF DISCUSSING DELICATE *MORAL* QUESTIONS! THIS GUY'S GONE OVER THE EDGE--AND WE'VE GOT TO STOP HIM BEFORE HE TAKES THIS WHOLE ISLAND WITH HIM!

BEAST...OUR OWN DESIRE FOR EASY ANSWERS DROVE US TO TAKE THE MIRACLE MAN AT FACE VALUE. NOW WE ASK THAT WE MAY BE THE ONES TO PUT A SWIFT END TO HIS INSANITY.

MAKES SENSE, O.M.! MIRACLE MAN'S POWER COMES FROM HIS MIND... AND YOU'RE THE BEST MIND-ZAPPER WE'VE GOT, SO...

...GO GET 'IM!

THE UNITED MINDS OF SIX OF EARTH'S MOST POWERFUL TELEPATHS CALL UP PSIONIC ENERGIES THAT COULD LAY WASTE A MOUNTAIN...

SHRAKKKK

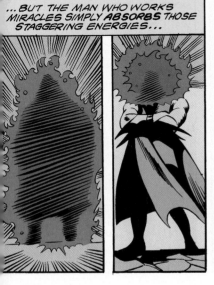

...BUT THE MAN WHO WORKS MIRACLES SIMPLY *ABSORBS* THOSE STAGGERING ENERGIES...

...AND SPITS THEM *BACK* IN THE OVER-MIND'S *FACE!*

SHOOOOM!

16

313

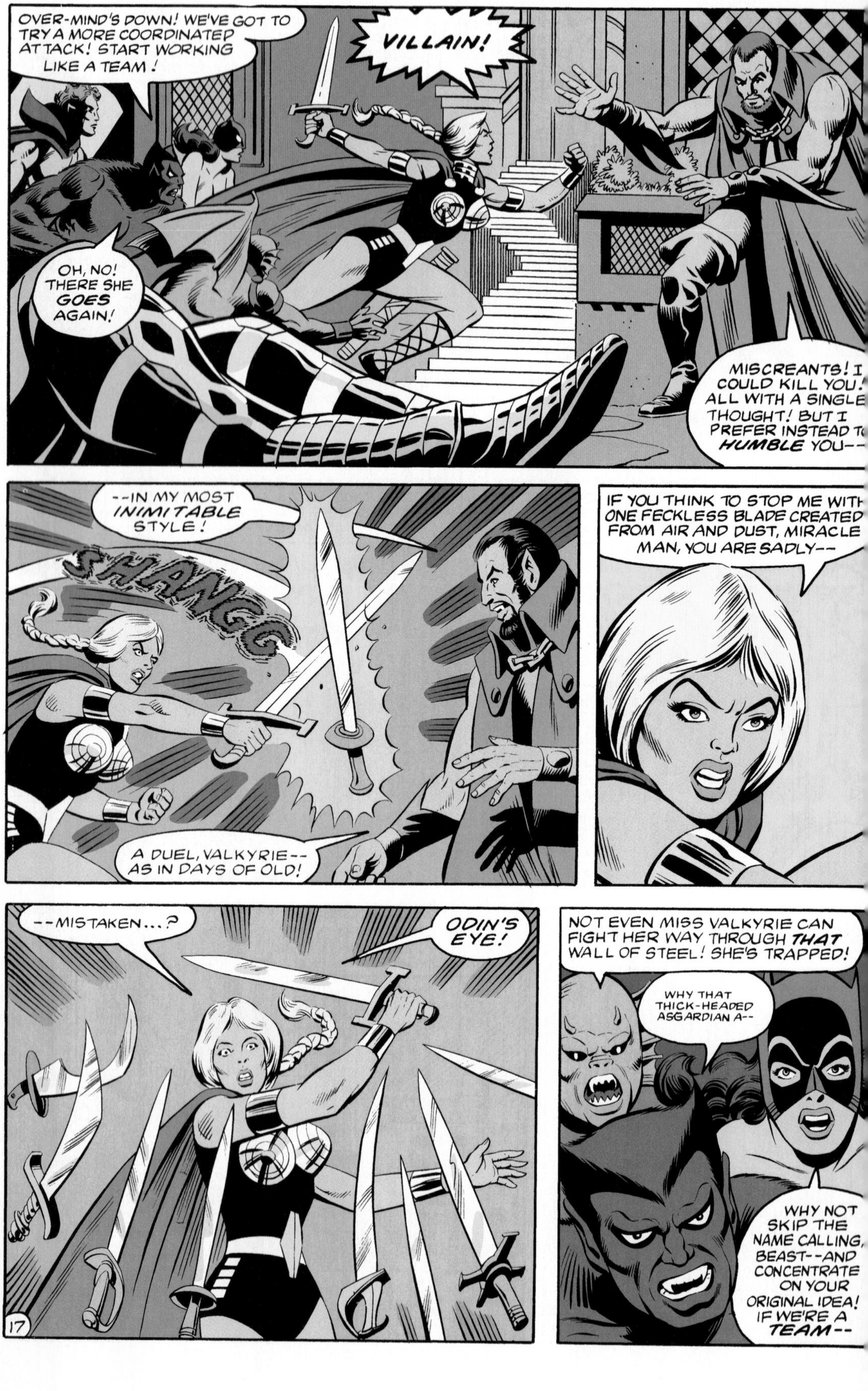
OVER-MIND'S DOWN! WE'VE GOT TO TRY A MORE COORDINATED ATTACK! START WORKING LIKE A TEAM!
VILLAIN!
OH, NO! THERE SHE GOES AGAIN!
MISCREANTS! I COULD KILL YOU! ALL WITH A SINGLE THOUGHT! BUT I PREFER INSTEAD TO HUMBLE YOU--
--IN MY MOST INIMITABLE STYLE!
SHANGG
A DUEL, VALKYRIE-- AS IN DAYS OF OLD!
IF YOU THINK TO STOP ME WITH ONE FECKLESS BLADE CREATED FROM AIR AND DUST, MIRACLE MAN, YOU ARE SADLY--
--MISTAKEN...?
ODIN'S EYE!
17
NOT EVEN MISS VALKYRIE CAN FIGHT HER WAY THROUGH THAT WALL OF STEEL! SHE'S TRAPPED!
WHY THAT THICK-HEADED ASGARDIAN A--
WHY NOT SKIP THE NAME CALLING, BEAST--AND CONCENTRATE ON YOUR ORIGINAL IDEA! IF WE'RE A TEAM--

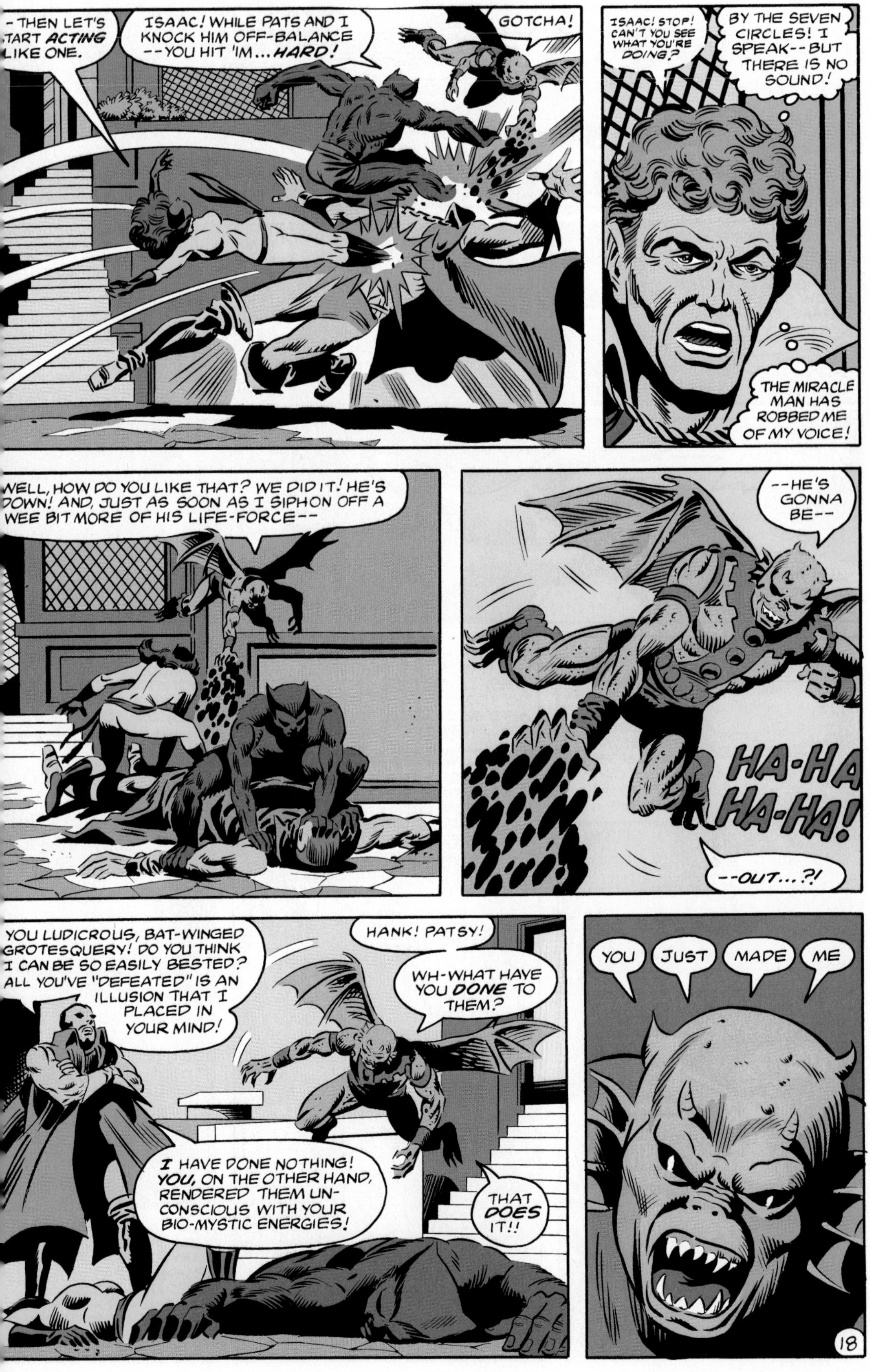
-THEN LET'S START ACTING LIKE ONE.
ISAAC! WHILE PATS AND I KNOCK HIM OFF-BALANCE --YOU HIT 'IM... HARD!
GOTCHA!
ISAAC! STOP! CAN'T YOU SEE WHAT YOU'RE DOING?
BY THE SEVEN CIRCLES! I SPEAK--BUT THERE IS NO SOUND!
THE MIRACLE MAN HAS ROBBED ME OF MY VOICE!
WELL, HOW DO YOU LIKE THAT? WE DID IT! HE'S DOWN! AND, JUST AS SOON AS I SIPHON OFF A WEE BIT MORE OF HIS LIFE-FORCE--
--HE'S GONNA BE--
HA-HA HA-HA!
--OUT...?!
YOU LUDICROUS, BAT-WINGED GROTESQUERY! DO YOU THINK I CAN BE SO EASILY BESTED? ALL YOU'VE "DEFEATED" IS AN ILLUSION THAT I PLACED IN YOUR MIND!
HANK! PATSY!
WH-WHAT HAVE YOU DONE TO THEM?
I HAVE DONE NOTHING! YOU, ON THE OTHER HAND, RENDERED THEM UN-CONSCIOUS WITH YOUR BIO-MYSTIC ENERGIES!
THAT DOES IT!!
YOU
JUST
MADE
ME
18

MAD!!!

WHAMM!!

I WAS NEVER MUCH FOR FISTICUFFS--AND I'M ONLY *BEGINNING* TO FIGURE OUT *JUST* HOW STRONG THIS GARGOYLE'S BODY REALLY *IS* --

BASSSH!

--BUT I'M BETTING IT'S STRONG ENOUGH TO BELT YOU CLEAN BACK TO MASSACHUSSETS.

YOU... HURT... ME!

AND, FOR SUCH AN UNFORGIVABLE TRANSGRESSION--

"--YOU MUST PAY THE PRICE OF THE DAMNED!"

HIS VOICE RETURNED, DAIMON HELLSTROM CALLS OUT TO HIS FRIEND...

...BUT THERE IS NO REPLY.

FOR WHEN DID *STONE* EVER SPEAK.?

"HEAVEN HELP US," HELLSTROM THINKS. "THE DARKSOUL HAS RISEN COMPLETELY TO THE FORE! THE MIRACLE MAN'S VERY FEATURES HAVE BEEN TWISTED INTO A DAEMONIC MASK!

"HE BELLOWS AND RAGES-- AND THIS... PARADISE OF HIS--ERUPTS!"

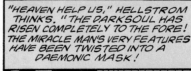

SO IT DOES.

THE EARTH SHAKES AND SPLITS WIDE. THE SKIES DARKEN AND SPIT LIGHTNING.

BUT PERHAPS MOST CURIOUS OF ALL IS THE MOMENTARY *CONFUSION* THAT SEEMS TO COME OVER THE MIRACLE MAN.

FOR AN INSTANT, DAIMON HELLSTROM SWEARS HE CAN SEE THE PAINED, PLEADING EYES OF *BROTHER JOSHUA*, STARING OUT AT HIM; THE EYES OF A MAN TRAPPED IN A HELL OF HIS OWN MAKING.

19

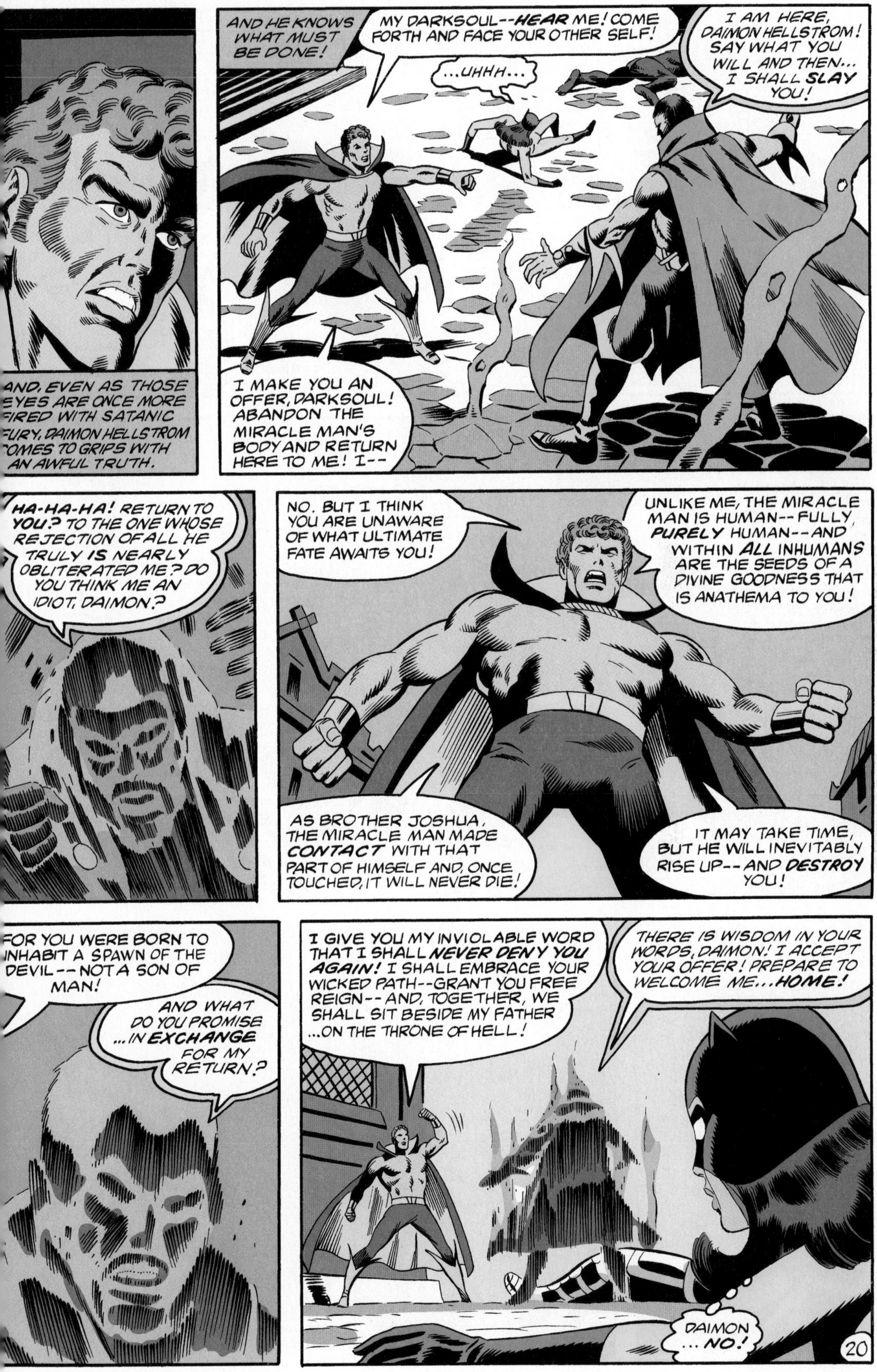
AND HE KNOWS WHAT MUST BE DONE!
MY DARKSOUL--HEAR ME! COME FORTH AND FACE YOUR OTHER SELF!
...UHHH...
I AM HERE, DAIMON HELLSTROM! SAY WHAT YOU WILL AND THEN... I SHALL SLAY YOU!
AND, EVEN AS THOSE EYES ARE ONCE MORE FIRED WITH SATANIC FURY, DAIMON HELLSTROM COMES TO GRIPS WITH AN AWFUL TRUTH.
I MAKE YOU AN OFFER, DARKSOUL! ABANDON THE MIRACLE MAN'S BODY AND RETURN HERE TO ME! I--
HA-HA-HA! RETURN TO YOU? TO THE ONE WHOSE REJECTION OF ALL HE TRULY IS NEARLY OBLITERATED ME? DO YOU THINK ME AN IDIOT, DAIMON?
NO. BUT I THINK YOU ARE UNAWARE OF WHAT ULTIMATE FATE AWAITS YOU!
UNLIKE ME, THE MIRACLE MAN IS HUMAN--FULLY, PURELY HUMAN--AND WITHIN ALL INHUMANS ARE THE SEEDS OF A DIVINE GOODNESS THAT IS ANATHEMA TO YOU!
AS BROTHER JOSHUA, THE MIRACLE MAN MADE CONTACT WITH THAT PART OF HIMSELF AND, ONCE TOUCHED, IT WILL NEVER DIE!
IT MAY TAKE TIME, BUT HE WILL INEVITABLY RISE UP--AND DESTROY YOU!
FOR YOU WERE BORN TO INHABIT A SPAWN OF THE DEVIL--NOT A SON OF MAN!
AND WHAT DO YOU PROMISE ...IN EXCHANGE FOR MY RETURN?
I GIVE YOU MY INVIOLABLE WORD THAT I SHALL NEVER DENY YOU AGAIN! I SHALL EMBRACE YOUR WICKED PATH--GRANT YOU FREE REIGN--AND, TOGETHER, WE SHALL SIT BESIDE MY FATHER ...ON THE THRONE OF HELL!
THERE IS WISDOM IN YOUR WORDS, DAIMON! I ACCEPT YOUR OFFER! PREPARE TO WELCOME ME...HOME!
DAIMON ...NO!
20

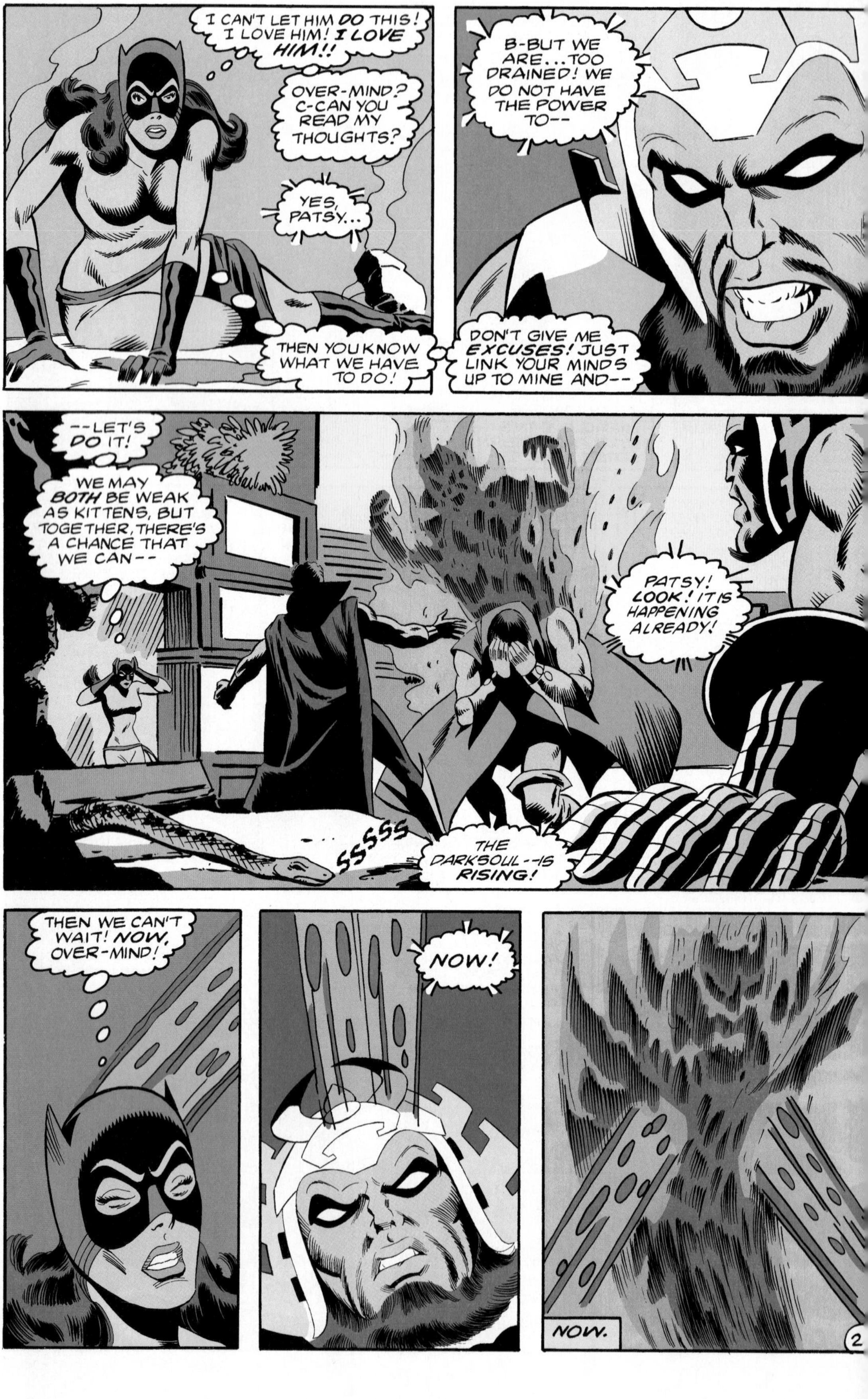
I CAN'T LET HIM DO THIS! I LOVE HIM! I LOVE HIM!!
OVER-MIND? C-CAN YOU READ MY THOUGHTS?
YES, PATSY...
THEN YOU KNOW WHAT WE HAVE TO DO!
B-BUT WE ARE...TOO DRAINED! WE DO NOT HAVE THE POWER TO--
DON'T GIVE ME EXCUSES! JUST LINK YOUR MINDS UP TO MINE AND--
--LET'S DO IT!
WE MAY BOTH BE WEAK AS KITTENS, BUT TOGETHER, THERE'S A CHANCE THAT WE CAN--
PATSY! LOOK! IT IS HAPPENING ALREADY!
SSSSS
THE DARKSOUL--IS RISING!
THEN WE CAN'T WAIT! NOW, OVER-MIND!
NOW!
NOW.
2

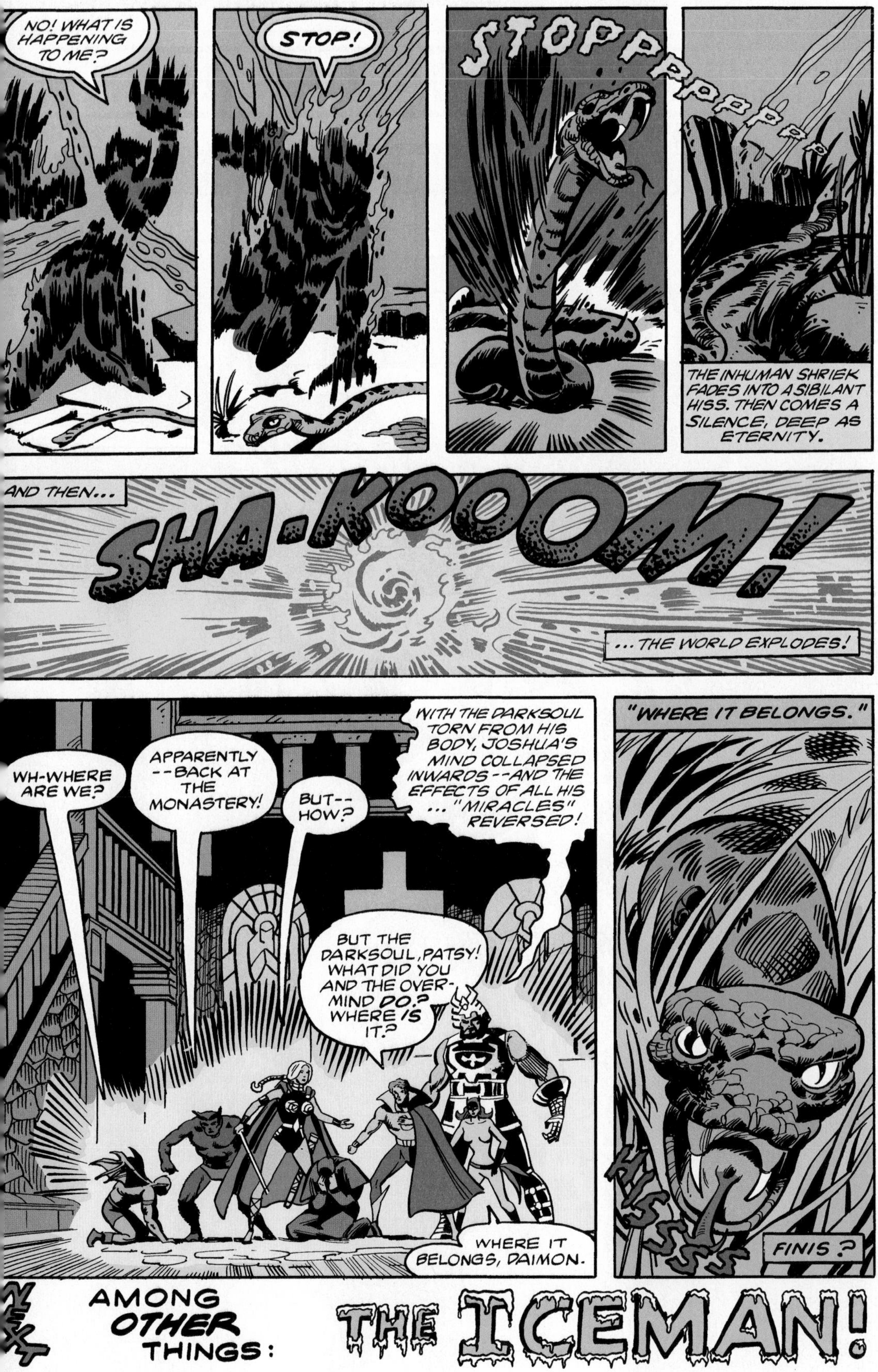
NO! WHAT IS HAPPENING TO ME?
STOP!
STOPPPPPPPPPP
THE INHUMAN SHRIEK FADES INTO A SIBILANT HISS. THEN COMES A SILENCE, DEEP AS ETERNITY.
AND THEN...
SHA-KOOOM!
...THE WORLD EXPLODES!
WH-WHERE ARE WE?
APPARENTLY --BACK AT THE MONASTERY!
BUT-- HOW?
WITH THE DARKSOUL TORN FROM HIS BODY, JOSHUA'S MIND COLLAPSED INWARDS--AND THE EFFECTS OF ALL HIS ... "MIRACLES" REVERSED!
BUT THE DARKSOUL, PATSY! WHAT DID YOU AND THE OVER-MIND DO? WHERE IS IT?
WHERE IT BELONGS, DAIMON.
"WHERE IT BELONGS."
HISSSS
FINIS?
NEXT
AMONG OTHER THINGS:
THE ICEMAN!

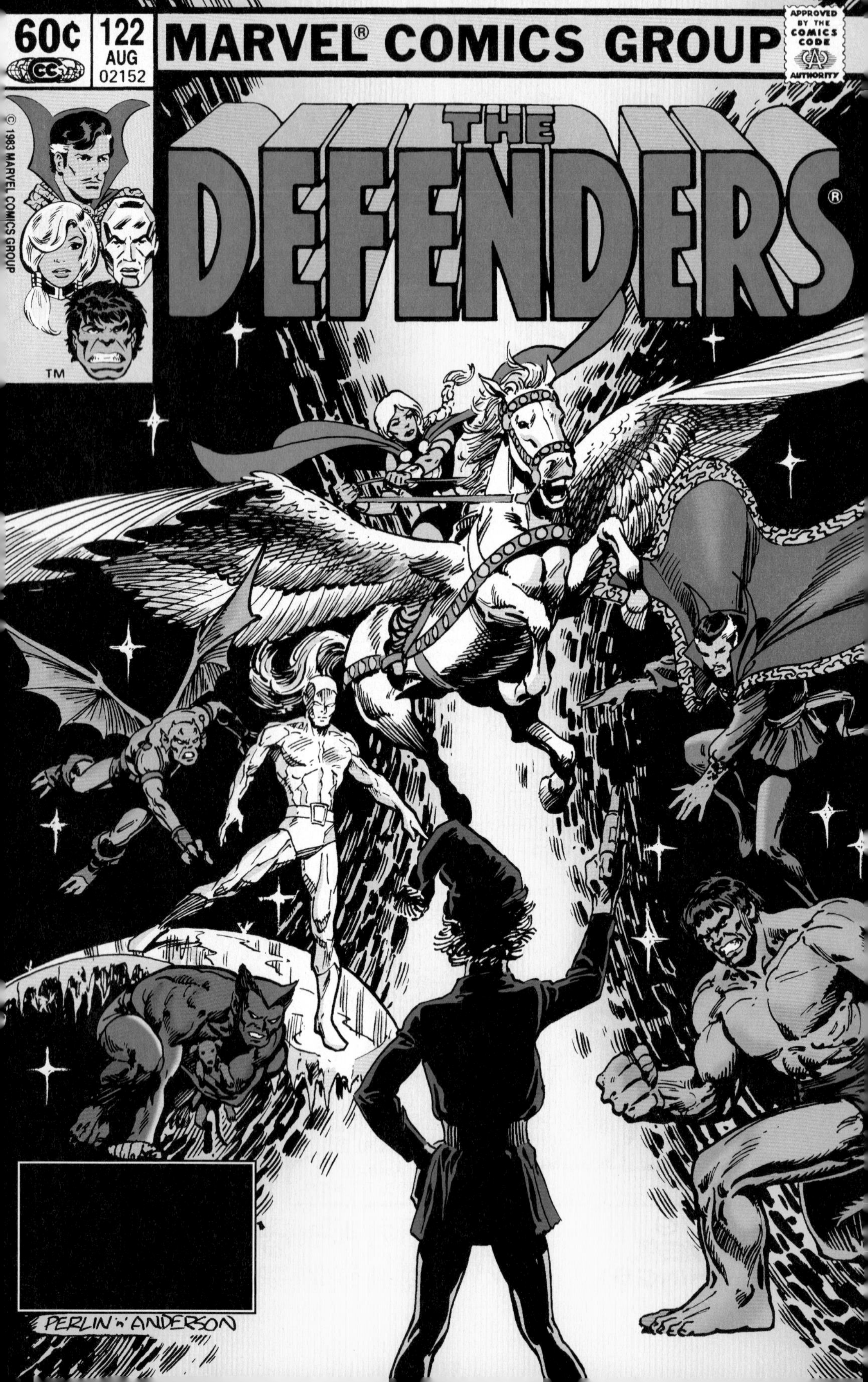
60¢
122
AUG
02152
MARVEL® COMICS GROUP
APPROVED BY THE COMICS CODE AUTHORITY
THE DEFENDERS®
© 1983 MARVEL COMICS GROUP
TM
PERLIN 'n' ANDERSON

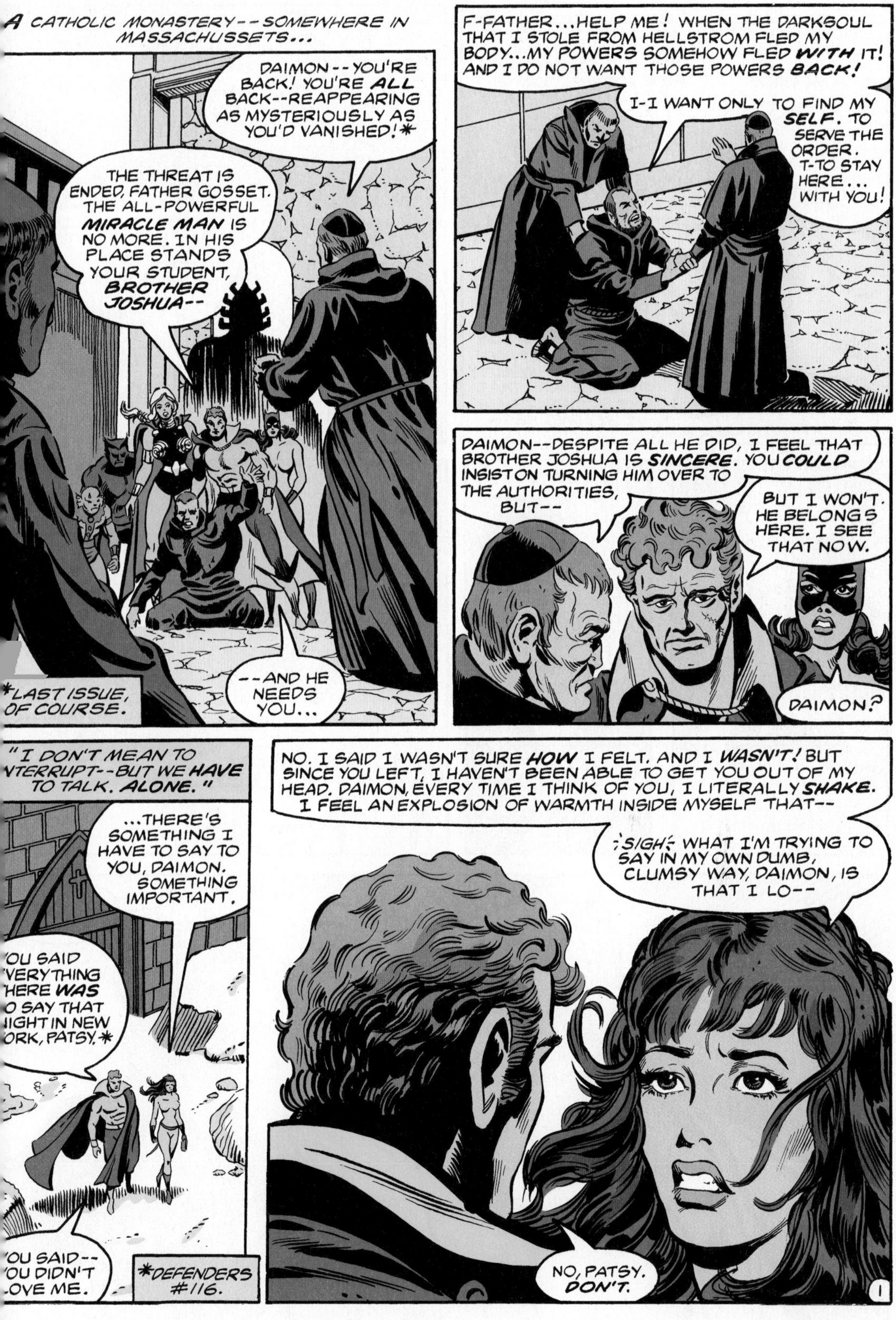
A CATHOLIC MONASTERY--SOMEWHERE IN MASSACHUSSETS...
DAIMON--YOU'RE BACK! YOU'RE ALL BACK--REAPPEARING AS MYSTERIOUSLY AS YOU'D VANISHED!*
THE THREAT IS ENDED, FATHER GOSSET. THE ALL-POWERFUL MIRACLE MAN IS NO MORE. IN HIS PLACE STANDS YOUR STUDENT, BROTHER JOSHUA--
--AND HE NEEDS YOU...
*LAST ISSUE, OF COURSE.
F-FATHER...HELP ME! WHEN THE DARKSOUL THAT I STOLE FROM HELLSTROM FLED MY BODY...MY POWERS SOMEHOW FLED WITH IT! AND I DO NOT WANT THOSE POWERS BACK!
I-I WANT ONLY TO FIND MY SELF. TO SERVE THE ORDER. T-TO STAY HERE... WITH YOU!
DAIMON--DESPITE ALL HE DID, I FEEL THAT BROTHER JOSHUA IS SINCERE. YOU COULD INSIST ON TURNING HIM OVER TO THE AUTHORITIES, BUT--
BUT I WON'T. HE BELONGS HERE. I SEE THAT NOW.
DAIMON?
"I DON'T MEAN TO NTERRUPT--BUT WE HAVE TO TALK. ALONE."
...THERE'S SOMETHING I HAVE TO SAY TO YOU, DAIMON. SOMETHING IMPORTANT.
OU SAID VERYTHING HERE WAS O SAY THAT IGHT IN NEW ORK, PATSY.*
OU SAID-- OU DIDN'T OVE ME.
*DEFENDERS #116.
NO. I SAID I WASN'T SURE HOW I FELT. AND I WASN'T! BUT SINCE YOU LEFT, I HAVEN'T BEEN ABLE TO GET YOU OUT OF MY HEAD. DAIMON, EVERY TIME I THINK OF YOU, I LITERALLY SHAKE. I FEEL AN EXPLOSION OF WARMTH INSIDE MYSELF THAT--
-SIGH- WHAT I'M TRYING TO SAY IN MY OWN DUMB, CLUMSY WAY, DAIMON, IS THAT I LO--
NO, PATSY. DON'T.
1

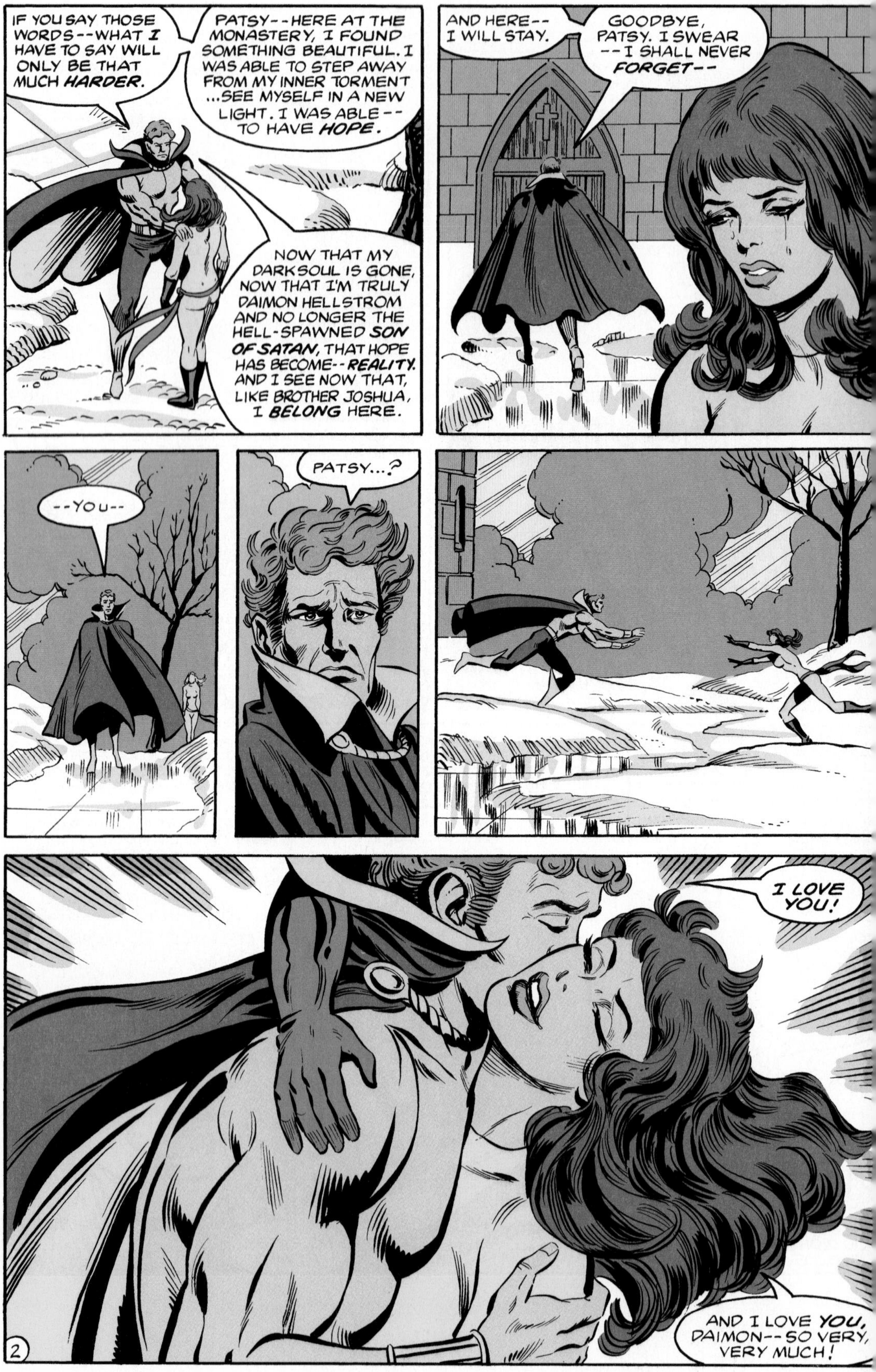
IF YOU SAY THOSE WORDS--WHAT I HAVE TO SAY WILL ONLY BE THAT MUCH HARDER.
PATSY--HERE AT THE MONASTERY, I FOUND SOMETHING BEAUTIFUL. I WAS ABLE TO STEP AWAY FROM MY INNER TORMENT ...SEE MYSELF IN A NEW LIGHT. I WAS ABLE-- TO HAVE HOPE.
NOW THAT MY DARKSOUL IS GONE, NOW THAT I'M TRULY DAIMON HELLSTROM AND NO LONGER THE HELL-SPAWNED SON OF SATAN, THAT HOPE HAS BECOME--REALITY. AND I SEE NOW THAT, LIKE BROTHER JOSHUA, I BELONG HERE.
AND HERE-- I WILL STAY.
GOODBYE, PATSY. I SWEAR --I SHALL NEVER FORGET--
--YOU--
PATSY...?
I LOVE YOU!
AND I LOVE YOU, DAIMON--SO VERY, VERY MUCH!
2

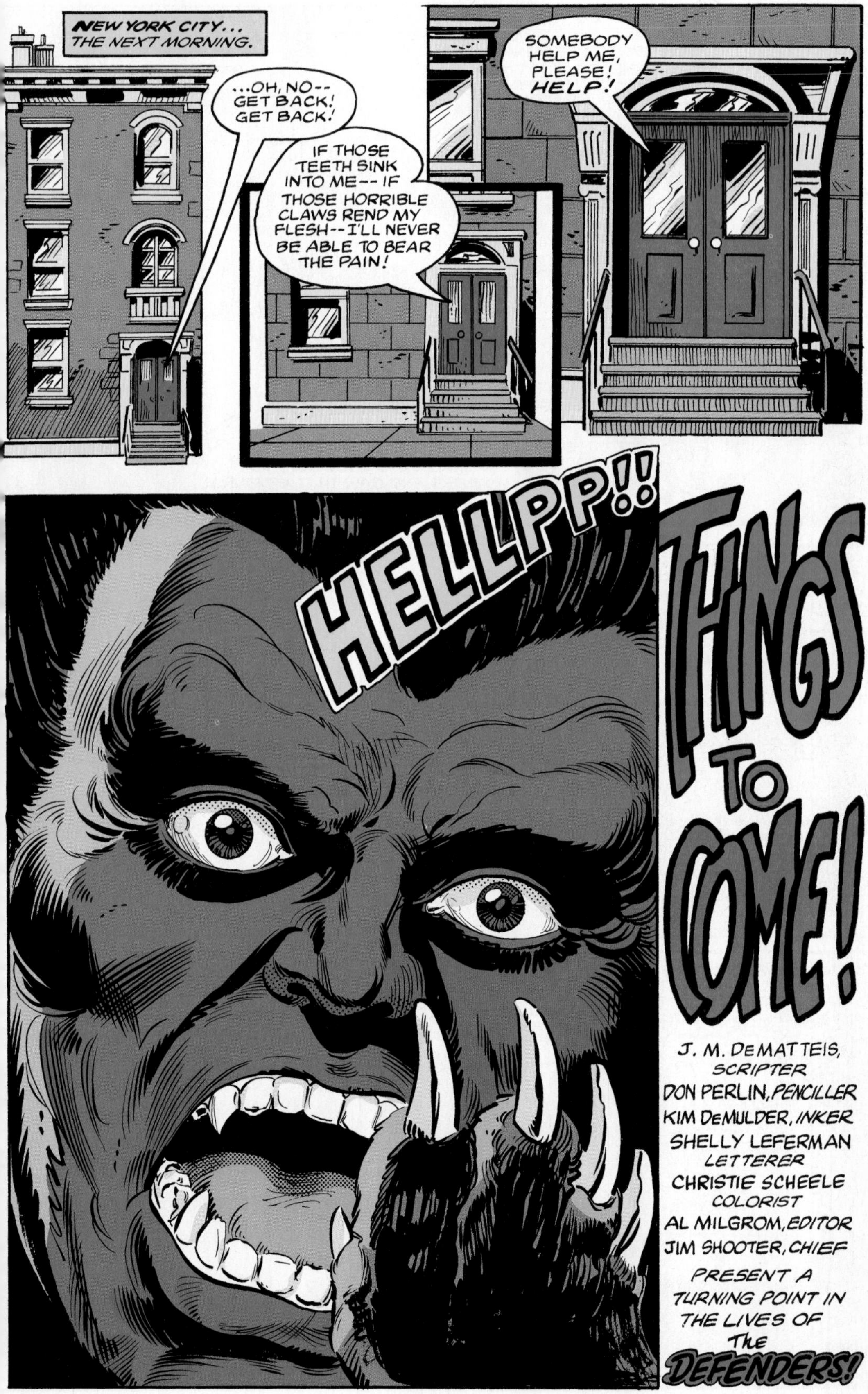

NEW YORK CITY... THE NEXT MORNING.
...OH, NO-- GET BACK! GET BACK!
IF THOSE TEETH SINK INTO ME-- IF THOSE HORRIBLE CLAWS REND MY FLESH--I'LL NEVER BE ABLE TO BEAR THE PAIN!
SOMEBODY HELP ME, PLEASE! HELP!
HELLPP!!
THINGS TO COME!
J. M. DEMATTEIS, SCRIPTER
DON PERLIN, PENCILLER
KIM DEMULDER, INKER
SHELLY LEFERMAN LETTERER
CHRISTIE SCHEELE COLORIST
AL MILGROM, EDITOR
JIM SHOOTER, CHIEF
PRESENT A TURNING POINT IN THE LIVES OF The DEFENDERS!

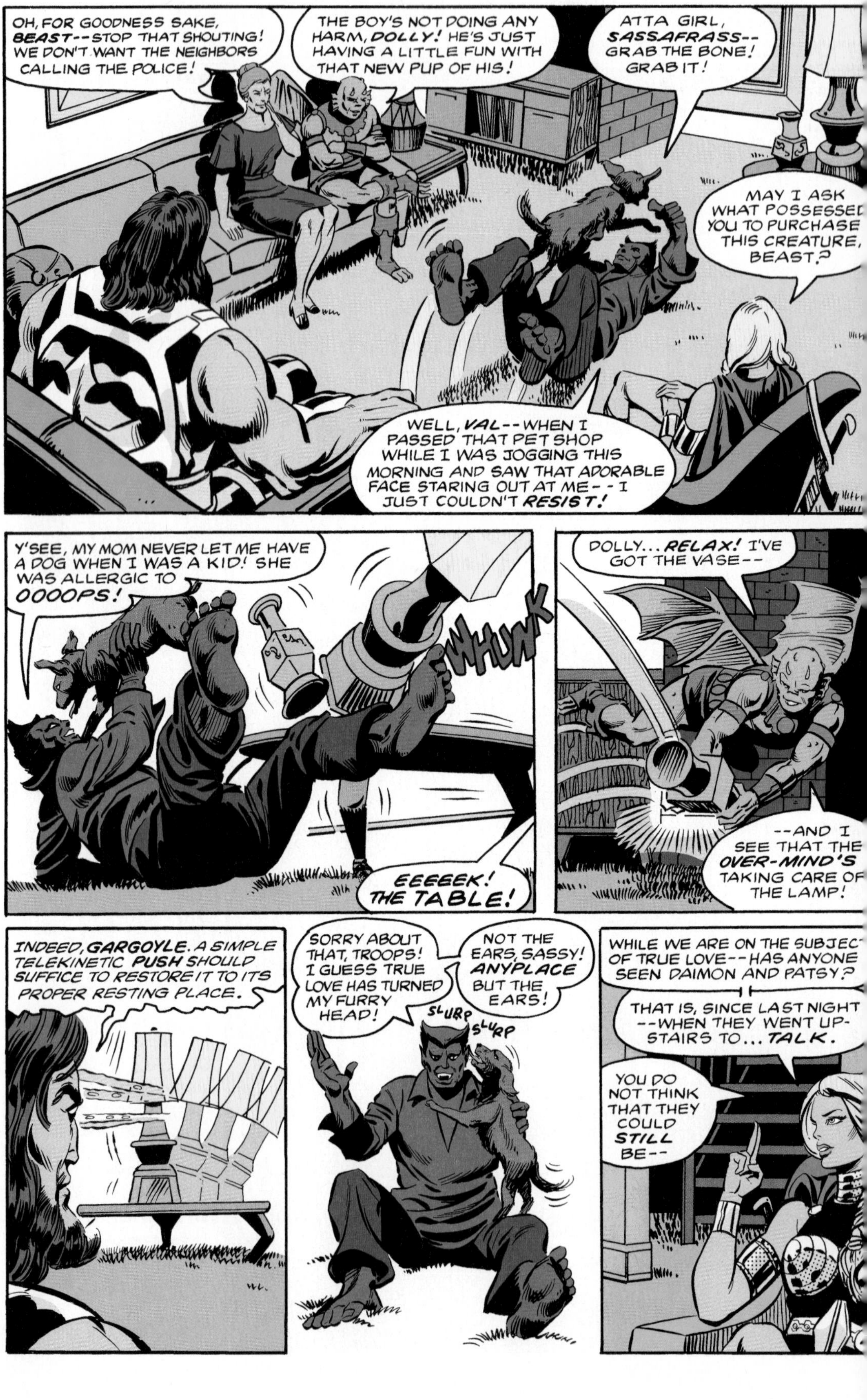

OH, FOR GOODNESS SAKE, BEAST--STOP THAT SHOUTING! WE DON'T WANT THE NEIGHBORS CALLING THE POLICE!
THE BOY'S NOT DOING ANY HARM, DOLLY! HE'S JUST HAVING A LITTLE FUN WITH THAT NEW PUP OF HIS!
ATTA GIRL, SASSAFRASS--GRAB THE BONE! GRAB IT!
MAY I ASK WHAT POSSESSED YOU TO PURCHASE THIS CREATURE, BEAST?
WELL, VAL--WHEN I PASSED THAT PET SHOP WHILE I WAS JOGGING THIS MORNING AND SAW THAT ADORABLE FACE STARING OUT AT ME--I JUST COULDN'T RESIST!
Y'SEE, MY MOM NEVER LET ME HAVE A DOG WHEN I WAS A KID! SHE WAS ALLERGIC TO OOOOPS!
WHUNK
EEEEEK! THE TABLE!
DOLLY... RELAX! I'VE GOT THE VASE--
--AND I SEE THAT THE OVER-MIND'S TAKING CARE OF THE LAMP!
INDEED, GARGOYLE. A SIMPLE TELEKINETIC PUSH SHOULD SUFFICE TO RESTORE IT TO ITS PROPER RESTING PLACE.
SORRY ABOUT THAT, TROOPS! I GUESS TRUE LOVE HAS TURNED MY FURRY HEAD!
NOT THE EARS, SASSY! ANYPLACE BUT THE EARS!
SLURP
SLURP
WHILE WE ARE ON THE SUBJECT OF TRUE LOVE--HAS ANYONE SEEN DAIMON AND PATSY?
THAT IS, SINCE LAST NIGHT--WHEN THEY WENT UPSTAIRS TO... TALK.
YOU DO NOT THINK THAT THEY COULD STILL BE--

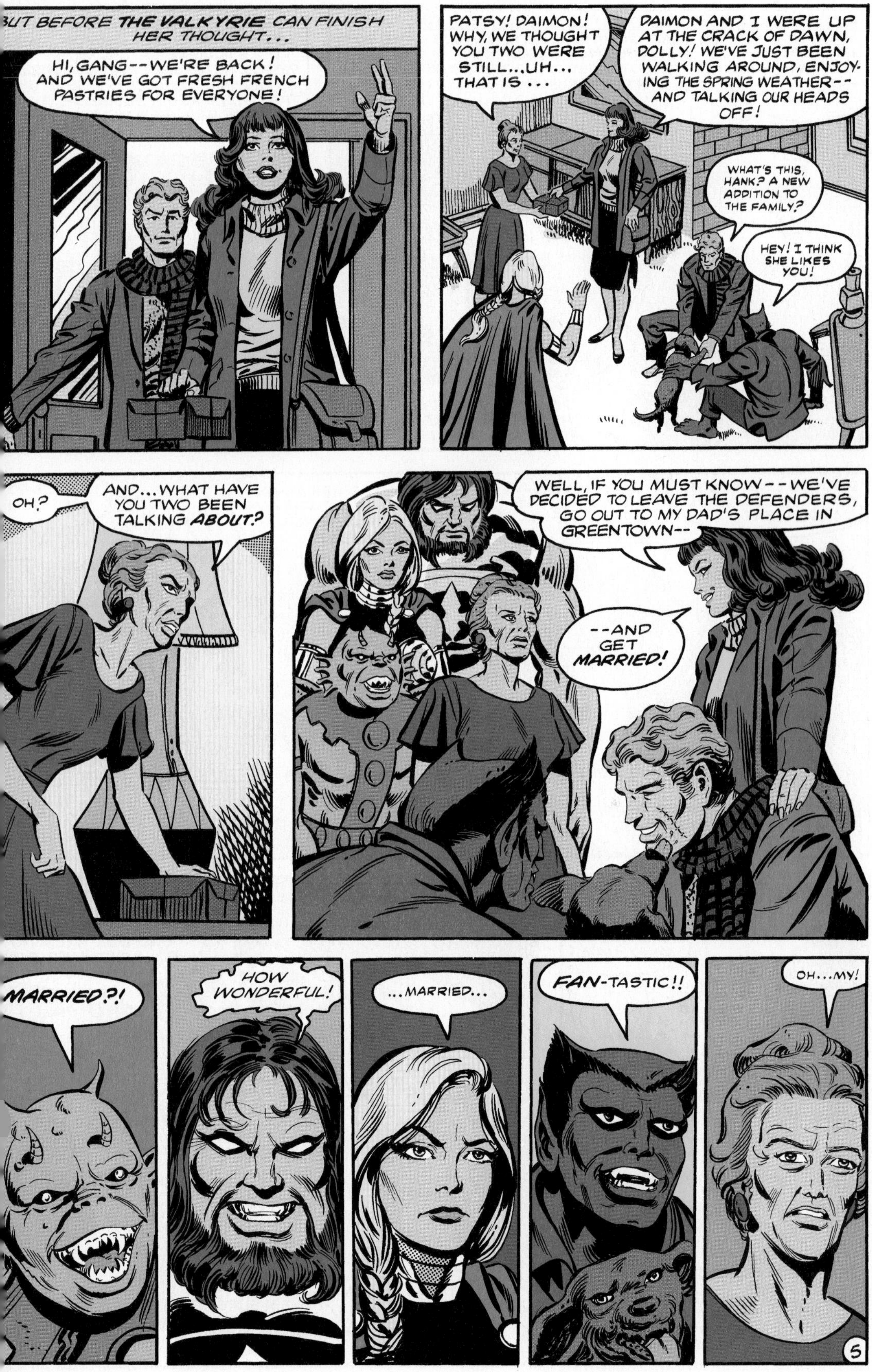
BUT BEFORE THE VALKYRIE CAN FINISH HER THOUGHT...
HI, GANG--WE'RE BACK! AND WE'VE GOT FRESH FRENCH PASTRIES FOR EVERYONE!
PATSY! DAIMON! WHY, WE THOUGHT YOU TWO WERE STILL...UH... THAT IS...
DAIMON AND I WERE UP AT THE CRACK OF DAWN, DOLLY! WE'VE JUST BEEN WALKING AROUND, ENJOYING THE SPRING WEATHER--AND TALKING OUR HEADS OFF!
WHAT'S THIS, HANK? A NEW ADDITION TO THE FAMILY?
HEY! I THINK SHE LIKES YOU!
OH?
AND...WHAT HAVE YOU TWO BEEN TALKING ABOUT?
WELL, IF YOU MUST KNOW--WE'VE DECIDED TO LEAVE THE DEFENDERS, GO OUT TO MY DAD'S PLACE IN GREENTOWN--
--AND GET MARRIED!
MARRIED?!
HOW WONDERFUL!
...MARRIED...
FAN-TASTIC!!
OH...MY!
5

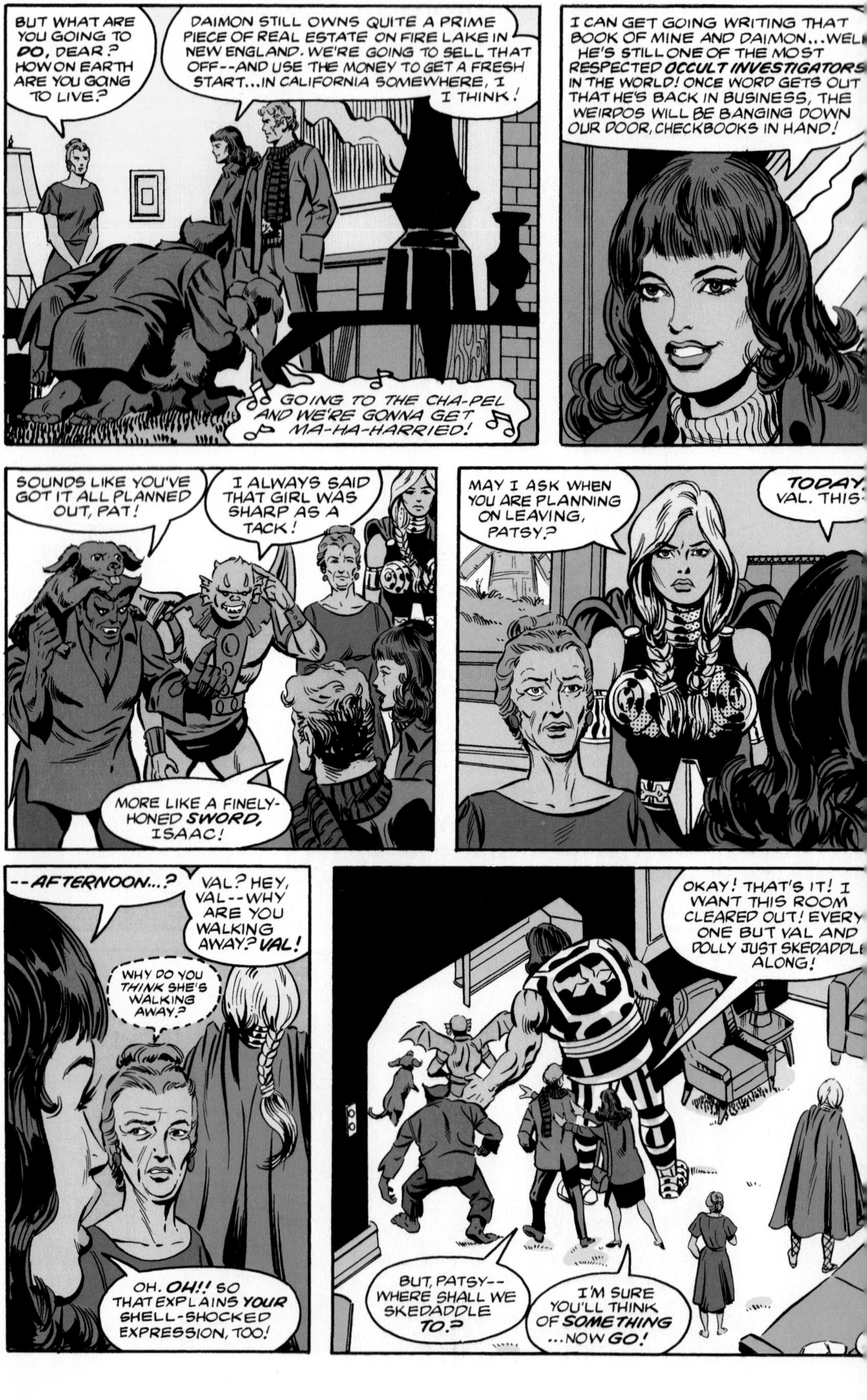

BUT WHAT ARE YOU GOING TO DO, DEAR? HOW ON EARTH ARE YOU GOING TO LIVE?
DAIMON STILL OWNS QUITE A PRIME PIECE OF REAL ESTATE ON FIRE LAKE IN NEW ENGLAND. WE'RE GOING TO SELL THAT OFF--AND USE THE MONEY TO GET A FRESH START...IN CALIFORNIA SOMEWHERE, I I THINK!
GOING TO THE CHA-PEL AND WE'RE GONNA GET MA-HA-HARRIED!
I CAN GET GOING WRITING THAT BOOK OF MINE AND DAIMON...WEL HE'S STILL ONE OF THE MOST RESPECTED OCCULT INVESTIGATORS IN THE WORLD! ONCE WORD GETS OUT THAT HE'S BACK IN BUSINESS, THE WEIRDOS WILL BE BANGING DOWN OUR DOOR, CHECKBOOKS IN HAND!
SOUNDS LIKE YOU'VE GOT IT ALL PLANNED OUT, PAT!
I ALWAYS SAID THAT GIRL WAS SHARP AS A TACK!
MORE LIKE A FINELY-HONED SWORD, ISAAC!
MAY I ASK WHEN YOU ARE PLANNING ON LEAVING, PATSY?
TODAY. VAL. THIS
--AFTERNOON...?
VAL? HEY, VAL--WHY ARE YOU WALKING AWAY? VAL!
WHY DO YOU THINK SHE'S WALKING AWAY?
OH. OH!! SO THAT EXPLAINS YOUR SHELL-SHOCKED EXPRESSION, TOO!
OKAY! THAT'S IT! I WANT THIS ROOM CLEARED OUT! EVERY ONE BUT VAL AND DOLLY JUST SKEDADDLE ALONG!
BUT, PATSY-- WHERE SHALL WE SKEDADDLE TO?
I'M SURE YOU'LL THINK OF SOMETHING ...NOW GO!

ALL RIGHT, YOU TWO--WHAT'S GOING ON HERE? VAL LOOKS LIKE *MISS STONEFACE* OF 1983--AND YOU, DOLLY--! YOU LOOK LIKE YOUR WHOLE WORLD JUST CAME TO AN END!

MAYBE IT DID.

COME ON, GIRL--SPIT IT OUT!

IT'S THAT DAIMON HELLSTROM, PATSY. I DON'T ...APPROVE OF HIM.

OH, REALLY? IT NEVER BOTHERED YOU THAT I HUNG AROUND WITH *THE HULK*--BUT YOU DON'T APPROVE OF *DAIMON*?

I KNOW MY OPINION DOESN'T MATTER... I'M JUST YOUR *HOUSEKEEPER*, NOT YOUR MOTHER... BUT HE *FRIGHTENS* ME.

DOLLY, I'VE KNOWN YOU PRACTICALLY MY WHOLE LIFE! I'M CLOSER TO YOU THAN I *EVER* WAS TO MOM.

OF *COURSE* YOUR OPINION MATTERS.

BUT, DOLLY, THE VERY FACT THAT I LOVE DAIMON SO--THAT I WANT TO SPEND MY LIFE WITH HIM--SHOULD BE ENOUGH TO CONVINCE YOU THAT THERE'S NOTHING TO BE FRIGHTENED OF!

HE'S NOT THE *SON OF SATAN* ANY MORE! HE'S A *MAN*! A VERY DEAR, VERY LOVING *MAN*!

AND THAT MAN IS TAKING YOU THREE THOUSAND MILES AWAY FROM ME!

FIRST OF ALL, YOU'LL BE SEEING ME AGAIN IN A FEW WEEKS FOR THE WEDDING AT DAD'S! SECOND OF ALL, AS SOON AS WE'RE SETTLED IN CALIFORNIA I'M *SENDING* FOR YOU! I'VE HAD YOU IN MY LIFE TOO LONG TO LET YOU SLIP AWAY NOW!

OH, PATSY --CAN YOU EVER FORGIVE AN OLD FOOL?

ONLY IF THE OLD FOOL *HUGS* ME!

IT'S A SHAME YOUR MOTHER DIDN'T LIVE TO SEE YOU SO HAPPY!

IF MOM *WERE* ALIVE-- CHANCES ARE SHE'D *BOYCOTT* THE WEDDING!

BUT THAT'S NOT IMPORTANT.

I'M MORE CONCERNED WITH WHAT'S BUGGING OUR RESIDENT NORSE GODDESS! COME ON, VAL --IT'S *YOUR* TURN TO SPILL THE--

7

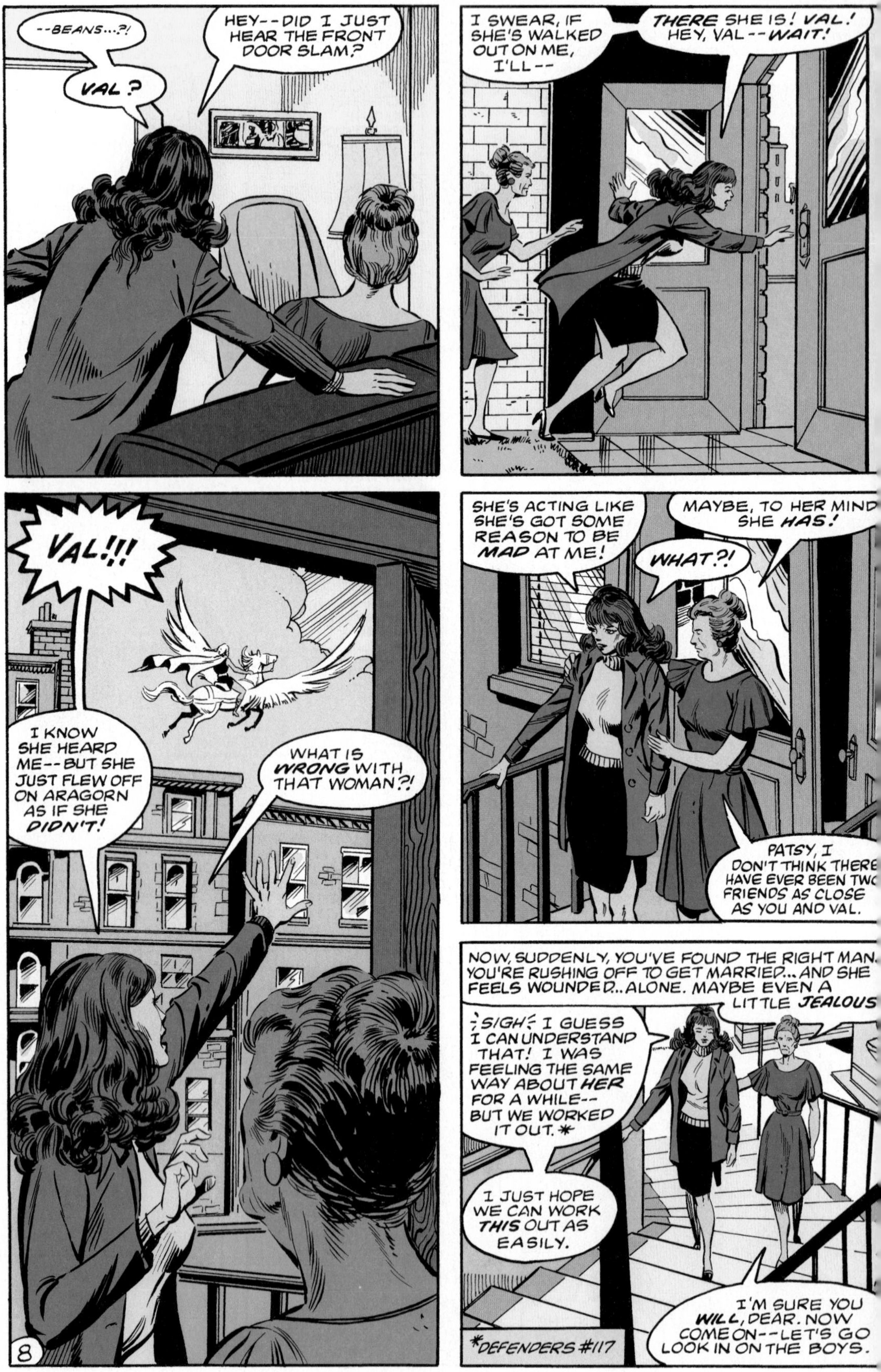
--BEANS...?!
VAL?
HEY--DID I JUST HEAR THE FRONT DOOR SLAM?
I SWEAR, IF SHE'S WALKED OUT ON ME, I'LL--
THERE SHE IS! VAL! HEY, VAL--WAIT!
VAL!!!
I KNOW SHE HEARD ME--BUT SHE JUST FLEW OFF ON ARAGORN AS IF SHE DIDN'T!
WHAT IS WRONG WITH THAT WOMAN?!
8
SHE'S ACTING LIKE SHE'S GOT SOME REASON TO BE MAD AT ME!
MAYBE, TO HER MIND SHE HAS!
WHAT?!
PATSY, I DON'T THINK THERE HAVE EVER BEEN TWO FRIENDS AS CLOSE AS YOU AND VAL.
NOW, SUDDENLY, YOU'VE FOUND THE RIGHT MAN. YOU'RE RUSHING OFF TO GET MARRIED... AND SHE FEELS WOUNDED... ALONE. MAYBE EVEN A LITTLE JEALOUS.
-SIGH- I GUESS I CAN UNDERSTAND THAT! I WAS FEELING THE SAME WAY ABOUT HER FOR A WHILE--BUT WE WORKED IT OUT.*
I JUST HOPE WE CAN WORK THIS OUT AS EASILY.
*DEFENDERS #117
I'M SURE YOU WILL, DEAR. NOW COME ON--LET'S GO LOOK IN ON THE BOYS.

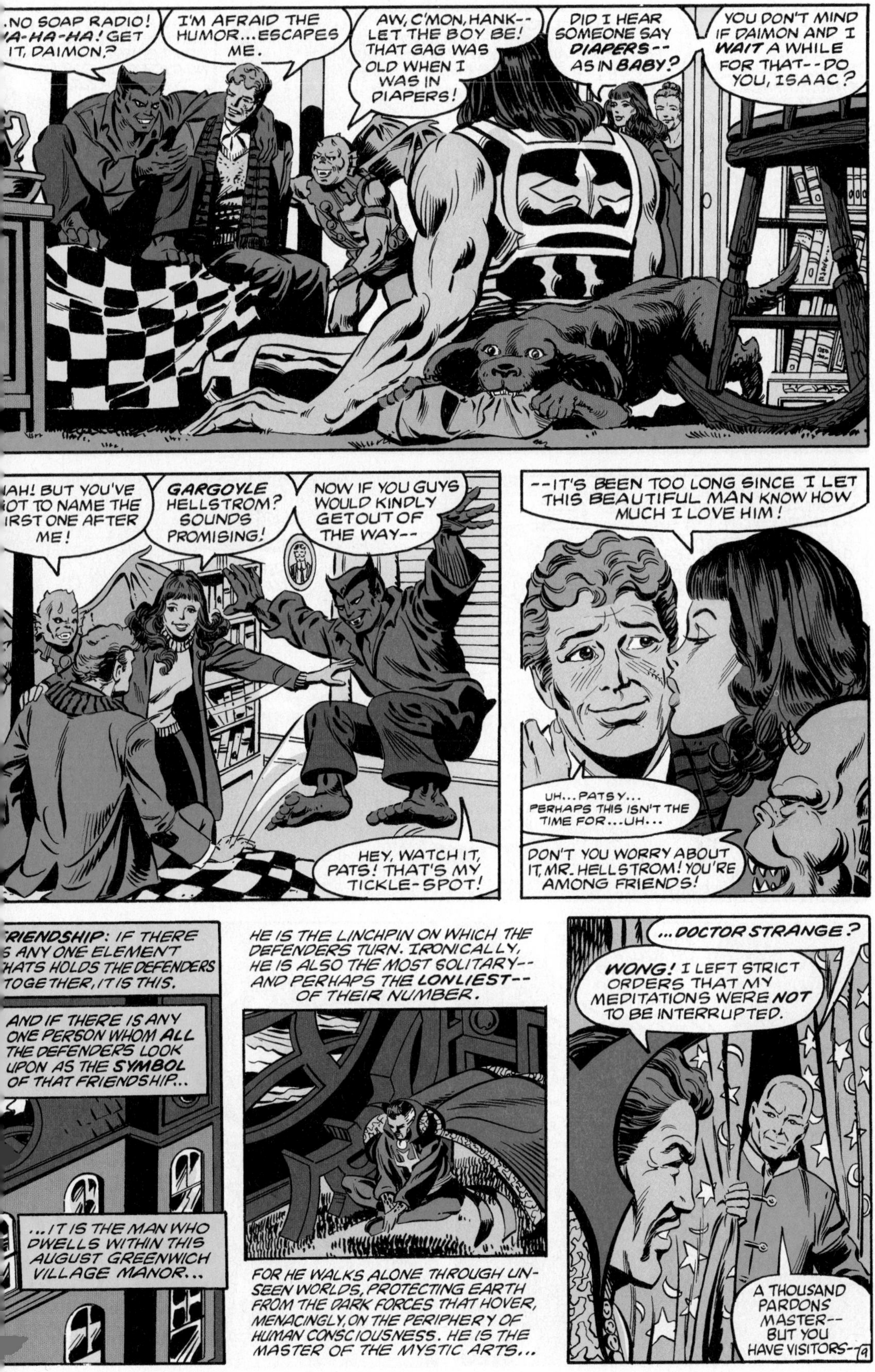
.NO SOAP RADIO! HA-HA-HA! GET IT, DAIMON?
I'M AFRAID THE HUMOR...ESCAPES ME.
AW, C'MON, HANK-- LET THE BOY BE! THAT GAG WAS OLD WHEN I WAS IN DIAPERS!
DID I HEAR SOMEONE SAY DIAPERS-- AS IN BABY?
YOU DON'T MIND IF DAIMON AND I WAIT A WHILE FOR THAT--DO YOU, ISAAC?
AH! BUT YOU'VE GOT TO NAME THE FIRST ONE AFTER ME!
GARGOYLE HELLSTROM? SOUNDS PROMISING!
NOW IF YOU GUYS WOULD KINDLY GET OUT OF THE WAY--
HEY, WATCH IT, PATS! THAT'S MY TICKLE-SPOT!
--IT'S BEEN TOO LONG SINCE I LET THIS BEAUTIFUL MAN KNOW HOW MUCH I LOVE HIM!
UH...PATSY... PERHAPS THIS ISN'T THE TIME FOR...UH...
DON'T YOU WORRY ABOUT IT, MR. HELLSTROM! YOU'RE AMONG FRIENDS!
FRIENDSHIP: IF THERE IS ANY ONE ELEMENT THATS HOLDS THE DEFENDERS TOGETHER, IT IS THIS.
AND IF THERE IS ANY ONE PERSON WHOM ALL THE DEFENDERS LOOK UPON AS THE SYMBOL OF THAT FRIENDSHIP...
...IT IS THE MAN WHO DWELLS WITHIN THIS AUGUST GREENWICH VILLAGE MANOR...
HE IS THE LINCHPIN ON WHICH THE DEFENDERS TURN. IRONICALLY, HE IS ALSO THE MOST SOLITARY-- AND PERHAPS THE LONLIEST-- OF THEIR NUMBER.
FOR HE WALKS ALONE THROUGH UNSEEN WORLDS, PROTECTING EARTH FROM THE DARK FORCES THAT HOVER, MENACINGLY, ON THE PERIPHERY OF HUMAN CONSCIOUSNESS. HE IS THE MASTER OF THE MYSTIC ARTS...
...DOCTOR STRANGE?
WONG! I LEFT STRICT ORDERS THAT MY MEDITATIONS WERE NOT TO BE INTERRUPTED.
A THOUSAND PARDONS MASTER-- BUT YOU HAVE VISITORS--
9

--OF A MOST ...*PERSISTENT* NATURE!

PRINCE NAMOR! DOCTOR BANNER! THIS IS SOMETHING OF A SURPRISE!

YOUR ASTRAL FORM APPEARS TO ME IN ATLANTIS--BEGGING FOR *THE SUB-MARINER'S* AID --AND YOU ARE *SURPRISED?*

I RECEIVED A SIMILAR VISITATION, DOCTOR-- SO I IMMEDIATELY CHANGED INTO *THE HULK* AND RUSHED RIGHT OVER! NOW--WHAT'S THE CRISIS?

I'M AFRAID I AM AS MUCH IN THE DARK AS YOU GENTLEMEN ARE--SINCE NO SUCH CALL FOR HELP WAS EVER *SENT!*

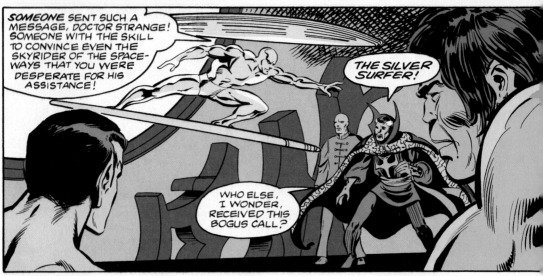

SOMEONE SENT SUCH A MESSAGE, DOCTOR STRANGE! SOMEONE WITH THE SKILL TO CONVINCE EVEN THE SKYRIDER OF THE SPACE-WAYS THAT YOU WERE DESPERATE FOR HIS ASSISTANCE!

THE SILVER SURFER!

WHO ELSE, I WONDER, RECEIVED THIS BOGUS CALL?

JUST THE *FOUR* OF YOU, MAGIC-MAN! AND I SHOULD KNOW--

--SINCE *I'M* THE BAD LITTLE BOY WHO *DID* IT!

PLEASANT DREAMS, SUCKERS!

BLAM

MORE ON THE ENIGMATIC ELF *NEXT* MONTH. BUT, FOR NOW...

10

330

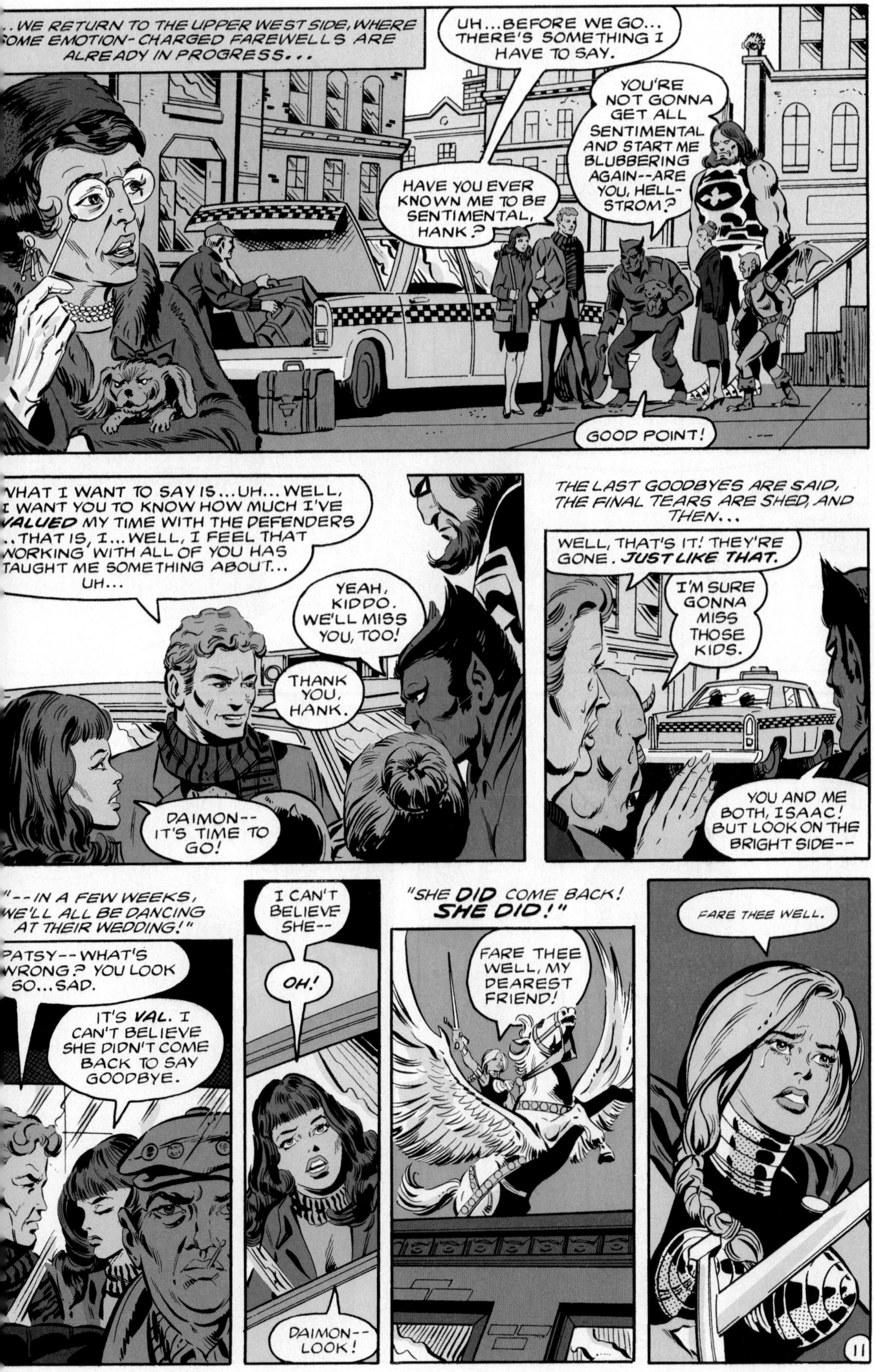

...WE RETURN TO THE UPPER WEST SIDE, WHERE SOME EMOTION-CHARGED FAREWELLS ARE ALREADY IN PROGRESS...
UH...BEFORE WE GO... THERE'S SOMETHING I HAVE TO SAY.
YOU'RE NOT GONNA GET ALL SENTIMENTAL AND START ME BLUBBERING AGAIN--ARE YOU, HELLSTROM?
HAVE YOU EVER KNOWN ME TO BE SENTIMENTAL, HANK?
GOOD POINT!
WHAT I WANT TO SAY IS...UH...WELL, I WANT YOU TO KNOW HOW MUCH I'VE VALUED MY TIME WITH THE DEFENDERS ...THAT IS, I...WELL, I FEEL THAT WORKING WITH ALL OF YOU HAS TAUGHT ME SOMETHING ABOUT... UH...
YEAH, KIDDO. WE'LL MISS YOU, TOO!
THANK YOU, HANK.
DAIMON-- IT'S TIME TO GO!
THE LAST GOODBYES ARE SAID, THE FINAL TEARS ARE SHED, AND THEN...
WELL, THAT'S IT! THEY'RE GONE. JUST LIKE THAT.
I'M SURE GONNA MISS THOSE KIDS.
YOU AND ME BOTH, ISAAC! BUT LOOK ON THE BRIGHT SIDE--
"--IN A FEW WEEKS, WE'LL ALL BE DANCING AT THEIR WEDDING!"
PATSY--WHAT'S WRONG? YOU LOOK SO...SAD.
IT'S VAL. I CAN'T BELIEVE SHE DIDN'T COME BACK TO SAY GOODBYE.
I CAN'T BELIEVE SHE--
OH!
DAIMON-- LOOK!
"SHE DID COME BACK! SHE DID!"
FARE THEE WELL, MY DEAREST FRIEND!
FARE THEE WELL.
11

SOME HOURS LATER, AFTER THE DEFENDERS' HOUSEHOLD HAS RETURNED TO SOME SEMBLANCE OF NORMALCY...

SASSAFRASS! HOW COULD YOU?!

...THE BEAST FINDS HIMSELF ON THE RECEIVING END OF A PECULIAR BRAND OF CANINE AFFECTION...

HAVEN'T YOU BEEN LISTENING TO ME? ON THE PAPER, I SAID! ON THE PAPER!

DING-DONG!

WHY DOES THE DOORBELL ALWAYS RING AT THE MOST EMBARRASSING TIMES?

DING-DONG! DING-DONG!

OKAY! I'M COMING! I'M COMING!

AND WHAT CAN I DO FOR YOU, MISTER MERRY MAILMAN?

HEY, MAN-- YOU RUNNIN' A KENNEL IN THERE? SNIFF! SOMETHIN' SMELLS REAL FUNKY!

NEVER MIND THAT -- WHAT DO YOU WANT?

WE'RE LOOKIN' FOR THE BEAST... AN' YOU SURE FIT THE DESCRIPTION!

I'M THE BEAST! WHAT'S IT TO YOU?

U.S. MAIL

THIS IS THE PLACE, GUYS! BACK 'ER UP!

HEY! WAIT A MINUTE!

THIS STUFF'S BEEN FORWARDED FROM AVENGERS MANSION, PAL--

FIFTEEN BAGS OF IT!

U.S. MAIL

USE EXPRESS MA

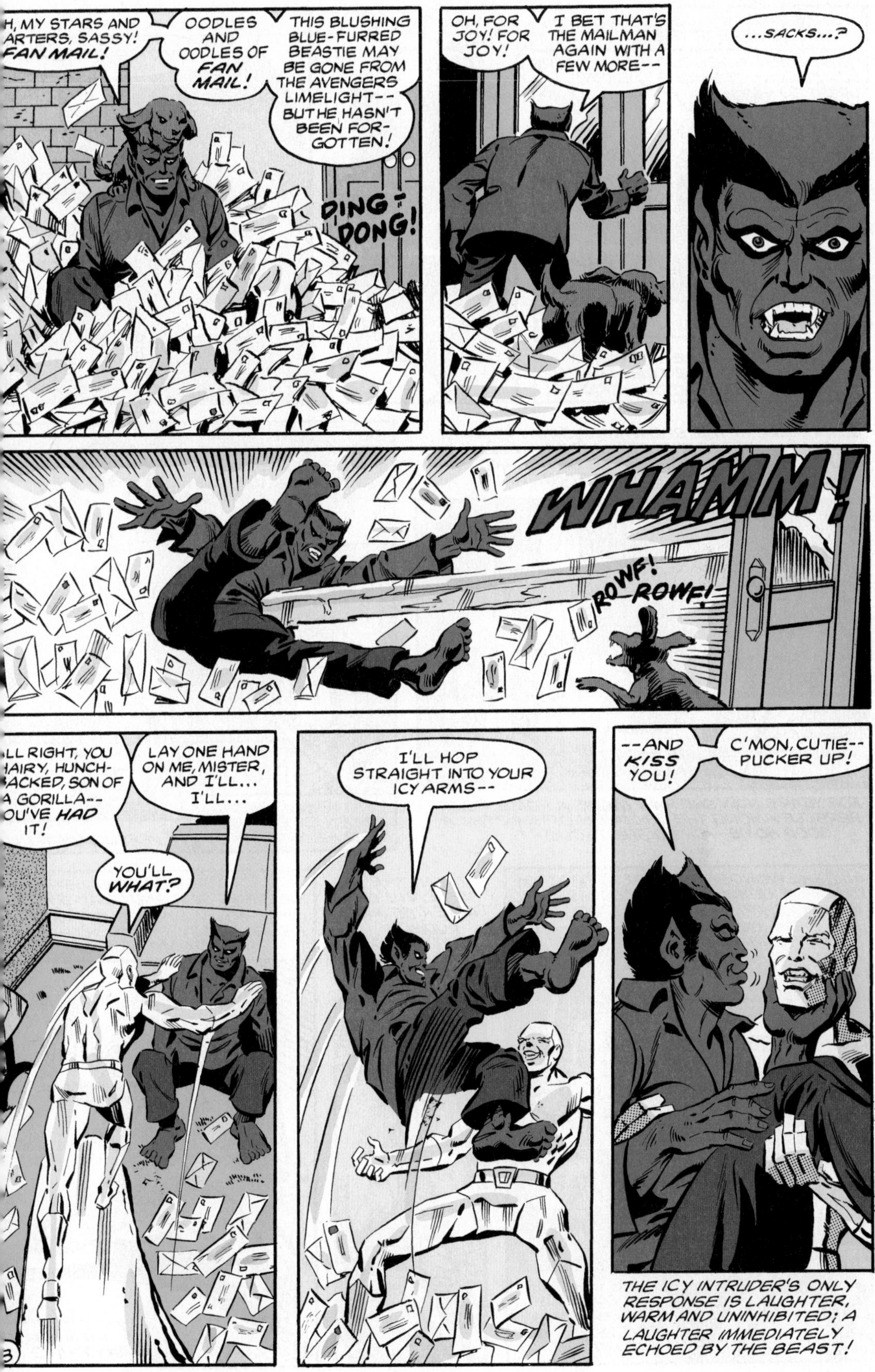
H, MY STARS AND ARTERS, SASSY! FAN MAIL!
OODLES AND OODLES OF FAN MAIL!
THIS BLUSHING BLUE-FURRED BEASTIE MAY BE GONE FROM THE AVENGERS LIMELIGHT-- BUT HE HASN'T BEEN FOR-GOTTEN!
DING-DONG!
OH, FOR JOY! FOR JOY!
I BET THAT'S THE MAILMAN AGAIN WITH A FEW MORE--
...SACKS...?
WHAMM!
ROWF! ROWF!
LL RIGHT, YOU HAIRY, HUNCH-BACKED, SON OF A GORILLA-- OU'VE HAD IT!
LAY ONE HAND ON ME, MISTER, AND I'LL... I'LL...
YOU'LL WHAT?
I'LL HOP STRAIGHT INTO YOUR ICY ARMS--
--AND KISS YOU!
C'MON, CUTIE-- PUCKER UP!
THE ICY INTRUDER'S ONLY RESPONSE IS LAUGHTER, WARM AND UNINHIBITED; A LAUGHTER IMMEDIATELY ECHOED BY THE BEAST!

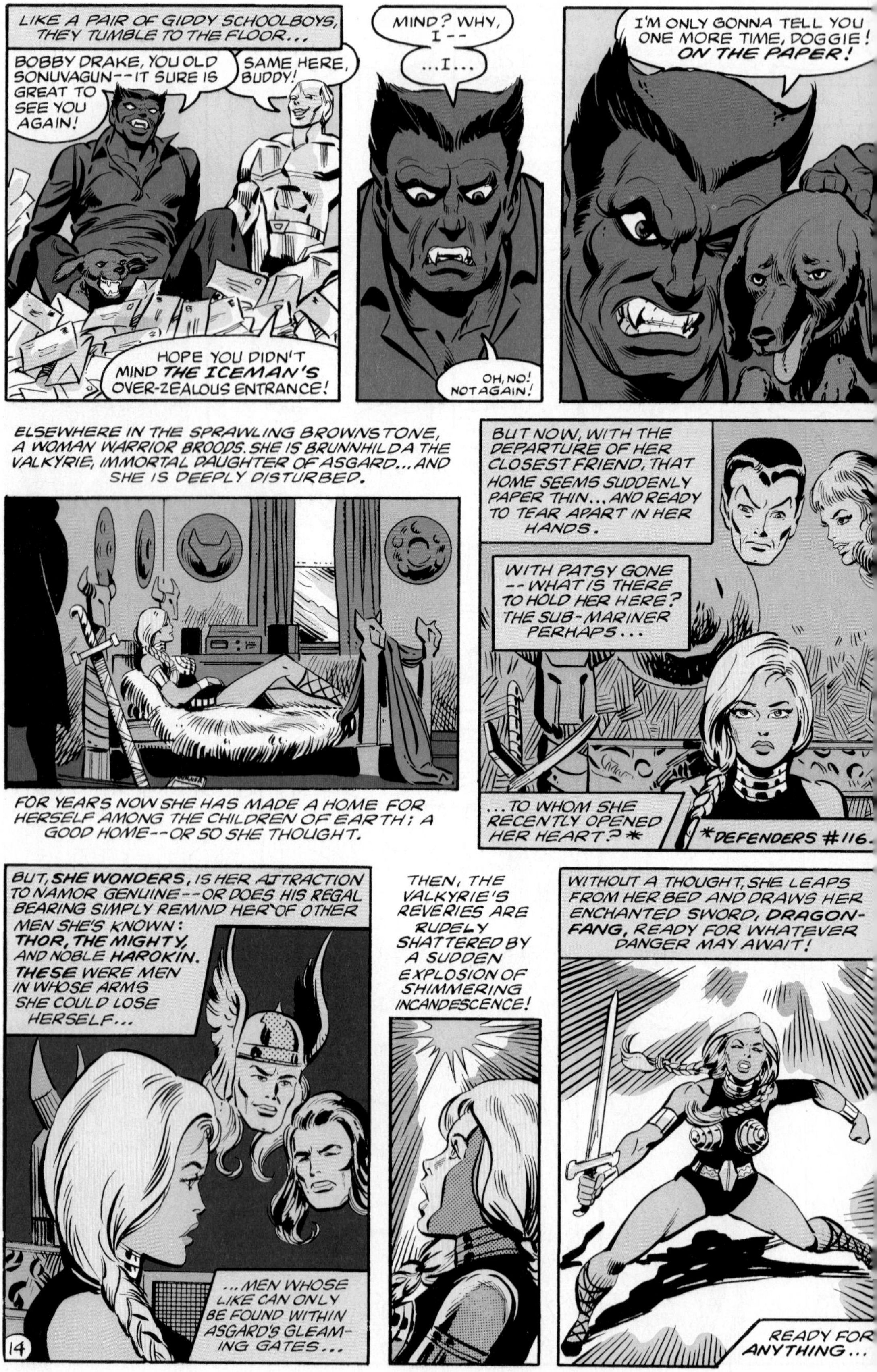
LIKE A PAIR OF GIDDY SCHOOLBOYS, THEY TUMBLE TO THE FLOOR...
BOBBY DRAKE, YOU OLD SONUVAGUN--IT SURE IS GREAT TO SEE YOU AGAIN!
SAME HERE, BUDDY!
HOPE YOU DIDN'T MIND THE ICEMAN'S OVER-ZEALOUS ENTRANCE!
MIND? WHY, I--
...I...
OH, NO! NOT AGAIN!
I'M ONLY GONNA TELL YOU ONE MORE TIME, DOGGIE! ON THE PAPER!
ELSEWHERE IN THE SPRAWLING BROWNSTONE, A WOMAN WARRIOR BROODS. SHE IS BRUNNHILDA THE VALKYRIE, IMMORTAL DAUGHTER OF ASGARD... AND SHE IS DEEPLY DISTURBED.
FOR YEARS NOW SHE HAS MADE A HOME FOR HERSELF AMONG THE CHILDREN OF EARTH: A GOOD HOME--OR SO SHE THOUGHT.
BUT NOW, WITH THE DEPARTURE OF HER CLOSEST FRIEND, THAT HOME SEEMS SUDDENLY PAPER THIN... AND READY TO TEAR APART IN HER HANDS.
WITH PATSY GONE --WHAT IS THERE TO HOLD HER HERE? THE SUB-MARINER PERHAPS...
...TO WHOM SHE RECENTLY OPENED HER HEART? *
*DEFENDERS #116.
BUT, SHE WONDERS, IS HER ATTRACTION TO NAMOR GENUINE--OR DOES HIS REGAL BEARING SIMPLY REMIND HER OF OTHER MEN SHE'S KNOWN: THOR, THE MIGHTY, AND NOBLE HAROKIN. THESE WERE MEN IN WHOSE ARMS SHE COULD LOSE HERSELF...
...MEN WHOSE LIKE CAN ONLY BE FOUND WITHIN ASGARD'S GLEAMING GATES...
14
THEN, THE VALKYRIE'S REVERIES ARE RUDELY SHATTERED BY A SUDDEN EXPLOSION OF SHIMMERING INCANDESCENCE!
WITHOUT A THOUGHT, SHE LEAPS FROM HER BED AND DRAWS HER ENCHANTED SWORD, DRAGON-FANG, READY FOR WHATEVER DANGER MAY AWAIT!
READY FOR ANYTHING...

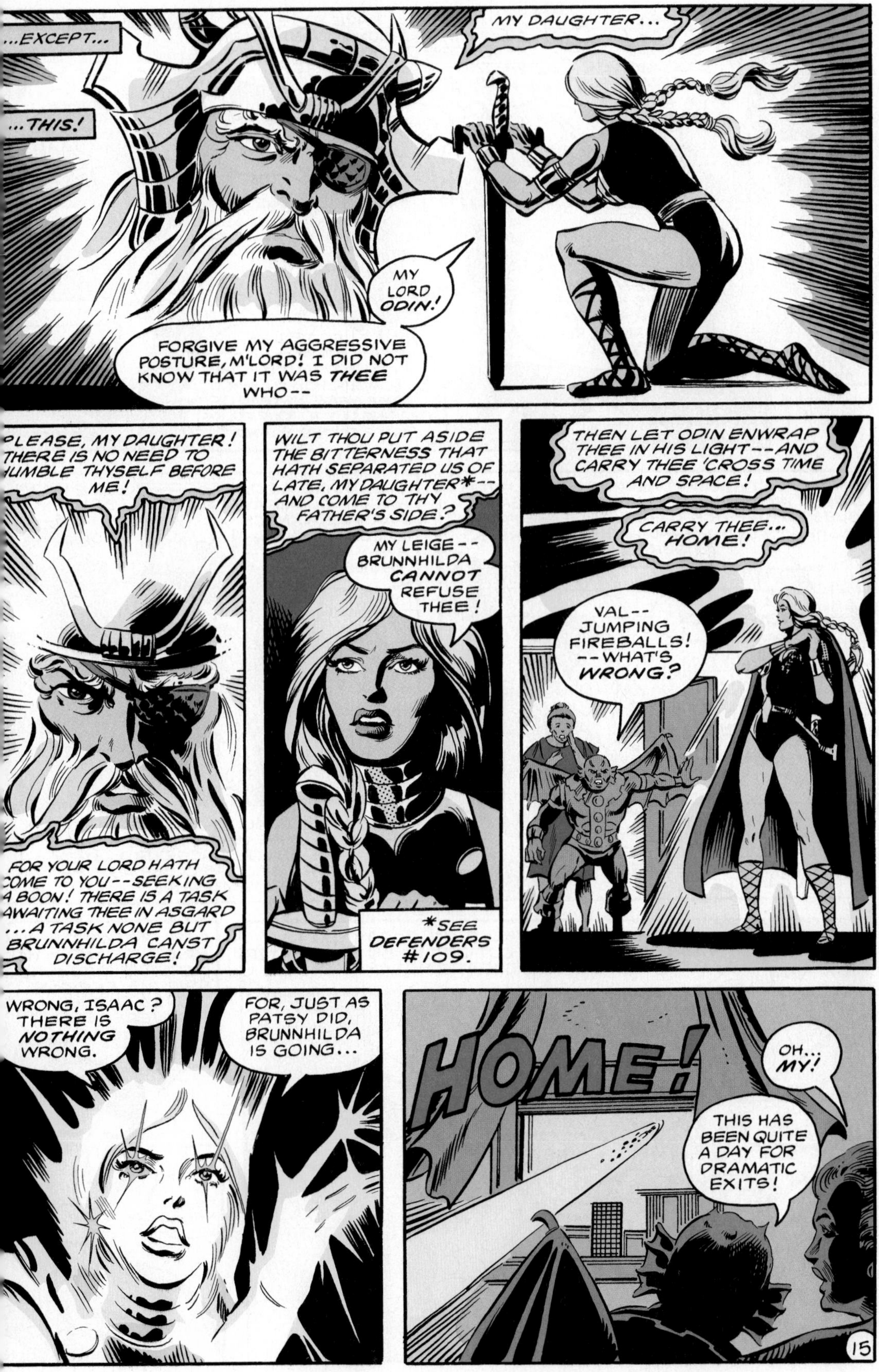
...EXCEPT...
...THIS!
MY DAUGHTER...
MY LORD ODIN!
FORGIVE MY AGGRESSIVE POSTURE, M'LORD! I DID NOT KNOW THAT IT WAS THEE WHO--
PLEASE, MY DAUGHTER! THERE IS NO NEED TO HUMBLE THYSELF BEFORE ME!
FOR YOUR LORD HATH COME TO YOU--SEEKING A BOON! THERE IS A TASK AWAITING THEE IN ASGARD ...A TASK NONE BUT BRUNNHILDA CANST DISCHARGE!
WILT THOU PUT ASIDE THE BITTERNESS THAT HATH SEPARATED US OF LATE, MY DAUGHTER*-- AND COME TO THY FATHER'S SIDE?
MY LEIGE-- BRUNNHILDA CANNOT REFUSE THEE!
*SEE DEFENDERS #109.
THEN LET ODIN ENWRAP THEE IN HIS LIGHT--AND CARRY THEE 'CROSS TIME AND SPACE!
CARRY THEE... HOME!
VAL-- JUMPING FIREBALLS! --WHAT'S WRONG?
WRONG, ISAAC? THERE IS NOTHING WRONG.
FOR, JUST AS PATSY DID, BRUNNHILDA IS GOING...
HOME!
OH... MY!
THIS HAS BEEN QUITE A DAY FOR DRAMATIC EXITS!
15

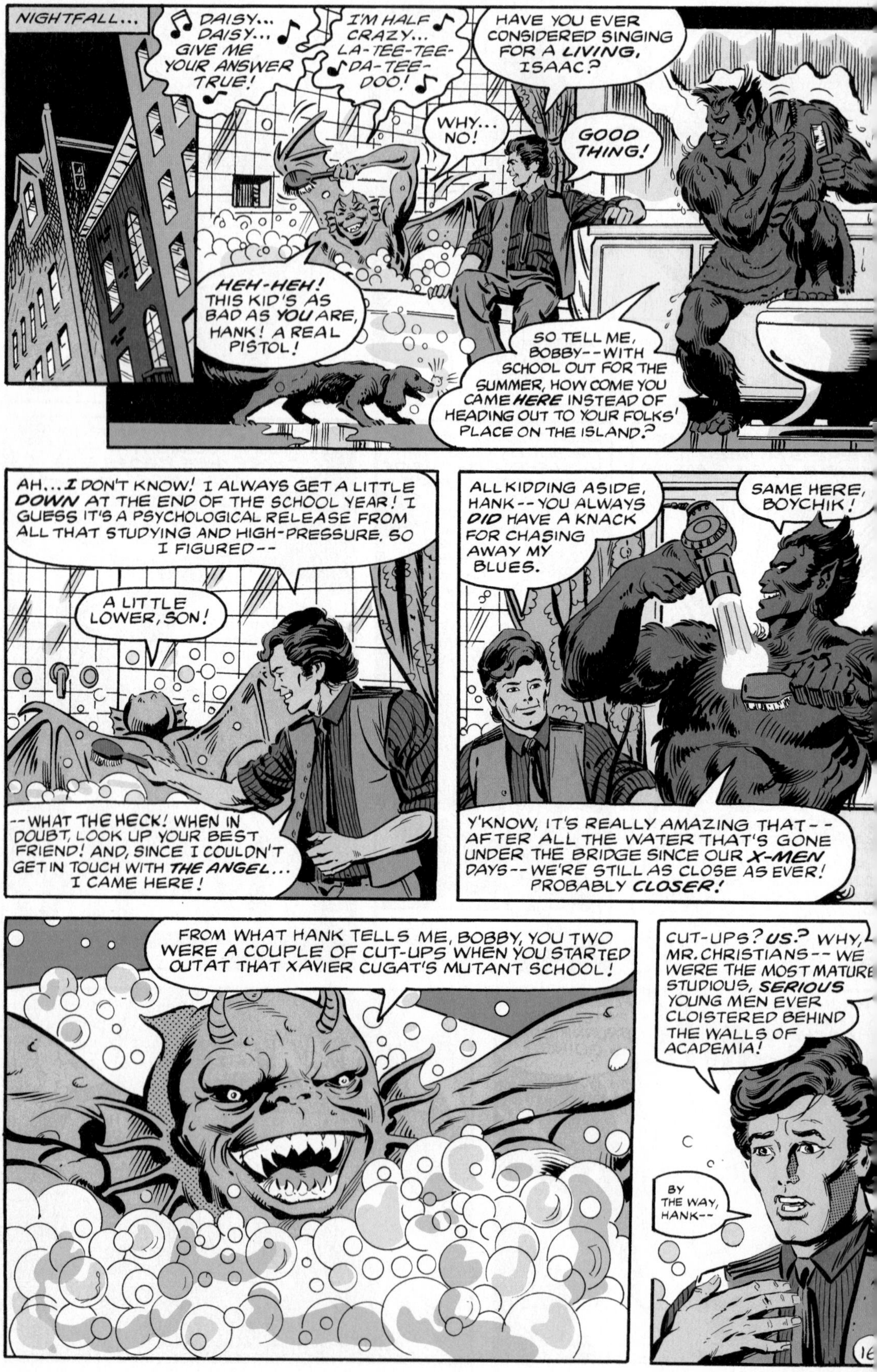
NIGHTFALL...
DAISY... DAISY... GIVE ME YOUR ANSWER TRUE!
I'M HALF CRAZY... LA-TEE-TEE-DA-TEE-DOO!
HAVE YOU EVER CONSIDERED SINGING FOR A LIVING, ISAAC?
WHY... NO!
GOOD THING!
HEH-HEH! THIS KID'S AS BAD AS YOU ARE, HANK! A REAL PISTOL!
SO TELL ME, BOBBY--WITH SCHOOL OUT FOR THE SUMMER, HOW COME YOU CAME HERE INSTEAD OF HEADING OUT TO YOUR FOLKS' PLACE ON THE ISLAND?
AH... I DON'T KNOW! I ALWAYS GET A LITTLE DOWN AT THE END OF THE SCHOOL YEAR! I GUESS IT'S A PSYCHOLOGICAL RELEASE FROM ALL THAT STUDYING AND HIGH-PRESSURE. SO I FIGURED--
A LITTLE LOWER, SON!
--WHAT THE HECK! WHEN IN DOUBT, LOOK UP YOUR BEST FRIEND! AND, SINCE I COULDN'T GET IN TOUCH WITH THE ANGEL... I CAME HERE!
ALL KIDDING ASIDE, HANK--YOU ALWAYS DID HAVE A KNACK FOR CHASING AWAY MY BLUES.
SAME HERE, BOYCHIK!
Y'KNOW, IT'S REALLY AMAZING THAT--AFTER ALL THE WATER THAT'S GONE UNDER THE BRIDGE SINCE OUR X-MEN DAYS--WE'RE STILL AS CLOSE AS EVER! PROBABLY CLOSER!
FROM WHAT HANK TELLS ME, BOBBY, YOU TWO WERE A COUPLE OF CUT-UPS WHEN YOU STARTED OUTAT THAT XAVIER CUGAT'S MUTANT SCHOOL!
CUT-UPS? US? WHY, MR. CHRISTIANS--WE WERE THE MOST MATURE STUDIOUS, SERIOUS YOUNG MEN EVER CLOISTERED BEHIND THE WALLS OF ACADEMIA!
BY THE WAY, HANK--
16

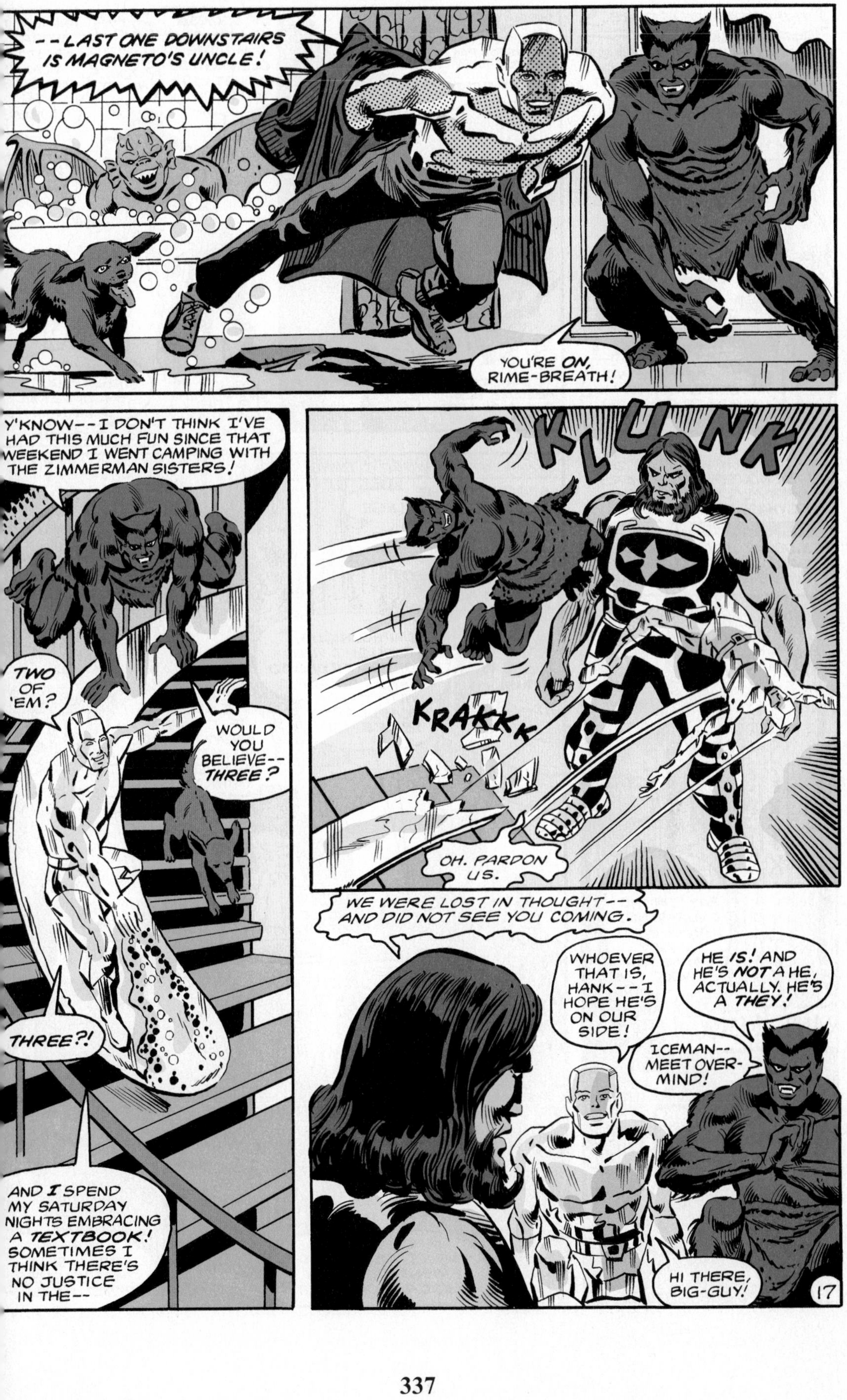
--LAST ONE DOWNSTAIRS IS MAGNETO'S UNCLE!
YOU'RE ON, RIME-BREATH!
Y'KNOW--I DON'T THINK I'VE HAD THIS MUCH FUN SINCE THAT WEEKEND I WENT CAMPING WITH THE ZIMMERMAN SISTERS!
TWO OF 'EM?
WOULD YOU BELIEVE--THREE?
THREE?!
AND I SPEND MY SATURDAY NIGHTS EMBRACING A TEXTBOOK! SOMETIMES I THINK THERE'S NO JUSTICE IN THE--
KLUNK
KRAKKK
OH. PARDON US.
WE WERE LOST IN THOUGHT--AND DID NOT SEE YOU COMING.
WHOEVER THAT IS, HANK--I HOPE HE'S ON OUR SIDE!
HE IS! AND HE'S NOT A HE, ACTUALLY. HE'S A THEY!
ICEMAN--MEET OVERMIND!
HI THERE, BIG-GUY!
17

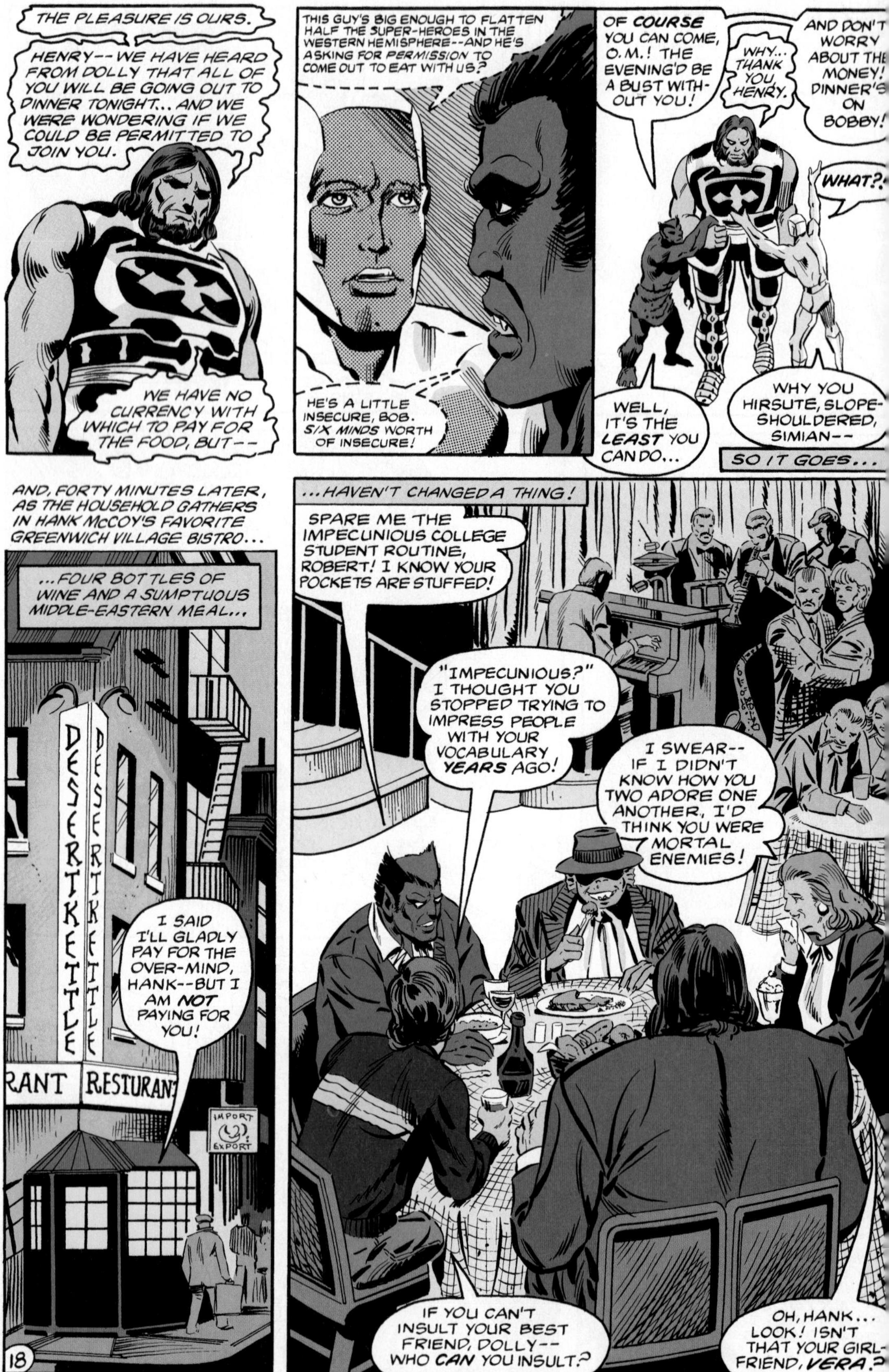
THE PLEASURE IS OURS.
HENRY-- WE HAVE HEARD FROM DOLLY THAT ALL OF YOU WILL BE GOING OUT TO DINNER TONIGHT... AND WE WERE WONDERING IF WE COULD BE PERMITTED TO JOIN YOU.
WE HAVE NO CURRENCY WITH WHICH TO PAY FOR THE FOOD, BUT--
THIS GUY'S BIG ENOUGH TO FLATTEN HALF THE SUPER-HEROES IN THE WESTERN HEMISPHERE--AND HE'S ASKING FOR PERMISSION TO COME OUT TO EAT WITH US?
HE'S A LITTLE INSECURE, BOB. SIX MINDS WORTH OF INSECURE!
OF COURSE YOU CAN COME, O.M.! THE EVENING'D BE A BUST WITH-OUT YOU!
WHY... THANK YOU, HENRY.
AND DON'T WORRY ABOUT THE MONEY! DINNER'S ON BOBBY!
WHAT?!
WELL, IT'S THE LEAST YOU CAN DO...
WHY YOU HIRSUTE, SLOPE-SHOULDERED, SIMIAN--
SO IT GOES...
AND, FORTY MINUTES LATER, AS THE HOUSEHOLD GATHERS IN HANK McCOY'S FAVORITE GREENWICH VILLAGE BISTRO...
...FOUR BOTTLES OF WINE AND A SUMPTUOUS MIDDLE-EASTERN MEAL...
DESERT KETTLE
RANT
RESTURANT
IMPORT EXPORT
I SAID I'LL GLADLY PAY FOR THE OVER-MIND, HANK--BUT I AM NOT PAYING FOR YOU!
18
...HAVEN'T CHANGED A THING!
SPARE ME THE IMPECUNIOUS COLLEGE STUDENT ROUTINE, ROBERT! I KNOW YOUR POCKETS ARE STUFFED!
"IMPECUNIOUS?" I THOUGHT YOU STOPPED TRYING TO IMPRESS PEOPLE WITH YOUR VOCABULARY YEARS AGO!
I SWEAR-- IF I DIDN'T KNOW HOW YOU TWO ADORE ONE ANOTHER, I'D THINK YOU WERE MORTAL ENEMIES!
IF YOU CAN'T INSULT YOUR BEST FRIEND, DOLLY-- WHO CAN YOU INSULT?
OH, HANK... LOOK! ISN'T THAT YOUR GIRL-FRIEND, VERA?

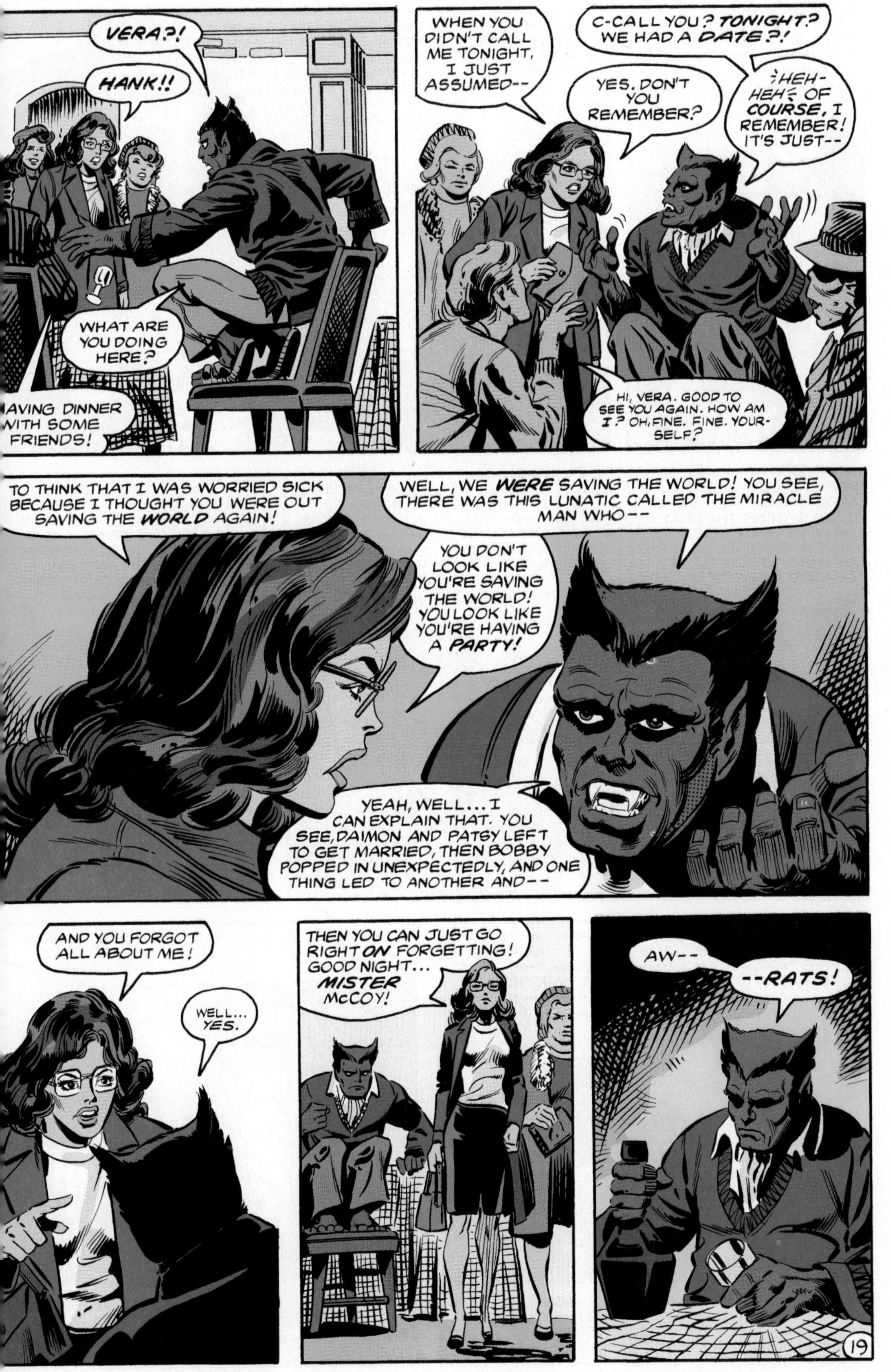
VERA?!
HANK!!
WHAT ARE YOU DOING HERE?
AVING DINNER WITH SOME FRIENDS!
WHEN YOU DIDN'T CALL ME TONIGHT, I JUST ASSUMED--
C-CALL YOU? TONIGHT? WE HAD A DATE?!
YES. DON'T YOU REMEMBER?
HEH-HEH OF COURSE, I REMEMBER! IT'S JUST--
HI, VERA. GOOD TO SEE YOU AGAIN. HOW AM I? OH, FINE. FINE. YOURSELF?
TO THINK THAT I WAS WORRIED SICK BECAUSE I THOUGHT YOU WERE OUT SAVING THE WORLD AGAIN!
WELL, WE WERE SAVING THE WORLD! YOU SEE, THERE WAS THIS LUNATIC CALLED THE MIRACLE MAN WHO--
YOU DON'T LOOK LIKE YOU'RE SAVING THE WORLD! YOU LOOK LIKE YOU'RE HAVING A PARTY!
YEAH, WELL... I CAN EXPLAIN THAT. YOU SEE, DAIMON AND PATSY LEFT TO GET MARRIED, THEN BOBBY POPPED IN UNEXPECTEDLY, AND ONE THING LED TO ANOTHER AND--
AND YOU FORGOT ALL ABOUT ME!
WELL... YES.
THEN YOU CAN JUST GO RIGHT ON FORGETTING! GOOD NIGHT... MISTER McCOY!
AW--
--RATS!
19

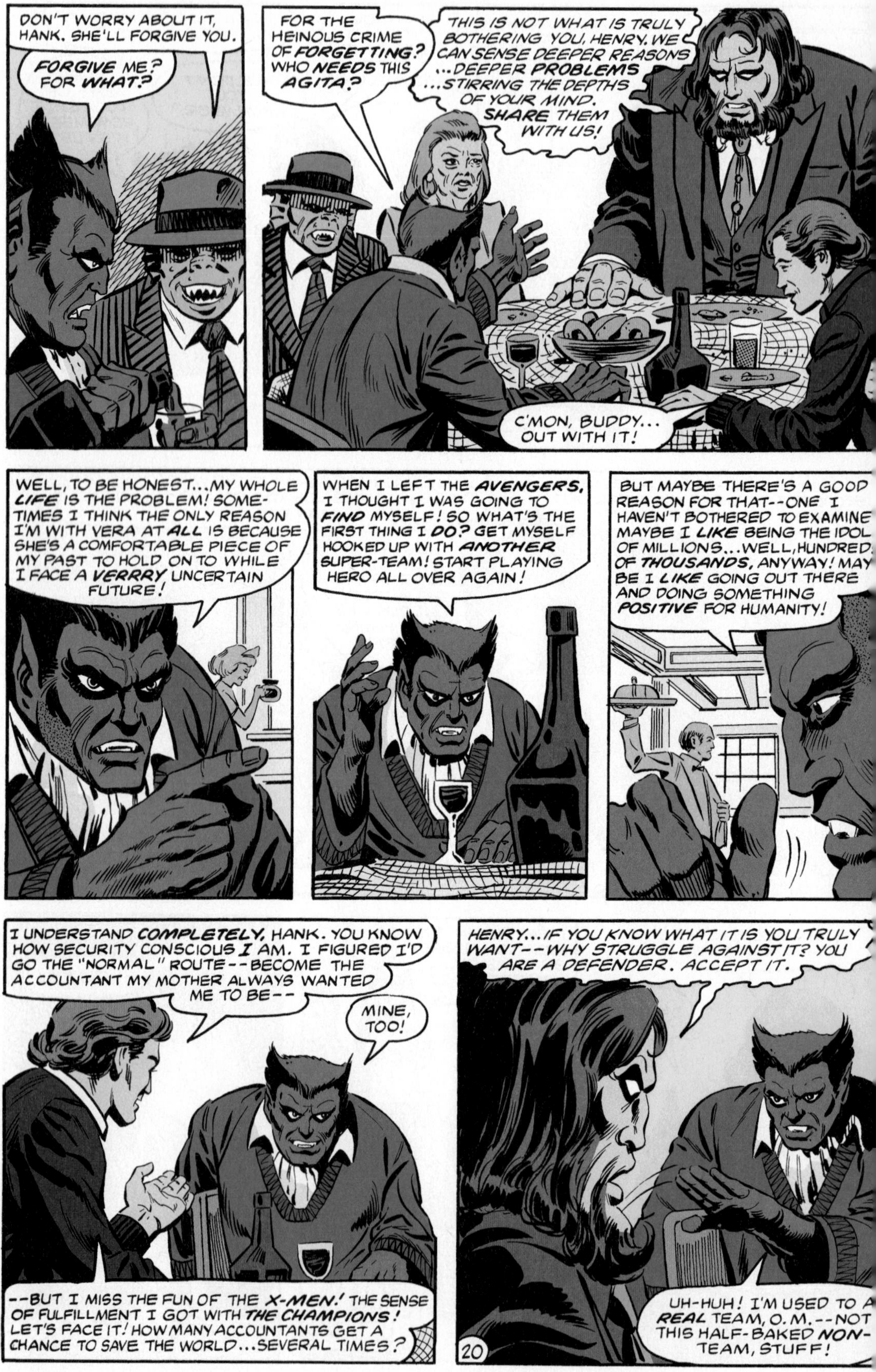
DON'T WORRY ABOUT IT, HANK. SHE'LL FORGIVE YOU.
FORGIVE ME? FOR WHAT?
FOR THE HEINOUS CRIME OF FORGETTING? WHO NEEDS THIS AGITA?
THIS IS NOT WHAT IS TRULY BOTHERING YOU, HENRY. WE CAN SENSE DEEPER REASONS ...DEEPER PROBLEMS ...STIRRING THE DEPTHS OF YOUR MIND. SHARE THEM WITH US!
C'MON, BUDDY... OUT WITH IT!
WELL, TO BE HONEST...MY WHOLE LIFE IS THE PROBLEM! SOMETIMES I THINK THE ONLY REASON I'M WITH VERA AT ALL IS BECAUSE SHE'S A COMFORTABLE PIECE OF MY PAST TO HOLD ON TO WHILE I FACE A VERRRY UNCERTAIN FUTURE!
WHEN I LEFT THE AVENGERS, I THOUGHT I WAS GOING TO FIND MYSELF! SO WHAT'S THE FIRST THING I DO? GET MYSELF HOOKED UP WITH ANOTHER SUPER-TEAM! START PLAYING HERO ALL OVER AGAIN!
BUT MAYBE THERE'S A GOOD REASON FOR THAT--ONE I HAVEN'T BOTHERED TO EXAMINE MAYBE I LIKE BEING THE IDOL OF MILLIONS...WELL, HUNDRED OF THOUSANDS, ANYWAY! MAY BE I LIKE GOING OUT THERE AND DOING SOMETHING POSITIVE FOR HUMANITY!
I UNDERSTAND COMPLETELY, HANK. YOU KNOW HOW SECURITY CONSCIOUS I AM. I FIGURED I'D GO THE "NORMAL" ROUTE--BECOME THE ACCOUNTANT MY MOTHER ALWAYS WANTED ME TO BE--
MINE, TOO!
--BUT I MISS THE FUN OF THE X-MEN! THE SENSE OF FULFILLMENT I GOT WITH THE CHAMPIONS! LET'S FACE IT! HOW MANY ACCOUNTANTS GET A CHANCE TO SAVE THE WORLD...SEVERAL TIMES?
HENRY...IF YOU KNOW WHAT IT IS YOU TRULY WANT--WHY STRUGGLE AGAINST IT? YOU ARE A DEFENDER. ACCEPT IT.
UH-HUH! I'M USED TO A REAL TEAM, O.M.--NOT THIS HALF-BAKED NON-TEAM, STUFF!
20

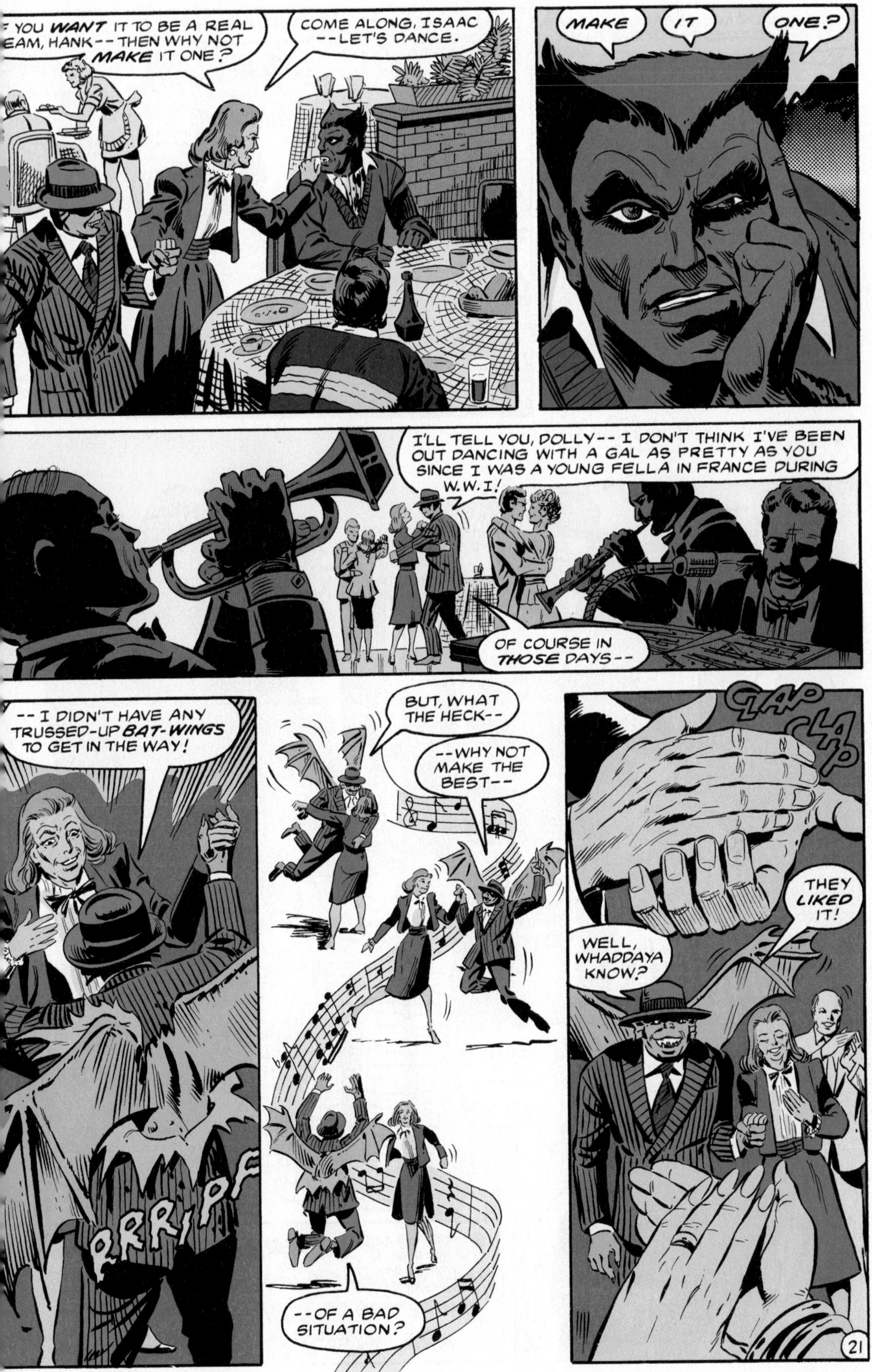
F YOU WANT IT TO BE A REAL
EAM, HANK--THEN WHY NOT MAKE IT ONE?
COME ALONG, ISAAC --LET'S DANCE.
MAKE
IT
ONE?
I'LL TELL YOU, DOLLY-- I DON'T THINK I'VE BEEN OUT DANCING WITH A GAL AS PRETTY AS YOU SINCE I WAS A YOUNG FELLA IN FRANCE DURING W.W.I!
OF COURSE IN THOSE DAYS--
--I DIDN'T HAVE ANY TRUSSED-UP BAT-WINGS TO GET IN THE WAY!
RRRIPP
BUT, WHAT THE HECK--
--WHY NOT MAKE THE BEST--
--OF A BAD SITUATION?
CLAP CLAP
THEY LIKED IT!
WELL, WHADDAYA KNOW?
21

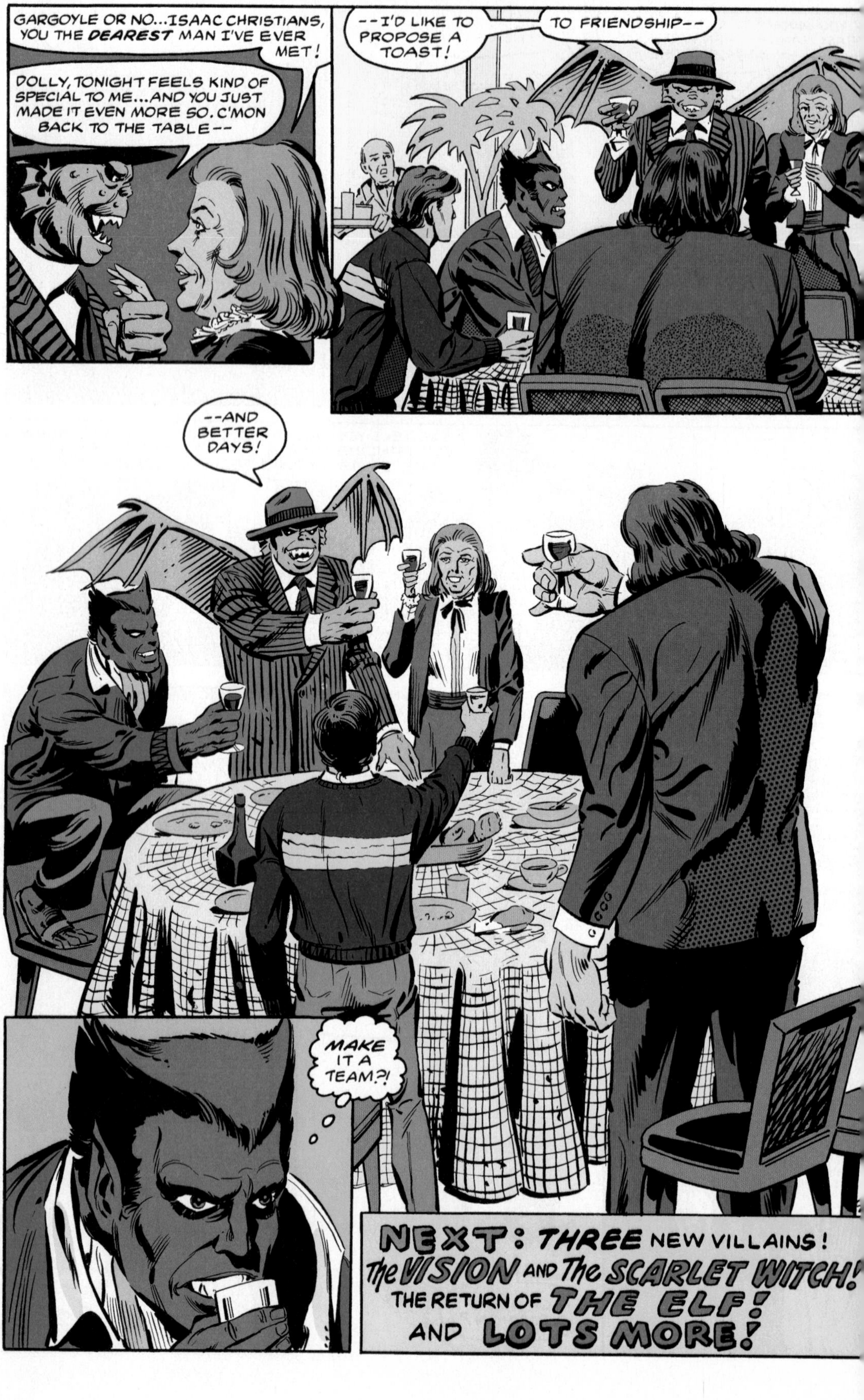
GARGOYLE OR NO...ISAAC CHRISTIANS, YOU THE DEAREST MAN I'VE EVER MET!
DOLLY, TONIGHT FEELS KIND OF SPECIAL TO ME...AND YOU JUST MADE IT EVEN MORE SO. C'MON BACK TO THE TABLE--
--I'D LIKE TO PROPOSE A TOAST!
TO FRIENDSHIP--
--AND BETTER DAYS!
MAKE IT A TEAM?!
NEXT: THREE NEW VILLAINS! The VISION AND The SCARLET WITCH! THE RETURN OF THE ELF! AND LOTS MORE!

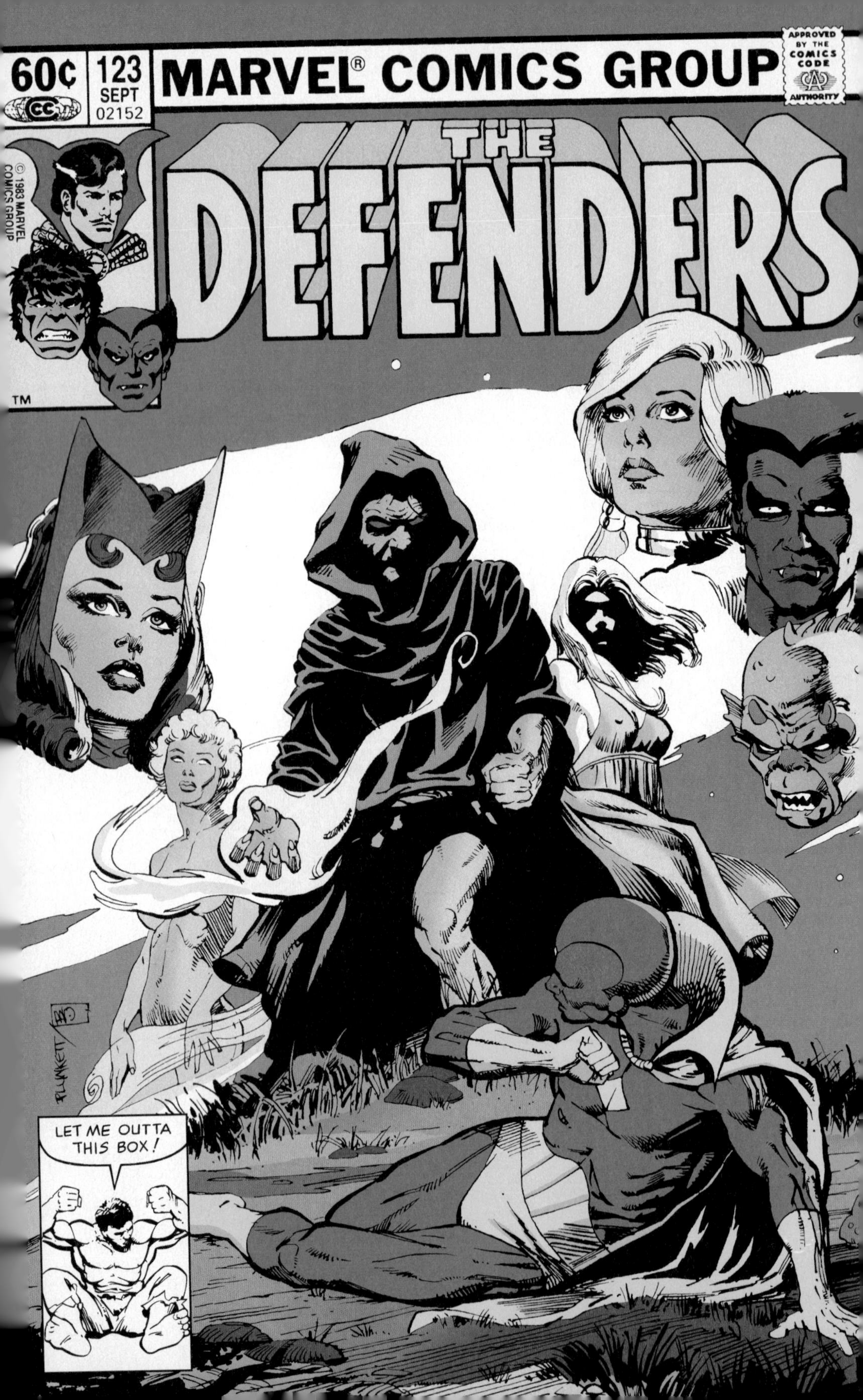
60¢
123
SEPT
02152
MARVEL® COMICS GROUP
APPROVED BY THE COMICS CODE AUTHORITY
THE DEFENDERS
© 1983 MARVEL COMICS GROUP
TM
LET ME OUTTA THIS BOX!

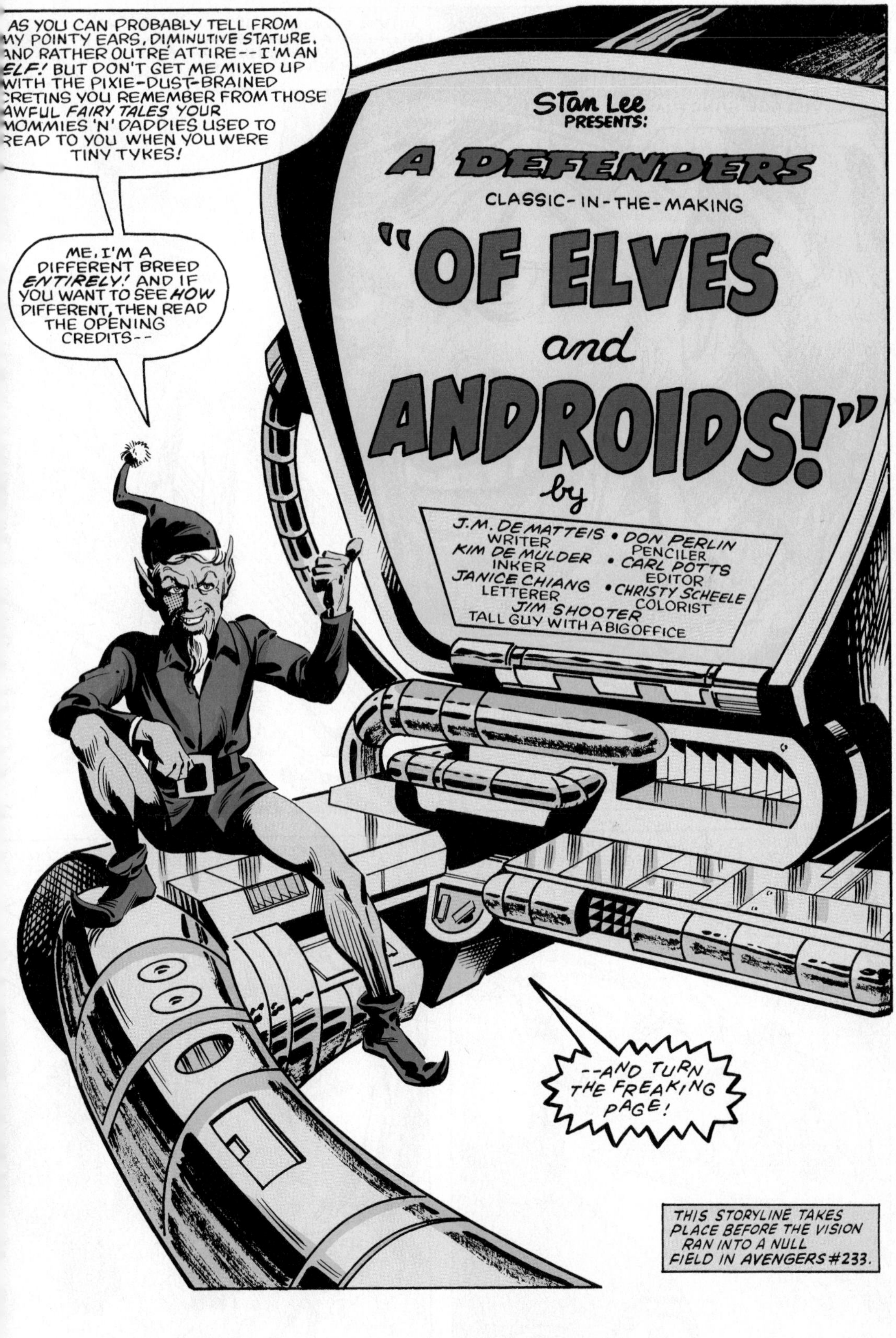
AS YOU CAN PROBABLY TELL FROM MY POINTY EARS, DIMINUTIVE STATURE, AND RATHER OUTRÉ ATTIRE-- I'M AN ELF! BUT DON'T GET ME MIXED UP WITH THE PIXIE-DUST-BRAINED CRETINS YOU REMEMBER FROM THOSE AWFUL FAIRY TALES YOUR MOMMIES 'N' DADDIES USED TO READ TO YOU WHEN YOU WERE TINY TYKES!
ME, I'M A DIFFERENT BREED ENTIRELY! AND IF YOU WANT TO SEE HOW DIFFERENT, THEN READ THE OPENING CREDITS--
STAN LEE PRESENTS:
A DEFENDERS CLASSIC-IN-THE-MAKING
"OF ELVES and ANDROIDS!"
by
J.M. DEMATTEIS • WRITER
DON PERLIN • PENCILER
KIM DE MULDER • INKER
CARL POTTS • EDITOR
JANICE CHIANG • LETTERER
CHRISTY SCHEELE • COLORIST
JIM SHOOTER • TALL GUY WITH A BIG OFFICE
--AND TURN THE FREAKING PAGE!
THIS STORYLINE TAKES PLACE BEFORE THE VISION RAN INTO A NULL FIELD IN AVENGERS #233.

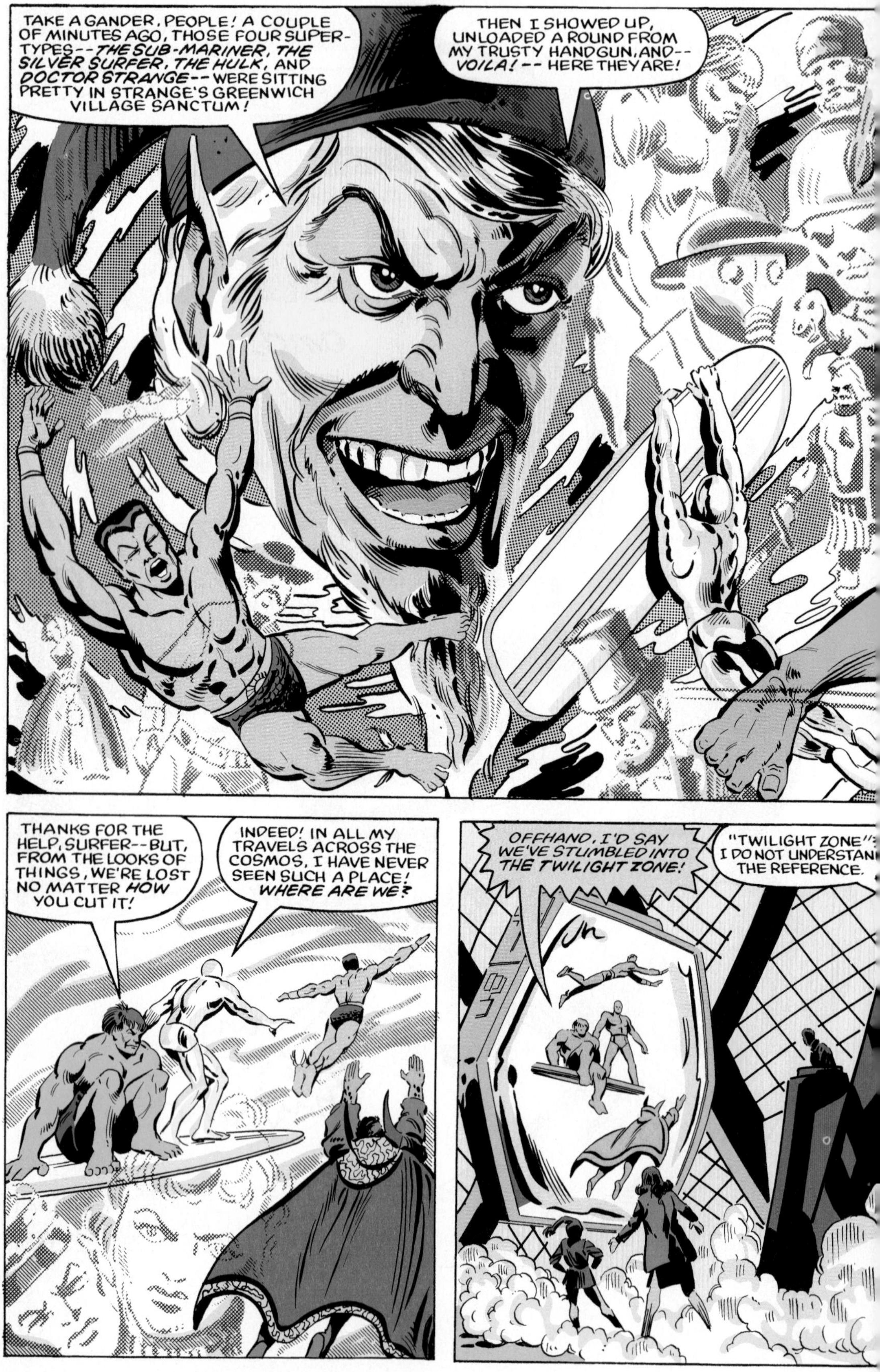
TAKE A GANDER, PEOPLE! A COUPLE OF MINUTES AGO, THOSE FOUR SUPER-TYPES-- *THE SUB-MARINER, THE SILVER SURFER, THE HULK,* AND *DOCTOR STRANGE*-- WERE SITTING PRETTY IN STRANGE'S GREENWICH VILLAGE SANCTUM!
THEN I SHOWED UP, UNLOADED A ROUND FROM MY TRUSTY HANDGUN, AND-- *VOILA!* -- HERE THEY ARE!
THANKS FOR THE HELP, SURFER-- BUT, FROM THE LOOKS OF THINGS, WE'RE LOST NO MATTER *HOW* YOU CUT IT!
INDEED! IN ALL MY TRAVELS ACROSS THE COSMOS, I HAVE NEVER SEEN SUCH A PLACE! *WHERE ARE WE?*
OFFHAND, I'D SAY WE'VE STUMBLED INTO *THE TWILIGHT ZONE!*
"TWILIGHT ZONE"? I DO NOT UNDERSTAN THE REFERENCE.

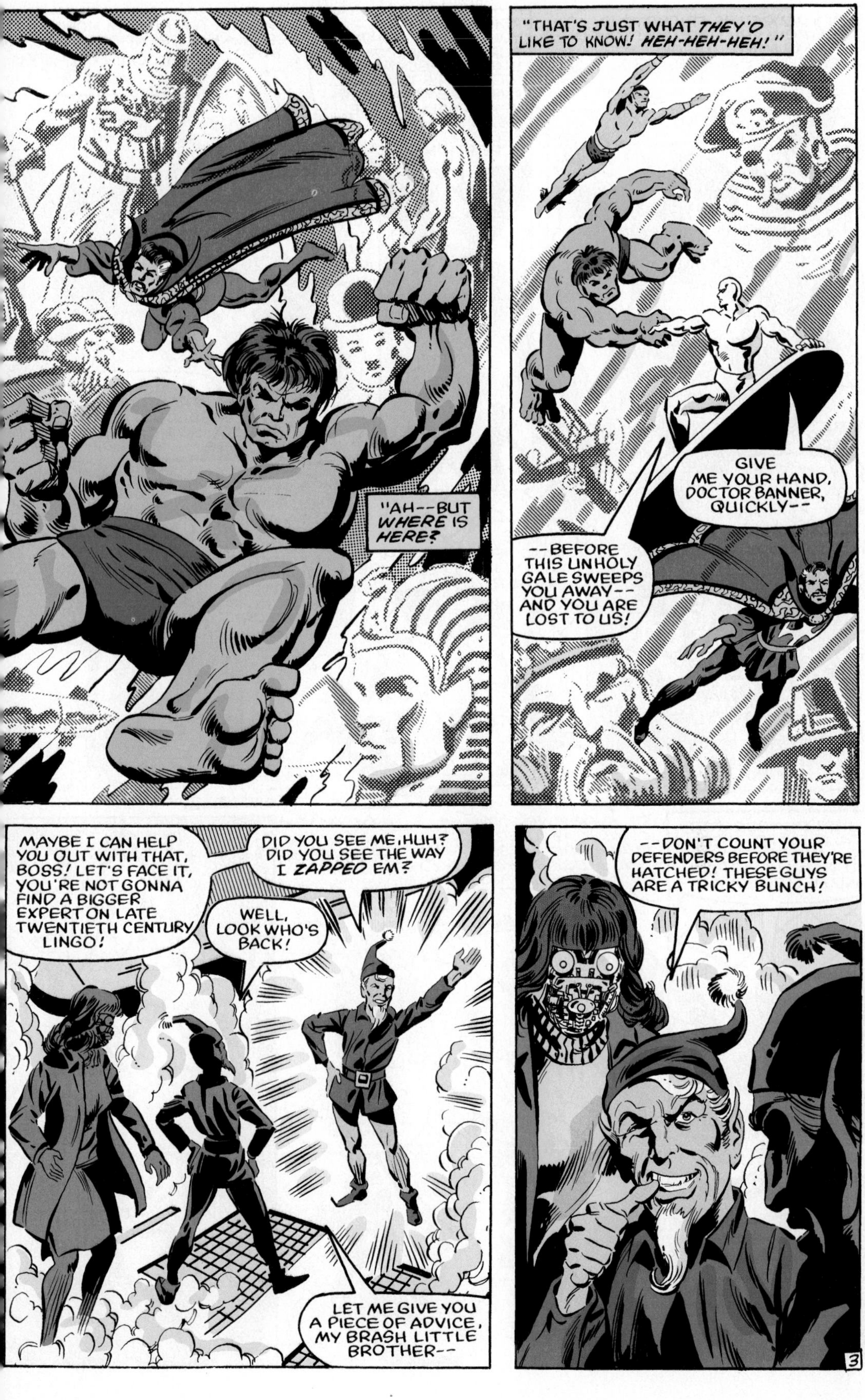
"AH--BUT WHERE IS HERE?
"THAT'S JUST WHAT THEY'D LIKE TO KNOW! HEH-HEH-HEH!"
GIVE ME YOUR HAND, DOCTOR BANNER, QUICKLY--
--BEFORE THIS UNHOLY GALE SWEEPS YOU AWAY-- AND YOU ARE LOST TO US!
MAYBE I CAN HELP YOU OUT WITH THAT, BOSS! LET'S FACE IT, YOU'RE NOT GONNA FIND A BIGGER EXPERT ON LATE TWENTIETH CENTURY LINGO!
WELL, LOOK WHO'S BACK!
DID YOU SEE ME, HUH? DID YOU SEE THE WAY I ZAPPED EM?
LET ME GIVE YOU A PIECE OF ADVICE, MY BRASH LITTLE BROTHER--
--DON'T COUNT YOUR DEFENDERS BEFORE THEY'RE HATCHED! THESE GUYS ARE A TRICKY BUNCH!
3

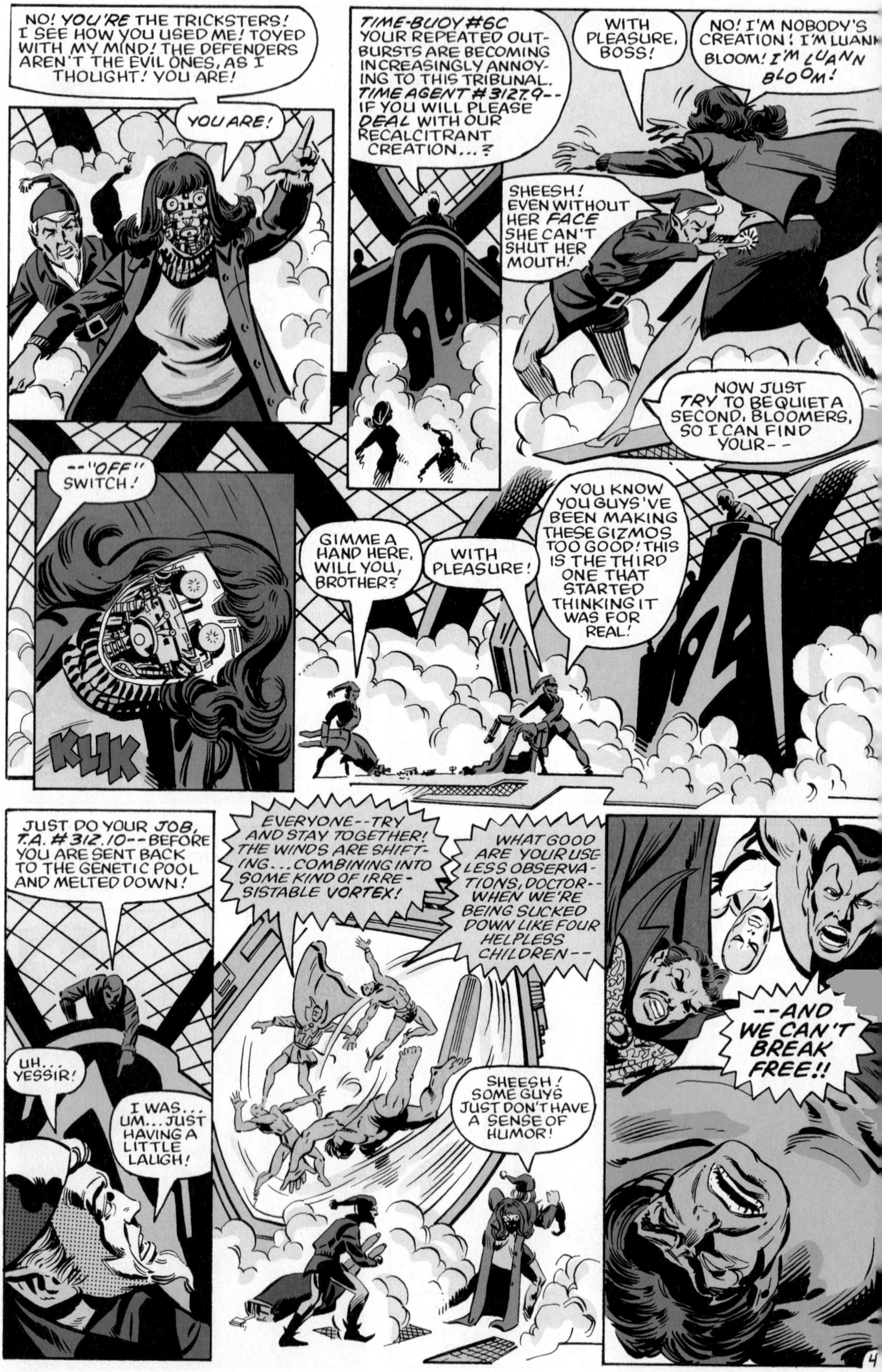

NO! YOU'RE THE TRICKSTERS! I SEE HOW YOU USED ME! TOYED WITH MY MIND! THE DEFENDERS AREN'T THE EVIL ONES, AS I THOUGHT! YOU ARE!
YOU ARE!
TIME-BUOY #6C YOUR REPEATED OUTBURSTS ARE BECOMING INCREASINGLY ANNOYING TO THIS TRIBUNAL. TIME AGENT #3127.9-- IF YOU WILL PLEASE DEAL WITH OUR RECALCITRANT CREATION...?
WITH PLEASURE, BOSS!
NO! I'M NOBODY'S CREATION! I'M LUANN BLOOM! I'M LUANN BLOOM!
SHEESH! EVEN WITHOUT HER FACE SHE CAN'T SHUT HER MOUTH!
NOW JUST TRY TO BE QUIET A SECOND, BLOOMERS, SO I CAN FIND YOUR--
--"OFF" SWITCH!
KLIK
GIMME A HAND HERE, WILL YOU, BROTHER?
WITH PLEASURE!
YOU KNOW YOU GUYS'VE BEEN MAKING THESE GIZMOS TOO GOOD! THIS IS THE THIRD ONE THAT STARTED THINKING IT WAS FOR REAL!
JUST DO YOUR JOB, T.A. #312.10--BEFORE YOU ARE SENT BACK TO THE GENETIC POOL AND MELTED DOWN!
UH... YESSIR!
I WAS... UM... JUST HAVING A LITTLE LAUGH!
EVERYONE--TRY AND STAY TOGETHER! THE WINDS ARE SHIFTING... COMBINING INTO SOME KIND OF IRRESISTABLE VORTEX!
WHAT GOOD ARE YOUR USELESS OBSERVATIONS, DOCTOR-- WHEN WE'RE BEING SUCKED DOWN LIKE FOUR HELPLESS CHILDREN--
SHEESH! SOME GUYS JUST DON'T HAVE A SENSE OF HUMOR!
--AND WE CAN'T BREAK FREE!!
4

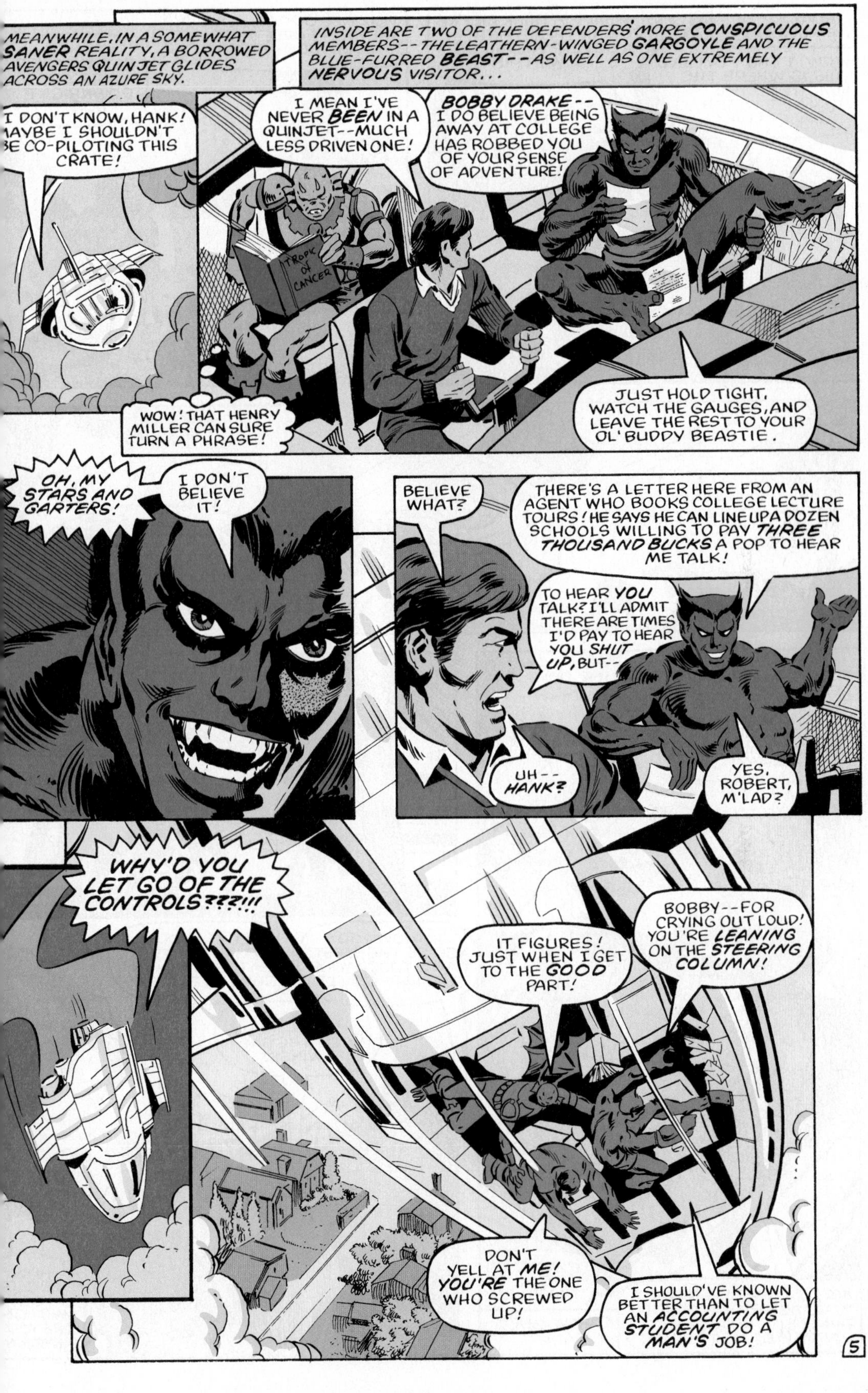

MEANWHILE, IN A SOMEWHAT SANER REALITY, A BORROWED AVENGERS QUINJET GLIDES ACROSS AN AZURE SKY.
INSIDE ARE TWO OF THE DEFENDERS' MORE CONSPICUOUS MEMBERS--THE LEATHERN-WINGED GARGOYLE AND THE BLUE-FURRED BEAST--AS WELL AS ONE EXTREMELY NERVOUS VISITOR...
I DON'T KNOW, HANK! MAYBE I SHOULDN'T BE CO-PILOTING THIS CRATE!
I MEAN I'VE NEVER BEEN IN A QUINJET--MUCH LESS DRIVEN ONE!
BOBBY DRAKE--I DO BELIEVE BEING AWAY AT COLLEGE HAS ROBBED YOU OF YOUR SENSE OF ADVENTURE!
TROPIC OF CANCER
WOW! THAT HENRY MILLER CAN SURE TURN A PHRASE!
JUST HOLD TIGHT, WATCH THE GAUGES, AND LEAVE THE REST TO YOUR OL' BUDDY BEASTIE.
OH, MY STARS AND GARTERS!
I DON'T BELIEVE IT!
BELIEVE WHAT?
THERE'S A LETTER HERE FROM AN AGENT WHO BOOKS COLLEGE LECTURE TOURS! HE SAYS HE CAN LINE UP A DOZEN SCHOOLS WILLING TO PAY THREE THOUSAND BUCKS A POP TO HEAR ME TALK!
TO HEAR YOU TALK? I'LL ADMIT THERE ARE TIMES I'D PAY TO HEAR YOU SHUT UP, BUT--
UH--HANK?
YES, ROBERT, M'LAD?
WHY'D YOU LET GO OF THE CONTROLS???!!!
IT FIGURES! JUST WHEN I GET TO THE GOOD PART!
BOBBY--FOR CRYING OUT LOUD! YOU'RE LEANING ON THE STEERING COLUMN!
DON'T YELL AT ME! YOU'RE THE ONE WHO SCREWED UP!
I SHOULD'VE KNOWN BETTER THAN TO LET AN ACCOUNTING STUDENT DO A MAN'S JOB!
5

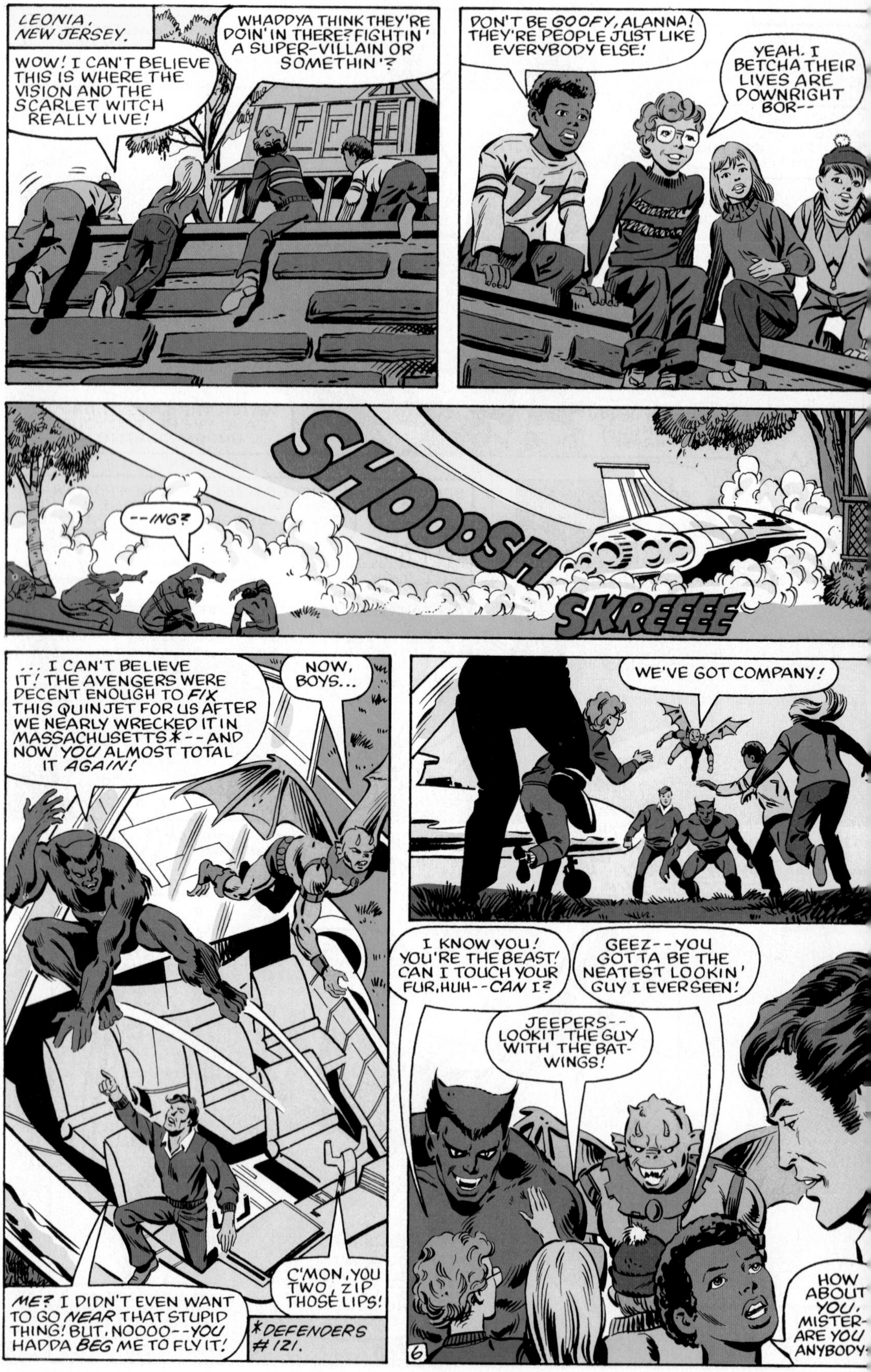

LEONIA, NEW JERSEY.
WOW! I CAN'T BELIEVE THIS IS WHERE THE VISION AND THE SCARLET WITCH REALLY LIVE!
WHADDYA THINK THEY'RE DOIN' IN THERE? FIGHTIN' A SUPER-VILLAIN OR SOMETHIN'?
DON'T BE GOOFY, ALANNA! THEY'RE PEOPLE JUST LIKE EVERYBODY ELSE!
YEAH. I BETCHA THEIR LIVES ARE DOWNRIGHT BOR--
--ING?
SHOOOSH
SKREEEEE
... I CAN'T BELIEVE IT! THE AVENGERS WERE DECENT ENOUGH TO FIX THIS QUINJET FOR US AFTER WE NEARLY WRECKED IT IN MASSACHUSETTS*--AND NOW YOU ALMOST TOTAL IT AGAIN!
NOW, BOYS...
ME? I DIDN'T EVEN WANT TO GO NEAR THAT STUPID THING! BUT, NOOOO--YOU HADDA BEG ME TO FLY IT!
C'MON, YOU TWO, ZIP THOSE LIPS!
*DEFENDERS #121.
WE'VE GOT COMPANY!
I KNOW YOU! YOU'RE THE BEAST! CAN I TOUCH YOUR FUR, HUH--CAN I?
GEEZ--YOU GOTTA BE THE NEATEST LOOKIN' GUY I EVER SEEN!
JEEPERS--LOOKIT THE GUY WITH THE BAT-WINGS!
HOW ABOUT YOU, MISTER-ARE YOU ANYBODY-
6

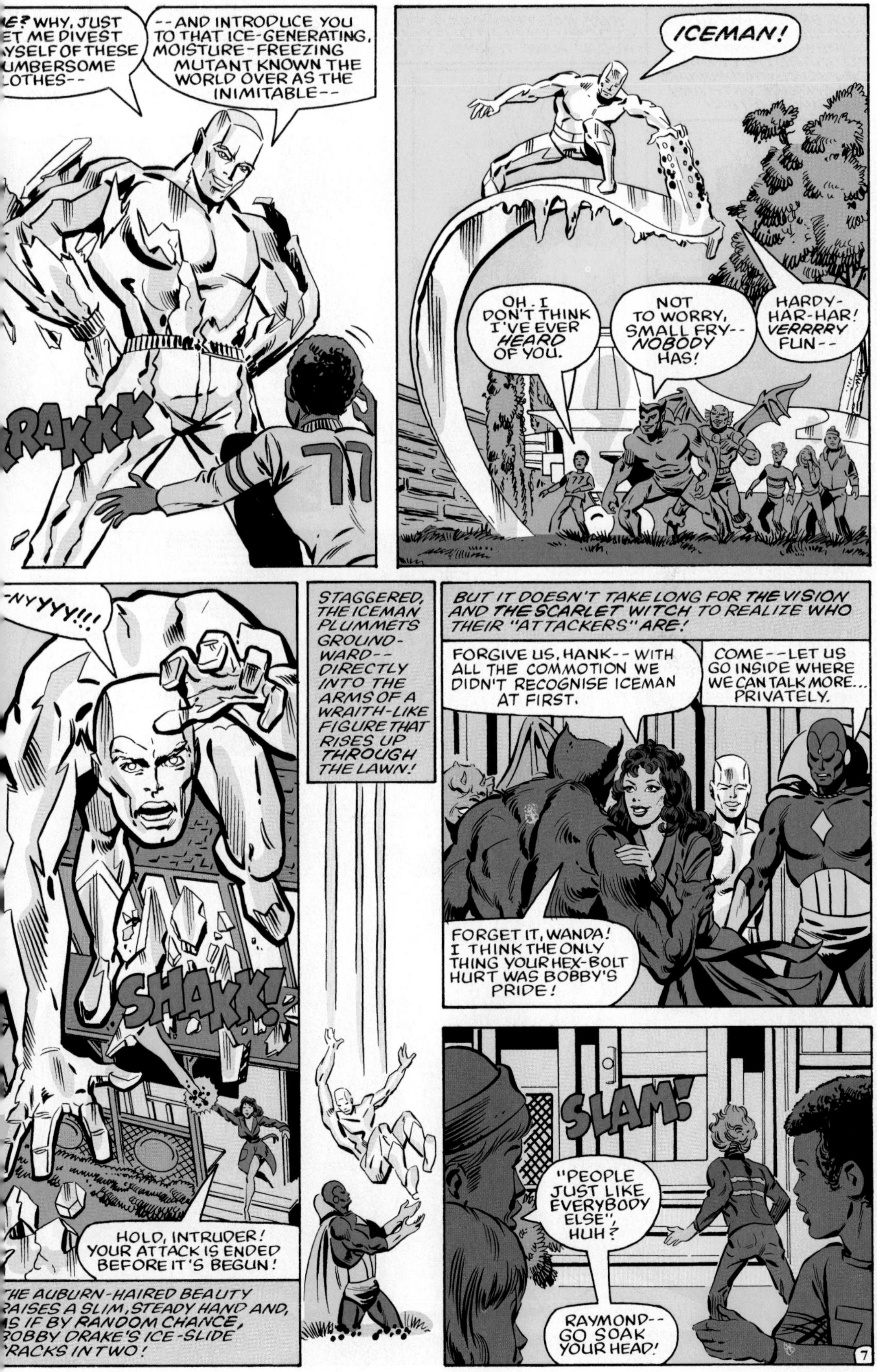

WHY, JUST ET ME DIVEST YSELF OF THESE UMBERSOME LOTHES--
--AND INTRODUCE YOU TO THAT ICE-GENERATING, MOISTURE-FREEZING MUTANT KNOWN THE WORLD OVER AS THE INIMITABLE--
RAKKK
ICEMAN!
OH. I DON'T THINK I'VE EVER HEARD OF YOU.
NOT TO WORRY, SMALL FRY-- NOBODY HAS!
HARDY-HAR-HAR! VERRRRY FUNNY--
NYYYY!!!
SHAKK!
HOLD, INTRUDER! YOUR ATTACK IS ENDED BEFORE IT'S BEGUN!
THE AUBURN-HAIRED BEAUTY RAISES A SLIM, STEADY HAND AND, AS IF BY RANDOM CHANCE, BOBBY DRAKE'S ICE-SLIDE CRACKS IN TWO!
STAGGERED, THE ICEMAN PLUMMETS GROUNDWARD-- DIRECTLY INTO THE ARMS OF A WRAITH-LIKE FIGURE THAT RISES UP THROUGH THE LAWN!
BUT IT DOESN'T TAKE LONG FOR THE VISION AND THE SCARLET WITCH TO REALIZE WHO THEIR "ATTACKERS" ARE!
FORGIVE US, HANK-- WITH ALL THE COMMOTION WE DIDN'T RECOGNISE ICEMAN AT FIRST.
COME--LET US GO INSIDE WHERE WE CAN TALK MORE... PRIVATELY.
FORGET IT, WANDA! I THINK THE ONLY THING YOUR HEX-BOLT HURT WAS BOBBY'S PRIDE!
SLAM!
"PEOPLE JUST LIKE EVERYBODY ELSE", HUH?
RAYMOND-- GO SOAK YOUR HEAD!
7

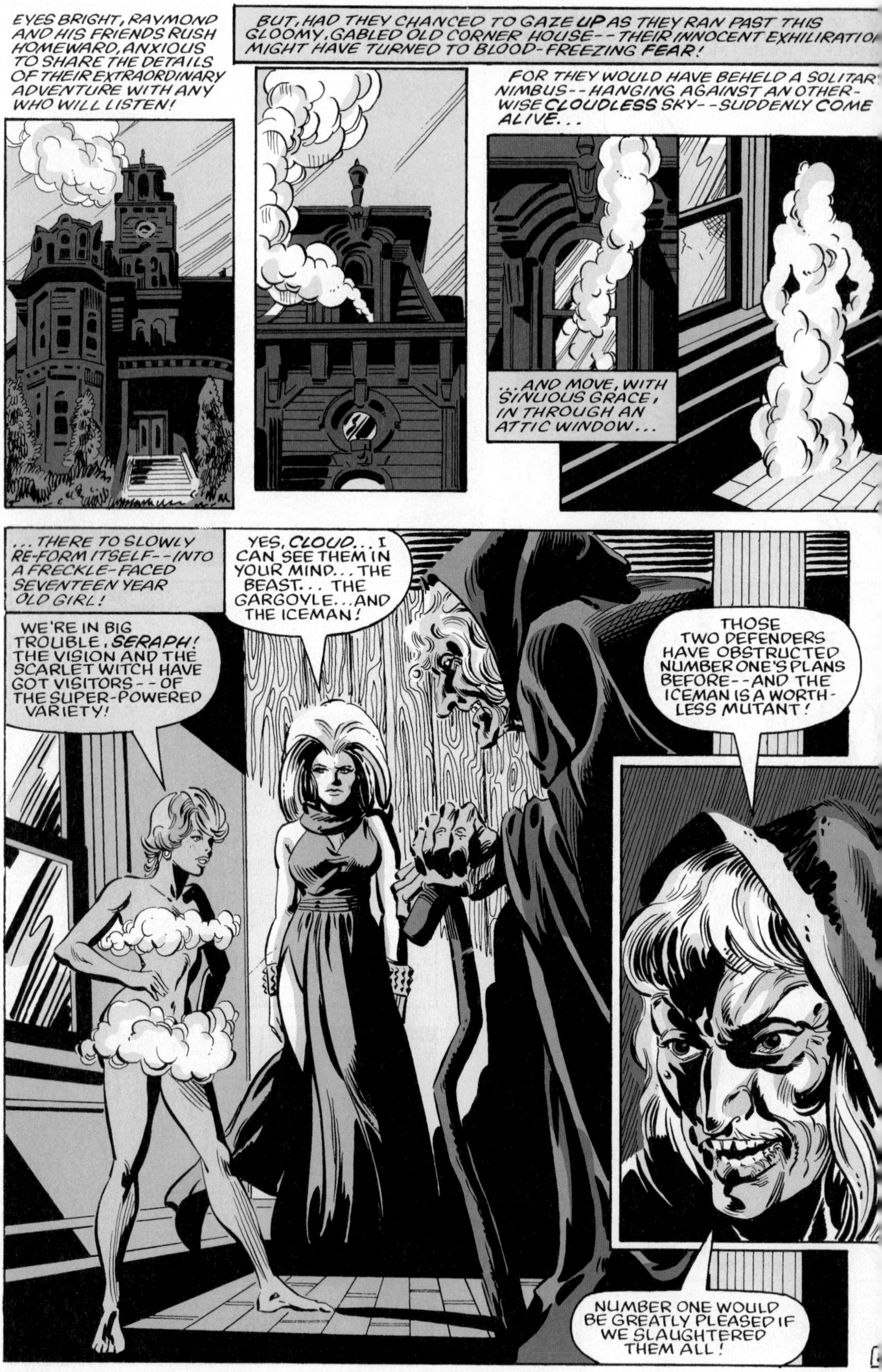

EYES BRIGHT, RAYMOND AND HIS FRIENDS RUSH HOMEWARD, ANXIOUS TO SHARE THE DETAILS OF THEIR EXTRAORDINARY ADVENTURE WITH ANY WHO WILL LISTEN!
BUT, HAD THEY CHANCED TO GAZE UP AS THEY RAN PAST THIS GLOOMY, GABLED OLD CORNER HOUSE-- THEIR INNOCENT EXHILIRATIO MIGHT HAVE TURNED TO BLOOD-FREEZING FEAR!
FOR THEY WOULD HAVE BEHELD A SOLITAR NIMBUS--HANGING AGAINST AN OTHER-WISE CLOUDLESS SKY--SUDDENLY COME ALIVE...
...AND MOVE, WITH SINUOUS GRACE, IN THROUGH AN ATTIC WINDOW...
...THERE TO SLOWLY RE-FORM ITSELF--INTO A FRECKLE-FACED SEVENTEEN YEAR OLD GIRL!
WE'RE IN BIG TROUBLE, SERAPH! THE VISION AND THE SCARLET WITCH HAVE GOT VISITORS--OF THE SUPER-POWERED VARIETY!
YES, CLOUD... I CAN SEE THEM IN YOUR MIND... THE BEAST... THE GARGOYLE... AND THE ICEMAN!
THOSE TWO DEFENDERS HAVE OBSTRUCTED NUMBER ONE'S PLANS BEFORE--AND THE ICEMAN IS A WORTH-LESS MUTANT!
NUMBER ONE WOULD BE GREATLY PLEASED IF WE SLAUGHTERED THEM ALL!

CALM YOURSELF, OLD WOMAN. OUR INSTRUCTIONS ARE EXPLICIT. WE ARE TO CAPTURE THE SYNTHEZOID--AND ONLY THE SYNTHEZOID--SO THAT NUMBER ONE'S SCIENTISTS MAY STUDY HIM.

NO UNNECESSARY BLOOD IS TO BE SPILLED.

NO ONE BUT NUMBER ONE HIMSELF ORDERS ME, SERAPH--SO I SUGGEST YOU STILL YOUR WAGGING TONGUE--

--BEFORE THE LETHAL HANDS OF HARRIDAN DRAW THE VERY LIFE FROM THAT LOVELY YOUNG BODY!

FOR AN INSTANT, A DARK FEAR SWIMS IN THE ALBINO'S EYES...

..BUT THE FEAR IS QUICKLY DISPELLED BY AN AMBER LIGHT-- AND A GENTLE, HYPNOTIC TRILLING.

IN RESPONSE, THE HAG CALLED HARRIDAN SAGS TO HER KNEES, A VACUOUS SMILE ON HER LIPS.

TRY THAT AGAIN, WITCH-- AND I'LL GRIND THOSE AGED BONES OF YOURS TO DUST!

OH, WILL YOU TWO KNOCK IT OFF! WE'VE GOT A JOB TO DO, RIGHT? SO LET'S DO IT!

LET'S GO KIDNAP-- THE VISION!

9

353

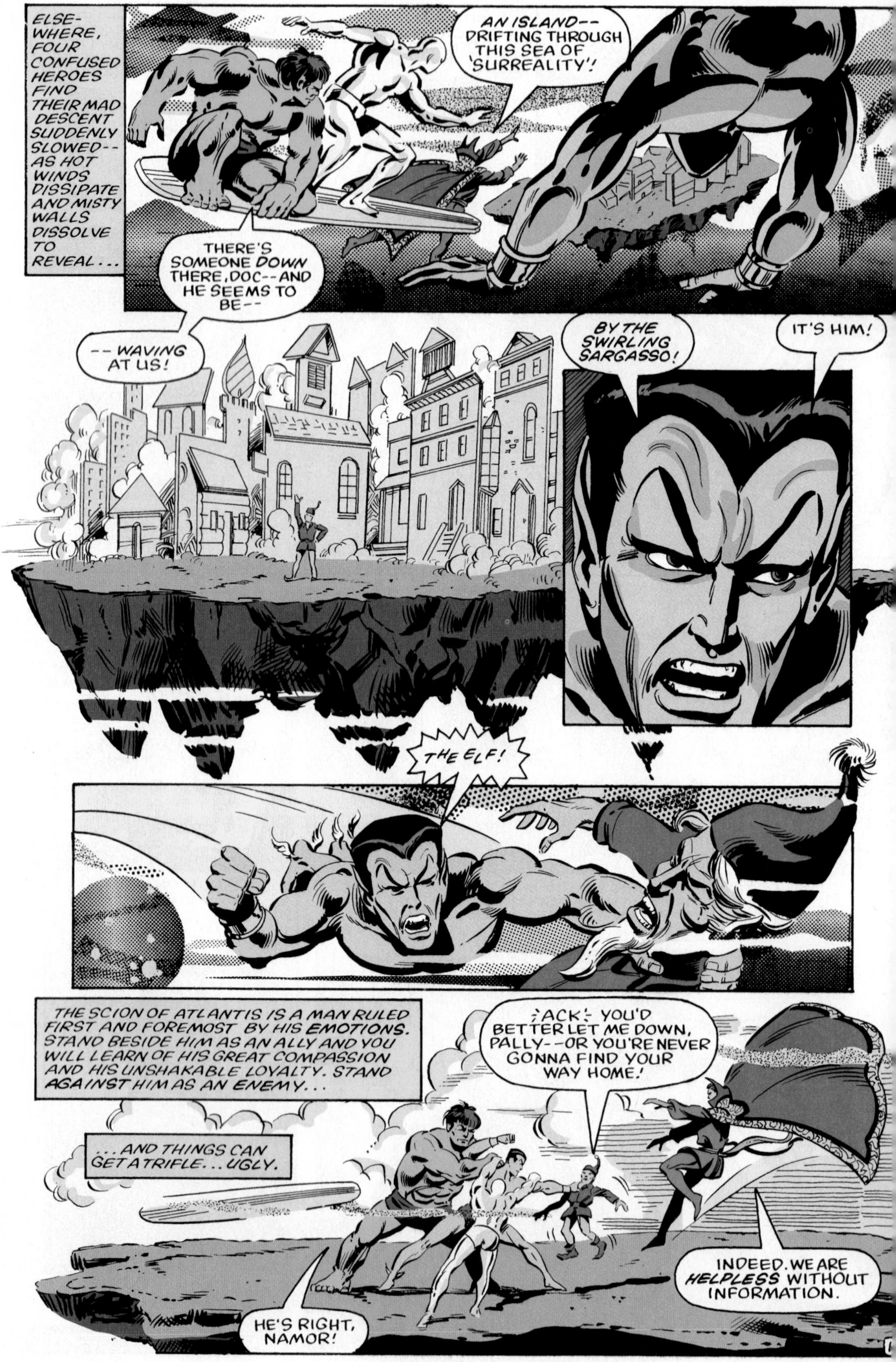
ELSE-WHERE, FOUR CONFUSED HEROES FIND THEIR MAD DESCENT SUDDENLY SLOWED-- AS HOT WINDS DISSIPATE AND MISTY WALLS DISSOLVE TO REVEAL...
AN ISLAND-- DRIFTING THROUGH THIS SEA OF 'SURREALITY'!
THERE'S SOMEONE DOWN THERE, DOC--AND HE SEEMS TO BE--
--WAVING AT US!
BY THE SWIRLING SARGASSO!
IT'S HIM!
THE ELF!
THE SCION OF ATLANTIS IS A MAN RULED FIRST AND FOREMOST BY HIS EMOTIONS. STAND BESIDE HIM AS AN ALLY AND YOU WILL LEARN OF HIS GREAT COMPASSION AND HIS UNSHAKABLE LOYALTY. STAND AGAINST HIM AS AN ENEMY...
;ACK;- YOU'D BETTER LET ME DOWN, PALLY--OR YOU'RE NEVER GONNA FIND YOUR WAY HOME!
...AND THINGS CAN GET A TRIFLE... UGLY.
INDEED. WE ARE HELPLESS WITHOUT INFORMATION.
HE'S RIGHT, NAMOR!

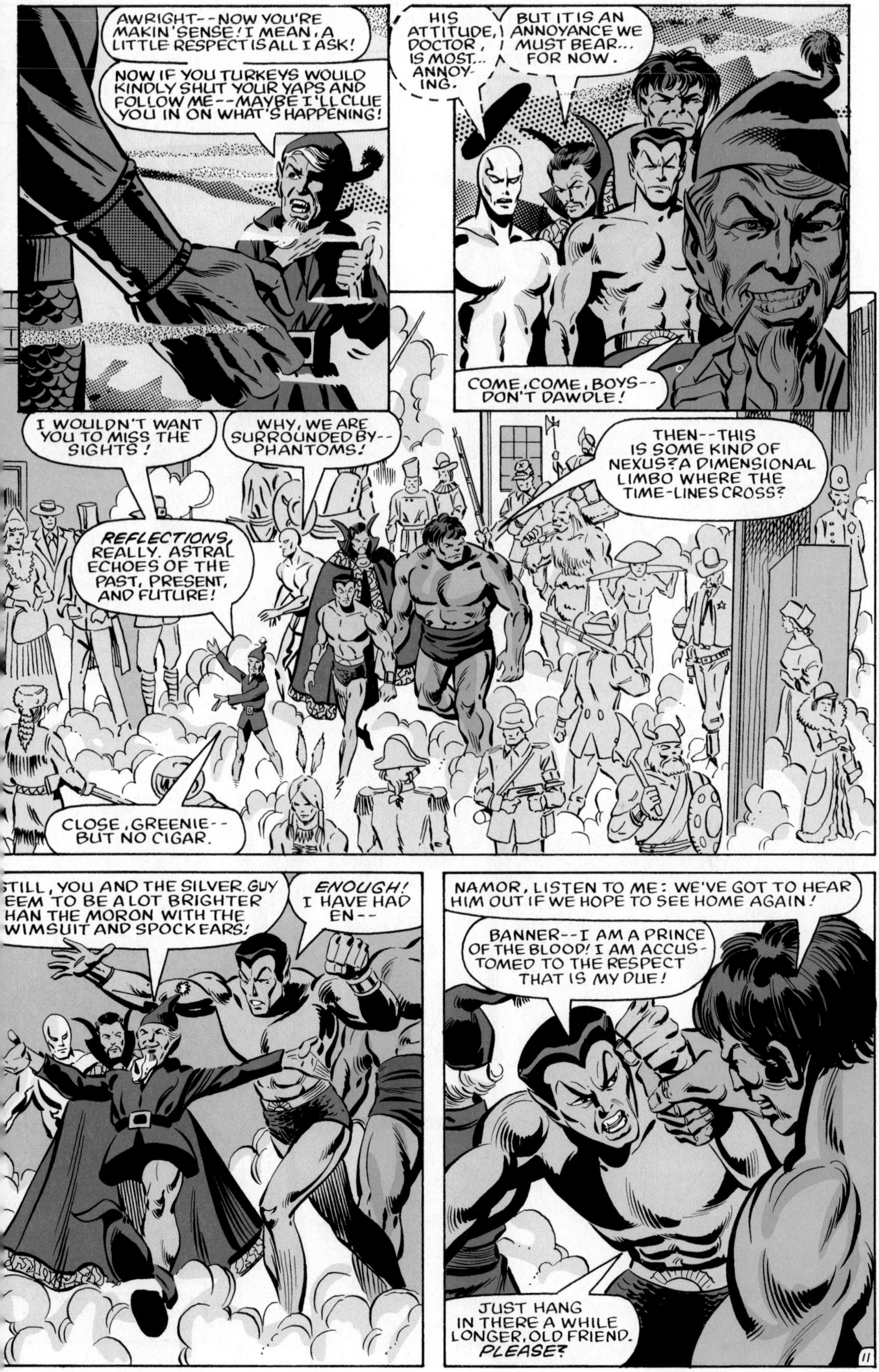

AWRIGHT--NOW YOU'RE MAKIN' SENSE! I MEAN, A LITTLE RESPECT IS ALL I ASK!
NOW IF YOU TURKEYS WOULD KINDLY SHUT YOUR YAPS AND FOLLOW ME--MAYBE I'LL CLUE YOU IN ON WHAT'S HAPPENING!
HIS ATTITUDE, DOCTOR, IS MOST... ANNOY-ING.
BUT IT IS AN ANNOYANCE WE MUST BEAR... FOR NOW.
COME, COME, BOYS--DON'T DAWDLE!
I WOULDN'T WANT YOU TO MISS THE SIGHTS!
WHY, WE ARE SURROUNDED BY--PHANTOMS!
REFLECTIONS, REALLY. ASTRAL ECHOES OF THE PAST, PRESENT, AND FUTURE!
THEN--THIS IS SOME KIND OF NEXUS? A DIMENSIONAL LIMBO WHERE THE TIME-LINES CROSS?
CLOSE, GREENIE--BUT NO CIGAR.
STILL, YOU AND THE SILVER GUY SEEM TO BE A LOT BRIGHTER THAN THE MORON WITH THE SWIMSUIT AND SPOCK EARS!
ENOUGH! I HAVE HAD EN--
NAMOR, LISTEN TO ME: WE'VE GOT TO HEAR HIM OUT IF WE HOPE TO SEE HOME AGAIN!
BANNER--I AM A PRINCE OF THE BLOOD! I AM ACCUS-TOMED TO THE RESPECT THAT IS MY DUE!
JUST HANG IN THERE A WHILE LONGER, OLD FRIEND. PLEASE?
11

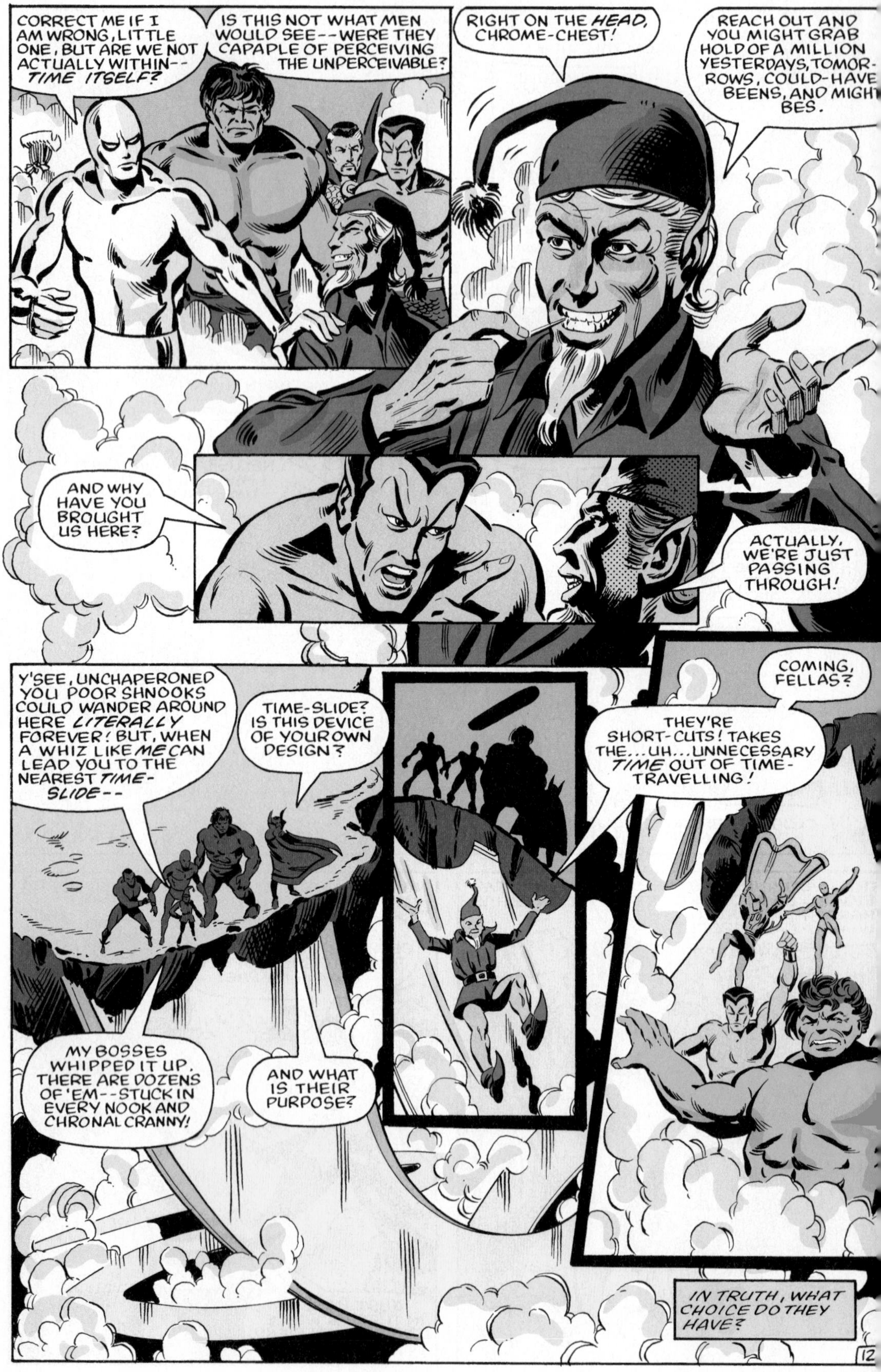

CORRECT ME IF I AM WRONG, LITTLE ONE, BUT ARE WE NOT ACTUALLY WITHIN-- TIME ITSELF?
IS THIS NOT WHAT MEN WOULD SEE--WERE THEY CAPAPLE OF PERCEIVING THE UNPERCEIVABLE?
RIGHT ON THE HEAD, CHROME-CHEST!
REACH OUT AND YOU MIGHT GRAB HOLD OF A MILLION YESTERDAYS, TOMORROWS, COULD-HAVE BEENS, AND MIGHT BES.
AND WHY HAVE YOU BROUGHT US HERE?
ACTUALLY, WE'RE JUST PASSING THROUGH!
Y'SEE, UNCHAPERONED YOU POOR SHNOOKS COULD WANDER AROUND HERE LITERALLY FOREVER! BUT, WHEN A WHIZ LIKE ME CAN LEAD YOU TO THE NEAREST TIME-SLIDE--
TIME-SLIDE? IS THIS DEVICE OF YOUR OWN DESIGN?
MY BOSSES WHIPPED IT UP. THERE ARE DOZENS OF 'EM--STUCK IN EVERY NOOK AND CHRONAL CRANNY!
AND WHAT IS THEIR PURPOSE?
THEY'RE SHORT-CUTS! TAKES THE...UH...UNNECESSARY TIME OUT OF TIME-TRAVELLING!
COMING, FELLAS?
IN TRUTH, WHAT CHOICE DO THEY HAVE?
12

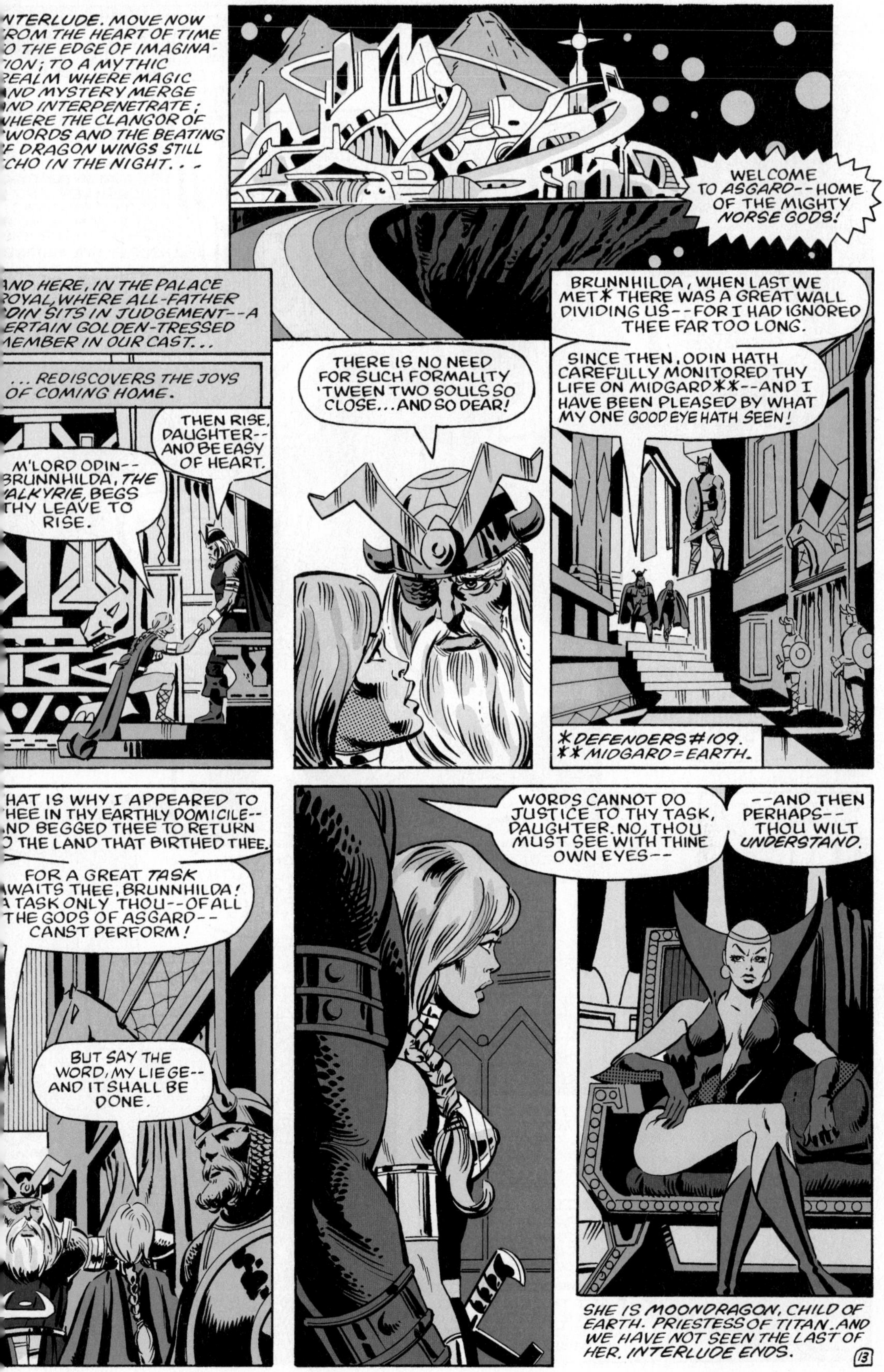
NTERLUDE. MOVE NOW FROM THE HEART OF TIME TO THE EDGE OF IMAGINATION; TO A MYTHIC REALM WHERE MAGIC AND MYSTERY MERGE AND INTERPENETRATE; WHERE THE CLANGOR OF SWORDS AND THE BEATING OF DRAGON WINGS STILL ECHO IN THE NIGHT. . .
WELCOME TO ASGARD--HOME OF THE MIGHTY NORSE GODS!
AND HERE, IN THE PALACE ROYAL, WHERE ALL-FATHER ODIN SITS IN JUDGEMENT--A CERTAIN GOLDEN-TRESSED MEMBER IN OUR CAST...
... REDISCOVERS THE JOYS OF COMING HOME.
M'LORD ODIN--BRUNNHILDA, THE VALKYRIE, BEGS THY LEAVE TO RISE.
THEN RISE, DAUGHTER--AND BE EASY OF HEART.
THERE IS NO NEED FOR SUCH FORMALITY 'TWEEN TWO SOULS SO CLOSE... AND SO DEAR!
BRUNNHILDA, WHEN LAST WE MET* THERE WAS A GREAT WALL DIVIDING US--FOR I HAD IGNORED THEE FAR TOO LONG.
SINCE THEN, ODIN HATH CAREFULLY MONITORED THY LIFE ON MIDGARD**--AND I HAVE BEEN PLEASED BY WHAT MY ONE GOOD EYE HATH SEEN!
*DEFENDERS #109.
**MIDGARD=EARTH.
THAT IS WHY I APPEARED TO THEE IN THY EARTHLY DOMICILE--AND BEGGED THEE TO RETURN TO THE LAND THAT BIRTHED THEE.
FOR A GREAT TASK AWAITS THEE, BRUNNHILDA! A TASK ONLY THOU--OF ALL THE GODS OF ASGARD--CANST PERFORM!
BUT SAY THE WORD, MY LIEGE--AND IT SHALL BE DONE.
WORDS CANNOT DO JUSTICE TO THY TASK, DAUGHTER. NO, THOU MUST SEE WITH THINE OWN EYES--
--AND THEN PERHAPS--THOU WILT UNDERSTAND.
SHE IS MOONDRAGON, CHILD OF EARTH. PRIESTESS OF TITAN. AND WE HAVE NOT SEEN THE LAST OF HER. INTERLUDE ENDS.
13

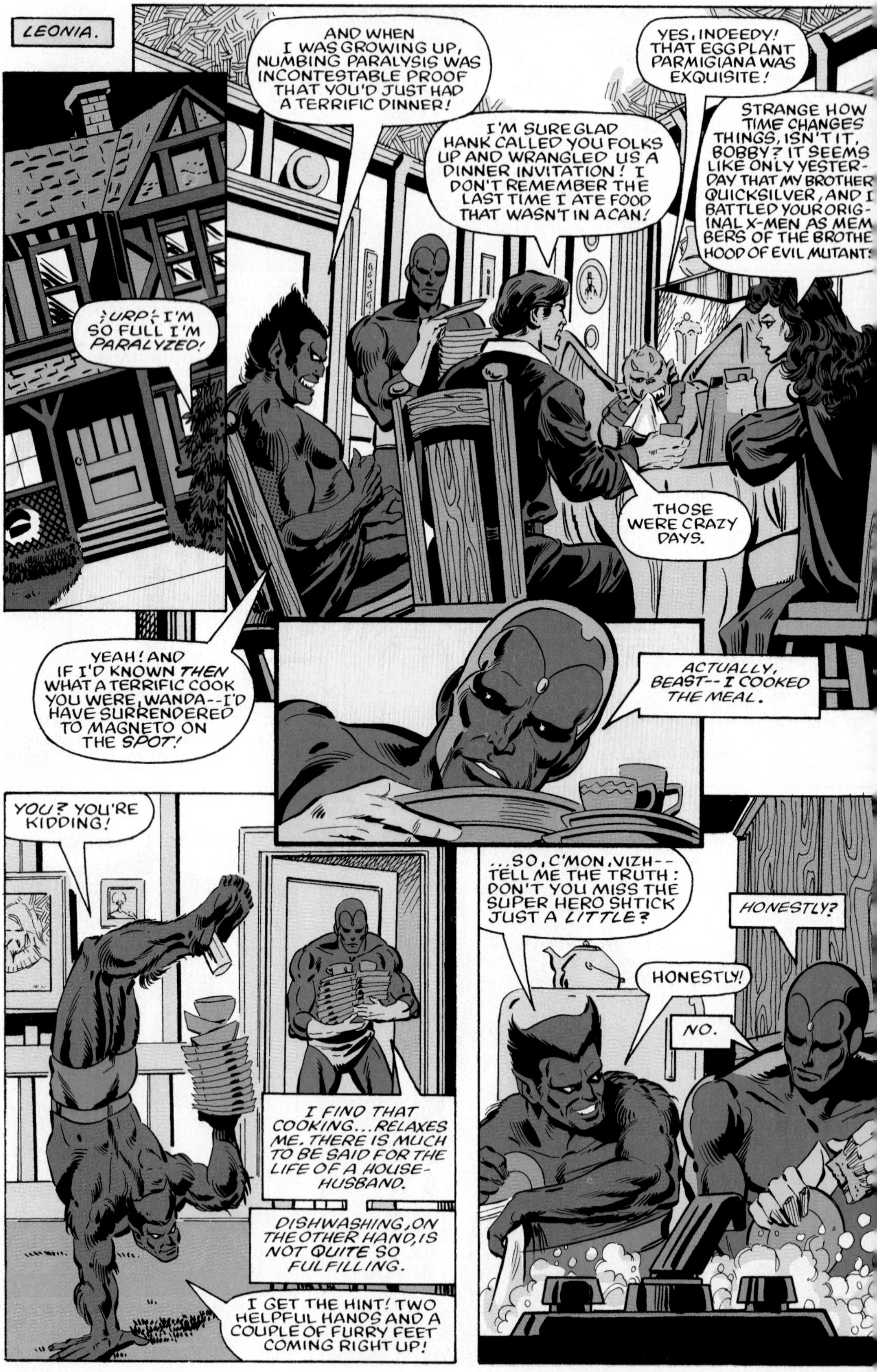
LEONIA.
AND WHEN I WAS GROWING UP, NUMBING PARALYSIS WAS INCONTESTABLE PROOF THAT YOU'D JUST HAD A TERRIFIC DINNER!
URP I'M SO FULL I'M PARALYZED!
I'M SURE GLAD HANK CALLED YOU FOLKS UP AND WRANGLED US A DINNER INVITATION! I DON'T REMEMBER THE LAST TIME I ATE FOOD THAT WASN'T IN A CAN!
YES, INDEEDY! THAT EGGPLANT PARMIGIANA WAS EXQUISITE!
STRANGE HOW TIME CHANGES THINGS, ISN'T IT, BOBBY? IT SEEMS LIKE ONLY YESTERDAY THAT MY BROTHER QUICKSILVER, AND I BATTLED YOUR ORIGINAL X-MEN AS MEMBERS OF THE BROTHE HOOD OF EVIL MUTANT
THOSE WERE CRAZY DAYS.
YEAH! AND IF I'D KNOWN THEN WHAT A TERRIFIC COOK YOU WERE, WANDA--I'D HAVE SURRENDERED TO MAGNETO ON THE SPOT!
ACTUALLY, BEAST--I COOKED THE MEAL.
YOU? YOU'RE KIDDING!
I FIND THAT COOKING...RELAXES ME. THERE IS MUCH TO BE SAID FOR THE LIFE OF A HOUSE-HUSBAND.
DISHWASHING, ON THE OTHER HAND, IS NOT QUITE SO FULFILLING.
I GET THE HINT! TWO HELPFUL HANDS AND A COUPLE OF FURRY FEET COMING RIGHT UP!
...SO, C'MON, VIZH--TELL ME THE TRUTH: DON'T YOU MISS THE SUPER HERO SHTICK JUST A LITTLE?
HONESTLY?
HONESTLY!
NO.

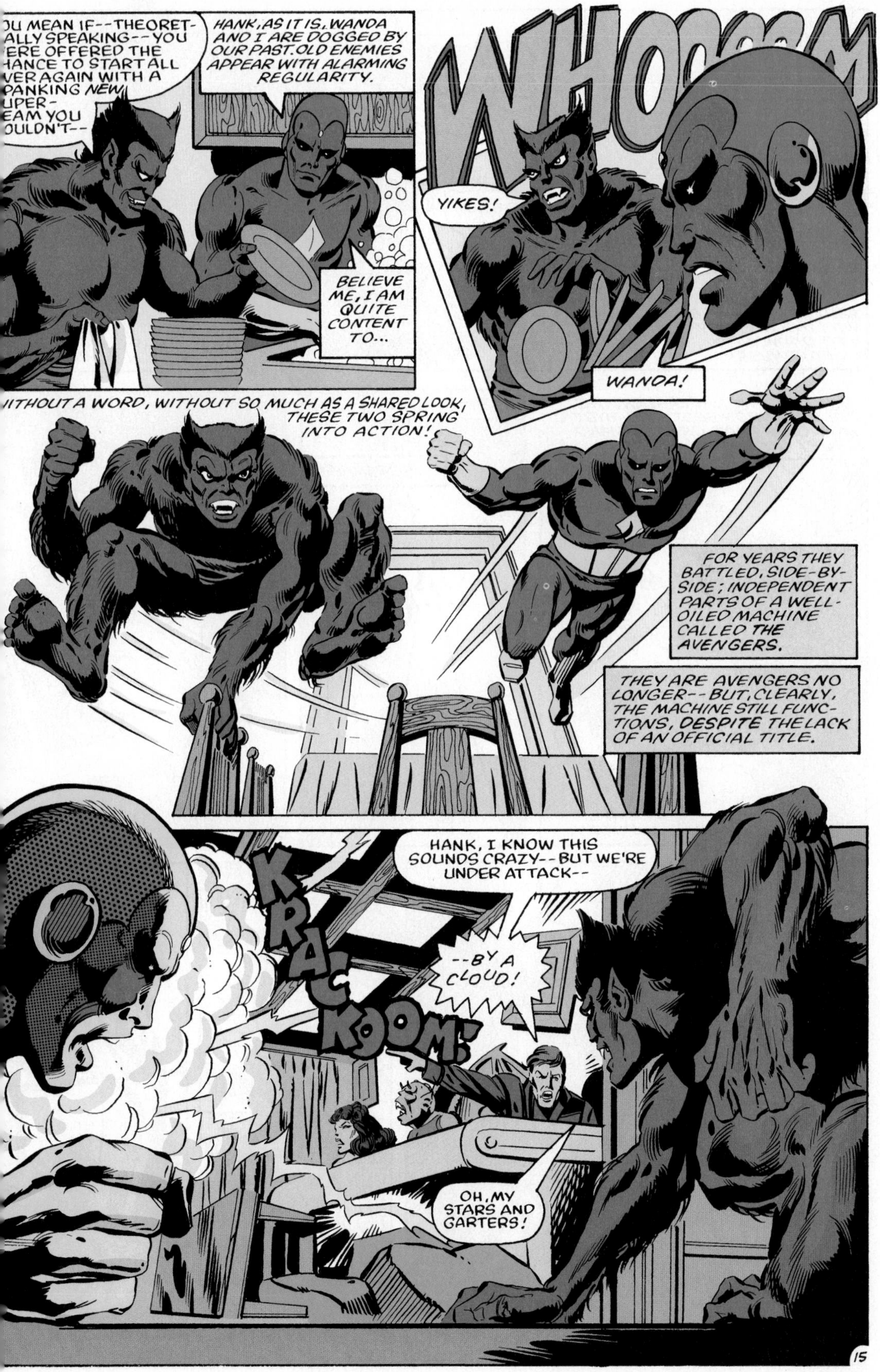

OU MEAN IF--THEORET-ALLY SPEAKING--YOU ERE OFFERED THE HANCE TO START ALL VER AGAIN WITH A PANKING NEW UPER-EAM YOU OULDN'T--
HANK, AS IT IS, WANDA AND I ARE DOGGED BY OUR PAST. OLD ENEMIES APPEAR WITH ALARMING REGULARITY.
BELIEVE ME, I AM QUITE CONTENT TO...
WHOOOOOM
YIKES!
WANDA!
ITHOUT A WORD, WITHOUT SO MUCH AS A SHARED LOOK, THESE TWO SPRING INTO ACTION!
FOR YEARS THEY BATTLED, SIDE-BY-SIDE; INDEPENDENT PARTS OF A WELL-OILED MACHINE CALLED THE AVENGERS.
THEY ARE AVENGERS NO LONGER--BUT, CLEARLY, THE MACHINE STILL FUNCTIONS, DESPITE THE LACK OF AN OFFICIAL TITLE.
HANK, I KNOW THIS SOUNDS CRAZY--BUT WE'RE UNDER ATTACK--
KRACKOOOM!
--BY A CLOUD!
OH, MY STARS AND GARTERS!
15

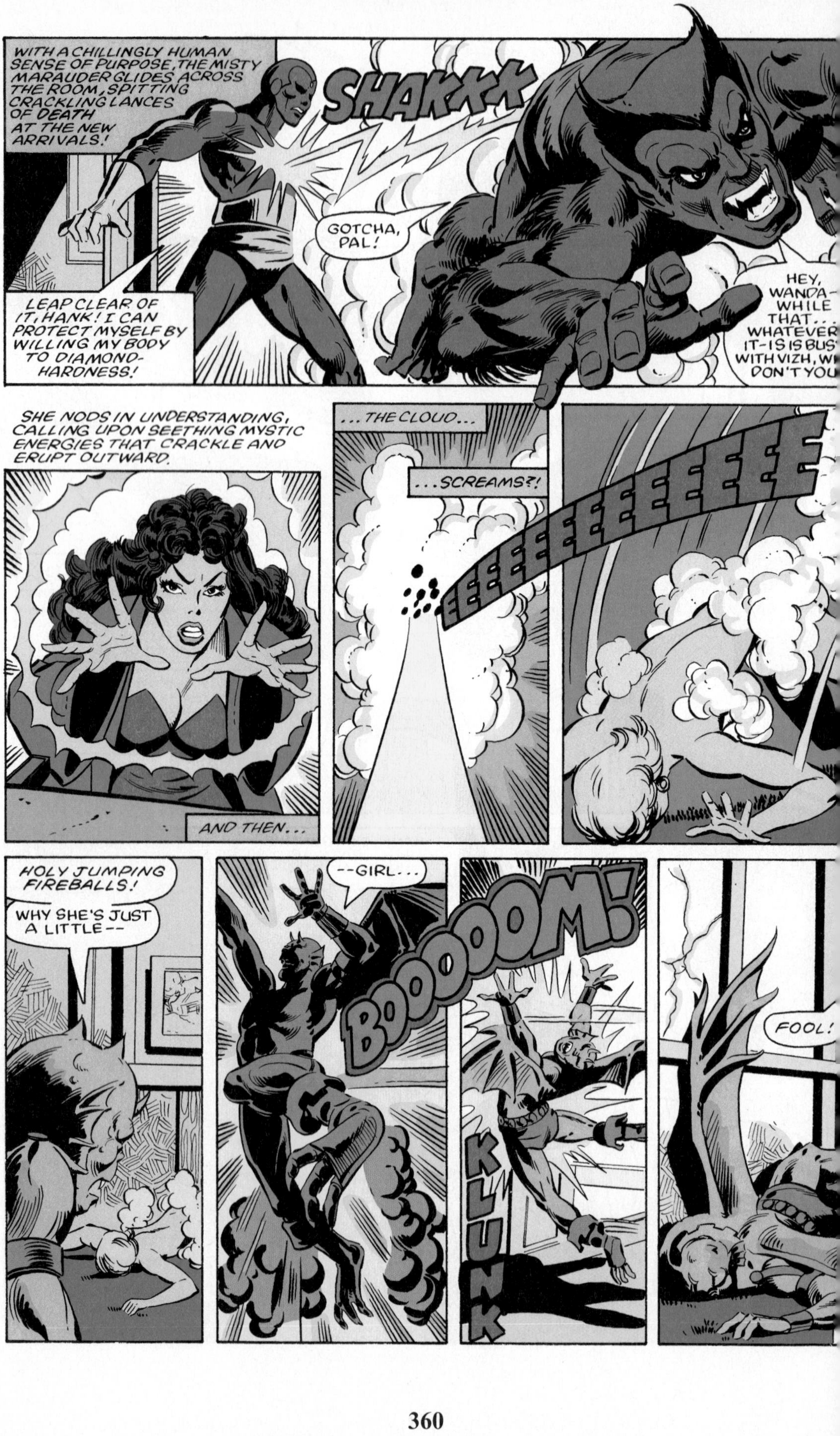
WITH A CHILLINGLY HUMAN SENSE OF PURPOSE, THE MISTY MARAUDER GLIDES ACROSS THE ROOM, SPITTING CRACKLING LANCES OF DEATH AT THE NEW ARRIVALS!
SHAKKK
GOTCHA, PAL!
LEAP CLEAR OF IT, HANK! I CAN PROTECT MYSELF BY WILLING MY BODY TO DIAMOND-HARDNESS!
HEY, WANDA-- WHILE THAT... WHATEVER IT-IS IS BUS WITH VIZH, W DON'T YOU
SHE NODS IN UNDERSTANDING, CALLING UPON SEETHING MYSTIC ENERGIES THAT CRACKLE AND ERUPT OUTWARD.
AND THEN...
...THE CLOUD...
...SCREAMS?!
EEEEEEEEEEEEEEEEEEE
HOLY JUMPING FIREBALLS!
WHY SHE'S JUST A LITTLE--
--GIRL...
BOOOOOOM!
KLUNK
FOOL!

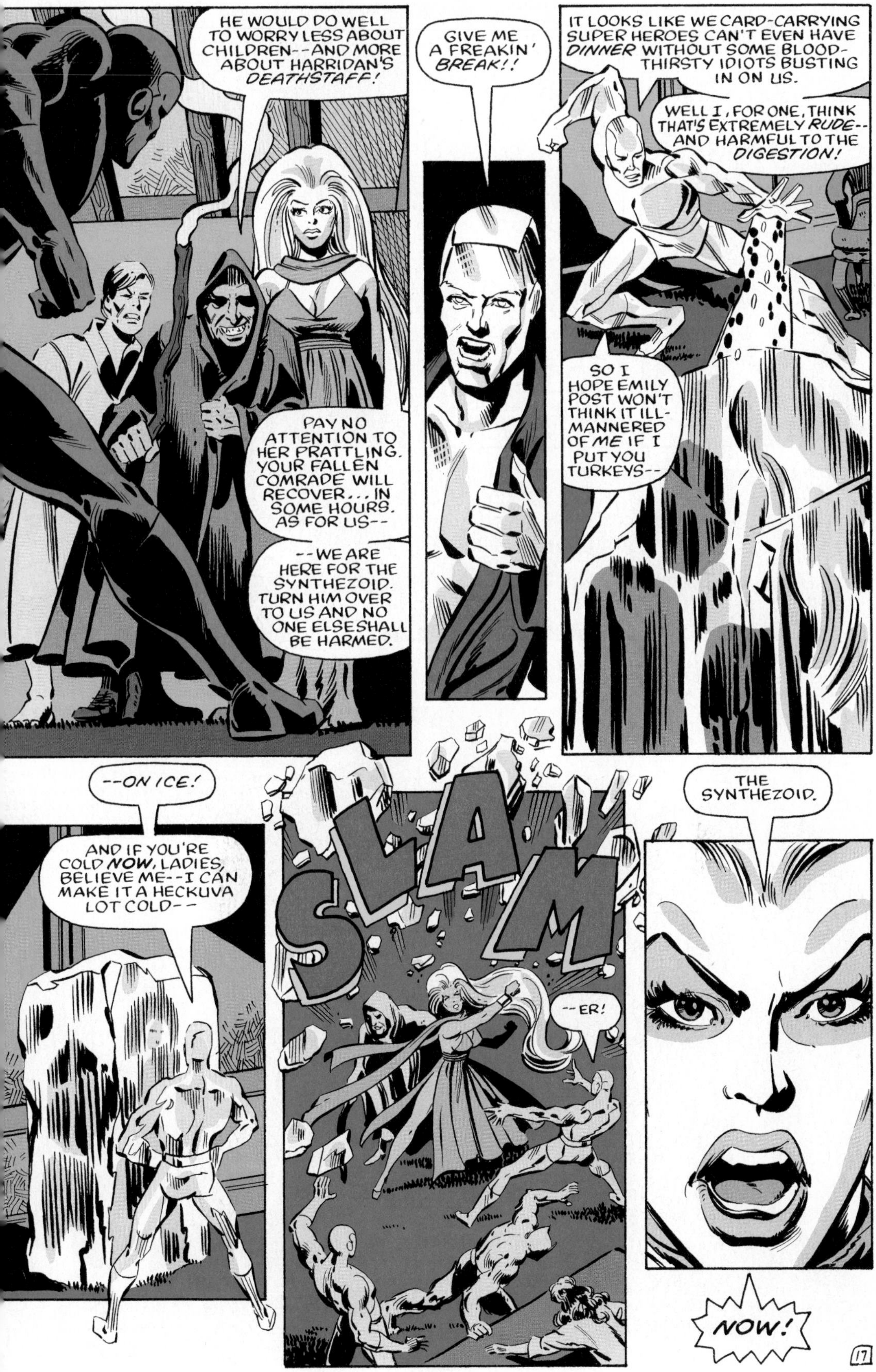

HE WOULD DO WELL TO WORRY LESS ABOUT CHILDREN--AND MORE ABOUT HARRIDAN'S *DEATHSTAFF!*
PAY NO ATTENTION TO HER PRATTLING. YOUR FALLEN COMRADE WILL RECOVER... IN SOME HOURS. AS FOR US--
--WE ARE HERE FOR THE SYNTHEZOID. TURN HIM OVER TO US AND NO ONE ELSE SHALL BE HARMED.
GIVE ME A FREAKIN' *BREAK!!*
IT LOOKS LIKE WE CARD-CARRYING SUPER HEROES CAN'T EVEN HAVE *DINNER* WITHOUT SOME BLOOD-THIRSTY IDIOTS BUSTING IN ON US.
WELL I, FOR ONE, THINK THAT'S EXTREMELY *RUDE*--AND HARMFUL TO THE *DIGESTION!*
SO I HOPE EMILY POST WON'T THINK IT ILL-MANNERED OF *ME* IF I PUT YOU TURKEYS--
--ON ICE!
AND IF YOU'RE COLD **NOW**, LADIES, BELIEVE ME--I CAN MAKE IT A HECKUVA LOT COLD--
SLAM
--ER!
THE SYNTHEZOID.
NOW!
17

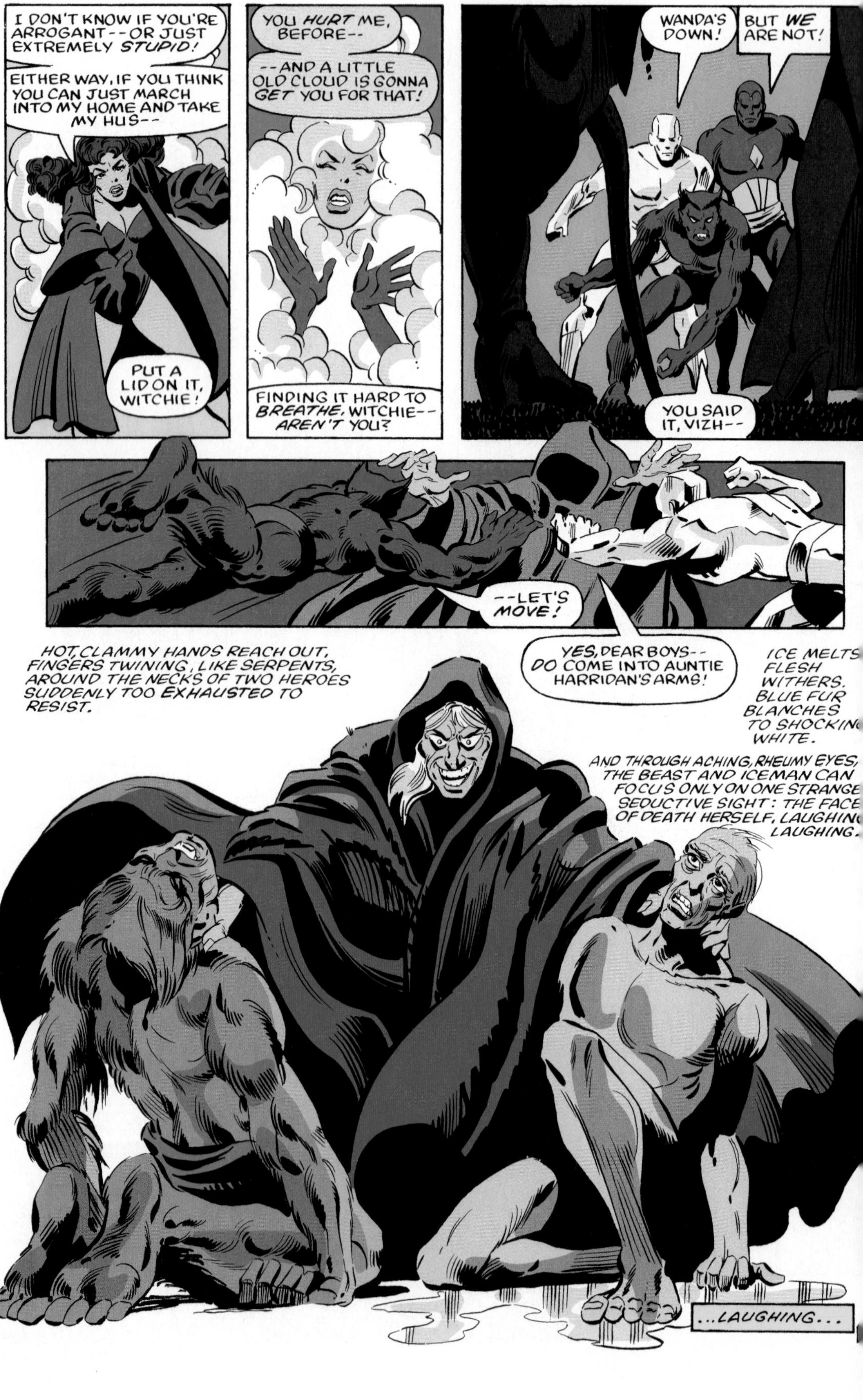

I DON'T KNOW IF YOU'RE ARROGANT--OR JUST EXTREMELY STUPID!
EITHER WAY, IF YOU THINK YOU CAN JUST MARCH INTO MY HOME AND TAKE MY HUS--
PUT A LID ON IT, WITCHIE!
YOU HURT ME, BEFORE--
--AND A LITTLE OLD CLOUD IS GONNA GET YOU FOR THAT!
FINDING IT HARD TO BREATHE, WITCHIE--AREN'T YOU?
WANDA'S DOWN!
BUT WE ARE NOT!
YOU SAID IT, VIZH--
--LET'S MOVE!
YES, DEAR BOYS--DO COME INTO AUNTIE HARRIDAN'S ARMS!
HOT, CLAMMY HANDS REACH OUT, FINGERS TWINING, LIKE SERPENTS, AROUND THE NECKS OF TWO HEROES SUDDENLY TOO EXHAUSTED TO RESIST.
ICE MELTS. FLESH WITHERS. BLUE FUR BLANCHES TO SHOCKING WHITE.
AND THROUGH ACHING, RHEUMY EYES, THE BEAST AND ICEMAN CAN FOCUS ONLY ON ONE STRANGE SEDUCTIVE SIGHT: THE FACE OF DEATH HERSELF, LAUGHING LAUGHING.
...LAUGHING...

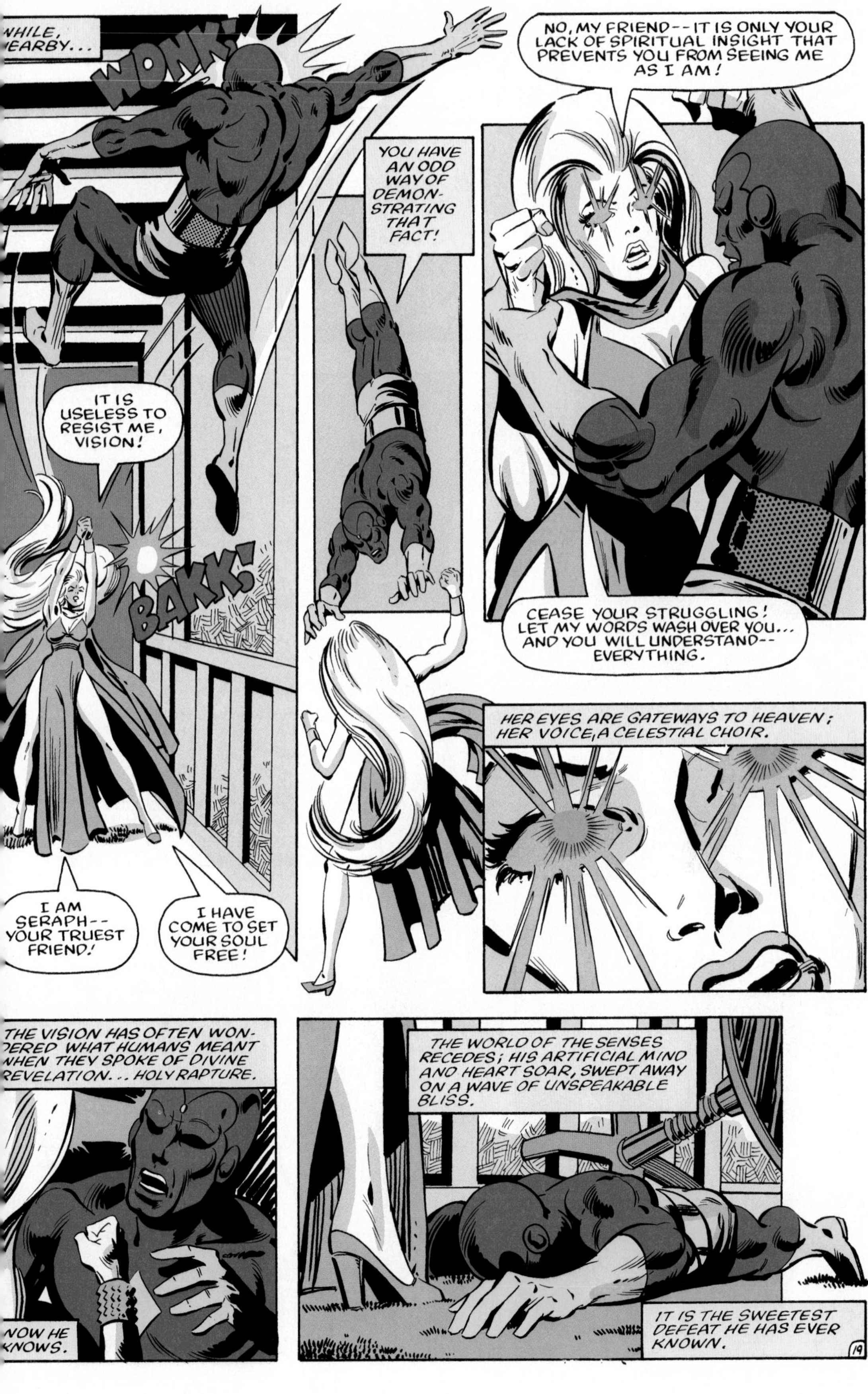
WHILE, NEARBY...
WONK!
IT IS USELESS TO RESIST ME, VISION!
BAKK!
I AM SERAPH-- YOUR TRUEST FRIEND!
I HAVE COME TO SET YOUR SOUL FREE!
YOU HAVE AN ODD WAY OF DEMON-STRATING THAT FACT!
NO, MY FRIEND--IT IS ONLY YOUR LACK OF SPIRITUAL INSIGHT THAT PREVENTS YOU FROM SEEING ME AS I AM!
CEASE YOUR STRUGGLING! LET MY WORDS WASH OVER YOU... AND YOU WILL UNDERSTAND-- EVERYTHING.
HER EYES ARE GATEWAYS TO HEAVEN; HER VOICE, A CELESTIAL CHOIR.
THE VISION HAS OFTEN WONDERED WHAT HUMANS MEANT WHEN THEY SPOKE OF DIVINE REVELATION... HOLY RAPTURE.
NOW HE KNOWS.
THE WORLD OF THE SENSES RECEDES; HIS ARTIFICIAL MIND AND HEART SOAR, SWEPT AWAY ON A WAVE OF UNSPEAKABLE BLISS.
IT IS THE SWEETEST DEFEAT HE HAS EVER KNOWN.
19

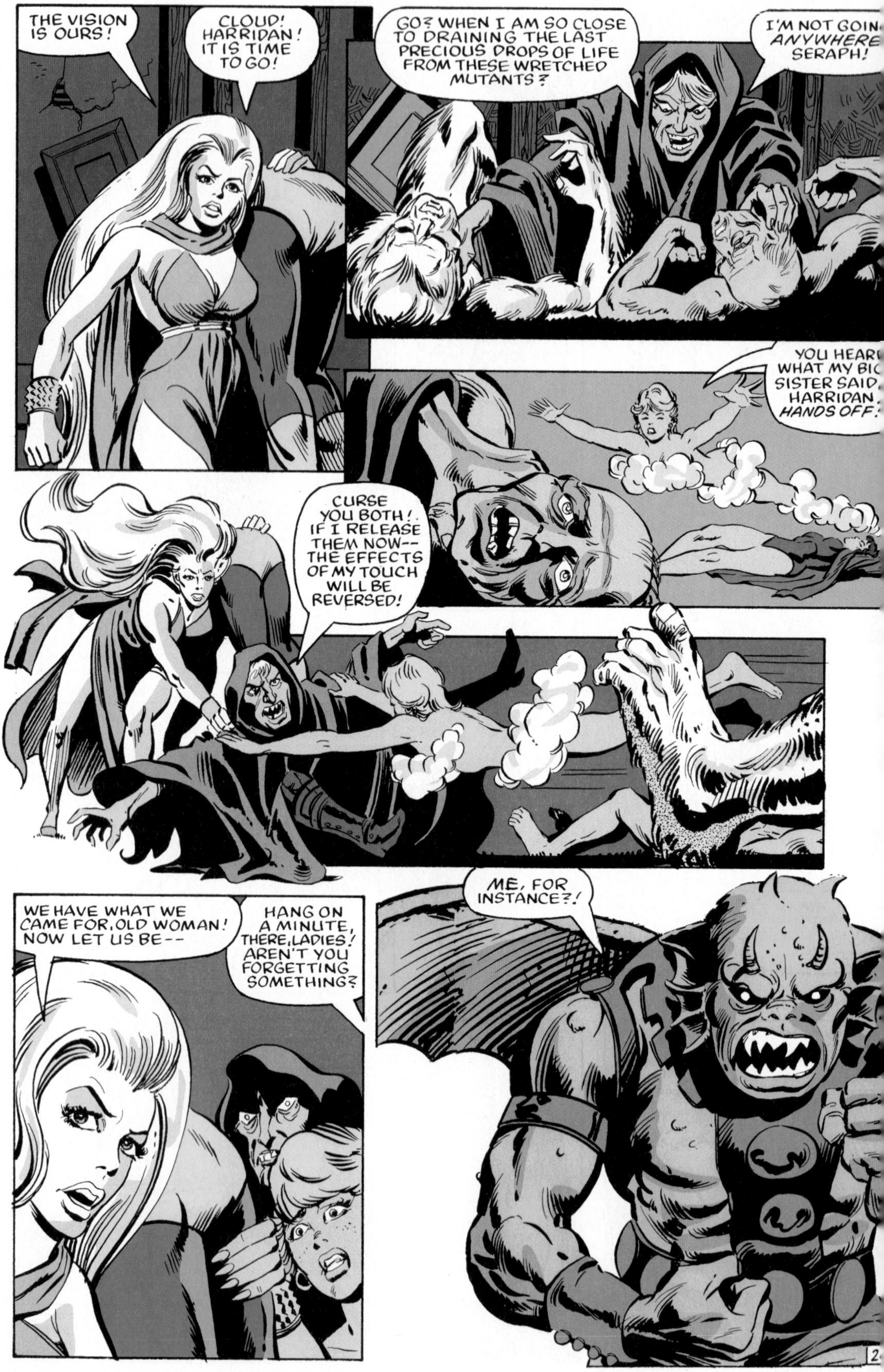
THE VISION IS OURS!
CLOUD! HARRIDAN! IT IS TIME TO GO!
GO? WHEN I AM SO CLOSE TO DRAINING THE LAST PRECIOUS DROPS OF LIFE FROM THESE WRETCHED MUTANTS?
YOU HEAR WHAT MY BIG SISTER SAID, HARRIDAN. HANDS OFF!
CURSE YOU BOTH! IF I RELEASE THEM NOW-- THE EFFECTS OF MY TOUCH WILL BE REVERSED!
WE HAVE WHAT WE CAME FOR, OLD WOMAN! NOW LET US BE--
HANG ON A MINUTE, THERE, LADIES! AREN'T YOU FORGETTING SOMETHING?
ME, FOR INSTANCE?!

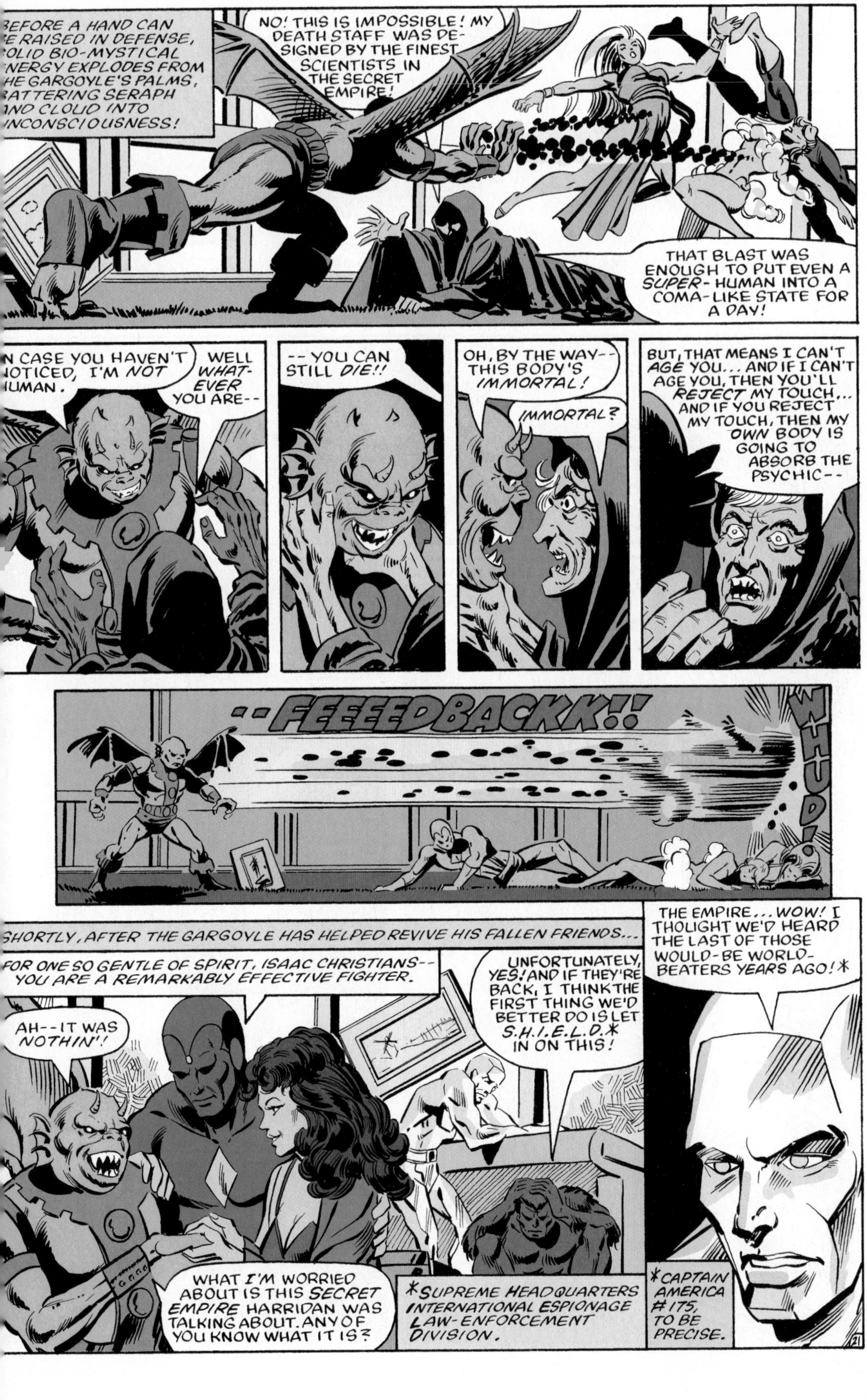
BEFORE A HAND CAN BE RAISED IN DEFENSE, SOLID BIO-MYSTICAL ENERGY EXPLODES FROM THE GARGOYLE'S PALMS, BATTERING SERAPH AND CLOUD INTO UNCONSCIOUSNESS!
NO! THIS IS IMPOSSIBLE! MY DEATH STAFF WAS DESIGNED BY THE FINEST SCIENTISTS IN THE SECRET EMPIRE!
THAT BLAST WAS ENOUGH TO PUT EVEN A SUPER-HUMAN INTO A COMA-LIKE STATE FOR A DAY!
IN CASE YOU HAVEN'T NOTICED, I'M NOT HUMAN.
WELL WHATEVER YOU ARE--
--YOU CAN STILL DIE!!
OH, BY THE WAY--THIS BODY'S IMMORTAL!
IMMORTAL?
BUT, THAT MEANS I CAN'T AGE YOU... AND IF I CAN'T AGE YOU, THEN YOU'LL REJECT MY TOUCH... AND IF YOU REJECT MY TOUCH, THEN MY OWN BODY IS GOING TO ABSORB THE PSYCHIC--
--FEEEEDBACKK!!
WHUD!
SHORTLY, AFTER THE GARGOYLE HAS HELPED REVIVE HIS FALLEN FRIENDS...
FOR ONE SO GENTLE OF SPIRIT, ISAAC CHRISTIANS--YOU ARE A REMARKABLY EFFECTIVE FIGHTER.
AH--IT WAS NOTHIN'!
UNFORTUNATELY, YES! AND IF THEY'RE BACK, I THINK THE FIRST THING WE'D BETTER DO IS LET S.H.I.E.L.D.* IN ON THIS!
WHAT I'M WORRIED ABOUT IS THIS SECRET EMPIRE HARRIDAN WAS TALKING ABOUT. ANY OF YOU KNOW WHAT IT IS?
*SUPREME HEADQUARTERS INTERNATIONAL ESPIONAGE LAW-ENFORCEMENT DIVISION.
THE EMPIRE... WOW! I THOUGHT WE'D HEARD THE LAST OF THOSE WOULD-BE WORLD-BEATERS YEARS AGO!*
*CAPTAIN AMERICA #175, TO BE PRECISE.
21

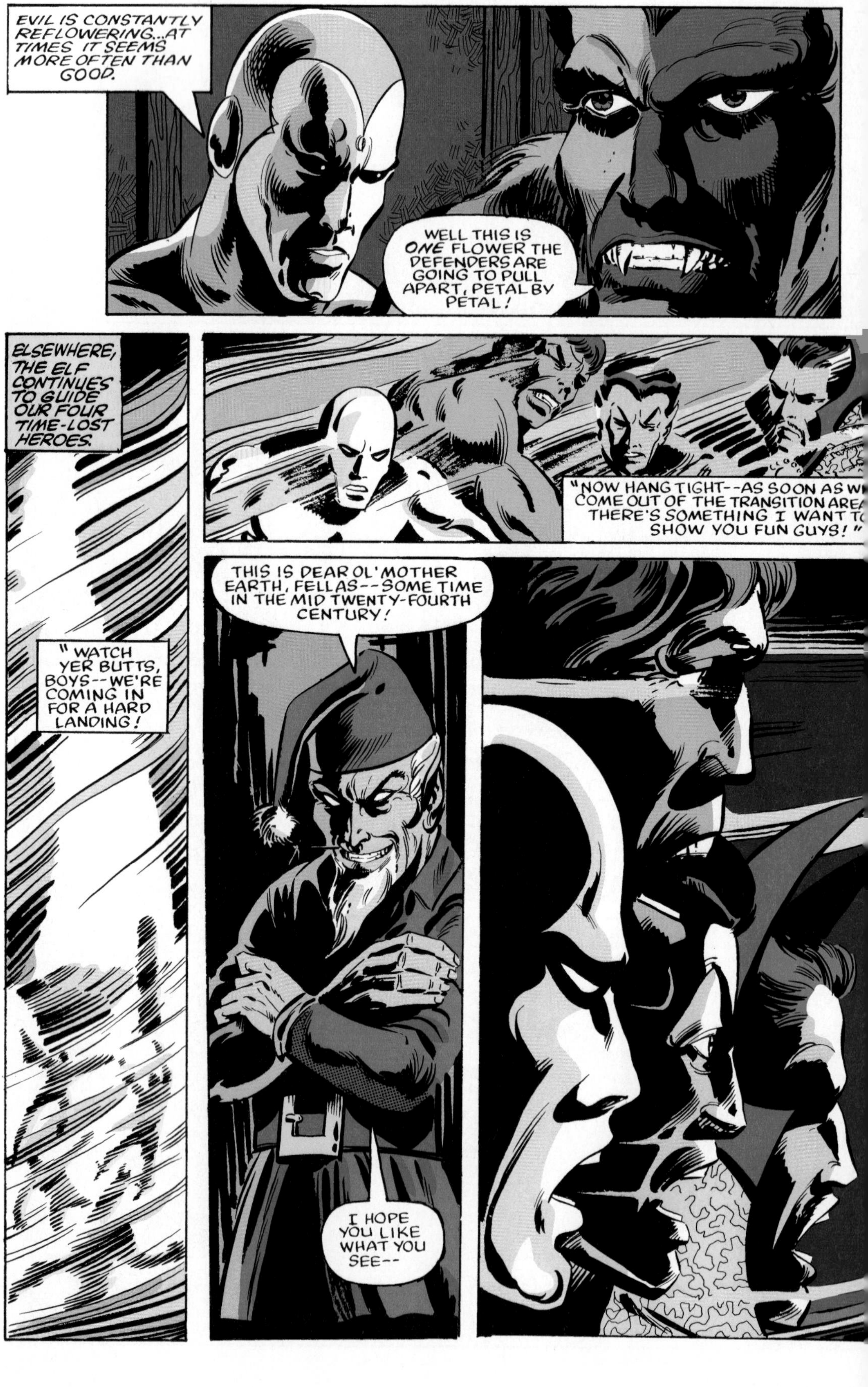
EVIL IS CONSTANTLY REFLOWERING...AT TIMES IT SEEMS MORE OFTEN THAN GOOD.
WELL THIS IS ONE FLOWER THE DEFENDERS ARE GOING TO PULL APART, PETAL BY PETAL!
ELSEWHERE, THE ELF CONTINUES TO GUIDE OUR FOUR TIME-LOST HEROES.
"NOW HANG TIGHT--AS SOON AS W COME OUT OF THE TRANSITION ARE THERE'S SOMETHING I WANT T SHOW YOU FUN GUYS!"
"WATCH YER BUTTS, BOYS--WE'RE COMING IN FOR A HARD LANDING!
THIS IS DEAR OL' MOTHER EARTH, FELLAS--SOME TIME IN THE MID TWENTY-FOURTH CENTURY!
I HOPE YOU LIKE WHAT YOU SEE--

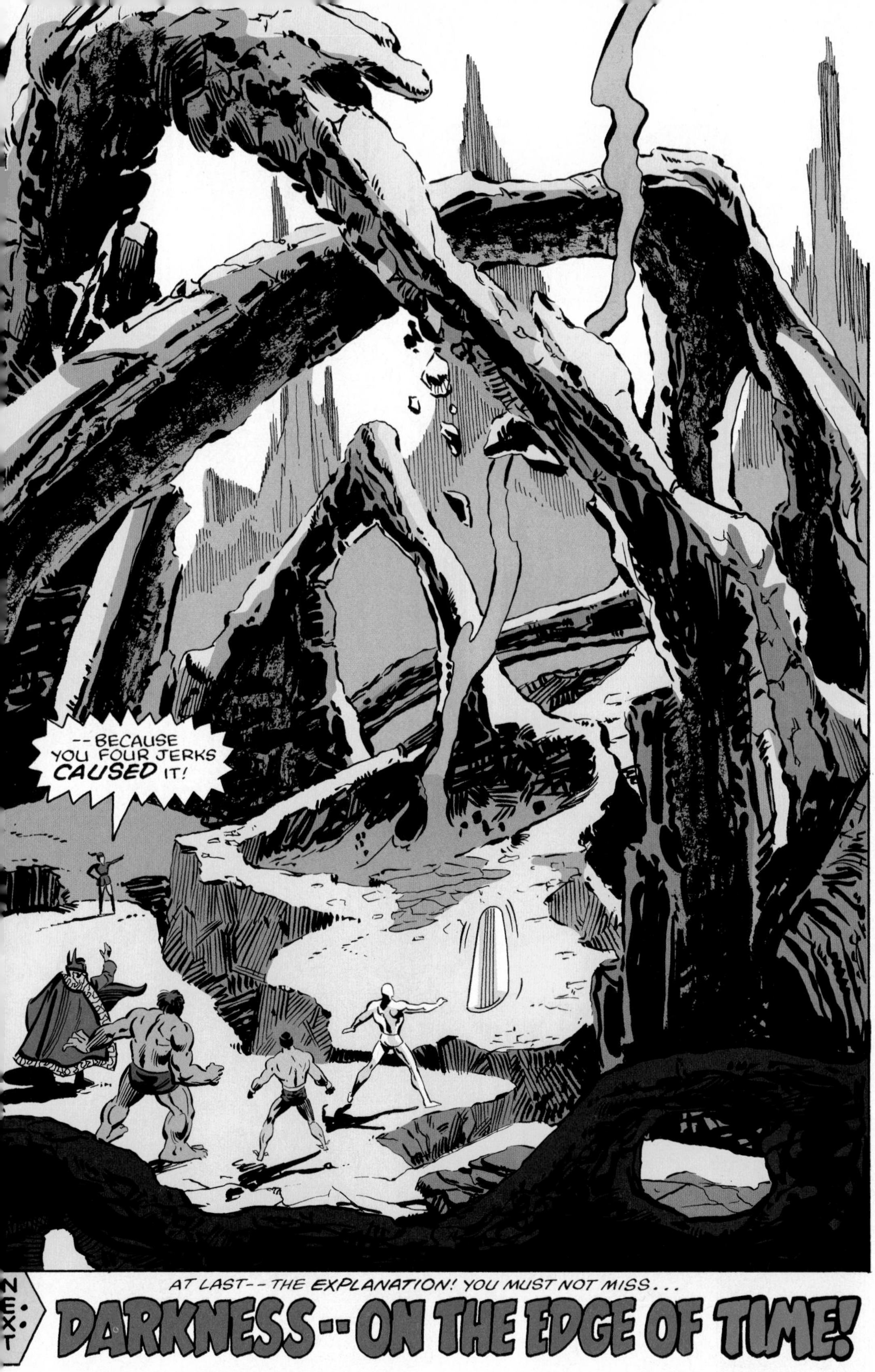

--BECAUSE YOU FOUR JERKS CAUSED IT!
NEXT:
AT LAST-- THE EXPLANATION! YOU MUST NOT MISS...
DARKNESS--ON THE EDGE OF TIME!

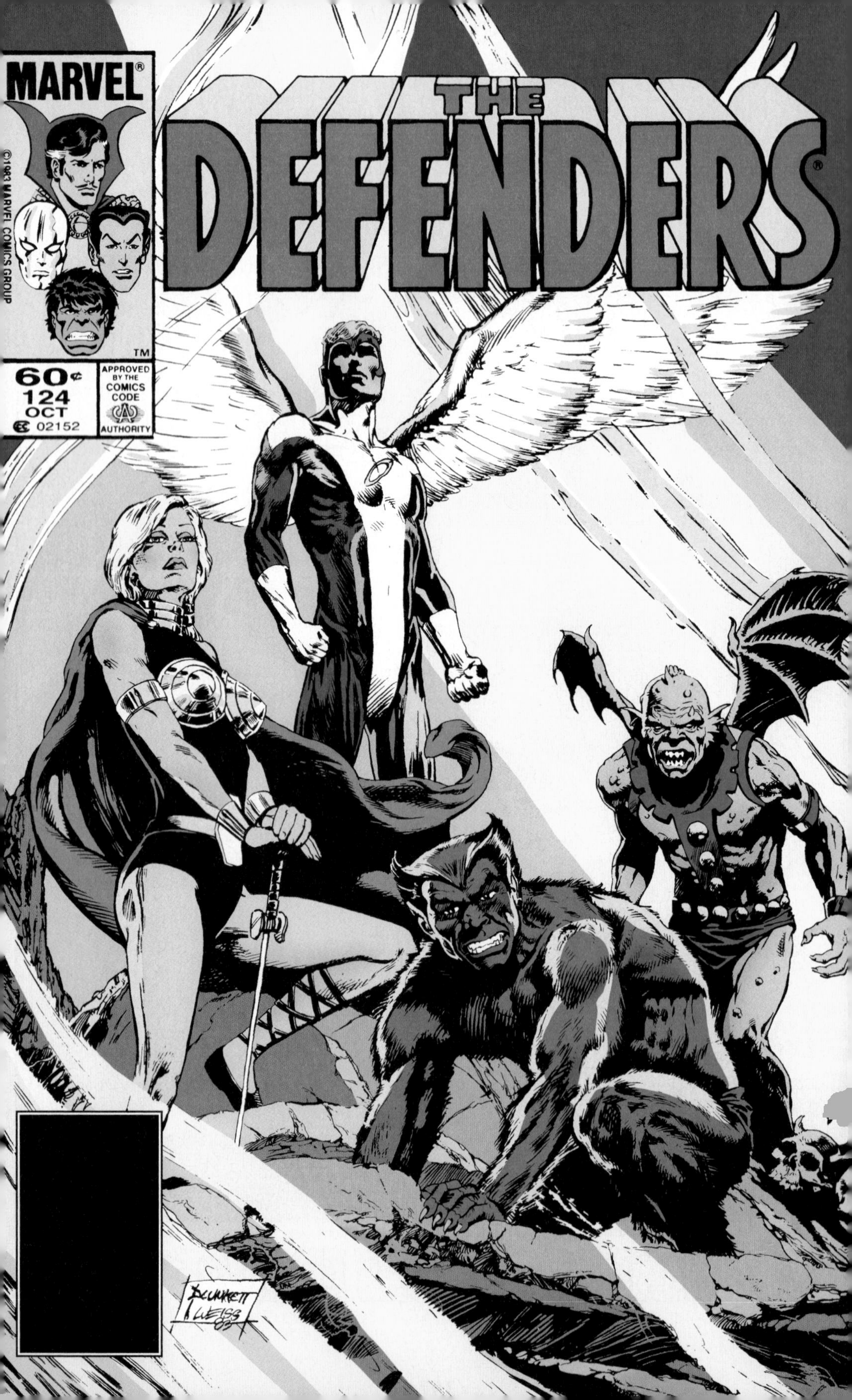

MARVEL®
THE DEFENDERS®
©1983 MARVEL COMICS GROUP
TM
60¢
124
OCT
02152
APPROVED BY THE COMICS CODE AUTHORITY

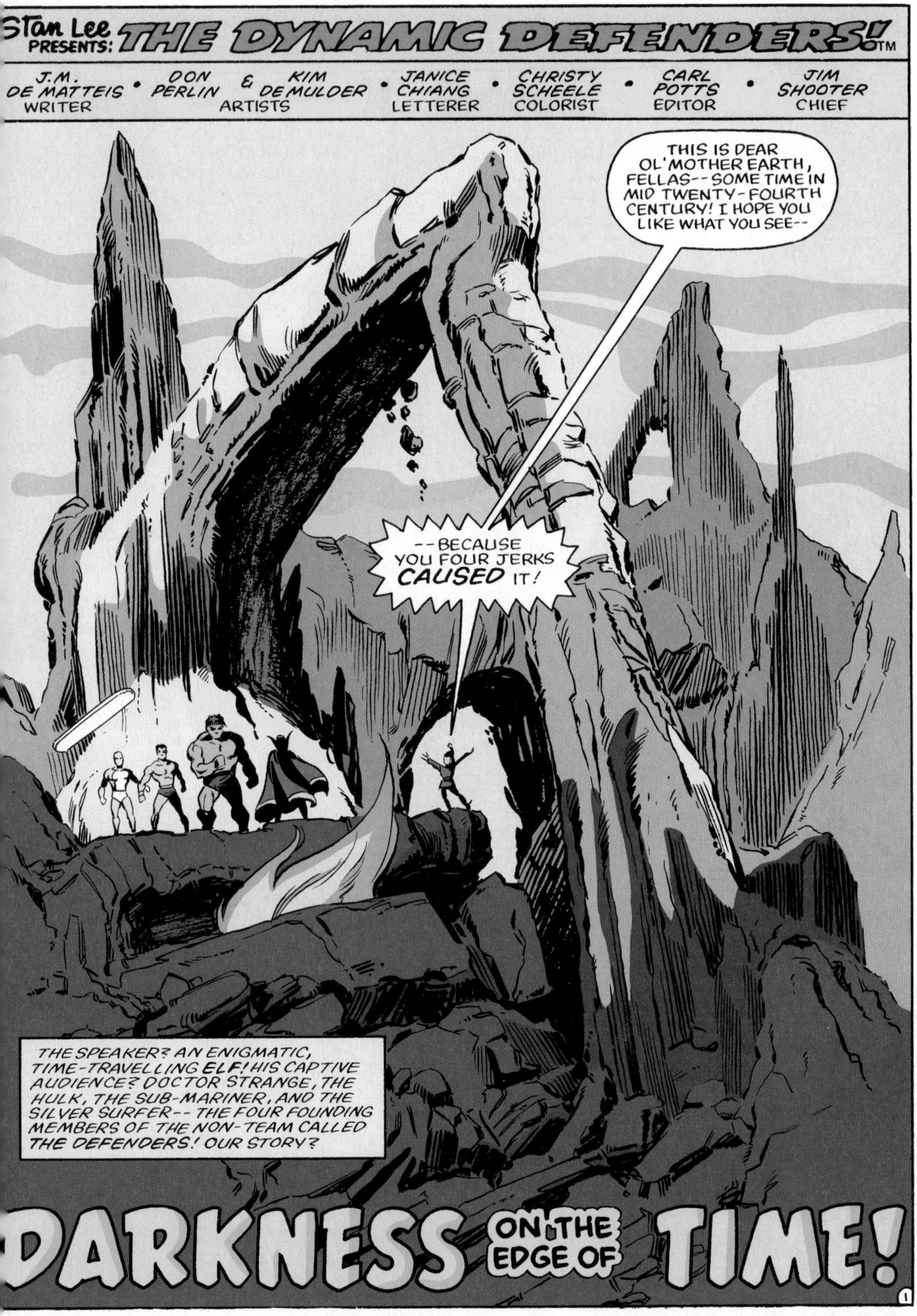
Stan Lee PRESENTS: THE DYNAMIC DEFENDERS! TM
J.M. DE MATTEIS WRITER • DON PERLIN & KIM DE MULDER ARTISTS • JANICE CHIANG LETTERER • CHRISTY SCHEELE COLORIST • CARL POTTS EDITOR • JIM SHOOTER CHIEF
THIS IS DEAR OL' MOTHER EARTH, FELLAS--SOME TIME IN MID TWENTY-FOURTH CENTURY! I HOPE YOU LIKE WHAT YOU SEE--
--BECAUSE YOU FOUR JERKS CAUSED IT!
THE SPEAKER? AN ENIGMATIC, TIME-TRAVELLING ELF! HIS CAPTIVE AUDIENCE? DOCTOR STRANGE, THE HULK, THE SUB-MARINER, AND THE SILVER SURFER--THE FOUR FOUNDING MEMBERS OF THE NON-TEAM CALLED THE DEFENDERS! OUR STORY?
DARKNESS ON THE EDGE OF TIME!
1

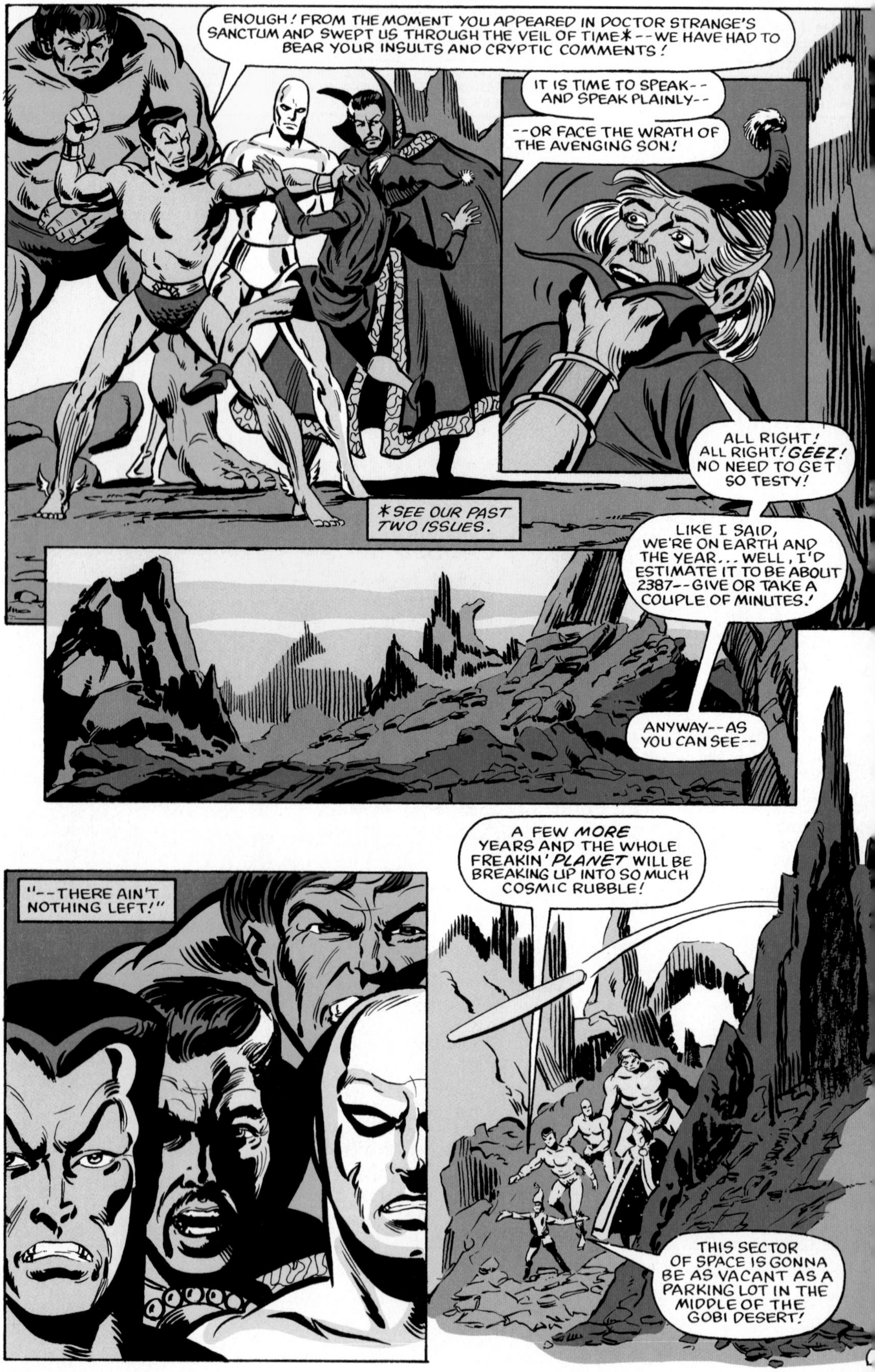
ENOUGH! FROM THE MOMENT YOU APPEARED IN DOCTOR STRANGE'S SANCTUM AND SWEPT US THROUGH THE VEIL OF TIME* --WE HAVE HAD TO BEAR YOUR INSULTS AND CRYPTIC COMMENTS!
*SEE OUR PAST TWO ISSUES.
IT IS TIME TO SPEAK-- AND SPEAK PLAINLY--
--OR FACE THE WRATH OF THE AVENGING SON!
ALL RIGHT! ALL RIGHT! GEEZ! NO NEED TO GET SO TESTY!
LIKE I SAID, WE'RE ON EARTH AND THE YEAR... WELL, I'D ESTIMATE IT TO BE ABOUT 2387--GIVE OR TAKE A COUPLE OF MINUTES!
ANYWAY--AS YOU CAN SEE--
"--THERE AIN'T NOTHING LEFT!"
A FEW MORE YEARS AND THE WHOLE FREAKIN' PLANET WILL BE BREAKING UP INTO SO MUCH COSMIC RUBBLE!
THIS SECTOR OF SPACE IS GONNA BE AS VACANT AS A PARKING LOT IN THE MIDDLE OF THE GOBI DESERT!

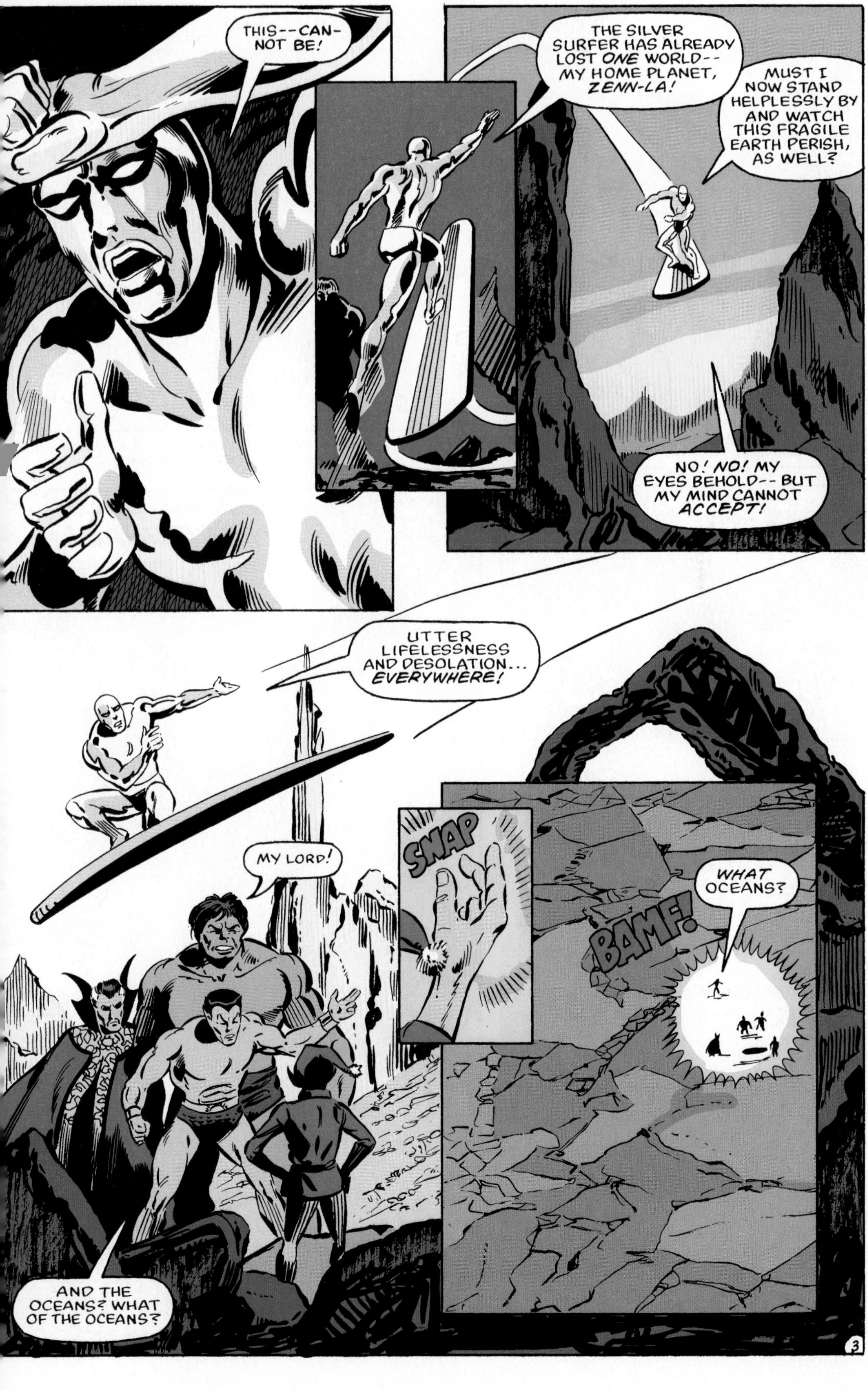
THIS--CAN-NOT BE!
THE SILVER SURFER HAS ALREADY LOST ONE WORLD--MY HOME PLANET, ZENN-LA!
MUST I NOW STAND HELPLESSLY BY AND WATCH THIS FRAGILE EARTH PERISH, AS WELL?
NO! NO! MY EYES BEHOLD--BUT MY MIND CANNOT ACCEPT!
UTTER LIFELESSNESS AND DESOLATION... EVERYWHERE!
MY LORD!
AND THE OCEANS? WHAT OF THE OCEANS?
SNAP
BAMF!
WHAT OCEANS?
3

EXALTED NEPTUNE-- DISPENSER OF THE LAW-- WHERE IS THE JUSTICE IN *THIS?*

YOUR HALLOWED SEAS-- REDUCED TO *DUST!*

THE CROWN PRINCE OF ATLANTIS SITS BROODING-- LOST IN DARK THOUGHTS...

... WHILE EARTH'S SORCERER SUPREME STRIDES SOLEMNLY FORWARD, RAISES A TREMBLING HAND...

... AND ENTRAPS THE GRINNING, GREEN-GARBED ELF WITHIN THE MYSTIC *SPHERE* OF SUFINDUM!

HOW?

ONE WORD-- BUT IT CARRIES WITH IT A HUNDRED SWELLING EMOTIONS-- AND AN UNYIELDING DEMAND FOR ANSWERS...

... THAT *MUST* BE MET!

IF YOU WOULD UNLOCK THE DOOR TO THIS MYSTERY, STEPHEN STRANGE-- THEN YOU MUST STAND BEFORE--

-- THE TRIBUNAL!

HIYA, PALLY-- I'M BACK!

GEE, I JUST CAN'T CONTAIN MY EXCITEMENT

372

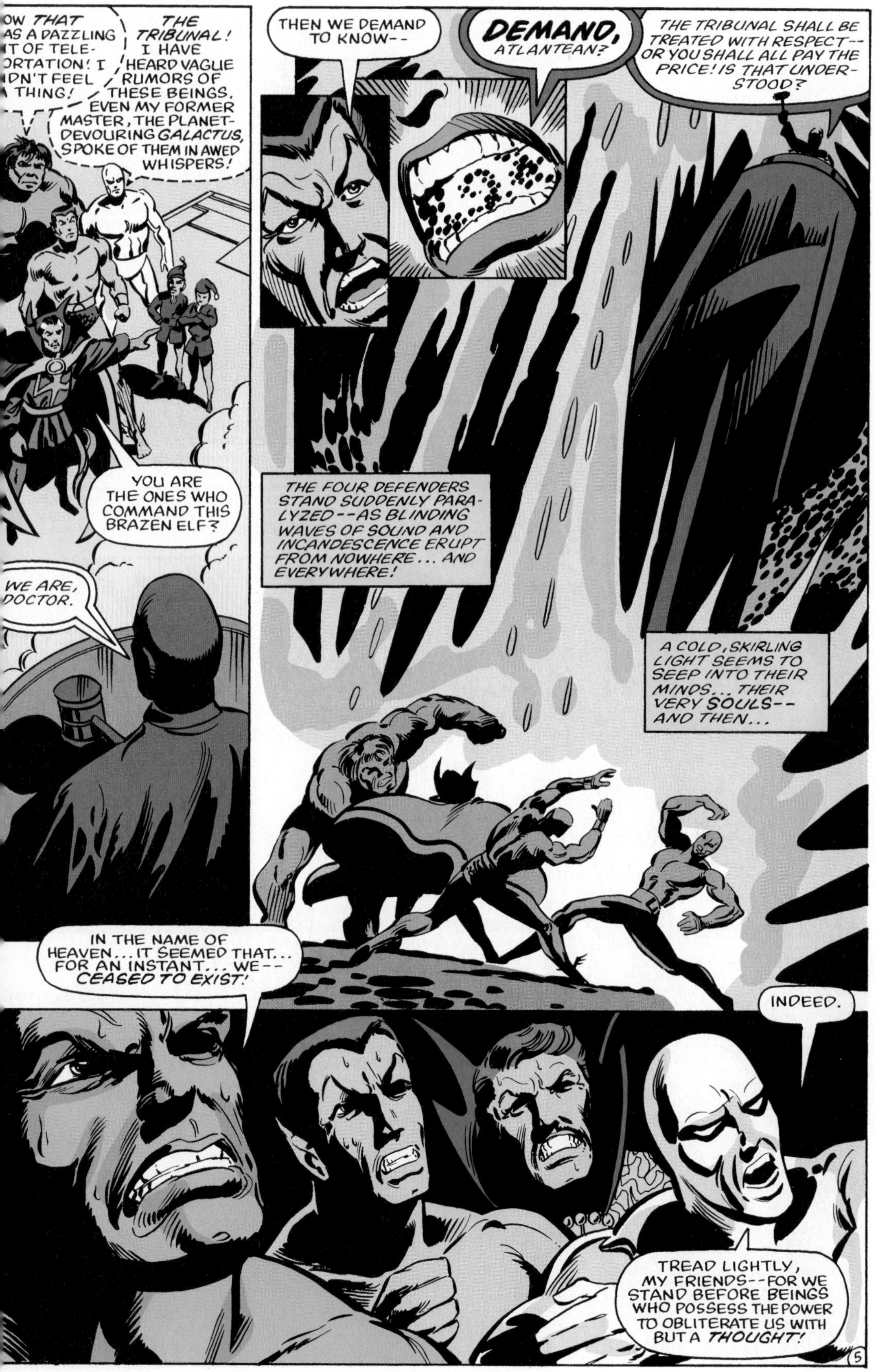
OW THAT AS A DAZZLING IT OF TELE-ORTATION! I DN'T FEEL THING!
THE TRIBUNAL! I HAVE HEARD VAGUE RUMORS OF THESE BEINGS. EVEN MY FORMER MASTER, THE PLANET-DEVOURING GALACTUS, SPOKE OF THEM IN AWED WHISPERS!
YOU ARE THE ONES WHO COMMAND THIS BRAZEN ELF?
WE ARE, DOCTOR.
THEN WE DEMAND TO KNOW--
DEMAND, ATLANTEAN?
THE TRIBUNAL SHALL BE TREATED WITH RESPECT--OR YOU SHALL ALL PAY THE PRICE! IS THAT UNDERSTOOD?
THE FOUR DEFENDERS STAND SUDDENLY PARALYZED--AS BLINDING WAVES OF SOUND AND INCANDESCENCE ERUPT FROM NOWHERE... AND EVERYWHERE!
A COLD, SKIRLING LIGHT SEEMS TO SEEP INTO THEIR MINDS... THEIR VERY SOULS--AND THEN...
IN THE NAME OF HEAVEN... IT SEEMED THAT... FOR AN INSTANT... WE--CEASED TO EXIST!
INDEED.
TREAD LIGHTLY, MY FRIENDS--FOR WE STAND BEFORE BEINGS WHO POSSESS THE POWER TO OBLITERATE US WITH BUT A THOUGHT!
5

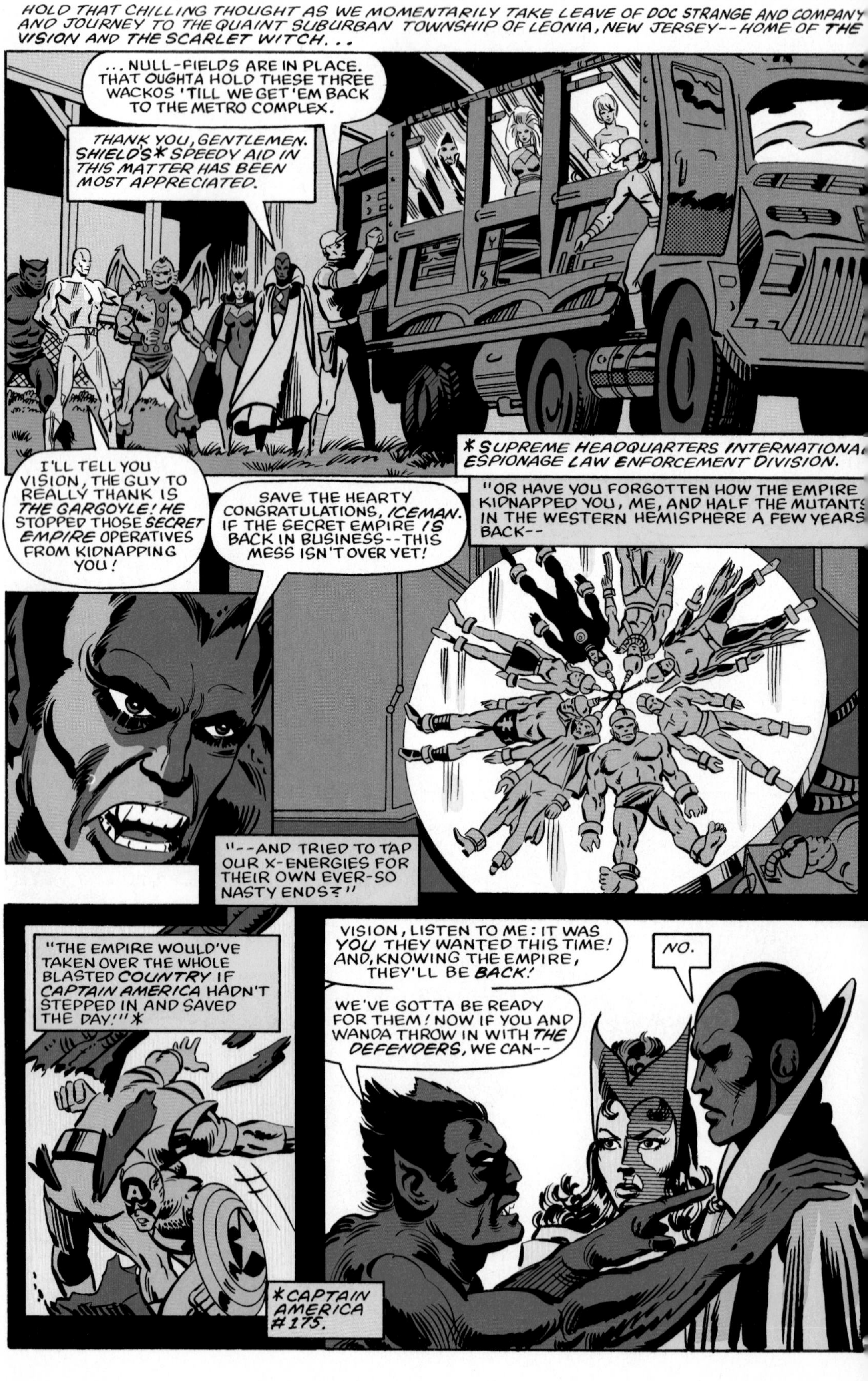
HOLD THAT CHILLING THOUGHT AS WE MOMENTARILY TAKE LEAVE OF DOC STRANGE AND COMPANY AND JOURNEY TO THE QUAINT SUBURBAN TOWNSHIP OF LEONIA, NEW JERSEY--HOME OF THE VISION AND THE SCARLET WITCH...
...NULL-FIELDS ARE IN PLACE. THAT OUGHTA HOLD THESE THREE WACKOS 'TILL WE GET 'EM BACK TO THE METRO COMPLEX.
THANK YOU, GENTLEMEN. SHIELD'S* SPEEDY AID IN THIS MATTER HAS BEEN MOST APPRECIATED.
*SUPREME HEADQUARTERS INTERNATIONAL ESPIONAGE LAW ENFORCEMENT DIVISION.
I'LL TELL YOU VISION, THE GUY TO REALLY THANK IS THE GARGOYLE! HE STOPPED THOSE SECRET EMPIRE OPERATIVES FROM KIDNAPPING YOU!
SAVE THE HEARTY CONGRATULATIONS, ICEMAN. IF THE SECRET EMPIRE IS BACK IN BUSINESS--THIS MESS ISN'T OVER YET!
"OR HAVE YOU FORGOTTEN HOW THE EMPIRE KIDNAPPED YOU, ME, AND HALF THE MUTANTS IN THE WESTERN HEMISPHERE A FEW YEARS BACK--
"--AND TRIED TO TAP OUR X-ENERGIES FOR THEIR OWN EVER-SO NASTY ENDS?"
"THE EMPIRE WOULD'VE TAKEN OVER THE WHOLE BLASTED COUNTRY IF CAPTAIN AMERICA HADN'T STEPPED IN AND SAVED THE DAY!"*
*CAPTAIN AMERICA #175.
VISION, LISTEN TO ME: IT WAS YOU THEY WANTED THIS TIME! AND, KNOWING THE EMPIRE, THEY'LL BE BACK!
WE'VE GOTTA BE READY FOR THEM! NOW IF YOU AND WANDA THROW IN WITH THE DEFENDERS, WE CAN--
NO.

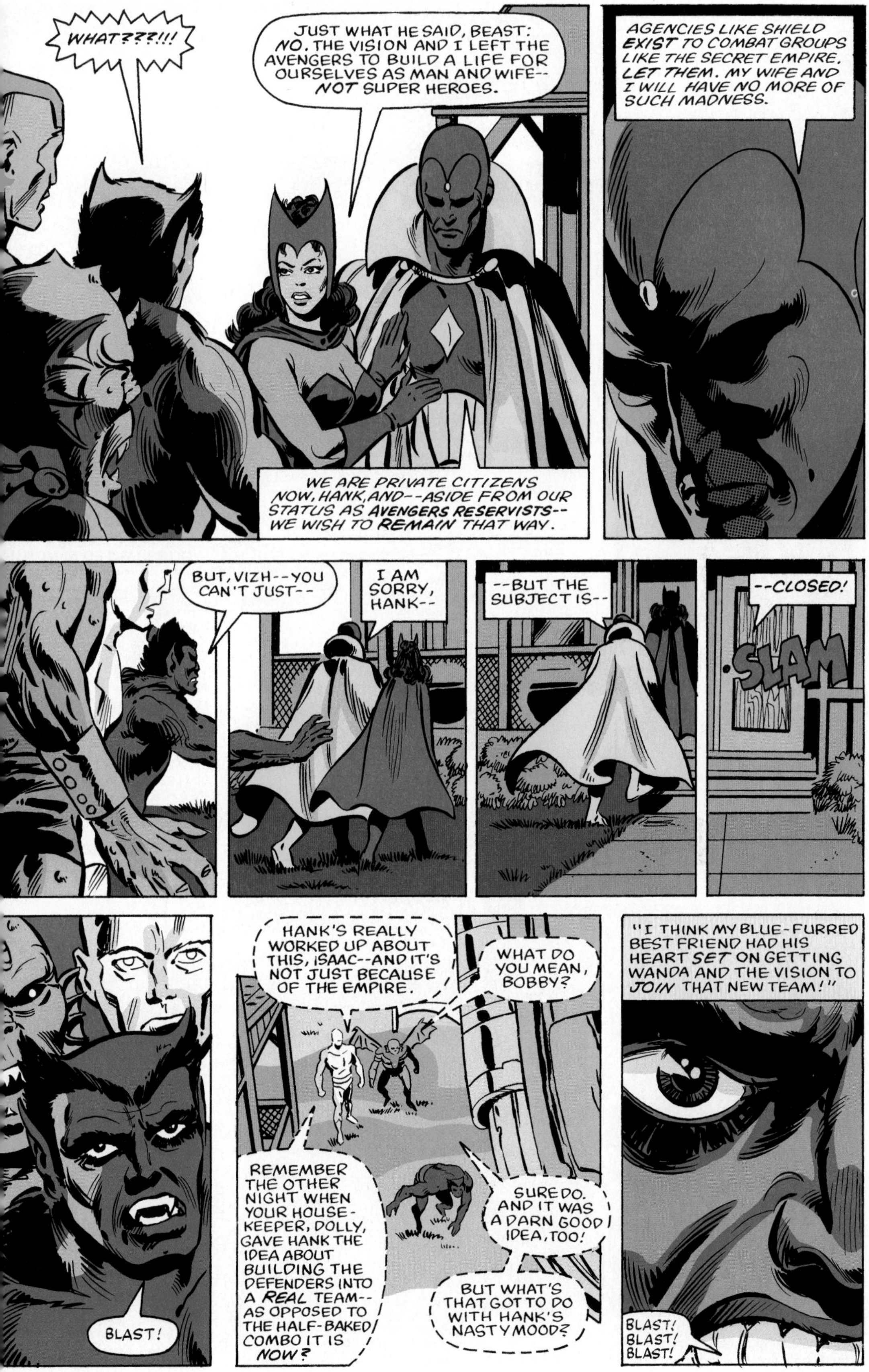
WHAT???!!!
JUST WHAT HE SAID, BEAST: NO. THE VISION AND I LEFT THE AVENGERS TO BUILD A LIFE FOR OURSELVES AS MAN AND WIFE-- NOT SUPER HEROES.
WE ARE PRIVATE CITIZENS NOW, HANK, AND--ASIDE FROM OUR STATUS AS AVENGERS RESERVISTS-- WE WISH TO REMAIN THAT WAY.
AGENCIES LIKE SHIELD EXIST TO COMBAT GROUPS LIKE THE SECRET EMPIRE. LET THEM. MY WIFE AND I WILL HAVE NO MORE OF SUCH MADNESS.
BUT, VIZH--YOU CAN'T JUST--
I AM SORRY, HANK--
--BUT THE SUBJECT IS--
--CLOSED!
SLAM
BLAST!
HANK'S REALLY WORKED UP ABOUT THIS, ISAAC--AND IT'S NOT JUST BECAUSE OF THE EMPIRE.
WHAT DO YOU MEAN, BOBBY?
REMEMBER THE OTHER NIGHT WHEN YOUR HOUSE-KEEPER, DOLLY, GAVE HANK THE IDEA ABOUT BUILDING THE DEFENDERS INTO A REAL TEAM-- AS OPPOSED TO THE HALF-BAKED COMBO IT IS NOW?
SURE DO. AND IT WAS A DARN GOOD IDEA, TOO!
BUT WHAT'S THAT GOT TO DO WITH HANK'S NASTY MOOD?
"I THINK MY BLUE-FURRED BEST FRIEND HAD HIS HEART SET ON GETTING WANDA AND THE VISION TO JOIN THAT NEW TEAM!"
BLAST! BLAST! BLAST!

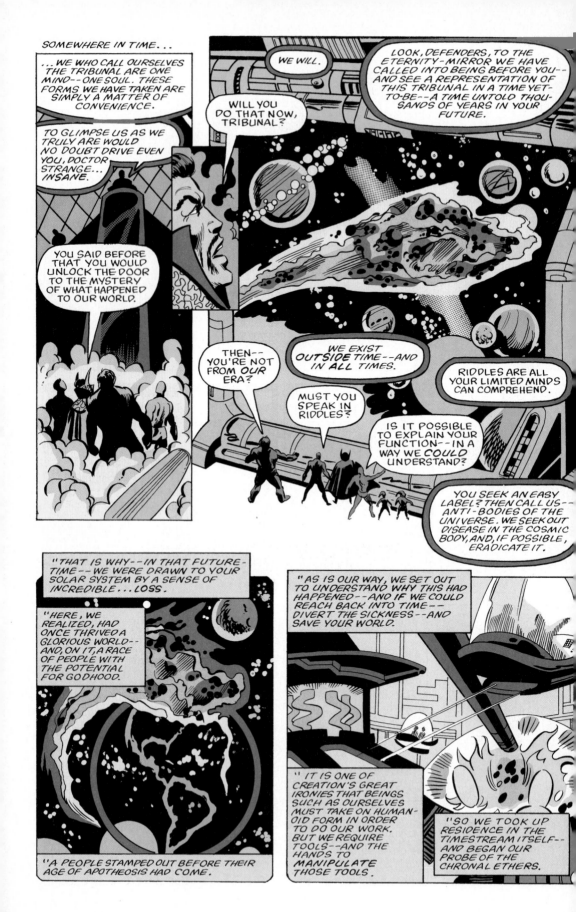

SOMEWHERE IN TIME...

...WE WHO CALL OURSELVES THE TRIBUNAL ARE ONE MIND--ONE SOUL. THESE FORMS WE HAVE TAKEN ARE SIMPLY A MATTER OF CONVENIENCE.

TO GLIMPSE US AS WE TRULY ARE WOULD NO DOUBT DRIVE EVEN YOU, DOCTOR STRANGE... INSANE.

YOU SAID BEFORE THAT YOU WOULD UNLOCK THE DOOR TO THE MYSTERY OF WHAT HAPPENED TO OUR WORLD.

WE WILL.

WILL YOU DO THAT NOW, TRIBUNAL?

LOOK, DEFENDERS, TO THE ETERNITY-MIRROR WE HAVE CALLED INTO BEING BEFORE YOU-- AND SEE A REPRESENTATION OF THIS TRIBUNAL IN A TIME YET-TO-BE--A TIME UNTOLD THOUSANDS OF YEARS IN YOUR FUTURE.

THEN-- YOU'RE NOT FROM OUR ERA?

WE EXIST OUTSIDE TIME--AND IN ALL TIMES.

MUST YOU SPEAK IN RIDDLES?

RIDDLES ARE ALL YOUR LIMITED MINDS CAN COMPREHEND.

IS IT POSSIBLE TO EXPLAIN YOUR FUNCTION--IN A WAY WE COULD UNDERSTAND?

YOU SEEK AN EASY LABEL? THEN CALL US-- ANTI-BODIES OF THE UNIVERSE. WE SEEK OUT DISEASE IN THE COSMIC BODY, AND, IF POSSIBLE, ERADICATE IT.

"THAT IS WHY--IN THAT FUTURE-TIME--WE WERE DRAWN TO YOUR SOLAR SYSTEM BY A SENSE OF INCREDIBLE...LOSS.

"HERE, WE REALIZED, HAD ONCE THRIVED A GLORIOUS WORLD-- AND, ON IT, A RACE OF PEOPLE WITH THE POTENTIAL FOR GODHOOD.

"A PEOPLE STAMPED OUT BEFORE THEIR AGE OF APOTHEOSIS HAD COME.

"AS IS OUR WAY, WE SET OUT TO UNDERSTAND WHY THIS HAD HAPPENED--AND IF WE COULD REACH BACK INTO TIME-- DIVERT THE SICKNESS--AND SAVE YOUR WORLD.

"IT IS ONE OF CREATION'S GREAT IRONIES THAT BEINGS SUCH AS OURSELVES MUST TAKE ON HUMAN-OID FORM IN ORDER TO DO OUR WORK. BUT WE REQUIRE TOOLS--AND THE HANDS TO MANIPULATE THOSE TOOLS.

"SO WE TOOK UP RESIDENCE IN THE TIMESTREAM ITSELF-- AND BEGAN OUR PROBE OF THE CHRONAL ETHERS.

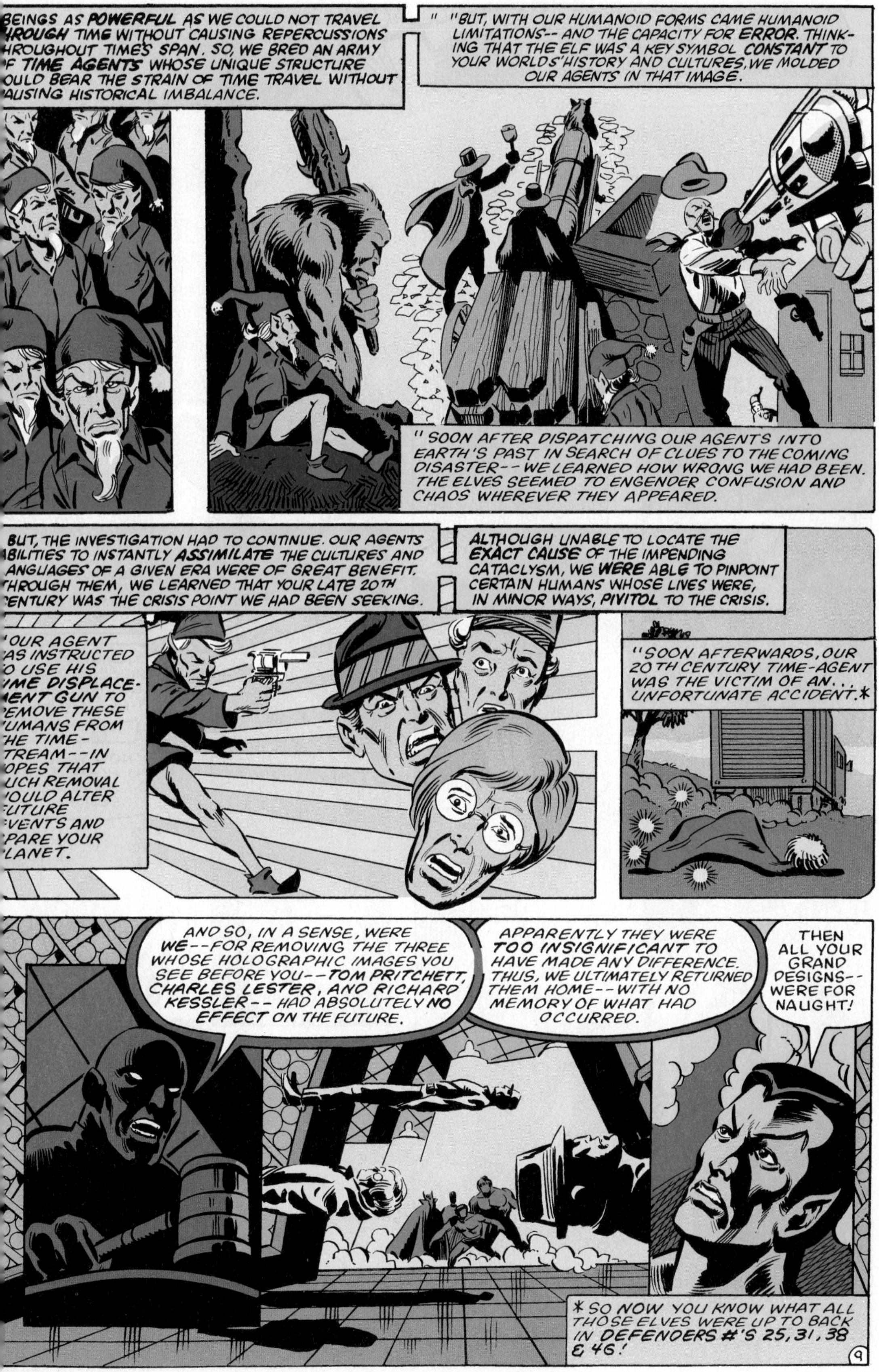
BEINGS AS POWERFUL AS WE COULD NOT TRAVEL THROUGH TIME WITHOUT CAUSING REPERCUSSIONS THROUGHOUT TIME'S SPAN. SO, WE BRED AN ARMY OF TIME AGENTS WHOSE UNIQUE STRUCTURE COULD BEAR THE STRAIN OF TIME TRAVEL WITHOUT CAUSING HISTORICAL IMBALANCE.
"BUT, WITH OUR HUMANOID FORMS CAME HUMANOID LIMITATIONS-- AND THE CAPACITY FOR ERROR. THINKING THAT THE ELF WAS A KEY SYMBOL CONSTANT TO YOUR WORLDS' HISTORY AND CULTURES, WE MOLDED OUR AGENTS IN THAT IMAGE.
"SOON AFTER DISPATCHING OUR AGENTS INTO EARTH'S PAST IN SEARCH OF CLUES TO THE COMING DISASTER-- WE LEARNED HOW WRONG WE HAD BEEN. THE ELVES SEEMED TO ENGENDER CONFUSION AND CHAOS WHEREVER THEY APPEARED.
BUT, THE INVESTIGATION HAD TO CONTINUE. OUR AGENTS ABILITIES TO INSTANTLY ASSIMILATE THE CULTURES AND LANGUAGES OF A GIVEN ERA WERE OF GREAT BENEFIT. THROUGH THEM, WE LEARNED THAT YOUR LATE 20TH CENTURY WAS THE CRISIS POINT WE HAD BEEN SEEKING.
ALTHOUGH UNABLE TO LOCATE THE EXACT CAUSE OF THE IMPENDING CATACLYSM, WE WERE ABLE TO PINPOINT CERTAIN HUMANS WHOSE LIVES WERE, IN MINOR WAYS, PIVITOL TO THE CRISIS.
"OUR AGENT WAS INSTRUCTED TO USE HIS TIME DISPLACEMENT GUN TO REMOVE THESE HUMANS FROM THE TIME-STREAM--IN HOPES THAT SUCH REMOVAL WOULD ALTER FUTURE EVENTS AND SPARE YOUR PLANET.
"SOON AFTERWARDS, OUR 20TH CENTURY TIME-AGENT WAS THE VICTIM OF AN... UNFORTUNATE ACCIDENT.*
AND SO, IN A SENSE, WERE WE--FOR REMOVING THE THREE WHOSE HOLOGRAPHIC IMAGES YOU SEE BEFORE YOU--TOM PRITCHETT, CHARLES LESTER, AND RICHARD KESSLER-- HAD ABSOLUTELY NO EFFECT ON THE FUTURE.
APPARENTLY THEY WERE TOO INSIGNIFICANT TO HAVE MADE ANY DIFFERENCE. THUS, WE ULTIMATELY RETURNED THEM HOME--WITH NO MEMORY OF WHAT HAD OCCURRED.
THEN ALL YOUR GRAND DESIGNS--WERE FOR NAUGHT!
*SO NOW YOU KNOW WHAT ALL THOSE ELVES WERE UP TO BACK IN DEFENDERS #'S 25, 31, 38 & 46!
9

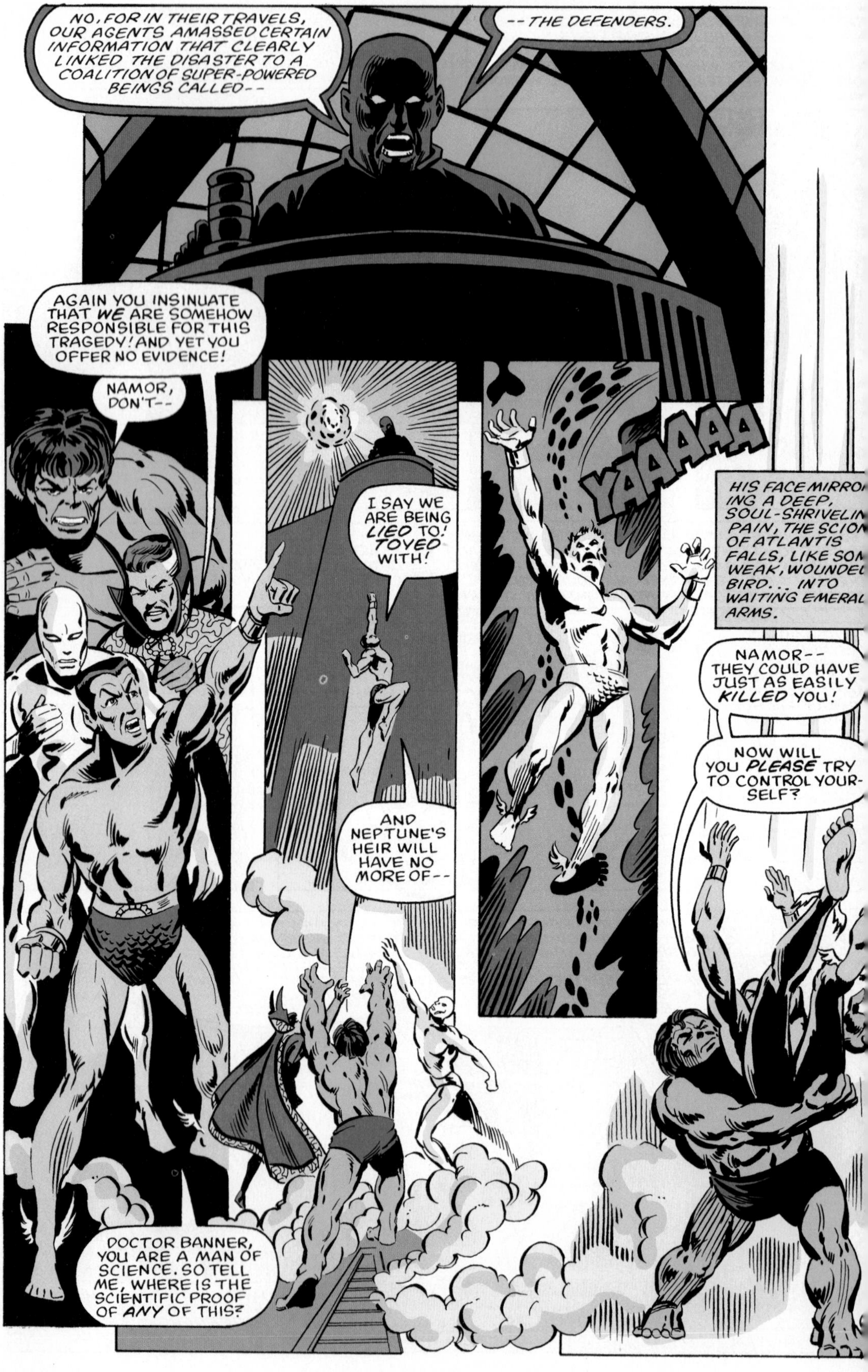
NO, FOR IN THEIR TRAVELS, OUR AGENTS AMASSED CERTAIN INFORMATION THAT CLEARLY LINKED THE DISASTER TO A COALITION OF SUPER-POWERED BEINGS CALLED--
--THE DEFENDERS.
AGAIN YOU INSINUATE THAT WE ARE SOMEHOW RESPONSIBLE FOR THIS TRAGEDY! AND YET YOU OFFER NO EVIDENCE!
NAMOR, DON'T--
DOCTOR BANNER, YOU ARE A MAN OF SCIENCE. SO TELL ME, WHERE IS THE SCIENTIFIC PROOF OF ANY OF THIS?
I SAY WE ARE BEING LIED TO! TOYED WITH!
AND NEPTUNE'S HEIR WILL HAVE NO MORE OF--
YAAAAA
HIS FACE MIRRORING A DEEP, SOUL-SHRIVELING PAIN, THE SCION OF ATLANTIS FALLS, LIKE SOME WEAK, WOUNDED BIRD... INTO WAITING EMERALD ARMS.
NAMOR-- THEY COULD HAVE JUST AS EASILY KILLED YOU!
NOW WILL YOU PLEASE TRY TO CONTROL YOURSELF?

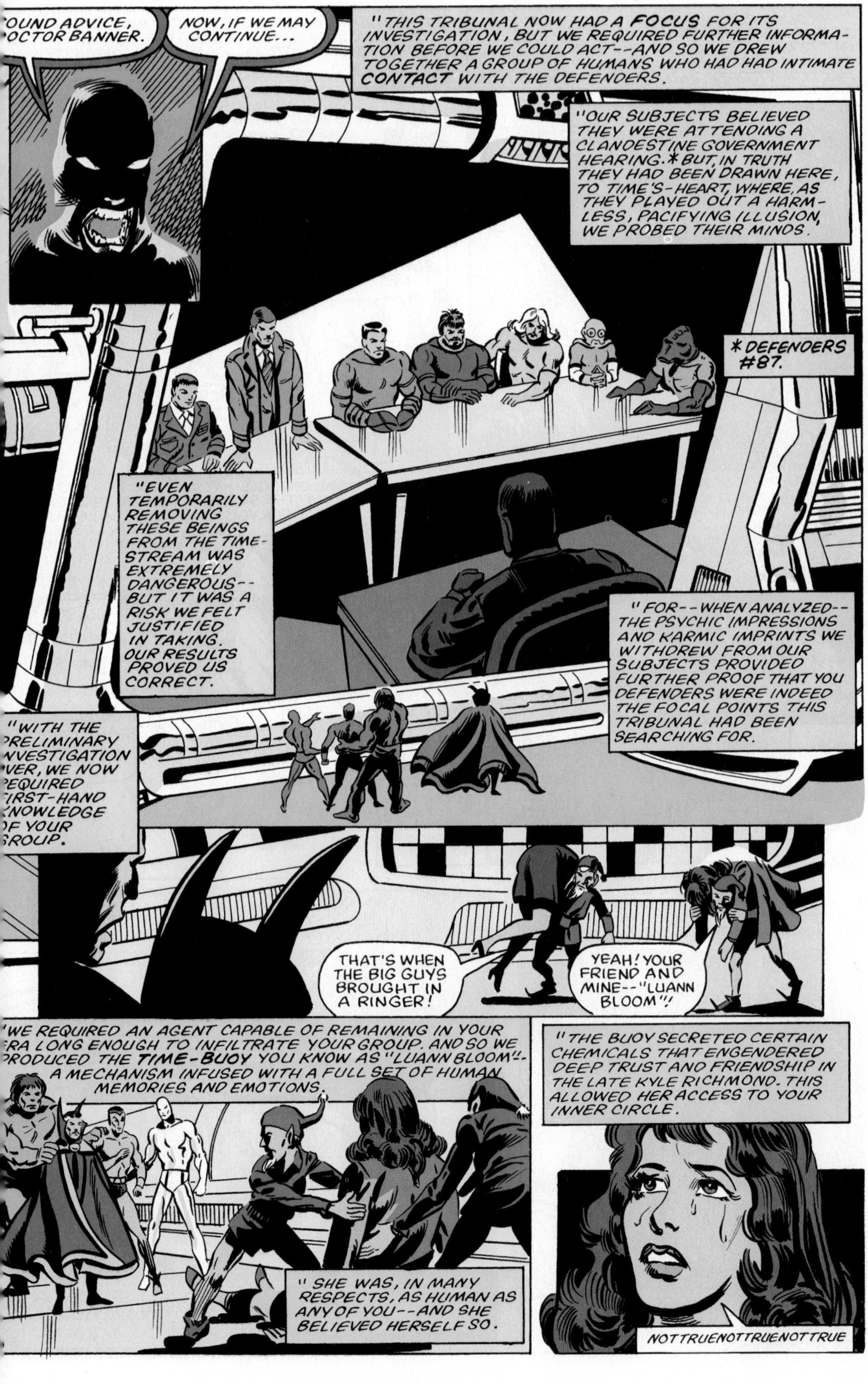
OUND ADVICE, OCTOR BANNER.
NOW, IF WE MAY CONTINUE...
"THIS TRIBUNAL NOW HAD A FOCUS FOR ITS INVESTIGATION, BUT WE REQUIRED FURTHER INFORMATION BEFORE WE COULD ACT--AND SO WE DREW TOGETHER A GROUP OF HUMANS WHO HAD HAD INTIMATE CONTACT WITH THE DEFENDERS.
"OUR SUBJECTS BELIEVED THEY WERE ATTENDING A CLANDESTINE GOVERNMENT HEARING.* BUT, IN TRUTH THEY HAD BEEN DRAWN HERE, TO TIME'S-HEART, WHERE, AS THEY PLAYED OUT A HARMLESS, PACIFYING ILLUSION, WE PROBED THEIR MINDS.
*DEFENDERS #87.
"EVEN TEMPORARILY REMOVING THESE BEINGS FROM THE TIME-STREAM WAS EXTREMELY DANGEROUS--BUT IT WAS A RISK WE FELT JUSTIFIED IN TAKING. OUR RESULTS PROVED US CORRECT.
"FOR--WHEN ANALYZED--THE PSYCHIC IMPRESSIONS AND KARMIC IMPRINTS WE WITHDREW FROM OUR SUBJECTS PROVIDED FURTHER PROOF THAT YOU DEFENDERS WERE INDEED THE FOCAL POINTS THIS TRIBUNAL HAD BEEN SEARCHING FOR.
"WITH THE PRELIMINARY NVESTIGATION VER, WE NOW EQUIRED IRST-HAND NOWLEDGE OF YOUR ROUP.
THAT'S WHEN THE BIG GUYS BROUGHT IN A RINGER!
YEAH! YOUR FRIEND AND MINE--"LUANN BLOOM"!
"WE REQUIRED AN AGENT CAPABLE OF REMAINING IN YOUR RA LONG ENOUGH TO INFILTRATE YOUR GROUP. AND SO WE PRODUCED THE TIME-BUOY YOU KNOW AS "LUANN BLOOM"--A MECHANISM INFUSED WITH A FULL SET OF HUMAN MEMORIES AND EMOTIONS.
"SHE WAS, IN MANY RESPECTS, AS HUMAN AS ANY OF YOU--AND SHE BELIEVED HERSELF SO.
"THE BUOY SECRETED CERTAIN CHEMICALS THAT ENGENDERED DEEP TRUST AND FRIENDSHIP IN THE LATE KYLE RICHMOND. THIS ALLOWED HER ACCESS TO YOUR INNER CIRCLE.
NOTTRUENOTTRUENOTTRUE

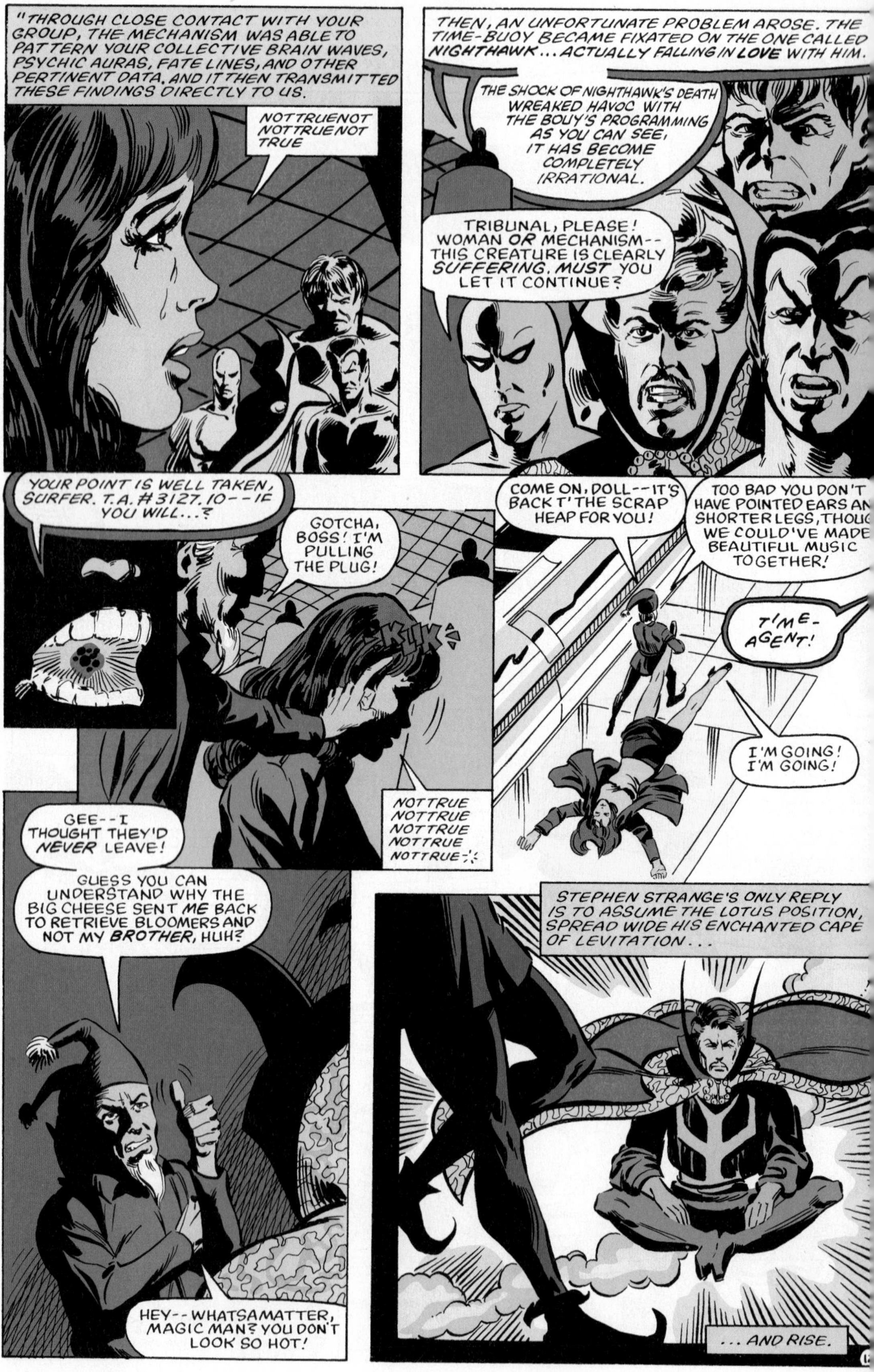
"THROUGH CLOSE CONTACT WITH YOUR GROUP, THE MECHANISM WAS ABLE TO PATTERN YOUR COLLECTIVE BRAIN WAVES, PSYCHIC AURAS, FATE LINES, AND OTHER PERTINENT DATA, AND IT THEN TRANSMITTED THESE FINDINGS DIRECTLY TO US.
NOTTRUENOT NOTTRUENOT TRUE
THEN, AN UNFORTUNATE PROBLEM AROSE. THE TIME-BUOY BECAME FIXATED ON THE ONE CALLED NIGHTHAWK... ACTUALLY FALLING IN LOVE WITH HIM.
THE SHOCK OF NIGHTHAWK'S DEATH WREAKED HAVOC WITH THE BOUY'S PROGRAMMING AS YOU CAN SEE, IT HAS BECOME COMPLETELY IRRATIONAL.
TRIBUNAL, PLEASE! WOMAN OR MECHANISM-- THIS CREATURE IS CLEARLY SUFFERING. MUST YOU LET IT CONTINUE?
YOUR POINT IS WELL TAKEN, SURFER. T.A. #3127.10-- IF YOU WILL...?
GOTCHA, BOSS! I'M PULLING THE PLUG!
KLIK
NOTTRUE NOTTRUE NOTTRUE NOTTRUE NOTTRUE
COME ON, DOLL--IT'S BACK T' THE SCRAP HEAP FOR YOU!
TOO BAD YOU DON'T HAVE POINTED EARS AN SHORTER LEGS, THOUG WE COULD'VE MADE BEAUTIFUL MUSIC TOGETHER!
TIME-AGENT!
I'M GOING! I'M GOING!
GEE--I THOUGHT THEY'D NEVER LEAVE!
GUESS YOU CAN UNDERSTAND WHY THE BIG CHEESE SENT ME BACK TO RETRIEVE BLOOMERS AND NOT MY BROTHER, HUH?
HEY--WHATSAMATTER, MAGIC MAN? YOU DON'T LOOK SO HOT!
STEPHEN STRANGE'S ONLY REPLY IS TO ASSUME THE LOTUS POSITION, SPREAD WIDE HIS ENCHANTED CAPE OF LEVITATION...
...AND RISE.

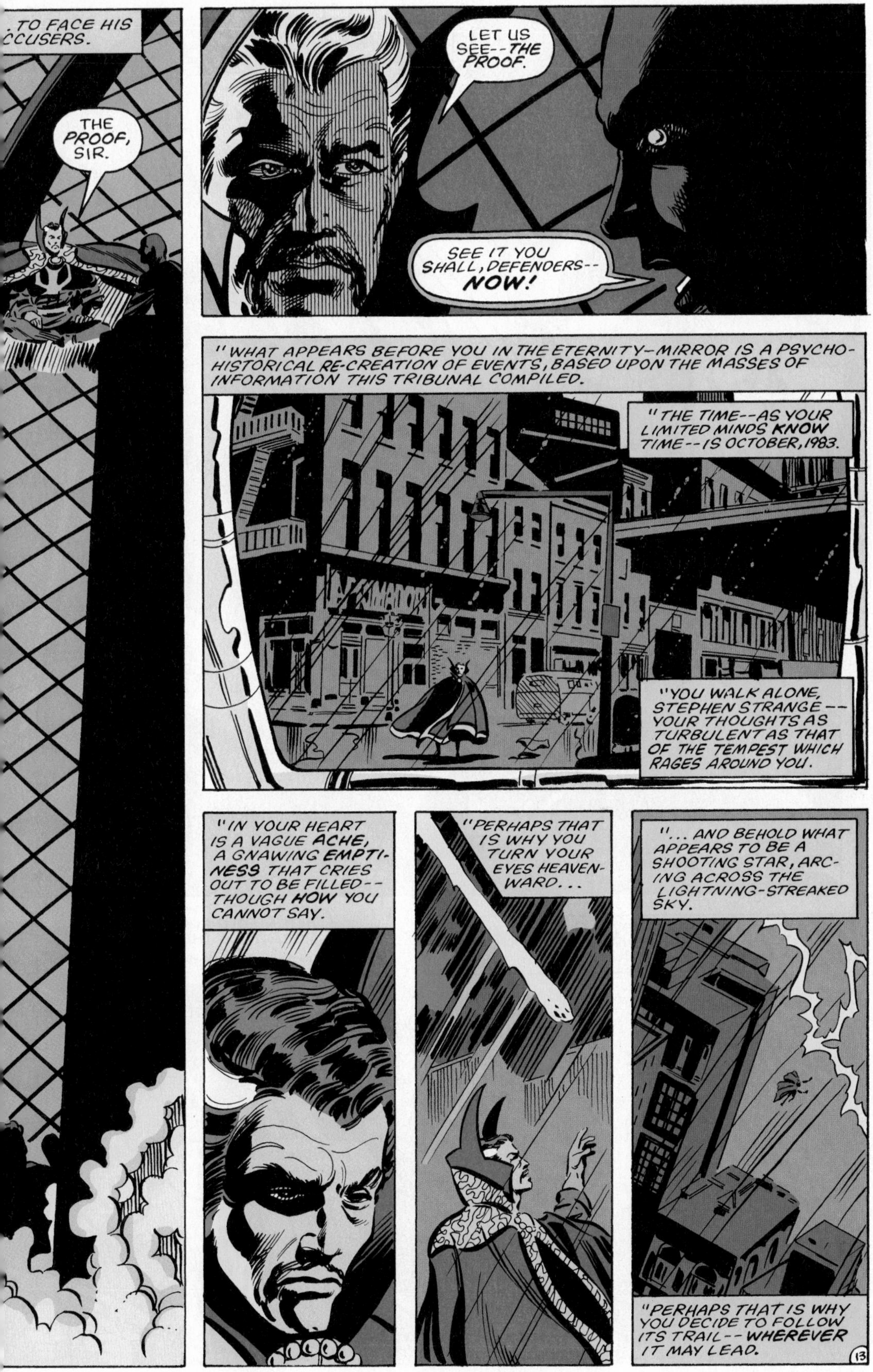

...TO FACE HIS ACCUSERS.
THE PROOF, SIR.
LET US SEE--THE PROOF.
SEE IT YOU SHALL, DEFENDERS--NOW!
"WHAT APPEARS BEFORE YOU IN THE ETERNITY-MIRROR IS A PSYCHO-HISTORICAL RE-CREATION OF EVENTS, BASED UPON THE MASSES OF INFORMATION THIS TRIBUNAL COMPILED.
"THE TIME--AS YOUR LIMITED MINDS KNOW TIME--IS OCTOBER, 1983.
"YOU WALK ALONE, STEPHEN STRANGE--YOUR THOUGHTS AS TURBULENT AS THAT OF THE TEMPEST WHICH RAGES AROUND YOU.
"IN YOUR HEART IS A VAGUE ACHE, A GNAWING EMPTINESS THAT CRIES OUT TO BE FILLED--THOUGH HOW YOU CANNOT SAY.
"PERHAPS THAT IS WHY YOU TURN YOUR EYES HEAVENWARD...
"...AND BEHOLD WHAT APPEARS TO BE A SHOOTING STAR, ARCING ACROSS THE LIGHTNING-STREAKED SKY.
"PERHAPS THAT IS WHY YOU DECIDE TO FOLLOW ITS TRAIL--WHEREVER IT MAY LEAD.
13

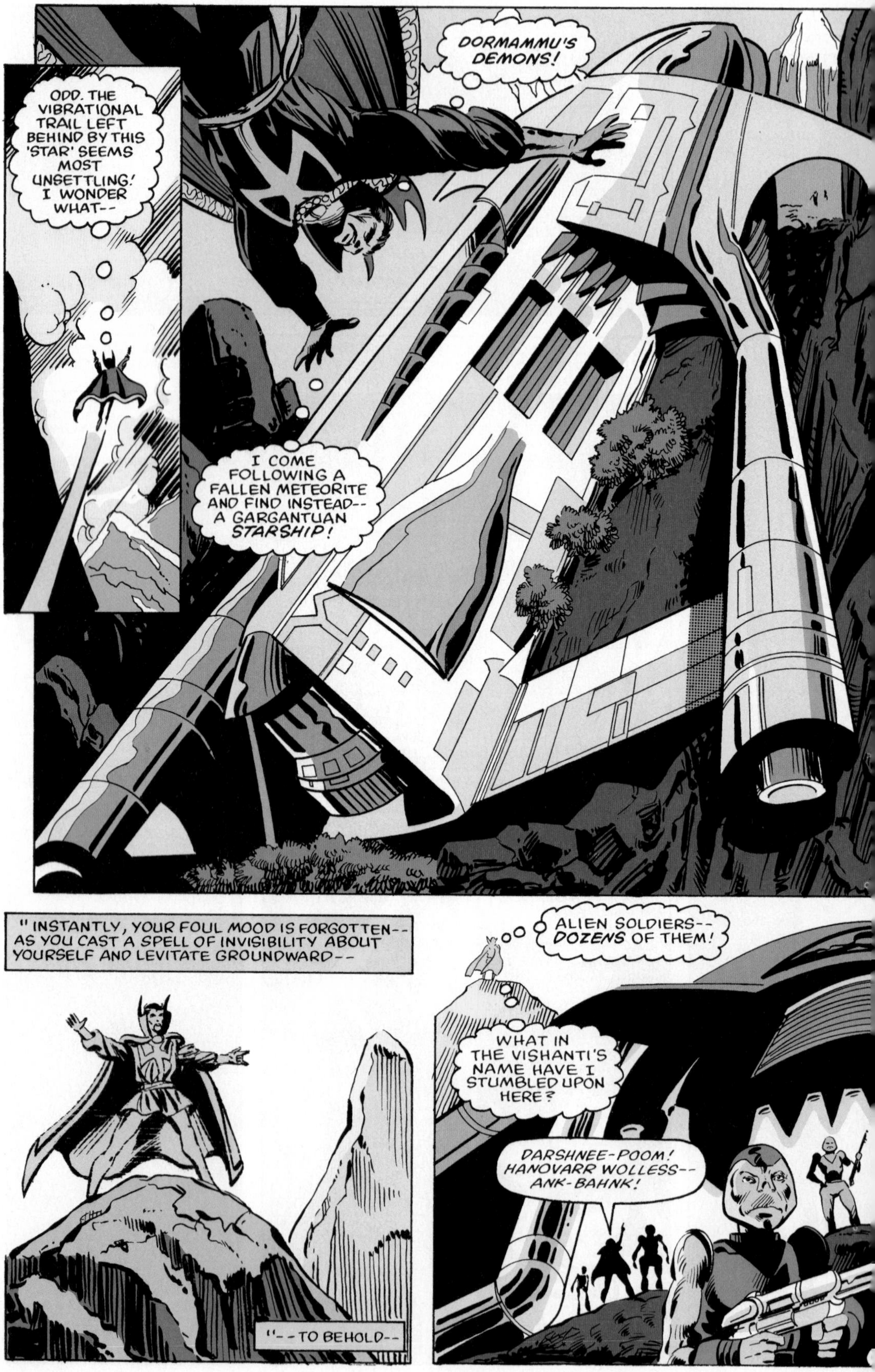

ODD. THE VIBRATIONAL TRAIL LEFT BEHIND BY THIS 'STAR' SEEMS MOST UNSETTLING! I WONDER WHAT--
DORMAMMU'S DEMONS!
I COME FOLLOWING A FALLEN METEORITE AND FIND INSTEAD-- A GARGANTUAN STARSHIP!
"INSTANTLY, YOUR FOUL MOOD IS FORGOTTEN-- AS YOU CAST A SPELL OF INVISIBILITY ABOUT YOURSELF AND LEVITATE GROUNDWARD--
"--TO BEHOLD--
ALIEN SOLDIERS-- DOZENS OF THEM!
WHAT IN THE VISHANTI'S NAME HAVE I STUMBLED UPON HERE?
DARSHNEE-POOM! HANOVARR WOLLESS-- ANK-BAHNK!

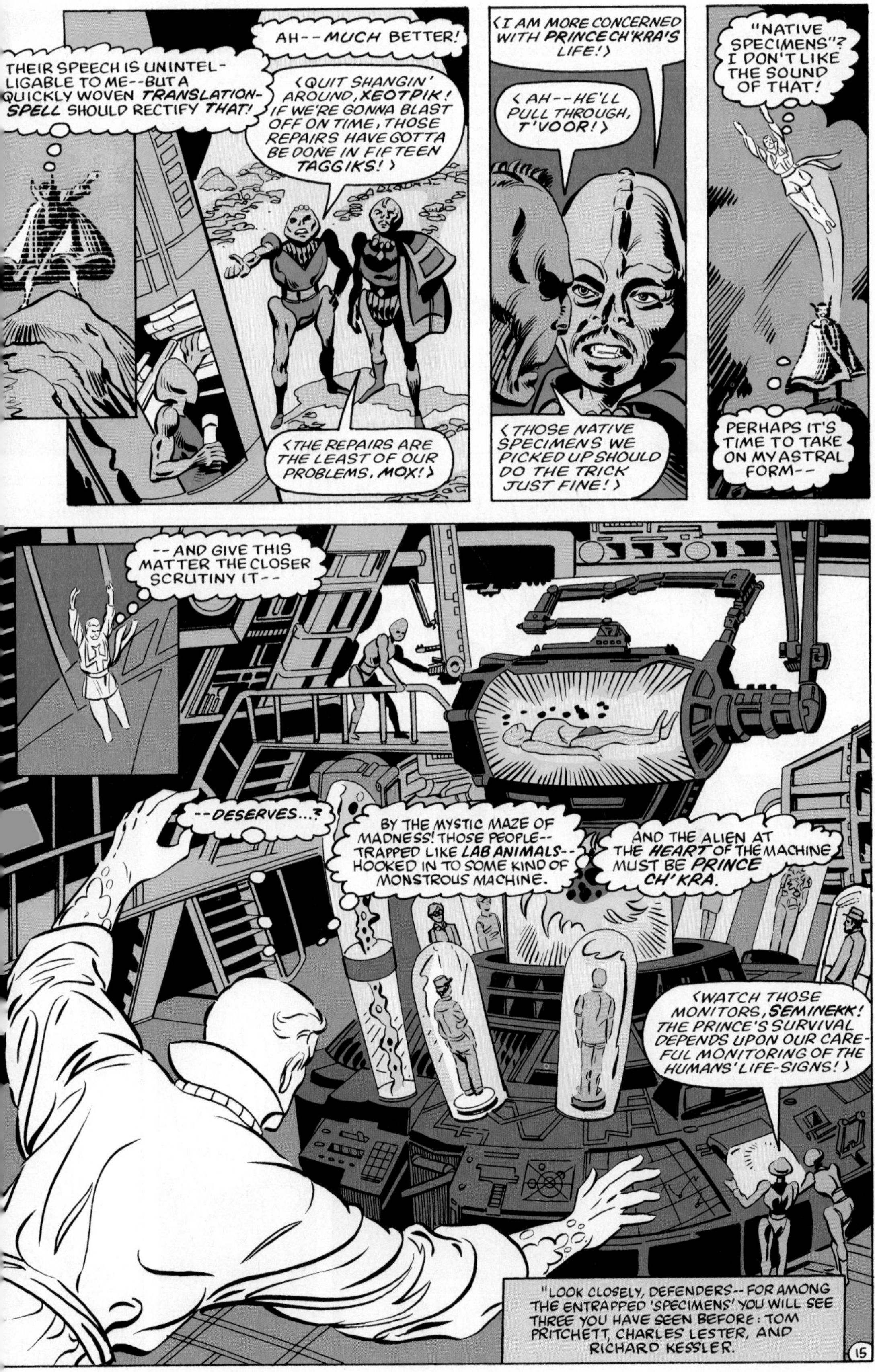
THEIR SPEECH IS UNINTEL-LIGABLE TO ME--BUT A QUICKLY WOVEN TRANSLATION-SPELL SHOULD RECTIFY THAT!
AH--MUCH BETTER!
<QUIT SHANGIN' AROUND, XEOTPIK! IF WE'RE GONNA BLAST OFF ON TIME, THOSE REPAIRS HAVE GOTTA BE DONE IN FIFTEEN TAGGIKS!>
<THE REPAIRS ARE THE LEAST OF OUR PROBLEMS, MOX!>
<I AM MORE CONCERNED WITH PRINCE CH'KRA'S LIFE!>
<AH--HE'LL PULL THROUGH, T'VOOR!>
<THOSE NATIVE SPECIMENS WE PICKED UP SHOULD DO THE TRICK JUST FINE!>
"NATIVE SPECIMENS"? I DON'T LIKE THE SOUND OF THAT!
PERHAPS IT'S TIME TO TAKE ON MY ASTRAL FORM--
--AND GIVE THIS MATTER THE CLOSER SCRUTINY IT--
--DESERVES...?
BY THE MYSTIC MAZE OF MADNESS! THOSE PEOPLE--TRAPPED LIKE LAB ANIMALS--HOOKED IN TO SOME KIND OF MONSTROUS MACHINE.
AND THE ALIEN AT THE HEART OF THE MACHINE MUST BE PRINCE CH'KRA.
<WATCH THOSE MONITORS, SEMINEKK! THE PRINCE'S SURVIVAL DEPENDS UPON OUR CARE-FUL MONITORING OF THE HUMANS' LIFE-SIGNS!>
"LOOK CLOSELY, DEFENDERS--FOR AMONG THE ENTRAPPED 'SPECIMENS' YOU WILL SEE THREE YOU HAVE SEEN BEFORE: TOM PRITCHETT, CHARLES LESTER, AND RICHARD KESSLER.
15

‹I DON'T LIKE THIS, ZIMM. TAPPING THE HUMANS' BIO-ENERGIES TO CURE OUR DYING PRINCE GOES AGAINST EVERYTHING WE BELIEVE!›

‹DON'T YOU THINK I KNOW THAT? BUT WITHOUT THE PRINCE TO LEAD US...GUIDE US...WE ARE LOST! WE MUST HAVE HIM BACK-- NO MATTER THE COST!›

‹FUNNY. I DON'T SEE ANY OF US RUSHING FORWARD TO HOOK IN THE RESURRECTONN!›

‹THE PRINCE IS SUFFERING FROM A DISEASE CONTRACTED ON THIS PLANET. ONLY THE NATURAL BIO-ENERGIES OF THE NATIVES CAN SAVE HIM!›

I HAVE HEARD ENOUGH!

THESE ALIENS ARE FRIGHTENED... DESPERATE... BUT FAR FROM EVIL!

‹I MUST RETURN TO MY CORPOREAL BODY-- AND RISK CONFRONTING THEM!›

IF I CAN CONVINCE THEM THAT I CAN BE TRUSTED--THAT I CAN FIND AID FOR THEIR STRICKEN PRINCE--

--THEN PERHAPS THEY WILL FREE THE CAPTURED "SPECIMENS" WITHOUT A STRUGGLE!

BUT I MUST BE EXTREMELY CAREFUL--

--FOR FEAR CAN OFTEN MAKE EVEN THE GENTLEST OF SOULS--

--MAD...?

‹WHAT IN THE NAME OF THE SACRED DUALITY?›

‹AN INTRUDER?›

‹HE COULD BE AN AGENT OF THE EMPIRE! STOP HIM!›

‹BUT WE CAN'T JUST--›

‹I SAID STOP HIM!›

BEEEEE

"YOU REPEL THEIR FIRST ATTACK, DOCTOR STRANGE, WITH AN EFFORTLESSLY-CONJURED MYSTIC SHIELD.

"BUT, WHILE YOU ARE ATTENDING TO ONE FLANK--

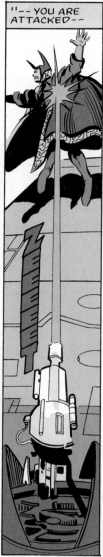

"--YOU ARE ATTACKED--

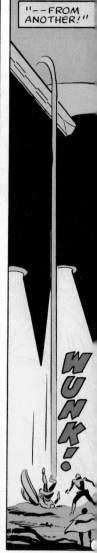

"--FROM ANOTHER!"

WUNK!

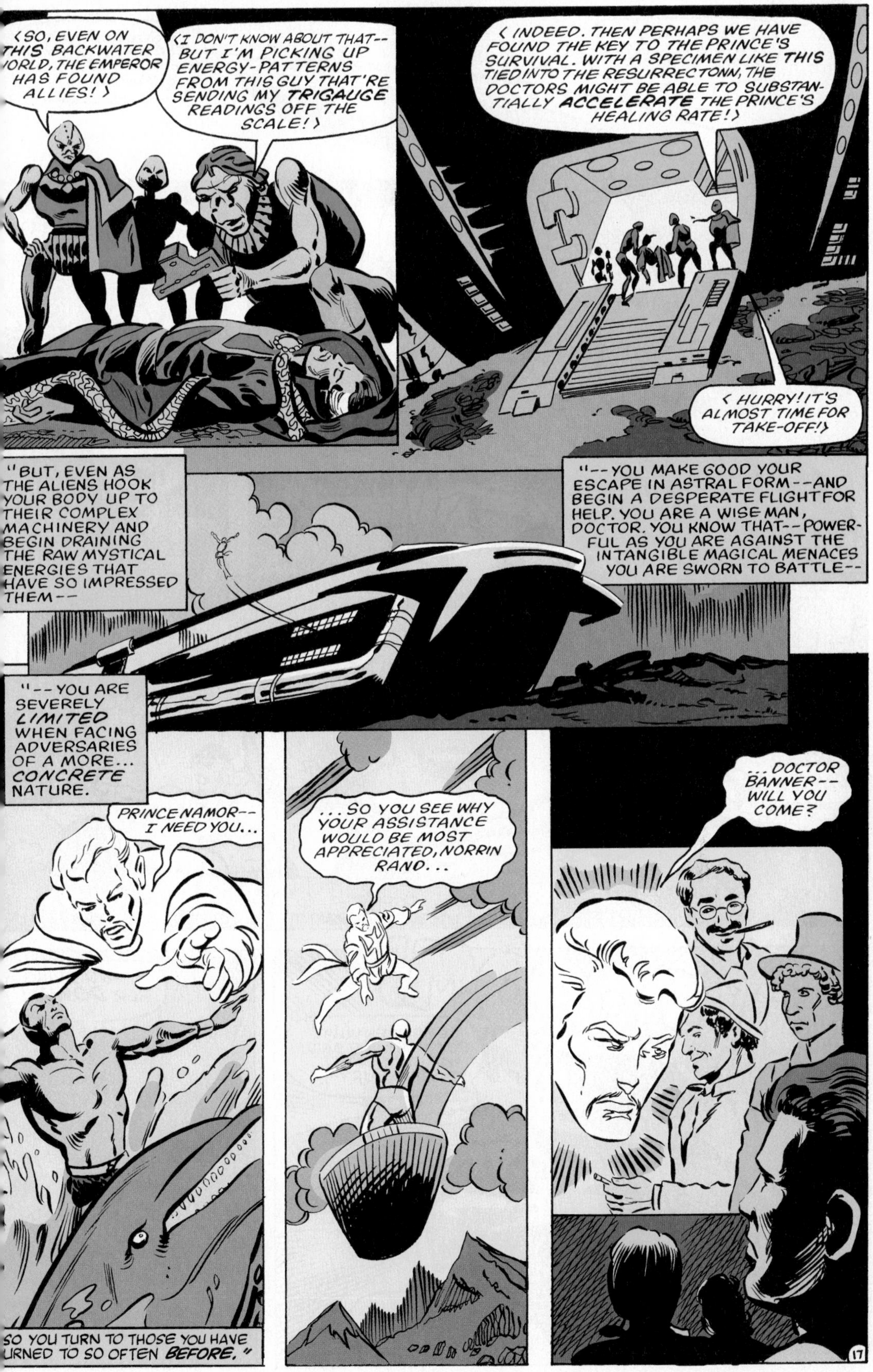
⟨SO, EVEN ON THIS BACKWATER WORLD, THE EMPEROR HAS FOUND ALLIES!⟩
⟨I DON'T KNOW ABOUT THAT-- BUT I'M PICKING UP ENERGY-PATTERNS FROM THIS GUY THAT'RE SENDING MY TRIGAUGE READINGS OFF THE SCALE!⟩
⟨INDEED. THEN PERHAPS WE HAVE FOUND THE KEY TO THE PRINCE'S SURVIVAL. WITH A SPECIMEN LIKE THIS TIED INTO THE RESURRECTONN, THE DOCTORS MIGHT BE ABLE TO SUBSTANTIALLY ACCELERATE THE PRINCE'S HEALING RATE!⟩
⟨HURRY! IT'S ALMOST TIME FOR TAKE-OFF!⟩
"BUT, EVEN AS THE ALIENS HOOK YOUR BODY UP TO THEIR COMPLEX MACHINERY AND BEGIN DRAINING THE RAW MYSTICAL ENERGIES THAT HAVE SO IMPRESSED THEM--
"--YOU MAKE GOOD YOUR ESCAPE IN ASTRAL FORM--AND BEGIN A DESPERATE FLIGHT FOR HELP. YOU ARE A WISE MAN, DOCTOR. YOU KNOW THAT--POWERFUL AS YOU ARE AGAINST THE INTANGIBLE MAGICAL MENACES YOU ARE SWORN TO BATTLE--
"--YOU ARE SEVERELY LIMITED WHEN FACING ADVERSARIES OF A MORE... CONCRETE NATURE.
PRINCE NAMOR-- I NEED YOU...
SO YOU TURN TO THOSE YOU HAVE URNED TO SO OFTEN BEFORE."
...SO YOU SEE WHY YOUR ASSISTANCE WOULD BE MOST APPRECIATED, NORRIN RAND...
...DOCTOR BANNER-- WILL YOU COME?
17

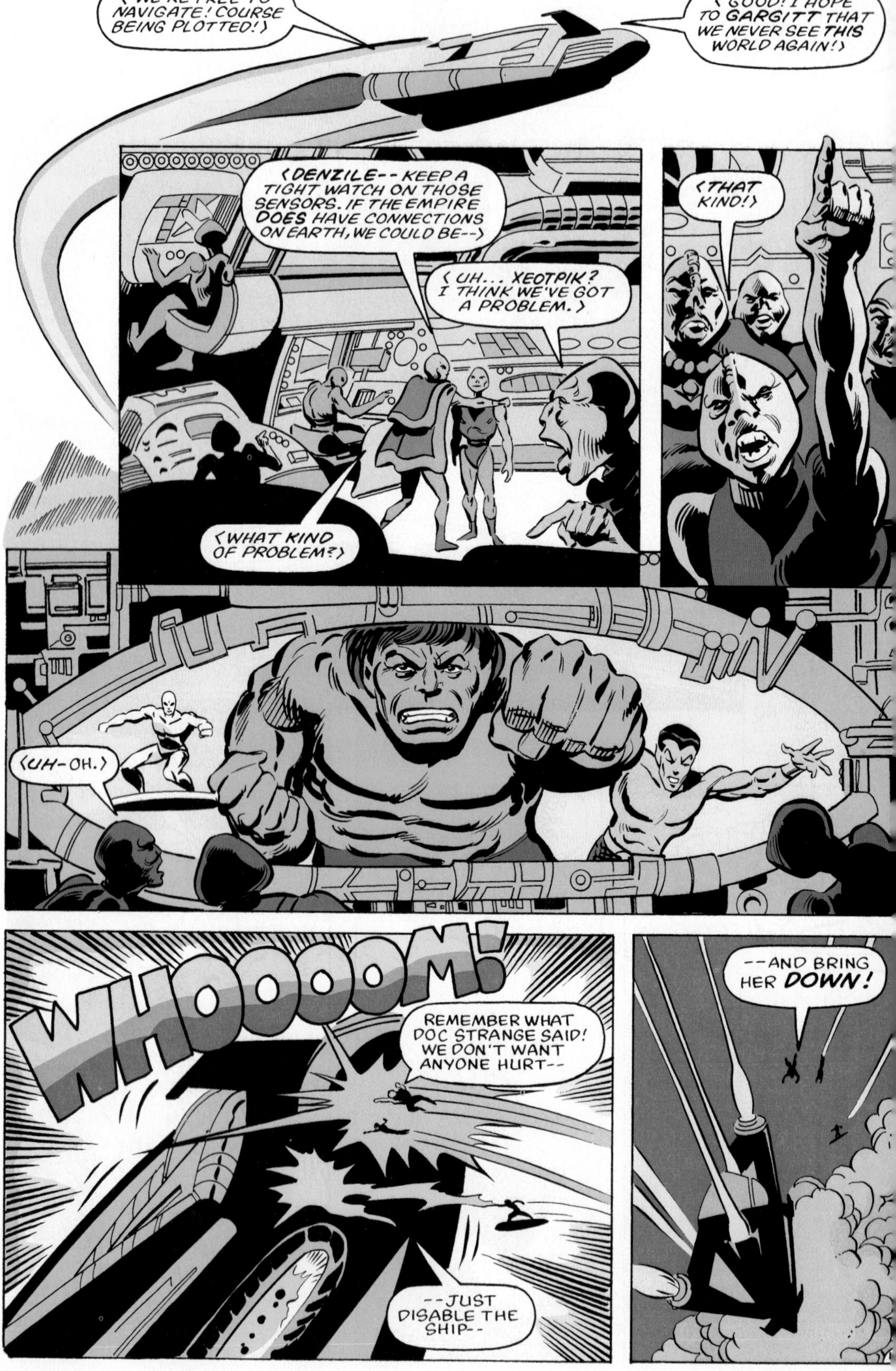
⟨WE'RE FREE TO NAVIGATE! COURSE BEING PLOTTED!⟩
⟨GOOD! I HOPE TO GARGITT THAT WE NEVER SEE THIS WORLD AGAIN!⟩
⟨DENZILE-- KEEP A TIGHT WATCH ON THOSE SENSORS. IF THE EMPIRE DOES HAVE CONNECTIONS ON EARTH, WE COULD BE--⟩
⟨UH... XEOTPIK? I THINK WE'VE GOT A PROBLEM.⟩
⟨WHAT KIND OF PROBLEM?⟩
⟨THAT KIND!⟩
⟨UH-OH.⟩
WHOOOOM!
REMEMBER WHAT DOC STRANGE SAID! WE DON'T WANT ANYONE HURT--
--JUST DISABLE THE SHIP--
--AND BRING HER DOWN!

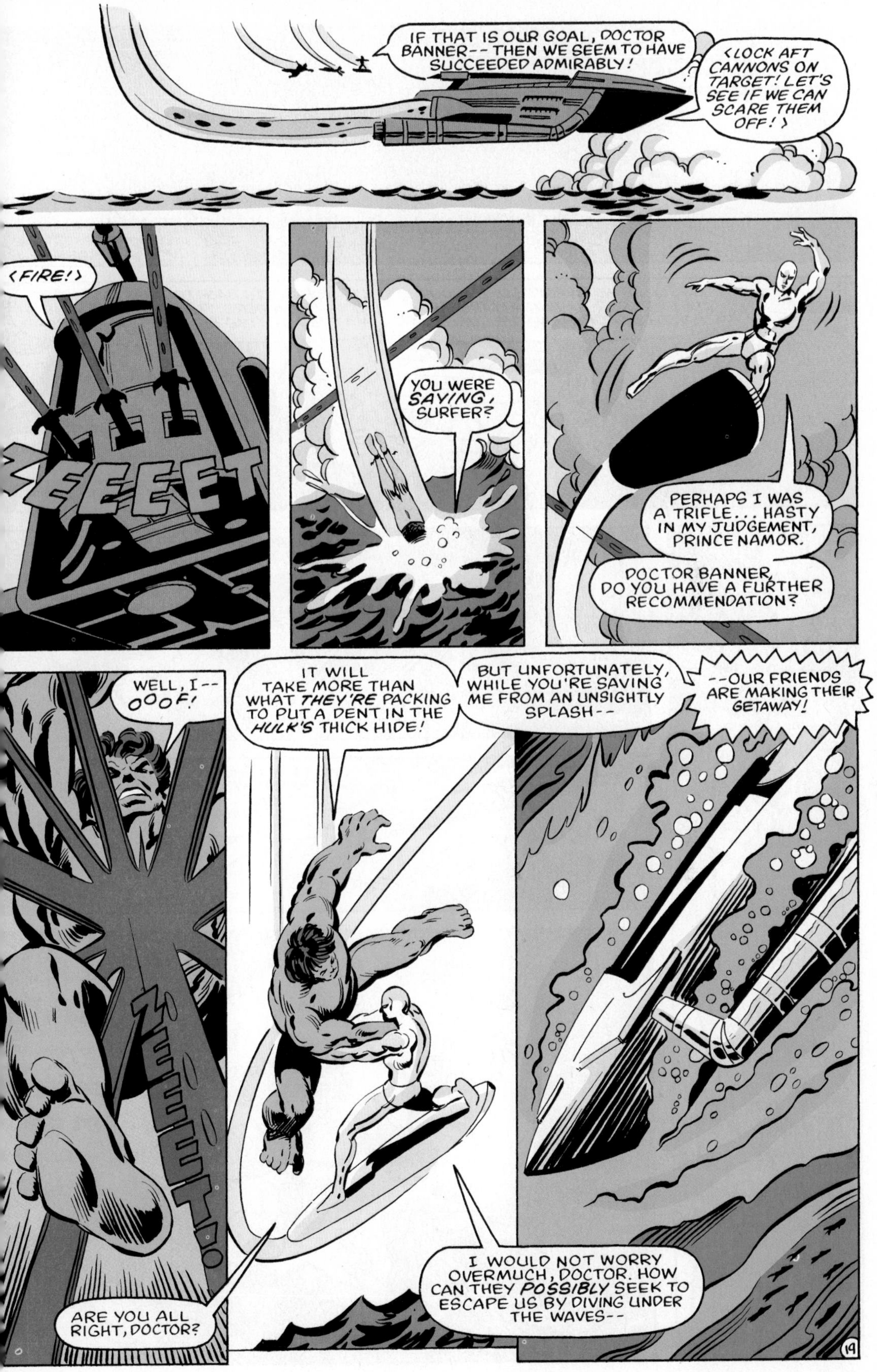
IF THAT IS OUR GOAL, DOCTOR BANNER-- THEN WE SEEM TO HAVE SUCCEEDED ADMIRABLY!
<LOCK AFT CANNONS ON TARGET! LET'S SEE IF WE CAN SCARE THEM OFF!>
<FIRE!>
ZEEEET
YOU WERE SAYING, SURFER?
PERHAPS I WAS A TRIFLE... HASTY IN MY JUDGEMENT, PRINCE NAMOR.
DOCTOR BANNER, DO YOU HAVE A FURTHER RECOMMENDATION?
WELL, I-- OOOF!
ZEEEET
ARE YOU ALL RIGHT, DOCTOR?
IT WILL TAKE MORE THAN WHAT THEY'RE PACKING TO PUT A DENT IN THE HULK'S THICK HIDE!
BUT UNFORTUNATELY, WHILE YOU'RE SAVING ME FROM AN UNSIGHTLY SPLASH--
--OUR FRIENDS ARE MAKING THEIR GETAWAY!
I WOULD NOT WORRY OVERMUCH, DOCTOR. HOW CAN THEY POSSIBLY SEEK TO ESCAPE US BY DIVING UNDER THE WAVES--
19

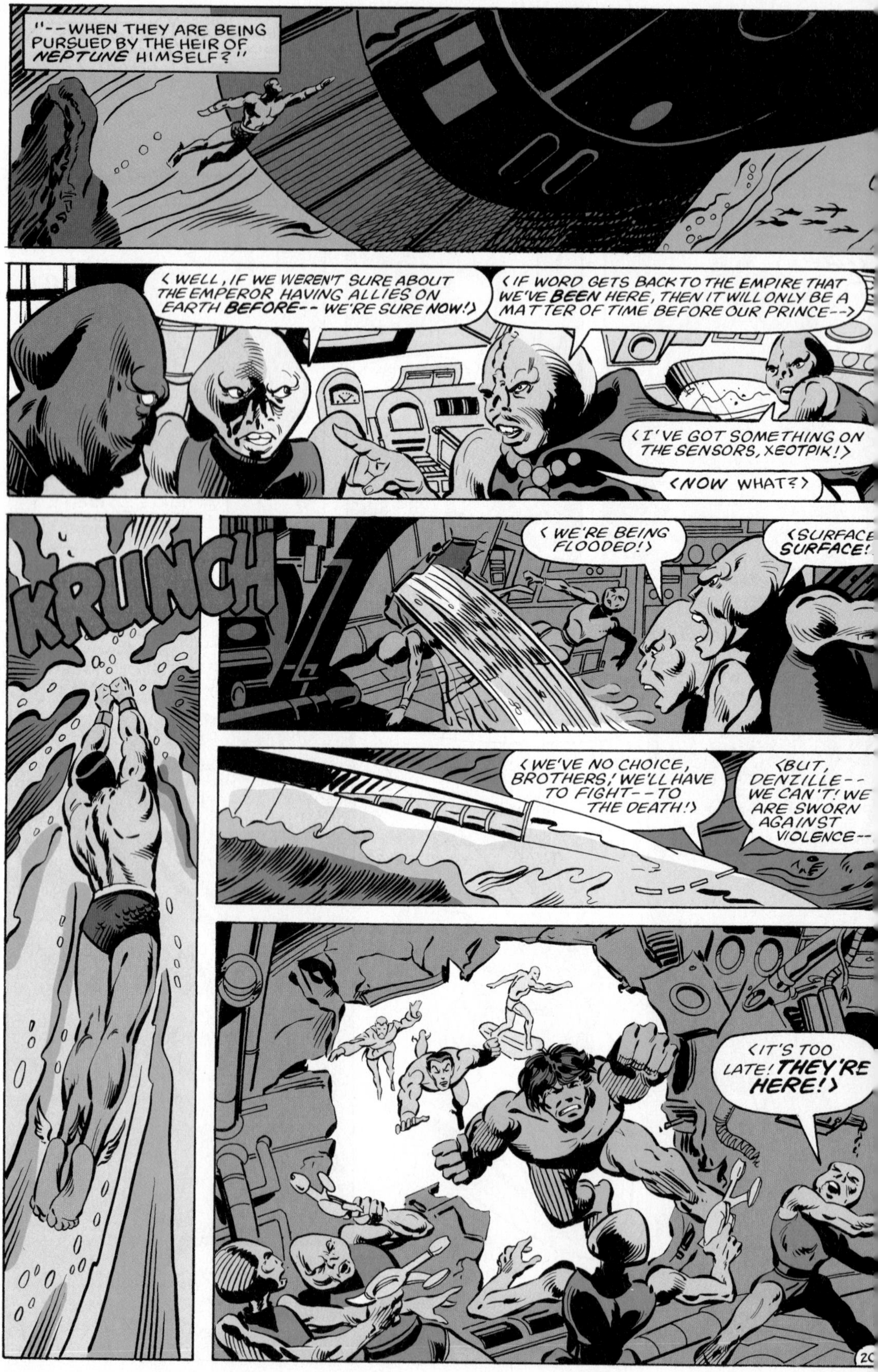
"--WHEN THEY ARE BEING PURSUED BY THE HEIR OF NEPTUNE HIMSELF?"
<WELL, IF WE WEREN'T SURE ABOUT THE EMPEROR HAVING ALLIES ON EARTH BEFORE-- WE'RE SURE NOW!>
<IF WORD GETS BACK TO THE EMPIRE THAT WE'VE BEEN HERE, THEN IT WILL ONLY BE A MATTER OF TIME BEFORE OUR PRINCE-->
<I'VE GOT SOMETHING ON THE SENSORS, XEOTPIK!>
<NOW WHAT?>
KRUNCH
<WE'RE BEING FLOODED!>
<SURFACE SURFACE!
<WE'VE NO CHOICE, BROTHERS, WE'LL HAVE TO FIGHT--TO THE DEATH!>
<BUT, DENZILLE-- WE CAN'T! WE ARE SWORN AGAINST VIOLENCE--
<IT'S TOO LATE! THEY'RE HERE!>
20

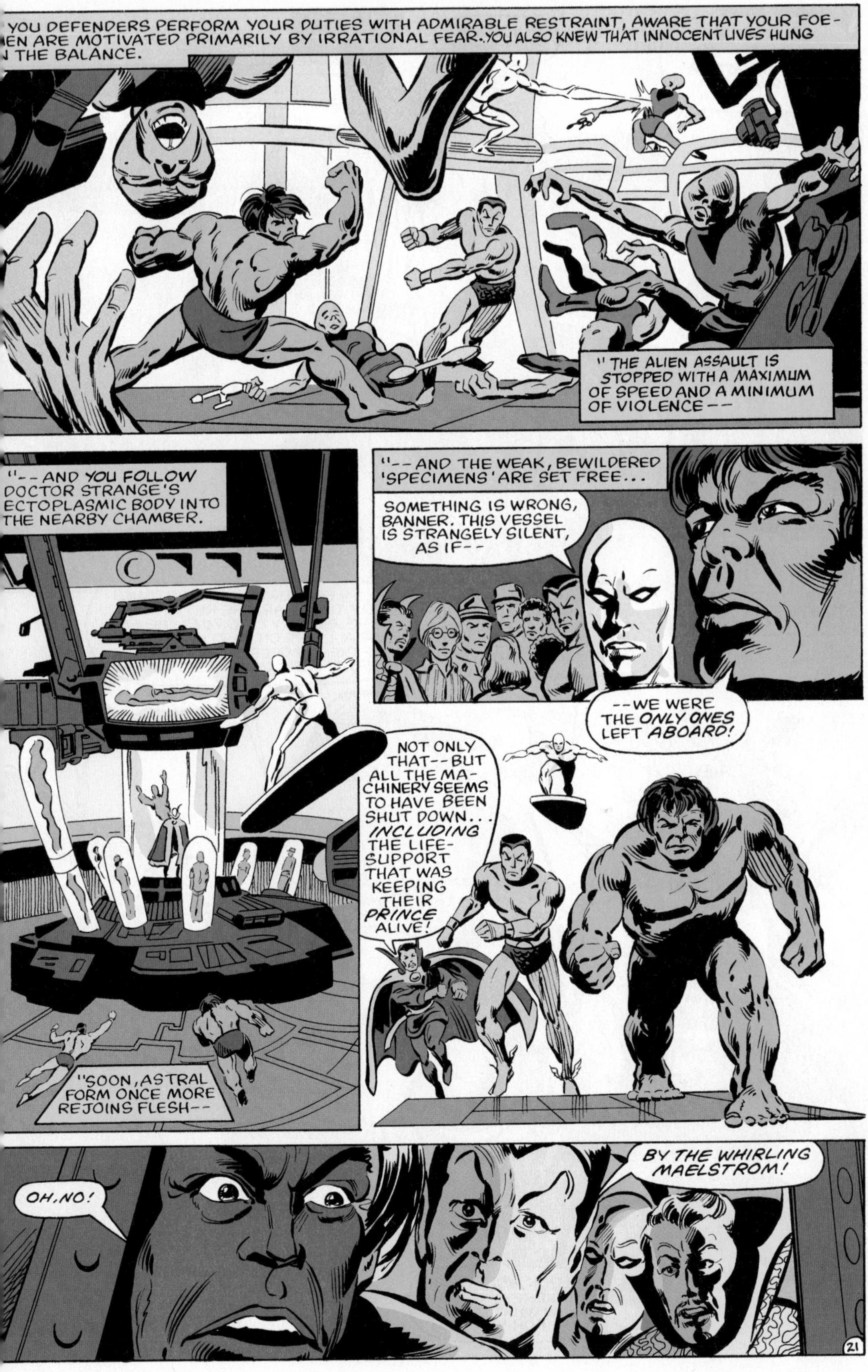
YOU DEFENDERS PERFORM YOUR DUTIES WITH ADMIRABLE RESTRAINT, AWARE THAT YOUR FOE-EN ARE MOTIVATED PRIMARILY BY IRRATIONAL FEAR. YOU ALSO KNEW THAT INNOCENT LIVES HUNG N THE BALANCE.
"THE ALIEN ASSAULT IS STOPPED WITH A MAXIMUM OF SPEED AND A MINIMUM OF VIOLENCE--
"--AND YOU FOLLOW DOCTOR STRANGE'S ECTOPLASMIC BODY INTO THE NEARBY CHAMBER.
"SOON, ASTRAL FORM ONCE MORE REJOINS FLESH--
"--AND THE WEAK, BEWILDERED 'SPECIMENS' ARE SET FREE...
SOMETHING IS WRONG, BANNER. THIS VESSEL IS STRANGELY SILENT, AS IF--
--WE WERE THE ONLY ONES LEFT ABOARD!
NOT ONLY THAT--BUT ALL THE MACHINERY SEEMS TO HAVE BEEN SHUT DOWN... INCLUDING THE LIFE-SUPPORT THAT WAS KEEPING THEIR PRINCE ALIVE!
OH, NO!
BY THE WHIRLING MAELSTROM!
21

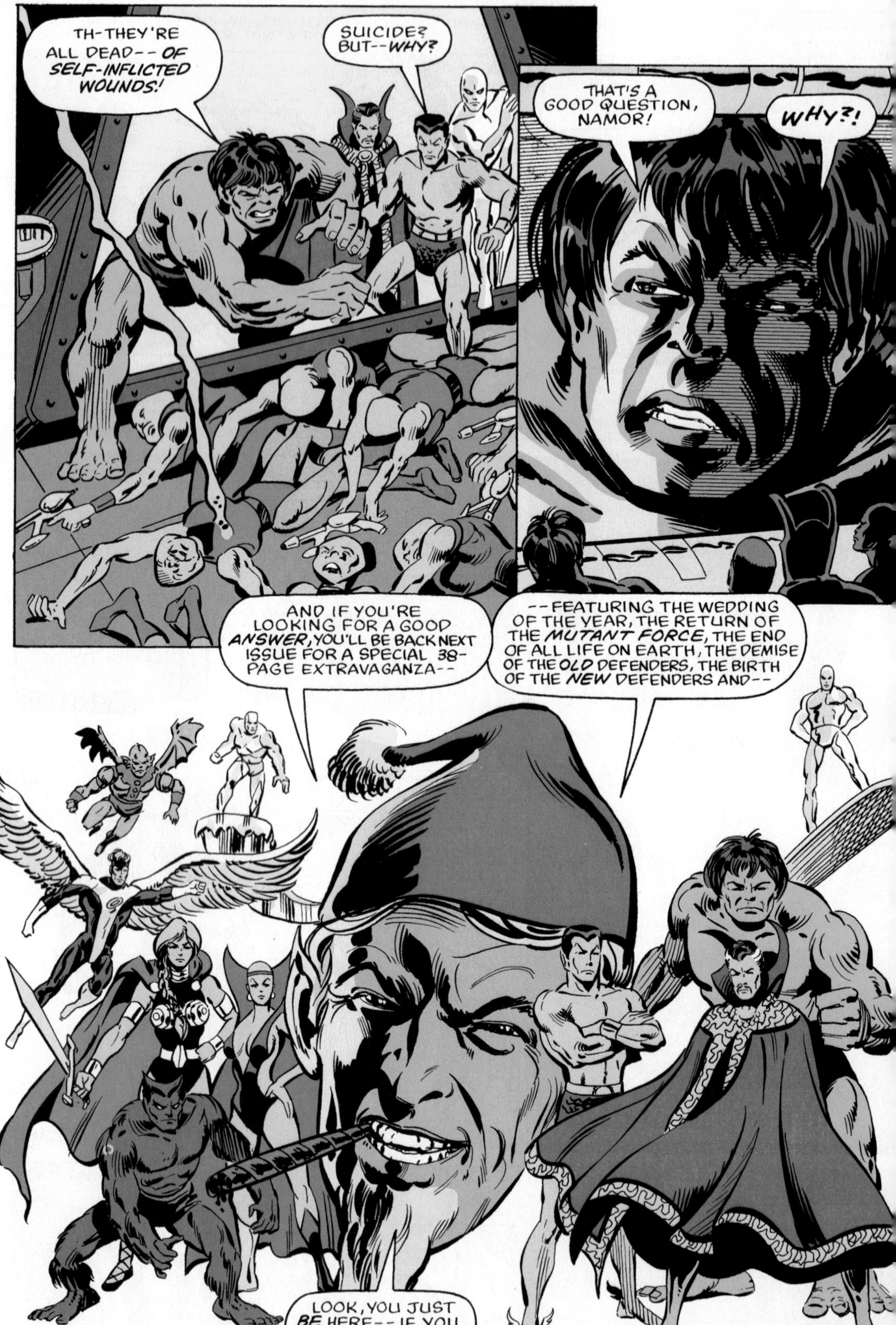
TH-THEY'RE ALL DEAD-- OF SELF-INFLICTED WOUNDS!
SUICIDE? BUT--WHY?
THAT'S A GOOD QUESTION, NAMOR!
WHY?!
AND IF YOU'RE LOOKING FOR A GOOD ANSWER, YOU'LL BE BACK NEXT ISSUE FOR A SPECIAL 38-PAGE EXTRAVAGANZA--
--FEATURING THE WEDDING OF THE YEAR, THE RETURN OF THE MUTANT FORCE, THE END OF ALL LIFE ON EARTH, THE DEMISE OF THE OLD DEFENDERS, THE BIRTH OF THE NEW DEFENDERS AND--
LOOK, YOU JUST BE HERE-- IF YOU KNOW WHAT'S GOOD FOR YA!
the end.

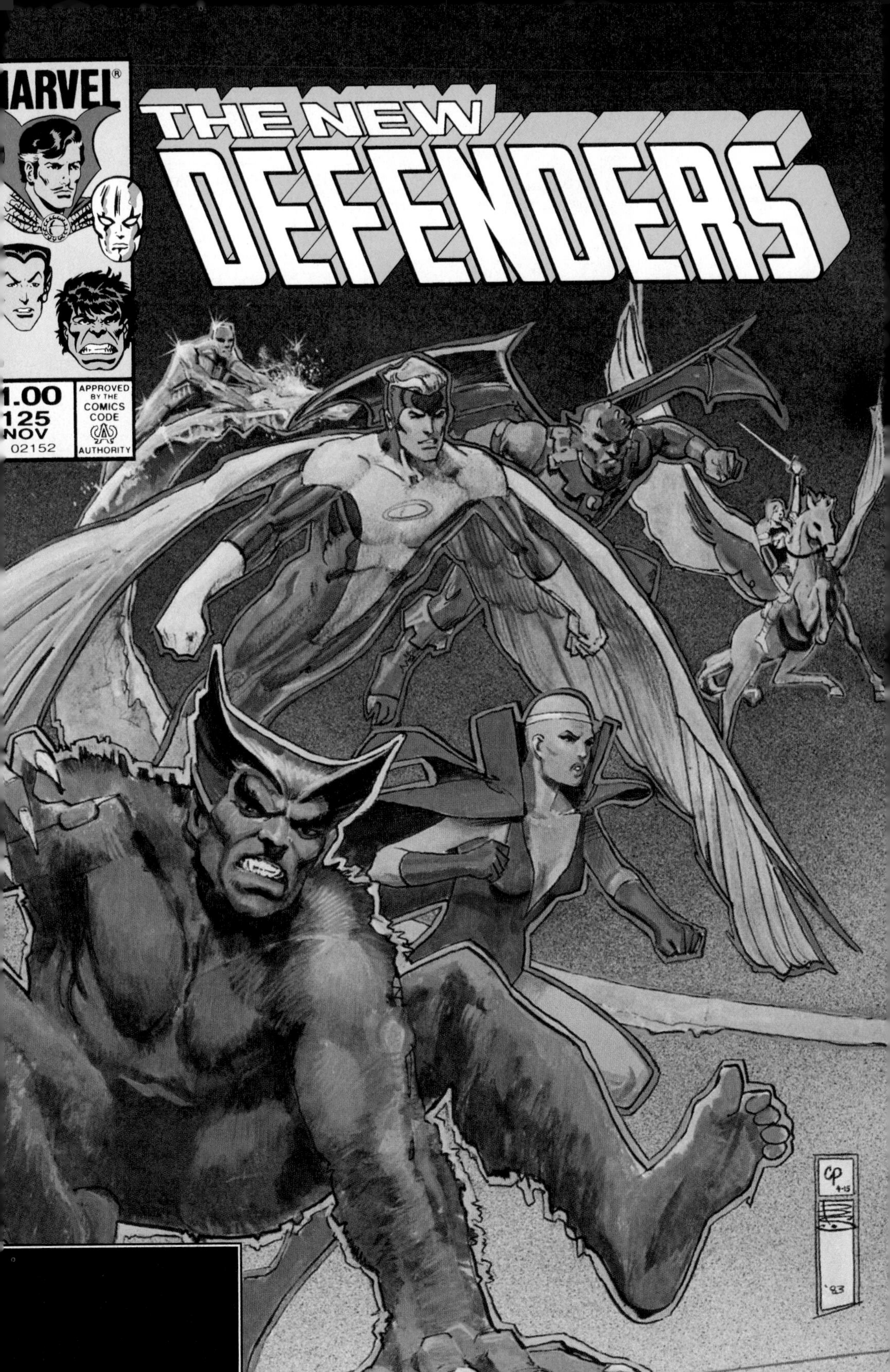
MARVEL®
THE NEW
DEFENDERS
1.00
125
NOV
02152
APPROVED BY THE COMICS CODE AUTHORITY
CP
'83

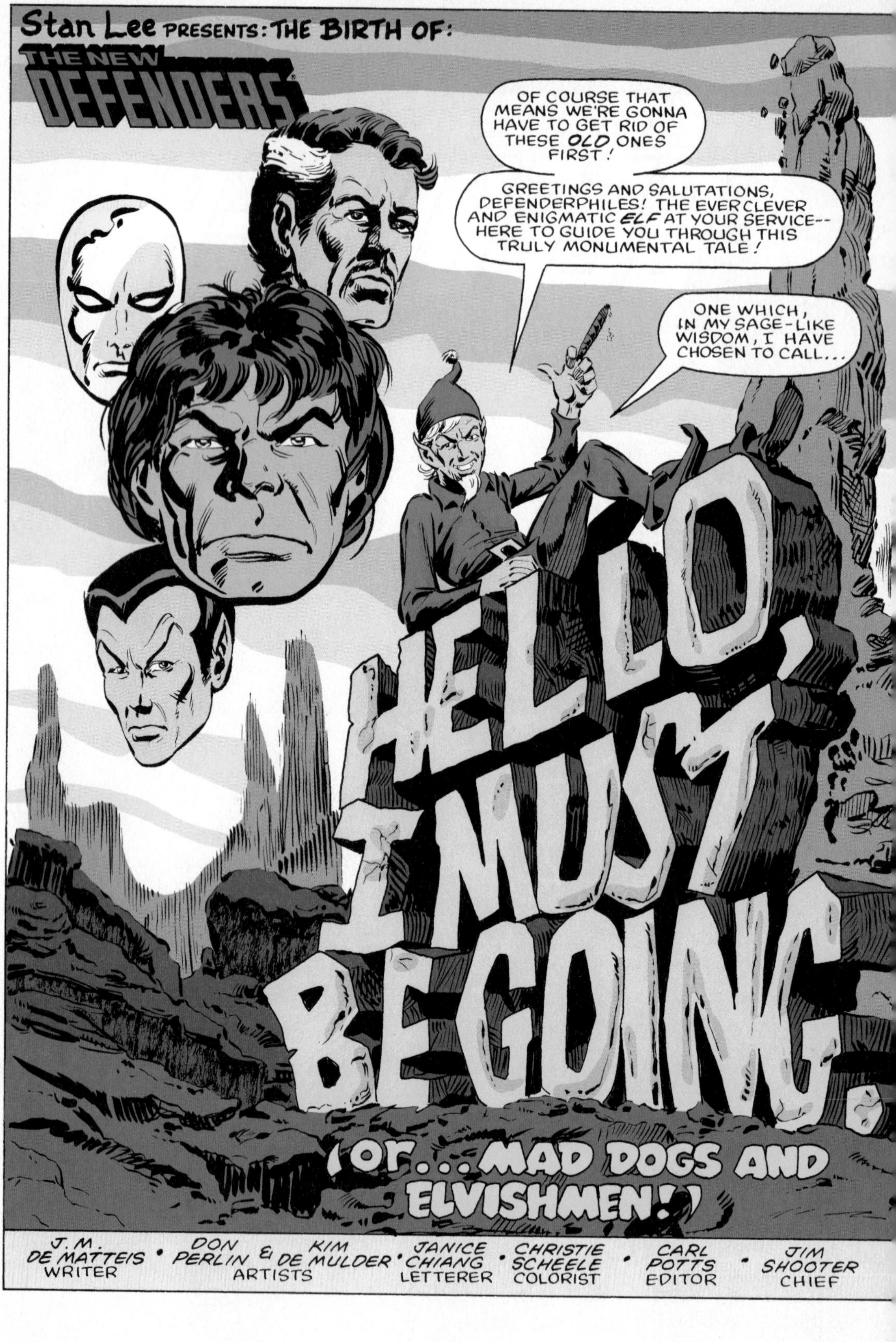
Stan Lee PRESENTS: THE BIRTH OF:
THE NEW DEFENDERS
OF COURSE THAT MEANS WE'RE GONNA HAVE TO GET RID OF THESE OLD ONES FIRST!
GREETINGS AND SALUTATIONS, DEFENDERPHILES! THE EVER CLEVER AND ENIGMATIC ELF AT YOUR SERVICE-- HERE TO GUIDE YOU THROUGH THIS TRULY MONUMENTAL TALE!
ONE WHICH, IN MY SAGE-LIKE WISDOM, I HAVE CHOSEN TO CALL...
HELLO, I MUST BE GOING.
(OR... MAD DOGS AND ELVISHMEN!)
J.M. DE MATTEIS WRITER • DON PERLIN & KIM DE MULDER ARTISTS • JANICE CHIANG LETTERER • CHRISTIE SCHEELE COLORIST • CARL POTTS EDITOR • JIM SHOOTER CHIEF

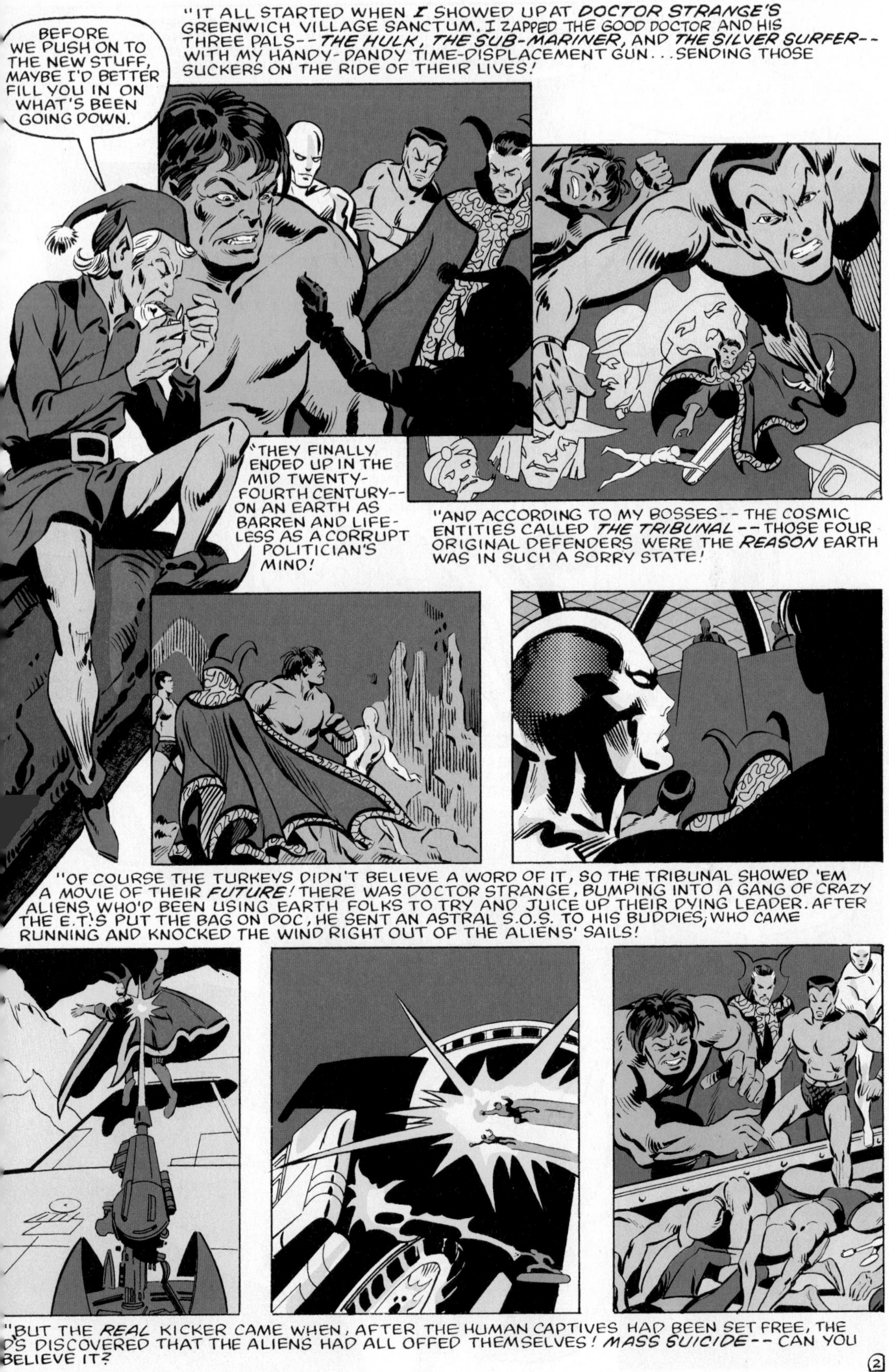
"IT ALL STARTED WHEN I SHOWED UP AT DOCTOR STRANGE'S GREENWICH VILLAGE SANCTUM. I ZAPPED THE GOOD DOCTOR AND HIS THREE PALS--THE HULK, THE SUB-MARINER, AND THE SILVER SURFER--WITH MY HANDY-DANDY TIME-DISPLACEMENT GUN. . . SENDING THOSE SUCKERS ON THE RIDE OF THEIR LIVES!
BEFORE WE PUSH ON TO THE NEW STUFF, MAYBE I'D BETTER FILL YOU IN ON WHAT'S BEEN GOING DOWN.
"THEY FINALLY ENDED UP IN THE MID TWENTY-FOURTH CENTURY--ON AN EARTH AS BARREN AND LIFELESS AS A CORRUPT POLITICIAN'S MIND!
"AND ACCORDING TO MY BOSSES--THE COSMIC ENTITIES CALLED THE TRIBUNAL--THOSE FOUR ORIGINAL DEFENDERS WERE THE REASON EARTH WAS IN SUCH A SORRY STATE!
"OF COURSE THE TURKEYS DIDN'T BELIEVE A WORD OF IT, SO THE TRIBUNAL SHOWED 'EM A MOVIE OF THEIR FUTURE! THERE WAS DOCTOR STRANGE, BUMPING INTO A GANG OF CRAZY ALIENS WHO'D BEEN USING EARTH FOLKS TO TRY AND JUICE UP THEIR DYING LEADER. AFTER THE E.T.'S PUT THE BAG ON DOC, HE SENT AN ASTRAL S.O.S. TO HIS BUDDIES, WHO CAME RUNNING AND KNOCKED THE WIND RIGHT OUT OF THE ALIENS' SAILS!
"BUT THE REAL KICKER CAME WHEN, AFTER THE HUMAN CAPTIVES HAD BEEN SET FREE, THE D'S DISCOVERED THAT THE ALIENS HAD ALL OFFED THEMSELVES! MASS SUICIDE--CAN YOU BELIEVE IT?
2

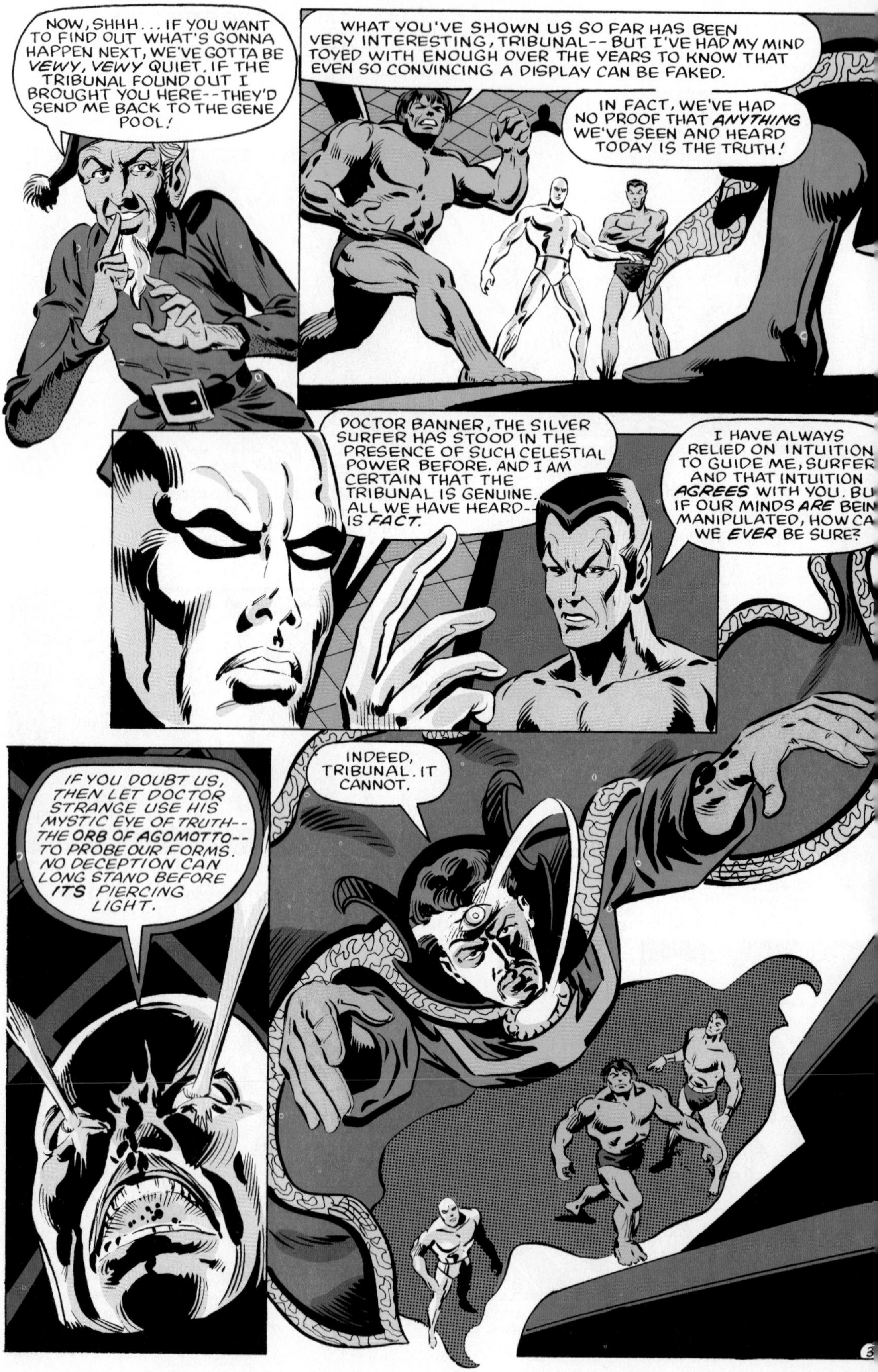

NOW, SHHH... IF YOU WANT TO FIND OUT WHAT'S GONNA HAPPEN NEXT, WE'VE GOTTA BE VEWY, VEWY QUIET. IF THE TRIBUNAL FOUND OUT I BROUGHT YOU HERE--THEY'D SEND ME BACK TO THE GENE POOL!
WHAT YOU'VE SHOWN US SO FAR HAS BEEN VERY INTERESTING, TRIBUNAL-- BUT I'VE HAD MY MIND TOYED WITH ENOUGH OVER THE YEARS TO KNOW THAT EVEN SO CONVINCING A DISPLAY CAN BE FAKED.
IN FACT, WE'VE HAD NO PROOF THAT ANYTHING WE'VE SEEN AND HEARD TODAY IS THE TRUTH!
DOCTOR BANNER, THE SILVER SURFER HAS STOOD IN THE PRESENCE OF SUCH CELESTIAL POWER BEFORE. AND I AM CERTAIN THAT THE TRIBUNAL IS GENUINE. ALL WE HAVE HEARD-- IS FACT.
I HAVE ALWAYS RELIED ON INTUITION TO GUIDE ME, SURFER AND THAT INTUITION AGREES WITH YOU. BU IF OUR MINDS ARE BEIN MANIPULATED, HOW CA WE EVER BE SURE?
IF YOU DOUBT US, THEN LET DOCTOR STRANGE USE HIS MYSTIC EYE OF TRUTH-- THE ORB OF AGOMOTTO-- TO PROBE OUR FORMS. NO DECEPTION CAN LONG STAND BEFORE ITS PIERCING LIGHT.
INDEED, TRIBUNAL. IT CANNOT.

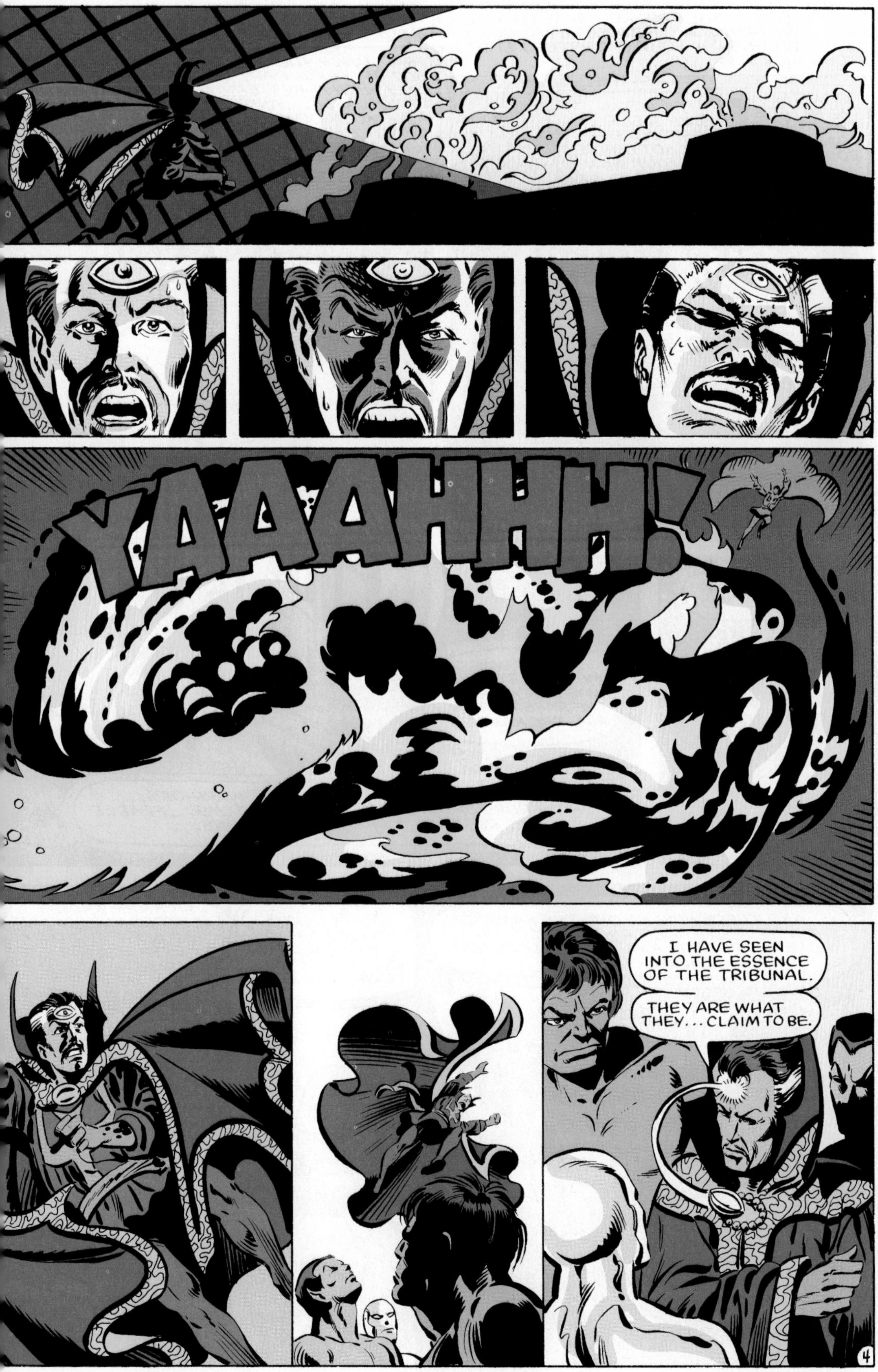
YAAAHHH!
I HAVE SEEN INTO THE ESSENCE OF THE TRIBUNAL.
THEY ARE WHAT THEY... CLAIM TO BE.
4

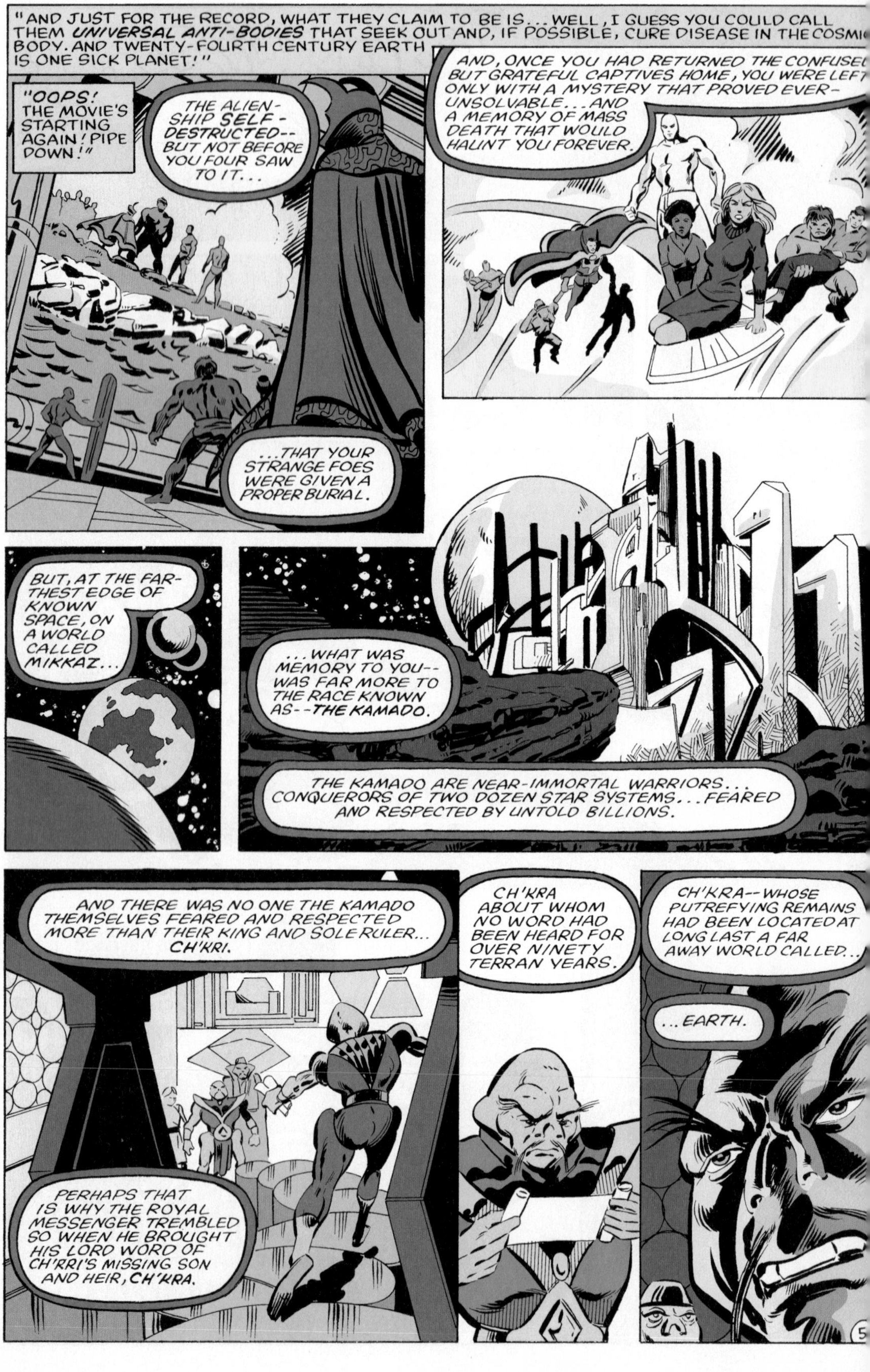
"AND JUST FOR THE RECORD, WHAT THEY CLAIM TO BE IS... WELL, I GUESS YOU COULD CALL THEM UNIVERSAL ANTI-BODIES THAT SEEK OUT AND, IF POSSIBLE, CURE DISEASE IN THE COSMIC BODY. AND TWENTY-FOURTH CENTURY EARTH IS ONE SICK PLANET!"
"OOPS! THE MOVIE'S STARTING AGAIN! PIPE DOWN!"
THE ALIEN-SHIP SELF-DESTRUCTED--BUT NOT BEFORE YOU FOUR SAW TO IT...
...THAT YOUR STRANGE FOES WERE GIVEN A PROPER BURIAL.
AND, ONCE YOU HAD RETURNED THE CONFUSED BUT GRATEFUL CAPTIVES HOME, YOU WERE LEFT ONLY WITH A MYSTERY THAT PROVED EVER-UNSOLVABLE... AND A MEMORY OF MASS DEATH THAT WOULD HAUNT YOU FOREVER.
BUT, AT THE FARTHEST EDGE OF KNOWN SPACE, ON A WORLD CALLED MIKKAZ...
...WHAT WAS MEMORY TO YOU--WAS FAR MORE TO THE RACE KNOWN AS--THE KAMADO.
THE KAMADO ARE NEAR-IMMORTAL WARRIORS... CONQUERORS OF TWO DOZEN STAR SYSTEMS... FEARED AND RESPECTED BY UNTOLD BILLIONS.
AND THERE WAS NO ONE THE KAMADO THEMSELVES FEARED AND RESPECTED MORE THAN THEIR KING AND SOLE RULER... CH'KRI.
PERHAPS THAT IS WHY THE ROYAL MESSENGER TREMBLED SO WHEN HE BROUGHT HIS LORD WORD OF CH'RRI'S MISSING SON AND HEIR, CH'KRA.
CH'KRA ABOUT WHOM NO WORD HAD BEEN HEARD FOR OVER NINETY TERRAN YEARS.
CH'KRA--WHOSE PUTREFYING REMAINS HAD BEEN LOCATED AT LONG LAST A FAR AWAY WORLD CALLED...
...EARTH.
5

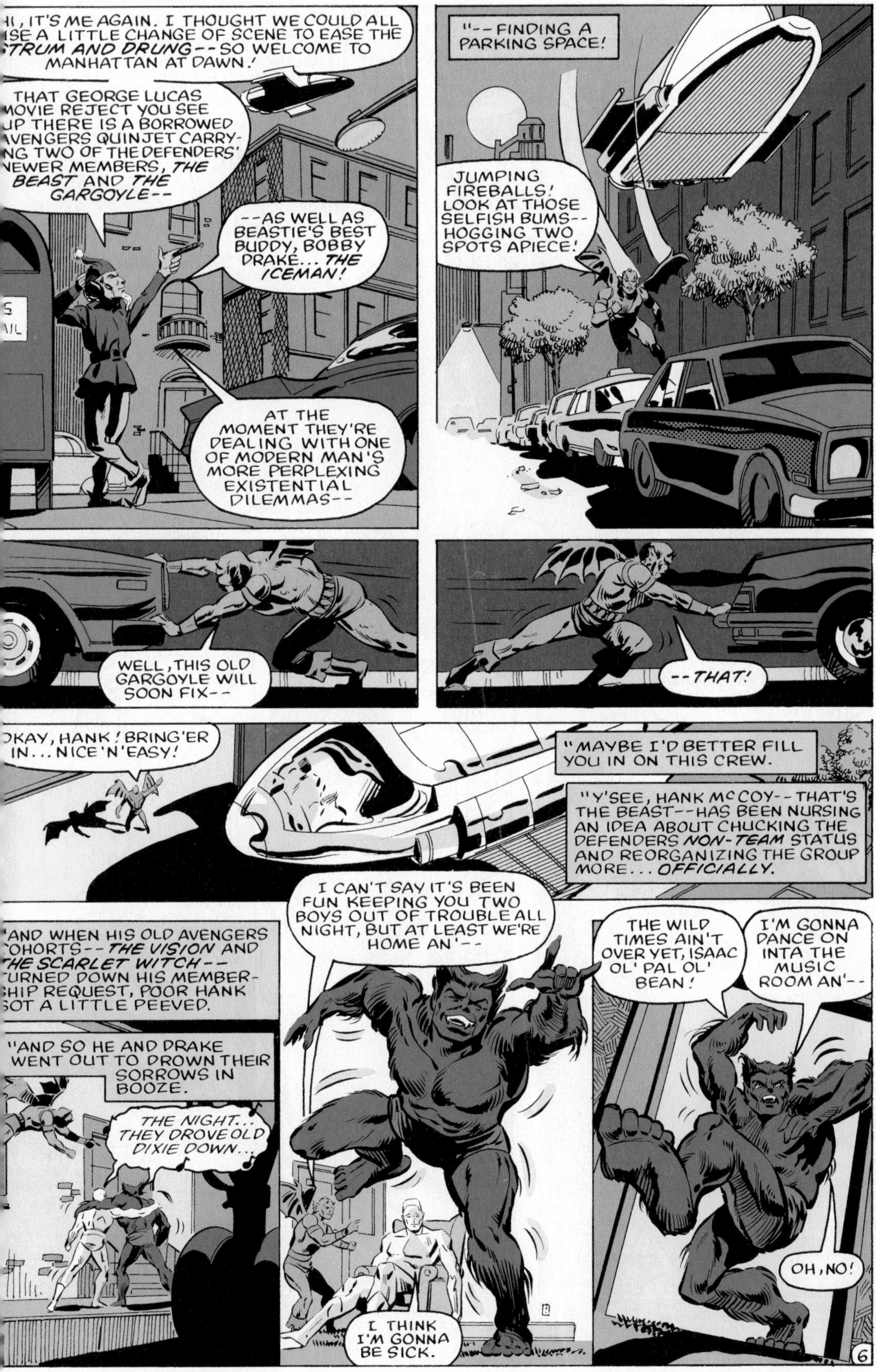

HI, IT'S ME AGAIN. I THOUGHT WE COULD ALL USE A LITTLE CHANGE OF SCENE TO EASE THE STRUM AND DRUNG-- SO WELCOME TO MANHATTAN AT DAWN!
THAT GEORGE LUCAS MOVIE REJECT YOU SEE UP THERE IS A BORROWED AVENGERS QUINJET CARRYING TWO OF THE DEFENDERS' NEWER MEMBERS, THE BEAST AND THE GARGOYLE--
--AS WELL AS BEASTIE'S BEST BUDDY, BOBBY DRAKE... THE ICEMAN!
AT THE MOMENT THEY'RE DEALING WITH ONE OF MODERN MAN'S MORE PERPLEXING EXISTENTIAL DILEMMAS--
"--FINDING A PARKING SPACE!
JUMPING FIREBALLS! LOOK AT THOSE SELFISH BUMS-- HOGGING TWO SPOTS APIECE!
WELL, THIS OLD GARGOYLE WILL SOON FIX--
--THAT!
OKAY, HANK! BRING'ER IN... NICE'N'EASY!
"MAYBE I'D BETTER FILL YOU IN ON THIS CREW.
"Y'SEE, HANK McCOY--THAT'S THE BEAST--HAS BEEN NURSING AN IDEA ABOUT CHUCKING THE DEFENDERS NON-TEAM STATUS AND REORGANIZING THE GROUP MORE... OFFICIALLY.
"AND WHEN HIS OLD AVENGERS COHORTS-- THE VISION AND THE SCARLET WITCH-- TURNED DOWN HIS MEMBERSHIP REQUEST, POOR HANK GOT A LITTLE PEEVED.
"AND SO HE AND DRAKE WENT OUT TO DROWN THEIR SORROWS IN BOOZE.
THE NIGHT... THEY DROVE OLD DIXIE DOWN...
I CAN'T SAY IT'S BEEN FUN KEEPING YOU TWO BOYS OUT OF TROUBLE ALL NIGHT, BUT AT LEAST WE'RE HOME AN'--
I THINK I'M GONNA BE SICK.
THE WILD TIMES AIN'T OVER YET, ISAAC OL' PAL OL' BEAN!
I'M GONNA DANCE ON INTA THE MUSIC ROOM AN'--
OH, NO!
6

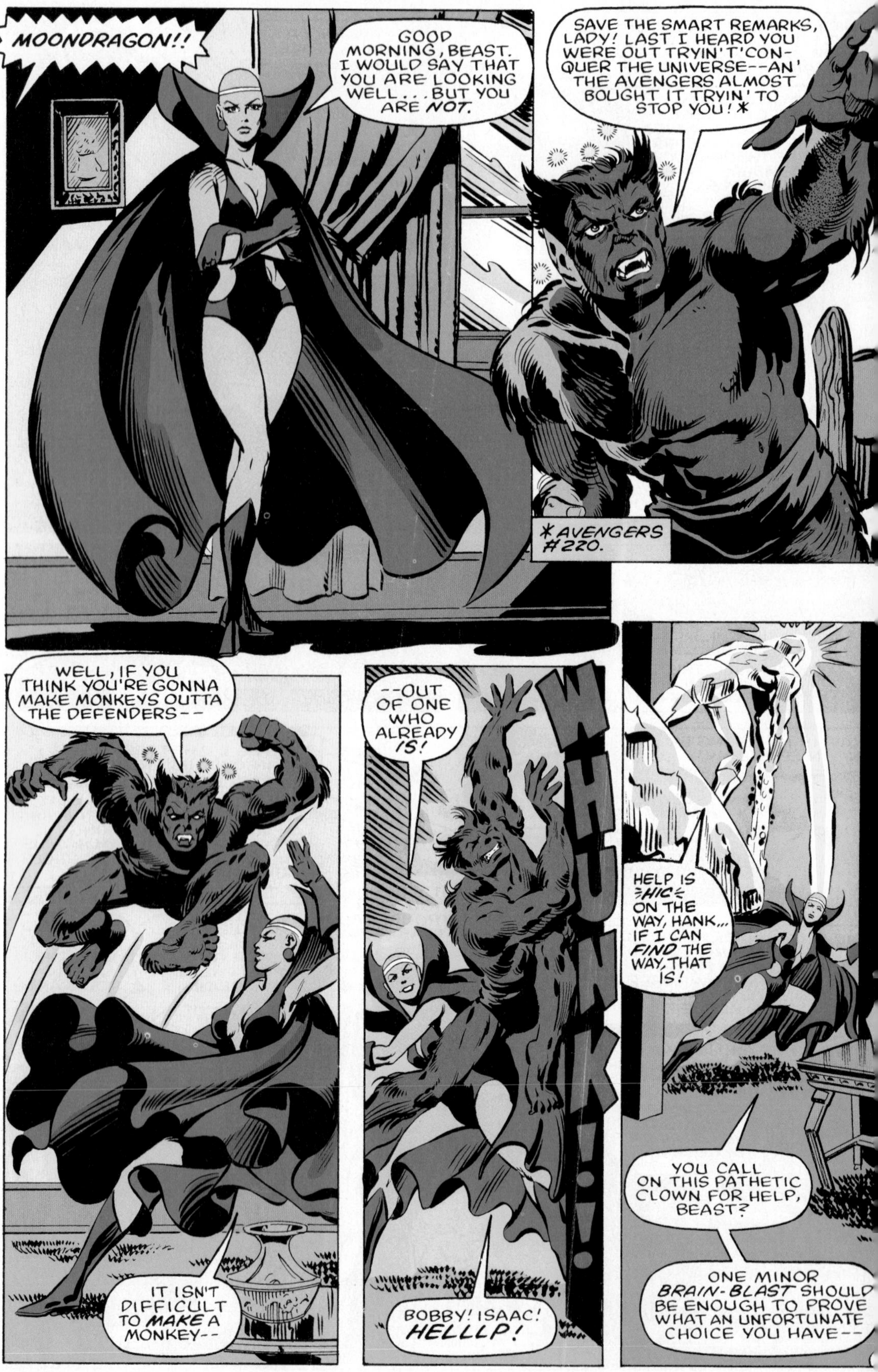
MOONDRAGON!!
GOOD MORNING, BEAST. I WOULD SAY THAT YOU ARE LOOKING WELL . . . BUT YOU ARE NOT.
SAVE THE SMART REMARKS, LADY! LAST I HEARD YOU WERE OUT TRYIN' T'CONQUER THE UNIVERSE--AN' THE AVENGERS ALMOST BOUGHT IT TRYIN' TO STOP YOU! *
* AVENGERS #220.
WELL, IF YOU THINK YOU'RE GONNA MAKE MONKEYS OUTTA THE DEFENDERS--
IT ISN'T DIFFICULT TO MAKE A MONKEY--
--OUT OF ONE WHO ALREADY IS!
WHUNK!!
BOBBY! ISAAC! HELLLP!
HELP IS HIC ON THE WAY, HANK... IF I CAN FIND THE WAY, THAT IS!
YOU CALL ON THIS PATHETIC CLOWN FOR HELP, BEAST?
ONE MINOR BRAIN-BLAST SHOULD BE ENOUGH TO PROVE WHAT AN UNFORTUNATE CHOICE YOU HAVE--

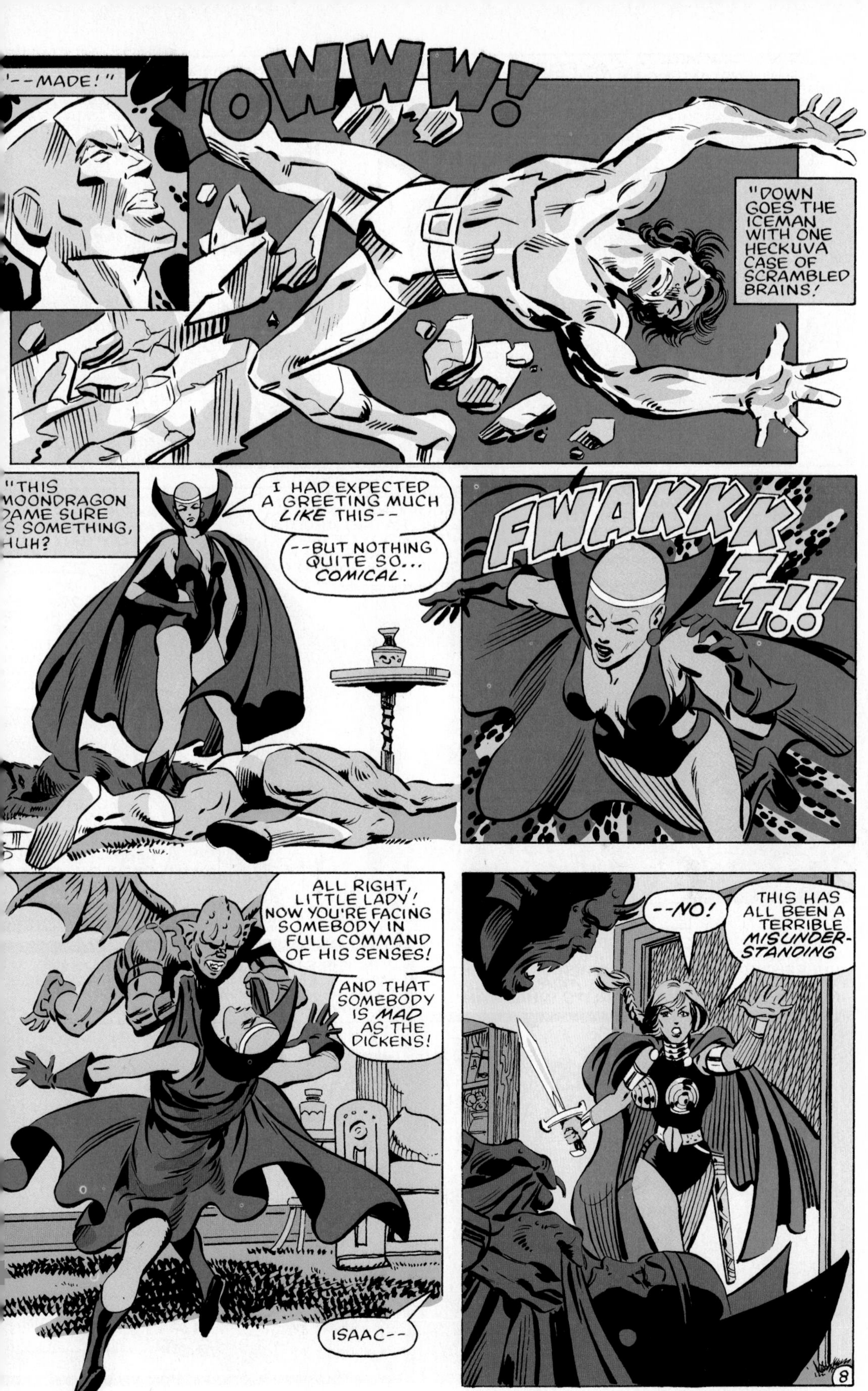
'--MADE!"
YOWWWW!
"DOWN GOES THE ICEMAN WITH ONE HECKUVA CASE OF SCRAMBLED BRAINS!
"THIS MOONDRAGON DAME SURE IS SOMETHING, HUH?
I HAD EXPECTED A GREETING MUCH LIKE THIS--
--BUT NOTHING QUITE SO... COMICAL.
FWAKKKTT!!
ALL RIGHT, LITTLE LADY! NOW YOU'RE FACING SOMEBODY IN FULL COMMAND OF HIS SENSES!
AND THAT SOMEBODY IS MAD AS THE DICKENS!
ISAAC--
--NO!
THIS HAS ALL BEEN A TERRIBLE MISUNDERSTANDING
8

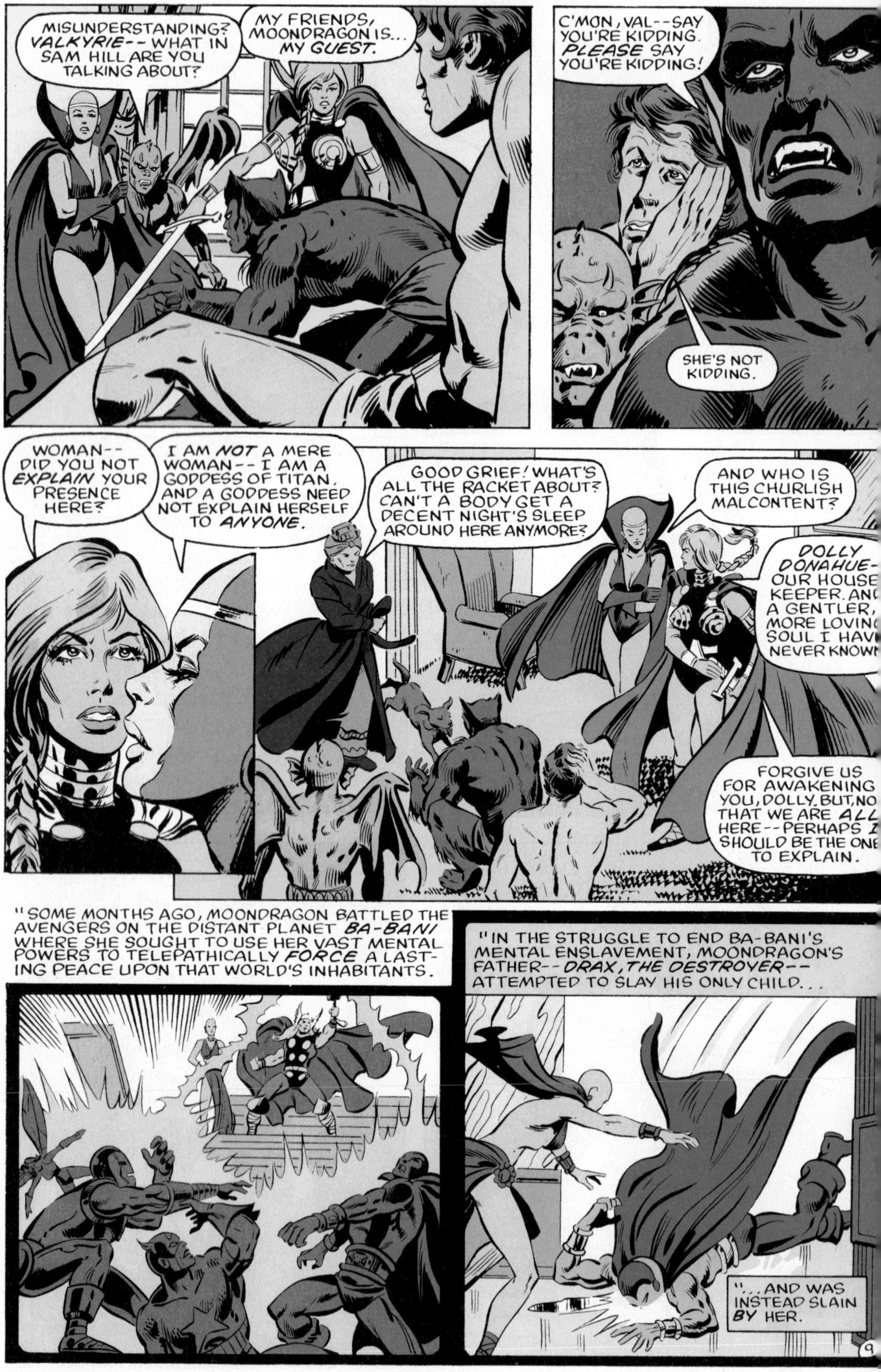
MISUNDERSTANDING? VALKYRIE-- WHAT IN SAM HILL ARE YOU TALKING ABOUT?
MY FRIENDS, MOONDRAGON IS... MY GUEST.
C'MON, VAL--SAY YOU'RE KIDDING. PLEASE SAY YOU'RE KIDDING!
SHE'S NOT KIDDING.
WOMAN-- DID YOU NOT EXPLAIN YOUR PRESENCE HERE?
I AM NOT A MERE WOMAN-- I AM A GODDESS OF TITAN, AND A GODDESS NEED NOT EXPLAIN HERSELF TO ANYONE.
GOOD GRIEF! WHAT'S ALL THE RACKET ABOUT? CAN'T A BODY GET A DECENT NIGHT'S SLEEP AROUND HERE ANYMORE?
AND WHO IS THIS CHURLISH MALCONTENT?
DOLLY DONAHUE- OUR HOUSE KEEPER. AN A GENTLER, MORE LOVIN SOUL I HAV NEVER KNOWN
FORGIVE US FOR AWAKENING YOU, DOLLY. BUT, NO THAT WE ARE ALL HERE--PERHAPS I SHOULD BE THE ONE TO EXPLAIN.
"SOME MONTHS AGO, MOONDRAGON BATTLED THE AVENGERS ON THE DISTANT PLANET BA-BANI WHERE SHE SOUGHT TO USE HER VAST MENTAL POWERS TO TELEPATHICALLY FORCE A LASTING PEACE UPON THAT WORLD'S INHABITANTS.
"IN THE STRUGGLE TO END BA-BANI'S MENTAL ENSLAVEMENT, MOONDRAGON'S FATHER--DRAX, THE DESTROYER--ATTEMPTED TO SLAY HIS ONLY CHILD...
"...AND WAS INSTEAD SLAIN BY HER.
9

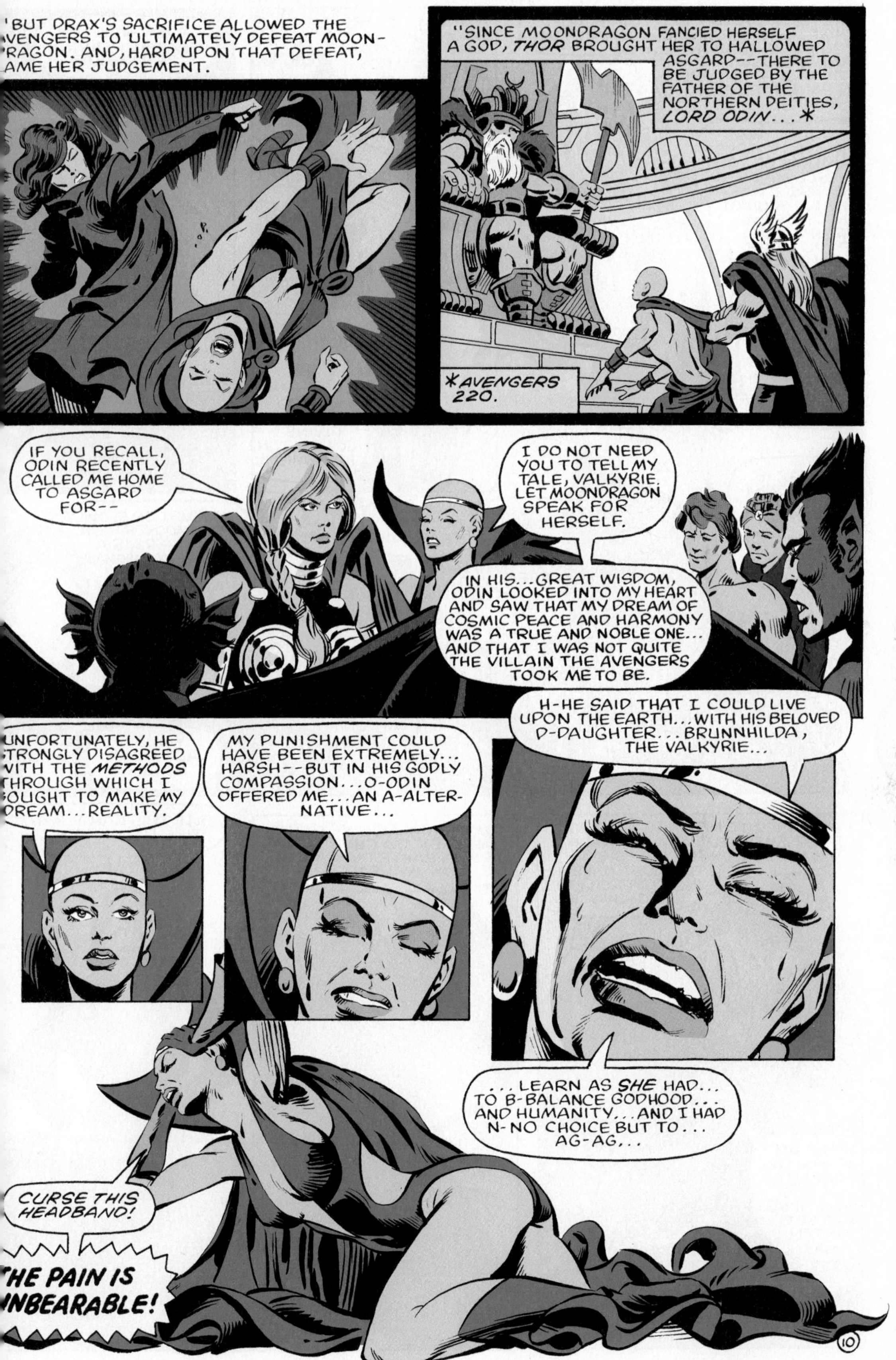

'BUT DRAX'S SACRIFICE ALLOWED THE AVENGERS TO ULTIMATELY DEFEAT MOON-DRAGON. AND, HARD UPON THAT DEFEAT, CAME HER JUDGEMENT.
"SINCE MOONDRAGON FANCIED HERSELF A GOD, THOR BROUGHT HER TO HALLOWED ASGARD--THERE TO BE JUDGED BY THE FATHER OF THE NORTHERN DEITIES, LORD ODIN...*
*AVENGERS 220.
IF YOU RECALL, ODIN RECENTLY CALLED ME HOME TO ASGARD FOR--
I DO NOT NEED YOU TO TELL MY TALE, VALKYRIE. LET MOONDRAGON SPEAK FOR HERSELF.
IN HIS...GREAT WISDOM, ODIN LOOKED INTO MY HEART AND SAW THAT MY DREAM OF COSMIC PEACE AND HARMONY WAS A TRUE AND NOBLE ONE... AND THAT I WAS NOT QUITE THE VILLAIN THE AVENGERS TOOK ME TO BE.
UNFORTUNATELY, HE STRONGLY DISAGREED WITH THE METHODS THROUGH WHICH I SOUGHT TO MAKE MY DREAM...REALITY.
MY PUNISHMENT COULD HAVE BEEN EXTREMELY... HARSH--BUT IN HIS GODLY COMPASSION...O-ODIN OFFERED ME...AN A-ALTER-NATIVE...
H-HE SAID THAT I COULD LIVE UPON THE EARTH...WITH HIS BELOVED D-DAUGHTER...BRUNNHILDA, THE VALKYRIE...
...LEARN AS SHE HAD... TO B-BALANCE GODHOOD... AND HUMANITY...AND I HAD N-NO CHOICE BUT TO... AG-AG,..
CURSE THIS HEADBAND!
THE PAIN IS UNBEARABLE!
10

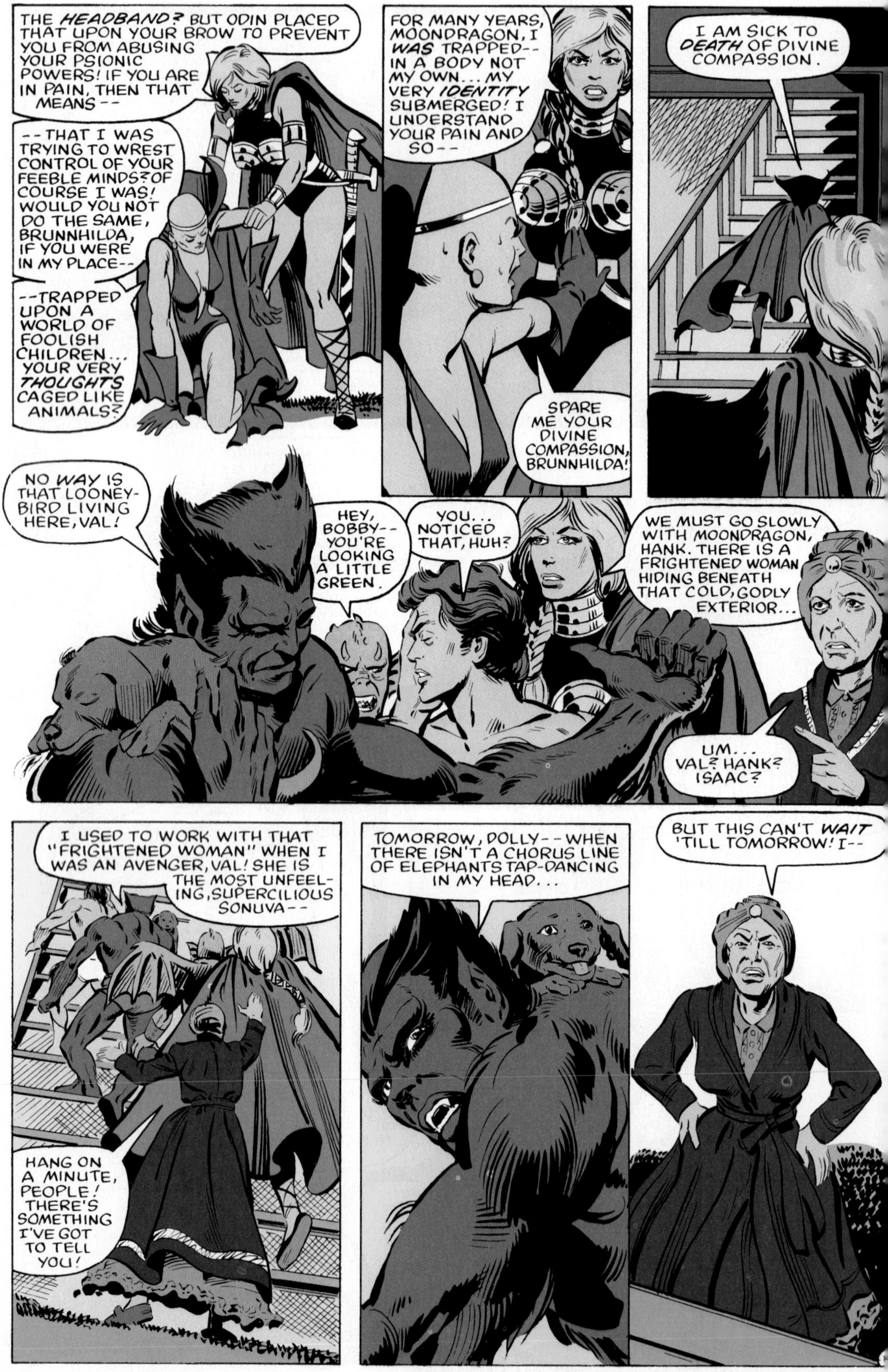
THE *HEADBAND?* BUT ODIN PLACED THAT UPON YOUR BROW TO PREVENT YOU FROM ABUSING YOUR PSIONIC POWERS! IF YOU ARE IN PAIN, THEN THAT MEANS --
-- THAT I WAS TRYING TO WREST CONTROL OF YOUR FEEBLE MINDS? OF COURSE I WAS! WOULD YOU NOT DO THE SAME, BRUNNHILDA, IF YOU WERE IN MY PLACE--
--TRAPPED UPON A WORLD OF FOOLISH CHILDREN... YOUR VERY *THOUGHTS* CAGED LIKE ANIMALS?
FOR MANY YEARS, MOONDRAGON, I *WAS* TRAPPED-- IN A BODY NOT MY OWN... MY VERY *IDENTITY* SUBMERGED! I UNDERSTAND YOUR PAIN AND SO--
SPARE ME YOUR DIVINE COMPASSION, BRUNNHILDA!
I AM SICK TO *DEATH* OF DIVINE COMPASSION.
NO *WAY* IS THAT LOONEY-BIRD LIVING HERE, VAL!
HEY, BOBBY-- YOU'RE LOOKING A LITTLE GREEN.
YOU... NOTICED THAT, HUH?
WE MUST GO SLOWLY WITH MOONDRAGON, HANK. THERE IS A FRIGHTENED WOMAN HIDING BENEATH THAT COLD, GODLY EXTERIOR...
UM... VAL? HANK? ISAAC?
I USED TO WORK WITH THAT "FRIGHTENED WOMAN" WHEN I WAS AN AVENGER, VAL! SHE IS THE MOST UNFEELING, SUPERCILIOUS SONUVA--
HANG ON A MINUTE, PEOPLE! THERE'S SOMETHING I'VE GOT TO TELL YOU!
TOMORROW, DOLLY-- WHEN THERE ISN'T A CHORUS LINE OF ELEPHANTS TAP-DANCING IN MY HEAD...
BUT THIS CAN'T *WAIT* 'TILL TOMORROW! I--

GOOD GRIEF! WHAT A SORRY LOOKING PAIR YOU TWO ARE!

NOW, LOOK, MOONDRAGON-- WE'VE HAD ENOUGH OF--

IF YOU'VE GOT *ME* CONFUSED WITH MOONDRAGON--IT'S NO *WONDER* YOU CAN'T GET A DATE ON SATURDAY NIGHT!

WARREN?

WARREN?!

"WARREN WORTHINGTON III TO BE PRECISE... AKA *THE ANGEL:* FORMER X-MAN, FORMER CHAMPION--AND CURRENT MULTI-MILLIONAIRE.

WHOOP-DEE-DOO! THIS IS LIKE OLD HOME WEEK! FIRST, BOBBY--NOW YOU!

GIMME A HUG, BUDDY! IT'S BEEN A LONG TIME!

"THE BIRD-MAN SHOWED UP DURING THE NIGHT FOR A SURPRISE VISIT. OLD LADY DONAHUE SHOWED 'IM TO ONE OF THE GUEST ROOMS--AND THE REST IS HISTORY. OR IS THAT--

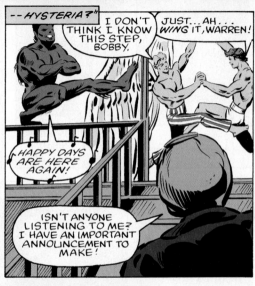

--HYSTERIA?"

I DON'T THINK I KNOW THIS STEP, BOBBY.

JUST...AH... *WING* IT, WARREN!

HAPPY DAYS ARE HERE AGAIN!

ISN'T ANYONE LISTENING TO ME? I HAVE AN IMPORTANT ANNOUNCEMENT TO MAKE!

HEY-- REMEMBER THAT TIME BACK AT SCHOOL WHEN WE BUSTED INTO SCOTT'S ROOM IN THE MIDDLE OF THE NIGHT AND STARTED DOING OUR *ROCKETTES* ROUTINE?

COULD I EVER FORGET?

ALL TOGETHER NOW: ONE, TWO, THREE... KICK! ONE, TWO THREE... KICK!

I WANT QUIET!!!

AH... NOW THAT'S *MUCH* BETTER!.

12

403

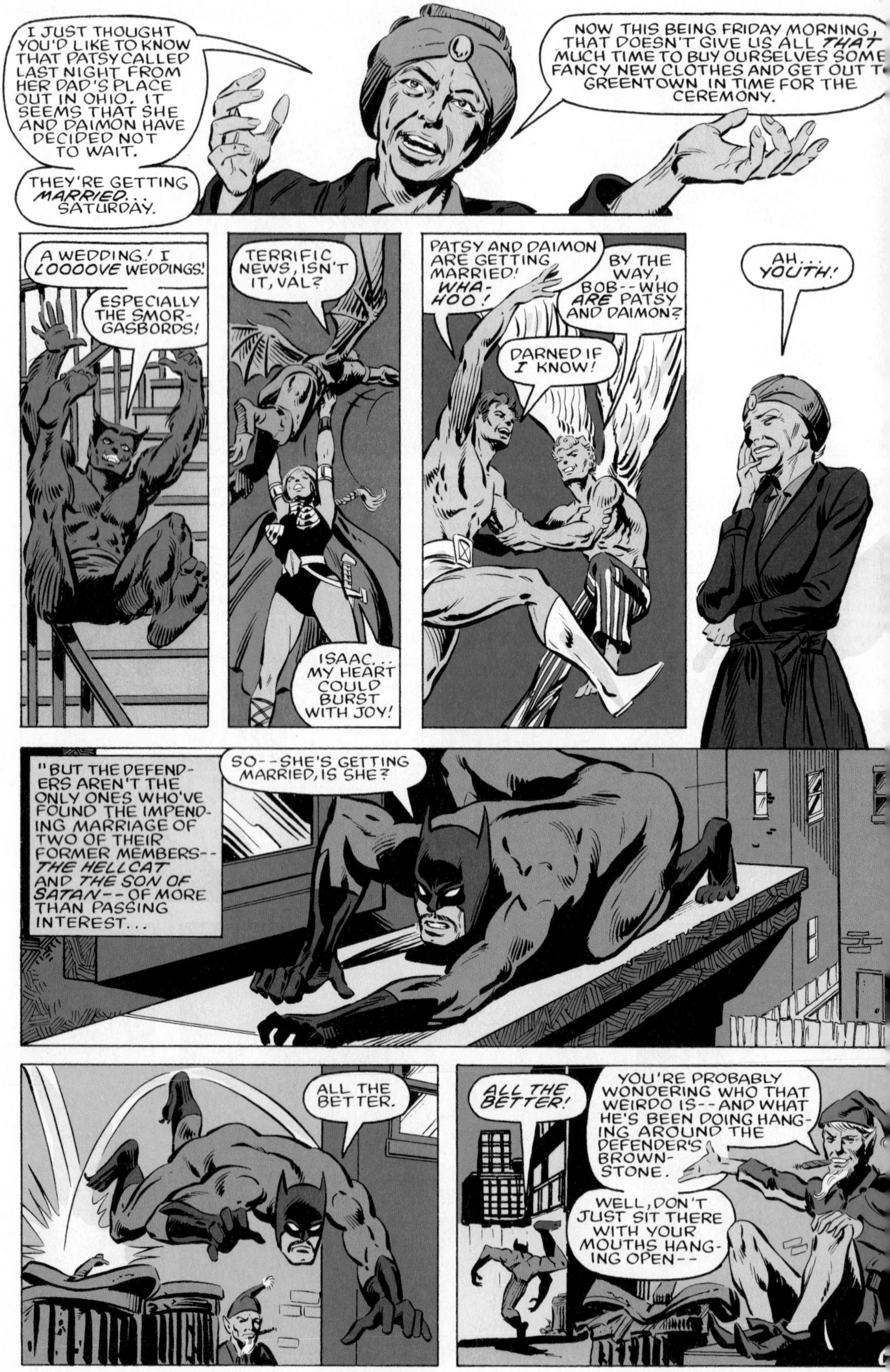
I JUST THOUGHT YOU'D LIKE TO KNOW THAT PATSY CALLED LAST NIGHT FROM HER DAD'S PLACE OUT IN OHIO. IT SEEMS THAT SHE AND DAIMON HAVE DECIDED NOT TO WAIT.
THEY'RE GETTING MARRIED... SATURDAY.
NOW THIS BEING FRIDAY MORNING, THAT DOESN'T GIVE US ALL THAT MUCH TIME TO BUY OURSELVES SOME FANCY NEW CLOTHES AND GET OUT T GREENTOWN IN TIME FOR THE CEREMONY.
A WEDDING! I LOOOOVE WEDDINGS!
ESPECIALLY THE SMORGASBORDS!
TERRIFIC NEWS, ISN'T IT, VAL?
ISAAC... MY HEART COULD BURST WITH JOY!
PATSY AND DAIMON ARE GETTING MARRIED! WHA-HOO!
BY THE WAY, BOB--WHO ARE PATSY AND DAIMON?
DARNED IF I KNOW!
AH... YOUTH!
"BUT THE DEFENDERS AREN'T THE ONLY ONES WHO'VE FOUND THE IMPENDING MARRIAGE OF TWO OF THEIR FORMER MEMBERS--THE HELLCAT AND THE SON OF SATAN--OF MORE THAN PASSING INTEREST...
SO--SHE'S GETTING MARRIED, IS SHE?
ALL THE BETTER.
ALL THE BETTER!
YOU'RE PROBABLY WONDERING WHO THAT WEIRDO IS--AND WHAT HE'S BEEN DOING HANGING AROUND THE DEFENDER'S BROWNSTONE.
WELL, DON'T JUST SIT THERE WITH YOUR MOUTHS HANGING OPEN--

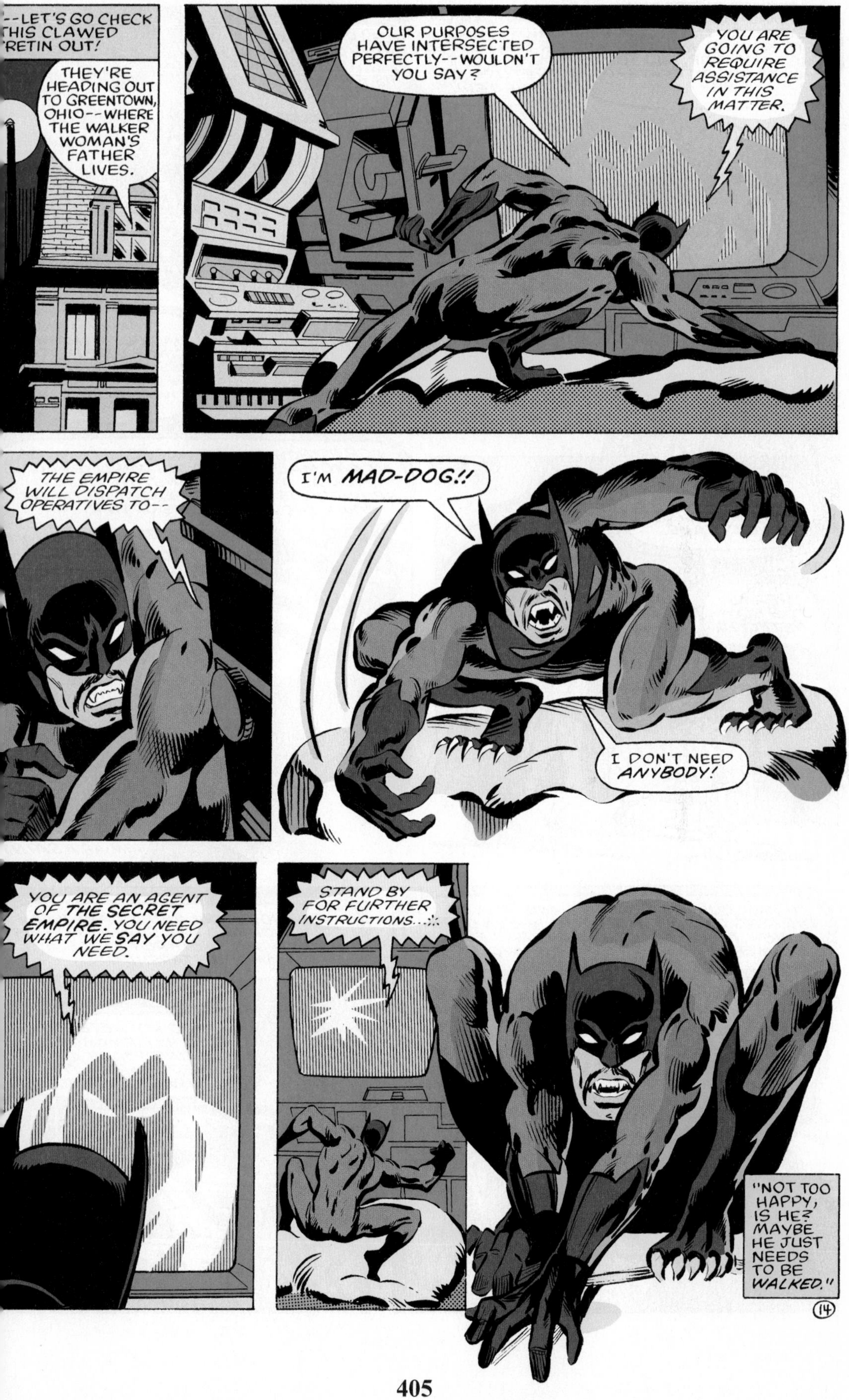

--LET'S GO CHECK THIS CLAWED 'RETIN OUT!
THEY'RE HEADING OUT TO GREENTOWN, OHIO--WHERE THE WALKER WOMAN'S FATHER LIVES.
OUR PURPOSES HAVE INTERSECTED PERFECTLY--WOULDN'T YOU SAY?
YOU ARE GOING TO REQUIRE ASSISTANCE IN THIS MATTER.
THE EMPIRE WILL DISPATCH OPERATIVES TO--
I'M MAD-DOG!!
I DON'T NEED ANYBODY!
YOU ARE AN AGENT OF THE SECRET EMPIRE. YOU NEED WHAT WE SAY YOU NEED.
STAND BY FOR FURTHER INSTRUCTIONS...
"NOT TOO HAPPY, IS HE? MAYBE HE JUST NEEDS TO BE WALKED."
14

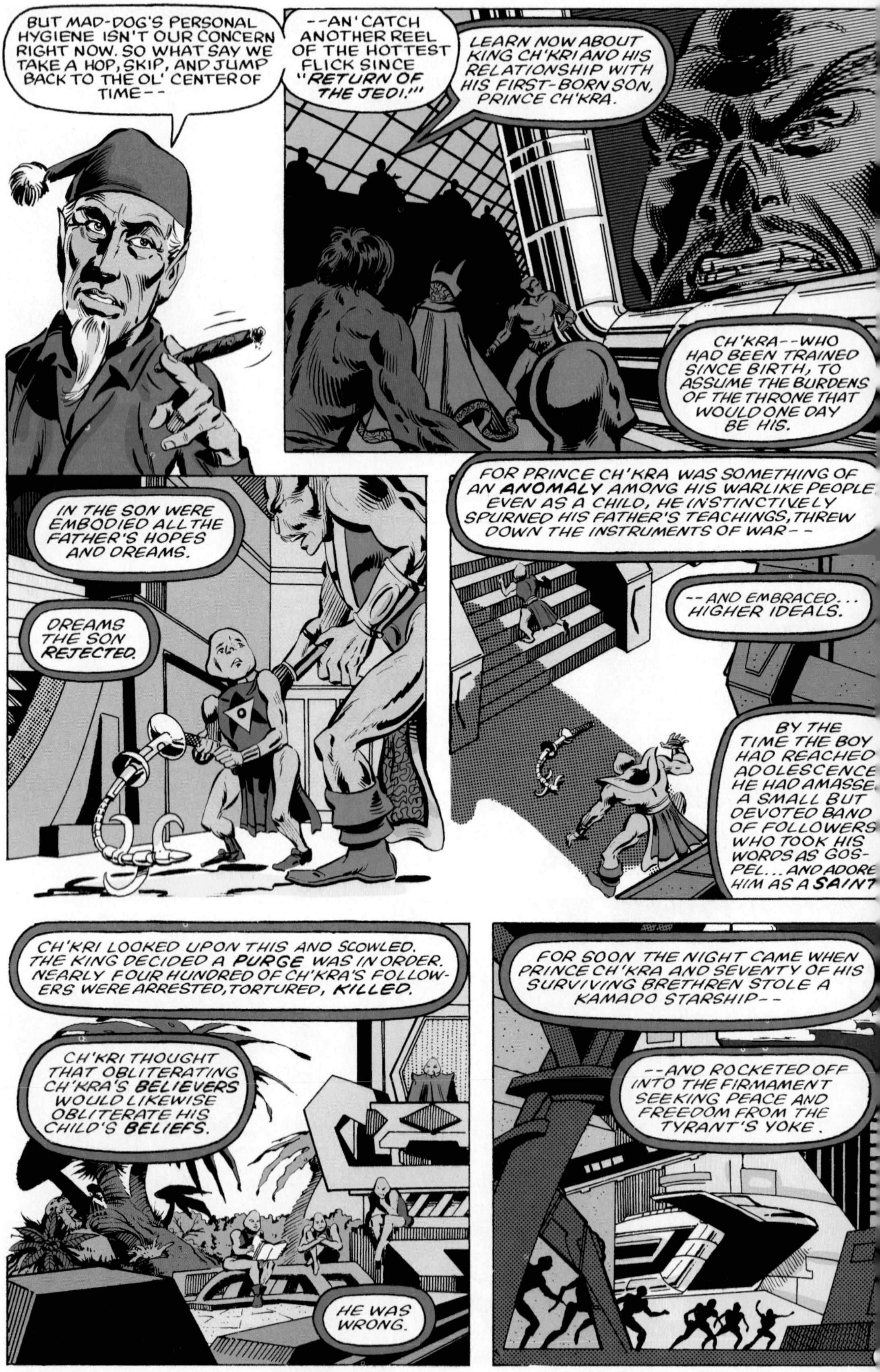
BUT MAD-DOG'S PERSONAL HYGIENE ISN'T OUR CONCERN RIGHT NOW. SO WHAT SAY WE TAKE A HOP, SKIP, AND JUMP BACK TO THE OL' CENTER OF TIME--
--AN' CATCH ANOTHER REEL OF THE HOTTEST FLICK SINCE "RETURN OF THE JEDI."
LEARN NOW ABOUT KING CH'KRI AND HIS RELATIONSHIP WITH HIS FIRST-BORN SON, PRINCE CH'KRA.
CH'KRA--WHO HAD BEEN TRAINED SINCE BIRTH, TO ASSUME THE BURDENS OF THE THRONE THAT WOULD ONE DAY BE HIS.
IN THE SON WERE EMBODIED ALL THE FATHER'S HOPES AND DREAMS.
DREAMS THE SON REJECTED.
FOR PRINCE CH'KRA WAS SOMETHING OF AN ANOMALY AMONG HIS WARLIKE PEOPLE. EVEN AS A CHILD, HE INSTINCTIVELY SPURNED HIS FATHER'S TEACHINGS, THREW DOWN THE INSTRUMENTS OF WAR--
--AND EMBRACED... HIGHER IDEALS.
BY THE TIME THE BOY HAD REACHED ADOLESCENCE HE HAD AMASSE A SMALL BUT DEVOTED BAND OF FOLLOWERS WHO TOOK HIS WORDS AS GOSPEL... AND ADORE HIM AS A SAIN
CH'KRI LOOKED UPON THIS AND SCOWLED. THE KING DECIDED A PURGE WAS IN ORDER. NEARLY FOUR HUNDRED OF CH'KRA'S FOLLOWERS WERE ARRESTED, TORTURED, KILLED.
CH'KRI THOUGHT THAT OBLITERATING CH'KRA'S BELIEVERS WOULD LIKEWISE OBLITERATE HIS CHILD'S BELIEFS.
HE WAS WRONG.
FOR SOON THE NIGHT CAME WHEN PRINCE CH'KRA AND SEVENTY OF HIS SURVIVING BRETHREN STOLE A KAMADO STARSHIP--
--AND ROCKETED OFF INTO THE FIRMAMENT SEEKING PEACE AND FREEDOM FROM THE TYRANT'S YOKE.

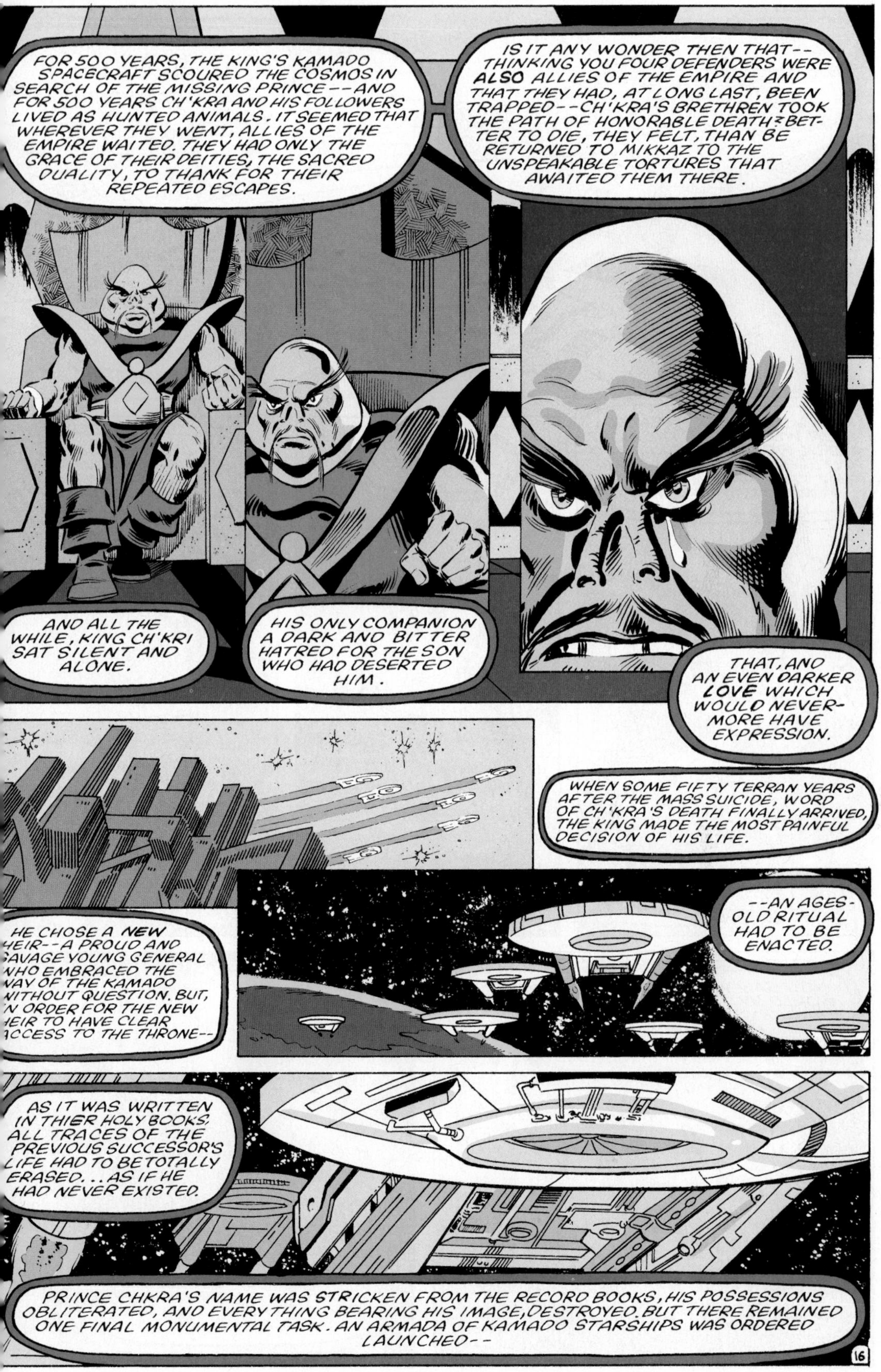
FOR 500 YEARS, THE KING'S KAMADO SPACECRAFT SCOURED THE COSMOS IN SEARCH OF THE MISSING PRINCE--AND FOR 500 YEARS CH'KRA AND HIS FOLLOWERS LIVED AS HUNTED ANIMALS. IT SEEMED THAT WHEREVER THEY WENT, ALLIES OF THE EMPIRE WAITED. THEY HAD ONLY THE GRACE OF THEIR DEITIES, THE SACRED DUALITY, TO THANK FOR THEIR REPEATED ESCAPES.
IS IT ANY WONDER THEN THAT--THINKING YOU FOUR DEFENDERS WERE ALSO ALLIES OF THE EMPIRE AND THAT THEY HAD, AT LONG LAST, BEEN TRAPPED--CH'KRA'S BRETHREN TOOK THE PATH OF HONORABLE DEATH? BETTER TO DIE, THEY FELT, THAN BE RETURNED TO MIKKAZ TO THE UNSPEAKABLE TORTURES THAT AWAITED THEM THERE.
AND ALL THE WHILE, KING CH'KRI SAT SILENT AND ALONE.
HIS ONLY COMPANION A DARK AND BITTER HATRED FOR THE SON WHO HAD DESERTED HIM.
THAT, AND AN EVEN DARKER LOVE WHICH WOULD NEVERMORE HAVE EXPRESSION.
WHEN SOME FIFTY TERRAN YEARS AFTER THE MASS SUICIDE, WORD OF CH'KRA'S DEATH FINALLY ARRIVED, THE KING MADE THE MOST PAINFUL DECISION OF HIS LIFE.
HE CHOSE A NEW HEIR--A PROUD AND SAVAGE YOUNG GENERAL WHO EMBRACED THE WAY OF THE KAMADO WITHOUT QUESTION. BUT, IN ORDER FOR THE NEW HEIR TO HAVE CLEAR ACCESS TO THE THRONE--
--AN AGES-OLD RITUAL HAD TO BE ENACTED.
AS IT WAS WRITTEN IN THIER HOLY BOOKS, ALL TRACES OF THE PREVIOUS SUCCESSOR'S LIFE HAD TO BE TOTALLY ERASED...AS IF HE HAD NEVER EXISTED.
PRINCE CHKRA'S NAME WAS STRICKEN FROM THE RECORD BOOKS, HIS POSSESSIONS OBLITERATED, AND EVERYTHING BEARING HIS IMAGE, DESTROYED. BUT THERE REMAINED ONE FINAL MONUMENTAL TASK. AN ARMADA OF KAMADO STARSHIPS WAS ORDERED LAUNCHED--
16

--TOWARD EARTH.

FOR IF EVERY TRACE OF PRINCE CH'KRA'S *LIFE* WAS TO BE STAMPED OUT--

--THEN SO WOULD EVERY TRACE OF HIS *DEATH.*

THE GAS THAT SATURATED YOUR WORLD WAS THE MOST AWFUL WEAPON THE KAMADO HAD EVER DEVISED; SO AWFUL THAT THEY HAD NEVER BEFORE DARED TO USE IT.

BUT USE IT THEY DID.

ALL LIVING THINGS DIED SLOWLY, OVER THE COURSE OF A CENTURY, AND IT TOOK ANOTHER *TWO* CENTURIES FOR THE RUINS LEFT STANDING IN MAN'S WAKE TO BE CONSUMED AND LEVELLED.

YOU SAW WHAT WAS LEFT OF YOUR WORLD BY THE MID TWENTY-FOURTH CENTURY. YOU DID *NOT* SEE WHAT HAPPENED LATER--

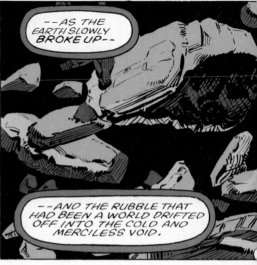

--AS THE EARTH SLOWLY *BROKE UP--*

--AND THE RUBBLE THAT HAD BEEN A WORLD DRIFTED OFF INTO THE COLD AND MERCILESS VOID.

NO! NO! HOW COULD SUCH HORROR HAVE RESULTED FROM ONE SIMPLE ACT OF COMPASSION?

TRIBUNAL, *WHAT* IS TO BE DONE?

CAN WE RETURN TO OUR OWN TIME AND SOMEHOW *PREVENT* THIS TRAGEDY? PERHAPS IF WE FIND PRINCE CH'KRA *BEFORE* HE SUC- CUMBS TO--

NO. THE DANCE OF THE KARMIC LINES IS TOO INTRICATE. IN ONE FORM OR ANOTHER-- ALL THAT YOU HAVE SEEN IS DESTINED TO OCCUR.

WHAT ARE YOU SAYING? OF *COURSE* WE CAN GO BACK! OF *COURSE* WE CAN CHANGE IT! WE *HAVE* TO!

NO, BRUCE. IT ISN'T THAT SIMPLE.

AH... DOCTOR. YOU BEGIN TO SEE. THE IMAGES AND THOUGHTS THAT ASSAILED YOU WHEN YOU PEERED INTO US WITH YOUR MYSTIC EYE ARE BEGINNING TO COALESCE.

PERHAPS YOU WOULD BE GOOD ENOUGH TO EXPLAIN TO YOUR COMPANIONS.

WELL, STEPHEN?

18

409

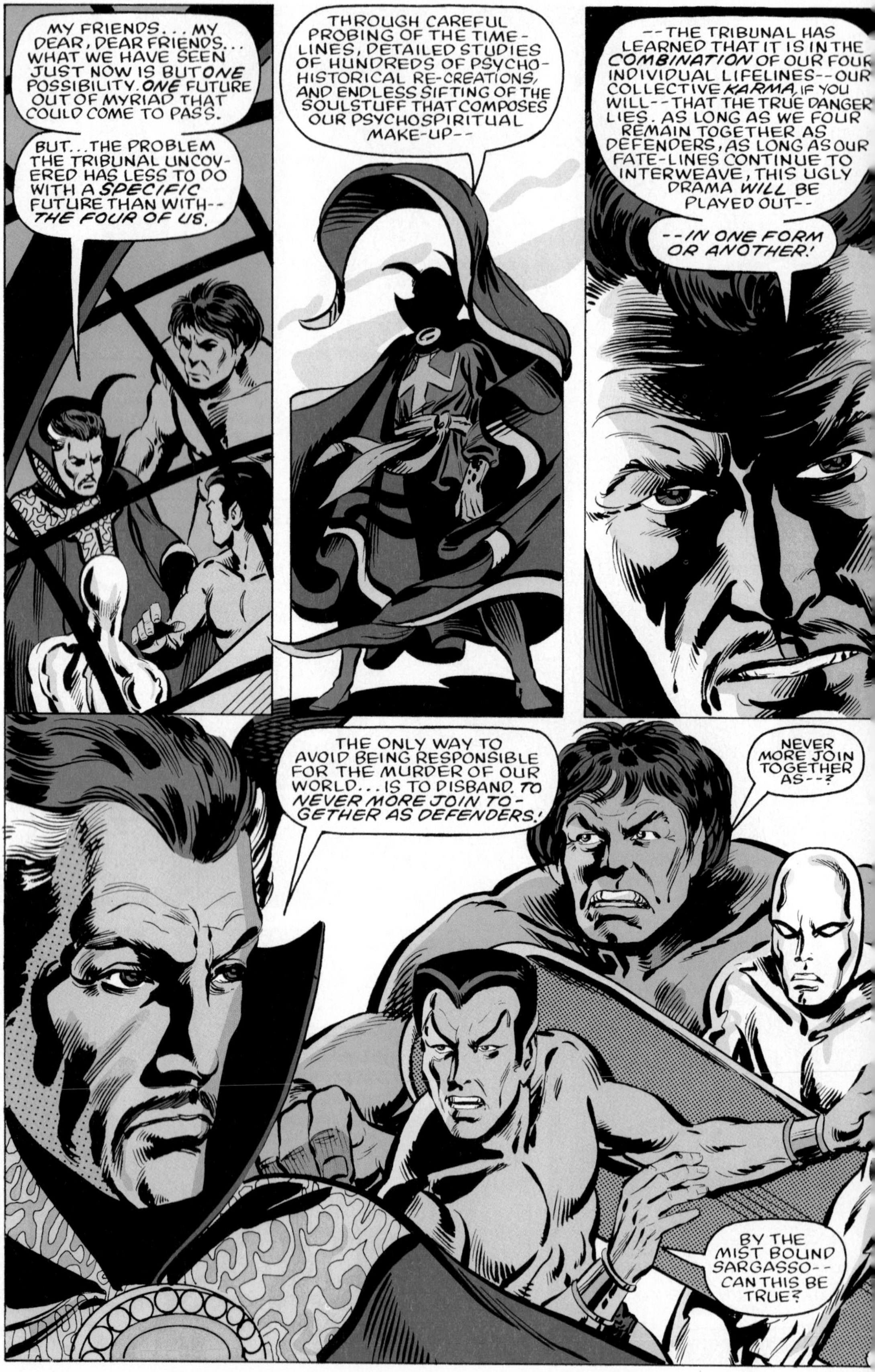

MY FRIENDS... MY DEAR, DEAR FRIENDS... WHAT WE HAVE SEEN JUST NOW IS BUT ONE POSSIBILITY. ONE FUTURE OUT OF MYRIAD THAT COULD COME TO PASS.
BUT...THE PROBLEM THE TRIBUNAL UNCOVERED HAS LESS TO DO WITH A SPECIFIC FUTURE THAN WITH-- THE FOUR OF US.
THROUGH CAREFUL PROBING OF THE TIME-LINES, DETAILED STUDIES OF HUNDREDS OF PSYCHO-HISTORICAL RE-CREATIONS, AND ENDLESS SIFTING OF THE SOULSTUFF THAT COMPOSES OUR PSYCHOSPIRITUAL MAKE-UP--
--THE TRIBUNAL HAS LEARNED THAT IT IS IN THE COMBINATION OF OUR FOUR INDIVIDUAL LIFELINES--OUR COLLECTIVE KARMA, IF YOU WILL--THAT THE TRUE DANGER LIES. AS LONG AS WE FOUR REMAIN TOGETHER AS DEFENDERS, AS LONG AS OUR FATE-LINES CONTINUE TO INTERWEAVE, THIS UGLY DRAMA WILL BE PLAYED OUT--
--IN ONE FORM OR ANOTHER!
THE ONLY WAY TO AVOID BEING RESPONSIBLE FOR THE MURDER OF OUR WORLD... IS TO DISBAND. TO NEVER MORE JOIN TOGETHER AS DEFENDERS!
NEVER MORE JOIN TOGETHER AS--?
BY THE MIST BOUND SARGASSO-- CAN THIS BE TRUE?

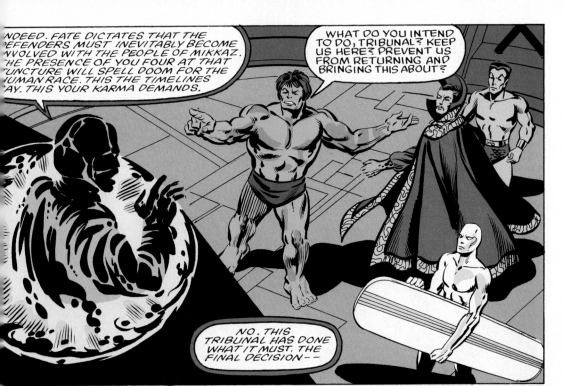

INDEED. FATE DICTATES THAT THE DEFENDERS MUST INEVITABLY BECOME INVOLVED WITH THE PEOPLE OF MIKKAZ. THE PRESENCE OF YOU FOUR AT THAT JUNCTURE WILL SPELL DOOM FOR THE HUMAN RACE. THIS THE TIMELINES SAY. THIS YOUR KARMA DEMANDS.

WHAT DO YOU INTEND TO DO, TRIBUNAL? KEEP US HERE? PREVENT US FROM RETURNING AND BRINGING THIS ABOUT?

NO. THIS TRIBUNAL HAS DONE WHAT IT MUST. THE FINAL DECISION--

--RESTS-- WITH YOU!

AN' JUST LIKE THAT, THEY'RE BACK AT THE DOC'S DIGS IN THE VILLAGE. LOOKS LIKE THE BEST THING *WE* CAN DO AT THIS POINT IS LEAVE THESE POOR SHNOOKS ALONE!

THEY'VE GOT A *LOT* TO THINK ABOUT!

20

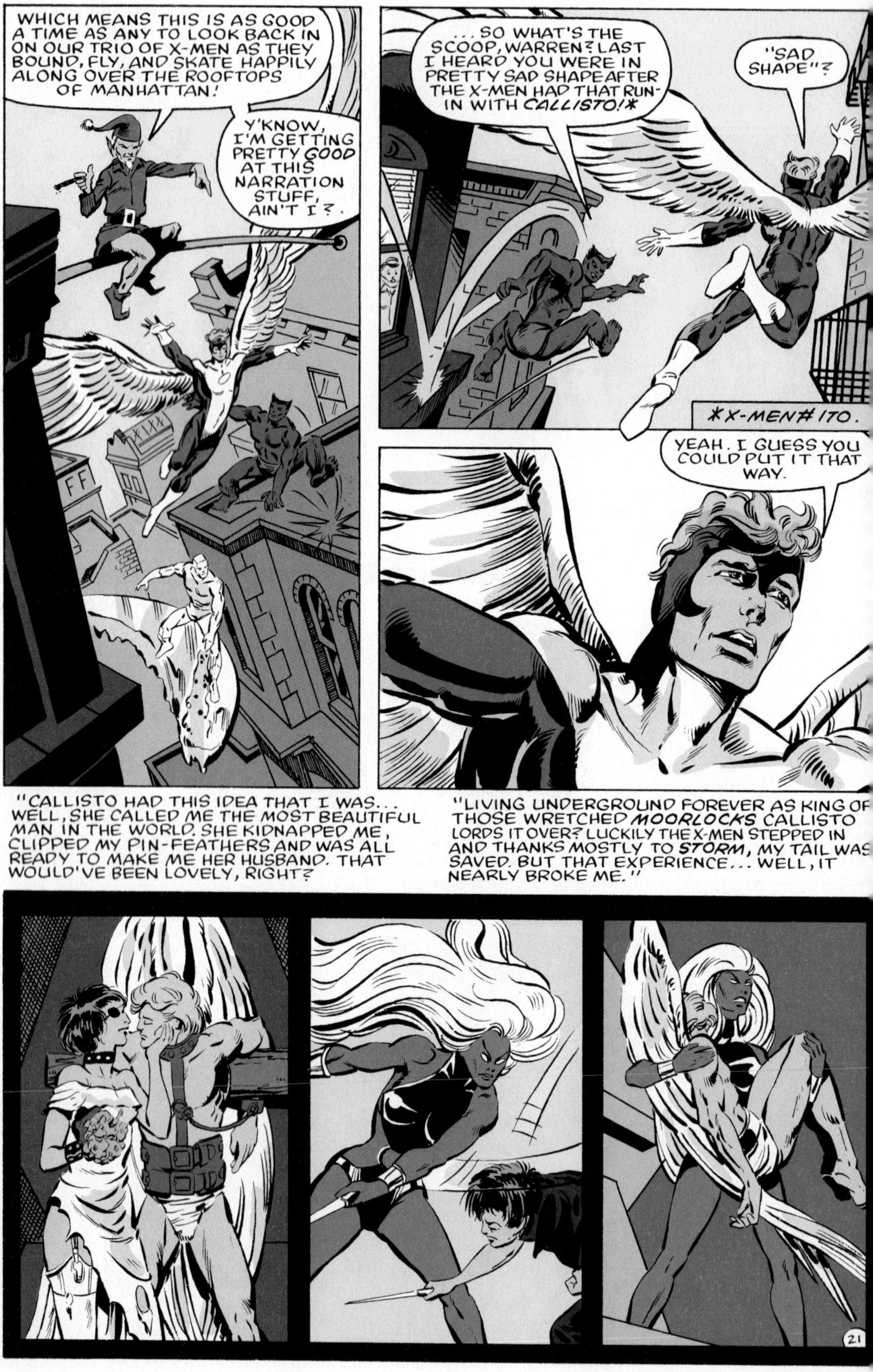

WHICH MEANS THIS IS AS GOOD A TIME AS ANY TO LOOK BACK IN ON OUR TRIO OF X-MEN AS THEY BOUND, FLY, AND SKATE HAPPILY ALONG OVER THE ROOFTOPS OF MANHATTAN!
Y'KNOW, I'M GETTING PRETTY GOOD AT THIS NARRATION STUFF, AIN'T I?
...SO WHAT'S THE SCOOP, WARREN? LAST I HEARD YOU WERE IN PRETTY SAD SHAPE AFTER THE X-MEN HAD THAT RUN-IN WITH CALLISTO!*
"SAD SHAPE"?
*X-MEN #170.
YEAH. I GUESS YOU COULD PUT IT THAT WAY.
"CALLISTO HAD THIS IDEA THAT I WAS... WELL, SHE CALLED ME THE MOST BEAUTIFUL MAN IN THE WORLD. SHE KIDNAPPED ME, CLIPPED MY PIN-FEATHERS AND WAS ALL READY TO MAKE ME HER HUSBAND. THAT WOULD'VE BEEN LOVELY, RIGHT?
"LIVING UNDERGROUND FOREVER AS KING OF THOSE WRETCHED MOORLOCKS CALLISTO LORDS IT OVER? LUCKILY THE X-MEN STEPPED IN AND THANKS MOSTLY TO STORM, MY TAIL WAS SAVED. BUT THAT EXPERIENCE... WELL, IT NEARLY BROKE ME."
21

I WAS ASHAMED. I FELT AS IF I'D BEEN... *VIOLATED.* MORE THAN THAT, IT WAS AS IF CALLISTO HAD PUSHED A BUTTON AND BROUGHT ALL THE PSYCHOLOGICAL SLUDGE UP FROM MY SUB-CONS-CIOUS -- AS IF EVERY WEAK LINK IN MY MENTAL ARMOR HAD JUST... *SNAPPED.*

I WAS FORCED TO LOOK AT MY LIFE IN A WAY I NEVER *HAD* BEFORE. THERE I WAS, THE MAN WHO HAD EVERYTHING -- LOOKS, WEALTH, POWER. *EVERYTHING!*

AND WHAT HAD I ACCOMPLISHED? *ZILCH!*

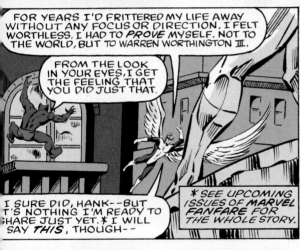

FOR YEARS I'D FRITTERED MY LIFE AWAY WITHOUT ANY FOCUS OR DIRECTION. I FELT WORTHLESS. I HAD TO *PROVE* MYSELF. NOT TO THE WORLD, BUT TO WARREN WORTHINGTON III.

FROM THE LOOK IN YOUR EYES, I GET THE FEELING THAT YOU DID JUST THAT.

I SURE DID, HANK -- BUT IT'S NOTHING I'M READY TO SHARE JUST YET.✱ I WILL SAY *THIS*, THOUGH --

✱ SEE UPCOMING ISSUES OF MARVEL FANFARE FOR THE WHOLE STORY.

-- FOR THE FIRST TIME IN YEARS, MAYBE IN MY WHOLE *LIFE*, I FEEL WHOLE AND CONFIDENT. I'M READY TO TAKE ON WHATEVER LIFE DISHES OUT.

THINK YOU COULD SPARE A CUP OR TWO OF THAT CONFIDENCE, BUDDY?

I'LL SEE WHAT I CAN DO, BOB!

HI, FOLKS! WE'RE BACK! NO, NO -- DON'T ALL COME RUSHING TO GREET US AT ONCE!

HOWDY, BOYS!

H'LLO, SASSY DARLIN'! HOWZABOUT A KISS?

I TRUST YOU THREE OLD FRIENDS ENJOYED YOUR AFTERNOON TOGETHER?

22

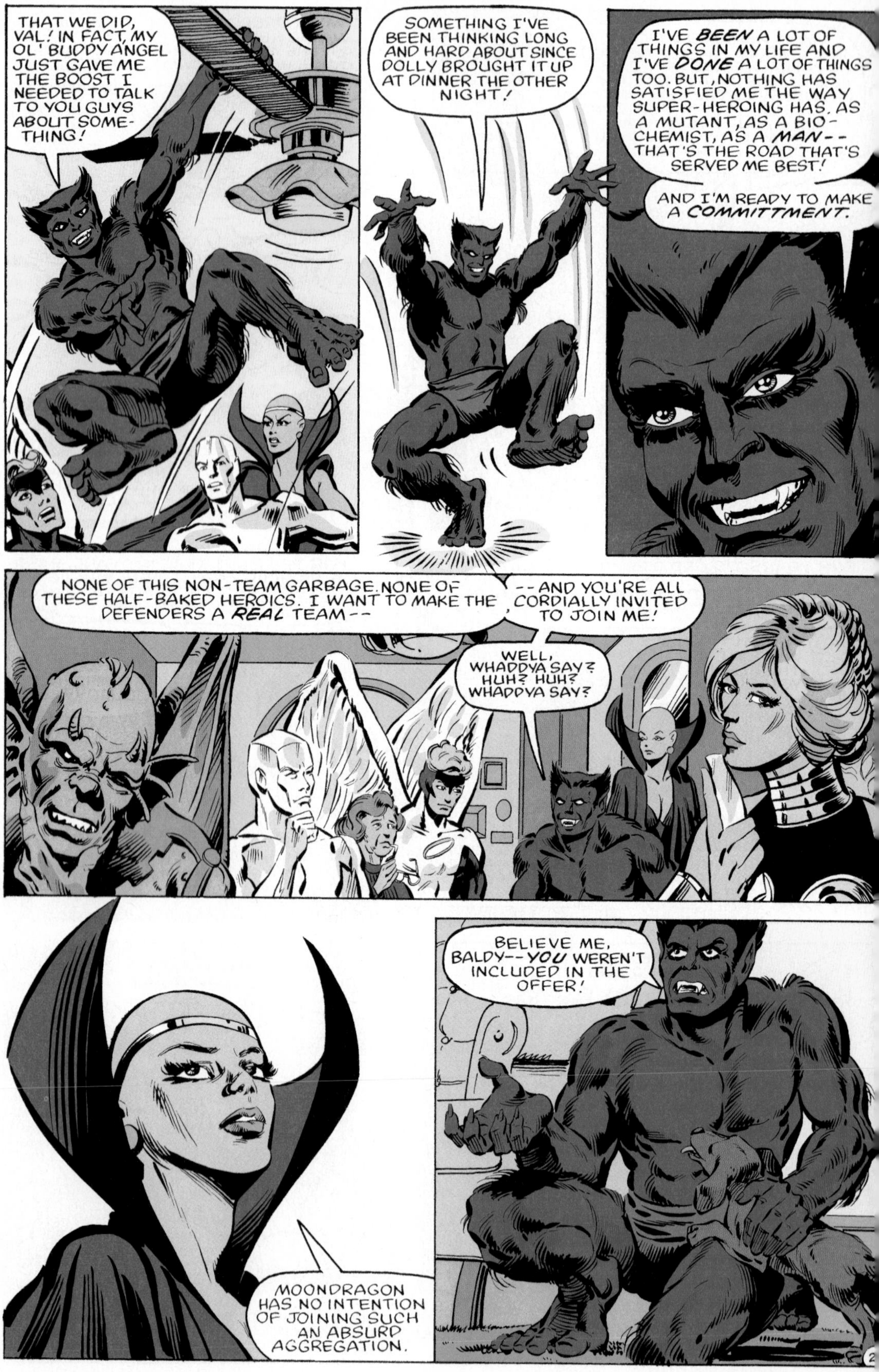
THAT WE DID, VAL! IN FACT, MY OL' BUDDY ANGEL JUST GAVE ME THE BOOST I NEEDED TO TALK TO YOU GUYS ABOUT SOME-THING!
SOMETHING I'VE BEEN THINKING LONG AND HARD ABOUT SINCE DOLLY BROUGHT IT UP AT DINNER THE OTHER NIGHT!
I'VE BEEN A LOT OF THINGS IN MY LIFE AND I'VE DONE A LOT OF THINGS TOO. BUT, NOTHING HAS SATISFIED ME THE WAY SUPER-HEROING HAS. AS A MUTANT, AS A BIO-CHEMIST, AS A MAN--THAT'S THE ROAD THAT'S SERVED ME BEST!
AND I'M READY TO MAKE A COMMITTMENT.
NONE OF THIS NON-TEAM GARBAGE. NONE OF THESE HALF-BAKED HEROICS. I WANT TO MAKE THE DEFENDERS A REAL TEAM--
--AND YOU'RE ALL CORDIALLY INVITED TO JOIN ME!
WELL, WHADDYA SAY? HUH? HUH? WHADDYA SAY?
MOONDRAGON HAS NO INTENTION OF JOINING SUCH AN ABSURD AGGREGATION.
BELIEVE ME, BALDY--YOU WEREN'T INCLUDED IN THE OFFER!

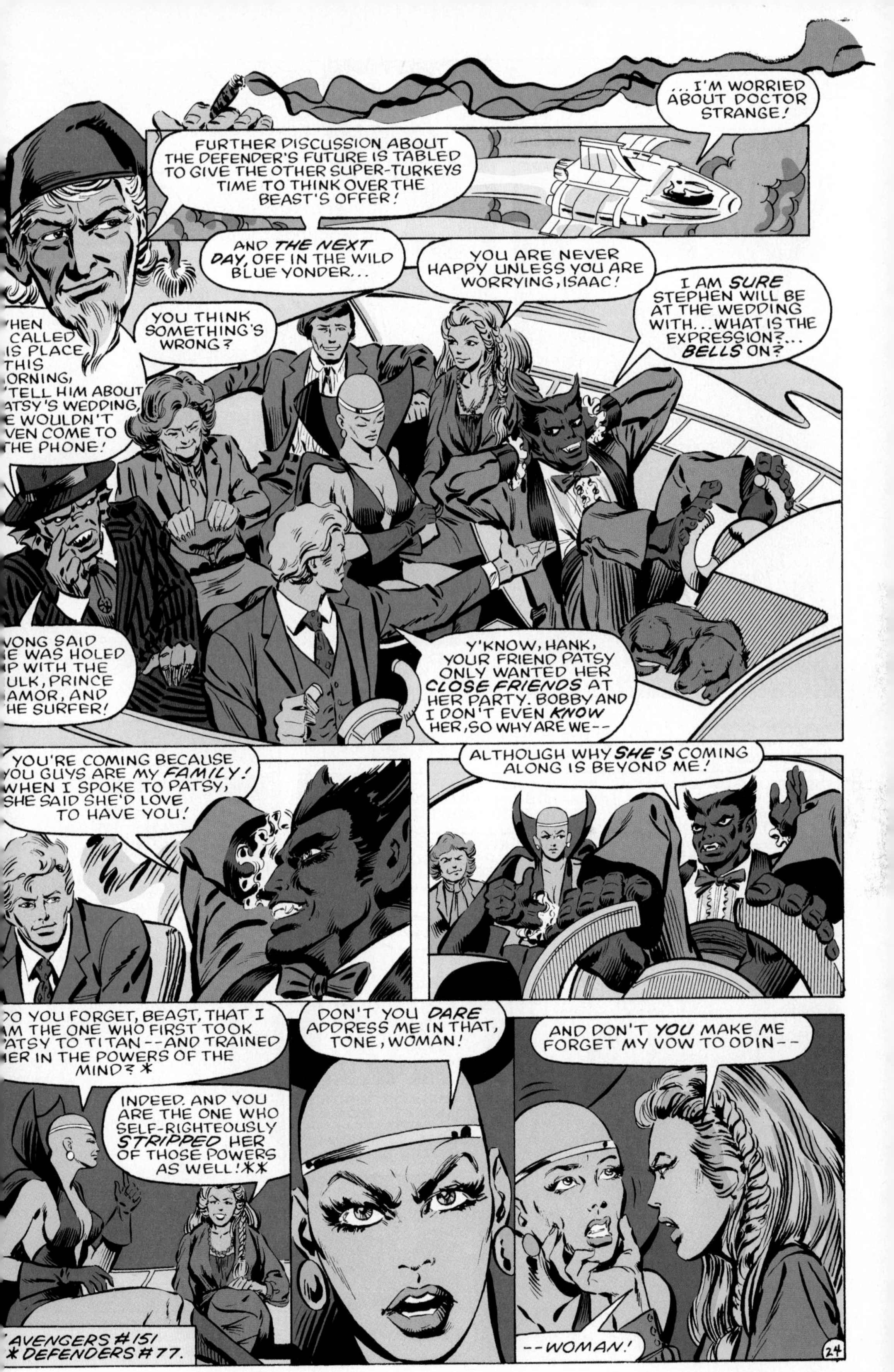

FURTHER DISCUSSION ABOUT THE DEFENDER'S FUTURE IS TABLED TO GIVE THE OTHER SUPER-TURKEYS TIME TO THINK OVER THE BEAST'S OFFER!
...I'M WORRIED ABOUT DOCTOR STRANGE!
AND THE NEXT DAY, OFF IN THE WILD BLUE YONDER...
YOU ARE NEVER HAPPY UNLESS YOU ARE WORRYING, ISAAC!
I AM SURE STEPHEN WILL BE AT THE WEDDING WITH...WHAT IS THE EXPRESSION?...BELLS ON?
YOU THINK SOMETHING'S WRONG?
HEN CALLED IS PLACE THIS ORNING, TELL HIM ABOUT PATSY'S WEDDING, E WOULDN'T VEN COME TO THE PHONE!
WONG SAID E WAS HOLED P WITH THE ULK, PRINCE AMOR, AND HE SURFER!
Y'KNOW, HANK, YOUR FRIEND PATSY ONLY WANTED HER CLOSE FRIENDS AT HER PARTY. BOBBY AND I DON'T EVEN KNOW HER, SO WHY ARE WE--
YOU'RE COMING BECAUSE YOU GUYS ARE MY FAMILY! WHEN I SPOKE TO PATSY, SHE SAID SHE'D LOVE TO HAVE YOU!
ALTHOUGH WHY SHE'S COMING ALONG IS BEYOND ME!
O YOU FORGET, BEAST, THAT I AM THE ONE WHO FIRST TOOK PATSY TO TITAN--AND TRAINED HER IN THE POWERS OF THE MIND? *
INDEED. AND YOU ARE THE ONE WHO SELF-RIGHTEOUSLY STRIPPED HER OF THOSE POWERS AS WELL! **
DON'T YOU DARE ADDRESS ME IN THAT, TONE, WOMAN!
AND DON'T YOU MAKE ME FORGET MY VOW TO ODIN--
--WOMAN!
AVENGERS #151
* DEFENDERS #77.
24

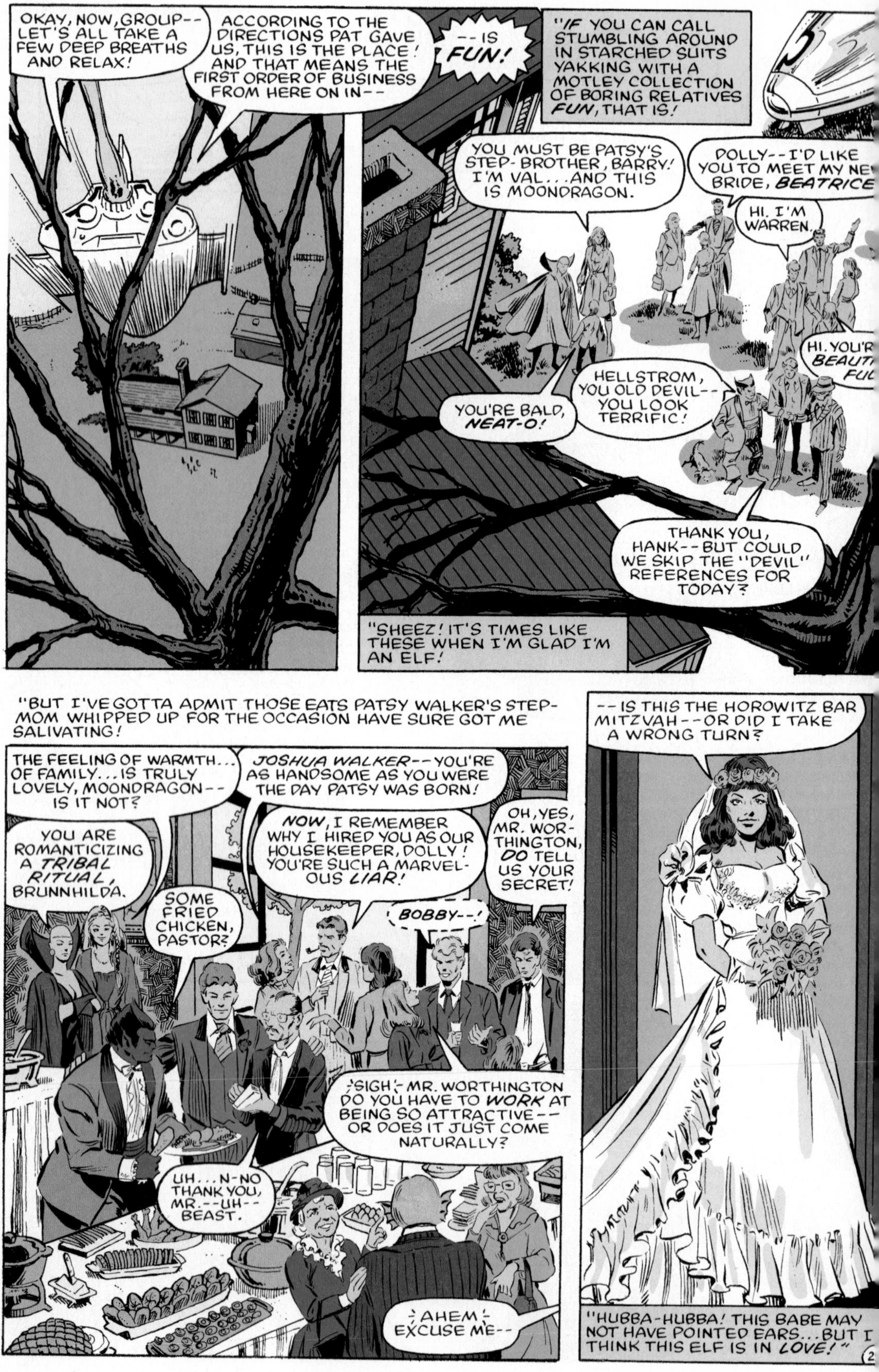
OKAY, NOW, GROUP-- LET'S ALL TAKE A FEW DEEP BREATHS AND RELAX!
ACCORDING TO THE DIRECTIONS PAT GAVE US, THIS IS THE PLACE! AND THAT MEANS THE FIRST ORDER OF BUSINESS FROM HERE ON IN--
--IS FUN!
"IF YOU CAN CALL STUMBLING AROUND IN STARCHED SUITS YAKKING WITH A MOTLEY COLLECTION OF BORING RELATIVES FUN, THAT IS!
YOU MUST BE PATSY'S STEP-BROTHER, BARRY! I'M VAL... AND THIS IS MOONDRAGON.
DOLLY--I'D LIKE YOU TO MEET MY NE BRIDE, BEATRICE
HI. I'M WARREN.
HI. YOU'R BEAUTI FU
YOU'RE BALD, NEAT-O!
HELLSTROM, YOU OLD DEVIL-- YOU LOOK TERRIFIC!
THANK YOU, HANK--BUT COULD WE SKIP THE "DEVIL" REFERENCES FOR TODAY?
"SHEEZ! IT'S TIMES LIKE THESE WHEN I'M GLAD I'M AN ELF!
"BUT I'VE GOTTA ADMIT THOSE EATS PATSY WALKER'S STEP-MOM WHIPPED UP FOR THE OCCASION HAVE SURE GOT ME SALIVATING!
THE FEELING OF WARMTH... OF FAMILY... IS TRULY LOVELY, MOONDRAGON-- IS IT NOT?
JOSHUA WALKER--YOU'RE AS HANDSOME AS YOU WERE THE DAY PATSY WAS BORN!
YOU ARE ROMANTICIZING A TRIBAL RITUAL, BRUNNHILDA.
NOW, I REMEMBER WHY I HIRED YOU AS OUR HOUSEKEEPER, DOLLY! YOU'RE SUCH A MARVELOUS LIAR!
OH, YES, MR. WORTHINGTON, DO TELL US YOUR SECRET!
SOME FRIED CHICKEN, PASTOR?
BOBBY--!
-SIGH- MR. WORTHINGTON DO YOU HAVE TO WORK AT BEING SO ATTRACTIVE-- OR DOES IT JUST COME NATURALLY?
UH... N-NO THANK YOU, MR.--UH-- BEAST.
-AHEM- EXCUSE ME--
--IS THIS THE HOROWITZ BAR MITZVAH--OR DID I TAKE A WRONG TURN?
"HUBBA-HUBBA! THIS BABE MAY NOT HAVE POINTED EARS... BUT I THINK THIS ELF IS IN LOVE!"

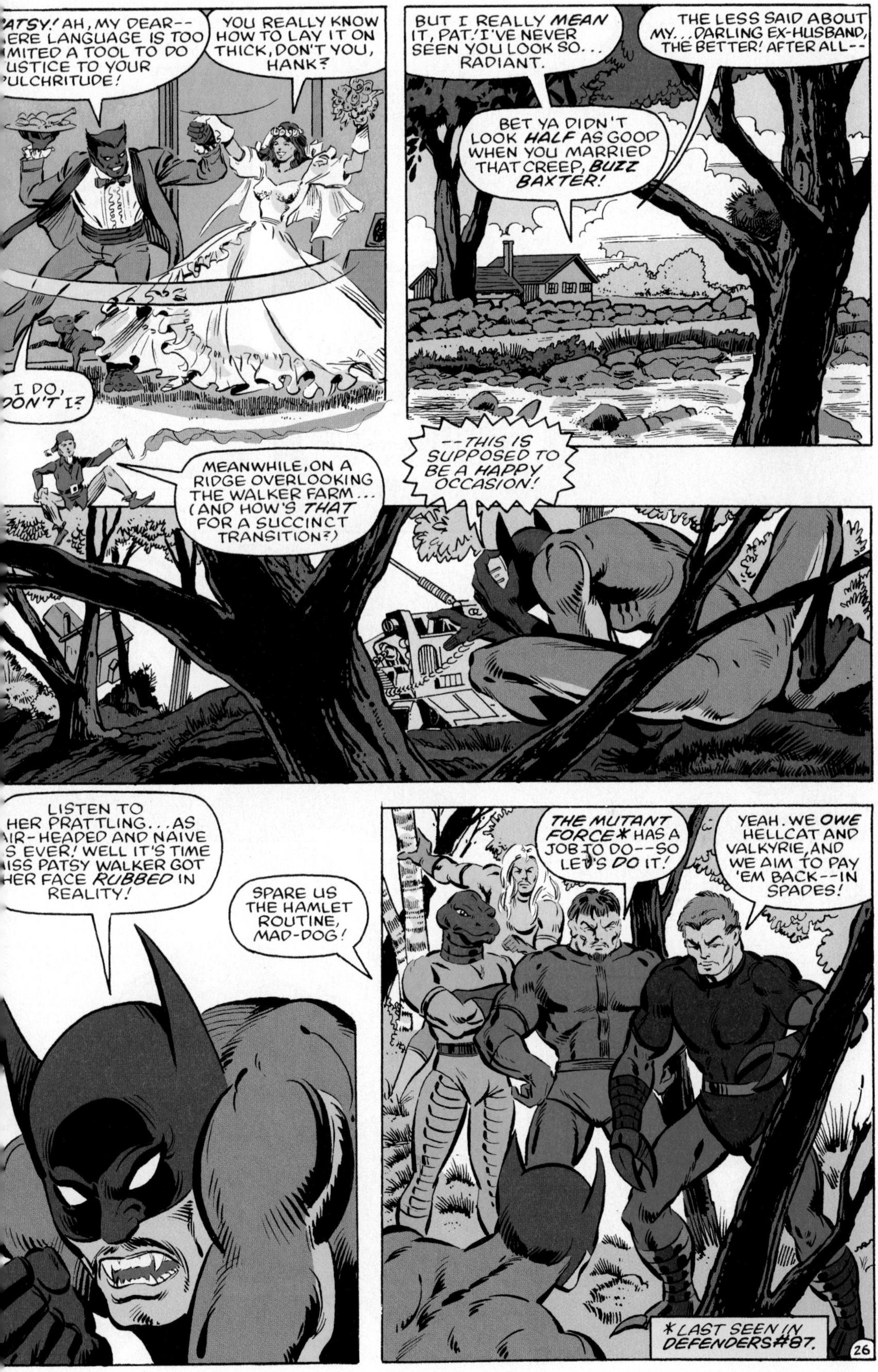
ATSY! AH, MY DEAR-- ERE LANGUAGE IS TOO MITED A TOOL TO DO USTICE TO YOUR ULCHRITUDE!
YOU REALLY KNOW HOW TO LAY IT ON THICK, DON'T YOU, HANK?
I DO, DON'T I?
BUT I REALLY MEAN IT, PAT! I'VE NEVER SEEN YOU LOOK SO... RADIANT.
THE LESS SAID ABOUT MY... DARLING EX-HUSBAND, THE BETTER! AFTER ALL--
BET YA DIDN'T LOOK HALF AS GOOD WHEN YOU MARRIED THAT CREEP, BUZZ BAXTER!
--THIS IS SUPPOSED TO BE A HAPPY OCCASION!
MEANWHILE, ON A RIDGE OVERLOOKING THE WALKER FARM... (AND HOW'S THAT FOR A SUCCINCT TRANSITION?)
LISTEN TO HER PRATTLING... AS AIR-HEADED AND NAIVE S EVER! WELL IT'S TIME ISS PATSY WALKER GOT HER FACE RUBBED IN REALITY!
SPARE US THE HAMLET ROUTINE, MAD-DOG!
THE MUTANT FORCE* HAS A JOB TO DO--SO LET'S DO IT!
YEAH. WE OWE HELLCAT AND VALKYRIE, AND WE AIM TO PAY 'EM BACK--IN SPADES!
*LAST SEEN IN DEFENDERS #87.
26

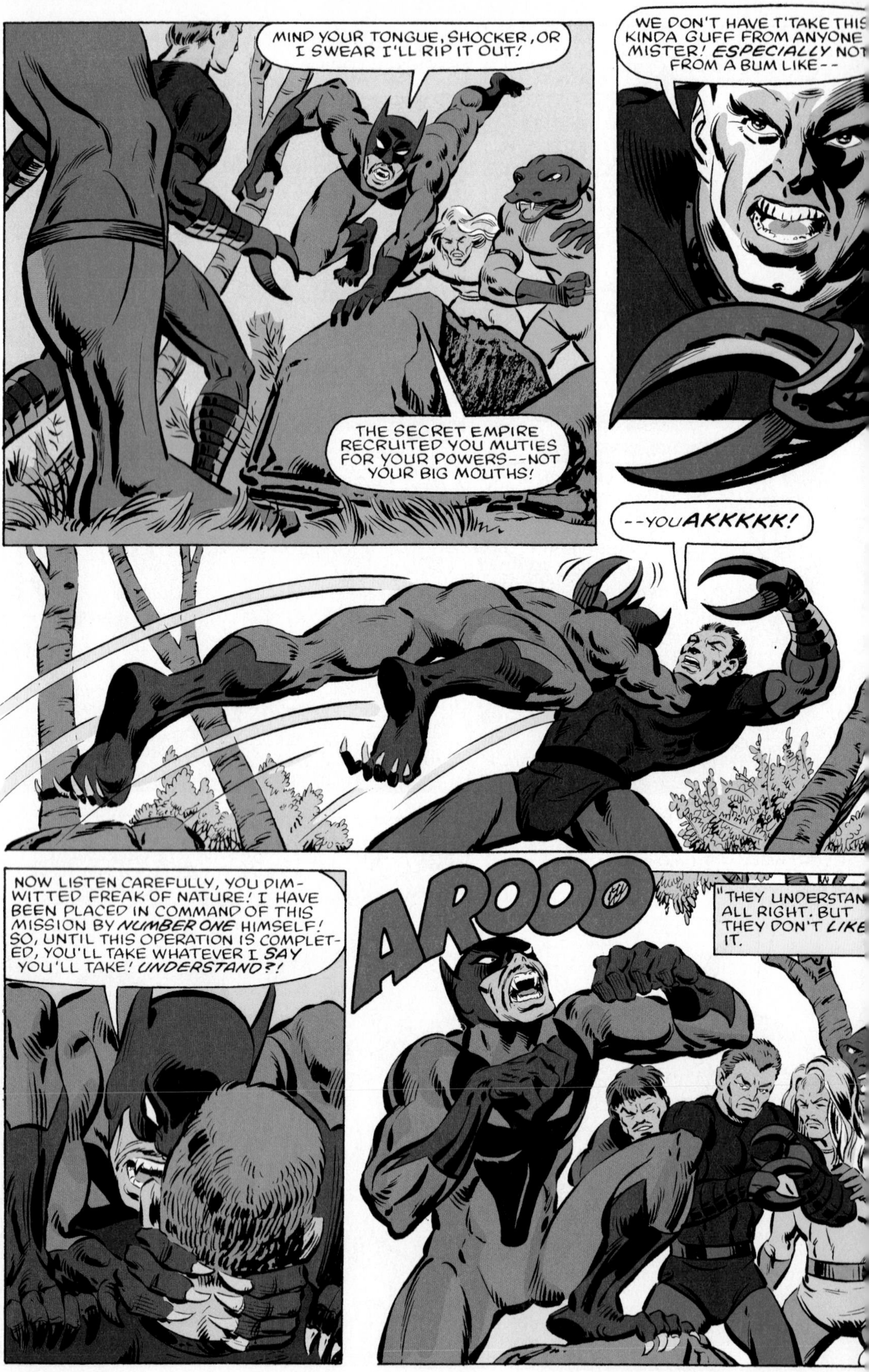
MIND YOUR TONGUE, SHOCKER, OR I SWEAR I'LL RIP IT OUT!
THE SECRET EMPIRE RECRUITED YOU MUTIES FOR YOUR POWERS--NOT YOUR BIG MOUTHS!
WE DON'T HAVE T'TAKE THIS KINDA GUFF FROM ANYONE MISTER! ESPECIALLY NOT FROM A BUM LIKE--
--YOU AKKKKK!
NOW LISTEN CAREFULLY, YOU DIM-WITTED FREAK OF NATURE! I HAVE BEEN PLACED IN COMMAND OF THIS MISSION BY NUMBER ONE HIMSELF! SO, UNTIL THIS OPERATION IS COMPLETED, YOU'LL TAKE WHATEVER I SAY YOU'LL TAKE! UNDERSTAND?!
AROOO
"THEY UNDERSTAN ALL RIGHT. BUT THEY DON'T LIKE IT.

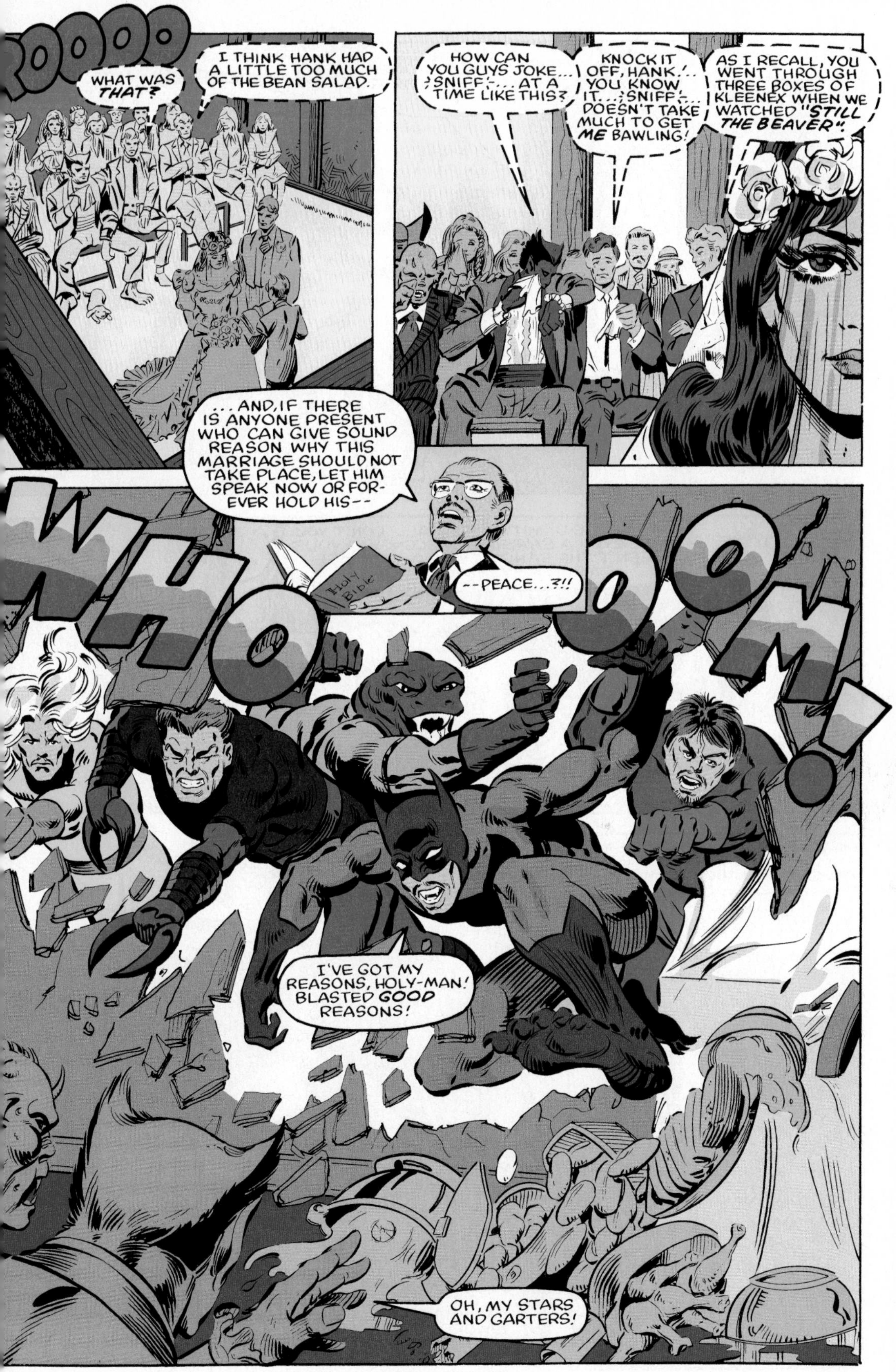
ROOOO
WHAT WAS THAT?
I THINK HANK HAD A LITTLE TOO MUCH OF THE BEAN SALAD.
HOW CAN YOU GUYS JOKE... SNIFF... AT A TIME LIKE THIS?
KNOCK IT OFF, HANK! YOU KNOW IT... SNIFF... DOESN'T TAKE MUCH TO GET ME BAWLING!
AS I RECALL, YOU WENT THROUGH THREE BOXES OF KLEENEX WHEN WE WATCHED "STILL THE BEAVER".
...AND, IF THERE IS ANYONE PRESENT WHO CAN GIVE SOUND REASON WHY THIS MARRIAGE SHOULD NOT TAKE PLACE, LET HIM SPEAK NOW OR FOREVER HOLD HIS--
--PEACE...?!!
Holy Bible
WHOOOM!
I'VE GOT MY REASONS, HOLY-MAN! BLASTED GOOD REASONS!
OH, MY STARS AND GARTERS!

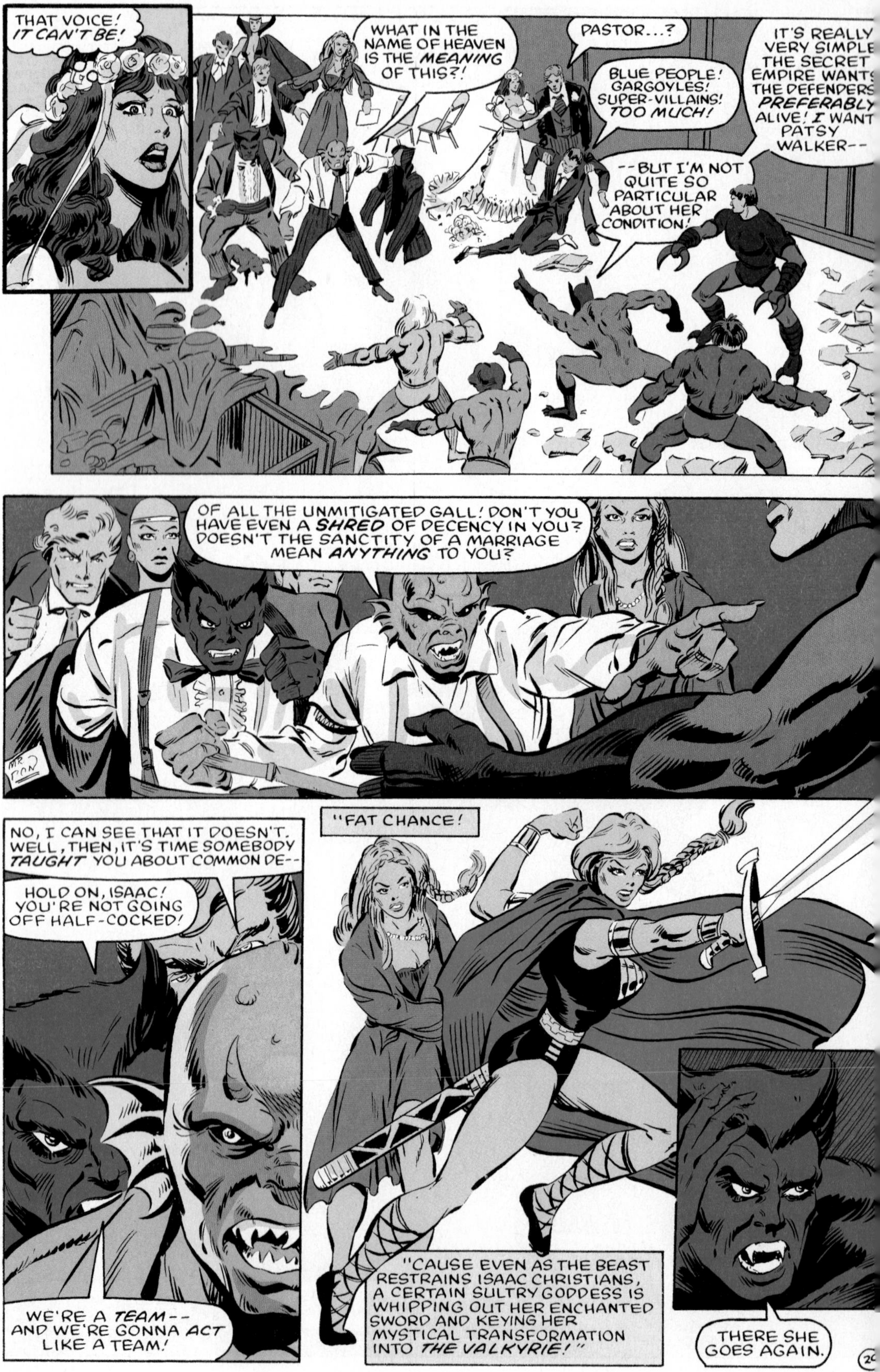
THAT VOICE! IT CAN'T BE!
WHAT IN THE NAME OF HEAVEN IS THE MEANING OF THIS?!
PASTOR...?
BLUE PEOPLE! GARGOYLES! SUPER-VILLAINS! TOO MUCH!
IT'S REALLY VERY SIMPLE THE SECRET EMPIRE WANTS THE DEFENDERS PREFERABLY ALIVE! I WANT PATSY WALKER--
--BUT I'M NOT QUITE SO PARTICULAR ABOUT HER CONDITION!
OF ALL THE UNMITIGATED GALL! DON'T YOU HAVE EVEN A SHRED OF DECENCY IN YOU? DOESN'T THE SANCTITY OF A MARRIAGE MEAN ANYTHING TO YOU?
NO, I CAN SEE THAT IT DOESN'T. WELL, THEN, IT'S TIME SOMEBODY TAUGHT YOU ABOUT COMMON DE--
HOLD ON, ISAAC! YOU'RE NOT GOING OFF HALF-COCKED!
WE'RE A TEAM-- AND WE'RE GONNA ACT LIKE A TEAM!
"FAT CHANCE!
"CAUSE EVEN AS THE BEAST RESTRAINS ISAAC CHRISTIANS, A CERTAIN SULTRY GODDESS IS WHIPPING OUT HER ENCHANTED SWORD AND KEYING HER MYSTICAL TRANSFORMATION INTO THE VALKYRIE!"
THERE SHE GOES AGAIN.

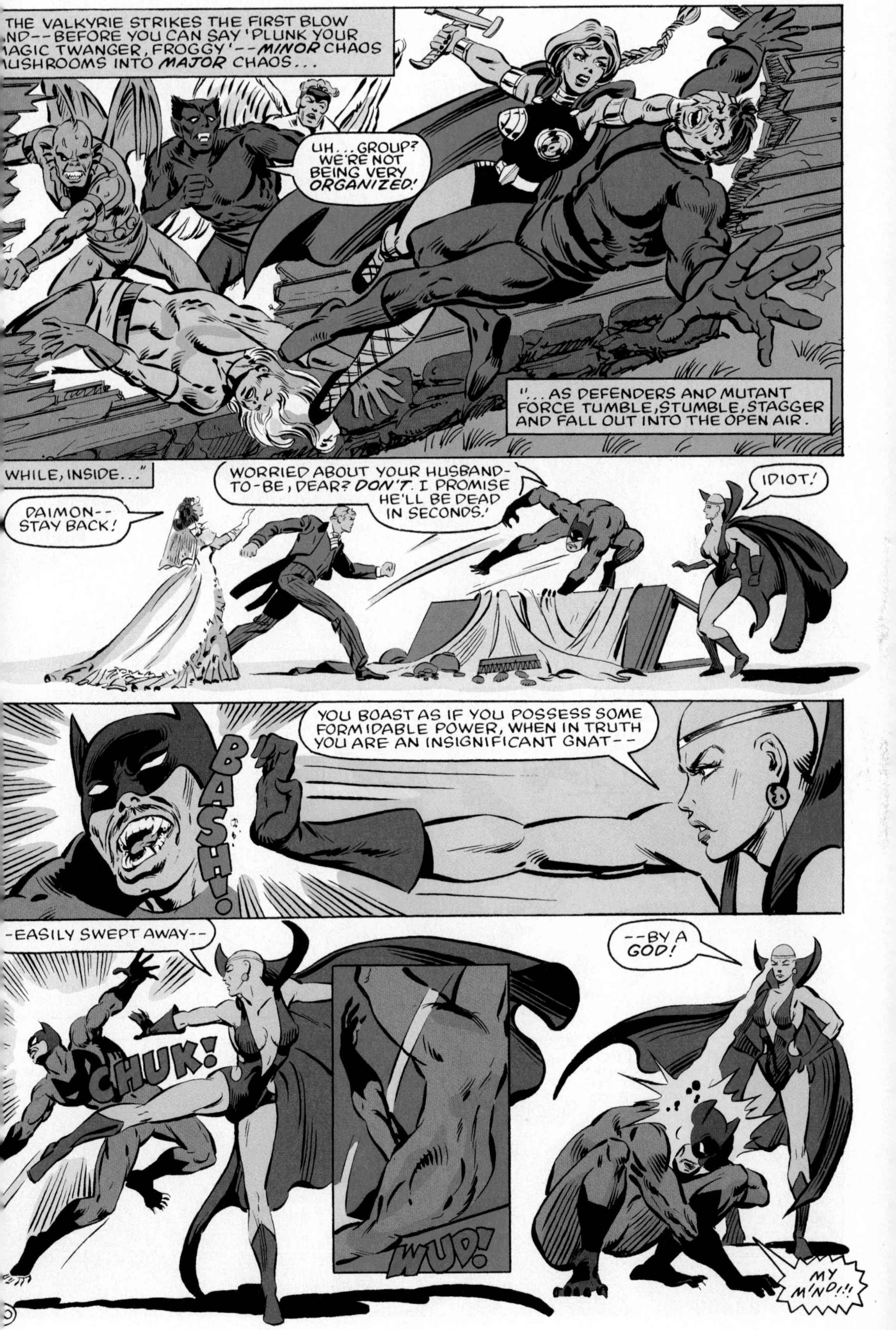
THE VALKYRIE STRIKES THE FIRST BLOW
ND--BEFORE YOU CAN SAY 'PLUNK YOUR
AGIC TWANGER, FROGGY'--MINOR CHAOS
USHROOMS INTO MAJOR CHAOS...
UH...GROUP? WE'RE NOT BEING VERY ORGANIZED!
"...AS DEFENDERS AND MUTANT FORCE TUMBLE, STUMBLE, STAGGER AND FALL OUT INTO THE OPEN AIR.
WHILE, INSIDE..."
DAIMON-- STAY BACK!
WORRIED ABOUT YOUR HUSBAND-TO-BE, DEAR? DON'T. I PROMISE HE'LL BE DEAD IN SECONDS!
IDIOT!
YOU BOAST AS IF YOU POSSESS SOME FORMIDABLE POWER, WHEN IN TRUTH YOU ARE AN INSIGNIFICANT GNAT--
BASH!
-EASILY SWEPT AWAY--
CHUK!
WUD!
--BY A GOD!
MY M'ND!!!

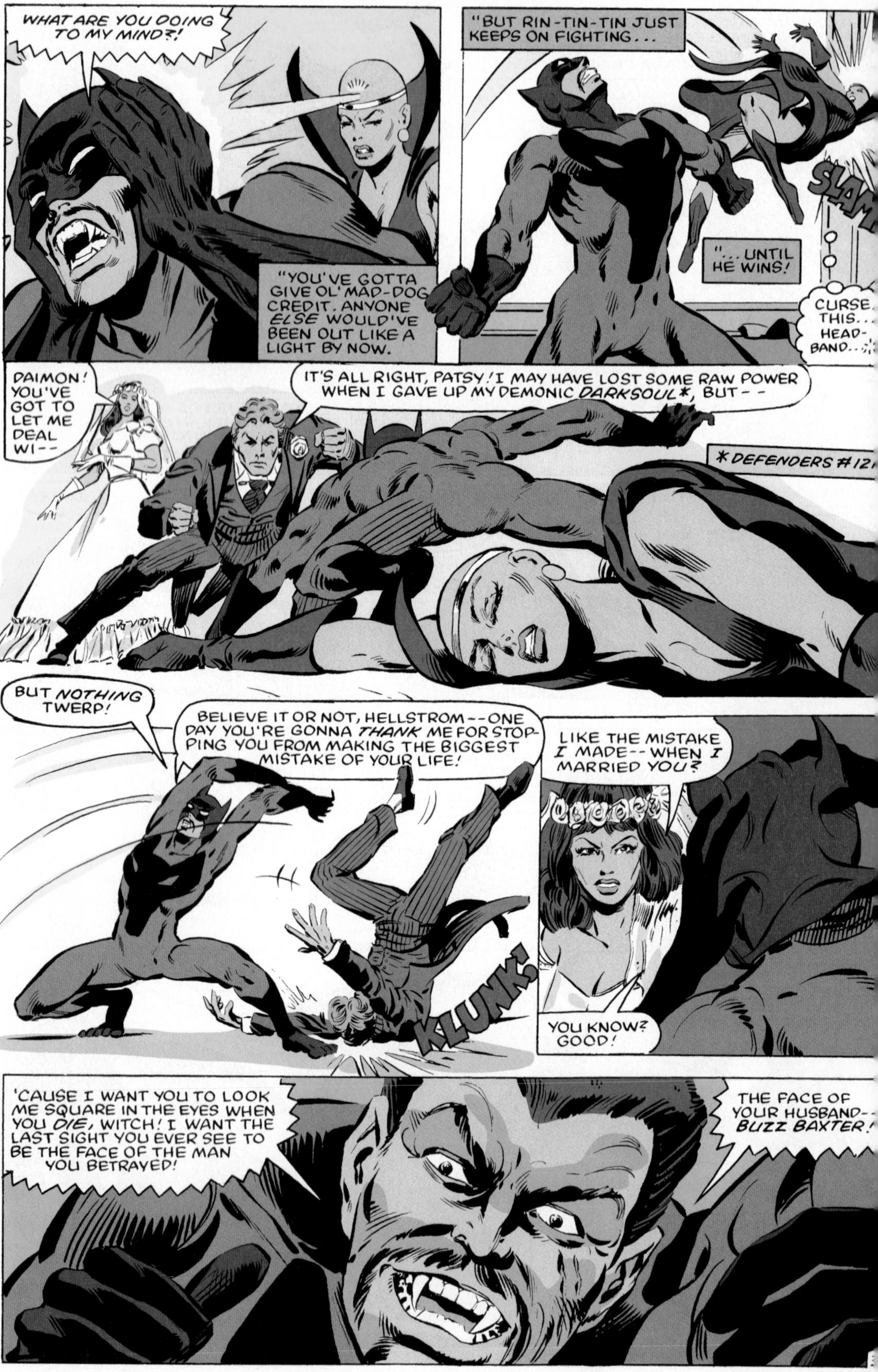
WHAT ARE YOU DOING TO MY MIND?!
"YOU'VE GOTTA GIVE OL' MAD-DOG CREDIT. ANYONE ELSE WOULD'VE BEEN OUT LIKE A LIGHT BY NOW.
"BUT RIN-TIN-TIN JUST KEEPS ON FIGHTING...
SLAM
"...UNTIL HE WINS!
CURSE... THIS... HEAD-BAND...
DAIMON! YOU'VE GOT TO LET ME DEAL WI--
IT'S ALL RIGHT, PATSY! I MAY HAVE LOST SOME RAW POWER WHEN I GAVE UP MY DEMONIC DARKSOUL*, BUT--
*DEFENDERS #12
BUT NOTHING TWERP!
BELIEVE IT OR NOT, HELLSTROM--ONE DAY YOU'RE GONNA THANK ME FOR STOPPING YOU FROM MAKING THE BIGGEST MISTAKE OF YOUR LIFE!
KLUNK!
LIKE THE MISTAKE I MADE--WHEN I MARRIED YOU?
YOU KNOW? GOOD!
'CAUSE I WANT YOU TO LOOK ME SQUARE IN THE EYES WHEN YOU DIE, WITCH! I WANT THE LAST SIGHT YOU EVER SEE TO BE THE FACE OF THE MAN YOU BETRAYED!
THE FACE OF YOUR HUSBAND--BUZZ BAXTER!

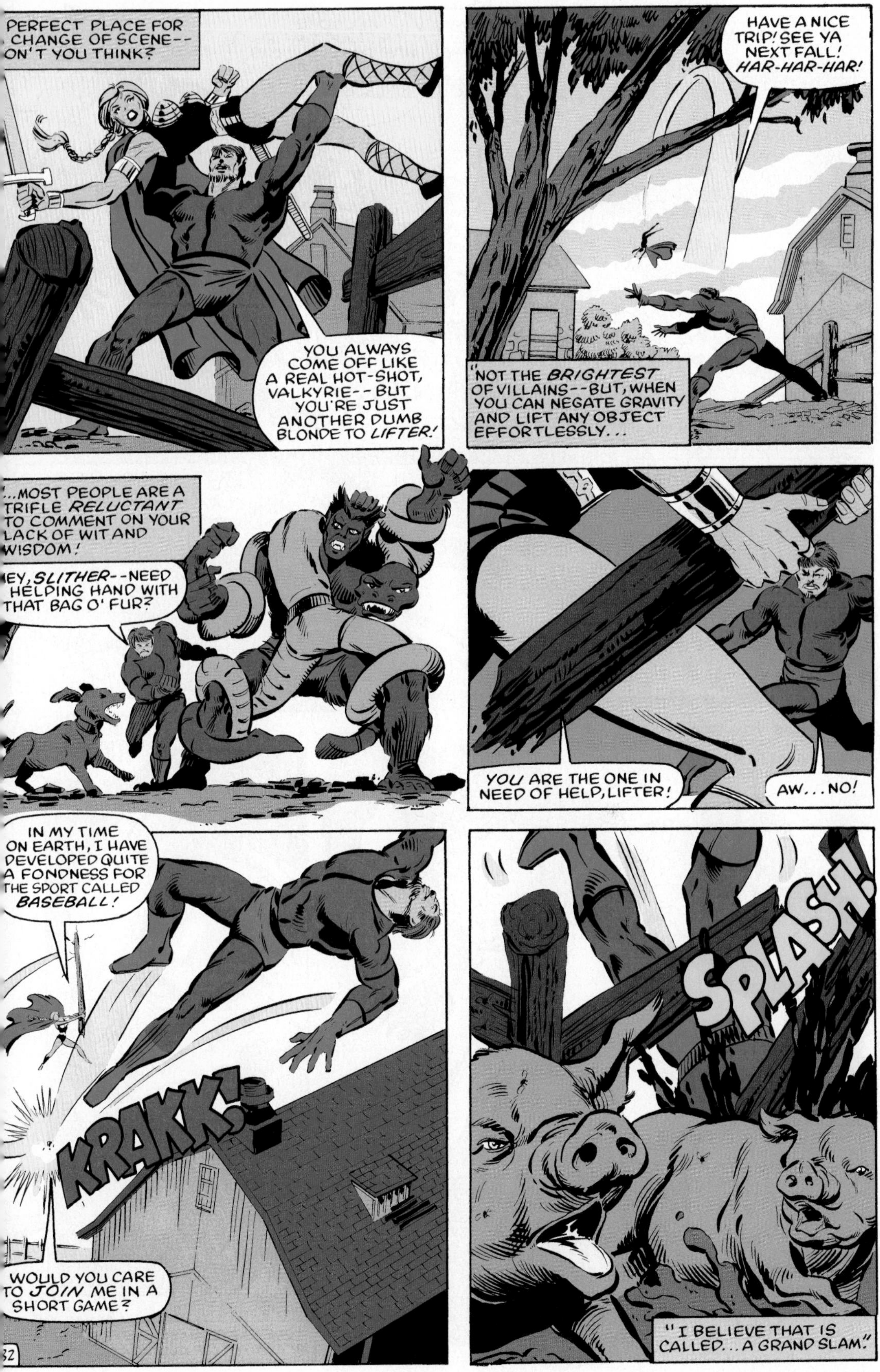

PERFECT PLACE FOR CHANGE OF SCENE-- ON'T YOU THINK?
YOU ALWAYS COME OFF LIKE A REAL HOT-SHOT, VALKYRIE--BUT YOU'RE JUST ANOTHER DUMB BLONDE TO LIFTER!
HAVE A NICE TRIP! SEE YA NEXT FALL! HAR-HAR-HAR!
"NOT THE BRIGHTEST OF VILLAINS--BUT, WHEN YOU CAN NEGATE GRAVITY AND LIFT ANY OBJECT EFFORTLESSLY...
...MOST PEOPLE ARE A TRIFLE RELUCTANT TO COMMENT ON YOUR LACK OF WIT AND WISDOM!
EY, SLITHER--NEED HELPING HAND WITH THAT BAG O' FUR?
YOU ARE THE ONE IN NEED OF HELP, LIFTER!
AW...NO!
IN MY TIME ON EARTH, I HAVE DEVELOPED QUITE A FONDNESS FOR THE SPORT CALLED BASEBALL!
KRAKK!
WOULD YOU CARE TO JOIN ME IN A SHORT GAME?
32
SPLASH!
"I BELIEVE THAT IS CALLED...A GRAND SLAM."

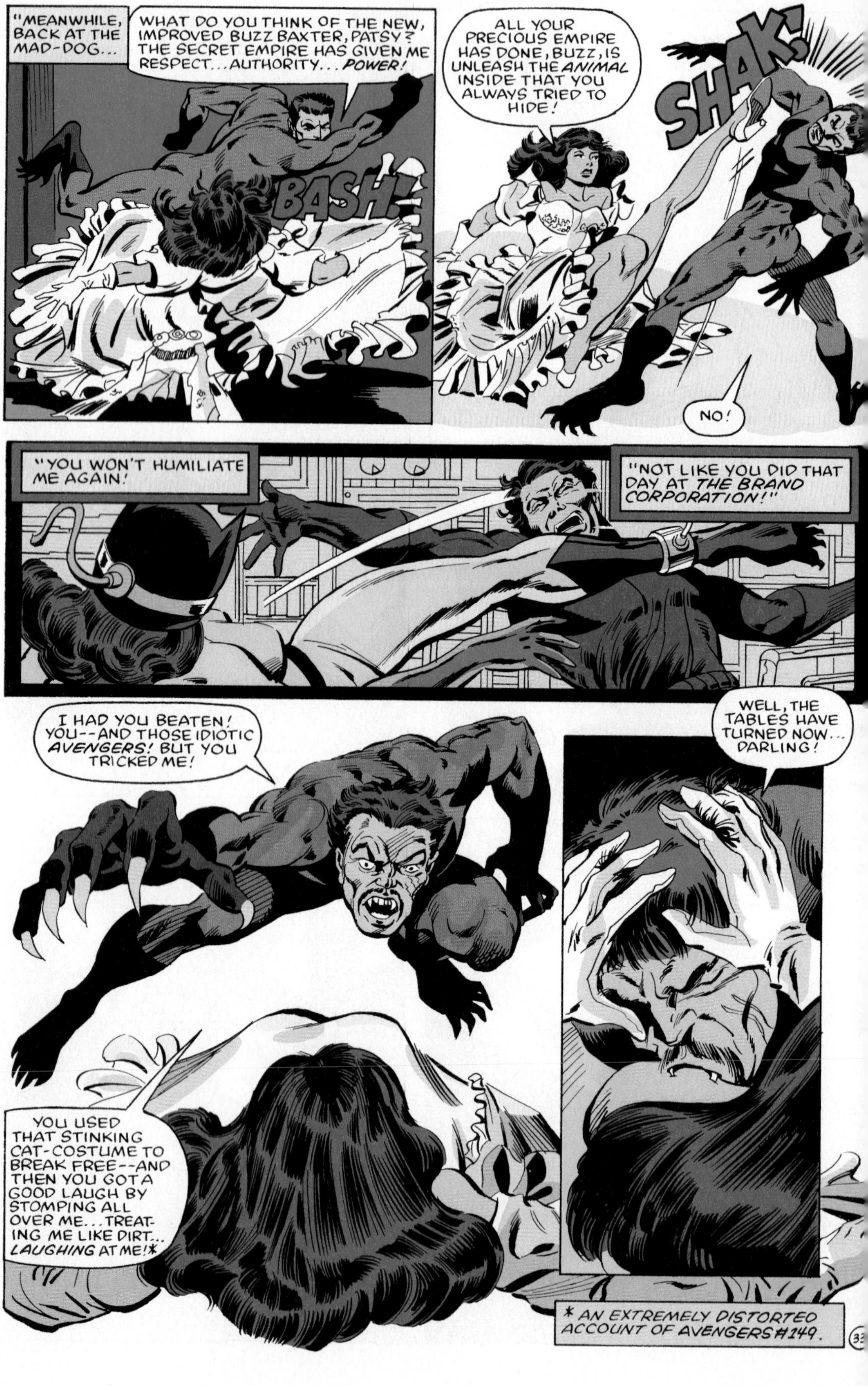
"MEANWHILE, BACK AT THE MAD-DOG...
WHAT DO YOU THINK OF THE NEW, IMPROVED BUZZ BAXTER, PATSY? THE SECRET EMPIRE HAS GIVEN ME RESPECT... AUTHORITY... POWER!
BASH!
ALL YOUR PRECIOUS EMPIRE HAS DONE, BUZZ, IS UNLEASH THE ANIMAL INSIDE THAT YOU ALWAYS TRIED TO HIDE!
SHAK!
NO!
"YOU WON'T HUMILIATE ME AGAIN!
"NOT LIKE YOU DID THAT DAY AT THE BRAND CORPORATION!"
I HAD YOU BEATEN! YOU--AND THOSE IDIOTIC AVENGERS! BUT YOU TRICKED ME!
YOU USED THAT STINKING CAT-COSTUME TO BREAK FREE--AND THEN YOU GOT A GOOD LAUGH BY STOMPING ALL OVER ME... TREATING ME LIKE DIRT... LAUGHING AT ME!*
WELL, THE TABLES HAVE TURNED NOW... DARLING!
* AN EXTREMELY DISTORTED ACCOUNT OF AVENGERS #149.
33

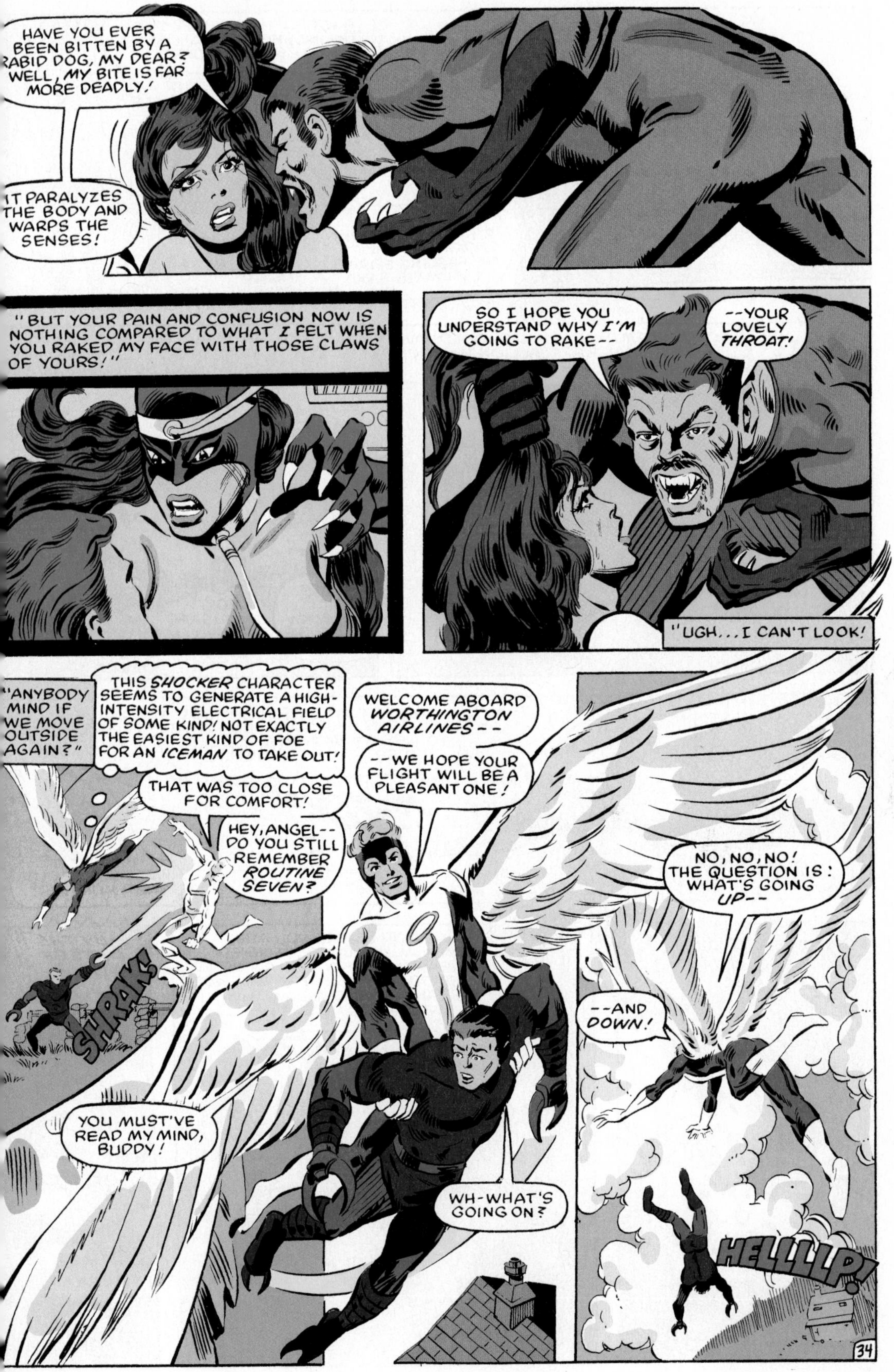
HAVE YOU EVER BEEN BITTEN BY A RABID DOG, MY DEAR? WELL, MY BITE IS FAR MORE DEADLY!
IT PARALYZES THE BODY AND WARPS THE SENSES!
"BUT YOUR PAIN AND CONFUSION NOW IS NOTHING COMPARED TO WHAT I FELT WHEN YOU RAKED MY FACE WITH THOSE CLAWS OF YOURS!"
SO I HOPE YOU UNDERSTAND WHY I'M GOING TO RAKE--
--YOUR LOVELY THROAT!
"UGH... I CAN'T LOOK!
"ANYBODY MIND IF WE MOVE OUTSIDE AGAIN?"
THIS SHOCKER CHARACTER SEEMS TO GENERATE A HIGH-INTENSITY ELECTRICAL FIELD OF SOME KIND! NOT EXACTLY THE EASIEST KIND OF FOE FOR AN ICEMAN TO TAKE OUT!
THAT WAS TOO CLOSE FOR COMFORT!
HEY, ANGEL-- DO YOU STILL REMEMBER ROUTINE SEVEN?
SHRAK!
YOU MUST'VE READ MY MIND, BUDDY!
WELCOME ABOARD WORTHINGTON AIRLINES--
--WE HOPE YOUR FLIGHT WILL BE A PLEASANT ONE!
WH-WHAT'S GOING ON?
NO, NO, NO! THE QUESTION IS: WHAT'S GOING UP--
--AND DOWN!
HELLLLP!
34

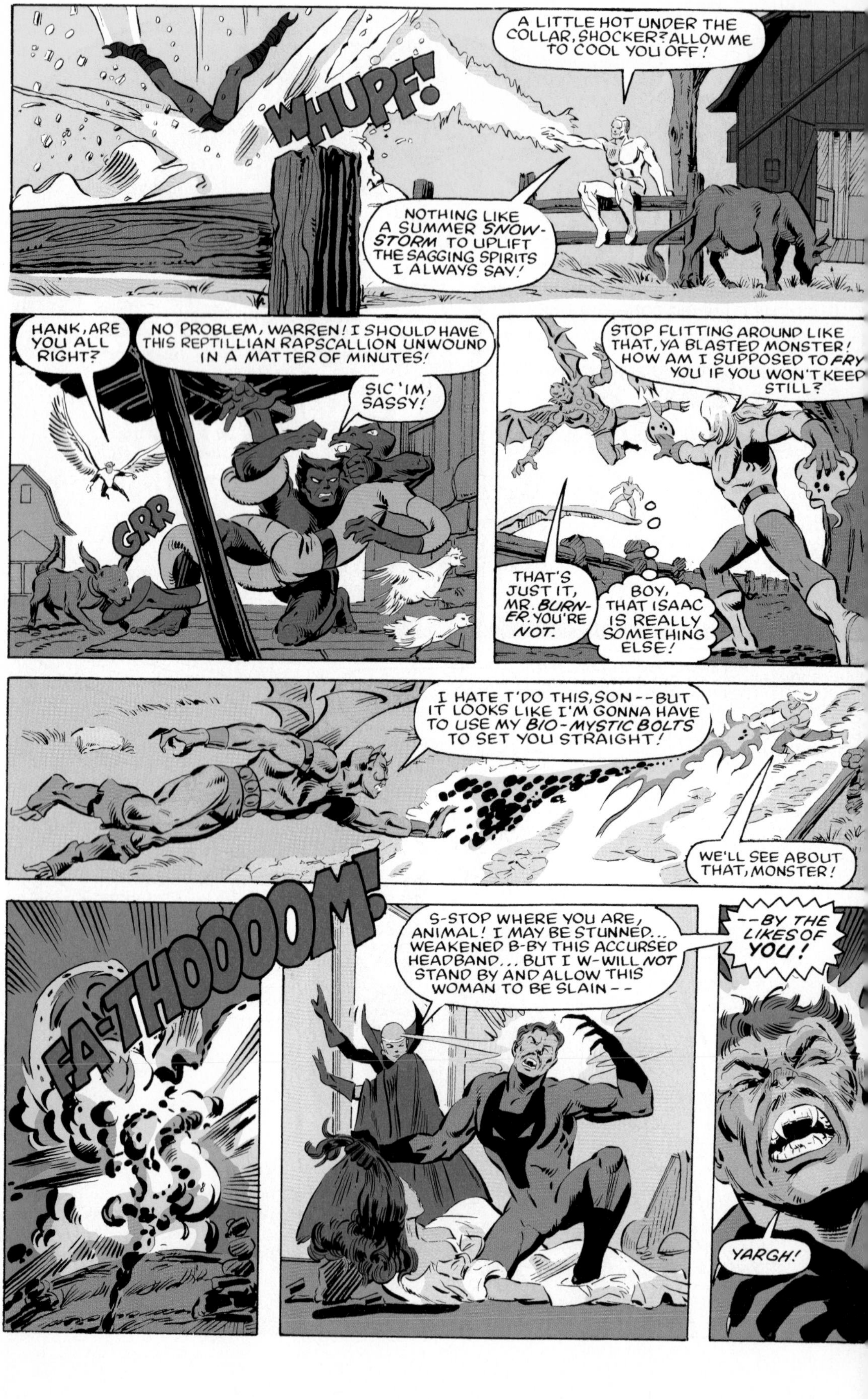
A LITTLE HOT UNDER THE COLLAR, SHOCKER? ALLOW ME TO COOL YOU OFF!
WHUPF!
NOTHING LIKE A SUMMER SNOW-STORM TO UPLIFT THE SAGGING SPIRITS I ALWAYS SAY!
HANK, ARE YOU ALL RIGHT?
NO PROBLEM, WARREN! I SHOULD HAVE THIS REPTILLIAN RAPSCALLION UNWOUND IN A MATTER OF MINUTES!
SIC 'IM, SASSY!
GRR
STOP FLITTING AROUND LIKE THAT, YA BLASTED MONSTER! HOW AM I SUPPOSED TO FRY YOU IF YOU WON'T KEEP STILL?
THAT'S JUST IT, MR. BURNER. YOU'RE NOT.
BOY, THAT ISAAC IS REALLY SOMETHING ELSE!
I HATE T'DO THIS, SON--BUT IT LOOKS LIKE I'M GONNA HAVE TO USE MY BIO-MYSTIC BOLTS TO SET YOU STRAIGHT!
WE'LL SEE ABOUT THAT, MONSTER!
FA-THOOOOM!
S-STOP WHERE YOU ARE, ANIMAL! I MAY BE STUNNED... WEAKENED B-BY THIS ACCURSED HEADBAND... BUT I W-WILL NOT STAND BY AND ALLOW THIS WOMAN TO BE SLAIN--
--BY THE LIKES OF YOU!
YARGH!

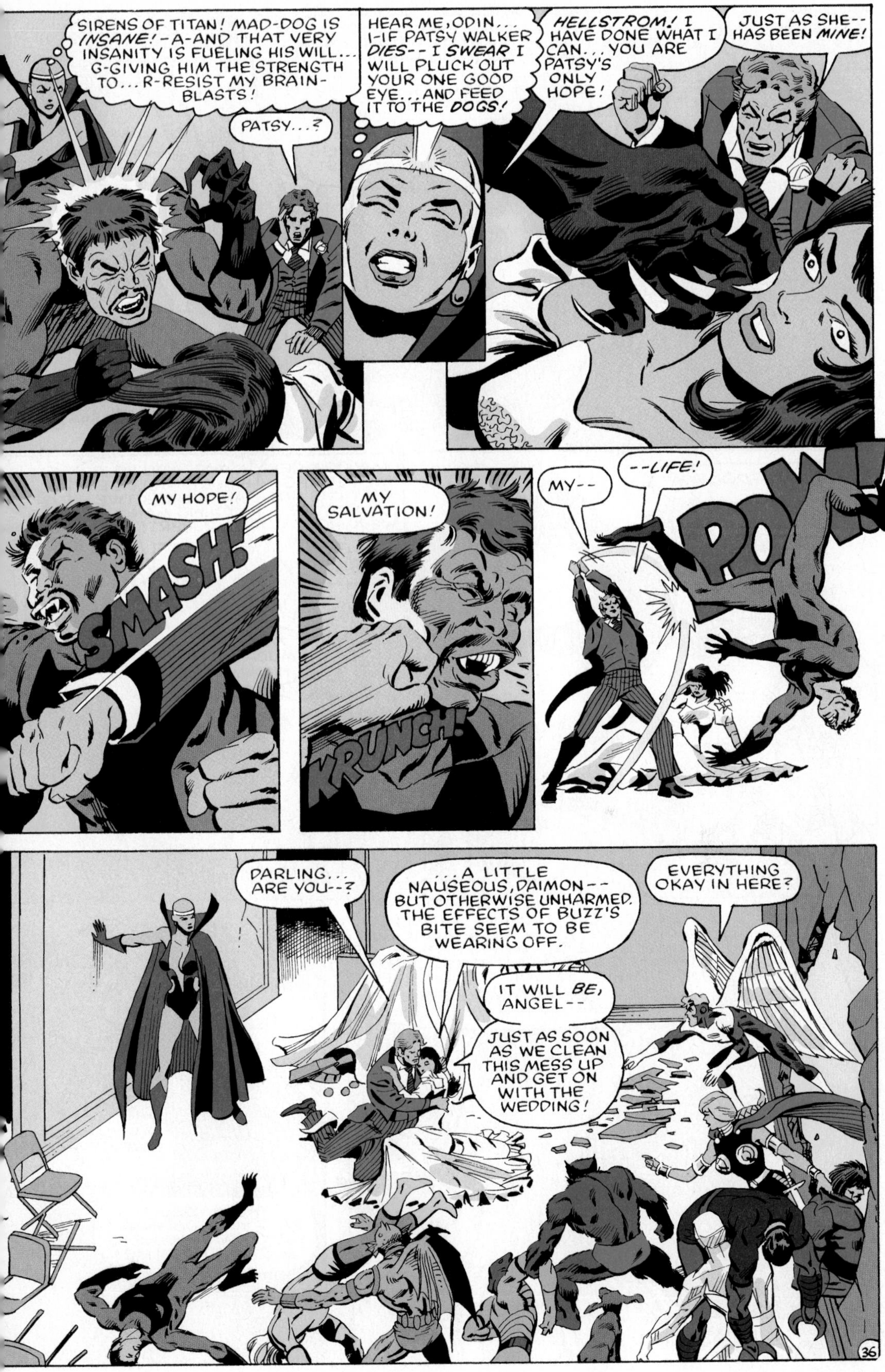

SIRENS OF TITAN! MAD-DOG IS INSANE! -A-AND THAT VERY INSANITY IS FUELING HIS WILL... G-GIVING HIM THE STRENGTH TO... R-RESIST MY BRAIN-BLASTS!
PATSY...?
HEAR ME, ODIN... I-IF PATSY WALKER DIES-- I SWEAR I WILL PLUCK OUT YOUR ONE GOOD EYE... AND FEED IT TO THE DOGS!
HELLSTROM! I HAVE DONE WHAT I CAN... YOU ARE PATSY'S ONLY HOPE!
JUST AS SHE-- HAS BEEN MINE!
MY HOPE!
SMASH!
MY SALVATION!
KRUNCH!
MY--
--LIFE!
POW!
DARLING... ARE YOU--?
...A LITTLE NAUSEOUS, DAIMON-- BUT OTHERWISE UNHARMED. THE EFFECTS OF BUZZ'S BITE SEEM TO BE WEARING OFF.
EVERYTHING OKAY IN HERE?
IT WILL BE, ANGEL--
JUST AS SOON AS WE CLEAN THIS MESS UP AND GET ON WITH THE WEDDING!
36

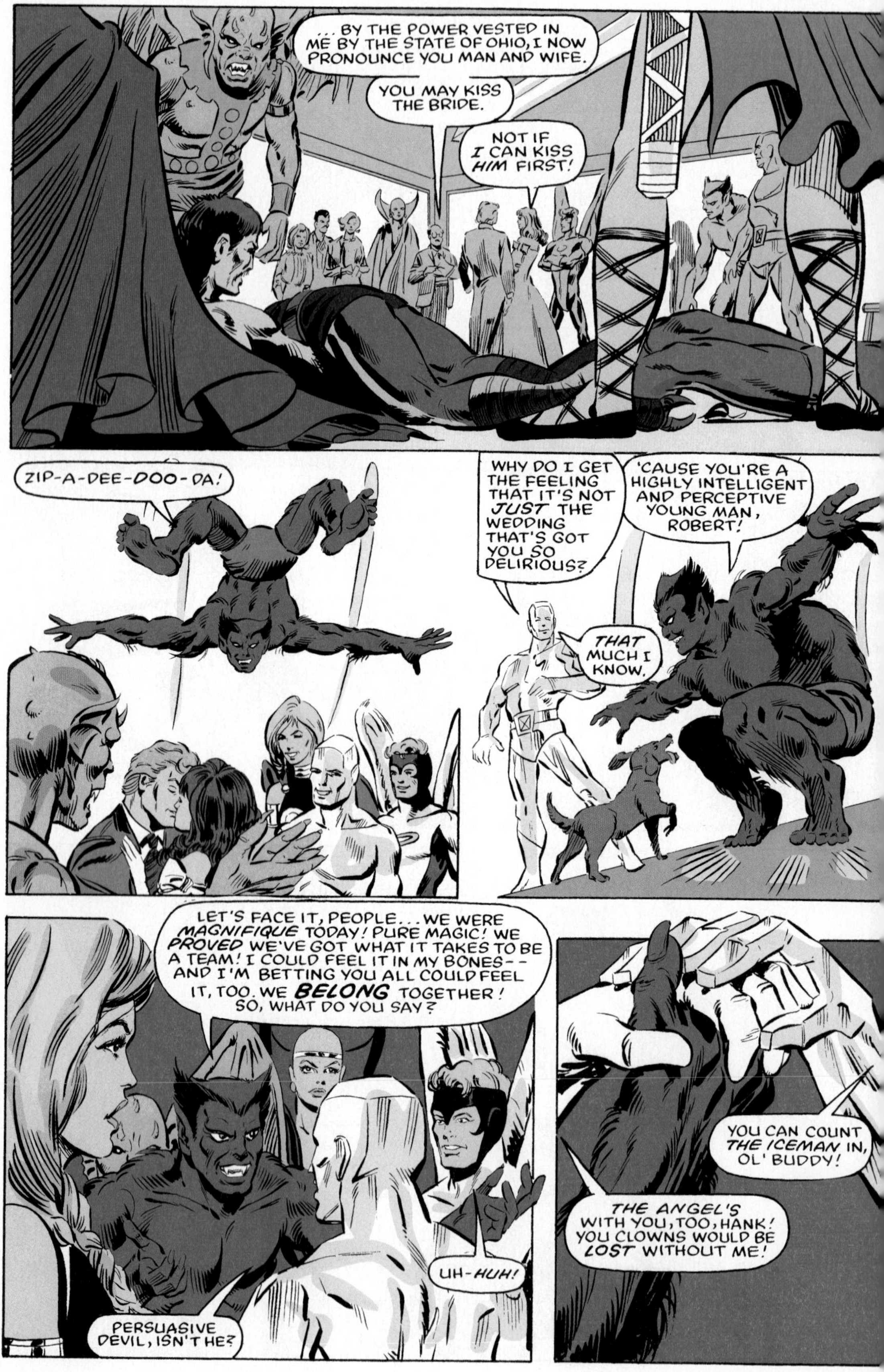
...BY THE POWER VESTED IN ME BY THE STATE OF OHIO, I NOW PRONOUNCE YOU MAN AND WIFE.
YOU MAY KISS THE BRIDE.
NOT IF I CAN KISS HIM FIRST!
ZIP-A-DEE-DOO-DA!
WHY DO I GET THE FEELING THAT IT'S NOT JUST THE WEDDING THAT'S GOT YOU SO DELIRIOUS?
'CAUSE YOU'RE A HIGHLY INTELLIGENT AND PERCEPTIVE YOUNG MAN, ROBERT!
THAT MUCH I KNOW.
LET'S FACE IT, PEOPLE... WE WERE MAGNIFIQUE TODAY! PURE MAGIC! WE PROVED WE'VE GOT WHAT IT TAKES TO BE A TEAM! I COULD FEEL IT IN MY BONES-- AND I'M BETTING YOU ALL COULD FEEL IT, TOO. WE BELONG TOGETHER! SO, WHAT DO YOU SAY?
UH-HUH!
PERSUASIVE DEVIL, ISN'T HE?
YOU CAN COUNT THE ICEMAN IN, OL' BUDDY!
THE ANGEL'S WITH YOU, TOO, HANK! YOU CLOWNS WOULD BE LOST WITHOUT ME!

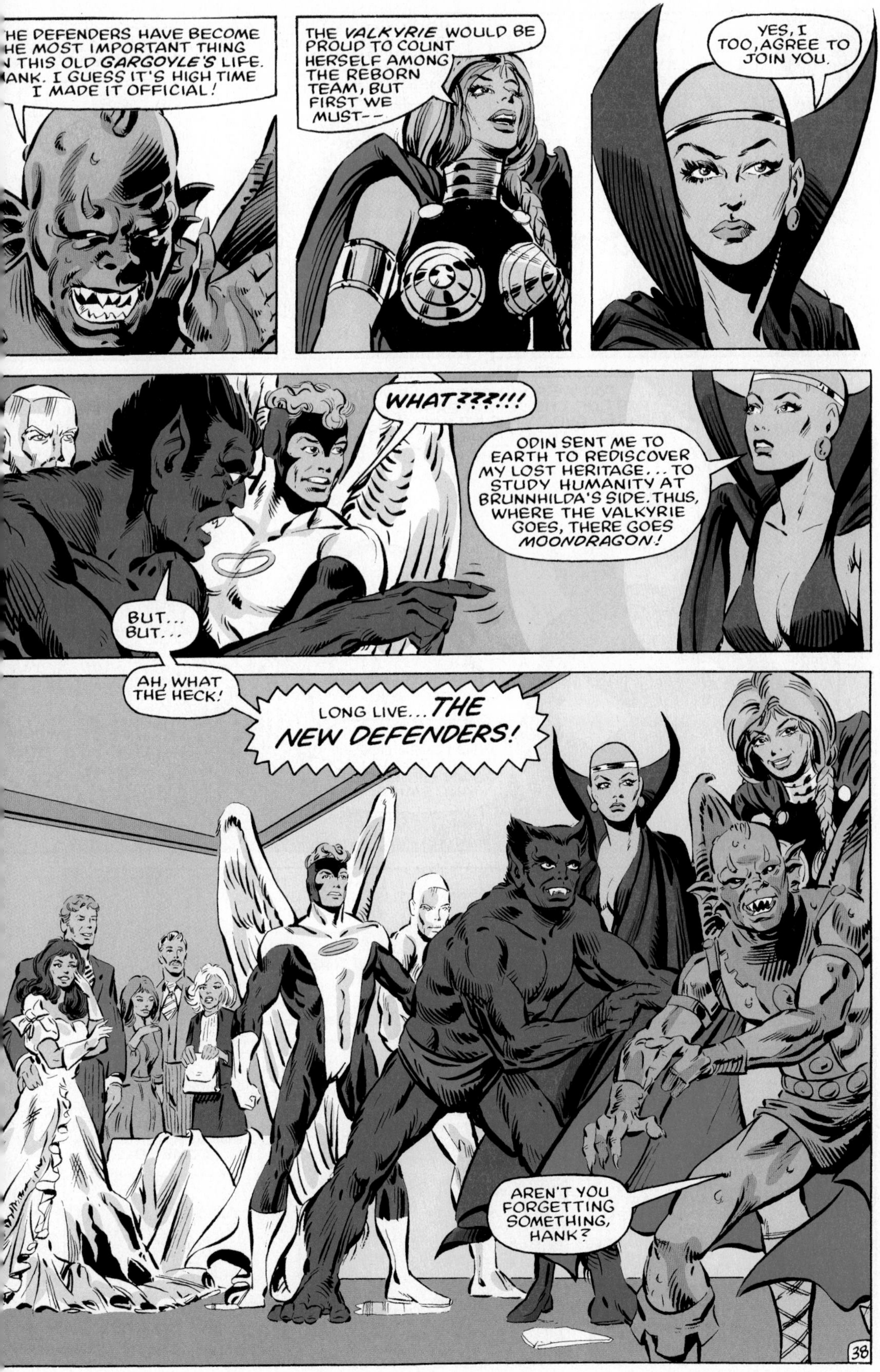
HE DEFENDERS HAVE BECOME HE MOST IMPORTANT THING N THIS OLD GARGOYLE'S LIFE. ANK. I GUESS IT'S HIGH TIME I MADE IT OFFICIAL!
THE VALKYRIE WOULD BE PROUD TO COUNT HERSELF AMONG THE REBORN TEAM, BUT FIRST WE MUST--
YES, I TOO, AGREE TO JOIN YOU.
WHAT???!!!
ODIN SENT ME TO EARTH TO REDISCOVER MY LOST HERITAGE... TO STUDY HUMANITY AT BRUNNHILDA'S SIDE. THUS, WHERE THE VALKYRIE GOES, THERE GOES MOONDRAGON!
BUT... BUT...
AH, WHAT THE HECK!
LONG LIVE... THE NEW DEFENDERS!
AREN'T YOU FORGETTING SOMETHING, HANK?
38

WHAT OF THE **OLD** DEFENDERS?

DOC! AW, GEEZ--I'M SORRY! Y'KNOW, I NEVER EVEN CONSIDERED--

DON'T GIVE IT A SECOND THOUGHT, HANK. AS IT IS, YOURS WAS THE WISEST DECISION THAT COULD HAVE BEEN MADE!

IN FACT, ONE MIGHT EVEN SAY--

--IT WAS... **KARMA**.

FOR WE FOUR ARE PART OF THE DEFENDERS' **PAST**--AND CAN NEVER MORE MOLD THEIR FUTURE!

THAT **FUTURE** WE NOW HAND OVER TO YOU, TO DO WITH AS YOU WILL.

GOOD LUCK, FRIENDS. REMEMBER US. THINK **WELL** OF US.

AND MAY WHATEVER GODS YOU HOLD DEAR LOOK DOWN UPON YOU... AND SMILE.

NOW WHAT WAS **THAT** ALL ABOUT?

I THINK... THEY JUST GAVE US THEIR **BLESSINGS!**

Y'KNOW, I THINK YOU'RE **RIGHT!**

SO THAT'S THE SCOOP, LADIES AND GENTS! OUT WITH THE OLD, IN WITH THE NEW! I'M NOT MAKING ANY GUESSES ABOUT THIS NEW NEW TEAM'S CHANCES FOR SUCCESS--

--BUT YOU CAN BET I'LL BE HERE NEXT ISSUE TO NARRATE IN MY OWN INIMATABLE STYLE, INTER-JECTING SUBTLE HUMOR PROFOUND WISDOM AN--

SO **THERE** YOU ARE!

THE TRIBUNAL HAD ME LOOKING ALL OVER FOR YOU--BUT SOMEHOW I JUST **KNEW** YOU'D BE HERE!

GO **WAY**, WILL YA? YOU'RE CRAMPIN' MY STYLE!

I'LL GIVE YOU A CRAMP IN THAT FAT **HEAD** OF YOURS IF YOU DON'T COME WITH ME RIGHT **NOW!** AND AS FOR **YOU** OUT THERE... GO SOAK YOUR HEADS OR SOMETHING? DON'T YOU KNOW WHEN A STORY'S COME TO...

THE END?

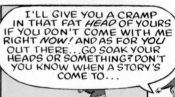

430

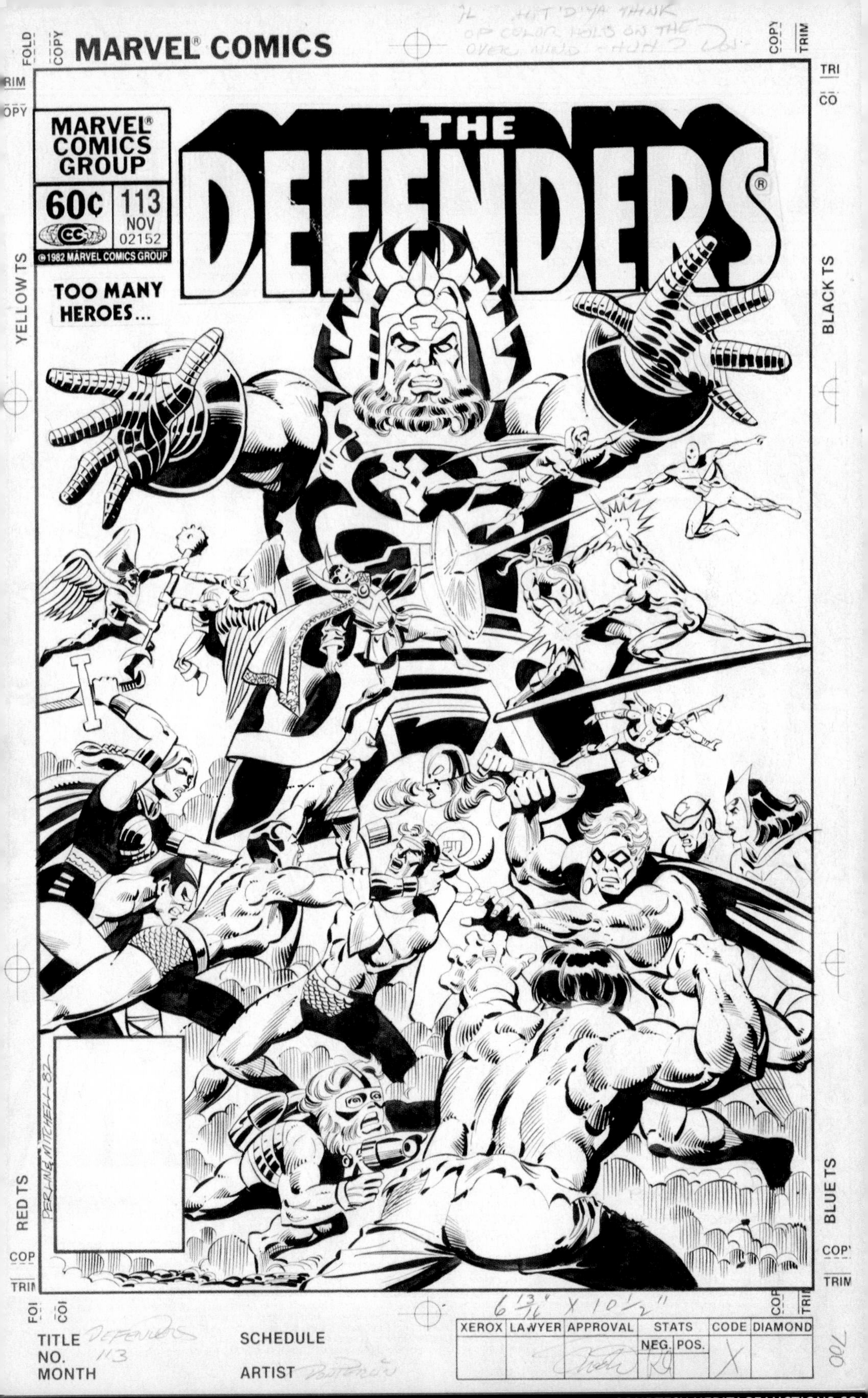
MARVEL COMICS
MARVEL COMICS GROUP
60¢
113
NOV
02152
©1982 MARVEL COMICS GROUP
THE DEFENDERS
TOO MANY HEROES...
PERLIN & MITCHELL 82
TITLE
NO.
MONTH
SCHEDULE
ARTIST
XEROX
LAWYER
APPROVAL
STATS
NEG.
POS.
CODE
DIAMOND

DEFENDERS #113 COVER ORIGINAL ART BY DON PERLIN & STEVE MITCHELL

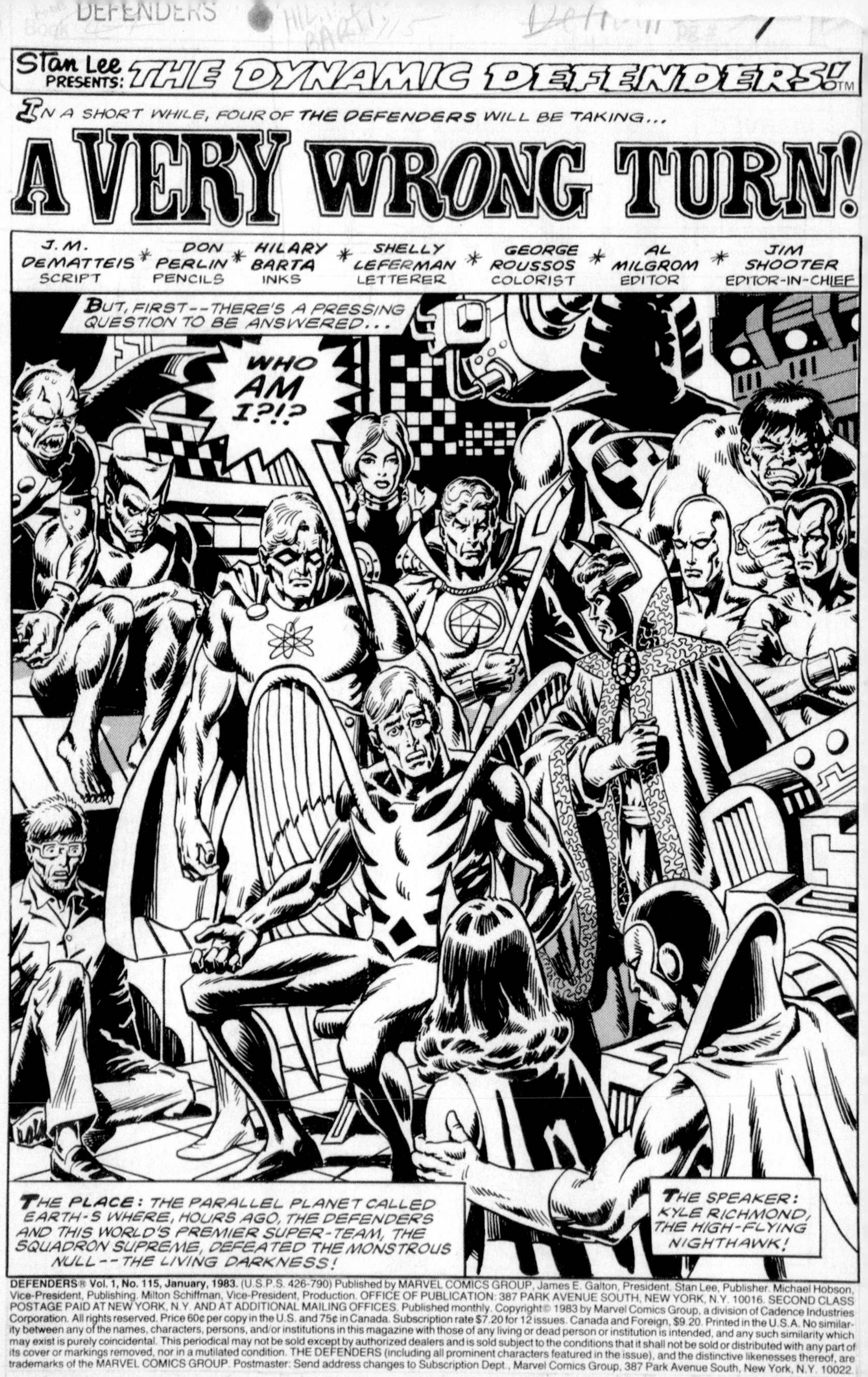

DEFENDERS
Stan Lee PRESENTS: THE DYNAMIC DEFENDERS!™
IN A SHORT WHILE, FOUR OF THE DEFENDERS WILL BE TAKING...
A VERY WRONG TURN!
J. M. DEMATTEIS SCRIPT * DON PERLIN PENCILS * HILARY BARTA INKS * SHELLY LEFERMAN LETTERER * GEORGE ROUSSOS COLORIST * AL MILGROM EDITOR * JIM SHOOTER EDITOR-IN-CHIEF
BUT, FIRST--THERE'S A PRESSING QUESTION TO BE ANSWERED...
WHO AM I?!?
THE PLACE: THE PARALLEL PLANET CALLED EARTH-S WHERE, HOURS AGO, THE DEFENDERS AND THIS WORLD'S PREMIER SUPER-TEAM, THE SQUADRON SUPREME, DEFEATED THE MONSTROUS NULL--THE LIVING DARKNESS!
THE SPEAKER: KYLE RICHMOND, THE HIGH-FLYING NIGHTHAWK!
DEFENDERS® Vol. 1, No. 115, January, 1983. (U.S.P.S. 426-790) Published by MARVEL COMICS GROUP, James E. Galton, President. Stan Lee, Publisher. Michael Hobson, Vice-President, Publishing. Milton Schiffman, Vice-President, Production. OFFICE OF PUBLICATION: 387 PARK AVENUE SOUTH, NEW YORK, N.Y. 10016. SECOND CLASS POSTAGE PAID AT NEW YORK, N.Y. AND AT ADDITIONAL MAILING OFFICES. Published monthly. Copyright © 1983 by Marvel Comics Group, a division of Cadence Industries Corporation. All rights reserved. Price 60¢ per copy in the U.S. and 75¢ in Canada. Subscription rate $7.20 for 12 issues. Canada and Foreign, $9.20. Printed in the U.S.A. No similarity between any of the names, characters, persons, and/or institutions in this magazine with those of any living or dead person or institution is intended, and any such similarity which may exist is purely coincidental. This periodical may not be sold except by authorized dealers and is sold subject to the conditions that it shall not be sold or distributed with any part of its cover or markings removed, nor in a mutilated condition. THE DEFENDERS (including all prominent characters featured in the issue), and the distinctive likenesses thereof, are trademarks of the MARVEL COMICS GROUP. Postmaster: Send address changes to Subscription Dept., Marvel Comics Group, 387 Park Avenue South, New York, N.Y. 10022.

COURTESY HERITAGEAUCTIONS.C

DEFENDERS #115, PAGE 1 ORIGINAL ART BY DON PERLIN & HILARY BARTA

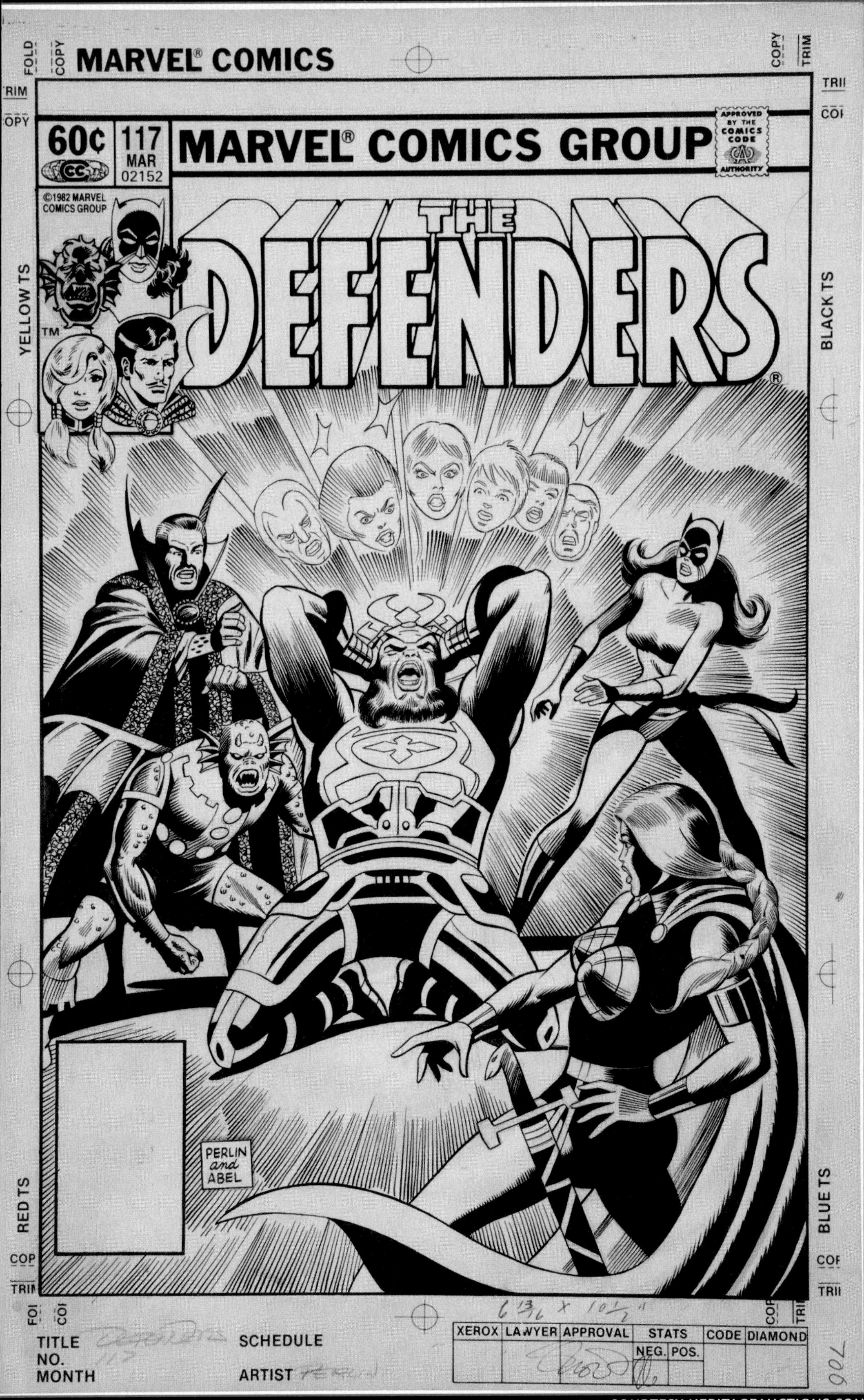
MARVEL COMICS
60¢
117
MAR
02152
MARVEL COMICS GROUP
APPROVED BY THE COMICS CODE AUTHORITY
©1982 MARVEL COMICS GROUP
THE DEFENDERS
PERLIN and ABEL
TITLE
NO.
MONTH
SCHEDULE
ARTIST
XEROX
LAWYER
APPROVAL
STATS
NEG.
POS.
CODE
DIAMOND

DEFENDERS **#117, COVER ORIGINAL ART, BY DON PERLIN & JACK ABEL**

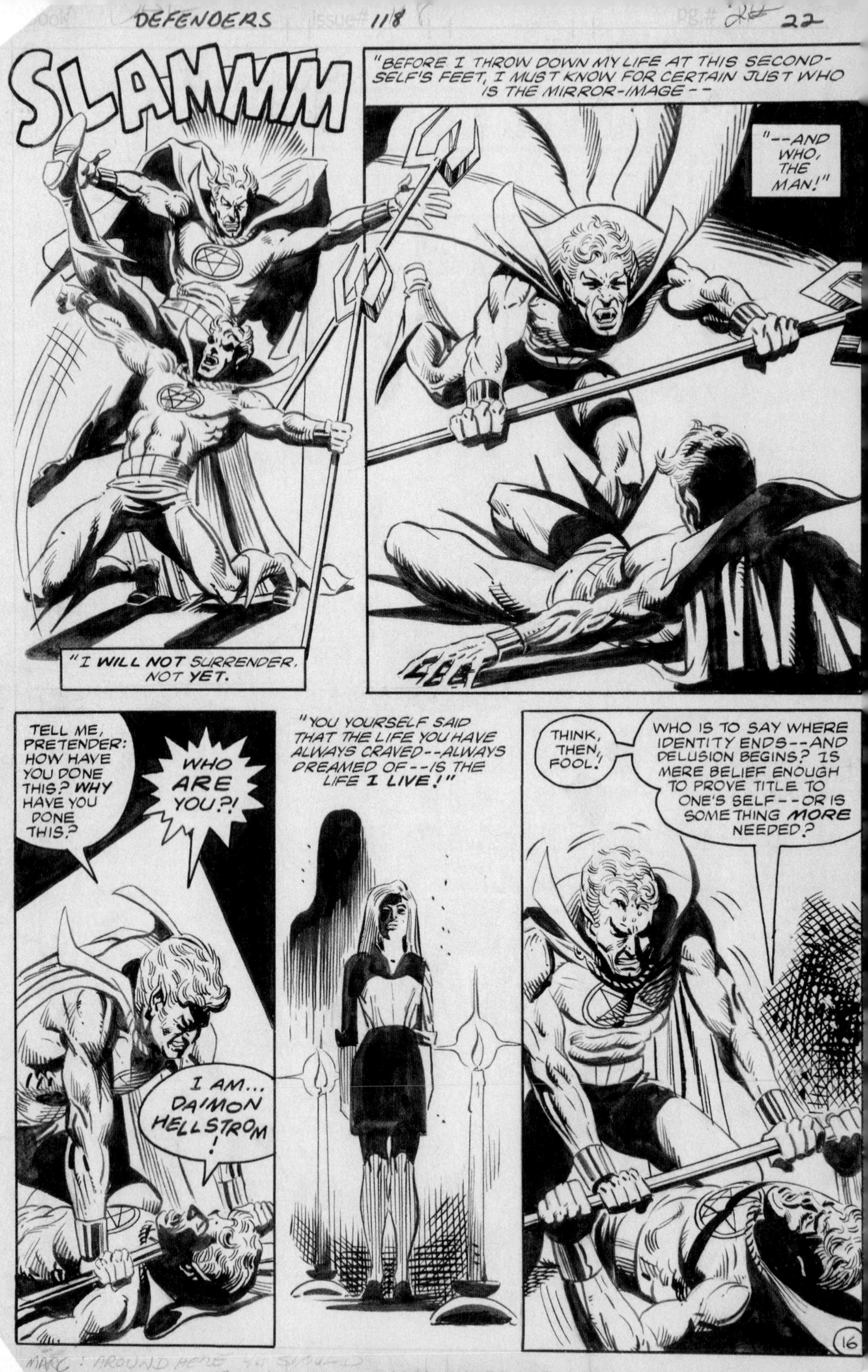
DEFENDERS issue# 118 pg.# 22
SLAMMMM
"BEFORE I THROW DOWN MY LIFE AT THIS SECOND-SELF'S FEET, I MUST KNOW FOR CERTAIN JUST WHO IS THE MIRROR-IMAGE--
"--AND WHO, THE MAN!"
"I WILL NOT SURRENDER. NOT YET.
TELL ME, PRETENDER: HOW HAVE YOU DONE THIS? WHY HAVE YOU DONE THIS?
WHO ARE YOU?!
I AM... DAIMON HELLSTROM!
"YOU YOURSELF SAID THAT THE LIFE YOU HAVE ALWAYS CRAVED--ALWAYS DREAMED OF--IS THE LIFE I LIVE!"
THINK, THEN, FOOL!
WHO IS TO SAY WHERE IDENTITY ENDS--AND DELUSION BEGINS? IS MERE BELIEF ENOUGH TO PROVE TITLE TO ONE'S SELF--OR IS SOMETHING MORE NEEDED?
16

DEFENDERS #118, PAGE 16 ORIGINAL ART BY DON PERLIN & AL MILGROM

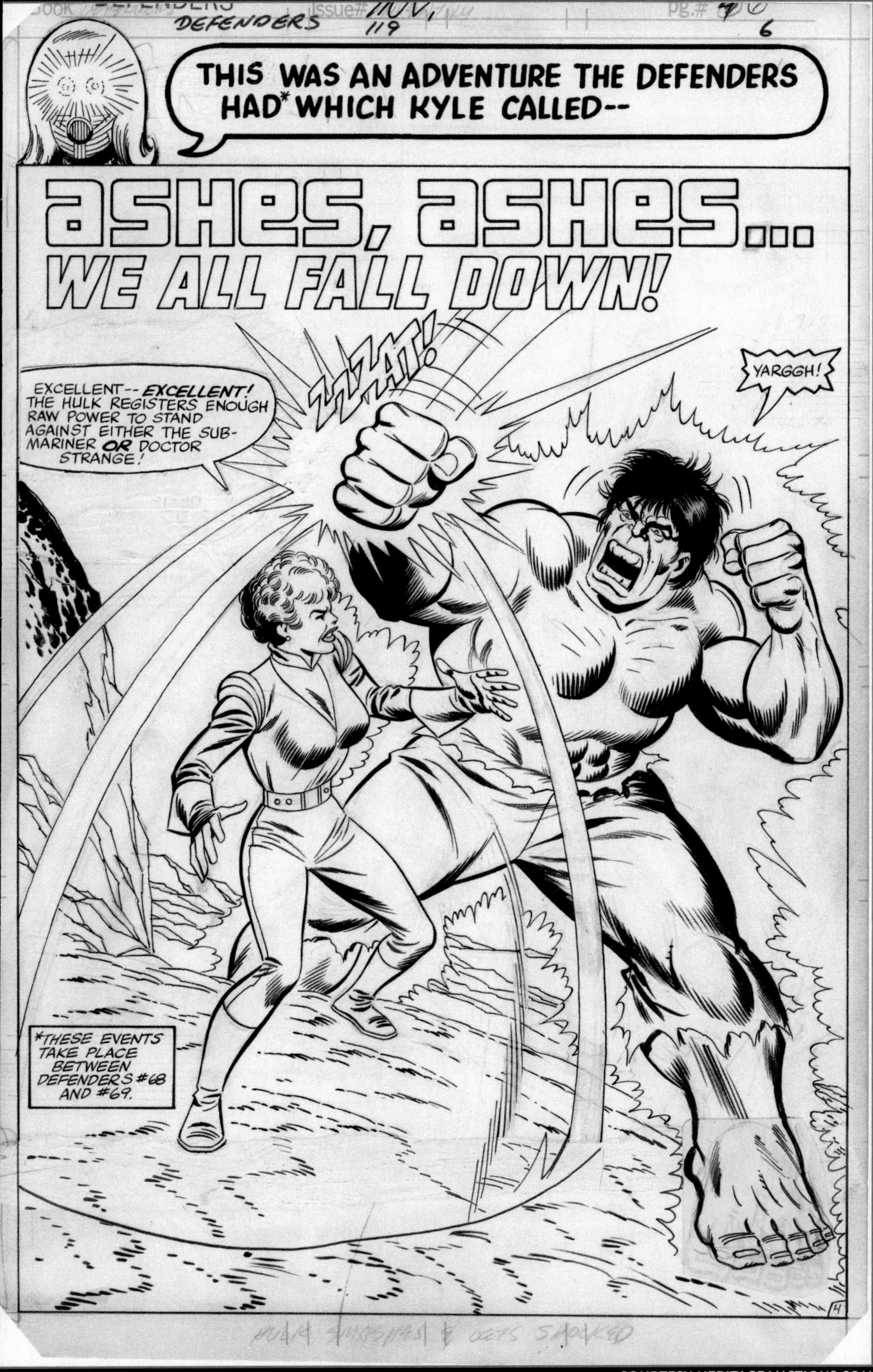

DEFENDERS 119 6
THIS WAS AN ADVENTURE THE DEFENDERS HAD* WHICH KYLE CALLED--
ASHES, ASHES... WE ALL FALL DOWN!
EXCELLENT-- EXCELLENT! THE HULK REGISTERS ENOUGH RAW POWER TO STAND AGAINST EITHER THE SUB-MARINER OR DOCTOR STRANGE!
ZZZAT!
YARGGH!
*THESE EVENTS TAKE PLACE BETWEEN DEFENDERS #68 AND #69.
4

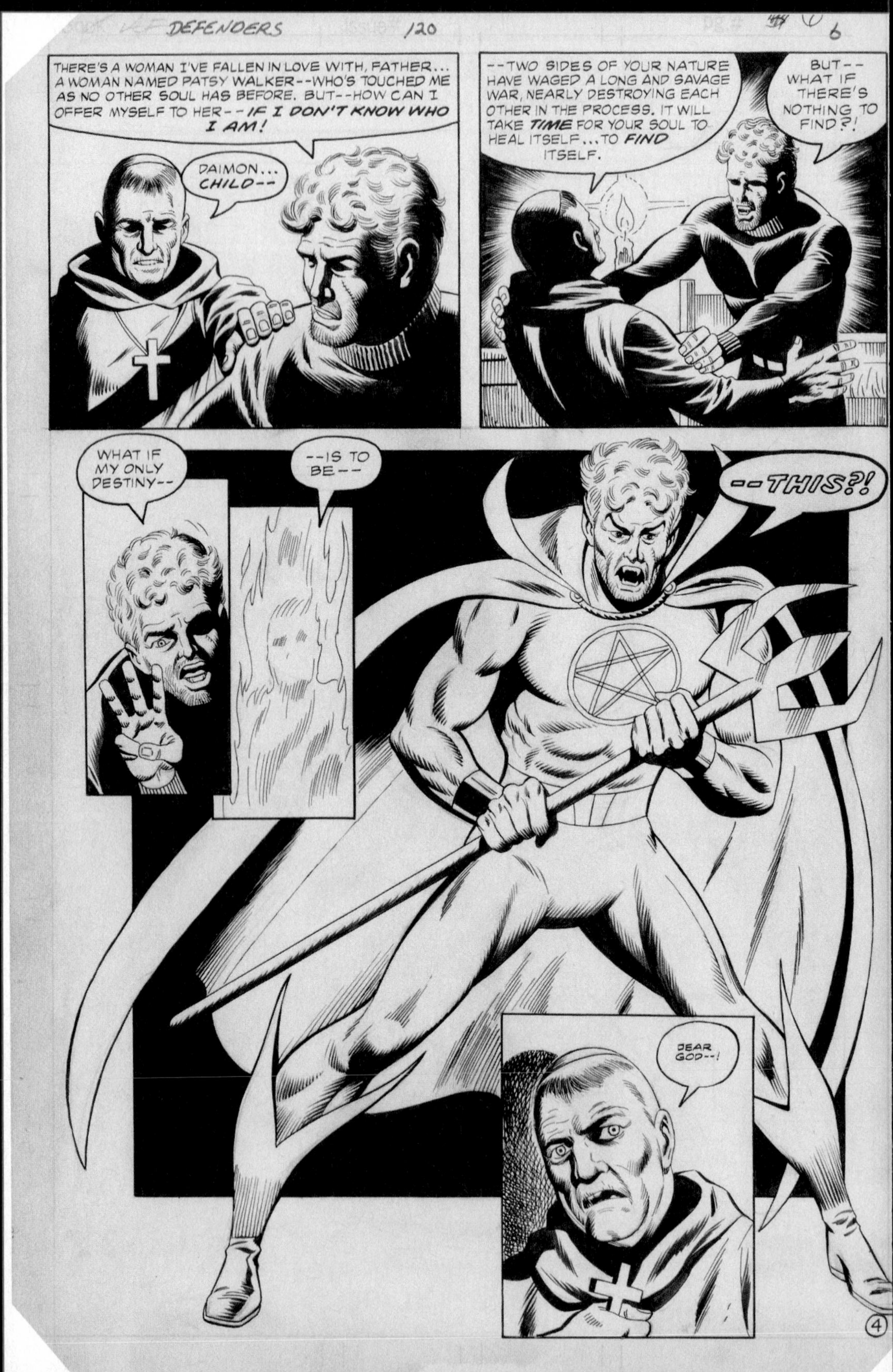
DEFENDERS
120
6
THERE'S A WOMAN I'VE FALLEN IN LOVE WITH, FATHER... A WOMAN NAMED PATSY WALKER--WHO'S TOUCHED ME AS NO OTHER SOUL HAS BEFORE. BUT--HOW CAN I OFFER MYSELF TO HER--IF I DON'T KNOW WHO I AM!
DAIMON... CHILD--
--TWO SIDES OF YOUR NATURE HAVE WAGED A LONG AND SAVAGE WAR, NEARLY DESTROYING EACH OTHER IN THE PROCESS. IT WILL TAKE TIME FOR YOUR SOUL TO HEAL ITSELF...TO FIND ITSELF.
BUT-- WHAT IF THERE'S NOTHING TO FIND?!
WHAT IF MY ONLY DESTINY--
--IS TO BE--
--THIS?!
DEAR GOD--!
4

COURTESY HERITAGEAUCTIONS.C

DEFENDERS #120, PAGE 4 ORIGINAL ART, BY DON PERLIN & ANDY MUSHYNSKY

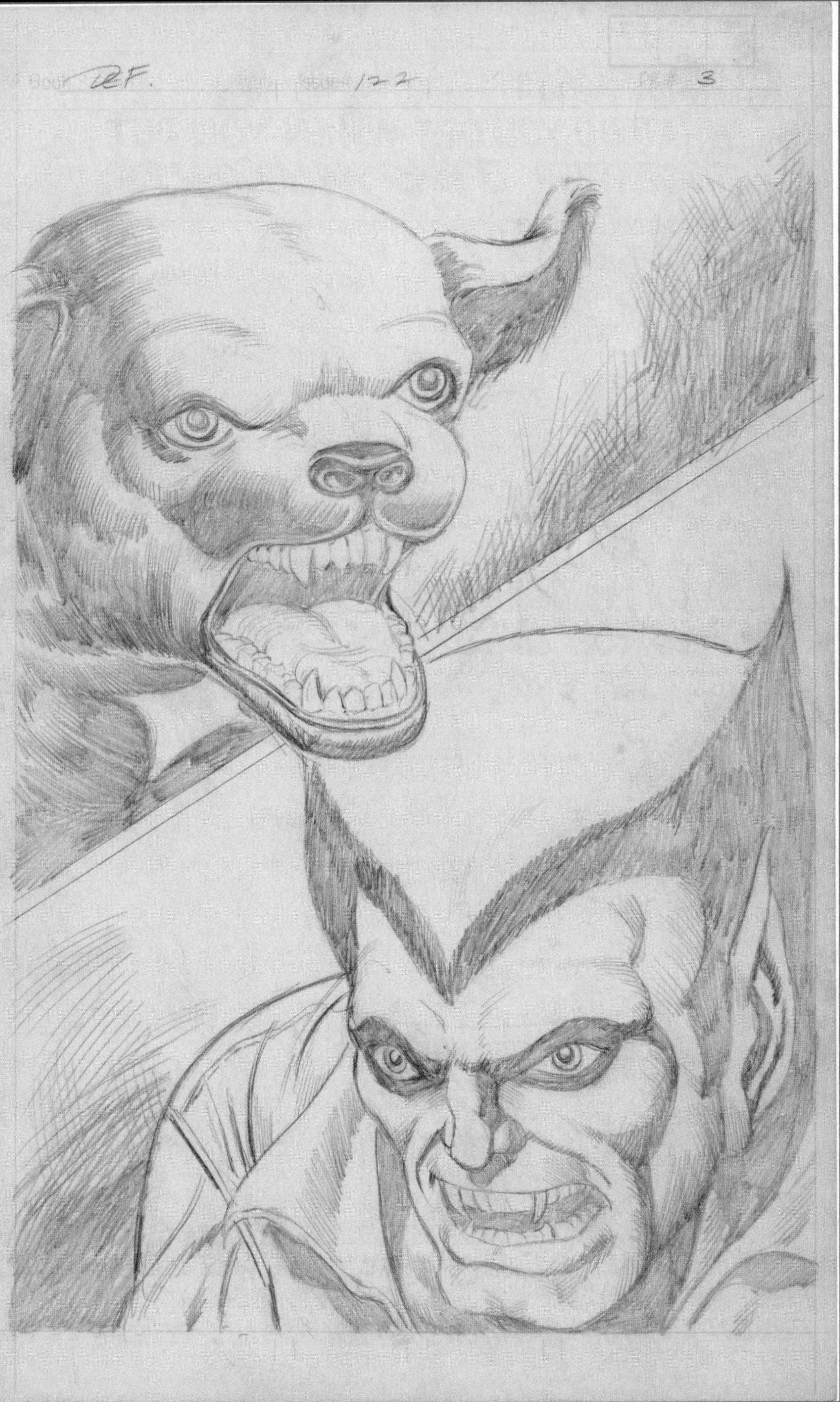
Book DEF.
Issue 122
3

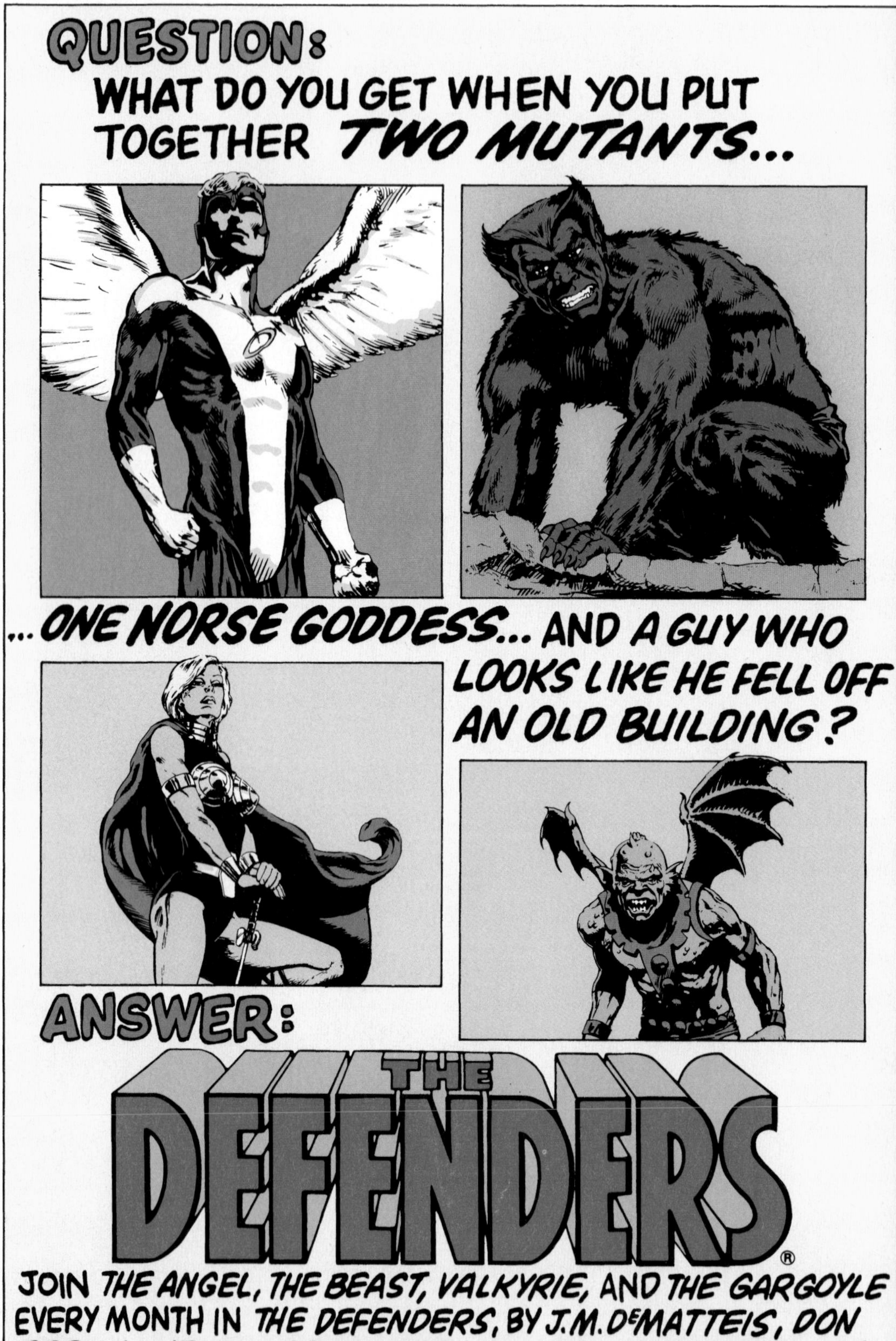
QUESTION:
WHAT DO YOU GET WHEN YOU PUT TOGETHER TWO MUTANTS...
...ONE NORSE GODDESS... AND A GUY WHO LOOKS LIKE HE FELL OFF AN OLD BUILDING?
ANSWER:
THE DEFENDERS®
JOIN THE ANGEL, THE BEAST, VALKYRIE, AND THE GARGOYLE EVERY MONTH IN THE DEFENDERS, BY J.M. DeMATTEIS, DON PERLIN AND KIM DeMULDER! YOU WON'T REGRET IT!

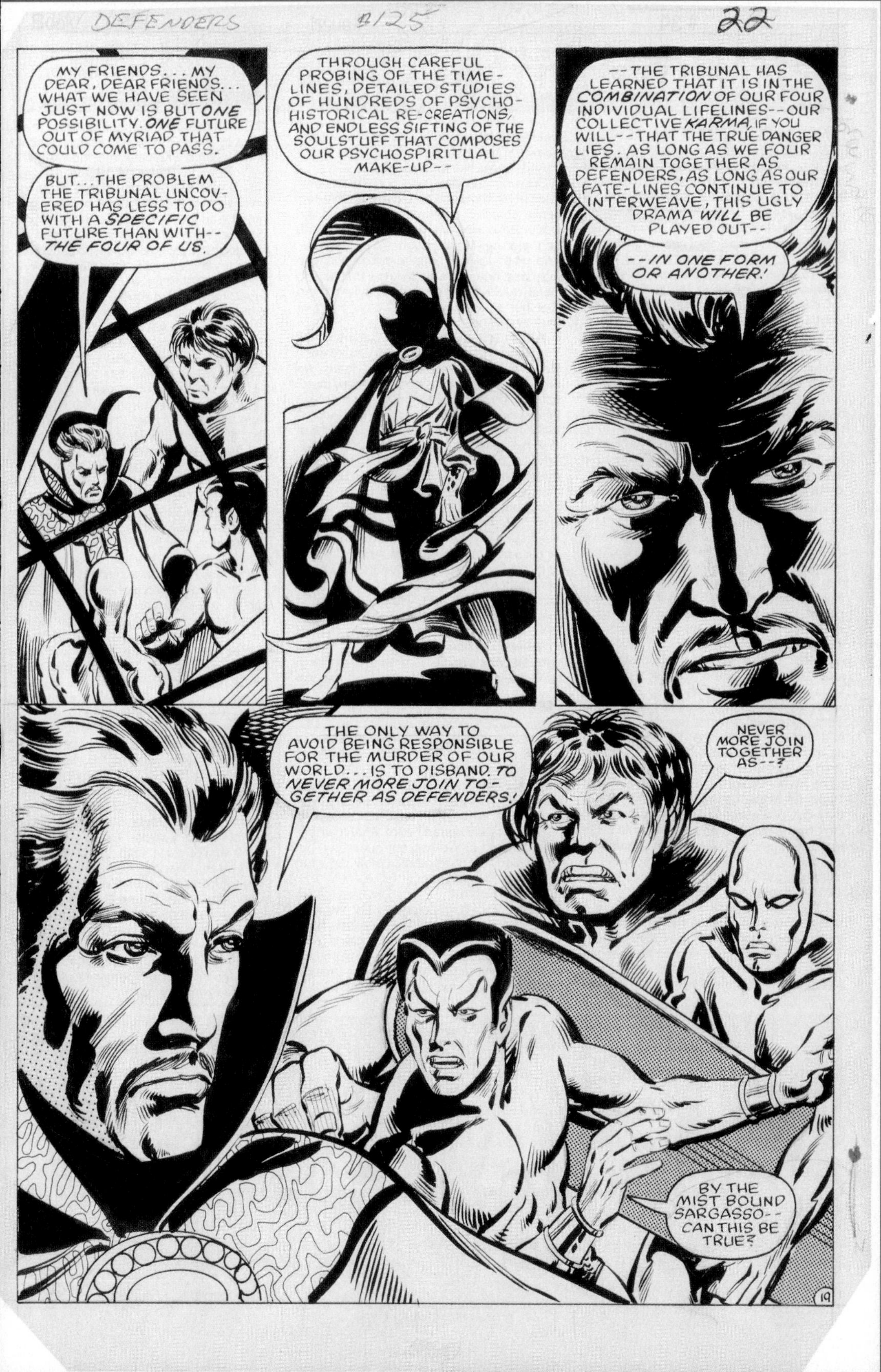
DEFENDERS #125 22
MY FRIENDS... MY DEAR, DEAR FRIENDS... WHAT WE HAVE SEEN JUST NOW IS BUT ONE POSSIBILITY. ONE FUTURE OUT OF MYRIAD THAT COULD COME TO PASS.
BUT... THE PROBLEM THE TRIBUNAL UNCOVERED HAS LESS TO DO WITH A SPECIFIC FUTURE THAN WITH-- THE FOUR OF US.
THROUGH CAREFUL PROBING OF THE TIME-LINES, DETAILED STUDIES OF HUNDREDS OF PSYCHO-HISTORICAL RE-CREATIONS, AND ENDLESS SIFTING OF THE SOULSTUFF THAT COMPOSES OUR PSYCHOSPIRITUAL MAKE-UP--
--THE TRIBUNAL HAS LEARNED THAT IT IS IN THE COMBINATION OF OUR FOUR INDIVIDUAL LIFELINES--OUR COLLECTIVE KARMA, IF YOU WILL--THAT THE TRUE DANGER LIES. AS LONG AS WE FOUR REMAIN TOGETHER AS DEFENDERS, AS LONG AS OUR FATE-LINES CONTINUE TO INTERWEAVE, THIS UGLY DRAMA WILL BE PLAYED OUT--
--IN ONE FORM OR ANOTHER!
THE ONLY WAY TO AVOID BEING RESPONSIBLE FOR THE MURDER OF OUR WORLD... IS TO DISBAND. TO NEVER MORE JOIN TOGETHER AS DEFENDERS!
NEVER MORE JOIN TOGETHER AS--?
BY THE MIST BOUND SARGASSO-- CAN THIS BE TRUE?
19

COURTESY HERITAGEAUCTIONS.COM

***DEFENDERS* #125, PAGE 10 ORIGINAL ART, BY DON PERLIN & KIM DeMULDER**

DEFENDERS DIALOGUE

% MARVEL COMICS GROUP
387 Park Avenue South
New York, New York 10016

CARL POTTS
EDITOR
ANN NOCENTI
ASSISTANT EDITOR

Welcome to issue #1 of THE NEW DEFENDERS. Oh, sure, our cover says #125 – but don't pay any attention to that. As far as our creative crew is concerned, as of this issue, it's a completely new ballgame! If you've already read "Hello, I Must Be Going," you know what we're talking about. If you haven't, read it right now and then get back here pronto. All done? Good! What was it we were saying? Oh, yeah. Welcome to issue #1 of THE NEW DEFENDERS.

First, let's explain *why* the Big Changes. Contrary to what you have read elsewhere, we weren't prompted by flagging sales or floundering direction. If you're a regular reader of the DeMatteis/Perlin DEFENDERS you know that, if nothing else, J.M. and Don have always been driven by unique demons. This book has had its own distinctive voice, look, and philosophy for as long as our two stalwarts have labored on it (actually, just about *every* DEFENDERS creative team has had an extremely unique and personal outlook.) If you're a regular reader you'll also know this: Our characters have a strange habit of running away from us, taking control of their own lives. Much as we've tried to beat Doc Strange and Company into submission, they've proven, time and again, that they're going to do what *they* want, when *they* want... and there's nothing we can do about it. And what they want now – what they *demand* – is the turn of the cards that's begun this very issue.

Listen: You've seen it happen here before. Devil-Slayer dropped in for a guest-spot, stuck around for months, and then, just when we were getting used to him, the guy went crazy, had a minor revelation or two, and turned himself over to the police to atone for past crimes. Then there are Daimon Hellstrom and Patsy Walker. We never even thought those two would get along, let *alone* fall in love. But fall in love they did. They chose their own direction, their own destiny. It was all we could do to wave goodbye. The list goes on and on and on. But, if you're looking for someone to blame (or praise) for this issue's events, lay it on the Beast.

It's clear that Hank McCoy has been a trifle uncomfortable since he first arrived in these pages, back in DEFENDERS #103. These past months, we've seen the reasons for that discomfort and the birth of his new obsession; his intransigent desire to turn the Defenders into an honest-to-gosh, no-holds barred, super-team.

And it looks like he's done it.

But who could've predicted the appearance of Moondragon on the scene? We certainly couldn't have guessed that Odin would be calling Valkyrie back to Asgard and placing Moondragon in her charge! And, when Iceman popped in for a post-college visit, how were we to know that he and Hank would find the bond that's held them together since their X-MEN days stronger than ever. And...

What's that you're saying? Cut the *what?* You know that characters don't make decisions all by themselves. You know we thought long and hard about the new direction this book is taking. "How naive do you think we are?" Is *that* what you're shouting? Well, listen, folks – we'll admit that some of this did happen on the *conscious* level. When it became clear that the Defenders *themselves* were taking things in a direction that would put an end to the non-team status that's been our theme since 1971, writer J.M. DeMatteis *did* sit down with a list of every single hero in the Marvel Universe. And it's true that DeMatteis, being a *big* fan of the original, 1960'-era X-MEN, jumped at the chance to bring the Angel and Iceman into these pages. And, yes, the concept of dropping a wild card like Moondragon into the midst of this new team did make DeMatteis's eyes dance with a positively lunatic light. But that's as far as it went. From there on in, the characters took over (and who's to say just who tossed those ideas into DeMatteis's head in the *first* place?). When Iceman came skating in a few months back, J.M. and Don were as surprised as everyone else to discover how his presence altered the chemistry of the whole book. And how about this? Up until the time the Vision and the Scarlet Witch turned down the Beast's offer to join THE NEW DEFENDERS (in issue #124), we really weren't sure *what* their answer would be! We had our guesses – but the Vision and Wanda ultimately did what they *wanted* to do.

Get the picture?

A couple of final points. 1) For the next three issues, Don Perlin will be catching his breath (wouldn't *you* want to catch your breath after laboring over 38 pages as crammed with characters and action as these?) and getting started on the BEAST/DAZZLER mini-series he's co-creating along with NEW DEFENDERS assistant editor, Ann Nocenti. Stepping into the breach to help us out next issue (and again in issue #128) is Alan Kupperberg. Alan has turned in what we think are the *best* jobs of his comics career – and we think you'll agree with us. In fact, we like Alan's work *so* much that he'll be back here yet again for issue #131, penciling a very special – (and very wacky) – story guest-starring a certain web-footed super hero who's been making Spider-Man's life miserable over in MARVEL TEAM-UP and AMAZING SPIDER-MAN. You can also look for Alan's work on our ICEMAN mini-series, which is just getting under way as we write this. NEW DEFENDERS #127 has been penciled by the ever-speedy – and ever terrific – Sal Buscema. Judging from your mail, you loved Sal's fill-in back in issue #119. Prepare to love again. Sal, as you know, can be found regularly in the pages of THE HULK, ROM and THE NEW MUTANTS. 2) WE WANT YOUR COMMENTS!!! *We're* crazy about THE NEW DEFENDERS – but will *you* be? We hope so – but we won't know until you write. The address is at the top of this page. Don't delay – write today!

This really is a new beginning for this title. It's a little scary – and a whole lot of fun. Stick with us in the months (make that *years*) to come. We promise that we'll do our best to see that you readers are *never* disappointed. All of us, super heroes and pencil pushers alike, intend to keep forging ahead to new horizons!

J.M., Don, Kim, Carl and Ann

NEXT ISSUE: Just what *do* you do after you've decided you're a super-team? Especially when you're having second thoughts? Will the new team chemistry work? What about when a *new* X-factor is mixed in?! Be here next issue as Beast, Iceman, Angel, Moondragon, Gargoyle and Valkyrie ponder those questions. You'll also take a visit to S.H.I.E.L.D.'s Manhattan Headquarters, say hello to stogie-chomping Nick Fury, learn more about the reborn Secret Empire and their dastardly plans, *and* come face-to-face with a brand new super-villain who's bound to knock your socks off: *Leviathan!* All this plus 22 pages of glorious Alan Kupperberg artwork. A steal at 60¢! Be there. *Aloha!*

EDITORIAL ON THE DEFENDERS' NEW DIRECTION, FROM *DEFENDERS* #125